ANIMATION ON DVD

The Ultimate Guide

ANDY MANGELS

Foreword by Mark Hamill

Stone Bridge Press • Berkeley, California

Published by
Stone Bridge Press, P.O. Box 8208, Berkeley, CA 94707
tel 510-524-8732 • sbp@stonebridge.com • www.stonebridge.com

The publisher would like to extend its thanks to the many studios and companies that cooperated in the publication of this book. Every effort has been made to provide information that is accurate as of the date of publication. Please send (polite!) comments, corrections, and updates to the author at animationcorrections@andymangels.com.

Book design and layout by Linda Ronan.

Front cover artwork and animation figures by Christopher Taylor.

Examples of box art throughout this book are used for exemplary and review purposes. All characters and art are copyright or trademark their respective owners, and no infringement is intended.

Printed in the United States of America.

10 9 8 7 6 5 4 3 2 1   2008 2007 2006 2005 2004 2003

LIBRARY OF CONGRESS CATALOGING-IN-PUBLICATION DATA
Mangels, Andy.
Animation on DVD: the ultimate guide / Andy Mangels.
    p. cm.
Includes bibliographical references and index.
ISBN 1-880656-68-X.
1. Animated films—Catalogs. 2. DVD-Video discs—Catalogs. I. Title.
NC1765.M34 2003

016.79143'75—dc21
                2003000292

ANIMATION
ON DVD

DEDICATION

My lifelong love of animation is entwined with my lifelong love of comic books, with 1973's *Super Friends* and its thirteen years of follow-ups keeping me a fan of Saturday mornings.

Stuart P. Heimdal was an animator for Marvel Productions in the early 1980s, and it was while he was working on such series as *Spider-Man and His Amazing Friends* and *The Incredible Hulk* that we met. He taught me a lot about the art of animation, and I still own the sketches of Hulk and Spider-Man that he drew for me on his animation table.

I dedicate this book to William Hanna and Joseph Barbera and the creative team behind *Super Friends*—and especially to Stuart Heimdal, who made the art of animation personal. This book might not exist without you, nor would generations of kids and adults around the world have as many fond memories of animated fun.

Contents

Animation on DVD

Foreword

Cartoons are among my favorite things in life. As a child I was devoted to them, much preferring them to most live-action programs. I knew all the characters and exactly what studio produced them. They inspired in me a lifelong love of drawing, as well as a compulsion to try to duplicate nearly every cartoon voice I heard. My friends and I would spend hours debating such seemingly crucial questions as "Who came first—Jackie Gleason or Fred Flinstone?" And long before I had any idea how it was done, I even fantasized about growing up to be an artist who made cartoons.

I've never outgrown my love of animation, and over the years I've acquired a fairly extensive collection, but nearly all of it is on videotape. Which brings us to Andy Mangels's *Animation on DVD*, a superb reference guide with a purpose as direct as its title. If it's animated and it's on DVD, it's in this book! Whether you are a casual fan or a serious collector, it belongs on a bookshelf near you.

I feel a certain sense of accomplishment that at least a portion of my dream has come true. I may not have been a good enough artist to become an animator, but I have been able to perform in hundreds of cartoons. For a character actor who missed out on radio's Golden Age, it doesn't get much more fun than this. Not being seen liberates you to play parts that would be otherwise inconceivable, to make bold choices you would never dare make if the audience could actually see you. Long before the drawings are done, it's just you, a microphone, and your imagination. It seems a bit ironic that one of the most complex and satisfying characters I've ever played in any medium is the deliciously demented Joker on the animated version of *Batman*, a part I've played for over ten years! That show is a good example of the composite nature of modern animation—the writing, the direction, the animation, the music, and the vocal performance all coming together to create a thrilling whole!

From *Gertie the Dinosaur* to *The Simpsons*, the sheer diversity of animated films will astound you, and chances are . . . they're all listed within these pages, thanks to the talented Mr. Mangels.

MARK HAMILL
February 2003

Preface

It *seemed* like such a good idea at the time. The DVD market was booming. The animation market was booming. I'm a writer who's known for doing research-intensive nonfiction books on pop culture phenomena (or fiction novels). So when I approached Stone Bridge Press about doing *Animation on DVD: The Ultimate Guide*, it was the closest to a slam-dunk great book idea that I've ever had.

Right now, the DVD market is growing exponentially. Between 150 and 250 new DVD titles are released weekly! Prices are still being kept low, despite a planned scale-up. DVD players are quickly becoming the new must-have feature of any household that considers itself a part of the 21st century.

As quickly as the DVD market is growing, the animation on DVD market is growing even faster. More than any other genre, animation is succeeding in sales volume precisely because most animated properties have volumes to spare. While the number of *Aliens* or James Bond movies is finite, the multiple *Scooby-Doo, Pokémon*, or Mickey Mouse releases are just the tip of the proverbial iceberg. From Disney films and Warner Bros. cartoons to Japanese anime and cutting-edge Computer Generated Imagery (CGI) creations . . . there's lots of "ink and paint" being digitized.

• • •

Animation fans are an interesting breed. There's an element that sets them apart and that contributes to the high sales and strong release schedule for the genre. Rare is the fan who will buy just one volume of a series. Much more plentiful is the fan who simply *must* own not only that whole series, but seeks out similar fare or other properties by the same creators.

Note that I'm not separating the anime (Japanese animation) fans from traditional animation aficionados. There are as many teens and adults who are rabid about Disney films or Don Bluth–related releases as there are teens and adults who are crazy for Hayao Miyazaki or CLAMP-inspired releases. And among children, tantrums are thrown equally as often to watch *Pokémon* or *Dragon Ball Z* as they are to watch *Arthur, Madeline*, or Dr. Seuss tales.

Given the mind-boggling array of animation titles on the DVD market, where can a fan look for more information? What is available? What extras do the DVDs offer? Is a title safe for kids or better for older viewers? Who released the product? Where does a viewer find it? There are excellent encyclopedias for both anime and U.S. animation. There are lots of websites for DVDs. But is there one comprehensive, illustrated, detail-filled guide to animation on DVD?

That was a rhetorical question. You're holding that guide in your hands.

• • •

Work began on this volume early in 2002 when there were about 1,200 animated titles available on DVD in the Region 1 (North American) market. As work on this book is winding up, there are more than 1,800, with many more announced!

Early on, I made a decision that each DVD covered in this volume would have an entry based upon a physical viewing. The information for the volumes is taken directly from the discs themselves, not from press materials or websites. The covers for each volume were hand-scanned.

That was well and good for the many companies out there who understood that this book would be a publicity goldmine for their products, but what about the titles that I didn't have in hand? If I couldn't get a copy of the DVD sent to me (and there were a few companies who didn't cooperate), the title got only a brief listing, and a note that it wasn't available for review.

Ten months of mind-bending, eye-searing labor began, as I started viewing and cataloguing 1,800 titles (while simultaneously co-writing several *Star Trek* and *Roswell* novels,

multiple magazine articles, DVD supplemental materials, and more). By summer it became clear that I wouldn't be able to write all the entries on time, so a half-dozen "outsource" writers were brought aboard to handle about 300 entries.

By the end, I've personally written over a thousand individual entries, and my Philips DVD player has held up beautifully to about 5,000 insertions and reinsertions of discs as I watched, checked, and double-checked information. My mind is so full of animated images and trivia now that it will likely never be cleansed. Some of it is fine and fun—the *Battle of the Planets* theme was also used as a *Super Friends* theme!—but other images are dreary and depressing (tentacle porn, anyone?).

• • •

It seemed like such a good idea at the time. And you know what? It's *still* a good idea!

You, dear reader, holding this *doorstop* of a book, are about to get immersed in the biggest, most graphics-heavy, comprehensive volume ever published on this subject.

Not to give you the hard cel (ugh!), but there's a reason this book was called *Animation on DVD: The Ultimate Guide*. And that's because it lives up to its title. Every word of it.

ANDY MANGELS
February 2003

Acknowledgments

A book of this size and scope is an incredible amount of work, which could not have been accomplished without a great deal of help and support. The following people provided plenty of both over the many months I worked on this project. For that, they deserve my thanks and appreciation!

For his help pulling technical information from over a thousand of the DVDs: Kehvan Zydhek.

For their help scanning the covers of each DVD volume and for general support, big thanks go to Howard Robertson and Cindy Okumoto, plus Kathy Putnam, Peter Fagnant, Debbie Fagnant, and Shawn Brooks, of Excalibur Comics (www.excaliburcomics.net).

For their opinions on anime titles: Mike Steele of Things From Another World (www.tfawatsandy.com), Kevin McIntyre, Aimee Eng, Alan Olsen, and Monica Olsen.

For his help with online research: Jai Sen of Shoto Press (www.shotopress.com).

For his help cataloguing writer and director credits: Jon Sauer.

The genesis of this project came from a series of DVD articles for *Comics Buyer's Guide*, some of which were cowritten by Richard Scott, and all of which were edited by Maggie Thompson and Brent Frankenhoff.

For their very nice promotional blurbs about this project: Mark Evanier, Doug Goldstein, Harry Knowles (www.aintitcool.news), Brian McGeehan, Brad Rader.

For his Foreword and the many years of entertainment he's provided: Mark Hamill.

For his fabulous cover image and designs: Christopher Taylor.

For their pressure-relieving help with outsourced reviews: Brett Rogers, Gerry Poulos, Jennifer Marie Contino, Michael Toole, Roman J. Martel, Wolfen Moondaughter, and Paul Guinan.

For rescuing my computer and helping to get the new one to work effectively: Rory Bowman of www.macrory.com.

For computer research help and support: Paul Tucker, Gary Gelardo, John Jenkins. For his editing help: Paul Smalley. For getting me to Stone Bridge for my contract meetings: Bill Byrne.

For help with DVD research: Ron Rich of *The DVD Guide* (www.thedvdguide.com) and Aaron Barnard, manager of Portland's best Suncoast store.

For agreeing to the project and putting up with the long process: publisher Peter Goodman and editor Barry Harris of Stone Bridge Press.

For several hundred trips up three flights of stairs to my apartment for deliveries of DVDs: my FedEx man Rick Williams, USPS men Dan and Kris, UPS men Norman Davis and Charlie, and Airborne driver Norm.

And as always, for his support: my partner Don Hood (plus our dog, Bela!).

The following companies and individuals provided DVD screener copies, press materials, artwork, and more. Thanks go to:

A&E (Suzanne Dobson), Acorn Media (Brian Clucas), AD Vision (Ken Wiatrek, Corey Henson, Andrew Nelson, Valerie Harper), Alpha Omega Publications (Christina Henderson, Jill Fishburn, Peggy Koehler), Anchor Bay (Donna Creighton, Jay Marks of Blue Underground), AnimEigo (Luray Carroll), Artisan/Republic/Live (Ashley Stanford), Bandai Entertainment (Jerry Chu), BBC (Deepa Shah, Marnie Lawler), Bender/Helper Impact PR (Pamela Grant, Shawna Lynch, Melisa Gotto, Steven Solomon, Jay Weisberger), BFS Entertainment (Leigh Ross), Big Idea (Elizabeth Fields), Blackboard Entertainment (Sharon Huikko), BMG (Todd Johnson, Rob Settler), Brentwood/Eclipse (Patricia Morgan), Buena Vista/Disney/Miramax (Roger Saunden), Central Park Media (Tim Altman, Joey Zerbo), Culture Q/Ariztical Entertainment Group (Michael Shoel), Digital Leisure (Elizabeth Foster), Dreamworks (Cheryl Glenn, Missy Davy), DVD International (David and Joan Goodman), First Run Features (Kelly Hargraves, Lisa Cacace), GoodTimes (Amy Lee), HBO (Laura Freeman Young), Hen's Tooth (Steve Newmark), HIT Entertainment (Denise Landry, Jackie Smith), Image Entertainment (Spencer Savage), Kino International (Gabriele Caroti), Liberty International (Noel Gimble), Madacy (Marisa Galuppo), Manga Entertainment/Palm Pictures (Danielle Opyt), Marengo (Philip E. Hopkins), Media Blasters/Kitty (Rachel Gluckstern, Mike Pascuzzi, Andrew Vidal, Carl Morano), MGM/UA (Steve Wegner, Stacy Studebaker), MMG Anime (Sally), Mondo Media (Christina Chavez), MPRM Public Relations (Gerald Opp, Chris Reichert, Diane Tang), Multimedia 2000/M2K (Greg Hutcheson, Nancy Rockwood), Naxos of America (Rebecca Pyle), New Concorde (Tony Pines), NuTech (Eric Zigler), Paramount (Liz Haggar), Pioneer (Chad Kime, Lori Johnson, Kevin Chu), Ralph Edwards Productions/Steeplechase (Risa Jewell), Retro Media (Fred Olen Ray, Elizabeth), Rhino (Lana Berman), Right Stuf International (Shawne and Kris Kleckner), Slingshot Entertainment (Jennifer Kahn), Sony/Sony Wonder (John Singh, Randy Koshinskie, Allison Ennis), SSA Public Relations (Brian Hershey), Sue Procko PR (Sue Procko, Krista, Maral), SVE/Churchill Media/Clearvue (Kelly Campbell, Jill Goorsky), Synch-Point (Ardith Santiago), Tai Seng (Frank Djeng), 10% Productions (Drew Pokorny, Ron Miller), Terry Hines and Associates PR (Nancy Jenkins, Mac), TokyoPop (Kristien Brada-Thompson), TriMark/Lion's Gate (Deborah Schonfeld, Jeyran Abtahi), UAV Entertainment (Jamie Campbell), Universal (Matt Kalinowski, Craig Radow), Urban Vision (Rhona Medina), Viz Communications (Matthew Lopez, Elena Ontiveros, Dallas Middaugh, Renee Soldberg), Voyager Entertainment (Barry Winston, Dianne Malmgren), Warner Bros. (Janet Brown-Keller, Josh), Wellspring Media/Winstar/Fox Lorber (Kim Rubin, David Samra), Whirlwind Media (Jane Newman), Xenon Studios (Dee Amamura).

Introduction

Few people in the English-speaking world—and America in particular—have lived in a time when animation was not a part of their lives. Animation grew out of toys from the 1800s, including the phenakistoscope from 1832 (invented by the Belgian scientist Joseph Antoine Plateau), a handle-mounted wheel that had drawings on one side. When the wheel was spun in front of a mirror, the drawings appeared to move. The concept was also instrumental in the development of live-action motion pictures.

In 1899, Englishman Arthur Melbourne-Cooper created a stop-motion short film using matchsticks. In 1906, newspaper cartoonist J. Stuart Blackton created the first animated short, called *Humorous Phases of Funny Faces*, which featured handmade drawings filmed frame-by-frame. French cartoonist Emile Cohl began producing animated shorts in 1908, and American newspaper cartoonist Winsor McCay followed soon thereafter, exhibiting his first *Little Nemo* film (based on his fantastical comic strip) in New York City in 1911.

Though Cohl was an important pioneer, McCay's work had more impact on the growing field of animation. Not only was his work more detailed and sophisticated, but the characters had personalities. In 1914, McCay released *Gertie the Dinosaur*, the lead character of which became the first animation "star."

That same year, animators John Randolph Bray, Earl Hurd, and others began to streamline the production process. One of the most important early innovations was the introduction of clear plastic "cels" on which were painted the animated characters. The cels could be laid over a background, thus saving animators from having to draw the background over and over.

Studios began assembling animation staffs to produce more of the animated shorts that were such a hit with movie audiences (shorts were shown prior to feature films in this pre-television era). Many of the animated shorts were based upon comic strip characters such as *Felix the Cat, The Katzenjammer Kids, Happy Hooligan, Mutt and Jeff*, and others.

Max Fleischer, with his brother Dave, combined live action and animation in their *Out of the Inkwell* series and later made stars of Ko-Ko the Clown, Betty Boop, and Popeye the Sailor. They developed a new style of animation called "rotoscoping," in which the movements of live actors were filmed, then traced over to provide naturalistic animation; although they used it early on, rotoscoping was most famously used in their classic *Superman* shorts from 1941 to 1943.

Other early animation pioneers included Paul Terry, Walter Lantz, and Walt Disney. Though Disney and his crew had been producing cartoons since the early 1920s, it was his 1928 black-and-white "Steamboat Willie" that sent shockwaves through the industry. In addition to introducing Mickey Mouse, it was the first cartoon with synchronized sound. Soon, studios were all touting their own sound cartoons—Warner's *Looney Tunes* and MGM's *Happy Harmonies,* to name but a few—to compete with Disney's *Silly Symphonies*.

Disney and his animators had other lasting effects on the industry. Disney characters, with their clearly identifiable personalities, led to the age of cartoon stars like Donald Duck (1934) and Goofy (1932); Paramount's Betty Boop (1930) and Popeye (1933); Walter Lantz's Woody Woodpecker (1941); Warner Bros.' Porky Pig (1936), Daffy Duck (1938), and Bugs Bunny (1940); Universal's Casper (1945); and others.

Color cartoons were another Disney innovation, the first being a 1932 *Silly Symphonies* cartoon called "Flowers and Trees" (though some previous cartoons had been tinted or had used a two-color process). Those innovations were only a warm-up for Disney's 1937 release of *Snow White and the Seven Dwarfs*, the first full-length animated motion picture.

Even as U.S. animators developed characters, many European animators worked at developing different forms of animation. Puppets, paper cut-outs, abstract shapes, pastel and charcoal drawings, pixelation, clay models (later known as "claymation") . . . all became tools of animation for creators in Poland, Russia, Germany, France, and England.

Animation remained popular during World War II (a series of *Private Snafu* training films were even shown to servicemen) and beyond.

In 1953, Paramount produced the first pair of 3D animated shorts, starring Popeye and Casper. By now, some producers were using a form of "limited animation," which used fewer cels to tell the same stories and only moved portions of the characters instead of the full figures. This helped recoup some of the rising animation costs. But in 1949, when a Supreme Court ruling said that studios could not require the purchase of shorts with their feature films, theatrical animation took another big hit. Newsreels, live-action shorts, and animated shorts began to get fewer bookings. What could save short-form animation?

Flash back a few years: In 1928, the Radio Corporation of America (RCA) tested its long-range broadcasts by filming a Felix the Cat statue rotated on a pedestal. Animation didn't really catch on on television during the 1930s and 1940s, largely because broadcasters were still working out technical aspect of the nascent technology, and the emphasis was on live events, sports, and news stories. When shown at all, cartoons were used as filler, since copyright laws at the time provided that whoever owned a 16mm print of a theatrical cartoon could broadcast it on television at no extra cost (theatrical showings were subject to a cut of the public exhibition profits). As television networks began expanding their programming in the late 1940s and early 1950s, children's shows that repurposed theatrical animated shorts into a programming block became a staple of most stations. They were inexpensive, and, once a children's show was established it could seek sponsorship and advertiser money.

The first animated series created specifically for television was the limited animation show *Crusader Rabbit*, created by Jay Ward in 1949. In the following years, other animation studios followed suit, including Walt Disney, Terrytoons, and others. William Hanna and Joe Barbera (the creators of *Tom and Jerry*) perfected the limited animation technique, repackaging theatrical shorts with new cartoons for the half-hour cartoon program *Ruff and Ready* (1957). In 1960, Hanna-Barbera's *The Flintstones* became the first newly animated primetime series, popular because its humor was aimed at adult audiences as well as at children.

By the mid-1960s, animation on television was a booming industry, and foreign animation was being imported from Japan and England. Saturday mornings were the almost exclusive domain of animation, and new forms and genres blossomed, from the realistic adventuring of *Jonny Quest* and the musical-comedy adventures of *The Archies*, to superheroes and space heroes like Space Ghost, Superman, and Spider-Man.

Animated films continue to be released—almost solely by Disney until the 1990s—but TV is where most animation has been seen in the last thirty years. The proliferation of networks and cable channels has led to plentiful choices for animation fans. Cable networks like Nickelodeon, The Disney Channel, MTV, and even premium channels like HBO have all introduced groundbreaking new series, while syndicated "superstations" offer repackaged older material from throughout film and television animation's history. The Cartoon Network launched in October 1992 as the first twenty-four-hour all-animation channel.

Today, the world of animation is a multi-billion-dollar business, tied in to toy licensing, fast food, advertising, and more. Animated characters have truly become stars of popular culture, as well as opinion makers. Could the animation pioneers ever have imagined how Bart Simpson's saucy naughtiness on *The Simpsons* would inspire public debate in that show's early years?

The technical side of animation has continued to progress, too, culminating in today's modern computer-generated imagery (CGI), animation that is indistinguishable at times from real-world live-action film. Although the dinosaurs in the *Jurassic Park* films are more realistic than the star of *Gertie the Dinosaur*, they're just as much the creations of modern animators as Gertie was of Winsor McCay. And, as if to close the circle, on the *South Park* series, CGI is even used in a way that approximates a cruder, paper-cut-out animation style that harkens back to the field's beginnings.

JAPANESE ANIME

In Japan, comic books are known as manga, and the animated adventures that result from them (as well as from original stories) are known as anime. From the 1960s until now, the popularity of manga and anime has steadily grown; today, the market for both entertainment forms is expanding substantially faster than the equivalent U.S. comic book or animation market. Anime is a multimillion-dollar industry in Japan and one of the most valued forms of popular entertainment. Besides the animated programs themselves, the ancillary merchandising, manga, and fan participation make anime's celebrity and status unrivaled by perhaps any pop culture product in the world today.

The term manga was first used in the 1800s by the famous Japanese artist Katsushika Hokusai for his numerous drawings and caricatures. Today, the word is usually used to describe illustrated stories in comic book form. Manga titles are published weekly, biweekly, or monthly, and an average issue might contain 200–400 pages and 10–15 different storylines. Most manga stories are serialized, and the most popular of these are generally collected into paperback or hardcover volumes. Manga account for over a third of all printed material in Japan!

Unlike American or European comics,

Japanese manga are formatted to read from right to left. Manga that are translated for American audiences by companies such as Viz, TokyoPop, and Dark Horse are usually "flopped" during translation for a more conventional left-to-right read. In recent years, several U.S. publishers have published some manga in their original right-to-left orientation, but with English translations.

Manga are read by a large percentage of the Japanese population and are published in a variety of genres, including *kodomo* (children's stories), *shonen* (boys), *shojo* (girls), *seinen* (young men), *redisu* (young women), *josei* (older women), *seijin* (adult-oriented), *yaoi/ shonen ai* (gay male-oriented, not necessarily adult), and *hentai* (adult-oriented heterosexual stories). There are basketball manga, police manga, funny manga, legal manga, historical manga, and even manga used as technical manuals. Several things account for manga's extreme popularity in Japan: the diverse subject matter means there's something for every taste; the size of most manga books lends itself to a hefty reading experience, but with multiple short, serialized stories; manga books are readily available on every newsstand, and even in vending machines next to the candy and cigarettes; and most importantly, the comic book style of manga is respected as a valid art form in Japan, avoiding the "comic books are for children" stigma that has crippled the American comic book industry.

Anime is the Japanese term for cel-based or computer-generated animation. The word is pronounced "ah-nee-may" (some pronounce it "ann-im-ay"). Among the earliest animated TV series in Japan was *Tetsuwan Atomu*, which debuted on Fuji TV on January 1, 1963. The series was based on Osamu Tezuka's ultrapopular manga series and newspaper strip of the same name. Later that year, U.S. network NBC bought a syndicated package of the series and renamed it *Astro Boy*. The edited and dubbed series was a hit, and other Japanese anime properties were soon hitting U.S. airwaves, including *The 8th Man* (1965), *Gigantor* (1966), *Kimba the White Lion* (1966), *Marine Boy* (1966), and *Speed Racer* (1967).

Anime made a U.S. resurgence in the late 1970s and early 1980s with such fare as *Battle of the Planets* (1978), *Starblazers* (1979), *Mobile Suit Gundam* (1979), *Force Five* (1980), and *Captain Harlock* (1980). By then, much of U.S. animation was inked overseas, so the styles and pacing of U.S. and Japanese animation matched more closely at times. But anime retained some of its big-eyed, big-haired imagery even as its fan base grew. Many of those fans resent the nickname the genre was given: "Japanimation."

The popularity of videotape gave rise to a wider collector mentality among anime fanatics (known as "otaku"), and soon the importing of Japanese videos and bootleg taping of many series became widespread. Anime fan clubs were founded on high school and college campuses and in comic book stores. It wasn't until the late 1980s, however, that anime-oriented companies began springing up in the U.S. Today, there are many companies that regularly release anime on VHS tapes and DVD.

Anime is often more complex—in both theme and artwork—than most traditional U.S. animated series. Characters experience tragedy alongside humor, have intimate relationships, and sometimes die. Sure, there are a lot of big robots, but that's not all that anime offers. Beyond its diversity of subject, the art styles used in anime are tremendously varied, and the animation form itself has been pushed forward on a technological level with computer animation and cel-based animation sharing the screen.

Traditionally, manga have provided the

source material for most of the anime produced (original stories, novel adaptations, and video games account for the remainder). However, like their American comic-based movie/TV counterparts, anime do not always stay true to their manga roots. Some anime productions take numerous liberties with the characters and stories. Others stay so faithful that knowledge of the original manga storylines is a boon to the viewer.

There are a few concepts that are unique to the anime domain. "Chibi" is a character that has a child's body, but often a full-sized head and adult actions. A similar and often-shared concept is "SD" or "super-deformed," wherein the character can be chibi or stretched into other odd shapes. "Idol" is a popular girl singer, generally one who is manufactured for the media, like Britney Spears. Finally, "mecha" refers to any type of mechanism, but is often used to describe giant robots or mobile suits of armor that make the wearer look like a giant robot.

In Japan, anime is released in one of three forms: as a TV series, as a feature film, or as an Original Video Animation or OVA. (The term Original Animated Video or OAV is just as common.) OVAs began appearing in 1983. Often a popular property may be found in multiple forms at once, including spin-offs or variations on a theme (such as the various *Sailor Moon* series).

In the U.S. market today, anime is one of the fastest-growing categories in video and DVD entertainment, as well as television syndication and toy licensing. As demonstrated by this book, there are over a thousand anime DVDs available on the market, allowing fans to obtain their favorites with near-perfect images and all the bells and whistles.

A DVD PRIMER

So what are DVDs? The acronym stands for Digital Versatile Disc (or, according to some sources, Digital Video Disc). It's a disk 4¾ inches in diameter, exactly the same size as a standard compact disc (CD). Each side of a DVD can contain two data layers, allowing for the storage of huge amounts of information, such as video images and audio, in an unprecedentedly crisp fashion. The DVD technology was introduced in late 1996 in Japan, and by the close of the 20th century the technology for both players and discs was rapidly gaining popularity worldwide.

What makes a DVD so special? Unlike VHS video, the picture and audio are recorded digitally, which means almost crystal-clear images and sound. Additionally, most DVDs showcase feature films in "widescreen" (with black bars across the top and bottom), meaning that you see it as you would in a theater instead of in the half-the-picture-is-missing "pan and scan" transfer that films generally receive for video and television.

Many DVDs also feature a lot of "extras" including director and star commentaries that can be played over the film, isolated music scores, deleted scenes, outtakes, uncensored footage, behind-the-scenes clips, alternate endings, music videos, foreign-language subtitles, and more.

"As CDs are to music, DVDs are to films," says Ron Rich, publisher of the quarterly *DVD Guide*. "It basically has replaced what was the highest quality home video device (the laserdisc). It is clearly the best medium for appreciating home video entertainment."

DVDs have already begun to replace VHS as the dominant form for entertainment media, with several companies announcing that they are already phasing out video releases and intend to move exclusively to DVD within 2003. With the introduction of home-based DVD recorders in 2002, the age of the DVD has begun.

Key to Entries

All entries in this book have been reviewed from physical copies of the DVDs. Every effort was made to check and double-check all credits, special features, and technical features.

The main DVD player used in this effort was a Philips DVD953; multichannel audio data and formats, screen ratios, and regional coding features (for the majority of titles) were checked by Kehvan Zydhek on a Samsung SD-616F DVD-ROM Drive with PowerDVD XP, as well as a JVC XV-501 DVD player. Some technical features were checked on an eMac G4 with DVD Player v3.2.

MAIN ENTRIES

Title: The title as listed on the cover or spine. Volume number is sometimes not shown, so I have bracketed it if appropriate. All titles were first sorted on a word-by-word basis, then by volume number. Thus, a volume that might come first alphabetically is listed third because it is volume 3. Additionally, leading articles (A, An, The) are ignored for all titles; that is, *An All Dogs Christmas Carol* is listed under "All Dogs," and *The Land Before Time* is listed in the "L" section. For consistency, I have replaced the ampersand (&) with the word "and," although box typography and official titles may vary. While it would have been nice, from

an editorial standpoint, to be consistent in our rendering of titles, the reality is that punctuation varies wildly among DVD manufacturers. Our primary goal was to render the title in text as you would find it on the cover of the DVD. In many cases, however, typography and layout indicate the title, subtitle, and volume number. As a general rule, titles are separated from subtitles by a colon; sub-subtitles follow an em-dash. Unfortunately, this system could not be applied consistently because some manufacturers have applied their own incompatible punctuation system. We did the best we could, but we don't write in a tidy world.

Company: The releasing company/companies. Contact information can be found in the section "Companies and Resources."

Year of Release: The year the DVD was released, not the year the program was released.

Running Time: The length of the main portion of DVD. This often differs from the time listed on the packaging, and we've pointed out a few of the most egregious errors.

Catalog Number: The order number listed on the spine, or if none was available, the UPC (Universal Product Code) number.

Director Credit: Taken from screen when

possible, in the manner it was presented onscreen. Some DVDs did not list a specific director, but listed "Animation directed by." Note that I have listed Japanese names in Western style with given name first, surname last. Releasing companies are seldom consistent in their romanization of Japanese names into English. Indeed, some well-known writers and directors insist on a quirky spelling all their own. I have opted for simplicity: extended vowels, usually indicated by a macron or spelled out as *ou* or *oo*, have been eliminated.

Writer Credit: Taken from screen when possible, in the manner it was presented onscreen. Some credits used "Screenplay by," "Script by," or "Written by." Story credits are listed separately.

Source Material: If the project is based on comic books, manga, novels, or short stories, I tried to list such sources here.

Byline: If an entry was written by an outside writer, that person's initials are included in brackets at the end of the text portion of the entry. Outside writers are: [BR] Brett Rogers; [GP] Gerry Poulos; [JMC] Jennifer Marie Contino; [MT] Michael Toole; [PVG] Paul Guinan; [RJM] Roman J. Martel; and [WM] Wolfen Moondaughter.

SPECIAL FEATURES

Here I list all the special features included on the disc, including many that are not advertised. Note that I have not included Web links or the ever-popular "Interactive Menus," neither of which is a Special Feature in any DVD collector's book. Also, note that Easter eggs are detailed in a separate section at the end of the book.

TECHNICAL FEATURES

Aspect Ratio: Here I have indicated whether a film is Widescreen (with black bars at the top and bottom) or Fullscreen. Some Widescreen releases have been enhanced for 16x9 televisions.

Subtitles/Closed Captions: English subtitles are listed first, followed alphabetically by other languages. In some cases, there are two English tracks, with the second being a "Dubtitle" track that represents the text of the Dub script.

Languages: The original language is listed first followed by the dubbed languages, English first and others arranged alphabetically.

Sound: The majority of DVDs feature some iteration of the Dolby Digital sound format. Some are surround sound, others aren't. Some discs feature one format for the English-language track and another for the foreign-language tracks. In such cases, I have only listed the English track. There may also be alternate sound tracks in DTS (Digital Theater System) or PCM (Pulse Code Modulation) audio on the disc.

Packaging: There are four main packaging types for DVDs, including keepcases (the most traditional), snapcases (cardboard, used mostly by Warner, HBO, and for some Image titles), multikeepcases (which hold multiple discs), and boxes. A few odd packaging types are also mentioned in this book.

Disc Number: The number of discs in the package.

Region Encoding: This lists the region or regions in which the DVD can be played. DVDs can be encoded for one or more of eight geographical regions. The codes mean that the DVD can only be played on a DVD player that is encoded for that Region. Thus, a U.S./Canadian Region 1 player cannot play a U.K./Japan Region 2 DVD. There are "multi-region" players available that will play any DVD. Some DVDs are encoded only for

Regions 1–6, while others are encoded for All Regions.

REGION 1: USA, Canada

REGION 2: Europe, Japan, Middle East, Egypt, South Africa

REGION 3: South Korea, Taiwan, Hong Kong, Southeast Asia

REGION 4: Australia, New Zealand, South America, Mexico, Pacific Islands, Caribbean

REGION 5: Russian Federation, Mongolia, North Korea, India, Pakistan, Africa (except Egypt)

REGION 6: China

REGION 7: Reserved

REGION 8: International Territories (airplanes, cruise ships, etc.)

GENRE & RATING

Here I have tried to provide several keywords that will help you find or identify genres of interest. I have also listed the rating, if one is provided, by either the MPAA (Motion Picture Association of America) or printed on the packaging itself. If a rating is not provided, I have listed age appropriateness.

Note regarding Mature/Adult titles: Due to the mature nature of these titles and covers, any title rated 17+, R or above, or MA/Mature has been placed in a separate section of the book. If you are likely to be offended by such material, please do not open this section. Also be aware that not all Mature/Adult titles are pornography; but if a film received an R rating (such as *Waking Life* or the *South Park* movie), it is included here.

REGARDING THE REVIEWS

First and foremost, I have tried to be informative in my reviews. The first paragraph is generally a synopsis of the stories contained on the disc. The following paragraphs include some historical information, trivia, and DVD-specific comments.

Because viewer tastes are so subjective, and the types of animation covered in this book are so broad, I have kept editorial opinions to a minimum. While *Pokémon* may not be my cup of tea, it has millions of fans; snarky critical comments interjected into the entries would serve few readers.

That's not to say that I have not been critical in my reviews, but I have tried to single out the good and bad points depending on your tastes (i.e., if you like a certain type of material, this DVD would be to your liking). I have also tried to point out certain titles that rate among the best examples of the animation form, as well as some that rank among the worst.

I have also tried to flag certain hot-button issues, some of which include: super-deformed art in anime titles, religious themes, gay themes, historical racist themes, and violence (sexual and otherwise). This enables viewers who wish to avoid—or view—these subjects to find out where they are.

I have tried to keep spoilers to a minimum, though this is sometimes difficult with multi-disc series. In my opinion, the plot should be enjoyed while viewing a DVD, not while reading a review.

I have included some titles that mix live action and animation, while excluding other titles. Why review *Mary Poppins* but not *Cats and Dogs*, or *Who Framed Roger Rabbit* and not *Star Wars Episode I: The Phantom Menace*? Given that a growing number of modern films incorporate some CGI elements, this was largely a judgment call based on multiple factors—and personal taste. First and foremost, I asked myself whether the animated sequences contained interaction between live characters and animated characters, that is, animation as more than just a background or special effect.

Another factor was whether the animated character was *meant* to be a cartoon and not a realistic-looking-character-that-happens-to-be-animated.

Some DVDs arrived too late for a full review. In such cases I have listed the key data and features for the release and included the promotional copy as it was provided by the releasing company.

Some DVDs were unavailable, due to their rarity or to companies failing to provide them for review. Rather than list what could be erroneous information on DVDs I did not have in hand, most entries where the DVD was not provided list only the title, releasing company information, and a few minor details.

Finally, I have tried to keep fan-specific terms to a minimum. This is especially true in the anime entries. Non-anime fans who might be drawn to an anime title might not be familiar with terms that fans take for granted. Thus, instead of "fan service," I use "cheesecake," and "robot" is generally used more than "mecha," and so on.

CORRECTIONS

Although every effort has been made to include correct data for all the entries, in a book of this size, and with this many entries, mistakes or errors can crop up. I'll make every effort to correct these in future printings or future volumes if you send a polite note informing me of any errors. You can send corrections to:

animationcorrections@andymangels.com

ANIMATION ON DVD

Ace Ventura, Pet Detective: The Case of the Serial Shaver

Slingshot, 2000, #BDVD9112. Directed by Safina Uberoi. Written by Jack Feldstein.

Ace Ventura is a pet detective who has a most unusual case: someone is shaving the animals at the zoo! Aided by his pet monkey, Spike, and with gawky veterinarian Angelica and beautiful zoo guide Erica, Ace must stop the Serial Shaver, and he needs your help to do it!

This DVD is a combination of game and story, which, if it were a book, would be called some variation of "Choose Your Own Adventure." However, Slingshot calls it a "Multipath Adventure." At various points in the story, viewers can use the remote to choose Ace's next decision, thus controlling (to an extent) the outcome of the story.

Based on the 1993 live-action Jim Carrey movie (and its 1995 sequel), this DVD captures some of the irreverent humor of the film without the gross-out PG-13 comedy, though Slingshot does warn of "suggestive themes." Unfortunately, the CGI animation is fairly ugly; video game fans will find it tolerable, but animation fans will cringe.

SPECIAL FEATURES Other Title Trailers TECHNICAL FEATURES Widescreen (1.85:1) • Languages: Eng. • Sound: Dolby Digital 5.1 • Keepcase • 1 Disc • Region 1 GENRE & RATING CGI/Comedy/Interactive • Not Rated (Teens)

Action Man in Space

Trimark/Lion's Gate, 2001, 70 mins., #78530. Written by Phil Harnage, Mike Medlock, Jesse Winfield, Reed Shelly, Bruce Shelly.

Action Man doesn't know who he is, but he knows who does: his archenemy, the evil Doctor X. So, it's up to Action Man and the other members of Team X-Treme to foil the dastardly plots of Doctor X. Whether it means saving the world's richest men from a hijacked shuttle or escaping a trap set for him at a space station, Action Man is ready to go. And when Doctor X captures the Stealth Satellite and trains its particle beam weapon on a major city, guess who opposes him? So how does Doctor X escape to take over Station X-Treme in orbit?

One in a never-ending line of toy-based animation series, *Action Man* was modeled after a popular Hasbro toy line and first aired in 1995. The four episodes on this DVD are "Space Walk"; "Peril at Perigee"; "Space Wars"; and "Skynap." The animation is competent, and the picture crisp, but the series is relatively generic.

SPECIAL FEATURES • Game • DVD "How-To" with Inspector Gadget. TECHNICAL FEATURES Fullscreen (1.33:1) • Subtitles/CC: Eng. • Languages: Eng., Span. dub • Sound: Dolby Digital Stereo 2.0 • Keepcase • 1 Disc • Region 1 GENRE & RATING Science Fiction/Adventure • Not Rated (Teens)

A.D. Police: To Protect and Serve

ADV Films, 2002, 300 mins., #DAP001. Directed by Hidehito Ueda, Naoyuki Konno, Jiro Fujimoto, Shintaro Itoga, Hidekazu Sato, Shigeki Hatakeyama, Satoshi Nakagawa, Nobuaki Nakanishi. Written by Taiko Hoshikawa, Hiroshi Onogi, Toshizo Nemoto.

Already destabilized after a major earthquake, Genom City is now troubled by a high crime rate. The high-tech specialists on the city's police force are an elite squad called "A.D. Police" (A.D. stands for "ADvanced"). Two of its six members are Takeru Sasaki (a robot crime specialist) and his new partner Hans Krief, a German with no long-term memory. In 2020, they encounter trouble in the form of mutating cyborgs called "Voomers." And not all of their police squadmates will emerge from the coming conflict alive....

This DVD collects all twelve twenty-five-minute episodes of the 1999 television series, which in turn followed up a trio of 1990 OAV stories (two others were planned but canned). The premise is a prequel spin-off from *Bubblegum Crisis*, and the revival was largely due to the popularity of 1998's *Bubblegum Crisis 2040* series. Featuring decent animation and some nice action sequences, this DVD set should appeal to fans of both *Blade Runner* and *NYPD Blue*. Be aware that the first few episodes are a bit predictable, but it gets better as it moves along.

SPECIAL FEATURES Character and Art Galleries • Production Notes • Clean Credits • Other Title Trailers TECHNICAL FEATURES Fullscreen (1.33:1) • Subtitles/CC: Eng. • Languages: Jap., Eng. dub • Sound: Dolby Digital 2.0 • Multikeepcase • 2 Discs • Region 1 GENRE & RATING Science Fiction/Action • Rated 12+

Adventures of Cheburashka and Friends, The

Jove.

This DVD was not available for review. It is a Russian-language disc.

Adventures of Curious George, The

SVE/Churchill Media, 2000, 30 mins., #62164-DVD. Directed by John Matthews. Written by H. A. Rey, Margret Rey. Based on the books by H. A. Rey, Margret Rey.

Many people grew up reading the adventures of the monkey known as Curious George and his keeper, the Man in the Yellow Hat. Here are two of their stories, telling how the pair met and what happens when George has to go to a hospital. Along the way there are misadventures in Africa, on a ship, and in jail, plus encounters with firemen and a pack of balloons.

This DVD contains the 1983 episodes "Curious George" and "Curious George Goes to the Hospital," both directly adapted from their source books. The stop-motion puppetry works wonderfully for the fuzzy George, though the Man (and other humans) looks a little wonky at times. Animation queen June Foray narrates the tales, and a charming old five-minute featurette explains how armature puppets and stop-motion works.

A sweet delight for kids and their parents, this classic is only hampered by its lackluster CD case. The print quality is sharp and the colors are superb.

SPECIAL FEATURES "Making of" Featurette TECHNICAL FEATURES Fullscreen (1.33:1) • Languages: Eng. • Sound: Dolby Digital 2.0 • CD Case • 1 Disc • Region 1 GENRE & RATING Stop-Motion/Puppet/Family • Not Rated (All Ages)

Adventures of Fat Albert and the Cosby Kids Collection, The

Time-Life, 2002.

Time-Life has published nine DVD volumes of Bill Cosby's popular *Fat Albert and the Cosby Kids* series. The DVDs contain episodes not included on their corresponding VHS tapes. The titles are: *Fat Albert: Creativi-*

ty/Moving, Fat Albert: Fat Albert Meets Dan Cupid/Lying; Fat Albert: The Newcomer/Suede Simpson; Fat Albert: Tomboy/The Fuzz; Fat Albert: Stage Fright/The Hero; Fat Albert: The Bully/TV or Not TV; Fat Albert: Readin', Ritin' and Rudy/The Prankster; Fat Albert: Smoke Gets In Your Hair/Little Business; and *The Fat Albert Christmas Specials and The Fat Albert Halloween Special.*

These DVDs were not available for review.

Adventures of Ichabod and Mr. Toad, The [Gold Collection]

Disney, 2001, 68 mins., #19581. Directed by Jack Kinney, Clyde Geronimi, James Algar. Story by Erdman Penner, Winston Hibler, Joe Rinaldi, Ted Sears, Homer Brightman, Harry Reeves. Based on the books *The Legend of Sleepy Hollow* by Washington Irving, and *The Wind in the Willows* by Kenneth Grahame.

J. Thaddeus Toad is convicted of stealing a motorcar, and it's up to his friends—Mole, Rat, and Angus MacBadger—to find a way to prove his innocence! Then, Ichabod Crane is a schoolmaster who wants to woo the beautiful Katrina Van Tassel, but first he must face down the bully Brom Bones and survive the terror of the Headless Horseman.

This 1949 feature from Disney was released by RKO Radio Pictures. Although the two stories make an odd pairing, audiences were charmed by the film. Basil Rathbone sonorously intones the narration for the *Willows* segment, while Bing Crosby is the narrator for the *Sleepy Hollow* story. The film's original title was "Two Fabulous Characters." Both segments were later released as shorts: *The Legend of Sleepy Hollow* in 1958, and *The Madcap Adventures of Mr. Toad* in 1975.

The DVD is crisply presented with nice sound, and it features the bonus "Lonesome Ghost" cartoon from 1937 starring Mickey Mouse, Donald Duck, and Goofy. Another cartoon bonus is an Easter egg presentation of "Susie, the Little Blue Coupe" from 1952.

SPECIAL FEATURES Storybook • Sing-Along • Game • Other Title Trailers • Easter Egg TECHNICAL FEATURES Fullscreen (1.33:1) • Languages: Eng., Fren. dub, Span. dub • Sound: Dolby Digital 5.0 • Keepcase • 1 Disc • Region 1 GENRE & RATING Animals/Horror/Music • Rated G

Adventures of Little Mouse

The following Adventures of Little Mouse titles, from Facets, were not available for review: Adventures of Little Mouse [#1], Adventures of Little Mouse [#2].

Adventures of Mini-Goddess, The: The Gan-Chan Files [#1]

Pioneer, 2002, 100 mins., #11639. Directed by Yasuhiro Matsumura. Teleplay by Shoji Yonemura, Chinatsu Hojo, Atsuhiro Tomioka, Shinzo Fujita, Kazuaki Mori, Kiyotaka Isako, Minoru Senboku. Based on the manga series by Kosuke Fujishima in *Afternoon Magazine*.

Keiichi is a student who has some very unusual live-in friends; goddesses Belldandy, Urd, and Skuld, and their pet rat, Gan-Chan. When Keiichi leaves the house, the three magical girls shrink themselves down for fun and adventures, often at the expense of put-upon Gan-Chan.

There are a dozen shorts on this DVD: "Let's Tell a Fortune"; "Secret Treasure in the Attic (I and II)"; "Let's Fly in the Sky"; "Let's Fly into Space"; "Slimming Down! Go!"; "Gabira, the Giant Monster—The Birth"; "Gabira, the Giant Monster—The Final Battle"; "For Whom the Bell Tolls—The Mysterious Can of Food"; "For Whom the Bell Tolls—The Secret of the Diamond"; "Gabira, the Giant Monster—The Strike Back"; and "Let's Play Baseball!"

These shorts were originally produced in 1998, spinning off from characters established in *Ah! My Goddess!* By changing the goddesses into super-deformed versions of themselves, the animators were able to escalate the cartoonish silliness into *Looney Tunes*-esque territory. The series often spoofs itself, other anime, and aspects of Japanese pop culture (meaning that some jokes may be lost on American audiences). Viewers who can't tolerate cute are advised to stay away; those who can handle higher cuteness levels may have a lot of fun. Fans might want to watch the episodes a few at a time rather than all at once. Like most comedy shows, it's better viewed in small doses than as a marathon.

SPECIAL FEATURES Character Bios • Art Galleries. TECHNICAL FEATURES Fullscreen (1.33:1) • Subtitles/CC: Eng. • Languages: Jap., Eng. dub • Sound: Dolby Digital Stereo 2.0 • Keepcase • 1 Disc • Region 1 GENRE & RATING Fantasy/Girls • Rated 13+

Adventures of Mini-Goddess, The: The Belldandy Files [#2]

Pioneer, 2002, 100 mins., #11640. Directed by Yasuhiro Matsumura. Teleplay by Shoji Yonemura, Chinatsu Hojo, Atsuhiro Tomioka, Shinzo Fujita, Kazuaki Mori, Kiyotaka Isako, Minoru Senboku. Based on the manga series by Kosuke Fujishima in *Afternoon Magazine*.

NOTE: This DVD arrived too late for a full review. The following text is promotional copy provided by the releasing company:

"Whenever Keichi leaves the house, Belldandy, Urd, and Skuld shrink themselves to play with the other residents of the area—including their clueless rat sidekick, Gan. Whether it's a quest to start a rock band or adventures in baby-sitting, the goddess adventures are dangerously funny!"

This disc contains episodes #13–24.

SPECIAL FEATURES Character Bios • Art Galleries • Clean Credits • Insert: Mini Poster TECHNICAL FEATURES Fullscreen (1.33:1) • Subtitles/CC: Eng. • Languages: Jap., Eng. dub • Sound: Dolby Digital 2.0 • Keepcase • 1 Disc • Region 1 GENRE & RATING Fantasy/Girls • Rated 13+

Adventures of Mini-Goddess, The: The Urd Files [#3]

Pioneer, 2002, 100 mins., #11641. Directed by Yasuhiro Matsumura. Teleplay by Shoji Yonemura, Atsuhiro Tomioka, Shinzo Fujita, Tetsuo Tanaka. Based on the manga series by Kosuke Fujishima in *Afternoon Magazine*.

NOTE: This DVD arrived too late for a full review. The following text is promotional copy provided by the releasing company:

"Whenever Keichi leaves the house, Belldandy, Urd, and Skuld shrink themselves to play with the other residents of the area—including their clueless rat sidekick, Gan. Whether it's fishing lessons by Gan or the case files of Detective Skuld, the goddess adventures are dangerously funny!"

This disc contains episodes #25–36.

SPECIAL FEATURES Character Bios • Art Galleries • Insert: Mini Poster TECHNICAL FEATURES Fullscreen (1.33:1) • Subtitles/CC: Eng. • Languages: Jap., Eng. dub • Sound: Dolby Digital 2.0 • Keepcase • 1 Disc • Region 1 GENRE & RATING Fantasy/Girls • Rated 13+

Adventures of Mini-Goddess, The: The Skuld Files [#4]

Pioneer, 2002, 100 mins., #11642. Directed by Yasuhiro Matsumura. Teleplay by Michiko Yokote, Chinatsu Hojo, Atsuhiro Tomioka, Shinzo Fujita, Tetsuo Tanaka. Based on the manga series by Kosuke Fujishima in *Afternoon Magazine*.

NOTE: This DVD arrived too late for a full review. The following text is promotional copy provided by the releasing company:

"Whenever Keichi leaves the house, Belldandy, Urd, and Skuld shrink themselves to play with the other residents of the area—including their clueless rat sidekick, Gan. Whether it's life trapped in a jar of miso paste or the revolt of Urd's clones, the goddess adventures are dangerously funny!"

This disc contains episodes #37–48.

SPECIAL FEATURES Character Bios • Art Galleries • Clean Credits • Insert: Mini Poster TECHNICAL FEATURES Fullscreen (1.33:1) • Subtitles/CC: Eng. • Languages: Jap., Eng. dub • Sound: Dolby Digital 2.0 • Keepcase • 1 Disc • Region 1 GENRE & RATING Fantasy/Girls • Rated 13+

Adventures of Pinocchio, The

Liberty International, 2001, 90 mins., #LIP0100. Directed by Jim Terry. Story by Donald J. Paonessa. Written by Angelo Grillo. Based on the book by Carlo Lorenzini (aka Collodi).

Geppetto the woodcarver has fashioned a wooden puppet that he names Pinocchio and treats as his son. One evening, the magical blue Fairy Godmother appears to Pinocchio and promises to make him a real boy someday. Determined to become real, Pinocchio sets out for a series of adventures with his sidekick Timothy the Cricket along for the ride.

Although parts of this film will be recognizable to those who know the commonly told story of Pinocchio, the disjointedness of the rest of it—including circuses, mermaids, a beautiful young girl, and a Christmas snowstorm—will strike many viewers as odd. A clue might be found in the credits: this film is based on the Japanese anime series *Mock* by Kenji Yoshida, directed by Ippei Kuri. This implies that the product may actually be several episodes of the anime haphazardly stitched together.

The art style is certainly anime, although it is bad anime. Despite the cheery front cover, don't confuse this with the superior Disney film or the live-action 1996 New Line Cinema film of the same name. As for quality, this disc has one of the most horrible transfers I've ever seen in animation. It's full of digital artifacts. I'd suggest it only for hardcore anime fans who follow Yoshida or Kuri's work.

SPECIAL FEATURES None TECHNICAL FEATURES Fullscreen (1.33:1) • Languages: Eng. dub, Span. dub • Sound: Dolby Digital Stereo 2.0 • Keepcase • 1 Disc • Region All GENRE & RATING Fantasy/Family • Not Rated (All Ages)

Adventures of Rocky and Bullwinkle, The

Universal, 2000, 92 mins., #20927. Directed by Des McAnuff. Written by Kenneth Lonergan.

It's been thirty-five years since *The Bullwinkle Show* was canceled, and Rocket J. Squirrel (Rocky) and Bullwinkle J. Moose are bored of their cartoon existence in Frostbite Falls.

But when Fearless Leader (Robert DeNiro) figures out a way to bring his villainous henchpeople, Boris Badenov (Jason Alexander) and Natasha Fatale (Rene Russo) out of the 2D world and into the real world, Rocky and Bullwinkle must become 3D characters, too. Teaming with a female FBI agent (Piper Perabo), they have to stop the evil trio from zombifying the world with bad TV.

Rocky and Bullwinkle debuted in 1959 on ABC-TV, the creation of animation legend Jay Ward (with help from Alex Anderson and Bill Scott). The series of shorts were known for bad puns mixed with sophisticated satire, meaning adults loved the program as much as kids. Unfortunately, while the movie tries to replicate the humor of the original toons, it lacks much charm, due largely to DeNiro and Alexander's embarrassing performances, and the incongruous and unbelievable character that Perabo plays. There are some fun and funny moments—enough to watch it at least once—but one wishes that a "Director's Cut" had been put on the disc—one that cut out all the bad performances.

Look for film appearances by comedians such as Janeane Garofalo, Billy Crystal, Whoopi Goldberg, Carl Reiner, Jonathan Winters, John Goodman, and others, but the real treat is hearing the tones of the original Rocky—June Foray—once again provide the flying squirrel's voice. The CGI animation of the leads is integrated seamlessly, though seeing Rocky and Bullwinkle "in the flesh" takes a bit of getting used to.

SPECIAL FEATURES "Making of" Featurette • Cast & Crew Filmographies • Production Notes • Trailer • DVD-ROM Features: Voice-activated Interactive Features TECHNICAL FEATURES Widescreen (1:85:1 enhanced for 16x9) • Subtitles/CC: Eng. • Languages: Eng., Fren. • Sound: Dolby Digital Surround 5.1, DTS 5.1 • Keepcase • 1 Disc • Region 1 GENRE & RATING Live & Animation/Comedy • Rated PG

Adventures of Tom Thumb and Thumbelina, The

Buena Vista, 2002, 75 mins., #27498. Directed by Glenn Chaika. Screenplay by Willard Carroll. Based on the story by Hans Christian Andersen.

NOTE: This DVD arrived too late for a full review. The following text is promotional copy provided by the releasing company:

"For the first time ever, two tiny fairy tale legends meet in one fun-filled, action-packed musical adventure. Trying to find their way in a great big world, Tom Thumb and Thumbelina join forces and face towering odds in a remarkable journey to find their true home. When the comically conniving Mole King takes Thumbelina into his underground lair and tries to claim her as his wife, Tom must call upon his friends in the forest for a daring rescue. But Thumbelina already has escape plans of her own. It's nonstop laughs and thrills as Tom and Thumbelina find excitement around every corner in their search for family and others like them.

"Featuring a stellar cast of voice talent—including Elijah Wood, Jennifer Love Hewitt, Peter Gallagher, Bebe Neuwirth, Robert Guillaume, Jane Leeves, Emma Samms, and Jon Stewart—and six irresistible new songs, *The Adventures of Tom Thumb and Thumbelina* is a heartwarming story of courage, friendship, and belonging."

SPECIAL FEATURES Sing-Alongs • Other Title Trailers TECHNICAL FEATURES Fullscreen (1.33:1) • Subtitles/CC: Eng. • Languages: Eng. • Sound: Dolby Digital 2.0 • Keepcase • 1 Disc • Region 1 GENRE & RATING Music/Fantasy/Family • Rated G

Aeon Flux

Sony, 1997, 120 mins., #LDV49810. Directed by Howard E. Baker, Peter Chung.

Aeon Flux is a leather-clad sexy secret agent and sometimes assassin who faces clones, mind control, robots, and viruses in this surreal series. Adding to the weirdness is the almost complete lack of dialogue (especially in the shorts), and the propensity for the lead character to die at many a story's denouement. Originally aired as shorts on MTV's Liquid Television, Aeon Flux debuted in 1991 and garnered a half-hour series in 1995. This DVD contains four long episodes, four shorts, and one medium-length show.

This DVD was not available for review.

Affairs, The ☞ see Mature/Adult Section

Agent Aika: Naked Missions [#1]

U.S. Manga Corps, 2001, 120 mins., #2038. Directed by Katsuhiko Nishijima. Written by Kenichi Kanemaki, Katsuhiko Nishijima.

Where James Bond had his own kind of supergadgets, secret agent Aika Sumeragi has a superbattle bustier that's loaded with power. She's going to need every weapon at her disposal to stop Neena Hagen and her brother Rudolf from getting access to the Ragu, a source of energy that might have caused the sinking of Tokyo thirty years before. Aided by two sidekicks—and in competition with male agent Gust Turbulence—Agent Aika hopes to bust crime, literally.

The DVD contains two storylines in four parts: "Naked Missions" and "Lace in Space." Although this is an action-and-spy story at its heart, the "plot" is really only a MacGuffin. The real purpose of the series is to have as many panty shots, bra shots, and sexual posing as possible in the allotted time. The crotch-and-cleavage

angles become distracting, so much so that this could almost be the dictionary definition of gratuitous. Some nudity also peppers the series, but not quite enough to take it into the adult category. While this is a plus for some viewers, concerned parents should take note.

SPECIAL FEATURES Character Bios • Music Video • DVD-ROM Features: Art Gallery, Script, Cast, Reviews TECHNICAL FEATURES Fullscreen (1.33:1) • Subtitles/CC: Eng. • Languages: Jap., Eng. dub • Sound: Dolby Digital Stereo 2.0 • Keepcase • 1 Disc • Region 1 GENRE & RATING Action/Adventure/Cheesecake • Rated 16+

Agent Aika: Final Battle [#2]

U.S. Manga Corps, 2001, 90 mins., #2044. Directed by Katsuhiko Nishijima. Written by Katsumi Terahigashi.

Aika is back, along with busty sidekick Rion Aida, for more underwear-themed adventuring. This time out, they accompany Rion's father and an annoying boy to a beautiful island for rest and relaxation. Unfortunately for them, the female underlings of Hagen are out for revenge, even if their leader is gone.

More panties, more cleavage, and lots of girl-fights between Aika and the villains . . . most of whom are dressed in fetishistic paramilitary outfits. Three episodes complete the 1997 series.

SPECIAL FEATURES Trailer • Promotional Footage • Music Video • Clean Credits • Other Title Trailers • DVD-ROM Features: Art Gallery, Script, Cast, Reviews TECHNICAL FEATURES Fullscreen (1.33:1) • Subtitles/CC: Eng. • Languages: Jap., Eng. dub • Sound: Dolby Digital Stereo 2.0 • Keepcase • 1 Disc • Region 1 GENRE & RATING Action/Adventure/Cheesecake • Rated 16+

Ah! My Goddess: The Movie

Pioneer, 2001, 106 mins., #11638. Directed by Hiroaki Goda. Screenplay by Michiko Yokote, Yoshihiko Tomisawa. Based on the manga series by Kosuke Fujishima in *Afternoon*.

It's been three years since Keiichi Morisato met Belldandy, the goddess who granted his wish that she be his girlfriend. They live together, with fellow goddess sisters Urd and Skuld hanging around, as well. When Belldandy's old mentor, Celestin, appears on Earth, he casts an amnesia spell on Belldandy and disrupts the entire goddess network. Heaven is closed off, and Urd and Skuld must find a way to help Belldandy regain her memory. Plus, who is the woman known as Morgan Le Fay, and what is her motive?

Following a 1993 OVA series *Oh My Goddess!*, this film was in the works for years before completion in

2000. The title is different here: AnimEigo released the OVA series as *Oh! My Goddess!*, whereas Pioneer uses the traditional Japanese name of *Ah! My Goddess*. The DVD features a bonus episode of *The Adventures of Mini-Goddess*, "Let's Tell Your Fortune" (see entry for that series).

Although it's much easier to follow the film if you're familiar with the history of the characters in the manga or video releases, beginners will understand *Ah! My Goddess* if they just let the epic nature of the story wash over them. The cel/CGI animation and backgrounds are breathtaking, the sound design and dubs are excellent, and the characters are nicely fleshed out. One of few anime that deserves the hype around it, this is a nice DVD package for fans.

SPECIAL FEATURES Art Galleries • Trailer • Promotional Footage • Inserts: Mini Pencil Board, Liner Notes TECHNICAL FEATURES Widescreen (1.85:1 enhanced for 16x9) • Fullscreen (1.33:1) • Subtitles/CC: Eng. • Languages: Jap., Eng. dub • Sound: Dolby Digital 5.1, Dolby Surround • Keepcase with Cardboard Slipcover • 1-3 Discs • Region 1 GENRE & RATING Fantasy/Girls • Rated 13+

Akira ☛ see Mature/Adult Section

Aladdin and the Adventure of All Time

New Horizons Home Video, 2000, 81 mins., #NH20544D. Directed by Cirio H. Santiago. Screenplay by Craig J. Nevius.

Paige is a bookworm who would rather read than interact with people, a fact that bothers her grandfather, even though he owns a bookstore. One evening, Paige reads the story of Aladdin, unaware that it was rewritten by the evil Scheherazade eons ago after she took Aladdin prisoner. The magic lamp is brought forward in time, and it falls into Paige's hands, whereupon she brings Aladdin to the present. He is pursued by Scheherazade, who reclaims the lamp and disappears to hide it in the time stream. Aladdin, Paige, and a talking world history book named Wordsworth must find a way through time to stop Scheherazade before she rewrites history.

Although copyrighted in 1999, the songs in the film are all copyright 1994, so clearly some time had passed before the project was completed. Initially, the story steals bits from other kids movies: the bookworm kid and grandpa from *The NeverEnding Story*; the town song about the bookworm kid from *Beauty and the Beast*; and the fairy-tales-come-to-life sequence from *The Pagemaster*. But none of these familiar elements do a disservice to the plot, which hangs together nicely.

The animation is eclectic, with computer-painted backgrounds mixed with what appears to be CGI and hand-drawn animation. The style works well, with the exception of Scheherazade, who seems to have wandered in from another film. Given that Roger Corman is the producer, it's no surprise that the barely dressed femme fatale can't act, even in animation! None of the songs are groundbreaking, but they feature a nice array of Broadway talents, including Michelle Nicastro, Susanne Blakeslee, and Rick Logan, while E.G. Daily and Jim Cummings are among the comfortable voice cast members in the lead roles. This *Aladdin* doesn't measure up to Disney's, but it is an enjoyable filler for an afternoon.

SPECIAL FEATURES Producer Bio • Trailer • Other Title Trailers TECHNICAL FEATURES Fullscreen (1.33:1) • Languages: Eng. • Sound: Dolby Digital Stereo 2.0 • Keepcase • 1 Disc • Region 1–6 GENRE & RATING Fantasy/Family/Music • Rated G

Alice

First Run Features, 2000, 93 mins., #FRF909266D. Directed by Jan Svankmajer. Scripted by Jan Svankmajer. Based on the book by Lewis Carroll.

In her room, young Alice is startled when a taxidermized rabbit awakens, dresses itself, and breaks free of its glass enclosure. Alice follows the rabbit through a drawer in a desk, entering a bizarre world that leaves her feeling ever more trapped. Whether shrinking or growing, floating in a pool of her own tears or attending a horrific tea party, Alice keeps her wits about her. But what happens when the Red Queen orders that Alice be beheaded?

Czechoslovakian filmmaker Jan Svankmajer (aided by animator Bedrich Glaser) conjures up the most surreal vision of *Alice in Wonderland* ever put to film. Released in 1988, this combines a live-action girl with stop-motion puppets. But whether it's the rabbit constantly losing his stuffing every time he pulls his watch out of his chest or the mobile bird skull and skeleton creatures that try to evict an overgrown Alice from a house, the images are creepy and disturbing. Svankmajer's caterpillar is a sock come to life, which uses a set of false teeth and false eyes to communicate. At one point, Alice bursts out of her own chest after she's been transformed into a doll!

While *Alice* is definitely on the must-see list for mature audiences, those who show it to their kids do so at the risk of damaging their psyche . . . or at least giving them a nightmare or three. The DVD also contains a seven-minute short by Svankmajer called "Darkness Light Darkness." In this inventive and humorous tale, two green clay hands use body parts to build themselves into a man. With some clay genitalia, I suppose this could qualify as nudity, but if you survived *Alice*, you can handle this.

SPECIAL FEATURES None TECHNICAL FEATURES Fullscreen (1.33:1) • Languages: Eng. • Sound: Dolby Digital 2.0 • Keepcase • 1

Disc • Region 1–6 GENRE & RATING Live/Stop Motion/Surreal • Not Rated (Teens)

Alice in Wonderland [Collector's Edition]

Digital Versatile Disc, 1999, 50 mins., #175. Directed by Richard Trueblood. Screenplay by Paul Leadon. Based on the book by Lewis Carroll.

While studying her *Principles of Modern Calculus* book by a river, Alice gets bored and follows a white rabbit down his rabbit hole. She finds herself in a series of adventures, encountering the Cheshire Cat, the Mad Hatter and his tea party, the Queen of Hearts, and more familiar characters.

Produced by Burbank Films Australia in 1978, this adaptation of Lewis Carroll's 1865 novel *Alice's Adventures in Wonderland* is colorfully animated and nicely voiced, even if it does seem at times to have been designed by somebody who'd eaten a little too much of the caterpillar's mushroom (if you know what I mean). Not as good as Disney's perhaps, but not a waste of time either. As with other DVD releases, there is a bio of the author on the disc.

SPECIAL FEATURES Author Bio • Game TECHNICAL FEATURES Fullscreen (1.33:1) • Languages: Eng. • Sound: Dolby Digital 5.1, DTS 5.1 • Keepcase • 1 Disc • Region All GENRE & RATING Fantasy/Family • Not Rated (All Ages)

Alice in Wonderland [Gold Collection]

Disney, 2001, 75 mins., #14372. Directed by Clyde Geronimi, Hamilton Luske, Wilfred Jackson. Story by Winston Hibler, Bill Peet, Joe Rinaldi, Bill Cottrell, Joe Grant, Del Connell, Ted Sears. Erdman Penner, Milt Banta, Dick Kelsey, Dick Huemer, Tom Oreb, John Walbridge. Based on the book by Lewis Carroll.

Alice is daydreaming in a tree, talking to her cat, Dinah. When a white rabbit with a pocket watch runs by, she follows him into his hole where a cornucopia of adventures awaits her. She runs a dodo's race, listens to Tweedledee and Tweedledum recite "The Walrus and the Carpenter," eats mushrooms upon the suggestion of a hookah-smoking caterpillar, attends the Mad Hatter's Tea Party, and goes on trial after beating the Red Queen at a game of croquet.

Based on segments from both of Lewis Carroll's *Alice* books, Disney's animated version was released in 1951. Walt Disney had done a series of shorts in the 1920s called *Alice in Cartoonland* in which a live girl cavorted with cartoons. A 1937 Mickey Mouse cartoon, *Thru the Mirror*, also paid homage to Wonderland, and Disney planned a live *Alice* feature, registering the title in 1938

and announcing it for Ginger Rogers to star in during 1945. The following year however, the decision was made to make the feature animated, and although the designers had planned on using Sir John Tenniel's original book illustrations as models, they ended up adapting them into a more clear Disney style instead.

A live-action film was shot using most of the voice actors, from which the animation team worked. Five years and $3 million later, the animated feature was ready for release. Today, on DVD, it has been digitally remastered and the print is clean and sharp. Besides other extras, the disc features a black-and-white featurette called "Operation Wonderland," which was originally broadcast as a segment of NBC's *Ford Star Review* on June 14, 1951. The short contains some of the live footage, as well as pencil roughs. This DVD release is by far the best *Alice* of the bunch, and recommended for all families.

SPECIAL FEATURES "Making of" Featurette • Trailer • Storybook • Sing-Alongs • Game • Other Title Trailers TECHNICAL FEATURES Fullscreen (1.33:1) • Languages: Eng., Span. dub • Sound: Dolby Digital Surround 5.0 • Keepcase • 1 Disc • Region 1, 4 GENRE & RATING Fantasy/Girls/Music • Rated G

Alice Through the Looking Glass

Liberty International, 2001, 73 mins., #LIP0114. Directed by Andrea Bresciani, Richard Slapczynski. Written by Jameson Brewer. Based on the book by Lewis Carroll.

Set in modern times, young Alice goes into a fantasy world, but this isn't Wonderland. Instead, she has to make her way across Chessland, and every move she makes leads to an adventure . . . and sometimes danger. Along her travels, she meets a helpful jester, a centaur with attitude, a man made of newspapers, the arguing midget twins Tweedledee and Tweedledum, the dinosaur egg Humpty Dumpty, an aging knight in armor, and the Jabberwocky.

Fourth in the alphabetical line of *Alice* reviews, this 1987 feature has the most eclectic voice cast, including Mr. T, Phyllis Diller, Jonathan Winters, George Gobel, and Clive Revill. The designs owe nothing to any past *Alice* illustrations and are fairly generic. The DVD transfer is mostly solid with bright colors, but there's an odd ghosting/flutter to some of the movements that is likely a digital glitch instead of an animation problem. While it's appropriate for all ages, this production is going to be best for viewers under six, or older viewers who watch it in smaller doses.

SPECIAL FEATURES None TECHNICAL FEATURES Fullscreen (1.33:1) • Languages: Eng., Fren., Germ., Span. • Sound: Dolby Digital 2.0 • Keepcase • 1 Disc • Region 1–6 GENRE & RATING Fantasy/Girls/Music • Not Rated (All Ages)

Alien Adventure

Slingshot, 2001, 85 mins., #SDVD9264. Directed by Ben Stassen. Written by Ben Stassen.

The Glagoliths have come through space in their search for a new home, arriving at the rather uninteresting—or so they think—planet we know as Earth. Sending two of their ships down to investigate what they believe to be a typical city, they instead land at the yet-to-be-opened amusement park known as "Adventure Planet." After enduring a number of theme rides, will the Glagoliths decide Earth is too much fun or just right?

Originally presented as an IMAX large-format film, *Alien Adventure* was also shot in 3D with some live background plates. Thus, whenever the aliens are on the ride, viewers see what they see, which is rather like a roller coaster in a spectacular environment (arctic wastes, underwater, toyland, ancient Arabia, etc.). Although there is some narration, most of the dialogue is spoken in an alien language, so the slight story mainly exists to bring viewers along for the rides.

Transferred from digital files, the print on the DVD is unusually crisp and pristine. Extra functions give you the option of watching in 2D or 3D (if you have the correct kind of 3D glasses), and other supplementals give the background behind the project. The only downsides to the disc are that viewers are forced to watch the trailers to get to either the menu or the movie itself, and that the package does not come with its own set of 3D glasses (or even an offer to order them). Still, *Alien Adventures* is a zoomingly fun CGI ride with some cool visuals.

SPECIAL FEATURES "Making of" Featurette • Commentary track by Ben Stassen • Photo Galleries • Trailer • Electronic Press Kit • Option of 2D or 3D Viewing • Other Title Trailers TECHNICAL FEATURES Fullscreen (1.33:1 modified from IMAX ratio) • Languages: Eng. • Sound: Dolby Digital 5.1, DTS • Keepcase • 1 Disc • Region 1–6 GENRE & RATING CGI/Science Fiction • Not Rated (All Ages)

All Dogs Christmas Carol, An

MGM, 1998, 73 mins., #907034. Directed by Paul Sabella. Written by Jymn Magon.

The dogs at the Flea Bite Cafe are getting ready for Christmas, and holiday cheer fills the air, despite the ailment of poor Timmy, whose leg is in need of an operation. When bad-boy bulldog Carface Carruthers muscles his way into the cafe, he brings his humbugged Christmas-hating attitude with him. It's up to Charlie B. Barkin and Itchy Itchiford to earn their guardian angel stripes once again, by showing the scro-ogy Carface the error of his ways.

Third in the line of *All Dogs* features, this 1998 tale is an odd amalgamation of *All Dogs Go to Heaven* and Charles Dickens's *A Christmas Carol*. With each installment, this series gets a little less entertaining, but the mixture is still good for younger audiences. Older viewers will appreciate Bebe Neuwirth's villainous take as demon dog Belladonna, complete with spiked collar. The DVD features a sing-along that kids will enjoy, but it is no-frills otherwise.

SPECIAL FEATURES Sing-Alongs • Insert: Booklet TECHNICAL FEATURES Fullscreen (1.33:1) • Subtitles/CC: Eng., Fren. • Languages: Eng., Fren. dub • Sound: Dolby Digital 2.0 • Keepcase • 1 Disc • Region 1 GENRE & RATING Holiday/Animals/Music • Rated G

All Dogs Go to Heaven

MGM, 2001, 85 mins., #1001599. Directed by Don Bluth. Screenplay by David Weiss.

It's 1939 in New Orleans, and a German Shepherd that used to be a con man—er, con dog—finds out that although all dead dogs go to Heaven, he still wants revenge on the one that killed him. Returning to Earth determined to also make good on some of his past evils, Charlie B. Barkin and his sidekick, Itchy Itchiford, become guardian angels of a sort to orphan girl Anne-Marie. In the process, Charlie plans to show his double-crossing old partner, Carface Carruthers, the error of his evil ways.

During production of this film, Don Bluth moved his animation studio from Hollywood to Dublin, Ireland, where his animators created over 1.5 million frames for the camera! While the voice cast reads like an episode of "Burt Reynolds, This Is Your Life"—with Burt Reynolds, Dom DeLuise, Loni Anderson, and Charles Nelson Reilly—the vocal troupe all perform well together, injecting some humor into the songs by *Annie* composer Charles Strouse. The DVD has only a single extra and a pan-and-scan transfer, but kids adore the film, so it would make a good addition to parental libraries.

SPECIAL FEATURES Theatrical Trailer. TECHNICAL FEATURES Fullscreen (1.33:1, modified from Widescreen) • Subtitles/CC: Fren., Span. • Languages: Eng., Fren. dub • Sound: Dolby Digital 2.0 • Keepcase • 1 Disc • Region 1 GENRE & RATING Animals/Adventure/Music • Rated G

All Dogs Go to Heaven 2

MGM, 2001, 83 mins., #1001600. Directed by Paul Sabella, Larry Leker. Story by Mark Young, Kelly Ward. Screenplay by Arne Olsen, Kelly Ward, Mark Young.

The dogs from the first film are back, this time in modern-day San Francisco. When Gabriel's horn is stolen from Heaven, Charlie B. Barkin gets on the trail to retrieve it, aided by his trusty old pal, Itchy Itchiford, a foxy Irish setter named Sasha, and a runaway boy. But, it seems as if Carface Carruthers is up to some of his bad tricks again, and this time, he's not the only villain in town . . . he's teamed up with a demonic cat named Red!

This 1996 sequel was made without the participation of Don Bluth or his animators, and with all the voice actors changed except Dom DeLuise (Charlie Sheen takes over Charlie's voice). Although it fared miserably at the box office, the sequel has done better business on video, and is popular among the youngsters. Besides being offered as a single pan-and-scan DVD, the disc was also included as part of an early 2002 two-pack set, its keepcase shrink-wrapped back-to-back with *The Secret of NIMH 2.*

SPECIAL FEATURES Theatrical Trailer. TECHNICAL FEATURES Fullscreen (1.33:1, Modified from Widescreen) • Subtitles/CC: Fren., Span. • Languages: Eng., Fren. dub, Span. dub • Sound: Dolby Digital 5.1 • Keepcase • 1 Disc • Region 1 GENRE & RATING Animals/Adventure/Music • Rated G

Allosaurus: A Walking With Dinosaurs Special

BBC Video/Warner, 2001, 60 mins., #E1552. Produced by BBC and Discovery Channel.

Narrated by Kenneth Branagh, this 2000 special appeared in the U.S. on the Discovery Channel. Combining fantastically detailed CGI dinosaurs with live nature backgrounds, this follows an allosaurus from his birth to his death as a six-year-old. A secondary program titled "Big Al Uncovered" features scientists discussing the true story behind the discovery of the complete bones of this particular allosaurus—"Big Al"—in the northwestern U.S.

This DVD is highly recommended for anyone with any interest in dinosaurs, and it is appropriate for children and adults. It's much more educational than Jurassic Park, but loaded with just as much (or more) dino-fun! See also *Walking With Dinosaurs.*

SPECIAL FEATURES Photo Galleries • Storyboards • DVD-ROM Features: Sounds, Wallpaper, Stills, Icons, Cursors, Videos

TECHNICAL FEATURES Widescreen (1.85:1 enhanced for 16x9) • Languages: Eng. • Sound: Dolby Digital 2.0 • Foldout Box • 1 Disc • Region 1 GENRE & RATING CGI/Dinosaurs/History • Not Rated (Kids)

Amazing Feats of Young Hercules, The [plus "Young Pocahontas"]

UAV Entertainment, 1997, 65 mins., #40088. Directed by Skinny Wen, Bill Hutten, Ed Love. "Hercules" Story Adapted by Bill Schwartz. Written by Jan Strnad, Ken Koonce, Michael Merton.

Hercules has misused his mighty powers, so Zeus banishes him from Mount Olympus and orders him to perform four challenges to prove his worth. With his ferret companion, Hercules is soon fighting the stony Gorgon, the multi-headed Hydra, vicious winged creatures, and a huge snake that guards the golden apple. In a second storyline, young Pocahontas romps with the animals of the woods and meets the light-skinned newcomers to America's shore and the hunky Captain Smith.

At thirty-two minutes each, these films are meant to cash in on the bigger Disney releases of *Hercules* and *Pocahontas,* though these don't contain quite the charm of those films or the talent behind the scenes. Still, the animation is competent and the stories move swiftly, meaning younger viewers should enjoy them.

SPECIAL FEATURES Other Title Trailers TECHNICAL FEATURES Fullscreen (1.33:1) • Languages: Eng. • Sound: Dolby Digital 2.0 • Snapcase • 1 Disc • Region All GENRE & RATING Fantasy/Historical/Music • Not Rated (All Ages)

Amazing Nurse Nanako: Memories of You [#1]

Pioneer, 2000, 60 mins., #10437. Directed by Hiroshi Negishi. Story by Rasputin Yano. Original Story by Taro Mako, Takumi Tsukumo.

Dr. Kyoji Ogami is supposedly the world's leading surgeon, but he's also a semi-mad scientist who is involved in a government conspiracy of some sort. He plans to transplant the brain of his bouncy big-breasted nurse, Nanako Schichigusa, into the body of the Venus 2000, a cybernetic combat robot. But things don't always go as planned. . . .

This series seems to exist purely to be about breasts (and the occasional up-the-skirt shot). And while there is some plot shoehorned in around the bust-shots, it's hard to see the story with all the immature sexuality in the way. The OVA adventures do feature some decent animation (with a bit of CGI mixed in), and the sound is nice, but Nanako's high-pitched voice may grate on some viewers.

In the DVD menu, Nanako's breasts bounce comically every few seconds, just in case you didn't get the point(s) earlier. The disc features two 1999 OVAs: "Operation 1: The First Spiral" and "Operation 2: Memories of You." The first release DVD also contained an insert plastic stand-up of Nanako.

SPECIAL FEATURES Character Galleries • Promotional Footage • Music Video TECHNICAL FEATURES Fullscreen (1.33:1) • Subtitles/CC: Eng. • Languages: Jap., Eng. dub • Sound: Dolby Digital 2.0 • Keepcase • 1 Disc • Region 1, 4 GENRE & RATING Adventure/Comedy/Cheesecake • Rated 16+

Amazing Nurse Nanako: Fire-Crackers [#2]

Pioneer, 2000, 60 mins., #10438. Directed by Hiroshi Negishi. Story by Rasputin Yano. Original Story by Taro Mako, Takumi Tsukumo.

Dr. Ogami is back with more mad plans for heaving-chested nurse Nanako. This time around, the pair must contend with Mr. Hyde, who doesn't remember the murders he's accused of committing, but who is hiding a monster inside. Plus, Nanako must don a mecha battle suit for Ogami's exhibit at a high-tech weapons exhibition.

More fun with cleavage and panties—plus some mecha battles—make this a must-see for some fans. Others may take that as a warning. The DVD contains two more 1999 OVAs: "Operation 3: Psycho Patient" and "Operation 4: Fire-Crackers."

SPECIAL FEATURES Character Galleries • Trailer • Insert: Plastic Standee TECHNICAL FEATURES Fullscreen (1.33:1) • Subtitles/CC: Eng. • Languages: Jap., Eng. dub • Sound: Dolby Digital 2.0 • Keepcase • 1 Disc • Region 1, 4 GENRE & RATING Comedy/Science Fiction • Rated 16+

Amazing Nurse Nanako: The Last Spiral [#3]

Pioneer, 2000, 60 mins., #10439. Directed by Hiroshi Negishi. Story by Rasputin Yano. Original Story by Taro Mako, Takumi Tsukumo.

The conspiracy Dr. Ogami is involved in is finally revealed, and it has to do with him designing a super weapon for the government from alien DNA and cloning Jesus Christ for the Vatican! Plus, Ogami's rival wants to gain immortality. What part could the jiggly nurse Nanako play in these serious affairs, and what does she have to do with Ogami's mother?

Finally working up some plot, the series should per-haps have started with these final episodes and combined the previous four into a shorter form. Or gone in a comedic direction totally and dumped the conspiracy. Either way, the final two OVA episodes round out this DVD: "Operation 5: The Last Spiral [Former Part]" and "Operation 6: The Last Spiral [Latter Part]."

SPECIAL FEATURES Character Timeline • Character Galleries • Clean Credits TECHNICAL FEATURES Fullscreen (1.33:1) • Subtitles/CC: Eng. • Languages: Jap., Eng. dub • Sound: Dolby Digital 2.0 • Keepcase • 1 Disc • Region 1, 4 GENRE & RATING Comedy/Science Fiction • Rated 16+

American Pop

Columbia/TriStar, 1998, 95 mins., #19599. Directed by Ralph Bakshi. Screenplay by Ronnie Kern.

Four generations in a Jewish-American family are involved in the music business. From turn-of-the-century vaudeville through the big-band era, to jazz, folk, 60s rock, and finally punk, a multitude of musical styles are represented in the story, which shows the dark side of the industry, filled with crime, sex, and addiction.

Bakshi's 1981 film polarized fans and critics. Naysayers complained the movie was historically inaccurate, mocked punk, and tied too much of musical history together. Those who liked the film contend that its roto-scoped animation was expressive and gorgeous, the stories realistic, and the music sharply chosen. Singers and musicians whose songs are represented in the film included Benny Goodman, Ira Gershwin, Jimi Hendrix, Bob Dylan, Janis Joplin, Pat Benatar, Lou Reed, Jefferson Airplane, Lynrd Skynrd, Elvis Presley, Fabian, The Doors, and dozens of others.

SPECIAL FEATURES Trailer • Insert: Liner Notes TECHNICAL FEATURES Widescreen (1.85:1 enhanced for 16x9) • Fullscreen (1.33:1) • Subtitles/CC: Eng., Fren., Span. • Languages: Eng., Span. dub • Sound: Dolby Digital 3.0 • Keepcase • 1 Disc • Region 1 GENRE & RATING Music/Drama • Rated PG

Amon Saga

Manga Entertainment, 2001, 90 mins., #4073-2. Directed by Shunji Oga. Written by Noboru Shiroyama. Based on the manga series by Baku Yumemakura and Yoshitaka Amano in *Ryu*.

Long ago, the evil Valhiss killed Amon's mother. Now, Valhiss is the emperor of a city that exists on the back of a giant turtle, and Amon wants revenge. This white-haired warrior joins with a mercenary group and falls for the captive Princess Lichia, but every step he takes toward vengeance is dangerous. Amon encounters werewolves and other monsters, but even a stint in the dungeons won't keep him from stopping Valhiss.

Sword and sorcery fans will enjoy this OVA, but even they will have to admit that the plot sounds familiar, having been used in *Conan the Barbarian*, *The Beastmaster*, and just about every barbarian-with-a-sword film ever made (at least in the U.S.). Still, the film is not without its good points, including great visuals inspired by the manga work of Yoshitaka Amano (he also provides the stunning cover art) and some nice surreal action. The DVD picture is mostly good, though it blurs at times.

SPECIAL FEATURES Character Bios • Art Galleries • Other Title Trailers TECHNICAL FEATURES Fullscreen (1.33:1) • Subtitles/CC: Eng. • Languages: Jap., Eng. dub • Sound: Dolby Digital 2.0, Dolby Digital 5.1 • Keepcase • 1 Disc • Region 1, 2, 4 GENRE & RATING Fantasy/Sorcery • Not Rated (Teens)

Anastasia

Fox, 1999, 97 mins., #4112601. Directed by Don Bluth, Gary Goldman. Screenplay by Susan Gauthier, Bruce Graham, Bob Tzudiker, Noni White.

When the evil Rasputin causes the death of Czar Nicholas and his family, daughter Anastasia is spirited away. Years later and now a teenage girl who doesn't know her true past, the tomboyish Anastasia gets involved in the plot of two con men, Dimitri and Vladimir. They want her to pretend to be the long-lost Anastasia to get the reward offered by the Dowager Empress Marie, her grandmother. But even though Rasputin is dead, Hell can't hold him, and he intends to stop Anastasia in Paris and kill the last surviving Romanov.

This 1997 feature didn't score highly in theaters, but it is a beautiful and enchanting piece of work. Don Bluth and his animation team produced flawless character designs, gorgeous backgrounds, and fluid movement. They were abetted by lush songs from Lynn Ahrens and Stephen Flaherty and a score by David Newman, which netted the feature two Academy Award nominations and a pair of Golden Globe nominations. The voice cast, which includes Meg Ryan, John Cusack, Kelsey Grammer, Christopher Lloyd, and Angela Lansbury, is all excellent, with Hank Azaria taking top honors for his hilarious turn as a bat named Bartok. Although the story came under some fire for historical inaccuracy, critics seemed to miss the point that fantasy musicals are rarely realistic.

The DVD release includes lots of features for kids, but this is more than a children's film. Adults should find themselves laughing, crying, and singing along as well. One of Bluth's best films ever, *Anastasia* rates highly on the must-own DVD list.

SPECIAL FEATURES "Making of" Featurettes • Trailer • Game • Sing-Alongs • Other Title Trailers TECHNICAL FEATURES Widescreen (2:35.1) • Fullscreen (1:48.1) • Subtitles/CC: Eng. • Languages: Eng., Fren. dub, Span. dub • Sound: Dolby Digital Surround 5.1 • Keepcase • 1 Disc • Region 1 GENRE & RATING Historical/Fantasy/Music • Rated G

Angel Cop: The Collection ☞ see Mature/Adult Section

Angelina Ballerina: Rose Fairy Princess

Big Idea, 2002, 48 mins.

This DVD was not available for review.

Angel Links, Vol. 1: Avenging Angel

Bandai, 2000, 100 mins., #0985. Directed by Yuji Yamaguchi. Written by Jiro Takayama, Masaharu Amiya. Based on the book *Guardian Force Angel Links* by Hideaki Ibuki and the manga series by Takehiko Ito in *Young Jump*.

When Meifon Li's grandfather died, he left her in charge of the Links Group Corporation, a major company. His only requirement was that Meifon use the money to start a free interstellar service to fight space pirates, keeping safe those who can't afford protection. Meifon gathers together a ragtag crew including a human man named Losei Hida, a warrior woman named Valeria Vertone, and a hulking Dragonite warrior named Duuz Delax Rex. Using the ship—and her catlike creature Taffei that can transform into Meifon's battle sword—Mefion plans to clean up space and stop piracy!

This 1999 series spins off from the popular *Outlaw Star* show; the characters first appeared there (in "Law and Lawlessness," a segment rerun in this disc's extras). *Angel Links* features some nice action sequences and fun characters, though Meifon's enhanced chest will be reason enough for some viewers to watch. The DVD features the first four episodes, and it is complete and unedited (the version on the Cartoon Network has been edited).

SPECIAL FEATURES First Appearance Clip • Clean Credits • Other Title Trailers • Insert: Character Notes TECHNICAL FEATURES Fullscreen (1.33:1) • Subtitles/CC: Eng. • Languages: Jap., Eng. dub • Sound: Dolby Digital 2.0 • Keepcase • 1 Disc • Region 1 GENRE & RATING Science Fiction/Adventure/Comedy • Rated 13+

Angel Links, Vol. 2: Fallen Angel

Bandai, 2000, 75 mins., #0986. Directed by Yuji Yamaguchi. Written by Yasuko Kobayashi. Based on the book *Guardian Force Angel Links* by Hideaki Ibuki and the manga series by Takehiko Ito in *Young Jump.*

Meifon and the crew of the Angel Links are back again, fighting more pirates in the Oracian star system. This time out, Kosei meets a cute pirate girl, Meifon has a date and hides something in her past, and the secret origin of the Angel Links crew is shared.

Another trio of episodes is shared on this disc: "The Rain Upon the Stars"; "Crossroads"; and "The Angel and the Fallen Angel."

SPECIAL FEATURES Promotional Footage • Clean Credits • Other Title Trailers • Insert: Character Notes TECHNICAL FEATURES Fullscreen (1.33:1) • Subtitles/CC: Eng. • Languages: Jap., Eng. dub • Sound: Dolby Digital 2.0 • Keepcase • 1 Disc • Region 1 GENRE & RATING Science Fiction/Adventure/Comedy • Rated 13+

Angel Links, Vol. 3: Broken Angel

Bandai, 2000, 75 mins., #0987. Directed by Yuji Yamaguchi. Written by Yasuko Kobayashi, Jiro Takayama. Based on the book *Guardian Force Angel Links* by Hideaki Ibuki and the manga series by Takehiko Ito in *Young Jump.*

The lives of the Angel Links crew are becoming more entwined, meaning further complications. First, Meifon and Kosei face a Tao master when a shipment is stolen from just outside the gates of the Links Group. Then, Valeria gets an intriguing offer from an old military friend in the Einhorn Empire, and a plot against the Angel Links is hatched. And Meifon meets her uncle, but tragedy—and mystery about Meifon's future—waits just around the corner.

The third *Angel Links* disc contains three episodes. Unfortunately, episodes #8–9—"My Ship" and "A Pheasant Chooses Its Tree"—both feature shoddier animation than their predecessors. Thankfully, the final episode on this disc, #10, "The Ones Who Were Left," begins to answer all the questions about Meifon's past, present, and future, tying together all the episodes so far and setting the story up for its conclusion.

SPECIAL FEATURES Spaceship Footage • Other Title Trailers • Insert: Character Notes TECHNICAL FEATURES Fullscreen (1.33:1) • Subtitles/CC: Eng. • Languages: Jap., Eng. dub • Sound: Dolby Digital 2.0 • Keepcase • 1 Disc • Region 1 GENRE & RATING Science Fiction/Adventure/Comedy • Rated 13+

Angel Links, Vol. 4: Eternal Angel

Bandai, 2000, 75 mins., #0988. Directed by Yuji Yamaguchi. Written by Jiro Takayama. Based on the book *Guardian Force Angel Links* by Hideaki Ibuki and the manga series by Takehiko Ito in *Young Jump.*

Tormented by the revelations from the previous storyline, Meifon disbands the Angel Links group and hides away with Kosei in a small village. But the forces that have conspired against Meifon and her future won't wait, and she is drawn into battle and destiny once again. Meifon will have to face the evil pirate Goryu, but only one of them will walk away from the fight.

The *Angel Links* series wraps up with its final three episodes: "At the Binary Interval," "All My Soul," and "Fragment of an Angel." Although the middle episode feels a bit like filler, the bookend shows complete the "mytharc" for the series. The disc's main extra is a look at designs for the ships, with the viewer guided through the tour by a super-deformed version of Meifon.

SPECIAL FEATURES Art Galleries • Other Title Trailers • Insert: Character Notes TECHNICAL FEATURES Fullscreen (1.33:1) • Subtitles/CC: Eng. • Languages: Jap., Eng. dub • Sound: Dolby Digital 2.0 • Keepcase • 1 Disc • Region 1 GENRE & RATING Science Fiction/Adventure/Comedy • Rated 13+

Angel of Darkness ☞ see Mature/Adult Section

Angel Sanctuary

U.S. Manga Corps, 2001, 90 mins., #USMD2047. Directed by Kiyoko Sayama. Screenplay by Kiyoko Sayama, Kenichi Kanemaki. Based on the manga series by Kaori Yuki.

Organic Angel Alexiel, a fallen member of the seraphim, was cast out of Heaven for defying God. Her soul imprisoned in a crystal, Alexiel is endlessly reincarnated, always dying a painful death at an early age. But in the present day, she is reborn into the body of Setsuna Muda, a teenage boy who has a little trouble with the law. When Alexiel realizes that God is dead and that the world will be coming to an end, s/he must make a decision about whose side to join in the final battle between Heaven and Hell.

Although it sounds religious, this story only uses the Christian concepts of Heaven and angels for story purposes, not for any form of theological message. Some viewers might be bothered by the incestuous themes that pop up, and by the bloody violence perpetrated by the angels and demons. Androgyny is the name of the game for the lead characters, and homosexual themes crop up as well.

The DVD contains a good print of the three-episode OVA series from 2000, and the figural animation is sharp. Unfortunately, the backgrounds and props aren't always given as much attention, but with beautiful winged people and ugly golems/demons to watch, who really cares about the cars and buildings?

SPECIAL FEATURES "Making of" Featurettes • Character Bios • Character and Art Galleries • Production Notes • Trivia Game • DVD-ROM Features: Art Gallery, Credits, Scripts) • Other Title Trailers • Easter Egg TECHNICAL FEATURES Fullscreen (1.33:1) • Subtitles/CC: Eng. • Languages: Jap., Eng. dub • Sound: Dolby Digital Stereo 2.0 • Keepcase • 1 Disc • Region 1 GENRE & RATING Action/Adventure/Supernatural • Rated 16+

Angels in the Court ☞ see Mature/Adult Section

Animaland

Image, 1998, 69 mins., #ID4393CEDVD. Directed by Bert Felstead. Story by Reg Parlett, Peter Griffiths, Nobby Clark.

Nine short films spotlight the silly world of forest animals—and a few jungle ones—in this compilation film. Ginger Nutt, a stealthy squirrel, shares four of the tales, while creatures of the world engage in high jinks in the other stories. Titles for the eight shorts include: "The Australian Platypus"; "Ginger Nutt's Christmas Circus"; "Ginger Nutt's Forest Dragon"; "The Cuckoo"; "Ginger Nutt's Bee-Bother"; "The Lion (felis leo)"; "The Ostrich"; "The House Cat (felis vulgaris)"; and "Ginger Nutt in It's A Lovely Day."

Although there aren't any liner notes or text materials, a closer look at the eight-minute Technicolor films shows that all of them were made from 1941 to 1947 at a studio in England's Cookham-on-Thames. David D. Hand produced the series, working with British writers and animators. In previous years, Hand worked for the U.S. company Bray Productions in the 1920s and directed early Disney shorts throughout the 1930s. He was also supervising director on two of Disney's classic films, *Snow White and the Seven Dwarfs* and *Bambi*. It was during the time of *Bambi* that Hand began work on the shorts seen in *Animaland*. When a U.S. distribution deal for the cartoons fell through, the series was shelved.

Although they lack the wackiness of Warner's *Looney Tunes*, the *Animaland* tales compare favorably to some of the *Silly Symphonies* and other kid's toons of the period. The DVD transfer is mostly excellent, though the age of the material means it carries a certain grain. British animation—especially from this period—is rare in the U.S., so animation fans will want to pay close attention to this release. Parents who want something fun and non-offensive for their kids should pick it up as well.

SPECIAL FEATURES None TECHNICAL FEATURES Fullscreen (1.33:1) • Languages: Eng. • Sound: Dolby Digital Mono 2.0 • Snapcase • 1 Disc • Region All GENRE & RATING Animals/Comedy • Not Rated (All Ages)

Animated Hero Classics

The following *Animated Hero Classics* titles, from Living Scriptures, were not available for review: *Christopher Columbus* [#1]; *William Bradford—The First Thanksgiving* [#2]; *George Washington* [#3]; *Benjamin Franklin* [#4]; *Abraham Lincoln* [#5]; *Thomas Edison* [#6]; *Florence Nightingale* [#7]; *Pocahontas* [#8]; *Louis Pasteur* [#9]; *Alexander Graham Bell* [#10]; *Maccabees: The Story of Hanukkah* [#11]; *Harriet Tubman* [#12]; *The Wright Brothers* [#13]; *Helen Keller* [#14]; *Leonardo da Vinci; Joan of Arc; Marco Polo; Galileo; Marie Curie.*

Animated New Testament

The following *Animated New Testament* titles, from Living Scriptures, were not available for review: *The King Is Born* [#1]; *John the Baptist* [#2]; *The Prodigal Son* [#3]; *The Miracles of Jesus* [#4]; *The Lost Is Found* [#5]; *The Greatest Is the Least* [#6]; *He Is Risen* [#7]; *Jesus the Son of God* [#8]; *Bread from Heaven* [#9]; *Lazarus Lives* [#10]; *Lord, I Believe* [#11]; *The Lord's Prayer* [#12]; *The Kingdom of Heaven* [#13]; *The Good Samaritan* [#14]; *Saul of Tarsus* [#15]; *The Ministry of Paul* [#16]; *The Righteous Judge* [#17]; *Treasures in Heaven* [#18]; *Forgive Us Our Debts* [#19].

Animated Old Testament

The following *Animated Old Testament* titles, from Living Scriptures, were not available for review: *Abraham and Isaac* [#1]; *Joseph in Egypt* [#2]; *Samuel, the Boy Prophet* [#3]; *Elijah* [#4]; *Daniel* [#5]; *Esther* [#6]; *Moses* [#7]; *Elisha* [#8]; *Ruth* [#9]; *David and Goliath* [#10]; *Solomon* [#11]; *Joseph's Reunion* [#12].

Animated Stories from the Book of Mormon

The following *Animated Stories from the Book of Mormon* titles, from Living Scriptures, were not available for review: *Nephi and the Brass Plates* [#1]; *Journey to the Promised Land* [#2]; *Abinadi and King Noah* [#3]; *The Conversion of Alma the Younger* [#4]; *Ammon, Missionary to the Lamanites* [#5]; *The Brother of Jared* [#6]; *The Savior in America* [#7]; *Samuel the Lamanite* [#8]; *Helaman's Stripling Warriors* [#9]; *Alma and the Zoramites* [#10]; *The Tree of Life* [#11]; *Mormon and Moroni* [#12]; *The Joseph Smith Story* [#13].

Animation Greats!

Slingshot, 1998, 71 mins., #9812. Produced by the National Film Board of Canada.

While the use of the term "Greats" in the title lends itself to almost immediate suspicion, the eight toons presented on this disc are representative of some of the best offered by the National Film Board of Canada. Animation styles are all cel-drawn, with the exception of a live-and-stop-motion piece and a collage entry.

Regular attendees of *Spike and Mike's Festival of Animation* will recognize several shorts here, including "The Cat Came Back" (by Cordell Barker), "Blackfly" (an Oscar-nominated short by Christopher Hinton), and "The Lump" (by John Weldon). Stylistically similar to Tex Avery's Warner Bros. toons is "Get A Job" (by Brad Caslor). The other four titles are: "Special Delivery" (by Eunice Macaulay and John Weldon); "Getting Started" (by Richard Condie); "The Big Snit" (by Richard Condie); and "Juke Bar" (by Martin Barry). Whether you'll conclude these are great or not is up to you. If not, blame Canada!

Note: This was previously released from Lumivision (#DVD0497), and it is credited as one of the first three commercially released DVDs!

SPECIAL FEATURES None TECHNICAL FEATURES Fullscreen (1.33:1) • Languages: Eng. • Sound: Dolby Digital 2.0 • Large CD-Style Case • 1 Disc • Region 1–6 GENRE & RATING Anthology/Live/Puppet/Collage • Not Rated (Teens)

Animation Legend: Winsor McCay

Slingshot, 1998, 100 mins., #DVD9817. Directed by Winsor McCay. Written by Winsor McCay.

One of the greatest artists in comic strip history and a pioneer of early animation is Winsor McCay, best known for his creations of "Little Nemo in Slumberland" and "Gertie the Dinosaur." This disc collects every single animated work of McCay's, giving each one a deluxe restoration from original archival 35mm prints. Although the pictures are still grainy and scratchy, it's unimaginable that you'll ever see them more clearly.

The eleven shorts—some of which are fragments and not finished pieces—include: "Little Nemo" (1911); "How a Mosquito Operates" (1912); "Gertie the Dinosaur" (1914); "The Sinking of the Lusitania" (1918); "The Centaurs" (1918–21); "Gertie on Tour" (1918–21); "Flip's Circus" (1918–21); "Bug Vaudeville" (1921); "The Pet" (1921); and "The Flying House" (1921).

The disc contains extensive liner notes and historical material about McCay. To put it succinctly, this DVD is an absolute necessity if you're a serious film buff, animation fan, or cartoon historian. This early classic animation does indeed earn McCay the title of "Legend."

SPECIAL FEATURES None TECHNICAL FEATURES Fullscreen (1.33:1 window-boxed) • Languages: Eng. • Sound: Dolby Digital 2.0 • Keepcase • 1 Disc • Region All GENRE & RATING Anthology/Live • Not Rated (All Ages)

Anime Fiction ☞ see Mature/Adult Section

Anime Guide: 2002 DVD Catalog

Bandai, 2002, 55 mins.

This DVD catalogue was given out at conventions in the summer of 2002 with a keepcase cover. The disc includes previews of thirty Bandai titles (some of which have yet to be released), as well as some cool extras. One of those extras is a complete episode of the series *Arjuna*, while another is a complete and complex timeline following the *Gundam* Saga.

The disc was also included with each copy of *Newtype-USA #1* magazine (see entry), though there it was in a paper envelope, not a DVD keepcase.

SPECIAL FEATURES Gundam Saga Timeline • Distributor Information • Ratings Guide • Other Title Trailers TECHNICAL FEATURES Widescreen (1.78:1) • Fullscreen (1.33:1) • Subtitles/CC: Eng. • Languages: Jap., Eng. dub • Sound: Dolby Digital Surround 5.1 • Keepcase • 1 Disc • Region 1 GENRE & RATING Catalog/Fantasy • Not Rated (Teens)

Annabelle's Wish

Ralph Edwards Films, 1997, 54 mins., #DVD 10252. Directed by Roy Wilson. Written by Jane Baer, John Bettis, Ken Blackwell, John Couch, Gary Edwards, Bruce Faulk, Kathy Grover, Riki Hobin, Jay Johnson, Jamie Barton Klein, George Larrimore, John Lewis, Barbara Dunn-Leonard, Sheryl Scarborough. Based on a short story by Dan Henderson.

Annabelle is a calf born on Christmas Eve. As she grows, she wishes more than anything that she could fly like one of Santa's reindeer. Annabelle makes friends with a young mute boy named Billy and joins with others of the barnyard animals to keep Billy safe from the mean neighborhood bullies and a cranky aunt. Will Annabelle's faithful and unselfish acts cause Santa to grant her wish?

Originally aired on Fox TV on November 30, 1997,

this animated Christmas story is better known than I had anticipated. Almost everyone I knew who saw the disc immediately knew what it was, from youngsters to oldsters. Not quite old enough to be called a classic, this is still a heartwarming holiday musical that will be popular with families.

The voice cast includes Cloris Leachman, Jerry Van Dyke, Jim Varney, Rue McClanahan, and Clancy Brown, as well as Randy Travis, who sings some of the songs along with other country croonsters Alison Krauss and Beth Nielsen Chapman. Although the disc cover says it's 105 minutes, the feature is only fifty-four minutes, which is still longer than its aired length. There are also a host of extras to keep kids happy.

SPECIAL FEATURES Cast Interviews • Deleted Scenes • Read-Along • Games • DVD-ROM Features: Puzzles, Coloring Pages, Stories, Soundtrack TECHNICAL FEATURES Fullscreen (1.33:1) • Languages: Eng., Fren. dub, Span. dub • Sound: Dolby Digital Stereo 2.0 • Keepcase • 1 Disc • Region 1 GENRE & RATING Christmas/Family • Rated 4+

Antz [Signature Selection]

DreamWorks, 1999, 83 mins., #84199. Directed by Eric Darnell, Tim Johnson. Screenplay by Todd Alcott, Chris Weitz, Paul Weitz.

Z is one of thousands of ants that lives deep in an anthill. Each day, he and all his fellow worker ants perform the same tasks. But Z is beginning to develop a personality, and it's one that questions the status quo. When Z trades places with Weaver, his soldier ant friend, the timid insect not only finds himself wooing the beautiful Princess Bala, but also preparing for conflict under the command of the ruthless General Mandible. Z and Bala soon escape the colony and embark on a quest to find the fabled Insectopia, not knowing what plans Mandible has for the ants back home. . . .

Antz is the second all-CGI feature film released (following *Toy Story* and predating the similarly themed *A Bug's Life*). But although this DreamWorks film has some startling and realistic animation, the brownish bodies and flat carapaces of the ants really do all begin to look alike. The voice cast—which includes Woody Allen, Sylvester Stallone, Sharon Stone, Christopher Walken, and Gene Hackman—is first-rate. The actors often riff on their own "star" personalities in their performances.

The DVD is packed with lots of extras that will fascinate fans of the CGI process, and therein lies part of the problem that befell *Antz* in theaters. Unlike *Toy Story*, in which the technology to create it took a back seat to an all-ages fable, *Antz* reaches to appeal to a much older audience and seems at times to be all about showing off the technology. Given a choice, kids will likely choose *A*

Bug's Life, but *Antz* will appeal to adults because it is funny and hip.

SPECIAL FEATURES "Making of" Featurettes • Commentary Track by Directors • Crew Bios • Character Galleries • Production Notes • Trailer • Promotional Footage • Insert: Liner Notes • Easter Egg TECHNICAL FEATURES Widescreen (1.85:1 enhanced for 16x9) • Subtitles/CC: Eng. • Languages: Eng. • Sound: Dolby Digital Surround 5.1 • Keepcase • 1 Disc • Region 1 GENRE & RATING Insects/Comedy • Rated PG

Apocalypse Zero: Kakugo Complete

Anime Works, 2001, 90 mins., #AWDVD-0110. Directed by Toshihiro Hirano. Screenplay by Akiyoshi Sakai. Based on the manga series "Kakugo no Susume" by Takayuki Yamaguchi in *Shonen Champion Comics*.

Two extraordinary warriors are heading for battle in a postapocalyptic world where monsters of the flesh and mind prey on the surviving humans. Harara and his brother Kakugo have both been taught the fighting art known as "Zero Form." But when Harara turns to the dark side and creates an army of evil, Kakugo must find a way to stop his brother, with some help from his special Tactical Zero armored suit.

This two-part 1996 story is so filled with unrelenting gore that audiences may feel as if they truly are drowning in a river of blood and grue. Although some wispy morals about honor make it through the charnel-packed plot, *Apocalypse Zero* is meant to appeal mostly to fans of violence and perverse mayhem.

Despite its dark subject matter, the disc contains a clean print of the film, with the apocalyptic backgrounds easily visible and the slightly cartoony art crisp. But really, be sure you want the ultragraphic visions included here in your mind before you rent or buy it. This author is a horror fan, and some of *Apocalypse Zero* even grossed me out.

SPECIAL FEATURES Character and Art Galleries • Other Title Trailers TECHNICAL FEATURES Fullscreen (1.33:1) • Subtitles/CC: Eng. • Languages: Jap., Eng. dub • Sound: Dolby Digital 2.0 • Keepcase • 1 Disc • Region 1 GENRE & RATING Horror/Gore • Rated 16+

Appleseed

Manga Entertainment, 2001, 68 mins., #4079-2. Directed by Kazuyoshi Katayama. Screenplay by Kazuyoshi Katayama. Based on the manga series by Masamune Shirow in *Seishinsha*.

Following the devastation of World War III, the cyberpunk megacity of Olympus is a veritable utopia, controlled by a computer called Gaia. Synthetic humanoids known as "bioroids" roam the streets, and the real humans have started getting tired of Gaia's careful control of their lives. When terrorists plot to destroy the computer, Olympus's E-SWAT team is called in to help. But should paradise be maintained? That's the question on the minds of the lead characters, a mix of cyborgs, human police officers, and freedom-fighters/terrorists.

Masamune Shirow's detailed designs are greatly simplified in this 1988 OVA feature, but although the film seems a bit dated now, it mostly stands the test of time. The character designs and technology are sharp, and the animation and story style have definitely influenced manga and anime since *Appleseed*'s release. If you want to see some of Shirow's beautifully toned artwork, check out the cover (although the image is flipped, a fact that is glaringly obvious due to backward lettering on the police patch) and the menu screens on the DVD.

Viewers may want to give this a few viewings—not at all a chore, mind you—to get the complete story, part of the message of which is to question our own dependence on emerging technology. The dub used is the original British-produced track; many fans have complained that the track inserts a significant amount of profanity and verbal abuse that isn't in the original Japanese text. Unfortunately, the subtitles are very low on the screen, making them tough to read at times. Still, this is a seminal anime release, and—for now—this is the only DVD version.

SPECIAL FEATURES Character Bios • Other Title Trailers • Easter Egg TECHNICAL FEATURES Fullscreen (1.33:1) • Subtitles/CC: Eng. • Languages: Jap., Eng. dub • Sound: Dolby Digital 2.0, Dolby Digital Surround 5.1 • Keepcase• 1 Disc • Region 1, 2, 4 GENRE & RATING Science Fiction/Action • Not Rated (Teens)

Arc the Lad: Hunters and Monsters [#1]

ADV Films, 2000, 75 mins., #DAR001. Directed by Itsuro Kawasaki. Script by Akemi Omode, Manabu Ishikawa. Based on the video game series.

Elk is the youngest member of the Hunter's Guild and the last survivor of a tribe of sorcerers. Now he roams an apocalyptic world as a mercenary, joined in his adventures by the mysterious monster-controlling Lieza, and the warrior Shu, who raised Elk from childhood. Together, they're searching for the outlaw known as Arc the Lad, whom Elk believes is responsible for the destruction of his people. Along the way, Elk has an adventure on a hijacked airship and fights monsters known as Chimeras.

This 26-part series is based on the PlayStation role-playing video game *Arc the Lad* and *Arc the Lad II*. There's a bit of *Mad Max* in here, and some medieval touches, as well as traces of other sword-and-sorcery heroes whose

original purpose was to avenge the deaths of their families. The story is a bit underwhelming and predictable, but the character designs and animation are all very modern, given that this series was created in 1999. The first disc contains three episodes, although the packaging makes it hard to figure that out.

SPECIAL FEATURES Other Title Trailers TECHNICAL FEATURES Fullscreen (1.33:1) • Subtitles/CC: Eng. • Languages: Jap., Eng. dub • Sound: Dolby Digital 2.0 • Keepcase • 1 Disc • Region 1 GENRE & RATING Action • Rated 15+

Arc the Lad: Fireball! [#2]

ADV Films, 2001, 75 mins., #DAR002. Directed by Itsuro Kawasaki. Script by Yasuo Yamabe, Masaharu Amiya, Akemi Omode. Based on the video game series.

When the bounty on Lieza's wolf-monster Pandit is lifted, Elk thinks a trap is in the making. Pursued by the henchmen of the Mayor, the trio of Elk, Shu, and Lieza must plan a counteroffensive. But it seems that someone else is also planning on eliminating the evil mayor! After an aerial battle between a blimp and the mayor's car, Elk comes face-to-face with the man he's been hunting—Arc the Lad.

So, Arc is finally found. Too bad he's not very interesting. This second DVD contains three more episodes, but with the exception of some hints of things-not-being-what-they-seem with Arc, it might fail to hold much attention.

SPECIAL FEATURES Other Title Trailers TECHNICAL FEATURES Fullscreen (1.33:1) • Subtitles/CC: Eng. • Languages: Jap., Eng. dub • Sound: Dolby Digital 2.0 • Keepcase • 1 Disc • Region 1 GENRE & RATING Action • Rated 15+

Arc the Lad: Wanted! [#3]

ADV Films, 2001, 125 mins., #DAR003. Directed by Itsuro Kawasaki. Script by Manabu Ishikawa, Yasuo Yamabe, Akemi Omode. Based on the video game series.

Elk and Lieza have been stranded on an island until they can fix the airship, but they find an ancient robot that tells them about eons-old battles. The humans eventually return to civilization, only to discover that there is a bounty on Elk's head! It seems that the bounty is a ploy for the villains to strike at Lieza through her new friend and protector Elk and they dispatch an assassin to find them. The killer is a chimera named Gene, who used to be a friend of Elk's.

With lots of flashbacks and a bit of modern revelation, the story finally seems to be going somewhere, even if it's in a meandering way. This disc is a meatier buy, with five episodes on it, though still no significant extras.

SPECIAL FEATURES Other Title Trailers TECHNICAL FEATURES Fullscreen (1.33:1) • Subtitles/CC: Eng. • Languages: Jap., Eng. dub • Sound: Dolby Digital 2.0 • Keepcase • 1 Disc • Region 1 GENRE & RATING Action • Rated 15+

Arc the Lad: Alliance [#4]

ADV Films, 2001, 125 mins., #DAR004. Directed by Itsuro Kawasaki. Script by Masaharu Amiya, Manabu Ishikawa, Akemi Omode, Yasuo Yamabe. Based on the video game series.

Elk and Lieza attack the White House aboard the *Silver Noah* airship, then team up with Arc to travel to Smeria in an effort to stop the spreading Chimera Plan before it's too late. But the line between friend and enemy becomes even blurrier in Smeria; the priestess Kukuru clearly wants Elk, but can she be trusted? Smeria's current leader is Andel, but he's not afraid of manipulating others, and he often lets his assistant Clive do the dirty work.

The first two episodes of this disc mostly wrap up the first thirteen-part arc (so to speak), while the remaining three shows start a new storyline.

SPECIAL FEATURES Other Title Trailers TECHNICAL FEATURES Fullscreen (1.33:1) • Subtitles/CC: Eng. • Languages: Jap., Eng. dub • Sound: Dolby Digital 2.0 • Keepcase • 1 Disc • Region 1 GENRE & RATING Action • Rated 15+

Arc the Lad: Oath of Vengeance [#5]

ADV Films, 2001, 125 mins., #DAR005. Directed by Itsuro Kawasaki. Script by Akemi Omode, Masaharu Amiya, Yasuo Yamabe, Manabu Ishikawa. Based on the video game series.

In the battle against Andel, Elk loses his flame powers, but with the help of Arc, Andel is routed, and Sumeria is now in Arc's hands. The storyline switches again, as Elk tries to deal with the loss of his powers by aiding a blind girl and a soldier infected with Chimera. Plus, Shu returns, Clive kidnaps Lieza, and Andel is preparing to unleash something very evil....

The story from the previous disc wraps up quickly, and the next few episodes are filler, before the final plot comes into view. Still, the five episodes on this disc are probably the meatiest of the lot so far, even if the adventures lurch around a bit haphazardly.

SPECIAL FEATURES Other Title Trailers TECHNICAL FEATURES Fullscreen (1.33:1) • Subtitles/CC: Eng. • Languages: Jap., Eng. dub • Sound: Dolby Digital 2.0 • Keepcase • 1 Disc • Region 1 GENRE & RATING Action • Rated 15+

Arc the Lad: Day of Reckoning [#6]

ADV Films, 2001, 125 mins., #DAR006. Directed by Itsuro Kawasaki. Script by Yasuo Yamabe, Masaharu Amiya, Akemi Omode. Based on the video game series.

Clive plans to use Lieza in his plans to unleash darkness and horror upon the world, but things don't go quite as he planned. As Chimeras attack, Arc and Elk and their allies must find a way to stop Clive and the Lords of Darkness. But will goodness come at the cost of Lieza's life? Or will Arc make the ultimate sacrifice?

The *Arc* series wraps up with the final five episodes, and although the series so far has been a bit spotty, the finale wraps things up pretty well. The action sequences are nice and the animation is fun.

SPECIAL FEATURES Other Title Trailers TECHNICAL FEATURES Fullscreen (1.33:1) • Subtitles/CC: Eng. • Languages: Jap., Eng. dub • Sound: Dolby Digital 2.0 • Keepcase • 1 Disc • Region 1 GENRE & RATING Action • Rated 15+

Area 88—The Blue Skies of Betrayal

U.S. Manga Corps, 1998, 50 mins., #USMD1727. Directed by Eiko Toriumi. Screenplay by Akiyoshi Sakai. Based on the manga series by Kaoru Shintani in *Shoga Kukan*.

Shin Kazama has recently graduated from Yamato Airlines as a pilot, but when a friend takes him out drinking, Shin signs a contract he'll come to regret. Duped into joining the Asran Air Force for three years, Shin is sent to the Middle East to fight in their civil war as a mercenary. If he can bring down enough enemy planes, he can buy his way out of his contract. Meanwhile, his fiancée doesn't know what's become of Shin, and his "friend" is making moves on her—and Shin's job as a commercial pilot.

Although this 1985 OVA feature is a bit dated, it is still a high-water mark in technical design. The attention to detail on the fighter jets is remarkable, and the aerial combat sequences are spectacular. Beyond the tech, the characterization and story are extremely well done, examining the effect that war and combat has on a young pilot's psyche. Even the incongruously soft look of the humans works in context, giving them an innocence when compared to the ultradetailed weapons of war.

Oddly enough, only the first of four *Area 88* OVAs has been released on DVD. Let's hope that USMC releases the rest sometime soon.

Besides being offered as a single DVD, the disc was also included as part of a 2002 "Combat Pack" set, along with *Silent Service*.

SPECIAL FEATURES Character Bios • Battle Scenes • Other Title Trailers TECHNICAL FEATURES Fullscreen (1.33:1) • Subtitles/CC: Eng. • Languages: Jap., Eng. dub • Sound: Dolby Digital Stereo 2.0 • Keepcase • 1 Disc • Region All GENRE & RATING Aerial Combat/Action • Not Rated (Teens)

Aristocats, The [Gold Collection]

Disney, 2000, 79 mins., #19536. Directed by Wolfgang Reitherman. Story by Larry Clemmons, Vance Gerry, Frank Thomas, Julius Svendsen, Ken Anderson, Eric Cleworth, Ralph Wright, Tom McGowan, Tom Rowe.

When their well-heeled owner leaves them a great sum of money upon her death, it appears that Duchess (a pampered cat) and her three kittens, Berlioz, Toulouse, and Marie, will continue to live the life of luxury. Unfortunately for them, the butler is next in line for the inheritance, and he dumps the feline quartet in the countryside. With the help of rough-around-the-paws alley cat Thomas O'Malley, they make their way back to Paris.

This 1970 release was the first animated feature produced without any direct participation from the late Walt Disney (though he did approve plans for the pic). The voice cast is excellent, with Eva Gabor taking the lead. Disney tried to get Louis Armstrong to do the voice of the jazzy Scat Cat, but Scatman Crothers stepped in to perform instead. The plot moves nicely, and there is some fun jazz along the way. The DVD features a fine print of the pic, and some cool extras, including a "Music Appreciation" booklet for the liner notes.

SPECIAL FEATURES Trailer • Game • Read-Along • Other Title Trailers • Insert: Liner Notes TECHNICAL FEATURES Fullscreen (1.33:1) • Subtitles/CC: Eng. • Languages: Eng., Fren. dub, Span. dub • Sound: Dolby Digital Surround 2.0 • Keepcase • 1 Disc • Region 1, 4 GENRE & RATING Animals/Adventure/Music • Rated G

Arjuna, Vol. 1: Rebirth

Bandai, 2002, 75 mins., #2220. Directed by Shoji Kawamori. Screenplay by Shoji Kawamori, Sumio Watanabe, Eiichi Sato, Hiroshi Onogi, Kazuharu Sato.

NOTE: This DVD arrived too late for a full review. The following text is promotional copy provided by the releasing company:

"High school, archery club, and boys were the things that filled Juna's daily life. But when an accident leaves her clinging tenuously between life and death, fate intervenes as she becomes the sole witness to scenes of Earth's destruction along with humanity's reckless pollution of the sky, the Earth, and

water. It is here in which Juna is given a new chance at life and bestowed the powers of the Earth, a power she must wield in order to stop an evil bent on Earth's destruction."

SPECIAL FEATURES Interviews with Cast • Arjuna Dictionary • Promotional Footage • Isolated Score • Other Title Trailers TECHNICAL FEATURES Widescreen (1.78:1 enhanced for 16x9) • Subtitles/CC: Eng. • Languages: Jap., Eng. dub • Sound: Dolby Digital 2.0, Dolby Digital Surround 5.1 • Keepcase • 1 Disc • Region 1 GENRE & RATING Fantasy/Action • Rated 13+

Armitage III

Pioneer, 2002, 140 mins., #11485. Directed by Hiroyuki Ochi. Screenplay by Chiaki Konaka.

NOTE: This DVD arrived too late for a full review. The following text is promotional copy provided by the releasing company:

"Mars 2046: The murder of a celebrity reveals the existence of a secret 'Third Type' robot so intelligent and sophisticated that they can pass as humans. The continuing public slaughter of these 'Thirds' by the hate-spewing D'anclaude fans the anti-robot sentiments of the human population into a firestorm of hate and violence. Assigned to the case, Ross Sylibus and his partner Naomi Armitage uncover a conspiracy of government-sponsored murder and forbidden technology that threatens to kill them both—especially once D'anclaude discovers Armitage's secret: Armitage is a 'Third.'"

SPECIAL FEATURES Promotional Art Galleries • Other Title Trailers• Easter Egg TECHNICAL FEATURES Fullscreen (1.33:1) • Subtitles/CC: Eng. • Languages: Jap., Eng. dub • Sound: Dolby Digital 2.0 • Keepcase • 1 Disc • Region 1, 4 GENRE & RATING Science Fiction/Action • Rated 16+

Armitage III: Poly-Matrix the Movie

Pioneer, 1997, 90 mins., #PIDA-1370V. Directed by Hiroyuki Ochi. Written by Chiaki Konaka.

By the year 2179, Mars has been colonized by Earth, and the huge city of Saint Lowell straddles the Marineris Trench on the red planet. Living there are humans, as well as "Second Type" robots that perform menial labor tasks. Although they're illegal, there are also "Third Type" robots among the populace, and they're almost identical to real humans. When a man named Rene D'anclaude declares war on the Thirds, bodies begin piling up. Cop Ross Sylibus—who hates robots because one killed his last partner—is assigned to work with Naomi Armitage to stop D'anclaude's killing spree. What he doesn't know yet is that she is also a Third, so her battle is personal. Then tragedy strikes Ross, bringing him closer than he ever wanted to be to the collision of man and machine.

This is a solid cyberpunk action feature, with a touch of romance, and some philosophical underpinnings about the nature of humanity and its relation to technology. With echoes of both *Blade Runner* and *Total Recall*, the technical and character designs are very strong and nicely detailed, though the animation is a little stiff at times. There is quite a bit of violence, and some nudity, so it isn't appropriate for kids. The dub version includes the voices of Kiefer Sutherland as Ross and Elizabeth Berkley as Naomi, and they do a credible job.

The movie version is cut together from four episodes of the OVA series, meaning almost thirty minutes of material is missing. An all-new ending was created as well, which differed significantly from the original. It was also given a letterbox treatment by adding black bands at the top and bottom, thus cutting off some of the original picture. The disc contains cool menus but not many extras.

Pioneer rereleased *Armitage III* in August 2002, packaged along with the sequel, *Armitage III: Dual Matrix*.

SPECIAL FEATURES Crew Bios • Trailer. TECHNICAL FEATURES Widescreen (1:85:1, altered from original 1.33:1) • Subtitles/CC: Jap., Eng.) • Languages: Jap., Eng. dub • Sound: Dolby Digital Surround 5.1 • Keepcase • 1 Disc • Region 1, 4 GENRE & RATING Science Fiction • Not Rated (Teens)

Armitage III: Poly-Matrix/Armitage: Dual Matrix [2-Disc Set]

Pioneer, 2002, 180 mins., #11688.

This multikeepcase set includes the *Armitage III: Poly-Matrix* and *Armitage: Dual Matrix—Special Edition* discs exactly as they appeared in the individual editions. See individual entries for the Special and Technical Features listings.

TECHNICAL FEATURES Multikeepcase • 2 Discs • Region 1 GENRE & RATING Science Fiction/Action • Rated 16+

Armitage: Dual Matrix

Pioneer, 2002, 90 mins., #11687. Directed by Katsuhito Akiyama. Screenplay by Hideki Kakinuma, Satoshi Wada, Naoko Hasegawa.

NOTE: This DVD arrived too late for a full review. The following text is promotional copy provided by the releasing company:

"The Bad Girl Returns! Naomi Armitage (voiced by Juliette Lewis) and Ross Sylibus have changed their names and live with their daughter Yoko as a happy and normal family on Mars—until a robot riot breaks out at an antimatter plant on Earth. Armitage learns the riot is a plot to suppress evidence of illegal research and development of more 'Third Robots' and decides to go to Earth to find out who is behind this heinous act. What Armitage discovers is the most powerful enemy she has ever encountered—replicas of herself!"

SPECIAL FEATURES Other Title Trailers • Inserts: Liner Notes • Easter Egg TECHNICAL FEATURES Fullscreen (1.33:1) • Subtitles/CC: Eng. • Languages: Jap., Eng. dub • Sound: Dolby Digital Surround 5.1 • Keepcase • 1 Disc • Region 1, 4 GENRE & RATING Science Fiction/Action • Rated 16+

Armitage: Dual Matrix—Special Edition

Pioneer, 2002, 90 mins., #11708. Directed by Katsuhito Akiyama. Screenplay by Hideki Kakinuma, Satoshi Wada, Naoko Hasegawa.

This Special Edition version of the *Armitage: Dual Matrix* disc features a host of extras, including an isolated score, behind the scenes footage, and a cool art-filled booklet. It also features an eye-catching chrome cover.

SPECIAL FEATURES "Making of" Featurette • Character and Art Galleries • Trailer • Isolated Soundtrack • Other Title Trailers • Inserts: Booklet • Easter Egg TECHNICAL FEATURES Fullscreen (1.33:1) • Subtitles/CC: Eng. • Languages: Jap., Eng. dub • Sound: Dolby Digital Surround 5.1 • Keepcase • 1 Disc • Region 1, 4 GENRE & RATING Science Fiction/Action • Rated 16+

Armored Trooper Votoms

In the Astragius Galaxy, warring star systems have been in conflict for years. One of the soldiers in the war is Chirico Cuvie, a young special forces power-armor mecha pilot on the verge of burn-out. He's been bred to be a Perfect Soldier, but as the war winds down, Chirico finds himself questioning his past, present, and future. He isn't a machine, but he doesn't feel strictly human. Assigned to engage in some espionage, Chirico is separated from his unit and thrown into a galaxy of danger and chaos, where robotic gladiator battles, slavery, and torture are in his future. Through it all, he is haunted by the image of a mysterious bald woman, but he has no clue who she is or what she means to him.

The *Votoms* story began in 1983 as a 52-episode television series (represented in this DVD series). Three hour-long OVAs were released from 1985 to 1987, followed in 1994 by a four-part half-hour OVA series that was set three decades after the original. A 1988 TV series sequel followed, introducing an entirely new cast. The original mecha designs by Kunio Okawara were functional, gritty, and realistic, while the storyline treated the robot soldiers as weaponry manipulated by the military or politicians. "VOTOMS" is an acronym for Vertical One-man Tank for Offensive Maneuvers.

The following *Armored Troopers Votoms* titles, from NuTech, were not available for review (NuTech catalogue numbers are in parentheses): *Stage 1—Uoodo City Vol. 1* (#187); *Stage 1—Uoodo City Vol. 2* (#188); *Stage 1—Uoodo City Vol. 3* (#189); *Stage 1—Uoodo City Vol. 4* (#190); *Stage 1—Uoodo City* [Box Set #1–4] (#203); *Stage 2—Kummen Jungle Wars Vol. 1* (#191); *Stage 2— Kummen Jungle Wars Vol. 2* (#192); *Stage 2—Kummen Jungle Wars Vol. 3* (#193); *Stage 2—Kummen Jungle Wars Vol. 4* (#194); *Stage 2—Kummen Jungle Wars* [Box Set #1–4] (#204); *Stage 3—Deadworld Sunsa Vol. 1* (#195); *Stage 3—Deadworld Sunsa Vol. 2* (#196); *Stage 3—Deadworld Sunsa Vol. 3* (#197); *Stage 3—Deadworld Sunsa Vol. 4* (#198); *Stage 3—Deadworld Sunsa* [Box Set #1–4] (#205); *Stage 4—God Planet Quent Vol. 1* (#199); *Stage 4—God Planet Quent Vol. 2* (#200); *Stage 4—God Planet Quent Vol. 3* (#201); *Stage 4—God Planet Quent Vol. 4* (#202); *Stage 4—God Planet Quent* [Box Set #1–4] (#206).

Around the World in 80 Days [Collector's Edition]

Digital Versatile Disc, 2000, 48 mins., #176. Screenplay by Leonard Lee. Based on the book by Jules Verne.

Adventurer Phileas Fogg sets off in a balloon with his manservant, Jean Passepartout, to explore the world. But as they visit Cairo, Bombay, and Hong Kong, a detective from Scotland Yard pursues them, believing Fogg is a bank robber. Much adventuring ensues, as boat, train, elephant, and other conveyances take the trio around the world.

This adaptation of Jules Verne's 1872 novel was produced by Burbank Films Australia in the mid-1980s. The print doesn't include a director's credit, and I'm not surprised. Almost devoid of charm, and animated with anthropomorphic animals instead of humans, this version is a disappointment. It's not horrible, but neither is it good, and the monkey/pig creature used as Passepartout's design will likely offend anyone with French ancestry. Better animated versions of this story exist (including another Australian-animated series from 1973), though none are available on DVD. The DVD does include a biographical section on Verne's life, but it's not enough to recommend this.

SPECIAL FEATURES Author Bio • Game TECHNICAL FEATURES Fullscreen (1.33:1) • Languages: Eng. • Sound: Dolby Digital 5.1, DTS 5.1 • Keepcase • 1 Disc • Region All GENRE & RATING Historical/Adventure/Animals • Not Rated (All Ages)

Art and Jazz in Animation: The Cosmic Eye

Image, 1999, 245 mins., #ID4709LYDVD. Directed by Faith and John Hubley.

This collection of 12 short films produced by the husband-and-wife team of Faith and John Hubley is an expressionistic lot, showcasing a wide range of animation and musical styles. The longest segment is "The Cosmic Eye" (71 mins., 1985), produced by Faith, in which a trio of alien musicians discuss their view of Earth's diverse cultures. Musicians and actors used for this include Dizzy Gillespie, Maureen Stapleton, Benny Carter, and others.

Three longer shorts include: "Voyage to Next" (10 mins., 1974), an Academy Award–nominated project; "Of Men and Demons" (10 mins., 1969), in which a farmer's life is disrupted by nature, with a score by Quincy Jones; and "The Hole" (15 mins., 1962), a whimsical discussion of life from the improvised dialogue of Dizzie Gillespie and George Mathews. This latter short was an Academy Award winner.

Eight other shorts are included on the disc: "Tender Game" (6 mins., 1958, with music by Ella Fitzgerald); "Eggs" (10 mins., 1970); "Urbanissimo" (6 mins., 1966); "Harlem Wednesday" (10 mins., 1958); "The Adventures of ★" (10 mins., 1957); "The Hat" (18 mins., 1964, with music and voice by Dizzy Gillespie and Dudley Moore); "Dig" (25 mins., 1972); and "Of Stars and Men" (53 mins., 1962).

This overstuffed disc is a tremendous bargain for both jazz and experimental animation lovers. Fans should look for further Hubley work under "The Hubley Collection" listings.

SPECIAL FEATURES Liner Notes TECHNICAL FEATURES Fullscreen (1.33:1) • Languages: Eng. • Sound: Dolby Digital Mono 1.0 • Snapcase • 1 Disc • Region 1–6 GENRE & RATING Anthology/ Music • Not Rated (All Ages)

Arthur's Best School Days

Sony Wonder, 2002, 40 mins., #LVD 55395. Directed by Greg Baily. Written by Ken Scarborough. Based on the children's books by Marc Brown.

NOTE: This DVD arrived too late for a full review. The following text is promotional copy provided by the releasing company:

"Join Arthur, D.W., and all their pals in a fun-filled animated series based on Mark Brown's best-selling children's books. In 'Arthur and the Square Dance,' does Francine have a crush on Arthur? That's what Binky thinks, and soon even Arthur is beginning to wonder. Can Arthur avoid Francine, and her cooties, for the rest of his life? In 'Team Trouble,' Arthur, Francine, and Buster have to do a report on ancient Rome, but can they work as a team to complete the assignment? And in 'Buster Hits the Books,' Buster has one week to finish a whole, entire book—with CHAPTERS—and write about it! Since he's gotten through school without ever reading a book will he live to tell the tale?"

Note that although the disc cover claims it is closed captioned, it is not.

SPECIAL FEATURES Other Title Trailers TECHNICAL FEATURES Fullscreen (1.33:1) • Languages: Eng. • Sound: Dolby Digital • Keepcase • 1 Disc • Region 1 GENRE & RATING Animal/Family • Not Rated (Kids)

Arthur Goes to the Doctor

Sony Wonder, 2002, 40 mins., #LVD 55396. Directed by Greg Baily. Written by Ken Scarborough. Based on the children's books by Marc Brown.

NOTE: This DVD arrived too late for a full review. The following text is promotional copy provided by the releasing company:

"Join Arthur, D.W., and all their pals in a fun-filled animated series based on Mark Brown's best-selling children's books. In 'Arthur's Knee,' Arthur's hurt his knee but he won't tell his mom because then she'd know he'd been playing down at the dump (where he was not allowed to go). Can the Brain and D.W. convince Arthur to face up to it and take his tetanus shot like a man—umm, an aardvark? In 'Buster's Breathless,' will Buster's friends ever treat him the same after they learn that he has asthma? Find out on a guided tour through Buster's lungs! And in 'The Lousy Week,' an army of lice has descended upon the heads of Lakewood Elementary. Who or what is strong enough to defeat them? Principal Haney? Nurse Flynn? Mayonnaise?"

Note that although the disc cover claims it is closed captioned, it is not.

SPECIAL FEATURES Other Title Trailers TECHNICAL FEATURES Fullscreen (1.33:1) • Languages: Eng. • Sound: Dolby Digital • Keepcase • 1 Disc • Region 1 GENRE & RATING Animal/Family • Not Rated (Kids)

Arthur's Great Summer

Sony Wonder, 2002, 40 mins., #LVD 54216. Directed by Greg Baily. Written by Ken Scarborough, Joe Fallon.

NOTE: This DVD arrived too late for a full review. The following text is promotional copy provided by the releasing company:

"Join Arthur, D.W., and all their

pals in a fun-filled animated series based on Marc Brown's best-selling children's books. In ' Arthur Goes to Camp,' Arthur and his friends go to sleepaway camp where it's strictly The Boys vs. The Girls. In all of their contests, who will come out the winner? In 'The Shore Thing,' Arthur and D.W. beg their Dad to take them to Aqualand, the coolest water park ever! He says that he knows an even better place: Ocean Zone. How cool can it be if Arthur and D.W. haven't even heard of it? And in 'The Short Quick Summer,' Arthur is shocked to find that summer vacation is over when it seems like it just started! What about all of those great, fun things he intended to do?"

Note that although the disc cover claims it is closed captioned, it is not.

SPECIAL FEATURES Other Title Trailers TECHNICAL FEATURES Fullscreen (1.33:1) • Languages: Eng. • Sound: Dolby Digital • Keepcase • 1 Disc • Region 1 GENRE & RATING Animal/Family • Not Rated (Kids)

Arthur's Perfect Christmas

Sony Wonder, 2002, 60 mins., #LVD 55399. Directed by Greg Baily. Written by Peter K. Hirsch. Based on the children's books by Marc Brown.

NOTE: This DVD arrived too late for a full review. The following text is promotional copy provided by the releasing company:

"This hour-long special finds Arthur, D.W., and their friends and family frantically making preparations for 'the perfect holiday season,' including perfect gifts, perfect parties, and perfect family traditions for Christmas, Hanukkah, and Kwanzaa. Arthur soon discovers, however, that perfection is hard to come by, and that the joy of Christmas isn't found in an artificial vision of the 'perfect holiday,' but in the wonderfully imperfect world in which he lives."

Note that although the disc cover claims it is closed captioned, it is not.

SPECIAL FEATURES Other Title Trailers TECHNICAL FEATURES Fullscreen (1.33:1) • Languages: Eng. • Sound: Dolby Digital • Keepcase • 1 Disc • Region 1 GENRE & RATING Holiday/Animal/ Family • Not Rated (Kids)

Arthur's Scary Stories

Sony Wonder, 2002, 40 mins., #LVD 55391. Directed by Greg Baily. Written by Ken Scarborough, Joe Fallon. Based on the children's books by Marc Brown.

NOTE: This DVD arrived too late for a full review. The following text is promotional copy provided by the releasing company:

"Join Arthur, D.W., and all their pals in a fun-filled animated series based on Marc Brown's best-selling children's books. In 'Night Fright,' big, brave Binky Barnes would be toast if people ever discovered he can't sleep without a night light. It's his deepest, darkest secret. When Arthur spends the night, and discovers the truth, Binky has no choice but to try bribery. In 'What Scared Sue Ellen?' Sue Ellen's not afraid of much, but when she encounters a really creepy, howling noise in the woods, she's scared for real. She gathers the gang for a show-down. Will they face their fears and learn the source of the mysterious howls? And in 'The Fright Stuff,' prankster poltergeists have arrived in Elwood City—and just in time for the 'Scare Your Pants Off' costume party! It's boys versus girls in what becomes a great big battle of pranks, until the kids learn a lesson about practical jokes—from a spooky source."

Note that although the disc cover claims it is closed captioned, it is not.

SPECIAL FEATURES Other Title Trailers TECHNICAL FEATURES Fullscreen (1.33:1) • Languages: Eng. • Sound: Dolby Digital • Keepcase • 1 Disc • Region 1 GENRE & RATING Animal/Family • Not Rated (Kids)

Arthur: The Good Sport

Sony Wonder, 2002, 40 mins., #LVD 54217. Directed by Greg Baily. Based on the children's books by Marc Brown.

NOTE: This DVD arrived too late for a full review. The following text is promotional copy provided by the releasing company:

"Join Arthur, D.W., and all their pals in a fun-filled animated series based on Marc Brown's best-selling children's books. In 'The Good Sport,' when the Athlete of the Year Award doesn't go to Francine, she makes no effort to hide her hurt feelings from Jenna, the recipient. Michelle Kwan, world champion figure skater and graduate of Lakewood Elementary, guest stars to teach Francine about being a good sport. In 'Muffy's Soccer Shocker,' Muffy's proud that her dad is the new soccer coach until he exhausts the team with demanding drills like the shock absorber! Even if Muffy survives playing goalie in the big game, will the team survive her dad? And in 'Francine Frensky, Olympic Rider,' all her life, Francine has dreamed of owning a horse. Her secret goal is to be an Olympic equestrienne but first she has to learn to ride!"

Note that although the disc cover claims it is closed captioned, it is not.

SPECIAL FEATURES Other Title Trailers TECHNICAL FEATURES Fullscreen (1.33:1) • Languages: Eng. • Sound: Dolby Digital • Keepcase • 1 Disc • Region 1 GENRE & RATING Animal/Family • Not Rated (Kids)

Art of Fighting

Image/U.S. Manga Corps, 1998, 46 mins., #ID4413CTDVD. Directed by Hiroshi Fukutomi. Screenplay by Nobuaki Kishima. Based on the video game.

Robert and Ryo are out looking for a lost cat when they witness something they wish they hadn't, a mob hit. Now the mob is after them and will do anything to erase these witnesses—permanently. Mr. Big kidnaps Ryo's sister and offers the two men a way to stay alive. If they can find a diamond that the murdered man was hiding, they'll be free. But Rob and Ryo have no clue where the diamond is, so their only choice is to go on the offensive against the mob and Mr. Big's best assassin, the beautiful King.

Adapted from a video game, the tone of this is supposed to be serious, but it comes off as silly much of the time. Even the music sounds like a bad seventies TV show (and at times like the theme to *Saturday Night Live!*). The fight scenes aren't nearly as complex or effects-heavy as the game, so those expecting slam-bang action will only get the "slam" part. In addition to the weak story, the colors in this disc are rather flat and uninspired. There are better—and artier—fight discs to be found.

SPECIAL FEATURES None TECHNICAL FEATURES Fullscreen (1.33:1) • Subtitles/CC: Eng. • Languages: Jap., Eng. dub • Sound: Dolby Digital Stereo 2.0 • Snapcase • 1 Discs • Region 1–6 GENRE & RATING Martial Arts/Action • Not Rated (Teens)

Assemble Insert

Right Stuf, 2001, 60 mins., #RSDVD9008. Directed by Ayumi Chibuki. Script by Matsura Shimado. Based on the manga series by Masami Yuki in *Out*.

The city is in chaos due to the dastardly crimes of the Demon Seed, a group of bad guys who wear power suits. The police don't seem to be able to stop them, but the brilliant Professor Shimakobe offers them a power suit if they can find the right champion. The dimwitted police chief Hattori holds auditions to find a singing girl who the police can turn into an idol for the public and will fit into the suit to fight crime. The auditions net them teenage Maron Namikaze, a girl who already has incredible strength and the looks to become a pop star. Unfortunately, she's as uncoordinated as a newborn calf, but that doesn't stop her from trying to bring the Demon Seed to justice.

If this 1989 series doesn't sound completely serious, you're correct. *Assemble Insert* is a parody of anime's conventions, from mecha to pop singers to pop culture. Manga creator Masami Yuki even wrote parts in the story for characters modeled after his coworkers. You'll have to understand Japanese pop culture to get all of the jokes, but even beginning anime viewers will understand the inherent silliness in the concept. The DVD contains both produced OVA episodes and is well worth a look for a chuckle or three.

SPECIAL FEATURES Promotional Footage TECHNICAL FEATURES Fullscreen (1.33:1) • Subtitles/CC: Eng. • Languages: Jap., Eng. dub • Sound: Dolby Digital 2.0 • Keepcase • 1 Disc • Region 1–6 GENRE & RATING Comedy/Action/Robots • Not Rated (Kids)

Atlantis: The Lost Empire

Disney, 2002, 96 mins., #24084. Directed by Kirk Wise, Gary Trousdale. Story by Kirk Wise, Gary Trousdale, Joss Whedon, Bryce Zabel, Jackie Zabel, Tab Murphy. Screenplay by Tab Murphy.

Lingustics expert Milo Thatch is convinced that if he can find the mysterious Shepherd's Journal his grandfather told him about, he'll be able to find the fabled lost kingdom of Atlantis. He gets the chance to fulfill his dream when an eccentric billionaire offers him not only the journal, but also a state-of-the-1914-art submarine and a specialized crew. Milo and the crew of the *Ulysses*—led by the crusty Commander Rourke—plunge deep into the ocean depths, but they barely escape with their lives when a monster attacks them. But the attack leads them to discover the subterranean approach to Atlantis, and Milo finds that civilization still exists in this city powered by magic crystals. Unfortunately, not everyone on Rourke's crew is what they seem, and a threat to Atlantis soon looms. . . .

Disney's underwater epic, released in the summer of 2001, underwhelmed audiences, but it's a stunning-looking lost gem. With designs based on the darkly art deco work of comic artist Mike Mignola, and a combination of 2D traditional and 3D CGI animation, the look of the film is at turns spooky and magical. An excellent voice cast is headed by Michael J. Fox and James Garner, with Leonard Nimoy, Claudia Christian, Jim Varney, Phil Morris, and others taking up supporting roles.

Although the producers don't credit any anime or manga source material, some fans have noted similarities between *Atlantis* and *Nadia*, but those comparisons aren't entirely correct. At the same time, the story itself—and the secrets of Atlantis—does seem more like something from the Eastern world rather than traditional Western animation plotting.

The main DVD offers an excellent mixture of extras, definitely giving fans value for their dollar. There is a problem with some DVD players having a language compatibility issue with the discs (such as the author's Philips deck), but a quick call to Disney's toll-free tech-

nical support and a few minor input changes solved that problem and didn't affect play on any other discs. *Atlantis* deserved to have been seen by a bigger audience and gets a good recommendation here.

SPECIAL FEATURES Commentary Track by the Directors and Producer Don Hahn • Deleted Scene • 3D Turnarounds • Linguistics Lessons • Historical Text TECHNICAL FEATURES Widescreen (2.35:1 enhanced for 16x9) • Fullscreen (1.33:1) • Subtitles/CC: Eng. • Languages: Eng., Fren. dub, Span. dub • Sound: Dolby Digital Surround 5.1 • Keepcase • 1 Disc • Region 1 GENRE & RATING CGI/Fantasy/Adventure • Rated PG

Atlantis: The Lost Empire [Collector's Edition]

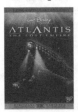

Disney, 2002, 96 mins., #24084. Directed by Kirk Wise, Gary Trousdale. Story by Kirk Wise, Gary Trousdale, Joss Whedon, Bryce Zabel, Jackie Zabel, Tab Murphy. Screenplay by Tab Murphy.

Disney once again provides an excellent collector's set for true cinephiles, stocking the discs with hours of extras and cool features. Interestingly enough, the first disc is not the same as the regular edition; some of the regular disc's extras have been moved to the second disc, and more behind-the-scenes footage has been added (make sure to watch the visual commentary for several extra deleted scenes and in-jokes).

The second disc is exhaustive in its tracking of *Atlantis* from concept to screen, with features on history, story and editorial, art direction, animation production, digital production, music and sound, and publicity! And not only are all these features available in an "explore" capacity, allowing viewers to choose from subjects, but there is a "tour" function that plays the entire set-up in proper order (a two-hour affair). Add in more deleted scenes, a CGI-readable model of the Shepherd's Journal, and more, and you've got an elaborate winner with this set.

SPECIAL FEATURES "Making of" Featurettes • Commentary and Visual Commentary Track by the Directors and Producer • Character and Art Galleries • Production Notes • Deleted Scenes and Abandoned Sequences • Storyboards • 3D Turnarounds • Linguistics Lessons • Historical Text • Story Treatment • Theatrical Trailers • Promotional Footage • Other Title Trailers TECHNICAL FEATURES Widescreen (2.35:1 enhanced for 16x9) • Fullscreen (1.33:1) • Subtitles/CC: Eng. • Languages: Eng., Fren. dub • Sound: Dolby Digital Surround 5.1, DTS 5.1 • Multikeepcase • 2 Discs • Region 1 GENRE & RATING CGI/Fantasy/Adventure • Rated PG

Ayane's High Kick

U.S. Manga Corps, 1998, 60 mins., #USMD 1731. Directed by Takahiro Okao. Story by Takahiro Okao. Written by Isao Shizuya.

High school student Ayane Mitsui wants to become a wrestling champion, but during her auditions, she fails to make a positive impression on the judges. She is soon recruited by Kunimitsu Tangay though, who begins training her in private. Although she thinks the training is in wrestling, he's actually preparing her to be a kickboxing champion. Ayane doesn't like kickboxing, but at her first match, she wins. Unfortunately, her high school vice principal is in the audience, and violent sports are against school rules. When she's challenged by the kickboxing champion, everything's on the line for Ayane; if she wins, she stays in school, but if she loses, she'll be expelled!

With a plot that sounds like *Rocky* crossed with *The Karate Kid* (and just about every other sports underdog film), *Ayane's High Kick* is predictable from start to finish. Not only is the story trite, but the animation isn't particularly up to standard, and the characters feel underdeveloped. Even the attempts at humor mostly fall flat. The DVD's dub (like the tape) is awful, with only Debbie Rabbai in the lead role sounding at all involved in the process. The disc contains both 1996 OVA episodes.

Besides being offered as a single DVD, the disc was also included as part of a 2002 "Martial Arts Pack" set, along with *Grappler Baki*.

SPECIAL FEATURES Character Bios • Fight Scenes • Other Title Trailers TECHNICAL FEATURES Fullscreen (1.33:1) • Subtitles/CC: Eng. • Languages: Jap., Eng. dub • Sound: Dolby Digital Stereo 2.0 • Keepcase • 1 Disc • Region All GENRE & RATING Kickboxing/Girls • Not Rated (Teens)

Babar: King of the Elephants

HBO, 1999, 78 mins., #91567. Directed by Davian Bobrowska, Amelie Bouchard, H. Grace Waddington B. Screenplay by Raymond Jafelice, Peter Sauder. Based on the *Babar* book series by Jean De Brunhoff and Laurent de Brunhoff.

Orphaned as a young elephant, Babar flees to the big city, where he is raised by a sweet old lady. Gaining all the grace and elegance of the upper crust of human culture, Babar returns to the jungle and becomes King of the Elephants. He marries Celeste and builds the town of Celesteville in her honor, but as they rule their kingdom and raise their children, lots of adventures will come into play.

Although the cover of this DVD is a little plain, the series is much better than that. Based on a series of French books that have delighted children and adults alike since 1931, *Babar* is worthwhile entertainment for the entire family. The stories have morals but are not overly preachy. Though there have been several *Babar* incarnations, this disc contains a 1989 feature by Nelvana, as well as the bonus episode "An Elephant's Best Friend," taken from the 1989–93 HBO series. The series won a CableAce award in 1989.

SPECIAL FEATURES Other Title Trailers TECHNICAL FEATURES Fullscreen (1.33:1) • Subtitles/CC: Eng. • Languages: Eng. • Sound: Dolby Digital Surround 2.0 • Snapcase • 1 Disc • Region 1 GENRE & RATING Animals/Music • Rated G

Babel II: Beyond Infinity—Call to the Gods [#1]

AnimeWorks, 2002, 100 mins., #AWDVD-0224. Directed by Takeshi Ushigusa. Screenplay by Takayuki Masuda. Based on the manga series by Kentaro Miura.

NOTE: This DVD arrived too late for a full review. The following text is promotional copy provided by the releasing company:

"Fall beneath the wave of exploding psychic powers! Koichi is an ordinary youth given extraordinary powers to fight a shadowy underworld of renegade psychics. Hidden in a forgotten desert lies the tower of Babel, created by an unknown force. As its successor, Koichi summons three psychic guardians and challenges Yomi, Leon and any other renegades brave enough to stand in his path."

This disc contains episodes #1–4.

SPECIAL FEATURES Clean Credits • Outtakes • Other Title Trailers TECHNICAL FEATURES Fullscreen (1.33:1) • Subtitles/CC: Eng. • Languages: Jap., Eng. dub • Sound: Dolby Digital 2.0 • Keepcase • 1 Disc • Region 1 GENRE & RATING Psychic/Action • Rated 13+

Babel II: Perfect Collection

Image, 1998, 111 mins., #ID1141EFDVD. Directed by Yoshihisa Matsumoto, Kazuhiro Ozawa. Screenplay by Masashi Namiki. Based on the manga series by Mitsuteru Yokoyama.

Koichi is a high school student who is hearing voices in his head and seeing visions of a tower in the desert. When he encounters a psychic girl named Juju, his own formidable psychic powers begin to manifest themselves. Unfortunately, Juju lures him into an evil cult run by Yomi, who plans to use his armies of psychics and zombies for evil. Koichi is aided in his battle against Yomi by a dragon, a robot, and a shapeshifter, all sent to him by the powers of the Tower of Babel, which his ancestor built.

Babel II mixes in Biblical concepts with aliens, telepaths, and cults for a crammed story that still seems to move a little slowly. The DVD contains four episodes of the 1992 series (which followed the 1973 series but changed the character designs). Some fans felt this new *Babel II* was a diluted version of the original. The disc has absolutely no frills but features a nice picture transfer. Episode titles are "The Awakening," "First Blood," "Crossroads," and "Final Conflict."

SPECIAL FEATURES Other Title Trailers TECHNICAL FEATURES Fullscreen (1.33:1) • Languages: Jap., Eng. dub • Sound: Dolby Digital Stereo 2.0 • Keepcase • 1 Disc • Region 1 GENRE & RATING Psychic/Adventure • Not Rated (Teens)

Balto

Universal, 2002, 78 mins., #20014. Directed by Simon Wells. Story by Cliff Ruby, Elana Lesser. Screenplay by Cliff Ruby, Elana Lesser, David Steven Cohen, Roger S. H. Schulman.

Based on a true story from 1925, *Balto* tells the tale of a courageous dog (wolf/husky mix), the leader of a team of sled dogs on the first Iditarod crossing. But this isn't a 600-mile race for glory; the dogs (and their human master) must deliver a diphtheria antitoxin to the stricken people of Nome, Alaska.

A solid and entertaining piece of British-American animation, *Balto* has some nice scruffy designs and isn't overly preachy or sweet. A team of good voice actors are on hand, including Kevin Bacon in the lead role, plus Bob Hoskins, Bridget Fonda, Jim Cummings, and Phil Collins. Director Simon Wells reunited with producer Steve Hickner, bringing the *Who Framed Roger Rabbit?* team back together again. Although the film wasn't a huge success in theaters, it has flourished on video and DVD.

Unfortunately, though the original was released in widescreen, the DVD only features a full-frame version. Other than that, all technical elements are solid.

SPECIAL FEATURES Trailer • Games • DVD-ROM Features • Other Title Trailers TECHNICAL FEATURES Fullscreen (1.33:1) • Subtitles/CC: Eng. • Languages: Eng., Fren. dub, Span. dub • Sound: Dolby Digital Surround 5.1 • Keepcase • 1 Disc • Region 1 GENRE & RATING Animal/Adventure • Rated G

Balto II: Wolf Quest

Universal, 2002, 76 mins., #21102. Directed by Phil Weinstein. Screenplay by Dev Ross.

Balto has a headstrong daughter named Aleu who seems closer to her wolf heritage than her husky side. Aleu sets off into the Alaskan wilderness on her own, but when she makes an enemy of a renegade wolf pack leader, it will be up to Balto and his snow goose and polar bear friends to help her.

A direct-to-video production, *Balto II* isn't quite as polished as the original, but that's to be expected with a lower budget. Still, it remains a solid piece of family entertainment with a reasonable moral lesson: be true to yourself. The voice actors are all different this time around, with David Carradine, Lacey Chabert, Mark Hamill, and Peter MacNicol stepping into animated character. The one complaint most viewers have is that the musical elements absent from the original, intrude here, making it tougher viewing for older audiences.

SPECIAL FEATURES Trailer • Games • DVD-ROM Features: Rescue Heroes Game • Other Title Trailers TECHNICAL FEATURES Fullscreen (1.33:1) • Subtitles/CC: Eng. • Languages: Eng., Fren. dub, Span. dub • Sound: Dolby Digital Surround 5.1 • Keepcase • 1 Disc • Region 1 GENRE & RATING Animal/Adventure/Music • Rated G

Baoh ☞ see Mature/Adult Section

Barbie: In The Nutcracker

Artisan, 2001, 78 mins., #12061. Directed by Owen Hurley. Written by Linda Engelsiepen, Hilary Hinkle, Rob Hudnut. Based on the story by E.T.A. Hoffman.

The famous ballet comes to CGI-animated life in this direct-to-video release. Barbie plays Clara, a girl who gets a wooden nutcracker as a gift from her aunt. While she sleeps, the Nutcracker comes to life to protect her from the villainous Mouse King. Barbie/Clara and the Nutcracker Prince are shrunk down and they must find the magical Sugarplum Princess to end the evil enchantment.

It's hard to fault the animation style here, which is motion-captured CGI based on the movements of real-life dancers from the New York City Ballet. And while one does have to ask why animation was important for the story, some of the more fantastic elements in the tale would be hard to replicate in live-action (plus, Mattel wouldn't get all the Barbie money if it were done live).

Appropriate for the entire family, the DVD will likely be most beloved by little girls. Picture and quality are excellent, and a few spare extras are nice. Oddly, the thirty-minute documentary about real-life ballerinas is available to view only from the first "original" menu, not the main menu. Most of the voice actors are relative unknowns, but Tim Curry is dangerous and campy as the Mouse King.

SPECIAL FEATURES Ballerina Featurette • "Act with Barbie" Segments. TECHNICAL FEATURES Widescreen (1.85:1 enhanced for 16:9) • Fullscreen (1.33:1) • Subtitles/CC: Eng. • Languages: Eng. • Sound: Dolby Digital Surround 2.0, Dolby Digital Surround 5.1 • Keepcase • 1 Disc • Region 1 GENRE & RATING CGI/Ballet/Music • Not Rated (All Ages)

Barefoot Gen

Image, 1999, 83 mins., #ID4649SEDVD. Directed by Masaki Mori. Written by Keiji Nakazawa. Based on the manga series by Keiji Nakazawa in *Boys Weekly*.

Keiji Nakazawa's boyhood experiences come to autobiographical animated life in this harrowing film about the bombing of Hiroshima in the summer of 1945. Six-year-old Gen Nakaoka is in the second grade, and he is looking forward to the upcoming birth of a sibling. But when the atomic bomb is dropped on Hiroshima, Gen's world crumbles. Unable to prevent the death of his father, brother, and sister, Gen helps his mother give birth to his premature sister, Tomoko. How will the two children survive the devastation in a world now filled with radiation poisoning and death?

Released in 1983, *Barefoot Gen* is regarded as one of the classics of animation, Eastern or Western. The true horror of war and what happened to Nakazawa is often disturbing, and sometimes poignant. Never has animation so accurately portrayed such dark moments of despair, and parents are warned that the violent aftermath of the bomb may result in nightmares for young viewers (and some older ones).

The DVD has no extras, but it features a clean print of the film. Some points are lost due to the poorly acted English dub, which is entirely replicated in the subtitles. Still, this film is a classic and should be seen. A 1986 sequel is yet to be released on DVD, but those interested in similar excellent fare should see the entry for *Grave of the Fireflies*.

SPECIAL FEATURES None TECHNICAL FEATURES Fullscreen (1.33:1) • Subtitles/CC: Eng. • Languages: Jap., Eng. dub • Sound: Dolby Digital Stereo 2.0 • Snapcase • 1 Disc • Region 1–6 GENRE & RATING Post-War/Autobiography • Not Rated (Teens)

Bartok The Magnificent

Fox, 1999, 68 mins., #4112600. Directed by Don Bluth, Gary Goldman. Screenplay by Jay Lacopo.

The diminutive albino bat from *Anastasia* returns, but this time the adventure is pure fantasy. Prince Ivan Romanoff is kidnapped, and Bartok, accompanied by a pink snake and a bear, must rescue him from the evil Russian witch Baba Yaga.

Bearing little connection to *Anastasia*—the film in which Bartok first appeared—this isn't quite a sequel as much as it is a fairy tale using the same character. Don't look for heavy morals or deep themes, just silliness, adventure, and a few fun songs. Hank Azaria returns to voice the excitable Bartok, and his vocal performance alone is worth viewing this direct-to-video feature. Other voice cast members include Jennifer Tilly and Kelsey Grammer, while the ever-present Tim Curry lends his tones to a riddle-asking skull.

SPECIAL FEATURES Trailer • Games • Sing-Alongs • Other Title Trailers TECHNICAL FEATURES Fullscreen (1.33:1) • Subtitles/CC: Eng., Span. • Languages: Eng., Fren. dub • Sound: Dolby Digital Surround 2.0 • Keepcase • 1 Disc • Region 1 GENRE & RATING Animal/Humor/Music • Rated G

Bastard: Complete Collection

Pioneer, 2001, 180 mins., #10371. Directed by Katsuhiko Akiyama. Screenplay by Hiroshi Yamaguchi. Based on the manga series by Kazushi Hagiwara in *Weekly Shonen Jump*.

Fifteen years ago, a powerful warlock named Dark Schneider was imprisoned, but now the people of Meta-Rikana must free him because they need his help. The Lords of Havoc, who once were allies of Schneider, are preparing to conquer Meta-Rikana. Schneider's essence has been contained in the body of a young man named Rushe, and when the warlock is freed, he contains some of the same feelings as Rushe— including the love of Yoko, daughter of the Meta-Rikana high priest. But what Schneider really wants from the battles to come is revenge—and fun.

Bastard collects the complete six-episode OVA series from 1992–93. The animation is a mixture of standard action fare punctuated with super goofy faces during comedy moments set against intense backgrounds. While the original Japanese names for characters, cities, and spells referred to heavy metal rock bands such as Metallica, Anthrax, Megadeath, Bon Jovi and the like, the English dub has removed this element (though it's audible on the Japanese track). The DVD is a nice transfer, but purists will be frustrated that the ending is cut from each odd-numbered episode.

SPECIAL FEATURES Art Galleries • Action Figure Ads. TECHNICAL FEATURES Fullscreen (1.33:1) • Subtitles/CC: Eng. • Languages: Jap., Eng. dub • Sound: Dolby Digital 2.0 • Keepcase • 1 Disc • Region 1 GENRE & RATING Sorcery/Fantasy/Action • Rated 16+

Bastard: Complete Collection [Limited Edition with Figure]

Pioneer, 2001, 180 mins., #11543. Directed by Katsuhiko Akiyama. Screenplay by Hiroshi Yamaguchi. Based on the manga series by Kazushi Hagiwara in *Weekly Shonen Jump*.

This release contains the exact DVD and keepcase as the regular edition. However, the keepcase is inset in a cardboard box/tray measuring 9.5 in. wide by 13 in. high. The art on the box continues the art from the DVD cover, a clever move that inspired many fans to keep the unwieldy box.

Shrinkwrapped to the back of the package was a 10-in. variant Dark Schneider action figure, though with limited poseability the term "action" is a bit of a misnomer. Still, this set is highly sought by fans, as it was originally released in a limited edition of only 5,000 copies.

SPECIAL FEATURES Art Galleries • Action Figure Ads. TECHNICAL FEATURES Fullscreen (1.33:1) • Subtitles/CC: Eng. • Languages: Jap., Eng. dub • Sound: Dolby Digital 2.0 • Keepcase • 1 Disc • Region 1 GENRE & RATING Fantasy/Action • Rated 16+

Batman and Mr. Freeze: SubZero

Warner, 2002, 70 mins., #14996. Directed by Boyd Kirkland. Written by Randy Rogel, Boyd Kirkland. Based on the comic book characters from DC Comics.

Batman, Robin, and Batgirl tangle with Mr. Freeze once again, as he returns to Gotham to kidnap Batgirl to aid in his quest to revive his wife. Batman and Robin must embark on a chilly high-tech rescue mission.

Released direct-to-video in March 1998 (and aired as three episodes on TV in May of that year), *SubZero* was timed to coincide with the feature film *Batman and Robin*, starring Arnold Schwarzenegger as Mr. Freeze. While the live-action film was widely regarded as awful, the animated feature got good reviews for continuing its portrayal of the villain as a sympathetic and important character. The story moves forward in a logical fashion, and there are some nice set pieces, though the use of some inserted CGI animation is not always smooth.

SPECIAL FEATURES Trailer • How to Draw Batman • Music and Art Montage • Other Title Trailers • Game TECHNICAL FEATURES Fullscreen (1.33:1) • Subtitles/CC: Eng., Fren., Port., Span. • Languages: Eng., Fren. dub, Port. dub, Span. dub • Sound: Dolby Digital 2.0 • Snapcase • 1 Disc • Region 1–4 GENRE & RATING Superhero/Action • Not Rated (Kids)

Batman Beyond: Return of the Joker [The Original, Uncut Version]

Warner, 2002, 77 mins., #22355. Directed by Curt Geda. Story by Paul Dini, Glen Murakami, Bruce Timm. Screenplay by Paul Dini. Based on the comic book characters from DC Comics.

This is the uncensored version of *Return of the Joker*, with all of the naughty bits put back in. Though they only add a few more minutes to the running time, the previously scissored scenes make plot points more clear and the danger to Batman, Robin, and Batgirl more real. However, you will actually see *less* picture during most of the movie; the producers added black bars on the top and bottom of the fullscreen frame. Although this technically letterboxed the feature, it also cut off much of the art.

The packaging is only slightly different, although the DVD features some added extras.

SPECIAL FEATURES "Making of" Featurette • Commentary Track

by Director and Writers • Character Bios • Storyboards and Animatics • Deleted Scenes • Trailer • Music Video • Game • Other Title Trailers TECHNICAL FEATURES Widescreen (1.85:1) • Subtitles/CC: Eng., Fren. • Languages: Eng., Fren. dub • Sound: Dolby Digital 5.1 • Snapcase • 1 Disc • Region 1–4 GENRE & RATING Superhero/Action • Not Rated (Teens)

Batman Beyond: The Movie

Warner, 1998, 132 mins., #17848. Directed by Curt Geda, Butch Lukic, Dan Riba, Yukio Suzuki. Story by Alan Burnett, Stan Berkowitz, Paul Dini, Hilary J. Bader. Based on the comic book characters from DC Comics.

Not technically a "movie," this combines the original two-part pilot "Rebirth" with four other episodes. In "Rebirth," young Terry McGinnis stumbles onto the secrets of the Batcave and the long-retired Batman/Bruce Wayne. Using futuristic technology and a black body suit equipped with red glider wings, Terry becomes the Batman of the future. Commissioner Barbara Gordon (once Batgirl) isn't always pleased with the exploits of young Batman.

The other four stories include: "Golem" (episode #4, misidentified as "Gotham Golem" on the cover), in which Batman faces a robotic drone controlled by a young social outcast; "The Winning Edge" (episode #9), in which Batman faces the Joker's gang again; "Dead Man's Hand" (episode #8), in which the new Royal Flush Gang attacks; and "Meltdown" (episode #5), in which the decapitated head of Mr. Freeze returns to life.

Batman Beyond debuted on the WB Network in January 1999 and was an immediate critical and public success story. The designs are sharp, and the animation features a techno-punk style that borrows heavily from anime while still retaining the original *Batman*'s "dark noir" flavor. Voice actors include Will Friedle, Kevin Conroy, Teri Garr, George Takei, Seth Green, Stockard Channing, and Linda Hamilton. Highly recommended for both anime and superhero fans.

SPECIAL FEATURES Trailer • Liner Notes: Inside Cover TECHNICAL FEATURES Fullscreen (1.33:1) • Subtitles/CC: Eng., Fren. • Languages: Eng., Fren. • Sound: Dolby Digital Stereo 2.0 • Snapcase • 1 Disc • Region 1 GENRE & RATING Superhero/Action • Not Rated (Kids)

Batman: Mask of the Phantasm

Warner, 1999, 76 mins., #15502. Directed by Eric Radomski, Bruce Timm. Screenplay by Alan Burnett, Paul Dini, Martin Pasko, and Michael Reaves. Based on the comic book characters from DC Comics.

Gotham City's gangsters are under siege, but it's not Batman who's taking them out. Instead, the mysterious cloaked figure known as Phantasm is terrorizing the criminal underground. Blamed for the murders of the gangsters, Batman sets out to clear his name because even though Phantasm's goals are positive, his methods are criminal. Phantasm has secret ties to Bruce Wayne's past, and soon the one-time love of Bruce's life resurfaces, and the Joker decides it's time to make his own strike of terror on Gotham.

Based on the "dark noir" designs of the Fox television series, *Mask of the Phantasm* was Warner's first full-length animated feature film of Batman, and it was released theatrically for a brief time around Christmas 1993. With a bigger budget and a PG rating, the producers were able to be darker than the television series allowed, but the same combination of gritty gloom and airbrushed glow pervaded the backgrounds. The angular and sharp character designs stayed much the same as well. The lead TV voice cast—including Kevin Conroy and Mark Hamill—made the jump to the project, along with newcomers Dana Delany, Hart Bochner, Stacey Keach, and Abe Vigoda.

The DVD contains almost no extras, which is a shame since HBO produced a nice "Making of" special prior to the film's release. And oddly, nowhere in the film is the inspiration for this specific story mentioned: 1987's *Detective Comics* #575–78's "Year Two" storyline by Mike W. Barr and artists Alan Davis, Paul Neary, Todd McFarlane, and Alfredo Alcala, where the vigilante character was named "The Reaper."

SPECIAL FEATURES Theatrical Trailer. TECHNICAL FEATURES Widescreen (1.85:1 enhanced for 16:9) • Fullscreen (1.33:1) • Subtitles/CC: Eng., Fren. • Languages: Eng., Fren. • Sound: Dolby Digital Surround 2.0 • Snapcase • 1 Disc • Region 1 GENRE & RATING Superhero/Action • Rated PG

Batman/Superman Movie, The

Warner, 2002, 80 mins., #16351. Directed by Toshihiko Masuda. Screenplay by Alan Burnett, Paul Dini, Rich Fogel, Steve Gerber, Stan Berkowitz. Based on the comic book characters from DC Comics.

After the Joker steals a statue made of Kryptonite in Gotham City, he heads to Metropolis where he's made a deal with Lex Luthor: $1 billion to kill

Superman. Batman follows the Joker to Metropolis, and in his secret identity of Bruce Wayne, discusses a joint venture with Luthor for a series of military devices. In his downtime, Bruce begins wooing Lois Lane, much to the consternation of Clark Kent. Batman and Superman soon discover each other's secret identities and—despite their animosity for each other—learn that they must work together to stop the evil duo of Joker and Luthor.

The "movie" is actually a three-part episode of *Superman* entitled "World's Finest," which aired in October 1997. All the regular voice actors are along for the ride: Timothy Daly, Kevin Conroy, Dana Delany, Mark Hamill, and Clancy Brown. Fans were ecstatic over the storyline, which paired the two iconic superheroes while spotlighting their very divergent methods of fighting crime. And although Lex Luthor is supposed to be a criminal mastermind, he comes up a little short when trying to outsmart Joker and his sidekick Harley Quinn. The print on the DVD isn't as sharp as it could be, but this is a nice inexpensive package for superhero fans.

SPECIAL FEATURES Interview with Bruce Timm • How to Draw Batman • How to Draw Superman • Music and Art Montage • Trailer • Game • Other Title Trailers . TECHNICAL FEATURES Fullscreen (1.33:1) • Subtitles/CC: Eng., Span. • Languages: Eng., Fren. dub, Port. dub, Span. dub • Sound: Dolby Digital 2.0 • Snapcase • 1 Disc • Region 1–4 GENRE & RATING Superhero/Action • Not Rated (Kids)

Batman: The Animated Series—The Legend Begins

Warner, 2002, 110 mins., #22319. Directed by Kevin Altieri, Kent Butterworth, Boyd Kirkland. Written by Mitch Brian, Eddie Gorodetsky, Henry Gilroy, Sean Catherine Derek, Carl Swenson, Paul Dini, Michael Reaves, Tom Ruegger. Based on the comic book characters from DC Comics.

Bruce Wayne faced the nightmare of his parents' murder and used it to build himself into a crime-fighting machine. Working outside the law, he now protects Gotham City from murderers and thieves, mobsters and monsters, and more than a few supervillains. He has been called "the Dark Knight" and "the Caped Crusader," but those who fear him most know him as . . . Batman.

Batman: The Animated Series debuted on Fox TV in 1992, the work of producers Bruce Timm, Eric Radomski, and others. The show was a critical smash, taking the darkest components from the comic book series' origins and combining them with other elements from Tim Burton's 1989 feature film.

The look of *Batman: TAS* was "dark deco," with Gotham's architecture and style a mixture of the 1930s and the 1960s. The animation was done over backgrounds painted on black paper (unlike traditional backgrounds painted on white paper), giving it an eerie feel. The characters were all stylized, closer to the artwork of *Batman* creator Bob Kane—and *Superman* animators, the Fleischer brothers—than to later versions of the comic book character. With moody music and an all-star cast of voice talent, the film noirish elements of *Batman* won over audiences and critics alike.

This DVD collects five of the earliest episodes of *Batman*: "On Leather Wings" introduces Man-Bat, a scientist whose experiments turn him into a monster; "Christmas with the Joker" features the Joker kidnapping Commissioner Gordon; "Nothing to Fear" debuts horror villain The Scarecrow; "The Last Laugh" is another Joker story set on April Fools' Day; and "Pretty Poison" introduces green-hued femme fatale Poison Ivy. Extras include interviews with cocreator Bruce Timm discussing the characters and settings for the episodes, and providing insight into the styles chosen on the acclaimed series. The one downside is the game; once started, you can't escape from it without stopping the DVD. Collectors can only hope Warner continues to put out more discs in this excellent line.

SPECIAL FEATURES Interviews with Bruce Timm • How to Draw Batman • Game SPECIAL FEATURES Fullscreen (1.33:1) • Subtitles/CC: Eng., Fren., Port., Span. • Languages: Eng., Fren. dub, Port. dub, Span. dub • Sound: Dolby Digital 2.0 • Snapcase • 1 Disc • Region 1–4 GENRE & RATING Superhero/Action • Not Rated (Kids)

Battle Angel ☞ see Mature/Adult Section

Battle Arena Toshinden [Uncut Version]

U.S. Manga Corps, 1997, 60 mins., #DUSM1630. Directed by Masami Obari. Screenplay by Jiro Takayama, Masaharu Amiya. Based on the video game by Sega.

Once a year, a secret tournament of the greatest martial artists is held to decide who is the world's most powerful fighter. At Battle Area Toshinden, eleven top warriors will compete against each other. Eiji Shinjo is a master swordsman who was denied victory in the last tournament when his battle against the renegade Gaia was cut short. Now it appears that Eiji's long-lost brother, Sho, may be back and out to eliminate all the competition at Toshinden, but the evil "Organization" might have other plans for all the fighters.

Not the best example of either anime or storytelling, this two-part 1996 OVA series exists mainly to cash in on the video game. The DVD was a very early release, and besides a sluggish menu, it exhibits problems in some players. The DVD-ROM drive used to double

check features for this book could not read the disc, and other problems have been reported by fans.

SPECIAL FEATURES Character Galleries • Other Title Trailers TECHNICAL FEATURES Fullscreen (1.33:1) • Subtitles/CC: Eng. • Languages: Jap., Eng. dub • Sound: Dolby Digital 2.0 • Snapcase • 1 Disc • Region All GENRE & RATING Fantasy/Action • Not Rated (Teens)

Battle Athletes: On Your Mark [#1]

Pioneer, 1998, 75 mins., #PIDA-1570V. Directed by Kazuhiro Ozawa. Written by Hideyuki Kurata.

In the year 4999, teenage Akari Kanzaki wants to follow in her mother's footsteps and enroll in the famous University Satellite. There, her mother had once held the title of Cosmo Beauty, and Akari is determined to train hard at the interstellar sports club and earn the respect of her peers. But the sports meets that the girls compete in are bound to get weird since they sometimes have to compete against sports-loving aliens!

This 1997 series is geared toward a younger crowd, despite its rating. The animation is decent, but it depends heavily on a cuteness factor, with gigantic eyes and triangle mouths all around. The messages delivered aren't bad, including lessons in self-confidence and living up to expectations. Another plus is the fact that the cast is multicultural and diverse, although the lack of males at the school shows that segregation of the sexes is apparently prevalent in the future.

The first DVD contains two episodes: "Chronicle Beginning" and "Oath Entrant." The worst element about the disc is its slow-moving menu, which doesn't show the chapter stops. The bright colors and red-white-and-blue color scheme of the keepcase might lead buyers to believe it's more American than it is, but it's an entertaining enough piece of fluff. The first-run DVDs featured a trio of stickers, but these are missing from later editions.

SPECIAL FEATURES Character Galleries. TECHNICAL FEATURES Fullscreen (1.33:1) • Subtitles/CC: Eng. • Languages: Jap., Eng. dub • Sound: Dolby Digital 2.0 • Keepcase • 1 Disc • Region 1, 4 GENRE & RATING Sports/Science Fiction/Comedy • Rated 13+

Battle Athletes: Ready . . . [#2]

Pioneer, 1999, 60 mins., #PIDA-1571V. Directed by Kazuhiro Ozawa. Written by Hideyuki Kurata.

Akari Kanzaki and her fellow sports competitors at the University Satellite are back. This time out they must face their midterms in an orbital elevator full of obstacles. Then, it's girls versus boys as the students from the Boy's School challenge the girls in a game of Acro Spike. But Akari has lost faith in herself, and a surprise is just around the corner. . . .

More comedy-sports action is showcased here in episodes #3 and #4: "Screaming Advance" and "Match Unexpected." A scene set at a hot springs is sexy, but not so much that parents will gasp.

SPECIAL FEATURES Promotional Footage. TECHNICAL FEATURES Fullscreen (1.33:1) • Subtitles/CC: Eng. • Languages: Jap., Eng. dub • Sound: Dolby Digital 2.0 • Keepcase • 1 Disc • Region 1, 4 GENRE & RATING Sports/Science Fiction/Comedy • Rated 13+

Battle Athletes: Go! [#3]

Pioneer, 1999, 60 mins., #PIDA-1572V. Directed by Kazuhiro Ozawa. Written by Hideyuki Kurata.

The Great Competition for the title of Cosmo Beauty is getting closer and Akari's main opponent is Kris. But while each girl does her best, two more competitors, the champion Lahrri and the ruthless Mylandah, make this a four-way race to the finish.

This final disc contains episodes #5 and #6: "Objective Tension" and "Stage Yonder." While the story wraps up most of its loose threads, some elements are left open for further exploration.

SPECIAL FEATURES Character Galleries. TECHNICAL FEATURES Fullscreen (1.33:1) • Subtitles/CC: Eng. • Languages: Jap., Eng. dub • Sound: Dolby Digital 2.0 • Keepcase • 1 Disc • Region 1, 4 GENRE & RATING Sports/Science Fiction/Comedy • Rated 13+

Battle Athletes Victory: Training [#1]

Pioneer, 1999, 85 mins., #PIDA-7141V. Directed by Katsuhito Akiyama. Written by Hideyuki Kurata.

Set in 4998, this series finds a younger Akari Kanzaki trying to get into the famous University Satellite (which we already saw her enter in the previous Battle Athletes series). Only three stu-

dents from each school can win entry, so Akari and her friends must triumph in a series of wacky physical trials. If only Akari's luck wasn't quite so bad. . . .

A prequel to *Battle Athletes*, this 1997 TV series is mostly similar to its predecessor, that is to say it has cute girls with big eyes and mouths, and lots of messages about believing in yourself and winning the day. It also contains some lesbian overtones. The DVD features episodes #1–4: "Ready, Go!"; "Kowloon's Attack!"; "The Night of Woong-A-Ji"; and "My Rival." Some fans won't be happy that the opening and closing credits for the middle episodes are missing (in all eight discs).

SPECIAL FEATURES None TECHNICAL FEATURES Fullscreen (1.33:1) • Subtitles/CC: (CC & Eng.) • Languages: Jap., Eng. dub • Sound: Dolby Digital 2.0 • Keepcase • 1 Disc • Region 1, 4 GENRE & RATING Sports/Science Fiction/Comedy • Rated 13+

Battle Athletes Victory: Doubt and Conflict [#2]

Pioneer, 1999, 65 mins., #PIDA-7142V. Directed by Katsuhito Akiyama. Written by Hideyuki Kurata, Yosuke Kuroda.

When Akari is humiliated during a race, she decides to quit; after all, she can't possibly live up to the legend of her mother! Akari's friends don't want her to leave though, and they'll do whatever it takes to keep her around.

Revealing more about Akari's mother, and containing some sad sequences, the DVD contains episodes #5–7: "Arrogance"; "The Return Home"; and "Lamentation."

SPECIAL FEATURES None TECHNICAL FEATURES Fullscreen (1.33:1) • Subtitles/CC: (CC & Eng.) • Languages: Jap., Eng. dub • Sound: Dolby Digital 2.0 • Keepcase • 1 Disc • Region 1, 4 GENRE & RATING Sports/Science Fiction/Comedy • Rated 13+

Battle Athletes Victory: Tragedy and Triumph [#3]

Pioneer, 1999, 65 mins., #PIDA-7143V. Directed by Katsuhito Akiyama. Written by Hideyuki Kurata, Yosuke Kuroda.

Akari has been training for the triathlon, since only a trio of winners will get into the University Satellite. But when her friend and trainer Itchan gets injured, Akari loses faith in herself and her sporting abilities.

Another trio of episodes are presented on this DVD, with shows #8–10: "The Sinking Talent"; "The Thing on the Other Side"; and "The Promise Resurrected." This group wraps up the first arc of the TV series.

SPECIAL FEATURES None TECHNICAL FEATURES Fullscreen (1.33:1) • Subtitles/CC: (CC & Eng.) • Languages: Jap., Eng. dub •

Sound: Dolby Digital 2.0 • Keepcase • 1 Disc • Region 1, 4
GENRE & RATING Sports/Science Fiction/Comedy • Rated 13+

Battle Athletes Victory: Spaceward Ho! [#4]

Pioneer, 1999, 65 mins., #PIDA-7144V. Directed by Katsuhito Akiyama. Written by Hideyuki Kurata, Yosuke Kuroda.

Akari is on the way to the University Satellite Sports Academy in space, when a trio of odd hijackers bars the way. Later, Akari finds she has a very weird roommate and a coach with a chocolate fetish. Plus, the physical tests at the University are much tougher than Akari expected.

A new storyline begins with episodes #11–13: "Girl Meets Girls"; "There Go the Three!"; and "There Go the Three Again!" This set of episodes is also more humorous than the preceding ten.

SPECIAL FEATURES None TECHNICAL FEATURES Fullscreen (1.33:1) • Subtitles/CC: (CC & Eng.) • Languages: Jap., Eng. dub • Sound: Dolby Digital 2.0 • Keepcase • 1 Disc • Region 1, 4 GENRE & RATING Sports/Science Fiction/Comedy • Rated 13+

Battle Athletes Victory: No Looking Back [#5]

Pioneer, 1999, 65 mins., #PIDA-7145V. Directed by Katsuhito Akiyama. Written by Hideyuki Kurata, Yosuke Kuroda.

Although Akari and her teammates are finally working together well, their entry into the Cosmo Beauty competition is far from clinched (especially after a day off goes very wrong). Plus, Akari's old rival Jessie is massacred in a competition and may not be able to rebuild her pluck and drive.

This DVD contains another three episodes, this time #14–16: "There Go the New Three!"; "Light"; and "Shadows."

SPECIAL FEATURES None TECHNICAL FEATURES Fullscreen (1.33:1) • Subtitles/CC: (CC & Eng.) • Languages: Jap., Eng. dub • Sound: Dolby Digital 2.0 • Keepcase • 1 Disc • Region 1, 4 GENRE & RATING Sports/Science Fiction/Comedy • Rated 13+

Battle Athletes Victory: Willpower [#6]

Pioneer, 1999, 65 mins., #PIDA-7146V. Directed by Katsuhito Akiyama. Written by Hideyuki Kurata, Yosuke Kuroda.

Akari and Kris are getting squashed in the sports competitions. To beat Lahrri and Mylandah, they're going to have to double their training regimen, but the semifinals for the Great Competition are coming soon.

Episodes #17–19 are showcased on this disc: "I'm Sorry"; "Reason to Fight"; and "From Heart, To Heart."

SPECIAL FEATURES None TECHNICAL FEATURES Fullscreen (1.33:1) • Subtitles/CC: (CC & Eng.) • Languages: Jap., Eng. dub • Sound: Dolby Digital 2.0 • Keepcase • 1 Disc • Region 1, 4 GENRE & RATING Sports/Science Fiction/Comedy • Rated 13+

Battle Athletes Victory: The Last Dance [#7]

Pioneer, 1999, 65 mins., #PIDA-7147V. Directed by Katsuhito Akiyama. Written by Hideyuki Kurata.

Akari and Kris are still being defeated in the finals by Lahrri's mechanically smooth performance and Mylandah's anger-fueled energy. The 100-meter dash is coming soon, but will Akari and Kris stay in the race? Two of the four girls will be eliminated by the finals, and something strange is about to arrive at the University. . . .

Another trio of episodes are presented on this DVD, with shows #20–22 veering away from comedy and more into the "sports drama" arena: "Friend"; "Save the Last Dance for Me"; and "Farewell and Introductions."

SPECIAL FEATURES None TECHNICAL FEATURES Fullscreen (1.33:1) • Subtitles/CC: (CC & Eng.) • Languages: Jap., Eng. dub • Sound: Dolby Digital 2.0 • Keepcase • 1 Disc • Region 1, 4 GENRE & RATING Sports/Science Fiction/Comedy • Rated 13+

Battle Athletes Victory: The Human Race [#8]

Pioneer, 1999, 85 mins., #PIDA-7148V. Directed by Katsuhito Akiyama. Written by Hideyuki Kurata.

The true purpose of the Cosmo Beauty competition is revealed when a group of hostile aliens arrives to pit their skills against humankind's greatest athletes! If Akari and the others don't triumph, Earth will fall to the Nerili Queen and her alien army! Plus, the secret identity of Akari's father is discovered.

The final four episodes of the series, #21–24, are contained on this DVD: "Day of Resurrection"; "Cultural Catastrophe"; "Oh God! The Evil Trap of the Nerilians"; and "Goat!"

SPECIAL FEATURES None TECHNICAL FEATURES Fullscreen (1.33:1) • Subtitles/CC: (CC & Eng.) • Languages: Jap., Eng. dub • Sound: Dolby Digital 2.0 • Keepcase • 1 Disc • Region 1, 4 GENRE & RATING Sports/Science Fiction/Comedy • Rated 13+

Battle of the Planets: Vol. 1

Rhino, 2001, 120 mins., #R2 970008. Directed by Alan Dinehart, David E. Hanson. Written by Jameson Brewer, Peter B. Germano, Jack Paritz, Helen Sosin, Richard Shaw, Howard Post, William Bloom, Harry Winkler, Muriel Germano, Kevin Coates, Sid Morse.

Battle of the Planets is the 1978 syndicated U.S. version of the 1972–74 Japanese series *Gatchaman*. In the *Gatchaman* series, the Earth was being invaded by the evil Gallacter, but his threats were always repelled by five heroes aboard a giant God-Phoenix spaceship. Dressed in bird costumes and cool helmets were leader Eagle Ken, romantic interest Swan June, tubby Owl Ryu, aggressive bad boy Condor Joe, and fireplug Swallow Jinpei.

In post–*Star Wars* America, TV producers were scrambling to get science fiction on the air. Gameshow distributor Sandy Frank hired Hanna-Barbera veterans Alan Dinehart and Jameson Brewer to rework the *Gatchaman* series for U.S. audiences. Names were changed—Ken/Mark Venture, June/The Princess, Joe/Jason, Tiny/Ryu, and Keyop/Jinpei—and the premise of the series was reworked as well. "G-Force" was now based in Center Neptune, underneath the Earth's oceans, and the villain Zoltar (from the planet Spectra) sought to conquer many worlds, not just Earth. Newly created animation sequences included robot 7-Zark-7 (whose narration helped bridge any excised materials) and more shots of the *Phoenix*. Out were some of the series's more violent elements and death scenes. Eighty-five shows were created from the 105 of the Japanese series.

Rhino has done a great job on this DVD series, showcasing not only the Americanized version of the show, but also including the original *Gatchaman* source episodes, and one show each of the sequel series *G-Force* (in which the characters are renamed yet again, and some animation is restored). The film transfers are relatively grainy, but the look has a nostalgic feel that adults will find comfortable. The DVD contains a humorous FBI warning at the beginning and an insert trading card.

Note: The titles for the episodes appear in three different forms in the DVD packaging. One title is on the back cover, a second is on the liner page and menu, and a third is subtitled onscreen. We have chosen the on-screen version to list below, except the *G-Force* title that comes from the menu because there is no on-screen title.

The *Battle of the Planets* episodes are "Attack of the Space Terrapin," in which Zoltar attacks Earth to gain access to the soil-renewing Vitaluman, and "Rescue of the Astronauts," in which the G-Force team must find two astronauts who discovered underwater alien bases on Mars! Corresponding *Gatchaman* episodes are "Gatchaman vs. Turtle King" and "A Demonic Aircraft Carrier." Capping the disc is the *G-Force* episode "Robot Stegasus."

See also the entry for *Gatchaman*.

SPECIAL FEATURES Insert: Trading Card "Mark" TECHNICAL FEATURES Fullscreen (1.33:1) • Subtitles/CC: Eng. • Languages: Jap., Eng. dub, Port. dub, Span. dub • Sound: Dolby Digital 2.0, Dolby Digital Surround 5.1 • Keepcase • 1 Disc • Region 1 GENRE & RATING Science Fiction/Action • Not Rated (Kids)

Battle of the Planets: Vol. 2

Rhino, 2001, 120 mins., #R2 970009. Directed by David E. Hanson. Written by Jameson Brewer, Peter B. Germano, Jack Paritz, Helen Sosin, Richard Shaw, Howard Post, William Bloom, Harry Winkler, Muriel Germano, Kevin Coates, Sid Morse.

Another superb set of the anime and Americanized animation favorite. The first *Battle of the Planets* episode is "The Space Mummy," in which G-Force investigates a new Earth-like planet hidden behind Venus and a giant mummy powered by Plutonium X! In "The Space Serpent," Zoltar has sent a giant space serpent that eats crude oil to ravage Earth. Corresponding *Gatchaman* episodes are "A Giant Mummy Calls the Storms" and "For Revenge on the Monster Mechadegon." Rounding out the disc is the *G-Force* episode "Blast at the Bottom of the Sea."

SPECIAL FEATURES Insert: Trading Card "Princess" TECHNICAL FEATURES Fullscreen (1.33:1) • Subtitles/CC: Eng. • Languages: Jap., Eng. dub, Port. dub, Span. dub • Sound: Dolby Digital 2.0, Dolby Digital Surround 5.1 • Keepcase • 1 Disc • Region 1 GENRE & RATING Science Fiction/Action • Not Rated (Kids)

Battle of the Planets: Vol. 3

Rhino, 2002, 125 mins., #R2 970010. Directed by David E. Hanson. Written by Jameson Brewer, Peter B. Germano, Jack Paritz, Helen Sosin, Richard Shaw, Howard Post, William Bloom, Harry Winkler, Muriel Germano, Kevin Coates, Sid Morse.

More Gatcha-fun with the team of the *Phoenix* ship. The *Battle of the Planets* episodes are "Ghost Ship of Planet Mir," in which G-Force is called back from vacation to stop Zoltar and a deposed ruler from destroying the planet Mir's natural resources, and "Big Robot Gold Grab," wherein Zoltar and the forces of Spectra intend to steal all of the galaxy's gold to cause economic collapse!

Corresponding *Gatchaman* episodes are "The Ghost Fleet from Hell" and "The Grand Mini–Robot Operation." Wrapping up the disc is the *G-Force* episode "The Strange White Shadow."

SPECIAL FEATURES None TECHNICAL FEATURES Fullscreen (1.33:1) • Subtitles/CC: Eng. • Languages: Jap., Eng. dub, Port. dub, Span. dub • Sound: Dolby Digital 2.0, Dolby Digital Surround 5.1 • Keepcase • 1 Disc • Region 1 GENRE & RATING Science Fiction/Action • Not Rated (Kids)

Battle of the Planets: Vol. 4

Rhino, 2002, 125 mins., #R2 970011. Directed by David E. Hanson. Written by Jameson Brewer, Peter B. Germano, Jack Paritz, Helen Sosin, Richard Shaw, Howard Post, William Bloom, Harry Winkler, Muriel Germano, Kevin Coates, Sid Morse.

Excitement and adventure face the G-Force team once again. The opening *Battle of the Planets* episode is "Ace from Outer Space," in which Mark and an experimental spacecraft he's flying are menaced by Captain Doon from the planet Urgos. In "Fearful Sea Anemone," Zoltar sends a Sea Anemone sub to destroy a top-secret submarine base.

Corresponding *Gatchaman* episodes are "Galactor's Grand Airshow" and "The Secret of the Crescent Coral Reef." Capping the disc is the *G-Force* episode "The Giant Centipod."

SPECIAL FEATURES None TECHNICAL FEATURES Fullscreen (1.33:1) • Subtitles/CC: Eng. • Languages: Jap., Eng. dub, Port. dub, Span. dub • Sound: Dolby Digital 2.0, Dolby Digital Surround 5.1 • Keepcase • 1 Disc • Region 1 GENRE & RATING Science Fiction/Action • Not Rated (Kids)

Battle of the Planets: Vol. 5

Rhino, 2002, 125 mins., #R2 970012. Directed by David E. Hanson. Written by Jameson Brewer, Peter B. Germano, Jack Paritz, Helen Sosin, Richard Shaw, Howard Post, William Bloom, Harry Winkler, Muriel Germano, Kevin Coates, Sid Morse.

G-Force is back in business protecting the galaxy in another set of stories. The first *Battle of the Planets* episode is "Juniper Moon Menace." The villainous Commander Typhon has launched a shower of meteors toward Earth, and G-Force must stop them! In "A Swarm of Robot Ants," the inhabitants of planet Trimulus have sent an army of robotic insects to invaded the Earth.

Corresponding *Gatchaman* episodes are "A Demon from the Moon" and "The Big Battle of the Underground Monsters." Rounding out the disc is the *G-Force* episode "Phantom Fleet."

SPECIAL FEATURES None TECHNICAL FEATURES Fullscreen (1.33:1) • Subtitles/CC: Eng. • Languages: Jap., Eng. dub, Port. dub, Span. dub • Sound: Dolby Digital 2.0, Dolby Digital Surround 5.1 • Keepcase • 1 Disc • Region 1 GENRE & RATING Science Fiction/Action • Not Rated (Kids)

Battle of the Planets: Vol. 6

Rhino, 2002, 125 mins., #R2 970078. Directed by David E. Hanson. Written by Jameson Brewer, Peter B. Germano, Jack Paritz, Helen Sosin, Richard Shaw, Howard Post, William Bloom, Harry Winkler, Muriel Germano, Kevin Coates, Sid Morse.

Mark Venture leads G-Force into more adventure against evil forces in this sixth volume. The first *Battle of the Planets* episode is "Space Rocket Escort," in which the *Phoenix* escorts a powerful new fighter but ends up on a collision course with an active volcano! In "Beast With a Sweet Tooth," a giant robotic beetle is destroying the Dominican Republic's sugar cane crop, leaving Earth with no sweetener for its coffee and breakfast cereal. G-Force gets cranky, especially when they find out Spectra is behind the sour plan.

Corresponding *Gatchaman* episodes are "The Mysterious Red Impulse" and "The Greedy Monster Ibukuron." Rounding out the disc is the *G-Force* episode "The Micro-Robots."

SPECIAL FEATURES None TECHNICAL FEATURES Fullscreen (1.33:1) • Subtitles/CC: Eng. • Languages: Jap., Eng. dub, Port. dub, Span. dub • Sound: Dolby Digital 2.0, Dolby Digital Surround 5.1 • Keepcase • 1 Disc • Region 1 GENRE & RATING Science Fiction/Action • Not Rated (Kids)

Battle Skipper: The Movie

U.S. Manga Corps, 2002, 90 mins., #USMD 1826. Directed by Takashi Watanabe. Screenplay by Hidemi Kamata.

The girls at St. Ignacio Catholic School are typical high-spirited teenagers, except for those who belong to the Debutante Club or the Etiquette Club. The Debs are run by a spoiled rich girl named Sayaka, but even her riches and haughty attitude can't quite compare to the quintet of freshman Etiquette clubbers who command mecha Battle Skippers from a secret base!

Three 1995 OVAs—based on a Tomy toy line—have been condensed to a feature-length "movie" for U.S.

audiences. A good choice for fans of *Sailor Moon* or *Project A-Ko*, this project does feature some nudity.

SPECIAL FEATURES Character and Art Galleries • Character Bios • Storyboards • Promotional Footage • Games • DVD-ROM Features: Art, Scripts • Other Title Trailers TECHNICAL FEATURES Fullscreen (1.33:1) • Subtitles/CC: Eng. • Languages: Jap., Eng. dub • Sound: Dolby Digital 2.0 • Keepcase • 1 Disc • Region All GENRE & RATING Robots/Girls/Comedy • Rated 13+

Beast City ☞ see Mature/Adult Section

Beast Wars: Classic Episodes [#1]

Alliance Atlantis (Canadian), 2001, 140 mins. Directed by Ian Pearson, Steve Ball, C. Michael Easton, TW Peacocke, Andrew Doucette, Nick Kendall. Written by Bob Forward, Larry D. Tillio, Greg Johnson, Jesse Winfield.

See the listing for Rhino's *Beast Wars: Transformers* for a complete description of this series. Fitting for a series animated in Canada, *Beast Wars* had a DVD release there almost a year prior to its U.S. release. Because Canada is Region 1, the disc is watchable on all U.S. players.

The DVD features the first seven episodes of the series, all of which aired in September 1996: "Beast Wars—Part 1"; "Beast Wars—Part 2"; "The Web"; "Equal Measures"; "Chain of Command"; "Power Surge"; and "Fallen Comrades."

This DVD was not available for review.

Beast Wars: Classic Episodes [#2]

Alliance Atlantis (Canadian), 2001.

See the following listing for Rhino's *Beast Wars: Transformers* and a description of the U.S.-release DVD.

Episodes #8–14 of the CGI series are presented in correct airing order: "Double Jeopardy"; "The Probe"; "Gorilla Warfare"; "A Better Mouse Trap"; "Victory"; "Dark Designs"; and "Double DinoBot."

This DVD was not available for review.

Beast Wars: Transformers—Vol. 1

 Rhino, 2001, 140 mins., #R2 976070. Directed by Ian Pearson, Steve Ball, C. Michael Easton, TW Peacocke, Andrew Doucette, Nick Kendall. Written by Bob Forward, Larry D. Tillio, Greg Johnson, Jesse Winfield.

Based on the revived Hasbro toy line, *Beast Wars* features the battles between the evil Predacons and heroic Maximals, two "races" that consist of giant animals that transform into giant robots. The creatures war over a supply of the fuel Energon and generally battle each other. Creatures on display include Rhinox, Cheetor, Tarantu-

las, Optimus Primal, Terrorsaur, Dinobot, Scorponok, Inferno, Tigatron, Rattrap, Waspinator, Silverbolt, Sentinel, Megatron, Airazor, and Blackarachnia.

The 3D CGI animation is by Mainframe Entertainment, and while it's slick and functional, neither the story nor the animation bear any resemblance to actual reality. The DVD features the first six episodes of the series, all of which aired in September 1996: "Beast Wars—Part 1"; "Beast Wars—Part 2"; "The Web"; "Equal Measures"; "Chain of Command"; and "Power Surge."

SPECIAL FEATURES None TECHNICAL FEATURES Fullscreen (1.33:1) • Languages: Eng. • Sound: Dolby Digital 2.0, Dolby Digital Surround 5.1 • Keepcase • 1 Disc • Region 1 GENRE & RATING CGI/Robot/Science Fiction • Not Rated (Kids)

Beast Wars: Transformers—Vol. 2

Rhino, 2001, 140 mins., #R2 976070.

More adventures of the Maximals versus the Predacons. This time out, Rattrap pretends to be a traitor to find out what the Predacons are planning, a probe from the planet Cybertron arrives, and a virus turns Optimus Primal into a vicious battle monkey. Then, Rattrap is trapped and the Predacons try to invade the Maximal base, an explosion rocks the Predacon base, and Rhinox is reprogrammed to fulfill an evil agenda. Finally, Megatron clones Dinobot, leading to a confrontation between the twins at the Maximal base.

This DVD was not available for review.

Beauty and the Beast

Madacy, 1999, 30 mins.

This DVD was not available for review.

Beauty and the Beast: Special Edition [Platinum Edition]

 Disney, 2002, 90 mins., #24962. Directed by Gary Trousdale, Kirk Wise. Screenplay by Linda Woolverton.

A book-loving townsgirl named Belle dreams of a life beyond her small provincial town, where her eccentric father is seen as a buffoon, and Gaston, the town Lothario, wants to make her his wife. But Belle gets more than she bargained for when—due to her father's actions—she's confined to a castle with a monstrous Beast and his walking, talking household furnishings. What she doesn't know is that if he doesn't find love soon, the curse put upon him and his castle will be permanent. But with his angry temperament, how can Belle ever learn to love . . . a beast?

Disney originally planned a darker, nonmusical version of *Beauty and the Beast* but wisely changed their plans and produced what is now seen as one of their masterpieces. The 1991 film was the first to earn over $100 million, blasting all previous Disney releases completely out of the town. With stunning animation, an awesome soundtrack, and a bravura vocal cast, the film was nominated for six Academy Awards, including Best Picture (a first for an animated film). Its only trophy was Best Song for its title tune, but more importantly, it won the hearts of families and animation fans worldwide.

This two-disc set is awash with extra features, but the movie itself has been given the best extras. Viewers have a choice of three versions of the film: a restored and remastered version with a new animated sequence added in; a restored and remastered version of the original theatrical print; and a "work-in-progress" version screened for critics and at a film festival which includes pencil test footage and early animation!

Beauty and the Beast deserved a *Special Edition* and Disney delivers. Highly recommended!

Note that some copies came with a CD-ROM preview of the *Beauty and the Beast: Magical Ballroom* game. The enveloped containing the disc was attached with double-stick tape to the outer box sleeve holding the keepcase. It was also promoted with a sticker on the front of the package.

SPECIAL FEATURES "Making of" Featurettes • Commentary Track with Filmmakers • Cast and Crew Bios • Character and Art Galleries • Production Notes • Deleted Scenes and Abandoned Sequences • Storyboards • Story Treatment • Trailers • Promotional Footage • Music Videos • Broadway Musical Footage • Awards • Games • Other Title Trailers • Inserts: Liner Notes TECHNICAL FEATURES Widescreen (1.85:1, enhanced for 16x9) • Subtitles/CC: Eng. • Languages: Eng. • Sound: Dolby Digital Surround 5.1 • Foldout Box with Multikeepcase • 2 Discs • Region 1 GENRE & RATING Music/Fantasy/Romance • Rated G

Beauty and the Beast: The Enchanted Christmas

Disney, 1998, 72 mins., #15282. Directed by Andy Knight. Written by Flip Kobler, Cindy Marcus, Bill Motz, Bob Roth.

This DVD was not available for review. The very first animated DVD released by Disney, it is currently on moratorium. A "Special Edition" version was released in 2002.

SPECIAL FEATURES Other Title Trailers TECHNICAL FEATURES Fullscreen (1.33:1)• Subtitles/CC: Eng. • Languages: Eng., Fren. dub • Sound: Dolby Digital Surround 5.1 • Keepcase • 1 Disc • Region 1 GENRE & RATING Holiday/Fantasy/Music • Not Rated (Kids)

Beauty and the Beast: The Enchanted Christmas [Special Edition]

Disney, 2002, 72 mins., #25277. Directed by Andy Knight. Screenplay by Flip Kobler, Cindy Marcus, Bill Motz, Bob Roth.

In this holiday story set during Disney's "tale as old as time," Belle decides to warm the heart of the Beast by showing him the warmth and joy of Christmas. Belle asks all the enchanted household objects to help, including Angelique, the Christmas ornament who used to be the castle's decorator before the curse. But an evil pipe organ named Forte gets wind of Belle's plans, and vows to put a halt to any forthcoming holiday cheer.

Although this is a direct-to-video release, it features the same voice cast as the big-budget film, including Robbie Benson, Paige O'Hara, Angela Lansbury, and others, while adding the over-the-top villainous voice of Tim Curry, plus Paul (Pee Wee Herman) Reubens and Haley Joel Osment. There are five new songs, and the animation is a mixture of traditional cel work and CGI, just as in the original film. There are some scary moments, including Belle imperiled in the Black Forest and imprisoned again, so parents of younger children might be wary.

The *Special Edition* features remastered picture and a better sound mix, plus a handful of enjoyable extras.

NOTE: This DVD is now on moratorium.

SPECIAL FEATURES "Making of" Featurette • Music Video • Games • Other Title Trailers TECHNICAL FEATURES Fullscreen (1.33:1) • Subtitles/CC: Eng. • Languages: Eng., Fren. dub, Span. dub • Sound: Dolby Digital Surround 5.1, DTS • Keepcase • 1 Disc • Region 1 GENRE & RATING Holiday/Music/Fantasy • Rated G

Beavis and Butt-Head Do America

Paramount, 2002, 82 mins., #15561. Directed by Mike Judge. Written by Mike Judge, Joe Stillman.

The barely animated, perpetually stupid stars of MTV's *Beavis and Butt-Head* cartoon awaken one morning to find that their precious television has been stolen. Attempting to find it, they set off on a cross-country trip, becoming the FBI's most-wanted men along the way. Whether you'll want to take this journey with B and B depends on whether or not you can handle puerile humor, mostly about sex, flatulence, sex, heavy metal bands, sex, and . . . sex.

Creator Mike Judge (who also provides the voices for both Beavis and Butt-Head) first debuted his two malcontents on MTV's *Liquid Television* in 1992. Eventually awarded their own half-hour show, B and B became a major part of American pop culture, with kids emulating the laughs and catch phrases of the characters. Parents and schools reacted with horror at the series, but this only fueled the popularity of the show. The series aired from 1993 to 1997, with the *Beavis and Butt-Head Do America* feature film released in December 1996.

Listen for a plethora of famous guest voices in the film, including David Letterman, Robert Stack, Cloris Leachman, Bruce Willis, Demi Moore, Greg Kinnear, David Spade, and others. Produced for $12 million, the movie would eventually gross over $63 million in theaters alone!

This DVD was not available for review.

Beavis and Butt-Head Do Christmas

Sony, 2001, 45 mins., #LVD49807.

This DVD was not available for review.

Beavis and Butthead: The Final Judgement

Sony, 1997, 42 mins.

This DVD was not available for review.

Bedknobs and Broomsticks [30th Anniversary Edition]

Disney, 2001, 139 mins., #19608. Directed by Robert Stevenson. Screenplay by Bill Walsh, Don DaGradi. Based on the book by Mary Norton.

Angela Lansbury plays an amateur witch who takes a stuffy professor (David Tomlinson) and three orphan children on the ride of their lives on a bed with an enchanted bed knob. It conveys them to the Isle of Naboombu, where animated animals rule. The humans interact with the denizens of Naboombu, including the undersea fish at the Beautiful Briny Ballroom, and the players at the lion king's Royal Cup soccer match.

One of the quaint magic-and-animation-mixed-with-reality films that Disney produced decades before *Who Framed Roger Rabbit?*, *Bedknobs and Broomsticks* is charming and fun. It won the 1971 Academy Award for Best Visual Effects and was nominated for four other Oscars. Walt Disney bought the rights to Mary Norton's novel in the early 1960s, and although development began concurrently with the similarly themed *Mary Poppins*, the project eventually stalled until 1970. The animated sequence was directed by Ward Kimball.

The 30th Anniversary DVD contains the restored edition of the film, which was released on video for the 25th anniversary. It includes almost half an hour of "lost" footage and a deleted song. The disc also contains a wealth of extras, including two animated shorts: Mickey

Mouse in "The Worm Turns" (1937) and Donald Duck in "The Vanishing Private" (1942).

SPECIAL FEATURES "Making of" Featurette • Character and Art Galleries • Production Notes • Deleted Song • Trailer • Promotional Footage • Recording Session • Other Trailers. TECHNICAL FEATURES Widescreen (1.66:1) • Subtitles/CC: Eng., Fren. • Languages: Eng. • Sound: Dolby Digital Surround 5.1 • Keepcase • 1 Disc • Region 1 GENRE & RATING Live/Animated • Rated G

Beetle Bailey/Hagar the Horrible/Betty Boop

Rhino/Image, 2000, 103 mins., ID9705RHDVD. Directed by Seymour Kneitel, Geoff Pike, Glen Kennedy (HH), Georg Evelyn (BBP). Written by Dennis Marks, Sidney Reznick, Willy Shawn, Howard Post, David Vern, Al Brodax, Les Colodny, Jack Mendelsohn, Bruce Howard, Paul Mason, Douglas Wyman (HH), Ali Marie Matheson (BBP). *Beetle Bailey* based on the comic strip series by Mort Walker. *Hagar the Horrible* based on the comic strip series by Dik Browne.

Three of King Features' popular comic strip characters are teamed up for this trilogy DVD release. Beetle Bailey gets the lion's share of the stories, with ten episodes of his 1963 syndicated adventures at Camp Swampy. All the regular characters are present: General Halftrack, Sergeant Orville Snorkel, Zero, Cosmo, Rocky, and the curvaceous Miss Buxley.

Hagar the Horrible's entry is a CBS television special from 1989, entitled "Hagar Knows Best." In it, the Viking dad returns home to find his daughter dating a traveling minstrel and his son writing poetry! Finally, "Betty Boop's Hollywood Mystery" shows what happens when Betty and Koko the Clown come to Hollywood to become movie stars. Instead, they get embroiled in a search for missing jewels, but a chance meeting with movie mogul Mr. Maxwell Moviola could change everything for them.

The transfers on the DVD are nice—especially given the age of some of the *Beetle Bailey* source material—but comic strip fans might be disappointed with the simplistic style used for the *Hagar* segment. The full-color *Betty Boop* story was created by modern animators; it isn't one of the classic Fleischer cartoons, although it tries to keep its designs similar.

SPECIAL FEATURES None TECHNICAL FEATURES Fullscreen (1.33:1) • Languages: Eng. • Sound: Dolby Digital Mono) • Snapcase • 1 Disc • Region 1–6 GENRE & RATING Comedy • Not Rated (All Ages)

Behind the Music That Sucks ☞ see
Mature/Adult Section

Berserk: War Cry [#1]

AnimeWorks, 2002, 125 mins., #BKDVD6001. Directed by Naohito Takahashi. Script by Atsuhiro Tomioka, Yukiyoshi Ohashi, Makoto Itakura, Shoji Yonemura, Shinzo Fujita. Based on the manga series by Kentaro Miura in *Young Animal.*

The Black Swordsman has come to the castle town of Midland, and his arrival does not sit well with the evil king. Newly seated upon the throne, the monarch has used treachery to get to where he is, and the Black Swordsman intends to bring him down. But the giant muscular mystery man—whose name is Guts—has problems of his own to contend with as well, mostly in the form of demonic tattoos that are trying to use him to further their own goals.

The disc contains five episode of the violent 1997 series: "The Black Swordsman"; "The Band of the Hawk"; "First Battle"; "The Hand of God"; and "A Wind of Swords."

SPECIAL FEATURES Character and Art Galleries • Outtakes • Other Title Trailers TECHNICAL FEATURES Fullscreen (1.33:1) • Subtitles/CC: Eng. • Languages: Jap., Eng. dub • Sound: Dolby Digital 2.0 • Keepcase • 1 Disc • Region 1 GENRE & RATING Fantasy/Action • Rated 16+

Berserk: Immortal Soldier [#2]

AnimeWorks, 2002, 100 mins., #BKDVD-6002. Directed by Naohito Takahashi. Script by Atsuhiro Tomioka, Yukiyoshi Ohashi, Makoto Itakura, Shoji Yonemura. Based on the manga series by Kentaro Miura in *Young Animal.*

NOTE: This DVD arrived too late for a full review. The following text is promotional copy provided by the releasing company:

"Led by Griffith and Guts, the Band of the Hawk has become the most powerful military force in the Kingdom of Midland. However, it is the fate of those who succeed to attract the ire of those who do not. Griffith walks freely among the King's court, but the ministers and nobles each have their own betraying schemes.

"On the battlefield, the natural element of the mercenary, supremacy is unreachable for the Hawks. They are superior in terms of tactics, mobility, and striking power. However, some soldiers are beyond the rules of war, and the limits of human comprehension. A monster guards the path Guts and Griffith must travel. Known as Zodd the Immortal, he is notorious for harvesting thousands of heads in battles during a span of nearly three hundred years. His appetite for blood and murder is unquenchable."

This disc contains episodes #6–9.

SPECIAL FEATURES Character and Art Galleries • Clean Credits • Outtakes • Other Title Trailers • Easter Egg TECHNICAL FEATURES Fullscreen (1.33:1) • Subtitles/CC: Eng. • Languages: Jap., Eng. dub • Sound: Dolby Digital 2.0 • Keepcase • 1 Disc • Region 1 GENRE & RATING Fantasy/Action • Rated 16+

Berserk: Box of War [DVD Collector Box with #1]

AnimeWorks, 2002, #BKDVD-6000.

This very cool cardboard box set is sized to fit six volumes of *Berserk*, but it contains only volume #1, plus an insert to fill out the rest of the box. Collectors can fill out their own box collection. See individual entries for the Special and Technical Features listings.

TECHNICAL FEATURES Cardboard Box with 1 Keepcase • 1 Disc GENRE & RATING Fantasy/Action • Rated 16+

Best of Beavis and Butt-Head, The

Time-Life, 2002.

Time-Life has published three DVD volumes of *The Best of Beavis and Butt-Head*: *Beavis and Butt-Head: Innocence Lost/Chicks n' Stuff*; *Beavis and Butt-Head: Troubled Youth/Feel Our Pain*; and *Beavis and Butt-Head: Butt-O-Ween/Beavis and Butt-Head Do Christmas*.

These DVDs were not available for review.

Best of Bulgarian Animation, The

Image, 2000, 50 mins., #ID9001ASDVD. Produced by Sofia Animation Studio.

Founded in 1948 in Bulgaria, the Sofia Animation Studio has produced a wide range of animated projects. This DVD collection contains eleven shorts, most of which have no dialogue, and all of which are appropriate for children and adults.

"Baby Dreams at the Airport" and "Baby Dreams at the Automobile Factory" are episodes in a twelve-part series in which a young child is miraculously unharmed, despite the death-defying adventures it embarks upon. In "De Facto," a town's leaders attempt to find someone to blame for a house's collapse. A quartet of shorts featuring a trio of idiots and their mishaps follows: "Three Fools and the Automobile"; "Three Fools and the Hat"; "Three Fools and the Tent"; and "Three Fools and the Hammer Throw."

"Beach" tells the story of an epic waterside war between frogs and ducks, while "Caw!" finds a crow attempting to join a choral group. In "Left, Right . . ." a young bird learns that the military is not for him, and the disc rounds out with "The Intelligent Village," in which a town is overrun by snakes.

SPECIAL FEATURES None TECHNICAL FEATURES Fullscreen (1.33:1) • Languages: Bulg. • Sound: Dolby Digital Mono • Snapcase • 1 Disc • Region 1–6 GENRE & RATING Anthology • Not Rated (All Ages)

Best of Kitty, The ☞ see Mature/Adult Section

Best of the Best: Especially for Kids!

Image, 2000, 82 mins., #ID0220NFDVD. Compiled by National Film Board of Canada.

The National Film Board of Canada has released some excellent fare over the years, and this disc contains nine Academy Award winners and nominees, all appropriate for children. While most of them are traditional animation, some are stop-motion or other forms.

The 1979 Oscar-winner "Every Child" tells the story of a baby abandoned on a busy executive's doorstep, while "The Tender Tale of Cinderella Penguin" (1981) transports the traditional fairy tale into the realm of the Antarctic birds. "Blackfly" (1991) is the tale of a folk singer's battle against an insect, and "The Cat Came Back" (1988) recounts a similar battle between a man and a little yellow cat that refuses to leave.

"Sandcastle," winner of the 1977 Oscar, shows what happens when the wind begins blowing at the Sandman's sand castles, while "The Owl Who Married a Goose" recounts an Inuit Indian legend. "Evolution" (1971) traces humankind's rise in a humorous manner, and "Christmas Cracker" (1964) gives a trio of holiday chuckles. "Monsieur Pointu" (1975) wraps up the collection with a mostly live-action story about a virtuoso violinist, "told" by a mime.

Note that the title on the disc itself reads "Especially for Children!" but the outer DVD packaging reads "Especially for Kids!"

SPECIAL FEATURES None TECHNICAL FEATURES Fullscreen (1.33:1) • Languages: Eng. • Sound: Dolby Digital 2.0 • Snapcase • 1 Disc • Region 1–6 GENRE & RATING Anthology • Not Rated (All Ages)

Best of the Best: Romantic Tales and Other Whimsical Relationships

Image, 2000, 97 mins., #ID0232NFDVD. Compiled by National Film Board of Canada.

Another set of animated shorts from the National Film Board of Canada, this disc contains ten stories that were either Academy Award winners or nominees. The animation styles range from traditional to collage to other forms.

Shorts include: "A Chairy Tale" (1957); "George and Rosemary" (1987); "Strings" (1991); "Bob's Birthday" (Oscar 1994); "The Street" (1976); "Walking" (1969); "Pas de Deux" (1968); "The Romance of Transportation in Canada" (1952); "The Drag" (1963); and "The Family That Dwelt Apart" (1974).

SPECIAL FEATURES None TECHNICAL FEATURES Fullscreen (1.33:1) • Languages: Eng. • Sound: Dolby Digital 2.0 • Snapcase • 1 Disc • Region 1–6 GENRE & RATING Anthology • Not Rated (All Ages)

Best of the Best: Strange Tales of the Imagination

Image, 2001, 90 mins., #ID0239NFDVD. Compiled by National Film Board of Canada.

The National Film Board of Canada offers another collection of ten animated shorts, all Academy Award winners or nominees. The subject matter this time is the bizarre and strange, with traditional animation, plus CGI and more.

The set includes: "The Big Snit" (1985); "This Is the House That Jack Built" (1968); "Special Delivery" (1978 Oscar); "My Financial Career" (1963); "Neighbors" (1952 Oscar); "Paradise" (1984); "Hunger" (1974); "The Bead Game" (1977); "La Salla" (1996); and "What On Earth!" (1967).

SPECIAL FEATURES None TECHNICAL FEATURES Fullscreen (1.33:1) • Languages: Eng. • Sound: Dolby Digital 2.0 • Snapcase • 1 Disc • Region 1–6 GENRE & RATING Anthology • Not Rated (All Ages)

Best of the Web, The ☞ see Mature/Adult Section

Best of Zagreb Film, The: Be Careful What You Wish For and The Classic Collection

Image, 2000, 114 mins., #ID9002ASDVD. Produced by Zagreb Film.

In the latter half of the twentieth century, the Yugoslavian animation studio Zagreb Films produced over 600 cartoon shorts. Unlike some studios, the animators at Zagreb wrote, designed, and directed their own films rather than relying on a group effort.

This DVD contains two programs, sorting the shorts into similar themes and tones. "Be Careful What You Wish For" has fourteen tales of irony, double-cross, and mystery. The selection includes: "Big Time"; "Curiosity"; "Musical Pig"; "Okay!"; "Elegy"; "The Fifth One"; "The Wall"; "Prayer"; "Paranoia"; and "The Ceremony." Of these, "Paranoia" is a standout; in a sleek and bold comic book style, a hero is hunted through a city.

"The Classic Collection" contains seven of Zagreb's unique offerings: "Ersatz"; "Diary"; "Mask of the Red Death"; "Butterflies"; "Last Waltz in the Old Mill"; "Fisheye"; and "Mass in A Minor." In 1961, "Ersatz" won the Best Animated Short Film Oscar, but both "Mask of the Red Death" and "Butterflies" are also very cool visual extravaganzas. You might want to keep kids away from the creepy "Fisheye," however.

SPECIAL FEATURES Production Notes. TECHNICAL FEATURES Fullscreen (1.33:1) • Languages: Russ. • Sound: Dolby Digital Mono) • Snapcase • 1 Disc • Region 1 GENRE & RATING Anthology • Not Rated (Teens)

Best of Zagreb Film: Laugh At Your Own Risk and For Children Only

Image, 2000, 109 mins., #ID9003ASDVD. Produced by Zagreb Film.

Another anthology of shorts from the Yugoslavian animation studio Zagreb Films, this collection is an odd mixture of both surreal and childlike stories.

This DVD contains two programs, sorting the shorts into similar themes and tones. "Laugh At Your Own Risk" features eight bits of black humor, surrealism, and comic irony, including: "The Tower of Babel"; "Exciting Love Story"; "The Devil's Work"; "Of Holes and Corks"; "Learning To Walk"; "Home Is the Best"; "Largo"; and the troika "Maxicat in Tennis/Maxicat in Rope/Maxicat in Door."

"For Children Only" has eight more offerings geared toward the younger set but no less imaginative: "Cow On the Moon"; "Strange Bird"; "Octave of Fear"; "Little and Big"; "Anna Goes To Buy Some Bread"; "Well Done

Job"; "Krek"; and another trilogy, "Maxicat in Ball of Yarn/Maxicat in Door/Maxicat in Fishing."

SPECIAL FEATURES Production Notes. TECHNICAL FEATURES Fullscreen (1.33:1) • Languages: Russ. • Sound: Dolby Digital Mono) • Snapcase • 1 Disc • Region 1 GENRE & RATING Anthology • Not Rated (Teens)

Best of Zagreb Film, The: Nudity Required

☛ see Mature/Adult Section

BetterMan: Vol. 1—The Awakening

Bandai, 2002, 125 mins., #1475. Directed by Yoshitomo Yonetani. Written by Hiroshi Yamaguchi.

The year is 2006, and nerdy Keita Aono loves to play video games. He's also got the hots for his old friend Hinoki who has just moved back into town. Following a massacre at an underground amusement park, Keita and Hinoki are drawn into a web of technology and intrigue. They both have the necessary genetic traits to pilot the "Awakeners," neuronoid robots created by Akamatsu Industries. That ability is a good thing since it appears that trouble is brewing. While battling a mysterious monster named Algernon, they come in contact with a rainbow-haired being, Betterman Lamia, who can also transform into other creatures. Though Betterman appears to be an ally, they can't be sure.

This DVD contains the first five episodes of the 1999 TV series from Japan (fourteen episodes were produced in all). Although the animation is grainy, it appears to be for effect rather than a bad DVD transfer. The story has some creepy elements and violence, so concerned parents will want to pay attention to the rating. Its keepcase mechanism for holding the DVD in place was almost impossible to use.

SPECIAL FEATURES Character Bios • Character and Art Galleries • Clean Credits • Other Title Trailers • Inserts: Liner Notes • Reversible Cover. TECHNICAL FEATURES Widescreen (1.85:1) • Subtitles/CC: Eng. • Languages: Jap., Eng. dub • Sound: Dolby Digital • Keepcase • 1 Disc • Region 1 GENRE & RATING Robots/Suspense • Rated 13+

BetterMan: Vol. 2—Metamorphosis

Bandai, 2002, 125 mins., #1476. Directed by Yoshitomo Yonetani. Written by Hiroshi Yamaguchi.

NOTE: This DVD arrived too late for a full review. The following text is promotional copy provided by the releasing company:

"Reunited with his childhood

friend Hinoki, Keita has joined the battle against Algernon as a Head Diver in the Kakuseijin No. 1, a multipurpose, state-of-the-art attack mecha. Danger abounds as the Akamatsu team travels around the world in search of Algernon! Meanwhile, Betterman continues to monitor the Akamatsu team's progress and comes to the rescue on more than one occasion. But even he has secrets that no one has even guessed. Will discovering them cost the Akamatsu team their lives?"

This disc contains episodes #6–10.

SPECIAL FEATURES Character Bios • Character and Art Galleries • Clean Credits • Other Title Trailers • Inserts: Liner Notes, Postcard • Reversible Cover TECHNICAL FEATURES Widescreen (1.85:1) • Subtitles/CC: Eng. • Languages: Jap., Eng. dub • Sound: Dolby Digital 2.0 • Keepcase • 1 Disc • Region 1 GENRE & RATING Robots/Suspense • Rated 13+

BetterMan: Vol. 3—Seeds of Death

Bandai, 2002, 100 mins., #1477. Directed by Yoshitomo Yonetani. Written by Hiroshi Yamaguchi.

NOTE: This DVD arrived too late for a full review. The following text is promotional copy provided by the releasing company:

"The mystery surround Algernon continues to thicken as the fight against this growing menace escalates. Having discovered the mysterious Animus Flower in the Ajanta caves in India, the team has a new lead in their quest against Algernon, but Keita and the group are faced with more questions than answers! When the rest of the team arrives at the BPL facility, they soon face a new breed of genetically engineered creatures, and among them is . . . Chandy? As the defeat of Betterman by the hands of these evil creations continues to linger, just when all looks lost, a new hope shines in the darkness. Could it be . . . another Betterman?"

This disc contains episodes #11–14.

SPECIAL FEATURES Character Bios • Character and Art Galleries • Other Title Trailers • Inserts: Liner Notes, Postcard • Reversible Cover TECHNICAL FEATURES Widescreen (1.85:1) • Subtitles/CC: Eng. • Languages: Jap., Eng. dub • Sound: Dolby Digital • Keepcase • 1 Disc • Region 1 GENRE & RATING Robots/Suspense • Rated 13+

Beyond the Mind's Eye [Gold Series Collector's Edition]

Unapix, 2000, 45 mins., #UPX72060. Directed by Michael Boydston.

One of the earliest examples of eye-candy CGI set to music—not to mention alphabetically the first of the sort in this book—*Beyond the Mind's Eye* is the granddaddy of them all. Released in 1992, it featured electronic and acoustic music by Jan Hammer, hot off his work on *Miami Vice*. Dozens of animation companies contributed bits and pieces to the video, with Michael Boylston and his crew weaving them together to create surreal storylines.

For most viewers, this was likely the first glimpse they had of full-on 3D CGI animation, as the video was popular as "background noise" at parties; even if one were stone cold sober, the hallucinatory nature of the segments took you on a trip. With alien plants growing from spores, metal chips that constantly flow and reform, and a bumblebee pursuit that resembles a cop show car chase, the feature has enough diversity that if you don't like something, it will have morphed to something different within seconds.

Though it doesn't tout it on the packaging, the program contains several CGI segments from *The Lawnmower Man*, a 1992 feature film very loosely based on a Stephen King short story. The DVD has an excellent picture and sound, even if the menus are a bit plain.

Snatch up this DVD if you see it. Unapix has gone out of business, and no other company has brought *Beyond the Mind's Eye* back into print—yet.

SPECIAL FEATURES None TECHNICAL FEATURES Fullscreen (1.33:1) • Languages: Eng. • Sound: PCM Audio • Keepcase • 1 Disc • Region 1 GENRE & RATING CGI/Music • Not Rated (Teens)

BFG, The: The Big Friendly Giant

Celebrity, 1999, 95 mins.

This DVD was not available for review.

Bible Black ☞ see Mature/Adult Section

Big O, The: Vol. 1

Bandai, 2001, 100 mins., #1835. Directed by Kazuyoshi Katayama, Kenji Hayama. Written by Chiaka Konaka. Based on the manga series by Hajime Yatate in *Monthly Magazine Z*.

Forty years ago, the citizens of Paradigm City lost their memories, all of them. Now the citizens have rebuilt their lives, relatively safe in their gloomy art deco city due to the imposition of martial law. Cocky Roger Smith is a Negotiator, and he's brought in whenever a dispute arises. Whatever Roger can't handle isn't a problem; he's got a giant Megadeus robot called "The Big O" to do his bidding. Aided by his faithful butler, Norman, and an eccentric girl android named R. Dorothy Wainwright, Roger makes sure the nights are safe for the city's citizens.

If this series sounds suspiciously like *Batman: The Animated Series*, wait until you've seen it, then you'll really think "homage" has been taken to the extreme with a lead character that is Bruce Wayne's spitting image and a "dark deco" city that harbors bizarre criminals. The Batman character isn't the only element that's been borrowed, the lead theme is almost note for note the *Flash Gordon* film theme by Queen, and the end credits feature a Disneyesque duet.

Thankfully, *The Big O* is entertaining and clever despite (or because of) its obvious origins, and the mixture of robots with crime-fighting and film noir mystery is a fun one. The scripts are very American in nature, meaning the English dub doesn't seem intrusive at all. The first disc features the initial quarter of episodes: "Roger the Negotiator"; "Dorothy, Dorothy"; "Electric City"; and "Underground City."

The only complaint about the DVD is its very screwed-up menu. You can't find items on it unless you direct the cursor over the correct area onscreen. Hey, Bandai: Easter eggs are supposed to be hidden, but the menu is not!

SPECIAL FEATURES Text Interview • Clean Credits • Other Title Trailers • Insert: Liner Notes TECHNICAL FEATURES Fullscreen (1.33:1) • Subtitles/CC: Eng. • Languages: Jap., Eng. dub • Sound: Dolby Digital Surround 2.0 • Keepcase • 1 Disc • Region 1 GENRE & RATING Action/Robots/Science Fiction • Rated 13+

Big O, The: Vol. 2

Bandai, 2001, 75 mins., #1836. Animation directed by Takuro Shinbo, Madoka Hirayama, Kami Horii. Written by Keiichi Hasegawa, Masanao Akahoshi, Chiaka Konaka. Based on the manga series by Hajime Yatate in *Monthly Magazine Z*.

Roger Smith is back on the case finding more trouble in Paradigm City to squash. This time he faces the cop-murdering ghost of a Military Policeman, a mad musician, and secrets from the past bringing trouble with them as they bubble to the surface from a long-submerged section of the city.

This DVD features episode #5–7: "Bring Back My Ghost"; "A Legacy of Amadeus"; and "The Call from the Past." Once again, the only thing not fun about the disc is the menu.

SPECIAL FEATURES Art Galleries • Text Interview • Other Title Trailers • Insert: Liner Notes TECHNICAL FEATURES Fullscreen (1.33:1) • Subtitles/CC: Eng. • Languages: Jap., Eng. dub • Sound: Dolby Digital Surround 2.0 • Keepcase • 1 Disc • Region 1 GENRE & RATING Action/Robots/Science Fiction • Rated 13+

Big O, The: Vol. 3

Bandai, 2001, 75 mins., #1837. Animation directed by Takuro Shinbo, Kenji Hayama. Written by Keiichi Hasegawa, Shin Yoshida. Based on the manga series by Hajime Yatate in *Monthly Magazine Z*.

The supporting cast members of *The Big O* get a bit more play here, although Roger Smith is still the lead.

When Dorothy brings home a stray pet, it brings mystery and danger with it. Next, cop Dan Dastun works a kidnapping case, even as an old arch-villain is sprung from jail. Finally, Dastun is involved in Smith's affairs again when he dreams of a woman being murdered on a dock.

More dark noir action is showcased here in episodes #8–10: "Missing Cat"; "Beck Comes Back"; and "Winter Night Phantom." The series continues to be entertaining, with a nice balance of humor, action, and suspense.

SPECIAL FEATURES Art Galleries • Text Interview • Other Title Trailers • Insert: Liner Notes TECHNICAL FEATURES Fullscreen (1.33:1) • Subtitles/CC: Eng. • Languages: Jap., Eng. dub • Sound: Dolby Digital Surround 2.0 • Keepcase • 1 Disc • Region 1 GENRE & RATING Action/Robots/Science Fiction • Rated 13+

Big O, The: Vol. 4

Bandai, 2001, 75 mins., #1838. Animation directed by Kenji Hayama, Madoka Hirayama, Keiichi Sato. Written by Shin Yoshida, Masanao Akahoshi, Keiichi Hasegawa. Based on the manga series by Hajime Yatate in *Monthly Magazine Z*.

A bizarre plant may cause trouble for the denizens of Paradigm City, even as they plan to celebrate Heaven Day (their version of Christmas). Then, Roger Smith's nemesis Schwarzwald returns, and he's got his own giant Megadeus—known as The Big Duo—to battle the Big O with. Finally, Roger is the target of a murderer who has ties to Smith's past—and may hold the key to Paradigm City's past.

This final disc contains episodes #11–13: "Daemonseed"; "Enemy Is Another Big"; and "A.D." Unfortunately, there was no second season of *The Big O* in Japan, so this disc concludes the series. Too bad. It's definitely a keeper.

SPECIAL FEATURES Art Galleries • Text Interview • Other Title Trailers • Insert: Liner Notes • Easter Egg TECHNICAL FEATURES Fullscreen (1.33:1) • Subtitles/CC: Eng. • Languages: Jap., Eng. dub • Sound: Dolby Digital Surround 2.0 • Keepcase • 1 Disc • Region 1 GENRE & RATING Action/Robots/Science Fiction • Rated 13+

Big Wars ☞ see Mature/Adult Section

Biohunter ☞ see Mature/Adult Section

Black Arrow, The [Collector's Edition]

Digital Versatile Disc, 2000, 48 mins., #177. Animation Directed by Alex Nicholas. Screenplay by Paul Leadon. Based on the book by Robert Louis Stevenson.

The 16th-century War of the Roses is the historical backdrop of this adventure story that pits archer Richard Shelton against the evil nobleman Sir Daniel Brackley. Young Shelton has many wrongs to avenge, not the least of which is the death of his father, and using his crossbow and other weapons, he'll get revenge.

Produced by Burbank Films Australia in 1988, this adaptation of Robert Louis Stevenson's novel follows its source material relatively well. The Robin Hoodesque nature of the story will appeal to adventure fans, and the animation features some nice character designs and backgrounds. The DVD producers not only included

information on Stevenson's life, but also historical notes about the real War of the Roses.

SPECIAL FEATURES Author Bio • Game TECHNICAL FEATURES Fullscreen (1.33:1) • Subtitles/CC: Eng. • Languages: Eng. • Sound: Dolby Digital 5.1, DTS • Keepcase • 1 Disc • Region All GENRE & RATING Historic/Adventure • Not Rated (All Ages)

Black Beauty [Collector's Edition]

Digital Versatile Disc, 1999, 49 mins., #178. Animation Directed by Warwick Gilbert. Screenplay by J. L. Kane and P. Jennings. Based on the book by Emma Sewell.

Young Polly is given a horse named "Black Beauty," and the two soon form an unbreakable bond of love. But hardships and danger stand in the way of their happiness on a lush country estate, and Polly and Black Beauty must work together to triumph over adversity.

Another production of Burbank Films Australia, this adaptation of Emma Sewell's beloved book has had lots of live-action treatments but relatively few animated versions. While the animation itself is OK, the designs look like Don Bluth on a really bad day. Still, for children who like horses, this will call to be collected in your DVD corral. It won't make you quite as weepy as some of the live versions, but it will tug at the heartstrings. As with other DVD releases, there is a bio of the author on the disc.

SPECIAL FEATURES Author Bio • Game TECHNICAL FEATURES Fullscreen (1.33:1) • Subtitles/CC: Eng. • Languages: Eng. • Sound: Dolby Digital 5.1, DTS 5.1 • Keepcase • 1 Disc • Region All GENRE & RATING Animal/Adventure • Not Rated (All Ages)

Black Cauldron, The [Gold Collection]

Disney, 2001, 80 mins., #19607. Directed by Ted Berman, Richard Rich. Story by David Jonas, Vance Gerry, Al Wilson, Roy Morita, Ted Berman, Peter Young, Richard Rich, Art Stevens, Joe Hale. Based on the book series *The Chronicles of Prydain* by Lloyd Alexander.

Taran lives in the mystical kingdom of Prydain, and when not playing with his psychic pig Hen Wen, he dreams of swordplay, adventure, and glory. Unexpectedly, he gets his wish, and he's soon on a quest to stop the evil Horned King from getting his claws on the fabled Black Cauldron. If the villain wins, the world will be overrun! But even with help from a magical sword and the comely princess Eilonwny, Taran's way isn't an easy one; he still has to battle dragons, monsters, a trio of witches, and more.

This was Disney's 25th animated feature film, and the first to garner a PG rating. It was also very expensive, costing $25 million and ten years of production time, plus it featured the first major use of CGI in an all animated film. It's only the second Disney cartoon to be shot in 70 millimeter (following 1959's *Sleeping Beauty*). So why did *The Black Cauldron* bomb on release in 1985, netting only $21 million? The true reason likely lay in its dark subject matter, which didn't make it a favorite of parents and "family film" watchdogs, even though the comedy relief sidekicks appealed to the young'uns.

The DVD is a competent job with only a few extras, but one of those is the 1952 Donald Duck cartoon "Trick or Treat." Even if just to see the innovations and Disney's newer set of animators breaking out of the "Old Guard" cocoon, *The Black Cauldron* is worth a look.

SPECIAL FEATURES Art Galleries • Trailer • Games • Other Title Trailers TECHNICAL FEATURES Widescreen (2.35:1) • Fullscreen (1.33:1) • Subtitles/CC: Eng. • Languages: Eng., Fren. dub, Span. dub • Sound: Dolby Digital Surround 5.1 • Keepcase • 1 Discs • Region 1 GENRE & RATING Magic/Fantasy • Rated PG

Black Jack ☞ see Mature/Adult Section

Black Magic M66 ☞ see Mature/Adult Section

Blackmail, The ☞ see Mature/Adult Section

Blood Reign: Curse of the Yoma

ADV Films, 2001, 80 mins., #DCY001. Directed by Takashi Anno. Screenplay by Sho Aikawa. Based on the manga series by Kei Kusunoki in *Ribbon Mascot Comics*.

Two young ninjas—Maro and Hikage—have been friends for a long time, in battle and in peace. When Hikage is told to kill his buddy, Maro goes on the run. His path leads both ninjas to a village where the inhabitants are stalked by a spider-creature known as a "Yoma." But what does the Yoma have to do with Maro, and how will a female ninja complicate matters?

This 1988 OVA two-parter is a decent historical fantasy set in feudal Japan, pitting giant spiders and demons against semi-heroic characters. For a show with this dark a storyline, the animation is clean and bright, although the DVD transfer is a bit lackluster at times. The disc contains two episodes: "Hikagi in an Evil World" and "Maro with Crazy Fang." The coolest thing about this disc is the insert, which gives the translation of a gruesome Japanese counting song taught to children.

SPECIAL FEATURES Character Bios • Trailer • Other Title Trailers • Insert: Song Lyrics TECHNICAL FEATURES Fullscreen (1.33:1) • Subtitles/CC: Eng. • Languages: Jap., Eng. dub • Sound: Dolby Digital 2.0 • Keepcase • 1 Disc • Region 1 GENRE & RATING Martial Arts/Historical/Horror • Rated 15+

Blood: The Last Vampire ☞ see Mature/Adult Section

Blue's Clues: Blue's Big Musical Movie

Paramount, 2000, 78 mins., #83972. Directed by Todd Kessler. Written by Angela C. Santomero, Michael T. Smith.

Nickelodeon's small-screen sensation makes the jump to DVD in this movie, in which Blue (the dog) and her various friends (ranging from a cat to a mailbox to a bar of soap) plan a musical in their back yard. Human buddy Steve helps Blue, and G-Clef (voiced by Ray Charles) sings a new song in this bouncy feature preschoolers will love.

Extras on the DVD include a "backstage" feature that shows how Steven Burns does all his scenes in front of a green screen, before Blue, his friends, and all the backgrounds are added in digitally. Several music videos are also offered, meaning kids will be able to sing along with their favorite characters. *Blue's Clues* is imaginative and cute, and it teaches some good lessons in music and self esteem without being preachy. Parents who want their kids to be musical prodigies would do better renting this than other big-budget adventure musicals.

SPECIAL FEATURES "Making of" Featurette • Music Videos • Games • DVD-ROM Features: Game TECHNICAL FEATURES Fullscreen (1.33:1) • Subtitles/CC: Eng. • Languages: Eng. • Sound: Dolby Digital Surround 2.0 • Keepcase • 1 Disc • Region 1 GENRE & RATING Children/Music/Live & Animation • Not Rated (All Ages)

Blue Gender

The following *Blue Gender* titles, from Funimation, were not available for review: *Blue Gender #1, Blue Gender #2, Blue Gender #3, Blue Gender #4, Blue Gender #5, Blue Gender #6, Blue Gender #7*.

Blue Seed: The Nightmare Begins [#1]

ADV Films, 2001, 180 mins., #DBS001. Directed by Jun Kamiya. Screenplay by Masaharu Amiya, Toshihisa Arakawa, Aoba Fujimiya, Yoshimasa Takahashi, Naruhisa Arakawa. Based on the manga series by Yuzo Takada in *Comic Gamma*.

Humankind's oldest enemies have been held in check thanks to continued human sacrifices, and now, special agents around the world prepare for battle. TAC agent Mamoru Kusanagi has serious plans for schoolgirl Momiji Fujimiya, who is the heir to the priestess bloodline of the Kushinada. The monstrous Aragami demons are wreaking havoc on Earth, and Mamoru has the ability to stop them. Unfortunately, Mamoru's sister has already disappeared in battle, meaning that the teen girl may be humankind's last hope against the forces of darkness.

If this 1994 Japanese TV series sounds suspiciously familiar, try substituting the words "Watcher," "Rupert Giles," "Buffy Summers," and "Slayer" for "TAC Agent," "Mamoru Kusanagi," "Momiji Fujimiya," and "priestess." Still, the show can't be considered a rip-off of *Buffy the Vampire Slayer* due to its timing, but fans of that popular show might find something to enjoy in *Blue Seed*. Each episode, Momiji fights another monster or demon, all while trying to return to her normal high school life. A similar mixture of humor, drama, and horror is present, although the stories are a bit more simplistic than *Buffy*'s. The animation is competent but can be very cutesy.

The first DVD contains seven episodes, all with extremely long titles such as "Complicated and Hard to Understand! Being a Man Puts You in Such a Difficult Position!" The disc contains an extra super-deformed chibi short "Omake Theatre" that is a parody of the main storyline. Note that the "Textless Opening" extras feature promised on the DVD cover is not on the disc.

SPECIAL FEATURES Character Bios • Additional Footage "Omake Theatre" • Other Title Trailers TECHNICAL FEATURES Fullscreen (1.33:1) • Subtitles/CC: Eng. • Languages: Eng. dub, Span. dub, Jap. • Sound: Dolby Digital 2.0 • Keepcase • 1 Disc • Region 1, 4 GENRE & RATING Horror/Action/Comedy • Rated 12+

Blue Seed: Descent Into Terror [#2]

ADV Films, 2001, 180 mins., #DBS002. Directed by Jun Kamiya. Screenplay by Naruhisa Arakawa, Yoshimasa Takahashi, Kenichi Araki, Ryoei Tsukimura, Yuzo Takada. Based on the manga series by Yuzo Takada in *Comic Gamma*.

A new part-Aragami character arrives on the scene, making things difficult for Mamoru, and another female warrior is introduced. The DVD contains seven more episodes, plus two additional omake parodies.

SPECIAL FEATURES Character Bios • Story Summary • Additional Footage "Omake Theatre" • Other Title Trailers TECHNICAL FEATURES Fullscreen (1.33:1) • Subtitles/CC: Eng. • Languages: Jap., Eng. dub, Span. dub • Sound: Dolby Digital 2.0 • Keepcase • 1 Disc • Region 1, 2, 4 GENRE & RATING Horror/Action/Comedy • Rated 12+

Blue Seed: Prelude to Sacrifice [#3]

ADV Films, 2001, 150 mins., #DBS003. Directed by Jun Kamiya. Screenplay by Yoshimasa Takahashi, Kenichi Araki, Naruhisa Arakawa, Yuzo Takada, Akimori Tsukimura, Masaharu Amiya, Naruhisa Arakawa. Based on the manga series by Yuzo Takada in *Comic Gamma*.

Sakura Yamazaki, the powerful Shinto Princess from America, helps the TAC teams and Momiji fight the Aragami. But the public is beginning to suspect the truth about the monsters in their midst, and a new soldier appears on the scene whose loyalties are unknown.

Another six episodes are presented on this DVD, along with five more omake.

SPECIAL FEATURES Character Bios • Story Summary • Additional Footage "Omake Theatre" • Other Title Trailers TECHNICAL FEATURES Fullscreen (1.33:1) • Subtitles/CC: Eng. • Languages: Jap., Eng. dub, Span. dub • Sound: Dolby Digital 2.0 • Keepcase • 1 Disc • Region 1, 2, 4 GENRE & RATING Horror/Action/Comedy • Rated 12+

Blue Seed: Nightfall [#4]

ADV Films, 2001, 150 mins., #DBS004. Directed by Jun Kamiya. Screenplay by Masaharu Amiya, Naruhisa Arakawa. Based on the manga series by Yuzo Takada in *Comic Gamma*.

The Aragami can be stopped for good, but it will take the sacrifice of Momiji's blood to do it! Now, she's on the run from monsters, the public, and her former allies, even as the final confrontation looms ever nearer.

The final five episodes round out this DVD, which also presents four more omake for fun.

SPECIAL FEATURES Character Bios • Story Summary • Additional Footage "Omake Theatre" • Other Title Trailers TECHNICAL FEATURES Fullscreen (1.33:1) • Subtitles/CC: Eng. • Languages: Jap., Eng. dub, Span. dub • Sound: Dolby Digital 2.0 • Keepcase • 1 Disc • Region 1, 2, 4 GENRE & RATING Horror/Action/Comedy • Rated 12+

Blue Seed: Perfect Collection

ADV Films, 2002, 650 mins., #DBS/100.

This multikeepcase set includes the four *Blue Seed* discs exactly as they appeared in the individual editions. See individual entries for the Special and Technical Features listings.

TECHNICAL FEATURES Multikeepcase • 4 Discs • Region 1 GENRE & RATING Horror/Action/Comedy • Rated 12+

Blue Submarine No. 6: Blues [#1]

Bandai, 2000, 30 mins., #0940. Directed by Mahiro Maeda. Screenplay by Hiroshi Yamaguchi. Based on the manga series by Satoru Ozawa in *Akita Shoten Sunday*.

The world has been flooded due to the shift of the planetary poles, and villain Zorndyke and his sea-based genetically altered mutant creations are waging war against what's left of humanity. *Blue Submarine No. 6* and her crew must lead the charge to save all humankind from Zorndyke's beasts. Among the crew are Tetsu Hayami, an angry young ex-submarine pilot, and Mayumi Kino, the young officer who persuades him to come back to duty.

Although this 1998 series has been aired on Cartoon Network's Toonami, it was edited for television. The DVD series contains the full uncut shows, and what shows they are! The beautiful animation is a combination of CG and cel work that seems all the more gorgeous due to its underwater setting. The character designs are sharp, and though clearly recognizable as anime, are unique enough not to look overly familiar. While the story is a little disjointed at times—information is doled out only when necessary—this also means that viewers who pay close attention are rewarded.

Fans have complained that Bandai only included a half-hour episode on each DVD in this series, but few have said that the show isn't well worth owning. Combined with the content, an excellent print and a nicely mixed stereo track make this a great example of both the anime form and DVD technology.

SPECIAL FEATURES Other Title Trailers • Easter Egg TECHNICAL FEATURES Fullscreen (1.33:1) • Subtitles/CC: Eng. • Languages: Jap., Eng. dub • Sound: Dolby Digital 2.0, Dolby Digital Surround 5.1 • Keepcase • 1 Disc • Region 1 GENRE & RATING Underwater/Action/Science Fiction • Rated 13+

Blue Submarine No. 6: Pilots [#2]

Bandai, 2000, 30 mins., #0941. Directed by Mahiro Maeda. Screenplay by Hiroshi Yamaguchi. Based on the manga series by Satoru Ozawa in *Akita Shoten Sunday*.

Zorndyke's forces attack the Blue Submarine base in this second DVD, and he announces an evil plot. As before, the animation, sound, and picture quality are excellent, even if the sole thirty-minute episode on the disc seems miserly.

SPECIAL FEATURES Other Title Trailers TECHNICAL FEATURES Fullscreen (1.33:1) • Subtitles/CC: Eng. • Languages: Jap., Eng. dub • Sound: Dolby Digital 2.0, Dolby Digital Surround 5.1 • Keepcase • 1 Disc • Region 1 GENRE & RATING Underwater/Action/Science Fiction • Rated 13+

Blue Submarine No. 6: Hearts [#3]

Bandai, 2000, 30 mins., #0942. Directed by Mahiro Maeda. Screenplay by Hiroshi Yamaguchi. Based on the manga series by Satoru Ozawa in *Akita Shoten Sunday*.

Tetsu Hayami, adrift in the ocean, is taken in by mysterious mermaid creatures. Meanwhile, Mayumi is determined to find Tetsu, with or without the help of the *Blue Submarine* crew. Another excellent DVD, though the pre-menu trailers can't be skipped (unlike others in the series).

SPECIAL FEATURES Other Title Trailers TECHNICAL FEATURES Fullscreen (1.33:1) • Subtitles/CC: Eng. • Languages: Jap., Eng. dub • Sound: Dolby Digital 2.0, Dolby Digital Surround 5.1 • Keepcase • 1 Disc • Region 1 GENRE & RATING Underwater/Action/Science Fiction • Rated 13+

Blue Submarine No. 6: Minasoko [#4]

Bandai, 2000, 50 mins., #0943. Directed by Mahiro Maeda. Screenplay by Hiroshi Yamaguchi. Based on the manga series by Satoru Ozawa in *Akita Shoten Sunday*.

Zorndyke's plans and motivations are revealed, and Hayami faces his enemy in battle. Mutant whale battleships, sharkmen, underwater warfare in Antarctica—it's all here. This extra-length episode wraps the series up nicely.

SPECIAL FEATURES Text Interview With Creator • Plot Summary • Other Title Trailers • Easter Egg TECHNICAL FEATURES Fullscreen (1.33:1) • Subtitles/CC: Eng. • Languages: Jap., Eng. dub • Sound: Dolby Digital 2.0, Dolby Digital Surround 5.1 • Keepcase • 1 Disc • Region 1 GENRE & RATING Underwater/Action/Science Fiction • Rated 13+

Blue Submarine No. 6: The Movie [Toonami Version]

Bandai, 2001, 115 mins., #0946. Directed by Mahiro Maeda. Screenplay by Hiroshi Yamaguchi. Based on the manga series by Satoru Ozawa in *Akita Shoten Sunday*.

This movie version combines the four OVA episodes into a shorter storyline, as edited for Toonami on the Cartoon Network. Approximately twenty minutes have been excised (much of that is missing episodic end credits), as well as some other alterations. The picture quality suffers a bit due to compression. Still an excellent choice, this one's a bit more kid-friendly, but adults will be better off with the uncensored versions.

SPECIAL FEATURES Other Title Trailers TECHNICAL FEATURES Fullscreen (1.33:1) • Languages: Eng. dub • Sound: Dolby Digital 2.0, Dolby Digital Surround 5.1 • Keepcase • 1 Disc • Region 1 GENRE & RATING Underwater/Action/Science Fiction • Not Rated (All Ages)

Bob Clampett's Beany and Cecil: The Special Edition

Image, 1999, 220 mins., #ID5660BBDVD. Produced by Bob Clampett, Bob Clampett, Jr., Greg Carson.

Beany is a seasick sea serpent who befriends Beany Boy and his uncle, Captain Horatio Huffenpuff, the skipper of the ship *Leakin' Lena*. Begun as a series of puppet shows for Los Angeles TV broadcast in 1949, the show was picked up for national airing in 1950 by Paramount. It won three Emmy awards during its run, and inspired a film cartoon series in 1959, followed by a prime-time ABC cartoon series in 1962.

The stories found Beany and Cecil meeting such imaginative (and sometimes irreverent) characters as Homer the Baseball-Playing Octopus, The Terrible Three-Headed Threep, Tear-a-long the Dotted Lion, and the bad-guy Dishonest John. Adults liked the series for its pop-culture references and sly humor that sometimes went over the heads of youngsters who were entertained by the silliness and action. Beany's propeller cap became a popular item among youth in America, and the series lasted until 1968, then continued in syndication to 1976.

This DVD is a treasure trove of classic animation for collectors, with a large variety of never-before-seen material. Over a dozen cartoons include bumper segments and extras, while live/puppet segments of *Time For Beany* from 1949–51 are presented as well. There are also several dozen other components, including shorts, interview segments, test footage, promotional films, and more. Other work of *Beany and Cecil* creator Bob Clampett is profiled, including material from a planned *John Carter of Mars* project, early stop motion, and much more.

This DVD harkens back to a simpler age but uses modern technology to offer a bounty of material. It is highly recommended for both its entertainment and historical value.

SPECIAL FEATURES Commentary track by Bob Clampett and Performers • Character and Art Galleries • Unaired Footage • Promotional Footage • Audio Recording Session • Unfinished/Lost Clips and Galleries • Insert: Liner Notes • Easter Egg TECHNICAL FEATURES Fullscreen (1.33:1) • Languages: Eng. • Sound: Dolby Digital Mono) • Keepcase • 1 Disc • Region 1–6 GENRE & RATING Family/Comedy • Not Rated (All Ages)

Bolek and Lolek [#1]

Facets, 2002, 48 mins.

This DVD was not available for review.

Bolek and Lolek [#2]

Facets, 2002, 48 mins.

This DVD was not available for review.

Bondage Mansion ☞ see Mature/Adult Section

Bondage Queen Kate: Complete ☞ see Mature/Adult Section

Boogiepop Phantom: Evolution 1

Right Stuf, 2001, 85 mins., #RSDVD2021. Directed by Takashi Watanabe. Screenplay by Sadayaki Murai, Seishi Minakami. Based on the novels by Kohei Kadono.

A ghost—or is it an angel of death?—named Boogiepop haunts the world of high school students. As their lives intertwine through the years, the realm of the supernatural and reality blur together. A boy can see bugs inside people's hearts, but if he removes the bug and consumes it, the people change. A girl witnesses ghosts, while another girl spreads the words and philosophies of a student who might never have existed. A serial killer lurked in the shadows five years ago . . . or is he here now?

A Japanese TV series in 2000, *Boogiepop Phantom* is a combination of *Serial Experiments Lain*, crossed with the *Twilight Zone, Buffy the Vampire Slayer*, existentialism, and goth posturing, with just a bit of the film *Memento* and the works of director David Lynch thrown in. As layered as an onion, *Boogiepop* jumps backward and forward in time, utilizing alienated characters fully in one episode and relegating them to background cameos in others. Basically, the plot is a gloomy fabric; the threads intersect with each other to make a whole, but each has its own path as well.

It would be hard to imagine an American animated project as unique as *Boogiepop Phantom*, and viewers used to more linear storytelling may find it difficult to follow. Those who do will be rewarded, though. The look of the series is grainy and washed out, with muted colors and halo flares around characters. The choice is an aesthetic one, and while it might look much worse on VHS, on DVD even the foggy grain is sharp. The DVD contains the first three episodes. Note that the commentary track is in the Set-Up menu, not in the Extra Features section.

SPECIAL FEATURES Commentary Track by American Producers/Directors • Promotional Footage • Music Video. TECHNICAL FEATURES Fullscreen (1.33:1) • Subtitles/CC: Eng. • Languages: Jap., Eng. dub • Sound: Dolby Digital Surround 2.0, Dolby Digital Surround 5.1 • Keepcase • 1 Disc • Region 1 GENRE & RATING Horror • Not Rated (15+)

Boogiepop Phantom: Evolution 2

Right Stuf, 2001, 85 mins., #RSDVD2022. Directed by Takashi Watanabe. Screenplay by Yasuyuke Nojiri, Sadayaki Murai. Based on the novels by Kohei Kadono.

Pushed to succeed by an overbearing father, a boy retreats into a fantasy life, perfecting his computer girlfriend. Fueled by what might be a drug, he becomes determined to remake a coworker into his cyberfantasy lover. The serial killer of the past stopped abruptly, but is a policeman hiding the reason why? A girl who fell prey to the serial killer five years ago was estranged from her mother—now, when mom discovers her diary, secrets emerge.

The second DVD features three more episodes, plus a very creepy "Fruits Video" filled with dissection and blood in both live-action and animation.

SPECIAL FEATURES Commentary Track by American Producers/Directors • Promotional Footage • Music Video. TECHNICAL FEATURES Fullscreen (1.33:1) • Subtitles/CC: Eng. • Languages: Jap., Eng. dub • Sound: Dolby Digital Surround 2.0, Dolby Digital Surround 5.1 • Keepcase • 1 Disc • Region 1 GENRE & RATING Horror • Not Rated (15+)

Boogiepop Phantom: Evolution 3

Right Stuf, 2001, 85 mins., #RSDVD2024. Directed by Takashi Watanabe. Screenplay by Seishi Minakami, Sadayaki Murai, Yasuyuke Nojiri. Based on the novels by Kohei Kadono.

A violent young man discovers he doesn't have much in common with humanity, on any level, and his mysterious powers are known only to him, his sister, and those he uses them on. A girl attempts to rid the world of evil based on the theories of her late father, and she and a magazine writer encounter the truth about Boogiepop. A gifted pianist reaches a crossroads and must decide if she wants to continue to sacrifice her life to music or seek another path.

Although it appears a lot of answers are given in this DVD's trio of episodes, the resolution and true framework of the story is still very much a mystery.

SPECIAL FEATURES Commentary Track by American Producers/Directors • Promotional Footage • Music Video. TECHNICAL FEATURES Fullscreen (1.33:1) • Subtitles/CC: Eng. • Languages: Jap., Eng. dub • Sound: Dolby Digital Surround 2.0, Dolby Digital Surround 5.1 • Keepcase • 1 Disc • Region 1 GENRE & RATING Horror • Not Rated (15+)

Boogiepop Phantom: Evolution 4

Right Stuf, 2001, 85 mins., #RSDVD2023. Directed by Takashi Watanabe. Screenplay by Seishi Minakami, Rokuro Nigi, Sadayaki Murai. Based on the novels by Kohei Kadono.

A magical world where children with special powers live without fear or pain. A girl experiences what lies beyond death, and learns of the next stage of evolution. Time unwinds and darkness retreats. But are the ghost stories of the past real?

The final DVD wraps up the series with three episodes. Some viewers may still wonder what the heck the whole thing was about; others will find it deep and meaningful.

SPECIAL FEATURES Commentary Track by American Producers/Directors • Character Notes • Art Galleries • Production Notes • Promotional Footage TECHNICAL FEATURES Fullscreen (1.33:1) • Subtitles/CC: Eng. • Languages: Jap., Eng. dub • Sound: Dolby Digital Surround 2.0, Dolby Digital Surround 5.1 • Keepcase • 1 Disc • Region 1–6 GENRE & RATING Horror • Not Rated (15+)

Boogiepop Phantom: Evolution 1–4 Complete [Set]

Right Stuf, 2002, 340 mins., #RSDVD2020. Directed by Takashi Watanabe. Screenplay by Sadayaki Murai, Seishi Minakami, Yasuyuke Nojiri, Rokuro Nigi. Based on the novels by Kohei Kadono.

This DVD set is not technically a box set, but instead a rather large keepcase edition. It contains the same four discs as the individual releases, plus a bonus music CD with two tracks totaling 9:56 minutes. The first track is the longer orchestral/choral/synthesizer mix of Wagner's "Die Meistersinger Von Nurnberg" (8:50), while the second track is an eerie whistled version of the same overture at 1:06.

Please see individual entries for Special and Technical Features.

TECHNICAL FEATURES Multikeepcase • 5 Discs • Region 1 GENRE & RATING Horror • Not Rated (15+)

Book of Pooh, The: Stories from the Heart

Disney, 2001, 77 mins., #22477. Directed by Mitchell Kriegman, Dean Gordon. Written by Mitchell Kriegman, Andy Yerkes, Jymn Magon, Claudia Silver, Mark Zaslove. Based on the book series by A. A. Milne.

All the creatures from the Hundred Acre Wood are present, including Winnie the Pooh, Tigger, Eeyore, Rabbit, Owl, and little Piglet. When the gang discovers "The Book of Pooh" in Christopher Robin's room, they delight in reading about their own adventures.

This DVD collects six stories from the Disney Channel series. The familiar friends aren't hand-animated but are instead a combination of rod puppetry with green screens, CGI, and other techniques. The effect mostly works, though at times it's a bit jarring for older eyes. Children, however, should absolutely love the show, and it will both entertain them and teach them values in a non-preachy fashion. An interesting extra featurette talks about Pooh's real-world beginnings and shows the actual stuffed animals that A. A. Milne based his stories on.

See also *The Many Adventures of Winnie the Pooh* and *The Tigger Movie* for more Pooh fun.

SPECIAL FEATURES "Making of" Featurette • Character Bios • Games • Other Title Trailers TECHNICAL FEATURES Fullscreen (1.33:1) • Subtitles/CC: Eng. • Languages: Eng. • Sound: Dolby Digital Surround 5.1 • Keepcase • 1 Disc • Region 1 GENRE & RATING CGI/Puppet/Family • Rated G

Brain Powered: Vol. 1—Birth

Bandai, 2002, 225 mins., #1420. Directed by Yoshiyuki Tomino. Written by Yoshiyuki Tomino.

Earth is in serious trouble. The environment has deteriorated and the population has expanded, leaving food, energy, and natural resources at a premium. A series of earthquakes would seem to seal humankind's fate, but instead, it produces a series of Organic Plates: energy being Antibodies of two types, Grand Chers and Brain Powereds. The strength of the Grand Chers comes from a centuries-old relic called Orphen; its followers want to leave Earth a dead husk and go into space to colonize. The Brain Powereds energy comes from the Earth itself, and those who ally themselves with the BP believe Earth has a chance. A young orphan named Hime Utsumiya becomes a pilot of a Brain Powered, even as Reclaimer pilot Yu Isami is questioning the motives of his leaders.

Nine episodes of this 1998 TV series are collected on the first two-disc set of *Brain Powered*. The series is tremendously convoluted, and while explanations seem to make sense at times, thinking about the plot elements too hard might cause headaches. Appealing to the same crowd as *Neon Genesis Evangelion*, *Brain Powered* has a bit of romance, some nice organic robots designs, and music by composer Yoko Kanno that will either have fans cheering or booing depending on musical tastes.

Note that despite the multiple nude women floating through the air in the opening credits, the show itself is not rife with nudity or sex.

SPECIAL FEATURES Clean Credits • Other Title Trailers • Inserts: Liner Notes TECHNICAL FEATURES Fullscreen (1.33:1) • Subtitles/CC: Eng. • Languages: Jap., Eng. dub • Sound: Dolby Digital • Keepcase • 2 Discs • Region 1 GENRE & RATING Robots/Science Fiction/Action • Rated 13+

Brain Powered: Vol. 2—Family Feuds

Bandai, 2002, 225 mins., #1421. Directed by Yoshiyuki Tomino. Written by Hajime Yatate and Yoshiyuki Tomino.

NOTE: This DVD arrived too late for a full review. The following text is promotional copy provided by the releasing company:

"Not wanting to join Novis Noah or the Reclaimers, Yu Isami has continued to work mostly independently. But with the increasing ferocity of the battles with the Grand Chers, and time running out until Orphan resurfaces, Yu finally joins the *Novis Noah* crew. With the critical data he can provide, Irene's drastic plan to contain Orphan just might work.

"But Yu pays a price. Accusing him of betraying his family, his sister Quincy continues to attack. And there is more pain in store for the Isami family when Jonathan Glen reveals a devastating secret. The battles intensify and the stakes have become much more personal. How much more suffering lies ahead for those who would defend the world?"

This disc contains episodes #10–18.

SPECIAL FEATURES Text Interview with Director and Composer • Character and Art Galleries • Clean Credits: Karaoke • Other Title Trailers • Inserts: Liner Notes TECHNICAL FEATURES Fullscreen (1.33:1)• Subtitles/CC: Eng. • Languages: Jap., Eng. dub • Sound: Dolby Digital 2.0 • Multikeepcase • 2 Discs • Region 1 GENRE & RATING Robots/Science Fiction/Action • Rated 13+

Brain Powered: Vol. 3—Resolutions

Bandai, 2002, 200 mins., #1422. Directed by Yoshiyuki Tomino. Written by Hajime Yatate and Yoshiyuki Tomino.

NOTE: This DVD arrived too late for a full review. The following text is promotional copy provided by the releasing company:

"With Commander Geybridge gone and Yu still missing in action, the *Novis Noah* feels a little empty. But what they don't know is that one of their own is planning to destroy *Novis Noah* and everyone aboard. Meanwhile, Yu finds himself in China after the tragic death of Nelly, a girl who saved him and gave him a newly revived Brain Powered. But before he can recover and get back to *Novis Noah*, he is imprisoned and his Brain Powered stolen! But a rescue attempt is on the horizon.

"The final battle is at hand, and the crew of the *Novis Noah* find themselves going up against the Grand Chers of the United States. Amidst all the chaos, Quincy is injured and taken aboard *Novis Noah* for treatment. She and Yu seem to be getting along, but how long will it last? And if it does, how much time do they have together before all the Earth is destroyed?"

This disc contains episodes #19–26.

SPECIAL FEATURES Text Interview with Director and Composer • Character and Art Galleries • Other Title Trailers • Inserts: Liner Notes TECHNICAL FEATURES Fullscreen (1.33:1)• Subtitles/CC: Eng. • Languages: Jap., Eng. dub • Sound: Dolby Digital 2.0 • Multikeepcase • 2 Discs • Region 1 GENRE & RATING Robots/Science Fiction/Action • Rated 13+

Brave Frog, The

Image, 1999, 91 mins., #ID5692PZDVD. Directed by Michael Reynolds. Written by Ilene Chase. Based on episodes directed by Tatsuo Yoshida and written by Jinzo Toriumi.

Tree frog Jonathon Jumper moves to Rainbow Pond in the woods, only to find it's not a very friendly place. Armed with his musical reed pipe and aided by his giggly girlfriend Pookie, Jonathon faces snakes, water monsters, cats, and the selfish King Leopold. Using music and rhymes, Jonathon must triumph and teach the residents of Rainbow Pond a happier way of life.

This DVD adventure is cannibalized from a 1973 Japanese TV series, with bits and pieces from multiple episodes making up the plot. The animation is so cute that it could almost induce sugar shock, and the film transfer to DVD is ultragrainy. While some small children might like this story, parents will have to decide if they can stand to be in the room long enough to push "Play."

SPECIAL FEATURES None TECHNICAL FEATURES Fullscreen (1.33:1) • Languages: Jap., Eng. dub • Sound: Dolby Digital Mono) • Snapcase • 1 Disc • Region 1–6 GENRE & RATING Animals/Adventure • Rated G

Bremenski Musicanti [Bremen's Musicians]

Jove/Stellar.

This DVD was not available for review. It is a Russian-language disc.

Bride of Darkness ☞ see Mature/Adult Section

Brothers Quay Collection, The

Kino, 2000, 123 mins., #K170 DVD. Directed by The Brothers Quay.

Eleven of the most bizarre and imaginative stop-motion film shorts you'll likely ever see are collected in this DVD volume. The Brothers Quay are a pair of identical twins whose first film, "Nocturna Artificialia," was created in 1978. It's included in this set, as well as "The Cabinet of Jan Svankmajer," a tribute to the famed Czechoslovakian animator, and others, spanning 1984–93. Included are two music videos for the British band His Name Is Alive.

The Quay's stop-motion work almost defines the term "surreal," but the pair's manipulation of the camera is as close as one gets on film to actual magic. Marvel at how they single-frame animated a real moving bullet, or kept pearls in mid-air, all without the use of CGI tricks. Props and characters collide, as the Quay's world of the living contains bones, moldy dolls, insect wings, nuts and bolts, and rusted scissors, all of which move with story-telling purpose. Disturbing and twisted, while still dreamlike and cool, the Brothers Quay shorts are beautifully transferred to disc. Highly recommended, but too spooky for the young 'uns.

SPECIAL FEATURES Creator Interview • Other Title Trailers • Liner Notes: Inside Cover TECHNICAL FEATURES Fullscreen (1.33:1) • Languages: Eng. • Sound: Dolby Digital 2.0 • Keepcase • 1 Disc • Region All GENRE & RATING Stop-Motion/Puppet/Anthology • Not Rated (Teens)

Bubblegum Crash: Total Crash Collection

AnimEigo, 2002, 135 mins., #AV201-065. Directed by Hiroshi Ishiodori, Hiroyuki Fukushima. Screenplay by Emu Ari.

The Knight Sabers have broken up, but the city still needs them. The AD Police aren't tough enough to contend with the combat-suited Illegal Army or the Boomers on their own, much less the Sabers' mysterious and deadly foe. So, it's up to four beautiful woman to don their hardsuits once again to defend MegaTokyo.

This three-part sequel was produced in 1989. Due to a split between the producers of the original *Bubblegum Crisis* series, this series was renamed *Bubblegum Crash*, even though the characters and settings remained functionally the same. Not as successful as the *Bubblegum Crisis 2040* series, *Crash* remains as dated looking as its predecessor. Still, fans of Priss, Sylia, Nene, and Linna will want this DVD to complete their collection.

The DVD contains three episodes: "Illegal Army"; "Geo Climbers"; and "Meltdown."

SPECIAL FEATURES Character and Art Galleries • Insert: Song Lyrics TECHNICAL FEATURES Fullscreen (1.33:1) • Subtitles/CC: Eng. • Languages: Jap., Eng. dub • Sound: Dolby Digital Stereo) • Keepcase • 1 Disc • Region 1 GENRE & RATING Robots/Action/Music • Not Rated (Teens)

Bubblegum Crisis: Episodes 1, 2, and 3

M2K/AnimEigo, 2000, 101 mins., #BCADV101. Directed by Katsuhito Akiyama. Screenplay by Kenichi Matsuzaki, Hideki Kakinuma, Shinji Aramaki, Katsuhito Akiyama.

The year is 2032, post-apocalypse. Genom is the world's biggest corporation, and its presence in Neo-Tokyo is maintained by giant androids called "Boomers." Four young women—Sylia Stingray, Nene,

Linna, and Priss—use their technical and combat skills to supplement the power of their own armored hardsuits. Now as Genom works toward its evil goals, the quartet of Knight Sabers begins its battle against the corporation.

One of the most popular anime series ever, *Bubblegum Crisis* has girls, guns, robots, action, and catchy pop music. Its cyberpunk tone doesn't take itself too seriously at all times, lending a sense of fun to an entertaining story with strong action and characterization. The art is slick and easy on the eyes, with an emphasis on bright colors.

The first DVD features three episodes: "Tinsel City," introduces the characters and setting; "Born to Kill" finds the girls battling a SuperBoomer; and "Blow Up" showcases the Knight Saber's battle alongside the AD Police against the Boomers. The DVD case itself has both reflective silver material and hot-pink lettering and trim, making it a bit of an eye-burner even as it stands out on the shelf.

SPECIAL FEATURES DVD-ROM Features TECHNICAL FEATURES Fullscreen (1.33:1) • Subtitles/CC: Eng., Fren. • Languages: Jap., Eng. dub • Sound: Dolby Digital 2.0 • Keepcase • 1 Disc • Region All GENRE & RATING Robots/Action/Music • Not Rated (Teens)

Bubblegum Crisis: Episodes 4, 5, and 6

M2K/AnimEigo, 2000, 132 mins., #BCBDV101. Directed by Hiroki Hayashi, Masami Obari. Screenplay by Emu Ari, Toshimichi Suzuki.

Three more adventures of the Knight Sabers on the second disc of this ultra-popular series. "Revenge Road" finds Priss endangered by a mysterious black car that is taking revenge on a biker gang; "Moonlight Rambler" features a space station crash and a vampiric Boomer that runs on human blood; and "Red Eyes" sees the Knight Sabers turn toward evil . . . or are they lookalike imposters?

SPECIAL FEATURES DVD-ROM Features TECHNICAL FEATURES Fullscreen (1.33:1) • Subtitles/CC: Eng., Fren. • Languages: Jap., Eng. dub • Sound: Dolby Digital 2.0 • Keepcase • 1 Disc • Region All GENRE & RATING Robots/Action/Music • Not Rated (Teens)

Bubblegum Crisis: Episodes 7, 8, and Music

M2K/AnimEigo, 2000, 116 mins., #BCCDV101. Directed by Fumihiko Takayama, Hiroaki Goda. Screenplay by Hidetoshi Yoshida, Toshimichi Suzuki.

Two more episodes of *Bubblegum Crisis* bring this series to an end: "Double Vision" features an American pop singer whose tour in Neo-Tokyo is connected to the deaths of Boomer engineers; and in "Scoop Chase" an ambitious reporter tries to get footage of the Knight Sabers at any cost, while a final battle against the Boomers might cost the girls their secret identities—if they survive at all!

The DVD also features four music videos with pop songs and footage from the anime series. Songs include "Rock Me," "Mad Machine," "Soldier of Roses," and "Victory."

SPECIAL FEATURES Character and Art Galleries • Music Videos • DVD-ROM Features TECHNICAL FEATURES Fullscreen (1.33:1) • Subtitles/CC: Eng., Fren. • Languages: Jap., Eng. dub • Sound: Dolby Digital 2.0 • Keepcase • 1 Disc • Region All GENRE & RATING Robots/Action/Music • Not Rated (Teens)

Bubblegum Crisis: Hurricane Live!

M2K/AnimEigo, 2000, 54 mins., #BCDDV101. Directed by Shinji Aramaki, Shizuki Fujieda.

An interesting meld of anime and live action, "Hurricane Live!" is a music video compilation featuring the tunes of Priss and the Replicants. Some of the songs have previously seen footage from the anime series, while others have new animation. Three songs are performed live in concert, featuring the voice actresses from the series singing at a "Tinsel City Rhapsody" concert.

Thirteen songs are presented, including repeats of the four from the third *Bubblegum Crisis* DVD.

SPECIAL FEATURES Character and Art Galleries • Music Videos • DVD-ROM Features TECHNICAL FEATURES Fullscreen (1.33:1) • Subtitles/CC: Eng., Fren. • Languages: Jap., Eng. dub • Sound: Dolby Digital 2.0 • Keepcase • 1 Disc • Region All GENRE & RATING Robots/Action/Music • Not Rated (Teens)

Bubblegum Crisis: Megaseries [Box Set]

M2K/AnimEigo, 1998, 403 mins., #BC2DV101.

This box set features all four *Bubblegum Crisis* DVDs in their keepcases. There aren't any extra features besides the cardboard box sleeve, although its bright pink and mirrored silver edges glow enough to light a darkened room. See individual entries for Special and Technical Features.

TECHNICAL FEATURES Cardboard Box with 4 Keepcases • 4 Discs • Region All GENRE & RATING Robots/Action/Music • Not Rated (Teens)

Bubblegum Crisis: Collector's Edition [Oversize Box Set]

M2K/AnimEigo, 1998, 349 mins., #BC2DV101.

Released largely to video game stores, this box version of the *Bubblegum Crisis* series only contains the first three discs, as also released individually. Each disc is packaged in a CD jewel case, not a keepcase. The 10.5 in. x 9 in. box is tremendously oversized for the material it contains. See individual entries for Special and Technical Features.

TECHNICAL FEATURES Cardboard Box with 3 Discs in CD Cases • Region All GENRE & RATING Robots/Action/Music • Not Rated (Teens)

Bubblegum Crisis: Tokyo 2040—Genesis [#1]

ADV Films, 2000, 100 mins., #DVDBG001. Directed by Hiroki Hayashi. Script by Chiaki Konaka, Sadayuki Murai.

The Knight Sabers are back to take on the Genom Corporation in Megalocity (formerly Tokyo). Suiting up in their armored hardsuits are lingerie-shop owner Sylia Stingray, cop Nene Romanova, country girl office worker Linna Yamazaki, and tomboy techno-grunge music star Priss Asagiri. New to the supporting cast is bike mechanic Nigel, who has the know-how to build more hardsuits. The vigilante Sabers are sometimes at odds with the AD Police, but mostly they're battling robotic Boomers.

This 1998 TV revival of *Bubblegum Crisis* was created in the wake of *Neon Genesis Evangelion*'s popularity. Still featuring cyberpunk action and girls in tight robot suits, the stories are a bit more cynical and dark, eschewing humor for sexuality. The ultra-slick animation is better than the original series, and the show is paced better

The first DVD features four episodes: "Can't Buy a Thrill"; "Fragile"; "Keep Me Hanging On"; and "Machine Head."

SPECIAL FEATURES Character Bios • Other Title Trailers TECHNICAL FEATURES Fullscreen (1.33:1) • Subtitles/CC: Eng. • Languages: Jap., Eng. dub, Span. dub • Sound: Dolby Digital Surround 2.0 • Keepcase • 1 Disc • Region 1–6 GENRE & RATING Robots/Action/Music • Rated 15+

Bubblegum Crisis: Tokyo 2040—Crusade [#2]

ADV Films, 2000, 100 mins., #DVDBG002. Directed by Hiroki Hayashi. Script by Chiaki Konaka, Sadayuki Murai.

This time out, Linna's hardsuit malfunctions, deadly new mutating Boomers are rampaging in the city and underwater, and the Knight Sabers become targets of the AD Police. Plus, Sylia's younger brother Mackey joins the Knight team, and Mason, a part of Genom, takes a particular interest in the hardsuits. Finally, Priss gives an interview.

More backstory for Priss and Sylia are established in the four episodes on this DVD: " Rough and Ready"; "Get It On"; "Look at Yourself"; and "Fireball."

SPECIAL FEATURES Character Bios • Other Title Trailers TECHNICAL FEATURES Fullscreen (1.33:1) • Subtitles/CC: Eng. • Languages: Jap., Eng. dub, Span. dub • Sound: Dolby Digital Surround 2.0 • Keepcase • 1 Disc • Region 1–6 GENRE & RATING Robots/Action/Music • Rated 15+

Bubblegum Crisis: Tokyo 2040—Leviathans [#3]

ADV Films, 2001, 100 mins., #DVDBG003. Directed by Hiroki Hayashi. Script by Chiaki Konaka, Sadayuki Murai.

Something in the deeply buried underground of the city is capturing Boomers and citizens, and everyone wants it stopped: the Knight Sabers, the AD Police, and even the Genom Corporation. Linna returns to her country home for a bittersweet reunion, and later, Priss must face a huge military Boomer on her own. Plus, Nene and Sylia are having problems, and Nene finds out something important about Sylia's past that could change the Knight Sabers forever.... Lots of secrets are revealed and mysteries deepened in this DVD's four episodes: "My Nation Underground"; "Woke Up with a Monster"; "Sheer Heart Attack"; and "Made in Japan."

SPECIAL FEATURES Character Bios • Other Title Trailers • Easter Egg TECHNICAL FEATURES Fullscreen (1.33:1) • Subtitles/CC: Eng. • Languages: Jap., Eng. dub, Span. dub • Sound: Dolby Digital Surround 2.0 • Keepcase • 1 Disc • Region 1–6 GENRE & RATING Robots/Action/Music • Rated 15+

Bubblegum Crisis: Tokyo 2040—Buried Secrets [#4]

ADV Films, 2001, 100 mins., #DVDBG004. Directed by Hiroki Hayashi. Script by Chiaki Konaka, Sadayuki Murai.

Sylia's past comes back to haunt her and the secrets of her family—and the origin of the hardsuits—may tear apart the Knight Sabers. Deep in the ruins of Old Tokyo, Genom's Brian Mason finds the buried creation of Sylia's father, Galatea, and unleashes it. Plus, the AD Police may be disbanded. . . .

Revelations about some characters may radically alter viewer perceptions as the series passes its halfway mark in four more episodes: "Atom Heart Mother"; "Shock Treatment"; "Minute by Minute"; and "I Surrender."

SPECIAL FEATURES Vehicle Art Galleries • Other Title Trailers TECHNICAL FEATURES Fullscreen (1.33:1) • Subtitles/CC: Eng. • Languages: Jap., Eng. dub, Span. dub • Sound: Dolby Digital Surround 2.0 • Keepcase • 1 Disc • Region 1–6 GENRE & RATING Robots/Action/Music • Rated 15+

Bubblegum Crisis: Tokyo 2040—Blood and Steel [#5]

ADV Films, 2001, 125 mins., #DVDBG005. Directed by Hiroki Hayashi. Script by Chiaki Konaka, Sadayuki Murai.

The Boomers are taking over AD Police headquarters, and Priss goes to help Nene and the officers. Meanwhile, the wave of bio-organic Boomers invading the city causes carnage and an eventual evacuation, and Galatea's maturation continues, promising destruction to come. The Knight Sabers can choose to fight in their new hardsuits, but the weaponry comes with a very high price. And did I mention there's a giant metal worm?

Upping the ante to five episodes, this set turns the plot fully serious: "Moving Waves"; "We Built This City"; "Are You Experienced?"; "One of Those Nights"; and "Close to the Edge."

SPECIAL FEATURES Character Galleries • Other Title Trailers TECHNICAL FEATURES Fullscreen (1.33:1) • Subtitles/CC: Eng. • Languages: Jap., Eng. dub, Span. dub • Sound: Dolby Digital Surround 2.0 • Keepcase • 1 Disc • Region 1–6 GENRE & RATING Robots/Action/Music • Rated 15+

Bubblegum Crisis: Tokyo 2040—For All Mankind [#6]

ADV Films, 2001, 125 mins., #DVDBG006. Directed by Hiroki Hayashi. Script by Chiaki Konaka, Sadayuki Murai.

Galatea and the monstrous Dragon Line have crushed human resistance, and Megalocity (Tokyo) has been abandoned. Now, four women in hardsuits must face Galatea and the Boomer hordes or all will be lost. But is their fight a suicide mission? And what happens when they must face Galatea in space?

The final quintet of episodes wraps up the Bubblegum Crisis saga: "Physical Graffiti"; "Hydra"; "Light My Fire"; "Walking on the Moon"; and "Still Alive and Well." The final two segments were actually released in Japan as OVAs, forcing fans to buy the conclusion rather than watch it on TV.

SPECIAL FEATURES Cast Filmographies • Other Title Trailers TECH-NICAL FEATURES Fullscreen (1.33:1) • Subtitles/CC: Eng. • Languages: Jap., Eng. dub, Span. dub • Sound: Dolby Digital Surround 2.0 • Keepcase • 1 Disc • Region 1–6 GENRE & RATING Robots/Action/Music • Rated 15+

Bubblegum Crisis: Tokyo 2040—Perfect Collection

ADV Films, 2002, 650 mins., #DBG/100.

This multikeepcase set includes the six *Bubblegum Crisis: Tokyo 2040* discs exactly as they appeared in the individual editions. See individual entries for Special and Technical Features.

SPECIAL FEATURES Insert: Liner Notes TECHNICAL FEATURES Multikeepcase • 6 Discs • Region 1 GENRE & RATING Robots/Action/Music • Rated 15+

Bug's Life, A [Gold Collection]

Disney, 2000, 95 mins., #19818. Directed by John Lasseter, Andrew Stanton. Story by John Lasseter, Andrew Stanton, Joe Ranft. Screenplay by Andrew Stanton, Donald McEnery, Bob Shaw.

The ants are tired of the grasshoppers feeding on their food supplies, but no one is willing to stand up to them. That's when one ant named Flik decides to gather together a group of warriors to defend his colony. But instead of tough and hearty fighters, what Flik gets are a group of flea circus performers who are a bit down on their luck. Now, with the grasshoppers preparing to attack once again, can Flik stand against them with a pair of pillbugs, a caterpillar, a walking stick, a surly male ladybug, and a handful of other insects?

A Bug's Life was Pixar's second CGI feature film for Disney, following *Toy Story*. For many animation fans, this runs even with that film in terms of quality. Certainly, the voice talents are impeccable, including Dave Foley, Kevin Spacey, Julia Louis-Dreyfus, Phyllis Diller, Richard Kind, David Hyde Pierce, Roddy McDowell, and others. The CGI work is flawless no matter which way you view the film (some scenes, but not all, have been digitally recomposed for full frame images). Plus, when you combine all of that with a hilarious script loosely based on the acclaimed Akira Kurosawa film *The Seven Samurai*, you're bound to come up with a winner.

The DVD contains a direct digital-to-digital print of the film (the first-ever DVD to feature this), as well as both sets of "outtakes" that were shown during the closing credits in theaters. "Geri's Game," an Oscar-winning short film by Pixar is also presented. *A Bug's Life* is a gem in any DVD collection, but if you can afford it, get the Collector's Edition.

SPECIAL FEATURES Outtakes • Other Title Trailers TECHNICAL FEATURES Widescreen (2.35:1) • Fullscreen (1.33:1) • Subtitles/CC: Eng. • Languages: Eng. • Sound: Dolby Digital Surround 5.1 • Keepcase • 1 Disc • Region 1 GENRE & RATING Insects/Comedy • Rated G

Bug's Life, A [Collector's Edition]

Disney, 2000, 202 mins., #21562. Directed by John Lasseter, Andrew Stanton. Story by John Lasseter, Andrew Stanton, Joe Ranft. Screenplay by Andrew Stanton, Donald McEnery, Bob Shaw.

Disney presents another jam-packed DVD set for cinephiles, as well as students and artists interested in CGI. The first disc contains two versions of the film (widescreen and recomposed standard), as well as a highly entertaining commentary track. It's topped off with isolated sound tracks for Randy Newman's score and the film's sound effects!

The second disc contains a thorough look at *A Bug's Life* from preproduction up through its video release. Along the way are early presentation reels, details on the story, treatment, script, design, concept, character, and location artwork. Plus, there's more on the sound, voice actors, the making of the outtakes, and advertising/trailer campaigns for the film in theaters and on video/DVD.

As good as *A Bug's Life* is, the Collector's Edition is even better.

SPECIAL FEATURES "Making of" Featurettes • Commentary Track by the Directors and Producer • Character and Art Galleries • Production Notes • Deleted Scenes and Abandoned Sequences • Storyboards • Story Treatment • Theatrical

Trailers • Promotional Footage • Outtakes • Isolated Music and Sound Effects Tracks • Other Title Trailers TECHNICAL FEATURES Widescreen (2.35:1 enhanced for 16x9) • Fullscreen (1.33:1) • Subtitles/CC: Eng. • Languages: Eng. • Sound: Dolby Digital Surround 5.1 • Multikeepcase • 2 Discs • Region 1 GENRE & RATING Insects/Comedy • Rated G

Burn Up Excess: To Serve and Protect! [#1]

ADV Films, 2002, 100 mins., #DBX/001. Directed by Shinichiro Kimura. Screenplay by Masataka Tsuchiya, Toshifumi Takizawa.

NOTE: This DVD arrived too late for a full review. The following text is promotional copy provided by the releasing company:

"Ready, aim, and fire up for animated adventure with Team Warrior! Join rowdy Rio and her friends—the machine-gun maniac Maya, the lovely Lilica, tech talent Nanvel, guy Friday Yuji, and their boss Maki—as they take on four of their hottest cases ever! Mechanical insects, firefighting jewel robbers, panty thieves, sexy sheiks, and fawning fathers—there's never a dull moment when the babes of Burn Up Excess are on the job!"

SPECIAL FEATURES Character and Art Galleries • Jiggle Counter • Trailer • Clean Credits • Other Title Trailers TECHNICAL FEATURES Fullscreen (1.33:1) • Subtitles/CC: Eng. • Languages: Jap., Eng. dub, Span. dub • Sound: Dolby Digital 2.0 • Keepcase • 1 Disc • Region 1 GENRE & RATING Action/Science Fiction • Rated 15+

Burn Up Excess: Crimes and Missed Demeanors [#2]

ADV Films, 2002, 75 mins., #DBX/002. Directed by Shinichiro Kimura. Screenplay by Yasuhito Kikuchi, Masanori Tsuchiya, Yoshihiro Yamaguchi.

NOTE: This DVD arrived too late for a full review. The following text is promotional copy provided by the releasing company:

"Polish your badge and grab your nightstick! It's time for more curious cases with your favorite babes in blue—Team Warrior! When a famous pop star is being stalked, racy cop-for-hire Rio is ordered to protect her. But when the singer comes into possession of a mysterious DNA pen, they find a stalker is nothing compared to the pen's dangerous owner! Later, Maki remembers how she first came to meet the craziest cop on the Team. And when Maki takes a vacation, it's up to the Team to solve a series of strange crimes on their own. But can they manage without their fearless leader?"

SPECIAL FEATURES Character and Art Galleries • Jiggle Counter • Trailer • Clean Credits • Other Title Trailers TECHNICAL FEATURES

Fullscreen (1.33:1) • Subtitles/CC: Eng. • Languages: Jap., Eng. dub, Span. dub • Sound: Dolby Digital 2.0 • Keepcase • 1 Disc • Region 1 GENRE & RATING Action/Science Fiction • Rated 15+

Burn Up Excess: Under the Gun [#3]

ADV Films, 2002, 75 mins., #DBX/003. Directed by Shinichiro Kimura. Screenplay by Shuji Sakamoto, Yasuhiro Shimosu, Kiyotaka Ohata.

NOTE: This DVD arrived too late for a full review. The following text is promotional copy provided by the releasing company:

"The bullet-blasting babes from Team Warrior are in real trouble this time! When a group of killer drag queens get out of jail, they've got their eye shadow fixed on Nanvel's new 'makeover' device that renders the wearer beautiful or, on high setting, invisible! Then, in an exciting cliffhanger, Rio and Team Warrior must escort a top-secret tank across the globe. But when the transport plane is attacked, Rio finds herself alone in a hostile desert, with the supertank as her only ally—and her only hope of survival! Don't miss the wildest, sexiest, strangest Team Warrior adventure yet!"

SPECIAL FEATURES Character and Art Galleries • Jiggle Counter • Trailer • Clean Credits • Other Title Trailers TECHNICAL FEATURES Fullscreen (1.33:1) • Subtitles/CC: Eng. • Languages: Jap., Eng. dub, Span. dub • Sound: Dolby Digital 2.0 • Keepcase • 1 Disc • Region 1 GENRE & RATING Action/Science Fiction • Rated 15+

Burn Up Excess: The Case of the Black Diamonds [#4]

ADV Films, 2002, 75 mins., #DBX/004. Directed by Shinichiro Kimura. Screenplay by Ko Ofuna, Susumu Ishizaki, Shinichiro Kimura.

NOTE: This DVD arrived too late for a full review. The following text is promotional copy provided by the releasing company:

"When an army of mecha cops are put on patrol, it looks as if the women of Team Warrior—ravishing Rio, Machiavellian Maki, munitions-happy Maya, intellectual Lillica and slightly neurotic Nanvel—might be out of a job. That is until the electronic enforcers start breaking the laws they're supposed to protect. But while the cops are in for repair, the Team finds a connection to Maki's past. This mysterious link to the Black Diamond Case proves dangerous for the entire team as Maki discovers the truth about her team's emergence, and the girls face their most dangerous, deadly enemy ever!"

This disc contains three episodes.

SPECIAL FEATURES Character and Art Galleries • Jiggle Counter • Trailer • Clean Credits • Other Title Trailers TECHNICAL FEATURES Fullscreen (1.33:1) • Subtitles/CC: Eng. • Languages: Eng. dub, Span. dub, Jap. • Sound: Dolby Digital 2.0 • Keepcase • 1 Disc • Region 1 GENRE & RATING Action/Science Fiction • Rated 15+

Burn-Up W: On the Case and In Your Face

ADV Films, 2000, 120 mins., #DVDBW001. Directed by Hiroshi Negishi. Screenplay by Katsuhiko Chiba, Sumio Uetake.

Team Warrior is a group of tough women (and one man) in the Neo-Tokyo police force. Attired in tight outfits and packing futuristic firepower, the top secret force of Rio, Maya, Maki, Lilica, and Yuji work to restrain the criminals of the city. Whether fighting giant mecha, virtual drugs, kidnappers, or rescuing a virtual idol, Team Warrior loves the chance to jump into action.

All four 1996 OVAs are collected in this DVD volume, which excels as a bit of anime parody mixed with action and liberal doses of cheesecake. The ultra-angular and goofy art design might not be to everyone's tastes, but those who like cartoony anime with big-busted girls with guns will find exactly what they desire. The menus are fun as well.

SPECIAL FEATURES Character and Art Galleries • Other Title Trailers TECHNICAL FEATURES Fullscreen (1.33:1) • Subtitles/CC: Eng. • Languages: Jap., Eng. dub, Span. dub • Sound: Dolby Digital 2.0 • Keepcase • 1 Disc • Region 1–6 GENRE & RATING Action/Science Fiction • Not Rated (Teens)

Buster and Chauncey's Silent Night

Columbia/TriStar, 2001, 49 mins.

This DVD was not available for review.

Butt-Ugly Martians: Best of the Bad Guys [#1]

Universal, 2002, 66 mins., #22120. Animation Directed by Egidio V. Dal Chele. Written by Richard Albreicht, Casey Keller, Pamela Hickey, Dennys McCoy.

NOTE: This DVD arrived too late for a full review. The following text is promotional copy provided by the releasing company:

"Butt-Ugly Martians is set in the year 2053 and features three Martian heroes—B-Bop-A-Luna, 2-T-Fru-T, and Do-Wah-Diddy. The heroes land on planet Earth having been sent on a mission to invade by their evil leader Emperor Bog. There's just one thing:

they really have no intention of taking over! In fact, they fought for the assignment because they wanted to experience Earth's great pop culture of fast food, video games, and TV!

"The Butt-Ugly's new mission includes keeping their three Earth friends—Mikey, Angela and Cedric—safe from other space invaders and evading Emperor Bog by sending phony taped progress reports of themselves 'conquering' the planet. Earth's invaders become its protectors . . . and that's where the adventure really begins!

"Presenting the *Butt-Ugly Martians*, as seen on their hit TV series on Nickelodeon! Emperor Bog launches an all-out attack after discovering that the Martians have been making friends on our planet instead of conquering it! Who will save the day? It's up to Do-Wah, B-Bop, and 2T as they draw upon their wits—and lots of Quantum burgers—while battling an invasion of the baddest, and ugliest meanies in the universe. The Butt-Ugly Martians have their four-fingered hands full in an exciting, fun-filled mini-feature, plus one action-packed bonus episode!"

SPECIAL FEATURES Character Bios • DVD-ROM Features: Game • Other Title Trailers TECHNICAL FEATURES Fullscreen (1.33:1) • Subtitles/CC: Eng., Fren., Span. • Languages: Eng. • Sound: Dolby Digital Surround 2.0 • Keepcase • 1 Disc • Region 1 GENRE & RATING CGI/Comedy/Science Fiction • Not Rated (Kids)

Butt-Ugly Martians: Hoverboard Heroes [#2]

Universal, 2002, 70 mins., #22250. Animation Directed by Egidio V. Dal Chele. Written by Kelly Ward, Pamela Hickey, Dennys McCoy, Richard Albreicht, Casey Keller.

NOTE: This DVD arrived too late for a full review. The following text is promotional copy provided by the releasing company:

"Mars' wackiest trio of warriors came to conquer Earth but they're having so much fun they've changed their minds! Now the Martians are protecting our planet from Emperor Bog and his alien baddies with the help from their secret weapon, Dog, and Earth kids Mike, Angela, and Cedric. Do-Wah, B-Bop, and 2T star in three action-packed adventures filled with out-of-this-world excitement! They can fool Bog, but can the Butt-Ugly Martians avoid crafty alien hunter Stoat Muldoon?"

SPECIAL FEATURES Character Bios • DVD-ROM Features: Game • Other Title Trailers TECHNICAL FEATURES Fullscreen (1.33:1) • Subtitles/CC: Eng., Fren., Span. • Languages: Eng. • Sound: Dolby Digital Surround 2.0 • Keepcase • 1 Disc • Region 1 GENRE & RATING CGI/Comedy/Science Fiction • Not Rated (Kids)

Butt-Ugly Martians: Boyz to Martians [#3]

Universal, 2002, 70 mins., #22251. Animation Directed by Egidio V. Dal Chele. Written by Pamela Hickey and Dennys McCoy, Richard Albreicht, Casey Keller, David Garber.

NOTE: This DVD arrived too late for a full review. The following text is promotional copy provided by the releasing company:

"Martians just wanna have fun as Do-Wah, B-Bop and 2T make a music video while trying to convince Emperor Bog that their fun-loving adventures are part of a master plan to 'rule' our planet! They can sing and dance, but can the Butt-Ugly Martians survive Dr. Damage and his evil plans? Join Earth kids Mike, Angela, and Cedric—along with Dog, the ultimate robotic secret weapon—as they rock and roll with the wackiest trio of aliens ever!"

SPECIAL FEATURES Character Bios • DVD-ROM Features: Game • Other Title Trailers TECHNICAL FEATURES Fullscreen (1.33:1) • Subtitles/CC: Eng., Fren., Span. • Languages: Eng. • Sound: Dolby Digital Surround 2.0 • Keepcase • 1 Disc • Region 1 GENRE & RATING CGI/Comedy/Science Fiction • Not Rated (Kids)

Buttobi CPU: I Dream of Mimi ☞ see

Mature/Adult Section

Buzz Lightyear of Star Command: The Adventure Begins

Disney, 2000, 70 mins., #19574. Directed by Tad Stones. Screenplay by Mark McCorkle, Robert Schooley, Bill Motz, Bob Roth.

One of the pleasant conceits of *Toy Story* was that spaceman Buzz Lightyear thought he was real, partially because he had his own TV show. So, it's no surprise that Disney would create a *Buzz Lightyear* series, with this project serving as its pilot. Buzz gathers his fearless team of Space Ranger Cadets to fight the evil Zurg and his henchmen. The bad guys have overrun the planet of the little green men, and teamed with mystical Mira Nova, bumbling giant Booster, and robot XR, Buzz has to send the villains back to infinity and beyond.

An opening sequence with the CGI-animated *Toy Story 2* stars settling down to watch Buzz on TV is a rousing start, but unfortunately, it showcases just how flat the cel animation is by comparison. Still, the adventures of Buzz and company are fun and cute, and fans of the little green men won't be disappointed either. The voice cast includes Tim Allen, Nicole Sullivan, Wayne Knight,

Patrick Warburton, Sean P. Hayes (as Brain Pod #13), and a cameo by Jim Hanks (Tom's brother) as Woody.

If you're a *Toy Story* fan or like campy science fiction you won't need any more prompting to check out this DVD, but I'll give you one more reason to love it or leave it: William Shatner performs the end-credit song, "To Infinity and Beyond," backed by The Star Command Chorus.

SPECIAL FEATURES Digital Comic Book • Games • Other Title Trailers TECHNICAL FEATURES Widescreen (1.78:1) • Subtitles/CC: Eng. • Languages: Eng. • Sound: Dolby Digital Surround 5.1 • Keepcase • 1 Disc • Region 1 GENRE & RATING Comedy/Science Fiction • Not Rated (All Ages)

C

C-Bear and Jamal

Xenon, 2000, 189 mins., #XE XX-4042DVD. Directed by Emory Myrick, Michael Lyman, Bill Hutten, Brian Hogan, David Brain, Leo Sullivan. Written by Al Sonja L. Rice, Todd R. Jones, Earl Richey Jones, Sib Ventress, Lee Gaither, Kevin Donahue.

Ten-year-old Jamal lives with his loving father, sister, and grandparents in south central Los Angeles, but the one who teaches him the most good lessons in life is C-Bear, his sunglasses-wearing teddy bear. The adults don't know it, but C-Bear can come magically to life, and he teaches Jamal life lessons. Each episode has a moral about topics such as money, changing yourself to please friends, hard work, why bullies are mean, the importance of truth, the value of old people, and why education is more important than sleep.

This DVD contains nine episodes of the top-rated and critically acclaimed 1996 Fox animated series. The show spreads good messages without being preachy and features a multicultural cast (though most are African-American). The voice cast is excellent, including rapper Tone-Loc as C-Bear, comedienne Margaret Cho, and Paul Rodriguez among others. Watch for a funny parody clip for "Def Comedy Zoo" in one episode. Though the DVD case lists an intro by Tone-Loc and a trailer, neither of them appeared to be on the disc I received.

SPECIAL FEATURES None TECHNICAL FEATURES Fullscreen (1.33:1) • Languages: Eng. • Sound: Dolby Digital 2.0 • Keepcase • 1 Disc • Region 1–6 GENRE & RATING African-American/Family • Not Rated (Kids)

Call, The: A Computer Animated Vision

DVD International, 2002, 46 mins., #DVDI0861. Directed by Beny Tchaicovsky.

Nine synthesized musical selections are accompanied by mind-tripping CGI computer animation. There's really no plot to speak of, just humans, robots, animals, and objects moving about in a surreal atmosphere while the camera swirls around them. Nice eye-candy for a short time, but I don't think many viewers will want to watch it straight through in one sitting, unless they're—ahem—chemically enhanced.

SPECIAL FEATURES Other Title Trailers TECHNICAL FEATURES Fullscreen (1.33:1) • Sound: Dolby Digital 2.0, Dolby Digital Surround 5.1, DTS 5.1 • Keepcase • 1 Disc • Region All GENRE & RATING CGI/Music • Not Rated (Teens)

Camelot

Madacy, 1999, 50 mins.

This DVD was not available for review.

Cameraman's Revenge and Other Fantastic Tales, The

Image, 2000, 80 mins., #ID9407MLSDVD. Directed by Ladislaw Starewicz, France Starewicz, Irene Starewicz.

Six astonishing short films are presented on this DVD, most of them stop-motion or puppet productions. Ladislaw Starewicz was a Lithuanian and Russian filmmaker who loved to film insects, but when he couldn't get them to perform as he wanted them to, he painstakingly stop-motion animated insect carcasses! The 1912 title film, "The Cameraman's Revenge" is one such short, showing bugs going about their lives in a very human fashion.

The six shorts range from black-and-white work to tinted and hand-colored projects, all created in Moscow and Paris. Other titles include "The Insects' Christmas" (1913), "The Frog Who Wanted a King" (1922), "Voice of the Nightingale" (1923), "The Mascot" (1933), and "Winter Carousel" (1958). Given the age of these shorts, the DVD contains an excellent transfer of this rare material. For those who enjoy slightly creepy stop motion films such as those Tim Burton has produced, here's the chance to see the work of his most excellent predecessor.

SPECIAL FEATURES Liner Notes: Inside Cover TECHNICAL FEATURES Fullscreen (1.33:1) • Sound: Dolby Digital 2.0 • Snapcase • 1

Disc • Region 1 GENRE & RATING Stop-Motion/Puppet/Anthology • Not Rated (Teens)

Campus ☞ see Mature/Adult Section

Captain Scarlet

A&E, 2002, 832 mins., #AAE70470. Directed by Desmond Saunders, David Lane, Brian Burgess, Alan Perry, Robert Lynn, Ken Turner, Leo Eaton. Written by Gerry Anderson, Sylvia Anderson, Tony Barwick, Shane Rimmer, Peter Curran, David Williams, Alan Pattillo, Richard Conway, Stephen J. Mattick, Bill Hedley, Ralph Hart, Bryan Cooper, Leo Eaton, David Lee.

The year is 2068, and when a Spectrum mission from Earth to Mars accidentally destroys an ancient civilization's computers, the Mysterons declare war on Earth. Using "retrometabolism," the Mysterons can reconstruct Spectrum agents to follow them, making them a difficult group to contain, and their attacks all the more insidious. Into the fray comes Captain Scarlet, the number one agent of Spectrum. When he gains powers of his own, he's able to withstand any attack by the Mysterons, and he soon leads Earth's battle against the attacking alien forces. He's aided by other color-coded agents, as well as a group of beautiful women known as "The Angels."

Aired in England from 1967 to 1968, *Captain Scarlet and the Mysterons* was the fifth science fiction puppet series created by Gerry Anderson. Using a process he called "Supermarionation," Anderson and his crew created the most realistic puppets televised to that date. Mechanics for the puppets were hidden within the body, while the heads were proportional, and the eyes were photographs of real eyes superimposed onto the puppet eyeballs! The hardware and technology used by the characters were all finely detailed as well, and very hi-tech for the era.

A&E's set of DVDs showcases the complete *Captain Scarlet* series, with all 32 episodes, plus a wealth of extras. Picture quality is excellent, and the shows are presented uncut. Gerry Anderson even chimes in with commentary on two episodes! As with A&E's presentation of the *Thunderbirds* series, this set is a must-have for any fan.

SPECIAL FEATURES Commentary Track by Gerry Anderson • Creator Bio and Filmography • Character Bios • Character and Technology Photo Galleries • Production Stills • Spectrum ID Cards • Vehicle Guides • History Notes • DVD-ROM Features: Interactive Vehicle Diagrams TECHNICAL FEATURES Fullscreen (1.33:1) • Languages: Eng. • Sound: Dolby Digital Surround 5.1 • Multikeepcase • 4 Discs • Region 1 GENRE & RATING Stop-Motion/Marionettes/Science Fiction • Not Rated (Kids)

Cardcaptor Sakura: The Clow [#1]

Pioneer, 2000, 100 mins., #10562. Directed by Morio Asaka, Yorimichi Nakano, Sunao Katabuchi, Nabuaki Nakanishi. Script by Nanase Okawa, Jiro Kaneko. Based on the manga series by CLAMP in *Nakayoshi*.

Ten-year-old schoolgirl Sakura Kinomoto didn't mean to cause trouble, but like Pandora and her box, when she opens the magical book of Clow, she accidentally unleashes a series of evil Clow cards into the world. Cerberus, the Guardian of the Cards, tells her she must become a "Cardcaptor" to catch all of the cards before they can cause death and destruction. Each card represents a different spirit or magical creature, and if she captures them, Sakura can control their powers. Sakura is both aided and hindered by her rich best friend Tomoyo Daidoji, and her Chinese rival Cardcaptor Li Shaoran. But as they face their sometimes dangerous adventures regaining the Clow, might something more sweet blossom between Sakura and Li, or does he prefer someone more masculine?

Created in 1998 by ultrapopular manga team CLAMP, *Cardcaptor Sakura* came to the U.S. on Kids WB! in 2000. Although the televised version was significantly edited (one of the big elements excised was a subtle thread of homosexuality), this DVD series collects the original uncut Japanese episodes. The animation is quite beautiful, even striking at times, and the stories make much more sense than their American counterparts. Still, the action and characters sometimes lapse into silliness. Note that there is no English dubbing on these discs, only subtitles.

The four episodes presented on the debut DVD are: "Sakura and the Mysterious Magic Book"; "Sakura's Wonderful Friend"; "Sakura's Heart-Racing First Date"; and "Sakura's Tiring Sunday."

SPECIAL FEATURES Character Bios • Promotional Footage • Clean Credits. TECHNICAL FEATURES Fullscreen (1.33:1) • Subtitles/CC: Eng. • Languages: Jap. • Sound: Dolby Digital 2.0 • Keepcase • 1 Disc • Region 1 GENRE & RATING Magic/Girls • Rated 13+

Cardcaptor Sakura: Everlasting Memories [#2]

Pioneer, 2001, 100 mins., #10563. Directed by Mamoru Kanbe, Akio Sakai, Kazunori Mizuno, Sunao Katabuchi. Script by Hiroshi Ishii, Nanase Okawa, Jiro Kaneko. Based on the manga series by CLAMP in *Nakayoshi*.

Four more magical girl adventures: Sakura and her friends go to a toy store and face possessed plush dolls in "Sakura, Panda, and the Cute Shop"; the ghost of Sakura's mother appears in the woods near the school in "Sakura and Memories of Her Mother"; Sakura has to break into an art museum to catch a Clow card in "Sakura's First Attempt As a Thief!?!"; and the punky Li makes his debut in "Sakura's Rival Appears."

SPECIAL FEATURES Clean Credits • Insert: Valentine Postcard TECHNICAL FEATURES Fullscreen (1.33:1) • Subtitles/CC: Eng. • Languages: Jap. • Sound: Dolby Digital 2.0 • Keepcase • 1 Disc • Region 1 GENRE & RATING Magic/Girls • Rated 13+

Cardcaptor Sakura: Friends Forever [#3]

Pioneer, 2001, 100 mins., #10564. Directed by Mamoru Kanbe, Akio Sakai, Junichi Sakata. Script by Nanase Okawa, Hiroshi Ishii, Jiro Kaneko. Based on the manga series by CLAMP in *Nakayoshi*.

More Clow cards are hunted down in four DVD adventures. While shopping, Sakura's friend Rika is possessed by a Clow card–controlled brooch in "Sakura and the Mysterious Brooch." Tomoya's mother comes to a sports meet in "Sakura and the Sports Day of Flowers." The mothers of Sakura and Tomoya were once best friends and their past relationship is explored in "Sakura, Tomoya, and a Mansion." Sakura and Li try to fight a card that can turn back time—on school test day no less—in "Sakura's Never-Ending Day."

SPECIAL FEATURES Art Galleries • Insert: Girl's Day Postcard TECHNICAL FEATURES Fullscreen (1.33:1) • Subtitles/CC: Eng. • Languages: Jap. • Sound: Dolby Digital 2.0 • Keepcase • 1 Disc • Region 1 GENRE & RATING Magic/Girls • Rated 13+

Cardcaptor Sakura: Sakura Fight [#4]

Pioneer, 2002, 100 mins., #10565. Directed by Kazunori Mizuno, Shoji Yabushita, Masaru Kitao, Mamoru Kanbe. Script by Nanase Okawa, Hiroshi Ishii, Jiro Kaneko. Based on the manga series by CLAMP in *Nakayoshi*.

The capturing of Clow cards continues with episodes #13–16 on this DVD. When Sakura and Li battle over the Power Card at a field trip to a zoo, things go badly in "Sakura and the Elephant's Test of Strength." Sakura's brother is the lead in a gender-bending production of a fairy tale play in "Sakura, Toya, and Cinderella." Tiny Kero runs away and becomes friends with a new little girl in "Sakura and Kero's Big Fight!." An old man in a mansion holds haunting secrets in "Sakura and the Rainbow of Memories." This latter episode may lead to some discussions between parents and kids about the dangers of befriending strangers.

SPECIAL FEATURES Art Galleries • Insert: Clow Card TECHNICAL FEATURES Fullscreen (1.33:1) • Subtitles/CC: Eng. • Languages: Jap. • Sound: Dolby Digital 2.0 • Keepcase • 1 Disc • Region 1 GENRE & RATING Magic/Girls • Rated 13+

Cardcaptor Sakura: Vacation Daze [#5]

Pioneer, 2001, 100 mins., #10566. Directed by Ken Ando, Shoji Yabushita, Mamoru Kanbe, Junichi Sakata. Script by Nanase Okawa, Jiro Kaneko. Based on the manga series by CLAMP in *Nakayoshi*.

It's summertime, and magical girl adventures continue with four more episodes. At a beach camp, all of Sakura's friends are disappearing in caves in "Sakura's Scary Tests of Courage." Sakura and her brother go to the local shrine, where a Clow card causes trouble in "Sakura, Yukito, and the Summer Festival." A trip to the library ends up with a dip in the lake with Li in "Sakura and the Summer Holiday Homework." In "Transfer Student vs. Sakura," Li's troubling cousin, Li Meilin, comes to town, and she's not fond of Sakura.

SPECIAL FEATURES Art Galleries • Insert: Fun in Sun Postcard TECHNICAL FEATURES Fullscreen (1.33:1) • Subtitles/CC: Eng. • Languages: Jap. • Sound: Dolby Digital 2.0 • Keepcase • 1 Disc • Region 1 GENRE & RATING Magic/Girls • Rated 13+

Cardcaptor Sakura: Friends and Family [#6]

Pioneer, 2001, 100 mins., #10567. Directed by Mamoru Kanbe, Kazunori Mizuno, Hitoyuki Matsui, Akira Mano. Script by Jiro Kaneko, Hiroshi Ishii, Nanase Okawa. Based on the manga series by CLAMP in *Nakayoshi*.

Cuteness reigns as Sakura and Li capture more Clow cards and face four more adventures. The Loop Card keeps the cast running forever in "Sakura's Long Marathon Race." Dad's going to have trouble when Sakura messes with his teaching in "Sakura and her Kind Father." The Song Card keeps the music playing in "Sakura, Tomoya, and a Wonderful Song." Guess who gets shrunk down in "Sakura's Little Adventure"?

SPECIAL FEATURES Art Galleries • Insert: Gunbattle Postcard TECHNICAL FEATURES Fullscreen (1.33:1) • Subtitles/CC: Eng. • Languages: Jap. • Sound: Dolby Digital 2.0 • Keepcase • 1 Disc • Region 1 GENRE & RATING Magic/Girls • Rated 13+

Cardcaptor Sakura: Magical Mystery [#7]

Pioneer, 2002, 100 mins., #10568. Directed by Mamoru Kanbe, Kazunori Mizuno, Hitoyuki Matsui. Script by Tomoko Ogawa, Tomoyasu Okubo, Nanase Okawa. Based on the manga series by CLAMP in *Nakayoshi*.

Mysterious women highlight the four episodes on this disc. A Clow card becomes Sakura's naughty twin in "Two Sakuras." Li senses that a beautiful substitute teacher might be trouble in "Sakura and the Wonderful Teacher." While the teacher is connected to the Maze card in "Sakura and the Shrine of Memories." Trading card mania causes hilarious trouble at school when the collectibles look like Clow cards in "Sakura and the Enchanted Cards."

SPECIAL FEATURES Art Galleries • Insert: Happy Holidays Postcard TECHNICAL FEATURES Fullscreen (1.33:1) • Subtitles/CC: Eng. • Languages: Jap. • Sound: Dolby Digital 2.0 • Keepcase • 1 Disc • Region 1 GENRE & RATING Magic/Girls • Rated 13+

Cardcaptor Sakura: Sweet Trouble [#8]

Pioneer, 2002, 100 mins., #10569. Directed by Akira Mano, Mamoru Kanbe, Kazunori Mizuno, Hitoyuki Matsui. Script by Tomoko Ogawa, Jiro Kaneko, Nanase Okawa, Tomoyasu Okubo. Based on the manga series by CLAMP in *Nakayoshi*.

Nastiness is cooked up in the four episodes on this disc. Baking a cake isn't usually so much trouble until a Clow card gets involved in "Sakura's Sweet Cooking." Rei learns a valuable lesson in "Sakura and the Injured Card." A monster cat and a dragon bedevil Sakura in "Sakura and the Nameless Book." Kero and Li switch bodies in "Sakura, Kero, and Shaoran."

SPECIAL FEATURES Art Galleries • Insert: Night Flight Postcard TECHNICAL FEATURES Fullscreen (1.33:1) • Subtitles/CC: Eng. • Languages: Jap. • Sound: Dolby Digital 2.0 • Keepcase • 1 Disc • Region 1 GENRE & RATING Magic/Girls • Rated 13+

Cardcaptor Sakura: Winter Wonderland [#9]

Pioneer, 2002, 75 mins., #10570. Directed by Mamoru Kanbe, Akira Mano, Kazunori Mizuno. Script by Tomoko Ogawa, Nanase Okawa. Based on the manga series by CLAMP in *Nakayoshi*.

NOTE: This DVD arrived too late for a full review. The following text is promotional copy provided by the releasing company:

"Fire and Ice! Learning how to ice skate can be a lot of fun. However, the lesson turns into a crash course when the Freeze Card appears. Later, Sakura and Yukito team up in a city-wide search for clues to a hidden prize that ends up in a death-defying drop! Then the Firey Card attacks and Sakura must learn a new technique with her Clow Cards in order to pull her friends out of the fire!"

This disc contains episodes #33–35.

SPECIAL FEATURES Art Galleries • Insert: April Showers Postcard TECHNICAL FEATURES Fullscreen (1.33:1) • Subtitles/CC: Eng. • Languages: Jap. • Sound: Dolby Digital 2.0 • Keepcase • 1 Disc • Region 1 GENRE & RATING Magic/Girls • Rated 13+

Cardcaptor Sakura: School Daze [#10]

Pioneer, 2002, 100 mins., #10571. Directed by Akira Mano, Kumiko Takahashi, Hitoyuki Matsui, Yasumi Miyamoto. Script by Nanase Okawa, Tomoyasu Okubo. Based on the manga series by CLAMP in *Nakayoshi*.

NOTE: This DVD arrived too late for a full review. The following text is promotional copy provided by the releasing company:

"Sakura starts the fifth grade on a high note with a beautiful new teacher, Kaho, and a precious birthday gift from Yukito. However, the Clow Cards make sure to remind her that she still has her duty as Cardcaptor in addition to her school work. The Snow Card's storm, the Voice Card's theft of Tomoyo's voice, and the Lock Card's attack on her school field trip, are just a few of the problems she has to deal with. Not an easy task when she's home sick with a high fever, but without Sakura, how can the Cloud Card be captured?"

This disc contains episodes #36–39.

SPECIAL FEATURES Art Galleries • Clean Credits • Insert: Baseball Postcard TECHNICAL FEATURES Fullscreen (1.33:1) • Subtitles/CC: Eng. • Languages: Jap. • Sound: Dolby Digital 2.0 • Keepcase • 1 Disc • Region 1 GENRE & RATING Magic/Girls • Rated 13+

Cardcaptor Sakura: Trust [#11]

Pioneer, 2002, 100 mins., #10573. Directed by Kumiko Takahashi, Akira Mano, Fushio Takase. Script by Nanase Okawa. Based on the manga series by CLAMP in *Nakayoshi*.

NOTE: This DVD arrived too late for a full review. The following text is promotional copy provided by the releasing company:

"The Dream Card pulls Sakura into a prophetic dream where she meets another Sakura who tells her

'Everything's going to be just fine.' Of course, that only makes her nervous. However, not quite as nervous as Li gets after he is cast as the princess in Sleeping Beauty! With Sakura cast as the Prince, they resolve to do their best, but they certainly couldn't have expected the Clow Cards to attack them on stage. Still, their troubles are only beginning. The Light and Dark Cards warn Sakura about the arrival of Yue the Judge, just as Mei Lin is forced to return to Hong Kong!"

This disc contains episodes #40–43.

SPECIAL FEATURES Art Galleries • Clean Credits • Insert: Beach Postcard TECHNICAL FEATURES Fullscreen (1.33:1) • Subtitles/CC: Eng. • Languages: Jap. • Sound: Dolby Digital 2.0 • Keepcase • 1 Disc • Region 1 GENRE & RATING Magic/Girls • Rated 13+

Cardcaptor Sakura: Final Judgement [#12]

Pioneer, 2002, 100 mins., #11754. Directed by Mamoru Kanbe, Yorifusa Yamaguchi, Shigehito Takayanagi. Script by Nanase Okawa. Based on the manga series by CLAMP in *Nakayoshi*.

NOTE: This DVD arrived too late for a full review. The following text is promotional copy provided by the releasing company:

"Mysteries Revealed! Kero confronts Sakura's teacher, Kaho Mizuki, to discover that the final judgement is upon them and the fate of the world is in balance! Then the earth splits open introducing the final card, the Earth Card. If Sakura can capture it, she will have captured all of the Clow Cards and Kero will regain his true form. However, will Sakura be ready for the final judgement? Will Sakura be ready to face the judge, Yue, when he appears? How will she be able to fight someone she loves?"

This disc contains episodes #44–47.

SPECIAL FEATURES Art Galleries • Insert: Autumn Postcard TECHNICAL FEATURES Fullscreen (1.33:1) • Subtitles/CC: Eng. • Languages: Jap. • Sound: Dolby Digital 2.0 • Keepcase • 1 Disc • Region 1 GENRE & RATING Magic/Girls • Rated 13+

Cardcaptor Sakura: The Movie

Pioneer, 2002, 86 mins., #11743. Directed by Morio Asaka. Script by Nanase Okawa. Based on the manga series by CLAMP in *Nakayoshi*.

Sakura wins a trip to Hong Kong for herself and four others, but danger lurks there. Those who controlled the Clow in ages past once lived in Hong Kong, and their legacy lingers on. Sakura will be forced to battle ancient foes—and a woman who lives in the water—to free her family

and friends, or they will be trapped in a phantom city forever!

This is the first *Cardcaptor Sakura* movie, released in Japan in 1999. Unlike the regular series, this features a dub track that on the whole is badly translated, and oddly, most of the names have been altered! For fans of the series, this adventure is a bit darker and more serious than others, but the animators make full use of the larger budget with richer art and backgrounds. Note that this adventure takes place chronologically between DVD volumes #9 and #10.

SPECIAL FEATURES Trailer • Promotional Footage • Alternate Angles • Insert: Character Chart, Plastic Card • Reversible Cover • Easter Eggs. TECHNICAL FEATURES Widescreen (1.85:1 enhanced for 16x9) • Subtitles/CC: Eng. • Languages: Jap., Eng. dub • Sound: Dolby Digital Surround 2.0, Dolby Digital 5.1 • Keepcase • 1 Disc • Region 1 GENRE & RATING Magic/Girls • Not Rated (Teens)

Cardcaptors: Tests of Courage [#1]

Pioneer, 2000, 65 mins., #10558. Based on the manga series by CLAMP in *Nakayoshi*.

This is the kid-friendly version of *Cardcaptor Sakura*, as edited by Nelvana for Kids WB! television. While the story and characters remain substantially the same, each episode is edited together from several of the original *Cardcaptor Sakura* episodes. This means that some of the stories verge on the nonsensical, especially as scenes and subtexts are edited out. Kids seem to love it, particularly because of its bright colors, cute animation, and silliness, but adults may find it difficult to watch, especially if they've ever seen the more coherent "non-kids" version.

Note that due to the complex cut-and-paste editing job for the series, providing director or writer credits is nearly impossible, so we've dispensed with them for these listings. As for titles and plots, the *Cardcaptors* titles listed as follows generally correspond with the second *Cardcaptor Sakura* titles; the episodes don't correspond perfectly due to editing, but most of the plots are the same.

This DVD contains episodes corresponding to: "Sakura's Rival"; "Sakura's Rival Appears"; "Time and Again"; "Sakura's Tiring Sunday"; "The Cave"; and "Sakura's Scary Tests of Courage."

SPECIAL FEATURES Character Bios • Promotional Footage • Insert: Plastic Standee TECHNICAL FEATURES Fullscreen (1.33:1) • Subtitles/CC: Eng. • Languages: Eng. • Sound: Dolby Digital 2.0 • Keepcase • 1 Disc • Region 1 GENRE & RATING Magic/Girls • Rated TV7

Cardcaptors: Power Match [#2]

Pioneer, 2001, 65 mins., #10559. Based on the manga series by CLAMP in *Nakayoshi*.

This DVD contains episodes episodes corresponding to "Power's Ploy"; "Sakura and the Elephant's Test of Strength"; "Double-edged Sword"; "Sakura and the Mysterious Brooch"; "The New Rival"; and "Transfer Student vs. Sakura."

SPECIAL FEATURES Character Bios • Promotional Footage TECHNICAL FEATURES Fullscreen (1.33:1) • Subtitles/CC: Eng. • Languages: Eng. • Sound: Dolby Digital 2.0 • Keepcase • 1 Disc • Region 1 GENRE & RATING Magic/Girls • Rated TV7

Cardcaptors: Misdirections [#3]

Pioneer, 2001, 65 mins., #10560. Based on the manga series by CLAMP in *Nakayoshi*.

This DVD contains episodes corresponding to "Double Take"; "Two Sakuras";"No Way Out";"Sakura and the Wonderful Teacher";"The Race"; and "Sakura and the Injured Card."

SPECIAL FEATURES Character Bios • Insert: Plastic Standee TECHNICAL FEATURES Fullscreen (1.33:1) • Subtitles/CC: Eng. • Languages: Eng. • Sound: Dolby Digital 2.0 • Keepcase • 1 Disc • Region 1 GENRE & RATING Magic/Girls • Rated TV7

Cardcaptors: New Lessons [#4]

Pioneer, 2001, 65 mins., #10561. Based on the manga series by CLAMP in *Nakayoshi*.

This DVD contains episodes corresponding to "Dragon Slayer";"Sakura and the Nameless Book"; "The Switch";"Sakura, Kero, and Shaoran"; "Ice Breaker"; and "Sakura's Freezing Ice Skating."

SPECIAL FEATURES Character Bios • Insert: Plastic Standee TECHNICAL FEATURES Fullscreen (1.33:1) • Subtitles/CC: Eng. • Languages: Eng. • Sound: Dolby Digital 2.0 • Keepcase • 1 Disc • Region 1 GENRE & RATING Magic/Girls • Rated TV7

Cardcaptors: Firestorm [#5]

Pioneer, 2001, 65 mins., #11468. Based on the manga series by CLAMP in *Nakayoshi*.

This DVD contains episodes corresponding to "The Third Element"; "Sakura's Wonderful Christmas"; "Buyer Beware"; "Sakura and the Enchanted Cards"; "Stormy Weather"; and "Sakura and the Snowy School Team."

SPECIAL FEATURES Character Bios • Insert: Plastic Standee TECHNICAL FEATURES Fullscreen (1.33:1) • Subtitles/CC: Eng. • Languages: Eng. • Sound: Dolby Digital 2.0 • Keepcase • 1 Disc • Region 1 GENRE & RATING Magic/Girls • Rated TV7

Cardcaptors: The Best of Friends [#6]

Pioneer, 2001, 65 mins., #11469. Based on the manga series by CLAMP in *Nakayoshi*.

This DVD contains episodes corresponding to "Allies";"Sakura's Heart-Racing First Date";"Meilin's Story"; "Sakura and Farewell to Meilin"; "The Last Card-Part One"; and "Sakura, Kero, and the Mysterious Teacher."

SPECIAL FEATURES Character Bios • Insert: Plastic Standee TECHNICAL FEATURES Fullscreen (1.33:1) • Subtitles/CC: Eng. • Languages: Eng. • Sound: Dolby Digital 2.0 • Keepcase • 1 Disc • Region 1 GENRE & RATING Magic/Girls • Rated TV7

Cardcaptors: End of Days [#7]

Pioneer, 2002, 65 mins., #11470. Based on the manga series by CLAMP in *Nakayoshi*.

This DVD contains episodes corresponding to "The Last Card—Part Two"; "Sakura and the Final Clow Card"; "The Final Judgement"; "Sakura and the Final Judgement"; "One Fateful Day"; and "Sakura and the Mysterious Magic Book."

SPECIAL FEATURES Character Bios • Clean Credits TECHNICAL FEATURES Fullscreen (1.33:1) • Subtitles/CC: Eng. • Languages: Eng. • Sound: Dolby Digital 2.0 • Keepcase • 1 Disc • Region 1 GENRE & RATING Magic/Girls • Rated TV7

Cardcaptors: Times of Need [#8]

Pioneer, 2002, 75 mins., #11471. Based on the manga series by CLAMP in *Nakayoshi*.

This DVD contains the corresponding episodes: "Under the Weather" is the same as "Sakura's Dizzy Fever Day"; "The Mysterious Painting" is the same as "Sakura's First Attempt As a Thief!?!"; and "The Past, the Present, and the Future" is a clips episode.

SPECIAL FEATURES Character Bios • Clean Credits TECHNICAL FEATURES Fullscreen (1.33:1) • Subtitles/CC: Eng. • Languages: Eng. • Sound: Dolby Digital 2.0 • Keepcase • 1 Disc • Region 1 GENRE & RATING Magic/Girls • Rated TV7

Cardcaptors: Star Power [#9]

Pioneer, 2002, 75 mins., #11472. Based on the manga series by CLAMP in *Nakayoshi*.

This DVD contains the corresponding episodes: "A Strange New Beginning" is the same as "Sakura and the Mysterious Transfer Student"; "Running Out of Time" is the same as "Sakura and the Awakened Key"; and "A New Set of Wings" is the same as both "Sakura, Shaoran, and the Invisible Thread" and "Sakura and the Big Teddy Bear."

SPECIAL FEATURES Character Bios TECHNICAL FEATURES Fullscreen (1.33:1) • Subtitles/CC: Eng. • Languages: Eng. • Sound: Dolby Digital 2.0 • Keepcase • 1 Disc • Region 1 GENRE & RATING Magic/Girls • Rated TV7

Cardcaptors: The Movie

Pioneer, 2002, 86 mins., #11744. Directed by Morio Asaka. Script by Nanase Okawa. Based on the manga series by CLAMP in *Nakayoshi*.

This is the slightly edited version of the first *Cardcaptor Sakura* movie. It has been pan-and-scanned from its original widescreen image.

SPECIAL FEATURES Trailer • Music Video TECHNICAL FEATURES Standard (modified to 1.33:1) • Languages: Eng. dub • Sound: Dolby Digital Surround 2.0 • Keepcase • 1 Disc • Region 1 GENRE & RATING Magic/Girls • Not Rated (Kids)

Care Bears Movie, The

MGM, 2002, 76 mins., #1003821. Directed by Arna Selznick. Screenplay by Peter Sauder.

NOTE: This DVD arrived too late for a full review. The following text is promotional copy provided by the releasing company:

"The world is in trouble . . . and it's up to the Care Bears to save it! Starring everyone's favorite animated characters and featuring the voices of Mickey Rooney and George Engel, as well as songs performed by Carole King, *The Care Bears Movie* will dazzle and delight viewers of all ages. Way up high where the clouds and rainbows live, the Care Bears watch over the Earth and make sure everyone is kind and friendly to one another. So when they see an evil spirit trick a lonely boy into helping make people mean, the huggable heroes jump into action! They come to the rescue with the animals from the Forest of Feelings . . . but it's going to take an awful lot of love to defeat the spirit's powerful spell."

Besides being offered as a single DVD, the disc was also included as part of a 2002 two-pack set, its keepcase banded back-to-back with *The Water Babies*.

SPECIAL FEATURES Trailer TECHNICAL FEATURES Fullscreen (1.33:1) • Subtitles/CC: Eng., Fren., Span. • Languages: Eng., Fren. dub, Span. dub • Sound: Dolby Digital 1.0 • Keepcase • 1 Disc • Region 1 GENRE & RATING Music/Fantasy/Animals • Rated G

Cartoon Crack-Ups

Warner, 2001, 124 mins., #H1788. Directed by Hanna-Barbera. Written by Warren Foster, Michael Maltese, Arthur Phillips, Tony Benedict, Larz Bourne, Tom Dagenais, Bill Lutz, Kin Platt.

The Hanna-Barbera cartoon characters are longtime television favorites, and this is the only DVD collection that features any of them (except for *Scooby-Doo* collections with their own entries in this book). This oversight will hopefully be remedied in the future, but for now you have to make due with complete, clean prints of early episodes of *The Flintstones*, *The Jetsons*, and more. There are also six music tracks and the pilot episode of *The Flintstones*, under its original name.

Family friendly episodes on the DVD include: "The Flagstones" (1960); *The Flintstones* "The Swimming Pool" (1960); *The Jetsons* "A Date with Jet Screamer" (1962); *Scooby-Doo . . . Where Are You?* "Jeepers, It's the Creeper" (1970); *Huckleberry Hound* "Spud Dud" (1960); *Yogi Bear* "Bear-Faced Disguise" (1960); *Pixie and Dixie* "Heavens to Jinksy" (1959); and *Top Cat* "The Maharajah of Pookajee" (1967).

SPECIAL FEATURES Music Videos. TECHNICAL FEATURES Standard (1.33:1) • Subtitles/CC: Eng., Fren., Span. • Languages: Eng. • Sound: Dolby Digital Mono) • Snapcase • 1 Disc • Region 1 GENRE & RATING Comedy/Animals • Rated G

Cartoon Crazys [#1]

Winstar, 1997, 100 mins., #WHE73002.

The *Cartoon Crazy's* collections feature a wide variety of 1930s to 1950s cartoons, most of which are believed to be in the public domain. Each of the shorts are given a restoration treatment that makes them look as good as they can for their age (although print quality still varies widely from excellent to nearly unwatchable), and on many discs, full credits and synopses are offered, as well as some historically themed extra features. The downside for many collectors is the soundtrack, which in addition to being restored, features new sound effects on many cartoons, some of which overwhelm and cheapen the original.

Titles on the disc include: Bugs Bunny in "Falling Hare" (1943); Daffy Duck in "Yankee Doodle Daffy" (1943); Tweety in "Tale of Two Kitties" (1942); Felix the Cat in "Neptune Nonsense" (1936); Foghorn Leghorn in "Crowing Pains" (1947); "Robin Hood Makes Good" (1939); Bugs Bunny and Elmer Fudd in "Fresh Hare" (1942); Daffy Duck in "Daffy the Commando" (1943); "Have You Got Any Castles?" (1938); Gabby in "Gabby Goes Fishing" (1941); and Elmer Fudd and Porky Pig in "Corny Concerto" (1943).

Besides being offered as a single DVD, the disc was also included as part of a 1999 two-pack set, its keepcase wrapped with *Cartoon Crazys 2*.

This DVD was not available for review.

Cartoon Crazys 2

Winstar, 1998, 100 mins., #WHE73009.

Titles on the disc include: "Doggone Tired" (1949); Daffy Duck in "To Duck or Not To Duck" (1943); "Inki and the Mynah Bird" (1943); "It's A Greek Life" (1936); Bugs Bunny in "The Wacky Wabbit" (1942); "The Goose That Laid the Golden Egg"; "Egghead"; "King for a Day"; Bugs Bunny in "The Wabbit Who Came to Supper" (1942); "The Early Worm Gets the Bird" (1940); "Toonerville Trolley" (1936); and "Fifth Column Mouse" (1943).

Aside from being offered as a single DVD, the disc was also included as part of a 1999 two pack set, its keepcase wrapped with *Cartoon Crazys*.

This DVD was not available for review.

Cartoon Crazys: And the Envelope, Please

Winstar, 1999, 120 mins., #WHE73045.

Titles on the disc include: "Popeye the Sailor Meets Sinbad the Sailor" (1936); Betty Boop in "Poor Cinderella" (1934); Superman in "The Mad Scientist" (1941); Porky Pig in "Pigs in a Polka" (1943); "The Hole"; Superman in "The Mechanical Monsters" (1941); "The Dover Boys" (1942); "MoonBird" (1959); "Hunky and Spunky" (1938); and "Summertime (1935)."

This DVD was not available for review.

Cartoon Crazys: Banned and Censored

Winstar, 2000, 110 mins., #WHE73118.

The *Banned and Censored* DVD features thirteen color and black-and-white shorts produced by such animation studios and directors as Ub Iwerks, Van Beuren, Walter Lantz, and Fleischer. There's also a good essay on the Hays Commission and old-time ratings boards, as well as a true-but-humorous listing of why each cartoon was banned or censored. There is quite a bit in the cartoons that might offend some audiences, including elements of racist stereotyping (mainly against African-Americans, Chinese, and Japanese), drug use, and some sexual elements. These are worth seeing for their historical value, but parents might want to discuss them with their children.

The thirteen shorts include: Betty Boop in "Be Human" (1936); Sambo in "Little Black Sambo" (1935); Private Snafu in "Booby Traps" (1944); Betty Boop and Koko in "Ha Ha Ha!" (1934); "Cupid Gets His Man" (1936); "Opening Night" (1933); "Scrub Me Momma With a Boogie Beat" (1941); Private Snafu in "Spies" (1943); "Fresh Vegetable Mystery" (1939); Betty Boop in "Making Stars" (1935); Little King in "Christmas Night" (1933, aka "Pals"); "In a Cartoon Studio" (1931); and "Easy Does It (1946)."

SPECIAL FEATURES Production Notes TECHNICAL FEATURES Fullscreen (1.33:1) • Languages: Eng. • Sound: Dolby Digital Surround 2.0, Dolby Digital 5.1 • Keepcase • 1 Disc • Region 1–6 GENRE & RATING Comedy/Adventure/Historical • Not Rated (Teens)

Cartoon Crazys: Christmas

Winstar, 1998, 100 mins., #WHE73017.

The thirteen titles on the disc include: "Rudolph the Red-Nosed Reindeer" (1944); "A Waif's Christmas Welcome" (1936); Bugs Bunny and Elmer Fudd in "Fresh Hare" (1942); "The Christmas Circus" (1949); "The Pup's Christmas" (1936); Popeye in "Private Eye Popeye" (1954); Little Audrey in "Santa's Surprise" (1947); "Hawaiian Birds Christmas" (1936); "Snow Foolin'" (1949); Grampy in "Christmas Comes But Once a Year (1936); Little Audrey in "Tarts and Flowers" (1950);

"Shanty Where Santy Claus Lives" (1933); and Little King in "Christmas Night" (1933, aka "Pals").

Besides being offered as a single DVD, the disc was also included as part of a 1999 three-pack set, packaged with *Cartoon Crazys: Kid's All-Time Favorites* and *Cartoon Crazys: Sci-Fi.*

This DVD was not available for review.

Cartoon Crazys: Comic Book Heroes

Winstar, 2000, 100 mins., #WHE73078.

The title of the "Comic Book Heroes" DVD is a bit of a misnomer, as only two characters are actually superheroes, unless you count Popeye. The disc features twelve color and black-and-white shorts produced by such animation studios and directors as Halas and Batchelor, Van Beuren, Harvey Films, and Fleischer. There's also a history feature, a selection on memorabilia, toys and artwork, and full credits and synopses. There is even one Japanese anime episode. Despite the listing on the back cover, there is no restoration demo or *Superman* preview on the disc.

The twelve shorts include: Superman in "The Underground World" (1943); Popeye in "I Don't Scare" (1956); Felix the Cat in "Bold King Cole" (1936); DoDo—The Kid from Outer Space in "Dodo in Japan" (1965); Superman in "Electronic Earthquake" (1942); "Toonerville Trolley" (1936); Little Audrey in "The Seapreme Court" (1954); Raggedy Ann in "Suddenly It's Spring" (1944); Betty Boop in "Henry, The Funniest Living American" (1935); Tobor the 8th Man in "The Case of the Numbers Gang" (1965); "Little Nemo" (1911); and Popeye in "Out to Punch" (1956).

SPECIAL FEATURES Production Notes • Synopsis TECHNICAL FEATURES Fullscreen (1.33:1) • Languages: Eng. • Sound: Dolby Digital Surround 2.0, Dolby Digital 5.1 • Keepcase • 1 Disc • Region All GENRE & RATING Comedy/Superhero/Historical • Not Rated (Kids)

Cartoon Crazys: Fairy Tales

Winstar.

This DVD was not available for review.

Cartoon Crazys: Goes to War

Winstar, 1998, 115 mins., #WHE73018.

Titles on the disc include: Bugs Bunny in "Bugs Bunny Bond Rally" (1942); Daffy Duck in "Daffy the Commando" (1943); Superman in "The Eleventh Hour" (1942); "Ding Dog Daddy" (1942); Bugs Bunny in "Falling Hare" (1943); "Jerky Turkey" (1945); Tweety in

"Tale of Two Kitties" (1942); Superman in "Jungle Drums" (1943); "Fifth Column Mouse" (1943); "Foney Fables" (1942); Daffy Duck in "Scrap Happy Daffy" (1943); "Hell Bent for Election" (1944); Private Snafu in "Snafuperman" (1944); Private Snafu in "Booby Traps" (1944); and Private Snafu in "Spies" (1943).

Besides being offered as a single DVD, the disc was also included as part of a two-pack set, its keepcase wrapped with *Cartoon Crazys: Sci-Fi.*

This DVD was not available for review.

Cartoon Crazys: The Great Animation Studios—Famous Studios

Winstar, 2000, 100 mins., #WHE73119.

In 1942, Paramount Studios caused the shutdown of Fleischer Studios, the animation unit it had sponsored until that time. Paramount immediately set up its own animation division, known as Famous Studios, and hired most of the Fleischer staff—including animation director Seymour Kneitel—to work for them directly. Famous Studios/Paramount produced cartoons up through 1967, and this DVD collects shorts from throughout that twenty-five year span.

The twelve shorts include: Little Lulu in "Bargain Counter Attack" (1946); Baby Huey in "Quack A Doodle Doo" (1950); Dog Face in "Self Made Mongrel" (1945); "Base Brawl—The Bouncing Ball Movie" (1948); Popeye in "Out to Punch" (1956); Little Audrey in "Seapreme Court" (1954); "Golden State—The Bouncing Ball Movie" (1948); Casper in "A-Haunting We Will Go" (1949); Raggedy Ann in "Suddenly It's Spring" (1944); Little Lulu in "A Scout with the Gout" (1947); "The Mild West—The Bouncing Ball Movie" (1947); and Henry in "Scrappily Married" (1945).

SPECIAL FEATURES Production Notes TECHNICAL FEATURES Fullscreen (1.33:1) • Languages: Eng. • Sound: Dolby Digital Surround 2.0, Dolby Digital 5.1 • Keepcase • 1 Disc • Region 1–6 GENRE & RATING Comedy/Adventure/Historical • Not Rated (Kids)

Cartoon Crazys: The Great Animators

Winstar, 2000, 100 mins., #WHE73120.

Three of early animation's pioneers are given the spotlight in this DVD collection, which features four shorts each from directors/animators Myron Waldman, Tom Palmer, and Seymour Kneitel. Much of these works was done for either Van Beuren or Fleischer Studios. There's also a history feature about the men and their cartoons.

The four Waldman shorts include: "Hawaiian Birds" (1936); "Hunky and Spunky" (1938); "Ants in the Pants" (1940); and Little Lulu in "A Bout with a Trout" (1947). The four Palmer shorts include "A Waif's Welcome" (1936); "Toonerville Trolley" (1936); "Molly Moo Cow and Robinson Crusoe" (1936); Felix the Cat in "Bold King Cole" (1936). The four Seymour Kneitel shorts include: Popeye in "Customers Wanted" (1939); Betty Boop in "Poor Cinderella" (1934); "Dancing on the Moon" (1935); and "The Song of the Birds" (1934).

SPECIAL FEATURES Director Bios TECHNICAL FEATURES Fullscreen (1.33:1) • Languages: Eng. • Sound: Dolby Digital Surround 2.0, Dolby Digital 5.1 • Keepcase • 1 Disc • Region 1–6 GENRE & RATING Comedy/Adventure/Historical • Not Rated (Kids)

Cartoon Crazys: Kid's All-Time Favorites

Winstar, 2000, 110 mins., #WHE73028.

Titles on the disc include: Bugs Bunny in "Wackiki Rabbit" (1943); "Bars and Stripes Forever" (1939); Daffy Duck in "Daffy Duck and the Dinosaur" (1939); Gabby in "Two for the Zoo" (1941); "The Dover Boys" (1942); Felix the Cat in "Bold King Cole" (1936); Bugs Bunny in "The Case of the Missing Hare" (1942); Porky Pig in "Pigs in a Polka" (1943); Casper in "Boo Moon" (1954); "Barnyard Showdown"; "Sports Chumpions" (1941); and "Popeye the Sailor Meets Ali Baba's Forty Thieves" (1947).

Besides being offered as a single DVD, the disc was also included as part of a 1999 three-pack set with *Cartoon Crazys: Sci-Fi* and *Cartoon Crazys: Christmas*.

This DVD was not available for review.

Cartoon Crazys: Sci-Fi

Winstar, 1999, 120 mins., #WHE73027.

Titles include: "Prest-O Change-O"; "To Spring" (1936); Superman in "Arctic Giant" (1942); Daffy Duck in "The Impatient Patient" (1942); "All's Fair at the Fair" (1938); "Cupid Gets His Man" (1936); "Dancing on the Moon" (1935); Superman in "The Magnetic Telescope" (1942); "The Sunshine Makers" (1935); "Cobweb Hotel" (1936); "Cooking With Gas"; Betty Boop in "House Cleaning Blues" (1937); "Crazy Inventions"; and the Puppetoon "John Henry and the Inky-Poo" (1946).

Besides being offered as a single DVD, the disc was also included as part of a two-pack set, its keepcase wrapped with *Cartoon Crazys: Goes to War*. It was also available as a 1999 three-pack set with *Cartoon Crazys: Kid's All-Time Favorites* and *Cartoon Crazys: Christmas*.

This DVD was not available for review.

Cartoon Crazys: Spooky Toons

Winstar, 2000, 90 mins., #WHE73111.

Twelve scary shorts from animation's yesteryear are presented, with color and black-and-white work from such animation studios and directors as Ub Iwerks, Fleischer, and Famous. There's even a George Pal Puppetoon ("Jasper in a Jam")! There are no historical notes, but the slime-dripping menus are fun.

The twelve shorts include: Casper in "There's Good Boos Tonight" (1948); Popeye in "Fright to the Finish" (1954); "Jasper in a Jam" (1946); "Jack Frost" (1934); "The Lunar Luger" (1957); "Balloon Land" (1935); Casper in "Spooking about Africa" (1957); Betty Boop in "The Scared Crows" (1939); "The Huffless, Puffless Dragon"; Betty Boop in "Is My Palm Read?" (1933); "Wot a Night" (1931); and Out of the Inkwell's "Ouija Board" (1917–20).

SPECIAL FEATURES None TECHNICAL FEATURES Fullscreen (1.33:1) • Languages: Eng. • Sound: Dolby Digital Surround 2.0, Dolby Digital 5.1 • Keepcase • 1 Disc • Region 1–6 GENRE & RATING Comedy/Horror/Historical • Not Rated (Kids)

Cartoon Explosion

The following *Cartoon Explosion* titles, from Front Row Entertainment, were not available for review: *Cartoon Explosion Vol. 1* [Corny Concerto/Jerky Turkey]; *Cartoon Explosion Vol. 2* [Henpecked Duck/Popeye]; *Cartoon Explosion's Collectors Classics* [Box Set].

Cartoon Noir ☞ see Mature/Adult Section

Cartoons of Halas and Batchelor, The

Hen's Tooth, 2000, 55 mins., #4073.

An animation apprentice to George Pal in the early 1930s, John Halas and his wife Joy Batchelor produced wartime propaganda art and movies during World War II. Their company, Halas and Batchelor Animation Ltd., was founded in 1940, and it eventually grew to be England's largest producer of animation. Of the approximately 2,000 shorts they produced over the years, 7 shorts are collected on this DVD. The print and sound are both excellent, especially given the age of some of the material.

Each of the cartoons represents a different art style, including stop-motion, 3D pixelization, and even some of the earliest-produced CGI work. Titles include: "The

Figurehead" (1935); "Owl and the Pussycat" (1952); "The Magic Canvas" (1948); "The Butterfly Ball" (1974); "Automania 2000" (1963); "The History of Cinema" (1957); and "Dilemma" (1981).

SPECIAL FEATURES None TECHNICAL FEATURES Fullscreen (1.33:1) • Languages: Eng. • Sound: Dolby Digital 2.0 • Keepcase • 1 Disc • Region 1–6 GENRE & RATING Anthology • Not Rated (Kids)

Cartoons That Time Forgot: The Ub Iwerks Collection, Vol. 1

Image, 1999, 236 mins., #ID4679DSDVD.

Who was the creator of Mickey Mouse? While most people would guess Walt Disney, the actual character design and original animated shorts featuring Mickey were the work of Ub Iwerks (birth name Ubbe Ert Iwwerks), the man who was Disney's close friend and very first employee. Iwerks remained at Disney from the early 1920s until 1930, when Disney's distributor, Pat Powers, offered to back Iwerks with a studio of his own. The studio lasted until 1936, producing seventy-six cartoon shorts starring such characters as Flip the Frog and Willie Whopper, as well as the fable-oriented ComiColor Cartoons.

This first DVD contains thirty-two of Iwerks cartoons, with some restoration work done to make the prints as attractive as possible. The shorts range in time from 1931 to 1936, and include mostly ComiColor Cartoons. Iwerks has been called "animation's forgotten man" by some animation historians; this DVD (and its follow-up) collect almost the entirety of Iwerks' output. They nicely showcase both his talent and the talent of those who worked in his studio (including Carl Stalling, Shamus Culhane, and the young Chuck Jones). Extensive fold-out liner notes are a nice addition as well.

SPECIAL FEATURES Liner Notes: Inside Cover TECHNICAL FEATURES Fullscreen (1.33:1) • Languages: Eng. • Sound: Dolby Digital Mono • Snapcase • 1 Disc • Region 1–6 GENRE & RATING Anthology • Not Rated (All Ages)

Cartoons That Time Forgot: The Ub Iwerks Collection, Vol. 2

Image, 1999, 190 mins., #ID4680DSDVD.

This second volume of Ub Iwerks cartoons feature another twenty-six historically important shorts, including stories of Flip the Frog, Willie Whopper, and ComiColor Cartoons. This second volume features some ethnic caricatures and a small amount of sexual innuendo, so it may not

be appropriate for younger audiences without parental discussion.

SPECIAL FEATURES Liner Notes: Inside Cover TECHNICAL FEATURES Fullscreen (1.33:1) • Languages: Eng. • Sound: Dolby Digital Mono • Snapcase • 1 Disc • Region 1–6 GENRE & RATING Anthology • Not Rated (Teens)

Cartoons That Time Forgot: From the Van Beuren Studio

Image, 1998, 236 mins., #ID4681DSDVD.

The Van Beuren Studio was the creation of Amadee J. Van Beuren, who bought an animation production company known as "Aesop's Fables Studios" in 1928. Although they produced a number of short films over the following few years, VBS really hit its stride when director Burt Gillett was hired away from the Disney Studios. Under Gillett's guidance, both production and quality flourished, and cartoons featuring Felix the Cat and Toonerville Trolley soon became popular. Van Beuren Studio produced over a hundred animated shorts until 1936, when their distributor, RKO Pictures, made a deal with Walt Disney to only carry Disney films. The decision spelled the end for Van Beuren Studio, and its animators dispersed to other companies.

Despite a cover design that shouts "13 Technicolor Extravaganzas," there are twenty-one cartoons on this DVD (fourteen color, seven black-and-white) including many Molly the Moo Cow shorts, plus Felix the Cat, Toonerville Trolley, and others. All selections have been copied from good quality prints and restored to look their best. A nice set of liner notes is another bonus. As with some other historical cartoons, there may be some troubling ethnic humor in some of the selections.

SPECIAL FEATURES Liner Notes: Inside Cover TECHNICAL FEATURES Fullscreen (1.33:1) • Languages: Eng. • Sound: Dolby Digital Mono • Snapcase • 1 Disc • Region 1–6 GENRE & RATING Anthology • Not Rated (All Ages)

Casper's Haunted Christmas

Universal, 2000, 84 mins., #20921. Directed by Owen Hurley. Written by Ian Boothby, Roger Fredericks. Based on the comic book series from Harvey Comics.

Casper has always been a friendly ghost, but when Kibosh, the head ghost of all ghosts, delivers an ultimatum, things will have to change. Now, Casper must truly scare someone before Christmas Day arrives, or he—along with the Ghostly Trio—will be banished to eternal darkness!

Unfortunately, Casper isn't very good at scaring, so the Ghostly Trio brings in a ringer for the job, grumpy cousin Spooky.

Unlike the 1995 feature film, this direct-to-video show is an all-CGI affair. While the ghosts and backgrounds look fine, the human characters look like plastic dolls. Still, the humor is funny at times, and kids (and some adults) should love it. Perfect to play when you want a "Scary Christmas and Happy Boo Year!"

SPECIAL FEATURES "Making of" Featurette • Character Bios • DVD-ROM Features: Game • Other Title Trailers TECHNICAL FEATURES Widescreen (1.78:1 enhanced for 16x9) • Fullscreen (1.33:1) • Subtitles/CC: Eng., Fren. • Languages: Eng. • Sound: Dolby Digital Surround 5.1 • Keepcase • 1 Disc • Region 1 GENRE & RATING CGI/Comedy/Holiday • Rated G

Casper the Friendly Ghost

Digital Disc, 1999, 30 mins., #501

The disc contains four episodes: "Casper the Friendly Ghost" (1945), "A-Haunting We Will Go" (1949), "There's Good Boos Tonight" (1948), and "Boo Moon" (1954).

This DVD was not available for review. The releasing company is out of business.

Castle of Cagliostro, The

Manga Entertainment, 2000, 109 mins., #Mang4051-2 Wr02. Directed by Hayao Miyazaki. Screenplay/Written by Hayao Miyazaki, Haruya Yamazaki. Based on the manga series by Monkey Punch (Kazuhiko Kato) in *Manga Action Weekly*.

While following a double-crossing counterfeiter, master thief Lupin III crosses paths with the evil Count Cagliostro. The Count is trying to force marriage on Princess Clarice (the last living heir to the Cagliostro name), and Lupin helps her. Now, the angry Count is trying to bump off Lupin at every turn. Rather than staying safe, Lupin and his bumbling-but-useful sidekicks decide to break into the castle to save Clarice and steal the Cagliostro fortune!

This film is adapted from the manga series by Monkey Punch using the Lupin III character, which was a character "borrowed" from French author Maurice Leblanc's novels of the early 1900s. Most U.S. video versions of *Lupin III* stories use the name "Rupan" or "The Wolf" to avoid copyright problems. A classic and silly movie presented with a nearly pristine print on DVD, this also has some suspenseful, almost Hitchcockian moments; it's clear that a lot of fun was had by director Hayao Miyazaki (creator of *Princess Mononoke*). Years later, Disney would "borrow" a fight scene from this as the template for a scene in *The Great Mouse Detective*.

See *Lupin the Third* for more adventures with these characters.

SPECIAL FEATURES Other Title Trailers TECHNICAL FEATURES Widescreen (1.85:1) • Subtitles/CC: Eng. • Languages: Jap., Eng. dub • Sound: Dolby Digital 2.0 • Keepcase • 1 Disc • Region 1, 2, 4 GENRE & RATING Action/Comedy/Suspense • Not Rated (Teens)

Cat City

Image, 1999, 95 mins., #ID5694PZDVD. Directed by Bela Ternovszky. Screenplay by Joseph Nepp.

The mice that live in Cat City have a difficult time surviving, until one of their own—a famous scientist—creates a weapon that shrinks cats down to mouse size, leveling the playing field. Intermaus, a spy agency, sends its top agent, Grabowski, to make sure that everything goes as planned.

This odd 1987 feature film apparently pressed censor buttons in its day—the DVD contains a parental advisory—but today it appears fairly tame. Although it has an intermittently interesting visual style, *Cat City* is incoherent at times, and even as it tries to be edgy or satirical about politics and class struggles, it runs the risk of losing its audience. The film was animated by Budapest's top animation studio, Paranoia.

SPECIAL FEATURES None TECHNICAL FEATURES Fullscreen (1.33:1) • Languages: Eng. dub • Sound: Dolby Digital 2.0 • Snapcase • 1 Disc • Region 1–6 GENRE & RATING Animal/Action/Satire • Not Rated (Teens)

Catnapped!

Pioneer, 2000, 75 mins., #PICT 0001V. Directed by Takashi Nakamura. Screenplay by Chiaki Konaka, Takashi Nakamura. Based on a story by Takashi Nakamura.

Young Toriyasu and Meeko are transported to the magical land of Banipal Witt, ostensibly to find Toriyasu's missing dog. But they're soon caught up in a feline plot to stop an evil sorceress cat whose touch turns anything into a balloon. Now they only have a few days to stop the sorceress Buburina, or they and their dog will be trapped as monsters.

It would be hard to come up with a more psychedelic and bizarre movie than this, though other entries in the book will try. A children's movie, this movie features cutesy animation and weird storylines that will make a parent's—or sober viewer's—head hurt. But if you want a kaleidoscope of colorful images of cats, dogs, balloons, and candy, with very little violence, here it is.

SPECIAL FEATURES Character Bios • Character and Art Galleries. TECHNICAL FEATURES Fullscreen (1.33:1) • Subtitles/CC: Eng. • Languages: Jap., Eng. dub • Sound: Dolby Digital 2.0 • Keepcase • 1 Disc • Region 1 GENRE & RATING Animal/Adventure • Rated 3+

Caught Between Worlds: A Computer Animated Vision

DVD International, 2002, 50 mins., #DVDI0862. Series Produced by Beny Tchaicovsky.

CGI computer animation that breaks all rules of perspective, sense, and reality is presented here, accompanied by ten synthesized musical selections. As with other CGI showcases, there's no plot, just lots of bizarre and pretty imagery meant to dazzle the eye and surrealize the mind.

SPECIAL FEATURES Other Title Trailers TECHNICAL FEATURES Fullscreen (1.33:1) • Sound: Dolby Digital 2.0, Dolby Digital Surround 5.1, DTS • Keepcase • 1 Disc • Region All GENRE & RATING CGI/Music • Not Rated (Teens)

Celebrity Deathmatch: Greatest Hits

Sony, 1999, 60 mins.

This DVD was not available for review.

Ceres, Celestial Legend: Destiny [#1]

Viz/Pioneer, 2001, 75 mins., #DAC01. Directed by Hajime Kamegaki, Susumu Nishizawa, Saeko Aoki, Takashi Takase, Juhei Matsuura, Aki Hayashi. Written by Yukiyoshi Ohashi, Sukehiro Tomita. Based on the manga series by Yu Watase in *Flower Comics Shogakukan*.

Aya and Aki Mikage are sixteen-year-old Japanese twins, a brother and sister who have no concept of their true lineage. Decades ago, a fisherman trapped a celestial angel into marrying him and bearing their children. Now, the resultant Mikage clan is very influential. When Aya begins manifesting signs that she holds the powers and vengeance of Ceres, the angel, the family isn't happy. In fact, at the twins' birthday party, they tell Aya that she must die! Now on the run from her family, Aya must find answers somehow, even if just from whispers and legends.

Creator Yu Watase also created *Fushigi Yugi*, and, like that series, *Ceres* is fairly addictive. The animation is pleasant, and even though the story has touches of romance, it is quickly paced. A modern setting also grounds it in a basic reality for viewers. The occasional use of super-deformed chibi moments may bother some fans, while draw others in.

The DVD contains a nice—though not exceptional—transfer and has three episodes of this 2000 TV series: "The Day the Moon and Sixteen Stars Align"; "The Angel's First Kiss"; and "The One Who Fell to Earth."

SPECIAL FEATURES Character Galleries • Creator Interview Clips • Easter Eggs TECHNICAL FEATURES Fullscreen (1.33:1) • Subtitles/CC: Eng. • Languages: Jap., Eng. dub • Sound: Dolby Digital Surround 2.0 • Keepcase • 1 Disc • Region 1 GENRE & RATING Magic/Intrigue/Romance • Not Rated (Teens)

Ceres, Celestial Legend: Past Unfound [#2]

Viz/Pioneer, 2001, 75 mins., #DAC02. Directed by Hajime Kamegaki, Susumu Nishizawa, Saeko Aoki, Takashi Takase, Juhei Matsuura, Aki Hayashi. Written by Yukiyoshi Ohashi, Sukehiro Tomita. Based on the manga series by Yu Watase in *Flower Comics Shogakukan*.

Aya is still on the run from her family and her brother in episodes #4–6: "The Stolen Hagoromo"; "Toya's Destiny"; and "The C Project." Ceres takes control of Aya's body once, leaving Aya's mother in the hospital, while Aki is the reincarnation of the fisherman who wronged Ceres generations ago. Plus, Aya is sheltered by another celestial descendant, and two new men in her life—Yuhi and the mysterious Toya—complicate matters.

SPECIAL FEATURES Character Galleries • Creator Interview Clips • Easter Eggs TECHNICAL FEATURES Fullscreen (1.33:1) • Subtitles/CC: Eng. • Languages: Jap., Eng. dub • Sound: Dolby Digital Surround 2.0 • Keepcase • 1 Disc • Region 1 GENRE & RATING Magic/Intrigue/Romance • Not Rated (Teens)

Ceres, Celestial Legend: C-Genome [#3]

Viz/Pioneer, 2001, 75 mins., #DAC03. Directed by Hajime Kamegaki, Susumu Nishizawa, Saeko Aoki, Takashi Takase, Juhei Matsuura, Aki Hayashi. Written by Yukiyoshi Ohashi, Sukehiro Tomita. Based on the manga series by Yu Watase in *Flower Comics Shogakukan*.

Another threat to Aya/Ceres arrives on the scene in the next three episodes of the series: "Celestial Awakening"; "The Mikage Conspiracy"; and "The Angel's Promise." Kagami Mikage, Aya's cousin, controls the international family business, and he plans to use genetic technology to siphon off the powers of those descended from celestial beings, including Yuhi, Suzumi, and Aya.

SPECIAL FEATURES Character and Art Galleries • Creator Interview Clips • Easter Eggs TECHNICAL FEATURES Fullscreen (1.33:1) • Subtitles/CC: Eng. • Languages: Jap., Eng. dub • Sound: Dolby Digital Surround 2.0 • Keepcase • 1 Disc • Region 1 GENRE & RATING Magic/Intrigue/Romance • Not Rated (Teens)

Ceres, Celestial Legend: Resolve [#4]

Viz/Pioneer, 2001, 75 mins., #DAC04.
Directed by Hajime Kamegaki, Susumu
Nishizawa, Saeko Aoki, Takashi Takase,
Juhei Matsuura, Aki Hayashi. Written by
Yukiyoshi Ohashi, Sukehiro Tomita.
Based on the manga series by Yu Watase
in *Flower Comics Shogakukan*.

Everyone must make hard decisions
in the next three episodes of *Ceres*:
"Chidori's Flight"; "Stir of Emotions"; and "The Silver
Choker." Aki is faced with the true intentions of the C-
Project conspiracy, while Aki struggles against the spirit
of his ancestor who may soon take over his mind and
body forever. Toya has to choose whether or not he'll aid
Aya or capture her to get the family's help to regain his
memories. Plus, was an entire populated area vaccinated
against a rare virus, or was it an experiment with the C-
Genome?

SPECIAL FEATURES Character Galleries • Trailer. TECHNICAL FEA-
TURES Fullscreen (1.33:1) • Subtitles/CC: Eng. • Languages:
Jap., Eng. dub • Sound: Dolby Digital Surround 2.0 • Keep-
case • 1 Disc • Region 1 GENRE & RATING
Magic/Intrigue/Romance • Not Rated (Teens)

Ceres, Celestial Legend: The Progenitor [#5]

Viz/Pioneer, 2001, 75 mins., #DAC05.
Directed by Hajime Kamegaki, Susumu
Nishizawa, Saeko Aoki, Takashi Takase,
Juhei Matsuura, Aki Hayashi. Written by
Yukiyoshi Ohashi, Sukehiro Tomita.
Based on the manga series by Yu Watase
in *Flower Comics Shogakukan*.

Halfway through the series, this DVD
continues with episodes #13–16:
"Relic of the Mikage"; "The Return of the First"; and
"Toya's Past." Aki is losing the battle to control his own
mind, but will the family really be happy with the violent actions of their ancestor if his spirit controls Aki's
body? Toya finds a way to recover his past, but it's not
without risks. And what grotesquery is hidden within
the Mikage clan's mansion?

SPECIAL FEATURES Character Galleries • Clean Credits . TECHNICAL
FEATURES Fullscreen (1.33:1) • Subtitles/CC: Eng. • Languages:
Jap., Eng. dub • Sound: Dolby Digital Surround 2.0 • Keep-
case • 1 Disc • Region 1 GENRE & RATING
Magic/Intrigue/Romance • Not Rated (Teens)

Ceres, Celestial Legend: Double [#6]

Viz/Pioneer, 2002, 75 mins., #DAC06.
Directed by Hajime Kamegaki, Susumu
Nishizawa, Saeko Aoki, Takashi Takase,
Juhei Matsuura, Aki Hayashi. Written by
Yukiyoshi Ohashi, Sukehiro Tomita.
Based on the manga series by Yu Watase
in *Flower Comics Shogakukan*.

It's double-duty time for Ceres,
although there are only three episodes
on this disc: "Another Ceres"; "Bewitching Affection";
and "Fleeting Happiness." Toya recovers his memory and
rediscovers a woman who could be Aya's twin. Could she
be another manifestation of Ceres? And what great
tragedy will strike?

SPECIAL FEATURES Character Galleries • Promotional Footage •
Clean Credits. TECHNICAL FEATURES Fullscreen (1.33:1) • Subti-
tles/CC: Eng. • Languages: Jap., Eng. dub • Sound: Dolby
Digital Surround 2.0 • Keepcase • 1 Disc • Region 1 GENRE &
RATING Magic/Intrigue/Romance • Not Rated (Teens)

Ceres, Celestial Legend: Requiem [#7]

Viz/Pioneer, 2002, 75 mins., #DAC07.
Directed by Hajime Kamegaki, Susumu
Nishizawa, Saeko Aoki, Takashi Takase,
Juhei Matsuura, Aki Hayashi. Written by
Yukiyoshi Ohashi, Sukehiro Tomita.
Based on the manga series by Yu Watase
in *Flower Comics Shogakukan*.

The penultimate disc of the series
contains episodes #19–21: "Chidori's
Confession"; "Toya's Death"; and "The Ancient Tennyo."
Aya makes a fateful decision about her future, while Aki
strikes at Toya with horrible consequences. The Mikage
family has made tremendous strides with their C-Project, and Yuhi decides to exact revenge against them.

SPECIAL FEATURES Character and Art Galleries • Clean Credits.
TECHNICAL FEATURES Fullscreen (1.33:1) • Subtitles/CC: Eng. •
Languages: Jap., Eng. dub • Sound: Dolby Digital Surround
2.0 • Keepcase • 1 Disc • Region 1 GENRE & RATING
Magic/Intrigue/Romance • Not Rated (Teens)

Ceres, Celestial Legend: Denouement [#8]

VIZ/Pioneer, 2002, 75 mins., #DAC08.
Directed by Hajime Kamegaki, Susumu
Nishizawa, Saeko Aoki, Takashi Takase,
Johei Matsuura, Aki Hayashi. Script by
Yujiyoshi Ohashi, Sukehiro Tomita. Based
on the manga series by Yu Watase in
Flower Comics Shogakukan.

NOTE: This DVD arrived too late for
a full review. The following text is
promotional copy provided by the releasing company:
"C-Project is literally falling apart! Planning a quick

getaway, Kagami takes Aya and the synthetically reconstructed Hagoromo aboard Mikage International's ship. Shuro Tsukasa, a pop-singer who happens to be a C-Genome, plans an act of revenge against Mikage and the walls come tumbling down. Adding to the chaos, Aki makes a complete physical transformation into the Progenitor. In the climactic conclusion to the series we find out what really happened to Ceres' Hagoromo!"

This disc contains episodes #22–24.

SPECIAL FEATURES Character And Art Galleries • Clean Credits TECHNICAL FEATURES Fullscreen (1.33:1) • Subtitles/CC: Eng. • Languages: Jap., Eng. dub • Sound: Dolby Digital Surround 2.0 • Keepcase • 1 Disc • Region 1 GENRE & RATING Magic/Intrigue/Romance • Not Rated (Teens)

Chance Pop Session: Session One

ADV Films, 2002, 125 mins., #DTR/001. Directed by Susumu Kuduo. Script by Sumino (or Sumio) Kawashima, Kazuhiko Soma, Tomoyasu Okubo.

NOTE: This DVD arrived too late for a full review. The following text is promotional copy provided by the releasing company:

"Three young girls, strangers to each other, share an instinctual passion and talent for music. Brought together from distinctly different worlds, the three meet by chance at the concert of their idol, the glamorous and sophisticated prodigy of an illustrious music school. The concert strikes a chord in each of their hearts and unites them with a common dream of stardom. Following their love of music, the girls each enroll in the school and are brought together again in a special class for exceptional talent. As their voices come together in harmony, the girls realize that they share more than just a passion for song.

"A mysterious blue stone, a hauntingly beautiful melody. . . what do these traces of the past have to do with the uncertain future of this gifted trio? Will the Angel of Music smile upon them and fulfill their dreams . . . Or will the challenges of music school tear them apart forever?"

This disc contains episodes #1–5.

SPECIAL FEATURES Character and Art Galleries • Clean Credits • Promotional Footage • Other Title Trailers • Inserts: "How to be a Pop Star" Booklet TECHNICAL FEATURES Fullscreen (1.33:1) • Subtitles/CC: Eng. • Languages: Jap., Eng. dub • Sound: Dolby Digital • Keepcase • 1 Disc • Region 1 GENRE & RATING Music/School/Girls • Rated 12+

Charlie Brown Christmas, A

Paramount, 2000, 48 mins., #15613. Directed by Bill Melendez. Written by Charles Schulz. Based on the comic strip by Charles Schulz.

Poor Charlie Brown is depressed, and to help him, "psychiatrist" Lucy Van Pelt sends him out to find the perfect Christmas tree for the Christmas play.

There are all sorts of trees available, but as Charlie discovers the true meaning of the holiday, he decides to pick the most unlikely tree of all. In a second episode, "It's Christmastime Again, Charlie Brown," it's time for another Christmas play, and this time, maybe Snoopy will get involved.

This is the very first *Peanuts* animated special, debuting on CBS in December 1965 and replaying almost every year since. The show is based on the beloved comic strip "Peanuts" by Charles Schulz, and the creator had a hand in producing, writing, and supervising the animated projects that came from his work. This special was the first prime-time cartoon that did not feature a laugh track, and it was also the first cartoon to feature the voices of real children playing children's roles!

A Charlie Brown Christmas won both the Emmy and Peabody awards for excellence. It would be hard to find a more family friendly or beloved holiday DVD to share with family members.

This disc was also included in the *Peanuts Classic Holiday Collection* box set.

SPECIAL FEATURES None TECHNICAL FEATURES Fullscreen (1.33:1) • Subtitles/CC: Eng. • Languages: Eng. • Sound: Dolby Digital Mono) • Keepcase • 1 Disc • Region 1 GENRE & RATING Holiday/Family • Not Rated (All Ages)

Charlie Brown Thanksgiving, A

Paramount, 2000, 49 mins., #15612. Directed by Bill Melendez, Phil Roman. Written by Charles Schulz. Based on the comic strip by Charles Schulz.

Charlie Brown hadn't planned on company on Thanksgiving Day, but then Peppermint Patty and all of their friends show up at the house wondering where the Thanksgiving feast is. With help from Snoopy and Woodstock, Charlie prepares a wonderful—though not very traditional—feast around the backyard Ping-Pong table. In a second cartoon, "The Mayflower Voyagers," Charlie Brown and his friends help the pilgrims celebrate their first Thanksgiving in the new land of America.

This 1973 CBS cartoon is another long-running family favorite and Emmy-award winner. It's excellent fare for the entire family, although parents may have to contend with young ones wanting a Thanksgiving feast like the one Charlie Brown prepares, complete with ice cream and jelly beans!

This disc was also included in the *Peanuts Classic Holiday Collection* box set.

SPECIAL FEATURES None TECHNICAL FEATURES Fullscreen (1.33:1) • Subtitles/CC: Eng. • Languages: Eng. • Sound: Dolby Digital Mono) • Keepcase • 1 Disc • Region 1 GENRE & RATING Holiday/Family • Not Rated (All Ages)

Charlotte's Web [Full Screen Edition]

Paramount, 2001, 94 mins. Directed by Charles A. Nichols, Iwao Takamoto. Written by Earl Hamner, Jr. Based on the book by E. B. White.

Little Fern rescues the runt of the pig litter and keeps him as a pet named Wilbur. As Fern grows older though, Wilbur is sold to Uncle Homer. Fern still comes to visit, but Wilbur is horrified to find out that he's being fattened up for slaughter. Enter Charlotte the spider who lives at the top of the barn. She feels badly for Wilbur and begins spinning words in her webbing, attracting attention to Wilbur and herself from far and wide. But will Charlotte's webs save Wilbur's life?

A wonderful and heart-breaking story based on E. B. White's 1952 children's story, the 1973 feature film of *Charlotte's Web* has been released in two different DVD versions. The voice cast includes such 1960s–1970s television favorites as Debbie Reynolds, Paul Lynde, Henry Gibson, Danny Bonaduce, and Agnes Moorehead.

This DVD was not available for review.

Charlotte's Web [Widescreen Edition]

Paramount, 2002, 94 mins., #15645. Directed by Charles A. Nichols, Iwao Takamoto. Written by Earl Hamner, Jr. Based on the book by E. B. White.

This absolutely enchanting film is available on this edition in widescreen. This is the one to get!

This DVD was not available for review.

Chicken Run

DreamWorks, 2000, 84 mins., #86453. Directed by Peter Lord, Nick Park. Story by Peter Lord, Nick Park. Screenplay by Karey Kirkpatrick.

All the chickens at Mrs. Tweedy's farm wish they could make an escape, but only clever Ginger is smart enough to devise a plan: they should fly over the fences. The only problem is, none of them can fly! Enter Rocky "The Flying Rooster," a slick American who might offer hope to the chickens. But is Rocky telling them the truth about his past? And what

evil plans does Mrs. Tweedy have for the chickens if they can't escape?

This 2000 film is a claymation masterpiece by Peter Lord and Nick Park, the men behind *Wallace and Gromit*. Although it isn't credited as such, it's based partially on the live-action 1963 film *The Great Escape*. Even in comparison to other stop-motion masterpieces, one would be hard pressed to find a more superb example of the form, which features dozens of individually moving chickens in most scenes. The script is both charming and hilarious, and there isn't a slow moment in the whole affair. Voices are top-notch, with Mel Gibson and Miranda Richardson leading an excellent, mostly British cast.

The DVD features a brilliant print, as well as a wealth of supplementals, including a dozen aptly named Easter eggs. Highly recommended.

SPECIAL FEATURES "Making of" Featurettes • Commentary Track by Directors • Cast and Crew Filmographies • Production Notes • Trailer • Promotional Footage • DVD-ROM Features • Read-Along • "Panic Button" Comedy Clip • Insert: Liner Notes • Easter Eggs TECHNICAL FEATURES Widescreen (1.85:1 Anamorphic) • Subtitles/CC: Eng. • Languages: Eng. • Sound: Dolby Digital Surround 2.0, Dolby Digital Surround 5.1, DTS 6.1 • Keepcase • 1 Disc • Region 1 GENRE & RATING Stop Motion/Animal/Comedy • Rated G

Chinese Ghost Story, A: The Tsui Hark Animation

Viz/Pioneer, 2000, 84 mins., #PEAD-010. Directed by Andrew Chin. Written by Tsui Hark.

Poor Ning has been jilted by the woman he loves, so he and his dog, Solid Gold, wander away to make money by collecting on outstanding debts. Unfortunately for him, the area he is dispatched to is infested with ghosts and monsters! And when a beautiful ghost girl seemingly falls in love with him, what will Ning do when the exorcists come calling?

A remake of the 1987 live-action feature film, this *Ghost Story* features a mix of traditional cel animation and CGI. The effect works at times but is jarring at others. The overall look is bright and unique, but the story feels both rushed and sluggish at the same time.

Despite the "full frame" promise on the packaging, the feature is actually presented in widescreen, with two Chinese-language tracks. The English subtitles are timed to the Cantonese track, so sub fans will want to watch that version. An interesting experiment, but you might also want to see the more complex live-action version.

SPECIAL FEATURES Character Bios • Trailer • Creator Text Interview. TECHNICAL FEATURES Widescreen (1.77:1) • Subtitles/CC: Eng. • Languages: Mandarin, Cantonese, Eng. dub • Sound: Dolby Digital 2.0, Dolby Digital Surround 5.1 • Keepcase • 1

Disc • Region 1 GENRE & RATING CGI/Horror/Romance • Not Rated (Teens)

Chinese Gods [The Golden Dragon Collection]

Entertainment Program, 2001, 90 mins., #70055. Directed by Chik Hoi Chang.

This DVD was not available for review.

Choose Your Own Nightmare: The Curse of the Mummy

Slingshot, 2000, #BDVD9154. Directed by Andrew Taylor. Written by Darin O'Connor. Based on the book series published by Bantam Doubleday Dell Books.

While at the museum working on a science project for school, teenagers Zach and Josh come face-to-face with an ancient Egyptian curse. When the secret to eternal life is stolen, an ancient Pharaoh returns from the dead to avenge its loss.

This is a "Multipath Adventure," which is a cross between a video game and traditional storytelling. As viewers watch the story, they are presented with choices of action every few minutes. Each choice (made using the DVD remote) branches the story off into a new direction, meaning there are multiple outcomes and storylines for the characters. The animation is rough 3-D CGI, which will probably be fine for video game enthusiasts but may hurt the eyes of traditional animation fans. There is mild violence in this story, but it's appropriate for younger teens and up.

SPECIAL FEATURES Other Title Trailers TECHNICAL FEATURES Widescreen (1.85:1) • Languages: Eng. • Sound: Dolby Digital Surround 5.1 • Keepcase • 1 Disc • Region 1–6 GENRE & RATING CGI/Comedy/Interactive • Not Rated (Teens)

Choose Your Own Nightmare: How I Became a Freak

Slingshot, 2000, #BDVD9306. Directed by Daniel Nettheim. Written by Anthony O'Conner. Based on the book series published by Bantam Doubleday Dell Books.

Teenagers always imagine that they look horrible in the mirrors, but for Tim Merrick, it's true. One morning he wakes up to find that his face is rotting away, his eyes are bulging, and he looks like a hideous freak! How did he get this way, and can he change back to normal?

This is a "Multipath Adventure," which is a cross between a video game and traditional storytelling. As

viewers watch the story, they are presented with choices of action every few minutes. Each choice (made using the DVD remote) branches the story off into a new direction, meaning there are multiple outcomes and storylines for the characters. The animation is rough 3-D CGI, which will probably be fine for video game enthusiasts but may hurt the eyes of traditional animation fans. There is mild violence in this story, but it's appropriate for younger teens and up.

SPECIAL FEATURES Other Title Trailers TECHNICAL FEATURES Widescreen (1.85:1) • Languages: Eng. • Sound: Dolby Digital Surround 5.1 • Keepcase • 1 Disc • Region 1–6 GENRE & RATING CGI/Horror/Interactive • Not Rated (Kids)

Choose Your Own Nightmare: Night of the Werewolf

Slingshot, 2000, #Bdvd9316. Directed by Daniel Nettheim. Adapted by Darin O'Connor, Bert Deling. Based on the book by Edward Packard.

The Storyteller has a nasty little tale to tell . . . about Bleeding Dog Creek and the dark forces that lurk within the forest there. When Lee goes to visit his cousin for summer vacation, he discovers the secrets and murderous dangers awaiting within the dark of the creek.

This is a "Multipath Adventure," which is a cross between a video game and traditional storytelling. As viewers watch the story, they are presented with choices of action every few minutes. Each choice (made using the DVD remote) branches the story off into a new direction, meaning there are multiple outcomes and storylines for the characters. The animation is rough 3-D CGI, which will probably be fine for video game enthusiasts but may hurt the eyes of traditional animation fans. There is mild violence in this story, but it's appropriate for younger teens and up.

SPECIAL FEATURES Other Title Trailers TECHNICAL FEATURES Widescreen (2.35:1) • Languages: Eng. • Sound: Dolby Digital Surround 5.1 • Keepcase • 1 Disc • Region 1–6 GENRE & RATING CGI/Comedy/Interactive • Not Rated (Teens)

Christmas Carol, A

Liberty International, 2001, 72 mins., #LIP0110. Animation Directed by Jean Tych. Adaption by Alex Buzo. Based on the book by Charles Dickens.

For those who don't yet know the story of miserly Ebenezer Scrooge and his night of haunting by three Christmas ghosts, here's another animated version of it. Led through his past, present, and future by apparitions, Scrooge must change his "humbug" attitude toward the holiday by Christmas morning or face a sad and lonely future.

A 1982 production by Australia's Burbank Films, this is a relatively faithful version of the story, though it's been brightened and lightened for children. The animation is passable, but there are too many bright primary colors on characters that clash with their drab backgrounds. And a scratched film print for the DVD transfer doesn't help. On the plus side, there are three Christmas carols to sing along with, and it is perhaps the only version of the story ever to feature a toga-wearing Ghost of Christmas Past! All this, plus voices by Mr. T, Phyllis Diller, Jonathan Winters, and others.

SPECIAL FEATURES Music Videos • Other Title Trailers TECHNICAL FEATURES Fullscreen (1.33:1) • Languages: Eng., Fren. dub, Span. dub • Sound: Dolby Digital 2.0, Dolby Digital Surround 5.1 • Keepcase • 1 Disc • Region 1–6 GENRE & RATING Holiday/Horror • Not Rated (All Ages)

Christmas Family Classics

American Home Treasures/BFS Entertainment, 2000, 104 mins., #82500D. Directed by Keith Scoble, Chris Randall. Written by John Broadhead, Joyce McAleer, Chris Randall, Keith Scoble.

Four animated half-hour shorts are presented on this DVD, all featuring songs by crooner Bing Crosby. "Silent Night" (1996) tells the story of a snowman brought to life by a tiny Ice Fairy, and the little girl he befriends who teaches him to sing and laugh. "Santa Claus' First Christmas" (1995) tells the origin story of Samuel Claus, a toymaker who decides to seek a new life and gets help from a magical fairy and elves in a peculiar forest.

The other two productions are "The Twelve Days of Christmas" (1995), in which Grandpa Billy tells his grandchildren how he won his Christmas bride in a twelve-day period with gifts; and "Good King Wenceslas" (1996), in which a gracious monarch delivers a holiday feast to the home of a poor peasant. Featuring clean-but-cute animation produced by the BBC, this DVD is appropriate for all ages.

SPECIAL FEATURES None TECHNICAL FEATURES Fullscreen (1.33:1) • Languages: Eng. • Sound: Dolby Digital 2.0 • Keepcase • 1 Disc • Region All GENRE & RATING Holiday/Music • Not Rated (All Ages)

Cinderella II: Dreams Come True

Disney, 2002, 73 mins., #22033. Directed by John Kafka. Screenplay by Jill Blotevogel, Tom Rogers, Jule Selbo.

The magic is back in the Prince's castle when he and Cinderella return from their honeymoon. But Cinderella finds it hard to be as stiff and proper as the Royal Court needs her to be, so a little magic from her Fairy Godmother and help from some familiar mischievous mice is welcomed. Plus, Anastasia, the former evil stepsister, finds love.

A direct-to-video sequel to Disney's classic 1950 feature film, *Cinderella II* tries hard to replicate the tone and feel of the original by using the same character models and approximating voices. The DVD is actually a trio of stories: "Aim To Please"; "Tall Tail"; and "An Uncommon Romance"— all of which deliver the message that being true to yourself is what it takes to win in life. A nice set of extras teaches the young 'uns about how movie music is made and allows them to play games in Cinderella's castle.

NOTE: This DVD is now on moratorium.

SPECIAL FEATURES "Making of" Featurettes • Music Video • Games • DVD-ROM Features: Games • Storybook • Other Title Trailers TECHNICAL FEATURES Widescreen (1.66:1 enhanced for 16x9) • Subtitles/CC: Eng. • Languages: Eng., Fren. dub, Span. dub • Sound: Dolby Digital Surround 5.1, DTS • Keepcase • 1 Disc • Region 1 GENRE & RATING Romance/Music/Family • Rated G

City Hunter: Secret Service

ADV Films, 2002, 90 mins., #DCH005. Directed by Kenji Kodama. Screenplay by Akinori Endo, Kenji Kodama. Based on the manga series by Tsukasa Hojo in *Weekly Shonen Jump*.

Ryo Saeba is the secret agent known as "City Hunter." He'll take on the most dangerous assignments around, even as he tries to romance the women (Fans have called him "James Bond on Viagra"). This time out, he's hired by James Maguire, a man whose past is catching up with him. Ryo must protect Maguire and his daughter, Anna, from those trying to kill them.

A popular and long-running spy TV series, *City Hunter* ran from 1987 to 1992, with multiple feature-length specials produced thereafter. *Secret Service* was the 1996 special. The animation is fairly realistic and sharp, though a handful of exaggerated and goofy scenes may bother some viewers. Be sure to stay until the end of the credits for a brief sequence. The extras feature also has a bonus three-minute short.

SPECIAL FEATURES Trailers • Promotional Footage • Clean Credits • Other Title Trailers TECHNICAL FEATURES Fullscreen (1.33:1) • Subtitles/CC: Eng. • Languages: Jap., Eng. dub • Sound: Dolby Digital 2.0 • Keepcase • 1 Disc • Region 1 GENRE & RATING Action/Spy • Rated 15+

City Hunter: The Motion Picture

ADV Films, 2002, 90 mins., #DCH/001. Directed by Kazuo Yamazaki. Script by Yuichi Higure. Based on the manga series by Tsukasa Hojo in *Weekly Shonen Jump*.

NOTE: This DVD arrived too late for a full review. The following text is promotional copy provided by the releasing company:

"A mysterious soldier known only as Professor takes his revenge on the government that betrayed him, and Tokyo is brought to its knees! Unless the government pays the Professor an impossible ransom, downtown Tokyo will be completely destroyed, and the Professor's beautiful sister will be the first to go! Only City Hunter Ryo Saeba, expert detective and shameless ladies' man, can keep Tokyo from blowing sky high!"

"The bullets fly furiously and the women have never been more tempting as City Hunter takes it to the edge in this action-packed animated feature. Explosive action will rock your senses as you witness City Hunter's greatest challenge ever!"

SPECIAL FEATURES Character Bios • Clean Credits • Promotional Footage • Other Title Trailers TECHNICAL FEATURES Fullscreen (1.33:1) • Subtitles/CC: Eng. • Languages: Jap., Eng. dub • Sound: Dolby Digital 2.0 • Keepcase • 1 Disc • Region 1 GENRE & RATING Action/Spy • Rated 15+

Cleopatra DC

AnimeWorks, 2002, 110 mins., #AWDVD0207. Directed by Naoyuki Yoshinaga, Hiroyuki Ebata. Screenplay by Kaoru Shintani. Based on the manga series by Kaoru Shintani in *Comic Burger*.

Sexy Cleopatra Corns is the head of the Corns Group, a multinational financial organization. Rather than spending time behind a desk, Cleo prefers to embark on a series of espionage adventures. When a plane crashes into her penthouse, Cleo is caught up in a plot involving damsels in distress, the Oil Minister, a turncoat assassin, satellite laser weapons, world domination, and androids.

Any film that opens with a plane crashing into a New York City skyscraper is probably not going to win friends in this day and age, and AnimeWorks might have done better to delay the title a while. The DVD contains

all three 1998 episodes of the TV series. The animation is very cutesy, and the women are so oversexualized that this almost lands in the "Adult" category. Astonishingly, the credits thank the show's National Security Advisor! Fans have complained that the disc features non-removable subtitles and only one language track.

SPECIAL FEATURES Other Title Trailers TECHNICAL FEATURES Fullscreen (1.33:1) • Subtitles/CC: Eng. • Languages: Jap. • Sound: Dolby Digital 2.0 • Keepcase • 1 Disc • Region 1 GENRE & RATING Action/Spy • Rated 16+

Clerks Uncensored ☞ see Mature/Adult Section

Clifford the Big Red Dog: Clifford Saves the Day! and Clifford's Fluffiest Friend Cleo [#1]

Artisan, 2001, 90 mins., #12370. Directed by John Over. Written by Anne-Marie Perrotta, Tean Schultz, Sindy Mckay, Scott Guy, Dev Ross, Dennis Haley, Marcy Brown, Kati Rocky. Based on the book series by Norman Bridwell.

Emily Elizabeth doesn't know that when she chooses a bright red puppy from its litter it will grow to be as big as a house! Soon, her family and the people in town come to recognize that having a supersized dog around can be fun and helpful. Charming and sweet, this cartoon series doesn't knock viewers over the head with morals and messages—although it still presents them in the midst of fun and frolics. *Clifford* is best for young kids.

This disc contains eight stories from the 2000 PBS animated series, separated into two themed sections (previously released on video). "Clifford Saves the Day!" features "Stormy Weather"; "Islander of the Year"; "Circus Stars"; and "Clifford on Parade." The second set is "Clifford's Fluffiest Friend Cleo," which includes "Fluffed-Up Cleo"; "Cleo's Fair Share"; "Friends, Morning, Noon and Night"; and "Two's Company." And given that last episode's title, it's ironic to find that John Ritter is the voice of Clifford.

The special features include brief animated segments focused on helping others and learning respect and sharing, followed by parental tips in text form. Another cute feature is real boys and girls talking about their own dogs in a mini "dogumentary."

SPECIAL FEATURES Morals Clips • Learn the Clifford Dance Clip • Live "Dog Friends" Clips. TECHNICAL FEATURES Fullscreen (1.33:1) • Languages: Eng. • Sound: Dolby Digital 2.0 • Keepcase • 1 Disc • Region 1 GENRE & RATING Animal/Family • Rated 3+

Clifford the Big Red Dog: Happy Birthday, Clifford! [#2]

Artisan, 2001, 90 mins., #12466. Directed by John Over. Written by Dennis Haley, Marcy Brown, Dean Stefan, Sheryl Scarborough, Kayle Kuche, Lois Becker, Mark Stratton, Baz Hawkins. Based on the book series by Norman Bridwell.

Another eight cartoons for kids showcase stories about friendship, sharing, surprises, and love. "Happy Birthday, Clifford!" features "The Best Party Ever"; "Clifford's Big Surprise"; "Potluck Party Pooper"; and "It's My Party." The disc's second half is "Puppy Love" and it contains "T-Bone, The Dog About Town"; "Clifford's Big Heart"; "Mimi's Back in Town"; and "The Best Gift."

SPECIAL FEATURES Game • Morals Clips • Live Dog Friends Clips. TECHNICAL FEATURES Fullscreen (1.33:1) • Languages: Eng. • Sound: Dolby Digital 2.0 • Keepcase • 1 Disc • Region 1 GENRE & RATING Animal/Family • Rated 3+

Complete Adventure Kid, The ☞ see
Mature/Adult Section

Complete Superman Collection, The [Diamond Anniversary Edition]

Image, 2000, 147 mins., #ID9574BKDVD.

Generally held up as one of the most lush action animation ever filmed, the *Superman* series by Fleischer Studios (and later, Famous Studios) began shortly after the comic book series itself had become a hit with audiences. Superman was introduced in Action Comics #1 in 1938, and Paramount licensed the series for theatrical cartoons shortly thereafter. The contract was given to Dave and Max Fleischer, who were just finishing work on the *Gulliver's Travels* animated movie.

The Fleischers spent around $50,000 on the pilot episode, three times the amount they regularly spent on a *Popeye* short. Eighteen total episodes of *Superman* were released from 1941 to 1943, and the series was a huge hit with audiences. The gorgeous airbrushed backgrounds and simple-but-realistic figures worked well together, and during World War II audiences needed to watch an escapist hero like Superman. The influence of the *Superman* cartoons is still felt today, with *Batman: The Animated Series*, *Superman*, *Justice League*, and even anime such as *The Big O* taking their cues from the deco-heavy designs and feel.

This DVD collects all seventeen color cartoons that were shot on 35mm prints. Unlike some Bosko Video titles for Image, these retain the complete shorts with all credits. The only addition is a subtitled release date on the screen during the start of each short. Purists will argue whether this single disc is better than the two Winstar DVDs (*Max Fleischer's Superman* and *Superman: The Lost Episodes*), which feature digitally restored prints, but both do a spectacular job of presenting the adventures of the hero from Krypton.

SPECIAL FEATURES Production Notes TECHNICAL FEATURES Fullscreen (1.33:1) • Languages: Eng. • Sound: Dolby Digital (Mono) • Snapcase • 1 Disc • Region 1–6 GENRE & RATING Superhero/Adventure • Not Rated (All Ages)

Complete Uncensored Private Snafu, The

Image, 1999, 130 mins., #ID5533BKDVD.

It's hard to think of a series of cartoons with a more gilt-edged Hollywood pedigree. In 1942, Col. Frank Capra (the famed director), then head of the Armed Forces Motion Picture Unit, put Dr. Theodor Geisel, better known as "Dr. Seuss," in charge of the animation division. Capra created a character named Private Snafu, whose name was an acronym for "Situation Normal All F•••ed Up" (though the word was shown as "Fouled," its appearance was a joke, because the actual military term was a little coarser). Capra wanted Snafu to appear in comedy shorts for the biweekly newsreel, "Army-Navy Screen Magazine."

Geisel wrote the shorts himself, each of which imparted a message to the troops. Some of animations' top comedy directors worked on the twenty-eight cartoons, including Chuck Jones, Friz Freleng, Bob Clampett, and others. Mel Blanc provided the voice of the title character. The cartoons are more risque and adult than most animated fare at the time, largely because they were targeted at World War II soldiers instead of kids and families. There are also a number of racist portrayals of Germans, Italians, and Japanese, among others.

This DVD collects all twenty-eight black-and-white cartoons from 1943 to 1946, including one never-released short. Although they have been restored as much as possible, the "Bosko Video" logo appears in the lower right-hand corner of the screen during the start of each short. The opening and end titles are cut from each episode as well. These blemishes are unfortunate on an otherwise, and even still, fascinating historical series.

SPECIAL FEATURES Production Notes TECHNICAL FEATURES Fullscreen (Window-boxed 1.33:1) • Languages: Eng. • Sound: Dolby Digital Mono • Snapcase • 1 Disc • Region 1–6 GENRE & RATING Military/Comedy • Not Rated (Teens)

Computer Animation Adventure

Image, 2001, 45 mins., #ID09350DDVD. Produced by Steven Churchill.

Another in the "Odyssey: The Mind's Eye Presents" series, this DVD collects twenty award-winning CGI short films. Each short is self-contained and presented by different studios and animators. Some are surreal, some are funny, some are sad, some are set to music, and others have dialogue.

Included among the shorts is a train determined not to be late, jumping its tracks in "Locomotion," while Captain Sarcastic gets a sidekick to help fend off alien invaders in "Grinning Evil Death." Todd Rundgren's lyrics and music join with animation in "Change Myself." The DVD has an excellent picture and sound.

SPECIAL FEATURES None TECHNICAL FEATURES Widescreen (Multi-Aspect) • Languages: Eng. • Sound: Dolby Digital 2.0 • Keepcase • 1 Disc • Region 1–6 GENRE & RATING CGI/Anthology • Not Rated (Kids)

Computer Animation Celebration

Sony, 1998, 50 mins.

This DVD was not available for review.

Computer Animation Classics

Sony, 1999, 55 mins.

This DVD was not available for review.

Computer Animation Experience

Image, 2001, 52 mins., #ID09360DDVD. Produced by Steven Churchill.

Another in the "Odyssey: The Mind's Eye Presents" series, this DVD collects twenty-one award-winning CGI short films. Picture and sound are superb.

Among the selections, Todd Rundgren's lyrics and music are back with a second music video, "Theology," and fellow musician Peter Gabriel presents "Liquid Selves." Tilting at windmills that might be dragons falls to the domain of CGI adventurer "Don Quichotte," while artificial intelligence and liquid color are explored in the Japanese-produced "Flora." And, if you think you can handle a rollercoaster without tracks, take the "Devil's Mine Ride."

SPECIAL FEATURES None TECHNICAL FEATURES Widescreen (Multi-Aspect) • Languages: Eng. • Sound: Dolby Digital 2.0 • Keepcase • 1 Disc • Region 1–6 GENRE & RATING CGI/Anthology • Not Rated (Kids)

Computer Animation Extravaganza

Image, 2000, 62 mins., #ID97540DDVD.

A number of famous digital effects houses contribute to this DVD volume in the "Odyssey: The Mind's Eye Presents" series, which collects eighteen short CGI films. Look for Pacific Data Images (the crew behind *Antz*) to contribute the hilarious "Fat Cat on a Diet," while Oscar-winners Digital Domain (of *Titanic* fame) jump in with "Tightrope," in which a harlequin and a tightrope walker duel to the death.

Other fun entries include a housewife who becomes one with her romance novels in "Ronin Romance Classics," and "Pings," in which a polar bear uses a fat yellow arctic bird to sit on, with disastrously funny results. Although the cover lists seventeen shorts, a bonus, "The Smell of Horror," rounds out the disc.

SPECIAL FEATURES None TECHNICAL FEATURES Widescreen (Multi-Aspect) • Languages: Eng. • Sound: Dolby Digital 2.0 • Snapcase • 1 Disc • Region 1–6 GENRE & RATING CGI/Anthology • Not Rated (Kids)

Computer Animation Festival

Sony, 1997, 58 mins.

This DVD was not available for review.

Computer Animation Marvels

Image, 1999, 57 mins., #ID70960DDVD. Produced by Steven Churchill.

An international entry in the "Odyssey: The Mind's Eye Presents" series, this DVD collects nineteen short CGI films from around the world, including one that is exclusive to the DVD (it wasn't on the corresponding video release).

Included among the shorts is a chance to hear what your pets really think in "Pets" (animated to the soundtrack of actual clips from a telephone dating line!), and a look at how animated characters do what they do in "The Physics of Cartoons–Part 1." Plus, a harried insect wife tries to get her husband ready to board Noah's ark in "Ticked Off," and a penguin discovers that fish make great skis in "The Hungry One." As with others in this series, style and content vary widely, but the entertainment value is high.

SPECIAL FEATURES None TECHNICAL FEATURES Widescreen (Multi-Aspect) • Languages: Eng. • Sound: Dolby Digital 2.0 • Keepcase • 1 Disc • Region 1–6 GENRE & RATING CGI/Anthology • Not Rated (Kids)

Computer Animation Showcase

Sony, 1999, 45 mins.

This DVD was not available for review.

Conspirators of Pleasure ☞ see Mature/Adult

Section

Cool Devices: Operations ☞ see Mature/Adult

Section

Cosmo Warrior Zero: Cold Steel Immortals [#1]

AnimeWorks, 2002, 100 mins., #AWDVD-0220. Directed by Kazuyoshi Yokota, Yukiyo Teramoto, Takeshi Yamaguchi, Itsuki Imazaki. Scripts by Nobuyuki Fujimoto, Mugi Kamio. Based on the manga series by Reiji Matsumoto

NOTE: This DVD arrived too late for a full review. The following text is promotional copy provided by the releasing company:

"The most famous pirate in the sea of stars is about to be brought to justice. The time of freedom and lawlessness in deep space is coming to a close. Men who have given up their souls to become robotic immortals have dominated Earth, and their cold grip is closing on the Sea of Stars. Warrius Zero, a battle-weary admiral, lost his family and his reason for living during the war for Earth. Now serving the mechanized victors, Zero carries out his orders without the will to resist. Then, he received one mission unlike any other. Zero was commanded to travel to the farthest reaches of the universe to hunt down a single wanted man, a mysterious space pirate, once known to all as Captain Harlock . . . and to Zero as his former best friend."

This disc contains episodes #1–4.

SPECIAL FEATURES Character Bios • Clean Credits • Outtakes • Other Title Trailers TECHNICAL FEATURES Fullscreen (1.33:1) • Subtitles/CC: Eng. • Languages: Jap., Eng. dub • Sound: Dolby Digital 2.0 • Keepcase • 1 Disc • Region 1 GENRE & RATING Science Fiction/Adventure • Rated 13+

Cosmo Warrior Zero: Sea of Stars [#2]

AnimeWorks, 2002, 100 mins., #AWDVD-0228. Directed by Kazuyoshi Yokota. Story by Reiji Matsumoto. Based on the manga series by Reiji Matsumoto

NOTE: This DVD arrived too late for a full review. The following text is promotional copy provided by the releasing company:

"Zero's unending search for Captain Harlock has brought him to the Wild West planet of Gun Frontier. But Zero isn't the only person looking for Harlock. The gun slinging bounty hunter, Sylvia, is hot on his trail and won't give up her prize so easily. Warrius is determined to bring the pirate to justice and Sylvia never loses a bounty. Fortunately for both, Harlock loves a good fight."

This disc contains episodes #5–8.

SPECIAL FEATURES Character Bios • Clean Credits • Outtakes • Other Title Trailers TECHNICAL FEATURES Fullscreen (1.33:1) • Subtitles/CC: Eng. • Languages: Jap., Eng. dub • Sound: Dolby Digital 2.0 • Keepcase • 1 Disc • Region 1 GENRE & RATING Science Fiction/Adventure • Rated 13+

Courageous Cat and Minute Mouse: The Complete Series [Box Set]

A&E, 2002, 720 mins., #AAE-70580. Directed by Sid Marcus, Ruben Timmins.

Which heroic superduo speeds out of a cave in their flashy car, fights gaudy supervillains, uses an amazing arsenal of weaponry they pull from their belts, and was created by Bob Kane? If you guessed Batman and Robin, you'd be partially correct. But here, we're talking about Courageous Cat and Minute Mouse, two animated superheroes Kane created for television in the late 1950s. Protecting Empire City, Courageous Cat and Minute Mouse stop the likes of Flat-Face Frog, Foxy Fox, Rodney Rodent, Black Cat, Professor Shaggy Dog, Professor Noodle Stroodle, Harry the Gorilla, Robber Rabbit, and others. Courageous Cat's versatile gun changes shape, style, and function moment-by-moment, becoming, among other things, a restorer gun, a parachute gun, a cannonball-interrupter gun, a refrigerator gun, and more.

Courageous Cat and Minute Mouse debuted in syndication in 1960, many years before Kane's Batman became a campy live-action hit. One hundred and thirty-five full-color five-minute shorts were produced. This four-disc set collects all of the episodes, though the quality of the film transfer varies. Some are incredibly grainy, but most have very bright, solid colors, and the soundtrack is relatively good. There is a very brief bio of Kane on all four discs.

For fans of superheroes or kitsch, it's unlikely you'll find a more pleasing set than this quartet from A&E. Just be sure to watch it in relatively small doses, lest the Cat-gun take over your mind.

SPECIAL FEATURES Creator Bio TECHNICAL FEATURES Fullscreen (1.33:1) • Languages: Eng. • Sound: Dolby Digital 1.0 • Cardboard Box with 4 Keepcases • 4 Discs • Region 1 GENRE & RATING Comedy/Superhero/Animals • Not Rated (Kids)

Cowboy Bebop: 1st Session

Bandai, 2000, 125 mins., #1290. Directed by Shinichiro Watanabe. Written by Keiko Nobumoto, Michiko Yokote, Ryota Yamaguchi, Sadayuki Murai.

The year is A.D. 2071, and humankind has long ago gone into space. Settled throughout the galaxy, humanity remains as diverse as it ever was, even as it interacts with alien races. Enter bounty hunter Spike Spiegel, an ex–Chinese mafia hitman now trying to forget his past and do what is right. Spike is aided by Jet Black, a cyborg ex-cop, and the pair reluctantly pick up other partners along their missions. Everywhere they go in their converted fishing ship named *Bebop*, Spike and Jet seem to get into trouble, but that's the risk of life in the future.

This 1998 series mixes a variety of styles to great effect, making it one of the anime world's most popular series ever. Spaghetti western characters duel in *Blade Runner* settings, all set to a cool jazzy soundtrack (which also dips into folk, blues, ska, classical, and other styles). Nothing seems out of place, whether it's pirates, hippies, the mafia, or hyperintelligent dogs. The character designs and animation are stylish, looking both retro-1970s and futuristic all at once. The fact that each story stands on its own while contributing to the greater whole is a plus as well. Heavy on action and violence, this airs late on the Cartoon Network, meaning parents might want to check it out with their children.

The DVD features five episodes: Spike and Jet target a drug dealer in "Asteroid Blues"; a mission to capture an unusual dog has some surprises in "Stray Dog Strut"; shady-but-beautiful criminal Faye Valentine enters the picture in "Honky Tonk Women"; an eco-terrorist prepares to unleash a virus in "Gateway Shuffle"; and in a John Woo homage, Spike faces a killer from his past in "Ballad of Fallen Angels."

The discs in the series are silk-screened to look like old 45 rpm record singles, which is a nice touch for a series that relies on music so heavily. The single-toned outer packaging also has some of the most striking anime covers produced for the Region 1 market. The only complaint about the *Cowboy Bebop* discs is that the menus tend to hold you hostage.

SPECIAL FEATURES Character Bios • Music Video • Insert: Liner

Notes TECHNICAL FEATURES Fullscreen (1.33:1) • Subtitles/CC: Eng. • Languages: Jap., Eng. dub • Sound: Dolby Digital 2.0 • Keepcase • 1 Disc • Region 1 GENRE & RATING Science Fiction/Action • Not Rated (Teens)

Cowboy Bebop: 2nd Session

Bandai, 2000, 125 mins., #1291. Directed by Shinichiro Watanabe. Written by Keiko Nobumoto, Michiko Yokote, Dai Soto, Akihiko Inari.

Five more jazzy episodes of *Cowboy Bebop* are presented on this second disc. A young musical prodigy hides a mystery in "Sympathy for the Devil." Spike makes both a friend and an enemy of butch female space trucker VT in "Heavy Metal Queen." Spike reluctantly takes on a young sidekick in "Waltz for Venus." A female hacker presents potential help—for a price—in "Jamming With Edward," while a visit to Jet's home planet brings back painful memories in "Ganymede Elegy."

SPECIAL FEATURES Crew Interviews • Other Title Trailers • Insert: Liner Notes TECHNICAL FEATURES Fullscreen (1.33:1) • Subtitles/CC: Eng. • Languages: Jap., Eng. dub • Sound: Dolby Digital 2.0 • Keepcase • 1 Disc • Region 1 GENRE & RATING Science Fiction/Action • Not Rated (Teens)

Cowboy Bebop: 3rd Session

Bandai, 2000, 100 mins., #1292. Directed by Shinichiro Watanabe. Written by Keiko Nobumoto, Michiko Yokote, Dai Soto.

Downshifting to four episodes, the third DVD features more *Bebop* action. An intruder on the ship means an *Alien* homage/parody in "Toys in the Attic." Faye leaves the crew of the Bebop without any money in "Jupiter Jazz, Part I," and confrontations abound as Spike, Jet, and Faye all find trouble in "Jupiter Jazz, Part II." A chess piece is a clue to a series of interstellar tollbooth robberies in "Bohemian Rhapsody."

SPECIAL FEATURES Crew Interviews • Other Title Trailers • Insert: Liner Notes TECHNICAL FEATURES Fullscreen (1.33:1) • Subtitles/CC: Eng. • Languages: Jap., Eng. dub • Sound: Dolby Digital 2.0 • Keepcase • 1 Disc • Region 1 GENRE & RATING Science Fiction/Action • Not Rated (Teens)

Cowboy Bebop: 4th Session

Bandai, 2000, 100 mins., #1293. Directed by Shinichiro Watanabe. Written by Keiko Nobumoto, Michiko Yokote, Shinichiro Watanabe, Akihiko Inari, Shoji Kawamori, Aya Yoshinaga.

The past comes back to haunt many of the Bebop's crew in four more episodes. Faye's origins are revealed in "My Funny Valentine," and Jet is on the trail of the criminal who cost him his arm in "Black Dog Serenade." Hacker Ed and Ein (the dog) set off to find food and get embroiled in strangeness in "Mushroom Samba." A mysterious Beta videotape offers more clues to Faye's beginnings on Earth in "Speak Like a Child."

SPECIAL FEATURES Music Video • Other Title Trailers • Insert: Liner Notes TECHNICAL FEATURES Fullscreen (1.33:1) • Subtitles/CC: Eng. • Languages: Jap., Eng. dub • Sound: Dolby Digital 2.0 • Keepcase • 1 Disc • Region 1 GENRE & RATING Science Fiction/Action • Not Rated (Teens)

Cowboy Bebop: 5th Session

Bandai, 2000, 100 mins., #1294. Directed by Shinichiro Watanabe. Written by Keiko Nobumoto, Shinichiro Watanabe, Akihiko Inari, Sadayuki Murai.

The penultimate disc in the series presents four more episodes. Space pirates and a computer virus cause trouble in "Wild Horses." A paranormal assassin hunts Spike in "Pierrot La Fou." Jet helps out an old friend in "Boogie Woogie Feng-Shui." Rival bounty hunter Cowboy Andy might stop Spike from catching the "Teddy Bomber" before the plush-clad killer can strike again in the silly "Cowboy Funk."

SPECIAL FEATURES Clean Credits • Other Title Trailers • Insert: Liner Notes TECHNICAL FEATURES Fullscreen (1.33:1) • Subtitles/CC: Eng. • Languages: Jap., Eng. dub • Sound: Dolby Digital 2.0 • Keepcase • 1 Disc • Region 1 GENRE & RATING Science Fiction/Action • Not Rated (Teens)

Cowboy Bebop: 6th Session

Bandai, 2000, 100 mins., #1295. Directed by Shinichiro Watanabe. Written by Keiko Nobumoto, Michiko Yokote, Dai Soto.

The *Cowboy Bebop* series comes to an end with the final four episodes. Faye joins a cult headed toward suicide in "Brain Scratch," while Ed is reunited with his father, but there's a bounty on his head in "Hard Luck Women."

Spike is finally reunited with Julia, the love of his life, in "The Real Folk Blues, Part I," but Spike's old enemy Vicious is determined not to let Spike and Julia live happily ever after in "The Real Folk Blues, Part II."

SPECIAL FEATURES Art Galleries • Other Title Trailers • Insert: Liner Notes • Easter Egg TECHNICAL FEATURES Fullscreen (1.33:1) • Subtitles/CC: Eng. • Languages: Jap., Eng. dub • Sound: Dolby Digital 2.0 • Keepcase • 1 Disc • Region 1 GENRE & RATING Science Fiction/Action • Not Rated (Teens)

Cowboy Bebop: The Perfect Sessions [Limited Edition Box Set]

Bandai, 2001, 650 mins., #1296.

A limited edition with a run of 10,000 copies (individually numbered on the bottom), this box set contained all six DVDs in the *Cowboy Bebop* series, as well as the original soundtrack CD. See individual entries for Special and Technical Features.

This DVD box set was not available for review.

TECHNICAL FEATURES Box with 6 keepcases and a jewel case • 7 Discs • Region 1 GENRE & RATING Science Fiction/Action • Not Rated (Teens)

Cowboy Bebop: Best Sessions

Bandai, 2002, 150 mins., #1297. Directed by Shinichiro Watanabe. Written by Keiko Nobumoto, Michiko Yokote, Ryota Yamaguchi, Sadayuki Murai, Dai Soto, Akihiko Inari, Shinichiro Watanabe, Shoji Kawamori, Aya Yoshinaga.

If you enjoyed the *Cowboy Bebop* series, now you'll have the chance to enjoy parts of it again . . . with a whole new sound! Six favorite episodes have been completely remixed with a Dolby Digital 5.1 soundtrack, all the better to hear the action with. Rejoin rag-tag bounty hunters Spike, Jet, Faye, Ed, and brainy dog Ein for a pair of mix discs in a cool package.

Disc One includes series director Shinichiro Watanabe's favorite trio of episodes: "Asteroid Blues" (#1), "Ballad of Fallen Angels" (#5), and "Wild Horses" (#19). Disc Two contains the three episodes that fans voted as their favorites: "Waltz for Venus" (#8), "Mushroom Samba" (#17), and "Hard Luck Woman" (#24).

SPECIAL FEATURES Character Bios • Clean Credits • Outtakes • Other Title Trailers • Inserts: Liner Notes • Reversible Cover TECHNICAL FEATURES Fullscreen (1.33:1) • Subtitles/CC: Eng. • Languages: Jap., Eng. dub • Sound: Dolby Digital Surround 5.1 • Multikeepcase in Plastic Sleeve • 2 Discs • Region 1 GENRE & RATING Science Fiction/Action • Rated 13+

Creature Comforts

Image, 2000, 35 mins., #ID0106CUDVD. Directed by Nick Park, Peter Lord, Boris Kossmehl. Written by Peter Lord, Boris Kossmehl, Andrea Friedrich.

This DVD contains four incredible and hilarious clay animation masterpieces produced by England's Aardman Animations, best known for its work on Wallace and Gromit and *Chicken Run*. Although it's a relatively short disc, the amount of sheer entertainment packed into its time frame is immense! Highly recommended.

"Creature Comforts" (1989) is an Oscar-winning short that details what animals in the zoo think about humans and their own lives in captivity. "Wat's Pig" (1996) is the Oscar-nominated story of a set of brothers separated at birth, one becoming a serf and the other blessed with royal wealth. The slightly ghoulish (but in a very good way) "Not Without My Handbag" (1993) is the longest entry. In it, dear dead Auntie won't go to Hell without her handbag, no matter what the devil has to say about it. The disc rounds out with "Adam" (1992), another Oscar nominee, which showcases the clay-formed early days of Earth's first man.

SPECIAL FEATURES None TECHNICAL FEATURES Widescreen (1.85:1 enhanced for 16x9) • Fullscreen (1.33:1) • Languages: Eng. • Sound: Dolby Digital 2.0 • Keepcase • 1 Disc • Region 1–6 GENRE & RATING Stop Motion/Puppet/Anthology • Not Rated (Kids)

Crest of the Stars #1: To the Stars

Bandai, 2001, 100 mins., #0680. Directed by Yasuchika Nagaoko. Written by Aya Yoshinaga. Based on a novel series by Hiroyuki Morioka.

On the planet of Martine, ten-year-old Jinto Lin is the son of the president. When their home world is overtaken by the Abh Empire, his father submits and is rewarded with a place in the Abh imperial court. Secretly, Jinto is schooled in the ways of the Abh, a race of elfin humanoids that was once genetically altered from Earth's inhabitants. When Jinto joins the Imperial Star Forces military group at seventeen, he makes his first Abh friend in a beautiful trainee named Lafiel. She's hiding a secret, though, about who and what she really is.

Based on a series of science fiction novels, the 1999 TV series *Crest of the Stars* reveals its story very slowly. It explores the alien cultures closely, even down to a specific alphabet (translated in the liner notes). While there are some excellent space battles, the story is very slow-going at times, bogging down in too many cultural debates. Overall, *Crest of the Stars* is pure modern science fiction.

The initial DVD features the first four episodes: "Invasion"; "Kin of the Stars"; "Daughter of Love"; and "Surprise Attack." The DVD authoring is rough in a few spots, pixilating and artifacting (something that's fixed in later volumes), and the menu may confuse some viewers. To navigate, just roll over the Abh lettering with the DVD controls, and English translations will appear.

SPECIAL FEATURES Text History • Clean Credits • Other Title Trailers • Insert: Liner Notes • Easter Egg TECHNICAL FEATURES Fullscreen (1.33:1) • Subtitles/CC: Eng. • Languages: Jap., Eng. dub • Sound: Dolby Digital 2.0 • Keepcase • 1 Disc • Region 1 GENRE & RATING Science Fiction/Action • Rated 13+

Crest of the Stars #2: The Politics of War

Bandai, 2001, 75 mins., #0681. Directed by Yasuchika Nagaoko. Written by Aya Yoshinaga. Based on a novel series by Hiroyuki Morioka.

On the run from enemy pursuers, the United Mankind fleet, Lafiel and Jinto are aboard the starship *Gosroth*. They make a run for the Baron Febdash Territory, where the ruling family offers every hospitality to Lafiel. But something odd is going on with the Baron and his son, and Lafiel and Jinto may have jumped out of the proverbial frying pan and into the fire.

A much cleaner transfer is welcome on this disc, which contains three more episodes full of political intrigue: "The Battle of Gosroth"; "Mysterious Conspiracy"; and "Fortunate Revolt."

SPECIAL FEATURES Text History • Clean Credits • Other Title Trailers • Insert: Liner Notes • Easter Eggs TECHNICAL FEATURES Fullscreen (1.33:1) • Subtitles/CC: Eng. • Languages: Jap., Eng. dub • Sound: Dolby Digital 2.0 • Keepcase • 1 Disc • Region 1 GENRE & RATING Science Fiction/Action • Rated 13+

Crest of the Stars #3: Wayward Soldiers

Bandai, 2001, 75 mins., #0682. Directed by Yasuchika Nagaoko. Written by Aya Yoshinaga. Based on a novel series by Hiroyuki Morioka.

Lafiel and Jinto are caught in the midst of a civil war in the Febdash Territory, and the Baron is determined to go forward with his own sinister plans. Later, Lafiel and Jinto encounter more enemy ships and are forced to land on a planet that is already overrun. Lafiel is completely unprepared for survival on the ground, leaving Jinto to protect her when the United Mankind forces come calling! Elsewhere, the Abh Empress makes an important decision. . . .

The penultimate disc features a trio of stories: "The

Style of the Abh"; "To the Battlefield"; and "Escape: Just the Two of Us."

SPECIAL FEATURES Text History • Clean Credits • Other Title Trailers • Insert: Liner Notes • Easter Eggs TECHNICAL FEATURES Fullscreen (1.33:1) • Subtitles/CC: Eng. • Languages: Jap., Eng. dub • Sound: Dolby Digital 2.0 • Keepcase • 1 Disc • Region 1 GENRE & RATING Science Fiction/Action • Rated 13+

Crest of the Stars #4: Into the Unknown

Bandai, 2001, 75 mins., #0683. Directed by Yasuchika Nagaoka. Written by Aya Yoshinaga. Based on a novel series by Hiroyuki Morioka.

In space, Admiral Trife prepares the Abh fleet for interstellar warfare against the United Mankind starships but when the battle is engaged, Rear Admiral Lady Spoor begins to deviate from the battle plans. Down on the hostile planet, Jinto and Lafiel are captured and must find a way to free themselves. But even if they escape, will there be an Abh Empire to return to?

The final three episodes conclude the story on this DVD: "Sufugnoff Gateway Battle"; "Lady of Chaos"; and "Trouble Soaring through Heaven." Be sure to watch the scenes after the final episode's credits for a six-minute preview of *Celestial Banner*, a sequel to *Crest of the Stars*. Though it was produced in 2000, DVD plans for that series have yet to be announced.

SPECIAL FEATURES Text History • Other Title Trailers • Insert: Liner Notes • Easter Eggs TECHNICAL FEATURES Fullscreen (1.33:1) • Subtitles/CC: Eng. • Languages: Jap., Eng. dub • Sound: Dolby Digital 2.0 • Keepcase • 1 Disc • Region 1 GENRE & RATING Science Fiction/Action • Rated 13+

Crimson Wolf ☞ see Mature/Adult Section

Cute Cavalcade of Classic Christmas Cartoons, A

Whirlwind, 2000, 90 mins., #WDVD2015. Although the cover screams cheesiness, this DVD contains a number of fun and funny cartoons from the 1930s to the 1950s. Quality of the prints vary, but most are reasonable given their age. Studios represented herein include Ub Iwerks, Warner Bros., Fleischer Studios, Van Beuren Studios, and Famous Studios. Although years are listed on both the packaging and the disc, a few of them are incorrect.

The eleven titles on the disc include: "Jack Frost" (1934); "Shanty Where Santy Claus Lives" (1933);

"Somewhere in Dreamland" (1936); Grampy in "Christmas Comes But Once a Year" (1936); Little King in "Christmas Night" (aka "Pals," 1933); Rudolph the Red-Nosed Reindeer" (1944); "Hector's Hectic Life" (1948); "Snow Foolin'" (1949); Tweety in "Gift Wrapped" (1952); Little Audrey in "Santa's Surprise" (1947); and the Russian short "Nobozodhee" (1959).

Besides being offered as a single DVD, the disc was also included as part of a two-pack set, packaged with the live-action *Christmas in New England*.

SPECIAL FEATURES None TECHNICAL FEATURES Fullscreen (1.33:1) • Languages: Eng. • Sound: Dolby Digital 2.0 • Keepcase • 1 Disc • Region All GENRE & RATING Holiday/Family • Not Rated (All Ages)

Cyber City Oedo 808: Vol. 1, 2, and 3

U.S. Manga Corps/Digital Versatile Disc, 1999, 149 mins., #DVD155. Directed by Yoshiaki Kawajiri. Script by Akinori Endo.

In the year 2808, a trio of criminals is offered the chance to be free from an orbital prison, but only if they do some dangerous dirty work for the police. Each is fitted with an explosive collar to keep them in line as they become bounty hunting special agents of the Cyber Police. Every job they successfully complete will lower their sentence, but if they fail, it's off with their heads! Each criminal has a specialty, all the better to help them battle terrorists, body part thieves, the military's ultimate killing machine, and even vampires!

This short-lived 1990 series is rather similar in concept to *The A-Team* or the comic book series *Suicide Squad*. While stylistically cyberpunk, this has echoes to older samurai adventures, and one criminal agent is even modeled after a famous kabuki character. The audio on the first of three episodes contains an echo, though the other two shows are fine. Despite a promise of liner notes on the reverse side of the cover, there are none. The picture is sharp.

SPECIAL FEATURES None TECHNICAL FEATURES Fullscreen (1.33:1) • Subtitles/CC: Eng. • Languages: Jap., Eng. dub • Sound: Dolby Digital 2.0 • Keepcase • 1 Disc • Region All GENRE & RATING Action/Horror/Science Fiction • Not Rated (Teens)

Cybernetics Guardian

U.S. Manga Corps, 2000, 45 mins., #USMD1774. Directed by Koichi Ohata. Screenplay by Mutsumi Sanjo.

The slums of the city are called "Cancer," and for good reason. Now two scientists work with the Central Guard Company to come up with an effective deterrent to crime. Leyla's answer is a non-violent Guard Suit, but Adler's response is a much more deadly Genocyber Killing Machine. When Leyla's assistant John tests the Guard Suit, Adler sends the Genocyber to take out the competition. Meanwhile, a secret organization is planning to ressurect the death god Saldor, and John gets caught up in the plot.

A very strange story, this contains lots of action and blood, alongside possession, weird cults, and robots. Note that although Koichi Ohata also directed the later *Genocyber* series, this does not have anything to do with it. *Cybernetics Guardian* is recommended for action and horror fans, and for followers of the *Guyver* series. The DVD contains the sole OVA and features good picture and sound. Unlike most discs, the DVD-ROM features are available for both PC and Mac!

Besides being offered as a single DVD, the disc was also included as part of a 2002 "Judgment Day Pack" set, along with *Judge*.

SPECIAL FEATURES Creator Bio • Character Galleries • DVD-ROM Features: Script, Storyboards, Character and Art Galleries, Storyboards • Other Title Trailers TECHNICAL FEATURES Fullscreen (1.33:1) • Subtitles/CC: Eng. • Languages: Jap., Eng. dub • Sound: Dolby Digital 2.0 • Keepcase • 1 Disc • Region All GENRE & RATING Robots/Horror/Science Fiction • Rated 13+

Cyberscape—A Computer Animation Vision

Sony, 1998, 45 mins., #LVD49925.

This DVD was not available for review.

Dai-Guard: Terrestrial Defense Corp.— Hostile Takeover [#1]

ADV Films, 2002, 125 mins., #DDG/001. Directed by Seiji Mizushima, Shinichiro Kimura, Yukio Suzuki, Yoshiaki Iwasaki, Shigeru Ueda. Script by Fuyuhiko Shimo, Hiroaki Kitajima, Akihio Inari, Manabu Ishikawa. Based on the manga series in *Gekkan Ace Next*.

NOTE: This DVD arrived too late for a full review. The following text is promotional copy provided by the releasing company:

"We only thought we were prepared . . . Twelve years ago, the Earth was attacked by giant invaders. To defend our planet, Earth's greatest minds and corporations assembled to design a giant robot of incredible power. Unfortunately, as with most government projects, the contract went to the lowest bidder. Fortunately, by the time the robot was ready, the mysterious invaders had already disappeared without a trace. The giant robot became first a curiosity, then a tourist attraction. But now the invaders are back and the only thing in their way is Dai-Guard and a young team of office workers who've been supplementing their regular incomes as part-time pilots and tour guides. Can these reluctant heroes halt their alien foes while simultaneously concealing the defects in their giant robot?"

This disc contains episodes #1–5.

SPECIAL FEATURES Character And Art Galleries • Clean Credits • Other Title Trailers TECHNICAL FEATURES Fullscreen (1.33:1) • Subtitles/CC: Eng. • Languages: Jap., Eng. dub • Sound: Dolby Digital 2.0 • Keepcase • 1 Disc • Region 1 GENRE & RATING Robots/Science Fiction • Rated 12+

Dai-Guard: Terrestrial Defense Corp.—To Serve and Defend but Not to Spend [#2]

ADV Films, 2002, 125 mins., #DDG/002. Directed by Seiji Mizushima, Yukio Suzuki, Takashi Sudo, Yusaku Itsukijo, Yoshiaki Iwasaki. Script by Junko Okazaki, Katsuhiko Koide, Manabu Ishikawa, Miho Sakai. Based on the manga series in *Gekkan Ace Next*.

NOTE: This DVD arrived too late for a full review. The following text is promotional copy provided by the releasing company:

"Everyone's worried about the bottom line. The Earth must be saved from the encroaching invaders, but has anyone bothered to add up the price tag for victory? Luckily for the human race, our trio of heroes has thrown the calculator out of the window. Can the mighty Dai-Guard save the world from certain destruction? Will the enemy discover our heroes' weaknesses? Who will be left standing after the smoke clears—and the accountants arrive?"

This disc contains episodes #6–9.

SPECIAL FEATURES Character and Art Galleries • Clean Credits • Other Title Trailers TECHNICAL FEATURES Fullscreen (1.33:1) • Subtitles/CC: Eng. • Languages: Jap., Eng. dub • Sound: Dolby Digital 2.0 • Keepcase • 1 Disc • Region 1 GENRE & RATING Robots/Science Fiction • Rated 12+

Dai-Guard: Terrestrial Defense Corp.— Checks and Balances of Terror [#3]

ADV Films, 2002, 125 mins., #DDG/003. Directed by Seiji Mizushima. Script by Tsuro Hatsuki, Manabu Ishikawa, Katsuhiko Koide. Based on the manga series in *Gekkan Ace Next*.

NOTE: This DVD arrived too late for a full review. The following text is promotional copy provided by the releasing company:

"In desperate times, the people of Earth search for a new hero. Hopefully one that comes fully loaded with a lifetime guarantee! What they have is Dai Guard. The Heterodyne invaders think they have the advantage, but they don't understand that it's not the age of the steel, but the spirit of the pilots that counts. Our daring trio is about to show their enemies that a good heart and a can-do attitude are stronger than the latest technology. Let's just hope they don't get laid off before the final battle!"

This disc contains episodes #10–13.

SPECIAL FEATURES "Making of" Featurette • Character and Art Galleries • Clean Credits • Other Title Trailers TECHNICAL FEATURES Fullscreen (1.33:1) • Subtitles/CC: Eng. • Languages: Jap., Eng. dub • Sound: Dolby Digital 2.0 • Keepcase • 1 Disc • Region 1 GENRE & RATING Robots/Science Fiction • Rated 12+

Dangaizer 3: Vol. 1

Right Stuf, 2002, 60 mins., #RSDVD8003. Directed by Masami Obari. Script by Reimu Aoki. Based on the manga series by Masami Obari and Reimu Aoki in *Comic Zip.*

NOTE: This DVD arrived too late for a full review. The following text is promotional copy provided by the releasing company:

"Hina loved high-tech battle, she just never thought her life would become one! Avid gamer Hina Mitsurugi loves the fast paced action of battle. Whether it's blasting away the competition on her favorite arcade game or watching the latest kickboxing match, she's always ready for a good fight. When an innocent outing with friends turns into an all-out battle for survival, Hina must put her virtual battle skills to the test in the real world—only this is no game and she doesn't get a second chance!

"Hunted by assassins and thrown into a battle between ancient gigantic robots, Hina is in for the shock of her life—it seems she's one of the pilots of Dangaizer, the most powerful robot of all time! Now she and her fellow pilots, Cindy and Reika, have been targeted for annihilation by Dangaizer's ancient enemies, the evil organization of Goma. Somehow the trio must awaken Hina's past memories and unlock her destiny before Goma manages to destroy Dangaizer and seize control of the entire planet!"

SPECIAL FEATURES Character and Art Galleries • Production Notes TECHNICAL FEATURES Fullscreen (1.33:1) • Subtitles/CC: Eng. • Languages: Jap., Eng. dub • Sound: Dolby Digital 2.0 • Keepcase • 1 Disc • Region 1 GENRE & RATING Robot/Science Fiction • Rated 16+

Dangaizer 3: Vol. 2

Right Stuf, 2002, 60 mins., #RSDVD8004. Directed by Masami Obari. Script by Reimu Aoki. Based on the manga series by Masami Obari and Reimu Aoki in *Comic Zip.*

NOTE: This DVD arrived too late for a full review. The following text is promotional copy provided by the releasing company:

"Hina Mitsurugi never imagined her life would end up like her favorite battle game! Even after piloting the monolithic robot Dangaizer, Hina can't seem to remember what her true purpose is or why Goma is trying to kill her. While Reika and Cindy struggle to restore her broken memories, Goma is targeting Neo Hong Kong for the next stage in their diabolical plans of destruction.

"When the three pilots knowingly rush headlong into a trap, the stakes have been raised! There's a new player in the game—Eileen, the Angel of Destruction! Her close resemblance to Hina could contain the answers to her mysterious memory lapse. But why is she so determined to destroy Dangaizer? It's an all out battle to Armageddon that no one may be able to stop!"

SPECIAL FEATURES Character and Art Galleries • Production Notes • Other Title Trailers TECHNICAL FEATURES Fullscreen (1.33:1) • Subtitles/CC: Eng. • Languages: Jap., Eng. dub • Sound: Dolby Digital 2.0 • Keepcase • 1 Disc • Region 1 GENRE & RATING Robot/Science Fiction • Rated 16+

Daria: Is It College Yet? An MTV Movie

Paramount, 2002, 66 mins., #87175. Directed by Karen Disher. Written by Glenn Eichler, Peggy Nicoll.

NOTE: This DVD arrived too late for a full review. The following text is promotional copy provided by the releasing company:

"All vile things must come to an end, and for Daria Morgendorffer that means it's time to look beyond high school to college. Our little girl has grown up so fast. It's time for higher learning, lowered expectations, and a heavy dose of sarcasm in this special movie presentation. Follow Daria as she visits a college campus, councils her friend Jane, sets things straight with her boyfriend Tom, and comforts her sister Quinn in a college controversy of her own. Dimwitted quarterback Kevin keeps his future plans a secret, but there's no silencing Brittany's dream of cheerleading in the big leagues. It's classic Daria melancholy as she considers her new path to higher learning. Life can't suck more after high school, can it?"

This disc also contains two bonus episodes: "Lucky Strike" and "Boxing Daria."

SPECIAL FEATURES Character Bios • Character and Art Galleries
TECHNICAL FEATURES Fullscreen (1.33:1) • Languages: Eng. •
Sound: Dolby Digital Surround 2.0 • Keepcase • 1 Disc •
Region 1 GENRE & RATING Teen/Comedy • Not Rated (Teens)

Daria Movie, The: Is It Fall Yet?

Paramount, 2002, 115 mins., #87189.
Directed by Karen Disher, Guy Moore, Pat
Smith, Ted Stearn. Written by Glenn Eich-
ler, Peggy Nicoll.

It's summer time, and Daria Morgendorffer is volunteering at the "OK to
Cry Corral" summer camp for the
overly sensitive, as well as dealing with
a new boyfriend and his rich family.
Meanwhile, sister Quinn is being tutored to help her
PSAT scores, and Jane Lane is trying to find her muse at
an artist colony.

The first feature-length production of *Daria*, this is
based on the 1997 MTV series that spun off from *Beavis
and Butt-Head*. The DVD also features the final two
episodes of the series—#412 "Fire!" and #413 "Dye,
Dye, My Darling"—that lead into the movie. Another
extra is a music video featuring Mystic Spiral and Trent.
Daria is recommended for anyone who was charmed
by *My So-Called Life* and other sardonic teen dramedies.

SPECIAL FEATURES Music Video TECHNICAL FEATURES Fullscreen
(1.33:1) • Languages: Eng. • Sound: Dolby Digital 2.0 • Keepcase • 1 Disc • Region 1–6 GENRE & RATING Teen/Comedy • Not
Rated (Teens)

Darkside Blues

U.S. Manga Corps, 1999, 83 mins.,
#USMD 1827. Directed by Nobuyasa
Furukawa. Screenplay by Masayori Sekijima. Based on the book and manga series
by Hideyuki Kikuchi, Yuho Ashibe.

It's the dark future, and the Persona
Century Corporation owns 99 percent of the world. The isolated area of
Tokyo known as "Kabuki Town" is
home to violent misfit and rebels. Stepping into the picture is Darkside, a mystic who plans to overthrow Persona, if he can organize the dangerous revolutionary
elements of Kabuki Town to help combat Persona's
superhuman assassins.

Although *Darkside Blues* has a flashy visual style, this
1994 movie is completely disjointed and confusing, with
characters and situations inadequately explained.
Although some things may become clearer with repeat
viewings, it seems much more likely that the source
novel and manga are the only places the answers can be
found. The show is quite violent in some places, and it
features seminudity.

SPECIAL FEATURES Character Scene Links • Other Title Trailers
TECHNICAL FEATURES Fullscreen (1.33:1) • Subtitles/CC: Eng. •
Languages: Eng. dub, Jap. • Sound: Dolby Digital 2.0 • Keep-
case • 1 Disc • Region All GENRE & RATING
Fantasy/Horror/Action • Rated 13+

Davey and Goliath [#1]

Image, 1999, 113 mins., #ID8825PWDVD.
Directed by Art Clokey, Ray Peck. Written
by Nancy Moore.

Modern fans may be familiar with
Davey and Goliath mainly from the
Mountain Dew "We've been hosed!"
commercials of 2002, but the stop-
motion Davey and his talking dog
Goliath were very popular in the syndicated 1960–65 series, which was rerun (and supplemented by specials) for decades after. The series was
produced by Art Clokey, familiar to stop motion fans for
his other famous creations, Gumby and Pokey. Although
the 8-in. figures look somewhat simple, the ultradetailed
miniature sets are almost unrivaled.

Sponsorship of the series came from the United
Lutheran Church in America, which means that the
shows have a religious feel to them, though they don't
advance a specific secular agenda. The stories feature
young Davey Hanson and his family encountering tests
of faith, friendship, and more. By the end of each fifteen-
minute short, Davey and Goliath learn a valuable lesson
about family values, morals, and the meaning of God in
their lives.

This DVD contains nice prints of eight of the short
films: "The Waterfall"; "The Parade," which features a
street parade with multiple vehicles and twenty-eight
moving figures; "Officer Bob"; "The Dog Show"; "The
New Skates"; "Cousin Barney"; "The Time Machine";
and "The Mechanical Man."

SPECIAL FEATURES Production Notes TECHNICAL FEATURES
Fullscreen (1.33:1) • Languages: Eng. • Sound: Dolby Digital
Mono) • Snapcase • 1 Disc • Region 1–6 GENRE & RATING Stop
Motion/Religious • Not Rated (All Ages)

Davey and Goliath [#2]

Image, 2001, 113 mins., #ID0521PWDVD.
Directed by Art Clokey, Ray Peck. Written
by Nancy Moore.

Eight more stop-motion shorts featuring young Davey Hanson and his
talking dog Goliath impart more
moral lessons: "Doghouse Dream-
house"; "Editor-in-Chief"; "Ready
or Not"; "Chicken"; "Lemonade
Stand"; "The Shoemaker," a story about prejudice
against foreigners; "Good Neighbor"; and "Bully up a

Tree." The DVD also contains a comprehensive text episode guide for the series of shorts.

Note that the covers to both *Davey and Goliath* DVDs have the same photo and no subtitle or number, although the backs have different material. Volume #1 has a green background, while volume #2 has a purple background.

SPECIAL FEATURES Production Notes • Episode Guides • Still Gallery • Games TECHNICAL FEATURES Fullscreen (1.33:1) • Languages: Eng. • Sound: Dolby Digital Mono • Snapcase • 1 Disc • Region 1–6 GENRE & RATING Stop Motion/Religious • Not Rated (All Ages)

Demon Beast Invasion ☞ see Mature/Adult Section

Demon City Shinjuku

U.S. Manga Corps, 1998, 82 mins., #USMD1732. Directed by Yoshiaki Kawajiri. Script by Kaori Okamura. Based on the manga series by Hideyuki Kikuchi.

The demon Rebi Rah kills his opponent, Izayoi, and turns part of Tokyo into a haven for monsters and demons. A decade later, Rah plans to open the portals of Hell and destroy the world. With only days to stop him, the streetwise son of Izayoi teams up with the beautiful daughter of a politician to defeat the dark sorcerer and rescue the politician.

A 1988 feature, *Demon City Shinjuku* will seem familiar to any viewer of anime horror or science fiction films. Most of the elements have been seen before, and even some new elements have been seen since (such as one scene that predates a look-alike in *Terminator 2*). Still, the story is relatively easy to follow and the designs and animation are nice and appropriately dark. Low marks though for the music, and the vocal dubs, which have odd accents and added cursing for no apparent reason.

SPECIAL FEATURES Character Scene Links • Other Title Trailers . TECHNICAL FEATURES Fullscreen (1.33:1) • Subtitles/CC: Eng. • Languages: Jap., Eng. dub • Sound: Dolby Digital 2.0 • Keepcase • 1 Disc • Region All GENRE & RATING Horror/Action • Not Rated (Teens)

Demon Fighter Kocho

AnimeWorks, 2000, 30 mins., #AWSDVD-0091. Directed by Toru Yoshida. Screenplay by Hiroshi Toda. Based on the manga series by Nonki Miyasu in *Weekly Young Jump*.

Life at Heian University can be fun, but not after angry spirits arrive to terrorize the students. That's when astrology student Kocho Enoki must use both her magical powers and her voluptuous body to stop the spirits. But Kocho's powers don't work on female demons, so how will she defeat a new femme menace?

This OVA verges on adult territory with extensive nudity and seminudity (both male and female), though little of it has specific sexual connotation or details. The brightly colored look of the show is extremely cutesy and silly. The DVD contains an extensive section called "Fun in the Studio," which showcases the vocal recording sessions for the disc.

SPECIAL FEATURES Voice Actor Footage • Cast Party Video. TECHNICAL FEATURES Fullscreen (1.33:1) • Subtitles/CC: Eng. • Languages: Jap., Eng. dub • Sound: Dolby Digital 2.0 • Keepcase • 1 Disc • Region 1 GENRE & RATING Cheesecake/Action/Comedy • Rated 16+

Demon Warrior Koji ☞ see Mature/Adult Section

Desert Island Story X, The ☞ see Mature/Adult Section

Desert Island Story XX, The ☞ see Mature/Adult Section

Detonator Orgun

U.S. Manga Corps, 2001, 159 mins., #USMD2059. Directed by Masami Obari. Screenplay by Hideki Kakinuma.

Tomoru Shindo is about to graduate, but his carefree life will soon be complicated. His dreams are disturbed by warnings of an alien invasion of Earth. Meanwhile, an Earth Defense Forces Military Researcher named Michi has almost unlocked the secrets of a suit of alien armor. But is something controlling the armor, and how does it relate to Tomoru?

Three episodes of this 1991 series were produced, and the DVD contains all of them. The story is fairly standard for the mecha/robots/invading aliens genre. One nice touch is Michi's computer interface, I-Zack, which resembles the old *Max Headroom* TV character. Unfortunately, the invader's *Death Star*–esque planet destroyer is way too familiar. The animation is rather washed-out looking, although it's tough to tell if this was intended or the result of a bad transfer.

Note that the back side of the DVD slipcover has some notes on it, but because the case isn't clear (as with many USMC cases) viewers may not realize this.

SPECIAL FEATURES Character Bios • Character and Art Galleries • Trailer • Games • Other Title Trailers • DVD-ROM Features: Art Gallery, Scripts, Credits TECHNICAL FEATURES Fullscreen (1.33:1) • Subtitles/CC: Eng. • Languages: Jap., Eng. dub • Sound: Dolby Digital 2.0 • Keepcase • 1 Disc • Region All GENRE & RATING Robots/Science Fiction/Action • Rated 13+

Devadasy

AnimeWorks, 2002, 90 mins., #AWDVD0216. Directed by Kondo Nobuhiro. Screenplay by Sho Tokimura.

Aliens attack Earth with robotic destroyers (what, that again?) and Earth must be defended by young male student Kei. But to activate the superpowered Devadasy weapon, Kei must be linked with a perfect female match, schoolgirl Misako. The fate of humanity rests on their "sexual energy" union.

A familiar story, told with a heaping helping of girls in short skirts. This 2001 OVA was released very soon after its Japanese premiere.

SPECIAL FEATURES Character Bios • Character and Art Galleries • Trailer • Games • Other Title Trailers • DVD-ROM Features: Art Gallery, Scripts, Credits TECHNICAL FEATURES Fullscreen (1.33:1) • Subtitles/CC: Eng. • Languages: Jap., Eng. dub • Sound: Dolby Digital 2.0 • Keepcase • 1 Disc • Region 1 GENRE & RATING Robots/Science Fiction/Action • Rated 16+

Devil Hunter Yohko ☛ see Mature/Adult Section

Devil Lady, The: The Awakening [#1] ☛ see Mature/Adult Section

Devil Man ☛ see Mature/Adult Section

Digimon: Digital Monsters

Fox, 2000, 273 mins., #2000995. Series Directed by Hiroyuki Kakudo. Written by Dayna Barron, Michael L. Reynolds, Michael McConnohie, John Ludin, J. M. Morris, R.D. Chamberlain, Rebecca Olkowski, Eddie Leiner, Mark Ryan, Sean Abley.

Several kids are enjoying summer camp, when suddenly it begins to snow! The kids soon discover several mysterious digivices that transport them through a vortex in the Digiworld. They're befriended by small digital monsters ("Digimon") and team up with them to fight the evil "black force" that threatens the Digiworld, turning Digimon into nastier versions of themselves.

Brought to the U.S. on Fox for airing in the 1999–2000 season, *Digimon* was an attempt to capitalize on the ultrapopular *Pokémon* phenomenon, utilizing plucky kids, creatures that must be collected, and more. It is, however, more entertaining for older audiences since it actually makes sense (in a relative way). The Fox version is also fairly true to the original anime, largely since it aired in America just after it aired in Japan.

The disc contains the entire first thirteen episodes as aired. Kids will appreciate the recap of previous events shown at the beginning of each episode. Also cute are some specially animated "bloopers."

SPECIAL FEATURES Promotional Footage • Outtakes. TECHNICAL FEATURES Fullscreen (1.33:1) • Subtitles/CC: Eng. • Languages: Eng. • Sound: Dolby Digital Surround 2.0 • Keepcase • 1 Disc • Region 1 GENRE & RATING Adventure/Kids • Not Rated (Kids)

Digimon: The Movie

Fox, 2000, 83 mins., #2001134. Directed by Takaaki Yamashita, Hisashi Nakayama, Masahiro Aizawa. Screenplay by Jeff Nimoy, Bob Buchholz.

The group of human kids, now known as the Digidestined, are called upon to save the digital world again when an evil Internet Digimon threatens to destroy worldwide communications! Using their Digimon and teaming up with children all over the globe, they attempt to stop the World Wide Web from ending up an error screen.

Three holiday-released 2000 specials were edited together to create the U.S. version of *Digimon: The Movie*. The "feature" has simpler character designs than the ongoing series, and features a lot of CGI animation. Oddly, this kids film was rated PG for U.S. theatrical release.

SPECIAL FEATURES Theatrical Trailer • Music Video. TECHNICAL FEATURES Fullscreen (Pan and Scan 1.33:1) • Subtitles/CC: Eng.,

Span. • Languages: Eng. dub • Sound: Dolby Digital Surround 2.0, Dolby Digital Surround 5.1 • Keepcase • 1 Disc • Region 1 GENRE & RATING Adventure/Kids • Rated PG

Dimensional Connections: A Computer Animated Vision

DVD International, 2001, 56 mins., #DVDI0863. Series Produced by Beny Tchaicovsky.

Seven more music tracks are set to a plethora of surreal CGI animation. No story here at all, just eye candy. Warning: the flashing lights and kaleidoscopic images may induce seizures in viewers prone to that medical condition.

SPECIAL FEATURES None TECHNICAL FEATURES Fullscreen (1.33:1) • Languages: Eng. • Sound: Dolby Digital 2.0, Dolby Digital 5.1, DTS • Keepcase • 1 Disc • Region All GENRE & RATING CGI/Music • Not Rated (Teens)

Dinosaur

Disney, 2002, 82 mins., #19572. Directed by Eric Leighton, Ralph Zondag. Original Screenplay by Walon Green. Screenplay by John Harrison, Robert Nelson Jacobs.

About 65 million years ago, the egg of an iguanadon is set on a journey across the land. Newborn iguanadon Aladar is raised by a clan of lemurs, and though he hopes to be reunited with his own kind eventually, Aladar loves his adopted family. When a meteor shower destroys their home and threatens the food and water supplies, Aladar and the lemurs set out to discover a new nesting ground. They soon find themselves befriending other dinosaurs and prehistoric creatures who are looking for a safe haven. But their journey is bedeviled by attacking carnotaurs and undermined by the scheming leader of their pack, Kron.

A visually gorgeous feature film released in 2000, *Dinosaur* combines CGI characters against live backgrounds. At times the effect is astonishing, such as the opening sequence in which Aladar's egg makes its cross-country journey. The CGI process is also adept at creating the leathery hides of the multiple species of dinosaurs used in the film. Although it's emotionally manipulative at times, *Dinosaur* has a strong story with characters that are ably voiced by actors such as D. B. Sweeney, Alfre Woodard, Julianna Margulies, and Della Reese.

SPECIAL FEATURES "Making of" Featurettes • Dinopedia • Games • DVD-ROM Features TECHNICAL FEATURES Widescreen (1.85:1 enhanced for 16x9) • Fullscreen (1.33:1) • Subtitles/CC: Eng.

• Languages: Eng., Fren. dub • Sound: Dolby Digital Surround 5.1, DTS • Keepcase • 1 Disc • Region 1 GENRE & RATING CGI/Animal/Adventure • Rated PG

Dinosaur [2-Disc Collector's Edition]

Disney, 2002, 82 mins., #21924. Directed by Eric Leighton, Ralph Zondag. Original Screenplay by Walon Green. Screenplay by John Harrison, Robert Nelson Jacobs.

Another in the line of Disney's collector's series, this set of discs offers hours of special behind-the-scenes features, tracking the development of the film from start to finish. The first disc contains the widescreen version of the film with two different commentary tracks and a sound-effects-only track, as well as multiple games and dinosaur facts. But the most interesting audio track is one that describes the onscreen action in detail for the visually impaired!

The second disc is a comprehensive look at the roots of *Dinosaur*, with early tests and presentation reels, 3D workbook segments, and character creation (including unused characters). Plus, there are features on history, digital production, music and sound, and publicity, as well as six abandoned scenes. Combined with the *A Bug's Life, Atlantis*, and the two *Toy Story* collector's editions, the *Dinosaur* set offers a wealth of information for CGI artists-to-be. On its own, it roars above the crowd.

SPECIAL FEATURES "Making of" Featurettes • Commentary Tracks by the Directors and Production Team • Character and Art Galleries • Production Notes • Abandoned Sequences • Storyboards • Dinopedia • Story Treatment • Theatrical Trailers • Promotional Footage • Games • Isolated Music and Sound Effects Tracks • Descriptive Audio Track for the Visually Impaired • Other Title Trailers • Easter Eggs TECHNICAL FEATURES Widescreen (1.85:1 enhanced for 16x9) • Subtitles/CC: Eng. • Languages: Eng., Fren. dub • Sound: Dolby Digital Surround 2.0, Dolby Digital Surround 5.1, DTS • Multikeepcase • 2 Discs • Region 1 GENRE & RATING CGI/Animal/Adventure • Rated PG

Dirty Duck ☞ see Mature/Adult Section

Dirty Pair Flash: Angels In Trouble [#1]

ADV Films, 2000, 160 mins., #DDF001. Directed by Tsukasa Sunaga. Written by Tsukasa Sunaga, Hisashi Tokimura. Based on the novels by Haruka Takachiho.

Kei and Yuri are two young trouble consultants codenamed "Lovely Angels." They zip around the galaxy in as little clothing as possible, fulfilling their missions for the World Welfare and Works Agency, an intergalactic peacekeeping force. Their propensity for getting into trouble and causing lots of property damage has earned them the nickname "Dirty Pair." Their adventures start when a dying man gives Yuri a computer card encoded with secrets. Soon, the duo are dodging an army of bad guys, and the police, in their effort to unlock the card.

Just in case you're wondering what the title "Dirty Pair" refers to, while you could say that Kei and Yuri are the object, it's really more their bouncing body parts. This 1994 series (a reworking of an earlier series) is basically all about ultracute good girls in ultratiny outfits with big guns. While it's definitely a fan favorite, whether you'll like *Dirty Pair* depends on your interest in (or tolerance for) animated girls as sex objects. Not quite *Charlie's Angels*, this is really "*Baywatch in Outer Space*" with slightly more realistic actors—and guns.

This first disc contains six episodes: "Runaway Angel"; "Darkside Angel"; "Frozen Angel"; "Sleeping Angel"; "Stray Angel"; and "Lovely Angel."

SPECIAL FEATURES Character Bios • Character and Art Galleries • Trailer • Clean Credits • Other Title Trailers • Easter Eggs TECHNICAL FEATURES Fullscreen (1.33:1) • Subtitles/CC: Eng. • Languages: Jap., Eng. dub • Sound: Dolby Digital 2.0 • Keepcase • 1 Disc • Region 1, 2, 4 GENRE & RATING Science Fiction/Cheesecake/Action • Rated 12+

Dirty Pair Flash: Angels at Worlds End [#2]

ADV Films, 2001, 125 mins., #DDF002. Directed by Tomomi Mochizuki. Script by Fuyunori Gobu. Based on the novels by Haruka Takachiho.

While acting as bodyguards for a techno-nerd hacker, Kei and Yuri are back and getting into more trouble on World's World, a pleasure planet where android hit-women and cross-dressing assassins make them long for a real vacation spot.

This "Mission 2" disc contains five episodes: "Tokyo Holiday Network"; "Seventeen Mysterious High School"; "Hot Springs Steamy Romantic Tour"; "Sparkle Bright Pure Love Flower Shop"; and "Hot Pursuit Tokyo Airport."

SPECIAL FEATURES Character Bios • Trailer • Clean Credits • Other Title Trailers TECHNICAL FEATURES Fullscreen (1.33:1) • Subtitles/CC: Eng. • Languages: Jap., Eng. dub • Sound: Dolby Digital 2.0 • Keepcase • 1 Disc • Region 1, 2, 4 GENRE & RATING Science Fiction/Cheesecake/Action • Rated 12+

Dirty Pair Flash: Random Angels [#3]

ADV Films, 2001, 125 mins., #DDF003. Directed by Tomomi Mochizuki. Script by Fuyunori Gobu. Based on the novels by Haruka Takachiho.

More property damage and mass destruction ensues on "Mission 3," as Kei and Yuri rescue a baby, face a teenage assassin girl whose family has sent her to kill them, and prepare to play in the Galaxy Cup volleyball tournament.

The third disc contains five episodes: "Snow White Chaser"; "Pink Sniper"; "The Winner in Summer Colors"; "My Boy in Rose Color"; and "Grey Colored Avenger."

SPECIAL FEATURES Character Bios • Trailer • Clean Credits • Other Title Trailers TECHNICAL FEATURES Fullscreen (1.33:1) • Subtitles/CC: Eng. • Languages: Jap., Eng. dub • Sound: Dolby Digital 2.0 • Keepcase • 1 Disc • Region 1, 2, 4 GENRE & RATING Science Fiction/Girls/Action • Rated PG

Disney's American Legends

Disney, 2002, 58 mins., #24239. Directed by Mark Henn, Wilfred Jackson, Les Clark, Jack Kinney. Screenplay by Shirley Pierce, Winston Hibler, Erdman Penner, Joe Rinaldi, Jesse Marsh, Lance Nolley, Ted Berman, Dick Kinney, Dick Shaw.

Four short films celebrate male heroes of America's past both real and fictional. First up is the story of "John Henry," the man who built railroads using his brawn and brains. Next, "Johnny Appleseed" plants fruit trees as he travels the country. Then comes the forest-clearing adventures of the giant lumberjack "Paul Bunyan" and his big blue ox, Babe. Finally, conductor Casey Jones is "The Brave Engineer" who won't let his mail train run late no matter what the obstacles!

Actor James Earl Jones introduces each of the four stories on a folksy pioneer-like set. Although the disc cover implies that this animated set is all-new, that's only partially true; the *collection* is all-new, but only one of the segments, "John Henry," is a newly created animation for this volume. "Paul Bunyan" is a 1958 short that was nominated for an Academy Award, "Johnny Appleseed" was part of the 1948 anthology feature *Melody Time*, and "The Brave Engineer" ran in 1950.

Each of the four stories is inspiring and fun, and it's nice to have an African-American hero added to the mix, but surely Disney might find a set of heroines for a more distaff volume?

SPECIAL FEATURES Vintage Intro by Walt Disney • Games • Other Title Trailers TECHNICAL FEATURES Fullscreen (1.33:1) • Subtitles/CC: Eng. • Languages: Eng. • Sound: Dolby Digital Surround 2.0 • Keepcase • 1 Disc • Region 1 GENRE & RATING Historical/Adventure • Not Rated (All Ages)

Dog of Flanders, The

Pioneer, 2000, 93 mins., #PIDA-0001V. Directed by Yoshio Kuroda. Screenplay by Miho Maruo. Based on the book by Marie-Louise de la Ramee (under the pseudonym Oui'da Sebestyen).

Nello, a young boy living in 19th-century Belgium, wants to be a painter. He adopts a dog named Patrash and works on his art, although obstacles bar his way to happiness. His grandfather dies, he can't see the girl he loves, and even his beloved dog may be taken from him.

Although there were two previous television series made in Japan of this touching-but-ultimately-morose tale, the version released on this DVD is a 1997 theatrical production. Oddly, the DVD features a version with over ten minutes of footage missing (the complete film is on the video version), and no original language track! The dub features the voices of Robert Loggia and Sean Young as grandfather and a nun, respectively. The art is simplistic for the characters and ultradetailed for their surroundings, a combination that works to the film's benefit.

The Dog of Flanders is a wonderful family film, except that it all ends badly. Parents may want to consider previewing the title on their own first or having a talk with children about death beforehand. Many tears will be shed before the end, and not just by the younger viewers.

SPECIAL FEATURES Trailer. TECHNICAL FEATURES Widescreen (1.85:1) • Languages: Eng. dub • Sound: Dolby Digital 2.0 • Keepcase • 1 Disc • Region 1, 4 GENRE & RATING Animals/Family/Historical • Not Rated (All Ages)

Dominion Tank Police

U.S. Manga Corps, 1998, 160 mins., #USMD1779. Directed by Koichi Mashimo, Takaaki Ishiyama. Screenplay by Koichi Mashimo. Based on the manga series by Masamune Shirow in *Comi Comi*.

It's 2010, and the bad guys are better armed than the police, but that doesn't mean that the police can't try harder. Enter the Newport City Tank Police, a squad of lunatics who will try anything to corral the bad guys, even if it means blowing up half the city they're supposed to protect. One of their newest members is Leona Ozaki, driver of the minitank Bonaparte, and if she doesn't get hip to the high jinks soon, she'll be left in the dust. The bad guys in the Buaku Gang include the may-

hem-loving cat-girls Annapuma and Unipuma, as well as other genetic misfits.

Lots of over-the-top mischief and goofy action make this a popular title, though the 1988 series is much simpler in form and content than the original manga work by Shirow. The tone tends to vary widely as well, with slapstick pervading the first two episodes on the DVD, and more serious tones overtaking the next two episodes. Still, for fans of lighthearted cyberpunk action, you won't find a lot on DVD that is this dependable.

SPECIAL FEATURES Text Commentary by Director • Character Scene Links • Other Title Trailers TECHNICAL FEATURES Fullscreen (1.33:1) • Subtitles/CC: Eng. • Languages: Jap., Eng. dub • Sound: Dolby Digital 2.0 • Keepcase • 1 Disc • Region All GENRE & RATING Action/Science Fiction • Not Rated (Teens)

Don Quixote [Collector's Edition]

Digital Versatile Disc, 2000, 50 mins., #163. Directed by Warwick Gilbert, Geoff Collins. Screenplay by MJ Kane. Based on the book by Miguel de Cervantes.

A Spanish nobleman dons armor and sets out for adventure as a knight in medieval Spain. Aided by his portly sidekick Sancho Panza, Don Quixote attempts to defend the helpless, but the fact that he's more than a little crazy means he's at a bit of a loss. Whether mistaking an inn for a castle or a group of windmills as attacking giants, Quixote's imagination often runs away with his senses. But he becomes beloved by the country people all the same.

Produced by Burbank Films Australia in 1987, this is an enjoyable adaptation of the 1604 book, and it is appropriate for kids and adults. As with this company's other releases, the DVD producers have included information on author Miguel de Cervantes' life and more of his literary works.

SPECIAL FEATURES Author Bio • Game TECHNICAL FEATURES Fullscreen (1.33:1) • Languages: Eng. • Sound: Dolby Digital 5.1, DTS • Keepcase • 1 Disc • Region All GENRE & RATING Historical/Adventure • Not Rated (All Ages)

Don't Leave Me Alone Daisy: DVD Collection

Bandai, 2000, 300 mins., #1310. Directed by Yuji Muto. Screenplay by Satoshi Nishizono, Ryota Yamaguchi, Kazuhisa Sakaguchi. Based on the manga series by Noriko Nagano.

Reijiro Techno has spent most of his life locked in his grandfather's bomb shelter. But when the neighbor girl's hat blows into the yard, Techno becomes obsessed with pretty young Hitomi Matsuzawa. Determined she will be his, the genius boy leaves the shelter, enrolls in school, and begins using technology to gain control of Hitomi, whom he renames "Daisy." Others who become involved with Techno and Hitomi include rebellious young man Yamakawa X, buxom teacher Miss Rarako, tough senior girl Annie, among others.

The complete thirteen-episode 1997 series is contained on two discs, labeled "Daisy Disc" and "Techno Disc." Although the series verges on cutesy, it doesn't tip over the edge too often. However, many viewers may find aspects of the series objectionable, as Techno's actions to "own" Hitomi/Daisy cross over into the sexual harassment and stalker territories. It's probably best that parents discuss issues of boundaries, consent, and appropriateness with their kids before allowing them to view the DVDs.

SPECIAL FEATURES Other Title Trailers TECHNICAL FEATURES Fullscreen (1.33:1) • Subtitles/CC: Eng. • Languages: Jap. • Sound: Dolby Digital Surround 2.0 • Multikeepcase • 2 Discs • Region 1 GENRE & RATING Romance/Comedy • Not Rated (Teens)

Doomed Megalopolis ☞ see Mature/Adult Section

Dot and the Kangaroo

Hen's Tooth, 2001, 72 mins., #4078. Directed by Yoram Gross. Screenplay by John Palmer. Based on the book by Ethel Pedley.

Dot is a young settler's daughter who wanders into the Australian bush and is frightened by the sounds and shadows. She's soon befriended by a kangaroo, who tucks the girl inside her pouch and takes her on a musical tour of the Australian countryside. Along the way, Dot meets up with animals indigenous to Australia, including a koala bear, a platypus, a kookaburra, and some dingos.

This 1977 Australian film features live-action background footage shot in the outback, over which Dot and the animal characters are animated. Cute and entertaining, this played regularly on cable channels such as HBO in the 1980s. It won many awards as well, and multiple Dot films followed. Parents should be cautioned, however, that the movie does contain a violent animal confrontation, a song about a spooky monster, and an ending that could cause some trauma if a child has not been properly prepared. Be ready to answer questions about fear and death, and keep some tissues handy.

SPECIAL FEATURES Theatrical Trailer TECHNICAL FEATURES Fullscreen (1.33:1) • Languages: Eng. • Sound: Dolby Digital 2.0 • Keepcase • 1 Disc • Region 1–6 GENRE & RATING Animal/Music/Family • Rated G

Dr. Jekyll and Mr. Hyde [Collector's Edition]

Digital Versatile Disc, 1999, 48 mins., #162. Directed by Warwick Gilbert, Geoff Collins. Screenplay by Marcia Hatfield. Based on the book by Robert Louis Stevenson.

Dr. Henry Jekyll is seeking the causes of good and evil, but his experimentation unleashes a madness inside him. Soon, Mr. Hyde is carving a swath of terror through Victorian London and killing those who cross him—or Jekyll. Will the good doctor be able to control his drug-induced evil side?

Scottish author Robert Louis Stevenson's cautionary tale of 1886 was animated by Burbank Films Australia in 1986. The adaptation doesn't pull many punches, and although the deaths are not presented in gory detail, they are shown. The animation is a bit cartoony for the dark subject matter, but that may make it easier for younger audiences to view without too many resulting nightmares. A biography of Stevenson and information about his works are included as well.

SPECIAL FEATURES Author Bio • Game TECHNICAL FEATURES Fullscreen (1.33:1) • Languages: Eng. • Sound: Dolby Digital 5.1, DTS • Keepcase • 1 Disc • Region All GENRE & RATING Historical/Horror/Adventure • Not Rated (Kids)

Dr. Seuss Green Eggs and Ham

Sony Wonder, 2002, 30 mins., #LVD 49348. Written by Theodor Geisel. Based on the books by Dr. Seuss/Theodor Geisel.

Most adults will likely look back on Dr. Seuss books fondly from their youth, with their clever rhymes, funny illustrations, and a deeper message of respect for others. This series from Sony Wonder takes Seuss's original books and gives them limited animation—falling rain, moving limbs, popping bubbles, bulging eyes, etc.—in a way that keeps the original books intact, yet animates them enough for young audiences. Older audiences may be charmed again as well.

This disc includes the silly culinary classic "Green Eggs and Ham," as well as a story of animals balancing fruit on their noggins in "Ten Apples Up on Top!" A lesser-known story teaches dental health in "The Tooth Book."

Note that although the disc cover claims it is closed captioned, it is not.

SPECIAL FEATURES Other Title Trailers TECHNICAL FEATURES Fullscreen (1.33:1) • Languages: Eng. • Sound: Dolby Digital • Keepcase • 1 Disc • Region 1 GENRE & RATING Family/Imagination • Not Rated (All Ages)

Dr. Seuss' How the Grinch Stole Christmas

Warner, 2000, 60 mins., #65409. Directed by Chuck Jones. Written by Dr. Seuss. Based on the books by Dr. Seuss/Theodor Geisel.

All the Whos down in Whoville are preparing for a wonderful Christmas celebration, but the mean old Grinch who lives up on the mountain wants to spoil their celebration. Dressing as Santa, he strips Whoville of its Christmas cheer, but one little girl, in the form of Cindy Lou Who, might just hold the power to melt the Grinch's icy heart.

This DVD contains the 1966 television special that is a classic in every sense of the word. Brilliantly animated and directed by Chuck Jones, the text is the work of Theodor Geisel, better known as Dr. Seuss. Unlike the crassly commercial live-action film of 2001, this *Grinch* is absolutely watchable and endearing, and it is a treat for all ages. Boris Karloff narrates, while June Foray provides the voice of Cindy Lou Who.

The print has been digitally cleaned up for the DVD, though the color of the Grinch seems a bit off. There are quite a number of extras, including an hour-long "Special Edition," which is supplemented by behind-the-scenes footage and interviews, and it is hosted by a smarmy Phil Hartman.

As if the disc didn't hold enough value, another Geisel treasure is included. *Dr. Seuss' Horton Hears a Who* is a half-hour 1970 tale about an elephant who discovers a microscopic civilization living on a speck of dust. This DVD gets top recommendations and belongs in every animation collection.

SPECIAL FEATURES "Making of" Featurettes • Commentary Track by June Foray and Phil Roman • Cast Filmographies • Pencil Tests • Games TECHNICAL FEATURES Fullscreen (1.33:1) • Subtitles/CC: Eng., Fren., Span. • Languages: Eng., Fren. dub, Span. dub • Sound: Dolby Digital Surround 2.0 • Snapcase • 1 Disc • Region 1 GENRE & RATING Holiday/Music/Family • Not Rated (All Ages)

Dr. Seuss How the Grinch Stole Christmas

Sony Wonder, 2002, 30 mins., #LVD 51268. Written by Theodor Geisel. Based on the books by Dr. Seuss/Theodor Geisel.

Here's another of Seuss's most famous creations: the green-furred Grinch. Don't confuse this with the older Warner version or the live-action version; this is a limited-animation version using the illustrations from the original book. Walter Matthau narrates the story. Bringing up the end of the disc is "If I Ran the Zoo," in which young Gerald McGrew runs a zoo that includes a tizzle-topped Tufted Mazurka and a scraggle-foot Mulligatawny.

Note that although the disc cover claims it is closed captioned, it is not.

SPECIAL FEATURES Other Title Trailers TECHNICAL FEATURES Fullscreen (1.33:1) • Languages: Eng. • Sound: Dolby Digital • Keepcase • 1 Disc • Region 1 GENRE & RATING Holiday/Family/Imagination • Not Rated (All Ages)

Dr. Seuss The Cat in the Hat

Sony Wonder, 2002, 30 mins., #LVD 49347. Written by Theodor Geisel. Based on the books by Dr. Seuss/Theodor Geisel.

One of Seuss's most famous creations grabs the spotlight in "The Cat in the Hat." The follow-up story, "Maybe You Should Fly a Jet! Maybe You Should Be a Vet!" will give kids some wacky suggestions as to what they might do when they grow up.

Note that although the disc cover claims it is closed captioned, it is not.

SPECIAL FEATURES Other Title Trailers TECHNICAL FEATURES Fullscreen (1.33:1) • Languages: Eng. • Sound: Dolby Digital • Keepcase • 1 Disc • Region 1 GENRE & RATING Family/Imagination • Not Rated (All Ages)

Dr. Seuss's A B C's

Sony Wonder, 2002, 30 mins., #LVD 51246. Written by Theodor Geisel. Based on the books by Dr. Seuss/Theodor Geisel.

Another set of Seussian classics is given the limited-animation treatment here. "Dr. Seuss's ABC's" will give the alphabet a funny and imaginative feel, with creatures such as a "duck-dog" or "quacking quackeroo" sure to bring a smile. In "I Can Read with My Eyes Shut!" the Cat in the Hat teaches Young Cat that reading is fun. And in "Mr. Brown Can Moo, Can You?" viewers are encouraged to make the same silly sounds as the talented Mr. Brown.

Note that although the disc cover claims it is closed captioned, it is not.

SPECIAL FEATURES Other Title Trailers TECHNICAL FEATURES Fullscreen (1.33:1) • Languages: Eng. • Sound: Dolby Digital • Keepcase • 1 Disc • Region 1 GENRE & RATING Family/Imagination • Not Rated (All Ages)

Dr. Seuss's My Many Colored Days: Notes Alive!

Minnesota Orchestra, 1999, 60 mins. Directed by Chris LaPalm. Written by Dr. Seuss. Based on the book by Dr. Seuss/Theodor Geisel.

This is a charming computer-animated musical adventure adapted from a book by Dr. Seuss. In the story, a dog and a young child move through a variety of emotions, each represented by a specific color for the day—Red, Blue, Brown, Yellow, Gray, Orange, Green, Purple, Pink, Black, and Mixed-Up.

Holly Hunter narrates this DVD, which features an original score by composer Richard Einhorn and lush music by the Minnesota Orchestra. The 3D animation was created using motion-capture technology and other methods, and it's fun to watch. There is an extensive selection of extras, with a "making of" segment, as well as background pieces on Dr. Seuss (including a tour of his house!), the animators, the Minnesota Orchestra, and the making of the music. Additionally, you can watch the multi-angle concert version of the score, showcasing the talented musicians involved.

The only downside to this little-known gem is an overly complicated menu in which it's quite easy to get lost and frustrated. Parents may want to help their kids navigate, but be warned that if you do, you'll soon be watching right along with them! There are other titles in the *Notes Alive!* concert series on video; here's hoping more DVD releases are forthcoming.

SPECIAL FEATURES "Making of" Featurettes • Orchestra Concert Version • Game • Other Title Trailers TECHNICAL FEATURES Fullscreen (1.33:1) • Languages: Eng. • Sound: Dolby Digital 2.0 • Keepcase • 1 Disc • Region 1–6 GENRE & RATING CGI/Music/Family • Not Rated (All Ages)

Dragon Ball: Mystical Adventure

Funimation, 2001, 50 mins.

This DVD was not available for review.

Dragon Ball: The Saga of Goku [Box Set]

Trimark, 1999, 337 mins., #VM7484D. Series Produced by Toei Animation. Based on the manga series by Akira Toriyama in *Shonen Jump*.

Goku is a brave young boy who has extraordinary powers and martial arts skills. When he gets involved with a slightly crazy old man, he's soon fighting shape-changing monsters, villains of every sort, and rescuing beautiful girls, all while searching for the seven legendary Dragon Balls. Plus, Goku must face the Eternal Dragon deep within his fiery lair under the Earth. This is the origin story of Goku, showing that he manages to get in as much trouble as any adventurer.

This two-DVD set includes thirteen 1986 "prequel" episodes, plus the full-length feature "Curse of the Blood Rubies." Buyers should be warned that these are apparently heavily edited from their original form. Still, they have cute animation, lots of action, and more humor and fun than the successor series.

SPECIAL FEATURES Promotional Footage • Games TECHNICAL FEATURES Fullscreen (1.33:1) • Subtitles/CC: Eng. • Languages: Eng. dub • Sound: Dolby Digital 2.0 • Box with 2 Keepcases • 2 Discs • Region 1 GENRE & RATING Martial Arts/Adventure/Fantasy • Rated 5+

Dragon Ball Z: Arrival [#1]

Pioneer, 1998, 80 mins., #PIDA-1330V. Series produced by Toei Animation. Based on the manga series by Akira Toriyama in *Shonen Jump*.

Still searching for the mystical Dragon Balls, Goku's grown up a bit and now has a son, Gohan. He also has a lot more enemies, including the Saiyan, an alien race bent on conquering Earth. When the Saiyan send their mightiest warrior, Radlitz, to Earth, he blackmails Goku into destroying a hundred humans or Gohan will be killed. Goku teams up with his enemy Piccolo to stop Radlitz, but will their combined powers be enough?

The *Dragon Ball* story spun out of a 1984 series of manga adventures by Akira Toriyama. The original series ran from 1986 to 1989, then was rebooted as *Dragon Ball Z* and set three years after its predecessor. Both *DB* series' were ultrapopular in Japan, and although the first series didn't perform as well on U.S. television, the second series was a substantial hit in U.S. syndication. There are over 500 episodes to release, meaning that *Dragon Ball* will be with us for some time. The episodes released on DVD have some nudity and violence excised to make them more "kid-friendly."

This DVD volume contains episodes #1–4.

SPECIAL FEATURES Episode Previews TECHNICAL FEATURES Fullscreen (1.33:1) • Languages: Eng. dub • Sound: Dolby Digital 2.0 • Keepcase • 1 Disc • Region 1 GENRE & RATING Martial Arts/Adventure/Fantasy • Rated 3+

Dragon Ball Z: The Saiyans [#2]

Pioneer, 1999, 65 mins., #PIDA-1331V. Series produced by Toei Animation. Based on the manga series by Akira Toriyama in *Shonen Jump.*

Gohan is taken to live in the wastelands by Piccolo, where he becomes a giant ape and befriends a dinosaur. Meanwhile, Saiyan warriors Vegeta and Nappa arrive on the planet Arlia and lay siege.

This DVD volume contains episodes #5–7.

SPECIAL FEATURES Episode Previews TECHNICAL FEATURES Fullscreen (1.33:1) • Languages: Eng. dub • Sound: Dolby Digital 2.0 • Keepcase • 1 Disc • Region 1 GENRE & RATING Martial Arts/Adventure/Fantasy • Rated 3+

Dragon Ball Z: Snake Way [#3]

Pioneer, 1999, 65 mins., #PIDA-1332V. Series produced by Toei Animation. Based on the manga series by Akira Toriyama in *Shonen Jump.*

Goku has to best two ogres in a competition, then falls into the clutches of the beautiful snake princess. Warriors gather to prepare for a fight against the Saiyans, while Gohan escapes the wilderness and washes up on an island.

This DVD volume contains episodes #8–10.

SPECIAL FEATURES Episode Previews TECHNICAL FEATURES Fullscreen (1.33:1) • Languages: Eng. dub • Sound: Dolby Digital 2.0 • Keepcase • 1 Disc • Region 1 GENRE & RATING Martial Arts/Adventure/Fantasy • Rated 3+

Dragon Ball Z: Pendulum Room [#4]

Pioneer, 1999, 65 mins., #PIDA-1333V. Series produced by Toei Animation. Based on the manga series by Akira Toriyama in *Shonen Jump.*

Mr. Popo trains Earth's warriors by sending them into a virtual reality fight against the Saiyans. Gohan turns into a giant ape again and menaces Piccolo, while Goku must catch another monkey on a high-gravity planet.

This DVD volume contains episodes #11–13.

SPECIAL FEATURES Episode Previews TECHNICAL FEATURES Fullscreen (1.33:1) • Languages: Eng. dub • Sound: Dolby Digital 2.0 • Keepcase • 1 Disc • Region 1 GENRE & RATING Martial Arts/Adventure/Fantasy • Rated 3+

Dragon Ball Z: Doom [#5]

Pioneer, 1999, 65 mins., #PIDA-1334V. Series produced by Toei Animation. Based on the manga series by Akira Toriyama in *Shonen Jump.*

Goku learns more about the history of the Saiyans and fights a grasshopper, while Vegeta and Nappa arrive on Earth. A confrontation is brewing, and the plant monsters known as Saibamen won't help matters.

This DVD volume contains episodes #14–16.

SPECIAL FEATURES Episode Previews TECHNICAL FEATURES Fullscreen (1.33:1) • Languages: Eng. dub • Sound: Dolby Digital 2.0 • Keepcase • 1 Disc • Region 1 GENRE & RATING Martial Arts/Adventure/Fantasy • Rated 3+

Dragon Ball Z: Immortals [#6]

Pioneer, 1999, 65 mins., #PIDA-1335V. Series produced by Toei Animation. Based on the manga series by Akira Toriyama in *Shonen Jump.*

Earth's Special Forces fight the plant monster Saibamen and then battle Vegeta and Nappa. But where is Goku?

This DVD volume contains episodes #17–19.

SPECIAL FEATURES Episode Previews TECHNICAL FEATURES Fullscreen (1.33:1) • Languages: Eng. dub • Sound: Dolby Digital 2.0 • Keepcase • 1 Disc • Region 1 GENRE & RATING Martial Arts/Adventure/Fantasy • Rated 3+

Dragon Ball Z: Destruction [#7]

Pioneer, 1999, 65 mins., #PIDA-1337V. Series produced by Toei Animation. Based on the manga series by Akira Toriyama in *Shonen Jump.*

The battle against Vegeta and Nappa costs some of our heroes their lives, and when Goku arrives, vengeance will be his!

This DVD volume contains episodes #20–22.

SPECIAL FEATURES Episode Previews TECHNICAL FEATURES Fullscreen (1.33:1) • Languages: Eng. dub • Sound: Dolby Digital 2.0 • Keepcase • 1 Disc • Region 1 GENRE & RATING Martial Arts/Adventure/Fantasy • Rated 3+

Dragon Ball Z: Showdown [#8]

Pioneer, 1999, 65 mins., #PIDA-0109V. Series produced by Toei Animation. Based on the manga series by Akira Toriyama in *Shonen Jump.*

Goku's battle against Vegeta could mean the destruction of the Earth, and when Vegeta transforms into a giant ape, only the dangerous "Spirit Bomb" might stand a chance at stopping him!

This DVD volume contains episodes #23–25.

SPECIAL FEATURES Episode Previews TECHNICAL FEATURES Fullscreen (1.33:1) • Languages: Eng. dub • Sound: Dolby Digital 2.0 • Keepcase • 1 Disc • Region 1 GENRE & RATING Martial Arts/Adventure/Fantasy • Rated 3+

Dragon Ball Z: Departure [#9]

Pioneer, 1999, 65 mins., #PIDA-1112V. Series produced by Toei Animation. Based on the manga series by Akira Toriyama in *Shonen Jump.*

Gohan transforms into a giant ape to attack Vegeta, and the Dragon Balls are taken away from Earth and scattered on the planet Namek. The crew of heroes boards a spaceship heading for Namek to recover the Balls, but they're waylaid in space.

This DVD volume contains episodes #26–28.

SPECIAL FEATURES Episode Previews TECHNICAL FEATURES Fullscreen (1.33:1) • Languages: Eng. dub • Sound: Dolby Digital 2.0 • Keepcase • 1 Disc • Region 1 GENRE & RATING Martial Arts/Adventure/Fantasy • Rated 3+

Dragon Ball Z: Rebirth [#10]

Pioneer, 1999, 65 mins., #PIDA-1113V. Series produced by Toei Animation. Based on the manga series by Akira Toriyama in *Shonen Jump.*

A band of space refugees believe that the Earth champions are working for the evil Frieza, but once they are convinced of the truth, they allow our heroes to continue on to Namek. Both Frieza and Vegeta are on their way to the planet to capture the Dragon Balls, while back on Earth, Goku begins training again.

This DVD volume contains episodes #29–31.

SPECIAL FEATURES Episode Previews TECHNICAL FEATURES Fullscreen (1.33:1) • Languages: Eng. dub • Sound: Dolby Digital 2.0 • Keepcase • 1 Disc • Region 1 GENRE & RATING Martial Arts/Adventure/Fantasy • Rated 3+

Dragon Ball Z: Namek [#11]

Pioneer, 1999, 65 mins., #PIDA-1114V. Series produced by Toei Animation. Based on the manga series by Akira Toriyama in *Shonen Jump.*

Gohan and the other Earth heroes mix it up with Frieza's forces on Namek, while Vegeta faces his rival, Cui. Plus, Frieza already has four of the Dragon Balls, and Goku learns Gohan may be in trouble.

This DVD volume contains episodes #32–34.

SPECIAL FEATURES Episode Previews TECHNICAL FEATURES Fullscreen (1.33:1) • Languages: Eng. dub • Sound: Dolby Digital 2.0 • Keepcase • 1 Disc • Region 1 GENRE & RATING Martial Arts/Adventure/Fantasy • Rated 3+

Dragon Ball Z: Betrayal [#12]

Pioneer, 1999, 65 mins., #PIDA-1115V. Series produced by Toei Animation. Based on the manga series by Akira Toriyama in *Shonen Jump.*

Gohan and Krillin fight against Frieza's henchmen, while Vegeta searches for the Dragon Balls, and Goku speeds his way toward Namek in a spaceship.

This DVD volume contains episodes #35–37.

SPECIAL FEATURES Episode Previews TECHNICAL FEATURES Fullscreen (1.33:1) • Languages: Eng. dub • Sound: Dolby Digital 2.0 • Keepcase • 1 Disc • Region 1 GENRE & RATING Martial Arts/Adventure/Fantasy • Rated 3+

Dragon Ball Z: Collision [#13]

Pioneer, 1999, 65 mins., #PIDA-1116V. Series produced by Toei Animation. Based on the manga series by Akira Toriyama in *Shonen Jump.*

Goku's ship has some trouble, and some old dead friends find new life. Plus, Vegeta gets a Dragon Ball and fights the monstrous Zarbon.

This DVD volume contains episodes #38–40.

SPECIAL FEATURES Episode Previews TECHNICAL FEATURES Fullscreen (1.33:1) • Languages: Eng. dub • Sound: Dolby Digital 2.0 • Keepcase • 1 Disc • Region 1 GENRE & RATING Martial Arts/Adventure/Fantasy • Rated 3+

Dragon Ball Z: Quest [#14]

Pioneer, 1999, 65 mins., #PIDA-1117V. Series produced by Toei Animation. Based on the manga series by Akira Toriyama in *Shonen Jump*.

Krillin's power is increased, and Vegeta plots to steal all five of Frieza's Dragon Balls.

This DVD volume contains episodes #41–43.

SPECIAL FEATURES Episode Previews TECHNICAL FEATURES Fullscreen (1.33:1) • Languages: Eng. dub • Sound: Dolby Digital 2.0 • Keepcase • 1 Disc • Region 1 GENRE & RATING Martial Arts/Adventure/Fantasy • Rated 3+

Dragon Ball Z: Trouble! [#15]

Pioneer, 1999, 65 mins., #PIDA-1118V. Series produced by Toei Animation. Based on the manga series by Akira Toriyama in *Shonen Jump*.

Extreme gravity may crush Goku in his spaceship, while Vegeta becomes even more powerful. Plus, Bulma must rescue one of the Dragon Balls from deep underwater.

This DVD volume contains episodes #44–46.

SPECIAL FEATURES Episode Previews TECHNICAL FEATURES Fullscreen (1.33:1) • Languages: Eng. dub • Sound: Dolby Digital 2.0 • Keepcase • 1 Disc • Region 1 GENRE & RATING Martial Arts/Adventure/Fantasy • Rated 3+

Dragon Ball Z: The Ginyu Force [#16]

Pioneer, 1999, 65 mins., #PIDA-1119V. Series produced by Toei Animation. Based on the manga series by Akira Toriyama in *Shonen Jump*.

Frieza's Ginyu Force brings trouble to the heroes of Earth and Namek, even as they close in on recapturing all of Vegeta's Dragon Balls.

This DVD volume contains episodes #47–49.

SPECIAL FEATURES Episode Previews TECHNICAL FEATURES Fullscreen (1.33:1) • Languages: Eng. dub • Sound: Dolby Digital 2.0 • Keepcase • 1 Disc • Region 1 GENRE & RATING Martial Arts/Adventure/Fantasy • Rated 3+

Dragon Ball Z: Super Saiyan?! [#17]

Pioneer, 1999, 85 mins., #PIDA-1120V. Series produced by Toei Animation. Based on the manga series by Akira Toriyama in *Shonen Jump*.

Members of the Ginyu Force challenge Gohan and Krillin, and even Vegeta gets involved in the fight against Frieza's thugs. Then, Frieza gets all seven Dragon Balls, but Goku has arrived, bringing with him a bold new power. . . .

This DVD volume contains episodes #50–53.

SPECIAL FEATURES Episode Previews TECHNICAL FEATURES Fullscreen (1.33:1) • Languages: Eng. dub • Sound: Dolby Digital 2.0 • Keepcase • 1 Disc • Region 1 GENRE & RATING Martial Arts/Adventure/Fantasy • Rated 3+

Dragon Ball Z: The Movie—Dead Zone [#1]

Pioneer, 1997, 45 mins., #PIDA-1336V. Directed by Daisuke Nishio. Screenplay by Takao Koyama. Based on the manga series by Akira Toriyama in *Shonen Jump*.

Garlic Jr. collects the seven Dragon Balls in a bid for immortality. He plans to take over the world to make humankind suffer for the death of Garlic Sr., but not if Goku and crew have anything to say about it! Gohan's hidden powers surface just in time to help fight Garlic's black hole "dead zone."

Seen on U.S. television in an edited form, this DVD features the uncut 1990 theatrical movie.

SPECIAL FEATURES Character Bios • Deleted TV Scenes • Other Title Trailers TECHNICAL FEATURES Fullscreen (1.33:1) • Subtitles/CC: Eng. • Languages: Jap., Eng. dub • Sound: • Keepcase • 1 Disc • Region 1 GENRE & RATING Martial Arts/Adventure/Fantasy • Not Rated (Teens)

Dragon Ball Z: The Movie—The World's Strongest [#2]

Pioneer, 1998, 60 mins., #PIDA-0123V. Directed by Daisuke Nishio. Screenplay by Takao Koyama. Based on the manga series by Akira Toriyama in *Shonen Jump*.

Dr. Wheelo has been freed from his ice entrapment, but his evil brain lives on in a jar. Wheelo sends his android minions out to capture several of the heroes so he can transfer his brain into the body of the world's strongest fighter. It's up to Goku and his allies to end the evil brain's plans by defeating him and his android crew. Goku must kick the brain's Medulla Oblongata!

Seen on U.S. television in an edited form, this DVD features the uncut 1990 theatrical movie.

SPECIAL FEATURES Character Bios • Battle/Fight Demos • Other Title Trailers TECHNICAL FEATURES Fullscreen (1.33:1) • Subtitles/CC: Eng. • Languages: Jap., Eng. dub • Sound: Dolby Digital 2.0 • Keepcase • 1 Disc • Region 1 GENRE & RATING Martial Arts/Adventure/Fantasy • Rated 13+

Dragon Ball Z: The Movie—Tree of Might [#3]

Pioneer, 1998, 60 mins., #PIDA-0110V. Directed by Daisuke Nishio. Screenplay by Takao Koyama. Based on the manga series by Akira Toriyama in *Shonen Jump*.

Space pirates plant a seed on good, old mother Earth; the tree that grows from it will drain all life from the planet. Goku and his pals try to stop the tree and its decimation of the planet, but they just aren't up to the task. Gohan gets captured by one of the pirates who turns out to be a tough alien warrior known as a Saiyan!

Seen on U.S. television in an edited form, this DVD features the uncut 1991 theatrical movie.

SPECIAL FEATURES Character Bios • Games • Other Title Trailers TECHNICAL FEATURES Fullscreen (1.33:1) • Subtitles/CC: (Eng. and CC) • Languages: Jap., Eng. dub • Sound: Dolby Digital 2.0 • Keepcase • 1 Disc • Region 1 GENRE & RATING Martial Arts/Adventure/Fantasy • Not Rated (Teens)

Dragon Ball Z: Uncut Movie Trilogy [Box Set]

Pioneer, 2001, 165 mins., #11601.

This box set features the first three uncut *Dragon Ball Z* movie DVDs in their keepcases. There are no extra features besides the cardboard box sleeve, which features two large images. See individual entries for Special and Technical Features.

TECHNICAL FEATURES Box with 3 Keepcases • 3 Discs • Region 1 GENRE & RATING Martial Arts/Adventure/Fantasy • Rated 13+

Dragon Ball Z: The Saiyan Conflict [Box Set #1]

Pioneer, 2001, 535 mins., #11602.

This box set features the first eight *Dragon Ball Z* DVDs in their keepcases. There aren't any extra features besides the cardboard box sleeve, which features a wraparound design of all the major characters. See individual entries for Special and Technical Features.

TECHNICAL FEATURES Box with 8 Keepcases • 8 Discs • Region 1 GENRE & RATING Martial Arts/Adventure/Fantasy • Rated 3+

Dragon Ball Z: The Namek Saga [Box Set #2]

Pioneer, 2001, 605 mins., #11603.

This box set features *Dragon Ball Z* DVDs #9–17 in their keepcases. There are no extra features except the cardboard box sleeve, which features a wraparound design of all the major characters. See individual entries for Special and Technical Features.

TECHNICAL FEATURES Box with 9 Keepcases • 9 Discs • Region 1 GENRE & RATING Martial Arts/Adventure/Fantasy • Rated 3+

Dragon Ball Z

The following *Dragon Ball Z* titles, from Funimation, were not available for review: *Captain Ginyu—Assault* [#18], episodes #54–56; *Captain Ginyu—Double Cross* [#19], episodes #57–60; *Frieza—The Summoning* [#20], episodes #61–63; *Frieza—Tranformation* [#21], episodes #64–66; *Frieza—Revealed* [#22], episodes #67–69; *Frieza—Death of a Prince* [#23], episodes #70–72; *Frieza—Clash* [#24], episodes #73–75; *Frieza—Desperation* [#25], episodes #76–78; *Frieza—Super Saiyan Goku* [#26], episodes #79–81; *Frieza—Eleventh Hour* [#27], episodes #82–85; *Frieza—Fall of a Tyrant* [#28], episodes #86–89; *Frieza—Namek's End* [#29], episodes #90–92; *Garlic Jr.—Black Water Mist* [#30], episodes #93–95; *Garlic Jr.—Sacred Water* [#31], episodes #96–98; *Garlic Jr.—Vanquished* [#32], episodes #99–102; *Trunks—Mysterious Youth* [#33], episode #103–5; *Trunks—Prelude To Terror* [#34–35], episodes #106–10; *Androids—Invasion* [#36], episodes #111–14; *Androids—Dr. Gero* [#37], episodes #115–17; *Androids—Assassins* [#38], episodes #118–20; *Androids—Invincible* [#39], episodes #121–24; *Imperfect Cell—Encounter* [#40], episodes #125–27; *Imperfect Cell—Discovery* [#41], episodes #128–30; *Imperfect Cell—Race Against Time* [#42], episodes #131–33;

Imperfect Cell—17's End [#43], episodes #134–37; *Perfect Cell—Hunt For 18* [#44], episodes #138–40; *Perfect Cell—Temptation* [#45], episodes #141–43; *Perfect Cell—Perfection* [#46], episodes #144–46; *Perfect Cell—Unstoppable* [#47], episodes #147–50; *Cell Games—Ultimatum* [#48], episodes #151–53; *World Tournament—Junior Division* [#62], episodes #195–97; *World Tournament—The Draw* [#63], episodes #198–200; *World Tournament—Blackout* [#64], episodes #201–4; *Babidi—Descent* [#65], episodes #205–7; *Babidi—Battle Royale* [#66], episodes #208–10; *Babidi—The Dark Prince Returns* [#67], episodes #211–13; *Babidi—Rivals* [#68], episodes #214–16; *Majin Buu—The Hatching* [#69], episodes #217–19; *Majin Buu—Atonement* [#70], episodes #220–22; *Majin Buu—Revival* [#71], episodes #223–25; *Majin Buu—Tactics* [#72], episodes #226–28; *Majin Buu—Defiance* [#73], episodes #229–31; *Majin Buu—A Hero's Farewell* [#74], episodes #232–34; *Majin Buu—Emergence* [#75], episodes #235–38; *Fusion—Evil Buu* [#76], episodes #239–41; *Fusion—Play For Time* [#77], episodes #242–44; *Fusion—Losing Battle* [#78], episodes #245–47; *Fusion—Ambush* [#79], episodes #248–50; *Fusion—Hope Returns* [#80], episodes #251–53; *Fusion—The Last Saiyan* [#81], episodes #254–56; *Fusion—Internal Struggle* [#82], episodes #257–60; *Kid Buu—Regression* [#83], episodes #261–63; *Kid Buu—Saiyan Pride* [#84], episodes #264–66; Feature #1: *The History of Trunks*; Feature#2: *Bardock the Father of Goku*; Feature #4: *Lord Slug* [Edited]; Feature #4: *Lord Slug* [Uncut]; Feature #5: *Cooler's Revenge* [Edited]; Feature #5: *Cooler's Revenge* [Uncut]; Feature #6: *Return of Cooler* [Edited]; Feature #6: *Return of Cooler* [Uncut].

Dragon Half

ADV Films, 2002, 50 mins., #DDH/001. Directed by Shinya Sadamitsu. Story by Shinya Sadamitsu. Based on the manga series by Ryusuke Mita in *Monthly Dragon Magazine*.

NOTE: This DVD arrived too late for a full review. The following text is promotional copy provided by the releasing company:

"So you think *you* have problems? Mink's mom is a dragon and her dad's a knight, and that's just the beginning of her list of teenage anxieties! After all, when you're part reptile and you're in love with a handsome singer who's also a dragon slayer, you just know somebody's going to get burned! So what's a lovestruck Dragon Half to do when the man of her dreams wants her head on a platter and Mom and Dad are too busy fighting to notice? Why, go to his concert all on your own, of course, even if it does mean a long, strange journey filled with sinister villains and bizarre encounters. It's a good thing Mink inherited wings and the ability to breathe fire from her mom's side of the family, because when you're half-dragon, you don't make friends easily...."

SPECIAL FEATURES Clean Credits • Other Title Trailers • Easter Egg TECHNICAL FEATURES Fullscreen (1.33:1) • Subtitles/CC: Eng. • Languages: Jap., Eng. dub • Sound: Dolby Digital • Keepcase • 1 Disc • Region 1 GENRE & RATING Fantasy/Comedy • Rated 15+

Dragon's Lair

Digital Leisure, 1998, #24719-99001. Directed by Don Bluth.

In the land of magic, brave knight Dirk the Daring must venture into the castle of Singe the Evil Dragon to rescue the beautiful Princess Daphne. Along the way he must defeat snakes, a smoke monster, a cloaked specter, purple Goons, the Black Knight, the Lizard King, the mudmen, and more.

Dragon's Lair was a 1983 arcade-style video game that featured stunning graphics by the animation team headed by Don Bluth. The popular game inspired a short-lived ABC TV series, but that's not what's collected here. This DVD contains the game itself, with all of the animation footage present and accounted for. In "watch mode," you can view the game as a complete adventure story, without the death scenes. In "play mode," you can use the DVD remote to control the character's choices, which leads to alternate story possibilities and, often, death.

An excellent picture transfer—and the chance to play the game without continually depositing quarters—will bring happiness to older fans. There's also a nice set of vintage interviews with Don Bluth and Rick Dyer, the game's cocreators. A very cool product, *Dragon's Lair* lets you get back in control of the adventure. Unfortunately, the DVD will not play on some Toshiba machines, so if that's your brand, be warned. Also, the front menu is very difficult to navigate because of the barely changing colors of the selections.

SPECIAL FEATURES Interview Clips • Other Title Trailers • Insert: Liner Notes and Game Hints TECHNICAL FEATURES Fullscreen (1.33:1) • Languages: Eng. • Sound: Dolby Digital 2.0 • Keepcase • 1 Disc • Region All GENRE & RATING Fantasy/Adventure/Interactive • Rated 6+

Dragon's Lair II: Time Warp

Digital Leisure, 1998, #24719-99005. Directed by Don Bluth.

The Evil Wizard Mordroc has pulled Princess Daphne through a wrinkle in time. He plans to marry her, but Dirk the Daring vows to save her using a bumbling old time machine. As he fights against dinosaurs, the Queen of Hearts, and the Snake Brothers, Dirk has less and less time to stop Mordroc from putting the Death Ring upon Daphne's finger and spiriting her away forever!

This sequel to the original playable arcade game was released in 1991. Like its predecessor, *Dragon's Lair II* can be watched or played on the DVD.

SPECIAL FEATURES "Work in Progress" Clips • Other Title Trailers • Insert: Liner Notes and Game Hints TECHNICAL FEATURES Fullscreen (1.33:1) • Languages: Eng. • Sound: Dolby Digital 2.0 • Keepcase • 1 Disc • Region 1–6 GENRE & RATING Fantasy/Adventure/Interactive • Rated 6+

Dragon's Lair 20th Anniversary Special Edition [Box Set]

Digital Leisure, 2002, #24719-99043.

This box set contains *Dragon's Lair, Dragon's Lair II: Timewarp*, and *Space Ace*. The discs are similar to the individual releases, though the keepcases have new covers, and the discs are silk-screened with the "20th Anniversary Special Edition" banner. There are also new unreleased scenes, which can be viewed in "watch" mode, or played in the interactive mode.

On the *Dragon's Lair* disc, there is a new merchandising section, creator bios, press clippings, new creator interviews, a featurette, an episode of the Canadian arcade game TV show *Starcade* (focusing on *Dragon's Lair*), and footage from the new *Dragon's Lair* 3D game. On the *Dragon's Lair II* disc is a preproduction video with scratch audio tracks, and some pencil test footage. See individual entries for the original Special and Technical Features listings.

SPECIAL FEATURES "Making of" Featurette • Creator Interviews • Creator Bios • Merchandising and Box Art Galleries • Deleted Scenes • Press Notes • Promotional Footage • Other Title Trailers • Insert: Booklet TECHNICAL FEATURES Cardboard Box with 3 Keepcases • 3 Discs • Region All GENRE & RATING Fantasy/Adventure/Interactive • Rated E

Dragon Rider ☛ see Mature/Adult Section

Dragon Tales: Adventures in Dragon Land! [#1]

Columbia/TriStar, 2000, 66 mins., #04611. Directed by Tim Eldred. Written by Bob Carrau, Cliff Ruby, Elana Lesser, Alicia Marie Schudt, Robert Schechter, Lisa Medway.

Emmy and Max are two young children with a wonderful secret: they can call on the dragons pictured on their wallpaper. The dragons come to life and transport them to a magical land where they have fantastic adventures.

Children's Television Workshop presents this gentle TV series that teaches life lessons in a non-preachy and entertaining manner. Appropriate for even the youngest children, *Dragon Tales* will entertain and delight, and it teaches kids to sing along to subtitled songs. The first DVD contains five episodes: "To Kingdom Come"; "Baby Troubles"; "Bad Share Day"; "Zak Takes a Dive"; and "The Forest of Darkness."

SPECIAL FEATURES Sing-Alongs • Other Title Trailers TECHNICAL FEATURES Fullscreen (1.33:1) • Subtitles/CC: Eng., Fren., Span. • Languages: Eng., Span. dub • Sound: Dolby Digital 2.0 • Keepcase • 1 Disc • Region 1, 3, 4 GENRE & RATING Dragons/Kids • Not Rated (All Ages)

Dragon Tales: Let's Share! Let's Play! [#2]

Columbia/TriStar, 2001, 65 mins., #07304. Directed by Tim Eldred. Written by Jeffrey Scott, Bob Carrau, Lane Raichert, James Greenberg.

Another quintet of adventures with Emmy, Max, and their dragon friends are included on this DVD: "Quetzal's Magic Pop-Up Book"; "The Fury Is Out On This One"; "Much Ado About Nodlings"; "Four Little Pigs"; and "Quibbling Siblings."

SPECIAL FEATURES Sing-Alongs • Other Title Trailers TECHNICAL FEATURES Fullscreen (1.33:1) • Subtitles/CC: Eng., Fren., Span. • Languages: Eng., Span. dub • Sound: Dolby Digital 2.0 • Keepcase • 1 Disc • Region 1, 3, 4 GENRE & RATING Dragons/Kids • Not Rated (All Ages)

Dragon Tales: Don't Give Up [#3]

Columbia/TriStar, 2002, 69 mins., #08090. Directed by Tim Eldred. Written by Jeffrey Scott, Bob Carrau, Mark Hoffmeier, Alicia Marie Schudt, Robert Schechter, Cliff Ruby, Elana Lesser.

Five more educational and entertaining dragon adventures include: "Pigment of Your Imagination"; "Backwards to Forwards"; "Sand Castle Hassle"; "Tails You Lose"; and "Bully for You."

SPECIAL FEATURES Sing-Alongs • Other Title Trailers TECHNICAL FEATURES Fullscreen (1.33:1) • Subtitles/CC: Eng., Fren., Span. • Languages: Eng., Span. dub • Sound: Dolby Digital Surround 2.0 • Keepcase • 1 Disc • Region 1, 3, 4 GENRE & RATING Dragons/Kids • Not Rated (All Ages)

Dragon Tales

The following Dragon Tales titles, from Columbia/TriStar, were not available for review: *It's Cool To Be Me!*; *Let's Stick To It!*; *Yes We Can!*

Dual: Parallel Trouble Adventure—Visions [#1]

Pioneer, 1999, 100 mins., #10398. Directed by Katsuhito Akiyama. Screenplay by Yosuke Kuroda, Hideki Shirane, Takashi Kobayashi. Based on the manga series by Masaki Kajishima in *Monthly Dragon Jr*.

Kazuki Yogutsa is a normal school kid whose mind is full of visions of giant robots fighting. When he gets sucked into a parallel Earth by a mad scientist, Kazuki discovers his visions are real. Soon, he's fighting as a Core Robot Pilot and getting the girls—alien and human both. It's robot fighting to the hilt! Joining him as a robot pilot on the Earth Defense Command is the scientist's original-Earth daughter, Mitsuki Sanada, who has also crossed over into the parallel Earth to fight the villainous forces of Rara.

This 1999 television series is a slickly made product, but its settings and plot all seem borrowed from anime such as *Neon Genesis Evangelion* and others. Still, the basic plot is enjoyable, and the show manages to be sexy at times without being vulgar (though there is some horny humor from Dr. Sanada and a bit of cross-dressing). The art is fairly simple, smooth, and uncluttered, and many of the robot sequences are done with CGI animation. There is some gentle humor as well.

The DVD contains the first four episodes: "Life Sympathy"; "My Home"; "Illegal Guy"; and "No Disguise." The first release included a window sticker of Mitsuki Sanada.

SPECIAL FEATURES Character Bios • Character and Art Galleries • Clean Credits • Insert: Recipe • Easter Egg TECHNICAL FEATURES Fullscreen (1.33:1) • Subtitles/CC: Eng. • Languages: Jap., Eng. dub • Sound: Dolby Digital 2.0 • Keepcase • 1 Disc • Region 1, 4 GENRE & RATING Robots/Adventure • Rated 13+

Dual: Parallel Trouble Adventure—Student Housing [#2]

Pioneer, 1999, 75 mins., #10399. Directed by Katsuhito Akiyama. Screenplay by Matsumi Nakano, Hideki Shirane, Takashi Kobayashi. Based on the manga series by Masaki Kajishima in *Monthly Dragon Jr*.

Now living with the Sanadas, Kazuki is rattled when a pretty girl named D moves in, while another girl moves in next door. Things get tense when Rara prepares to crash a robot into the airport, and Mitzuki and Kazuki must stop it.

This DVD contains the second set of three episodes: "Campus Life"; "Intrigue"; and "Hard Case." The initial release included another window sticker of Mitsuki Sanada.

SPECIAL FEATURES Character Bios • Character and Art Galleries • Insert: Recipe • Easter Egg TECHNICAL FEATURES Fullscreen (1.33:1) • Subtitles/CC: Eng. • Languages: Jap., Eng. dub • Sound: Dolby Digital 2.0 • Keepcase • 1 Disc • Region 1, 4 GENRE & RATING Robots/Adventure • Rated 13+

Dual: Parallel Trouble Adventure—Artifacts [#3]

Pioneer, 1999, 75 mins., #10400. Directed by Katsuhito Akiyama. Screenplay by Yosuke Kuroda, Matsumi Nakano, Hideki Shirane. Based on the manga series by Masaki Kajishima in *Monthly Dragon Jr*.

Downed behind enemy lines, Kazuki is taken in by Miss Rah and nursed back to health, only to find out that she is this world's version of a familiar face! She dotes on Kazuki, and even in the midst of occupied territory, he begins to feel like things can change for the better. But then he meets her parents—the villainous Rara and his evil wife!

The trio of episodes on this DVD ratchet up the tension: "Mitsuki"; "Escape"; and "Repatriate." The initial release included a window sticker of Miss Rah.

SPECIAL FEATURES Character Bios • Character and Art Galleries • Trailers • Promotional Footage • Insert: Recipe • Easter Eggs TECHNICAL FEATURES Fullscreen (1.33:1) • Subtitles/CC: Eng. • Languages: Jap., Eng. dub • Sound: Dolby Digital 2.0 • Keepcase • 1 Disc • Region 1, 4 GENRE & RATING Robots/Adventure • Rated 13+

Dual: Parallel Trouble Adventure—One Vision [#4]

Pioneer, 1999, 100 mins., #10401. Directed by Katsuhito Akiyama. Screenplay by Takashi Kobayashi, Matsumi Nakano, Yosuke Kuroda. Based on the manga series by Masaki Kajishima in *Monthly Dragon Jr*.

Kazuki and Mitsuki make it back to the real world, but Kazuki returns to the second Earth only to discover that Rara's army has won the battle and enslaved the world. Now, the barrier between the parallel Earths is breaking down, and to stabilize the dimensions, either the robot technology must be destroyed or Kazuki must die!

This final DVD contains the last four *Dual* episodes: "Real!"; "Ardent Desire"; "The World"; and "Final Frontier." The fourteenth episode was never broadcast on TV, but was an exclusive part of the laserdisc, video, and DVD releases. The initial release of this disc also included another window sticker of Mitsuki Sanada.

SPECIAL FEATURES Character Bios • Character and Art Galleries • Voice Actor Clips • Insert: Recipe • Easter Eggs TECHNICAL FEATURES Fullscreen (1.33:1) • Subtitles/CC: Eng. • Languages: Jap., Eng. dub • Sound: Dolby Digital 2.0 • Keepcase • 1 Disc • Region 1, 4 GENRE & RATING Robots/Adventure • Rated 13+

Dumbo [60th Anniversary Edition]

Disney, 2001, 64 mins., #21615. Directed by Ben Sharpsteen. Story by Helen Aberson, Harold Pearl, Joe Grant, Dick Huemer.

Circus entertainer Mrs. Jumbo is about to have a baby elephant, and when the stork makes his delivery, she names it Jumbo. The babe is adorable, except for its giant-sized ears, which quickly make the poor creature an object of the other elephant's scorn (they call him "Dumbo" instead). Dumbo becomes a part of the circus, but tragedy shadows the big top when his mother goes berserk upon seeing Dumbo's mistreatment by children. Later, with the help of Timothy Mouse, Dumbo learns to use his ears to fly. The circus will never be the same.

This 1941 film is Disney's shortest feature, but it is also one of the most beloved by critics and fans alike. Audiences young and old can relate to Dumbo's feelings of being different, as well as the joy he feels when he discovers his true talent. The hallucinatory "Pink Elephants on Parade" number is astonishing, and even the hardest-hearted Grinch will cry during Mrs. Jumbo's "Baby Mine" lullaby.

Dumbo is given a deluxe restoration on this DVD, as well as a plethora of extras, including audio commentary by animation historian John Canemaker, and lots of behind-the-scenes materials. The disc also features a preview of the now-in-production film *Dumbo II*, and two Disney animated shorts: "The Flying Mouse" (1934) and "Elmer Elephant" (1936). Be sure to buy this disc while you can; it belongs in every animation fan's library.

SPECIAL FEATURES "Making of" Featurette • Commentary Track • Character and Art Galleries • Sound Design Featurette • Storybook • Theatrical Trailer • Promotional Footage • Music Video • Sing-Alongs • Vintage Intro by Walt Disney • Other Title Trailers • DVD-ROM Features TECHNICAL FEATURES Fullscreen (1.33:1) • Subtitles/CC: Eng. • Languages: Eng., Fren. dub, Span. dub • Sound: Dolby Digital Surround 5.1 • Keepcase • 1 Disc • Region 1 GENRE & RATING Animal/Family/Music • Rated G

E

Earthian: Angelic Collection

AnimeWorks, 2001, 150 mins., #AWDVD-0194. Directed by Toshiyasu Kogawa, Tomoya Asano. Written by Toshiyasu Kogawa, Hiroyuki Kawasaki, Katsuhiko Takayama. Based on the manga series by Yun Koga.

Two angels have come to Earth from Planet Eden to judge humanity. The white-winged angel is Kagetsuya, the angel of vengeance, while the black-winged angel is Chihaya, an angel of compassion. As they explore humanity, as well as face biohumanoids, psychics, and corrupted angels, the true purpose of their mission becomes less clear.

Filled with lots of pretty men, flowing hair, and angel wings, *Earthian* is a slightly schizophrenic affair. The first two episodes on this DVD are from 1989, while the second pair are from 1996, and the stories jump all over the place. Viewers may be left unsure exactly where this is all leading, even up to the final episode.

SPECIAL FEATURES Interview with Creator Yun Koga • Art Gallery TECHNICAL FEATURES Fullscreen (1.33:1) • Subtitles/CC: Eng. • Languages: Jap., Eng. dub • Sound: Dolby Digital 2.0 • Keepcase • 1 Disc • Region 1 GENRE & RATING Fantasy/Science Fiction • Rated 13+

Easter in Bunnyland

Delta Entertainment, 2001, 49 mins., #82125. Animation Directed by Susan Beak, Geoff Beak. Story by Roddy Lee, Roz Phillips. Screenplay by Leonard Lee.

The Easter Bunny has been kidnapped by the evil Beau Rat and J.J., and it's up to his young friends Flip, Buck, and Bitsy Bunny to help rescue him, or Easter will have to be canceled.

Another feature from Australia's Burbank Animation, this is a cute story for the younger set, but its simplistic animation style and ultrapastel color palette will leave older viewers wanting something more substantial.

SPECIAL FEATURES None TECHNICAL FEATURES Fullscreen (1.33:1) • Languages: Eng. • Sound: Dolby Digital 2.0 • Keepcase • 1 Disc • Region All GENRE & RATING Holiday/Animals • Not Rated (All Ages)

Eat Man '98

Bandai/Pioneer, 2000, 3000 mins.

This two-disc DVD set was not available for review. It is out of print.

EL ☞ see Mature/Adult Section

Elf Princess Rane

AnimeWorks, 2001, 60 mins., #AWDV-0105. Directed by Heitaro Daichi. Script by Taishi Yamazaki.

NOTE: This DVD arrived too late for a full review. The following text is promotional copy provided by the releasing company:

"Go Takarada, an enthusiastic young treasure hunter, he has always dreamed of big adventure. When he meets the Elf Princess named Rane, he gets one! He and Rane have an unfortunate language barrier of titanic proportions. He charges onward, blissfully unaware that his quest is actually totally different than what he thinks!"

SPECIAL FEATURES Character and Art Galleries • Other Title Trailers TECHNICAL FEATURES Fullscreen (1.33:1) • Subtitles/CC: Eng. • Languages: Jap., Eng. dub • Sound: Dolby Digital 2.0 • Keepcase • 1 Disc • Region 1 GENRE & RATING Fantasy/Girls/Adventure • Rated 13+

El Hazard: The Alternative World—The Priestess of Water [#1]

Pioneer, 1999, 100 mins., #PIDA-1588V. Directed by Yasuhito Kikuchi. Screenplay by Akihiro Yamada, Hiroshi Yamaguchi.

Schoolboy Makoto, his friend Nanami, their teacher Mr. Fujisawa, and a few others had already been transported to another world from Earth once. Now, during a coronation ceremony in El Hazard for the new High Priestess of Water, Makato and the others are transported to a new alternate world known as Creteria. There, some of the characters are mistaken for sky goddesses, and other fantastic entities, and they come up against the mysterious Arjah, ruler of the universe.

With a setting that combines high adventure and fantasy with comedy, the *El Hazard* series is very popular with both Japanese and American audiences. The plots are generally very detailed, with smooth and exciting visuals. *El Hazard: The Alternative World* is the third in the line (see *El Hazard: The Magnificent World* and *The Wanderers: El Hazard*), representing a 1997 TV series. This series was not as popular as its predecessors, largely due to some shallow characterization and a sense of "been there, done that" to the story. Still, it's largely entertaining, though fans may want to watch the earlier series first to keep track of the characters. This DVD features the first four of thirteen episodes and brightly colored lively animation.

SPECIAL FEATURES Clean Credits TECHNICAL FEATURES Fullscreen (1.33:1) • Subtitles/CC: Eng. • Languages: Jap., Eng. dub • Sound: Dolby Digital 2.0 • Keepcase • 1 Disc • Region 1, 4 GENRE & RATING Fantasy/Adventure • Rated 13+

El Hazard: The Alternative World—The Spring of Life [#2]

Pioneer, 1999, 75 mins., #PIDA-1589V. Directed by Yasuhito Kikuchi. Screenplay by Akihiro Yamada, Hideki Mitsui.

Miz, Fujisawa, and Afura meet up with a farmer who is connected to Princess Rune Venus, while Makoto tries to find the secret of the Spring of Life, which could rejuvenate the kingdom and send him back home to Earth. Creteria's ruler, Dall Narciss, is infatuated with Water Priestess Qawoor, and he enlists Nanami's help to woo her. Love is also in the air for Fatora, who falls for Lady Gilda, the head of Creteria's militia, but a case of mistaken identity could cause problems. And Parnasse and Alielle run amok in the city.

This DVD contains episodes #5–7.

SPECIAL FEATURES None TECHNICAL FEATURES Fullscreen (1.33:1) • Subtitles/CC: Eng. • Languages: Jap., Eng. dub • Sound: Dolby Digital 2.0 • Keepcase • 1 Disc • Region 1, 4 GENRE & RATING Fantasy/Adventure • Rated 13+

El Hazard: The Alternative World—Ruler of the Universe! [#3]

Pioneer, 1999, 75 mins., #PIDA-1590V. Directed by Yasuhito Kikuchi. Screenplay by Akihiro Yamada.

A planned coup by Lady Gilda leads to an alliance with the villainous Jinnai against Dall Narciss. They blackmail Qawoor and Shayla-Shayla into breaking the seal on the Spring of Life, but the results aren't what anyone expected. Gilda's secret history with the Emperor is revealed, and Makoto is caught between several women who love him. Plus, more about the mystery of the Eye of God, and Arjah, ruler of the universe, is coming.

This DVD contains episodes #8–10.

SPECIAL FEATURES Humorous Audio Clips "Jinnai Rants!" TECHNICAL FEATURES Fullscreen (1.33:1) • Subtitles/CC: Eng. • Languages: Jap., Eng. dub • Sound: Dolby Digital 2.0 • Keepcase • 1 Disc • Region 1, 4 GENRE & RATING Fantasy/Adventure • Rated 13+

El Hazard: The Alternative World—Dreams of Tomorrow [#4]

Pioneer, 1999, 75 mins., #PIDA-1591V. Directed by Yasuhito Kikuchi. Screenplay by Akihiro Yamada.

Gilda and Makoto discover the secrets behind the Spring of Life, but when the password is spoken, disaster descends upon the floating colonies and farmlands! Now, all the characters will have to choose their alliances before Arjah and his helpers destroy Creteria. But even if they're victorious, will they make it back to the first Alternate World or Earth?

This DVD contains episodes #11–13. Oddly, the final episode was not originally aired in Japan, though it was later released on video.

SPECIAL FEATURES Art Galleries • Clean Credits TECHNICAL FEATURES Fullscreen (1.33:1) • Subtitles/CC: Eng. • Languages: Jap., Eng. dub • Sound: Dolby Digital 2.0 • Keepcase • 1 Disc • Region 1, 4 GENRE & RATING Fantasy/Adventure • Rated 13+

El Hazard: The Magnificent World [DVD Box Set]

Pioneer, 1999, 245 mins., #10405. Directed by Hiroki Hayashi, Yoshiaka Iwasaki. Screenplay by Ryoei Tsukimura, Kazuhisa Onishi, Mitsuhiro Yamada.

Three high school students—Makoto, his female pursuer Nanami, and his enemy Katsuhiko Jinnai—are transported to an alternate world along with their (usually drunken) teacher Mr. Fujisawa. There, they find themselves embroiled in adventures full of magic and menace, with lost technology, an army of sentient bugs, water priestesses, missing princesses, and more. In El Hazard, Princess Rune Venus enlists the help of Makoto and Fujisawa to retrieve three priestesses and help the kingdom of Roshtaria against the Bugrom Empire gain control of the floating super-weapon known as "The Eye of God." But Jinnai has already allied himself with the Bugrom and their queen, Diva, and determines a path to take over all of El Hazard! And behind the scenes, the Phantom Tribe may be manipulating all of the players against each other.

This multidisc set collects the original 1995 seven-episode OVA series on two discs and 1997's four-episode OVA second series on the third disc. Though the follow-up wasn't as well liked, the original stories made the series very popular with fans, as the characters, designs, and plots were new, imaginative, and funny. Two TV series with the *El Hazard* characters were also produced and are available on DVD (see *El Hazard: The Alternative World* and *The Wanderers: El Hazard*). The series contains a strong lesbian subplot, as well as cross-dressing. The dub tracks are particularly nice and considered by many fans to be among the best dubs ever recorded. The DVDs contain nice prints of the pretty and detailed animation, while the box and foldout sleeves are gorgeously produced.

SPECIAL FEATURES Character and Art Galleries • Geographical Features • Clean Credits • Other Title Trailers • Easter Eggs TECHNICAL FEATURES Fullscreen (1.33:1) • Subtitles/CC: Eng. • Languages: Jap., Eng. dub • Sound: Dolby Digital 2.0 • Foldout Box with 3 Discs and Slipcase • 3 Discs • Region 1 GENRE & RATING Fantasy/Adventure • Rated 13+

Elm-Chanted Forest, The

Image, #ID5697PZDVD. Directed by Milan Blazekovic. Screenplay by Fred P. Sharkey.

This DVD was not available for review.

Emperor's New Clothes, The

Delta Entertainment, 2001, 41 mins., #82102. Animation directed by Richard Slapczynski. Story by Peter Jennings. Screenplay by Leonard Lee. Based on the story by Hans Christian Andersen.

Emperor Louis is the vain monarch who loves his clothes, making him an easy mark for two "master tailors" who make him an exquisite set of invisible clothes for his birthday. But the tailors are swindlers, and the Emperor is embarrassed when he parades in public dressed in only his underwear. When a brave little girl tells the Emperor he's not really wearing any clothes, the monarch learns a valuable lesson and saves his own birthday celebration from ruin.

Produced by Australia's Burbank Animation, this features dull animation and flat backgrounds, though with some of the flaws it is difficult to tell if they're in the work itself or in the transfer to DVD. Kids will like it, and it has a good message that what's inside is more important than what one wears. This DVD was also part of the *Hans Christian Andersen: Fairy Tale Classics Boxed Set.*

SPECIAL FEATURES None TECHNICAL FEATURES Fullscreen (1.33:1) • Languages: Eng. • Sound: Dolby Digital 2.0 • Keepcase • 1 Disc • Region All GENRE & RATING Comedy/Fantasy • Not Rated (All Ages)

Emperor's New Clothes, The: 30th Anniversary Edition

Sony Wonder, 2002, 60 mins., #LVD 54259. Directed by Arthur Rankin, Jr., Jules Bass. Written by Romeo Muller. Based on the story by Hans Christian Andersen.

NOTE: This DVD arrived too late for a full review. The following text is promotional copy provided by the releasing company:

"Emperor Klonkenlocker of Bibbentucker is the best-dressed man in the land, and has offered one million grinklens to the winning tailor for the Emperor's new clothes. Marmaduke and his loyal partner Musty decide that becoming tailors will enhance their chances to win the competition. First premiering on ABC as a network special in February 1972, *The Enchanted World of Danny Kaye* stars Danny as the character Marmaduke telling the classic story of a magical musical adaptation of Hans Christian Andersen's *The Emperor's New Clothes.*

"Filmed in live action from a small town in Denmark, Danny sings and tells the story surrounded by children. This one-of-a-kind Rankin and Bass production features live action, cel animation, and 'Animagic,' the studio's trademark stop-motion animation technique."

Note that although the disc cover claims it is closed captioned, it is not.

SPECIAL FEATURES "Making of" Featurette TECHNICAL FEATURES Fullscreen (1.33:1) • Languages: Eng. • Sound: Dolby Digital • Keepcase • 1 Disc • Region 1 GENRE & RATING Music/Fantasy/Family • Not Rated (All Ages)

Emperor's New Groove, The

Disney, 2001, 77 mins., #21617. Directed by Mark Dindal. Story by Chris Williams and Mark Dindal. Screenplay by David Reynolds.

Emperor Kuzco is a self-centered jerk who plans to build his summer home atop a mountain overlook that is already home to Pancha, Pancha's family, and other village peasants. After Kuzco's evil advisor Yzma turns him into a llama so she can usurp the throne, Kuzco must rely Pancha to return to the city from the wilderness and find a way to restore his true form. But if Kuzco regains the throne, will he still demolish Pancha's home?

Although the genesis of this 2000 feature film was convoluted, and much of it was reworked during the process, the resulting film is sly, silly, and a lot of fun. Superb voice work by David Spade, John Goodman, Eartha Kitt, and Patrick Warburton (who plays Yzma's dimwitted assistant) brings the characters a modern feel, even though the story takes place in ancient South America. The animation on the film is stylistically goofy, incorporating Mayan and Aztec motifs into more traditional Disney designs. The film didn't do as well as most Disney films in the theaters (perhaps audiences hated the idea of David Spade getting work as much as this author did), but it deserves to get an audience on DVD.

SPECIAL FEATURES "Making of" Featurettes • Commentary Track by Director and Production Team • Deleted Scenes • Music Videos • Games • DVD-ROM Features: Games • Other Title Trailers TECHNICAL FEATURES Widescreen (1.66:1 enhanced for 16x9)• Fullscreen (1.33:1)• Subtitles/CC: Eng. • Languages: Eng., Fren. dub • Sound: Dolby Digital Surround 5.1, DTS • Keepcase • 1 Disc • Region 1 GENRE & RATING Comedy/Historical • Rated G

Emperor's New Groove, The: The Ultimate Groove [2-Disc Collector's Edition]

Disney, 2001, 77 mins., #22311. Directed by Mark Dindal. Story by Chris Willllams and Mark Dindal. Screenplay by David Reynolds.

Once again, Disney pulls out all the stops for this two-DVD set, which contains the feature film plus a huge number of extras. The commentary

track by the director, producer, and multiple department heads is a heady exploration about exactly how a film with a genesis so dark and moody can end up so bright and funny. Two track levels take you in separate-but-convergent directions; "The Studio Groove" showcases the entire process of making the film, while "The Animation Groove" uses split-screen comparisons and other techniques to show the stages in progress.

Although it doesn't spotlight all the behind-the-scenes drama, the discs do show some of the deleted and excised footage that was cut when *Groove* was retooled. Fortunately, none of the additional Sting songs recorded for the feature are included. It will take hours to go through all the supplementals in this package, so fans of that material will find it here (excuse the pun) in spades.

SPECIAL FEATURES "Making of" Featurettes • Commentary Track • Character and Art Galleries • Production Notes • Deleted Scenes and Abandoned Sequences • Storyboards • Story Treatment • Trailers • Promotional Footage • Music Video • Games • DVD-ROM Features: Games, Online Content • Other Title Trailers • Inserts: Liner Notes • Easter Eggs TECHNICAL FEATURES Widescreen (1.66:1 enhanced for 16x9) • Fullscreen (1.33:1)• Subtitles/CC: Eng. • Languages: Eng., Fren. dub • Sound: Dolby Digital Surround 5.1, DTS • Multisnapcase • 2 Discs • Region 1 GENRE & RATING Comedy/Historical • Rated G

Enchanted Crayon, The #1

Facets, 2002.

This DVD was not available for review.

Enchanted Crayon, The #2

Facets, 2002.

This DVD was not available for review.

Enchanted Tales: An Easter Bunny Adventure

Sony, 2002, 48 mins.

This DVD was not available for review.

Escaflowne: Dragons and Destiny [#1]

Bandai, 2000, 100 mins., #0430. Directed by Kazuki Akane. Written by Hajime Yatate, Shoji Kawamori, Ryota Yamaguchi, Akihiko Inari.

Hitomi Kanzaki, a high school girl, is whisked away through arcane means to the medieval realm of Gaea by Van Fanel, a swordsman who saves her from a dragon. On Gaea, Hitomi learns to help Van control a mecha suit of armor known as "Escaflowne." They're going to need the suit's firepower to help them survive, since Gaea is being torn apart by a colossal war and Van's kingdom of Fanelia is threatened. They're soon opposed by Dilandau's forces, and the other mecha suits known as "guymelefs," each powered by the crystallized heart of a dragon! Other cast members include Merle, a catgirl who is overly protective of Van, Allen Schezar, a knight of Asturia, and the villains Folken and Emperor Dornkirk.

As seen on Fox Kids in an edited form, *Escaflowne* is an extremely popular fantasy series that features some absolutely wonderful character designs and a nice mixture of CGI and traditional animation, mostly in muted, natural colors. Yuko Kanno, who also worked on *Cowboy Bebop,* produces another great soundtrack here. This DVD contains the first four episodes of the series. Viewers should be warned that some of the music videos contain plot spoilers.

SPECIAL FEATURES Music Video • Other Title Trailers • Clean Credits • Inserts: Liner Notes • Easter Egg TECHNICAL FEATURES Fullscreen (1.33:1)• Subtitles/CC: Eng. • Languages: Jap., Eng. dub • Sound: Dolby Digital Surround 2.0 • Keepcase • 1 Disc • Region 1 GENRE & RATING Fantasy/Adventure • Rated 13+

Escaflowne: Betrayal and Trust [#2]

Bandai, 2000, 75 mins., #0431. Directed by Kazuki Akane. Written by Hiroaki Kitajima, Ryota Yamaguchi, Akihiko Inari.

Zaibach's forces are marching across Gaea, spreading destruction, and now Van has been captured by Dilandau's troops. Hitomi and Allen mount a rescue mission based on visions that Hitomi has of Van's impending doom. Later, Allen learns that the kingdom he is defending has already been betrayed from within, an arranged marriage may lead to trouble, and the truth about Van's origins.

This DVD contains episodes #5–8. The lead extra feature for this disc is called "Club Escaflowne," and in it the Japanese voice actors for the series participate in a live-action segment in which they "interview" each other. Bandai does have a spoiler warning on this segment, which gives away secrets almost up to the end of the series.

SPECIAL FEATURES "Club Escaflowne" Live Segment • Other Title Trailers • Inserts: Liner Notes TECHNICAL FEATURES Fullscreen (1.33:1)• Subtitles/CC: Eng. • Languages: Jap., Eng. dub • Sound: Dolby Digital Surround 2.0 • Keepcase • 1 Disc • Region 1 GENRE & RATING Fantasy/Adventure • Rated 13+

Escaflowne: Angels and Demons [#3]

Bandai, 2000, 75 mins., #0432. Directed by Kazuki Akane. Written by Ryota Yamaguchi, Hiroaki Kitajima.

Hitomi's powers give her a glimpse into Van's past and the background of the Fanel family. Later, Van, Hitomi, and Merle are discovered by the guymelefs, and Allen is hurt trying to stop Zaibach from capturing Escaflowne. Folken sends a doppelganger assassin to kill a captured Zaibach guymelef pilot. Plus, who is the Prince Child, ruler of Freid, and what is his connection to Allen? And a prophecy of death comes true.

Not quite halfway through the series, this disc collects episodes #9–11. It also features another humorous interview segment with cast members.

SPECIAL FEATURES "Club Escaflowne" Live Segment • Other Title Trailers • Inserts: Liner Notes TECHNICAL FEATURES Fullscreen (1.33:1)• Subtitles/CC: Eng. • Languages: Jap., Eng. dub • Sound: Dolby Digital Surround 2.0 • Keepcase • 1 Disc • Region 1 GENRE & RATING Fantasy/Adventure • Rated 13+

Escaflowne: Past and Present [#4]

Bandai, 2000, 75 mins., #0433. Directed by Kazuki Akane. Written by Ryota Yamaguchi, Akihiko Inari, Hiroaki Kitajima.

The Duke of Fried returns to discover the trouble his son has wrought, but Folken and his armies are invading Fried anyhow, on a search for a dragon and more power. As scores of guymelefs ready for battle, tension builds. Princess Millerna learns a shocking secret about her daughter and nephew, while a link is found to ancient Atlantis, and Van's relationship with Escaflowne deepens. Dilandau faces loss, while a new power in the land shows up: Dryden, a man whose workers can "heal" mecha—even the damaged Escaflowne.

This DVD contains episodes #12–14. The "Club Escaflowne" segment switches from cast member interviews to staff and crew interviews.

SPECIAL FEATURES "Club Escaflowne" Live Segment • Other Title Trailers • Inserts: Liner Notes • Easter Egg TECHNICAL FEATURES Fullscreen (1.33:1)• Subtitles/CC: Eng. • Languages: Jap., Eng. dub • Sound: Dolby Digital Surround 2.0 • Keepcase • 1 Disc • Region 1 GENRE & RATING Fantasy/Adventure • Rated 13+

Escaflowne: Paradise and Pain [#5]

Bandai, 2000, 75 mins., #0434. Directed by Kazuki Akane. Written by Ryota Yamaguchi, Akihiko Inari.

Escaflowne is defeated and Van hovers between life and death, but that doesn't stop his enemies from pursuing him, including ghosts of those he's killed in the past, as well as Folken and his duo of catgirl minions. Hitomi finds out that one of her own ancestors crossed over from Gaea to Earth, and Allen's father's legacy catches up with him. And when Dryden finds the location to Atlantis, everything may change. . . .

This disc contains episodes #15–17, plus more staff and crew interviews at "Club Escaflowne."

SPECIAL FEATURES "Club Escaflowne" Live Segment • Other Title Trailers • Inserts: Liner Notes TECHNICAL FEATURES Fullscreen (1.33:1)• Subtitles/CC: Eng. • Languages: Jap., Eng. dub • Sound: Dolby Digital Surround 2.0 • Keepcase • 1 Disc • Region 1 GENRE & RATING Fantasy/Adventure • Rated 13+

Escaflowne: Fate and Fortune [#6]

Bandai, 2000, 75 mins., #0435. Directed by Kazuki Akane. Written by Akihiko Inari, Ryota Yamaguchi.

When Hitomi, Allen, and Van finally come face-to-face with Zaibach Emperor Dornkirk, the meeting—and his plan for Gaea—isn't quite what they expected. Meanwhile, a marriage is soon to occur to bring unity to the land, but Hitomi's tarot reading reveals ominous future tidings and an invasion is about to begin.

This fast-paced volume contains episodes #18–20, plus more staff and crew interviews at "Club Escaflowne."

SPECIAL FEATURES "Club Escaflowne" Live Segment • Other Title Trailers • Inserts: Liner Notes TECHNICAL FEATURES Fullscreen (1.33:1)• Subtitles/CC: Eng. • Languages: Jap., Eng. dub • Sound: Dolby Digital Surround 2.0 • Keepcase • 1 Disc • Region 1 GENRE & RATING Fantasy/Adventure • Rated 13+

Escaflowne: Light and Shadow [#7]

Bandai, 2000, 75 mins., #0436. Directed by Kazuki Akane. Written by Hiroaki Kitajima, Ryota Yamaguchi, Akihiko Inari.

Hitomi is captured by Folken's catgirls, but she learns more about their backgrounds and motivations. Van and Folken meet in some ruins where they are set upon by dragons and dark memories. Hitomi, Van, and Allen

begin to explore their true feelings for each other, and Van faces Dilandu in a savage battle.

This penultimate DVD contains episodes #21–23, plus the final set of staff and crew interviews at "Club Escaflowne."

SPECIAL FEATURES "Club Escaflowne" Live Segment • Other Title Trailers • Inserts: Liner Notes TECHNICAL FEATURES Fullscreen (1.33:1)• Subtitles/CC: Eng. • Languages: Jap., Eng. dub • Sound: Dolby Digital Surround 2.0 • Keepcase • 1 Disc • Region 1 GENRE & RATING Fantasy/Adventure • Rated 13+

Escaflowne: Forever and Ever [#8]

Bandai, 2000, 75 mins., #0437. Directed by Kazuki Akane. Written by Hiroaki Kitajima, Akihiko Inari, Ryota Yamaguchi.

Hitomi makes a fateful decision that could save her life but doom Gaea. On the other world, the war rages on, with the Doomsday Weapon coming into play. Friends turn on friends, enemies may be saviors, and a dragon and a mystic girl may hold the answer to the fate of the land.

The final DVD features episodes #24–26, as well as a peek at the *Escaflowne* movie.

SPECIAL FEATURES Music Video: Concert • Playstation Game Footage • Other Title Trailers • Inserts: Liner Notes • Easter Eggs TECHNICAL FEATURES Fullscreen (1.33:1)• Subtitles/CC: Eng. • Languages: Jap., Eng. dub • Sound: Dolby Digital Surround 2.0 • Keepcase • 1 Disc • Region 1 GENRE & RATING Fantasy/Adventure • Rated 13+

Escaflowne: The Movie—Ultimate Edition [Box Set]

Bandai, 2002, 166 mins., #0437. Directed by Kazuki Akane. Screenplay by Ryota Yamaguchi, Kazuke Akane .

Hitomi Kanzaki is a depressed high school girl who is pulled into the medieval realm of Gaea. There, she is heralded as the "Wing Goddess," who supposedly can summon Escaflowne. She soon finds herself caught up in the battles of roguish young warrior Van, as he fights to avenge his fallen kingdom against the Black Dragon Clan. Other familiar characters appear including Lord Folken, Dilandau, Merle, and Allen. The storyline for the movie is similar to the series in its basic building blocks, though not the same in its execution. The animation is gorgeous, with less anime stylization and yet, at the same time, a more Far Eastern feel.

Released theatrically in Japan in 2000, *Escaflowne: The Movie* gets a beautiful treatment in this deluxe set. The main disc features the movie, as well as an insert-screen realtime storyboard track and an isolated score audio track. The second disc offers a variety of extras, most of which are interviews and premiere footage (from both the Japanese and American premieres). The third disc is the complete soundtrack on CD, with twenty-five tracks (including five vocal selections).

For those who liked the original *Escaflowne*, here's the bigger, bolder, more beautiful, pumped-up version. Not a remake, but a reimagining.

SPECIAL FEATURES Cast and Crew Interviews • Character, Weapons, and Vehicles Art Galleries • Storyboards • Trailer • Promotional Footage • Isolated Score • Premiere Footage • Other Title Trailers • Inserts: Booklet, Production Notes, Song Lyrics TECHNICAL FEATURES Widescreen (1.85:1) • Subtitles/CC: Eng. • Languages: Jap., Eng. dub • Sound: Dolby Digital Surround 5.1, DTS • Cardboard Box with 3 Keepcases • 3 Discs • Region 1 GENRE & RATING Fantasy/Adventure • Rated PG-13

Evil Toons ☞ see Mature/Adult Section

Evolution: The Animated Movie

Trimark, 2002, 60 mins., #VM7877D. Written by Michael Ryan.

After defeating the alien menace once, Dr. Ira Kane and his eccentric crew expected a little bit of downtime. Unfortunately, a new outerspace menace has arrived, and it's out for revenge. Using a bloodhound-like alien named Gassie to help them track their enemy, Kane and his gang of Alienators set out to save Earth one more time.

Three episodes of *Evolution: The Animated Series* are presented here as a "movie." The TV series spun off from the 2001 live-action film starring David Duchovny and Julianne Moore. None of the film actors have reprised their roles vocally, and while the animation is clean-cut and pleasant, the product isn't much funnier or more entertaining than the feature, which bombed with audiences. Kids will probably like the DVD though, as it is pseudohip and full of corny one-liners, big monsters, and slime.

SPECIAL FEATURES Game TECHNICAL FEATURES Fullscreen (1.33:1) • Subtitles/CC: Eng. • Languages: Eng. • Sound: Dolby Digital 2.0 • Keepcase • 1 Disc • Region 1 GENRE & RATING Science Fiction/Comedy • Rated 6+

Excel Saga ☞ see Mature/Adult Section

Ex-Driver #1: Downshift

AnimeWorks, 2002, 90 mins., # AWDVD-0222. Directed by Jun Kawagoe. Screenplay by Shinzo Fujita. Story by Kosuke Fujishima.

NOTE: This DVD arrived too late for a full review. The following text is promotional copy provided by the releasing company:

"The cars are hot but the girls are hotter! Pull over, highway patrol. Lorna Endou and Lisa Sakakino have eX-Driver licenses, assigned only to the best of the best. They are authorized to drive fast, drive recklessly, and hunt down malfunctioning AI-controlled cars that endanger the populace. With tricked-out cars and tricked-out moves, Lorna and Lisa rule the road!"

This disc contains episodes #1–3. The menu is nearly impossible to navigate. Note that the DVD cover says the screenwriter is Kenichi Hamazaki, but the onscreen credit is for Shinzo Fujita.

SPECIAL FEATURES "Making of" Featurette • Interviews with Crew • Clean Credits • Other Title Trailers • Easter Eggs TECHNICAL FEATURES Fullscreen (1.33:1) • Subtitles/CC: Eng. • Languages: Jap., Eng. dub • Sound: Dolby Digital • Keepcase • 1 Disc • Region 1 GENRE & RATING Racing/Adventure • Rated 13+

Ex-Driver #2: Crossroads

AnimeWorks, 2002, 90 mins., #AWDVD-0230. Directed by Jun Kawagoe. Screenplay by Shinzo Fujita. Story by Kosuke Fujishima.

NOTE: This DVD arrived too late for a full review. The following text is promotional copy provided by the releasing company:

"Lorna and Lisa ride again! In the near future, automated cars are standard, and most citizens don't even know how to drive. The eX-Drivers were created to stop malfunctioning AI cars, but their latest threat is something new. An unknown terrorist is controlling cars by remote, trashing the city and seriously injuring Lisa! Will the other eX-Drivers be able to defeat the mysterious driver without her?"

This disc contains episodes #4–6. The menu is nearly impossible to navigate.

SPECIAL FEATURES "Making of" Featurette • Interviews with Crew • Clean Credits • Promotional Footage • Other Title Trailers TECHNICAL FEATURES Fullscreen (1.33:1) • Subtitles/CC: Eng. • Languages: Jap., Eng. dub • Sound: Dolby Digital • Keepcase • 1 Disc • Region 1 GENRE & RATING Racing/Adventure • Rated 13+

Extremely Goofy Movie, An

Disney, 2000, 76 mins., #19146. Directed by Douglas McCarthy. Screenplay by Scott Gorden, Hillary Carlip.

Goofy's son Max is headed off to college, but dad doesn't want to cut the leash just yet. He heads to school right alongside Max, resulting in extreme sports skateboarding disasters, a love affair with a librarian, and a sequence of pure disco inferno. Will Goofy's antics drive his son away or bring the two of them even closer as a family?

If you didn't know that Disney characters even *could* reproduce, you didn't catch this feature's predecessor, *A Goofy Movie*. Adults will likely find that *An Extremely Goofy Movie* tries much to painfully hard to be hip, but early teens and kids will likely find much humor in the "dad's so dorky" situations. Voice actors include Bebe Neuwirth, Jo Anne Worley, and (Heaven help us!) Pauly Shore. In the disco scene, one character finally answers *Stand By Me*'s age-old question when she refers to Goofy as one of the "pretty cool canines."

SPECIAL FEATURES Music Video • Jokes • Games • DVD-ROM Features: Games, Art Studio, Read-Along • Other Title Trailers TECHNICAL FEATURES Widescreen (1.66:1) • Subtitles/CC: Eng. • Languages: Eng. • Sound: Dolby Digital Surround 5.1 • Keepcase • 1 Disc • Region 1 GENRE & RATING Animals/Comedy • Rated G

F

Fake

AnimeWorks, 2000, 60 mins., #AWDVD-0093. Directed by Iku Suzuki. Script by Akinori Endo. Based on the manga series by Sanami Mato in *Be-Boy*.

Dee Laytner and Randy (Ryo) McLane are a pair of New York police detectives who share more in common than a badge. They're gay and attracted to each other. So when they take a trip to England for a relaxing vacation, they really don't expect to get caught up in a series of murders.

Based on a popular manga series, *Fake* was originally released as a 1996 OVA. The first of a very few gay male anime projects to be released on DVD in the U.S., *Fake* is groundbreaking in one sense but stereotypical in others. Randy/Ryo is a bit too feminine and maternal, undermining his effectiveness as both a character and a detective. The project can't quite decide if it wants to be a detective drama or a comedy, and there are lots of characters from the manga that non-readers may not recognize or understand what they mean to the plot. Still, it's an entertaining hour.

Although the disc does depict gay characters, it does not feature sex, so it's appropriate for most audiences, excepting smaller children and those intolerant of diversity.

SPECIAL FEATURES None • Other Title Trailers TECHNICAL FEATURES Fullscreen (1.33:1) • Subtitles/CC: Eng. • Languages: Jap., Eng. dub • Sound: Dolby Digital 2.0 • Keepcase • 1 Disc • Region 1 GENRE & RATING Detective/Gay • Rated 13+

Fancy Lala: Vol. 1—A Star Is Born

Bandai, 2002, 125 mins., #1330. Directed by Takahiro Omari.

NOTE: This DVD arrived too late for a full review. The following text is promotional copy provided by the releasing company:

"Miho was just an ordinary elementary school student until she met a pair of miniature dinosaur fairies. It's hard to believe but the fairies gave her a magic sketchbook and a pen that enables her to transform into a fifteen-year-old Fancy Lala! On her way to stardom, Lala is scouted by a talent agency and starts working as a model. But it's not easy for Miho to juggle both work and school. According to her best friend Akiru, idol stars rarely have any time to have a boyfriend. Oh, no! With the help of two dinosaur fairies, Miho makes it through all sorts of troubles. But who is this Mystery Man?"

This disc contains episodes #1–5.

SPECIAL FEATURES Clean Credits • Other Title Trailers • Inserts: Liner Notes TECHNICAL FEATURES Fullscreen (1.33:1) • Subtitles/CC: Eng. • Languages: Jap., Eng. dub • Sound: Dolby Digital • Keepcase • 1 Disc • Region 1 GENRE & RATING Fantasy/Girls • Rated 7+

Fancy Lala: Vol. 2—Sharing the Spotlight

Bandai, 2002, 125 mins., #1331. Directed by Takahiro Omari.

NOTE: This DVD arrived too late for a full review. The following text is promotional copy provided by the releasing company:

"Now that Miho is getting used to being 15-year-old Lala, she learns it's not all fun and games! As Lala becomes more popular, it begins to affect Miho's social life. But that's not all! Lyrical Production's president Yumi has a grudge against the president of rival company Five Star, and in her anger, she commits Lala to work on a weekday. How is Miho going to juggle home, work, and school?"

This disc contains episodes #6–10.

SPECIAL FEATURES Text Interview with Director and Crew • Clean Credits • Other Title Trailers • Inserts: Liner Notes TECHNICAL FEATURES Fullscreen (1.33:1) • Subtitles/CC: Eng. • Languages: Jap., Eng. dub • Sound: Dolby Digital • Keepcase • 1 Disc • Region 1 GENRE & RATING Fantasy/Girls • Rated 7+

Fancy Lala: Vol. 3—Taking Center Stage

Bandai, 2002, 100 mins., #1332. Directed by Takahiro Omari.

NOTE: This DVD arrived too late for a full review. The following text is promotional copy provided by the releasing company:

"With Lala's debut CD a hot seller, she is very busy throwing the first pitch for a regional baseball tournament and appearing on various television shows. But just when things are going well, Miho encounters all sorts of troubles when there's a hitch in the Memories of Time. No one seems to remember who she is anymore! She also travels through toyland with a stuffed bear to rescue a princess. Is this real or is Miho dreaming?"

This disc contains episodes #11–14.

SPECIAL FEATURES Cover Art with Illustrator Notes • Other Title Trailers • Inserts: Liner Notes TECHNICAL FEATURES Fullscreen (1.33:1) • Subtitles/CC: Eng. • Languages: Jap., Eng. dub • Sound: Dolby Digital • Keepcase • 1 Disc • Region 1 GENRE & RATING Fantasy/Girls • Rated 7+

Fantasia [Special 60th Anniversary Edition]

Disney, 2000, 125 mins., #18268. Directed by Samuel Armstrong, James Algar, Bill Roberts, Paul Satterfield, Hamilton Luske, Jim Handley, Ford Beebe, T. Hee, Norman Ferguson, Wilfred Jackson. Story by Lee Blair, Elmer Plummer, Phil Dike, Sylvie Moberly-Holland, Norman Wright, Albert Heath, Bianca Majolie, Graham Heid, Perce Pearce, Carl Fallberg, William Martin, Leo Thiele, Robert Sterner, John Fraser McLeish, Otto Englander, Webb Smith, Erdman Penner, Joseph Sabo, Bill Peet, George Stallings, Campbell Grant, Arthur Heinemann.

In 1940, Disney released *Fantasia*, a bold experiment in animation. The film features eight segments animated in a wide variety of techniques, all set to classical music played by the Philadelphia Orchestra as conducted by Leopold Stokowski. Johann Sebastian Bach's "Toccata and Fugue in D Minor" is given an abstract treatment, whereas Peter Ilich Tchaikovsky's "The Nutcracker Suite" features fairies, dancing mushrooms, floating flower petals, wriggling fish, and more. The film's centerpiece is Paul Dukas' "The Sorceror's Apprentice," in which Mickey Mouse magically animates brooms to do his work, only to end up flooding his wizard's keep.

The other segments include: Igor Stravinsky's "The Rite of Spring," which depicts the creation of the world and the birth of dinosaurs; Ludwig van Beethoven's "Pastoral Symphony," which revels in elements of Greek mythology and tells the love story of a centaur pair;

Amilcare Ponchielli's "Dance of the Hours," with ostriches and hippos performing a ballet; and a medley of Modest Mussorgsky's "Night on Bald Mountain" and Franz Schubert's "Ave Maria" that tells of a frightening struggle of good and evil as demons and spirits rule the night until church bells ring the morning call (this latter selection may scare children).

The DVD features a stunning transfer of the remastered film, and all of the original introductions, narration, and even intermission. There are a number of nice extras as well. *Fantasia* is one of the top animated features of all time, in terms of quality, style, and entertainment. This DVD is a must-own (although if you can afford the box set, buy it).

SPECIAL FEATURES "Making of" Featurette • Commentary track • Archival Interviews with Walt Disney • Trailer TECHNICAL FEATURES Fullscreen (1.33:1) • Subtitles/CC: Eng., Fren. • Languages: Eng. • Sound: Dolby Digital Surround 5.0, DTS • Keepcase • 1 Disc • Region 1 GENRE & RATING Anthology/Music • Rated G

Fantasia 2000

Disney, 2000, 74 mins., #19571. Directed by Pixote Hunt, Hendel Butoy, Eric Goldberg, James Algar, Francis Glebas, Gaetan Brizzi, Paul Brizzi, Don Hahn. Story by Eric Goldberg, Gaetan Brizzi, Paul Brizzi, Perce Pearce, Carl Fallberg, Don Hahn, Irene Mecchi, David Reynolds.

Roy E. Disney presented this sequel to one of his uncle's most enduring animated films. Nine years in production, *Fantasia 2000* followed the lead of its 1940 predecessor. With the changes in technology, CGI effects, and a bigger budget, it could be argued that the sequel outdid the original, but purists might scoff at that, and truly, the pair of films complement each other very nicely.

This time out, conductor James Levine leads the Chicago Symphony Orchestra, while movie stars Steve Martin, Bette Midler, James Earl Jones, Angela Lansbury, Penn and Teller, and others handle the introductions. Ludwig van Beethoven's "Symphony No. 5" is given an abstract pastel battlefield; Ottorino Respighi's "Pines of Rome" presents the CGI journey of whales in ecstatic flight; and George Gershwin's "Rhapsody in Blue" is spectacularly played based on the caricature style of Al Hirschfeld.

Dmitri Shostakovich is represented by "Piano Concerto No. 2, Allegro, Opus 102" in a CGI sequence that tells Hans Christian Andersen's story of "The Steadfast Tin Soldier"; Camille Saint-Saens' "Carnival of the Animals, Finale" shows what happens if you give a flamingo a yo-yo; a rerun of "The Sorceror's Apprentice" follows; Sir Edward Elgar's "Pomp and Circumstance—Marches 1, 2, 3, and 4" is told with Donald Duck playing the part of Noah the ark-builder; and Igor Stravinsky's "Firebird Suite—1919 Version" is the embodiment of rebirth as a wood sprite and an elk work to rebuild a forest ravaged by a volcano.

The DVD features a variety of extras, including two 1953 shorts—"Melody" (Disney's first 3D cartoon) and the Oscar-winning "Toot, Whistle, Plunk, and Boom" (Disney's "first CinemaScope cartoon)—as well as a pair of commentary tracks by the producers, conductor, and segment directors. Highly recommended.

SPECIAL FEATURES 2 Commentary tracks • Promotional Footage • Insert: Booklet TECHNICAL FEATURES Widescreen (1.85:1 enhanced) • Subtitles/CC: Eng., Fren. • Languages: Eng., Fren. dub • Sound: Dolby Digital Surround 5.1, DTS • Keepcase • 1 Disc • Region 1 GENRE & RATING Anthology/Music • Rated G

Fantasia Anthology, The [Box Set]

Disney, 2000, 360 mins., #21269.

This box set features both the traditional *Fantasia* and *Fantasia 2000* DVDs (with no differences from the individual versions) as well as a third disc, *Fantasia Legacy*, which is exclusive to this set. Once again, Disney pulls out all the stops on supplementals, though this time they've got material from two classic films created sixty years apart!

On *Fantasia Legacy*, the *Fantasia* section shows visual development, production photos, story reels, deleted animation, character design, special effects demonstrations, and a whole section on segments that were considered or developed for *Fantasia* but never made it through. The *Fantasia 2000* section has significantly more material for each of the segments, including early concepts, animation stage comparisons, abandoned concepts, publicity, and more.

If you can find this box set, buy it!

SPECIAL FEATURES "Making of" Featurettes • Commentary tracks • Archival Interviews with Walt Disney • Composer and Crew Filmographies • Character and Art Galleries • Production Notes • Deleted and Abandoned Scenes • Storyboards • Story Reels • Notes about the Music • Trailer • Promotional Footage • Other Title Trailers • Insert: Booklet, Map, Liner Notes TECHNICAL FEATURES Widescreen (1.85:1 enhanced for 16x9) • Fullscreen (1.33:1) • Subtitles/CC: Eng., Fren. • Languages: Eng., Fren. dub • Sound: Dolby Digital 2.0, Dolby Digital Surround 5.1, DTS • Cardboard Box with 3 Keepcases • 3 Discs • Region 1 GENRE & RATING Anthology/Music • Rated G

Fantastic Planet

Anchor Bay, 1999, 72 mins., #DV10702. Directed by Rene Laloux. Screenplay by Roland Topor, Rene Laloux. Based on the book *Om En Seire* by Stefan Wul.

On the planet of Ygam live two races: the humanoid Oms, and their keepers, the blue-skinned giant Traags. The Oms are kept as pets for the Traag children and are purposely left uneducated. When Terr escapes from his Traag oppressors, he takes with him one of their learning devices and begins educating the other Oms. With their new knowledge, the Oms rise up and revolt against their exploiters. The key to freedom lies on a moon orbiting their world.

Anchor Bay added a subtitle to the back cover of this DVD, calling it "The psychedelic animated classic," and they're absolutely correct. The film, based on the works of a French novelist, is disturbingly animated with paper cutouts and surreal backgrounds and features a sometimes-incomprehensible story. *Fantastic Planet* has often been compared to *Yellow Submarine*, and though it doesn't contain as many drug references, watching it may give the viewer the sense that they *are* on drugs. Or, as one friend put it, "letting young kids watch this could mess them up."

The film was created as an allegory about the Soviet invasion of Czechoslovakia, and political pressure forced the animators to move production from Prague to Paris to finish their work. It was released in 1973, and won the Grand Prix Award at the Cannes Film Festival. The DVD also includes three early short subjects by director Laloux: "Monkey's Teeth" (1960); "Dead Times" (1964), and "The Snails" (1965). The one drawback to the DVD is that the English subtitles cannot be removed from either the French or English tracks.

SPECIAL FEATURES Director Filmography and Bios • Theatrical Trailer TECHNICAL FEATURES Widescreen (1.85:1) • Subtitles/CC: Eng. • Languages: Fren., Eng. dub • Sound: Dolby Digital 1.0 • Keepcase • 1 Disc • Region 1–6 GENRE & RATING Science Fiction/Psychedelia • Rated PG

Fantasy Film Worlds of George Pal, The

Image, 2000, 93 mins., #ID5866ALDVD. Directed by Arnold Leibovit. Written by Arnold Leibovit.

One of the most celebrated fantasy filmmakers and animators of the 20th century is George Pal, whose work includes not only the early Academy Award-winning Puppetoons from 1941–47, but also such science fiction classics as *The War of the Worlds* (1953), *The Time Machine* (1959), and many others.

This documentary—labeled the "Director's Cut Expanded Edition"—includes much footage from Pal's animated and live-action projects, as well as a wealth of cool extras. Excerpts from "Mr. Strauss Takes a Walk" and "Tulips Shall Grow" (1942) are remarkable expressions about World War II, while the "John Henry and the Inky Poo" short from 1946 was probably the first animated project to gave African-American characters any dignity.

Included in both the film and the extensive extras section are interviews with Puppetoon animators, plus footage of the Wah Chang hand puppets from *The Seven Faces of Dr. Lao*, and much more. This is a great look into the making of some classic animated and science fiction fare.

SPECIAL FEATURES Kinescope Segments • Film Premiere Footage • Home Movies • Photos and Art Galleries • Trailer • Promotional Footage • Other Title Trailers TECHNICAL FEATURES Fullscreen (1.33:1) • Languages: Eng. • Sound: Dolby Digital 1.0 • Snapcase • 1 Disc • Region 1 GENRE & RATING Stop-Motion/Puppets/Live Documentary • Not Rated (Kids)

Farewell to Space Battleship Yamato: In the Name of Love

Voyager, 2002, 151 mins., #69071-00629. Directed by Tosho Masuda. Screenplay by Toshio Masuda, Keisuke Fujikawa, Hideaki Yamamoto.

NOTE: This DVD arrived too late for a full review. The following text is promotional copy provided by the releasing company:

"Earth has been revived from its near-destruction at the hands of the Gamilons, but now a new danger appears at the edge of the Milky Way, and the crew of the *Space Battleship Yamato* must reunite to confront it! Mysterious signals from the distant planet Telezart warn them of interstellar terror. An enormous dreadnaught, disguised as a massive white comet, is on a rampage of conquest. The power-hungry Emperor Zordar enslaves entire planets and destroys others . . . and Earth is his next target! This the second feature film in the now-legendary *Space Battleship Yamato* series, shattered all previous Japanese box office records. Now, follow the crew of Yamato to the very edge of existence . . . and beyond!"

SPECIAL FEATURES Text interviews with Producer and Cast • Production Notes & Program Book • Trailer • Promotional Materials TECHNICAL FEATURES Fullscreen (1.33:1) • Subtitles/CC: Eng. • Languages: Jap. • Sound: Dolby Digital 1.0 • Keepcase • 1 Disc • Region 1 GENRE & RATING Science Fiction/Action • Not Rated (Kids)

Fatal Fury: Double Impact

Pioneer/Viz, 2000, 120 mins., #10413. Directed by Hiroshi Fukutomi, Kazuhiro Furuhashi. Screenplay by Takashi Yamada.

When their father, a martial arts champion, is murdered in front of them by Geese Howard, young Terry and Andy Bogard spend their lives training in the martial arts and waiting for revenge. Though they pursue different disciplines, Terry and Andy both want to learn the legendary *Hakkyokuseiken* technique—but only one of them can learn it. Later, Terry brings together a gang that includes Andy, a kickboxer, a redheaded ninja girl, and a street punk to take on the deadly German nobleman Wolfgang Krauser.

This DVD contains the OVA adventures *Fatal Fury: Legend of the Hungry Wolf* (1992) and *Fatal Fury 2: The New Battle* (1993). Both are based on the video game by SNK. With starkly clean animation, this is one of the more Americanized pieces of anime on the market, most likely due to crossover appeal rather than adherence to story goals. Still, these are pretty decent, mindless action stories.

SPECIAL FEATURES Character and Art Galleries • Trailer • Other Title Trailers • Easter Egg TECHNICAL FEATURES Fullscreen (1.33:1) • Subtitles/CC: Eng. • Languages: Jap., Eng. dub • Sound: Dolby Digital Surround 2.0 • Keepcase • 1 Disc • Region 1 GENRE & RATING Martial Arts/Action • Not Rated (Teens)

Fatal Fury: The Motion Picture

Viz/Pioneer, 1999, 100 mins., #DVD-FF01. Directed by Masami Obari. Screenplay by Takashi Yamada, Trish Ledoux.

Now that they've exacted their revenge, Terry and Andy Bogard are free to use their martial arts skills to go adventuring. Beautiful Sulia hires Terry and his friends to stop her estranged twin brother, Laocorn Gaudeamus, and his gang of villains. He's searching for the fabled "Armor of Mars," which supposedly has godlike powers. If he finds all the pieces of the armor, he'll be invincible, so it's up to Terry and company to stop him by any means necessary.

The third of the *Fatal Fury* projects, this 1994 movie is full of flashy visuals and nice action, but it still feels a little less fresh than its predecessors. Perhaps that's because moments of it feel like an Indiana Jones or James Bond film—with a lot more kicking.

SPECIAL FEATURES Character Bios • Character and Art Galleries • Series Notes • Trailer • Promotional Footage • Other Title

Trailers TECHNICAL FEATURES Widescreen (1.85:1) • Subtitles/CC: Eng. • Languages: Jap., Eng. dub • Sound: Dolby Digital 2.0 • Keepcase • 1 Disc • Region 1 GENRE & RATING Martial Arts/Action • Rated 13+

Faust

Kino, 1999, 97 mins., #K122DVD. Directed by Jan Svankmajer. Written by Jan Svankmajer.

Two of Lucifer's followers lure Faust, an everyman living in a city, to an abandoned building. There, he finds an old theater and a copy of Goethe's *Faust*. As he reads the book, Lucifer appears and offers to grant him his heart's desire in exchange for his soul. Soon, Faust is trapped in a set of multiple existences: as a puppet in a play, as an opera singer, and as himself. As the wilds of the world are opened before him, Faust meets demons and desires, and he learns that if he tries to escape the story of his life, he is doomed.

As with his other films (see *Alice* and *Conspirators of Pleasure*), Jan Svankmajer mixes live action with stop motion, claymation, and puppet effects in this 1994 feature. The look is startling and unsettling, but always engaging. Full of fantastic elements, *Faust* plays as much with the concept of reality within the film as it does with the reality that our eyes see as we watch the film. The soundtrack is in English, Latin, and Czech, without subtitles; astonishingly, one actor—Andrew Sachs—performs all the voices for the English dub! Recommended for those who want to experience something foreign and creepy from a highly skilled craftsman.

SPECIAL FEATURES Inserts: Liner Notes TECHNICAL FEATURES Fullscreen (1.33:1) • Languages: Eng. • Sound: Dolby Digital 2.0 • Snapcase • 1 Disc • Region 1–6 GENRE & RATING Live/Stop-Motion/Surreal • Not Rated (Teens)

Felix!

Slingshot, 1998, 51 mins., #DVD9816. Directed by Pat Sullivan.

Created in 1919 by Pat Sullivan, Otto Messmer, and John King, for the short "Feline Follies," Felix the Cat (originally named Tom) was an adventurous scamp whose tail helped him out of many a problem. The character became ultrapopular with both American and British audiences and appeared in more than eighty silent films, plus many sound cartoons and revivals up through the 1960s and beyond. A Felix toy was the first picture ever broadcast on a TV signal in 1928.

Included on this DVD are: "Feline Follies" (1919);

"Felix Saves the Day" (1922); "Felix in Hollywood" (1923); "Felix Dopes It Out" (1924); "Futuritzy" (1928); "Comicalamities" (1928); "Felix Woos Whoopee" (1930); and rare footage of Felix animator Otto Messmer at work. Some of the cartoons are straight-out comedy, while at least one of them is exceedingly surreal, and another guest-stars famous Hollywood celebrities of the silent film era. The films are all black-and-white and silent, with title cards and word balloons conveying the dialogue and narration. Transfer quality is excellent given the age of the source material, and a musical soundtrack is included as well. There are several racial stereotypes of African-Americans in the cartoons, so those who may be offended are warned. That fault aside, this is an excellent historical disc for animation enthusiasts.

SPECIAL FEATURES None TECHNICAL FEATURES Fullscreen (1.33:1) • Sound: Dolby Digital • Keepcase • 1 Disc • Region 1 GENRE & RATING Animals/Comedy • Not Rated (All Ages)

Felix the Cat: Collector's Edition

Sony Wonder , 2001, 105 mins., #LVD 54064.

NOTE: This DVD arrived too late for a full review. The following text is promotional copy provided by the releasing company:

"Whenever he gets into a fix . . . he reaches into his bag of tricks! From the original 1958–1959 television releases, Felix the Cat stars in his greatest adventures, complete and uncut for the first time ever on DVD. You can enjoy the original classic cartoon supercat in a whole new way! Digitally remastered and beautifully restored. Ten unedited and full-color episodes make any collection complete for Felix fans one and all! Felix the Cat is back, still full of mischief, and creating a twist with his provocative bag of tricks. You never know what he'll do next! Join Felix and his zany cast of familiar characters, featuring the brainy Poindexter, his greedy nemesis The Professor, Rock Bottom, and that creepy metal menace from the moon—the Master Cylinder, plus many more. Includes a bonus 1920 short, 'Feline Follies.'"

Note that although the disc cover claims it is closed captioned, it is not.

SPECIAL FEATURES Interview with Historian • Promotional Footage • Sing-Along • Game • DVD-ROM Features: Audio Clips, Screensavers TECHNICAL FEATURES Fullscreen (1.33:1) • Languages: Eng. • Sound: Dolby Digital • Keepcase • 1 Disc • Region 1 GENRE & RATING Animals/Comedy • Not Rated (All Ages)

Fencer of Minerva ☛ see Mature/Adult Section

FernGully: The Last Rainforest

Fox, 2002, 80 mins., #2003297. Directed by Bill Kroyer. Screenplay by Jim Cox. Based on the *FernGully* stories by Diana Young.

Deep in the rain forest is the enchanted hidden world of FernGully. When Crysta, a tree fairy, ventures outside her confines, she discovers that the rainforest is being demolished. Together with a human named Zak, some other fairies, a bat, a lizard, and the rough-and-tumble Beetle Boys, Crysta makes it her mission to stop the evil Hexxa and his plans to destroy both the rainforest and FernGully.

Released in 1992, *FernGully* features an all-star voice cast, including Robin Williams, Tim Curry, and Cheech Marin, and showcases some nice songs by Elton John, Sheena Easton, Tone Loc, and others. The movie is great for kids and environmental activists, but the average viewer might get tired of getting hit over the head by preachy eco-friendly messages and the thinly disguised antitechnology slant. Though the DVD doesn't have much in the way of extras, both the widescreen and pan-and-scan versions are presented.

SPECIAL FEATURES Trailer • Other Title Trailers TECHNICAL FEATURES Widescreen (1.85:1) • Fullscreen (1.33:1) • Subtitles/CC: Eng., Fren., Span. • Languages: Eng., Fren. • Sound: Dolby Digital Surround 2.0, Dolby Digital 5.1 • Keepcase • 1 Disc • Region 1 GENRE & RATING: Animals/Environmental/Music • Rated G

FernGully 2: The Magical Rescue

Image/Fox, 2000, 73 mins., #ID9167CUDVD. Directed by Phil Robinson, David Marshall. Screenplay by Richard Tulloch. Based on the *FernGully* stories by Diana Young.

FernGully is once again threatened, but this time it's by a group of poachers who work with a carnival. When three baby animals under Crysta's care are taken by the humans, all the magical creatures of FernGully band together to rescue them. Aiding them in their rescue attempt are a little girl named Budgie and her grandfather.

This 1998 direct-to-video sequel lacks most of the charm and features none of the voice cast or musical talent of the original. While younger viewers will likely still be entranced by the magical creatures, anyone older than a decade will likely search for the remote rather quickly.

SPECIAL FEATURES None TECHNICAL FEATURES Fullscreen (1.33:1) • Languages: Eng. • Sound: Dolby Digital Surround 2.0 • Snapcase • 1 Disc • Region 1–6 GENRE & RATING Animals/Environmental/Music • Rated G

Fight!! Spirit of the Sword

AnimeWorks, 2001, 30 mins., #AWDVD-0118. Directed by Ryo Yasumura. Screenplay by Ryo Yasumura. Based on the manga series by Pink Aomata in *Wings*.

Although Yonosuke Hikura is only sixteen, he is heir to a family legacy that protects Earth from demons and other menaces. Using his enchanted sword Chitentai, Yonosuke is also aided by a female Protector sent by the high priests of the Earth to battle by his side.

This 1993 OVA features some nice action sequences and smooth character designs, but it is disappointingly short, and relatively humorless. With only a half-hour on the DVD, this is an expensive short.

SPECIAL FEATURES Interview with Voice Actor • Other Title Trailers TECHNICAL FEATURES Widescreen (1.85:1) • Subtitles/CC: Eng. • Languages: Jap., Eng. dub • Sound: Dolby Digital 2.0 • Keepcase • 1 Disc • Region 1 GENRE & RATING Martial Arts/Action • Rated 13+

Final Fantasy: The Spirits Within

Columbia/TriStar, 2002, 106 mins., #09429.

This DVD was not available for review.

Final Fantasy: The Spirits Within [Special Edition]

Columbia/TriStar, 2001, 106 mins., #06249. Directed by Hironobu Sakaguchi, Moto Sakakibara. Screenplay by Al Reinert, Jeff Vintar.

By the year 2065, humankind faces extinction on its home planet. Alien spirits have infested the world, and Dr. Sid and scientist Aki Ross have a plan to purge them. With the help of the military Deep Eyes Squadron, Aki hopes to capture eight of the spirits and harness their power to make the alien presence leave Earth. But even as Aki and the ever-dwindling Squadron race to their goals, the plot unravels around them.

Although this 2001 film is technically based on the ultrapopular video game franchise, it has little to do with the actual "plot" of the game, even though the game's creator was also the film's director. In development and production for four years, *Final Fantasy* is the first film to realistically render human beings completely in CGI. Indeed, the computer animation is absolutely breathtaking and stunning in most cases, hitting a high mark that other films will have trouble topping for years to come. The voice cast is also nice, with Alec Baldwin, James

Woods, Donald Sutherland, and Ving Rhames on the mikes.

Unfortunately, the story is a confusing mess. When this author saw it in the theater, the majority of the audience was asking what it all meant when they left. On DVD, you'll have the chance to ponder that question again, and multiple commentary tracks may help illuminate the answers for you. The beautiful DVD set is crammed with extra features, showcasing the incredible work and development that went into creating the film. Visually, *Final Fantasy* is a masterpiece. Intellectually and emotionally it's a train wreck.

SPECIAL FEATURES "Making of" Featurettes • Multiple Commentary Tracks • Isolated Score with Commentary • Character and Art Galleries • Production Notes • Deleted Scenes • Storyboards • Workshops • Scene Editing Feature • Trailer • Promotional Footage • DVD-ROM Features: Screenplay, Virtual Tour • Other Title Trailers • Inserts: Liner Notes • Easter Eggs TECHNICAL FEATURES Widescreen (1.85:1 enhanced for 16x9) • Subtitles/CC: Eng., Fren. • Languages: Eng., Fren. • Sound: Dolby Digital Surround 2.0, Dolby Digital 5.1 • Multikeepcase • 2 Discs • Region All GENRE & RATING CGI/Science Fiction • Rated PG-13

Fist of the North Star

Image, 1998, 110 mins., #ID4661SEDVD. Directed by Toyo Ashida. Written by Susumu Takahisa. Based on the manga series by Buronson and Tetsu Hara in *Shonen Jump*.

This DVD was not available for review. It is out of print.

Five Card ☞ see Mature/Adult Section

Flashback ☞ see Mature/Adult Section

FLCL (Fooly Cooly) #1

Digital Manga, 2002, 60 mins.

This DVD was not available for review.

Flint: The Time Detective—The Blast from the Past [#1]

Right Stuf, 2000, 66 mins., #RSDVD2101. Directed by Hitoshi Nagao, Hiroshi Fukutomi, Koichi Takada, Shinji Okuda. Written by Hideki Sonoda, Steve Apostolina, Rebecca Olkowski, Mark Ryan.

In the 25th century, time travel has become a reality, but the Bureau of Time and Space Investigations polices the time stream to avoid any mishaps. The Old-Timer keeps things relatively safe as well, with the aid of TimeShifters—creatures with magical powers

who help keep the fabric of time from unraveling. But the Dark Lord wants to mess up history, so he dispatches Petra Fina (along with sidekick animals Dyno and Might) through time to catch all of the little TimeShifters. Petra freezes a caveman named Flint, but the Old-Timer thaws Flint out and makes the diminutive Cro-Magnon a time cop, charged with keeping the time stream safe from Petra Fina. Flint is often accompanied on his adventures by twins Sarah and Tony, whose uncle Bernie Goodman works for the BTSI.

This 1998 TV series in Japan hit at just the right time, mixing together the collecting elements of *Pokémon* with time travel fun. Squarely aimed at youthful viewers, *Flint* is goofily animated in the big-mouth/big-eyed style, and all sense of reality goes out the window the moment the disc goes into the machine. The DVD contains three edited episodes, as seen in the U.S. on Fox Kids and the Fox Family Channel.

The first disc contains: "Hammerhead Rock," which introduces Flint and the others; "Jitter Bug," which finds Petra going to 2nd-century Japan to retrieve the title creature; and "Eldora," in which a TimeShifter that can turn things to gold brings the cast to 16th-century South America and an adventure with chief Inca Dinka.

SPECIAL FEATURES Trailer TECHNICAL FEATURES Fullscreen (1.33:1) • Languages: Eng. dub • Sound: Dolby Digital 1.0 • Keepcase • 1 Disc • Region All GENRE & RATING Time Travel/Comedy • Not Rated (Kids)

Flint: The Time Detective—The Power of Good [#2]

Right Stuf, 2000, 66 mins., #RSDVD2102. Directed by Hitoshi Nagao, Hiroshi Fukutomi, Koichi Takada, Shinji Okuda. Written by Hideki Sonoda, Steve Apostolina, Bridget Hoffman, Tom Wyner, Mark Ryan.

The second time-traveling comedy disc contains episodes #4-6 of *Flint:* "Talen" finds Petra Fina capturing a TimeShifter that allows her to enter 8th-century fairy tales; "Mosbee" tells the story of a TimeShifter that can freeze anything, including Napoleon Bonaparte; and "Coconaut" showcases the search for a TimeShifter on the sailing vessel captained by Christopher Columbus.

SPECIAL FEATURES Trailer TECHNICAL FEATURES Fullscreen (1.33:1) • Languages: Eng. dub • Sound: Dolby Digital 1.0 • Keepcase • 1 Disc • Region All GENRE & RATING Time Travel/Comedy • Not Rated (Kids)

Flint: The Time Detective—The Sands of Time [#3]

Right Stuf, 2001, 66 mins., #RSDVD2103. Directed by Hitoshi Nagao, Hiroshi Fukutomi, Koichi Takada, Shinji Okuda. Written by Hideki Sonoda, Steve Apostolina, Tom Wyner, Rebecca Olkowski, Michael McConnohie.

Flint and his friends return for three more episodes: "Bubblegum" finds the crew in 16th-century Japan to face a Shogun; "Lynx" jumps the crew back to ancient Egypt to stop Petra from becoming queen; and "Artie" is a cute story set in Paris of 1950, in which Flint helps a preteen boy named Rodin discover where his artistic talents lie.

SPECIAL FEATURES Trailer TECHNICAL FEATURES Fullscreen (1.33:1) • Languages: Eng. dub • Sound: Dolby Digital 1.0 • Keepcase • 1 Disc • Region All GENRE & RATING Time Travel/Comedy • Not Rated (Kids)

Flint: The Time Detective—Can't We All Get Along? [#4]

Right Stuf, 2001, 88 mins., #RSDVD2104. Directed by Hitoshi Nagao, Hiroshi Fukutomi, Koichi Takada, Shinji Okuda. Written by Hideki Sonoda, Steve Apostolina, Tom Wyner, Michael McConnohie.

A quartet of stories bumps this *Flint* volume up in time and value: "Go Getalong" has Petra chasing a TimeShifter with the power of love; "Batterball" is the hidden story about Babe Ruth and his time-traveling allies; "Bindi" features a trip to Transylvania and introduces another Time Police detective named Merlock Holmes; and "Miss Iknow Makes a House Call" has Petra getting Flint in trouble while in her secret identity as a schoolteacher.

SPECIAL FEATURES Trailer TECHNICAL FEATURES Fullscreen (1.33:1) • Languages: Eng. dub • Sound: Dolby Digital 1.0 • Keepcase • 1 Disc • Region All GENRE & RATING Time Travel/Comedy • Not Rated (Kids)

Forgotten Toys, The

Sony Wonder, 2002, 30 mins., #LVD 497222. Directed by Graham Ralph. Written by Mark Holloway, Graham Ralph. Based on the book *The Night After Christmas* by James Stevenson.

NOTE: This DVD arrived too late for a full review. The following text is promotional copy provided by the releasing company:

"It's the night after Christmas and in a dark, cold alley an old, worn teddy bear and a raggedy rag doll find themselves tossed in the trash, abandoned by their owner in favor of the brand new toys they've received for the holidays. After narrowly escaping being carted away with the trash, Teddy and Annie set off on a perilous journey, wandering the big city in search of another child to love them. *The Forgotten Toys*, featuring the vocal talents of Bob Hoskins, is a heartwarming tale of love, friendship and the true meaning of Christmas."

Note that although the disc cover claims it is closed captioned, it is not.

SPECIAL FEATURES None TECHNICAL FEATURES Fullscreen (1.33:1) • Languages: Eng. • Sound: Dolby Digital • Keepcase • 1 Disc • Region 1 GENRE & RATING Holiday/Toys • Not Rated (All Ages)

Fortune Quest: Journey to Terrason [#1]

AnimeWorks, 2002, 125 mins., #EFDVD-8906. Directed by Eiichi Sato, Yoshizo Hamada. Written by Yumi Kageyama. Based on the works by Michio Fukuzawa and Natsumi Mukai.

Pastel, a poet and navigator, leads a group of heroes in adventures throughout a land of magic. They are a mismatched lot, including Clay, a young knight that doesn't fight much; Trapp, a thief who doesn't steal much; Rumi, a child-sized lisping elf wizard; and their pet white baby dragon, Shiro. The plot—such as it is—concerns the kidnapping of Trapp, the group traveling to Mount Terrason, the truth about baby Shiro's dragon ancestry, and a giant rampaging centipede.

Fortune Quest is so terminally cute and sweet that you'll almost need to brush your teeth after watching it. The animation is all over the map in terms of quality, the jokes are half-hearted, and there doesn't really seem to be much in the way of danger or action, despite promises on the cover copy. Overall, this series feels like a tryout for a video game and is really mostly suitable for children. The DVD contains episodes #1–5 of the 1997 TV series.

SPECIAL FEATURES Other Title Trailers TECHNICAL FEATURES Fullscreen (1.33:1) • Subtitles/CC: Eng. • Languages: Jap., Eng. dub • Sound: Dolby Digital 2.0 • Keepcase • 1 Disc • Region 1 GENRE & RATING Fantasy/Adventure • Rated 7+

Fox and the Hound, The [Gold Collection]

Disney, 2000, 83 mins., #18453. Directed by Art Stevens, Ted Berman, Richard Rich. Story by Larry Clemmons, Ted Berman, Peter Young, Steve Hulett, David Michener, Burny Mattinson, Earl Kress, Vance Gerry. Based on the book by Daniel P. Mannix.

Widow Tweed adopts an orphaned fox cub and names him Tod. The forest creature soon becomes best friends with a nearby hound puppy named Copper. Despite the hound's cranky owner and grumpy older dog Chief, Tod and Copper grow up adventuring together on the farm and in the woods. But as they get older, the natural antagonism between the fox and the hound grows, leading to an ultimate test of their friendship and a spectacular battle against an angry bear.

Nobody does cute animal stories as well as Disney, as this 1981 feature film shows. There's little not to like about this story, which hammers home the messages about friendship, respect, and love with little subtlety but great affection. The film was a hit with audiences, and even as it marked a return to "classic" Disney style in tone and animation, it also was a turning point for the studio, which began developing edgier and more experimental features thereafter.

The DVD doesn't have a lot of frills, and it features a grainy and sometimes-flawed picture. It's unfortunate that Disney didn't digitally remaster the picture. Still, it's a great disc to own, and something even the most hard-hearted will warm to.

SPECIAL FEATURES Trailer • Read-Along • Game • Insert: Booklet TECHNICAL FEATURES Fullscreen (1.33:1) • Subtitles/CC: Eng. • Languages: Eng., Fren. dub, Span. dub • Sound: Dolby Digital Surround 2.0 • Keepcase • 1 Disc • Region 1, 4 GENRE & RATING Animals/Adventure/Music • Rated G

Fraidy Cat

Brentwood, 2001, 60 mins., #44067-9. Directed by Don Towsley. Written by Mike O'Connor.

Every cat has nine lives, and eight of Fraidy Cat's have already gone to the Great Beyond. Now, he lives in fear because he only has one life left, but he just can't help getting into trouble. If he says the numbers 1–8 in any form, the ghosts of his past life appear, and though they sometimes help, more often they're trying to get Fraidy killed so he can join them in the afterlife. In his various misadventures he befriends a dog, finds a girlfriend, goes to jail, gets mixed up with the mob, falls in with thieves, and gets into the clutches of fat horny birds.

Fraidy Cat appeared as a segment in ABC's 1975 series *Uncle Croc's Block*, with animation by Filmation (though you wouldn't know it as almost all credits are missing). The series echoes the studio's earlier *Secret Lives of Waldo Kitty*, but isn't as funny. The show comes with a laugh track, which is peculiar since little of it is in any way humorous. In fact, this is one of the poorest examples of American animation released on DVD, and given a transfer that looks as if it was taken from a second-generation VHS copy, I can find little to recommend it. Well, there are a few nice extras that have nothing to do with *Fraidy Cat*.

SPECIAL FEATURES DVD Dictionary • Movie Trivia Game TECHNICAL FEATURES Fullscreen (1.33:1) • Languages: Eng. • Sound: Dolby Digital 2.0 • Keepcase • 1 Disc • Region 1–6 GENRE & RATING Animals/Adventure • Rated G

Franklin and the Green Knight: The Movie

USA, 2000, 75 mins., #963060-050-2. Directed by John Van Bruggen. Screenplay by Betty Quan. Based on the books by Paulette Bourgeois and Brenda Clark.

Franklin is a fun-loving young turtle who likes adventures, but sometimes he has to learn from his mistakes. He lives in Woodland, along with many other forest creatures. Worried that his parents won't have time for him after a new baby is born, Franklin sets out to bring Spring to the Woodland which is caught in the cold grip of Winter. As the "Green Knight," he takes Snail as his squire and sets out on his quest.

The star of a popular Nelvana-animated series, *Franklin* is very popular among the younger set. The stories are cute but not treacly, and they teach valuable lessons to children while avoiding being too preachy. This film, for instance, would be great to show children who are about to welcome (or resent) a new brother or sister in the family.

Although the DVD transfer and extras are nice, the one major drawback to *Franklin* is the packaging. The glowing lime-green keepcase is made of a plastic that sucks up the sticky residue from the security labels. You'll want to take the cover out and ditch the keepcase for another one as soon as possible.

SPECIAL FEATURES "Making of" Featurette • Music Videos • DVD-ROM Features: Games • Insert: Liner Notes TECHNICAL FEATURES Fullscreen (1.33:1) • Languages: Eng., Fren. dub, Span. dub • Sound: Dolby Digital Surround 5.1 • Keepcase • 1 Disc • Region 1–6 GENRE & RATING Animals/Adventure/Music • Not Rated (All Ages)

Fritz the Cat ☛ see Mature/Adult Section

Frog and Toad Are Friends

SVE/Churchill Media, 2000, 18 mins., #62162-DVD. Directed by John Matthews. Written by Arnold Lobel. Based on the book by Arnold Lobel.

Mr. Frog and Mr. Toad are friends. living out in the woods. Although Frog is usually cheerful and Toad is usually grumpy, they still manage to get along well. In five short segments, Frog and Toad welcome springtime, look for a lost button, take a swim (all the forest animals laugh at Toad's bathing suit), and wait for a letter to arrive by snail mail (literally!).

This DVD contains all the stop-motion shorts of *Frog and Toad* by John Matthews. Created in 1985, these were later licensed to HBO. The stories are sweet and the animation is well done. And it's a nice touch to have the original book's author as the narrator. An extra nine-minute featurette explains how armature puppets are created and stop-motion animation is shot.

Although the shortness of the actual footage may give buyers pause, this is an excellent example of independent stop-motion animation, and both kids and their parents will like it. Also licensed for school use, this "Home Edition" DVD comes in a CD case.

SPECIAL FEATURES "Making of" Featurette TECHNICAL FEATURES Fullscreen (1.33:1) • Languages: Eng. • Sound: Dolby Digital 2.0 • CD Case • 1 Disc • Region 1 GENRE & RATING Stop-Motion/Puppet/Family • Not Rated (All Ages)

Frosty the Snowman

Sony Wonder, 2002, 70 mins., #LVD 54401. Directed by Arthur Rankin, Jr., Jules Bass, Bill Melendez, Evert Brown. Written by Romeo Muller, Oliver Goldstick. "Frosty Returns" based on a story by Jim Lewis.

NOTE: This DVD arrived too late for a full review. The following text is promotional copy provided by the releasing company:

"Featuring the vocal talents of Jackie Vernon, *Frosty the Snowman* has been a holiday tradition for over thirty years! When Frosty the Snowman comes to life, he must weather a storm of adventures and the dastardly plans of an evil magician before he can find safety and happiness at the North Pole.

"Then, in *Frosty Returns*, join John Goodman and Jonathan Winters in the tuneful winter adventure of a little girl named Holly and her very special friend— Frosty the Snowman! When a power-hungry tycoon invents a new product that will eliminate snow, Holly has to convince the people of Beansboro to save the magical winter dust . . . and Frosty!"

Note that although the disc cover claims it is closed captioned, it is not.

SPECIAL FEATURES Introduction by Producer • Pencil Test • Foreign Language Songs TECHNICAL FEATURES Fullscreen (1.33:1) • Languages: Eng. • Sound: Dolby Digital • Keepcase • 1 Disc • Region 1 GENRE & RATING Holiday/Music • Not Rated (All Ages)

Fun and Fancy Free [Gold Collection]

Disney, 2001, 73 mins., #19693. Directed by William Morgan, Jack Kinney, Bill Roberts, Hamilton Luske. Story by Homer Brightman, Harry Reeves, Ted Sears, Lance Nolley, Eldon Dedini, Tom Oreb. "Bongo" based on the story by Sinclair Lewis.

Jiminy Cricket introduces a pair of tales on this DVD, sharing stories with dolls, teddy bears, and live-action ventriloquist's dummies (including famed ventriloquist Edgar Bergen). First up is the story of Bongo, a circus bear, who flees to the woods where he finds his true love . . . and she slaps him. Then Mickey Mouse, Donald Duck, and Goofy are the main characters in the fairy tale *Mickey and the Beanstalk*. Can the trio raid the giant's castle and rescue the beautiful singing harp?

Most of Walt Disney's most famous characters came together for this theatrical feature in 1947, the studio's ninth full-length animated release. This was also Walt's swan song as the voice of Mickey Mouse. Watch for a pair of chipmunks that will ultimately become Chip 'n' Dale in animated shorts from the same time period.

Although there aren't a lot of bonus features, the "making of" section is very well done, and the print is extremely crisp. This is a nice DVD for animation lovers, and a must-have for Disney collectors. Look in the extras section for an unannounced music video, "Disney's Mambo 5" by Lou Bega.

SPECIAL FEATURES "Making of" Featurette • Music Video • Game • Storybook • Other Title Trailers TECHNICAL FEATURES Fullscreen (1.33:1) • Subtitles/CC: Eng. • Languages: Eng., Fren. dub, Span. dub • Sound: Dolby Digital 2.0 • Keepcase • 1 Disc • Region 1, 4 GENRE & RATING Animals/Comedy/Music • Rated G

Fushigi Yugi: The Mysterious Play [#1— Suzaku/Red Box Set]

Pioneer, 1999, 650 mins., #PIFY-0001V. Directed by Hajime Kamegaki. Screenplay by Yoshio Urasawa, Kazuhisa Sakaguchi, Genki Yoshimura. Based on the manga series by Yu Watase in *Shojo Comic.*

Schoolgirl Yuki Miaka discovers a book called *The Universe of the Four Gods* that transports her and her friend Yui Hongo to Ancient China. There, Yuki must become the world's savior priestess by finding seven Celestial Warriors to defend the Konan Empire. If she accomplishes her task, she'll be able to awaken Suzaku, a flaming bird god that protects China from evil . . . and she'll be granted any wish. Her quest includes love triangles, betrayals, martial arts, pretty boys, pretty girls, magic, and action.

A very popular 1995 TV series, *Fushigi Yugi* was one of the earliest DVD sets released, containing twenty-six of the fifty-two episodes. The story is mainly aimed at female viewers, but is broad enough to be enjoyed by all. The animation is well done and extremely colorful, but some viewers will be put off by the overabundance of super-deformed scenes. In fact, with this series, that's a make-it-or-break-it feature; if you don't like super-deformed, stay away. If it doesn't bother you, you'll find a slow but richly detailed fantasy series, with lots of injections of goofy fun.

The DVD packaging is exquisite, and each disc—containing six to seven episodes—is attractively presented. There are a number of cool extras and a highly informative booklet with episode summaries and character notes for all the leads.

SPECIAL FEATURES Crew Interviews • Character and Art Galleries • Clean Credits • Relationship Chart • Footnotes • Insert: Booklet TECHNICAL FEATURES Fullscreen (1.33:1) • Subtitles/CC: Eng. • Languages: Jap., Eng. dub • Sound: Dolby Digital Surround 2.0 • Foldout Box with 4 Discs and Plastic Slipcase • 4 Discs • Region 1 GENRE & RATING Fantasy/Adventure • Not Rated (Teens)

Fushigi Yugi: The Mysterious Play [#2— Seiryu/Blue Box Set]

Pioneer, 2000, 650 mins., #10282. Directed by Hajime Kamegaki. Screenplay by Kazuhisa Sakaguchi, Yoshio Urasawa, Genki Yoshimura. Based on the manga series by Yu Watase in *Shojo Comic.*

Priestess/schoolgirl Yuki Miaka is still in the fantasy world of the Konan Empire, and she remains involved with the seven Celestial Warriors. But the more Miaka tries to meet her goals, the more obstacles are placed in her way. Things get a bit darker this time, as Miaka is betrayed by a close friend, the Suzaku Seven take on other Celestial Warriors, a major character is sexually assaulted, characters enter the real world outside the book, war is waged and death is delivered, a wedding is held, and wishes are granted.

Pioneer's second DVD set is as beautifully packaged as the first. The four discs contain episodes #27–52, rounding out the entire TV series. There have been some minor formatting changes to the DVD menu layouts and content, but the package is a solid set in every way. The quality of the picture and sound is once again impeccable. As mentioned above, this set is a bit darker than the previous one, and features more sexual material, but older viewers won't find it objectionable.

SPECIAL FEATURES Character and Art Galleries • Promotional Footage • Music Videos • Insert: Booklet • Easter Egg TECHNICAL FEATURES Fullscreen (1.33:1) • Subtitles/CC: Eng. • Languages: Jap., Eng. dub • Sound: Dolby Digital Surround 2.0 • Foldout Box with 4 Discs and Plastic Slipcase • 4 Discs • Region 1 GENRE & RATING Fantasy/Adventure • Not Rated (Teens)

Fushigi Yugi: The Mysterious Play [#3— Oni/Green Box Set]

Pioneer, 2001, 295 mins., #10553. Directed by Hajime Kamegaki. Screenplay by Genki Yoshimura, Ukiyoshi Ohashi. Based on the manga series by Yu Watase in *Shojo Comic.*

A short time after the events of the TV series, the world of the Konan Empire reaches back into the lives of Yuki Miaka and others who are living in the real world. Tamahome is faced with a difficult choice about his future, while the Suzaku Seven are reunited against a new villain. Then, the Jewel of Memory becomes a target for multiple factions, as revenge, obsession, and magic strike against Miaka and Tamahome.

This third box set of *Fushigi Yugi* contains the three-part and six-part 1996–97 OVA sequels to the TV series. Production values for the box set, and the animation and extras on the DVDs, are as high as the previous two volumes. There are also "omake" at the end of each episode (they aren't hidden, so they are not technically Easter eggs) that feature the gang in humorous and often super-deformed continuing adventures. The only problem found on the discs was in the English credits in the extras section; they cannot be stopped, paused, or rewound without turning off the DVD player.

SPECIAL FEATURES Character and Art Galleries • Insert: Booklet TECHNICAL FEATURES Fullscreen (1.33:1) • Subtitles/CC: Eng. • Languages: Jap., Eng. dub • Sound: Dolby Digital Surround

2.0 • Foldout Box with 2 Discs and Plastic Slipcase • 2 Discs • Region 1 GENRE & RATING Fantasy/Adventure • Not Rated (Teens)

Fushigi Yugi: The Mysterious Play—Eikoden [#4]

Pioneer, 2002, 120 mins., #11707. Directed by Nanako Shimazaki. Screenplay by Hiroaki Sato. Based on the manga series by Yu Watase in *Shojo Comic*.

NOTE: This DVD arrived too late for a full review. The following text is promotional copy provided by the releasing company:

"Miaka and Taka are now happily married and expecting their first child. Unfortunately, Mayo, a jealous young girl infatuated with Taka, finds the Universe of the Four Gods and uses the power of Suzaku to steal their unborn baby! Now Taka must return to Konan to save his new family and save Konan from an unknown menace that threatens to destroy the book and all that live within."

This disc contains all four OVAs.

SPECIAL FEATURES Character and Art Galleries • Clean Credits • Promotional Footage • Insert: Booklet TECHNICAL FEATURES Fullscreen (1.33:1) • Subtitles/CC: Eng. • Languages: Jap., Eng. dub • Sound: Dolby Digital Surround 2.0 • Keepcase with Plastic Slipcase • 1 Disc • Region 1 GENRE & RATING Fantasy/Adventure • Not Rated (Teens)

Future Sight Collection [Box Set]

Simitar, 2000, 232 mins.

This DVD box set was not available for review. The company is out of business. It contains the keepcase editions of the animated films *Beyond the Mind's Eye*, *The Gate to the Mind's Eye*, and *Televoid*. It also contains three live-action films/documentaries.

Gadget Trips: Mindscapes

Image, 2002, 79 mins., #ID0937ODDVD. Directed by Haruhiko Shono. Text by Hirokazu Nabekura.

Are Japanese CGI experimental music video sequences substantially different from their American counterparts? Not really, it seems. There apparently is a story in here about a war between the Empire and the Republic (no, not the *Star Wars* versions) and the hallucinations produced by the Sensorama machine. There are lots of subways, statues, ghosts, kaleidoscopes, and branching tree roots. The music is by Koji Ueno, and while some of it is interesting New Age stuff, parts of it are discordant and unpleasant.

SPECIAL FEATURES None TECHNICAL FEATURES Fullscreen (1.33:1) • Languages: Eng. • Sound: Dolby Digital Surround 2.0 • Keepcase • 1 Disc • Region 1–6 GENRE & RATING CGI/Music • Not Rated (Teens)

Galaxy Fraulein Yuna

ADV Films, 2002, 125 mins., #DGY/001. Directed by Yorifusa Yamaguchi, Akiyuki Shinbo. Screenplay by Saturo Akahuri, Masashi Noro, Sumio Uetake, Masashi Kubota.

NOTE: This DVD arrived too late for a full review. The following text is promotional copy provided by the releasing company:

"How many girls does it take to save the universe? Start with Yuna, Savior of the Light, Galaxy Defender, and the number one fan of Polyina, who not only plays a superhero on TV but actually is one in her spare time. Add Yuna's friend, Yuri, an android with an astonishing appetite. Multiply by Misaki, the new girl in class, who is actually a spy from the Galactic Council, sent to assess a charge that Yuna is trying to take over the galaxy. Divide by the sinister Fraulein D, who is using Misaki as a pawn in a larger game to put Yuna, Yuri, the mechanical sprite Elner, and the slow-talking Shiori out of commission, so

that she can take over the galaxy. Confused? Then we won't factor in the cooking contest, the lost puppy, Fraulein D's hench-women, or any of the other girls who help Yuna save the universe. It all adds up to great fun in *Galaxy Fraulein Yuna*!"

SPECIAL FEATURES Easter Egg TECHNICAL FEATURES Fullscreen (1.33:1) • Subtitles/CC: Eng. • Languages: Jap., Eng. dub • Sound: Dolby Digital 2.0 • Keepcase • 1 Disc • Region 1 GENRE & RATING Robots/Girls/Science Fiction • Rated 12+

Gall Force—Eternal Story

U.S. Manga Corps, 1998, 86 mins., #USMD1724. Directed by Katsuhito Akiyama. Screenplay by Sukehiro Tomita. Based on the manga series by Hideki Kakinuma.

An ongoing war is under way between the Solnoids and the Paranoids; which of them will control Chaos, the newly terraformed planet? Drafted into the battle is the all-female crew of the starship *Starleaf*, but when the ship is crippled and cut off from the rest of the armada, secrets are revealed. Are they being betrayed by the Solnoid high command? Why is their computer withholding data? Is there a new race about to be born?

This 1986 film was based on both manga and a photo series of model ships in *Model Graphics* magazine. It's full of big-haired, big-eyed girls who look like children and nicely designed mecha technology. Looking a little soft and old-style, the hard science fiction story of *Gall Force* has echoes of the film *Alien* and its sequels. There is some nudity, though it isn't overly gratuitous. The DVD reproduces the pastel-toned animation well.

See also the entry for *Rhea Gall Force*. In addition to being offered as a single DVD, the disc was also included as part of a 2002 "Girlpower Pack" set, along with *Virgin Fleet*.

SPECIAL FEATURES Character Bios • Comic Book Covers • Other Title Trailers • Liner Notes TECHNICAL FEATURES Fullscreen (1.33:1) • Subtitles/CC: Eng. • Languages: Jap., Eng. dub • Sound: Dolby Digital 2.0 • Keepcase • 1 Disc • Region All GENRE & RATING Science Fiction/Robots • Not Rated (Teens)

Garaga

U.S. Manga Corps, 2001, 100 mins., #USMD2063. Directed by Hidemi Kubo. Screenplay by Hidemi Kubo. Based on the manga series by Satomi Mikuriya.

A starship of explorers is lost through a warp-ring wormhole. They land on a hostile planet full of hostile apes, dinosaurs, and other monsters. As the crew tries to stay alive, they find out what the hidden agenda of their mission is and what a race of psychics will mean to their futures.

If this 1989 OVA sounds like a cross between *Planet of the Apes* and *Farscape*, you've hit it on the head (though it predates the latter series). But it's not just an action story; most of the plot is full of spies, double agents, and political intrigue. The DVD presents the simple, clean animation well.

SPECIAL FEATURES Character Bios • Trailer • Other Title Trailers • DVD-ROM Features: Art, Script TECHNICAL FEATURES Fullscreen (1.33:1) • Subtitles/CC: Eng. • Languages: Jap., Eng. dub • Sound: Dolby Digital 2.0 • Keepcase • 1 Disc • Region 1–6 GENRE & RATING Science Fiction/Action • Rated 13+

Garzey's Wing

U.S. Manga Corps, 1999, 90 mins., #USMD1878. Directed by Yoshiyuki Tomino. Screenplay by Yoshiyuki Tomino.

Chris, a half-Japanese, half-American teenager, is transported to another world. There, he is proclaimed the holy warrior "Garzey's Wing," savior of an enslaved humanoid tribe. The tribe wants him to lead them in battle against the slavers and using his knowledge of Earth weapons like gunpowder, Chris agrees to lead them. Battle ensues, involving knights, dragons, and fairies.

This DVD contains all three 1996 episodes of this series. For those who like fantasy that mixes time periods, here's another disc for you, but the stories are bland and uninteresting. The animation lines are so thin in places that they drop out on the transfer to DVD, meaning the picture isn't great. And fans have roundly criticized the dub as one of the industry's worst.

Besides being offered as a single DVD, the disc was also included as part of a 2002 "Fantasy Pack" set, along with *Legend of Lemnear.*

SPECIAL FEATURES Director Bio • Other Title Trailers • DVD-ROM Features: Art, Script TECHNICAL FEATURES Fullscreen (1.33:1) • Subtitles/CC: Eng. • Languages: Jap., Eng. dub • Sound: Dolby Digital 2.0 • Keepcase • 1 Disc • Region All GENRE & RATING Fantasy • Not Rated (Teens)

Gasaraki #1: The Summoning

ADV Films, 2000, 100 mins., #DVDGK001. Directed by Ryosuke Takahashi, Hideki Okamoto. Screenplay by Toru Nozaki, Yuichiro Takeda. Story by Hajime Yatate, Ryosuke Takahashi.

The time is now, but the world is a very different place. Giant robot weapons are real, but they're only as good in battle as their drivers. These Tactical Armors come into play when military action in the Middle Eastern country of Belgistan heats up. Yushiro Gowa is the fourth son of a powerful Japanese clan—the Gowa family—that has ties to the military, computer systems, and the government. Yushiro controls a TA better than anyone else, but does he also have ties to a secret ancestral power? Plus, who is the mysterious psychic girl, Miharu, and for which side is she fighting?

This 1997 series has a complex storyline with nice characterization and mechanical design. The simplistic nondetailed human characters are nicely shadowed and complementary to the modern mecha. As for the story, the viewer is dropped into the middle of the action with little explanation at the start, meaning that viewers need to pay attention to understand the relationships and plot (this may alienate more casual watchers). The Belgistan war has numerous parallels to the Gulf War, including familiar media and news reports used in the series.

A nice DVD package all around, *Gasaraki* has some very cool menu designs. The only real complaint is that neither the episode numbers nor titles are listed on the outer cover or interior sheets. Episodes #1–4 are: "On the Ancient Stage of Stone"; "Opening Movements"; "Tantric Circle"; and "Mirage."

SPECIAL FEATURES Text Interviews • Character and Art Galleries • Production Notes • Glossary • Other Title Trailers • Insert: Relationship Chart • Easter Egg TECHNICAL FEATURES Fullscreen (1.33:1) • Subtitles/CC: Eng. • Languages: Jap., Eng. dub • Sound: Dolby Digital Surround 2.0) • Keepcase • 1 Disc • Region 1 GENRE & RATING Robots/War • Rated 12+

Gasaraki #2: The Circle Opens . . .

ADV Films, 2000, 75 mins., #DVDGK002. Directed by Ryosuke Takahashi, Hideki Okamoto. Screenplay by Chiaki Konaka, Toru Nozaki, Yuichiro Takeda. Story by Hajime Yatate, Ryosuke Takahashi.

All-out war erupts in Belgistan, and the TAs are caught in the battle. Yushiro and Miharu meet on the battlefield, while all the players and events are manipulated from behind the scenes by the covert group known as Symbol. Double-crosses, conspiracies, surprising allies. . . . Is this still only disc two?

The DVD contains episodes #5–7: "The Touching"; "The Puppet"; and "Return."

SPECIAL FEATURES Text Interviews • Character and Art Galleries • Production Notes • Glossary • Other Title Trailers • Insert: Schematics TECHNICAL FEATURES Fullscreen (1.33:1) • Subtitles/CC: Eng. • Languages: Jap., Eng. dub • Sound: Dolby Digital Surround 2.0 • Keepcase • 1 Disc • Region 1 GENRE & RATING Robots/War • Rated 12+

Gasaraki #3: Betrayal

ADV Films, 2000, 75 mins., #DVDGK003. Directed by Ryosuke Takahashi, Hideki Okamoto. Screenplay by Toru Nozaki, Chiaki Konaka. Story by Hajime Yatate, Ryosuke Takahashi.

The war may be over for now, but the battle for the TAs and Yushiro's loyalty is still ongoing. The involvement of the TAs in the war may violate Japan's constitution and disgrace its pilots. Can the Gowa clan protect its own? Symbol launches a series of raids on Gowa City, and revelations about the past have Yushiro doubting everything he's ever known. What lies within the vault in the family shrine? Plus, the next generation of TA pilots are given experimental drugs. . . .

The DVD contains episodes #8–10: "Inferno"; "Storehouse"; and "Kugai."

SPECIAL FEATURES Text Interviews • Voice Actor Footage • Character and Art Galleries • Glossary • Other Title Trailers • Insert: Schematics TECHNICAL FEATURES Fullscreen (1.33:1) • Subtitles/CC: Eng. • Languages: Jap., Eng. dub • Sound: Dolby Digital Surround 2.0 • Keepcase • 1 Disc • Region 1 GENRE & RATING Robots/War • Rated 12+

Gasaraki #4: From the Ashes . . .

ADV Films, 2001, 75 mins., #DVDGK004. Directed by Ryosuke Takahashi, Hideki Okamoto. Screenplay by Toru Nozaki, Yuichiro Takeda. Story by Hajime Yatate, Ryosuke Takahashi.

Yushiro and Miharu are both being pursued now—by the military, the Gowa, and other forces. Can they uncover the secret of the Kai and the Kugutsu before Japan is threatened? Yushiro's ex-TA teammates also find themselves targeting an out-of-control TA from the second generation!

The DVD contains episodes #11–13: "Ties"; "Unravel"; and "Disembark."

SPECIAL FEATURES Text Interviews • Sketch Video Footage • Character and Art Galleries • Glossary • Other Title Trailers • Insert: Schematics TECHNICAL FEATURES Fullscreen (1.33:1) • Subtitles/CC: Eng. • Languages: Jap., Eng. dub • Sound: Dolby Digital Surround 2.0) • Keepcase • 1 Disc • Region 1 GENRE & RATING Robots/War • Rated 12+

Gasaraki #5: Revelations

ADV Films, 2001, 75 mins., #DVDGK005. Directed by Ryosuke Takahashi, Hideki Okamoto. Screenplay by Toru Nozaki. Story by Hajime Yatate, Ryosuke Takahashi.

Yushiro and Miharu are still being pursued, even as they follow the path of the Kai and try to unravel the secrets in their past lives. Meanwhile, the monstrous Kugai attack, and Kugutsu battle Kugutsu. War is on the horizon yet again, in both the past and the present. Questions are answered, but they only lead to more mysteries.

The DVD contains episodes #14–16: "Companions"; "The Threshold"; and "Karma."

SPECIAL FEATURES Text Interviews • Voice Actor Footage • Character and Art Galleries • Glossary • Other Title Trailers • Insert: Map TECHNICAL FEATURES Fullscreen (1.33:1) • Subtitles/CC: Eng. • Languages: Jap., Eng. dub • Sound: Dolby Digital Surround 2.0 • Keepcase • 1 Disc • Region 1 GENRE & RATING Robots/War • Rated 12+

Gasaraki #6: Fires of War . . .

ADV Films, 2001, 75 mins., #DVDGK006. Directed by Ryosuke Takahashi, Hideki Okamoto. Screenplay by Toru Nozaki, Yuichiro Takeda. Story by Hajime Yatate, Ryosuke Takahashi.

Yasuhiro and Miharu find refuge with a surprising group in the slumlike area known as "the Asian Vein." Meanwhile, the Gowa family makes preparations for their new vision of Japan; how will they take advantage of riots that are about to occur? The Gowa clan also sends a TA after Yasuhiro and Miharu, but will the Symbol's own mecha get to the two lead characters first?

The DVD contains episodes #17–19: "Chaos"; "Rear Window"; and "Wails."

SPECIAL FEATURES Text Interviews • Sketch Video Footage • Character and Art Galleries • Glossary • Other Title Trailers • Insert: Schematics TECHNICAL FEATURES Fullscreen (1.33:1) • Subtitles/CC: Eng. • Languages: Jap., Eng. dub • Sound: Dolby Digital Surround 2.0 • Keepcase • 1 Disc • Region 1 GENRE & RATING Robots/War • Rated 12+

Gasaraki #7: In the Spider's Web

ADV Films, 2001, 75 mins., #DVDGK007. Directed by Ryosuke Takahashi, Hideki Okamoto. Screenplay by Chiaki Konaka, Toru Nozaki. Story by Hajime Yatate, Ryosuke Takahashi.

Yushiro tries to free Miharu from her captors, while Japan stands once again at the brink of war against one of the world's superpowers. World markets are collapsing, rioters are in the streets, and the TA team is caught in the middle, not knowing which side is right. The apocalypse is coming. . . .

This penultimate DVD contains episodes #20–22: "Upheaval"; "Run"; and "Personification."

SPECIAL FEATURES Text Interviews • Voice Actor Footage • Character and Art Galleries • Glossary • Other Title Trailers • Insert: Schematics TECHNICAL FEATURES Fullscreen (1.33:1) • Subtitles/CC: Eng. • Languages: Jap., Eng. dub • Sound: Dolby Digital Surround 2.0 • Keepcase • 1 Disc • Region 1 GENRE & RATING Robots/War • Rated 12+

Gasaraki #8: To Be a Kai

ADV Films, 2001, 75 mins., #DVDGK008. Directed by Ryosuke Takahashi, Hideki Okamoto. Screenplay by Toru Nozaki. Story by Hajime Yatate, Ryosuke Takahashi.

Humankind is at the brink of its final battle, and the world's fate rests in the hands of a few people. Alliances are broken, new paths are forged, and the ultimate confrontation is coming. The series wraps up nicely, having been an engrossing, complex, and suspenseful political thriller mixed with mecha and magic.

The final DVD contains episodes #23–25: "Eternal"; "Punctuation"; and "Gasara." Check the extras for almost half an hour of textless opening and end credits.

SPECIAL FEATURES Text Interviews • Character and Art Galleries • Clean Credits • Glossary • Other Title Trailers • Insert: Schematics TECHNICAL FEATURES Fullscreen (1.33:1) • Subtitles/CC: Eng. • Languages: Jap., Eng. dub • Sound: Dolby Digital Surround 2.0 • Keepcase • 1 Disc • Region 1 GENRE & RATING Robots/War • Rated 12+

Gasaraki: Box Set

ADV Films, 2002, 650 mins., #DGK/100.

This box set features the eight commercially available keepcase editions of *Gasaraki*, in a cardboard box. It does not feature any additional extras. See individual entries for the Special and Technical Features listings.

TECHNICAL FEATURES Cardboard Box with 8 Keepcases • 8 Discs • Region 1 GENRE & RATING Robots/War • Rated 12+

Gatchaman: Collection DVD

Urban Vision, 2001, 135 mins., #UV1070. Directed by Hiroyuki Fukushima, Akihiko Nishiyama. Written by ART MIC.

The Gatchaman heroes are back, and they're still dressed in those cool bird costumes. Join eagle Ken, swan June, owl Ryu, condor Joe, and swallow Jinpei as they fight the forces of evil, most especially the Galactors. The crew of the Phoenix first defends the world's energy resources from Galactor attack, then gets in both an aerial and an undersea battle against the Jupiter Death Brigade and the BlackBird Battalion. And, as the Galactors begin their final assault on Earth, will the Gatchaman crew be able to trust its new ally, the Red Specter?

This DVD contains all three episodes of the 1994 OVA series of *Gatchaman*. It's a nice update/remake, with hipper jaggedy visuals, plus lots of plot mixed with lots of action. There is a bit more blood in the violent scenes than the original had, so squeamish viewers are warned. Urban Vision did a great job with this package, though the extras are a bit skimpy (the best one is an Easter egg music video).

See *Battle of the Planets* for the original (and Americanized) versions of the *Gatchaman* series.

SPECIAL FEATURES Other Title Trailer • Insert: Liner Notes • Easter Egg TECHNICAL FEATURES Fullscreen (1.33:1) • Subtitles/CC: Languages • Languages: Jap., Eng. dub • Sound: Dolby Digital 2.0 • Keepcase • 1 Disc • Region 1 GENRE & RATING Science Fiction/Action • Not Rated (Teens)

Gatekeepers: Open the Gate! [#1]

Pioneer, 2001, 80 mins., #11567. Directed by Shintaro Inokawa, Hirotoshi Takaya, Masahiro Hosoda. Written by Hiroshi Yamaguchi, Aya Matsui. Based on the manga series by Gonzo in *Ace Next*.

Some teenagers in 1969 Japan have secret powers. They are "Gate Keepers," able to open doorways into alternate dimensions. The Earth defense forces—known as AEGIS (Alien Exterminating Global Intercept System)—draft several young agents, including schoolboy Shun Ukiya and multiple schoolgirls to help him. The aliens they fight have powers of mind control, giving them the ability to turn normal humans into their pawns. And the "Invaders" have their own shape-changing abilities as well, making them all the harder to fight.

Aired in 2000 on television, *Gate Keepers* quickly made its way to American shores for its DVD release. The series features a bold, slick, uncluttered art style full of bright colors and big eyes. With regard to the story, these aren't terribly serious. The transfer is pristine, and the menus are very cool. Recommended for fans of *Men in Black* and *Sailor Moon*.

SPECIAL FEATURES Special Prologue & Ending • Promotional Footage • Clean Credits • Insert: Agent ID Cards • Reversible Cover TECHNICAL FEATURES Fullscreen (1.33:1) • Subtitles/CC: Eng. • Languages: Jap., Eng. dub • Sound: Dolby Digital 2.0 • Keepcase • 1 Disc • Region 1 GENRE & RATING Science Fiction/Comedy • Rated 13+

Gatekeepers: New Fighters [#2]

Pioneer, 2001, 80 mins., #11620. Directed by Yasuhiro Takemoto, Akio Sakai, Yasuhiro Matsumura, Shinichi Tokairin. Written by Hideki Mitsui, Hiroshi Yamaguchi, Aya Matsui. Based on the manga series by Gonzo in *Ace Next*.

AEGIS needs more agents to fight the alien Invaders, so they search for more teenage Gate Keepers. Unfortunately for them, young secret agents don't always get along well. Shun Ukiya, Ruriko Ikusawa, and Reiko Asagiri take a train trip out of Nagoya to find Bancho "Big Boss," a brash new male agent. Later, athletic girl Kaoru Konoe is tested by AEGIS, but she chooses not to join up until she gets proof of an Invaders plot while rescuing a bus full of school kids.

The second disc features three episodes: "Search for the New Fighter!"; "Charge Toward Your Dreams!"; and "Infiltrate the Haunted Female Dormitory!"

SPECIAL FEATURES Special Prologue & Ending • Character and Art Galleries • Japanese Box Art • Insert: Agent ID Cards • Reversible Cover TECHNICAL FEATURES Fullscreen (1.33:1) • Subtitles/CC: Eng. • Languages: Jap., Eng. dub • Sound: Dolby Digital 2.0 • Keepcase • 1 Disc • Region 1 GENRE & RATING Science Fiction/Comedy • Rated 13+

Gatekeepers: Infiltration! [#3]

Pioneer, 2002, 80 mins., #11614. Directed by Susumu Nishizawa, Shigeru Kimiya, Masahiro Hosoda. Written by Hideki Mitsui, Hiroshi Yamaguchi. Based on the manga series by Gonzo in *Ace Next*.

The plot thickens as more Invaders are discovered by the Gate Keeper team. The airline industry is in trouble, and the team finds out that one of the planes is a shape-changed Invader (wait until you see a plane with teeth!), and their new Gate Keeper ally is a monkey named Fei. Then a teacher at Ruriko's school is an Invader, but the battle leads to the discovery of another powerful teen, Megumi Kurogane. And which Gate Keeper is secretly working for the enemy?

This disc features episodes #7–9: "Shoot the Enemy

Out of the Sky!"; "Find the Infiltrator!"; and "Break Down the Gate of Darkness!"

SPECIAL FEATURES Character and Art Galleries • Special Ending • Insert: Agent ID Cards • Reversible Cover TECHNICAL FEATURES Fullscreen (1.33:1) • Subtitles/CC: Eng. • Languages: Jap., Eng. dub • Sound: Dolby Digital 2.0 • Keepcase • 1 Disc • Region 1 GENRE & RATING Science Fiction/Comedy • Rated 13+

Gatekeepers: The New Threat [#4]

Pioneer, 2002, 80 mins., #11615. Directed by Yasuhiro Takemoto, Yasuhiro Matsumura, Koichi Chigira. Written by Hideki Mitsui, Takashi Sadayama, Aya Matsui. Based on the manga series by Gonzo in *Ace Next*.

After the Gate Keepers help Apollo 11 land safely, their ship is forced to land on a tropical island by the evil Invader Baron Akuma. Is he controlling the heroes' minds? The Invaders hijacked a cargo ship six years ago, but how does that relate to Kaiser Kikai's attack on a bullet train headed for Tokyo? And a new member of the team is introduced in an episode in which the Gate Keepers search for a missing airplane, get involved in something supernatural, and fight a new form of flying Invader.

The fourth DVD contains episodes #10–12, reaching the halfway point for the series: "Shake Free from the Demonic Dream!"; "Stop That Bullet Train!"; and "Fly to the Northern Lands!"

SPECIAL FEATURES Special Prologue & Ending • Character and Art Galleries • Script Covers • Insert: Agent ID Cards • Reversible Cover TECHNICAL FEATURES Fullscreen (1.33:1) • Subtitles/CC: Eng. • Languages: Jap., Eng. dub • Sound: Dolby Digital 2.0 • Keepcase • 1 Disc • Region 1 GENRE & RATING Science Fiction/Comedy • Rated 13+

Gatekeepers: To The Rescue! [#5]

Pioneer, 2002, 80 mins., #11616. Directed by Koichi Chigira, Shinichi Tokairin, Yasuhiro Matsumura. Script by Hiroshi Yamaguchi, Aya Matsui. Based on the manga series by Gonzo in *Ace Next*.

NOTE: This DVD arrived too late for a full review. The following text is promotional copy provided by the releasing company:

"Internal Conflict! The AEGIS HQ in New York sends experienced agents to take over the defense of Japan! Immediately, Shun and the other Far East Branch agents protest, but after a near disaster in the field, they are forced to recognize their inexperience. However, are these new orders playing right into the Invaders' schemes? When self-doubt and internal conflicts become more of a threat than the Invaders plans, it's time for action both in the battlefield and in love!"

This disc contains episodes #13–15.

SPECIAL FEATURES Character and Art Galleries • Alternate Ending • Other Title Trailers • Inserts: ID card, Mini Poster • Reversible Cover TECHNICAL FEATURES Fullscreen (1.33:1) • Subtitles/CC: Eng. • Languages: Jap., Eng. dub • Sound: Dolby Digital 2.0 • Keepcase • 1 Disc • Region 1 GENRE & RATING Science Fiction/Comedy • Rated 13+

Gatekeepers: Discovery! [#6]

Pioneer, 2002, 80 mins., #11617. Directed by Koichi Chigira, Mitsuyoshi Yoneda, Masahiro Hosada, Yasuhiro Matsumura. Script by Aya Matsui, Hiroshi Yamaguchi. Based on the manga series by Gonzo in *Ace Next*.

NOTE: This DVD arrived too late for a full review. The following text is promotional copy provided by the releasing company:

"Spitzilla Attacks! Megumi's insults force Reiko to face her own incompetence, so Reiko attempts to improve by emulating each of the other Gate Keeper's training methods. Even though her efforts continuously fail, Reiko eventually discovers her own way to contribute to AEGIS just in time to meet new challenges from the Invaders! Then, the Far East Branch of AEGIS uncovers evidence that real people are being replaced by Invaders, but HQ refuses to devote more resources to help. With the discovery of a canine Invader, Spitzilla, will HQ be forced to regret their decision?"

This disc contains episodes #16–18.

SPECIAL FEATURES Character and Art Galleries • Alternate Ending • Other Title Trailers • Inserts: ID card, Mini Poster • Reversible Cover TECHNICAL FEATURES Fullscreen (1.33:1) • Subtitles/CC: Eng. • Languages: Jap., Eng. dub • Sound: Dolby Digital 2.0 • Keepcase • 1 Disc • Region 1 GENRE & RATING Science Fiction/Comedy • Rated 13+

Gatekeepers: The Shadow! [#7]

Pioneer, 2002, 80 mins., #11618. Directed by Koichi Chigira, Ukei Okada, Shinichi Tokairin, Keiji Goto, Akihiko Nishiyama. Script by Hiroshi Yamaguchi, Aya Matsui. Based on the manga series by Gonzo in *Ace Next*.

NOTE: This DVD arrived too late for a full review. The following text is promotional copy provided by the releasing company:

"The Dark Plan. Reiji Kageyama revealed his radical political theories on national TV, but an Invader attack forces AEGIS to jam the rest of the broadcast to prevent widespread panic. Christmas and New Year's pass rela-

tively uneventfully, but the Shadow's plots weaken the AEGIS team. To further complicate the situation, the return of Kaiser Kikai (Kikai Shogun) and Count Akuma (Akuma Hakushaku) coincides with a threat against Ruriko's father—will the Gate Keepers be able to deal with the threat? Will they realize the true enemy before it is too late?"

This disc contains episodes #19–21.

SPECIAL FEATURES Character and Art Galleries • Alternate Ending • Other Title Trailers • Inserts: ID card, Mini Poster • Reversible Cover TECHNICAL FEATURES Fullscreen (1.33:1) • Subtitles/CC: Eng. • Languages: Jap., Eng. dub • Sound: Dolby Digital 2.0 • Keepcase • 1 Disc • Region 1 GENRE & RATING Science Fiction/Comedy • Rated 13+

Gatekeepers: For Tomorrow! [#8]

Pioneer, 2002, 80 mins., #11619. Directed by Yasuhiro Takemoto, Shinichi Tokairin, Koichi Chigira, Akihiko Nishiyama. Script by Hiroshi Yamaguchi. Based on the manga series by Gonzo in *Ace Next*.

NOTE: This DVD arrived too late for a full review. The following text is promotional copy provided by the releasing company:

"The Shadow commandeers the Tokyo Tower and broadcasts paranormal frequencies at 10,000 times the normal strength! The AEGIS commander scrambles the Gate Keepers to deal with the threat but Ruriko and Megumi remain missing. Unfortunately, the Gate Keepers are unable to stop the awakening of sleeper Invaders from all over Japan and the Shadow seizes control of the government! The fate of Japan rests on the shoulders of AEGIS, but even the HQ has been compromised. Only surprising revelations can provide the glimmer of hope necessary for survival!"

This disc contains episodes #22–24.

SPECIAL FEATURES Character and Art Galleries • Alternate Ending • Other Title Trailers • Inserts: Two ID cards, Mini Poster • Reversible Cover TECHNICAL FEATURES Fullscreen (1.33:1) • Subtitles/CC: Eng. • Languages: Jap., Eng. dub • Sound: Dolby Digital 2.0 • Keepcase • 1 Disc • Region 1 GENRE & RATING Science Fiction/Comedy • Rated 13+

Gate to the Mind's Eye, The

Simitar, 1997, 55 mins., #7321. Directed by Michael Boydston. Produced by Steven Churchill.

One of the earliest of the computer-animated musical anthologies was this disc. It features an original score by Thomas Dolby and nine segments. The "story" roughly follows an Alloy as he/it views the universe beginning again and the development of humankind. This gives the stories chronological latitude, including the ancient Egyptians and works of Leonardo da Vinci, all the way up to futuristic cities. Two tracks feature guest vocals by Dr. Fiorella Terenzi, a renowned Italian physicist.

As evidenced by its pathetic menu, this is an early DVD, but the picture quality still holds up. The releasing company is out of business, so this may be a difficult disc to find.

SPECIAL FEATURES None TECHNICAL FEATURES Fullscreen (1.33:1) • Languages: Eng. • Sound: Dolby Digital • Keepcase • 1 Disc • Region 1 GENRE & RATING CGI/Music/Anthology • Not Rated (Kids)

Gate to the Mind's Eye, The [Gold Series]

A-Pix, 2000, 55 mins. Directed by Michael Boydston. Produced by Steven Churchill.

This DVD was not available for review. The company is out of business. It contains the same feature as the Simitar version, with a slightly different cover.

General Chaos Uncensored Animation ☞ see
Mature/Adult Section

Generator Gawl: Vol. 1—Human Heart, Metal Soul

ADV Films, 2000, 75 mins., #DVDGG001. Directed by Seiji Mizushima, Yoshiaki Iwasaki, Ken Ando. Script by Manabu Ishikawa, Fumihiko Shimo. Based on the manga series by Hidefumi Kimura and Fumihiko Shimo in *Animedia*.

In the year 2007, the human genetic code has been unlocked, and humanity has been taken over by mutants known as Generators. Two young scientists, Ryo and Koji, travel into the past to stop future events from unfolding. They are accompanied by Gawl, who reluctantly became a Generator to fight the villains on their own terms. But even as they attempt to stop Professor Takuma Nekasa from fulfilling his scientific destiny—within the next three months—Generator agents from the future have come back in time to stop them!

This short-lived 1998 TV series only had twelve episodes, collected in four DVD volumes. The animation is adequate, with pastel colors, but some of the character designs are rather ugly. The storyline has a great resemblance to the *Terminator* films (and their SF predecessors), except with giant robots and giant bug creatures added to the mix. The DVD transfer is grainy enough that many fans have complained about its quality, but the biggest problem actually lies in the translation. Viewers should watch the dubbed English version with the Eng-

lish subtitles on to see the clearest example ever of what the dub vs. sub debate is all about. The difference in dialogue and script is astonishing. My suggestion: watch the Japanese track with subtitles.

SPECIAL FEATURES Character and Art Galleries • Schematics • Trailer • Clean Credits • Other Title Trailers TECHNICAL FEATURES: Fullscreen (1.33:1) • Subtitles/CC: Eng. • Languages: Jap., Eng. dub • Sound: Dolby Digital Surround 2.0 • Keepcase • 1 Disc • Region 1 GENRE & RATING Science Fiction/Robots • Rated 12+

Generator Gawl: Vol. 2—Future Memory

ADV Films, 2000, 75 mins., #DVDGG002. Directed by Seiji Mizushima, Shinichiro Kimura, Kiyotaka Ohata, Toshimasa Suzuki. Script by Manabu Ishikawa, Hidefumi Kimura, Akihiko Inari. Based on the manga series by Hidefumi Kimura and Fumihiko Shimo in *Animedia*.

Ryo confronts Professor Nekasa in order to stop the future developments, and secrets about Ryo's involvement with the creation of Gawl are revealed. The mysterious schoolteacher Ryuko Saito manipulates the future trio—and their friend Masami—while more powerful Generators come back in time to destroy Gawl and his allies.

Note that although the episodes listed on the back cover are numbered 1–3, they are actually episodes #4–6. The titles included are "Future Memory"; "The Best of Both Worlds"; and "Chameleons."

SPECIAL FEATURES Character and Art Galleries • Schematics • Trailer • Clean Credits • Other Title Trailers TECHNICAL FEATURES Fullscreen (1.33:1) • Subtitles/CC: Eng. • Languages: Jap., Eng. dub • Sound: Dolby Digital Surround 2.0 • Keepcase • 1 Disc • Region 1 GENRE & RATING Science Fiction/Robots • Rated 12+

Generator Gawl: Vol. 3—Secrets and Lies

ADV Films, 2001, 75 mins., #DVDGG003. Directed by Seiji Mizushima, Ichiro Miyoshi, Makoto Sokuza, Yoshiaki Iwasaki. Script by Fumihiko Shimo, Hidefumi Kimura, Manabu Ishikawa. Based on the manga series by Hidefumi Kimura and Fumihiko Shimo in *Animedia*.

Gawl's revelations to Masami lead to some tension, even as the surveillance of Ryuko Saito threatens the intent of the group's mission to the past. Much more is revealed about what actually happened/might happen in the future, and with only two weeks left to stop Professor Nekasa's experiments, Ryo, Koji, and Gawl must score a decisive victory soon—even if it means they will never exist.

Once again, the episodes listed on the back cover are numbered 1–3, but they are actually episodes #7–9. The titles included are "Secrets and Lies"; "Future Tense"; and "Storms."

SPECIAL FEATURES Character and Art Galleries • Schematics • Trailer • Clean Credits • Other Title Trailers TECHNICAL FEATURES Fullscreen (1.33:1) • Subtitles/CC: Eng. • Languages: Jap., Eng. dub • Sound: Dolby Digital Surround 2.0 • Keepcase • 1 Disc • Region 1 GENRE & RATING Science Fiction/Robots • Rated 12+

Generator Gawl: Vol. 4—Out of Time

ADV Films, 2001, 75 mins., #DVDGG004. Directed by Seiji Mizushima, Kiyotaka Ohata, Ichiro Miyoshi. Script by Fumihiko Shimo, Akihiko Inani. Based on the manga series by Hidefumi Kimura and Fumihiko Shimo in *Animedia*.

As the title of this volume suggests, Ryo, Koji, and Gawl have precious little time left to stop the future from being born. Help arrives from a surprising source, but sabotage and betrayal come from another person. And deadly new Generators come back in time to make sure the men from the future die in the past. There are lots of time paradoxes here, with mostly satisfying resolutions.

Again, the episodes listed on the back cover are numbered 1–3, but they are actually episodes #10–12. The final three titles included are "Rage within the Machine"; "Pleased to Meet Me"; and "Out of Time."

SPECIAL FEATURES Character and Art Galleries • Schematics • Trailer • Clean Credits • Other Title Trailers TECHNICAL FEATURES Fullscreen (1.33:1) • Subtitles/CC: Eng. • Languages: Jap., Eng. dub • Sound: Dolby Digital Surround 2.0 • Keepcase • 1 Disc • Region 1 GENRE & RATING Science Fiction/Robots • Rated 12+

Generator Gawl: Perfect Collection

ADV Films, 2002, 300 mins., #DGG/100.

This multikeepcase set includes the four *Generator Gawl* discs exactly as they appeared in the individual editions. See individual entries for the Special and Technical Features listings.

TECHNICAL FEATURES Multikeepcase • 4 Discs • Region 1 GENRE & RATING Science Fiction/Robots • Rated 12+

Genocyber: The Collection

U.S. Manga Corps, 1999, 156 mins., #USMD2007. Directed by Koichi Ohata. Script by Noboru Aikawa, Emu Ari, Koichi Ohata. Based on the manga series by Tony Takezaki in *Comic Shelf*.

Twin sisters Elaine and Diane Reed can join into one powerful being known as the Genocyber, but their wild nature leads to a rampage that destroys Tokyo in the 21st century. Many years later, the world is at war, and the Genocyber battles another deadly power suit creation in the Middle East. Jumping to the year 2400, a cult believes that the Genocyber is meant to cleanse the world and start humankind's destiny over again.

A trio of storylines compose this 1993 OVA series, with the second and third story split into two parts. The series looks fine but is very violent and bloody. The storyline isn't terribly involving, partially due to its 300-year arc, which means characters are less important than gory set pieces. Only recommended for those who like derivative violent B-movies.

SPECIAL FEATURES Character Bios • Other Title Trailers • Soundtrack Clips • DVD-ROM Features: Art, Storyboards, Models TECHNICAL FEATURES Fullscreen (1.33:1) • Subtitles/CC: Eng. • Languages: Jap., Eng. dub • Sound: Dolby Digital 2.0 • Keepcase • 1 Disc • Region All. GENRE & RATING Science Fiction/Horror • Rated 13+

Geo-Armor: Kishin Corps [Alien Defender]

Pioneer, 2001, 231 mins., #11488. Directed by Takaki Ishiyama. Based on books by Masaki Yamada.

In 1941, during the height of the second World War, an alien invasion of the Earth begins. Both the Axis and the Allies continue to fight each other, but the Kishin Corps and their four giant Geo-Armor robots take point in fighting the aliens. The Nazis are developing giant robots of their own, and they need a power device from the aliens. That device is being hidden by young Taishi, whose family is killed in the conflict. But will a woman whom Taishi trusts betray him to gain the alien control unit? And will the Kishin Corps be able to stand against the aliens even as the world battles around them?

One of the most original of the giant robot anime series, *Geo-Armor* is an alternate history story, putting its action not in a distant future or fantasy-based present, but squarely within World War II. The seven episodes were released in 1993–94, and although the final storylines may leave viewers a bit frustrated and wanting more resolution, the series is well worth watching. The animation style is at times cutesy and bulbous, but the steampunk look of the Kishins is very cool, as are the other retro designs. The extensive image gallery in the DVD extras section offers a closer look at those designs.

SPECIAL FEATURES Character and Art Galleries • Schematics • Easter Egg TECHNICAL FEATURES Fullscreen (1.33:1) • Subtitles/CC: Eng. • Languages: Jap., Eng. dub • Sound: Dolby Digital 2.0 • Multikeepcase • 2 Discs • Region 1, 4 GENRE & RATING War/Science Fiction/Retro Robots • Not Rated (Teens)

Geobreeders

U.S. Manga Corps, 1999, 90 mins., #USMD1874. Directed by Yuji Moriyama. Script by Yosuke Kuroda. Based on the manga series by Akihiro Ito in *Young King*.

A team of big-eyed pretty young girls are agents of the Kagura Total Security force. Their main job is to protect the world from phantom cats, ghostly creatures that haunt humanity. The phantoms can control magnetic data and be trapped by talismans and then deleted via computers. What do the cats have to do with a mysterious Russian cargo ship? Why do they attack an atomic power plant and a shopping mall? Those are questions the Kagura team must answer.

A short 1998 OVA series, *Geobreeders* is a female version of *Ghostbusters*, except it makes less sense. The logic behind the phantom cats and their actions takes a back seat to butt-kicking action and comic romps. Surprisingly fun and enjoyable at times, this does feature some brief nudity and lots of sight gags. Readers who are fond of catgirls are alerted that a few of them make an appearance here. This DVD features the first three episodes; the remaining four episodes have not yet been released on DVD.

SPECIAL FEATURES Other Title Trailers • Comic Book Covers • DVD-ROM Features: Art, Script, Storyboards, Comic Art • Easter Egg TECHNICAL FEATURES Fullscreen (1.33:1) • Subtitles/CC: Eng. • Languages: Jap., Eng. dub • Sound: Dolby Digital 2.0 • Keepcase • 1 Disc • Region All GENRE & RATING Girls/Action/Science Fiction • Rated 13+

Gestalt

AnimeWorks, 2000, 60 mins., #AWDVD0092. Directed by Osamu Yamazaki. Script by Mamiya Fujimura. Based on the manga series by Yun Koga in *G Fantasy*.

Father Olivier is a young priest of the Vasaria order, but his belief system is shaken when he saves a mute girl, Ohiri, from slavery. He takes her with

him to travel to the forbidden island of G, the supposed dwelling place of a powerful god. But as they travel, secrets about Ohiri's true nature are revealed, and battles with dark elves, elementals, and other magic obstacles await them.

Comprising two very short 1996 OVAs, *Gestalt* is really goofy. The art is total cheesecake, and the story vaguely silly. Digital painting doesn't quite help the picture, especially given the overly bright (some would say gaudy) colors chosen. Ohiri initially "talks" using onscreen text windows, but that device is gone shortly before it becomes really annoying. The story feels truncated, but fans can follow the pair's further adventures in the comics.

SPECIAL FEATURES Character and Art Galleries • Other Title Trailers TECHNICAL FEATURES Fullscreen (1.33:1) • Subtitles/CC: Eng. • Languages: Jap., Eng. dub • Sound: Dolby Digital • Keepcase • 1 Disc • Region 1 GENRE & RATING Fantasy/Adventure/Cheesecake • Rated 13+

Getter Robo: Transfiguration [Armageddon #1]

ADV Films, 2001, 100 mins., #DGR001. Directed by Yutaka Sato. Screenplay by Yutaka Sato, Yasuhiro Geshi, Keitaro Motonaga. Based on the manga series by Go Nagai and Ken Ishikawa.

During the lunar wars, a series of robots called "Getter Robo G" were created to defend mankind against alien threats. But in the years since then, the Getters have become fearsome weapons controlled by destructive forces. Now, the Getter creator—who everyone thought had been murdered—has created newer Getter Robos, as well as reanimating the dead and bringing back dinosaurs! The aliens may be gone (or are they?), but nuclear annihilation and destruction by giant robots are just a few of the things that humanity has to worry about now.

The original *Getter Robo* TV series was created in 1974, with *Getter Robo G* following in 1975 (dubbed for U.S. airing as *Starvengers*), plus a series of movies in 1975–76, and a third series, *Getter Robo Go!* in 1991. This DVD series collects the 1998 revival known as *Change Getter Robo*, which lasted for thirteen episodes. Some criticism has been leveled that the series "changed" too much by making several core characters and concepts evil—or at least vengeful. The animation is jagged, bumpy, and rather unattractive, though this is apparently intended to make it look like the older material. And as for the story, "convoluted" barely scratches the surface.

The DVD has nice production values and extras, but it's not without some problems. The "making of" segments, which highlight the ADR and voice actors, feature a camera that jiggles so much you'll think the camera operator was having a seizure. The menu takes forever to get to, as well. The four episodes here are: "From Beyond the Grave"; "Shin Dragon: God or Devil?"; "Goodbye Getters!"; and "After the Blast."

Note: some copies of *Getter Robo: Resurrection [Armageddon #1]* actually contained the pressing of volume #2, but ADV recalled most of them, so it's unlikely you'll get one.

SPECIAL FEATURES "Making of" Featurette • Character and Art Galleries • Clean Credits • Other Title Trailers • Laserdisc Covers TECHNICAL FEATURES Fullscreen (1.33:1) • Subtitles/CC: Eng. • Languages: Jap., Eng. dub • Sound: Dolby Digital 2.0 • Keepcase • 1 Disc • Region 1 GENRE & RATING Robots/Science Fiction • Rated 15+

Getter Robo: Resurrection [Armageddon #2]

ADV Films, 2001, 75 mins., #DGR002. Directed by Yutaka Sato. Screenplay by Masahiko Murata, Tomio Yamauchi, Yasuhiro Geshi. Based on the manga series by Go Nagai and Ken Ishikawa.

Thirteen years after humankind faced destruction, the survivors in Japan come back above ground to find the alien Invaders still fighting the forces of the Super Robot Army. The trio of Getter Robo pilots must try to stop the Invaders, even as the robots' own creator spurs on the coming apocalypse!

This DVD contains episodes #5–7: "The New Generation"; "The Awful Truth"; and "Into the Dragon."

SPECIAL FEATURES "Making of" Featurette • Character and Art Galleries • Clean Credits • Other Title Trailers • Easter Egg TECHNICAL FEATURES Fullscreen (1.33:1) • Subtitles/CC: Eng. • Languages: Jap., Eng. dub • Sound: Dolby Digital 2.0 • Keepcase • 1 Disc • Region 1 GENRE & RATING Robots/Science Fiction • Rated 15+

Getter Robo: Ascension [Armageddon #3]

ADV Films, 2001, 100 mins., #DGR003. Directed by Yutaka Sato. Screenplay by Nanako Shimazaki, Keitaro Motonaga, Kiyoshi Fukumoto. Based on the manga series by Go Nagai and Ken Ishikawa.

In the frozen tundra near Alaska, the Getter trio comes to the aid of a group of human survivors beset by Invader attacks. During the battle, they are joined by a new Black Getter Robo, whose silence makes his violent and deadly attacks against the Invaders more eerie. Then, the Getters go to New York to rescue some more survivors, but they're trapped, and only the Black Getter Robo can help them. And what disastrous evil is hidden in the cold of space?

Those who might be bothered by scenes of massive robot-battle destruction in New York City—including lower Manhattan and the World Trade Center buildings—might want to avoid this volume. It contains episodes #8–10: "Blood and Ice"; "Battleground Manhattan"; and "War in the Pacific."

SPECIAL FEATURES "Making of" Featurette • Clean Credits • Other Title Trailers • Laserdisc Insert Art TECHNICAL FEATURES Fullscreen (1.33:1) • Subtitles/CC: Eng. • Languages: Jap., Eng. dub • Sound: Dolby Digital 2.0 • Keepcase • 1 Disc • Region 1 GENRE & RATING Robots/Science Fiction • Rated 15+

Getter Robo: Salvation [Armageddon #4]

ADV Films, 2001, 75 mins., #DGR004. Directed by Yutaka Sato. Screenplay by Yutaka Sato, Yasuhiro Geshi, Jun Kawagoe. Based on the manga series by Go Nagai and Ken Ishikawa.

The Getter team battles the Shin Dragon, then prepares to take on the Invaders a final time. Though some attempt is made to make sense of the overall storyline, the flow soon gives way to more fighting. And let's just say that this contains perhaps the mother of all robot battles.

The final volume in this DVD series features episodes #11–13: "Overload!"; "Help from the Stars"; and "Evolution's End."

SPECIAL FEATURES "Making of" Featurette • Clean Credits • Other Title Trailers • Laserdisc Insert Art TECHNICAL FEATURES Fullscreen (1.33:1) • Subtitles/CC: Eng. • Languages: Jap., Eng. dub • Sound: Dolby Digital 2.0 • Keepcase • 1 Disc • Region 1 GENRE & RATING Robots/Science Fiction • Rated 15+

Getter Robo: Armageddon—Power Pack

ADV Films, 2002, 325 mins., #DGR/100.

This multikeepcase set includes the four *Getter Robo: Armageddon* discs exactly as they appeared in the individual editions. See individual entries for the Special and Technical Features listings.

TECHNICAL FEATURES Multikeepcase • 4 Discs • Region 1 GENRE & RATING Robots/Science Fiction • Rated 15+

Ghost in the Shell

Manga Entertainment, 1998, 82 mins., #800 635 529-2 WR02. Directed by Mamoru Oshii. Screenplay by Kazunori Ito. Based on the manga series by Masamune Shirow in *Young Magazine Kaizokuban*.

The year 2029: In a world controlled by the Internet, a cybernetic Puppet Master is replacing people's minds and memories with its own implanted evil. A group of government agents must stop the data thief before they lose their own minds. Enter cybernetic agent Major Motoko Kusanagi, a woman so heavily modified with implants that little of her remains except her own "ghost." She's aided by other cybercops as they try to trap the Puppet Master. But even as Kusanagi gets closer in her pursuit, she realizes that she may well be the target of the Puppet Master, and that a conspiracy between the government, security agencies, and the ghosts on the Internet may doom her.

Ghost in the Shell was released simultaneously in Japan, the U.S., and the UK in winter 1995, a first for an anime feature film. Its great hardcore science fiction/thriller plot melded perfectly with the CGI/cel animation merger to create an award-winning film that helped launch anime as a film art form as far as the popular media were concerned. In fact, the only other anime film as feted by the "world-at-large" is *Akira*, to which this compares favorably, even if style and tone are completely different.

The DVD is an excellent package, offering a bounty of extras. The "making of" video is a good starter for those who are new to anime as well as for seasoned pros. Multiple text pieces explore many of the complex ideas shown in the film, several of which presaged our society's massive reliance on the Internet and cyberspace. The film contains strong violence and nudity, but older viewers will want to watch this one again and again.

What does it mean to be human? Where does the soul come from? Can technology supplant a soul? These are questions to ponder while watching this highly recommended disc.

SPECIAL FEATURES "Making of" Featurettes • Cast and Crew Bios • Character Bios • Character and Art Galleries • Production Notes • Trailer • Synopsis • Glossary • Essays • Other Title Trailers TECHNICAL FEATURES Widescreen (1.85:1 enhanced for 16x9) • Subtitles/CC: Eng. • Languages: Jap., Eng. dub • Sound: Dolby Digital Surround 5.1 • Keepcase • 1 Disc • Region 1 GENRE & RATING Thriller/Science Fiction • Not Rated (Teens)

Ghost Sweeper Mikami

Manga Entertainment, 2002, 60 mins., #MANGA4115-2. Directed by Atsutoshi Umezawa. Scenario by Aya Matsui. Based on the manga series by Takashi Shiina in *Weekly Shonen Sunday*.

Reiko Mikami is the sexy leader of one of Japan's most unusual agencies. She and her team of exorcists will trap ghosts, fight demons, and even slay vampires—for a price. She'll need all her wits and weapons about her when an ancient spirit hires her to stop Nosferatu, the vampire lord who is draining the life, and souls, from his victims, turning Tokyo into a city of the living dead. Aided by a lovelorn assistant used for bait, a beautiful ex-ghost, a half-vampire, a priest, a voodoo woman, a young demon-beastmaster, a mad scientist/alchemist, and a robot, Mikami may get the upper hand—or she may lose her soul.

Mixing supernatural action with humor is a tough job, made even tougher in today's *Buffy the Vampire Slayer* era. This hour-long DVD contains the final two episodes of the popular Japanese TV series from 1993 to 1994. The animation is a bit cheap-looking and goofy, while Mikami herself suffers both from big-eye syndrome and unlikable character traits. Nevertheless, U.S. fans have waited a long time for the show to reach these shores, so these negatives aren't likely to dissuade fans of humor and horror. Be sure to stay after the end of the credits for a comedy moment.

SPECIAL FEATURES Character Bios • Character and Art Galleries • Other Title Trailers TECHNICAL FEATURES Widescreen (1.78:1) • Subtitles/CC: Eng. • Languages: Jap., Eng. dub • Sound: Dolby Digital Surround 5.1 • Keepcase • 1 Disc • Region 1–6 GENRE & RATING Horror/Action/Comedy • Not Rated (Teens)

G.I. Joe: The Movie

Rhino, 2000, 94 mins., #R2 976626. Directed by Don Jurwich. Written by Ron Friedman.

The forces of Cobra are back to their evil ways, and Serpentor, Destro, the Baroness, and Dr. Mindbender now have allies in the form of a race of 40,000-year-old snake people! Driven underground by the ice age, the snake people developed a spore that can turn humans into lesser beings. If they can take over the secret Broadcast Energy Emitter, the snake people can enslave mankind and rebuild Earth into a serpentine paradise. All that stands in their way are the heroic forces—and new recruits—of G.I. Joe!

In 1964, Hasbro Toys introduced a series of dolls for boys with a decidely militaristic bent. Highly popular, the G.I. Joe toys were discontinued in the late 1970s then revived again in 1982 as smaller action figures. A 1983 *G.I. Joe* animated pilot miniseries eventually led to a long-running syndicated action series, which led finally to this film in 1987.

Fans of the toys and series will want this DVD for the wave of nostalgia it inspires, but it's not terribly well-done despite its bigger budget. Voice actors on the feature included Don Johnson in the lead, as well as Burgess Meredith (the star of the 1945 live-action film *The Story of GI Joe*), and wrestler Sgt. Slaughter. The disc also features some cool-but-short extras, including twenty-five jaw-droppingly wonky "educational" public service announcements culled from the TV series.

SPECIAL FEATURES Trailers • Vintage Toy Commercials • Public Service Announcements TECHNICAL FEATURES Fullscreen (1.33:1) • Languages: Eng. • Sound: Dolby Digital Surround 5.1 • Keepcase • 1 Disc • Region 1 GENRE & RATING Action/Military • Not Rated (Kids)

Gigantor: Part 1—Episodes 1–26 [Box Set]

Rhino, 2002, 650 mins., #R2 976083. Based on the manga series by Mitsuteru Yokoyama in *Shonen Magazine*.

NOTE: This DVD arrived too late for a full review. The following text is promotional copy provided by the releasing company:

"Premiering in the mid-'60s, *Gigantor* blazed a trail for Japanese animation. The first of many shows featuring friendly giant robots, it achieved a distinctive look with cinematic touches and unusual camera angles. *Gigantor* is controlled by Jimmy Sparks, the son of his creator. Using a remote control joystick, Jimmy sends the huge fighting machine into battle, defending Earth against a never-ending assault by hostile aliens and enemy robots."

Transferred digitally from original 16mm film sources, these four DVDs contain episodes #1–26, plus lots of cool bonuses (including a few episodes of commentary on disc one). *Gigantor* also has one of the coolest box designs of any animated DVD yet!

SPECIAL FEATURES Interview with American Producer and Anime Historian • Commentary Track by Producer • Creator Bios • Character and Art Galleries • Other Title Trailers • Inserts: Episode Guide Booklet TECHNICAL FEATURES Fullscreen (1.33:1) • Languages: Eng. dub • Sound: Dolby Digital 1.0 • Plastic Box with Foldout Cardboard Case • 4 Discs • Region 1 GENRE & RATING Robot/Action • Not Rated (Kids)

Gokudo #1: Swordsman Extraordinaire

AnimeWorks, 2001, 125 mins., #EFDVD-8904. Directed by Kenichi Kasai. Script by Takeru Kirishima, Sumihiro Tomioka. Based on the book *Gokuda-Kun Mannyu-Ki* by Usagi Nakamura.

Gokudo is a greedy and obnoxious mullet-haired adventurer who travels the country searching for fame, fortune, and rascally good times. He soon gains allies in a drunken genie named Djinn, a tomboy princess named Rubette, and others. Early on, Gokudo is turned into a woman and captured by a king who wants virgin blood. Later, Gokudo and friends try to get him the job as king of a city . . . but things aren't quite as simple as they seem. But if Gokudo dies, how will they do a second disc?

Little in this comedy/action TV series from 1999 should be taken seriously, and it revels in overly cartoonish art and super-deformed sequences. Still, with a crude anti-hero and slapstick humor that crosses all boundaries (What? Fart jokes?), *Gokudo* will likely find fans searching for something lighthearted. With a generous five episodes on the disc, fans almost won't notice a lack of extras.

SPECIAL FEATURES Other Title Trailers TECHNICAL FEATURES Fullscreen (1.33:1) • Subtitles/CC: Eng. • Languages: Jap., Eng. dub • Sound: Dolby Digital 2.0 • Keepcase • 1 Disc • Region 1 GENRE & RATING Action/Fantasy/Comedy • Rated 13+

Gokudo #2: Magician Extraordinaire

AnimeWorks, 2002, 125 mins., #EFDVD-8909. Directed by Kenichi Kasai. Script by Sumihiro Tomioka. Based on the book by Usagi Nakamura.

Gokudo is betrayed by his fiancée, Princess Coco, even as he attempts to win the kingdom. But once in the hands of the Dumpling King, what will be Gokudo's fate? Plus, what happens when Gokudo meets a wizard prince who is a bigger jerk than himself?

The lowbrow humor continues with episodes #6–10 on this disc.

SPECIAL FEATURES Other Title Trailers • Easter Egg TECHNICAL FEATURES Fullscreen (1.33:1) • Subtitles/CC: Eng. • Languages: Jap., Eng. dub • Sound: Dolby Digital • Keepcase • 1 Disc • Region 1 GENRE & RATING Action/Fantasy/Comedy • Rated 13+

Gokudo #3: Goddess Extraordinaire

AnimeWorks, 2002, 100 mins., #EFDVD-8911. Directed by Kenichi Kasai. Script by Sumihiro Tomioka. Based on the book by Usagi Nakamura.

NOTE: This DVD arrived too late for a full review. The following text is promotional copy provided by the releasing company:

"A great war between the God world, the Magic world and the Buddha world? Not a problem for Gokudo, the greatest adventurer ever to serve himself and save the world. However, Gokudo is stuck babysitting the sun goddess, Nano. She's a spoiled brat with unbelievable cosmic powers, and if that combination doesn't give Gokudo a star-sized headache, nothing will."

This disc contains episodes #11–14.

SPECIAL FEATURES Character and Art Galleries • Clean Credits • Other Title Trailers TECHNICAL FEATURES Fullscreen (1.33:1) • Subtitles/CC: Eng. • Languages: Jap., Eng. dub • Sound: Dolby Digital • Keepcase • 1 Disc • Region 1 GENRE & RATING Action/Fantasy/Comedy • Rated 13+

Gokudo #4: Witches Extraordinaire

AnimeWorks, 2002, 100 mins., #EFDVD-8913. Directed by Kenichi Kasai. Script by Sumihiro Tomioka. Based on the book by Usagi Nakamura.

NOTE: This DVD arrived too late for a full review. The following text is promotional copy provided by the releasing company:

"The odds may be stacked against Gokudo, but he's not planning to slow down any time soon. This time, he's got a pair of bubble-headed Chinese witches to deal with, not to mention a spell-throwing talking panda. And if that isn't confusing enough, Gokudo wakes up one morning and finds that he's a girl again! Only this time, it's a specific girl, Rubette, and everyone else has changed places too. There's no justice in this world! What has a lying, cheating, sniveling weasel like Gokudo ever done to deserve all this?"

This disc contains episodes #15–18.

SPECIAL FEATURES Character and Art Galleries • Clean Credits • Other Title Trailers TECHNICAL FEATURES Fullscreen (1.33:1) • Subtitles/CC: Eng. • Languages: Jap., Eng. dub • Sound: Dolby Digital • Keepcase • 1 Disc • Region 1 GENRE & RATING Action/Fantasy/Comedy • Rated 13+

Gokudo #5: Lover Extraordinaire

AnimeWorks, 2002, 100 mins., #EFDVD-8916. Directed by Kenichi Kasai. Script by Sumihiro Tomioka. Based on the book by Usagi Nakamura.

NOTE: This DVD arrived too late for a full review. The following text is promotional copy provided by the releasing company:

"Gokudo and the gang have a new quest, to find the legendary Savior Device of the Buddha people! All they need to do is deal with the fact that their bodies and souls are still swapped around, Panda is giving birth to the monkey god, Goku, Jiki has become a turtle, the witch sisters have become snakes, and everyone has been recruited by the demon Ikkyu to be in a pop band. Luckily, they have help in the form of Nanya, a servant of the White Tiger God, but she's fallen hopelessly in love with Djinn's soul and Prince Niari's body. Even if they get all this straightened out and find the Savior Device, they still have to deal with the evil monk Sanzo, who has his own plans for it."

This disc contains episodes #19–22.

SPECIAL FEATURES Character and Art Galleries • Clean Credits • Other Title Trailers TECHNICAL FEATURES Fullscreen (1.33:1) • Subtitles/CC: Eng. • Languages: Jap., Eng. dub • Sound: Dolby Digital • Keepcase • 1 Disc • Region 1 GENRE & RATING Action/Fantasy/Comedy • Rated 13+

Golden Boy ☞ see Mature/Adult Section

Goldilocks and the Three Bears

Madacy, 1999, 30 mins.

This DVD was not available for review.

Golgo 13: Queen Bee—Special Edition ☞ see Mature/Adult Section

Gonad the Barbarian: Search for Uranus ☞ see Mature/Adult Section

Good Housekeeping Kids

The following *Good Housekeeping Kids* titles, from Simitar, were not available for review. The company is out of business. The titles are: *The Black Tulip; The Corsican Brothers; The Princess and the Pirate; A Tale of Two Kitties; The Three Musketeers;* and *5 Animated Adventures* [Box Set].

Goofy Movie, A [Gold Collection]

Disney, 2000, 78 mins., #19578. Directed by Kevin Lima. Story by Jymn Magon. Screenplay by Jymm Magon, Chris Matheson, Brian Pimenthal.

Single father Goofy just wants to bond with his teenage son, Max. Is that so wrong? The klutzy canine decides to take his offspring on a cross-country vacation, resulting in all sorts of accidents and misadventures, including a run-in with Bigfoot and a starring moment at a rock concert!

Goofy first appeared in 1932, though he was then called "Dippy Dawg." He starred in a variety of theatrical shorts, and even as part of a star trio in 1947's *Fun and Fancy Free*. In 1992, Disney spun him off into his own syndicated TV series called *Goof Troop*, wherein he gained Max and a suburban life filled with mishaps in Spoonerville. *A Goofy Movie* was his first starring role in a theatrical feature. Animated mainly in France and Australia, the 1995 film was a surprise hit, grossing over $35 million at the box office!

The disc offers a nice print of the film, as well as a twenty-two-minute *Goof Troop* cartoon from 1993, "Calling All Goofs." See *An Extremely Goofy Movie* for the animated sequel.

SPECIAL FEATURES Vintage Introduction • Trailer • Storybook • Music Video • Games • Other Title Trailers TECHNICAL FEATURES Fullscreen (1.33:1) • Subtitles/CC: Eng., Span. • Languages: Eng., Fren. dub, Span. dub • Sound: Dolby Digital Surround 2.0 • Keepcase • 1 Disc • Region 1, 4 GENRE & RATING Animals/Comedy/Music • Rated G

Goshogun: The Time Etranger

NuTech, 2001, 90 mins.

This DVD was not available for review.

Grandma Got Run Over by a Reindeer

Warner, 2001, 51 mins., #18652. Directed by Phil Roman. Story by Fred A. Rappaport, Elmo Shropshire, Jim Fisher, Jim Staahl. Screenplay by Jim Fisher, Jim Staahl.

Young Jake Spenkenheimer thinks he witnesses his grandmother being run over by Santa's sleigh on Christmas Eve. Now he's on a quest to prove that Santa is real and that Grandma is still alive, but his curvy and evil cousin Mel has more sinister plans. It will take a little elf magic, some flying reindeer, roundly hated fruitcake, and a day in court before this story is resolved.

Taking a novelty song written by Randy Brooks, the producers stretch it into an overly long 2000 holiday special for TV consumption. It tries very hard to please, but even with a twisted premise, the treacly message may be hard for adults to stomach. Kids will no doubt like it though, and there are a few gags for older audiences; check out the notes at the very end of the credit list.

SPECIAL FEATURES Songwriter Bio • Character Galleries • Trailer • Games TECHNICAL FEATURES Fullscreen (1.33:1) • Subtitles/CC: Eng. • Languages: Eng., Fren. dub, Span. dub • Sound: Dolby Digital Surround 2.0 • Snapcase • 1 Disc • Region 1 GENRE & RATING Holiday/Comedy/Music • Not Rated (Kids)

Grappler Baki: The Ultimate Fighter

U.S. Manga Corps, 1998, 45 mins., #USMD 1733. Directed by Yuji Asada. Screenplay by Yoshihisa Araki. Based on the manga series by Keisuke Itagake in *Shonen Champion*.

Baki Hanma is a mystery to the martial arts world. He seems to be able to predict his opponent's moves before they make them, blocking them and taking control of their weaknesses. And yet, he has a baby face and a body covered with scars. Now, he must enter the ShinShinkai organization's private arena for the fight of his life. His foe has left all of his previous opponents paralyzed or dead. Is Baki next in line for a body bag?

This 1994 OVA features a forgettable storyline, and some absolutely ugly, awful animation. I couldn't find a single redeeming quality in the DVD, other than perhaps the sheer relentlessness of the martial arts action.

Besides being offered as a single DVD, the disc was also included as part of a 2002 "Martial Arts Pack" set, along with *Ayane's High Kick*.

SPECIAL FEATURES Character Bios • History of Fighting • Other Title Trailers TECHNICAL FEATURES Fullscreen (1.33:1) • Subtitles/CC: Eng. • Languages: Jap., Eng. dub • Sound: Dolby Digital 2.0 • Keepcase • 1 Disc • Region All GENRE & RATING Wrestling/Martial Arts • Not Rated (Teens)

Grave of the Fireflies

Central Park Media, 1998, 88 mins., #CPMD1729. Directed by Isao Takahata. Written by Isao Takahata. Based on the autobiographical novel by Akiyuki Nosaka.

It is 1945 in Kobe, Japan, a city devastated during the war. Living within the rubble are orphaned children like young Seita and his little sister, Setsuko. As the two attempt to live in the shadows and ruined buildings, Seita learns to abandon his dignity if he wants to keep himself and his sister alive. And yet through all the hardships, he never abandons his love for little Setsuko, or the hope that his father will return. But sometimes love and hope are not enough to keep one anchored to life.

This 1988 movie, based on a semiautobiographical novel by a man whose little sister died of malnutrition during the war, is powerful and dramatic. The art for the animation uses brown lines instead of black, giving everything an earthy quality that implies either life or death depending on the scene. The story shows the hardship of life with constant air raids and bombing, and the threat of starvation that forces Seita to steal food to survive.

Having won multiple awards, *Grave of the Fireflies* belongs on every animation lover's viewing list. Not because the animation is drawn particularly well, but because it is a powerful example of great, dark, historic storytelling perhaps unrivaled by any other animated project (only *Barefoot Gen* comes close in this arena). American animators—and animation studios—would never be this bold. This is not a lighthearted film; it's grim and generally depressing, and parents should think twice about showing it to younger kids. But it *should* be seen, and it gets a high recommendation.

SPECIAL FEATURES: Character Bios • Other Title Trailers TECHNICAL FEATURES Widescreen (1.85:1) • Subtitles/CC: Eng. • Languages: Jap., Eng. dub • Sound: Dolby Digital 2.0 • Keepcase • 1 Disc • Region All GENRE & RATING Drama/War • Not Rated (Teens)

Grave of the Fireflies [Collector's Edition]

Central Park Media, 2002, 159 mins., #CPMD2206. Directed by Isao Takahata. Written by Isao Takahata. Based on the autobiographical novel by Akiyuki Nosaka.

Take everything I said above about *Grave of the Fireflies* and multiply it by two. There are two discs in this set, with some excellent features that shine a light on this animation diamond. Interviews with Isao Takahata, Akiyuki Nosaka, and film critic Roger Ebert are but a few of the cool extras, as is the option to watch the film with alternate angle storyboards!

Both the picture and soundtrack have been remastered, and the look is more vibrant than its predecessor. In fact, the only complaint one could have with this disc at all is that CPM has listed it as suitable for ages 3+! Unless you really want traumatized tots, stick with my recommendation that this is for older viewers.

SPECIAL FEATURES "Making of" Featurettes • Interviews with Director, Author, and Film Critic • Historical Commentary Featurette • Crew Bios • Character and Art Galleries • Storyboards • Trailers • Promotional Footage • DVD-ROM Features: Art, Scripts, Reviews, Awards • Other Title Trailers TECHNICAL FEATURES Widescreen (1.85:1) • Subtitles/CC: Eng. • Languages: Jap., Eng. dub • Sound: Dolby Digital 2.0 • Keep-

case • 1 Disc • Region All GENRE & RATING Drama/War • Rated 3+

Gravity Angels: Alien Discovery [#1]

Slingshot, 2000, #BDVD9305. Directed by Simon Klaebe. Written by Chris Wheeler and Damien Hogan.

On Jupiter's icy moon of Ganymede, a colony sponsored by corporate giant Miller-Western used to be the crown jewel of space life. But in 2098, it's a crumbling slum full of chemical spills and a mystery in need of a solution. Settlers keep turning up dead, and six outsiders must find out why.

This is a "Multipath Adventure," a cross between a video game and traditional storytelling. As viewers watch the story, they are presented with choices of action every few minutes. Each choice (made using the DVD remote) branches the story off in a new direction, meaning there are multiple outcomes and storylines for the characters. The animation is rough 3D CGI, which will probably be fine for video game enthusiasts, but it will hurt the eyes of traditional animation fans.

SPECIAL FEATURES Other Title Trailers TECHNICAL FEATURES Widescreen (2.35) • Languages: Eng. • Sound: Dolby Digital Surround 5.1 • Keepcase • 1 Disc • Region 1–6 GENRE & RATING Science Fiction/Interactive • Not Rated (Teens)

Gravity Angels: The Betrayal [#2]

Slingshot, 2000, #BDVD9319. Directed by Simon Klaebe. Written by Chris Wheeler and Damien Hogan.

Corporate giant Miller-Western will order the death of anyone who might expose its secrets. What are they hiding on Ganymede, Jupiter's moon, and how will it affect humanity's future? It's up to several characters—whose choices are controlled by you—to find the answers.

This is another "Multipath Adventure" with branching story choices. Like its predecessor, the animation is the rough 3D CGI appropriate for video games.

SPECIAL FEATURES Other Title Trailers TECHNICAL FEATURES Widescreen (2.35) • Languages: Eng. • Sound: Dolby Digital Surround 5.1 • Keepcase • 1 Disc • Region 1–6 GENRE & RATING Science Fiction/Interactive • Not Rated (Teens)

Great Animation Studios, The: Fleischer Studios

Winstar, 2000, 90 mins., #WHE73104.

One of the most innovative animation studios in history was Fleischer
Studios, founded by brothers Max
and Dave Fleischer. Max created the
rotoscoping process for the pair's first
cartoon, which featured Dave as
Koko the Clown, in 1914. Soon after,
they were creating "Out of the
Inkwell" cartoons for Paramount, many combining live-
action segments with animation. They also created the
"bouncing ball" technique that helped audiences follow
the lyrics of songs onscreen. Dozens of other innovations
followed, including the first long-form cartoon, and
more.

The Fleischers are best known for their work on such
characters as Koko the Clown, Betty Boop, Popeye, and
the luminescent *Superman* cartoons that still inspire
today's top animators. This disc contains prints of eleven
cartoon shorts from the 1920s to the 1940s. Print quality
varies, but restoration work on the cartoons has brightened and cleaned them considerably. It's a good selection
of classic animation, and fans would do well to check it
out.

Cartoons on the disc are: Koko and Max in "Tantaliz-
ing Fly" (1917–1920); Koko and Max in "Bubbles"
(1922); Betty Boop and Koko in "Betty Boop's Ker-
Choo" (1933); Betty Boop and Max in "More Pep"
(1936); "Song of the Birds" (1934); Popeye in "Little
Swee' Pea" (1936); Betty Boop and Grampy in
"Grampy's Indoor Outing" (1936); "Small Fry" (1939);
"Ants in the Pants" (1940); Gabby in "It's a Hap-Hap-
Happy Day" (1941); and "Popeye the Sailor Meets
Aladdin and His Wonderful Lamp" (1939).

SPECIAL FEATURES Production Notes and Bios TECHNICAL FEATURES
Fullscreen (1.33:1) • Languages: Eng. • Sound: Dolby Digital
Surround 2.0, Dolby Digital 5.1 • Keepcase • 1 Disc • Region
1–6 GENRE & RATING Comedy/Anthology • Not Rated (All Ages)

Great Mouse Detective, The

Disney, 2002, 74 mins., #21619. Directed
by John Musker, Ron Clements, Dave
Michener, Burny Mattinson. Story by Pete
Young, Vance Gerry, Steve Hulett, Ron
Clements, John Musker, Bruce M. Morris,
Matthew O'Callaghan, Burny Mattinson,
Dave Michener, Melvin Shaw. Based on
the book *Basil of Baker Street* by Eve
Titus.

In 1897 London, brave Olivia only
has one place to turn when her toymaker father disappears: to sleuth Basil of Baker Street, his assistant Dr.

Dawson, and their dog Toby. Their adventures—and the
clues—lead them to Professor Ratigan, a villain who
wants to control the world by using a robot rodent that
will help him dethrone the mouse queen!

This 1986 release by Disney was the first feature film
to have digital footage, and its use in the climactic battle
within London's Big Ben clock makes for a bravura
scene. Vincent Price turns in a chilling performance as
Ratigan. *The Great Mouse Detective* is a fun diversion of a
film, though not one of Disney's most memorable, or
profitable.

The disc contains a restored and remastered version of
the feature, as well as a nice trove of art from production.
There are also two animated shorts: the Academy
Award–nominated "Donald's Crime" (1945) and the
Mickey Mouse–starring "Clock Cleaners" (1937).

SPECIAL FEATURES "Making of" Featurette • Character and Art
Galleries • Trailer • Sing-Along • Other Title Trailers TECHNICAL
FEATURES Widescreen (1.66:1 enhanced for 16x9) •
Subtitles/CC: Eng. • Languages: Eng., Fren. dub, Span. dub •
Sound: Dolby Digital 5.1 Surround • Keepcase • 1 Disc •
Region 1 GENRE & RATING Music/Animal/Detective • Rated G

Green Legend Ran

Pioneer, 1998, 140 mins., #PIDA1131V.
Directed by Satoshi Saga. Screenplay by
Yu Yamato.

Six alien Rodo descend to Earth and
suck up most of its vegetation and
water. What's left of humanity lives in
the shadow of these "Holy Mothers,"
where crops still grow. A religion
based on alien worship becomes the
governing power over humanity, though groups of freedom fighters are trying to retake control. Young boy Ran
is caught between the opposing forces; he blames the
rebellious Hazzards for the death of his mother, but the
Rodoists are responsible for the planet's further decline.
If he and a silver-haired priestess can find the Holy
Green, they might bring the balance of nature back to
Earth.

A three-part OVA series from 1992, *Green Legend Ran*
mixes action with ecological messages, and more than
a touch of *Dune*. It's a thinking person's post-
apocalypse/alien invasion storyline. The DVD contains a
nice print, but the simplistic animation style on gritty
sandswept backgrounds isn't terribly attractive. Astonishingly enough, there are no menu functions at all! The
music video and director's comments have to be watched
by clicking forward to the 50th and 51st chapter segments. The subtitle feature allows two English tracks: a
translation of the Japanese script or the English script.

SPECIAL FEATURES Director Interview • Music Video TECHNICAL
FEATURES Fullscreen (1.33:1) • Subtitles/CC: Eng., CC • Languages: Jap., Eng. dub • Sound: Dolby Digital 2.0 • Keepcase

• 1 Disc • Region 1, 4 GENRE & RATING Science Fiction/Alien Invasion/Environmental • Not Rated (Teens)

GSC: Gunsmith Cats—Bulletproof!

ADV Films, 2001, 90 mins., #DGS001. Directed by Takeshi Mori. Screenplay by Atsuji Kaneko. Based on the manga series by Kenichi Sonoda in *Comic Afternoon*.

Rally Vincent and Minnie May Hopkins are two firepower-toting lethal ladies whose grasp of the law is far exceeded by their grasp on their firearms. Rally's into guns, Minnie's into grenades, and the two of them are bounty hunters on the streets of Chicago, often racing to the scene in their souped-up Shelby GT-500. Their missions include infiltrating a gun-smuggling operation, catching a psycho Russian assassin, and recapturing a load of illegal weapons that are connected with a politician.

Only three episodes of *Gunsmith Cats* were produced as 1995 OVAs, and that's a damn shame. The animation features strong visuals, nice technical design, clearly researched Chicago backgrounds, loads of humor, and great action. The slick pop-art opening credit sequence ranks as one of the best ever seen in anime. The stories are fairly faithful to the original manga, and although there is lots of violence, it isn't too strong for teens to view. Watching *Gunsmith Cats* is like scuffing your feet on the carpet; you know the jolt will be there but you want to do it anyhow. An extensive "making of" segment on the DVD makes this a must-own.

SPECIAL FEATURES "Making of" Featurette • Trailers • Other Title Trailers • Clean Credits TECHNICAL FEATURES Fullscreen (1.33:1) • Subtitles/CC: Eng. • Languages: Jap., Eng. dub • Sound: Dolby Digital 2.0 • Keepcase • 1 Disc • Region 1, 2, 4 GENRE & RATING Guns/Girls/Action • Rated 15+

GTO: Great Teacher Onizuka [#1]

TokyoPop, 2002, 125 mins., #TPDV-1322. Directed by Noriyuke Abi, Naoyasu Hanyu, Nao Okezawa, Hayato Date, Tomio Uchiyama. Written by Masashi Sogo, Yoshiyuki Suga, Satoru Nishizono. Based on the manga series by Toru Fujisawa in *Weekly Shonen Magazine*.

Twenty-two-year-old Eikichi Onizuka used to be a bike gang leader, but now he wants to teach high school so he can meet young girls. The road to a teaching degree, however, is paved with a class of dimwits who harass and blackmail him, a perverted vice principal who fondles girls on the train, bullied students who plan to roof-dive, and manipulated photos showing Onizuka in some compromising

situations. If Onizuka wasn't both a hard-ass and a heart-on-his-sleeve guy, he wouldn't survive high school. The word is still out on whether or not his juvenile delinquent students will live to see higher education.

An ultra-popular manga led to this 1999 television series (and a live-action series as well). Watching it, all I could think of was that it played like a WB sitcom starring bigoted rapper Eminem in a remake of *Welcome Back Kotter*. Onizuka is not a role model by any means, but his bad-boy antics do prompt some smiles. It's too bad that the figure animation is so ugly; *GTO* would pass with flying colors if it looked better. File this slickly produced DVD under "guilty pleasures" and show it to your friends, but *not* to your parents.

SPECIAL FEATURES Character and Art Galleries • Japanese Openings & Endings • Other Title Trailers • Insert: GTO Temporary Tattoo TECHNICAL FEATURES Fullscreen (1.33:1) • Subtitles/CC: Eng. • Languages: Jap., Eng. dub • Sound: Dolby Digital 2.0 • Keepcase • 1 Disc • Region 1 GENRE & RATING School/Humor/Action • Rated 16+

GTO: Great Teacher Onizuka—The Bully [#2]

TokyoPop, 2002, 125 mins., #TPDV-1332. Directed by Yoshiki Odaka, Hiroyuki Ishido, Akihiro Enomoto, Hayato Date, Naoyasu Hanyu. Written by Yoshiyuki Suga, Satoru Nishizono, Ryota Yamaguchi. Based on the manga series by Toru Fujisawa in *Weekly Shonen Magazine*.

Five more fun-filled episodes of *GTO* find the lewd and crude Onikuza still up to his pierced ears in troubled teens. This time out, the teacher-in-training bullies the bullies, gets targeted by the PTA, and becomes involved with the single mother of a student. Plus, bungee jumping and bowling figure prominently in the last two episodes.

Another nicely packed "guilty pleasure" DVD, this features an interesting set of insert footnotes, in which the series translator explains Japanese humor, spotlights the manga/anime in-jokes in the series, and explains the various "eye-catches" used as promotional spots.

SPECIAL FEATURES Character Galleries • "Onizuka Goes Wild" Clips • Japanese Openings & Endings • Promotional Footage • Other Title Trailers • Insert: Episodic Footnotes TECHNICAL FEATURES Fullscreen (1.33:1) • Subtitles/CC: Eng. • Languages: Jap., Eng. dub • Sound: Dolby Digital 2.0 • Keepcase • 1 Disc • Region 1 GENRE & RATING School/Humor/Action • Rated 16+

GTO: Great Teacher Onizuka—Outcasts [#3]

TokyoPop, 2002, 125 mins., #TPDV-1342. Directed by Hiroto Kato, Yutaka Kagawa, Yoshiki Odaka, Naoyasu Hanyu, Kazunori Mizuno. Written by Masashi Sogo, Ryota Yamaguchi, Yoshiyuki Suga. Based on the manga series by Toru Fujisawa in *Weekly Shonen Magazine.*

NOTE: This DVD arrived too late for a full review. The following text is promotional copy provided by the releasing company:

"Onizuka mentors a young (and very well-endowed) female student that has been ostracized by her classmates. The bad news is not everyone thinks this student/teacher relationship is healthy. The good news is that Great Teacher Onizuka doesn't care what other people think."

This disc contains episodes #11–14.

SPECIAL FEATURES Character and Art Galleries • "Onikuza Goes Wild" Clips • Clean Credits • Promotional Footage • Other Title Trailers • Inserts: Liner Notes TECHNICAL FEATURES Fullscreen (1.33:1) • Subtitles/CC: Eng. • Languages: Jap., Eng. dub • Sound: Dolby Digital • Keepcase • 1 Disc • Region 1 GENRE & RATING School/Humor/Action • Rated 16+

GTO: Great Teacher Onizuka—The Test [#4]

TokyoPop, 2002, 125 mins., #TPDV-1352. Directed by Hiroyuki Ishido, Shigeki Hatakeyama, Akihiro Enomoto, Naoyasu Hanyu, Hiroto Kato. Written by Yoshiyuki Suga, Satoru Nishizono. Based on the manga series by Toru Fujisawa in *Weekly Shonen Magazine.*

NOTE: This DVD arrived too late for a full review. The following text is promotional copy provided by the releasing company:

"Onizuka is in for his biggest challenge yet—not only must he pass a nationwide exam to keep teaching, but he's also introduced to mischief and mayhem, all wrapped up in the feminine form of notorious teacher killer Urumi. Using beauty, bombs and blackmail, this vicious vixen seems unstoppable. It's up to GTO to save the day."

This disc contains episodes #15–19.

SPECIAL FEATURES Interview with Creator • Character and Art Galleries • "Onikuza Goes Wild" Clips • Clean Credits • Promotional Footage • Other Title Trailers • Inserts: Liner Notes TECHNICAL FEATURES Fullscreen (1.33:1) • Subtitles/CC: Eng. • Languages: Jap., Eng. dub • Sound: Dolby Digital • Keepcase • 1 Disc • Region 1 GENRE & RATING School/Humor/Action • Rated 16+

Guardian of Darkness—Takegami: War God

U.S. Manga Corps, 1998, 130 mins., #USMD1748. Directed by Osamu Yamazaki. Screenplay by Osamu Yamazaki.

Koichi and Terumi are two youngsters who don't realize they're about to play a part in an ages-old war. A trio of ancient dragons are coming, and only the avatar that contains the spirit of a powerful warrior god from the past can defeat the beasts. Will Tokyo crumble beneath dragonfire, or will the ancient war god find his champion?

Three 1990 OVA episodes are collected on this DVD, which contains some brief-but-gratuitous nudity and quite a bit of violence. The animation style favors 1980s' big hair and big eyes, though the backgrounds are nice. The DVD cover art makes this look like a mecha-heavy project, but it really isn't. It also isn't very entertaining or memorable.

SPECIAL FEATURES Director Interview • Character Bios • Character and Art Galleries • Other Title Trailers TECHNICAL FEATURES Fullscreen (1.33:1) • Subtitles/CC: Eng. • Languages: Jap., Eng. dub • Sound: Dolby Digital 2.0 • Keepcase • 1 Disc • Region All GENRE & RATING Fantasy/Horror • Not Rated (Teens)

Gulliver's Travels [60th Anniversary]

Winstar, 1999, 110 mins., #WHE73044. Directed by Dave Fleischer. Story by Edmond Seward. Written by Dan Gordon, Ted Pierce, Izzy Sparber, Edmond Seward. Based on the book by Jonathan Swift.

Adventurer Lemuel Gulliver is swept off a sailing ship, and his body is tossed onto a beach. There, he is discovered by the tiny people of Lilliput, who consider him a giant. Although they fear Gulliver at first, the Lilliputians come to see him as their friend, especially when the neighboring kingdom of Blefuscu attacks. Even though the Lilliputian Princess Glory and the Blefuscuan Prince David are betrothed, it's going to take a big hand—in the form of Gulliver—to bring the kingdoms to peace and the lovers together.

In the late 1930s, Max and Dave Fleischer decided to mount a full-scale animated feature film in response to Walt Disney's classic *Sleeping Beauty.* Like that film, *Gulliver's Travels* used rotoscoping for much of its naturalistic animation, but since the Fleischers had invented the technique, they had higher claim to it. Over 700 artists worked on the film for eighteen months, and it premiered with great acclaim in theaters in December 1939. Although it did not win, it was nominated for Academy Awards for Best Song and Best Score.

There are three DVD versions of *Gulliver's Travels*, each offering something different. This disc from Winstar has the best picture, with a full digital restoration that makes it look a decade old instead of six. It offers multiple different soundtracks, from the state-of-the-art newly recorded tracks to the untouched original version. The beautiful picture quality is complemented by a documentary about the Fleischer Studios, as well as press kit and promotional materials that detail the film's extensive media campaign. Two Gabby cartoons are presented as well: "King for a Day" (1940) and "Swing Cleaning" (1941).

As much an American cartoon classic as any Disney film, *Gulliver's Travels* deserves watching by every animation fan.

SPECIAL FEATURES Fleischer Studios Documentary • Restoration Demo • Character and Art Galleries • Production Notes • Other Title Trailers TECHNICAL FEATURES Fullscreen (1.33:1) • Languages: Eng. • Sound: Dolby Digital 1.0 on Original Soundtrack, Dolby Digital 2.0, Dolby Digital 5.1 • Keepcase • 1 Disc • Region 1–6 GENRE & RATING Fantasy/Adventure/Music • Not Rated (All Ages)

Gulliver's Travels

Image, 2000, 83 mins., #HRS9447. Directed by Dave Fleischer. Story by Edmond Seward. Written by Dan Gordon, Ted Pierce, Izzy Sparber, Edmond Seward. Based on the book by Jonathan Swift.

The second DVD release for *Gulliver's Travels* is also the second in terms of quality. Although the print was apparently taken from a 35mm master and restored, it shows a lot of pops and scratches in the artwork. It does feature the original trailer, which is in beautiful shape, but it is presented badly framed with a significant part of the edges cut off. It includes an extra Gabby cartoon—"It's a Hap-Hap-Happy Day" (1941)—but you can't click to it. The only way to watch it is to wait until after the end credit sequence.

SPECIAL FEATURES Trailer TECHNICAL FEATURES Fullscreen (1.33:1) • Languages: Eng. • Sound: Dolby Digital 2.0 • Snapcase • 1 Disc • Region 1–6 GENRE & RATING Fantasy/Adventure/Music • Not Rated (All Ages)

Gulliver's Travels

GoodTimes, 2001, 76 mins., #05-81212. Directed by Dave Fleischer. Story by Edmond Seward. Written by Dan Gordon, Ted Pierce, Izzy Sparber, Edmond Seward. Based on the book by Jonathan Swift.

The third DVD release of the Fleischer film is, unfortunately, the worst. The film print is more scratched than the Image version, and there are no extras whatsoever. At least it has some nice liner notes on the back of the keepcase sleeve.

SPECIAL FEATURES None TECHNICAL FEATURES Fullscreen (1.33:1) • Languages: Eng. • Sound: Dolby Digital Mono • Keepcase • 1 Disc • Region All GENRE & RATING Fantasy/Adventure/Music • Not Rated (All Ages)

Gumby: Vol. 1

Rhino, 2002, 121 mins., #R2 976078. Directed by Art Clokey, Ray Peck, Pete Kleinow. Written by Ray Peck, Pete Kleinow.

Hey kids! Before there were Sims, there were marionettes and puppets, which only moved and talked with the help of humans. One of the most famous of these was Howdy Doody, a frightening-looking cowboy puppet. On TV's *The Howdy Doody Show* in 1956, a new cartoon star was born. Made of green clay, the maleable humanoid was known as Gumby. His orange horse was Pokey. Over the course of their adventures, other molded characters joined the cast, including the nasty Blockheads, Prickle the dinosaur, and the blue girl Goo.

So popular were these shorts that NBC debuted *The Gumby Show* in March 1957. The series stayed in syndication for decades and spawned a second series in 1988 titled *The All-New Gumby*. Through the years, the little green clayboy stretched and glided his way through over a hundred adventures, most split into two- to three-part stories. The *Gumby* tales were very imaginative, verging on the bizarre at times, Creator Art Clokey and his team tapped into the wonder and acceptance with which a child views the world, and streamlined it into morphing clay fun.

Rhino collects the first twenty-one *Gumby* episodes on this initial disc, with prints that show some scratches due to age but are generally very nice. There's even an all-new opening segment animated for the disc, featuring Gumby, Pokey, and the Kid Rhino mascot. Recommended for kids of all ages.

SPECIAL FEATURES Inserts: Liner Notes TECHNICAL FEATURES Fullscreen (1.33:1) • Languages: Eng. • Sound: Dolby Digital

• Keepcase • 1 Disc • Region 1 GENRE & RATING Stop
Motion/Puppet • Not Rated (All Ages)

Gumby [Box Set]

Rhino, 2002, #R2 970085. Directed by Art Clokey.

This DVD box set was not available for review. It also
contains a small Gumby figure.

Gundam Wing: The Movie—Endless Waltz [Special Edition]

Bandai, 2000, 180 mins., #1680. Directed
by Yasunao Aoki. Screenplay by Katsuyuki Sumizawa. Based on the manga
series by Hajime Yatate, Yoshiyuki Tomino in *Mobile Suit Gundam*.

It's AC 196 and a year of peace
between Earth and the space colonies
has everyone breathing easier. All but
one of the Gundam pilots are so sure
peace will last that they send their Gundam armor
hurtling into the sun. That's just when somebody decides
to break out her secret supply of custom Mobile Suits in
an effort to take over the world from the "Earth Sphere
Unified Nation." Now, with one friend held captive by
the villain, a pilot missing with his never-destroyed
armor, and their own Gundam suits about to get a major
sunburn, will the Gundam pilots be able to pull humanity back from the brink of war yet again?

Both the 1997 OVA mini-series (approximately 80
mins.) and its later reedited film version (94 mins.) are
available on this packed DVD that has had fans raving
since its release. The story handily continues the *MS
Gundam Wing* series for one more adventure, though
some have complained that it is an unnecessary story.
The script features some thoughtful exploration about
the purposes and reasons of war, while the animation is
some of the best ever seen on the series. Bold new Gundam designs and clean, nicely detailed art, with none of
the anime stereotypes, make this a visual treat. The packaging—with its metallic paper covers—lends an added
flair.

If you haven't watched *Mobile Suit Gundam* or any of
its various incarnations, you may be lost by events on this
disc and should start earlier in the series. But if you like
the *Gundam* series, here's a shining example of a DVD
that deserves its appellation "Special Edition."

SPECIAL FEATURES Character and Art Galleries • Mobile Suit
Encyclopedia • Clean Credits • Other Title Trailers • Easter
Egg TECHNICAL FEATURES Fullscreen (1.33:1) • Subtitles/CC: Eng.
• Languages: Jap., Eng. dub • Sound: Dolby Digital 2.0,
Dolby Digital 5.1 • Keepcase • 1 Disc • Region 1 GENRE & RAT-
ING Robots/Science Fiction • Rated 13+

Gundam Wing: The Movie—Endless Waltz [Toonami Version]

Bandai, 2000, 90 mins., #1681. Directed
by Yasunao Aoki. Screenplay by Katsuyuki Sumizawa. Based on the manga
series by Hajime Yatate, Yoshiyuki Tomino in *Mobile Suit Gundam*.

This is the Toonami version of the
Endless Waltz movie, as aired on the
Cartoon Network. There are some
slight edits to bring the running time
down and sanitize some of the violence. The Japanese-
language track has also been removed, as have, inexplicably, the subtitles.

SPECIAL FEATURES Other Title Trailers TECHNICAL FEATURES
Fullscreen (1.33:1) • Languages: Eng. dub • Sound: Dolby
Digital 2.0 • Keepcase • 1 Disc • Region 1 GENRE & RATING
Robots/Science Fiction • Rated 13+

H

Hades Project: Zeorymer

The following *Hades Project: Zeorymer* titles, from NuTech, were not available for review: *Hades Project: Zeorymer* [#1]; *Hades Project: Zeorymer* [#2]; *Hades Project: Zeorymer* [Box Set]

Haitoku no Shoujyo: Family of Debauchery

☛ see Mature/Adult Section

Hamtaro: Hamtaro and the Ham-Hams [#1]

VIZ/Pioneer, 2002, 60 mins., #DHA01. Directed by Osamu Nabeshima. Scripts by Yoshiyuki Suga, Michiru Shimada, Fumihiko Shimo, Toshiyasu Nagata, Miho Maruo, Koji Miura. Based on the manga series by Kentaro Miura.

NOTE: This DVD arrived too late for a full review. The following text is promotional copy provided by the releasing company:

"With over 20 million viewers since its U.S. debut on Cartoon Network, *Hamtaro* tells the heart-warming story of little hamsters and their big adventures. When ten-year-old Laura moves to a new town, she's not the only one who has to make new friends. Her pet hamster, Hamtaro, also needs to get used to his new surroundings and find new hamster friends. Meet Hamtaro and his gang of hamster pals, known as 'The Ham-Hams,' as they join forces to help Laura solve various problems and embark on countless adventures.

"In *Hamtaro: Hamtaro and the Ham-Hams*, Hamtaro and Laura move into their neighborhood and happily get used to their surroundings by both making new friends. One day after school, Hamtaro learns that Laura's new friends have pet hamsters of their own. He'll see them all soon at the new Ham-Ham Clubhouse! Unfortunately, when all the new Ham-Hams meet, there is some unexpected personality clashing!"

SPECIAL FEATURES None TECHNICAL FEATURES Fullscreen (1.33:1) • Subtitles/CC: Eng. • Languages: Eng. dub • Sound: Dolby Digital • Keepcase • 1 Disc • Region 1 GENRE & RATING Animals/Comedy • Not Rated (All Ages)

Hand Maid May: Maid to Order [#1]

Pioneer, 2000, 100 mins., #11556. Directed by Shinichiro Kimura. Screenplay by Mutsumi Nakano, Kenichi Yamada, Koichi Taki, Kazuki Matsui. Based on the manga series by Juzo Mutsuki and Wonder Farm in *AX*.

College engineering student Kazuya Saotome has an enemy in the flamboyant Nanbara, aka "Mr. Laaaaaarge!," but he never expects his rival to deliver his bitterness in such a delightful way. Nanbara's computer virus results in Kazuya getting an experimental cyborg maid from Cyberdine. She's only a foot tall, but she's sweet, sexy, and oh-so-cheerful. But will May the maid help or hinder Kazuya's goal of completing his own female cyborg? And what about the $1.5 million bill that Cyberdine expects Kazuya to pay?

Panty shots, cleavage, and lots of beautiful animated women throwing themselves at a geeky guy—where have we seen this before? A 2000 TV series, *Hand Maid May,* is yet another in a long line of Japanese comedies that feature women as objects to be ogled, rather like a cartoon *Playboy* channel. Nanbara is annoying as hell, especially in the premenu sequence in which you have to guess which words best describe him (it's the bottom right "Mr. Laaaaaarge!"). You then have to endure more clips of his antics before you're finally delivered to the menu.

This four-episode DVD is well-designed, except for the premenu Nanbara sequence and the fact that several extra features are blocked until future discs are released. Truthfully, the humor is kind of sweet and even entertaining at times. Fans of *Tenchi Muyo* or *Saber Marionette* will likely enjoy this.

SPECIAL FEATURES Character Bios • Appendix • Easter Eggs TECHNICAL FEATURES Fullscreen (1.33:1) • Subtitles/CC: Eng. • Languages: Jap., Eng. dub • Sound: Dolby Digital 2.0 • Keepcase • 1 Disc • Region 1, 4 GENRE & RATING Cheesecake/Comedy • Rated 13+

Hand Maid May: Product Recall [#2]

Pioneer, 2000, 75 mins., #11591. Directed by Shinichiro Kimura. Screenplay by Koichi Taki, Kazuki Matsui, Kenichi Yamada. Based on the manga series by Juzo Mutsuki and Wonder Farm in *AX*.

Kazuya hasn't paid Cyberdine's huge bill for May, and the corporation wants her back! Now, Kasumi selflessly helps Kazuya and May have one last day together. It's not hard to guess that May will be back though, but in the meantime, who is the mysterious Mami who has her eyes on Kazuya? Plus, Nanbara falls in lust with May, and a fireworks festival leads to some explosions of the heart.

Lots more panty shots and cutesy humor—plus some extensive Easter eggs—make this disc fun for fans of the genre. The three episodes included are: "Until Today, I've Really. . ."; "More! More!"; and "I Don't Have Much Time?"

SPECIAL FEATURES Character Bios • Appendix • Easter Eggs
TECHNICAL FEATURES Fullscreen (1.33:1) • Subtitles/CC: Eng. • Languages: Jap., Eng. dub) • Sound: Dolby Digital 2.0 • Keepcase • 1 Disc • Region 1, 4 GENRE & RATING Cheesecake/Comedy • Rated 13+

Hand Maid May: Memory Failure [#3]

Pioneer, 2001, 100 mins., #11592. Directed by Shinichiro Kimura. Screenplay by Koichi Taki, Mutsumi Nakano, Kazuki Matsui, Shinichiro Kimura. Based on the manga series by Juzo Mutsuki and Wonder Farm in *AX*.

A flesh-eating bacteria causes Kazuya to lose three of his limbs, forcing May into prostitution, and . . . what, you don't buy that? Well, there *is* a virus loose in one episode, but it only affects Cyberdine dolls. Plus, a typhoon blows ill winds, and Nanbara's descendant from the future comes back in time. Oh yeah, and there are a bunch of panty shots as well.

The final four episodes of the series are on this disc: "There's So Much I Want!"; "Besides That . . . I Believe You"; "My Best!"; and "Never Give Up."

SPECIAL FEATURES Character Bios • Appendix • Easter Eggs
TECHNICAL FEATURES Fullscreen (1.33:1) • Subtitles/CC: Eng. • Languages: Jap., Eng. dub • Sound (Dolby Digital 2.0) • Keepcase • 1 Disc • Region 1, 4 GENRE & RATING Cheesecake/Comedy • Rated 13+

Hans Christian Andersen: Fairy Tale Classics [Box Set]

Delta Entertainment, 2001, 123 mins., #89073. Based on the stories by Hans Christian Andersen.

This box set features the three individually available volumes *Thumbelina*, *The Little Mermaid*, and *The Emperor's New Clothes* in their original keepcases. See individual entries for the Special and Technical Features.

TECHNICAL FEATURES Fullscreen (1.33:1) • Languages: Eng. • Sound: Dolby Digital 2.0 • Cardboard Box with 3 Keepcases • 3 Discs • Region All GENRE & RATING Fantasy/Family/Comedy • Not Rated (All Ages)

Hansel and Gretel: An Opera Fantasy

View Video, 2001, 72 mins., #2421. Directed by Michael Meyerberg.

This DVD was not available for review. The opera was composed by Engelbert Humperdinck.

Happy Tree Friends: Vol. 1—First Blood ☞
see Mature/Adult Section

Harlock Saga

U.S. Manga Corps, 2001, 180 mins., #USMD2032. Directed by Yoshio Takeuchi. Screenplay by Megumi Hiyoshi. Based on the manga series by Reiji Matsumoto in *Shonen Sunday* and the opera *Der Ring des Nibelungen* by Richard Wagner.

He may traverse space in the pirate ship Arcadia, but Captain Phantom F. Harlock isn't really a bad guy. When a killer named Alberich steals a legendary treasure known as the "Rhein gold," he plans to turn it into a ring that will give him the power to conquer the galaxy. Accompanied by some old allies, Harlock must stop Alberich and recover the gold before the old gods awaken and humanity pays the price.

Although the story pays homage to Wagner's operatic cycle *Der Ring des Nibelungen*, the characters have been around since the 1970s. Harlock headlined his own TV series in 1978, followed by spin-offs and multiple reinterpretations of his story. The version contained on this disc is a six-part OVA series from 2000, and it is moody, well-drawn space opera. The character designs are a bit dated, but Harlock, *Queen Emeraldas*, and *Starblazer* fans will want to get it. The DVD itself is crammed with extras, more than perhaps any other single-sided DVD;

some of the special features alone make it worth the price.

Besides being offered as a single DVD, the disc was also included as part of a 2002 set, along with *Maetel Legend*.

SPECIAL FEATURES "Making of" Featurettes • Creator Interviews • Text Interviews • Character and Art Galleries • Historical Notes • Clean Credits • Other Title Trailers • DVD-ROM Features: Interviews, Scripts, Art, Reviews, Glossary TECHNICAL FEATURES Fullscreen (1.33:1) • Subtitles/CC: Eng. • Languages: Jap., Eng. dub • Sound: Dolby Digital 2.0 • Keepcase • 1 Disc • Region All GENRE & RATING Science Fiction/Action/Opera • Rated 13+

Harmagedon

U.S. Manga Corps, 1998, 132 mins., #USMD1723. Directed by Rintaro. Screenplay by Chiho Katsura, Makoto Naito, Masaki Mori. Based on the book series by Kazumasa Hirai and the manga series by Shotaro Ishinomori.

An evil force called Genma is loose in the universe and is on its way to destroy Earth. Princess Luna and cybernetic heroine Vega are determined to save humankind from Genma, but they'll have to gather a group of the world's most powerful psychics to accomplish the task. But Genma's agents are already on Earth, preparing the way to the coming darkness, and they'll kill anyone who stands in their way, psychic or not.

If you can get past the goofy first five minutes, you'll find a fun psychic apocalypse action film from 1983. The hyped character designs by Katsuhiro Otomo (*Akira*) aren't terribly interesting, but this is an enjoyable couple of hours. The ending theme music is by Keith Emerson of Emerson, Lake and Palmer, but you may want to hit mute when it comes on.

SPECIAL FEATURES Character Bios • Character and Art Galleries • Other Title Trailers TECHNICAL FEATURES Fullscreen (1.33:1) • Subtitles/CC: Eng. • Languages: Jap., Eng. dub • Sound: Dolby Digital 2.0 • Keepcase • 1 Disc • Region All GENRE & RATING Psychic/Science Fiction • Not Rated (Teens)

Haunted Castle

Slingshot, 2001, 132 mins., #SDVD9263. Directed by Ben Stassen. Written by Ben Stassen.

Years ago, a woman made a deal with Mephisto, trading her soul for fame and fortune. After her death, her young musician son Johnny is summoned to an ancient castle, where he is given the same offer. But as Johnny explores the castle, scare upon scare is heaped upon him.

He decides to rescue his mother's soul and all hell breaks loose!

Combining live action with CGI animation, *Haunted Castle* was originally created in 3D for IMAX theaters. The DVD contains two thirty-eight-minute versions of the film—2D and 3D—as well as a host of extras, including virtual image galleries and lots of behind-the-scenes material. This makes for good spooky fun that won't be too scary for younger audiences. It's too bad it doesn't come with 3D glasses, because the visuals are cool enough in 2D that they must look fantastic in three dimensions.

See *Alien Adventure* for similar fun from the same director.

SPECIAL FEATURES "Making of" Featurette • Commentary Track by Director • Virtual Character and Art Galleries • Trailer • Electronic Press Kit • Other Title Trailers TECHNICAL FEATURES Fullscreen (1.33:1) • Languages: Eng. • Sound: Dolby Digital Surround 5.1, DTS • Keepcase • 1 Disc • Region 1–6 GENRE & RATING CGI/Live/Horror • Rated PG

Haunted Junction

Bandai, 2000, 300 mins., #1130. Directed by Yuji Muto. Story by Nemu Mukudori. Screenplay by Kazuhisa Sakaguchi, Satoru Nishizono, Yuji Hashimoto. Based on the manga series book by Nemu Mukudori in *Dengeki Comics*.

A school with a secret: some of its students are dead! The son of a minister, Haruto Hojo is the president of the Holy Student Council at Saito High. His friends are Mutsuki Asahina, a Shinto priestess and exorcist, and Kazumi Ryudo, a Buddhist who's always getting possessed. Together, the three contend with all manner of weird—and sometimes dangerous—ghosts, goblins, and other spooks. There's a voluptuous woman who haunts the bathroom stalls, an anatomical model and tiny skeleton that haunt the science lab, an attention-seeking girl who lives in the mirrors, a giant pair of dancing legs in the school gym, fish monsters in the pool, walking statues. . . . High school is Hell, especially at Saito High.

A cross between *Buffy the Vampire Slayer* and *Harry Potter*, *Haunted Junction* first appeared on TV in 1997. It's very funny, though not for youngsters due to some nudity, swearing, and Ms. Mutsuki's predeliction for younger boys. The animation is pleasant, and most of the humor translates well, though some jokes (especially the names of some characters) will pass over the heads of Western audiences. With all twelve episodes on two discs, this is recommended for those who want their funny bones tickled.

SPECIAL FEATURES Character and Art Galleries • Easter Egg TECHNICAL FEATURES Fullscreen (1.33:1) • Subtitles/CC: Eng. • Languages: Jap., Eng. dub • Sound: Dolby Digital Surround 2.0 •

Multikeepcase • 2 Discs • Region 1 GENRE & RATING Comedy/Horror/Fantasy • Rated 13+

Headcandy: Sidney's Psychedelic Adventure

Victory Video, 1998, 60 mins.

This DVD was not available for review.

Heat for All Seasons, A ☞ see Mature/Adult Section

Heavy Metal ☞ see Mature/Adult Section

Heavy Metal 2000 ☞ see Mature/Adult Section

Heavy Traffic ☞ see Mature/Adult Section

Hello Kitty's Paradise: Pretty Kitty [#1]

ADV Films, 2002, 90 mins., #DHK/001.

NOTE: This DVD arrived too late for a full review. The following text is promotional copy provided by the releasing company:

"Hello Kitty's Paradise is a part of the wildly popular Hello Kitty franchise, built around the adorable, instantly recognizable kitten character. The title centers around the adventures of legendary character Hello Kitty, her best friend Mimmy and their friends from school. Hello Kitty's Paradise is a joyful take on childhood adventures, with a healthy smattering of educational content about such important skills as sharing, having good table manners, writing letters, and being polite."

The first DVD in this series includes the following episodes: "A Blooming Good Morning"; "A Storybook Adventure"; "Kitty's Clean Cuisine"; "A Day Out with Dad"; "Underground Kitty"; "Watch the Birdie"; "Minding Manners"; and "Streetwise."

SPECIAL FEATURES Other Title Trailers TECHNICAL FEATURES Fullscreen (1.33:1) • Subtitles/CC: Eng. • Languages: Jap. Eng. dub • Sound: Dolby Digital 2.0 • Keepcase • 1 Disc • Region 1 GENRE & RATING Animals/Girls • Not Rated (All Ages)

Hellsing: Impure Souls [#1]

Pioneer, 2002, 75 mins., #11813. Directed by Yasunori Urata, Kaoru Suzuki, Manabu Ono. Screenplay by Chiaki J. Konaka. Based on the manga series by Kota Hirano in *Monthly Young King Ours.*

NOTE: This DVD arrived too late for a full review. The following text is promotional copy provided by the releasing company:

"The worst enemy of the night—is one of its own . . . A secret war is brewing in the night—a war in which humanity is only a pawn. The mysterious Hellsing Organization deploys within the shadows to protect ordinary mortals from the undead legions that would prey upon us. Now, as the ghouls and vampires increase in number, they threaten the human police forces forcing the deployment of the Hellsing Organization's ultimate weapon—the rogue vampire, Arucard! After saving Victoria Seras Victoria, a special police operative, from death by transforming her into a vampire, Arucard must work with her to fight the undead army—as well as her own newfound hungers!"

This disc contains episodes #1–3.

SPECIAL FEATURES Character and Art Galleries • Trailer • Action Figure Photos • Clean Credits • Other Title Trailers • Inserts: Mini Poster TECHNICAL FEATURES Fullscreen (1.33:1) • Subtitles/CC: Eng. • Languages: Jap., Eng. dub • Sound: Dolby Digital 2.0 • Keepcase • 1 Disc • Region 1 GENRE & RATING Horror/Action • Rated 16+

Hellsing: Blood Brother [#2]

Pioneer, 2002, 75 mins., #11814. Directed by Yasunori Urata, Yutaka Takeda, Shinya Hanai, Ryoki Uetsobo. Screenplay by Chiaki J. Konaka. Based on the manga series by Kota Hirano in *Monthly Young King Ours.*

NOTE: This DVD arrived too late for a full review. The following text is promotional copy provided by the releasing company:

"Arucard and the Hellsing Organization face a twofold challenge! A traitor within begins leaking classified information about the Organization, and a TV journalist is out to expose Hellsing's secret mission! Then, the ruthless Valentine Brothers lead their undead army on a deadly raid against the Hellsing headquarters, interrupting the secret Round Table meeting . . ."

This disc contains episodes #4–6.

SPECIAL FEATURES Staff Interview • Character and Art Galleries • Action Figure Photos • Clean Credits • Other Title Trailers • Inserts: Mini Poster TECHNICAL FEATURES Fullscreen (1.33:1) • Subtitles/CC: Eng. • Languages: Jap., Eng. dub • Sound:

Dolby Digital 2.0 • Keepcase • 1 Disc • Region 1 GENRE & RAT-
ING Horror/Action • Rated 16+

Hellsing: Search and Destroy [#3]

Pioneer, 2002, 75 mins., #11815. Directed
by Kaoru Suzuki, Akihiko Nishiyama,
Tokio Yamauchi. Screenplay by Yuji
Hosono, Chiaki J. Konaka. Based on the
manga series by Kota Hirano in *Monthly
Young King Ours.*

NOTE: This DVD arrived too late for
a full review. The following text is
promotional copy provided by the
releasing company:

"The Hellsing Organization's war against the undead
intensifies! The organization suffers major losses in battle
and Arucard must face Paladin Alexander from Iscariot
again! Then, the stakes are raised as he prepares to face
one of the original undead, and Integra fights for her life
against her own sister?"

This disc contains episodes #7–9.

SPECIAL FEATURES Character and Art Galleries • Packaging Art •
Clean Credits • Other Title Trailers • Inserts: Mini Poster TECH-
NICAL FEATURES Fullscreen (1.33:1) • Subtitles/CC: Eng. • Languages: Jap., Eng. dub • Sound: Dolby Digital 2.0 • Keepcase
• 1 Disc • Region 1 GENRE & RATING Horror/Action • Rated 16+

Hellsing: Special Collector's Box

Pioneer, 2002, 75 mins., #11691.

This cardboard box set is sized to fit
four volumes of *Hellsing*, but it contains only the first volume, plus an
insert to fill out the rest of the box.
Collectors can fill out their own box
collection. See individual entries for
the Special and Technical Features
listings.

TECHNICAL FEATURES Cardboard Box with 1 Keepcase • 1 Disc
GENRE & RATING Horror/Action • Rated 16+

Hercules

Madacy, 1999, 50 mins., #DVD9 9141.

This DVD was not available for review.

Hercules [Collector's Edition]

Digital Versatile Disc, 2000, 48 mins.,
#174. Directed by Tim Forder. Written by
Leslie Sayle Scharf, Michael Eugene
Fairman.

Hercules is the son of Zeus, king of
the Greek gods. But Zeus's wife Hera
is jealous of Hercules, and she tricks
him into some destructive actions. To
make up for his misdeeds, Hercules is
given some labors to perform, including killing the
many-headed Hydra.

A 1997 production by Pure Magic, *Hercules* is a somewhat faithful retelling of the Greek myth, but the animation is atrocious. We're talking painfully bad, from awful
character designs to boring backgrounds; even the script
is putrid and sometimes anachronistic. While kids may
not mind watching it for a few minutes, its unlikely even
youngsters will be able to make it through this tripe.
Still, it might be good for an animated version of *Mystery
Science Theater 3000.*

SPECIAL FEATURES Mythology Notes • Games TECHNICAL FEATURES
Fullscreen 1.33:1 • Languages: Eng. • Sound: Dolby Digital
Surround 5.1, DTS • Keepcase • 1 Disc • Region All GENRE &
RATING Fantasy/Adventure • Not Rated (All Ages)

Hercules [Gold Collection]

Disney, 2001, 93 mins., #19708. Directed
by Ron Clements, John Musker. Story by
Barry Johnson. Screenplay by Ron
Clements, Don McEnery, Irene Mecchi,
John Musker, Bob Shaw.

Baby Hercules is the pride of daddy
Zeus, but Hades, Lord of the Underworld, is planning a takeover. He
sends his minions to kill Hercules, but
they mess up and only turn him mostly mortal. As his
parents watch from high above the Earth on Mount
Olympus, Hercules grows older and stronger. He eventually learns of his divine heritage, but if he ever wants to
claim his throne in the Greek pantheon, he has to go
from "zero to hero" and prove his worth through a series
of tasks. Along the way, he's helped by his childhood flying horse Pegasus, a feisty satyr named Phil, and a reluctant smart-mouthed beauty named Meg. But Hercules'
road to glory won't be easy; Hades is still determined to
see him dead!

Released in 1997, *Hercules* wasn't nearly as big a hit
with audiences as it should have been. Based on designs
by British caricaturist Gerald Scarfe—and images on
ancient Greek pottery—the animation is beautifully stylized, harkening back to some of the more experimental
elements of *Fantasia.* The voice cast is tremendous, with

stand-out James Woods (Hades) holding his own against Robin Williams's *Aladdin* genie for sheer ad-libbing bravura. Danny DeVito, Bobcat Goldthwait, Matt Frewer, and Rip Torn also chew the hell out of the scenery, and are all the funnier for it. The script is fast and lean, and even skewers modern movie merchandising such as that eventually done for *Hercules!* In-jokes and inventive dialogue abound, and the music—often sung by a literal Greek chorus—is mostly sensational.

The DVD of *Hercules* doesn't have many frills, but it does offer a perfect widescreen print (though it measures out at 1.85:1, not the 1.66:1 listed on the cover). A nice "making of" covers the basics, but the oddest component will probably be the Ricky Martin music video of the Oscar-nominated (and Golden Globe-winning) theme song "Go the Distance." What's so odd about it? It's the Spanish-language music video, with no English version or subtitles!

Hercules is one of the five best comedies ever made by Disney (including *Who Framed Roger Rabbit?, Aladdin, Toy Story*, and *A Bug's Life*). Go get a copy and see what you missed in theaters.

SPECIAL FEATURES "Making of" Featurettes • Music Video • Other Title Trailers TECHNICAL FEATURES Widescreen 1.66:1 • Subtitles/CC: Eng. • Languages: Eng., Fren. dub, Span. dub • Sound: Dolby Digital Surround 5.1 • Keepcase • 1 Disc • Region 1 GENRE & RATING Comedy/Fantasy/Music • Rated G

Hercules [Limited Edition]
Disney, 93 mins., #18010.

This DVD was not available for review. It is on moratorium. The contents are the same as the *Gold Collection* version, but it features a different cover.

Hercules and Xena: The Animated Movie—The Battle for Mount Olympus

Universal, 1998, 80 mins., #20160. Directed by Lynne Naylor. Written by John Loy.

Hercules and Xena, Warrior Princess, are joined by their young sidekicks, Iaolus and Gabrielle, in a new myth. Angry Hera, queen of the Greek gods, decides it is time for her to be in charge of the universe. She takes charge of the powerful Chronos Stone and frees the Titans, monstrous elemental proto-gods who have been imprisoned beneath the Earth's crust for millennia. Now, even with the muscles of Hercules and the chakram-throwing power of Xena, the supernatural power of the Titans may destroy all hope.

It must have sounded good on paper. Take two action characters at the top of the syndicated ratings charts, and combine them in a kid-friendly animated film. Add in a bit of singing to draw in those parents who fear it might be too violent, and voila, instant hit, right? Wrong. 1987's *Hercules and Xena: The Animated Movie* is poorly animated, and the character designs are ugly in the extreme, though the backgrounds do have a psychedelic retro-hippy chic. Even if the characters are voiced by their live-action counterparts Kevin Sorbo and Lucy Lawless, little of their charm or personality comes through. And even a dedicated showtunes fan will cringe at the songs (though Lawless sings her solo nicely). Sorry, folks, this one's for *Hercules* and *Xena* completists only.

This disc, in its original keepcase, was also included as part of the *Hercules Action Pack* box set from Universal.

SPECIAL FEATURES Cast Bios TECHNICAL FEATURES Fullscreen: 1.33:1 • Subtitles/CC: Eng., Fren., Span. • Languages: Eng., Fren. dub, Span. dub • Sound: Dolby Digital Surround 2.0 • Keepcase • 1 Disc • Region 1 GENRE & RATING Fantasy/Adventure/Music • Rated PG

Here Comes Peter Cottontail

Sony Wonder, 2002, 95 mins., #LVD 54187. Directed by Arthur Rankin, Jr., Jules Bass. Based on the book *The Easter Bunny That Overslept* by Priscilla and Otto Friedrich.

NOTE: This DVD arrived too late for a full review. The following text is promotional copy provided by the releasing company:

"Peter Cottontail wants to be the chief Easter Bunny, and everyone in April Valley agrees . . . except for evil Irontail. Peter must deliver more eggs than his archrival to earn the top spot . . . and save Easter for children everywhere! Hop along with Peter and his friend Seymour S. Sassafrass (the voice of Danny Kaye) as they race through time to overcome Irontail's terrible plans and restore the magic of Easter Sunday.

"Then, enjoy a classic bonus feature from *The Festival of Family Classics* by Rankin/Bass. In *Puss in Boots*, Jacques and the family cat Tabby strike out on their own to seek their fortune. When they buy a pair of lucky wishing boots, Tabby transforms into 'Puss in Boots,' with adventure and fun in store for everyone they encounter."

Note that although the disc cover claims it is closed captioned, it is not.

SPECIAL FEATURES Sing-Alongs TECHNICAL FEATURES Fullscreen (1.33:1) • Languages: Eng. • Sound: Dolby Digital • Keepcase • 1 Disc • Region 1 GENRE & RATING Holiday/Stop Motion/Animal • Not Rated (All Ages)

Herman and Catnip and Friends
Digital Disc Entertainment, 1999.

This DVD was not available for review. The company is out of business.

Hermes: Winds of Love

Image, 2001, 114 mins., #ID1015SIDVD. Directed by Tesuo Imazawa. Written by the Hermes Scenario Project.

Prince Hermes rescues and marries Princess Aphrodite, then plans to overthrow King Minos of Crete. After helpers Theseus and Ariadne face the Minotaur in Minos' labyrinth, Hermes kills the evil king. Learning he is the reincarnation of the head god Ophealis, Hermes then travels Greece doing good deeds and opening up free trade routes with the rest of the known world. Then he decides to banish unhappiness from the land!

Although this bears a tenuous resemblance to actual Greek mythology, this 1997 film makes a hash out of the old stories and even its own story. Blame for this can partially be laid on the producers, a neo-Buddhist religious movement called Kofuku no Kagaku (The Insitute for Research in Human Happiness), who wanted the anime story to reflect their belief system. The evangelical group's founder, Ryuho Okawa, claims that he is a reincarnation of the Hermes consciousness. Does this remind anyone else of the connection between Scientology and *Battlefield Earth*?

If you can get past the thinly disguised New Age religious elements, the animation and designs in this film are quite beautiful, and the DVD transfer is good as well. There is no English dub, so if you want to just enjoy the visuals without the evangelical "messages," turn off the subtitles and just let the Japanese language track play. There's also an isolated "music and sound effects" track, which means you don't have to listen to the dialogue at all! The extra segment listed on the packaging as an outtake is actually a deleted scene.

SPECIAL FEATURES Trailers • Deleted Scene TECHNICAL FEATURES Widescreen: 1.85:1 • Subtitles/CC: Eng. • Languages: Jap. • Sound: Dolby Digital Surround 2.0, Dolby Digital Surround 5.1 • Keepcase • 1 Disc • Region 1–6 GENRE & RATING Fantasy/Adventure • Not Rated (Kids)

Heroic Legend of Arslan: Age of Heroes

U.S. Manga Corps, 1998, 240 mins., #USMD1747. Directed by Mamoru Hamazu. Screenplay by Tomoya Miyashita, Kaori Takada, Megumi Sugihara. Based on the novel series by Yoshiki Tanaka.

In an ancient time, half-crocked King Andragoras defends his land against the Rucitanians, but he is captured by a mysterious man known as Silver Mask. Andragoras' son is Arslan, a blond heroic figure who searches the lands for allies. He raises a new army that includes legendary warriors and old friends. But as battles on the land and sea commence, Arslan learns of a connection between himself and Silver Mask . . . and the two of them are fated to clash over who will ascend to the country's throne.

Produced in 1991, this fantasy series is very nicely animated, with the first two parts in widescreen. Though the story does get a bit disjointed at times—partially due to the dub—it's easy enough to follow for any fan of medieval sword and sorcery (although the sorcery is *very* minor). The two-DVD set features all four parts of the original storyline, as well as the secondary *Age of Heroes* story. Unfortunately, the story ends without a firm resolution; viewers will have to get the novels or manga to find out what happens. One of the extras is an interesting segment of the DVD producers talking about name changes for the characters, as requested by the licensors. The first four parts feature British actors and one set of names, while *Age of Heroes* features a different voice cast and a second set of names.

SPECIAL FEATURES Character Bios • Character and Art Galleries • Trailer • Other Title Trailers TECHNICAL FEATURES Widescreen: 1.85:1 • Fullscreen: 1.33:1 • Subtitles/CC: Eng. • Languages: Jap., Eng. dub • Sound: Dolby Digital 2.0 • Multikeepcase • 2 Discs • Region All GENRE & RATING Fantasy/Adventure • Not Rated (Teens)

Highlander: The Animated Series—The Adventure Begins

Artisan, 2000, 77 mins.

This DVD was not available for review.

His and Her Circumstances: The Appearance of a Normal Life [#1]

Right Stuf, 2002, 180 mins., #RSDVD8011. Directed by Hideaki Anno. Screenplay by Hideaki Anno. Based on the manga series by Maami Tsuda and Hideaki Anno in *Monthly LaLa*.

NOTE: This DVD arrived too late for a full review. The following text is promotional copy provided by the releasing company:

"A high-tension story of the heart-rending rivalries of a first love. Like a drug, Yukino Miyazawa was addicted to admiration and praise from those around her. She worked hard to become the perfect student, the perfect girl. But that was before . . . him. Souichirou Arima. The instant she met him, she hated him. Without even trying, he snatched the very glory from her hands by easily acing the high school entrance exam that should have made her the class representative. To take back what is rightfully hers, Yukino is putting all her efforts into plotting her revenge, but was love part of the plan?"

This disc contains episodes #1–6.

SPECIAL FEATURES Character Bios • Producer Notes • Production Notes • Storyboards • Other Title Trailers • Easter Egg TECHNICAL FEATURES Fullscreen (1.33:1) • Subtitles/CC: Eng., Span. • Languages: Jap., Eng. dub • Sound: Dolby Digital 2.0 • Keepcase • 1 Disc • Region 1 GENRE & RATING Romance/Drama • Rated 13+

His and Her Circumstances: Love and War Under the Cherry Blossoms [#2]

Right Stuf, 2002, 150 mins., #RSDVD8012. Directed by Hideaki Anno. Screenplay by Hideaki Anno. Based on the manga series by Maami Tsuda and Hideaki Anno in *Monthly LaLa*.

NOTE: This DVD arrived too late for a full review. The following text is promotional copy provided by the releasing company:

"Happiness could be a fleeting thing for our two new high school sweethearts Yukino and Arima. With their hearts flying high, the couple has been spending a lot of time together. Finally the public masks of perfection that they've both maintained for so long are beginning to fall, but so are their grades.

"When the latest round of scores is posted, Yukino is mortified to discover that she's slipped all the way to 13th! She's not the only one that's angry—so are her teachers. When Yukino and Arima are dragged before their guidance counselor to explain their poor grades, the administration is determined that the pair stop seeing each other. Could this mean the end of their newfound love forever?"

This disc contains episodes #7–11.

SPECIAL FEATURES Actor Interviews • Character Bios • Production Notes • Other Title Trailers • Easter Egg TECHNICAL FEATURES Fullscreen (1.33:1) • Subtitles/CC: Eng., Span. • Languages: Jap., Eng. dub • Sound: Dolby Digital 2.0 • Keepcase • 1 Disc • Region 1 GENRE & RATING Romance/Drama • Rated 13+

His and Her Circumstances: Vol. 1 [with box]

Right Stuf, 2002, 180 mins.

This DVD was not available for review. It features the same version as the keepcase edition, but comes in a cardboard box intended to contain the whole set.

Hobbit, The

Warner, 2001, 78 mins., #566. Directed by Arthur Rankin, Jr., Jules Bass. Written by Romeo Muller. Based on the book by J.R.R. Tolkien.

Middle Earth is a land of elves, wizards, dragons, humans, and furry-footed short people known as Hobbits. One of these Hobbits is Bilbo Baggins, and when Gandalf the wizard asks his help in recovering the golden One Ring of Power, how can he refuse? Little does he know that the days ahead will be filled with giant spiders, the subterranean Gollum, killer trolls, the great fire-breathing dragon Smaug, and temptation.

This TV special first aired on NBC in 1977, predating Ralph Bakshi's *Lord of the Rings* film by less than a year. Although *The Hobbit* truncates the 1937 book significantly, it hits many of Tolkien's high points, and features a great voice cast including Orson Bean, John Huston, and "Theodore" as the creepily obsessed Gollum. The animation is gorgeous and lush, and translates well to DVD (though it does have a lot of scratches and fuzz). The oddest component of this version is the inclusion of songs, some of which are very intrusive, and some of which work in context. A little too scary for young kids, this is still a nice introduction to Tolkien's worlds, and will hopefully send viewers in the direction of the books.

This disc was also included as part of a 2001 three-pack set, its keepcase packaged with *Lord of Rings* and *Return of the King*.

SPECIAL FEATURES Author Bio & Trivia • Other Title Trailers TECHNICAL FEATURES Fullscreen: 1.33:1 • Subtitles/CC: Eng., Fren., Span. • Languages: Eng. • Sound: Dolby Digital 1.0 • Keepcase • 1 Disc • Region 1 GENRE & RATING Fantasy/Adventure/Music • Not Rated (Kids)

House of Morecock, The ☞ see Mature/Adult Section

Hubley Collection, The: Vol. 1

Image, 1999, 118 mins., #ID5855PIDVD. Produced by John Hubley, Faith Hubley, Emily Hubley.

Like other samplers of their work, this collection of thirteen short films produced by the husband-and-wife team of Faith and John Hubley is an expressionistic lot, showcasing a wide array of animation and musical styles. There isn't much traditional cel animation (if any), with most of the work appearing to be watercolor and washes, and paper cutouts. The Hubley's work is generally rather dreamlike, with music and philosophical vocal segments accompanying the artwork. Consider the work psychedelia for the intelligentsia.

"Enter Life" (1981) traces evolution and was coproduced by the Smithsonian Institution, while "Upside Down" (1991) was inspired by the work of an Indian poet. "Who Am I?" (1989) finds a child discovering her five senses, and "Blake Ball" (1988) pairs the poetry of William Blake with a baseball game. "Time of the Angels" (1987) has a South American flair, while "W.O.W. (Women of the World)" (1975) is a collage work about the changing nature of sexual roles. "People, People, People" (1975) is jazzily scored by Benny Carter and was produced for the American bicentennial celebrations, tracing North America from 17,760 B.C. to A.D. 1776.

"Amazonia" (1989) is a mythological exploration of the rain forests, and "Yes We Can" (1988) finds people uniting to save Mother Earth. "Moonbird" (1959) is an Academy Award-winning short about two brothers hunting an imaginary bird, while "Tall Time Tales" presents a surreal musical landscape. "Windy Day" (1967) tells two sister's views on life and marriage, and "Cloudland" (1993) is an Aboriginal exploration of culture.

Fans should look for more Hubley work under *Art and Jazz in Animation: The Cosmic Eye and Pigeon (And More) Within.*

SPECIAL FEATURES None TECHNICAL FEATURES Fullscreen: 1.33:1 • Languages: Eng. • Sound: Dolby Digital 1.0 • Snapcase • 1 Disc • Region 1–6 GENRE & RATING Anthology/Music • Not Rated (Teens)

Hubley Collection, The—Vol. 2

Image, 1999, 99 mins., #ID5856PIDVD. Produced by John Hubley, Faith Hubley, Emily Hubley.

Ten more surreal watercolor and mixed media shorts are in this collection. "Seers and Clowns" (1994) is a group of multicultural vignettes, with "Sky Dance" (1979) spotlighting prehistoric art, and "Cockaboody" (1973) animating the discussions of the Hubley's two preschool girls. "Hello" (1984) has aliens sending messages of peace, while "Step by Step" (1978) matches music with children from the past, present, and future.

"Rainbows of Hawaii" (1995) is based on a myth of the South Pacific, and "The Big Bang and Other Creation Myths" (1981) examines stories about the world's beginning from multiple cultures. "ZuckerKandl!" (1968) is a philosophical satire on getting through life, while "Whither Weather" (1977) is a parable about global warming. Rounding out the disc is "Her Grandmother's Gift" (1995), a short about menstruation.

SPECIAL FEATURES None TECHNICAL FEATURES Fullscreen: 1.33:1 • Languages Eng. • Sound: Dolby Digital 2.0 • Snapcase • 1 Disc • Region 1–6 GENRE & RATING Anthology/Music • Not Rated (Teens)

Hubley Collection, The: Everybody Rides the Carousel

Image, 1999, 123 mins., #ID5854PIDVD. Produced by John Hubley, Faith Hubley, Emily Hubley.

The third in *The Hubley Collection* series features three longer-form animations. "Everybody Rides the Carousel" (72 mins.) traces the eight different stages of life, as based on the theories and work of psychoanalyst Erik Erikson. "My Universe Inside Out" (25 mins.) is Faith Hubley's self-portrait about her life.

The disc's most traditional sequence is *A Doonesbury Special* (26 mins.), based on the comic strip by Garry Trudeau. Originally broadcast on NBC in November 1977, the special features Zonker Harris ruminating on the social and political issues he and the other characters have faced in the past. The Hubley's perfectly capture Trudeau's linework for the animation, and the work was nominated for an Academy Award (as a short film).

SPECIAL FEATURES None TECHNICAL FEATURES Fullscreen (1.33:1) • Languages: Eng. • Sound: Dolby Digital 2.0 • Snapcase • 1 Disc • Region 1–6 GENRE & RATING Anthology/Music/Political • Not Rated (Teens)

Hunchback of Notre Dame, The

Madacy, 1999, 50 mins., #DVD9 9140.

This DVD was not available for review.

Hunchback of Notre Dame, The [Collector's Edition]

Digital Versatile Disc, 2000, 52 mins., #168. Animation Directed by Warwick Gilbert. Written by Eddy Graham. Based on the book by Victor Hugo.

Raised in secrecy in the belltower of the Cathedral of Notre Dame, a misshapen, crippled bellringer named Quasimodo longs for a better life. When he is befriended by the dancing gypsy girl Esmerelda, he gains the courage and the strength to fight back against his oppressor and father figure, Frollo.

This 1985 production by Burbank Films Australia is pretty faithful to Hugo's original story, even down to Frollo's death scene. Although the character designs are only serviceable, the earthy watercolor backgrounds and grainy picture quality actually aid the storytellers. I've criticized many of this animation studio's discs; here's one that is actually a keeper. But why, oh why, do all the Parisians have British accents?

SPECIAL FEATURES Author Bio • Games TECHNICAL FEATURES Fullscreen (1.33:1) • Languages: Eng. • Sound: Dolby Digital Surround 5.1, DTS • Keepcase • 1 Disc • Region All. GENRE & RATING Historical/Fantasy/Romance • Not Rated (All Ages)

Hunchback of Notre Dame, The

Disney, 2002, 91 mins., #23315. Directed by Gary Trousdale, Kirk Wise. Story by Tab Murphy. Screenplay by Tab Murphy, Irene Mecchi, Bob Tzudiker, Noni White, Jonathan Roberts. Based on the book by Victor Hugo.

Pity poor Quasimodo, the hunchback bellringer of Notre Dame's cathedral. His only friends are a dancing, singing gargoyle trio—Victor, Hugo, and Laverne—until he meets Esmerelda, a bewitching gypsy. Unfortunately, Esmerelda has also caught the eye of the powerful Frollo, who plans to do whatever it takes to make her his . . . even if it means burning the gypsy population out of Paris! Can Quasi save his love, or will Phoebus of the royal guard be the hero of the day?

Disney's retelling of Hugo's 1831 novel received a tremendous amount of flack for its liberal "adaptation," but the 1996 film is a lot of fun on its own terms. The dizzying CGI work brings the towers of the cathedral to luscious life, and there's probably never been a Disney woman as hot as Esmerelda. Voice work is top-notch, with Demi Moore, Kevin Kline, and Jason Alexander chiming in, among others.

Adults will enjoy the comic relief gargoyles as much as the kids, but some material is aimed at older audiences; track #17 where Frollo sings "Hellfire" features perhaps the most erotic sequence Disney has ever animated, and it's creepy as well! The DVD contains some nice extras, including a fascinating multilingual version of the song "A Guy Like You," with the soundtrack switching between thirty-one different languages!

SPECIAL FEATURES "Making of" Featurettes • Commentary Track with Producer and Directors • Multilanguage Music Video • Sing-Along • Other Title Trailers • Games TECHNICAL FEATURES Widescreen (1.85:1 enhanced for 16x9) • Subtitles/CC: Eng. • Languages: Eng., Fren. dub, Span. dub • Sound: Dolby Digital Surround 5.1, DTS • Keepcase • 1 Disc • Region 1, 4 GENRE & RATING Historical/Romance/Music • Rated G

Hunchback of Notre Dame II, The

Disney, 2002, 68 mins., #21317. Directed by Bradley Raymond. Screenplay by Julie Selbo, Flip Kobler, Cindy Marcus. Based on characters in the book by Victor Hugo.

Quasimodo is still the bellringer at Notre Dame's cathedral, but now he's got new friends. Esmerelda and Phoebus have a son named Zephyr, and he likes Quasi and the gargoyle trio. A traveling circus comes to town, and its owner, the evil magician Sarousch, plans to steal a church bell. He uses pretty young Madellaine to help him win Quasimodo's trust, but what happens between them is a surprise to everyone.

This direct-to-DVD sequel tries hard to replicate the charm of the original, aided by the returning voice talents from all the principals (new additions include Jennifer Love Hewitt and Haley Joel Osment). Unfortunately, the animation is stiff, and somebody in quality-control should be fired; Esmerelda's skin color changes from scene to scene. Still, it's a nice diversion for the family, and it promotes the positive message of not judging people by their appearance. The DVD contains a behind-the-scenes featurette with Hewitt, plus a pair of games. My player got stuck on the games menu, but it's unclear if this is a common occurrence or not.

SPECIAL FEATURES "Making of" Featurette • Poetic Tribute to Gargoyles • Other Title Trailers • Games TECHNICAL FEATURES Widescreen (1.66:1 enhanced for 16x9) • Subtitles/CC: Eng. • Languages: Eng., Fren. dub, Span. dub • Sound: Dolby Digital Surround 5.1, DTS • Keepcase • 1 Disc • Region 1 GENRE & RATING Historical/Romance/Music • Rated G

Hyper Doll: Mew and Mica the Easy Fighters

Pioneer, 2000, 60 mins., #11487. Directed by Makoto Moriwaki. Screenplay by Ryo Motohira. Based on the manga series by Shinpei Ito in Tokuma Shoten.

Mew and Mica—the "Hyper Dolls" from another galaxy—must fight monstrous beings, all while posing as ordinary high school students. They bicker, goof off, and eat while the world is in dire peril from supersized jellyfish and a giant worm. Mew and Mica might save the world if they can just bring themselves to care.

You know that saying about 100 monkeys with typewriters pounding out the works of William Shakespeare if given enough time? Well, it's clear they snatched this script from the simians before they got around to *Romeo and Juliet. Hyper Doll,* first released in 1995, is meant to be a cute parody of superhero girl anime, but this just comes off as abuse of the audience. The monster worm with giant lips is exceedingly lame. Flee!

SPECIAL FEATURES None TECHNICAL FEATURES Fullscreen (1.33:1) • Subtitles/CC: Eng. • Languages: Jap., Eng. dub • Sound: Dolby Digital 2.0 • Keepcase • 1 Disc • Region 1, 4 GENRE & RATING Action/Girls/Superhero • Rated 13+

I Married a Strange Person! ☛ see
Mature/Adult Section

Ice Age [2-Disc Special Edition]

Fox, 2002, 81 mins., #2004664. Directed by Chris Wedge, Carlos Saldanha. Screenplay by Michael Berg, Michael J. Wilson, Peter Ackerman. Story by Michael J. Wilson.

Way back a long time ago, the Earth was being overrun by glaciers. It was the dawn of the Ice Age, and the pre-historic creatures were on the move to find warmer homelands. By chance, four unusual creatures learn they must work together for survival: devilish saber-tooth tiger Diego; a wooly mammoth named Manny; dim-witted sloth Sid; and Scrat, a saber-toothed squirrel whose passion for acorn's causes no end of trouble. So how much weirder can their journey get when this misfit group finds a human infant and decides to return the child to its tribe? Let's just say that their adventure has started down a slippery slope.

Released early in 2002, this all-CGI film had an unusual voice cast, with Ray Romano, Denis Leary, and John Leguizamo sharing the mic. Like the sometimes-pedestrian voice work, the animation is extremely effective at times, and less effective at others. Those looking for pretty, polished Pixar-style work will instead get edgy animation that at times looks similar to a video game. But if you don't mind the style, there are a number of good laughs to be had here, most of them at the expense of Scrat.

This two-disc set is loaded with extras, including multiple deleted scenes, behind-the-scenes featurettes, interstitials, and games. There's also an Academy Award–winning short cartoon called "Bunny" by director Chris Wedge, and a five-minute new short called "Scrat's Missing Adventure," in which the acorn-greedy creature picks up one nut too many.

SPECIAL FEATURES "Making of" Featurettes • Commentary Track by Directors • Scene-Specific Commentary by Character • Character and Art Galleries • Deleted Scenes • Storyboards •

Animation Progression Reels • Trailers • Promotional Footage • International Clips • Games • DVD-ROM Features: Games • Other Title Trailers TECHNICAL FEATURES Widescreen (1.85:1 enhanced for 16x9) • Fullscreen (1.33:1) • Subtitles/CC: Eng., Span. • Languages: Eng., Fren. dub, Span. dub • Sound: Dolby Digital 5.1 Surround • Multikeepcase • 2 Discs • Region 1 GENRE & RATING CGI/Animals/Comedy • Rated PG

I'm Gonna Be an Angel: Vol. 1—Earth Angel

Synch-Point, 2002, 125 mins., #SPTN-DVD2. Directed by Hiroshi Nishikiori. Script by Mamiko Ikeda, Hiroshi Nishikiori.

Yusuke is living on his own while his dad's away on business, so of course, trouble isn't far away. When he bumps into a naked Noelle in the woods on the way to school, he finds that she considers him to be her husband. The oh-so-chirpy girl is a newly transferred student at the school, but she's also an angel, complete with halo. Her "Demon World" family soon moves in with Yusuke: Dad's a Frankenstein–like monster, while the brother is a vampire, and the sisters are a mad scientist and an invisible girl. Then there's Grandma, a hag who doesn't much like Yusuke. To make matters more complicated, he secretly loves the girl next door, Natsume. Wackiness ensues.

What would you get if you crossed *The Addams Family* with any of the dozens of "dorky high school guy gets beautiful girl but doesn't want her" anime series? Something very similar to this silly, derivative television series from 1999. The animation is very pretty—except for the ugly stylized villain characters—with bright pastel colors and supercutesy faces. It appears the creators are having fun with the concept. Those who don't like cute stuff should stay far away though; Noelle's voice alone could shatter glass.

The DVD contains several nice extras, including some "outtakes" that appear to be deleted scenes. There's also a second English subtitle option, offering general or more specific subtitles.

SPECIAL FEATURES Character and Art Galleries • Translation Notes • Karaoke Songs • Audio Audition Clips • Deleted Scenes • Reversible Cover • Insert: Lyrics TECHNICAL FEATURES:

Fullscreen (1.33:1) • Subtitles/CC: Eng. • Languages: Jap., Eng. dub • Sound: Dolby Digital • Keepcase • 1 Disc • Region 1. GENRE & RATING Girls/Comedy • Not Rated (Kids)

Imma Youjo: The Erotic Temptress ☞ see
Mature/Adult Section

Immoral Sisters: Two Premature Fruits ☞ see
Mature/Adult Section

Incredible Adventures of Wallace and Gromit, The

BBC/Warner, 2000, 84 mins., #E1510. Directed by Nick Park. Written by Nick Park, Bob Baker.

Wallace is a bald Englishman who fiddles with elaborate inventions. Gromit is his dog, who often ends up in trouble because of Wallace's inventions. In "A Grand Day Out," Wallace blasts off to the moon to enjoy some cheese, only to find that an old lunar oven wants to spoil his fun. In "The Wrong Trousers," a gun-toting penguin plans a diamond robbery, and Wallace's Techno-Trousers may give him just the power he needs to execute the heist. And in "A Close Shave," Gromit is framed for a sheepnapping, and Wallace finds love. But who's really fleecing the city's sheep population?

It's rare that you find a series of modern animated shorts that appeal to just about everybody regardless of age, class, origin, sexual orientation, or shoe size, but *Wallace and Gromit* pretty much fit that bill. The stories are so inventive, charming, and funny that this disc belongs on every DVD shelf (or wish list). There are a bushel of bonus features on this disc, including over half an hour of behind-the-scenes footage, five early animated works by Nick Park, British TV "bumper segments," and much more.

There is an earlier disc for these chaps—see the entry for *Wallace and Gromit: The First Three Adventures*—but *The Incredible Adventures of Wallace and Gromit* actually features more extras than that disc. And for more work by Park and his cohorts, see *Chicken Run* and *Robbie the Reindeer*.

SPECIAL FEATURES "Making of" Featurettes • Commentary track • Crew Bios • Scrapbook • Invention Blueprints • Storyboards • Trailer • Other Title Trailers TECHNICAL FEATURES Fullscreen (1.33:1) • Languages: Eng., Fren. dub, Span. dub • Sound: Dolby Digital • Keepcase • 1 Disc • Region 1 GENRE & RATING Stop Motion/Animal/Comedy • Not Rated (All Ages)

Incredible Mr. Limpet, The
Warner, 2002, 99 mins.

This DVD was not available for review.

Infinity's Child

Winstar, 1999, 40 mins., #WHE73049. Produced by Jan Nickman.

A group of alien spacecraft travel through a gateway into another reality. The world they find there is a constantly shifting quicksilver-like planet, where nothing is solid and yet everything has form and substance. Welcome to another all-CGI mind trip with lots of eye candy and some decent techno-trip music.

As would be expected of a digital film, the DVD contains an excellent print, as well as a number of extras. The same producer/director was responsible for *Planetary Traveler*, which is related to this story somehow.

SPECIAL FEATURES: Artist Interviews • Art Galleries • Trailers • Promotional Footage • DVD-ROM Features (Demo Versions, Software) • Web Links. TECHNICAL FEATURES: Fullscreen (1.33:1) • Subtitles/CC (Fren., Germ., Jap., Kor., Span.) • Languages (Eng.) • Sound (Dolby Digital 2.0, Dolby Digital Surround 5.1) • Keepcase • 1 Disc • Region All GENRE & RATING: CGI/Music/Science Fiction • Not Rated (Teens)

Inhumanoids: The Evil that Lies Within [Episodes 1–5]

Rhino, 2001, 105 mins., #R2 976014. Directed by Ray Lee. Written by Flint Dille.

The Inhumanoids are a subterranean race of monstrous beings who want to destroy the surface world. Antienvironmentalist Blackthrone Shore aids the Inhumanoids for his own evil ends, but his wealthy sister Sandra underwrites the heroes who try to stop the horror. The good guys are known as the Earth Corps, and their weapons include armored mecha-suits and other high-tech equipment. But deep beneath the Earth's crust, will the Earth Corps win against the Inhumanoids?

This short-lived 1986 TV series was a product of Marvel Productions and Claster, and it tied in to an action figure toy line from Hasbro. The designs for the series are fairly good, and there is a lot of scary action going on, but it looks dated today. Did American toy-based action animation from the 1980s really *all* look alike? This DVD contains the first five *Inhumanoids* episodes.

SPECIAL FEATURES None TECHNICAL FEATURES Fullscreen (1.33:1) •

Languages: Eng. • Sound: Dolby Digital 2.0 • Keepcase • 1 Disc • Region 1–6 GENRE & RATING Action/Robots/Horror • Not Rated (Kids)

Inhumanoids: Vol. 3, Vol. 4

Rhino, 2001, 90 mins., #R2 976015. Directed by Ray Lee. Written by Flint Dille.

The final set of adventures of the Earth Corps vs. the Mutors are presented on this DVD. The four episodes include: "Cypheroid"; "Surma Plan"; "Cult of Darkness"; and "Negative Polarity." Look for more trouble from Metlar and his monstrous cronies, as they try to stomp the "Earth slugs."

Don't let the subtitle of the disc make you concerned that you missed a disc; Rhino titled them based on the VHS volumes. The first DVD had volumes one and two, and this DVD has volumes three and four.

SPECIAL FEATURES None TECHNICAL FEATURES Fullscreen (1.33:1) • Languages: Eng. • Sound: Dolby Digital 2.0 • Keepcase • 1 Disc • Region 1 GENRE & RATING Action/Robots/Horror • Not Rated (Kids)

Inma Seiden: The Legend of the Beast of Lust ☞ see Mature/Adult Section

Inmu: Feast of Victims ☞ see Mature/Adult Section

Inmu 2: The Wandering Flesh Slave ☞ see Mature/Adult Section

Iria: Zeiram the Animation

Image, 1998, 180 mins., #ID4407CTDVD.

This DVD was not available for review. It is out of print.

Iron Giant, The

Warner, 1999, 87 mins., #17644. Directed by Brad Bird. Screenplay by Brad Bird. Screenplay by Tim McCanlies. Based on the book *The Iron Giant* by Ted Hughes.

It is 1957 in Rockwell, Maine. Hogarth Hughes is a child with an active imagination, but what falls to Earth in the woods near his home is beyond his wildest dreams. After Hogarth finds a 50-foot-tall robot with a taste for metal, he hides it at the local scrapyard, much to the surprise of the beat-

nik artist/junkyard owner. When an overzealous government agent comes to town in search of the "alien invader," Hogarth and his oversized friend find themselves on the run from the military.

Lauded by critics, this retro fantasy was not a big hit in movie theaters, but it is loaded with charm, whimsy, and fun. Using modern CGI animation technology, *The Iron Giant* was created with no actual cel animation, although it resembles the 1940's Fleischer Bros. *Superman* shorts and the best of Disney's cartoons. Star voice talents in the feature include Jennifer Aniston, Harry Connick Jr., and Vin Diesel.

Despite its rating, *The Iron Giant* is appropriate for most ages, though a few sad tears may be shed near the end. This gets a high recommendation for both kids and adults.

SPECIAL FEATURES "Making of" Featurette • Cast Filmographies • Trailer • Music Video • DVD-ROM Features: Web links TECHNICAL FEATURES Widescreen (2.35:1 enhanced for 16x9) • Fullscreen (1.33:1) • Subtitles/CC: Eng. • Languages: Eng. • Sound: Dolby Digital Surround 5.1 • Snapcase • 1 Disc • Region 1 GENRE & RATING Retro Science Fiction/Robots/Family • Rated PG

Irresponsible Captain Tylor, The: Leave This to Me [TV #1]

Right Stuf, 2000, 175 mins., #RSDVD2001. Directed by Koichi Mashimo. Screenplay by Nato Kimura, Masami Watanabe, Hiroyuki Kawasaki. Based on the book series *The Most Irresponsible Man in Space* by Hitoshi Yoshioka.

The battered starship *Soyokaze* has a new captain, but he's a slacker who only joined the United Planets Space Force to have fun. It's a good thing that Captain Justy Ueki Tylor has the best dumb luck in the galaxy, because the galaxy is at the brink of war with the Raalgon Empire. Other than two stuffy commanding officers Sesshu Mifune and Susumu Fuji, Tylor's crew is a motley bunch, with cute Lieutenant Yuriko Star, airheaded twins Emi and Yumi Hanner, straight-laced Makoto Yamamoto, and others. Then there is Harumi Nakagawa, a female assassin who never kills her target (Tylor, naturally), and alien Empress Azalyn, who lusts after the good captain.

Tylor's life is a comedy of errors and goodwill, spotlit in this volume on stories about the Raalgon crisis, tensions between the Marines and the fighter pilots on board the *Soyokaze*, a new ship's officer that everyone falls in love with, and Yuriko's attempt to whip the ragtag crew into shape. *The Irresponsible Captain Tylor* is a 1992 TV series that adroitly combines humor and action for a fun space opera romp. The animation and designs are pleasant, and the tech design is great. The DVD transfer quality is also sharp.

Right Stuf has done a great job with this DVD series, cramming seven episodes on this disc along with a whole bunch of extra features. The bios are of *Soyokaze* crewmembers and UPSF leaders. In addition to the Easter eggs (which are literally a game to find), there are unadvertised liner notes as well. In the episode sections, click the <CHP> notice on the side to get to the subchapter menu; there you'll find a button for liner notes for each episode! Right Stuf also gives the fans a hearty thank you on the disc, listing the names of the first 750 people who pre-ordered the box set!

SPECIAL FEATURES Character Bios • Character and Art Galleries • Liner Notes • Easter Eggs TECHNICAL FEATURES Fullscreen (1.33:1) • Subtitles/CC: Eng. • Languages: Jap., Eng. dub, Span. dub • Sound: Dolby Digital 2.0 • Keepcase • 1 Disc • Region 1 GENRE & RATING Comedy/Science Fiction • Not Rated (Teens)

Irresponsible Captain Tylor, The: Did Somebody Say Luck? [TV #2]

Right Stuf, 2000, 175 mins., #RSDVD2002. Directed by Koichi Mashimo. Screenplay by Masami Watanabe, Hiroyuki Kawasaki. Based on the book series *The Most Irresponsible Man in Space* by Hitoshi Yoshioka.

The crew of the starship *Soyokaze* enlists for seven more adventures in this volume. Tylor's assassination is plotted, and the Miss *Soyokaze* contest is planned. United Planets Space Force Command decides to send the ship into the middle of nowhere, while Emi and Yumi throw in their lot as fighter pilots, much to the dismay of the real pilots. And speaking of dismay, Yuriko's getting very frustrated that nobody is following her new regulations.

Some of the *Soyokaze*'s past is revealed—the previous captain and crew all committed suicide—but will their ghosts return to haunt the new crew? Then, a Raalgon admiral sets his sights on Tylor, but the good captain's dumb luck prevails. Now he's *really* in the Raalgon fleet's crosshairs!

This DVD contains all the extra features detailed in the first disc's description. The bios this time out are of the Raalgon characters.

SPECIAL FEATURES Character Bios • Character and Art Galleries • Liner Notes • Easter Eggs TECHNICAL FEATURES Fullscreen (1.33:1) • Subtitles/CC: Eng. • Languages: Jap., Eng. dub, Span. dub • Sound: Dolby Digital 2.0 • Keepcase • 1 Disc • Region 1 GENRE & RATING Comedy/Science Fiction • Not Rated (Teens)

Irresponsible Captain Tylor, The: Little Azalyn, Eh? [TV #3]

Right Stuf, 2000, 150 mins., #RSDVD2003. Directed by Koichi Mashimo. Screenplay by Hiroyuki Kawasaki, Kenichi Kanemaki, Masami Watanabe. Based on the book series *The Most Irresponsible Man in Space* by Hitoshi Yoshioka.

The *Soyokaze* is infected with a deadly virus, and the Raalgon will only give them a cure in exchange for Tylor. But even in the hands of his enemy, Tylor's dumb luck continues. He meets someone very important and gets a reprieve that might just be the key to everything. Meanwhile, the *Soyokaze* is caught between the United Planets Space Force and the Raalgon fleet, Tylor gets an unwanted implant in his head, and dissension in the Raalgon ranks ratchets up the tension.

This penultimate DVD contains six more episodes, plus all the extra features detailed in the first disc's description.

SPECIAL FEATURES Ship Bios • Character and Art Galleries • Liner Notes • Easter Eggs TECHNICAL FEATURES Fullscreen (1.33:1) • Subtitles/CC: Eng. • Languages: Jap., Eng. dub, Span. dub • Sound: Dolby Digital 2.0 • Keepcase • 1 Disc • Region 1 GENRE & RATING Comedy/Science Fiction • Not Rated (Teens)

Irresponsible Captain Tylor, The: Let's Go! [TV #4]

Right Stuf, 2000, 150 mins., #RSDVD2001. Directed by Koichi Mashimo. Screenplay by Kenichi Kanemaki, Hiroyuki Kawasaki, Masami Watanabe. Based on the book series *The Most Irresponsible Man in Space* by Hitoshi Yoshioka.

The Raalgon Empress Azalyn is on board the *Soyokaze*, and she claims to be pregnant . . . with Tylor's child! Then Tylor is arrested and sentenced to death by firing squad, and the Raalgon fleet makes some major offensive pushes in the war, threatening the stability of the entire United Planets Space Force!

Still alive, Tylor manages to pull some tricks out of his hat, but when his saving graces net him possible command of a new ship, he disappears. The *Soyokaze* crew looks for him, even as reassignments are decided upon, and life-altering decisions are made.

This DVD contains the final six episodes of the original TV series, plus all the extra features detailed in the first disc's description. There is also an extra called "Melva Tour," which is actually diary entries about a ship and a debriefing.

Note: The first pressing of disc #4 had missing footage on episode #23, making it approximately sixteen minutes long instead of twenty-two minutes. Right Stuf has re-pressed and replaced as many defective copies as possible, but if you come across one, contact the company for a replacement disc.

SPECIAL FEATURES Ship Bios • Character and Art Galleries • "Melva Tour" • Liner Notes • Easter Eggs TECHNICAL FEATURES Fullscreen (1.33:1) • Subtitles/CC: Eng. • Languages: Jap., Eng. dub, Span. Dub • Sound: Dolby Digital 2.0 • Keepcase • 1 Disc • Region 1 GENRE & RATING Comedy/Science Fiction • Not Rated (Teens)

Irresponsible Captain Tylor, The: The Irresponsible TV DVD Collection [Box Set]

Right Stuf, 2000, 650 mins., #RSDVD2005.

This box set features all four DVD volumes of *The Irresponsible Captain Tylor* TV series, in a cardboard box. The keepcases are the same as the individual release cases. See individual entries for Special and Technical Features listings.

TECHNICAL FEATURES Cardboard Box with 4 Keepcases • 4 Discs • Region 1 GENRE & RATING Comedy/Science Fiction • Not Rated (Teens)

Irresponsible Captain Tylor, The: The OVA Collection—An Exceptional Episode [#1]

Right Stuf, 2001, 90 mins., #RSDVD2006. Directed by Koichi Mashimo. Screenplay by Koichi Mashimo. Based on the book series *The Most Irresponsible Man in Space* by Hitoshi Yoshioka.

Neither side is happy with the resolution of the war between the Raalgon Empire and the United Planets Space Force. The Raalgons have developed a superweapon, and Captain Tylor is assigned to take the crew of the *Soyokaze* into the heart of the Empire and defeat them. Only Tylor and his superiors know that this is a suicide mission, even if the crew is successful. But Tylor has a plan, if mutiny doesn't happen first.

This DVD contains the two-part 1994 OVA *An Exceptional Episode* . The animation is a bit stronger than the TV series, and the DVD transfer is just as nice. All of the extras from earlier volumes are here, including a blueprint of the "undefeated" *Soyokaze*. The liner notes are in the episodic scene selection pages, and there are four music videos.

SPECIAL FEATURES Ship Bio and Schematics • Music Videos • Liner Notes TECHNICAL FEATURES Fullscreen (1.33:1) • Subtitles/CC: Eng. • Languages Jap., Eng. dub, Span. dub •

Sound: Dolby Digital 2.0 • Keepcase • 1 Disc • Region 1 GENRE & RATING: Comedy/Science Fiction • Not Rated (Teens)

Irresponsible Captain Tylor, The: The OVA Collection—The Sidestory Collection [#2]

Right Stuf, 2001, 180 mins., #RSDVD2007. Directed by Takashi Yoshinaga. Screenplay by Akira Yamamura. Based on the book series *The Most Irresponsible Man in Space* by Hitoshi Yoshioka.

With the war officially "over," the crew of the *Soyokaze* is scattered across the galaxy, all assigned to different missions. Kojiro is testing out a new form of space fighter, while many of the Marines have been ordered to test out some new battle armor. Makoto Yamamoto is commanding his own ship, and Commander Yuriko Star is now an intelligence operative who just wants to spend a nice Christmas with Tylor. And on Raalgon, Azalyn attempts to take a vacation, but when she is reunited with a childhood friend, the political stability of Raalgon may be blown to pieces.

The six episodes on this DVD are the complete 1995 OVA series. As can be gleaned from the above plot summaries, the stories concentrate mainly on the supporting cast members of the series rather than on Tylor and the *Soyokaze*. This allows for quite a bit of character development, even if the mood is a bit more somber than in previous volumes. The DVD contains all the traditional extras for the series, plus five music videos.

SPECIAL FEATURES Music Videos • Liner Notes TECHNICAL FEATURES Fullscreen (1.33:1) • Subtitles/CC: Eng. • Languages: Jap., Eng. dub, Span. Dub • Sound: Dolby Digital 2.0 • Keepcase • 1 Disc • Region 1 GENRE & RATING Comedy/Science Fiction • Not Rated (Teens)

Irresponsible Captain Tylor, The: The OVA Collection—From Here to Eternity [#3]

Right Stuf, 2001, 90 mins., #RSDVD2008. Directed by Takashi Yoshinaga. Screenplay by Akira Yamamura. Based on the book series *The Most Irresponsible Man in Space* by Hitoshi Yoshioka.

Out on the frontier of space, United Planets Space Force ships are in trouble, and with the Raalgon Empire's military leadership destabilizing, it looks as if war may be imminent yet again. This time both sides have been preparing for battle, and if the fray is joined again, there will be tremendous casualties on all sides. But with the crew of the *Soyokaze* scattered across the galaxy, who will help find the solution to the impending crisis? Could the return of Captain Tylor be on the way?

The final animated adventures of Tylor and company are collected here with a two-part 1996 OVA set. The ending does have a sense of closure, but a lot of unanswered questions remain. Good thing there are extensive liner notes in the final chapter that explain what the future holds for all the characters in both the novels and manga. There's also four more music videos, just to round things out nicely.

SPECIAL FEATURES Character and Art Galleries • Music Video • Liner Notes TECHNICAL FEATURES Fullscreen (1.33:1) • Subtitles/CC: Eng. • Languages: Jap., Eng. dub, Span. dub • Sound: Dolby Digital 2.0 • Keepcase • 1 Disc • Region 1 GENRE & RATING Comedy/Science Fiction • Not Rated (Teens)

Irresponsible Captain Tylor, The: The OVA Collection—The Complete OVA Series

Right Stuf, 2001, 360 mins., #RSDVD2009. Directed by Koichi Mashimo, Takashi Yoshinaga. Screenplay by Koichi Mashimo, Akira Yamamura. Based on the book series *The Most Irresponsible Man in Space* by Hitoshi Yoshioka.

This box set is actually a multikeepcase that contains the same three discs found in the individual OVA keepcases. The back cover gives a brief synopsis, but there are no other extra features. See individual entries for Special and Technical Features.

SPECIAL FEATURES Multikeepcase • 3 Discs • Region 1 GENRE & RATING Comedy/Science Fiction • Not Rated (Teens)

It's the Great Pumpkin, Charlie Brown

Paramount, 2000, 25 mins., #15611. Directed by Bill Melendez. Written by Charles M. Schulz. Based on the *Peanuts* comic strip by Charles M. Schulz.

Halloween is a special time for Charlie Brown and his best friend Linus Van Pelt. According to Linus, it's the time when the Great Pumpkin visits the pumpkin patch, bringing toys and gifts to all the good children who believe in him. Plus, Charlie gets invited to a party! This 1966 special was nominated for an Emmy Award, and it features the first appearance of Snoopy's Red Baron character.

A second short on this DVD is *You're Not Elected, Charlie Brown*, a 1972 special in which the school has a class election and Linus is in the running for class president. Will Russell, Linus's opponent, vote for himself, or for Linus? Watch for some political frustration expressed by sister Sally.

For more *Peanuts* fun, check out *A Charlie Brown Christmas* and *A Charlie Brown Thanksgiving*, as well as the next entry. This disc was also included in the *Peanuts Classic Holiday Collection* box set.

SPECIAL FEATURES None TECHNICAL FEATURES Fullscreen (1.33:1) • Subtitles/CC: Eng. • Languages: Eng. • Sound: Dolby Digital Mono • Keepcase • 1 Disc • Region 1 GENRE & RATING Family • Rated G

It's the Pied Piper, Charlie Brown

Paramount, 2000, 25 mins.

This DVD was not available for review.

Ivanhoe [Collector's Edition]

Digital Versatile Disc, 1999, 50 mins., #164. Directed by Warwick Gilbert. Screenplay by Alex Nicholas, Kit Denton. Based on the book by Walter Scott.

It is the Dark Ages, when the Normans and the Saxons feuded, and the Crusades against the Saracens were underway. Into a web of romance, intrigue, and adventure steps Wilfred of Ivanhoe, a knight loyal to King Richard the Lionheart. In the days ahead, Wilfred will fall in love with the beauteous Lady Rowena, navigate the intrigues of English court politics, and help fight against King John, usurper of the throne.

A 1986 production by Burbank Films Australia, *Ivanhoe* is a decent medieval romp. The animation design resembles illuminated art from the era, with bright pastel colors and a slightly grainy picture. As with other discs from this company, there is an author bio and other historical information.

SPECIAL FEATURES Author Bio • Games TECHNICAL FEATURES Fullscreen (1.33:1) • Languages: Eng. • Sound: Dolby Digital Surround 5.1, DTS • Keepcase • 1 Disc • Region All GENRE & RATING Historical/Adventure • Not Rated (All Ages)

J

Jackie Chan Adventures: The Search for the Talismans [#1]

Columbia/TriStar, 2001, 63 mins., #07305. Directed by Bryan Andrews, Vincenzo Trippetti, Andy Thom. Written by John Rogers, David Slack, Duane Capizzi.

Jackie Chan voices Jackie, an expert on ancient artifacts and special agent for the government's top-secret Section 13. He lives in San Francisco with his eleven-year-old niece, Jade, and his cantankerous old uncle, an imperfect wizard and antique shop owner. When Jackie finds the ancient rooster talisman, which has secret powers, he becomes the target of villains and thugs. Now, Jackie embarks on a worldwide search for all twelve magical talismans—each based on a sign of the Chinese zodiac—to keep them from falling into the hands of the crime family The Dark Hand.

In this initial volume, which combines three episodes of the 2000 Kids WB! series into one adventure, Jackie and Jade go after the rooster talisman, then travel to Mexico and join up with the wrestler El Toro Fuerte to protect the ox talisman. Picture quality is crisp and clean, as can be expected from a show less than a year old, and the audio has a wide variety of languages and subtitles. Unlike most Eastern-themed animation, this series falls squarely in the realm of Chinese culture, with Jackie Chan lending his traditional air of martial artistry (even if it is animated) and heroic underdog humor.

The episodes combined for this disc—uncredited here—were originally titled: "The Dark Hand" (#1), "The Power Within" (#2), and "The Mask of El Toro Fuerte" (#3).

SPECIAL FEATURES Jackie Chan Interview • Other Title Trailers
TECHNICAL FEATURES Fullscreen (1.33:1) • Subtitles/CC: Eng., Chin., Fren., Kor., Port., Span., Thai • Languages: Eng., Fren. dub, Mand. dub, Port. dub, Span. dub • Sound: Dolby Digital 2.0 • Keepcase • 1 Disc • Region 1, 3, 4 GENRE & RATING Martial Arts/Comedy • Not Rated (Kids)

Jackie Chan Adventures: The Shadow of Shendu [#2]

Columbia/TriStar, 2002, 57 mins., #08362. Directed by Rick Del Carmen, Gloria Jenkins, Bryan Andrews. Written by Tom Pugsley, Greg Klein, David Slack, Alex Van Dyne.

Jackie and Jade travel to Istanbul to stop the famous thief Viper from stealing the snake talisman from a museum. Then, they get a ride from a turtle that holds the rabbit talisman within its shell. Finally, Jade learns the secrets of astral projection from the sheep talisman, and the dragon Shendu has some dastardly plans.

Three more episodes of WB's *Jackie Chan Adventures* are combined into one longer storyline in this DVD volume. The episodes combined for this disc—uncredited here—were originally titled: "Enter the Viper" (#4), "Project A, For Astral" (#5), and "Shell Game" (#6).

SPECIAL FEATURES Jackie Chan Interview • Other Title Trailers
TECHNICAL FEATURES Fullscreen (1.33:1) • Subtitles/CC: Eng., Fren., Port., Span. • Languages: Eng., Chin. dub, Fren. dub, Port. dub, Span. dub • Sound: Dolby Digital Surround 2.0 • Keepcase • 1 Disc • Region 1, 3, 4 GENRE & RATING Martial Arts/Comedy • Not Rated (Kids)

Jackie Chan Adventures: The Dark Hand Returns [#3]

Columbia/TriStar, 2002, 59 mins., #07505. Directed by Rick Del Carmen, Bryan Andrews, Andy Thom. Written by David Slack, Duane Capizzi.

The evil Valmont gains control of the dragon talisman, putting Section 13 special agent Captain Black in the hospital, and Jackie must come to the rescue. Then, the rat talisman brings one of Jade's action figures to life, and danger rears its head. Jackie is tricked into drinking a serum that will turn him into a statue, but Uncle and the powers of the horse talisman might save him if Valmont would only get out of the way!

Three more episodes of WB's *Jackie Chan Adventures* are combined into one longer storyline in this DVD volume.

SPECIAL FEATURES Jackie Chan Interview • Other Title Trailers TECHNICAL FEATURES Fullscreen (1.33:1) • Subtitles/CC: Eng., Port., Span. • Languages: Eng., Chin. dub, Fren. dub, Port. dub, Span. dub • Sound: Dolby Digital Surround 2.0 • Keepcase • 1 Disc • Region 1, 3, 4 GENRE & RATING Martial Arts/Comedy • Not Rated (Kids)

James and the Giant Peach [Special Edition]

Disney, 2001, 79 mins., #20100. Directed by Henry Selick. Screenplay by Karey Kirkpatrick, Jonathan Roberts, Steve Bloom. Based on the book by Roald Dahl.

Young James lives with his two evil guardians, but when an old man gives him a bag of magic crocodile tongues, a peach near his home grows to gigantic size. Entering the peach, James encounters a grasshopper, a spider, an earthworm, a glowworm, a centipede, and a ladybug. The giant peach gets launched into the ocean, and the group heads to New York City to find James's parents. Along the way, they have fantastic—and scary—adventures, and learn that by working together, they might just reach their goals.

This marvelous and imaginative 1996 film is a combination of live-action and stop-motion animation, with judicious use of CGI. Directed by the same man who directed *Tim Burton's The Nightmare Before Christmas*, this shares much of the same anything-goes style, and even features a guest appearance by Jack Skellington as an undersea pirate captain. Some sequences might by a little scary for young kids—after all, this is based on a book by Roald Dahl, whose *Willy Wonka and the Chocolate Factory* and *The Witches* weren't exactly devoid of scary moments—but if they watch it with parents or older viewers, youngsters should be fine.

As expected from Disney, this is a beautiful print of the film, but although the case lists it as widescreen ratio of 1.66:1, it measures out at 1.85:1. The voice cast is glorious, including Richard Dreyfuss, Susan Sarandon, David Thewlis, and others, and the music is by the ever-present-these-days Randy Newman (who was nominated for an Oscar for the score). Given the ultra-meticulous stop-motion work done here, this is an excellent disc with which to try the step-frame/slow motion feature on your DVD player while watching. Not as successful in theaters as it should have been, the audience on DVD deserves to be huge; it's an easy pun, but this *James* is a peach of a film.

Besides being offered as a single DVD, the disc was also included as part of a two-pack set, along with *The Nightmare Before Christmas*.

SPECIAL FEATURES "Making of" Featurette • Character and Art Galleries • Trailer • Music Video • Other Title Trailers TECHNICAL FEATURES Widescreen (1.85:1) • Fullscreen (1.33:1) • Subtitles/CC: Eng., Span. • Languages: Eng., Fren. dub, Span. dub • Sound: Dolby Digital Surround 5.1, DTS • Keepcase • 1 Disc • Region 1, 4 GENRE & RATING Stop-Motion/Live/Music • Rated G

Jay Jay the Jet Plane: Adventures in Learning

Columbia/TriStar, 2002, 65 mins., #07600. Directed by Hugh Martin. Written by John Semper Jr., Megan Brown.

Jay Jay is a jet plane stationed out of the small Tarrytown airport. He's friends with many of the other airplanes, as well as the helicopter, fire truck, and tow truck. In each storyline, Jay Jay and his friends learn valuable lessons about science, imagination, nature, and life itself. In one story, Jay learns that you don't always have to see something to believe it, while in another, he tags along with some butterflies during a winter journey.

Jay Jay the Jet Plane is an educational children's series on PBS that combines CGI characters with the occasional live-action background or guest star. The stories are cute and occasionally funny, but are mainly appropriate for younger children. This DVD contains five adventures: "A Trip to Skylandia"; "Jay Jay's Butterfly Adventure"; "Jay Jay and the Magic Books"; "Tuffy's Trip to Pangabula"; and "Tuffy's Adventure in Pangabula."

SPECIAL FEATURES Educational "Think About" Moments • Sing-Alongs • DVD-ROM Features: Games, Activities TECHNICAL FEATURES Fullscreen (1.33:1) • Subtitles/CC: Eng. • Languages: Eng., Span. dub • Sound: Dolby Digital Surround 2.0 • Keepcase • 1 Disc • Region 1 GENRE & RATING Educational/Aviation • Not Rated (Kids)

Jay Jay the Jet Plane: Supersonic Pals

Columbia/TriStar, 2002, 63 mins.

This DVD was not available for review.

Jewel BEM Hunter Lime

AnimeWorks, 2001, 90 mins., #AWDVD-0117. Directed by Tetsuro Amino. Written by Kenichiro Nakamura.

Once a month, a gateway from a magical dimension opens onto Earth. Bass, a three-eyed demon hunter, and sexy angelic hunter Lime, follow a demon through it. Unfortunately, before his demise, the demon unleashes multiple magic spheres on the world, each of them creating bizarre monsters. How bizarre? How about Mister Candle, a wax-shooting hardcase? Or Mister Purse and Mister Needle?

Only three episodes of this 1996 OVA , which was based on a video game character, were produced. It appears to exist solely for its cutesy, cartoony cheesecake. Your enjoyment of it will depend on how much of your brain you expect to be engaged. AnimeWorks labels it a "sexy comedy."

SPECIAL FEATURES Virtual "Dress-Up" Feature • Trailers TECHNICAL FEATURES Fullscreen (1.33:1) • Subtitles/CC: Eng. • Languages: Jap., Eng. dub • Sound: Dolby Digital 2.0 • Keepcase • 1 Disc • Region 1 GENRE & RATING Comedy/Cheesecake/Fantasy • Rated 16+

Jimmy Neutron: Boy Genius

Paramount, 2002, 82 mins., #33826. Directed by John A. Davis. Screenplay by John A. Davis, David N. Weiss, J. David Stem, Steve Oedekirk. Story by John A. Davis and Steve Oedekirk.

Jimmy Neutron is a boy genius whose inventions don't always make him popular. Sure he's got a superrobot dog named Goddard, but only sniffly nerd Carl will be his friend and launch into outer space with him. Cindy is jealous because, until Jimmy came along, she was the smartest girl in Retroville, and the other kids laugh at the predicaments Jimmy's inventions cause. Speaking of which, Jimmy's makeshift satellite draws an alien race to Earth, and while the kids have all snuck out to a carnival, all the grown-ups are abducted by the aliens! What at first seems to be heaven without parental control soon turns into chaos, and the kids all want Jimmy to help them get their parents back. Jimmy and the kids of Retroville soon launch an outer space rescue mission using the most unlikely means of space travel. But will they be able to stop the green gooey egg aliens?

Released in December 2001, *Jimmy Neutron: Boy Genius* was the feature-length version of a series of short cartoon interstitials on TV cable station Nickelodeon (the interstitials and film were animated concurrently). The character had been created in 1995 as "Johnny Quasar" by John A. Davis and his studio, but was substantially revamped for the new story. The CGI animation gives everything an otherworldly plastic sheen (at times resembling claymation), but the characters are cute and expressive, and the script and Jimmy's inventions are fun. The two best things about the film, though, are the villains voiced by Patrick Stewart and Martin Short (who also worked together in *The Prince of Egypt*), and the hyperdetail used for the outer space kid's armada and Jimmy's creations. Though the audience only sees bits and pieces of the "tech," it's clearly all been built in a multilayered and stunning way.

The DVD has a few cool extras, including a behind-the-scenes show, two music videos, seven DVD-ROM games, and twelve promotional spots. The film was nominated for Best Animated Feature Academy Award. Although it didn't win, many parents discovered—as did I—that this kid's film was a charming and fun way to spend some time.

SPECIAL FEATURES "Making of" Featurette • Trailer • Promotional Footage • Music Videos • DVD-ROM Features: Games • Other Title Trailers TECHNICAL FEATURES Widescreen (1.66:1 enhanced for 16x9) • Fullscreen (1.33:1) • Subtitles/CC: Eng. • Languages: Eng., Fren. dub • Sound: Dolby Digital 5.1 Surround • Keepcase • 1 Disc • Region 1 GENRE & RATING CGI/Science Fiction/Comedy • Rated G

Jin-Roh: The Wolf Brigade

Bandai/Viz, 2002, 105 mins., #1881. Directed by Hiroyuki Okiura. Screenplay by Mamoru Oshii. Based on the manga series *Hellhound: Panzer Corps* by Mamoru Oshii and Kamui Fujiwara.

Alternate history time: After World War II—and the German takeover — Japan is in a state of domestic turmoil, and as acts of terrorism and civil unrest besiege the police forces, a paramilitary police group is formed. Members of the Capitol Police work outside the law, mainly hunting down the rebel faction known as "The Sect." During riots, the rebels use young girls to deliver weapons and explosives. Constable Fuse of the Capitol Police catches one of these girls, but before he can find out more, she commits suicide. As Fuse explores the dead girl's past and motives, he meets her sister, a girl half his age. Fuse and Kei are drawn into a romance, even as their very natures struggle to tear them apart. And as a complex web of political intrigue closes around him, Fuse becomes a scapegoat . . . and perhaps, a wolf?

This 1999 feature film is an astonishingly well animated project; the characters and designs are so realistic that it almost appears as if rotoscoping was involved. The story has overtones—direct and subliminal—of the Little Red Riding Hood fairy tale, with Kei as Red, and Fuse as (potentially) the Big Bad Wolf. Full of earthy greys, olives, tans, and blacks, the film is often hazy, softly lit as if in a dark dream.

The story is full of metaphor, political intrigue, and a central philosophical question. It also has some strong action sequences—too strong for young viewers—but this is a thinking person's military romance, not an action story with tacked-on emotional baggage. Although some reviewers have carped about the story's similarity to previous works by Mamoru Oshii, many storytellers have thematic echoes, which, in my opinion, often make their stories more cohesive.

The DVD features a stunningly clear print of the film (an accomplishment in itself given the muted palette) and excellent sound, though it apparently does not play in some DVD-ROM drives. The single disc release is a nice bet if you want just the film, but the *Special Edition* set contains so much more. *Jin-Roh: The Wolf Brigade* raises the bar, both in terms of alternate history storytelling, and in terms of its naturalistic and realistic animation.

SPECIAL FEATURES Insert: Police/Character Chart TECHNICAL FEATURES Widescreen (1.85:1) • Subtitles/CC: Eng. • Languages: Jap., Eng. dub • Sound: Dolby Digital Surround 5.1, DTS • Keepcase* 1 Disc • Region 1 GENRE & RATING War/Romance/Intrigue • Rated 16+

Jin-Roh: The Wolf Brigade—Special Edition

Bandai/Viz, 2002, 105 mins., #1882. Directed by Hiroyuki Okiura. Screenplay by Mamoru Oshii. Based on the manga series *Hellhound: Panzer Corps* by Mamoru Oshii and Kamui Fujiwara.

This lush box set features a trio of discs in a nice foldout case. The initial disc is the film, essentially the same as in the keepcase edition. The second disc holds the extras, with a substantial amount of informative features. Over forty-five minutes of video interviews with the director, screenwriter, composer, and art director are followed by multiple Japanese trailers (and the U.S. spot). An extensive gallery showcases characters, vehicles, weapons, and backgrounds, with more than 100 illustrations.

The third disc is the CD soundtrack by Hajime Mizoguchi, an orchestral score dominated by strings but with choral underpinnings. Like the film, it does not rely overmuch on action setpieces; instead, it concentrates on emotional underscoring. A sixteen-page booklet profiles Mamoru Oshii and features an essay on history and its influence on filmmakers by Carl Gustav Horn, as well as a Police/Character Chart. Highly recommended.

SPECIAL FEATURES Interviews • Character and Art Galleries • Trailers • Soundtrack • Insert: Booklet TECHNICAL FEATURES Widescreen (1.85:1) • Subtitles/CC: Eng. • Languages: Jap., Eng. dub • Sound: Dolby Digital Surround 5.1, DTS • Plastic Slipcase with Fold-Out Box Set • 3 Discs • Region 1 GENRE & RATING War/Romance/Intrigue • Rated 16+

Joseph and the Coat of Many Colors

Delta Entertainment, 2001, 50 mins., #82 124. Animation Directed by Richard Slapczynski. Screenplay by Paul Leadon. Based on stories in the Old Testament.

Having been a bit too precocious for his brothers to handle, young Joseph was sold into slavery, eventually ending up in the dungeons of the Pharaoh. But Joseph's amazing ability to interpret dreams helps the Pharaoh and earns Joseph a favored place in his government. Given the chance, will he take revenge upon his brothers?

Once again, Australia's Burbank Studios turns in an embarrassing job on this 2000 project. Do they get worse on each project, or just those in the last decade? Most of the characters are unpleasantly cartoony, except Joseph, whose more natural look is a stark contrast. The anachronistic dialogue is grating. The DVD case contains the best art, but this is one of those discs best bought cheaply.

SPECIAL FEATURES None TECHNICAL FEATURES Fullscreen (1.33:1) • Languages: Eng. • Sound: Dolby Digital 2.0 • Keepcase • 1 Disc • Region All GENRE & RATING Religious/Family • Not Rated (Kids)

Joseph: King of Dreams—Special Edition

DreamWorks, 2000, 74 mins., #86452. Directed by Robert Ramirez, Rob LaDuca. Screenplay by Eugenia Bostwick-Singer, Raymond Singer, Joe Stillman, Marshall Goldberg. Based on stories in the Old Testament.

The story of Joseph from the book of Genesis is a familiar one (a synopsis of which is in the preceding review). From shepherd to slave to dream interpreter to pharaoh's confidant and beyond, Joseph's interesting life is reinterpreted here, by many of the same people who produced *The Prince of Egypt.*

Although this is a direct-to-video/DVD release, its production values are higher than most, perhaps because it was produced concurrently with *Prince.* Vocal talent is nice, including Ben Affleck in the lead role, supported by Mark Hamill, Judith Light, Rene Auberjonois, and Jodi Benson. The dream sequences are based on the works of Vincent Van Gogh (no, really!), brought to life with CGI. The result is a nice film that isn't overtly religious or preachy; its agenda seems to be to tell a sweeping saga of one man's life—with songs added in—and it does that very well.

Besides being offered as a single DVD, the disc was also included as part of a pack set, along with *The Prince of Egypt.*

SPECIAL FEATURES Cast Filmographies • Production Notes • Storyboards with Commentary • Trailer • Read-Along • Sing-Along • DVD-ROM Features: Coloring Book, Activities • Insert: Liner Notes TECHNICAL FEATURES Widescreen (1.85:1 enhanced for 16x9) • Subtitles/CC: Eng. • Languages: Eng. • Sound: Dolby DigitalSurround 2.0, Dolby Digital Surround 5.1 • Keepcase • 1 Disc • Region 1 GENRE & RATING Religious/Family/Music • Rated PG

Jubei-chan: Ninja Girl—Secret of the Lovely Eyepatch: A Legend Reborn [#1]

Bandai, 2000, 100 mins., #0970. Directed by Akitaro Daichi. Script by Akitaro Daichi. Based on the manga series by Akitaro Daichi in *AX*.

Three hundred years ago, legendary swordsmaster Yagyu Jubei gives his disciple Koinosuke Odago a heart-shaped talisman of power and tells him to find someone worthy of being Jubei the second . . . preferably someone with a curvy top and bottom. In modern times, Koinosuke finds a bouncy young schoolgirl named Jiyu "Jubei" Nanohana, and implores her to become Jubei the second. By donning the eyepatch, Jiyu is transformed into a sword-wielding warrioress, all the better to fight agents of the Ryujoji clan, whose feud with the Yagyu clan is revived when Jubei is "reborn." Now, Jiyu must balance boys, school, and cooking with reluctant swordplay, teachers who keep attacking her, and other excitement.

Jubei-chan: Ninja Girl is a hyperactive and frenetic muddle, with both art and story alternating between goofy and deformed cartoonish sub-humor and dark and grim samurai battles. The resulting mixture is popular in some areas of fandom, though others may find it schizophrenic and annoying. The 1999 TV series appeared almost concurrently with its manga version. It is based on speculative stories about an actual 17th-century swordsman named Yagyu Jubei, who has appeared in pulp stories, manga, and the *Ninja Scroll* and *Ninja Resurrection* OVAs.

This DVD features the initial four episodes of the series, and the transfer quality is fine. There is an automatic subtitle track that appears with the English-language version; it functions as a form of liner notes, translating some Japanese elements for better understanding by Western audiences.

SPECIAL FEATURES "Cooking with Jubei" • Trailers • Other Title Trailers • Insert: Character Notes • Easter Eggs TECHNICAL FEATURES Fullscreen (1.33:1) • Subtitles/CC: Eng. • Languages: Jap., Eng. dub • Sound: Dolby Digital 5.1 • Keepcase • 1 Disc • Region 1 GENRE & RATING Martial Arts/Girls • Not Rated (Teens)

Jubei-chan: Ninja Girl—Secret of the Lovely Eyepatch: Basic Ninja Training [#2]

Bandai, 2000, 75 mins., #0971. Directed by Akitaro Daichi. Script by Akitaro Daichi. Based on the manga series by Akitaro Daichi in *AX*.

Jiyu continues to try to deny her heritage, but Koinosuke won't let her. A husband and wife work their way into Jiyu's house while she and her father are away, and when Jiyu returns, she's surprised to find that her enemy resembles someone very important in her life. Next, Jiyu explores the secrets of her past, and learns about the weaknesses in her fighting style from kendo master Shiro Ryujoji. Then, Jiyu faces a group of men in black . . . make that *assassins* in black!

Three more *Jubei-chan* episodes are presented on this volume, which continues its style of annoyingly bizarre humor mixed with dark samurai action. The episodes are: "The Enemy Brought a Memory with Them"; "My Next Enemy Is Yesterday's Ally"; and "She Had Grasped the Secret Before She Knew It!"

SPECIAL FEATURES "Bantaro's Dating Tips" • Trailers • Other Title Trailers • Insert: Character Notes • Easter Eggs TECHNICAL FEATURES Fullscreen (1.33:1) • Subtitles/CC: Eng. • Languages: Jap., Eng. dub • Sound: Dolby Digital 5.1 • Keepcase • 1 Disc • Region 1 GENRE & RATING Martial Arts/Girls • Not Rated (Teens)

Jubei-chan: Ninja Girl—Secret of the Lovely Eyepatch: Heart of Steel [#3]

Bandai, 2000, 75 mins., #0972. Directed by Akitaro Daichi. Script by Akitaro Daichi. Based on the manga series by Akitaro Daichi in *AX*.

The last disc ended on a cliff-hanger, and it's resolved in this trio of stories. Jiyu's father performs a rather unorthodox healing method on his daughter, and we find out the history of Jiyu and how her mother died. Plus, lots of ninjas attack, and Shiro's evil brother, Hajime, the head of the Ryujoji clan, makes his move on Jiyu/Jubei, but things don't end as anyone expects them to. And someone new joins the Ruffians "gang."

Episodes #8–10 are presented on this DVD: "I Attached This Thing to My Head"; "Dad's Premonition of Love"; and "This Is Where to Make the Effort." The eighth episode contains some scenes that may make many viewers uncomfortable, as they have implications of incest (although that is not what is going on).

SPECIAL FEATURES "Ninja Fashion with Jubei-chan" • Trailers • Other Title Trailers • Insert: Character Notes • Easter Egg

TECHNICAL FEATURES Fullscreen (1.33:1) • Subtitles/CC: Eng. • Languages: Jap., Eng. dub • Sound: Dolby Digital 5.1 • Keepcase • 1 Disc • Region 1 GENRE & RATING Martial Arts/Girls • Not Rated (Teens)

Jubei-chan: Ninja Girl—Secret of the Lovely Eyepatch: Final Showdown! [#4]

 Bandai, 2000, 75 mins., #0973. Directed by Akitaro Daichi. Directed by Akitaro Daichi. Script by Akitaroh Daichi. Based on the manga series by Akitaro Daichi in *AX*.

Even as Jiyu finally comes to terms with her role as Jubei, the successor to the eyepatch talisman, she finds out that a close friend is really her enemy. And what will her father's reaction be when he discovers Jiyu's secret? There is one more battle to be fought in the 300-year-old clash between the Yagyu clan and the Ryujoji clan; will Jiyu/Jubei emerge victorious, and if so, at what cost?

The final three episodes are presented on this volume, which is more emotion-oriented than previous storylines: "But the Path Curves Ahead"; "I Had Met a Daughter That I Never Knew"; and "Night Gave Way to a Brand New Day."

SPECIAL FEATURES Trailers • Promotional Footage • Clean Credits • Insert: Character Notes • Easter Egg TECHNICAL FEATURES Fullscreen (1.33:1) • Subtitles/CC: Eng. • Languages: Jap., Eng. dub • Sound: Dolby Digital 5.1 • Keepcase • 1 Disc • Region 1 GENRE & RATING Martial Arts/Girls • Not Rated (Teens)

Judge

 U.S. Manga Corps, 1999, 50 mins., #USMD 1773. Directed by Hiroshi Negishi. Screenplay by Katsuhiko Chiba. Based on the manga series by Fujihiko Hosono.

What would happen if you were the judge in an afterlife courtroom in Hell? That's the concept behind this series, which features Hoichiro Oma as a man who metes out justice to those who have wronged others. From a corrupt and murderous executive to supernatural lawyers, Oma must deal with all types of scum as he adjudicates retribution. And if he can't make a decision, he can always appeal to the Ten Kings of Hell, who have final jurisdiction.

A 1991 OVA, *Judge* is an interesting concept, as if you have combined *The Crow* with *The Practice*. Really, how many other horror court dramas have you seen? Though some of the art is realistic, some is highly stylized in an unattractive manner. One interesting mystical battle is fought in a snowy wilderness, a nice change of pace from

the usual city-bound clashes. The DVD doesn't have a lot of extras, but when you've got a concept this odd, you might not need them.

Besides being offered as a single DVD, the disc was also included as part of a 2002 "Judgment Day Pack" set, along with *Cybernetics Guardian*.

SPECIAL FEATURES Character Intros • "Laws of Darkness" • Other Title Trailers • DVD-ROM Features: Web Links TECHNICAL FEATURES Fullscreen (1.33:1) • Subtitles/CC: Eng. • Languages: Jap., Eng. dub • Sound: Dolby Digital 2.0 • Keepcase • 1 Disc • Region All GENRE & RATING Horror/Thriller/Occult • Not Rated (Teens)

Jungle Book, The [Limited Edition]
Disney, 1999, 78 mins.

This DVD was not available for review. It is now on moratorium.

Jungle De Ikou!

 AnimeWorks, 2001, 90 mins., #AWDVD-0108. Directed by Yuji Moriyama. Story by Yuji Moriyama. Script by Haruo Takayama.

Nasumi is a young girl who is given an ancient statue by her archeologist father. She soon dreams of Ahem, the creator god, who tells her that she will need power to defeat Ongo, the god of destruction. Nasumi learns a creepily sexual dance from Ahem, which turns her into Mie, a flower spirit and fertility goddess with barely there clothes and humongous breasts. Now, using her "talents" and new powers, Nasumi will try her breast—ahem—best to defend Tokyo from Ongo (who isn't quite what she's been warned about), whales, and fighter pilots.

Just when you thought you couldn't see anything creepier than *Pokémon*'s popularity, along comes this embarrassing spectacle, released as three OVAs in 1997. Ahem is a grotesque tribal shaman type, clad only in a protruding horn-like spout on his crotch. His performance of the ritual power dance, complete with nipple twisting, is enough to put most viewers off solid food for a few days at least. The rest of this goofy "comedy" is equally filled with sexual innuendo, making it for an older audience than its rating would imply.

The DVD presents the material well, and its cover tells you all you need to know about the disc visually.

SPECIAL FEATURES Character and Art Galleries • Trailers TECHNICAL FEATURES Fullscreen (1.33:1) • Subtitles/CC: Eng. • Languages: Jap., Eng. dub • Sound: Dolby Digital 2.0 • Keepcase • 1 Disc • Region 1 GENRE & RATING Fantasy/Girls/Cheesecake • Rated 13+

Jungle Girl and the Lost Island of the Dinosaurs

Koch, 2002, 50 mins., #KOC-DV-6138.

This DVD was not available for review.

Justice League

Warner, 2002, 60 mins., #22236. Directed by Dan Riba, Butch Lukic. Written by Rich Fogel. Based on the comic book series published by DC Comics.

J'onn J'onnz, the Martian Manhunter, comes to warn the Earth about an impending alien invasion. Superman and Batman have already engaged in the fight, and soon others of the world's greatest superheroes are recruited as well. Wonder Woman, Hawkman, Flash, and Hawkgirl join the fray as the alien menace arrives. Will the newly formed Justice League have enough power and teamwork to save the day?

First things first: this ain't your parent's *Super Friends*. Brought to the Cartoon Network in 2001 by the team behind *Batman: The Animated Series* and *Superman*, this new *Justice League* is leaner, meaner, and more moody than its predecessor. The heroes don't always get along, and each has his own distinct personality. Although completely appropriate for young audiences, *Justice League* has become a hit among older viewers thanks to its quality art and storylines.

Justice League is aired on television in two versions: fullscreen and widescreen. The widescreen version is just the fullscreen version with black bars added in, meaning the viewer actually gets *less* picture (Batman's ears and characters' feet are constantly cut off). So, it's nice that this DVD retains the fullscreen version of the show. The first three-part episode, "Secret Origins," fills up this volume. Transfer quality—like the enjoyment factor—is excellent. Trivia note: Michael Rosenbaum, who plays proto-villain Lex Luthor on WB's *Smallville*, here voices Superman ally The Flash!

SPECIAL FEATURES Character Bios • Other Title Trailers • DVD-ROM Features: Web Links TECHNICAL FEATURES Fullscreen (1.33:1) • Languages: Eng. • Sound: Dolby Digital Surround 2.0 • Snapcase • 1 Disc • Region 1–4 GENRE & RATING Superheroes/Action • Not Rated (Kids)

Kamyla ☞ see Mature/Adult Section

Karakuri Ninja Girl ☞ see Mature/Adult Section

Karen ☞ see Mature/Adult Section

Key: The Metal Idol #1—Awakening

Pioneer/Viz, 2000, 210 mins., #D-KM001. Directed by Hiroaki Sato. Written by Hiroaki Sato.

Tokiko Mima is known as "Key" by all those who know her, but when her grandfather dies, he leaves her the truth about herself, and a real key to her future. She is an experimental robot that he has upgraded each year; after his death no one will work on her anymore and her batteries will eventually run dry. However, if she can win the love of 30,000 people, she will become a flesh-and-blood girl. Key goes to Tokyo, where she becomes the target of an unscrupulous pornography director, a strange scientist that makes robots, a snake cult, a disturbed school friend, and more. But to reach her goal of becoming human, she realizes she must become a pop music sensation . . . an idol.

A mix of the Pinocchio and Frankenstein stories, *Key: The Metal Idol* is unpredictable without being inscrutable. The plot-heavy tale appears on one level to be about the search for humanity, while on another it draws us into a struggle over technology and secrets. A 1994 OVA series, *Key* also has a lot of well-placed cliffhangers. The animation is nice—and fairly Western-looking—but some of the lines drop out a bit in the digital image. On the disc, the first episode has a few picture problems, but the rest of the shows are fine. Pioneer really crammed this DVD, putting seven episodes on it along with some nice extras. Despite the listed age rating, this is really for audiences 16 and older, due to some violence and nudity.

SPECIAL FEATURES Text Interview with Director • Character Bios • Character and Art Galleries • FAQ TECHNICAL FEATURES Fullscreen (1.33:1) • Subtitles/CC: Eng. • Languages: Jap., Eng. dub • Sound: Dolby Digital Surround 2.0 • Keepcase • 1 Disc • Region 1 GENRE & RATING Science Fiction/Girls/Music • Not Rated (Teens)

Key: The Metal Idol #2—Dreaming

Pioneer/Viz, 2000, 180 mins., #D-KM002. Directed by Hiroaki Sato. Written by Hiroaki Sato.

Key's attempts to become a pop singer don't go very well, since she hasn't been programmed to sing or dance, and someone is sabotaging her chances. Meanwhile, someone else is snooping around Key's childhood home town, and freakish scientist Ajo continues his disturbing robot experiments. Plus, Priest Snake Eyes has plans for Key within his cult. The story threads on this disc intersect at a concert by music idol Miho, but what could the pop princess have to do with Key?

Six more episodes are offered on the second DVD, along with extras. Like the first disc, there are some picture problems every now and then, but quality is relatively consistent.

SPECIAL FEATURES Text Interview with Director • Character Bios • Character and Art Galleries • Easter Egg TECHNICAL FEATURES Fullscreen (1.33:1) • Subtitles/CC: Eng. • Languages: Jap., Eng. dub • Sound: Dolby Digital Surround 2.0 • Keepcase • 1 Disc • Region 1 GENRE & RATING Science Fiction/Girls/Music • Not Rated (Teens)

Key: The Metal Idol #3—Singing

Pioneer/Viz, 2000, 180 mins., #D-KM003. Directed by Hiroaki Sato. Written by Hiroaki Sato.

The secrets of Key's past are exposed, and Ajo and Miho are linked to her. Now, as Miho prepares to give a major concert, the evil machinations of Ajo and his project may prove deadly to everyone in the cast . . . and all those in the concert audience!

The final two movie-length OVAs resolve the story. The first of these is more dialogue-heavy, while the second contains more action.

SPECIAL FEATURES Text Interview with Director • Character Bios • Character and Art Galleries TECHNICAL FEATURES Fullscreen (1.33:1) • Subtitles/CC: Eng. • Languages: Jap., Eng. dub • Sound: Dolby Digital Surround 2.0 • Keepcase • 1 Disc • Region 1 GENRE & RATING Science Fiction/Girls/Music • Not Rated (Teens)

Kidnapped [Collector's Edition]

Digital Versatile Disc, 2000, 49 mins., #165. Animation Directed by Warwick Gilbert. Screenplay by Leonard Lee. Based on the book by Robert Louis Stevenson.

After the death of his father, David Balfour goes to live with his Uncle Ebenezer, but doesn't realize that his relative has evil plans in store for him. David is soon shanghaied onto a sailing ship, where he is mistreated until he meets Alan Stewart, the survivor of a collision with another vessel. Swept into the sea, David is stranded on an island, but through a series of adventures, he finds his way back to Scotland and his friend Alan. Will he get even with his traitorous uncle?

A 1986 production of Burbank Films Australia, this contains grainy, washed-out animation that seems appropriate for the story it tells. Unfortunately, half of the story takes place at night, and the animators' shorthand for this is using only blue tones to replace the color palette instead of adding shadows. The adaptation streamlines the complex book, making it easier for younger audiences to follow. As with other DVD Ltd. releases, there is a bio of the author on the disc.

SPECIAL FEATURES Author Bio • Game TECHNICAL FEATURES Fullscreen (1.33:1) • Languages: Eng. • Sound: Dolby Digital 5.1, DTS • Keepcase • 1 Disc • Region All GENRE & RATING Historical/Adventure • Not Rated (Kids)

Kimagure Orange Road TV [Box Set]

AnimEigo, 2002, 1200 mins., #AV002-200. Directed by Kobayashi Osamu. Screenplay by Shikichi Ohashi, Isao Shizutani, Kenji Terada, Yoshihiro Tomita. Based on the manga series by Izumi Matsumoto and Kenji Terada in *Shonen Jump Weekly*.

NOTE: This DVD arrived too late for a full review. The following text is promotional copy provided by the releasing company:

"High school student Kasuga Kyosuke has problems with women. Big time! First, he thinks he's falling in love with the beautiful and somewhat mysterious Ayuka Madoka, but he's not at all sure if Madoka feels the same way about him. Second, he's being pursued by the exceedingly sweet, cute, and bubbly Hiyami Hikaru, who has taken to calling him 'Darling' and asking him if she'll make a good wife. The two girls are total opposites—and best friend since childhood. Which means that Kyosuke's love life is somewhat complicated.

"But wait: Kyosuke's woman troubles are far from over. He's got two bratty sisters to worry about, and his two sex-crazed buddies are stalking them! And one of the toughest guys in the Karate Club, who is rather annoyed about him 'stealing' Hikaru, is stalking him!

"Kyosuke does have one thing going for him. Both he and his sisters have inherited the family gift—paranormal powers! Teleportation, Telekinesis, Precognition, they can do it all. Unfortunately, if anyone catches them using their powers, they'll have to leave town. And it turns out that Kyosuke's powers are much better at getting him into trouble than they are at getting him out of it. All this means that life is rarely boring (and always hilarious) on Kimagure Orange Road."

This immense box set features all forty-eight episodes, and was originally available only from the AnimEigo website. See also the entry for *New Kimagure Orange Road: Summer's Beginning.*

SPECIAL FEATURES Inserts: 60-page Liner Note Booklet TECHNICAL FEATURES Fullscreen (1.33:1) • Subtitles/CC: Eng. • Languages: Jap. • Sound: Dolby Digital 2.0 • Cardboard Box with 12 Keepcases • 12 Discs • Region 1 GENRE & RATING Romance • Not Rated (Teens)

Kimera ☞ see Mature/Adult Section

King and I, The

Warner, 1999, 90 mins., #17468. Directed by Richard Rich. Screenplay by Peter Bakalian, Jacqueline Feather, David Seidler. Based on the novel "Anna and the King of Siam" by Margaret Landon and the stage musical by Richard Rodgers and Oscar Hammerstein II.

Prim British schoolteacher Anna Leonowens arrives in 19th-century Imperial Siam to be the governess to the King's multiple children. But even as Anna begins to teach the children about the ways of the world, she also catches the eye—and heart—of the arrogant King, who has never before encountered a woman so alive and full of contradictions. Meanwhile, the crown prince falls in forbidden love with a lowly servant girl named Tuptim, and the scheming Kralahome plans a coup to overthrow the King.

This cross-cultural story has enthralled audiences for years, with the Broadway musical garnering ten Tony Awards and the 1956 feature film capturing five Academy Awards. With a pedigree like that, you would think that the producers—once they decided that an animated version was absolutely necessary—would have left well enough alone and let the story and music carry the ball. Unfortunately, this was not the case, as this 1999 feature film version of *The King and I* features fire-breathing dragons, sorcery, kickboxing, and cute animals—a baby elephant, a mischevious monkey, and a regal black panther. And then there's the stunt casting: Barbra Streisand sings "I Have Dreamed" over the end credits.

Not to say the film is a total waste, as the combination of cel work and CGI make this glittering and magical Siam a wonder to behold. And the voice cast is nice, headed by Miranda Richardson and Christiane Noll as Anna's speaking and singing voice, respectively. Most of the cast members are Broadway stars, giving the soundtrack a showier quality than it might otherwise have had with Hollywood voice actors.

The DVD of *The King and I* is full of cool extras, making it quite a good value. For kids who've seen nothing but Disney musicals, this is a good introduction to "classic" musical theater and another culture. But afterward, you might try to interest them in the live-action version, and other Rodgers and Hammerstein masterpieces.

SPECIAL FEATURES "Making of" Featurette • Character Bios • Trailers • Sing-Alongs • Other Title Trailers • Games • DVD-ROM Features TECHNICAL FEATURES Widescreen (1.85:1 enhanced for 16x9) • Subtitles/CC: Eng., Fren., Span. • Languages: Eng., Fren. dub, Span. dub • Sound: Dolby Digital 5.1 • Snapcase • 1 Disc • Region 1 GENRE & RATING Historical/Romance/Music • Rated G

Kingdom Under the Sea: Return of the King [#1]

Bridgestone, 2001, 25 mins., #98273. Directed by David Mulhern. Story by Steve Engelbrite. Script by Steve Engelbrite, Betsy Hernandez.

Splash and his sister Coral are excited because they've heard that the great whale King Pacificus is returning, but Splash accidentally lets the secret slip to the evil Krakken. Soon, Pacificus must sacrifice himself to save the school of fish, but he is miraculously reborn, despite Krakken's misdeeds. Will Splash be forgiven?

Although the packaging clearly states that this is a religious series, *Kingdom Under the Sea* is really only religious in an allegorical sense. There aren't any leanings to any specific denomination beyond references to God and Jesus Christ on the packaging. The entire story is told in parable form, using fish. As for the animation, it's done with extremely fluid CGI, better than the majority of non-feature CGI. The extra featurette is a nice touch, too, especially given the show's short running time. One

of the scenes in the extras—an emotion/speech test for Splash—will have almost all viewers laughing out loud.

SPECIAL FEATURES "Making of" Featurette TECHNICAL FEATURES Fullscreen (1.33:1) • Languages: Eng. • Sound: Dolby Digital 2.0 • Keepcase • 1 Disc • Region All GENRE & RATING CGI/Religious/Animal • Not Rated (All Ages)

Kingdom Under the Sea: Red Tide [#2]

Bridgestone, 2001, 25 mins., #95733. Directed by David Mulhern. Script by Betsy Hernandez.

The evil Krakken has come up with another insidious plan, and Professor Pinch has helped him. They will release the "Red Tide" poison onto the coral ReefVillage during the next incoming tide, killing everything there. Naughty young Creeper and Crustin are almost caught in the deadly tide, but they're saved by the young fishes Squash and Coral. The ReefVillage inhabitants are protected by the enormous King Pacificus, and after the deadly tide has passed, they set about rebuilding their home. But will Creeper and Crustin accept forgiveness for their misdeeds, or rejoin the dark side?

Featuring better CGI animation than its predecessor, *The Red Tide* is again told in parable form. There is an insert in the package that gives parents Biblical citations for further study, mostly from the Old Testament. A different "Making of" feature takes viewers on an eight-minute behind-the-scenes trip.

SPECIAL FEATURES "Making of" Featurette • Character and Art Galleries • Insert: Parental Guide TECHNICAL FEATURES Fullscreen (1.33:1) • Languages: Eng. • Sound: Dolby Digital 2.0 • Keepcase • 1 Disc • Region All GENRE & RATING CGI/Religious/Animal • Not Rated (All Ages)

King Solomon's Mines [Collector's Edition]

Digital Versatile Disc, 1999, #166.

This DVD was not available for review.

KISS: Immortals

Slingshot, 2000, #BDVD9304. Directed by Jane Schneider. Written by Bruce Onder, Jefferey Sullivan.

The rock band KISS is playing another huge concert in Pittsburgh when something unexpected happens; the group is pulled through a wormhole into another dimension! In this surreal world, the Voice of Shadows asks the musicians to save her, but they soon discover that in this world music is outlawed. Being the rebels that they are, the members of KISS decide to take on the antimusic forces, including the trigger-happy, redheaded Domino!

This is a "Multipath Adventure," a cross between a video game and traditional storytelling. As viewers watch the story, they are presented with choices of action every few minutes. Each choice (made using the DVD remote) branches the story off in a new direction, meaning there are multiple outcomes and storylines for the characters. The animation is rough 3D CGI, which will probably be fine for video game enthusiasts but may hurt the eyes of traditional animation fans.

This adventure features performances and excerpts of four KISS songs: "Master and Slave," "Shout It Out Loud," "Strutter," and "Within." Other than *Pink Floyd: The Wall*, which is a combination of live-action and animation, *KISS: Immortals* is the only animated DVD of a rock band.

SPECIAL FEATURES Other Title Trailers TECHNICAL FEATURES Fullscreen (1.33:1) • Languages: Eng. • Sound: Dolby Digital 5.1 • Keepcase • 1 Disc • Region 1–6 GENRE & RATING Interactive/Horror/Music • Not Rated (Teens)

Kite

AnimeWorks, 2000, 45 mins., #AWDVD-0082. DIrected by Yasuoml Umezu. Script by Yasuomi Umezu.

Sawa is a young girl whose parents were brutally murdered years before. Taken in by Akai, the detective assigned to the case, she grows up to be his lover and protégé. Behind the scenes, Akai has trained her to be a cold-blooded assassin, using special exploding bullets to take out those who think they're above the law. But what will happen when little miss vigilante starts showing interest in another boy? And what is the secret that detective Akai never wants her to learn?

Exceedingly bloody and featuring some nudity, this is the censored version of the 1998 OVA series. While the animation and designs have a cool techno-crisp look, the gore and violence so overwhelm everything else that it almost becomes strange not to see spurting blood in some scenes. When released on video (and later on DVD) there was much controversy over *Kite* in fan communities, both because the OVAs had been edited together, and because so much footage had been removed. Few complained that the English dialogue and subtitles referred to Sawa as a college student, however; that at least removed the element of underaged sex.

The DVD contains a top-notch print, as well as several extras, including storyboard-to-animation split-screen comparisons. But those who are squeamish—or who are concerned about what their kids watch—should make sure this *Kite* doesn't fly into their DVD player. And truthfully, those who want to see this fare should probably get the *Kite: Director's Cut* version instead.

SPECIAL FEATURES Character and Art GallerIes • Storyboards • Music Video • Other Title Trailers TECHNICAL FEATURES Fullscreen (1.33:1) • Subtitles/CC: Eng. • Languages: Jap., Eng. dub • Sound: Dolby Digital 2.0 • Keepcase • 1 Disc • Region 1–6 GENRE & RATING Action/Adventure • Rated 16+

Kite: Director's Cut ☞ see Mature/Adult Section

Kizuna

Culture Q, 2001, 60 mins., #CQC502. Directed by Hiro Rin. Screenplay by Miyo Morita. Based on the manga series by Kazuma Kodaka in *Be-Boy*.

Ranmaru "Ran" Samejima is the college fencing champion, but when he saves his boyfriend, Kei Enjoji, from a hit-and-run car accident, his sports career is over. The accident is actually a murder plot to kill Enjoji, who is the son of the local yakuza don in Osaka. Although he's initially paralyzed, Ran is nursed back to health with the love and support of Enjoji. But their life is not going to be simple, as a sexually aggressive college professor and Enjoji's half-brother both make plans to steal Ran away as their lover.

A two-part 1994 OVA series, *Kizuna* was the first gay-themed anime to be released for the English-language market; it still remains one of a very few gay animated projects on DVD. The animation is smooth, though it occasionally jumps into goofy moments. It also has a lot of pans of still-frame manga drawings for scene transitions or moments of action. The story does gets a bit convoluted, but the characters are distinct enough if you pay attention.

Picture quality on the DVD is fine, though the story has a slightly grainy, hazy quality to it. It's hard to tell if that was intended. For those worried about exposure to gay relationships, this has much material that could offend, although sexual situations are kept to a minimum.

There is a second version of *Kizuna* available (#CQC503), but the contents of the disc are exactly the same. The cover, however, is different and aimed at a more mainstream anime audience, with no overt gay elements.

SPECIAL FEATURES None TECHNICAL FEATURES Fullscreen (1.33:1) • Subtitles/CC: Eng. • Languages: Jap. • Sound: Dolby Digital 2.0 • Keepcase • 1 Disc • Region 1–6 GENRE & RATING Gay/Romance/Adventure • Not Rated (Teens)

Kizuna

Culture Q, 2001, 60 mins., #CQC503. Directed by Hiro Rin. Screenplay by Miyo Morita. Based on the manga series by Kazuma Kodaka in *Be-Boy*.

This is the second version of *Kizuna*. The contents of the disc are exactly the same, but the cover image is different and is aimed at a more mainstream anime audience, with no overt gay elements.

SPECIAL FEATURES None TECHNICAL FEATURES Fullscreen (1.33:1) • Subtitles/CC: Eng. • Languages: Jap. • Sound: Dolby Digital 2.0 • Keepcase • 1 Disc • Region 1–6 GENRE & RATING Gay/Romance/Adventure • Not Rated (Teens)

Knight Hunters: Weiss Kreuz—Dead Ringer [#1]

AnimeWorks, 2002, 125 mins., #KHDVD-5001. Directed by Kiyoshi Egami. Story by Takehito Koyasu, Project Weiss. Screenplay by Shigeru Yanagawa, Isao Shizuna, Yuji Kawahara, Sukehiro Tomita. Based on the stories in *Animage*.

Florists by day, vigilante killers by night . . . Aya, Ken, Yoji, and Omi aren't your typical quartet of young guys. Aya is moody, Ken is an ex-athlete with Wolverine-like claws, Yoji is a ladies man, and Omi is a computer specialist. Together, they fight crime. Working under assignment from a mystery man known as Persia, the quartet patrols the streets of the city, meting out deadly justice to those who think themselves above the law. Assassins, hackers, and pimps beware: these boys may smell like roses, but they're sharp like thorns!

With the cool gothic covers on these DVDs, combined with the Germanic title, I was looking forward to a good horror/suspense series different from the traditional bloodbath anime horror. Well, these are *different*, all right. The premise of this 1998 TV series is bizarre, as if it were some Hollywood buddy movie gone awry. You can picture the pitch meeting: "There's these four guys who look like N'Sync, except they're killers who fight crime, but during the day, they're florists, but not gay florists! They're *Charlie's Angels*, but bloodier!"

The design work on the series is pretty and glam. The animation itself is stilted, however, and slips into cutesy moments, especially when the crush-heavy schoolgirls come around the flower shop. As for the stories, the scripts lack interest and coherence. The sloppiness in the plots and characterization extends to AnimeWorks' job on the special features: the Sketches section is misspelled "Sketchs."

The DVD itself is nicely done, with a great cover and some pleasant extras, including some very funny vocal outtakes, and voice actor bios of the Japanese cast. It features five episodes, untitled in the packaging, but titled onscreen: "Lockvogel—Sacred Banquet"; "Fort Laufen—The Awakened Runaway"; "Paradise—Heaven Is Hell"; "Verrat—Execution of Betrayal"; and "Shicksal—Fate of the Hunter."

SPECIAL FEATURES Cast Bios • Character and Art Galleries • Clean Credits • Outtakes • Other Title Trailers TECHNICAL FEATURES Fullscreen (1.33:1) • Subtitles/CC: Eng. • Languages: Jap., Eng. dub • Sound: Dolby Digital 2.0 • Keepcase • 1 Disc • Region 1 GENRE & RATING Action/Adventure • Rated 13+

Knight Hunters: Weiss Kreuz—Lost Boys [#2]

AnimeWorks, 2002, 125 mins., #KHDVD-5002. Directed by Kiyoshi Egami. Story by Takehito Koyasu, Project Weiss. Screenplay by Shigeru Yanagawa, Isao Shizuna, Yuji Kawahara, Sukehiro Tomita. Based on the stories in *Animage*.

Five more adventures of the killer florists (*snicker*) make up this volume.

Aya gets personally involved in a case in which the organs of kidnapped girls begin circulating on the black market. Another case involving missing boys conjures up Omi's memories of his own kidnapping. There's also a werewolf on the loose, and a group of powerful female assassins known as the Schreient.

Once again, the outtakes on this disc are almost as entertaining as all the stories put together, and a fabulous cover may lure unsuspecting buyers. The five episodes are: "Fraulein—The Image of a Girl"; "Entfuhren—The Memories Return"; "Raubtier—Howls in the Night"; "Schreient—Hopes"; and "Bruder—Bond of Darkness."

SPECIAL FEATURES Voice Actor Interviews • Character and Art Galleries • Clean Credits • Outtakes • Other Title Trailers TECHNICAL FEATURES Fullscreen (1.33:1) • Subtitles/CC: Eng. • Languages: Jap., Eng. dub • Sound: Dolby Digital 2.0 • Keepcase • 1 Disc • Region 1 GENRE & RATING Action/Adventure • Rated 13+

Knight Hunters: Weiss Kreuz—Lonely Heart [#3]

AnimeWorks, 2002, 125 mins., #KHDV-5003. Directed by Kiyoshi Egami. Written by Shigeru Yanagawa, Isao Shizuya, Yuji Kawahara, Sukehiro Tomita. Based on the stories in *Animage*.

NOTE: This DVD arrived too late for a full review. The following text is promotional copy provided by the releasing company:

"The secret connections between Weiss and the Takatori family are finally revealed. Hirofumi Takatori captures Omi, but will the youngest member of Weiss be able to fight back once he discovers their relationship? Aya is disillusioned by a discovery about Persia, and vows to leave the group forever. All this, and the final showdown between Weiss and their archnemesis, the assassin group Schwarz!"

This disc contains episodes #11–15.

SPECIAL FEATURES Actor Interviews • Cast Bios • Character and Art Galleries • Outtakes • Other Title Trailers TECHNICAL FEATURES Fullscreen (1.33:1) • Subtitles/CC: Eng. • Languages: Jap., Eng. dub • Sound: Dolby Digital • Keepcase • 1 Disc • Region 1 GENRE & RATING Action/Adventure • Rated 13+

Knight Hunters: Weiss Kreuz—Shining Cross [#4]

AnimeWorks, 2002, 125 mins., #KHDV-5004. Directed by Kiyoshi Egami. Written by Shigeru Yanagawa, Isao Shizuya, Yuji Kawahara, Sukehiro Tomita. Based on the stories in *Animage*.

NOTE: This DVD arrived too late for a full review. The following text is promotional copy provided by the releasing company:

"The assassins of Weiss have defeated every outside threat, but their worst enemies will always be themselves! Their group has finally fallen apart. However, just because they have gone their separate ways doesn't mean they can leave the life of killers behind. Their murderous past is catching up with them in the form of cleverly disguised assassins. But the worst is yet to come. Aya finds his sister has been kidnapped by an underground cult that burns women to death! Will the members of Weiss ever fight together again?"

This disc contains episodes #16–20.

SPECIAL FEATURES Actor Interviews • Character and Art Galleries • Outtakes • Other Title Trailers TECHNICAL FEATURES Fullscreen (1.33:1) • Subtitles/CC: Eng. • Languages: Jap., Eng. dub • Sound: Dolby Digital • Keepcase • 1 Disc • Region 1 GENRE & RATING Action/Adventure • Rated 13+

Knights of Ramune

Software Sculptors, 2000, 180 mins., #SSDVD-6081. Directed by Yoshitaka Fujimoto. Script by Katsumi Hasegawa.

Holy Virgin-in-training Parfait and Holy Virgin Cacao (she of the Psychic Saturation Power) have a job to do. First they must rescue children from an attacking space fleet. Then, they have to find a mythic Champion of the Galaxy or all of space will be destroyed. They're aided in their quest by Lemon, a young orphan girl, plus a giant robot, and their own magic powers.

Big boobs, armor, big butts, guns, big eyes, swords, crotches, explosions, bright colors, robots, and spaceships . . . it's easy to list what this show has on its agenda, and some fans will come a'running. But this silly and inconsequential story—made up of six 1997 OVAs, and based on a 1990 TV series—will send other anime viewers diving for the remote. With almost enough nudity (mainly topless) to dump it into the adult category, *Knights Of Ramune* is only for those who want titillation with a minimum of plot.

SPECIAL FEATURES Character Bios • Character and Art Galleries • Trailer • Other Title Trailers • DVD-ROM Features: Art, Scripts TECHNICAL FEATURES Fullscreen (1.33:1) • Subtitles/CC: Eng. • Languages: Jap., Eng. dub • Sound: Dolby Digital 2.0 • Keepcase • 1 Disc • Region All GENRE & RATING Fantasy/Action/Girls • Rated 16+

Koihime ☛ see Mature/Adult Section

Kokudo Oh: The Black Eye King ☛ see Mature/Adult Section

Kurogane Communication: #1—Wasteland Paradise

AnimeWorks, 2002, 120 mins., #AWDVD-0210. Directed by Yasuhito Kikuchi. Screenplay by Mitsuhiro Yamada. Based on the manga series by Hosei Takuma and Hideo Kato in *Dengeki Daid*.

Decades after a world war has devastated most of mankind, a group of thinking robots finds teenage Haruka in a cryogenic chamber. Unthawing her, they form a family and explore the ruins of Japan, keeping the girl safe from the other warlike robots who roam the streets intent on killing human survivors. The girl's metal family includes: Spike, a naive droid who looks like a little boy; Cleric, an intelligence robot that resembles a nun; Reeves, who looks like a Terminator robot but cooks and cleans; Trigger, a floating combat robot with impeccable aim; and Angela, a mysterious warrior droid who looks almost human.

A 1998 TV series, *Kurogane Communication* is a series of fifteen-minute short episodes (including credits and previews). The designs for the show are quite cool and cyberfunky, and the animation has a clean techno feel that plays out well against nicely detailed backgrounds. The pacing is more languid than most anime, but clearly, characterization is important to the writers; the shortness of the episodes means there's really no fat on the stories.

The DVD features some nice extras, as well as eight episodes: "Haruka"; "Lost Memories"; "Oasis"; "Machine (Non-Intelligent Fighting Machine)"; "Angela, Parts 1 and 2"; "Camping Trip"; and "The Incident." *Kurogane Communication* is recommended for those who are looking for a breather from the action to explore a postapocalyptic world with a girl and her robot family.

SPECIAL FEATURES Character and Art Galleries • Clean Credits • Mini-Comic • Outtakes • Other Title Trailers TECHNICAL FEATURES Fullscreen (1.33:1) • Subtitles/CC: Eng. • Languages: Jap., Eng. dub • Sound: Dolby Digital 2.0 • Keepcase • 1 Disc • Region 1 GENRE & RATING Science Fiction/Robots • Rated 13+

Kurogane Communication: #2—A Human Presence

AnimeWorks, 2002, 120 mins., #AWDVD-0212. Directed by Yasuhito Kikuchi. Screenplay by Mitsuhiro Yamada. Based on the manga series by Hosei Takuma and Hideo Kato in *Dengeki Daid*.

Haruka and her robot companions continue their journey through the devastated world, only to find that killer war machines aren't the only menace. A tsunami threatens their lives, and a dormant spacecraft may help them . . . or lead to more trouble. And as secrets of Haruka's past begin to be revealed, a surviving human boy named Kanoto is found!

Eight more episodes are included on this DVD: "Shelter"; "The Truth"; "Flyer"; "Taking Off"; "New Land"; "Kanato"; "Ruin"; and "Hate."

SPECIAL FEATURES Character and Art Galleries • Mini-Comic • Outtakes • Other Title Trailers TECHNICAL FEATURES Fullscreen (1.33:1) • Subtitles/CC: Eng. • Languages: Jap., Eng. dub • Sound: Dolby Digital 2.0 • Keepcase • 1 Disc • Region 1 GENRE & RATING Science Fiction/Robots • Rated 13+

Kurogane Communication #3: Future Horizons

AnimeWorks, 2002, 120 mins., #AWDVD-0214. Directed by Yasuhito Kikuchi. Screenplay by Mitsuhiro Yamada. Based on the manga series by Hosei Takuma and Hideo Kato in *Dengeki Daid*.

NOTE: This DVD arrived too late for a full review. The following text is promotional copy provided by the releasing company:

"Kanoto doesn't know what to make of Haruka and her friends. His profound disdain for robots makes him wary of their intentions. With his guardian robot, Honi, threatening everyone and Haruka trying desperately to befriend him, Kanoto is lost in a sea of emotion. Caught between the loss of his own parents, wavering trust for his robot servants and the dream of finding other humans, Kanoto must choose sides for a climactic battle."

This disc contains episodes #17–24.

SPECIAL FEATURES Character and Art Galleries • Mini Comic • Outtakes • Other Title Trailers TECHNICAL FEATURES Fullscreen (1.33:1) • Subtitles/CC: Eng. • Languages: Jap., Eng. dub • Sound: Dolby Digital • Keepcase • 1 Disc • Region 1 GENRE & RATING Science Fiction/Robots • Rated 13+

LA Blue Girl ☞ see Mature/Adult Section

LA Blue Girl Returns: Demon Seed ☞ see Mature/Adult Section

Labyrinth of Flames: Tales of a Wannabe Samurai . . .

U.S. Manga Corps, 2002, 60 mins., #USMD2151. Directed by Katsuhiko Nishijima. Story by Studio Fantasia. Scenario by Kenichi Kanemaki.

Galan has dreams of becoming a samurai. Wild, chaotic, frenzied dreams. When his girlfriend Natsu gives him a special gift and invites Galan to come to her house to "see her swords," things take a turn Galan could never have dreamed up. Returning with her to Russia, Galan finds that Natsu is the daughter of a powerful—and perverted—leader of a lost Japanese tribe in exile. Joined by the buxom Carrie, and Natsu's future husband Datenoshin, Galan finally starts to get a clue as to why he was invited. He must become the samurai he's always dreamed of being or lose Natsu's family's greatest treasure.

Labyrinth of Flames, first released in 2000, is an insanely zany production. At times silly and at others side-splitting, it is replete with hilarity. From Natsu's superanemic handmaid Kasumi's mud-puddle maneuver, to Datenoshin's rubber-man fencing moves, *Labyrinth of Flames* is one serious laugh after another. The film also sports a wide assortment of scantily (or even less) clad women to the point it's almost ludicrous—almost.

Laden with panty shots—very laden—*Labyrinth* contains frequent near-nudity, brief actual nudity, adult situations, and even fetish scenes. Very well animated, and with striking clarity, it seems to bounce from one up-skirt/cleavage shot to another, falling just shy of an adults-only rating. All in all, with good sturdy sound and some potent voice acting, *Labyrinth of Flames* is some solid cheesecake-filled eye candy and a genuinely funny disc. [GP]

SPECIAL FEATURES "Making of" Featurette • Text Interviews • Character and Art Galleries • Clean Credits • Other Title Trailers • DVD-ROM Features: Art, Scripts, Director Interview TECHNICAL FEATURES Fullscreen (1.33:1) • Subtitles/CC: Eng. • Languages: Jap., Eng. dub • Sound: Dolby Digital 2.0 • Keepcase • 1 Disc • Region 1 GENRE & RATING Comedy/Cheesecake/Action • Rated 16+

Lady and the Tramp [Limited Edition]

Disney, 1999, 76 mins., #17975.

This DVD was not available for review. It is now on moratorium.

Lady and the Tramp II: Scamp's Adventure

Disney, 2001, 70 mins., #21228. Directed by Darrell Rooney. Screenplay by Bill Motz, Bob Roth, Tom Rogers, Flip Kobler, Cindy Marcus.

Six months have passed since Lady and Tramp got together, and they still live with the Darlings. Lady has given birth to four new puppies: three girls, and a boy named Scamp who takes after Dad. But when Scamp decides to leave the house and become a "real dog" out on the streets, trouble comes barking at his door. Scamp has run-ins with the Junkyard Dogs's gangleader, as well as a persistent dog catcher, but he also meets a cute stray named Angel. Will they find puppy love in the streets? More importantly, what happens when they revisit that Italian diner where Scamp's folks fell in love?

Only half a year has passed for the dogs, but it took forty-six years to make a sequel to one of Disney's most popular animated feature films (Aren't dog years supposed to be a lot shorter than human years?). This cute story features some nice animation that mimics the mood and style of the original, while still capturing a bit of modern rebellion with Scamp. The story isn't all that engaging for adults, but younger viewers should love it, and some of the songs are fun. Voice actors include Scott Wolf, Alyssa Milano, and—hauled out of mothballs—Mickey Rooney!

Everything looks perfect on this DVD, and the vintage

featurette with Walt Disney talking about the making of the original *Lady and the Tramp* is a nice counterpoint to the filmmaker's commentary track. The DVD also features three classic Pluto cartoons to bring out the dog in everyone: "Bone Trouble" (1940), "Pluto Junior" (1942), and "Pluto's Kid Brother" (1946).

SPECIAL FEATURES "Making of" Featurette • Commentary track by Directors and Producers • Other Title Trailers • Games • DVD-ROM Features: Game TECHNICAL FEATURES Widescreen (1.66:1 enhanced for 16x9) • Subtitles/CC: Eng. • Languages: Eng., Fren. dub, Span. dub • Sound: Dolby Digital Surround 5.1, DTS • Keepcase • 1 Disc • Region 1 GENRE & RATING Animals/Romance/Music • Rated G

Lady Blue ☛ see Mature/Adult Section

Land Before Time, The

Universal, 1999, 69 mins., #20278. Directed by Don Bluth. Story by Judy Freudberg, Tony Geiss. Screenplay by Stu Krieger.

Journey back to prehistory with the animated dino-adventure that began a series. Orphaned brachiosaurus Littlefoot sets out on a quest to find the mythical feeding grounds of the Great Valley. Along the way, he meets four other young dinosaurs—triceratops Cera, stegosaur Spike, anatosaur Ducky, and pterodactyl Petrie—who decide to make the journey with him. But danger awaits them in this lost landscape, since some of the dinosaurs are predators. As they travel, the quintet learns to love and trust each other, and that friendship and cooperation will help them reach their goals.

Released as a feature film in 1988, this Don Bluth film resonates with *An American Tail*, with its themes of an orphaned child. But not since the earliest days of animation—when Winsor McCay unveiled Gertie the Dinosaur—had the prehistoric world been put on film. This charming story will appeal to kids and adults alike, though there are sad moments. The music, by James Horner, is superb.

The DVD is strictly a no-frills proposition, but the transfer is tight and the sound is good. Although the picture looks grainy, this had more to do with the original filmed animation than the digital transfer. Unlike its sequels, *The Land Before Time* is a widely praised film that will fit nicely in any DVD library.

SPECIAL FEATURES None TECHNICAL FEATURES Fullscreen (1.33:1) • Subtitles/CC: Eng. • Languages: Eng., Fren. dub, Span. dub • Sound: Dolby Digital Surround 2.0 • Keepcase • 1 Disc • Region 1 GENRE & RATING Animals/Adventure • Rated G

Land Before Time II, The: The Great Valley Adventure

Universal, 2002, 74 mins.

This DVD was not available for review.

Land Before Time, The: The Time of Great Giving [Vol. III]

Universal, 2002, 71 mins.

This DVD was not available for review.

Land Before Time, The: The Stone of Cold Fire [Vol. VII]

Universal, 2001, 75 mins., #20920. Directed by Charles Grosvenor. Screenplay by Len Uhley.

The gang's all here in prehistoric times, but only Littlefoot sees the blazing meteor that lit the night sky and landed in the Smoking Mountains. Petrie's devious uncle Pterano thinks Littlefoot is on to something, and that the flaming stone of cold fire may have magical properties that could help him rule the roost. Unfortunately, Petrie gets caught in the midst of his uncle's scheme, and the young flyer's friends must venture into the Mysterious Beyond to find him and bring him home safely.

This is the seventh installment in this series, but for some reason, #2–6 have not been released on DVD (and since this is numbered only on the spine, many buyers may be unaware of its predecessors). Created for the direct-to-video market, it utilizes the same designs and settings, though the voices and music are different. There isn't quite as much scary violence as in earlier episodes, though there is peril for the characters, and a bit of mystery.

Adults may find this adventure a little treacly, but it will teach younger viewers some pleasant lessons about people being not all bad inside, and reinforces the central theme of the series: that friendship and cooperation will win against all odds. The DVD-ROM content on the disc includes games with multiple age and skill levels.

SPECIAL FEATURES Other Title Trailers • DVD-ROM Features: Games, Activities TECHNICAL FEATURES Fullscreen (1.33:1) • Subtitles/CC: Eng. • Languages: Eng., Fren. dub • Sound: Dolby Digital 5.1 • Keepcase • 1 Disc • Region 1 GENRE & RATING Animals/Adventure • Rated G

Land Before Time VIII, The: The Big Freeze

Universal, 2001, 75 mins., #C21265. Directed by Charles Grosvenor. Screenplay by John Loy.

There's something cold and white on the ground when the dinosaurs of the Great Valley are buried under the first snow. The younger dinosaurs think it's fun to play in, but the older creatures know that food may become difficult to find if the cold weather continues. Spike decides to accompany a herd of adult Stegosauruses as they attempt to find a way out of the freeze, prompting Ducky to follow. Along with stuffy Mr. Thicknose, the other young dinos mount a rescue party to find their friends, leading to a confrontation with a T-Rex, plus icy blizzards and landslides, and the discovery of something that may save the dinosaurs.

The eighth volume in this series continues the trend of offering moral lessons—and a bit of science—mixed in with the adventures and musical numbers. Younger audiences will love it, though parents may start to drift off. There are also a host of interactive extras to entertain kids, both on the DVD and in the DVD-ROM content.

SPECIAL FEATURES Character Bios • Other Title Trailers • Sing-Alongs • DVD ROM Features: Sound Clips, Interviews TECHNICAL FEATURES Fullscreen (1.33:1) • Subtitles/CC: Eng. • Languages: Eng., Fren. dub • Sound: Dolby Digital 5.1 • Keepcase • 1 Disc • Region 1 GENRE & RATING Animals/Adventure • Rated G

Land Before Time, The: Journey to Big Water [Vol. IX]

Universal, 2002, 71 mins., #22126

This DVD was not available for review.

Landlock

Manga Entertainment, 2002, 90 mins., #MANGA4058-2. Directed by Yasuhiro Matsumura. Screenplay by Orca.

Luda is the heir of Mohg, the "Master of the Wind," on the war-ravaged planet of Zoro-earth. One peaceful night, Luda's small, quiet village barely notices it's under attack before it is destroyed by the technologically superior troopers of the Zaroan Army. Unable to stop the alluring Captain Agahali, leader of the Zaroan hoard, Luda watches as his sister Ansa is taken captive. With his home in ashes, his father dead, and his belief in himself shaken, Luda sets out on a journey to rescue Ansa. During his travels Luda learns much about himself, his powers, and his heritage, but can he save his sister, let alone his entire planet?

Originally released in 1995 as a two-part OVA series in Japan, this action-packed anime mixes technology and mystic forces into a spectacular yarn. Exotic character designs by famed artist Masamune Shirow, stunning colors, and high-tech equipment are all rolled up into an exquisite adventure tale. Note that the packaging spells the main character as "Lue'der," but the disc materials spell it as "Luda." Other similar changes abound in the Japanese-English translations.

With both parts of this striking story on one disc, *Landlock*'s animation is excellent, as is its picture quality. Though the soundtrack lacks any shining moments, it is clear, crisp, and befits the story. *Landlock* does contain brief nudity and abundant violence, but it is integral to the storyline and can hardly be called gratuitous. *Landlock* combines sorcery, science, and swashbuckling into an awe-inspiring dark epic, sure to please and excite. [GP]

SPECIAL FEATURES Character Bios • Character and Art Galleries • Other Title Trailers TECHNICAL FEATURES Fullscreen (1.33:1) • Subtitles/CC: Eng. • Languages: Jap., Eng. dub • Sound: Dolby Digital 2.0 • Keepcase • 1 Disc • Region 1, 2, 4 GENRE & RATING Fantasy/Action • Not Rated (Teens)

Larryboy: The Cartoon Adventures—The Angry Eyebrows [#1]

Big Idea, 2002, 60 mins., #BIDVD3000. Directed by Larry Whitaker, Jr. Written by Kent Redeker.

Larry the Cucumber works as a janitor at *The Daily Bumble*, but he's secretly the superhero Larryboy, defending Bumblyburg from evil! But the villainous Awful Alvin has released a swarm of Angry Eyebrows into the city, and the townspeople are all becoming ill-tempered. Can Larryboy use his plunger-powers to save his veggie friends?

This animated spin-off from the CGI *VeggieTales* series (see entry) is tremendously cute. The animation style is perfect for the humorous subject matter, and the plot and characters—including a cheese-breathing cow-dragon—are clever and imaginative. I'd compare *Larryboy* to *Powerpuff Girls* in quality, fun, and content. One factor may bother some viewers; its creators deliver a few religious messages along the way. None are secular—"God wants us to be nice to people" is the first example—but it's a little more blatant in its message than *Davey and Goliath*. However, unless you're a vehement atheist, the moments will pass by, and you'll be quickly absorbed into this charming and inventive series.

Although the running time of the actual episode is brief, it also contains a bonus short, and there are a multitude of cool extras on the disc. Kids will be entertained by the fun and games, while animation fans will enjoy the multiple behind-the-scenes options. And there are a bunch of Easter eggs as well, each decorated to look like Larryboy.

SPECIAL FEATURES "Making of" Featurettes • Director Interviews • Character and Art Galleries • Storyboards • Story Reels • Trailers • Other Title Trailers • Games • Sing-Along • DVD-ROM Features: Treatment, Script • Easter Eggs TECHNICAL FEATURES Fullscreen (1.33:1) • Subtitles/CC: Eng. • Languages: Eng. • Sound: Dolby Digital 2.0, Dolby Digital 5.1 • Keepcase • 1 Disc • Region 1 GENRE & RATING Vegetables/Comedy • Not Rated (All Ages)

Larryboy: The Cartoon Adventures—Leggo My Ego [#2]

Big Idea, 2002, 60 mins., #BIDVD3002. Directed by Larry D. Whitaker, Jr. Story by Brian Roberts. Scripts by Sean Gaffney, Tod Carter.

Pink, fluffy horror strikes at the Bumblyburg carnival when the cotton candy machine goes wild. Luckily, superhero Larryboy is there to plunge the carnival patrons out of trouble. But our hero is soon confronted by the evil antics of The Alchemist and his matron, Mother Pearl. The supervillain is powered by his ego, and every time he knocks someone else down, he grows stronger. If he can't stop him soon, Larryboy will have to face a villain with superpowers and a superego!

Like the first volume, this is cute and funny superhero parody, with vegetables. There are more non-secular religious messages and morals imparted, and the special features are once again chock full of fun. Kids are likely to love it.

SPECIAL FEATURES Character Bios • Character and Art Galleries • Storyboards • Trailers • Other Title Trailers • How to Draw • Games • Storybook • DVD-ROM Features: Games • Easter Eggs TECHNICAL FEATURES Fullscreen (1.33:1) • Subtitles/CC: Eng. • Languages: Eng. • Sound: Dolby Digital Surround 5.1 • Keepcase • 1 Disc • Region 1 GENRE & RATING Vegetables/Comedy • Not Rated (All Ages)

Last of the Mohicans, The [Collector's Edition]

Digital Versatile Disc, 1999, 51 mins., #169. Animation Directed by Warwick Davis. Screenplay by Leonard Lee. Based on the book by James Fenimore Cooper.

In the time before the American Revolution, the French and Indian War is raging on American soil. Scout Nathaniel "Hawkeye" Bummpo—a white man who is more comfortable

living with Native Americans than "civilized" people—makes friends with Chief Chingachgook and his son, Uncas. Hawkeye and Uncas must soon team up to rescue the daughters of the English commander of Fort William Henry from the Hurons, leading to a bloody stand-off.

Produced by Burbank Films Australia in 1987, this adaptation of James Fenimore Cooper's 1826 novel is surprisingly violent fare for animation aimed at children. Not that the story is an easy one to make into a pacifistic tome, but given the on-screen arrow, knife, and gunfire deaths, it's unlikely this would ever have gotten past U.S. Standards and Practices for TV airing. Following the book pretty closely, this disc features simple artwork and watercolor backgrounds, as well as some bold voice work. As with other DVD Ltd. releases, there is a bio of the author on the disc.

SPECIAL FEATURES Author Bio • Game TECHNICAL FEATURES Fullscreen (1.33:1) • Languages: Eng. • Sound: Dolby Digital 5.1, DTS • Keepcase • 1 Disc • Region All GENRE & RATING Historical/Action • Not Rated (Kids)

Leatherman ☛ see Mature/Adult Section

Legend of Black Heaven, The: Rock Bottom [#1]

Pioneer, 2000, 100 mins., #10505. Directed by Yasuhito Kikuchi. Screenplay by Toshihisa Arakawa, Takehiro Nakayama.

Oji Tanaka is a middle-aged office drone who is about to start his midlife crisis, big-time. An attractive female coworker named Layla Yuki lures him to her place one night, but instead of an affair, she offers him a chance to return to his glory. Oji used to be Gabriel, the guitarist of a heavy metal band called Black Heaven, but he gave up fame for a wife, kid, and a suburban home. Layla is an alien, and she gives him the chance to play guitar again, as his music gives her people the power they need to fight a battle for freedom.

The back covers claims "Hard Rock Saves Space!" and that's the quickest way to define this 1999 TV series. In today's post–*The Osbournes* world, in which a middle-aged rocker's domestic strife has been well-documented, the plot may not seem revolutionary, but when compared to the majority of anime, which features either cute high-schoolers or robots, *Black Heaven* is a refreshingly *older* take on things.

Those with nostalgic leanings for the music of Stryper, Scorpion, and other big-hair bands will love *Black Heaven*, which even features a theme by Whitesnake's John Sykes, among other guitar riffs. The animation is simple and clean, with CGI effects added in, but the story and music are the real draw here. The DVD contains the first four episodes, each named after a famous rock song.

SPECIAL FEATURES Character and Art Galleries • Clean Credits • Insert: Chrome Cover Card on first pressings TECHNICAL FEATURES Fullscreen (1.33:1) • Subtitles/CC: Eng. • Languages: Jap., Eng. dub • Sound: Dolby Digital 2.0 • Keepcase • 1 Disc • Region 1, 4 GENRE & RATING Music/Science Fiction/Comedy • Rated 13+

Legend of Black Heaven, The: Space Truckin' [#2]

Pioneer, 2000, 80 mins., #10502. Directed by Yasuhito Kikuchi. Screenplay by Hiroshi Onogi, Mizuhiro Yamada, Toshihisa Arakawa.

Oji's music is changing him, and those around him are worried. His wife thinks he's having an affair, and his boss is concerned about his attitude. Meanwhile, the bad aliens are getting stronger, and Oji's solo music isn't enough to stop them. Will they invade Earth next?

Adding complexity to the relationship between Oji and his wife, this DVD contains three more episodes.

SPECIAL FEATURES Character and Art Galleries • Clean Credits • Insert: Chrome Cover Card on first pressings TECHNICAL FEATURES Fullscreen (1.33:1) • Subtitles/CC: Eng. • Languages: Jap., Eng. dub • Sound: Dolby Digital 2.0 • Keepcase • 1 Disc • Region 1, 4 GENRE & RATING Music/Science Fiction/Comedy • Rated 13+

Legend of Black Heaven, The: All Right Now [#3]

Pioneer, 2000, 80 mins., #10503. Directed by Yasuhito Kikuchi. Screenplay by Hiroshi Onogi, Masaharu Amiya.

Oji needs more power to save the universe, so he entices the other band members of Black Heaven to come out of retirement and help him play music that will charge the ultimate weapon against the invaders. But each of them is living their own middle-aged lives as well, and their strange disappearances lead to problems. Layla's trio of assistants try to help, but only end up making matters worse.

A humorous guest appearance by a couple of FBI agents who look just like Mulder and Scully of The X-Files comes midway through the third episode on this penultimate DVD.

SPECIAL FEATURES Character and Art Galleries • Clean Credits • Promotional Footage • Insert: Chrome Cover Card on first pressings TECHNICAL FEATURES Fullscreen (1.33:1) • Subtitles/CC: Eng. • Languages: Jap., Eng. dub • Sound:

Dolby Digital 2.0 • Keepcase • 1 Disc • Region 1, 4 GENRE & RATING Music/Science Fiction/Comedy • Rated 13+

Legend of Black Heaven, The: Into the Arena [#4]

Pioneer, 2000, 80 mins., #10504. Directed by Yasuhito Kikuchi. Screenplay by Toshihisa Arakawa, Hiroshi Onogi.

The invader aliens are arming their deadliest weapons, and an ex-member of Black Heaven is somehow involved in their plans. It's up to the rest of the band to jam like there's no tomorrow, or there may not *be* a tomorrow! If one last concert is a success, maybe the universe can be saved. Can the band and their fans get their groove on?

The final trio of episodes are presented on this DVD, which features the music of both John Sykes and the Michael Schenker Group.

SPECIAL FEATURES Character and Art Galleries • Clean Credits • Insert: Chrome Cover Card on first pressings TECHNICAL FEATURES Fullscreen (1.33:1) • Subtitles/CC: Eng. • Languages: Jap., Eng. dub • Sound: Dolby Digital 2.0 • Keepcase • 1 Disc • Region 1, 4 GENRE & RATING Music/Science Fiction/Comedy • Rated 13+

Legend of Crystania: The Motion Picture [#1]

ADV Films, 1999, 85 mins., #DVDLC001. Directed by Ayutaro Nakamura. Based on the novels and game scenarios by Ryo Mizuno and Hiroshi Yasuda.

Set in the aftermath of the *Record of Lodoss Wars* anime series, we find that King Ashram has been tricked into selling his soul to the bloodthirsty Barbas, who wants to become Crystania's new king. In the world of Crystania 300 years after the earlier stories, amid a civil war waged by shapechanging were-warriors, the Dark Elf Pirotesse's love for Ashram leads her on a quest to find him. Together with Redon, a young prince seeking to avenge his murdered parents, she confronts Barbas. But in the battle to come against Barbas, not only is Ashram's soul at stake . . . so is Redon's innocence!

Originally released in 1995, *Legend of Crystania* is a nice idea—with its few nods to *Record of Lodoss War*—but it just isn't that well done; it is neither legendary nor spectacular. Only two characters from *Lodoss War* appear (Ashram and Pirotesse), but they don't do much to advance the *Lodoss* story. There are a few cool fight scenes, but the artwork isn't nearly as crisp or sharp as its predecessor and the coloring is quite flat and dull.

If you're a *Lodoss* fan, don't think you have to own this

DVD to have the complete story; it hardly has anything in common with that powerful anime series. The DVD has a parental guidance warning due to violent fight scenes, but the scenes aren't any worse than most modern video games. [JMC]

SPECIAL FEATURES Character Bios • Character and Art Galleries • Trailer TECHNICAL FEATURES Fullscreen (1.33:1) • Subtitles/CC: Eng., Span. • Languages: Jap., Eng. dub • Sound: Dolby Digital 2.0 • Keepcase • 1 Disc • Region 1–6 GENRE & RATING Fantasy/Adventure • Not Rated (Teens)

Legend of Crystania: The Chaos Ring [#2]

ADV Films, 2002, 135 mins., #DLC002. Directed by Ryutaro Nakamura. Screenplay by Akinori Endo. Based on the novels and game scenarios by Ryo Mizuno and Hiroshi Yasuda.

Even though peace has come to the land of Crystania, problems are on the horizon. The seals that protect the land are opening, the Bell of Wakening is tolling, and monsters roam the country. But even the tornadoes, basilisks, and Dragon Lords pale in comparison to the horrors King Barbas plans to inflict with his return. Even as villages are destroyed and the gods of Crystania are defeated, Prince Redon and the Dark Elf Pirotesse try to gain a portal home from the World of Chaos so that King Ashram can save his people from the coming Armageddon!

A collection of the three-part OVA miniseries originally released in 1996, *Chaos Ring* requires knowledge of both *Legend of Crystania: The Motion Picture* and the *Lodoss War* saga. A lot of assumptions are made that viewers are already familiar with the characters and situations that brought them to this point. This DVD should have included a character guide to introduce or reacquaint viewers with the characters, since most aren't even named until the second episode, and character designs are similar to existing *Lodoss War* characters.

Although very dry and longwinded in some parts, the action scenes make up for some of the lags in adventure. A lot of time is spent recapping information from prior episodes contained in this volume, but the anime would have been a lot better if those recaps were of information from *The Legend of Crystania*. The story has many violent fight scenes, and should appeal to fantasy fans due to the wide variety of elves, dragons, and fairies represented. [JMC]

SPECIAL FEATURES Trailers • Clean Credits • Other Title Trailers TECHNICAL FEATURES Fullscreen (1.33:1) • Subtitles/CC: Eng. • Languages: Jap., Eng. dub • Sound: Dolby Digital 2.0 • Keepcase • 1 Disc • Region 1 GENRE & RATING Fantasy/Adventure • Rated 12+

Legend of Hiawatha, The [Collector's Edition]

Digital Versatile Disc, 1999, #182. Screenplay by Paul Leadon. Based on the book by Henry Wadsworth Longfellow.

This DVD was not available for review.

Legend of Himiko: Sacred Fire [#1]

U.S. Manga Corps, 2002, 100 mins., #USMD2176. Directed by Ayumi Tomobuki. Screenplay by Sanshiro Kuramoto, Masumi Hirayanagi.

NOTE: This DVD arrived too late for a full review. The following text is promotional copy provided by the releasing company:

"In a world where the dead walk, where good and evil exist as palpable forces, a darkness is stirring. The undead march against the cities of light to capture the sacred fire that is the source of their power. But one hope remains. Called into this world by the magical flame, a young girl named Himiko is thrust into the maelstrom of danger, betrayal, and war. For she is heir to the sacred fire, and holds a power that could save its Guardians . . . if she survives!"

SPECIAL FEATURES Character Bios • Character and Art Galleries • Promotional Footage • Clean Credits • DVD-ROM Features: Art, Scripts • Other Title Trailers TECHNICAL FEATURES Fullscreen (1.33:1) • Subtitles/CC: Eng. • Languages: Jap., Eng. dub • Sound: Dolby Digital 2.0, Dolby Digital Surround 5.1 • Keepcase • 1 Disc • Region 1 GENRE & RATING Fantasy/Adventure • Rated 13+

Legend of Himiko: The Pendant [#2]

U.S. Manga Corps, 2002, 100 mins., #USMD2177. Directed by Ayumi Tomobuki. Screenplay by Sanshiro Kuramoto, Masumi Hirayanagi.

NOTE: This DVD arrived too late for a full review. The following text is promotional copy provided by the releasing company:

"War ignites among enemy camps, and both sides desperately seek Himiko, an Earth girl with the power to save, or destroy, them all. But even as a fugitive, Himiko has found allies, fierce warriors of great magic and swordfighting skill. She'll need all the help she can get to survive this alien world, and discover her true power! As armies march and treachery abounds, the fate of the world rests upon the shoulders of one girl!"

SPECIAL FEATURES Character Bios • Character and Art Galleries • Promotional Footage • Music Video • Outtakes • DVD-ROM Features: Art, Scripts • Other Title Trailers TECHNICAL FEATURES Fullscreen (1.33:1) • Subtitles/CC: Eng. • Languages: Jap.,

Eng. dub • Sound: Dolby Digital 2.0, Dolby Digital Surround 5.1 • Keepcase • 1 Disc • Region 1 GENRE & RATING Fantasy/Adventure • Rated 13+

Legend of Lemnear

U.S. Manga Corps, 1998, 45 mins., #USMD1742. Directed by Kinji Yoshimoto. Screenplay by Kinji Yoshimoto. Based on the manga series by Satoshi Ushihara.

The evil Dark Lord and his wizard minion Gardein have sent their monstrous legions across the land, devastating its people. In a burned village, one woman survives. She is Lemnear, the legendary Champion of Silver, and she is determined to have her revenge. Making her way to the city, she fights villainous forces and eventually encounters the Dark Lord's slave pits and flying fortress, not to mention a monster or two.

A 1989 OVA production, *Legend of Lemnear* is about as perfunctory as revenge-fantasy stories get. The last survivor of a holocaust fighting the person(s) who killed their loved ones? Where *haven't* we seen that one before? The animation is bright, and there are some nice special effects, but the backgrounds are mostly simplistic.

There is quite a bit of topless nudity in the story, and several gory moments punctuate the violence, so this is clearly not intended for younger viewers. The DVD has more extras than most of the early USMC titles, but none explains why this repetitive story is necessary.

Besides being offered as a single DVD, the disc was also included as part of a 2002 "Fantasy Pack" set, along with *Garzey's Wing*.

SPECIAL FEATURES Character Intros • Character and Art Galleries • Other Title Trailers • Comic Book Preview TECHNICAL FEATURES Fullscreen (1.33:1) • Subtitles/CC: Eng. • Languages: Jap., Eng. dub • Sound: Dolby Digital 2.0 • Keepcase • 1 Disc • Region All GENRE & RATING Fantasy/Action/Sorcery • Not Rated (Teens)

Legend of Mulan, The

Digital Versatile Disc, 1998, 42 mins., DVD101.

Chinese girl Mulan comes from a family of famous warriors, but girls are not allowed to fight. Because of a large-scale drought, war breaks out in China, and Mulan disguises herself as a male warrior to join the troops. As the years pass, Mulan gets promoted, but eventually she is captured by the enemy forces. Following her escape, Mulan must pass four tests, after which she'll be able to end the war and save the land from drought.

Taken from the same ancient story upon which Disney based its superior *Mulan*, this is still a nicely done version of the tale. The animation begins with clean, bright colors and cutesy elements, but gets darker as the battle wears on. And unlike much of Eastern animation, the characters look as if they belong in their homeland. Concerned parents should be warned that this version does contain strong violence and a few curses, but it is certainly a much more adult version of the story than Disney's.

The disc supposedly features a whole host of extras, but none are accessible from the DVD menu; they're all on DVD-ROM. Oddly, the story features no credits whatsoever, and one of the coming attractions is for an interactive animation project released by another company!

SPECIAL FEATURES Other Title Trailers • DVD-ROM Features: Isolated Score, Games, Picture Book, Coloring Book, Screen Savers TECHNICAL FEATURES Fullscreen (1.33:1) • Languages: Eng. • Sound: Dolby Digital 5.1, DTS • Keepcase • 1 Disc • Region All GENRE & RATING Historical/Fantasy/Adventure • Not Rated (Kids)

Legend of the Dog Warriors, The: The Hakkenden

Pioneer, 2001, 480 mins., #11486. Directed by Takashi Anno, Yukio Okamoto. Screenplay by Noboru Aikawa, Hidemi Kamata. Based on the serialized novels by Kyokutei Bakin.

It's 1478, during the "Warring States" period in Japan. Wandering samurai are common, but the warriors in this story aren't your typical swordsmen. They are the Dog Warriors, eight samurai who are linked together by a mysterious past, reincarnation, magic prayer beads, the virtues of bushido, and an uncertain destiny. This story is told in thirteen episodes that bring the Dog Warriors together to face off against powerful warlords and spirits bent on revenge.

This 1993 OVA series is basically the telling of an epic tale—originally serialized in ninety-six stories published between 1814 and 1841—but it's the CliffsNotes version. Characters and situations are introduced so quickly that it's hard to keep up with the pace of storytelling. It appears the creators were counting on the Japanese audience's familiarity with the story. Unfortunately for those of us who have never heard the tale, the episodes presented here can be difficult to follow on first viewing. The animation also goes through some interesting changes; episodes 12 and 13 look very good, but episodes 9 and 10 look like they got the short end of the budget. Viewers may be intrigued enough to seek out a translation of the story, but this particular telling is not overly impressive.

The set includes all thirteen episodes on three discs, plus a half-hour "digest version" of the story that is easier to follow than the full version. This is a violent series with some sexual situations, so it may appeal to more mature samurai fans. [RJM]

SPECIAL FEATURES Character and Art Galleries • Clean Credits TECHNICAL FEATURES Fullscreen (1.33:1) • Subtitles/CC: Eng. • Languages: Jap., Eng. dub • Sound: Dolby Digital 2.0 • Multi-keepcase • 3 Discs • Region 1, 4 GENRE & RATING Historical/Action/Samurai • Rated 16+

Legend of the Dragon Kings: Under Fire

U.S. Manga Corps, 2001, 94 mins., #USMD2061. Directed by Osamu Dezaki, Norio Kashima, Hisayuki Toriumi, Kiyosuke Mikurya. Screenplay by Akinori Endo. Based on the novels by Yoshiki Tanaka.

One of four brothers, Hajime Ryudo, has been having troubling dreams lately—dreams of dragons—and his speed and strength have increased far beyond that than normal men. Now it seems that there are forces working to capture and contain the four Ryudo brothers, even if the siblings don't know why. What could a rich old man want with them? And when their friends are kidnapped, will the beasts living within the brothers for 117 generations walk the Earth once more?

Released as a twelve-part TV series in 1991, this DVD does not contain the entire saga, but what it does contain is nice. The animation is done in a very realistic manga style, and the Japanese characters and settings actually look Japanese. While the story is intriguing, the dub isn't the best; fans should watch the subtitles instead. At this time, it is unknown if the rest of the story will be released on DVD.

SPECIAL FEATURES Character and Art Galleries • Other Title Trailers • Games • DVD-ROM Features: Art, Scripts TECHNICAL FEATURES Fullscreen (1.33:1) • Subtitles/CC: Eng. • Languages: Jap., Eng. dub • Sound: Dolby Digital 2.0 • Keepcase • 1 Disc • Region 1 GENRE & RATING Action/Fantasy • Rated 13+

Legend of the Last Labyrinth

AnimeWorks, 2000, 60 mins., #AWDVD-0084. Directed by Isato Date. Screenplay by Aoi Takeuchi.

High school student Yusuke is walking through the woods one day when a mysterious woman falls out of the sky and lands right in his lap! Who is the green-haired Rouge? Even she doesn't know, but when Yusuke offers her shelter, she moves in. Days later, two women who claim to be Rouge's sisters arrive, but what plans do

Kaige and Meige have for their sibling? As Yusuke and Rouge fall in love, magical underworld forces conspire to tear them apart.

When you see the opening of this series, you'll be forgiven if you think you've accidentally popped in the debut episodes of *Oh My Goddess!* Because it mirrors that series's plot so closely, I'm surprised no lawsuits were filed. The animation contains some super-deformed moments, and bright colors against pretty watercolor backgrounds.

The DVD has a few nice extras and a solid picture, but this magical love story seems so familiar you'll feel like you're caught in a rerun. This 1997 two-parter was supposed to be six parts, but no follow-ups were ever animated, leaving the story hanging.

SPECIAL FEATURES Character and Art Galleries • Music Video • Outtakes TECHNICAL FEATURES Fullscreen (1.33:1) • Subtitles/CC: Eng. • Languages: Jap., Eng. dub • Sound: Dolby Digital 2.0 • Keepcase • 1 Disc • Region 1–6 GENRE & RATING Fantasy/Adventure/Comedy • Rated 13+

Leonard Maltin's Animation Favorites from the National Film Board of Canada

Image, 2001, 95 mins., #ID0241NFDVD.

Famed movie critic and animation fan Leonard Maltin hosts and introduces nine specially chosen animated shorts from the vaults of the National Film Board of Canada. Ten years after the NFBC was formed, experimental animation pioneer Norman McLaren created his first animated short for them. "Begone Dull Care" (1949) is a pre-psychedelia music and art trip that was hand-painted on the film itself!

Others titles include "Mindscape," a black-and-white piece in which a painter steps into his own painting; "Log Driver's Waltz," a cute sing-along that segues seamlessly from live-action to animation; and McLaren's "Pas de Deux," in which live ballet dancers are hand-animated in a kind of non-rotoscoping process that today would be a slam-dunk with computers, but which was revolutionary at the time.

Also featured are: "The Cat Came Back"; "Getting Started"; "The Sweater"; "The Street"; and "Anniversary." The transfer onto disc of these many different types of animation is accomplished well, though there are no extras. The disc does win this book's award, though . . . for longest title.

SPECIAL FEATURES None TECHNICAL FEATURES Fullscreen (1.33:1) • Languages: Eng. • Sound: Dolby Digital 1.0 • Snapcase • 1 Disc • Region 1–6 GENRE & RATING Anthology • Not Rated (Kids)

Lesson of Darkness ☛ see Mature/Adult Section

Lilo and Stitch

Disney, 2002, 85 mins., #23989. Directed by Chris Sanders, Dean DeBlois. Story by Chris Sanders. Written by Chris Sanders, Dean DeBlois.

On a far-off planet, an alien scientist creates a creature whose sole purpose is to destroy. The miniature creature—Experiment 626—is deemed a bio-weapon and exiled to an asteroid. But the creature escapes to Earth and lands in Hawaii. There, he's adopted by mischievous troublemaker girl Lilo, who loves the odd "dog" and names him "Stitch." Lilo's sister, Nani, is under stress from her job, and from the social service worker that threatens to take Lilo away. When aliens come to Earth to recapture Stitch, Lilo and Nani are caught up in a surprising chase to keep their barely functional-but-loving family together.

Lilo and Stitch is Disney's forty-first animated film, and was one of Disney's few feature films in recent years to actually make a profit, despite a meager promotional push. The film is much more intimate and personal than most Disney features. Designed with a rounded big-foot style that comes from co-director Chris Sanders (but resembles some of Robert Crumb's work), the feature also employs some truly lush watercolor backgrounds that make the Hawaiian setting seem gorgeous and inviting. The aspects of Hawaiian culture worked into the story are both entertaining and educational, and the voice cast—including Tia Carrere, Kevin McDonald, and Ving Rhames—is exceptional.

The DVD features an excellent transfer from film, and a whole host of cool extras. These include a DisneyPedia travelogue of Hawaii narrated by cast members. Another featurette offers Hula dance lessons, along with some behind the scenes looks at the children's choir used in the film, how the Hula was animated, location scouting with the directors, and the designs of the film. There're four fun deleted scenes as well, but the cutest aspect of the extras are a segment showing Stitch inserted into art from historical Disney features, and a quartet of actual Theatrical Teaser Trailers—with Stitch interrupting and parodying trailers for *Beauty and the Beast, Aladdin, The Lion King,* and *The Little Mermaid.*

Adults should enjoy *Lilo and Stitch* along with their kids—it's a rare PG-rated Disney animation—as it's both a melancholy and adorably funny film.

SPECIAL FEATURES "Making of" Featurettes • Deleted Scenes • Trailers • Promotional Footage • Music Video • Game • Other Title Trailers TECHNICAL FEATURES Widescreen (1.66:1 enhanced for 16x9) • Subtitles/CC: Eng. • Languages: Eng., Fren. dub, Span. dub • Sound: Dolby Digital 5.1 Surround • Keepcase •

1 Disc • Region 1 GENRE & RATING Science Fiction/Comedy • Rated PG

Linnea in Monet's Garden

First Run, 1999, 30 mins., #CN99-41499. Directed by Lena Anderson, Christina Bjork. Written by Lena Anderson, Christina Bjork. Based on the book by Lena Anderson, Christina Bjork.

Linnea is a young Swedish girl whose interest in art is sparked by paintings she sees in a book shown to her by her friend, the elderly Mr. Bloom. Soon, the two of them travel to the Marmottan museum in Paris where Linnea is astonished by the collection of paintings by Impressionist painter Claude Monet. Up close, they're just "blobs and smears," but the brush strokes form flowers and gardens when seen at a distance. Mr. Bloom later takes Linnea to the gardens in Giverny so she can see the foliage that inspired Monet.

This 1993 story is a unique blend of cel animation in drab watercolors for the homebound settings, detailed photographs of the real paintings of Monet, and lush color work in the gardens. The story, based on a children's book, offers both the wonders of art and of nature, while teaching viewers about the history and Impressionist techniques of Monet.

There are few films that teach viewers in such an entertaining fashion, and both adults and children will be charmed and inspired by Linnea. It's too bad there aren't more DVDs of this sort.

SPECIAL FEATURES Interactive Games TECHNICAL FEATURES Fullscreen (1.33:1) • Languages: Eng. • Sound: Dolby Digital 2.0 • Keepcase • 1 Disc • Region 1–6 GENRE & RATING Historical/Art/Family • Not Rated (All Ages)

Lion King 2, The: Simba's Pride [Limited Issue]

Disney, 1999, 75 mins., #17976. Directed by Darrell Rooney, Rob LaDuca. Screenplay by Flip Kobler, Cindy Marcus, Jenny Wingfield, Linda Voorhees, Gregory Poirer, Bill Motz, Bob Roth, Mark McCorkle, Robert Schooley, Jonathan Cuba.

The Pridelands are about to get a new adventurer when King Simba and Nala reveal their daughter, Kiara, to the denizens of the wild. As a young cub, Kiara ventures outside the Pridelands, where she discovers another tribe of lions who were once loyal to the evil Scar, and who hate Simba for banishing them. After Kiara is forbidden to mingle with the outside lions again, one of them, a young male cub named Kovu, comes to live among the other animals. His mission is to eventually kill Simba, but

Kovu falls in love with Kiara, and now he may not follow through on his mother's evil plot of revenge.

It's hard to make a follow up to your biggest animated hit ever, but Disney did its best with this made-for-video sequel, reassembling almost the entire voice cast, and adding newcomers Suzanne Pleshette, Neve Campbell, Andy Dick, and others. The animation budget is clearly lower, and the story is just a gender-reversal of the original, but this still growls above the crowd. Although it has some dark and dangerous moments, this movie doesn't have quite the emotional darkness as the original had with Simba's father's death, so kids will likely be able to handle it a bit better. In addition to the comedy relief of Timon and Pumba, an oddball lion character is introduced as well.

The DVD offers an excellent picture and sound, all the better to hear the songs with. While not all are up to the level of the first film's, some of the songs are excellent, including music from the *Lion King* Broadway show, the original film's sequel album, and all new material. One song is even co-written by *Buffy the Vampire Slayer's* creator, Joss Whedon! This DVD is recommended for anyone who liked the original.

SPECIAL FEATURES Trailer • Music Video • Other Title Trailers TECHNICAL FEATURES Widescreen (1.66:1) • Subtitles/CC: Eng. • Languages: Eng., Fren. dub, Span. dub • Sound: Dolby Digital 5.1 • Keepcase • 1 Disc • Region 1, 4 GENRE & RATING Animal/Music/Family • Not Rated (Kids)

Lion of Oz

Sony Wonder, 2000, 90 mins., #LVD 55258. Directed by Tim Deacon. Written by Elana Lesser, Cliff Ruby. Based on the book *Lion of Oz and the Badge of Courage* by Roger S. Baum.

Oscar Diggs is a balloonist at the Omaha Magnificent Circus, but when he takes a lonely lion with him on a balloon ride, the craft is blown over the rainbow and into the magical Land of Oz. The lion is accidentally dropped into the forest, where he discovers that not only can he talk, but so can the trees and other magical creatures there. The Wicked Witch of the East and her evil pal Gloom soon cross his path, and he finds himself on an adventure with a little girl named Wimsik, as well as her magical companions, a doll, a toy soldier, and a hyperactive creature known as Silly Ozbul. Will the lion find the balloonist and his lost badge of courage, or does that adventure lie further down the road?

This 2000 production is a prequel to *The Wizard of Oz*, and is based on a book by the great-grandson of Oz creator, L. Frank Baum. *Lion of Oz* is full of imaginative and fantastical characters and situations. The character designs are pleasant for everyone except the Witch and Wimsik, though anyone expecting something that resembles the famous live-action film or the original Oz illustrations will probably be disappointed. Still, the animation is nice, and the script clever. An all-star voice cast includes Tim Curry, Jason Priestley. Bobcat Goldthwait, Lynn Redgrave, and others.

The DVD is a nice package with a few fun extras, but the transfer of the animation image is rough in spots, especially for crowd scenes. But for those with fond memories of Oz—especially the rich and imaginative world beyond the film—here's the best animation produced on the topic.

SPECIAL FEATURES "Making of" Featurette • Interviews with Author and Cast • Character and Art Galleries • Music Video • Sing-Alongs • Games • DVD-ROM Features: Art, Games, Coloring Pages • Other Title Trailers TECHNICAL FEATURES Fullscreen (1.33:1) • Subtitles/CC: Eng., Fren. • Languages: Eng., Fren. dub • Sound: Dolby Digital 2.0 • Keepcase • 1 Disc • Region 1 GENRE & RATING Fantasy/Family • Not Rated (Kids)

Little Bytes

Image, 2000, 54 mins., #ID71160DDVD.

Although most computer-animated anthologies are meant as visual/aural wallpaper—and tend to err on the side of mind-tripping psychedelia—*Little Bytes* has been gathered expressly for kids. Each of these CGI shorts is aimed at young audiences, though this hardly means that adults are exempt from the fun.

The biggest draw for some will be the appearance of two Luxo Jr. shorts from Pixar, the studio behind *Toy Story* and *A Bug's Life*. There's also a *ReBoot* short from Mainframe Entertainment, in which the entirety of season three's plot is told in an opera performance. Most of the shorts are humorous, with a few featuring music as well.

The animation is excellent on all but "Sharing," (which seems out of place here) with some of the tracks so resembling real 3D claymation that you'll believe it isn't CGI. The DVD also features "Why Does the Wind Blow?" a bonus film that wasn't on the video version. This title is highly recommended for anyone with young kids, as well as CGI lovers.

SPECIAL FEATURES None TECHNICAL FEATURES Widescreen (multiple aspects) • Fullscreen (1.33:1) • Languages: Eng. • Sound: Dolby Digital 2.0 • Snapcase • 1 Disc • Region 1–6 GENRE & RATING CGI/Anthology • Not Rated (All Ages)

Little Mermaid, The

Delta Entertainment, 2001, 41 mins., #82 100. Animation Directed by Susan and Geoff Beak. Screenplay by Leonard Lee. Based on the story by Hans Christian Andersen.

Princess Miranda is a mermaid with an astonishingly beautiful voice. On her fifteenth birthday, she glimpses the human world above the sea, and falls in love with a handsome prince. He, in turn, is trying to escape a marriage arranged for him by his father. To become human so that she can see the prince again, Miranda makes a pact with the evil Sea Witch. But as with all deals with the devil, things take a turn for the worse, and tragedy is coming.

Although credited to Burbank Animation Studios, this DVD is copyrighted 2000 to Anchor Bay, another DVD releasing company. It is a relatively faithful retelling of Andersen's original story, complete with the more tragic and depressing moments missing from Disney's far superior version. The animation is cute, and the colors are bright throughout.

SPECIAL FEATURES None TECHNICAL FEATURES Fullscreen (1.33:1) • Languages: Eng. • Sound: Dolby Digital 5.1, DTS • Keepcase • 1 Disc • Region All GENRE & RATING Fantasy/Romance • Not Rated (All Ages)

Little Mermaid, The [Limited Edition]

Disney, 1999, 82 mins., #18787.

This DVD was not available for review. It is now on moratorium.

Little Mermaid II, The: Return to the Sea

Disney, 2000, 75 mins., #19303. Directed by Jim Kammernia. Screenplay by Elizabeth Anderson, Temple Mathews, Elise D'Haene, Eddie Guzelian. Based on the story by Hans Christian Andersen.

Prince Eric and his wife Ariel have a daughter named Melody, but on the day of her christening, Ursula's vengeful sister Morgana arrives to threaten the child. Fearful of Morgana's dark magic, Ariel and Eric erect a sea wall around their palace and vow never to tell Melody about her heritage as the daughter of a mermaid. But Melody is instinctively drawn to the sea, and she is eventually pulled into Morgana's web. The witch turns her into a mermaid for a brief time, and promises her the change will be permanent if she steals King Triton's magic trident. But once Melody gets the trident, Morgana's inky true colors are revealed. . . .

Another in a line of Disney's direct-to-video sequels, this compares favorably to its predecessor, though it does split the focus a bit with two new comedic sidekicks for Melody, a trio of sidekicks for Ursula, plus appearances by just about every character from the original. The animation is slightly better than TV quality, but keeps the designs from the first *The Little Mermaid*; Prince Eric even wears the same clothes in some scenes! The music is nicely sung, though a bit forgettable. Parents might be a bit concerned about the "Mother lied to you" message the film imparts for its first two-thirds, but it's all smoothed out by the end.

The DVD contains a handful of nice extras, and a gorgeously drawn *Silly Symphonies* cartoon from 1938 entitled "Merbabies." The disc is almost worth the price just for this cartoon short alone, which is transferred so nicely you'd almost think it was only a few years old instead of a few decades. By the way, the case says that the lead film is letterboxed at a 1.66:1 ratio, but it measures out at 1.85:1 in comparison tests.

NOTE: This DVD is now on moratorium.

SPECIAL FEATURES Other Title Trailers • Games • Storybook TECHNICAL FEATURES Widescreen (1.85:1) • Fullscreen (1.33:1) • Subtitles/CC: Eng., Span. • Languages: Eng., Fren. dub, Span. dub • Sound: Dolby Digital 5.1 • Keepcase • 1 Disc • Region 1, 4 GENRE & RATING Fantasy/Family/Music • Rated G

Little Witch

Sony Wonder, 1999, 40 mins., #LVD 51590. Directed by Olaf Miller, Maurice Sherwood. Written by Nicholas Hollander. Based on the books by Deborah Hautzig

NOTE: This DVD arrived too late for a full review. The following text is promotional copy provided by the releasing company:

"Liddy, otherwise known as Little Witch, is a ten-year-old sorceress with a difference: she just wants to be 'normal' (which drives her witchy family bats!). But when Liddy wants to have a normal birthday party (with normal birthday guests), her mixed-up magic powers send her on a comical quest that zips from outer space to a pirate ship and beyond in search of the most magical thing on Earth: some 'Bestest Friends!'"

SPECIAL FEATURES Author Bio • Character Bios • Sing-Along • Games • Other Title Trailers TECHNICAL FEATURES Fullscreen (1.33:1) • Subtitles/CC: Eng. • Languages: Eng. • Sound: Dolby Digital 2.0 • Keepcase • 1 Disc • Region 1 GENRE & RATING Supernatural/Family • Not Rated (Kids)

Lord of the Rings, The

Warner, 2001, 134 mins., #37408. Directed by Ralph Bakshi. Screenplay by Chris Conkling, Peter S. Beagle. Based on the books *The Fellowship of the Ring* and *The Two Towers* by J.R.R. Tolkien.

The wizard Gandalf enlists hobbit Frodo Baggins to take the powerful and dangerous One Ring of magic to be destroyed in the fires of Mount Doom, but the quest is a long and frightful one. Frodo is joined in his journey by other hobbits, as well as a dwarf, an elf, and other human warriors. Along the way, they face Orcs, trolls, the Gollum, the monster Balrog, and the evil wizard Saruman's horsebound Black Rider ringwraiths.

Ralph Bakshi intended to film Tolkein's *Lord of the Rings* as a long-form project, covering all three of the books in the trilogy. Unfortunately, time and budget did not allow him to fully complete even one film to his satisfaction. Although it is relatively faithful to its origins, the story suffers in places by necessary cuts for time, and by assumptions that the audience will have some background as to who the characters are and why they're doing what they're doing. In other words, you have to already *know* the story to *understand* the story.

Much of the 1978 feature film is rotoscoped—the animation is traced over a film of live-action actors—and it looks utterly gorgeous initially. But as time and money began to run out, shortcuts were taken, so that by the end, the animation is nowhere near as grand as when it started. The story also ends abruptly—in midbattle!—partially into the second volume of Tolkein's trilogy. Still, despite these carpings, *Lord of the Rings* is a nice attempt, which Tolkien and fantasy fans should have in their animation library.

A sequel was created by Rankin-Bass, though none of this film's personnel took part. See the entry for *Return of the King*. This disc was also included as part of a 2001 three-pack set, its keepcase packaged with *The Hobbit* and *Return of the King*.

SPECIAL FEATURES "Of Elves & Other Races" Text • Tolkien Bio • Director Filmography • Trailer TECHNICAL FEATURES Widescreen (1.85:1 enhanced for 16x9) • Subtitles/CC: Eng., Chin., Fren., Jap., Kor., Port., Span., Thai • Languages: Eng., Fren. dub • Sound: Dolby Digital Surround 2.0 • Snapcase • 1 Disc • Region 1–4 GENRE & RATING Fantasy/Adventure • Rated PG

Lost Universe: Vol. 1—In Space . . . It's Very, Very Dark

ADV Films, 2000, 100 mins., #DVDLU001. Directed by Takashi Watanabe. Script by Yasunori Yamada, Jiro Takayama, Sumio Uetake. Based on the manga series by Hajime Kanzaka, Shoko Yoshinaka in *Dragon Junior*.

Kain Blueriver is a cape-wearing trouble consultant who handles cases too difficult or dangerous for the Universal Guardians, a law-enforcement service. Armed with a lightsaber-like weapon called a psi blade, and the occasional robotic armor, Kain and his pals—Canal, the holographic embodiment of the control system of his ship, the *Swordbreaker,* and Millie, a dead-eyed heroine looking to find her place in the universe—set out on adventures, taking on any and all jobs. Whether it's protecting an important person or retrieving stolen goods, they're on the case—even if they spend as much time bickering as solving problems. Unfortunately, the crew of the *Swordbreaker* usually gets stuck with really bad assignments, thanks to the mysterious Rail Claymore of the Universal Guardians.

Debuting on TV in 1997, *Lost Universe* is a twenty-six-episode anime series that combines familiar sci-fi elements with deadpan humor, bounty hunters, and lots of outer space mayhem. This series should appeal to viewers of all ages, but it does contain some violence and death of minor characters.

This first DVD contains episodes #1–4 of the anime series. The animation for the space scenes is a mix of CGI and painted cels. The work is choppy in some places and looks a little fake. However by the third volume of the series, the process appears to have been perfected and the space scenes look very realistic. [JMC]

SPECIAL FEATURES Other Title Trailers TECHNICAL FEATURES Fullscreen (1.33:1) • Subtitles/CC: Eng. • Languages: Jap., Eng. dub • Sound: Dolby Digital Surround 2.0 • Keepcase • 1 Disc • Region 1 GENRE & RATING Action/Comedy/Science Fiction • Not Rated (12+)

Lost Universe: Vol. 2—The Ultimate Fowl!

ADV Films, 2000, 100 mins., #DVDLU002. Directed by Takashi Watanabe. Script by Shoichi Sato, Go Tamai, Yasunori Yamada, Jiro Takayama. Based on the manga series by Hajime Kanzaka, Shoko Yoshinaka in *Dragon Junior*.

Another group of misadventures featuring the crew of the starship *Swordbreaker.* Kain, Canal, and Millie provide security on an asteroid, then protect the students at a nursing school from an internal conflict between two rival groups. They find a missing person who holds the secret to the Lost Ships, and guard a dignitary from the forces of an evil tribe who want to kill him. Just another typical week for these trouble consultants who laugh at danger, smile in the face of destruction, and usually can't get along to save their lives!

This DVD contains episodes #5–8, a collection of zany, outrageous episodes that feature a lot of chicken jokes. [JMC]

SPECIAL FEATURES Other Title Trailers TECHNICAL FEATURES Fullscreen (1.33:1) • Subtitles/CC: Eng. • Languages: Jap., Eng. dub • Sound: Dolby Digital Surround 2.0 • Keepcase • 1 Disc • Region 1 GENRE & RATING Action/Comedy/Science Fiction • Rated 12+

Lost Universe: Vol. 3—Flushed into Space!

ADV Films, 2000, 100 mins., #DVDLU003. Directed by Takashi Watanabe. Script by Sumio Uetake, Yasunori Yamada, Shoichi Sato, Go Tamai. Based on the manga series by Hajime Kanzaka, Shoko Yoshinaka in *Dragon Junior*.

When the crew members of the *Swordbreaker* rummage through an abandoned ship, one of their finds causes various rooms on the ship to change places, including the ship's only bathroom. The vessel becomes a giant maze that the crew must navigate before their bladders . . . or something else breaks. Rooms aren't the only thing changing places, though. Bored with an assignment, Kain swaps places with another Trouble Consultant for a different guarding gig. Unknown to Kain, this places his pal in jeopardy when an old enemy attacks.

This DVD contains episodes #9–12 and begins to advance the story's plots and subplots, revealing more information about the Lost Ships and the mysterious forces at work to thwart Kain, Millie, and Canal. [JMC]

SPECIAL FEATURES Other Title Trailers TECHNICAL FEATURES Fullscreen (1.33:1) • Subtitles/CC: Eng. • Languages: Jap., Eng. dub • Sound: Dolby Digital Surround 2.0 • Keepcase • 1 Disc • Region 1 GENRE & RATING Action/Comedy/Science Fiction • Rated 12+

Lost Universe: Vol. 4—Psyche Up! Freak Out!

ADV Films, 2000, 100 mins., #DVDLU004. Directed by Takashi Watanabe. Script by Sumio Uetake, Jiro Takayama, Go Tamai, Shoichi Sato. Based on the manga series by Hajime Kanzaka, Shoko Yoshinaka in *Dragon Junior*.

Kain's past is revisited as old debts come back to haunt him in several different forms, and karmic repayment is on the menu. First a newly awakened evil, the Dark Seeder, seeks his destruction due to a grudge against Kain's grandmother. Then Kain teams up with an old friend to help on a rescue mission. Next, another familiar face appears with a brand new ship that houses a unique power source. Finally, Millie begins to doubt her place on board the *Swordbreaker* and thinks about calling it quits. Can Kain convince her that the life of a trouble consultant is definitely still for her?

This revealing DVD contains episodes #13–16, and the revelation that someone might be a traitor. [JMC]

SPECIAL FEATURES Other Title Trailers TECHNICAL FEATURES Fullscreen (1.33:1) • Subtitles/CC: Eng. • Languages: Jap., Eng. dub • Sound: Dolby Digital 2.0 • Keepcase • 1 Disc • Region 1 GENRE & RATING Action/Comedy/Science Fiction • Rated 12+

Lost Universe: Vol. 5—Wanted Union of Evil

ADV Films, 2000, 125 mins., #DVDLU005. Directed by Takashi Watanabe. Script by Yasunori Yamada, Shoichi Sato, Sumio Uetake, Go Tamai. Based on the manga series by Hajime Kanzaka, Shoko Yoshinaka in *Dragon Junior*.

Friends? Who needs them! That's what Kain, Canal, and Millie are thinking when their contact in the Universal Guardians, Rail Claymore, turns out to be a spy who's telling secrets to the dark forces. Worse, since he was their associate, the Universal Guardians mark them as guilty also. Now the whole crew of the *Swordbreaker* is wanted for treason, with evil star cruisers breathing down their necks trying to destroy them. Can our heroes survive a long night of laser blasts, psychotic ships, and light whips?

This penultimate action-packed disc contains episodes #17–21, a wild roller coaster ride that sets the stage for the conclusion of this grand sci-fi series. [JMC]

SPECIAL FEATURES Other Title Trailers • Easter Eggs TECHNICAL FEATURES Fullscreen (1.33:1) • Subtitles/CC: Eng. • Languages: Jap., Eng. dub • Sound: Dolby Digital 2.0 • Keepcase • 1 Disc • Region 1 GENRE & RATING Action/Comedy/Science Fiction • Rated 12+

Lost Universe: Vol. 6—It's His Duty to Kick Some Booty

ADV Films, 2000, 125 mins., #DVDLU006. Directed by Takashi Watanabe. Script by Yasunori Yamada, Jiro Takayama, Sumio Uetake, Go Tamai. Based on the manga series by Hajime Kanzaka, Shoko Yoshinaka in *Dragon Junior*.

Kain's entire universe has been turned upside down! Rail Claymore is a traitor, Millie and Nina are lost in space, and the Universal Guardians, taken over by the evil Kali, want him for treason! Now, armed with his psi-blade, he must fight an invincible enemy or the crew and his ship are lost. Battles between good and evil, starship against starship, and intense revelations about the past, present, and future, bring to a close this space-faring anime series.

This final DVD contains episodes #22–26, a nice ending that brings closure to several situations and reveals many important pieces of information. Most of the puzzle pieces seem to fit nicely within the context of this last volume. [JMC]

SPECIAL FEATURES Other Title Trailers • Easter Eggs TECHNICAL FEATURES Fullscreen (1.33:1) • Subtitles/CC: Eng. • Languages: Jap., Eng. dub • Sound: Dolby Digital 2.0 • Keepcase • 1 Disc • Region 1 GENRE & RATING Action/Comedy/Science Fiction • Rated 12+

Love Hina: Moving In . . . [#1]

Bandai, 2002, 100 mins., #1900. Directed by Yoshiaki Iwasaki. Based on the manga series by Ken Akamatsu in *Shonen Magazine*.

Keitaro Urashima is a third-year ronin, a prep-school student trying to get into Tokyo University in order to fulfill a promise he made fifteen years before to a little girl. The only thing is, he has no idea who the girl is! To top that off, his parents have kicked him out. A visit to his grandmother's apartment building reveals that grandma's not there—but her young female charges are, and they don't appreciate a young man showing up in their bath. Can he convince the girls of the Hinata Apartments that he's not a pervert so they will let him stay and be their building manager? Will kendo-expert Mokoto kill him before he can pass his exams? Will sex-kitten Kitsune's seduction techniques distract him too much? Will crazy foreigner Su eat his homework? Will he make sensitive young Shinobu cry again? He made a bad first impression with Narusegawa, but she still seems willing to be his reluctant study partner. Could she be his long-lost love?

A mad-cap mix of *Ranma* meets *Tenchi Muyo*, this 2000 TV series is chock full of sex-comedy and sweet angst, all done with top-of-the-line animation. Great characterizations makes this a thoroughly enjoyable collection of four episodes on the first DVD! More sensitive viewers may be turned off by accusations of Keitaro getting fresh with the middle-schooler, Shinobu, while some avid fans may be perturbed at how much this has actually been toned down and rewritten compared to the manga it's based on. [WM]

SPECIAL FEATURES Character and Art Galleries (including "Keitaro's Sketchbook") • Other Title Trailers • Inserts: Liner/Character Notes TECHNICAL FEATURES Fullscreen (1.33:1) • Subtitles/CC: Eng. • Languages: Jap., Eng. dub • Sound: Dolby Digital Surround 2.0 • Keepcase • 1 Disc • Region 1 GENRE & RATING Romance/Comedy • Rated 13+

Love Hina: Moving In . . . [#1 with DVD Collector Box]

Bandai, 2002, 100 mins., #1906. Directed by Yoshiaki Iwasaki. Based on the manga series by Ken Akamatsu in *Shonen Magazine*.

This cardboard box set is sized to fit six volumes of *Love Hina*, but it contains only volume #1, plus a foam insert to fill out the rest of the box. Collectors will thus be able to fill out their own box collection.

SPECIAL FEATURES Character and Art Galleries • Other Title Trailers • Inserts: Liner/Character Notes TECHNICAL FEATURES Fullscreen (1.33:1) • Subtitles/CC: Eng. • Languages: Jap., Eng. dub • Sound: Dolby Digital Surround 2.0 • Box with 1 Keepcase • 1 Disc • Region 1 GENRE & RATING Romance/Comedy • Rated 13+

Love Hina: Go West! [#2]

Bandai, 2002, 100 mins., #1901. Directed by Yoshiaki Iwasaki. Based on the manga series by Ken Akamatsu in *Shonen Magazine*.

Keitaro and Naru have both left their home at the Hinata Apartments, and the others wonder if they're going to elope. Who is Otohime, and what is she to Keitaro? Who is *Ken*taro (as he stresses), and what has he to do with Naru? Plus, Su invents a device that can pluck the thoughts right out of your head and show them on TV, so Keitaro better watch what he's thinking! And is Motoko dreaming about all her friends becoming small-bodied, or is she really trapped in an RPG-style videogame?

Episodes #5–8 are on this disc. "Keitaro's Songbook" is a fun extra, giving a little background information to a song in episode eight, as well as romaji lyrics and the English translation. [WM]

SPECIAL FEATURES Character and Art Galleries • "Keitaro's Song-book" • Other Title Trailers • Inserts: Liner/Character Notes TECHNICAL FEATURES Fullscreen (1.33:1) • Subtitles/CC: Eng. • Languages: Jap., Eng. dub • Sound: Dolby Digital Surround 2.0 • Keepcase • 1 Disc • Region 1 GENRE & RATING Romance/Comedy • Rated 13+

SPECIAL FEATURES "Making of" Featurette • Character Bios • Character and Art Galleries • Other Title Trailers • Inserts: Liner Notes TECHNICAL FEATURES Fullscreen (1.33:1) • Subtitles/CC: Eng. • Languages: Jap., Eng. dub • Sound: Dolby Digital • Keepcase • 1 Disc • Region 1 GENRE & RATING Romance/Comedy • Rated 13+

Love Hina: Secret Lives [#3]

Bandai, 2002, 100 mins., #1902. Directed by Yoshiaki Iwasaki. Based on the manga series by Ken Akamatsu in *Shonen Magazine*.

Someone has stolen the rent money, but Detective Kitsune is on the case to recover the stolen goods. Who is the mysterious woman who keeps appearing every time the moon is red and full? Could it be that Su has grown up? Plus, Naru might fulfill her dream of being a pop star, but if she does, it might crush Keitaro's own dreams. And can it be true that if Motoko ever wears a dress, she will she lose her martial arts abilities?

This third DVD contains four episodes of fun and romantic goodness, as well as an interview with director Yoshiaki Iwasaki. This makes a nice bonus, offering insight into the making of the series. Sensitive viewers may object to innuendoes of incest and underage hanky-panky. [WM]

SPECIAL FEATURES Interview with Director • Character and Art Galleries • Other Title Trailers TECHNICAL FEATURES Fullscreen (1.33:1) • Subtitles/CC: Eng. • Languages: Jap., Eng. dub • Sound: Dolby Digital Surround 2.0 • Keepcase • 1 Disc • Region 1 GENRE & RATING Romance/Comedy • Rated 13+

Love Hina: Love Hurts [#4]

Bandai, 2002, 100 mins., #1903. Directed by Yoshiaki Iwasaki. Based on the manga series by Ken Akamatsu in *Shonen Magazine*.

NOTE: This DVD arrived too late for a full review. The following text is promotional copy provided by the releasing company:

"Shinobu searches for life's ultimate question! What would a person's first kiss be like? Meanwhile, the gang at the Hinata Inn have been partying a little too much these days! With a huge bill to pay, can they find a way to earn enough money and pay off their debts? The road of love can be a bumpy one—and between Keitaro and Naru, its only going to get bumpier! When Naru stumbles across her former tutor—who she had a crush on—she falls for him all over again. Get ready for an unforgettable summer at the beach!"

This disc contains episodes #13–16.

Love Hina: Summer by the Sea [#5]

Bandai, 2002, 100 mins., #1904. Directed by Yoshiaki Iwasaki. Based on the manga series by Ken Akamatsu in *Shonen Magazine*.

NOTE: This DVD arrived too late for a full review. The following text is promotional copy provided by the releasing company:

"It's summertime, and the gang of Hinata Inn winds up on a lush tropical island! Sounds like a fun time, right? Wrong! Supernatural mysteries run wild as our vacationers deal with Naru who is seemingly possessed by a spirit of the island! Plus, outrageous summer visits from Kaolla's relatives and more outrageous summer vacation mayhem!"

This disc contains episodes #17–20.

SPECIAL FEATURES Character Bios • Character and Art Galleries • Other Title Trailers • Inserts: Liner Notes TECHNICAL FEATURES Fullscreen (1.33:1) • Subtitles/CC: Eng. • Languages: Jap., Eng. dub • Sound: Dolby Digital • Keepcase • 1 Disc • Region 1 GENRE & RATING Romance/Comedy • Rated 13+

Love Hina: And the Winner Is . . . [#6]

Bandai, 2002, 100 mins., #1905. Directed by Yoshiaki Iwasaki. Based on the manga series by Ken Akamatsu in *Shonen Magazine*.

NOTE: This DVD arrived too late for a full review. The following text is promotional copy provided by the releasing company:

"Love is in the air! Could Naru finally be opening up to geeky Keitaro? The residents of Hinata Inn sure hope so. With the Inn under construction, the fun-loving gang must deal with time away from the Hinata Inn, but what will happen to the residents after Keitaro's shocking announcement? Will he finally fulfill his lifelong promise to enter Tokyo University or will he seek something . . . errr, *someone* new?!"

This disc contains episodes #21–24.

SPECIAL FEATURES Character Bios • Character and Art Galleries • Fan Art Gallery • Other Title Trailers • Inserts: Liner Notes TECHNICAL FEATURES Fullscreen (1.33:1) • Subtitles/CC: Eng. • Languages: Jap., Eng. dub • Sound: Dolby Digital • Keepcase • 1 Disc • Region 1 GENRE & RATING Romance/Comedy • Rated 13+

Love Hina: Christmas Movie [#7]

Bandai, 2002, 75 mins., #1910. Directed by Yoshiaki Iwasaki. Based on the manga series by Ken Akamatsu in *Shonen Magazine.*

NOTE: This DVD arrived too late for a full review. The following text is promotional copy provided by the releasing company:

"It's Christmas at Hinata Inn, which means gifts, parties, and utter chaos! While sneaking around for gifts, Su and Sara discover a letter in Naru's room: 'I Always Loved . . .' What does this mean? Who does Naru love? The plot thickens as Keitaro is spotted going out with Mutsumi! A day of celebration, a night of miracles . . . the holiday spirit is in the air and there's gonna be a whole lotta lovin' goin' on! Plus, a special bonus present: *Love Hina* Episode 25!"

SPECIAL FEATURES Clean Credits • Other Title Trailers • Inserts: Calendar TECHNICAL FEATURES Fullscreen (1.33:1) • Subtitles/CC: Eng. • Languages: Jap., Eng. dub • Sound: Dolby Digital • Keepcase • 1 Disc • Region 1 GENRE & RATING Holiday/Romance/Comedy • Rated 13+

Love Lessons ☞ see Mature/Adult Section

Luminous Visions

Sony, 1998, 50 mins., #LVD49484.

This CGI anthology DVD was not available for review.

Lupin III: The Mystery of Mamo

Image, 1998, 102 mins., #4653SEDVD.

This DVD was not available for review. It is out of print.

Lupin the Third #1: The Secret of Twilight Gemini [Edited Version]

Funimation, 2002, 85 mins.

This DVD was not available for review.

Lupin the Third #1: The Secret of Twilight Gemini [Uncut Feature]

Funimation, 2002, 90 mins.

This DVD was not available for review.

Luv Wave ☞ see Mature/Adult Section

M.D. Geist and M.D. Geist II

Image, 2000, 91 mins., #ID4412CTDVD.

This DVD was not available for review. It is out of print.

M.D. Geist: Director's Cut/Death Force [Collector's Series]

U.S. Manga Corps, 2002, 93 mins., #USMD2202. Directed by Hayato Ikeda, Koichi Ohata. Script by Riku Sanjo.

NOTE: This DVD arrived too late for a full review. The following text is promotional copy provided by the releasing company:

"Classified as too unstable, the genetically engineered soldier, Geist-02, was permanently imprisoned aboard an orbital satellite. But times change and the world that created him has become a wasteland devastated by war. The battle weary humans have unleashed their own destruction, a doomsday device that will annihilate all life. Now, Geist-02 must return to save the world that tried to destroy him!"

The second bonus disc included here is titled "The World of Koichi Ohata." It has lots of extra material on *M.D. Geist*, *Genocyber*, and *Cybernetics Guardian*.

SPECIAL FEATURES Text Interview with Co-Director • Commentary Track by Co-Director and Writer • Co-Director Retrospective • Character and Art Galleries • Storyboards • Trailer • Promotional Footage • Alternate Angle Manga • Music Video • Motorcycle and Model Photos • DVD-ROM Features: Art, Scripts, Storyboards, Manga, Soundtrack • Other Title Trailers TECHNICAL FEATURES Fullscreen (1.33:1) • Subtitles/CC: Eng. • Languages: Jap., Eng. dub • Sound: Dolby Digital 2.0 • Multikeepcase • 2 Discs • Region All GENRE & RATING Robots/Action • Rated 16+

Macross II: The Movie

Manga Entertainment, 2000, 160 mins., #MANGA4056-2. Directed by Kenichi Yatagai. Screenplay by Manabu Nakamura.

In the year 2089 (eighty years after the original Macross first took flight), Earth's military once again faces an encroaching alien threat. The forces of the Marduk aren't nearly as easy to defeat as the now-friendly Zentreadi; a failed "Minmay attack" (which actually involves disrupting the enemy's attacks by blaring pop music at them!) results in Earth's forces retreating in confusion. Hibiki Kanzaki, a tabloid reporter, is caught up in the conflict when an unauthorized flyby of the battlefield results in him crash-landing inside one of the Marduk ships. There, he meets Ishtar, a strange and beautiful girl. It falls to the pair to make a daring escape—and the only hope for ending the war lies in the dormant hulk of the superdimensional space fortress *Macross*.

Macross II was a 1992 attempt by Bandai Visual and Big West to revive the popular franchise. Initially released as six separate episodes and later presented as a theatrical film, *Macross II* failed to generate much enthusiasm from fans, despite the involvement of signature character designer Haruhiko Mikimoto. The plot actually contradicts other parts of the *Macross* saga, probably because series director and designer Shoji Kawamori was not involved in the production. (Kawamori would return to the *Macross* franchise to direct 1995's far superior *Macross Plus*.) *Macross II* is so inconsistent, in fact, that it's no longer considered part of the "official" *Macross* timeline.

The DVD contains a compilation of all six *Macross II* episodes, minus the repeating opening and ending sequences, so it's not really a proper "movie." However, the long running time and continuous presentation of the story makes it more or less indistinguishable from one. [MT]

SPECIAL FEATURES Character Bios • Character and Art • Trailers • Music Video • Other Title Trailers TECHNICAL FEATURES Fullscreen (1.33:1) • Subtitles/CC: Eng. • Languages: Jap., Eng. dub • Sound: Dolby Digital 2.0 • Keepcase • 1 Disc •

Region 1, 2, 4 GENRE & RATING Robots/Science Fiction • Not Rated (Teens)

Macross Plus [Movie Edition]

Manga Entertainment, 2002, 115 mins., #MANGA4113-2. Directed by Shoji Kawamori. Screenplay by Keiko Nobumoto.

This feature film condenses the story told in the *Macross Plus* OVAs into a single feature film. It can be viewed as a stand-alone movie (no prior knowledge of *Macross* is required), and also includes some new sequences to tempt *Macross* fans who are already familiar with the OVA series.

While the contents of the *Macross Plus* movie are as excellent as their OVA source material, demanding fans may be disappointed that this DVD contains "hard" subtitles that cannot be turned off. Beyond that, the DVD contains a fairly standard set of simple extras. [MT]

SPECIAL FEATURES Character and Art Galleries • Trailer • Other Title Trailers TECHNICAL FEATURES Fullscreen (1.33:1) • Subtitles/CC: Eng. • Languages: Jap., Eng. dub • Sound: Dolby Digital 2.0 • Keepcase • 1 Disc • Region 1, 2, 4 GENRE & RATING Robots/Science Fiction • Not Rated (Teens)

Macross Plus: Vol. 1—Parts 1 and 2

Manga Entertainment, 1999, 78 mins., #602 004 021 2. Directed by Shoji Kawamori. Screenplay by Keiko Nobumoto.

It's twenty-eight years after the original *Macross* saga, and daredevil military pilot Isamu Dyson is having some problems with authority. To punish him for his disobedience, Dyson's superiors banish him to planet Eden, where he's assigned to work as a test pilot. Unbeknownst to them, this is actually Dyson's dream job—he eagerly attacks the task of taking the experimental YF-19 fighter through competitive trials with another prototype fighter, the YF-21. Things get complicated when Dyson realizes that the YF-21's test pilot is the half-Zentreadi Guld Goa Bowman, an old friend turned adversary. Tension comes to a head when Eden is visited by interplanetary music sensation Sharon Apple, whose manager turns out to be an old flame of both test pilots.

Supported by a strong story that features the classic *Macross* love triangle, a buoyant orchestral score, and some of the most painstakingly realistic animation of aircraft ever created, *Macross Plus* is generally quite exceptional. It's sharper-looking and more vividly characterized than its predecessors, featuring production values that are easily on a par with most animated motion pictures. For fans of action, mecha, or character-driven drama, *Macross Plus* is hard to resist.

The DVD presentation of *Macross Plus* is strong. The series features an excellent Dolby 5.1 English mix, and a solid Japanese 2.0 mix. Video quality is pristine, and the usual small raft of extras are present. This disc contains the first two (of four total) OVA episodes. [MT]

SPECIAL FEATURES Other Title Trailers • Easter Egg TECHNICAL FEATURES Fullscreen (1.33:1) • Subtitles/CC: Eng. • Languages: Jap., Eng. dub • Sound: Dolby Digital 2.0, Dolby Digital 5.1 • Keepcase • 1 Disc • Region 1, 2, 4 GENRE & RATING Robots/Science Fiction • Not Rated (Teens)

Macross Plus: Vol. 2—Parts 3 and 4

Manga Entertainment, 1999, 78 mins., #602 004 034 2. Directed by Shoji Kawamori. Screenplay by Keiko Nobumoto.

The second volume of *Macross Plus* continues chronicling the tempestuous lives of test pilots Isamu Dyson and Guld Goa Bowman, as well as their mutual old flame Myung-fang Lone and "virtual" pop star Sharon Apple. The plot thickens as a strange connection between Myung and Sharon is revealed; meanwhile, Isamu and Guld seem destined to settle their rivalry in aerial combat.

The DVD continues the strong presentation of the first volume, with excellent audio and video. This volume contains episodes #3 and #4 of *Macross Plus*. [MT]

SPECIAL FEATURES Character and Art Galleries • Other Title Trailers • Easter Egg TECHNICAL FEATURES Fullscreen (1.33:1) • Subtitles/CC: Eng. • Languages: Jap., Eng. dub • Sound: Dolby Digital 2.0, Dolby Digital 5.1 • Keepcase • 1 Disc • Region 1, 2, 4 GENRE & RATING Robots/Science Fiction • Not Rated (Teens)

Madeline at the Eiffel Tower

Trimark, 2002, 65 mins., #VM 7926D. Directed by Judy Reilly. Written by Shelley Zellman, Betty G. Birney, Diane Fresco. Based on the book series by Ludwig Bemelmans.

Madeline is a little girl whose curiosity gets her into many adventures. She's the smallest girl at Miss Clavel's boarding school, but that doesn't stop her from exploring the world around her—sometimes with her friends Danielle, Chloe, Nicole, and Yvette— and learning important life lessons along the way. In this set of tales, Madeline learns about gravity and taking on dares at the Eiffel Tower. Then, in "Madeline at Versailles," she travels to the castle at Versailles, where the rascally boy Pepito's actions almost ruin a priceless antique.

And in "Madeline and the White Lie," the children learn the value of being completely truthful.

Madeline first appeared in 1939 in a series of children's books by author Ludwig Bemelmans. The little redheaded girl remained popular through the years, and was first animated in a 1952 UPA cartoon. In 1988, DIC Enterprises produced a *Madeline* special for HBO, followed in 1990 by a series of other specials for the Family Channel. A weekly series began in 1993 on the Family Channel, moving to ABC in 1995. Whereas the early specials were based on stories in the books, the weekly series featured new stories, all designed to be educational and fun.

The DVD features three Parisian adventures of Madeline and her friends, complete with songs and games.

SPECIAL FEATURES Other Title Trailers • Games TECHNICAL FEATURES Fullscreen (1.33:1) • Subtitles/CC: Eng. • Languages: Eng. • Sound: Dolby Digital 2.0 • Keepcase • 1 Disc • Region 1 GENRE & RATING Girls/Family • Rated 2+

Madeline at the North Pole

Trimark, 2001, 70 mins., #VM7815D. Directed by Judy Reilly. Written by Judy Rothman Rofe, Martha Moran, Betty G. Birney. Based on the book series by Ludwig Bemelmans.

Madeline and her friends travel to the North Pole for the Christmas season, but all of Santa's elves are sick with a bad case of flu! Will Christmas be canceled, or will the little girls help Santa finish the presents? Then, in "Madeline and Santa," the jolly Mr. Claus eats too many of Madeline's cookies and grows too fat to fit through the chimneys! How will he slim down in time?

These two holiday-themed episodes are joined by a third snowy episode, "Madeline and the Ice Skates," making this a packed winter DVD for young viewers.

SPECIAL FEATURES Other Title Trailers • Game TECHNICAL FEATURES Fullscreen (1.33:1) • Subtitles/CC: Eng. • Languages: Eng., Span. dub • Sound: Dolby Digital 2.0 • Keepcase • 1 Disc • Region 1 GENRE & RATING Girls/Family • Rated 2+

Madeline Best Manners

Trimark, 2002, 83 mins.

This DVD was not available for review.

Madeline's Christmas/Madeline and the Toy Factory

Sony Wonder, 2002, 50 mins., #LVD 54329. Directed by , Stephan Martiniere, Stan Phillips. Screenplay by Stephan Martiniere, Peter Landecker. Based on the book series by Ludwig Bemelmans.

NOTE: This DVD arrived too late for a full review. The following text is promotional copy provided by the releasing company:

"When her friends come down with the flu and can't make it home to their families for Christmas, it's a sad holiday for all. Or is it? Join in the magic of the season as a special friend shows Madeline that with love in your heart, wishes can come true! Then, while visiting a toy factory, Madeline becomes a living doll after she's accidentally boxed up and shipped out to a toy store! Play along as her pretending brightens up the lonely days of a sickly girl amazed at this miraculous new walking and talking toy! Both stories are narrated by Christopher Plummer."

Note that although the disc cover claims it is closed captioned, it is not.

SPECIAL FEATURES None TECHNICAL FEATURES Fullscreen (1.33:1) • Languages: Eng. • Sound: Dolby Digital • Keepcase • 1 Disc • Region 1 GENRE & RATING Girls/Family • Not Rated (All Ages)

Madeline Manners

Trimark, 2001, 75 mins., #VM7801D. Directed by Judy Reilly. Written by Susan Amerikaner, Shelley Zellman. Based on the book series by Ludwig Bemelmans.

Pepito is enticed by his cousin Pablito to practice bad manners. Pepito's ambassador father threatens to ban his son from a banquet honoring soccer star Pepe Pelota, unless his manners improve. Pepito soon joins Madeline and the girls in etiquette school to learn better table manners. Then, in "Madeline and the Show Off," young Yvette gets a swelled head after a painter chooses her to sit for him. Madeline and the others soon learn from Miss Clavel that each girl is beautiful in her own way, and Yvette finds out what an abstract painter is!

In addition to the two episodes, this DVD also features a compilation episode with almost a dozen sing-alongs.

SPECIAL FEATURES Other Title Trailers • Sing-Alongs • Games TECHNICAL FEATURES Fullscreen (1.33:1) • Subtitles/CC: Eng. • Languages: Eng., Span. dub • Sound: Dolby Digital 2.0 • Keepcase • 1 Disc • Region 1 GENRE & RATING Girls/Family • Rated 2+

Madeline: Sing-a-long Around the World with Madeline

Trimark, 2001, 60 mins., #VM 7924D. Directed by Judy Reilly. Based on the book series by Ludwig Bemelmans.

If you like the cheery and catchy tunes that Madeline and her friends sing in their various adventures, this DVD gathers eighteen songs from many episodes, spotlighting countries around the world, and teaching valuable lessons to young viewers. Unfortunately, of the two "musical clip" episodes here, one is a repeat of the compilation on the *Madeline Manners* DVD, which may make some buyers feel a bit cheated.

SPECIAL FEATURES Other Title Trailers • Interactive Games TECHNICAL FEATURES Fullscreen (1.33:1) • Subtitles/CC: Eng. • Languages: Eng. • Sound: Dolby Digital 2.0 • Keepcase • 1 Disc • Region 1 GENRE & RATING Girls/Family • Rated 2+

Madeline: The Best Episodes Ever, Vol. 1

Sony Wonder, 2002, 50 mins.

This DVD was not available for review. It features "Madeline at the Ballet" and "Madeline in New York."

Madeline: The Best Episodes Ever, Vol. 2

Sony Wonder, 2002, 50 mins.

This DVD was not available for review. It features "Madeline and the 40 Thieves" and "Madeline and the New House."

Madeline's Winter Vacation/Madeline in London

Sony Wonder, 2002, 50 mins., #LVD 54330. Directed by Stan Phillips, Stephan Martiniere. Screenplay by Susan Amerikaner, Stephan Martiniere, Peter Landecker. Based on the book series by Ludwig Bemelmans.

NOTE: This DVD arrived too late for a full review. The following text is promotional copy provided by the releasing company:

"The snowy fun of a Swiss Alps vacation turns into snowy trouble for Madeline and her friends after an avalanche cuts them off from outside help! Watch as Madeline helps everyone put their fears on ice and shows that, no matter what, you must never give up hope! Then, the adventures only begin as Madeline and her friends take off for London to visit their friend Pepito on his birthday and present him with a precious new

pet horse! Ride along as Madeline leads the Royal guard, meets the queen, and plays detective to solve the mystery of the ravaged garden. Both stories are narrated by Christopher Plummer."

Note that although the disc cover claims it is closed captioned, it is not.

SPECIAL FEATURES None TECHNICAL FEATURES Fullscreen (1.33:1) • Languages: Eng. • Sound: Dolby Digital • Keepcase • 1 Disc • Region 1 GENRE & RATING Girls/Family • Not Rated (All Ages)

Madonna

Anime Works, 1999, 104 mins., #AWDVD-0206. Directed by Akinori Nagaoka. Screenplay by Kaori Okamura. Based on the manga series by Ikuko Kujirai in *Big Comic Spirits*.

When pretty young Mako Domon agreed to teach at a rough technical high school, she never expected that she'd end up being the tough teen boys' rugby coach as well! But even though these bad news bears aren't a very good rugby team, Mako's influence begins to draw them together. But the road to victory—on the sporting field and in the classroom—won't be an easy one, and Mako may have a more difficult time reforming the juvenile delinquents than anyone thinks.

Riding a line between comedy and sports drama, this 1998 two-part OVA feels a bit mean-spirited at times, especially when the teens sexually harass their teacher. But its plot is certainly different from most anime. There is profanity and sexual talk, as well as some brief nudity, so parents may want to monitor the action. The DVD is strictly no-frills.

SPECIAL FEATURES None TECHNICAL FEATURES Fullscreen (1.33:1) • Subtitles/CC: Eng. • Languages: Jap. • Sound: Dolby Digital 2.0 • Keepcase • 1 Disc • Region 1 GENRE & RATING Sports/Comedy • Rated 13+

Maetel Legend

Central Park, 2002, 90 mins., #USMD 2146. Directed by Kazuyoshi Yokota. Screenplay by Mugi Kamio. Based on the manga series by Reiji Matsumoto.

The inhabitants of planet La Metal are facing a dire threat to their very existence. The planet's orbital cycle moves it through several different solar systems, taking an astonishing 1,000 years to complete a single cycle. But since the planet doesn't actually revolve around a star, it's deathly cold, and its inhabitants are gradually dying out. This problem vexes La Metal's ruler, Queen Promethium, but her chief scientist, the android Hard Gear, has a solution. He proposes that the only way the citizens of La Metal can survive the cold is to transfer their minds to new, indestructible machine bodies. Maetel and Emeraldas, Promethium's twin daughters, are dead set against this idea, but the queen reluctantly accepts Hard Gear's solution. It's up to Maetel and Emeraldas to defy their mother and save themselves—and hopefully the rest of La Metal—from a fate worse than death.

Maetel Legend was produced in 2000 to capitalize on the resurgent popularity of Reiji Matsumoto, creator of *Captain Harlock* and *Galaxy Express 999*. *Maetel Legend* is essentially a bridge between Matsumoto's *Queen Millennium* anime (as yet unreleased in the United States) and the *Galaxy Express 999* series (which is available on VHS, but not on DVD). With a murky story that can use prior knowledge of Matsumoto's universe, and animation that is subpar, *Maetel Legend* is a pretty tough sell. Still, longtime fans of Matsumoto's style will no doubt appreciate the new chapter in the story of the popular *Maetel*.

The DVD contains both episodes of *Maetel Legend*. Aside from being offered as a single DVD, the disc was also included as part of a 2002 pack set, along with *Harlock Saga*. [MT]

SPECIAL FEATURES Character Bios • Director Bio • DVD-ROM Trivia Game • Other Title Trailers TECHNICAL FEATURES Fullscreen (1.33:1) • Subtitles/CC: Eng. • Languages: Jap., Eng. dub • Sound: Dolby Digital 2.0 • Keepcase • 1 Disc • Region 1–6 GENRE & RATING Science Fiction/Action • Rated 13+

Magical Project S: Pretty Sammy Debut! [#1]

Pioneer, 2002, 325 mins., #11903. Directed by Katsuhito Akiyama.

NOTE: This DVD arrived too late for a full review. The following text is promotional copy provided by the releasing company:

"Drafted! Sasami Kawai suddenly finds herself transforming into a magical girl, teaming up with a talking rabbit (that claims to be a cat), wearing embarrassing clothes, and battling bizarre enemies. All of these are consequences of the coronation of Tsunami, the new queen of Juraihelm, who has chosen Sasami as her champion to restore the balance of good in the universe. Tsunami's rival has also selected a magical girl to cause trouble and discredit Tsunami, but no one knows that this Pixy Misa is really Sasami's best friend!"

These discs contains episodes #1–13 of this campy *Tenchi Muyo!* spin-off.

SPECIAL FEATURES Character and Art Galleries • Bonus Scenes • Clean Credits • Other Title Trailers • Inserts: Mini Poster, Pencil Board • Reversible Cover TECHNICAL FEATURES Fullscreen (1.33:1) • Subtitles/CC: Eng. • Languages: Jap. • Sound: Dolby Digital • Multikeepcase • 2 Discs • Region 1 GENRE & RATING Action/Girls • Rated 3+

Magical Project S: Pixy Misa Finale! [#2]

Pioneer, 2002, 325 mins., #11904. Directed by Katsuhito Akiyama.

NOTE: This DVD arrived too late for a full review. The following text is promotional copy provided by the releasing company:

"Each of Ramia's plots to destroy Pretty Sammy has failed and Tsunami comes ever closer to becoming the true queen of Juraihelm. Before Ramia could let this happen, she decides to get personally involved and creates the Team Lovely Madams to assist her champion, Pixy Misa. Even the third candidate for Queen of Juraihelm, Romio, helps through her champion, Love Me Eimi. Will Pretty Sammy be able to succeed against such powerful magical enemies? What will happen when Sasami discovers Pixy Misa's true identity and Ramia's ally reveals her true intentions?"

These discs contains episodes #14–26 of this campy *Tenchi Muyo!* spin-off.

SPECIAL FEATURES Character and Art Galleries • Bonus Scenes • Clean Credits • Trailer • Other Title Trailers • Inserts: Mini Poster, Pencil Board • Reversible Cover TECHNICAL FEATURES Fullscreen (1.33:1) • Subtitles/CC: Eng. • Languages: Jap. • Sound: Dolby Digital • Multikeepcase • 2 Discs • Region 1 GENRE & RATING Action/Girls • Rated 3+

Magic Knight Rayearth #1: Daybreak

Media Blasters, 2000, 100 mins., #MKKD-VD-1001. Directed by Toshihiro Hirano. Scripts by Nanase Okawa, Keiko Maruo, Osamu Nakamura. Based on the manga series by CLAMP in *Nakayoshi*.

Three junior high school friends meet at Tokyo Tower for a day of fun, not realizing that their lives are about to be changed forever. Hikaru Shido, Umi Ryuzaki, and Fu Ho-oji are beckoned by a mysterious voice belonging to Princess Emeraude the Pillar of Cephiro, imploring them to help save the magical land. Soon the trio are transported to Cephiro where monsters, mythical creatures, and other amazing beings roam free. Master Cleff, one of the land's greatest sorcerers, informs them they are the legendary Magic Knights destined to save the dying land, rescue the Princess from an evil priest, and restore Cephiro to glory. He tells the girls they must obtain weapons from the mysterious Presea and wake up the three Rune Gods to restore order. With magic armor and powers, the girls set out on a mission of peace and freedom, but the evil Zagato doesn't want them to succeed, and will go to any length to stop the Magic Knights. Will Zagato be successful or will the freshmen Knights be able to complete their quest?

Magic Knight Rayearth is an epic fantasy/magical Shojo (girls) series created by CLAMP in 1993 spanning six manga trade paperbacks, forty-nine anime episodes in 1994, and three later OVAs. This imaginative series features themes of loyalty, romance, honor, justice, betrayal, and redemption, all packaged nicely via CLAMP's beautiful artwork and spirited storytelling. This DVD contains episodes #1–4 and has some mature scenes and deaths of characters. This powerful anime leaves a lasting impression and will appeal to all romance and fantasy fans. [JMC]

SPECIAL FEATURES Cast Interviews • Character Bios • Character and Art Galleries • Magic Spell Index • Omake Ending • Other Title Trailers • Easter Egg TECHNICAL FEATURES Fullscreen (1.33:1) • Subtitles/CC: Eng. • Languages: Jap., Eng. dub • Sound: Dolby Digital 2.0 • Keepcase • 1 Disc • Region 1–6 GENRE & RATING Fantasy/Girls/Action • Rated 13+

Magic Knight Rayearth #2: Sunrise

Media Blasters, 2000, 100 mins., #MKKD-VD-1002. Directed by Toshihiro Hirano. Scripts by Nanase Okawa, Keiko Maruo, Osamu Nakamura. Based on the manga series by CLAMP in *Nakayoshi*.

All knights go through a series of tests to prove their merit and skill, and the Magic Knights are no different. On their magical journey, Hikaru, Umi, and Fu are being challenged by entities doubting their role as the legendary protectors. They pass one test only to be attacked by a magical brute immune to their powers, who forces the girls to rely on something other than magic to save the day. Finally their emotions are put through the gauntlet when a small helpless creature they save from a monster turns into a hideous, violent beast and attacks them the next day. It seems the price to continue on the path to freedom is high. How long will the Magic Knights be willing to pay it?

The tests and stakes are raised for the Magic Knights in this heartfelt second installment containing episodes #5–8. [JMC]

SPECIAL FEATURES Cast Interviews • Character and Art Galleries • Outtakes • Magic Spell Index • Omake Ending • Other Title Trailers TECHNICAL FEATURES Fullscreen (1.33:1) • Subtitles/CC: Eng. • Languages: Jap., Eng. dub • Sound: Dolby Digital 2.0 • Keepcase • 1 Disc • Region 1–6 GENRE & RATING Fantasy/Girls/Action • Rated 13+

Magic Knight Rayearth #3: Noon

Media Blasters, 2000, 100 mins., #MKRD-VD-1003. Directed by Toshihiro Hirano. Scripts by Nanase Okawa, Keiko Marua, Osama Nakamura. Based on the manga series by CLAMP in *Nakayoshi*.

The road to the Rune-God gets a little damp as the Knights find themselves traveling to an underwater shrine to free the dormant god. Once there, though, Hikaru, Fu, and Umi must pass a terrible test to prove they are worthy of disturbing its rest and protecting Cephiro. But unknown to the Magic Knights, their enemies stand ready to ambush them. Once freed, what secrets about the legends of the Magic Knights will the Rune-God reveal? Later, the Knights find out that their second target is in a shrine that floats in the sky. As they begin the climb to the sky city, they're attacked by a dangerous new enemy—a master of illusions—who has the girls doubting anything and everything they see.

This DVD contains wet and wild episodes #9–12, and furthers the quest as the girls attain one of their goals: the freeing of the Rune-God. Now there are just two deities and lots of adventures to go! [JMC]

SPECIAL FEATURES Cast Interviews • Text Interview with Director • Character and Art Galleries • Magic Spell Index • Omake Ending • Other Title Trailers TECHNICAL FEATURES Fullscreen (1.33:1) • Subtitles/CC: Eng. • Languages: Jap., Eng. dub • Sound: Dolby Digital 2.0 • Keepcase • 1 Disc • Region 1–6 GENRE & RATING Fantasy/Girls/Action • Rated 13+

Magic Knight Rayearth #4: Twilight

Media Blasters, 2000, 100 mins., #MKRDV-1004. Directed by Toshihiro Hirano. Scripts by Nanase Okawa, Keiko Marua, Osama Nakamura. Based on the manga series by CLAMP in *Nakayoshi*.

Still reeling from their fight with the illusionist, the girls press onward toward the shrine in the sky in search of the second Rune-God. Fu faces her biggest challenge yet when the illusionist returns and hypnotizes Umi and Hikaru, forcing them to fight against Fu. To save her friends, Fu must battle them, but will she be strong enough to hurt the ones she loves? Then, Hikaru is left on her own when a mysterious force nabs Fu and Umi. She must overcome her anxieties to save her friends. Later, after the three meet the challenge of the second Rune-God, Windim: Lord of the Skies, they are attacked by monsters, which almost kill Umi. A mysterious stranger rescues Umi and slays the creature, but then turns on the Magic Knights saying he's an agent of Zagato ordered to destroy them.

Managing separation anxiety seems to be the theme

of this penultimate installment of the *Magic Knight Rayearth* saga. This DVD contains nail-biting episodes #13–16. [JMC]

SPECIAL FEATURES Cast Interviews • Character and Art Galleries • Magic Spell Index • Alternate Opening Song • Omake Ending • Other Title Trailers TECHNICAL FEATURES Fullscreen (1.33:1) • Subtitles/CC: Eng. • Languages: Jap., Eng. dub • Sound: Dolby Digital 2.0 • Keepcase • 1 Disc • Region 1–6 GENRE & RATING Fantasy/Girls/Action • Rated 13+

Magic Knight Rayearth #5: Midnight

Media Blasters, 2000, 100 mins., #MKDVD-1005. Directed by Toshihiro Hirano. Scripts by Nanase Okawa, Keiko Marua, Osama Nakamura. Based on the manga series by CLAMP in *Nakayoshi*.

Searching for the last Rune-God, Rayearth: Lord of Fire, the Magic Knights face some of their toughest challenges and consequences yet. First they're powerless against the evil Inova and must find a way to overcome his shields. Then, tired and drained from that battle, they're easy pickings for Zagato. He defeats Fu and Umi leaving Hikaru—without the power of a Magic Knight—at his mercy. The girls recover, free their Princess, and prepare for a final battle with Zagato. The trio defeats Zagato, but the victory is hollow; the Princess is driven insane due to their actions! Now, the only way to restore the land will be to destroy its Pillar, Emeraude. Will the Magic Knights find the strength to kill the woman they fought so hard to rescue?

There are few happy endings in the conclusion of this heroic anime series. Episodes #17–20, the final four first-season shows of *Magic Knight Rayearth*, round out this heart-wrenching volume. [JMC]

SPECIAL FEATURES Cast Interviews • Character and Art Galleries • Magic Spell Index • Alternate Credits TECHNICAL FEATURES Fullscreen (1.33:1) • Subtitles/CC: Eng. • Languages: Jap., Eng. dub • Sound: Dolby Digital 2.0 • Keepcase • 1 Disc • Region 1–6 GENRE & RATING Fantasy/Girls/Action • Rated 13+

Magic Knight Rayearth: DVD Memorial Box 1 [Box Set #1–5]

Media Blasters, 2000, 500 mins., #AWDVD-0083.

This DVD box set features all five DVD keepcase volumes of *Magic Knight Rayearth*, housed in a top-opening cardboard box. There are no extras specific to the box set. See individual entries for the Special and Technical Features listings.

TECHNICAL FEATURES Cardboard Box with 5 Keepcases • 5 Discs • Region 1–6 GENRE & RATING Fantasy/Girls/Action • Rated 13+

Magic Knight Rayearth 2: DVD Memorial Box 2 [Box Set #6–12]

AnimeWorks, 2002, 812 mins., #MKRD-VD-0172. Directed by Toshihiro Hirano. Scripts by Nanase Okawa. Based on the manga series by CLAMP in *Nakayoshi*.

NOTE: This DVD arrived too late for a full review. The following text is promotional copy provided by the releasing company:

"*Magic Knight Rayearth* continues as Hikaru, Umi, and Fu defeat the very person they were sent to rescue, Princess Emeraude. Filled with regret, the three were finally able to leave Cephiro and return to their families in Tokyo. Now, the three girls have been summoned back to Cephiro by an unknown force, and they will have to complete a new quest if they ever want to return home again. Cephiro is crumbling without a Pillar, and the Magic Knights must find a new candidate before the world is completely destroyed!

"To make things worse, invaders from the three neighboring countries of Autozam, Chizeta, and Fahren have arrived in Cephiro with their eyes on the Pillar! Now the girls must fight, and once again their opponents are not only monsters, but desperate people with hopes and dreams of their own. Will they bring themselves to find someone for the most sorrowful position in Cephiro, or will the Magic Knights and the invaders alike be swallowed by the mysterious darkness known as Lady Debonair?"

The six discs of this set include episodes #21–49 (the entire second season of *Magic Knight Rayearth*), and are divided into the following seven discs: "Wake" (#6), "Rise" (#7), "Learn" (#8), "Grow" (#9), "Sleep" (#10), "Dream" (#11), and "Live" (#12).

SPECIAL FEATURES Commentary Track with Director (final episode) • Character Bios • Character and Art Galleries • Magic Spell Index • Omake Endings • Storyboards • Promotional Footage • Music Video • Outtakes • Clean Credits • Other Title Trailers TECHNICAL FEATURES Fullscreen (1.33:1) • Subtitles/CC: Eng. • Languages: Jap., Eng. dub • Sound: Dolby Digital • Cardboard Box with 7 Keepcases • 7 Discs • Region 1–6 GENRE & RATING Fantasy/Girls/Action • Rated 13+

Magic of Santa Claus, The

Delta Entertainment, 2001, 51 mins., #82122. Directed by Julian Tarrago. Script by Alicia Boardman.

Coco and Drila, two young lizard children, embark on a great adventure to deliver Santa's magic sack and boots to Rudolph on the day before Christmas. Along the way, they meet a snowman who comes to life, an evil witch, and lots of obstacles. But if they don't reach Rudolph, children all over the world will be sad.

Although it says *The Magic of Santa Claus* on the package, the actual video is entitled "The Magic Sack of Santa Claus." It is part of a series called *Coco and Drila Adventures*, animated in Spain. The animation is credible and voice dubs mostly pleasant, but the songs sprinkled throughout are awful. This DVD is appropriate for all ages, but younger viewers will likely enjoy it best.

SPECIAL FEATURES None TECHNICAL FEATURES Fullscreen (1.33:1) • Languages: Eng. dub • Sound: Dolby Digital 2.0 • Keepcase • 1 Disc • Region All GENRE & RATING Holiday/Animals • Not Rated (Kids)

Magic User's Club #1: I'll Follow You!

Anime Works, 2001, 60 mins., #MTTD-VD-4002. Animation Directed by Ikuko Ito, Tatsuya Oka. Screenplay by Akinori Endo, Junichi Sato. Based on the manga series by Tami Ota in *Monthly Asuka Fantasy DX*.

Giant robots have invaded Earth, and even though they don't seem to be particularly threatening to the general populace, the members of Kitanohashi High School's Magic Club decide to stop them. Leading the battle is president Takakura, who interprets every situation as fraught with sexual overtones, while the androgynous male vice-president, Aburatsubo, has a penchant for tight tennis shorts and prancing. Clueless Sae Sawanoguchi is an enthusiastic new recruit, and the club also includes Nanaka and Akane. When the members of the club aren't fighting shiny robots, they still have to deal with romantic entanglements and their rivals—the school's Manga Club—which wants to take over their meeting room.

The first pair of six 1996 OVAs are presented on this DVD, which combines cute character designs, goofy situations, and high school humor with robot-fighting action and magic. Older readers of *Harry Potter* and the like will have a ball with this, although the panty shots and gay overtones from Aburatsubo definitely move this one toward a teen audience. Note that the beginning of both episodes is silent, so don't adjust your volume. The DVD cover is clear, as is the slipcover itself, resulting in a pretty pastel-colored see-through package unlike any other animated DVD released to date.

SPECIAL FEATURES Character and Art Galleries • Clean Credits • Other Title Trailers TECHNICAL FEATURES Fullscreen (1.33:1) • Subtitles/CC: Eng. • Languages: Jap., Eng. dub • Sound: Dolby Digital 2.0 • Keepcase • 1 Disc • Region 1 GENRE & RATING Magic/Comedy/Girls • Rated 13+

Magic User's Club #2: Magic Is So Easy!

Anime Works, 2001, 60 mins., #MTTD-VD-4005. Animation Directed by Ikuko Ito, Hideki Takahashi, Shigeyuki Suga, Tatsuya Oka, Fumio Matsumoto. Screenplay by Akinori Endo, Junichi Sato. Based on the manga series by Tami Ota in *Monthly Asuka Fantasy DX*.

The mysterious alien Bell, which controls the invaders, takes a special interest in Akane, whose magical powers are the strongest. When the Bell sends some mechanical devices to capture her, Akane must make her escape through the streets of Tokyo, where she finds some unexpected help. Later, the Magic Club goes on vacation to a beach, where much discussion of their pasts and exploration of their powers takes place. But when the busty Miyama—president of the Manga Club—shows up, her rivalry with Takakura and Sae may well spoil the peaceful retreat.

This DVD contains two more OVA episodes. And although the cover design is nowhere near as interesting as the debut volume, the disc does have a fun selection of voice actor outtakes.

SPECIAL FEATURES Clean Credits • Outtakes • Other Title Trailers TECHNICAL FEATURES Fullscreen (1.33:1) • Subtitles/CC: Eng. • Languages: Jap., Eng. dub • Sound: Dolby Digital 2.0 • Keepcase • 1 Disc • Region 1 GENRE & RATING Magic/Comedy/Girls • Rated 13+

Magic User's Club #3: Believe in Yourself

Anime Works, 2001, 60 mins., #MTTD-VD-4008. Animation Directed by Ikuko Ito. Screenplay by Akinori Endo, Junichi Sato. Based on the manga series by Tami Ota in *Monthly Asuka Fantasy DX*.

At the urging of a reporter named Minawa, Akane attempts a dangerous spell that links her with the mind of the Bell. She soon finds that the Bell is very interested in tracking the members of the Magic Club! Meanwhile, things are a little unstable at the Club after Nanaka confesses her love for Aburatsubo—with unpredictable results—and Sae considers letting Takeo know how she really feels as well. When Sae is captured by the Bell, it's up to the remaining members of the Club to join forces to rescue her and make a final assault on the invaders . . . with the fate of the entire human race in jeopardy!

The finale of the OVA series is presented in this DVD's pair of episodes, and although it wraps up the story in an enjoyable manner, it does leave events open for the TV series that followed. Watch for some very funny—but rather risque—moments when the Club members need to replace their flying broomsticks with "human brooms."

SPECIAL FEATURES Promotional Footage • Clean Credits • Outtakes • End Slates • Other Title Trailers TECHNICAL FEATURES Fullscreen (1.33:1) • Subtitles/CC: Eng. • Languages: Jap., Eng. dub • Sound: Dolby Digital 2.0 • Keepcase • 1 Disc • Region 1 GENRE & RATING Magic/Comedy/Girls • Rated 13+

Magic User's Club #4: I Wanna Do More

Anime Works, 2001, 100 mins., #MTTD-VD-4011. Directed by Junichi Sato. Screenplay by Chiaki Konaka, Michiko Yokote. Based on the manga series by Tami Ota in *Monthly Asuka Fantasy DX*.

In the final battle against the Bell, a giant cherry tree was created by Sae in the midst of Tokyo. With blossoms and leaves getting everywhere, the Magic Club tries to move the obstruction, but the result is straight out of a Godzilla movie! Later, Aburatsubo's mother comes to school for a parent-teacher conference, and she's wild herself. And when the Club begins opening dimensional doorways, what weirdness will ensue?

The frothy fun from previous volumes continues here; rather than beginning a completely new storyline, the 1997 TV series picks up directly after the events of the OVA series. As expected, there's a bit of decline in the animation, but the feel and look of the show overall is pretty much the same. This DVD contains the first four episodes of the thirteen-episode run.

SPECIAL FEATURES Clean Credits • Outtakes • Sing-Along • End Slates • Other Title Trailers TECHNICAL FEATURES Fullscreen (1.33:1) • Subtitles/CC: Eng. • Languages: Jap., Eng. dub • Sound: Dolby Digital 2.0 • Keepcase • 1 Disc • Region 1 GENRE & RATING Magic/Comedy/Girls • Rated 13+

Magic User's Club #5: My Secret Wish

AnimeWorks, 2002, 75 mins., #MTTDVD-4014. Animation Directed by Yuichi Tanaka, Ikuko Ito. Based on the manga series by Tami Ota in *Monthly Asuka Fantasy DX*.

NOTE: This DVD arrived too late for a full review. The following text is promotional copy provided by the releasing company:

"Takeo has always had an eye and a heart for the ladies but never the luck to go with them! Now, however, it seems that he is skipping club meetings to go see Akane! If that's not enough, Takeo shows up later at Sae's window. Drifting up on a broom, he is cloaked in a dashing cape and the glow of moonlight. Has the Magic Club president finally become a real lady's man?"

This disc contains episodes #5–7.

SPECIAL FEATURES Clean Credits • Bonus Scenes • Outtakes • Other Title Trailers TECHNICAL FEATURES Fullscreen (1.33:1) • Subtitles/CC: Eng. • Languages: Jap., Eng. dub • Sound: Dolby Digital • Keepcase • 1 Disc • Region 1 GENRE & RATING Magic/Comedy/Girls • Rated 13+

Magic User's Club #6: A Magic Kiss

Anime Works, 2002, 75 mins., #MTTD-VD-4017. Directed by Junichi Sato. Screenplay by Sadayuki Murai, Michiko Yokote, Chiaki Konaka. Based on the manga series by Tami Ota in *Monthly Asuka Fantasy DX*.

The school is holding a Culture Festival, but the kids in the Magic Club can't let anyone see their magic powers! Although most of the members get involved with other clubs, poor Sae is stuck doing fortune-telling spells that lead to disappearances and floating Tarot cards. Then, Akane drags Sae and Nanaka to a Drama Club audition, and Sae catches a glimpse of the mysterious blond boy who appears whenever her magic backfires. Later, Sae goes to her home for a wedding, and while practicing a flying spell, she's startled by the mysterious boy. He kisses her and she soon learns his name is Jinno Jurachy. He's the newest member of the Magic Club, and his powers are very advanced. But there's something different about him . . .

Another trio of episodes on this DVD feature Sae learning to lighten up a bit and enjoy her magic. Viewers will also enjoy more of the voice actor outtakes.

SPECIAL FEATURES Outtakes • End Slates • Other Title Trailers TECHNICAL FEATURES Fullscreen (1.33:1) • Subtitles/CC: Eng. • Languages: Jap., Eng. dub • Sound: Dolby Digital 2.0 • Keepcase • 1 Disc • Region 1 GENRE & RATING Magic/Comedy/Girls • Rated 13+

Magic Users Club #7: Should I Do?

Anime Works, 2002, 75 mins., #MTTD-VD-4020. Directed by Junichi Sato. Screenplay by Sadayuki Murai, Michiko Yokote, Chiaki Konaka. Based on the manga series by Tami Ota in *Monthly Asuka Fantasy DX*.

Jinno has made himself an integral member of the Magic Club, but he's pushing himself into the other member's personal lives. He tries to get Nanaka, Aburatsubo, and Takeo to all deal with their secret loves, but when Jinno's spell on Akane works its magic, chaos ensues. Akane's unleashed wildness turns Tokyo upside-down with pandemonium, and the rest of the Magic Club must find a way to contain the spells. And if the festively decorated trees weren't enough of a hint, Christmas is on the way as well!

The final three episodes of the TV series wrap up this DVD, which brings to a close this familiar-but-funny series.

SPECIAL FEATURES Outtakes • End Slates • Other Title Trailers TECHNICAL FEATURES Fullscreen (1.33:1) • Subtitles/CC: Eng. • Languages: Jap., Eng. dub • Sound: Dolby Digital 2.0 • Keepcase • 1 Disc • Region 1 GENRE & RATING Magic/Comedy/Girls • Rated 13+

Magic Voyage, The

Image, 1999, 80 mins., #ID5701ZDVD. Directed by Michael Schoeman. Screenplay by Scott Santoro, David Reilly. Story by Ute Koll.

When his pet woodworm Pico gnaws his cube of the world round, Christopher Columbus becomes convinced that the world is a sphere and sets his sights on exploring. Given financing and ships by the angry King Ferdinand and the flirty Queen Isabella, Columbus sets out to cross the sea. Along the way, beautiful firefly Princess Marilyn is captured by the evil Swarm Lord and his army of bugs, and upon arriving in the New World, Columbus teams up with a beaver, a bird, and other animals to rescue Marilyn and gain a golden disc that will . . .

Excuse me, but do I really need to go on? Bavaria Film's first animated feature film is an abominable mess, with a story that makes absolutely no sense, character designs that evoke winces, and forgettable songs. It's really hard to tell who this film was aimed at, as I would imagine that even the youngest children could tell a more cohesive tale than this one. The only things not awful are the animation itself, and the American voice cast that dubbed the feature (including Dom DeLuise, Corey Feldman, Irene Cara, Dan Haggerty, and Mickey Rooney), even if their dialogue seems improvised after a three-day drunken bender.

Sorry to say, but the only reason I can think of to purchase *The Magic Voyage* DVD is to turn it into an animated version of *Mystery Science Theater 3000*.

SPECIAL FEATURES None TECHNICAL FEATURES Fullscreen (1.33:1) • Languages: Eng. • Sound: Dolby Digital 2.0 • Snapcase • 1 Disc • Region 1 GENRE & RATING Historical/Music/Adventure • Rated G

Magic Woman M ☞ see Mature/Adult Section

Magnos the Robot

Liberty International., 2001, 90 mins., #LIP0102. Written by L. Michael Haller, Collins Walker.

Here's a piece of cookie-cutter super-robot fare: When the earth is threatened by a mysterious race of aliens, scientific genius Sir Miles creates a pair of giant robots to combat the threat. He enlists world kung-fu champion Janis, along with his own daughter, Ester, to pilot his inventions. Janis pilots Magnon and Ester controls Magneta, and when the forces of evil prove too overwhelming, the pair combine their mighty robots to form Magnos, an even bigger robot with an even larger set of gimmicks.

It sounds silly because it is. This DVD contains a condensed 1984 version of the original 1976 Japanese TV series *Magno Robo Ga-Keen*. Since it's essentially a simple story, ninety minutes is plenty of time to summarize it, and the production is made even campier by some extremely bizarre name changes for the English adaptation (witness the fearsome villain, Xerxes Tire-Iron Dada!). This title is marketed for children, but adult fans of kitschy giant robots are more likely to enjoy this than kids, who will probably be bored by the lousy animation and goofy dubbing.

The DVD is lackluster, but that's to be expected considering the title's low profile and price point. Fans will be disappointed by the lack of a Japanese audio track, but there is a (somewhat muffled) Spanish-language track. Beyond that, the DVD is devoid of special features, and the footage looks like it could use some remastering, to boot. And note that although it says on the packaging that the sound mix is 5.1, it outputs as 2.0. [MT]

SPECIAL FEATURES None TECHNICAL FEATURES Fullscreen (1.33:1) • Languages: Eng. dub, Span. dub • Sound: Dolby Digital 2.0 • Keepcase • 1 Disc • Region All GENRE & RATING Robots/Science Fiction • Not Rated (Kids)

Maiden Diaries, The ☞ see Mature/Adult Section

Mail Order Maiden 28 ☞ see Mature/Adult Section

Make Mine Music [Gold Collection]

Disney, 2000, 67 mins., #19604. Directed by Jack Kinney, Clyde Geronimi, Hamilton Luske, Bob Cormack, Josh Meador. Story by Homer Brightman, Dick Huemer, Dick Kinney, John Walbridge, Tom Oreb, Dick Shaw, Erik Gurney, Sylvia Holland, T. Hee, Dick Kelsey, Roy Williams, Jesse Marsh, Erdman Penner, Jim Bodrero Cap Palmer, Erwin Graham.

Nine animated musical interludes make up this film collection, Disney's eighth full-length animated feature. Perhaps the most famous segment is "Peter and the Wolf," but you'll also enjoy "Blue Bayou"; "All the Cats Join In"; "Without You"; "Two Silhouettes"; "Johnny Fedora and Alice Bluebonnet"; and "The Whale Who Wanted to Sing at the Met." Each selection is animated in its own style, ranging from humans playing baseball in "Casey at the Bat," to anthropomorphic instruments taking a surreal trip in "After You've Gone."

Although this 1946 project is not technically a sequel to *Fantasia*, the spirit—and many of the people who worked on the film—remains the same. Though there are several classical pieces here, there are also a number of contemporary popular musicians, including Benny Goodman, Dinah Shore, the Andrews Sisters, and more. Inexplicably, a seven-minute sequence of hillbilly rivalry, "The Martins and the Coys" has been edited out of the DVD release (as has a title card for "A Music Fantasy in Ten Parts"). Reportedly, the animation to "All the Cats Join In" has also been altered, to tone down the larger breasts on some female characters.

Three *Silly Symphonies* cartoons with musical elements have been added to the disc as a bonus: "The Band Concert" (1935, the first Mickey Mouse cartoon in color); "Farmyard Symphony" (1938); and "Music Land" (1935). The picture transfer is excellent given the age of the source material, and fans of music, shorts, and Disney will want to make certain this is a part of their collection.

SPECIAL FEATURES "Making of" Featurette • Commentary Track • Cast Filmographies • Character Bios • Character and Art Galleries • Production Notes • Deleted Scenes • Storyboards • Trailer • Promotional Footage • Music Video • Outtakes • Games • DVD-ROM Features • Other Title Trailers • Inserts: Liner Notes • Other Title Trailers TECHNICAL FEATURES Fullscreen (1.33:1) • Subtitles/CC: Eng. • Languages: Eng., Span. dub • Sound: Dolby Digital 5.1, DTS • Keepcase • 1 Disc • Region 1, 4 GENRE & RATING Music/Animals/Adventure • Rated G

Mama, Do You Love Me?

Sony Wonder, 1999, 40 mins., #LVD 49507. Directed by Lee Young Gil, Shin Sung Ho. Written by Betty Birney. Based on the book written by Barbara M. Joose and illustrations of Barbara Lavallee.

NOTE: This DVD arrived too late for a full review. The following text is promotional copy provided by the releasing company:

"In a distant northern land, a little Inuit girl asks, 'Mama, do you love me?' The answer makes for a charming tale of affection, adventure, and wonder in this magically animated adaptation of the award-winning children's book. Set amid an arctic realm of spellbinding beauty, the story follows young Nyla as she disobeys her mother—and journeys from village to ice floe in search of her wayward puppy. But as Nyla discovers, no matter what mischief a child gets into, a mother's love is unconditional and enduring. With delightful details of Inuit life and breathtaking fantasy sequences, this universal story of the bond between mother and child will capture the imaginations—and the hearts—of your entire family."

SPECIAL FEATURES Author Bio • Sing-Along • Game • Other Title Trailers TECHNICAL FEATURES Fullscreen (1.33:1) • Subtitles/CC: Eng. • Languages: Eng. • Sound: Dolby Digital • Keepcase • 1 Disc • Region 1 GENRE & RATING Family/Arctic • Not Rated (Kids)

Man in the Iron Mask, The [Collector's Edition]

Digital Versatile Disc, 2000, 53 mins., #170. Animation Directed by Warwick Gilbert. Screenplay by Keith Dewhurst. Based on the novel by Alexander Dumas.

The famed Musketeers are nearing the end of their careers, but one final grand adventure awaits them. They learn that King Louis XIV of France has a twin brother, and that one of them is imprisoned within the walls of a dungeon. One brother is good and kind, while the other is unpleasant and cruel. Questions of loyalty and honor abound as the Musketeers must make a choice as to which brother they will help keep on the throne of France.

A 1985 production of Burbank Films Australia, this is a fairly straightforward telling of Dumas' classic tale, though it has far too many cutesy moments early on, and the entrance of the Musketeers takes much too long. There is one very nice sequence thirty minutes in: a hallucinogenic dance segment that would seem at home in a Baz Luhrman feature.

SPECIAL FEATURES Author Bio • Game TECHNICAL FEATURES Fullscreen (1.33:1) • Languages: Eng. • Sound: Dolby Digital

5.1, DTS • Keepcase • 1 Disc • Region All GENRE & RATING Historical/Adventure • Not Rated (Kids)

Many Adventures of Winnie the Pooh, The [25th Anniversary Edition]

Disney, 2002, 74 mins., #24452. Directed by Wolfgang Reitherman, John Lounsbery. Story by Larry Clemmons, Vance Gerry, Ken Anderson, Ted Berman, Ralph Wright, Xavier Atencio, Julius Svendsen, Eric Cleworth. Based on the books by A.A. Milne.

Winnie the Pooh lives in the Hundred Acre Wood with his friends Tigger, Eeyore, Piglet, Owl, Kanga, Roo, Rabbit, and Gopher. Their friend is the boy Christopher Robin, but the animals often get into trouble and adventures without him, especially when Pooh is on the search for more honey. That nose for sweets gets Pooh in trouble with a hive of bees in "Winnie the Pooh and the Honey Tree." Then, strong winds blow and Tigger bounces into town in "Winnie the Pooh and the Blustery Day." Finally, winter comes to the woods in "Winnie the Pooh and Tigger Too."

Milne's lovable characters make the jump from children's books to the feature film screen in this 1977 compilation film. The feature actually gathered three previously produced shorts (1966, 1968, and 1974 respectively) and combined them with new material. In their original release as theatrical shorts, "Blustery Day" won an Academy Award, and "Tigger Too" was nominated for one.

According to reports, almost half of Disney's current licensing empire is built on the *Winnie the Pooh* franchise, and it all started with these ultracharming stories. While some purists may carp that the character designs deviate from Milne and artist Ernest Shepard's originals, it's clear that the infectious sense of fun and camaraderie that Milne created has made it to the screen.

The DVD is packed with ten special features, including sneak peeks at two upcoming *Pooh* projects, as well as a bonus short film from 1983, "Winnie the Pooh and a Day for Eeyore." Not only is this disc appropriate for all ages, it's something that viewers young and old will enjoy.

SPECIAL FEATURES "Making of" Featurette • Pop-Up Facts • Character and Art Galleries • Music Video • Sing-Alongs • Games • Storybook • Other Title Trailers TECHNICAL FEATURES Fullscreen (1.33:1) • Subtitles/CC: Eng., Fren., Span. • Languages: Eng., Fren. dub, Span. dub • Sound: Dolby Digital 5.1 • Keepcase • 1 Disc • Region 1, 4 GENRE & RATING Animals/Family • Rated G

Marriage

Anime Works, 2001, 60 mins., #AWDVD-0115 Directed by Kazuhiro Ozawa. Script by Tesuro Amino, Akira Hitani.

Shizuka is one of a group of friends who've known each other since high school, and who now work together. As each of them searches for love, Maki enters the shy Shizuka into a dating service known as "The Wedding Club," to find a suitable mate. Shizuka doesn't initially meet the man of her dreams, but another man may be just around the corner. . . .

In a second story, five sisters, each a year apart, are either engaged or already married. All except Kiyomi, who can't seem to find the right man. Coworker Mikimaro asks Kiyomi out on a date, and wants to ask her to marry him, but Kiyomi's sisters' overeager meddling may put too much strain on the relationship.

These two OVAs were originally released in 1996, utilizing characters and situations based on a PC video game (and also used in a science fiction setting in *Sailor Victory*). The settings are straight-on romance, with no fantastic elements. The designs are all realistic, though there are a couple of super-deformed sequences. *Marriage* should appeal most to all hopeless romantics in the audience.

SPECIAL FEATURES Other Title Trailers TECHNICAL FEATURES Fullscreen (1.33:1) • Subtitles/CC: Eng. • Languages: Jap., Eng. dub • Sound: Dolby Digital 2.0 • Keepcase • 1 Disc • Region 1 GENRE & RATING Romance/Girls • Rated 13+

Martian Successor Nadesico: Chronicle 1— Invasion! [#1]

ADV Films, 2000, 100 mins., #DND/001. Directed by Tatsuo Sato. Script by Sho Aikawa, Naruhisa Arakawa. Based on the manga series by Kia Asamiya in *Monthly Shonen Ace*.

In 2195, Earth is colonizing outer space. Their settlements on the moon and Mars are attacked and nearly destroyed by invaders from Jupiter. The Jovian lizard creatures destroy most of the Earth Forces space fleet and then set their sights on a nearly defenseless Earth. A large corporation, Negral, takes charge of defending the Earth. Utilizing new gravitic technology, Negral creates a prototype battleship called *Nadesico*. The ship is piloted by twenty-year-old strategist Yurika Misamaru and an unorthodox ragtag crew of misfits and outcasts, including: Akito, a young pilot turned chef turned pilot again when circumstances force him into a giant defense mecha ship; Ryoko, a tomboy pilot with a crush on Akito; Ruri, a mysterious eleven-year-old computer genius sold to Negral as an infant; Minato, a former secretary; and Megumi, a former anime actress turned Bridge Communications Officer. Together, this odd group fights to protect the Earth from invaders.

Created in 1996, *Martian Successor Nadesico* is an epic dramatic comedy space soap opera spanning twenty-six episodes, one OVA, and a manga series. What makes this different from other sci-fi anime is the depth of characterizations: the good guys have dark secrets, the bad guys have redeeming qualities, and you can't judge any book by its cover. Also unique is the fact that standard themes such as loyalty, friendship, betrayal, and trust are presented in a non-clichéd fashion. Viewers will likely enjoy the fact that some of the crew are otaku (anime and manga fans), arguing and laughing over classic anime shows. This DVD volume contains episodes #1–4. [JMC]

SPECIAL FEATURES Character Bios • Translation Notes • Trailer • Clean Credits • Other Title Trailers TECHNICAL FEATURES Fullscreen (1.33:1) • Subtitles/CC: Eng. • Languages: Jap., Eng. dub • Sound: Dolby Digital 2.0 • Keepcase • 1 Disc • Region 1 GENRE & RATING Robots/Science Fiction • Rated 12+

Martian Successor Nadesico: Mission to Mars [#2]

ADV Films, 2000, 100 mins., #DND/002. Directed by Tatsuo Sato. Script by Takeshi Shudo, Sho Aikawa. Based on the manga series by Kia Asamiya in *Monthly Shonen Ace*.

Yurika is overseeing funeral services for the victims of the Jovian Chulip attacks as the *Nadesico* prepares to search for and rescue humans still trapped on Mars. The *Nadesico* crew discovers the gateways the Jovians created, and attempts to use one to return quickly to Earth, but it takes several months to pass through the gateway. During that time, Negral and the United Earth Forces team up and create new technologies, including a sister ship, the *Cosmos*. Now *Nadesico* has been reassigned to the Force's Far Eastern command, but what dangers await them there?

This DVD contains episodes #5–8 and introduces a few designers of the *Nadesico*, who talk about the inner workings of the ship and its capacities. [JMC]

SPECIAL FEATURES Character Bios • Trailer • Clean Credits • Other Title Trailers TECHNICAL FEATURES Fullscreen (1.33:1) • Subtitles/CC: Eng. • Languages: Jap., Eng. dub • Sound: Dolby Digital 2.0 • Keepcase • 1 Disc • Region 1 GENRE & RATING Robots/Science Fiction • Rated 12+

Martian Successor Nadesico: Danger Zones [#3]

ADV Films, 2001, 100 mins., #DND/003. Directed by Tatsuo Sato. Script by Naruhisa Arakawa, Satoru Akahori, Hiroyuki Kawasaki, Takeshi Shudo. Based on the manga series by Kia Asamiya in *Monthly Shonen Ace*.

Love is in the air as three women compete for Akito's attention, but is the way to his heart truly through his stomach, or will their attempts only bring indigestion, not affection? Speaking of indigestion, the crew is sick to their stomachs when they discover a new Jovian weapon: a gravity wave railgun that has the potential to destroy almost anything in its path. Will the *Nadesico* be able to avoid that wave, or will it be wiped out? Plus, the United Earth Forces think a computer glitch in the Nadesico is causing serious malfunctions, and they want to wipe the memory banks and destroy the ship's self-awareness. Horrified, Ruri appeals to Akito to help her save their sentient craft.

This DVD contains episodes #9–12, which use comedic satire with equal amounts of drama. [JMC]

SPECIAL FEATURES Character Bios • Trailer • Clean Credits • Other Title Trailers TECHNICAL FEATURES Fullscreen (1.33:1) • Subtitles/CC: Eng. • Languages: Jap., Eng. dub • Sound: Dolby Digital 2.0 • Keepcase • 1 Disc • Region 1 GENRE & RATING Robots/Science Fiction • Rated 12+

Martian Successor Nadesico: Paradigm Shifts [#4]

ADV Films, 2001, 100 mins., #DND/004. Directed by Tatsuo Sato. Scripts by Sho Aikawa, Tatsuo Sato, Mamoru Kanbe, Studio Yu. Based on the manga series by Kia Asamiya in *Monthly Shonen Ace*.

It's Christmas, and besides decking the halls, the military wants to deck the crew in fatigues and have everyone join up . . . well, all except Akito. While others are reminiscing about events that led to them being on the *Nadesico* and thinking about Christmas cheer, Akito's holiday gift is getting booted from the *Nadesico*. Megumi can't stand to see him leave and decides life on *Nadesico* isn't worth living without Akito, so she ditches the crew and joins him in civilian life. But Akito's civilian stint might be short-lived, as other sources have plans for the young pilot. Plus, secrets are revealed about the Jovian nation and a government conspiracy that will shock and stun the people of Earth.

This shocking DVD contains episodes #13–16, which further the story of the Jovians and reveal more about Akito's struggles to find his place on Earth. [JMC]

SPECIAL FEATURES Character Bios • Trailer • Clean Credits • Other Title Trailers TECHNICAL FEATURES Fullscreen (1.33:1) • Subtitles/CC: Eng. • Languages: Jap., Eng. dub • Sound: Dolby Digital 2.0 • Keepcase • 1 Disc • Region 1 GENRE & RATING Robots/Science Fiction • Rated 12+

Martian Successor Nadesico: Secrets and Lies [#5]

ADV Films, 2001, 125 mins., #DND/005. Directed by Tatsuo Sato. Scripts by Hiroyuki Kawasaki, Takeshi Sendo, Naruhisa Arakawa, Mitsuyasu Sakai, Sho Aikawa. Based on the manga series by Kia Asamiya in *Monthly Shonen Ace*.

With the Jovians revealed to be related to the human race, the *Nadesico* and its crew must now decide whether to continue the war, or find another solution. While the crew worries about these choices, Ruri learns the secret of her own past, and details about her connection with the mysterious place called Peaceland. Meanwhile the rest of the crew has a talent show to blow off steam, but things get weird when crewmembers start seeing ghosts!

This character-driven penultimate DVD contains episodes #17–21, adding insight into the precocious Ruri, and bringing closure to the issues surrounding the death of an early crew member. [JMC]

SPECIAL FEATURES Other Title Trailers TECHNICAL FEATURES Fullscreen (1.33:1) • Subtitles/CC: Eng. • Languages: Jap., Eng. dub • Sound: Dolby Digital 2.0 • Keepcase • 1 Disc • Region 1 GENRE & RATING Robots/Science Fiction • Rated 12+

Martian Successor Nadesico: Endgame [#6]

ADV Films, 2001, 125 mins., #DND/006. Directed by Tatsuo Sato. Scripts by Naruhisa Arakawa, Sho Aikawa, Tatsuo Sato, Hiroyuki Kawasaki. Based on the manga series by Kia Asamiya in *Monthly Shonen Ace*.

You never saw it coming. At least the crew of the *Nadesico* didn't: When a trusted pilot reveals a shocking secret, most of the crew quits the *Nadesico* on the spot. However, with the conflict raging and an outpost on Mars holding the key to the defeat of the Jovians and the end of the war, the remaining crew hijacks the *Nadesico* and sets off to Mars with a peaceful goal in mind. But with everyone against them, do they stand a chance?

This final DVD contains episodes #22–26, bringing a fitting end to a fantastic journey. [JMC]

SPECIAL FEATURES Other Title Trailers TECHNICAL FEATURES Fullscreen (1.33:1) • Subtitles/CC: Eng. • Languages: Jap., Eng. dub • Sound: Dolby Digital 2.0 • Keepcase • 1 Disc • Region 1 GENRE & RATING Robots/Science Fiction • Rated 12+

Martian Successor Nadesico: The Complete Chronicles

ADV Films, 2002, 650 mins., #DND/100.

This multikeepcase set includes the six *Martian Successor Nadesico* discs exactly as they appeared in the individual editions. See individual entries for the Special and Technical Features listings.

TECHNICAL FEATURES Multikeepcase • 6 Discs • Region 1 GENRE & RATING Robots/Science Fiction • Rated 12+

Mary Poppins [Widescreen]

Disney, 1998, 139 mins., #13854.

This DVD was not available for review. It is on moratorium. The *Gold Collection* version features the same movie, but with many added bonuses.

Mary Poppins [Gold Collection]

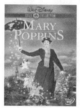

Disney, 2001, 139 mins., #20221. Directed by Robert Stevenson. Animation Directed by Hamilton Luske. Screenplay by Bill Walsh, Don DaGradi. Based on the book series by P. L. Travers.

When a London banker needs a new nanny for his pair of mischievous children, who should blow into town but the magical Mary Poppins? Full of songs and fun, Mary teaches the banker and his children that life can be an adventure, and even dull chores can be fun if one looks at them in the right frame of mind. Among Mary's magical treats is a segment wherein chimneysweep Bert dances with animated penguins, and Mary wins an animated horse race on an merry-go-round steed!

Disney's 1964 feature film starred Julie Andrews and Dick Van Dyke, and garnered five Academy Award wins out of thirteen nominations! Although most of the film is live-action, the animated segments stand out; characters interact fully with the animation, predating similar scenes in *Bedknobs and Broomsticks* and the entire feature film *Who Framed Roger Rabbit?*

The DVD transfer is one of the Disney company's best, and this is one of Uncle Walt's most magical films (many critics rate it as *the* best of his career). Combined with a slate of extra features—which provide both a vintage and modern view of the making of *Mary Poppins*—this DVD is, as they say, supercalifragilisticexpialidocious!

SPECIAL FEATURES "Making of" Featurette • Vintage Film Premiere Footage • Trailer • Game • Other Title Trailers TECHNICAL FEATURES Widescreen (1.85:1) • Subtitles/CC: Eng. • Languages: Eng., Fren. dub, Span. dub • Sound: Dolby Digital 5.1 • Keepcase • 1 Disc • Region 1, 4 GENRE & RATING Live/Music • Rated G

Masquerade ☞ see Mature/Adult Section

Master Q 2001

Tai Seng, 2001, 103 mins., #HF30108D. Directed by Herman Yau. Screenplay by Tsui Hark, Li Man Choi, Ray Szeto, Herman Yau. Based on the comic strip characters created by Alphonso Wong.

Cartoonist Mr. Wong decides to take a break and go on a fishing vacation, accompanied by Mr. Chun, one of his characters. This leaves the conservative Master Q and the dumpy Potato in a bit of a predicament. They're soon fired, and get in trouble with Kam, who is trying to bribe Fung, the man whom he believes will be police commissioner some day. When Master Q and Potato accidentally cause Fung and his girlfriend, Miss Cheung, to lose their memories, Kam takes Fung under his wing to brainwash him. Now, Master Q and Potato must try to undo all the trouble they've caused.

The above synopsis is crucial to any viewer who may try to figure out exactly what is going on in this film. Perhaps it's the cultural clashes that made it so inscrutable to my Western aesthetics, but I was very confused. The *Master Q* characters were created for comic strips in 1962 by Alphonso Wong, and they remain popular today in comics and merchandising all over China. The film uses a combination of puppets and CGI animation to have the trio (Master Q, Potato, and Mr. Chun) interact with the live-action characters, à la *Who Framed Roger Rabbit?* The effect is startlingly realistic, and is often better than the CGI work being produced for today's Hollywood films.

The DVD features a nice array of extras, including a behind-the-scenes short that illuminates how the film was shot. While some of the feature's slapstick comedy will translate for any audience, the actual story might leave viewers scratching their heads.

SPECIAL FEATURES "Making of" Featurette • Cast & Crew Filmographies • Synopsis • Trailer TECHNICAL FEATURES Widescreen (1.85:1 enhanced for 16x9) • Subtitles/CC: Eng., Chin. • Languages: Cant., Mand. • Sound: Dolby Digital 5.1, DTS • Keepcase • 1 Disc • Region All GENRE & RATING Live/CGI/Comedy • Not Rated (Teens)

Masters of Russian Animation, Vol. 1

Image, 2000, 133 mins., #ID5525FJDVD.

The Russian animation industry officially began in 1912, when Vladislav Starevish created a short film about insects. The form flourished following the Revolution, particularly in 1924, when Lenin authorized a series of animated Communist propaganda shorts. Following a festival of Walt Disney films in the 1930s, Moscow's Soyuzmultfilm Studios was founded in 1936, and animators had a home base from which to work. Early films were aimed at younger audiences, but beginning in the late 1950s—after Nikita Kruschev came into power—animation became more adult.

The *Masters of Russian Animation* project features films produced between 1962 and 1990, all of which were originally seen on the big screen, and many of which won film awards. The stories and styles vary widely: some use traditional cel animation, while others add live elements, collage, colored pencil, stop-motion, or other techniques. As might be expected, many of the films have subtle political messages, though some are amazingly overt as well. Some are humorous, others are musical, and still others are surreal.

This DVD features ten shorts from 1962 to 1968, ranging from one to twenty minutes in length: "Story of One Crime" (1962); "Man in the Frame" (1966); "My Green Crocodile" (1966); "There Lived Kozyavin" (1966); "Mountain of Dinosaurs" (1967); "Passion of Spies" (1967); "Glass Harmonica" (1968); "Ball of Wool" (1968); "Singing Teacher" (1968);" and "Film Film Film" (1968).

SPECIAL FEATURES Liner Notes on Foldout Cover TECHNICAL FEATURES Widescreen: Various Ratios • Subtitles/CC: Eng. • Languages: Russ. • Sound: Dolby Digital 2.0 • Snapcase • 1 Disc • Region 1 GENRE & RATING Anthology • Not Rated (Teens)

Masters of Russian Animation, Vol. 2

Image, 2000, 125 mins., #ID5526FJDVD.

Twelve more short films from 1969 to 1978 are presented in this volume, ranging from nine to seventeen minutes in length. Titles include: "Seasons" (1969); "Ballerina on the Boat" (1969); "Armoire" (1970); "Battle at Kerzhenets" (1971); "Butterfly" (1972); "Island" (1973); "Fox and Rabbit" (1973); "Heron and Crane" (1974); "Hedgehog in the Fog" (1975); "Crane Feathers" (1977); "Firing Range" (1975); and "Contact" (1978).

All of these films have been digitally restored from

new 35mm prints, though some show signs of wear or age. Of this selection the standout is "Battle at Kerzhenets," an astonishing piece done as if animated by the classical art masters. Other excellent selections include the surreal "Butterfly," the tapestry-like "Fox and Rabbit," the Japanese puppet short "Crane Feathers," and the pseudo-realist "Firing Range."

SPECIAL FEATURES Liner Notes on Foldout Cover TECHNICAL FEATURES Widescreen: Various Ratios • Subtitles/CC: Eng. • Languages: Russ. • Sound: Dolby Digital 1.0 • Snapcase • 1 Disc • Region 1 GENRE & RATING Anthology • Not Rated (Teens)

Masters of Russian Animation, Vol. 3

Image, 2000, 140 mins., #ID5527FJDVD.

Eleven more short films from 1979 to 1985 are presented in this volume, ranging from seven to thirty minutes in length. Titles include: "Tale of Tales" (1979); "Hunt" (1979); "Last Hunt" (1982); "There Once Was a Dog" (1982); "Travels of an Ant" (1983); "Lion and Ox" (1983); "Wolf and Calf" (1984); "Cabaret" (1984); "Old Stair" (1985); "King's Sandwich" (1985); and "About Sidorov Vova" (1985).

Top-notch entries in this set include the multiple award-winning "Tale of Tales"; the precursor to *A Bug's Life* called "Travels of an Ant"; an imaginative visit into a little boy's fantasies in "Old Stair"; and an adaptation of an A.A. Milne poem in "King's Sandwich."

SPECIAL FEATURES Liner Notes on Foldout Cover TECHNICAL FEATURES Widescreen: Various Ratios • Subtitles/CC: Eng. • Languages: Russ. • Sound: Dolby Digital 2.0 • Snapcase • 1 Disc • Region 1 GENRE & RATING Anthology • Not Rated (Teens)

Masters of Russian Animation, Vol. 4

Image, 2000, 141 mins., #ID5528FJDVD.

Twelve more short films from 1986 to 1990 are presented in this volume, each ranging from seven to twenty-one minutes in length. Titles include: "Door" (1986); "Boy Is a Boy" (1986); "Liberated Don Quixote" (1987); "Martinko" (1987); "Big Underground Ball" (1987); "Cat and Clown" (1988); "Dream" (1988); "Kele" (1988); "Alter Ego" (1989); "Girlfriend" (1989); "Croak x Croak" (1990); and "Cat and Company" (1990).

The films in this set were made around the time of the Soviet regime's collapse, an event that cut funding to the Soyuzmultfilm Studio. Of the offerings here, the stop-motion film "Door" is best-known, and its story of an apartment building full of people who won't go through

an open door was a satirical allegory for the plight of the Russian people. Other shorts recall the work of painters and illustrators, as well as surreal animator Jan Svankmajer. And prepare to be wowed by the detailed stop motion work on display in "Liberated Don Quixote," which rivals almost anything produced by Tim Burton, Henry Selick, or Will Vinton Studios.

SPECIAL FEATURES Liner Notes on Foldout Cover TECHNICAL FEATURES Widescreen: Various Ratios • Subtitles/CC: Eng. • Languages: Russ. • Sound: Dolby Digital 2.0 • Snapcase • 1 Disc • Region 1 GENRE & RATING Anthology • Not Rated (Teens)

Maze

Software Sculptors, 2000, 85 mins., #SSDVD-6080. Directed by Iku Suzuki. Script by Masashi Noro, Katsumi Hasegawa. Based on the stories by Satoru Akahori.

In a mysterious and magical land, a group of people is on the run from the Jaina Holy Group, which has overthrown the land's royalty. Princess Mill is among the refugees, and when she runs into a young girl named Maze, things start to get strange; at night, Maze transforms into a lecherous man. The group travels to Babylon to seek refuge, but they're falling into a trap.

This single disc includes the two 1996 OVA stories, as well as the first episode of the later TV series (also included in the box set). *Maze* is exceedingly silly most of the time, with lots of super-deformed action and goofy antics. There is also a lot of semi- and full-nudity and a bit of violence, almost enough to rate a higher age rating.

SPECIAL FEATURES Other Title Trailers • DVD-ROM Features: Art, Scripts TECHNICAL FEATURES Fullscreen (1.33:1) • Subtitles/CC: Eng. • Languages: Jap., Eng. dub • Sound: Dolby Digital 2.0 • Keepcase • 1 Disc • Region 1–6 GENRE & RATING Fantasy/Comedy • Rated 13+

Maze [DVD Collection—Box Set]

Software Sculptors, 2001, 625 mins., #SSDVD-6180. Directed by Iku Suzuki. Script by Yasunori Yamada, Sumio Uetake, Katsumi Hasegawa, Tsuyoshi Tamai. Based on the stories by Satoru Akahori.

Maze is just a nice college girl who got sucked into another world. Now she can shoot energy from her hands and operate a large robot called Dulger. Unfortunately there is a teensy-weensy side effect. When the sun goes down Maze changes from a shy, ultranice girl to a testosterone-charged man who hits on every girl around him.

Our gender-bending hero runs into Princess Mill and saves her life. So, of course, Mill falls head over heels in love with Maze . . . both versions. But war is brewing in this medieval/futuristic world, so Maze must help the princess return to her throne (and maybe get back home in the bargain).

Released in the late 1980s, this television series seems to have been influenced by several other Japanese animated stories. Unfortunately it ends up being a mishmash of plot and style. The comedy often falls flat and the adventure isn't adventurous. The basic premise is pretty amusing, but the whole thing gets stretched out over twenty-six episodes and it's been spread pretty thin by the final few installments. It has a bouncy end theme, but that's about the best part.

The complete *Maze* television series is on four discs. The special features include an entertaining behind-the-scenes documentary with the English dub cast. There's also a montage of Princess Mill saying her favorite line (in English); It is one of the funniest moments in the entire box set. This series has some heavy homosexual overtones, and lots of heterosexual groping and ogling, so concerned parents are hereby warned.

SPECIAL FEATURES "Making of" Featurette • Character Bios • Character and Art Galleries • Compilation Clip • DVD-ROM Features: Art, Scripts • Other Title Trailers • Easter Egg TECHNICAL FEATURES Fullscreen (1.33:1) • Subtitles/CC: Eng. • Languages: Jap., Eng. dub • Sound: Dolby Digital 2.0 • Cardboard Box with 4 Keepcases • 4 Discs • Region All GENRE & RATING Fantasy/Comedy • Rated 13+

Mecha Masters: Explosive Anime Classics [Box Set]

U.S. Manga Corps, 2002, 296 mins., #USMD2235.

This box set includes the *M.D. Geist: Director's Cut/Death Force, Genocyber: The Collection,* and *Cybernetics Guardian* discs exactly as they appeared in the individual keepcase editions. See individual entries for the Special and Technical Features listings.

It also features a fourth bonus keepcase that contains two CDs of the soundtracks to *M.D. Geist* and *Genocyber.*

TECHNICAL FEATURES Cardboard Box with 2 Keepcases and 2 Multikeepcases • 6 Discs • Region All GENRE & RATING Robots/Science Fiction/Action • Rated 13+ and 16+

Medabots: Transport Metabee! [#1]

ADV Films, 2002, 125 mins., #DME/001. Directed by Tensai Okamura.

Ten-year-old Ikki Tenryo is a poor child who gets picked on by the school bullies, doesn't get along with all his teachers, and dreams of someday owning an expensive Medabot and fighting in the World Robattle Tournament. However with the robots being so expensive, it looks as if his dream will never come true. A shop owner offers him a beat-up Medabot for next to nothing, but the 'bot still won't work unless Ikki can get an expensive medal to act as the Medabots brain. Ikki's dreams seem dashed, until he chances upon a Rare Medal, one that just happens to be the key to every Medabots' soul! Now the opportunity to become a Medabot fighter may be within his grasp. By challenging others to battles and besting their Medabots with his skilled Medabilities, it looks as if Ikki and his robot, the Metabee, might very well become champions.

Medabots began life as a popular computer game before being transformed into a 1999 televisions series and a serialized manga for Comic BomBom. In 2001, Fox Kids brought the series to the U.S. as part of its Saturday morning line-up. This DVD contains episodes #1–5 and introduces the main cast, plus the reasons why Ikki wants to be in the World Robattle Tournament.

The five episodes presented on this disc are: "Stung By a Metabee"; "Return of the Screws"; "Running Scared"; "The Legendary Medafighter"; and "The Old Man and the Sea Monster." [JMC]

SPECIAL FEATURES Character Bios • Other Title Trailers TECHNICAL FEATURES Fullscreen (1.33:1) • Languages: Eng. • Sound: Dolby Digital 2.0 • Keepcase • 1 Disc • Region 1 GENRE & RATING Robots/Science Fiction • Not Rated (Kids)

Medabots: Medabots, Robattle! [#2]

ADV Films, 2002, 100 mins., #DME/002. Directed by Tensai Okamura.

NOTE: This DVD arrived too late for a full review. The following text is promotional copy provided by the releasing company:

"Ikki knew it would take a lot of hard work and determination to get the chance to compete in the World Robattle Tournament, but he had no idea it would be this tough! Not only does the scrappy ten-year-old and his pet robot Metabee face challenges from other Medafighters, but they must also uncover the secret of the mysterious Medabot, the Phantom Renegade, and battle the bullying Screws and the dastardly Rubberobo

Gang, too! To make matters worse, the annual citywide Robattle competition is right around the corner, and Ikki and Metabee don't stand a chance of winning if they can't stop arguing long enough to work together!"

This disc contains episodes #6–9.

SPECIAL FEATURES Character Bios • Other Title Trailers TECHNICAL FEATURES Fullscreen (1.33:1) • Languages: Eng. • Sound: Dolby Digital 2.0 • Keepcase • 1 Disc • Region 1 GENRE & RATING Robots/Science Fiction • Not Rated (Kids)

Medabots: Time to Robattle! [#3]

ADV Films, 2002, 100 mins., #DME/003. Directed by Tensai Okamura.

NOTE: This DVD arrived too late for a full review. The following text is promotional copy provided by the releasing company:

"Ikki and Metabee are beginning to come to terms with each other. That's a good thing, because the Rubberobo Gang is stepping up their activities, and it's up to Ikki and his friends to stop them from taking over the world, or at least turning the neighborhood into a new-wave housing development. If that's not enough the local Parent-Teacher Organization has decided that Medabot's are a bad influence on the kids and is confiscating any Medabot found at school. That's not good, because the real leader of the Rubberobo Gang makes his appearance at last. Will the introduction of Dr. Meta-Evil turn the bumbling Rubberobo Gang into successful criminals?"

This disc contains episodes #10–13.

SPECIAL FEATURES Character Bios • Other Title Trailers TECHNICAL FEATURES Fullscreen (1.33:1) • Languages: Eng. • Sound: Dolby Digital 2.0 • Keepcase • 1 Disc • Region 1 GENRE & RATING Robots/Science Fiction • Not Rated (Kids)

Medabots: Medabot Wars [#4]

ADV Films, 2002, 100 mins., #DME/004. Directed by Tensai Okamura.

NOTE: This DVD arrived too late for a full review. The following text is promotional copy provided by the releasing company:

"As the Rubberobo Gang under the direction of Dr. Meta-Evil step up their plans for World Domination, Ikki and his friends are learning more about the history and origin of the Medabots. Dr. Aki takes them on a tour of Medabot Corporation as part of their education. But things get rough when Seaslug infiltrates the company in search of Rare Medals. Things have barely settled down when Rokusho becomes convinced that Dr. Aki is

responsible for killing his former medafighter. Will Metabee be able to save Dr. Aki from Rokusho's mistake? More importantly, will the distraction prove disastrous for all of them when the Rubberobo Gang attacks yet again?"

This disc contains episodes #14–17.

SPECIAL FEATURES Character Bios • Other Title Trailers TECHNICAL FEATURES Fullscreen (1.33:1) • Languages: Eng. • Sound: Dolby Digital 2.0 • Keepcase • 1 Disc • Region 1 GENRE & RATING Robots/Science Fiction • Not Rated (Kids)

Medabots: Use the Medaforce! [#5]

ADV Films, 2002, 100 mins., #DME/005. Directed by Tensai Okamura.

NOTE: This DVD arrived too late for a full review. The following text is promotional copy provided by the releasing company:

"The World Robattle Tournament is fast approaching and only the top three medafighters from each country advance to the Tournament. Guess who's on the list when the rankings are announced for Japan? The mysterious Space Medafighter X is ranked First; Koiji and Sumilidon are ranked Second; and to their surprise Ikki and Metabee are ranked Third! If they can hold on to that ranking for a few days, they'll be representing Japan in the Tournament, but it's not going to easy with every medafighter in Japan gunning for them. And the Rubberobo Gang isn't about to give up their plans for World Domination just because Ikki's got other things on his mind right now."

This disc contains episodes #18–21.

SPECIAL FEATURES Character Bios • Other Title Trailers TECHNICAL FEATURES Fullscreen (1.33:1) • Languages: Eng. • Sound: Dolby Digital 2.0 • Keepcase • 1 Disc • Region 1 GENRE & RATING Robots/Science Fiction • Not Rated (Kids)

Megazone 23, Vol. 1

Image, 1999, 81 mins., #ID5550SEDVD.

This DVD was not available for review. It is out of print.

MeiKing ☞ see Mature/Adult Section

Melody Time [Gold Collection]

Disney, 2000, 75 mins., #19603. Directed by Clyde Geronimi, Wilfred Jackson, Hamilton Luske, Jack Kinney. Story by Winston Hibler, Erdman Penner, Harry Reeves, Homer Brightman, Ken Anderson, Ted Sears, Joe Rinaldi, Bill Cottrell, Art Scott, Jesse Marsh, Bob Moore, John Walbridge. "Little Toot" based on the story by Hardie Gramatky.

Seven musical animated short films make up this animated feature, with Donald Duck starring in the Latin-flavored "Blame It on the Samba." Other famous entries are "The Legend of Johnny Appleseed" and "Pecos Bill," both of which received much television play ("Johnny Appleseed" also shows up on the *Disney's American Legends* DVD). Other segments include the adventures of a mischievous tugboat in "Little Toot"; plus "Once Upon a Wintertime"; "Bumble Boogie"; "Trees"; and "Blue Shadows on the Trail."

This is Disney's third music-based anthology followed *Fantasia* and *Make Mine Music*, but this 1948 feature was the least popular of the lot, even if the set of stories and styles of animation are as impressive as its predecessors. The musical numbers include songs by The Andrews Sisters and Dennis Day, and Roy Rogers makes a live-action appearance, telling the tale of Pecos Bill. The animation on "Pecos Bill" has been digitally altered—removing Bill's cigarette—to make the short fit into today's more politically correct climate.

The DVD also features three extra cartoons: "Casey Bats Again" (1954); Academy Award–nominated "Lambert the Sheepish Lion" (1952); and "Donald Applecore" (1952). As usual, Disney does a fine job with the picture and sound on this DVD.

SPECIAL FEATURES Other Title Trailers TECHNICAL FEATURES Fullscreen (1.33:1) • Subtitles/CC: Eng., Span. • Languages: Eng., Fren. dub, Span. dub • Sound: Dolby Digital 2.0 • Keepcase • 1 Disc • Region 1, 4 GENRE & RATING Anthology/Music • Rated PG

Metal Fighter Miku

Anime Works, 2001, 325 mins., #EFDVD-8901. Directed by Akiyuki Shinbo. Story Written by Daisaku Ogawa.

In the year 2061, a new form of entertainment has hit the sports world. Neo Wrestling is the hottest thing on the airwaves, with gorgeous girls in armored mecha suits getting it on tag-team style. Miku is the newest member of the Pretty Four, a team that also includes Ginko, Sayaka, and Nana. Despite having a drunken coach, the team sets out to beat their main opponent, Team Sapphire. Along the way, Miku learns some important lessons about life and combat thanks to her idol, grand champion Metal Fighter Aquamarine.

The plot for this 1994 television series is silly, but certainly no more silly than those story lines that take place in "real" professional wrestling. The characters are all a bit standard, and yet the writers do attempt to give each of them some personality. Even the adversaries of the bunch get some needed character development. The animation is pleasantly mainstream, colorful and energetic without assaulting the eyes.

The two-DVD set contains the entire television series, though, unfortunately, there are no extras. Despite the 3+ age rating, the coach's drunkenness and the action/violence quota make this more appropriate for older kids. But if you like wrestling, cute girls, and armored suits, this one has it all wrapped up in a comfortable package.

SPECIAL FEATURES Other Title Trailers TECHNICAL FEATURES Fullscreen (1.33:1) • Subtitles/CC: Eng. • Languages: Jap., Eng. dub • Sound: Dolby Digital 2.0 • Keepcase • 1 Disc • Region 1 GENRE & RATING Wrestling/Girls/Action • Rated 3+

Metropolis

Columbia/TriStar, 2002, 109 mins., #07796. Directed by Rintaro . Screenplay by Katsushiro Otomo. Based on the manga series by Osamu Tezuka.

In a modern megalopolis populated by both humans and robots, the evil Duke Red plots to gain control of the city. To accomplish this, the mad Dr. Lawton has created Tima, an android clone of Duke's dead daughter capable of controlling the city's computer systems from a throne within the Ziggurat, a soaring tower that dominates the Metropolis skyline. Duke's adopted son Rock hates robots and resents his father's plan to install Tima as ruler of Metropolis. Along with his uncle, an aging detective, young Kenichi arrives in the city and soon finds himself lost in a maze of subterranean levels beneath Metropolis with an innocent, just-activated Tima. The two become close friends, but when Rock's violent plots and Duke's visions of grandeur drive the two apart, all of Metropolis suffers.

When *Metropolis* hit movie theaters in 2001, critics were won over by the film's striking landscapes, the lush, luxuriant detail, and the unusual soundtrack featuring jazz and Dixieland. The character designs, based on the original Tezuka characters with cartoony features, short legs and fat arms may be distracting for those unfamiliar with his work, but the overlay of the quirky characters and their postmodern environs makes for a fascinating contrast. The story is enjoyable but not terribly inventive. As one of many films based loosely on Fritz Lang's 1926 masterpiece of the same name (though Tezuka had reportedly not seen Lang's film when he created the original manga), *Metropolis* explores common themes of humanity's relationship with technology and with divisions within its own societal constructs. In all, *Metropolis* is a triumph of animated art and a must-see in DVD format.

The special edition DVD comes with a mini disc that features a "making-of" documentary, information about the original manga, creator biographies, and an image gallery. [BR]

SPECIAL FEATURES "Making of" Featurette • Crew Interviews • Creator Bios • Character and Art Galleries • Production Notes • Multi-angle Scenes • Trailer • Other Title Trailers TECHNICAL FEATURES Widescreen (1.85:1) • Subtitles/CC: Eng., Chin., Fren., Kor., Port., Span., Thai • Languages: Eng. dub, Fren. dub, Jap. • Sound: Dolby Digital 5.1 • Cardboard Folding Case • 2 Discs • Region 1 GENRE & RATING Science Fiction/Action • Rated PG-13

Mezzo Forte

Media Blasters, 2001, 55 mins., #AWDVD-0120 Directed by Yasuomi Umezu. Script by Yasuomi Umezu.

Disgraced former police detective Mr. Kurosawa ("Mr. K" for short) anchors a trio of affable, capable mercenaries in near-future Tokyo. He's aided by ace mechanic Harada and the real star of the show, Mikura, a cute, good-humored young lady with lethal fighting skills. Things are looking up for the gang when a former Yakuza hitman arrives on their doorstep with an easy job and a big payoff. All they have to do is kidnap a local crime lord. But when the job goes awry, Mikura and her friends find themselves facing the most insane, vicious enemy possible—the boss's teenage daughter!

Mezzo Forte is the director's funny, sexy follow-up to the earlier and more depressing *Kite*. It features many of the same visual trademarks—odd character designs, wildly original costumes and color design, and a penchant for violence so ridiculous and over-the-top that it's almost reminiscent of *Looney Tunes*. Viewers might be turned off by the flimsy story, but they might be drawn back by the easygoing charm of Mikura and her friends, or the show's broad streak of comedy.

The DVD presentation of this two-part OVA series is solid. The video transfer is good, and there are some nice extras. There is also a separate "Director's Cut" DVD available, which has more adult scenes. [MT]

SPECIAL FEATURES Interview with Director • Storyboards • Other Title Trailers • Inserts: Liner Notes • Easter Egg TECHNICAL FEATURES Fullscreen (1.33:1) • Subtitles/CC: Eng. • Languages: Jap., Eng. dub • Sound: Dolby Digital 2.0 • Keepcase • 1 Disc • Region 1 GENRE & RATING Action/Comedy • Rated 16+

Mezzo Forte [Uncut] ☛ see Mature/Adult Section

Mickey's House of Villains

Disney, 2002, 70 mins., #25271. Directed by Jamie Mitchell. Written by Thomas Hart.

Oh, the House of Mouse is in trouble when villains from throughout the Disney pantheon show up to take over the club. Mickey relents and shows a bunch of spooky cartoons, but the villains want more. Can Mickey and his friends retake the club, or will a little magical help be needed? Now where did Mickey put that pointed hat and broom?

It's a joy to see so many beloved baddies show up, even if it's just to add padding to a Halloween grouping of toons. Historic shorts included are: Donald Duck in "Trick or Treat" (1952); Mickey, Donald, and Goofy in "Lonesome Ghosts" (1937); and "Donald Duck and the Gorilla" (1944). Other cartoons include "Mickey's Mechanical House"; "Dance of the Goofys"; "Donald's Halloween Scare"; "How to Haunt a House"; and Mickey and Minnie in "Hansel and Gretel."

Look for the following baddies to get a line or two—most villains are only glimpsed—in dialogue or a group sing-along: Captain Hook, Charnabog, Hades, Maleficent, Queen of Hearts, Jafar, Cruella DeVil, Ursula, Pain, Panic, and the Big Bad Wolf! In terms of extras, there's a puzzling segment called "Fright Delight" that shows you villain scenes with or without music or sound effects. I'm not sure what purpose it serves. And while they are not Easter eggs, you will want to click in the menu on the movie posters of Ursula, the Evil Queen, and Hades for some fun montages.

SPECIAL FEATURES Sound Effect Villain Clips • Games • Other Title Trailers TECHNICAL FEATURES Fullscreen (1.33:1) • Subtitles/CC: Eng. • Languages: Eng. • Sound: Dolby Digital 5.1 Surround • Keepcase • 1 Disc • Region 1 GENRE & RATING Anthology/Family • Not Rated (Kids)

Mickey's Magical Christmas: Snowed in at the House of Mouse

Disney, 2001, 84 mins., #22950. Directed by Tony Craig and Roberts Gannaway. Written by Thomas Hart, Jesse Winfield.

Imagine all your favorite Disney characters gathered in one place, celebrating Christmas. You don't have to travel to Disneyland to find that group. When many of Disney's famous characters are stranded by a snowstorm, Mickey's "House of Mouse" nightclub is filled to the rafters with guests. Besides Mickey and Minnie Mouse, look for Donald Duck and his nephews, Goofy, and Pluto, plus cast members from *The Little Mermaid, Lady and the Tramp, Bambi, Peter Pan, Pinocchio, The Lion King, Beauty and the Beast, Snow White, Aladdin, Alice in Wonderland, Dumbo*, and more!

The hour-long story includes the 1952 Pluto and Chip and Dale short "Pluto's Christmas Tree," and ends with the entire 1983 film, *Mickey's Christmas Carol* (nominated for an Academy Award, shown without credits here). It also includes a new telling of *The Nutcracker* starring Donald Duck (and narrated by John Cleese).

The DVD features a behind the scenes segment, detailing how sound effects are created for cartoons, as well as the half-hour premiere episode of "House of Mouse," a *Muppet Show*–like mixture of skits and old cartoons. While the older animation occasionally outshines the newer material on this disc, Disney fans will have a great time spotting old favorites in brief comedy gags, and kids will love it.

SPECIAL FEATURES "Making of" Featurette • Sing-Alongs • Other Title Trailers TECHNICAL FEATURES Fullscreen (1.33:1) • Subtitles/CC: Eng. • Languages: Eng. • Sound: Dolby Digital Surround 5.1, DTS • Keepcase • 1 Disc • Region 1 GENRE & RATING Holiday/Music/Family • Not Rated (All Ages)

Mickey's Once Upon a Christmas [Gold Collection]

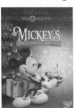

Disney, 1999, 72 mins., #20732. Directed by Bradley Raymond, Jun Falkenstein, Bill Speers, Toby Shelton. Screenplay by Charlie Cohen, Scott Gorden, Tom Nance, Carter Crocker, Richard Cray, Temple Mathews. Donald Duck segment inspired by "Christmas Every Day" by William Dean Howells. Mickey Mouse story based on "The Gift of the Magi" by O. Henry

Christmastime is a time for sharing and caring, and this year, Mickey and all his friends are gathering together to reminisce. Donald Duck and his nephews share a story in which the three ducklings find out what the holiday spirit really means, after they wish for Christmas every day. Mickey and Minnie tell a tale about how each of them sacrificed their own happiness for the other during one Christmas, while Goofy and his son Max tell their comedic disaster-filled holiday tale, complete with a visit from Santa Claus.

There's lots of sweetness and gentle humor in this direct-to-video project that is mostly appropriate for all ages. The music video of "Deck the Halls" by SHeDAISY, however, may not be interesting for younger viewers, given its funeral-dirge singing, disjointed editing, and slightly creepy beginning.

SPECIAL FEATURES Music Video • Sing-Alongs • Storybook • Other Title Trailers TECHNICAL FEATURES Fullscreen (1.33:1) • Subtitles/CC: Eng. • Languages: Eng., Fren. dub, Span. dub • Sound: Dolby Digital 5.1 • Keepcase • 1 Disc • Region 1, 4 GENRE & RATING Holiday/Music/Family • Not Rated (All Ages)

Midnight Panther ☞ see Mature/Adult Section

Mija: Beautiful Demon ☞ see Mature/Adult Section

Miracle Maker, The: The Story of Jesus

Artisan, 2001, 87 mins., #10348. Directed by Stanislav Sokolov, Derek Hayes. Screenplay by Murray Watts. Based on the New Testament.

A family in old Jerusalem who cross paths with Jesus Christ and his disciples begin to believe in his miracles as the Son of God. Jesus relates parables to teach important moral concepts, but he is seen as a threat by the Romans, who bring him to trial and ultimately crucify him. But death is not the end, and the King of the Jews who died for mankind's sins rises again.

The Miracle Maker took four years to create, with animators in Moscow assembling more than thirty sets and over 250 12-in.-tall models for stop-motion use. Six different sets and figures were filmed concurrently to meet the production deadline. Jesus's parables are told in more traditional 2D animation, to separate them from the rest of the film, and animators in Wales worked on these. The finished film debuted worldwide in 1999.

Although it streamlines the Biblical story of Jesus to his life after the age of thirty (with a few relevant flashbacks), this tale is relatively faithful to its roots. An all-star voice cast includes Ralph Fiennes, William Hurt, and Miranda Richardson, among others. The most astonishing element of the DVD is the animation itself. Mostly stop-motion puppetry with ultradetailed costumes, the lush realism of the picture is amazing.

For those looking for religious material, this is an excellent choice. Stop-motion animation fans will also want to track this down for a superb example of the art form.

SPECIAL FEATURES "Making of" Featurette • Cast & Crew Filmographies • Production Notes • Trailer • Insert: Liner Notes TECHNICAL FEATURES Widescreen (1.85:1 enhanced for 16x9) • Languages: Eng., Span. dub • Sound: Dolby Digital 5.1 • Keepcase • 1 Disc • Region 1 GENRE & RATING Stop-Motion/Puppet/Religious • Rated PG

Mission of Darkness ☛ see Mature/Adult Section

Miyuki-chan in Wonderland

ADV Films, 2002, 30 mins., #DMW/001. Directed by Seiko Sayama, Mamoru Hamazu. Screenplay by Nanase Okawa. Based on the manga series by CLAMP in *Newtype Magazine*.

Miyuki-chan awakens from a strange dream to find she's overslept. Rushing to school, she sprints from her house shouting, "I'm late! I'm late!" Just then, a tall woman in a bunny suit speeds past on a skateboard. Miyuki-chan hardly notices the company and follows her right through a hole in the sidewalk. What follows is an adventure full of surreal wackiness and lesbian nuance. After grabbing a woman's "knobs" to enter a magic door, and a fun "Drink Me" shrinking/growing episode, the Cheshire Cat offers to give Miyuki a sex-ed lesson. Night becomes day and Miyuki awakens to meet the dominatrix queen of the land, who promptly whips Miyuki into shape.

In the second featurette on this disc, *Miyuki-chan in Mirrorland*, Miyuki is getting ready for school when she's suddenly pulled through her mirror. Miyuki's carried to Mirrorland, where she is molested by wood nymphs and after meeting a strange butterfly girl, falls onto a giant chessboard. There, a sultry woman by the name of Humpty Dumpty forces Miyuki to play a game of strip chess against her mirror image. Certainly you've guessed by now that all the chess pieces are scantily clad women. Miyuki wins the game but realizes that beating her double means she'll have to strip one way or the other.

This strange 1995 CLAMP production is not your average "Alice in Wonderland" remake. The animation is quite impressive for such a short project, and though the disc exudes sexuality and kink, it's harmless and not at all in bad taste. Just to add to the oddness, this disc comes with an imbedded .pdf file of a printable paper Miyuki-chan doll with costumes. [BR]

SPECIAL FEATURES DVD-ROM Features: Paper Dolls TECHNICAL FEATURES Fullscreen (1.33:1) • Subtitles/CC: Eng. • Languages: Jap. • Sound: Dolby Digital 2.0 • Keepcase • 1 Disc • Region 1 GENRE & RATING Comedy/Cheesecake • Rated 15+

Mobile Fighter G Gundam: Round One

Bandai, 2002, 100 mins., #2130. Directed by Yasuhiro Imagawa. Written by Fuyunori Gobu. Based on the stories by Hajime Yatate, Yoshiyuki Tomino in *Mobile Suit Gundam*.

NOTE: This DVD arrived too late for a full review. The following text is promotional copy provided by the releasing company:

"The year is Future Century 60. It is time for the 'Gundam Fight' tournament! Each country sends a Gundam to Earth for this prestigious tournament in the hopes of winning power and glory for their homeland! But this time, there's an unseen evil lurking behind the scene. Domon Kasshu, Neo Japan's reluctant Fighter, is determined to uncover this evil and clear his family name! The fight to the top begins now!"

This disc contains episodes #1–4.

SPECIAL FEATURES Text Interview with Director • Other Title Trailers • Inserts: Character Bios TECHNICAL FEATURES Fullscreen (1.33:1) • Subtitles/CC: Eng. • Languages: Jap., Eng. dub • Sound: Dolby Digital • Cardboard Box with 3 Keepcases • 3 Discs • Region 1 GENRE & RATING Robots/Science Fiction • Rated 13+

Mobile Fighter G Gundam: Round Two

Bandai, 2002, 100 mins., #2131. Directed by Yasuhiro Imagawa. Written by Fuyunori Gobu. Based on the stories by Hajime Yatate, Yoshiyuki Tomino in *Mobile Suit Gundam*.

NOTE: This DVD arrived too late for a full review. The following text is promotional copy provided by the releasing company:

"Domon and Rain continue to travel the Earth, seeking out opponents to challenge in the Gundam Fight, and searching for clues to the whereabouts of Domon's brother Kyoji. When he arrives in Neo Russia, however, he is immediately thrown into prison. While there, he discovers that Neo Russia Gundam Fighter Argo Gulskii is also a prisoner. Then, after failing to perform up to his government's expectations, Domon is ordered to return home. But what awaits him there is a psychological test—to see if he will be able to battle his brother when the time comes!"

This disc contains episodes #5–8.

SPECIAL FEATURES Text Interview with Director • Other Title Trailers • Inserts: Character Bios TECHNICAL FEATURES Fullscreen (1.33:1) • Subtitles/CC: Eng. • Languages: Jap., Eng. dub • Sound: Dolby Digital • Cardboard Box with 3 Keepcases • 3 Discs • Region 1 GENRE & RATING Robots/Science Fiction • Rated 13+

Mobile Fighter G Gundam: Round Three

Bandai, 2002, 100 mins., #2132. Directed by Yasuhiro Imagawa. Written by Fuyunori Gobu. Based on the stories by Hajime Yatate, Yoshiyuki Tomino in *Mobile Suit Gundam*.

NOTE: This DVD arrived too late for a full review. The following text is promotional copy provided by the releasing company:

"Domon's quest to find his brother takes him to Neo England! He challenges the invincible Gentle Chapman, the man who's won the previous three Gundam Fight Tournaments! Afterwards, his travels lead him to the deserts of Neo Egypt, where he and Sai Saici confront the ghost of a former Gundam Fighter. Rain is reunited with an old flame, and learns the secret of the mysterious DG cells. Domon is also reunited with someone special—his martial arts teacher, the great Master Asia!"

This disc contains episodes #9–12.

SPECIAL FEATURES Text Interview with Director • Other Title Trailers • Inserts: Character Bios TECHNICAL FEATURES Fullscreen (1.33:1) • Subtitles/CC: Eng. • Languages: Jap., Eng. dub • Sound: Dolby Digital • Cardboard Box with 3 Keepcases • 3 Discs • Region 1 GENRE & RATING Robots/Science Fiction • Rated 13+

Mobile Fighter G Gundam: Collector's Box 1—The Earth Is the Ring! [Box Set]

Bandai, 2002, 300 mins., #2142.

This box set contains the three *Mobile Fighter G Gundam* discs exactly as they appeared in the individual keepcase editions. See individual entries for the Special and Technical Features listings.

TECHNICAL FEATURES Cardboard Box with 3 Keepcases • 3 Discs • Region 1 GENRE & RATING Robots/Science Fiction • Rated 13+

Mobile Suit Gundam: The Battle Begins! [#1]

Bandai, 2001, 125 mins., #1770. Directed by Yoshiyuki Tomino. Written by Hiroyuki Hoshiyama, Yoshihisa Araki, Masaru Yamamoto, Kenichi Matsuzaki, Yoshiyuki Tomino. Based on the stories by Hajime Yatate, Yoshiyuki Tomino in *Mobile Suit Gundam*.

In the near future, mankind deals with its overpopulation problem by building a series of enormous, cylindrical space colonies, nicknamed "sides." After a long period of growth and expansion in outer space, the human race has entered a new era, and the "Universal Century" is incorporated.

Seventy-nine years later, the first great war between the Earth Federation and a breakaway group of space colonists called the Principality of Zeon breaks out. The Zeon, outraged at Earth's poor treatment of the space colonies, quickly seize the advantage using new war machines known as Mobile Suits. The Federation soon develops Mobile Suits of its own, and after a surprise attack on a spacebound Federation base, fifteen-year-old civilian Amuro Ray finds himself thrust into war, drafted as the pilot of a Mobile Suit developed by his own father, code-named "Gundam."

Much has been made of the various *Gundam* series, and rightfully so. It's a cornerstone of both Japanese animation and Japanese science fiction. It was the first anime series to portray giant robots as simple tools of war rather than superpowered heroes, and its enormous, detailed ensemble cast and tough, gritty portrayal of war has won thousands of fans over the years. This first version of *Gundam*, a 1979 TV series totaling forty-two episodes, is not without problems; among them are some bad animation and poorly paced direction. Still, *Gundam* is worth seeing as a seminal example of Japanese animation and a well-crafted piece of science fiction.

The *Mobile Suit Gundam* TV DVDs have an enormous strike against them—each disc contains only English-language dialogue. The Japanese version that hardcore fans prize is conspicuously absent. However, the video quality is pristine, making *Gundam* appear younger than it actually is, and the English dubbed version is solid, if not excellent. Each *Gundam* TV disc contains a "Gundam Encyclopedia" that gives technical specs for a few of the show's Mobile Suits. Surprisingly, this DVD also features the show's original opening and ending sequences. This DVD contains episodes #1–5 of the original *Mobile Suit Gundam* TV series. [MT]

SPECIAL FEATURES Mobile Suit Encyclopedia • Other Title Trailers • Inserts: Sticker TECHNICAL FEATURES Fullscreen (1.33:1) • Languages: Eng. • Sound: Dolby Digital Surround 2.0 • Keepcase • 1 Disc • Region 1 GENRE & RATING Robots/Science Fiction • Rated 13+

Mobile Suit Gundam: The Red Comet [#2]

Bandai, 2001, 125 mins., #1771. Directed by Yoshiyuki Tomino. Written by Hiroyuki Hoshiyama, Yoshihisa Araki, Masaru Yamamoto, Kenichi Matsuzaki, Yoshiyuki Tomino. Based on the stories by Hajime Yatate, Yoshiyuki Tomino in *Mobile Suit Gundam*.

Amuro Ray is now firmly integrated into the young and confused crew of the *White Base*, a prototype ship that was forced to flee from the colony Side 7 in the wake of Zeon attacks. He's trying hard, but his constant duties as pilot of the powerful Gundam are exhausting him. Meanwhile, an ace

Zeon pilot named Char Aznable is making plans of his own—plans that may not bode well for either the Federation or the Zeon.

This DVD contains episodes #6–10. [MT]

SPECIAL FEATURES Mobile Suit Encyclopedia • Other Title Trailers • Inserts: Sticker TECHNICAL FEATURES Fullscreen (1.33:1) • Languages: Eng. • Sound: Dolby Digital Surround 2.0 • Keepcase • 1 Disc • Region 1 GENRE & RATING Robots/Science Fiction • Rated 13+

Mobile Suit Gundam: The Threat of Zeon [#3]

Bandai, 2001, 125 mins., #1772. Directed by Yoshiyuki Tomino. Written by Hiroyuki Hoshiyama, Yoshihisa Araki, Masaru Yamamoto, Kenichi Matsuzaki, Yoshiyuki Tomino. Based on the stories by Hajime Yatate, Yoshiyuki Tomino in *Mobile Suit Gundam.*

The *White Base* has managed to make planetfall on Earth, but they're still being pursued by relentless Zeon forces. Zeon ace Char Aznable continues with his own plans, as Zeon commander Garma Zabi places himself in extreme peril in order to bring down the *White Base* and the Gundam. Meanwhile, Amuro Ray's skills with the Gundam continue to progress, even as his relationship with the *White Base* crew—particularly the grim Ensign Bright Noah—sours.

This DVD contains episodes #11–14. [MT]

SPECIAL FEATURES Mobile Suit Encyclopedia • Other Title Trailers • Inserts: Sticker TECHNICAL FEATURES Fullscreen (1.33:1) • Languages: Eng. • Sound: Dolby Digital Surround 2.0 • Keepcase • 1 Disc • Region 1 GENRE & RATING Robots/Science Fiction • Rated 13+

Mobile Suit Gundam: Desert of Despair [#4]

Bandai, 2001, 100 mins., #1773. Directed by Yoshiyuki Tomino. Written by Hiroyuki Hoshiyama, Yoshihisa Araki, Masaru Yamamoto, Kenichi Matsuzaki, Yoshiyuki Tomino. Based on the stories by Hajime Yatate, Yoshiyuki Tomino in *Mobile Suit Gundam.*

As the *White Base* continues to fight its way across the surface of Earth, crewmember Sayla Mas makes some frightening discoveries about her own past. The friction between Amuro and the rest of the crew comes to a head, and he flees the ship just in time to encounter his toughest foe yet—the seasoned Zeon soldier, Ranba Ral!

This DVD contains episodes #15–18. [MT]

SPECIAL FEATURES Mobile Suit Encyclopedia • Other Title Trailers

• Inserts: Sticker TECHNICAL FEATURES Fullscreen (1.33:1) • Languages: Eng. • Sound: Dolby Digital Surround 2.0 • Keepcase • 1 Disc • Region 1 GENRE & RATING Robots/Science Fiction • Rated 13+

Mobile Suit Gundam: In Love and War [#5]

Bandai, 2001, 100 mins., #1774. Directed by Yoshiyuki Tomino. Written by Hiroyuki Hoshiyama, Yoshihisa Araki, Masaru Yamamoto, Kenichi Matsuzaki, Yoshiyuki Tomino. Based on the stories by Hajime Yatate, Yoshiyuki Tomino in *Mobile Suit Gundam.*

Ranba Ral and his men make a daring attack on the *White Base*. The crew desperately attempts to fend them off, but the battle exacts a terrible price. Just when it seems like the day has been saved, Ral's vengeful lover, Crowley Hamon, makes a devastating surprise attack—and it's up to one brave crewmember to make the ultimate sacrifice.

This DVD contains episodes #19–22. [MT]

SPECIAL FEATURES Mobile Suit Encyclopedia • Other Title Trailers • Inserts: Sticker TECHNICAL FEATURES Fullscreen (1.33:1) • Languages: Eng. • Sound: Dolby Digital Surround 2.0 • Keepcase • 1 Disc • Region 1 GENRE & RATING Robots/Science Fiction • Rated 13+

Mobile Suit Gundam: The Black Tri-Star [#6]

Bandai, 2002, 100 mins., #1775. Directed by Yoshiyuki Tomino. Written by Hiroyuki Hoshiyama, Yoshihisa Araki, Masaru Yamamoto, Kenichi Matsuzaki, Yoshiyuki Tomino. Based on the stories by Hajime Yatate, Yoshiyuki Tomino in *Mobile Suit Gundam.*

The beleaguered crew of the *White Base* has no time to relax as the ship is attacked by a trio of ace Zeon pilots in powerful new Mobile Suits. The *White Base* must face more new technology, as well as the return of a very angry and vengeful Char Aznable.

This DVD contains episodes #23–26. [MT]

SPECIAL FEATURES Mobile Suit Encyclopedia • Other Title Trailers TECHNICAL FEATURES Fullscreen (1.33:1) • Languages: Eng. • Sound: Dolby Digital Surround 2.0 • Keepcase • 1 Disc • Region 1 GENRE & RATING Robots/Science Fiction • Rated 13+

Mobile Suit Gundam: Return to Space [#7]

Bandai, 2002, 100 mins., #1776. Directed by Yoshiyuki Tomino. Written by Hiroyuki Hoshiyama, Yoshihisa Araki, Masaru Yamamoto, Kenichi Matsuzaki, Yoshiyuki Tomino. Based on the stories by Hajime Yatate, Yoshiyuki Tomino in *Mobile Suit Gundam.*

The *White Base*'s trials continue. A spy infiltrates the ship, and Mobile Suit pilot Kai Shiden has a battlefield experience that changes his view of the war completely. As the *White Base* returns to space, its ragged crew is finally officially enlisted by the military, and joined by a new veteran, the affable Lieutenant Sleggar Rowe.

This DVD contains episodes #27–30. [MT]

SPECIAL FEATURES Mobile Suit Encyclopedia • Other Title Trailers
TECHNICAL FEATURES Fullscreen (1.33:1) • Languages: Eng. •
Sound: Dolby Digital Surround 2.0 • Keepcase • 1 Disc •
Region 1 GENRE & RATING Robots/Science Fiction • Rated 13+

Mobile Suit Gundam: The Battle of Solomon [#8]

Bandai, 2002, 100 mins., #1777. Directed by Yoshiyuki Tomino. Written by Hiroyuki Hoshiyama, Yoshihisa Araki, Masaru Yamamoto, Kenichi Matsuzaki, Yoshiyuki Tomino. Based on the stories by Hajime Yatate, Yoshiyuki Tomino in *Mobile Suit Gundam.*

Amuro and the *White Base* find themselves drawn into an enormous battle between Federation forces and those of Zeon admiral Dozul Zabi. The *White Base* once again escapes, limping to a nearby colony for repairs. There, Amuro meets someone who will change his life forever.

This DVD contains episodes #31–34. [MT]

SPECIAL FEATURES Mobile Suit Encyclopedia • Other Title Trailers
TECHNICAL FEATURES Fullscreen (1.33:1) • Subtitles/CC: Eng. •
Languages: Jap., Eng. dub • Sound: Dolby Digital Surround
5.1 • Keepcase, Snapcase, Multikeepcase, Box • 1–3 Discs •
Region 1 GENRE & RATING Robots/Science Fiction • Rated 13+

Mobile Suit Gundam: Newtypes and the Future [#9]

Bandai, 2002, 100 mins., #1778. Directed by Yoshiyuki Tomino. Written by Hiroyuki Hoshiyama, Yoshihisa Araki, Masaru Yamamoto, Kenichi Matsuzaki, Yoshiyuki Tomino. Based on the stories by Hajime Yatate, Yoshiyuki Tomino in *Mobile Suit Gundam.*

Amuro comes to a great realization—his incredible aptitude with the Gundam might be more than just beginner's luck and pilot instinct! Federation technologists upgrade the Gundam to adapt it to what they believe are Amuro's emerging psychic powers, but more battles loom. The Federation forces successfully employ a new weapon, but Char and the rest of the Zeon forces are still at large.

This penultimate DVD contains episodes #35–38. [MT]

SPECIAL FEATURES Mobile Suit Encyclopedia • Other Title Trailers
TECHNICAL FEATURES Fullscreen (1.33:1) • Subtitles/CC: Eng. •
Languages: Jap., Eng. dub • Sound: Dolby Digital Surround
5.1 • Keepcase, Snapcase, Multikeepcase, Box • 1–3 Discs •
Region 1 GENRE & RATING Robots/Science Fiction • Rated 13+

Mobile Suit Gundam: Lalah's Fate [#10]

Bandai, 2002, 100 mins., #1779. Directed by Yoshiyuki Tomino. Written by Hiroyuki Hoshiyama, Yoshihisa Araki, Masaru Yamamoto, Kenichi Matsuzaki, Yoshiyuki Tomino. Based on the stories by Hajime Yatate, Yoshiyuki Tomino in *Mobile Suit Gundam.*

Amuro, now a seasoned veteran pilot and an apparent "Newtype" psychic, roars into battle as the Federation-Zeon war lurches toward an inevitable conclusion. On the battlefield, he's fated to have a brutal confrontation with the mysterious Lalah Sune—and a final battle with the equally skilled Char Aznable!

The final DVD of this series contains episodes #39–42. [MT]

SPECIAL FEATURES Mobile Suit Encyclopedia • Other Title Trailers
TECHNICAL FEATURES Fullscreen (1.33:1) • Subtitles/CC: Eng. •
Languages: Jap., Eng. dub • Sound: Dolby Digital Surround
5.1 • Keepcase, Snapcase, Multikeepcase, Box • 1–3 Discs •
Region 1 GENRE & RATING Robots/Science Fiction • Rated 13+

Mobile Suit Gundam 0080: War in the Pocket [#1]

Bandai, 2002, 90 mins., #0385. Directed by Fumihiko Takayama. Screenplay by Hiroyuki Yamaga. Based on the stories by Hajime Yatate, Yoshiyuki Tomino in *Mobile Suit Gundam.*

The momentous One-Year War between the forces of the Earth Federation and the Principality of Zeon is coming to a close. On Libot, a neutral space colony, a young boy named Alfred Izuruha harbors a typical kid's fascination with war. He's desperate for information about the war and Mobile Suits, both to satisfy his own curiosity and to impress his friends. His wish for action is soon granted—perhaps more than he'd hoped—when he discovers that the Federation is covertly developing a new Mobile Suit. Then, he meets and befriends Bernie Wiseman, an affable young man who turns out to be a Zeon spy. Al is too delighted by his new friendship to realize the danger he's in.

A 1990 addition to the sprawling *Gundam* saga, *Gundam 0080* is a surprisingly affecting side story. The six-part OVA is good looking, featuring the same distinctive character designs that made the original a hit, as well as new Mobile Suit designs. The story, a well-crafted drama with a central lesson about the fundamental evils of war, is sharp and intelligent. The animation and soundtrack are slightly dated, but *Gundam 0080* is still a solid science-fiction tale and a strong segment of the greater *Gundam* story.

The DVD looks excellent, and contains a few more extras than usual. Along with Dolby 5.1 mixes of both English and Japanese dialogue, the DVD includes textless "clean" opening and ending sequences, as well as a small collection of Japanese TV commercials for the series and a "Mobile Suit Encyclopedia" file detailing technical specs of some of the robots. The DVD contains episodes #1–3. [MT]

SPECIAL FEATURES Mobile Suit Encyclopedia • Promotional Footage • Clean Credits • Other Title Trailers • Reversible Cover • Inserts: Timeline Notes TECHNICAL FEATURES Fullscreen (1.33:1) • Subtitles/CC: Eng. • Languages: Jap., Eng. dub • Sound: Dolby Digital 5.1 • Keepcase • 1 Disc • Region 1 GENRE & RATING Robots/Science Fiction • Rated 13+

Mobile Suit Gundam 0080: War in the Pocket [#2]

Bandai, 2002, 90 mins., #0386. Directed by Fumihiko Takayama. Screenplay by Hiroyuki Yamaga. Based on the stories by Hajime Yatate, Yoshiyuki Tomino in *Mobile Suit Gundam.*

The situation on the colony Libot gets more dangerous. Al tries desperately to preserve his friendship with Bernie, but Bernie is intent on fulfilling his mission. Meanwhile, Al's friendly next-door neighbor, Christine McKenzie, is a Federation pilot—and to Al's horror, it seems probable that his two friends will meet on the battlefield!

This volume contains multiple extras such as the second "clean" ending sequence, a trio of music videos, and a promotional clip. The DVD contains the final episodes #4–6. [MT]

SPECIAL FEATURES Mobile Suit Encyclopedia • Promotional Footage • Music Video • Clean Credits • Other Title Trailers • Reversible Cover • Inserts: Timeline Notes TECHNICAL FEATURES Fullscreen (1.33:1) • Subtitles/CC: Eng. • Languages: Jap., Eng. dub • Sound: Dolby Digital 5.1 • Keepcase • 1 Disc • Region 1 GENRE & RATING Robots/Science Fiction • Rated 13+

Mobile Suit Gundam 0083: Stardust Memory [#1]

Bandai, 2002, 100 mins., #0365. Directed by Mitsuko Kase, Takashi Imanishi. Written by Fuyunori Gobu. Based on the stories by Hajime Yatate, Yoshiyuki Tomino in *Mobile Suit Gundam.*

It's three years after the devastating One-Year War between the Earth Federation and the Principality of Zeon. The Federation has stabilized, and the remaining Zeon forces are scattered and disorganized. All this doesn't matter much to the young Ko Uraki, a test pilot for the Federation. But Ko's life gets complicated with the arrival of Nina Purpleton, a bossy, demanding engineer from Anaheim Electronics. Nina brings two prototype Gundams with her, which attracts Ko's attention. However, Ko isn't the only one interested in the prototypes; one of them is promptly stolen by Anavel Gato, a legendary Zeon ace. Ko rushes to pursue Gato, but can the rookie stand up to a seasoned Zeon pilot?

Gundam 0083 is a popular segment of the *Gundam* saga, probably because it's well-animated and very action-packed. The thirteen-episode 1991 OVA series features a wealth of talent behind it. Many of the production staff would go on to produce the superlative *Cowboy Bebop.* Here, they introduce particularly memorable character and mechanical designs. The show's only drawback is probably its characters; Gato is an excellent villain, but both Ko and Nina come off as dull and foolish at times. *Gundam* fans will love it for its great action and flashy Mobile Suits, but regular science fiction fans might find it hard to take seriously.

The DVD looks excellent, with remastered video footage giving the animation a polished look. A Japanese Dolby 5.1 mix is included, though the English mix is only Dolby 2.0. The DVD also contains a physical extra: a reversible cover. This DVD contains episodes #1–4. [MT]

SPECIAL FEATURES Mobile Suit Encyclopedia • Clean Credits • Other Title Trailers • Reversible Cover • Inserts: Timeline Notes • Easter Egg TECHNICAL FEATURES Fullscreen (1.33:1) • Subtitles/CC: Eng. • Languages: Jap., Eng. dub • Sound: Dolby Digital 5.1 • Keepcase • 1 Disc • Region 1 GENRE & RATING Robots/Science Fiction • Rated 13+

Mobile Suit Gundam 0083: Stardust Memory [#2]

Bandai, 2002, 75 mins., #0366. Directed by Mitsuko Kase, Takashi Imanishi. Written by Akinori Endo, Asahide Okuma. Based on the stories by Hajime Yatate, Yoshiyuki Tomino in *Mobile Suit Gundam*.

Afraid of what Anavel Gato might do with his powerful stolen prototype, the Federation forces pursue him into space. There, the talented Ko experiences his first real defeat. Meanwhile, Gato meets up with the unpredictable pilot Cima, a former Zeon soldier leading a ragtag fleet of her own. She readily rejoins Gato and the rest of the Zeon forces, setting Ko up for an even tougher battle.

The high quality continues with this second volume. The disc is slimmer on extras than usual, though it still includes a reversible cover. It also has a four-minute side-story clip, called "The Mayfly of Space." This DVD contains episodes #5–7. [MT]

SPECIAL FEATURES Mobile Suit Encyclopedia • Promotional Footage • Other Title Trailers • Inserts: Timeline Notes TECHNICAL FEATURES Fullscreen (1.33:1) • Subtitles/CC: Eng. • Languages: Jap., Eng. dub • Sound: Dolby Digital 5.1 • Keepcase • 1 Disc • Region 1 GENRE & RATING Robots/Science Fiction • Rated 13+

Mobile Suit Gundam 0083: Stardust Memory [#3]

Bandai, 2002, 75 mins., #0367. Directed by Mitsuko Kase, Takashi Imanishi. Written by Ryosuke Takahashi. Based on the stories by Hajime Yatate, Yoshiyuki Tomino in *Mobile Suit Gundam*.

Ko's skills as a pilot continue to improve, but his mentor, Lieutenant Burning, is starting to feel his age. As the Federation prepares for a large-scale naval review, it's revealed that Anavel Gato is preparing a terrible counterattack for the Zeon's humiliating defeat at Solomon three years earlier!

This third volume looks and sounds as good as the previous two. The DVD contains episodes #8–10. [MT]

SPECIAL FEATURES Mobile Suit Encyclopedia • Clean Credits • Other Title Trailers • Reversible Cover • Inserts: Timeline Notes TECHNICAL FEATURES Fullscreen (1.33:1) • Subtitles/CC: Eng. • Languages: Jap., Eng. dub • Sound: Dolby Digital 5.1 • Keepcase • 1 Disc • Region 1 GENRE & RATING Robots/Science Fiction • Rated 13+

Mobile Suit Gundam 0083: Stardust Memory [#4]

Bandai, 2002, 75 mins., #0367. Directed by Mitsuko Kase, Takashi Imanishi. Written by Ryosuke Takahashi. Based on the stories by Hajime Yatate, Yoshiyuki Tomino in *Mobile Suit Gundam*.

The remaining Zeon forces continue their plans for ultimate revenge. Meanwhile, Ko and Gato continue to clash. As their conflict reaches a head, a startling discovery about engineer Nina Purpleton's past is made.

This final volume maintains the high video and audio quality of the prior three. The disc contains a collection of TV commercials, as well as the requisite Mobile Suit Encyclopedia and reversible cover. This DVD contains the final episodes #11–13. [MT]

SPECIAL FEATURES Mobile Suit Encyclopedia • Promotional Footage • Other Title Trailers • Reversible Cover • Inserts: Timeline Notes TECHNICAL FEATURES Fullscreen (1.33:1) • Subtitles/CC: Eng. • Languages: Jap., Eng. dub • Sound: Dolby Digital 5.1 • Keepcase • 1 Disc • Region 1 GENRE & RATING Robots/Science Fiction • Rated 13+

Mobile Suit Gundam: Char's Counterattack—The Motion Picture

Bandai, 2002, 124 mins., #2200. Directed by Yoshiyuki Tomino. Written by Yoshiyuki Tomino. Based on the stories by Hajime Yatate, Yoshiyuki Tomino in *Mobile Suit Gundam.*

The year is now Universal Century 0093, and it's been thirteen years since the events of the original *Mobile Suit Gundam* series. After simmering with indignation over Earth's oppression of its space colonies, Zeon pilot Char Aznable decides to make a final stand. He takes charge of a Neo Zeon army in an attempt to render Earth uninhabitable with a nuclear winter, forcing all of mankind into space! Char's arch-rival, Nu Gundam mobile suit pilot Amuro Ray, gathers allies in the Federation forces and prepares to defend humanity against Char . . . for the final time. Politics, vengeance, rivalry, and duty all make for an explosive climax.

This 1988 film serves as the conclusion to the trio of *Mobile Suit Gundam, Mobile Suit Zeta Gundam,* and *Mobile Suit Gundam Double Zeta Gundam* television series from 1979 to 1986. By wrapping up the longstanding feud between two of the lead characters, the creators cleared the slate for future endeavors with a conclusion that satisfied some fans and left others wanting more.

The DVD quality is excellent, and a number of nice extras are included. Fans will love the twelve-page booklet included, which maps out the entire *Gundam* storyline, history, and universe. And the foil-embossed slipcase is pretty cool as well.

SPECIAL FEATURES Creator Filmography • Trailer • Music Video • Other Title Trailers • Reversible Cover • Inserts: Booklet with Maps, Timeline, History TECHNICAL FEATURES Widescreen (1.85:1 enhanced for 16x9) • Subtitles/CC: Eng. • Languages: Jap., Eng. dub • Sound: Dolby Digital 2.0, Dolby Digital 5.1 • Keepcase with Embossed Cardboard Slipcase • 1 Disc • Region 1 GENRE & RATING Robots/Science Fiction • Rated 13+

Mobile Suit Gundam Wing: Operation 1

Bandai, 2000, 150 mins., #1670. Directed by Masashi Ikeda. Written by Katsuyuki Sumizawa. Based on the stories by Hajime Yatate, Yoshiyuki Tomino in *Mobile Suit Gundam.*

The year is 195 After Colony, in a time less than two centuries after mankind, due to overcrowding and overpopulation, looked to the stars and developed space colonies. War soon broke out in the settlements and, in an effort to unify Earth and its colonies, the United Earth Sphere Alliance was formed.

However, this organization, designed to keep the peace and instill order, soon turned into an oppressive dictatorship. Lady Une and Zechs Merquise rose through the ranks to become two of UESA's leading tacticians, acting as right hand man and woman to the evil Romefeller. Meanwhile, Minister Darlian, an influential politician, attempted to use his power to guarantee peace.

In a bid for independence from UESA's iron grip, a secret organization created five powerful tank-like Mobile Suits called "Gundams" and found five fifteen-year-old males to pilot each weapon. Heero Yuy (in his Wing Gundam), Duo Maxwell (in his Gundam Deathscythe), Trowa Barton (in his Gundam Heavyarms), Quatre Raberba Winner (in his Sandrock Gundam), and Wufei Chang (in his Shenlong Gundam), set out on a seek-and-destroy mission, called Operation Meteor, to cripple the UESA. Will these five brave, cunning, and sometimes-crazy teens be enough to paralyze an empire? And what role will Relena, the daughter of Minister Darlian, have in all their lives?

The second alternate-universe TV series based on *Mobile Suit Gundam, Gundam Wing* was first aired in 1995. In 2000, the Cartoon Network began airing a daily version of *Gundam Wing.* This DVD is the unedited pure anime as it was meant to be seen. *Mobile Suit Gundam Wing* is an exciting and compelling anime complete with philosophical debates, political intrigue, and lots of mecha action.

This disc contains episodes #1–5, a great introduction to the cast and the forces that motivate each young man to pilot his Gundam. [JMC]

SPECIAL FEATURES Character Bios • Mecha Technical Info • Other Title Trailers • Inserts: Liner Notes, Mecha Specs • Easter Egg TECHNICAL FEATURES Fullscreen (1.33:1) • Subtitles/CC: Eng. • Languages: Jap., Eng. dub • Sound: Dolby Digital Surround 2.0 • Keepcase • 1 Disc • Region 1 GENRE & RATING Robots/Science Fiction • Rated 13+

Mobile Suit Gundam Wing: Operation 2

Bandai, 2000, 150 mins., #1671. Directed by Masashi Ikeda. Written by Katsuyuki Sumizawa. Based on the stories by Hajime Yatate, Yoshiyuki Tomino in *Mobile Suit Gundam.*

Heero, Duo, Quatre, Wufei, and Trowa continue their attack on Earth. It appears war is inevitable, but Minister Darlian and his daughter, Relena, want to try one more time to reason with the colonies for peace. While on their journey, Relena learns a terrible secret about herself, and that revelation has a high price. Plus, the Gundams start to meet opposition from OZ, the secret society that controls UESA's military elite.

This action-packed disc contains episodes #6–10. [JMC]

SPECIAL FEATURES Character Bios • Mecha Technical Info • Other Title Trailers • Inserts: Liner Notes, Mecha Specs TECHNICAL FEATURES Fullscreen (1.33:1) • Subtitles/CC: Eng. • Languages: Jap., Eng. dub • Sound: Dolby Digital Surround 2.0 • Keepcase • 1 Disc • Region 1 GENRE & RATING Robots/Science Fiction • Rated 13+

Mobile Suit Gundam Wing: Operation 3

Bandai, 2000, 125 mins., #1672. Directed by Masashi Ikeda. Written by Katsuyuki Sumizawa. Based on the stories by Hajime Yatate, Yoshiyuki Tomino in *Mobile Suit Gundam.*

The conflict escalates and the battle rages on. The Gundam pilots are going strong, beating almost any foe, but their momentum is halted and they are forced to surrender when the colonies are held hostage by OZ. Lady Une has an ultimate weapon that will destroy all the colonies if the pilots oppose OZ. Rather than surrender his Suit, Heero sets it to self-destruct and the other young pilots go into hiding with their Mobile Suits, not knowing if Heero's alive or dead. With the pilots no longer a threat, OZ turns its attention to the colonies and conquest.

This disc contains episodes #11–15 and gives us more insight into the pilots. [JMC]

SPECIAL FEATURES Character Bios • Mecha Technical Info • Other Title Trailers • Inserts: Liner Notes, Mecha Specs, Trading Card TECHNICAL FEATURES Fullscreen (1.33:1) • Subtitles/CC: Eng. • Languages: Jap., Eng. dub • Sound: Dolby Digital Surround 2.0 • Keepcase • 1 Disc • Region 1 GENRE & RATING Robots/Science Fiction • Rated 13+

Mobile Suit Gundam Wing: Operation 4

Bandai, 2000, 125 mins., #1673. Directed by Masashi Ikeda. Written by Katsuyuki Sumizawa. Based on the stories by Hajime Yatate, Yoshiyuki Tomino in *Mobile Suit Gundam.*

As OZ continues to cripple the alliance military, Quatre and Duo return to their own colonies to warn them, but find that they have been declared enemies of their own nations. Angered, Duo begins a one-man war in space. Meanwhile Heero rebuilds his Wing Gundam and faces off against Zechs and the Tallgeese in a grand battle. After the fight, Heero attacks an OZ stronghold hoping to destroy its new Mobile Suits, but is amazed to find one of the other pilots there, fighting alongside OZ!

This shocking disc, filled with revelations and betrayals, contains episodes #16–20. [JMC]

SPECIAL FEATURES Character Bios • Mecha Technical Info • Other Title Trailers • Inserts: Liner Notes, Mecha Specs TECHNICAL

FEATURES Fullscreen (1.33:1) • Subtitles/CC: Eng. • Languages: Jap., Eng. dub • Sound: Dolby Digital Surround 2.0 • Keepcase • 1 Disc • Region 1 GENRE & RATING Robots/Science Fiction • Rated 13+

Mobile Suit Gundam Wing: Operation 5

Bandai, 2001, 125 mins., #1674. Directed by Masashi Ikeda. Written by Akemi Omode, Katsuhiko Chiba, Katsuyuki Sumizawa, Toshifumi Kawase. Based on the stories by Hajime Yatate, Yoshiyuki Tomino in *Mobile Suit Gundam.*

Romefeller's tactics have finally made Zechs see the light and begin to move against him. Lady Une learns of the Tallgeese's actions and sends Heero and Trowa to stop him, keeping Heero in line by threatening to self-destruct the new Mobile Suit he's piloting. While Trowa and Heero fight Zechs, Quatre returns to Earth after a terrible home visit, piloting a deadly new Mobile Suit, the Wing Gundam Zero. One problem—its operating system will drive its pilot mad!

This disc contains episodes #21–25. [JMC]

SPECIAL FEATURES Character Bios • Mecha Technical Info • Other Title Trailers • Inserts: Liner Notes, Mecha Specs TECHNICAL FEATURES Fullscreen (1.33:1) • Subtitles/CC: Eng. • Languages: Jap., Eng. dub • Sound: Dolby Digital Surround 2.0 • Keepcase • 1 Disc • Region 1 GENRE & RATING Robots/Science Fiction • Rated 13+

Mobile Suit Gundam Wing: Operation 6

Bandai, 2001, 125 mins., #1675. Directed by Masashi Ikeda. Written by Katsuyuki Sumizawa, Masashi Ikeda, Katsuhiko Chiba. Based on the stories by Hajime Yatate, Yoshiyuki Tomino in *Mobile Suit Gundam.*

There's conflict within OZ and it splits into two groups: one side is loyal to Romefeller, while the Treize Faction opposes him. The Treize Faction rescues Heero and Quatre after they are captured by OZ, and helps them escape with their Gundams. The secret of why the Wing Zero drives its pilot mad is revealed, but knowing might not be enough to save Heero's sanity when he's forced to pilot that Gundam to save his friends from OZ.

This disc contains episodes #26–30 and aside from the conflict with Wing Zero, this doesn't do a lot to advance the *Gundam* saga. Two of the episodes on this disc are flashback episodes recalling all the previous *Mobile Suit Gundam Wing* episodes so far. [JMC]

SPECIAL FEATURES Character Bios • Mecha Technical Info • Other Title Trailers • Inserts: Liner Notes, Mecha Specs TECHNICAL FEATURES Fullscreen (1.33:1) • Subtitles/CC: Eng. • Languages: Jap., Eng. dub • Sound: Dolby Digital Surround 2.0 • Keepcase • 1 Disc • Region 1 GENRE & RATING Robots/Science Fiction • Rated 13+

Mobile Suit Gundam Wing: Operation 7

Bandai, 2001, 125 mins., #1676. Directed by Masashi Ikeda. Written by Katsuyuki Sumizawa, Katsuhiko Chiba, Akemi Omode. Based on the stories by Hajime Yatate, Yoshiyuki Tomino in *Mobile Suit Gundam.*

Heero and Quatre try to help Relena achieve her goals of pacifism, but when OZ attacks, Relena is forced to ask for their defensive help. Meanwhile Duo continues to battle alone in space against the forces of OZ. The Treize Faction continues to oppose OZ, and after another fight, it reveals its ultimate weapon: the Gundam Epyon. Equipped with the same system as the Wing Zero, will Heero be able to pilot this and retain his wits, or will the Epyon drive him mad?

This disc contains episodes #31–35, and introduces a few more Gundam models. [JMC]

SPECIAL FEATURES Mecha Technical Info • Other Title Trailers • Inserts: Liner Notes, Mecha Specs TECHNICAL FEATURES Fullscreen (1.33:1) • Subtitles/CC: Eng. • Languages: Jap., Eng. dub • Sound: Dolby Digital Surround 2.0 • Keepcase • 1 Disc • Region 1 GENRE & RATING Robots/Science Fiction • Rated 13+

Mobile Suit Gundam Wing: Operation 8

Bandai, 2001, 125 mins., #1677. Directed by Masashi Ikeda. Written by Katsuhiko Chiba, Akemi Omode, Katsuyuki Sumizawa. Based on the stories by Hajime Yatate, Yoshiyuki Tomino in *Mobile Suit Gundam.*

Wufei fights alone as most of the other Gundam pilots begin a battle with OZ for control of the Space Fortress *Barge.* Zechs, the new leader of the White Fang section, is busy with projects of his own, including a deadly battleship his team has developed, the *Libra.* However, once it's ready for action, he doesn't attack OZ with the weapon but directs the *Libra* toward Earth. Duo discovers that Earth is in danger and that he might be the only one to protect the planet from the battleship.

This disc contains episodes #36–40 and adds more players and factions into the *Gundam* mix. [JMC]

SPECIAL FEATURES Historical Info • Other Title Trailers • Inserts: Liner Notes, Mecha Specs TECHNICAL FEATURES Fullscreen (1.33:1) • Subtitles/CC: Eng. • Languages: Jap., Eng. dub • Sound: Dolby Digital Surround 2.0 • Keepcase • 1 Disc • Region 1 GENRE & RATING Robots/Science Fiction • Rated 13+

Mobile Suit Gundam Wing: Operation 9

Bandai, 2001, 125 mins., #1678. Directed by Masashi Ikeda. Written by Akemi Omode, Katsuyuki Sumizawa, Katsuhiko Chiba. Based on the stories by Hajime Yatate, Yoshiyuki Tomino in *Mobile Suit Gundam.*

Treize removes Relena from power and attempts to use his influence to change the pacifist ways of her nation, the Sanc Kingdom. The Gundam pilots continue to fight for the Space Fortress *Barge.* Meanwhile OZ has created a variant of the Zero program and its new weapons are now programmed with the deadly template. Plus, Zechs and the *Libra* begin to fight against everyone, taking on the Gundams, OZ, and the Romefeller Foundation!

This penultimate disc contains episodes #41–45, a knock-down, drag-out slugfest. [JMC]

SPECIAL FEATURES Historical Info • Other Title Trailers • Inserts: Liner Notes, Mecha Specs TECHNICAL FEATURES Fullscreen (1.33:1) • Subtitles/CC: Eng. • Languages: Jap., Eng. dub • Sound: Dolby Digital Surround 2.0 • Keepcase • 1 Disc • Region 1 GENRE & RATING Robots/Science Fiction • Rated 13+

Mobile Suit Gundam Wing: Operation 10

Bandai, 2001, 100 mins., #1679. Directed by Masashi Ikeda. Written by Katsuyuki Sumizawa, Katsuhiko Chiba. Based on the stories by Hajime Yatate, Yoshiyuki Tomino in *Mobile Suit Gundam.*

Relena and Heero board the *Libra* but are unable to persuade Zechs to reconsider his attack. His enemy Treize also tries to convince Zechs to decide the fate of the war in a man-to-man duel, but Zechs still isn't interested. Now, the battleships *Libra* and *Peacemillion* are on a collision course in Earth's atmosphere. If the two ships strike each other, the resulting explosion could destroy all life on Earth! While most of the Gundam pilots attempt to stop both ships, Heero meets up with Zechs for a final battle.

This grand finale DVD contains episodes #46–49. There are some really cool extras, including textless openings and the ending, as well as a complete Mobile Suit Encyclopedia featuring all the Gundams and Mobile Suits seen in the show. These features alone are worth the price of the DVD. [JMC]

SPECIAL FEATURES Mobile Suit Encyclopedia • Clean Credits • Other Title Trailers • Inserts: Liner Notes, Mecha Specs TECHNICAL FEATURES Fullscreen (1.33:1) • Subtitles/CC: Eng. • Languages: Jap., Eng. dub • Sound: Dolby Digital Surround 2.0 • Keepcase • 1 Disc • Region 1 GENRE & RATING Robots/Science Fiction • Rated 13+

Mobile Suit Gundam Wing: The Complete Operations [Box Set]

Pioneer, 2002, 999 mins.

This 10-disc boxed set was not available for review.

Mobile Suit Gundam: The 08th MS Team [#1]

Bandai, 2001, 75 mins., #1710. Directed by Takeyuki Kanda. Written by Akira Okeya, Hiroaki Kitajima. Based on the stories by Hajime Yatate, Yoshiyuki Tomino in *Mobile Suit Gundam.*

In the heat of the One-Year War, a young ensign named Shiro Amada is assigned to the Federation's ground forces. However, before he reaches the planet, a battle in space leads to an unexpected encounter, and a surprising—and forbidden—friendship with a Zeon pilot. Shiro is eventually given the duty of leading the 08th MS Team, a squad consisting of three Mobile Suits and one hovercar. Shiro pilots a mass-production Gundam, and is backed up by the tough, no-nonsense Karen and the skilled Sanders, who carries a dark secret of his own. Manning the hovercar are the lazy, good-natured Eledore and the earnest Michel. As the ground campaign rages, it's up to Shiro to keep his young team alive, even as they team up with local guerillas to face the threat of a new, incredibly powerful Zeon prototype weapon.

Almost everything is done right in this 1996 incarnation of *Gundam.* The animation is splendid, and the mechanical designs are both streamlined and dirty-looking. Even the characters look great and are nicely fleshed-out. Another part of *08th MS Team*'s appeal is that it offers yet another aspect of the popular One-Year War story, from the point of view of a small, tightly knit ground combat group. *The 08th MS Team* is a solidly engaging piece of science fiction, and a must-have for *Gundam* fans.

The quality of the DVD is more or less perfect, and the extras include a nice reversible cover. This quality package contains the first three episodes of the total twelve. [MT]

SPECIAL FEATURES Promotional Footage • Clean Credits • Other Title Trailers • Reversible Cover • Inserts: Character Correspondence TECHNICAL FEATURES Fullscreen (1.33:1) • Subtitles/CC: Eng. • Languages: Jap., Eng. dub • Sound: Dolby Digital Surround 2.0 • Keepcase • 1 Disc • Region 1 GENRE & RATING Robots/Science Fiction • Rated 13+

Mobile Suit Gundam: The 08th MS Team [#2]

Bandai, 2001, 80 mins., #1711. Directed by Takeyuki Kanda. Written by Akira Okeya, Hiroaki Kitajima. Based on the stories by Hajime Yatate, Yoshiyuki Tomino in *Mobile Suit Gundam.*

Shiro continues to lead his team, but Sanders is really starting to dread the consequences of his unexplained secret. The 08th team finds itself hard-pressed to hold up against the Zeon's new weapon, the heavily armored Apsalus. Meanwhile, Eledore gets himself and Michel into an unexpected mess, and Shiro gains more trust and cooperation from Kiki, the *de facto* leader of a group of local guerillas.

Another exceptional DVD, this one containing episodes #4–6. [MT]

SPECIAL FEATURES Mobile Suit Encyclopedia • Promotional Footage • Clean Credits • Other Title Trailers • Reversible Cover • Inserts: Character Correspondence TECHNICAL FEATURES Fullscreen (1.33:1) • Subtitles/CC: Eng. • Languages: Jap., Eng. dub • Sound: Dolby Digital Surround 2.0 • Keepcase • 1 Disc • Region 1 GENRE & RATING Robots/Science Fiction • Rated 13+

Mobile Suit Gundam: The 08th MS Team [#3]

Bandai, 2001, 80 mins., #1712. Directed by Umanosuke Iida. Written by Akira Okeya, Hiroaki Kitajima. Based on the stories by Hajime Yatate, Yoshiyuki Tomino in *Mobile Suit Gundam.*

A strange set of circumstances leads Shiro back to Aina Sahalin, the Zeon pilot he met in the first volume. His experiences with her influence his own ideas about the war to the point that his superiors are afraid he might cause trouble. Meanwhile, the team's guerilla allies come under attack; with Shiro locked up and under threat of court martial, how will his team react to the new threat?

As usual, this DVD looks and sounds great. It contains episodes #7–9. [MT]

SPECIAL FEATURES Mobile Suit Encyclopedia • Promotional Footage • Other Title Trailers • Reversible Cover • Inserts: Character Correspondence TECHNICAL FEATURES Fullscreen (1.33:1) • Subtitles/CC: Eng. • Languages: Jap., Eng. dub • Sound: Dolby Digital Surround 2.0 • Keepcase • 1 Disc • Region 1 GENRE & RATING Robots/Science Fiction • Rated 13+

Mobile Suit Gundam: The 08th MS Team [#4]

Bandai, 2002, 90 mins., #1713. Directed by Umanosuke Iida. Written by Akira Okeya, Hiroaki Kitajima. Based on the stories by Hajime Yatate, Yoshiyuki Tomino in *Mobile Suit Gundam*.

Shiro, temporarily out of danger of a court martial, leads his team into a final assault against the Zeon forces and the powerful Apsalus prototype. He's desperate to end the conflict, keep his own team alive, and save the life of Aina, but how can he accomplish all three?

The final DVD of this series contains episodes #10–12. [MT]

SPECIAL FEATURES Mobile Suit Encyclopedia • Promotional Footage • Other Title Trailers • Reversible Cover • Inserts: Character Correspondence TECHNICAL FEATURES Fullscreen (1.33:1) • Subtitles/CC: Eng. • Languages: Jap., Eng. dub • Sound: Dolby Digital Surround 2.0 • Keepcase • 1 Disc • Region 1 GENRE & RATING Robots/Science Fiction • Rated 13+

Mobile Suit Gundam: The 08th MS Team— Miller's Report

Bandai, 2002, 55 mins., #1714. Directed by Takeyuki Kanda, Umanosuke Iida. Written by Akira Okeya, Hiroaki Kitajima. Based on the stories by Hajime Yatate, Yoshiyuki Tomino in *Mobile Suit Gundam*.

This "movie" was created to celebrate the twentieth anniversary of *Gundam*. It's essentially an alternate version of parts of episodes 7 and 8 of the regular *08th MS Team* OVA series, with new animation inserted at various points. The story is massaged to tell about Shiro's encounter with Aina from the point of view of Alice Miller, a bitter, chain-smoking Federation intelligence officer. It sheds a bit more light on Shiro's experiences, as well as introducing the interesting Miller herself.

This would be an excellent companion to the *08th M.S. Team* OVAs save for one thing; a disastrous problem with the English audio makes it practically unlistenable and heavily distorted. The Japanese audio is fine, and the disc also includes over twenty-five minutes of animation from the Playstation 2 game *Gundam: Journey to Jaburo*, but the severe technical problem with the English dub makes it difficult to recommend this disc. *Gundam* completists who can overlook the damaged English audio— and the ending scene, which some fans have found improbable and disappointing—will still want this disc; all others are hereby warned. [MT]

SPECIAL FEATURES Promotional Footage • Clean Credits • Other

Title Trailers • Reversible Cover • Inserts: Character Correspondence TECHNICAL FEATURES Fullscreen (1.33:1) • Subtitles/CC: Eng. • Languages: Jap., Eng. dub • Sound: Dolby Digital Surround 5.1 • Keepcase • 1 Disc • Region 1 GENRE & RATING Robots/Science Fiction • Rated 13+

Mobile Suit Gundam: Movie I

Bandai, 2002, 147 mins., #0310. Directed by Yoshiyuki Tomino. Written by Hiroyuki Hoshiyama, Yoshihisa Araki, Masaru Yamamoto, Kenichi Matsuzaki, Yoshiyuki Tomino. Based on the stories by Hajime Yatate, Yoshiyuki Tomino in *Mobile Suit Gundam*.

Teenager Amuro Ray is unwittingly yanked into a devastating war between Earth and a rogue colony, the Principality of Zeon, when he successfully tries to pilot the Gundam, an experimental weapon, in a bid to thwart a Zeon surprise attack. Along with several others, Amuro is drafted into service aboard the *White Base*, a prototype starship desperately fleeing through space toward earth. Amuro is forced to use his newfound skills against the Zeon, led by the ace pilot Char Aznable.

This 1981 movie, the first in a trilogy, was created as a successful attempt to popularize *Gundam* in Japan (the ratings of the original TV series were initially low). The movie features some TV animation, as well as a great deal of new animation created specifically for the theatrical release. It essentially condenses the first third of the TV series, filling in a few plot holes in the bargain. The movie is long and detailed, but some fans prefer it to the TV series, which features much more story but some poor animation and direction. The *Gundam* saga starts here, and watching these films is probably the best way for prospective viewers to introduce themselves to the story.

The DVD doesn't contain any extra features, but it's created from a newly remastered transfer, which makes for an excellent-looking picture. Purists might be ruffled to learn that the audio has been completely rebuilt, featuring newly recorded dialogue by the original cast, new sound design, and a slightly altered musical score. This is good, because the new audio sounds excellent on modern sound systems, but also not so good, because the original soundtrack is no longer available at all. Still, the DVD's quality is generally excellent. [MT]

SPECIAL FEATURES Inserts: Creator Bio TECHNICAL FEATURES Fullscreen (1.33:1) • Subtitles/CC: Eng. • Languages: Jap. • Sound: Dolby Digital 5.1 • Keepcase • 1 Disc • Region 1 GENRE & RATING Robots/Science Fiction • Rated 13+

Mobile Suit Gundam: Movie II—Soldiers of Sorrow

Bandai, 2002, 147 mins., #0311. Directed by Yoshiyuki Tomino. Written by Hiroyuki Hoshiyama, Yoshihisa Araki, Masaru Yamamoto, Kenichi Matsuzaki, Yoshiyuki Tomino. Based on the stories by Hajime Yatate, Yoshiyuki Tomino in *Mobile Suit Gundam.*

This 1981 film summarizes the second third of the original *Gundam* TV series story, in which the *White Base* reaches earth and makes a long journey across the surface to the Federation's headquarters at Jaburo. Amuro and the Gundam face a wide variety of tough foes, and the *White Base's* crew staunchly fends off constant attacks.

Once again, the DVD has an excellent new transfer and an all-new soundtrack—but no original soundtrack. [MT]

SPECIAL FEATURES Inserts: Designer Bio TECHNICAL FEATURES Fullscreen (1.33:1) • Subtitles/CC: Eng. • Languages: Jap. • Sound: Dolby Digital 5.1 • Keepcase • 1 Disc • Region 1 GENRE & RATING Robots/Science Fiction • Rated 13+

Mobile Suit Gundam: Movie III— Encounters in Space

Bandai, 2002, 147 mins., #0312. Directed by Yoshiyuki Tomino. Written by Hiroyuki Hoshiyama, Yoshihisa Araki, Masaru Yamamoto, Kenichi Matsuzaki, Yoshiyuki Tomino. Based on the stories by Hajime Yatate, Yoshiyuki Tomino in *Mobile Suit Gundam.*

This 1982 film summarizes the final story arc of the original *Gundam* television saga, in which the *White Base* joins the Federation forces in space. Amuro meets the mysterious Lalah, and hurtles toward a final confrontation with Zeon ace Char Aznable. A significant portion of this film is new animation, with some of it setting up plot points for the 1985 sequel series *Zeta Gundam.*

Once again, the DVD has an excellent new transfer and an all-new soundtrack, yet there's no alternate original soundtrack to be found. [MT]

SPECIAL FEATURES Inserts: Designer Bio TECHNICAL FEATURES Fullscreen (1.33:1) • Subtitles/CC: Eng. • Languages: Jap. • Sound: Dolby Digital 5.1 • Keepcase • 1 Disc • Region 1 GENRE & RATING Robots/Science Fiction • Rated 13+

Mobile Suit Gundam: Movie Box Set

Bandai, 2002, 441 mins., #0313.

This box set contains the three commercially available DVDs of the *Mobile Suit Gundam* movies in their original keepcases. It also contains a bonus twelve-page color booklet with character notes and series highlights. See individual entries for the Special and Technical Features listings.

SPECIAL FEATURES Inserts: Creator & Designer Bios • Booklet TECHNICAL FEATURES Cardboard Box with 3 Keepcases • 3 Discs • Region 1 GENRE & RATING Robots/Science Fiction • Rated 13+

Moldiver

Pioneer, 2001, 200 mins., #11490. Directed by Hiroyuki Kitazume. Screenplay by Manabu Nakamura.

It's the future, and the nerdy Hiroshi Ozora has developed an exciting new piece of technology; a molecular shield and transportation system that enables him to pull off superhuman feats of strength and speed. Trouble rears its head in the form of mad scientist Dr. Machinegal, a cackling old man flanked by a team of android beauties. Hiroshi uses his "Mol" technology to create a superhero identity for himself, but it isn't long before he's overshadowed by his cute sister Mirai, who uses his technology to transform into the heroic—and fashionable—superheroine Moldiver.

Moldiver is an entertainingly silly effort from one of the creators behind the original *Gundam* animation. This six-episode OVA series is lighthearted and goofy; even Dr. Machinegal, the show's chief villain, is more concerned with hoarding antiques than he is with hurting people. The cartoonish violence and less-than-serious tone may turn off some viewers, but overall the show is fun and inoffensive.

This DVD contains all six episodes of the *Moldiver* series. The quality isn't perfect; the footage is starting to show its age, with some dust and dirt visible. The extras, however, are quite substantial, including production art, a gallery of original laserdisc covers, and even a brief pseudo-documentary about the physics behind the "Mol" technology. The only problem is with the subtitles, which is simply the text of the dubbed dialogue rather than a literal translation from the Japanese (otherwise known as "dubtitles"). [MT]

SPECIAL FEATURES Character and Art Galleries • Promotional Footage • Clean Credits • Other Title Trailers • Inserts: Liner Notes TECHNICAL FEATURES Fullscreen (1.33:1) • Subtitles/CC: Eng. • Languages: Jap., Eng. dub • Sound: Dolby Digital 2.0

• Keepcase • 1 Disc • Region 1, 4 GENRE & RATING Robots/Science Fiction • Rated PG

Monkey Magic

The following *Monkey Magic* titles, from Bandai/Pioneer, were not available for review. They are out of print. *Enter Stone Monkey* [#1] (episodes #1–5); *The Celestial Heavens* [#2] (episodes #6–9); *The Quest Begins* [#3] (episodes #10–13).

Monkeybone

Fox, 2002, 100 mins., #2001935. Directed by Henry Selick. Written by Sam Hamm. Based on the comic book *Dark Town* by Kaja Blackley.

Stu Miley (Brendan Fraser) is a cartoonist whose infamous creation is an uninhibited simian named Monkeybone, whose personality comes from Stu's repressed sexual anxieties. Stu is on the cusp of success, with Monkeybone sold as an animated series and about to be launched as a toy franchise. But when Stu and his girlfriend Julie (Bridget Fonda) get into a car wreck, Stu goes into a coma. Stu's soul awakens in a bizarre and creepy waystation for lost souls called Down Town, which is home to many creatures of imagination and fear. Monkeybone is there as well, but the little stop-motion animated creature doesn't quite get along with his maker. Realizing that back in the real world his sister will soon pull the plug on his comatose body, Stu embarks on a plan to cheat Death herself (Whoopi Goldberg), but in the process, Monkeybone gains control of Stu's body. Now how will Stu's soul ever regain his body, what with a crazy monkey controlling him?

Loosely based on an unfinished graphic novel, the 2001 feature film *Monkeybone* was a flop in movie theaters. This is largely because it's nearly incomprehensibly goofy and full of so many bizarre set pieces that most non-chemically enhanced viewers will be glassy-eyed and scratching their heads by the end. The imaginative sequences in Down Town—realized with stop-motion, puppetry, CGI, and costumes—are too nightmarish for kids and too bizarre for most adults. It's as if Terry Gilliam were making *Baron Munchausen II* but fell asleep in the director's chair after eating bad clams.

At least the DVD allows you to stop and rewind to catch all the grotesqueries and strangeness on display. And lest it sound as if the movie is being completely panned, it isn't: *Saturday Night Live*'s Chris Kattan plays a gymnast with a broken neck who gets involved in the story and nearly saves the movie with his physical comedy alone. The DVD also has some extended scenes, which help make sense of the badly edited sequences in the actual film.

Sam Hamm is a crackerjack writer and Henry Selick an exceptional animator and filmmaker, but *Monkeybone* proved a bit too bizarre for theaters. On DVD, it may find an audience that will appreciate its crazy-quilt logic, impressionistic look, and whacked-out-on-cough-medication story.

SPECIAL FEATURES Commentary Track with Director • Still Galleries • Extended and Deleted Scenes • Animation Studies • Trailer • Promotional Footage • Easter Egg TECHNICAL FEATURES Widescreen (1.85:1 enhanced for 16x9) • Subtitles/CC: Eng., Span. • Languages: Eng., Fren. dub • Sound: Dolby Digital Surround 2.0, Dolby Digital 5.1, DTS • Keepcase • 1 Disc • Region 1 GENRE & RATING Live/Humor • Rated PG-13

Monster Rancher: Let the Games Begin! [#1]

ADV Films, 2000, 60 mins., #DVDMR001. Directed by Yuji Himaki, Yukio Okuwaki. Screenplay by Shoji Yonemura.

Genki is a video game genius, but when he wins a special CD-ROM in a Monster Battle tournament, he is transported into the world of Monster Rancher! He saves a girl named Holly—and her pet eyeball monster Suezo—from the sinister Black Dino Squad. Genki creates his own yellow monster named Mocchi, and the group is joined by a giant stone creature known as Golem, a wolf, and a rabbit, to fight the evil forces of Moo and his nasty Blue Gel Troops.

Debuting in 1999 in Japan, *Monster Rancher* swiftly made its way to America to air on Fox Kids. The series is very much in the vein of *Pokémon* and *Digimon*, the latter of which it was paired with for American airing. The animation is cute but barely up to standards, and the characters are bright, frenetic, and unabashedly aimed at the "buy-me-the-spinoff-toy-or-I'll-have-a-tantrum-in-the-store" set. The first DVD volume contains three episodes.

SPECIAL FEATURES None TECHNICAL FEATURES Fullscreen (1.33:1) • Languages: Eng. • Sound: Dolby Digital Surround 2.0 • Keepcase • 1 Disc • Region 1 GENRE & RATING Action/Adventure • Not Rated (Kids)

Monster Rancher: Catch a Tiger by the Tail! [#2]

ADV Films, 2000, 60 mins., #DVDMR002. Directed by Mihiro Yamaguchi, Makoto Fuchigami, Hiroki Negishi. Screenplay by Shinzo Fujita, Shoji Yonemura.

Searching for the Phoenix, which can defeat Moo's badness, Genki and his group encounter whip-wielding Allan and his frustrated monster worm. Will the worm betray his master to Moo and the Seed Sisters? Then it's the Tiger of the Wind versus the Hare. And why is Golem wearing a frilly dress?

Three more episodes are presented on this disc: "Eternal Worm"; "Tiger of the Wind"; and "Hare's Trick."

SPECIAL FEATURES None TECHNICAL FEATURES Fullscreen (1.33:1) • Languages: Eng. • Sound: Dolby Digital 2.0 • Keepcase • 1 Disc • Region 1 GENRE & RATING Action/Adventure • Not Rated (Kids)

Monster Rancher: Fast Friends and Fiendish Foes! [#3]

ADV Films, 2001, 75 mins., #DVDMR003. Directed by Nanako Shimazaki, Sachio Okazaki, Tomio Yamauchi. Screenplay by Osamu Nakamura, Shoji Yonemura, Shinzo Fujita.

Moo finally makes the scene, and he's after Genki and his crew. He even sends Pixie and her black hares after them! Holly's magical pendant has something to do with Moo's first evil attack, and its secrets will soon be revealed. Then, Genki and friends must create an Iron Bird to get across the perilous Heaven's Canyon, or they'll be caught by Captain Kudo!

Another trio of episodes on this DVD offers more kiddy fun: "The Courageous Seven"; "After the Rain"; and "The Iron Bird."

SPECIAL FEATURES Other Title Trailers TECHNICAL FEATURES Fullscreen (1.33:1) • Languages: Eng. • Sound: Dolby Digital 2.0 • Keepcase • 1 Disc • Region 1 GENRE & RATING Action/Adventure • Not Rated (Kids)

Monster Rancher: The Problem with Pixie [#4]

ADV Films, 2001, 75 mins., #DVDMR/004. Directed by Makoto Fuchigami, Tomio Yamauchi, Yukio Suzuki. Screenplay by Shoji Yonemura.

Genki and his crew have survived so far, but when they arrive at some ancient ruins, Pixie forces them to dig up some powerful and mysterious discs. The friends must battle Pixie, her own golem Big Blue, and the army of Clays to get free. But when Genki unlocks a disc, freeing Monol, the group learns all the secrets of the first battle between Moo and the Phoenix . . . and maybe the secret of how to defeat the evil monster!

This most recently released DVD features another three episodes of the series: "The Ruin's Secret"; "Pixie's Defeat"; and "Monol's Story."

SPECIAL FEATURES Other Title Trailers TECHNICAL FEATURES Fullscreen (1.33:1) • Languages: Eng. • Sound: Dolby Digital

2.0 • Keepcase • 1 Disc • Region 1 GENRE & RATING Action/Adventure • Not Rated (Kids)

Monsters, Inc.

Disney, 2002, 93 mins., #23968. Directed by Pete Docter, Lee Unkrich, David Silverman. Screenplay by Andrew Stanton, Daniel Gerson. Story by Pete Docter, Jill Culton, Jeff Pidgeon, Ralph Eggleston.

Mike and Sully work at Monsters, Inc., the plant that provides all of Monsteropolis with power. Said energy is captured when the monsters go through kid's closet doors, scare them, and bottle their powerful screams. Everything's just fine until Mike and Sully accidentally allow a child to follow them back to the monster realm! Now, as they try to hide "Boo," they learn of a suspicious plot being hatched by a slithery coworker. But what good will their knowledge do them if they get banished?

Released in 2001, *Monsters, Inc.* was the fourth feature film team-up of Pixar and Disney, and it became the second most profitable animated feature in history. Nominated for four Academy Awards, the movie is exceedingly clever, cute, and funny. And even though they're monsters, the characters are realistic and human, aided by impeccable CGI work (just watch Sully's fur move).

The two-DVD set was released in September 2002 and sold an astonishing five million units, making it the top first-day seller in history. The set is elaborate and packed with goodies. The picture is digitally transferred, meaning it's as close to perfection as one can find outside of the animator's computer screens. The sound is also flawless. In terms of extras, one of the coolest is a new animated short film, "Mike's New Car," and the film's commentary track is mighty enjoyable as well.

The DVDs are divided into two arenas. "The Human World" examines the making of the film and gives a tour through Pixar Animation Studios. There are oodles of 3D footage, artwork, deleted scenes, and hidden jokes, as well. "The Monster World" explores the city of Monsteropolis, giving you a chance to work at the scream factory, see outtakes, learn the history of monsters and humans, view the Company Play, and more. *Monsters, Inc.* is another highly recommended feature for animation fans of all ages.

SPECIAL FEATURES "Making of" Featurettes • Commentary Track with Filmmakers • Cast and Crew Bios • Character Bios • Character and Art Galleries • Production Notes • Deleted Scenes and Abandoned Sequences • Storyboards • Story Treatment • 3D Turnarounds • Trailers • Promotional Footage • Music Videos • Isolated Sound Effects Track • Outtakes • Guide to In-Jokes • Games • Other Title Trailers • Inserts: Liner Notes • Easter Eggs TECHNICAL FEATURES Widescreen (1.85:1 enhanced for 16x9) • Fullscreen (1.33:1) •

Subtitles/CC: Eng. • Languages: Eng. • Sound: Dolby Digital 5.1 Surround • Multikeepcase • 2 Discs • Region 1 GENRE & RATING CGI/Adventure/Comedy • Rated G

More! Animation Greats

Slingshot, 1998, 90 mins., #DVD 2197.

The vaults of the National Film Board of Canada are opened yet again for ten more short animated films. Included in the collection are: "Cactus Swing"; "La Salla"; "64 Million Years Ago"; "Evolution"; "Hot Stuff"; "Every Dog's Guide to Home Safety"; "The Family That Dwelt Apart"; "The Dingles"; "The Old Lady's Camping Trip"; and "Every Child."

The sound alternates from mono to stereo depending on the cartoon, but screen size and quality remain fairly consistent. "64 Million Years Ago," a short about dinosaurs, is the real stand-out of the bunch, although "The Family That Dwelt Apart" (based on a 1937 short story by E. B. White) and the baby-swapping "Every Child" are also nice. Don't judge this enjoyable DVD by its awful cover; the contents far surpass the plain outer wrapping.

SPECIAL FEATURES None TECHNICAL FEATURES Widescreen: Various Ratios • Fullscreen (1.33:1) • Languages: Eng. • Sound: Dolby Digital 1.0, Dolby Digital 2.0 • Keepcase • 1 Disc • Region 1–6 GENRE & RATING Anthology • Not Rated (Kids)

Mowgli [The Jungle Book]

Jove/Stellar, 83 mins.

This DVD was not available for review. It is a Russian-language disc.

Mr. Magoo's Christmas Carol

GoodTimes, 2001, 53 mins., #05-81239. Directed by Abe Levitow. Adapted by Barbara Chain. Based on *A Christmas Carol* by Charles Dickens.

The nearsighted Mr. Magoo takes on the role of Scrooge—literally—in this loosely adapted musical version of the Dickens classic. The story features Magoo as a famous actor portraying Scrooge on the Broadway stage, thus allowing elements of the original story and all the trademarks of Magoo's character to interplay nicely.

Aired on NBC in December 1962, *Mr. Magoo's Christmas Carol* was the first-ever animated-for-television special (as well as the first animated *musical* created for TV), and its huge ratings led not only to further holiday-themed specials for other characters, but a regular literary adaptation series called *The Famous Adventures of Mr. Magoo* in 1964. This special features five songs by Broadway songsters Jule Styne and Bob Merrill, as well as the always-terrific lead character voice of Jim Backus.

The DVD includes the complete special (some video versions omit the song "It's Great to Be Back on Broadway"), as well as a number of fun extras. Included is a complete history of Mr. Magoo on television and film, bios of the voice actors, lyricist, and composer, and the original movie poster. Fans will also likely go loopy for the vintage *Magoo* short "Magoo meets McBoing Boing." This is a terrific and fun DVD for all but the most Scroogy of animation connoisseurs.

SPECIAL FEATURES Crew Bios & Filmographies • History of Mr. Magoo • Promotional Art TECHNICAL FEATURES Fullscreen (1.33:1) • Languages: Eng. • Sound: Dolby Digital 2.0 • Keepcase • 1 Disc • Region 1–6 GENRE & RATING Holiday/Music/Comedy • Not Rated (All Ages)

Mulan

Madacy, 1999, 30 mins.

This DVD was not available for review.

Mulan [Gold Edition]

Disney, 1999, 88 mins., #17225. Directed by Barry Cook, Tony Bancroft. Screenplay by Rita Hsiao, Chris Sanders, Philip Lazebnik, Raymond Singer, Eugenia Bostwick-Singer.

When the Hun army comes to China's Great Wall, every available man is called to battle. But feisty young Mulan is worried; her father is aged and infirm, and he'll never be able to fight in his armor. Cutting her hair, Mulan disguises herself as a man and joins the Imperial Army, where she is befriended by a group of misfit soldiers. Mulan is aided by Mushu, a miniature guardian dragon sent by her ancestors, but she'll need all of her skills if she is going to stay alive long enough to help defeat the Huns. But when her deception is discovered, how will the Army treat a woman forbidden to be among them?

Disney's thirty-sixth animated feature film is based on an ancient Chinese legend, and it's a rousing and funny strike for girl power that garnered much-deserved critical praise. The animation is stellar at times—especially during a snow battle and a fireworks display—and the voice work from actors Ming Na, Eddie Murphy, Harvey Fierstein, June Foray, George Takei, and others, is excellent. A wonderful score and a set of memorable songs also complement the film. Sure, *Mulan* could have done without the comic-relief dragon sidekick—and possibly been stronger for it—but Murphy's lines are funny enough.

The *Mulan* DVD doesn't contain many extras, but it does contain both the widescreen and pan-and-scan versions of the film. And in a bizarre oddity, the trailer shown on the DVD is an unfinished version, with pencil-test animation in several parts!

NOTE: This DVD is now on moratorium.

SPECIAL FEATURES Trailer • Music Videos • Other Title Trailers TECHNICAL FEATURES Widescreen (1.85:1) • Fullscreen (1.33:1) • Subtitles/CC: Eng. • Languages: Eng., Fren. dub, Span. dub • Sound: Dolby Digital 5.1 • Keepcase • 1 Disc • Region 1, 4 GENRE & RATING Historical/Girl/Action • Rated G

Mummies Alive! The Real Beginning

Trimark, 2001, 103 mins., #VM 7722D. Directed by Seth Kearsley. Story by Mark Edens. Teleplay by Brooks Wachtel, Mathew Edens, Len Uhley, Steve Cuden

In the year 1525 B.C. the evil sorceror Scarab has defeated the Pharaoh's son and the four warriors who protected him. The Pharaoh entombs Scarab alive and curses him to live fifty lifetimes buried beneath the Egyptian sands. In modern day, Scarab has resurfaced, and lives in San Francisco with the wealth of the ages. But Prince Rapses has been reincarnated, and the four warriors rise again as armored Mummies to protect him. Soon, the forces of Scarab and Ja-Kal's quartet of Mummy warriors are at war, with the world's future hanging in the balance!

This 1997 DIC television series had at least one pedigreed name to its credit: producer Ivan Reitman (*Ghostbusters*). The DVD contains the first five episodes of the series, which has some scary moments and violence, but was shown on Saturday mornings, so it passed the Standards and Practices tests. It also has some goofy humor, and magical anime-style effects.

SPECIAL FEATURES Interview with Producer • Game • Other Title Trailers TECHNICAL FEATURES Fullscreen (1.33:1) • Subtitles/CC: Eng. • Languages: Eng., Span. dub • Sound: Dolby Digital 2.0 • Keepcase • 1 Disc • Region 1 GENRE & RATING Action/Horror/Comedy • Not Rated (Kids)

Mummy, The: Quest for the Lost Scrolls

Universal, 2002, 70 mins., #22125. Directed by Eddy Houchins. Written by Tom Pugsley, Greg Klein.

NOTE: This DVD arrived too late for a full review. The following text is promotional copy provided by the releasing company:

"Watch out for tumbling temples, monstrous sand worms, crashing trains, and invading armies of insects in this exciting adventure. After accidentally raising a Mummy from the dead, eleven-year-old Alex O'Connell is every kid's hero, as he narrowly escapes one disaster after another. He and his family must race across the globe to locate the lost scrolls that will unlock the powers of a magical manacle and send the Mummy back to his tomb for good! Will Alex take down the Mummy and save the future of our world?"

SPECIAL FEATURES Character Bios • Egyptology Notes • Trailer • Promotional Footage • Music Video • Games • Other Title Trailers TECHNICAL FEATURES Fullscreen (1.33:1) • Subtitles/CC: Eng., Fren., Span. • Languages: Eng. • Sound: Dolby Digital 2.0 • Keepcase • 1 Disc • Region 1 GENRE & RATING Action/Supernatural • Not Rated (Kids)

My Life As . . . ☛ see Mature/Adult Section

My My Mai ☛ see Mature/Adult Section

Mystery of the Necronomicon ☛ see Mature/Adult Section

N

Nadia: The Secret of Blue Water—The Adventure Begins [#1]

ADV Films, 2001, 100 mins., #DNS001. General Direction by Hideaki Anno. Screenplay by Hisao Okawa. Based on *20,000 Leagues Under the Sea* by Jules Verne.

Set near the turn of the century during the Industrial Revolution, *Nadia: The Secret of Blue Water* follows the adventures of two fourteen-year-olds and a lion cub named King. Nadia is an acrobat and circus performer who doesn't know much about her past. Jean is a precocious inventor, smitten with Nadia, and willing to do anything to help her discover the secrets surrounding her life and the reason that so many people are after the gem around her neck. The jewel, Blue Water, may hold the key to her past, the present, and the future, but only if Nadia and Jean can discover someone to help them interpret the mystery of the blue gem. As they travel through the land trying to unravel the secrets of Nadia's past, and meeting a variety of people both good and evil, the pair discover that the fate of the Earth rests with whoever controls the Blue Water. Joined by a young girl named Marie and former enemies Grandis, Sanson, and Hanson, they struggle to find the secret of the crystal. Will they be able to keep the gem away from the evil Gargoyle, who plans on using its power for nefarious ends?

Created in 1990 by the animation studio Gainax—based on an idea from Hayao Miyazaki—*Nadia* is an anime series that spanned thirty-nine episodes and one OVA, quickly becoming a fan favorite in Japan. The series is loosely based on Jules Verne's *20,000 Leagues Under the Sea*, and the legendary Captain Nemo and his submarine the *Nautilus* even make cameos in some episodes. The series combines steampunk technology with detailed and fun characterization, making for a property U.S. audiences enjoyed as well. It's too bad that *Nadia*'s 2001 release was marred a bit by Disney's film *Atlantis*, which shares some—ahem—very similar concepts.

This introduction to the series contains episodes #1–4, enough to tease viewers into wanting to go on a gem hunt of their own. [JMC]

SPECIAL FEATURES Clean Credits • Trailers • Promotional Footage • Other Title Trailers TECHNICAL FEATURES Fullscreen (1.33:1) • Subtitles/CC: Eng. • Languages: Jap., Eng. dub • Sound: Dolby Digital 2.0 • Keepcase • 1 Disc • Region 1 GENRE & RATING Fantasy/Historical/Action • Rated 13+

Nadia: The Secret of Blue Water—The Dark Kingdom [#2]

ADV Films, 2001, 100 mins., #DNS002. General Direction by Hideaki Anno. Screenplay by Hisao Okawa. Based on *20,000 Leagues Under the Sea* by Jules Verne.

After crash-landing on a mysterious island, Jean and Nadia find trouble awaits them. The pair find a murdered couple and a young survivor, Marie, who tells them a story of strange masked men attacking her village and taking anything they wanted. Nadia and Jean discover the masked men have a hidden city, with technology advanced far beyond the year 1889. The men want to rule the world, but they're starting small, with this island. Soon, they capture Nadia and King, and it's up to Jean and Marie, with some unlikely allies—the evil Grandis and her gang—to rescue Nadia and the Blue Water before the masked men learn that it may hold the key to their dreams of conquest.

The second volume of this delightful series contains episodes #5–8, and enough action, intrigue, and mystery to appeal to a broad range of anime fans. This disc could have made a great conclusion to the series, but *Nadia* is still in its beginning stages. [JMC]

SPECIAL FEATURES Clean Credits • Trailers • Promotional Footage • Other Title Trailers TECHNICAL FEATURES Fullscreen (1.33:1) • Subtitles/CC: Eng. • Languages: Jap., Eng. dub • Sound: Dolby Digital 2.0 • Keepcase • 1 Disc • Region 1 GENRE & RATING Fantasy/Historical/Action • Rated 13+

Nadia: The Secret of Blue Water—Aboard the Nautilus [#3]

ADV Films, 2001, 100 mins., #DNS003. General Direction by Hideaki Anno. Screenplay by Hisao Okawa. Based on *20,000 Leagues Under the Sea* by Jules Verne.

Nadia, Jean, Marie, King, and their two new allies (for the time being) Grandis and Sanson, are adrift in the damaged floating tank, *Katherine.* Captain Nemo and the *Nautilus* crew spot the craft and rescue the group, even though they have reservations about taking Grandis and Sanson aboard the sea vessel. Planning to repair the *Katherine,* Nemo guides them to a special area within the ship and tells them not to wander around. Curiosity gets the better of them, and soon the whole group is exploring the ship. What secrets and situations will the crew of the *Nautilus* reveal to these visitors? Do any of them know about the Blue Water?

This character-driven DVD contains episodes #9–12 and explores new facets of the relationships between the main characters, their allies, and their enemies.

SPECIAL FEATURES Clean Credits • Trailers • Promotional Footage • Other Title Trailers TECHNICAL FEATURES Fullscreen (1.33:1) • Subtitles/CC: Eng. • Languages: Jap., Eng. dub • Sound: Dolby Digital 2.0 • Keepcase • 1 Disc • Region 1 GENRE & RATING Fantasy/Historical/Action • Rated 13+

Nadia: The Secret of Blue Water—Battleground [#4]

ADV Films, 2001, 100 mins., #DNS004. General Direction by Hideaki Anno. Screenplay by Hisao Okawa, Hisao Okawa, Kaoru Umeno. Based on *20,000 Leagues Under the Sea* by Jules Verne.

After a long stay at sea, the crew of the *Nautilus* sets up camp on an island, not knowing the Neo Atlanteans are also there. A battle between the two groups ensues, with the crew of the *Nautilus* prevailing. Unfortunately, their victory is short lived. When they return to the water, Nadia and Marie contract a deadly illness that requires herbs from the ocean floor for treatment. When a group attempts to retrieve the plants, they are attacked by a group of Garfish submarines. The *Nautilus* suffers heavy damage and surfaces, but the American Naval Fleet is waiting for them. The Navy bombards the advanced submarine with cannon fire, and the vessel suffers further damage. Tough choices result in the ultimate sacrifice for some of the crew, but even if the *Nautilus* escapes, was it worth the cost in lives?

This gut-wrenching *Nadia* collection contains episodes #13–16. [JMC]

SPECIAL FEATURES Character Bios • Promotional Footage • Other Title Trailers TECHNICAL FEATURES Fullscreen (1.33:1) • Subtitles/CC: Eng. • Languages: Jap., Eng. dub • Sound: Dolby Digital 2.0 • Keepcase • 1 Disc • Region 1 GENRE & RATING Fantasy/Historical/Action • Rated 13+

Nadia: The Secret of Blue Water—Nemo's Fortress [#5]

ADV Films, 2001, 100 mins., #DNS005. General Direction by Hideaki Anno. Screenplay by Hisao Okawa, Kaoru Umeno. Based on *20,000 Leagues Under the Sea* by Jules Verne.

Now that Jean has discovered that the evil Gargoyle murdered his father, the youth wants to join the crew of the *Nautilus* and hunt Gargoyle down. Angry and ignoring his scientific tendencies for a while, he begins acting on his heightened emotions. Captain Nemo doubts that Jean has the killer instinct to exact revenge, and the vengeful Jean asks Grandis if she will kill Gargoyle for him. Will she help Jean with his request, or has this former bad girl truly turned over a new leaf?

Great character development and expression of emotions are contained within episodes #17–20.

SPECIAL FEATURES Character Bios • Promotional Footage • Other Title Trailers TECHNICAL FEATURES Fullscreen (1.33:1) • Subtitles/CC: Eng. • Languages: Jap., Eng. dub • Sound: Dolby Digital 2.0 • Keepcase • 1 Disc • Region 1 GENRE & RATING Fantasy/Historical/Action • Rated 13+

Nadia: The Secret of Blue Water—The Deep Blue Sea [#6]

ADV Films, 2002, 100 mins., #DNS006. General Direction by Hideaki Anno. Screenplay by Hisao Okawa, Kaoru Umeno. Based on *20,000 Leagues Under the Sea* by Jules Verne.

Surrounded by a dozen Garfish, the *Nautilus* fights frantically to avoid their torpedoes. From above, Gargoyle arrives in a huge flying fortress, with an ultimate weapon ready to destroy Nemo's submarine. As the fortress hovers atop the water, Gargoyle unleashes his weapon, a powerful magnet that wrenches the *Nautilus* from the ocean floor and brings it to the surface. The crew struggles to avoid capture, but the magnet's pull is too powerful. Once trapped, Gargoyle uses another weapon, an atomic vibrator powerful enough to rend the ship asunder bit by bit. Can anything or anyone save the *Nautilus*? What will happen to Jean, Marie, Nadia, and the rest of the crew?

Another powerful collection of *Nadia* episodes (#21–24) contains pulse-pounding excitement, guaranteed to make even the most stoic of viewers wonder what happens next! [JMC]

SPECIAL FEATURES Character Bios • Promotional Footage • Other Title Trailers TECHNICAL FEATURES Fullscreen (1.33:1) • Subtitles/CC: Eng. • Languages: Jap., Eng. dub • Sound: Dolby Digital 2.0 • Keepcase • 1 Disc • Region 1 GENRE & RATING Fantasy/Historical/Action • Rated 13+

Nadia: The Secret of Blue Water—Nadia's Island [#7]

ADV Films, 2002, 100 mins., #DNS007. General Direction by Hideaki Anno. Screenplay by Hisao Okawa, Kaoru Umeno. Based on *20,000 Leagues Under the Sea* by Jules Verne.

Alone and stranded on a strange island, Jean, Marie, King, and Nadia struggle to survive and learn if anyone else from the *Nautilus* is still alive after Gargoyle's attack. To aid in their search, Jean builds a giant kite, attaches King to it, then flies the lion cub up high for a bird's-eye view. Instead of spotting people, King sees a terrible storm raging in the distance and heading their way. They take cover from the typhoon and after it's over, discover a small island in the distance that was not there before. The group journeys to the island and finds amazing things: pine trees growing with palm trees, fruits and vegetables ripening when they shouldn't be, survivors from the American battleships and the *Nautilus* and, perhaps . . . a monster?

A character-driven story line that illustrates the value of teamwork, trust, and friendship is the focus of this DVD containing episodes #25–28. [JMC]

SPECIAL FEATURES Character Bios • Promotional Footage • Other Title Trailers TECHNICAL FEATURES Fullscreen (1.33:1) • Subtitles/CC: Eng. • Languages: Jap., Eng. dub • Sound: Dolby Digital 2.0 • Keepcase • 1 Disc • Region 1 GENRE & RATING Fantasy/Historical/Action • Rated 13+

Nadia: The Secret of Blue Water—The Secret Cave [#8]

ADV Films, 2002, 100 mins., #DNS007. General Direction by Hideaki Anno. Screenplay by Hisao Okawa, Kaoru Umeno. Based on *20,000 Leagues Under the Sea* by Jules Verne.

While searching the ocean bottom for the robotic lion cubs, Hanson and Sanson, who crashed into the water, Jean discovers a metal plate with circles carved into it. The next day while going through another section of the island with Nadia, Jean discovers another metal plate on the side of the mountain. Upon further exploration, the pair discover a passage to a secret

chamber. Once inside, Nadia's jewel glows, putting her in a trance. She soon disappears through a metal wall, with Jean unable to follow! Nadia finds herself with Red Noah, an Atlantean who wants to return her to Atlantis. To Nadia's horror, the island begins to sink, with her friends still on it! Nadia's friends are soon aloft in a giant balloon, but they're attacked by Gargoyle and his flying fortress. Crash-landing in Africa, they will soon find more secrets of Nadia's past . . . and Atlantis.

Our globetrotting heroes are the toast of the tribes in this exciting DVD containing episodes #29–32. [JMC]

SPECIAL FEATURES Voice Actress Interview • Promotional Footage • Other Title Trailers TECHNICAL FEATURES Fullscreen (1.33:1) • Subtitles/CC: Eng. • Languages: Jap., Eng. dub • Sound: Dolby Digital 2.0 • Keepcase • 1 Disc • Region 1 GENRE & RATING Fantasy/Historical/Action • Rated 13+

Nadia: The Secret of Blue Water—Nadia in Love [#9]

ADV Films, 2002, 100 mins., #DNS/009. Directed by Masatsuga Higuchi. Screenplay by Hisao Okawa, Kaoru Umeno. Based on *20,000 Leagues Under the Sea* by Jules Verne.

NOTE: This DVD arrived too late for a full review. The following text is promotional copy provided by the releasing company:

"The end draws near . . . With King in the evil clutches of Grandis's former love, it will take everything Nadia and the rest have to save him! But something more is in store for the adventurers as they finally draw near to Nadia's homeland. Sinister forces from the past pursue them, while the last pieces of Nadia's heritage come together. Will her fate doom them all? Or is there someone that can save them? Find out as Nadia's magical adventure approaches its ultimate conclusion!"

SPECIAL FEATURES Voice Actor Interview • Promotional Footage • Other Title Trailers TECHNICAL FEATURES Fullscreen (1.33:1) • Subtitles/CC: Eng. • Languages: Jap., Eng. dub • Sound: Dolby Digital • Keepcase • 1 Disc • Region 1 GENRE & RATING Fantasy/Historical/Action • Rated 12+

Nadia: The Secret of Blue Water—The Prophecy Fulfilled [#10]

ADV Films, 2002, 75 mins., #DNS/010. Directed by Masatsuga Higuchi. Screenplay by Hisao Okawa, Kaoru Umeno. Based on *20,000 Leagues Under the Sea* by Jules Verne.

NOTE: This DVD arrived too late for a full review. The following text is promotional copy provided by the releasing company:

"With the fate of the world at stake, will Nadia finally face her destiny? Gargoyle has seized Nadia and her Blue Water, and has resurrected the most terrible power of the ancient people of Atlantis! Will Jean and the crew of the *New Nautilus* be able to rescue Nadia and prevent Gargoyle's horrific plan to control the destiny of humanity? Who will survive the final battle of one of the world's most beloved animated series? Join Nadia and Jean one last time for the thrilling climax of *Nadia, Secret of Blue Water!*"

SPECIAL FEATURES Voice Actor Interview • Clean Credits • Promotional Footage • Other Title Trailers TECHNICAL FEATURES Fullscreen (1.33:1) • Subtitles/CC: Eng. • Languages: Jap., Eng. dub • Sound: Dolby Digital • Keepcase • 1 Disc • Region 1 GENRE & RATING Fantasy/Historical/Action • Rated 12+

Nadia: The Secret of Blue Water—The Motion Picture

ADV Films, 2002, 90 mins., #DNS/011. Directed by So Aono. Screenplay by Kaoru Umeno. Based on *20,000 Leagues Under the Sea* by Jules Verne.

NOTE: This DVD arrived too late for a full review. The following text is promotional copy provided by the releasing company:

"On the eve of a worldwide conflict, when businessmen, admirals and ministers of state are evaporating into thin air, a mysterious girl named Fuzzy reunites Nadia and Jean after years of separation. Together with the Grandis Gang, they must fight off the minions of a new nemesis—Giegar—bent on world domination. Giegar plots to use a mind control device to set the world ablaze with war, and in the ensuing chaos conquer the world with his own personal army. It's up to Jean and Nadia to stop him and save the day again. A final, feature-length adventure for the pair, with their tempestuous relationship tested even as they struggle to stop Giegar once and for all."

SPECIAL FEATURES Original Opening • Trailer • Clean Credits • Other Title Trailers TECHNICAL FEATURES Fullscreen (1.33:1) • Subtitles/CC: Eng. • Languages: Jap., Eng. dub • Sound: Dolby Digital • Keepcase • 1 Disc • Region 1 GENRE & RATING Fantasy/Historical/Action • Rated 12+

Nazca—Blades of Fate [#1]

Pioneer, 2000, 75 mins., #PIDA-7181V. Directed by Hiroko Tokita. Screenplay by Tsunehisa Ito. Original Story by Yoshihiko Inamoto.

Kyoji Miura is a practitioner of kendo who regards his teacher, Tate, with something approaching hero worship. But a strange turn of events during a kendo match reveals shocking secrets about both Tate and Kyoji himself, along with several of their schoolmates and friends, the pair begin having flashes of their past lives as soldiers in the Inca Empire. A whirlwind trip to Peru and an unexpected conflict later, Kyoji makes a terrible realization: his teacher, the man he admires most, is the one he must defeat in order to save the world and fulfill the destiny he established in his past life.

While sporting some extremely poor animation, *Nazca* is worth noting for the sheer originality and strength of its story and characters. The South American influence is strong, from the title itself (nazca are enormous ancient Inca murals, carved into the ground) to the show's music, straight through to the historical background of the story and the outfits and fighting styles of the characters. At the same time, the sheer complexity of the story and the large cast makes it difficult to follow at times. Put simply, *Nazca* is a straight-faced action story with a somewhat over-ambitious plot.

This DVD contains episodes #1–3 of the TV series from 1998. Sharp-eyed viewers might note some ugly video, but it's because of bad computer animation, not the disc itself. By the way, fans of the *Malcolm in the Middle* sitcom will recognize some of the *Nazca* animation from that series' opening credits. [MT]

SPECIAL FEATURES Character and Art Galleries TECHNICAL FEATURES Fullscreen (1.33:1) • Subtitles/CC: Eng. • Languages: Jap., Eng. dub • Sound: Dolby Digital 2.0 • Keepcase • 1 Disc • Region 1, 4 GENRE & RATING Action/Historical/Fantasy • Rated 13+

Nazca—Blood Rivals [#2]

Pioneer, 2000, 75 mins., #PIDA-7182V. Directed by Hiroko Tokita. Screenplay by Naruhisa Arakawa, Tsunehisa Ito. Original Story by Yoshihiko Inamoto.

Tate continues his relentless drive to unleash the power of the Inca God Iriyatesse; Kyoji, along with a growing number of allies awakening to their past lives, moves to thwart him. But Tate is gathering allies of his own, and enemies in past lives are horrified to learn that they've become friends in their current ones.

This disc maintains the series' ambitious storytelling and byzantine character relationships. One cool extra feature not usually found is a "mini manga" comic included on the disc itself. This DVD contains episodes #4–6. [MT]

SPECIAL FEATURES Mini Manga TECHNICAL FEATURES Fullscreen (1.33:1) • Subtitles/CC: Eng. • Languages: Jap., Eng. dub • Sound: Dolby Digital 2.0 • Keepcase • 1 Disc • Region 1, 4 GENRE & RATING Action/Historical/Fantasy • Rated 13+

Nazca—Betrayal of Humanity [#3]

Pioneer, 2000, 75 mins., #PIDA-7183V. Directed by Hiroko Tokita. Screenplay by Naruhisa Arakawa, Katsuyuki Kumazawa. Original Story by Yoshihiko Inamoto.

Kyoji and his allies stood by, horrified, as Tate revealed the terrifying power of Iriyatesse. Now, the reincarnated Inca warrior and his allies work even more furiously against the seemingly deranged Tate. But a newly awakened Inca god, Garos, threatens to upset the balance of power between the two sides.

This disc continues the the show's challenging story line, containing episodes #7–9. [MT]

SPECIAL FEATURES Mini Manga TECHNICAL FEATURES Fullscreen (1.33:1) • Subtitles/CC: Eng. • Languages: Jap., Eng. dub • Sound: Dolby Digital 2.0 • Keepcase • 1 Disc • Region 1, 4 GENRE & RATING Action/Historical/Fantasy • Rated 13+

Nazca—Eternal Power [#4]

Pioneer, 2000, 75 mins., #PIDA-7184V. Directed by Hiroko Tokita. Screenplay by Naruhisa Arakawa. Original Story by Yoshihiko Inamoto.

Tate is determined to destroy humanity in order to remake a perfect world, and Kyoji must stop him. But the battle is going badly, and if victory is to be achieved, the final sacrifice may need to be made. Will Kyoji sacrifice himself, or one of this allies? And who will betray Kyoji?

The final three episodes of the series, #10–12, are collected here, wrapping up a complex and unusual story. The animation for the final two episodes noticeably improves, especially in the fight sequences, although some cheesy CGI material still shows up.

SPECIAL FEATURES Mini Manga TECHNICAL FEATURES Fullscreen (1.33:1) • Subtitles/CC: Eng. • Languages: Jap., Eng. dub • Sound: Dolby Digital 2.0 • Keepcase • 1 Disc • Region 1, 4 GENRE & RATING Action/Historical/Fantasy • Rated 13+

Neon Genesis Evangelion—Collection 0:1

ADV Films, 2000, 100 mins., #DVDEV001. Directed by Hideaki Anno. Script by Hideaki Anno, Yoji Enoto, Akio Satsukawa. Based on the manga series by Hideaki Anno, Yoshiyuki Sadamoto in *Shonen Ace.*

Fifteen years after Earth suffered mass destruction at the hands of aliens dubbed "Angels," humanity has begun to rebuild and recover. Housed in cities that can disappear underground during attacks, mankind is turned upside down again when the Angels return. With superpowered robotic Evangelion Units that bond with their teenage pilots, the mysterious government organization NERV may well be humanity's last hope. That is, if the teen pilots—Shinji Ikari in Eva Unit 01, Rei Ayanami in Eva Unit 00, and Asuka Langley Soryu in Eva Unit 02—can handle the job. Matters are made tougher considering that emotionless Gendo Ikari, the Supreme Commander of NERV, has an estranged relationship with his son Shinji, yet shows plenty of emotion with Rei. Shinji's confusion and vacillation about his place in the world—and within NERV—may cost his teammates dearly. Luckily, Major Misato Katsuragi is ready to teach Shinji the life lessons all teens need to learn. But will her influence, and the power of the Eva Unit, be enough to help this confused teen defend the world?

Filled with intrigue, heartache, mecha action, mystery, religion, horror, and government conspiracies, this series created in 1995 is an epic twenty-six-episode anime, the conclusion of which spawned two OVAs and a movie. The show is extremely popular with fans, and the first disc, containing episodes #1–4, is an awesome introduction to the series. Animation is very sharp, and the story should appeal to all mecha, action, and sci-fi fans. It is, however a darker anime series and shouldn't be viewed by all ages, as there are mature themes and situations.

Note that the original release of *Collection 0:1* has the logo at the top of the front cover and is listed as 120 minutes on the package. [JMC]

SPECIAL FEATURES Character Bios • Other Title Trailers TECHNICAL FEATURES Fullscreen (1.33:1) • Subtitles/CC: Eng. • Languages: Jap., Eng. dub, Fren. dub, Span. dub • Sound: Dolby Digital 2.0 • Keepcase • 1 Disc • Region 1, 2, 4 GENRE & RATING Robots/Science Fiction • Not Rated (Teens)

Neon Genesis Evangelion—Collection 0:1 [Remastered]

ADV Films, 2001, 100 mins., #DVDEV001. Directed by Hideaki Anno. Script by Hideaki Anno, Yoji Enoto, Akio Satsukawa. Based on the manga series by Hideaki Anno, Yoshiyuki Sadamoto in *Shonen Ace.*

Note that the original release of *Collection 0:1* has the logo at the top of the front cover, and is listed as 120 minutes on the package. The December 2001 release (dated 2002) has the logo at the bottom of the front cover, and the time is listed as the correct 100 minutes.

The animation is substantially sharper and cleaner on this remastered disc, which also features a reformatted menu, matching the others in the series.

SPECIAL FEATURES Character Bios • Other Title Trailers • Easter Egg TECHNICAL FEATURES Fullscreen (1.33:1) • Subtitles/CC: Eng.

• Languages: Jap., Eng. dub, Fren. dub, Span. dub • Sound: Dolby Digital 2.0 • Keepcase • 1 Disc • Region 1, 2, 4 GENRE & RATING Robots/Science Fiction • Not Rated (Teens)

Neon Genesis Evangelion—Collection 0:2

ADV Films, 2000, 100 mins., #DVDEV002. Directed by Hideaki Anno. Script by Akio Satsukawa, Hideaki Anno. Based on the manga series by Hideaki Anno, Yoshiyuki Sadamoto in *Shonen Ace.*

Although Rei was injured while testing her Eva unit, at the first sign of trouble she's back in her unit, with Shinji piloting his Eva against a terrible Angel that is attacking Tokyo 3. With teamwork, they're able to best this Angel. Next Misato takes Shinji and his friends on a trip to an aircraft carrier where they're attacked by a renegade robot. Can Shinji/Eva Unit 01 defeat this robot and get his friends home in time for dinner, or are the teens destined to become fish food? And just how will all the Eva pilots lives change when Asuka Langely makes the scene? With a fiery personality to match her red hair, Asuka has problems getting along with anyone her age. If she and Shinji fight like cats and dogs out of Evas, how will they ever be able to get along in combat, when the stakes are high?

This character-driven disc contains episodes #5–8 and introduces some key characters, as well as laying the groundwork for plots and situations that will play out in future episodes. This volume also contains some nudity, so parents be warned! [JMC]

SPECIAL FEATURES Character Bios • Other Title Trailers TECHNICAL FEATURES Fullscreen (1.33:1) • Subtitles/CC: Eng. • Languages: Jap., Eng. dub, Fren. dub, Span. dub • Sound: Dolby Digital 2.0 • Keepcase • 1 Disc • Region 1, 2, 4 GENRE & RATING Robots/Science Fiction • Not Rated (Teens)

Neon Genesis Evangelion—Collection 0:3

ADV Films, 2001, 75 mins., #DVDEV003. Directed by Hideaki Anno. Script by Akio Satsukawa, Hideaki Anno. Based on the manga series by Hideaki Anno, Yoshiyuki Sadamoto in *Shonen Ace.*

The newest Angel has the power to duplicate itself, each of its parts moving in perfect harmony against any and all opponents. To combat this, Shinji and Asuka must learn to get along outside their Eva Units, so they can work as a team inside. If the two pilots can synchronize their movements perfectly, they will be able to defeat this Angel. Then things heat up for our Eva pilots when a dormant but powerful Angel is discovered inside a volcano. Can they stand the heat to retrieve and destroy the Angel before it "wakes up" and

wreaks havoc? Then all three young pilots are in for it when an Angel with an acid touch that can corrode anything—including their Evas—attacks Tokyo 3.

Teamwork and trust is key in this decisive volume of *Neon Genesis Evangelion,* containing episodes #9–11. As more and more pieces of the puzzle click into place, the characters learn not to judge all books by their covers. [JMC]

SPECIAL FEATURES Character Bios • Other Title Trailers TECHNICAL FEATURES Fullscreen (1.33:1) • Subtitles/CC: Eng. • Languages: Jap., Eng. dub, Fren. dub, Span. dub • Sound: Dolby Digital 2.0 • Keepcase • 1 Disc • Region 1, 2, 4 GENRE & RATING Robots/Science Fiction • Not Rated (Teens)

Neon Genesis Evangelion—Collection 0:4

ADV Films, 2001, 75 mins., #DVDEV004. Directed by Hideaki Anno. Script by Akio Satsukawa, Hideaki Anno, Mitsuo Iso. Based on the manga series by Hideaki Anno, Yoshiyuki Sadamoto in *Shonen Ace.*

An Angel has the potential to destroy all of Tokyo 3 just by touching the ground. It's up to Shinji, Rei, and Asuka to make sure this heavenly body never sets down. Next, an Angel with the ability to adapt, change, and evolve, has infiltrated NERV headquarters and is corrupting everything it touches. It's up to the scientists of NERV to combat this technologically advanced Angel, but will brains win out over brawn? Then, things slow down with an insightful character-driven episode that reveals some private thoughts of the young pilots.

Episodes #12–14 are a diverse group of episodes that illustrate the value of knowledge and wisdom alongside brute strength, and offer more perspective on the many facets of the pilots. [JMC]

SPECIAL FEATURES Character Bios • Other Title Trailers • Easter Egg TECHNICAL FEATURES Fullscreen (1.33:1) • Subtitles/CC: Eng. • Languages: Jap., Eng. dub, Fren. dub, Span. dub • Sound: Dolby Digital 2.0 • Keepcase • 1 Disc • Region 1, 2, 4 GENRE & RATING Robots/Science Fiction • Not Rated (Teens)

Neon Genesis Evangelion—Collection 0:5

ADV Films, 2001, 75 mins., #DVDEV/005. Directed by Hideaki Anno. Script by Akio Satsukawa, Hideaki Anno, Hiroshi Yamaguchi, Shinji Higuchi. Based on the manga series by Hideaki Anno, Yoshiyuki Sadamoto in *Shonen Ace.*

Kaji, a spy working at NERV, reveals to Misato a secret kept hidden for over fifteen years—the body of the first Angel is in NERV's headquarters! Misato, stunned by this information, now must decide where her loyalties lie: to the organization she works for that has lied . . . or to the organization that is trying to make this matter public knowledge. Meanwhile Shinji, after a confidence boost, takes on an Angel by himself and is gravely injured. Depressed and again in doubt, Shinji again questions his place within NERV. And, after Shinji's rash act, NERV decides that another pilot should be trained: Shinji's best friend, Toji. How will Toji's inclusion affect the rest of the young Eva commanders?

Not a lot of fighting, but the revelation of many dark secrets help to further the *Evangelion* saga. This shocking disc contains episodes #15–17. [JMC]

SPECIAL FEATURES Character Bios • Other Title Trailers • Easter Egg TECHNICAL FEATURES Fullscreen (1.33:1) • Subtitles/CC: Eng. • Languages: Jap., Eng. dub, Fren. dub, Span. dub • Sound: Dolby Digital 2.0 • Keepcase • 1 Disc • Region 1, 2, 4 GENRE & RATING Robots/Science Fiction • Not Rated (Teens)

Neon Genesis Evangelion—Collection 0:6

ADV Films, 2001, 75 mins., #DVDEV006. Directed by Hideaki Anno. Script by Shinji Higuchi, Hideaki Anno, Akio Satsukawa. Based on the manga series by Hideaki Anno, Yoshiyuki Sadamoto in *Shonen Ace.*

During Toji's first test with Eva Unit 03, something goes amiss. The Unit is revealed to be an Angel, and it proceeds to damage Unit 00 and Unit 02, forcing Shinji into battle. He doesn't want to use deadly force, because a human is piloting it. NERV overrides Shinji's control of Unit 01 and destroys the Eva, gravely injuring an old friend. Horrified, Shinji doesn't want to pilot anymore, but when another Angel strikes, he has no choice. During the battle Shinji achieves a perfect 100% synchronization ratio with the Eva unit and the two are now one, with the Eva in control. For Shinji to return to "reality" he has to want to, and after the events of the past few days, he's happy to stay in the dark. Can the others "ground" Shinji and convince him to return to reality?

This action-packed DVD contains episodes #18–20. [JMC]

SPECIAL FEATURES Character Bios • Other Title Trailers • Easter Egg TECHNICAL FEATURES Fullscreen (1.33:1) • Subtitles/CC: Eng. • Languages: Jap., Eng. dub, Fren. dub, Span. dub • Sound: Dolby Digital 2.0 • Keepcase • 1 Disc • Region 1, 2, 4 GENRE & RATING Robots/Science Fiction • Not Rated (Teens)

Neon Genesis Evangelion—Collection 0:7

ADV Films, 2001, 75 mins., #DVDEV007. Directed by Hideaki Anno. Script by Akio Satsukawa, Hideaki Anno, Hiroshi Yamaguchi. Based on the manga series by Hideaki Anno, Yoshiyuki Sadamoto in *Shonen Ace.*

Kaji frees one of NERV's important prisoners and reveals the secrets of the group, but then is caught and pays a high price for his betrayal. Misato is heart-broken, but presses on. An Angel attacks and gets the upper hand, giving Unit 02 a terrible pounding. Things look hopeless, until Gendo allows Unit 00 to use the first Angel's weapon against the creature. After the battle, another trusted member of NERV betrays the organization and destroys an important part of the Eva project.

This poignant—and penultimate—DVD collection includes episodes #21–23. [JMC]

SPECIAL FEATURES Character Bios • Other Title Trailers • Easter Eggs TECHNICAL FEATURES Fullscreen (1.33:1) • Subtitles/CC: Eng. • Languages: Jap., Eng. dub, Fren. dub, Span. dub • Sound: Dolby Digital 2.0 • Keepcase • 1 Disc • Region 1, 2, 4 GENRE & RATING Robots/Science Fiction • Not Rated (Teens)

Neon Genesis Evangelion—Collection 0:8

ADV Films, 2001, 75 mins., #DVDEV007. Directed by Hideaki Anno. Script by Akio Satsukawa, Hideaki Anno, Masayuki, Kazuya Tsurumaki. Based on the manga series by Hideaki Anno, Yoshiyuki Sadamoto in *Shonen Ace.*

New Eva pilot Kaoru is hiding an important secret, but that doesn't matter to Shinji, with whom he becomes fast friends. Things are made all the worse when Kaoru almost destroys NERV and Tokyo 3. Shinji must battle his new friend to the death. Then, in a whirlwind turn of events, the secret connection that Gendo shares with Rei is disclosed and other secrets are explained, just before Shinji makes a startling discovery.

This final collection contains episodes #24–26. The climax of the series was a letdown to hardcore *Evangelion* fans, who refused to believe that all the heart and emotion of the masterful series was so easily dispatched by a single revelation. It's unfortunate that the producers seem to have taken a page from the scripts of *Dallas* and *St. Elsewhere* to end this story. [JMC]

SPECIAL FEATURES Character Bios • Other Title Trailers • Easter Egg TECHNICAL FEATURES Fullscreen (1.33:1) • Subtitles/CC: Eng. • Languages: Jap., Eng. dub, Fren. dub, Span. dub • Sound: Dolby Digital 2.0 • Keepcase • 1 Disc • Region 1, 2, 4 GENRE & RATING Robots/Science Fiction • Not Rated (Teens)

Neon Genesis Evangelion—Perfect Collection [Box Set]

ADV Films, 2002, 650 mins., #DEVBX1.

This box set features all eight keep-case editions as they were individually released, with no new extras. The backs of the keepcase sleeves have the UPC code blacked out, however. See individual entries for the Special and Technical Features listings.

TECHNICAL FEATURES Cardboard Box with 8 Keepcases • 8 Discs • Region 1, 2, 4 GENRE & RATING Robots/Science Fiction • Not Rated (Teens)

Neon Genesis Evangelion: Death and Rebirth

Manga Entertainment, 2002, 115 mins., #MANGA4107-2. Directed by Kazuya Tsurumaki, Masayuki, Hideaki Anno. Written by Hideaki Anno, Yoji Enoto, Akio Satsukawa, Mitsuo Iso, Hiroshi Yamaguchi, Shinji Higuchi, Masayuki, Kazuya Tsurumaki. Based on the manga series by Hideaki Anno, Yoshiyuki Sadamoto in Shonen Ace.

Containing excerpts from the first twenty-four Neon Genesis Evangelion episodes as well as added footage, this powerful DVD provides an alternative ending to the story. The tale begins when Shinji kills Kaoru, an Angel disguised as an Eva pilot, sending him into a terrible depression. Nothing seems able to stir Shinji from his funk. Meanwhile another government organization, SEELE, has decided NERV has outlived its usefulness and seeks to destroy its facilities. SEELE slaughters most of the men, women, and children housed in the NERV complex. Asuka, in her Eva Unit, prepares to fight these forces. She's surrounded and outnumbered by tons of SEELE weapons as the DVD ends.

This action-packed double-sided DVD features a 1997 OVA alternative ending to the series but does not provide closure at the end. It leaves viewers anxiously waiting for the next installment, The End of Evangelion.

A cool extra feature of this DVD is the Mokuji (moku-ji means information) Interactive Feature. Once activated, this feature allows viewers to select from an on-screen, footnote-style, chapter-specific index of EVA-related terms and character descriptions. [JMC]

SPECIAL FEATURES Commentary Track with Voice Director/ Actress • Character and Concept Index and Bios • Character and Art Galleries • Trailers • Promotional Footage • Other Title Trailers • Inserts: Foldout Poster TECHNICAL FEATURES Widescreen (1.85:1) • Subtitles/CC: Eng. • Languages: Jap., Eng. dub • Sound: Dolby Digital Surround 5.1 • Keepcase • 1 Disc • Region 1 GENRE & RATING Robots/Science Fiction • Not Rated (Teens)

Neon Genesis Evangelion: The End of Evangelion

Manga Entertainment, 2002, 90 mins., #MANGA4109-2. Directed by Kazuya Tsurumaki. Story by Gainax, Hideaki Anno. Based on the manga series by Hideaki Anno and Yoshiyuki Sadamoto in Shonen Ace.

NOTE: This DVD arrived too late for a full review. The following text is promotional copy provided by the releasing company:

"At the dawn of the new millennium, mankind has awakened a threat unlike any faced before—the angels. Conventional weapons are useless against them. They can only be stopped by means of the Evangelion—bio-engineered vessels born from the Angels' own technology. But this forbidden knowledge is also the key to bringing about a startling new genesis for the human race. Placed in the hands of three young pilots, the final fate of humanity resting upon their shoulders, the Evas are the world's last hope . . .

"The mind-blowing finale to the incredible Neon Genesis Evangelion series, this stunning anime feature was comprised of two alternate episodes intended to take the place of episodes 25 and 26 of the original series. The visual tour de force resolves many questions about the epic series while also generating new ones."

SPECIAL FEATURES Commentary Track by Crew • Promotional Footage • Other Title Trailers TECHNICAL FEATURES Widescreen (1.85:1) • Subtitles/CC: Eng. • Languages: Jap., Eng. dub • Sound: Dolby Digital Surround 5.1, DTS) • Keepcase • 1 Disc • Region 1 GENRE & RATING Robots/Science Fiction • Not Rated (Teens)

Neurotica: Middle-Age Spread and Other Life Crises

Image, 2001, 113 mins., #ID0242NFDVD.

Here is another collection of short animated films from the National Film Board of Canada, but this one's for mature viewers. Or rather, it's about mature people. The theme for each of the eleven featurettes is getting older or the various perils that accompany aging. "Bob's Birthday" is an Oscar winner about a dentist facing his fortieth birthday with absolutely no grace, while "Special Delivery" is another Oscar winner, this time about the chain of disasters that befall a man who fails to shovel the steps.

Others in this charming anthology include Oscar nominees "George and Rosemary"; "Strings"; and "The Big Snit"; and Cannes nominee "No, Problem." Non-award-winning shorts include "Shyness"; "Getting Started"; "Special Delivery"; "Get a Job"; "Why Me?"; "Scant Sanity"; and an untitled bonus. There is some brief nudity on this DVD, but it's certainly appropriate for almost any viewer who will be interested in the subject matter.

SPECIAL FEATURES None TECHNICAL FEATURES Fullscreen (1.33:1) • Subtitles/CC: Eng. • Languages: Eng. • Sound: Dolby Digital 2.0 • Snapcase • 1 Disc • Region 1 GENRE & RATING Anthology/Comedy • Not Rated (Teens)

New Christmas Classics Series

Artisan, 1999, 144 mins., #11236. Directed by Bert Ring. Written by John Loy.

Three 1999 animated holiday specials are melded onto one jolly holly DVD. Each story is based on a popular song, and name actors provide the voices and music. "We Wish You a Merry Christmas" is sung by Travis Tritt and features the voices of Nell Carter and Lacey Chabert in a story about how a town came to embrace Christmas carols.

"Jingle Bells" is sung by Jason Alexander and stars the voices of Don Knotts and Shelley Long. In it, a family learns the true meaning of Christmas thanks to a set of sleighbells. Finally, Marie Osmond sings "O' Christmas Tree," with Edward Asner and Tim Conway vocally chiming in for a story about a Christmas tree, a nutcracker, and their animal friends.

The animation is cute, but relatively standard fare for American television. The DVD is a nice length though, each story being just long enough to entertain the young 'uns while Mom and Dad roast chestnuts.

SPECIAL FEATURES Games • Sing-Alongs • Inserts: Coloring Book TECHNICAL FEATURES Fullscreen (1.33:1) • Languages: Eng. • Sound: Dolby Digital 2.0 • Keepcase • 1 Disc • Region 1 GENRE & RATING Holiday/Music • Not Rated (All Ages)

New Cutey Honey ☞ see Mature/Adult Section

New Kimagure Orange Road: Summer's Beginning

ADV Films, 2001, 100 mins., #DOR001. Directed by Kunihiko Yuyama. Screenplay by Kenji Terada. Based on the manga series by Izumi Matsumoto, Kenji Terada in *Shonen Jump*.

Kyosuke Kasuga is a young man with psychic powers, but they barely help him after he's in an accident and wakes up three years later . . . to face his older self, now a photographer in Bosnia! Even in the future, Kyosuke is caught in a romantic triangle with Hikaru and Madoka, two girls who both want him, even

at the cost of their own friendship. Now, as summer begins, Kyosuke will finally have to make a choice between his loves.

Kimagure Orange Road spun out of a romance manga series into a 1987 TV series that included elements of psychic powers and some action. *Summer's Beginning* is the 1996 OVA conclusion to the series, and while the animation is nice and the story well-told, if you aren't familiar with the characters, you'll likely be a bit lost. Though fans expressed enjoyment of this story, many also decried the fact that the original character designs were not used. The DVD is no-frills, and there are moments of nudity and some sexual situations.

SPECIAL FEATURES Other Title Trailers TECHNICAL FEATURES Fullscreen (1.33:1) • Subtitles/CC: Eng. • Languages: Jap., Eng. dub • Sound: Dolby Digital 2.0 • Keepcase • 1 Disc • Region 1 GENRE & RATING Romance • Rated 15+

Newtype USA [Magazine]

Each issue of this magazine features a DVD insert in a paper envelope. The premiere issue (Nov. 2002) features the *Anime Guide: 2002 DVD Catalog* from Bandai. See that listing for contents and features. Issue #2 (Dec. 2002) has a *Chance Pop Session* episode and trailers from ADV. Vol. II #1 (Jan. 2003) has the first *Noir* episode and trailers from ADV.

Nick Jr. Holiday

Paramount, 2002, 116 mins., #87681. Directed by Koyalee Chanda, George Chialtas Jennifer Oxley, Olexa Hewryk. Written by Angela C. Santomero, Dr. Alice Wilder, Michael T. Smith, Chris Gifford, Chris Nee.

NOTE: This DVD arrived too late for a full review. The following text is promotional copy provided by the releasing company:

"Tis the season to make merry, and that's easy to do with Blue, Dora, and Little Bill! Play along with your preschool pals as they explore holiday traditions, sing songs, and celebrate the season in these three festive episodes. Episodes include: Blue's Clues in 'Blue's Big Holiday,' Dora the Explorer in 'A Present for Santa,' Little Bill in 'Merry Christmas, Little Bill,' and Rugrats in 'Babies in Toyland.' Celebrate three winter holidays—Christmas, Chanukah, and Kwanzaa!"

SPECIAL FEATURES Parent's Guide TECHNICAL FEATURES Fullscreen (1.33:1) • Subtitles/CC: Eng. • Languages: Eng. • Sound: Dolby Digital 2.0 • Keepcase • 1 Disc • Region 1 GENRE & RATING Holiday/Comedy/Family • Not Rated (All Ages)

NieA Under 7: Poor Girl Blues [#1]

Pioneer, 2001, 100 mins., #11560. Directed by Takuya Sato. Written by Takuya Sato. Based on the manga series by Yoshitoshi Abe in *Ace Next*.

Welcome to Japan of the near future. Aliens live among us, and people don't seem to mind. Well, most people. Poor Mayuko Chigasaki just happens to have one of the universe's laziest aliens living in her closet. Her name is NieA and she just wants to eat, build UFOs out of trash, and not do a lick of work. Mayuko is just trying to get through cram school and make enough money working in the bath house she lives over so that she can get into a decent college. But NieA keeps making trouble for our mild-mannered heroine.

This 2000 series is about as odd as you can get. It's your typical human-living-with-an-alien-in-her-closet comedy (see *Mork and Mindy* or *ALF*), with an even more offbeat flair. The characters are all pretty likable, but the pacing is a bit rough in places. Some episodes drag at times, while others move at a good pace. *NieA* has a unique feel, and is a refreshing change from typical genres found in other Japanese animated series.

This DVD contains four episodes and has a great extra: a glossary of Japanese terms used in the show. This is pretty handy for those who aren't familiar with Japanese language or customs.

SPECIAL FEATURES Character and Art Galleries • Production Notes/Footnotes/Glossary • Clean Credits TECHNICAL FEATURES Fullscreen (1.33:1) • Subtitles/CC: Eng. • Languages: Jap., Eng. dub • Sound: Dolby Digital 2.0 • Keepcase • 1 Disc • Region 1, 4 GENRE & RATING Comedy/Fantasy/Science Fiction • Rated 13+

NieA Under 7: Funky Water Blues [#2]

Pioneer, 2001, 75 mins., #11593. Directed by Takuya Sato. Written by Takuya Sato. Based on the manga series by Yoshitoshi Abe in *Ace Next*.

The bath house that Mayuko and NieA live over is in dire financial straits. It's time to drum up business, and what better way to do it than with a video game competition? Well, it sounded like a good idea at the time. And what's with the weird voice NieA hears from the alien mothership?

More strange situations and bizarre characters show up in this disc of *NieA*, which contains three episodes. The humor is still odd, and the pacing continues to be a little off. It almost feels like this series is going out of its way to be different, but in doing so, it's losing its focus on the characters. The final episode is a nice character study

of Mayuko, but it's tough to figure out if you like her or if you just think she's pathetic.

SPECIAL FEATURES Character and Art Galleries • Production Notes/Footnotes/Glossary • Clean Credits TECHNICAL FEATURES Fullscreen (1.33:1) • Subtitles/CC: Eng. • Languages: Jap., Eng. dub • Sound: Dolby Digital 2.0 • Keepcase • 1 Disc • Region 1, 4 GENRE & RATING Comedy/Fantasy/Science Fiction • Rated 13+

NieA Under 7: Sayonara Blues [#3]

Pioneer, 2001, 75 mins., #11594. Directed by Takuya Sato. Written by Takuya Sato. Based on the manga series by Yoshitoshi Abe in *Ace Next*.

The adventures of Mayuko, NieA, and the residents of Enohana continue. Mayuko feels guilty about fighting with her freeloading alien roommate, but receives some unexpected sage advice from the soft-spoken Genzo. As NieA continues to ponder the mysterious voice of the alien mothership, Mayuko dwells on her own past.

This DVD contains episodes #8–10 of the TV series. The disc's video quality is excellent, and the keepcase includes a couple of paper puppets printed on the insert. [MT]

SPECIAL FEATURES Character and Art Galleries • Production Notes/Footnotes/Glossary • Promotional Footage • Inserts: Diorama/Finger Puppets TECHNICAL FEATURES Fullscreen (1.33:1) • Subtitles/CC: Eng. • Languages: Jap., Eng. dub • Sound: Dolby Digital 2.0 • Keepcase • 1 Disc • Region 1, 4 GENRE & RATING Comedy/Fantasy/Science Fiction • Rated 13+

NieA Under 7: Under Seven Blues [#4]

Pioneer, 2002, 75 mins., #11595. Directed by Takuya Sato. Written by Takuya Sato. Based on the manga series by Yoshitoshi Abe in *Ace Next*.

The gang at Enohana are in low spirits; the bathhouse might have to be sold, and NieA is still missing. Mayuko is upset to find out that NieA's fellow aliens aren't even willing to admit that an "under seven" like her actually exists. Meanwhile, the mothership continues to broadcast its strange messages to NieA.

This DVD contains episodes #11–13, the conclusion of the TV series (although the slice-of-wacky-life story doesn't really conclude in any dramatic sense). Another set of cool finger puppets is included with the disc. [MT]

SPECIAL FEATURES Art Galleries • Production Notes/Footnotes/Glossary • Clean Credits • Music Videos • Inserts: Diorama/Finger Puppets TECHNICAL FEATURES Fullscreen (1.33:1) • Subtitles/CC: Eng. • Languages: Jap., Eng. dub • Sound: Dolby

Digital 2.0 • Keepcase • 1 Disc • Region 1, 4 GENRE & RATING
Comedy/Fantasy/Science Fiction • Rated 13+

Night on the Galactic Railroad

Central Park, 2001, 108 mins.,
#CPMD2071. Directed by Gisaburo Sugii.
Screenplay by Minoru Betsuyaku. Based
on the 1927 novel by Kenji Miyazawa.

This coming-of-age fable happens in
a world inhabited by cats who walk
and talk just like people. Young Giovanni is not the most well-liked in his
school, and he doesn't have any
friends except for Campanella, a charismatic older boy
who seems to be looking out for him. On the day of the
Festival of Stars, Giovanni climbs a lone hill and finds
himself boarding a car on the Galactic Railroad. Campanella appears and the two boys begin a journey across
the Milky Way, encountering fascinating passengers and
witnessing dazzling sights. But a dark shadow waits for
them too, something that neither boy is ready to face: the
end of childhood.

This film was released in 1985 and even though the
animation looks a bit dated, the style and story remain
topnotch. *Night on the Galactic Railroad* uses music, light,
shadow, sound, and pacing to create a dreamlike mood.
The movie's visual poetry might bore or confound some
viewers, but for those who are looking for something
different—and something that doesn't spoon-feed its
theme or plot—this is a gold mine.

The DVD includes interesting background information on the author of the original 1927 novel on which
the film is based, and a bit on his other stories. If you find
this film intriguing, see the entry for *Spring and Chaos*,
which is also based on the works of Miyazawa. There is
nothing in this movie that is inappropriate for children,
but the slow pace and dark tone may not hold the interest of younger viewers.

SPECIAL FEATURES Character and Art Galleries • Historical Notes
• Trailer • DVD-ROM Features: Art, Historical Notes, Scripts •
Other Title Trailers TECHNICAL FEATURES Widescreen (1.85:1) •
Subtitles/CC: Eng. • Languages: Jap., Eng. dub • Sound:
Dolby Digital 2.0 • Keepcase • 1 Disc • Region 1–6 GENRE &
RATING Animals/Fantasy/Drama • Rated 3+

Night Shift Nurses ☛ see Mature/Adult Section

Night Warriors: Darkstalker's Revenge [Alpha—#1]

Viz/Pioneer, 1999, 90 mins., #DVD-DS01.
Directed by Masahashi Ikeda. Screenplay
by Satoshi Ikeda, Tatsuhiko Urahata.

The world is plagued by darkness.
Supernatural creatures called Darkstalkers rule over humans . . . or seek
out and fight other Darkstalkers. In
this realm roams a hunter known as
Donovan who seeks out the creatures
of darkness so he can destroy them. Half Darkstalker
himself, he hunts the Darkstalkers to justify his own existence. Vampire Lord Demitiri Maximov is determined to
take over this dark world, as well as the world of demons.
Lady Morrigan decides to take on Demitiri herself and
put an end to his ambition. Looming above them all is
the dangerous being known as Pyron. His quest is simple: to take over the planet by battling the strongest warriors on it. But which Darkstalker will win the honor of
battling Pyron?

This OVA series was released in 1997 and is an anime
tie-in with the popular video game series from Capcom.
As a rule, anime based on video games tend to be weak
in the story department. This series is no exception;
however, it does fare better than most. The animation,
particularly in the fight scenes, is fluid and exciting. In
fact, the whole series has a very effective, dark atmosphere that makes things appropriately creepy. Even with
its weak plot, this series makes for some entertaining, no-
brain-required viewing. And the full 5.1 sound on the
Japanese track is pretty impressive for an OVA series.

Two OVAs are included on this disc, along with some
nice extra features.

SPECIAL FEATURES Character Bios • Character and Art Galleries •
Production Notes • Trailers • Promotional Footage • Other
Title Trailers TECHNICAL FEATURES Fullscreen (1.33:1) • Subti-
tles/CC: Eng. • Languages: Jap., Eng. dub • Sound: Dolby
Digital 2.0 • Keepcase • 1 Disc • Region 1 GENRE & RATING Hor-
ror/Action • Rated 13+

Night Warriors: Darkstalker's Revenge [Omega—#2]

Viz/Pioneer, 1999, 90 mins., #DVD-DS02.
Directed by Masahashi Ikeda. Screenplay
by Satoshi Ikeda, Tatsuhiko Urahata.

Your favorite Darkstalkers return for
an all-out battle against the deadly
being, Pyron. But will the forces of
darkness be enough to stop this
corrupted being of light? Can the
Darkstalkers stop fighting among
themselves long enough to counter the threat? If you

want some fast and furious final battles, this is the disc for you. Pyron is one tough customer, and the antiheroes are going to give it their best shot. But will it be enough?

The final two OVA episodes are on this disc, in 5.1 audio if you listen to the Japanese track. You also get some more conceptual art and a feature that lets you jump directly to the battle scenes.

SPECIAL FEATURES Character Bios • Character and Art Galleries • Trailer TECHNICAL FEATURES Fullscreen (1.33:1) • Subtitles/CC: Eng. • Languages: Jap., Eng. dub • Sound: Dolby Digital Surround 2.0 • Keepcase • 1 Disc • Region 1 GENRE & RATING Horror/Action • Rated 13+

Nightmare Before Christmas, The: Special Edition

Disney, 2001, 76 mins., #20102. Directed by Henry Selick. Screenplay by Caroline Thompson. Story by Tim Burton.

Jack Skellington is the grinning, ghoulish Pumpkin King of Halloween Town, but when he stumbles onto the entrance to Christmastown, he decides that Santa Claus has a pretty cool job. Jack's plan of replacing Santa goes bad when the scheming Oogie Boogie plots to not only get rid of Santa, but Jack as well!

This gothic creepshow from 1993 is one of the coolest and creepiest kids movies ever made. Based on a story and characters created by Tim Burton, *Nightmare* is like a Dr. Seuss story filtered through *The Addams Family* and then retold by a demented devil child. The stop-motion animation is astonishing, and the songs by Danny Elfman (who also sings Jack's songs) are memorable and fun.

The DVD is chock-a-chopping-block full of extras, more than almost any other DVD in this book. Also of special interest are two of Tim Burton's earliest short films, *Vincent* and *Frankenweenie*, both shown here in uncensored form. Few animated films deserve the appellation "classic": *The Nightmare Before Christmas* is indeed a classic, though some scenes may be a bit frightening for youngsters.

Besides being offered as a single DVD, the disc was also included as part of a two-pack set, along with *James and the Giant Peach*.

SPECIAL FEATURES "Making of" Featurettes • Commentary Track by Director • Character and Art Galleries (450+ images) • Deleted Scenes • Storyboards • Trailers • Promotional Footage and Art • Other Title Trailers • Inserts: Liner Notes TECHNICAL FEATURES Widescreen (1.66:1) • Subtitles/CC: Eng., Span. • Languages: Eng., Fren. dub • Sound: Dolby Digital 5.1, DTS • Keepcase • 1 Disc • Region 1, 4 GENRE & RATING Stop Motion/Holiday/Horror/Music • Rated PG

Nightmare Campus: A Total Nightmare ☞

see Mature/Adult Section

Nightwalker: Midnight Detective [#1]

U.S. Manga Corps, 2001, 180 mins., #USMD 2031. Directed by Kiyori Sasano, Yutaka Kagawa. Screenplay by Ryota Yamaguchi, Genki Yoshimura, Toji Gobu. Based on the manga series by Ayana Itsuki in *Dengeki Comic Gao.*

Shido is a half-vampire who specializes in finding those who commit supernatural murders, especially against others of the Nightbreed. Vowing never to take a human life, he isn't so careful when it comes to inhuman life. Aided by humans, Shido fights a possessed actress and her understudy, and other boogeys. Then, an old acquaintance named Caine shows up, with word of a forthcoming Golden Dawn . . . and ties to Shido's dark past.

This 1998 TV series could almost as easily be an animated version of the U.S. live-action TV series *Angel* with Tokyo sitting in for Los Angeles, and some similarities in the supporting characters and tone. The shows were developed independently, however. *Nightwalker* has some decent animation and fun stories, even if the monster-of-the-week aspect can get predictable. Fans have also expressed enthusiasm for the credit songs.

Although the cover sleeve doesn't tout it, the disc is bulging with episodes. Six, to be exact. Nice to see a hefty package instead of the traditional shorter discs.

SPECIAL FEATURES Character Clips • Storyboards • DVD-ROM Features: Art, Scripts, Reviews • Other Title Trailers TECHNICAL FEATURES Fullscreen (1.33:1) • Subtitles/CC: Eng. • Languages: Jap., Eng. dub • Sound: Dolby Digital 2.0 • Keepcase • 1 Disc • Region All GENRE & RATING Horror/Action • Rated 13+

Nightwalker: Eternal Darkness [#2]

U.S. Manga Corps, 2001, 180 mins., #USMD 2041. Directed by Kiyori Sasano, Yutaka Kagawa. Screenplay by Ryota Yamaguchi, Genki Yoshimura, Toji Gobu.

Shido has to save his friend from Caine, and secrets about Shido and Caine's mutual past are revealed. What links them together? What does it have to do with a woman who massacred her village long ago? And how did Shido end up with the miniature Guni?

The final six episodes of *Nightwalker* are presented on this disc, with some echoes of Anne Rice's *Interview with the Vampire.* Solid vampiric entertainment for horror fans, this doesn't delve too much into the old ultraviolence, though it does have a bit of brief nudity.

SPECIAL FEATURES Character Clips • Storyboards • DVD-ROM Features: Art, Scripts, Reviews • Other Title Trailers TECHNICAL FEATURES Fullscreen (1.33:1) • Subtitles/CC: Eng. • Languages: Jap., Eng. dub • Sound: Dolby Digital 2.0 • Keepcase • 1 Disc • Region 1–6 GENRE & RATING Horror/Action • Rated 13+

Nine Lives of Fritz the Cat, The ☛ see Mature/Adult Section

Nine O'Clock Woman ☛ see Mature/Adult Section

Ninja Cadets

Anime Works, 2000, 60 mins., #AWDVD-0080. Directed by Kiyori Sasano, Yutaka Kagawa. Script by Mitsuhiro Yamada. Story by Eiji Suganuma.

In feudal Japan, war rages between the Byakuro and evil Kabusu clans. As the Kabusu plan to kidnap the Byakuro princess, a ninja steals her away to be raised in secret. Years later, a group of excitable young Ninja Cadets is given an assignment: sneak into the Byakuro castle and steal a special scroll. But one of the cadets is actually the princess all grown up, and the Kabusu clan sends ninja assassins to find out which one it is . . . and kill her.

Although this is meant partially as a comedy, that doesn't really excuse the sheer stupidity of most of the characters, who don't so much solve problems and use skills as wander aimlessly into the right place at the right time. Both episodes of the 1996 OVA series are included on this disc, but viewers who find the ending unsatisfying won't have any more episodes to look forward to. Recommended mainly for fans of role-playing adventures such as *Dungeons and Dragons*, this also features lots of cheesecake.

SPECIAL FEATURES Character and Art Galleries • Outtakes • Other Title Trailers TECHNICAL FEATURES Fullscreen (1.33:1) • Subtitles/CC: Eng. • Languages: Jap., Eng. dub • Sound: Dolby Digital • Keepcase • 1 Disc • Region 1 GENRE & RATING Martial Arts/Comedy/Action • Rated 13+

Ninja Resurrection ☛ see Mature/Adult Section

Ninja Scroll

Manga Entertainment, 1998, 94 mins., #440 047 611-2. Directed by Yoshiaki Kawajiri. Screenplay by Yoshiaki Kawajiri. Based on the novels by Futaro Yamada.

Jubei Kibagami is your typical samurai wandering around medieval Japan. He's calm, cool, and a master swordsman, of course. Jubei gets duped into helping Dakuan, a tricky old man who's more dangerous than he looks. With them is the beautiful and deadly ninja Kagero. They're going to need all the skills they can muster when they face the deadly Devils of Kimon and their invincible leader, Lord Gemma. Can this trio of master warriors defeat eight supernatural demons whose powers range from electrocuting their enemies to having skin as tough as rock? Swords and blood (not to mention entrails) are about to fly, and not everyone is going to get out of this alive.

Ninja Scroll is an action-packed, supernatural samurai movie that was released in 1993. The plot and characterizations are fairly straightforward, but its action scenes are what grab your attention. Not only does this film sport some of the most creative supernatural powers you'll see, but the visual style keeps things exciting and intense. This film is a stylized action movie with over-the-top gore and acrobatics, and fans of fast and furious sword battles will not be disappointed. It's an entertaining visceral slash-fest, that will satisfy the bloodthirsty samurai in you.

This disc has a 5.1 English track that will give your speakers a workout. Keep in mind that this movie is full of blood, guts, and gore. Also be aware that there are some sexual situations and nudity, so the little samurai will have to leave the room. [RJM]

SPECIAL FEATURES Character and Art Galleries • Synopsis • Other Title Trailers TECHNICAL FEATURES Fullscreen (1.33:1) • Subtitles/CC: Eng. • Languages: Jap., Eng. dub • Sound: Dolby Digital 5.1 • Keepcase • 1 Disc • Region 1, 2, 4 GENRE & RATING Martial Arts/Action/Supernatural • Not Rated (Teens)

Now and Then, Here and There #1: Discord and Doom [#1]

U.S. Manga Corps, 2001, 125 mins., #USMD 2122. Directed by Akitaro Daichi. Script by Hideyuki Kurata.

One evening, Shu, a typical schoolboy, climbs a factory smokestack to view the scenery. Once atop the stack, Shu notices a girl sitting on an adjacent stack also admiring the sunset. As Shu starts a conversation with the girl, who calls herself LaLa-Ru, time freezes. Suddenly, two serpent-like ships appear intent on capturing

LaLa-Ru. As Shu responds to her plea for help, a time portal opens taking the raiders, Lala-Ru, and Shu to a time far in the future. In this world, the sun is swollen to many times its present size, and Earth is a wasteland ruled by warlords. Shu's continued attempts to rescue LaLa-Ru fail, and he is conscripted into an army in which children slave as foot soldiers in the constant battle for natural resources.

Now and Then, Here and There, which began airing in 1999 as a Japanese television series, is a story with an interesting mix of chivalry, loyalty, and brutality. Often very dramatic, the story's complicated plot twists move through a range of emotions as its very human characters come to understand not only themselves but their horrible circumstances.

The animation is well done with moments of surrealistic beauty. The soundtrack, with a vibrant score and haunting melodies, is well-timed, shifting the viewer's mood along with the story line. Containing episodes #1–5, *Now and Then, Here and There* is brutal in its depictions of rape, slavery, and children slaughtering children in savage battle scenes. It is also a well-directed DVD with a gripping story that will have you both disturbed and riveted. [GP]

SPECIAL FEATURES Character and Art Galleries • Storyboards • Clean Credits • DVD-ROM Features: Art, Scripts • Other Title Trailers TECHNICAL FEATURES Fullscreen (1.33:1) • Subtitles/CC: Eng. • Languages: Jap., Eng. dub • Sound: Dolby Digital 2.0, Dolby Digital 5.1 • Keepcase • 1 Disc • Region 1–6 GENRE & RATING Action/Adventure • Rated 16+

Now and Then, Here and There: Flight and Fall [#2]

U.S. Manga Corps, 2002, 100 mins., #USMD 2149. Directed by Akitaro Daichi. Script by Hideyuki Kurata.

Sara has been taken as a slave by a villain in the other world, but she manages to escape into the barren desert. There, she finds haven among other refugees, freedom fighters, drifters, and rebels.

The more mature themes and scenes in this second volume of four episodes could bump this up into an older age range, including a scene of attempted rape. Though the covers to the DVD are gorgeous and the story reminiscent of *El Hazard*, parents are warned that this may not be the best choice for kids.

SPECIAL FEATURES Character and Art Galleries • Storyboards • DVD-ROM Features: Art, Scripts • Other Title Trailers TECHNICAL FEATURES Fullscreen (1.33:1) • Subtitles/CC: Eng. • Languages: Jap., Eng. dub • Sound: Dolby Digital 2.0, Dolby Digital 5.1 • Keepcase • 1 Disc • Region 1–6 GENRE & RATING Action/Adventure • Rated 16+

Now and Then, Here and There: Conflict and Chaos [#3]

U.S. Manga Corps, 2002, 100 mins., #USMD2150. Directed by Akitaro Daichi. Written by Hideyuki Kurata.

NOTE: This DVD arrived too late for a full review. The following text is promotional copy provided by the releasing company:

"The desert explodes in an all-out war as a tyrant unleashes a flying battleship against a rebel army. Guns blaze and lives are lost in the devastation. No one will be left unscarred, or innocent. Young Shu, searching the wreckage for a captured friend, is swept into the battle fray. It's the ultimate challenge of survival in a world gone mad!"

SPECIAL FEATURES Character and Art Galleries • Storyboards • Promotional Footage • DVD-ROM Features: Art, Scripts • Other Title Trailers TECHNICAL FEATURES Fullscreen (1.33:1) • Subtitles/CC: Eng. • Languages: Jap., Eng. dub • Sound: Dolby Digital Surround 5.1 • Keepcase • 1 Disc • Region All GENRE & RATING Action/Adventure • Rated 16+

Now and Then, Here and There: DVD Collection [Box Set]

U.S. Manga Corps, 2002, 395 mins., #USMD2169.

This box set includes the three *Now and Then, Here and There* discs exactly as they appeared in the individual keepcase editions. See individual entries for the Special and Technical Features listings.

It also features a fourth exclusive bonus keepcase and disc that contains lots of extra artwork, trailers, storyboards, behind the scenes footage, and more.

SPECIAL FEATURES (bonus disc) "Making of" Featurette • Character and Art Galleries • Storyboards • Trailers • Promotional Footage • DVD-ROM Features: Art, Scripts • Other Title Trailers TECHNICAL FEATURES Cardboard Box with 4 Keepcases • 4 Discs • Region All GENRE & RATING Action/Adventure • Rated 16+

Nu Pugodi [I'll Get You]

Jove/Stellar.

This DVD was not available for review. It is a Russian-language disc.

Nuttiest Nutcracker, The

Columbia/TriStar, 1999, 48 mins., #25189. Directed by Harold Harris. Created by Diane Eskenazi.

Food and the holidays have always gone together, but this CGI movie takes it to an extreme. Teenage Marie falls asleep and enters the magical world of the Nutcracker Prince. This realm is also populated by talking nuts, vegetables, fruits, and other food groups, as well as mouse armies and toy soldiers. With help from the Sugarplum Fairy, can Marie assist the Nutcracker Prince to regain his throne from the Rat King?

This film is certainly nutty, and fruity as well. And if adults watch it, they may want to veg out. Most of the humor in this direct-to-video offering is pun-inspired, or purely visual; we're expected to laugh just because the characters are talking food items. Still, this is a fun trifle for kids, who will enjoy the bright colors, wisecracking voices, and roller-coaster plotting. There's some nice voice work by Cheech Marin, Phyllis Diller, and Jim Belushi, among others. The DVD has a few nice extras.

SPECIAL FEATURES Trailer • Sing-Along • Games • Other Title Trailers TECHNICAL FEATURES Fullscreen (1.33:1) • Subtitles/CC: Eng. • Languages: Eng. • Sound: Dolby Digital Surround 2.0, Dolby Digital 5.1 • Keepcase • 1 Disc • Region 1 GENRE & RATING CGI/Holiday/Comedy • Rated G

Odin: Photon Space Sailer Starlight

U.S. Manga Corps, 1999, 235 mins., #DVD153. Directed by Takeshi Shirado, Eiichi Yamamoto. Screenplay by Kazuo Kasahara, Toshio Masuda, Eiichi Yamamoto.

By 2099, mankind has entered an era of space travel; interstellar voyages are made possible through ships that 'sail' on a system of laser networks. The story opens with the shakedown cruise of the *Starlight*, Earth's mightiest and most impressive new cruiser. Immediately after hotheaded protagonist Akira Tsubaka boards, the ship receives a distress call. What they find is a derelict alien ship, a strange girl, and a clue that just might lead them to the genesis of human life. This possibility captures the imagination of the *Starlight*'s crew, and they rush off to investigate. Meanwhile, an alien armada is massing against them. . . .

Odin is a difficult film to summarize. It represents a second attempt by the original producer of *Star Blazers* to recreate his original success by essentially redoing *Star Blazers*'s story, right down to the flying boat in space. Individual aspects of the movie's production, like the design of the ship itself and the animation quality, are excellent, but *Odin* simply falls flat when taken as a whole. The characters are stale and idiotic, the story is too familiar, the movie takes more than two hours to lurch and stagger to its unsatisfying conclusion. Truly hardcore animation fans and *Star Blazers* buffs might find some satisfaction in *Odin*'s high production values, but all other comers would do better to avoid this turkey.

The *Odin* DVD really only has one "extra," and there's even a sad story behind that. When *Odin* was first marketed to English-speaking audiences, the dubbed version was shaved to 93 minutes—no uncut dub exists. As such, this DVD contains both the complete, subtitled *Odin* feature film (at 140 mins.), and the highly edited dubbed version, billed as an extra. [MT]

SPECIAL FEATURES Multiple Versions TECHNICAL FEATURES Fullscreen (1.33:1) • Subtitles/CC: Eng. • Languages: Jap., Eng. dub • Sound: Dolby Digital 2.0 • Keepcase • 1 Disc • Region All GENRE & RATING Science Fiction/Adventure • Not Rated (Kids)

Odyssey into the Mind's Eye

Sony, 1997, 62 mins.

This DVD was not available for review. It is a CGI anthology set to music.

Odyssey, The [Collector's Edition]

Digital Versatile Disc, 1999, 48 mins., #183. Animation directed by Warwick Gilbert. Screenplay by Paul Leadon. Adapted by Alex Nicholas. Based on *The Odyssey* by Homer.

After helping the Greeks conquer Troy, Odysseus, the King of Ithaca, fails to return home to his land. As his wife, Penelope, is tempted by suitors hungry to take over the throne, the Olympian Gods watch over the fate of Odysseus. His perilous travels include encounters with a deadly Cyclops, the sorceress Circe, Scylla and Charybdis, and the singing Sirens. Will Odysseus ever make it home, or will the whims of the Gods forever keep him adrift on Poseidon's stormy seas?

As can be expected from any attempt to adapt Homer's sprawling epic, this version of *The Odyssey* condenses the stories and trials of Odysseus into a mere handful of adventures (with a lot less death than in the original stories as well). The animation for this 1987 production of Burbank Films Australia is pleasant enough, with semi-authentic costume designs and settings, plus a touch of ancient Greco stylings for the characters. As with other DVD Ltd. releases, there is a bio of the author on the disc.

SPECIAL FEATURES Author Bio • Game TECHNICAL FEATURES Fullscreen (1.33:1) • Languages: Eng. • Sound: Dolby Digital Surround 5.1, DTS • Keepcase • 1 Disc • Region All GENRE & RATING Historical/Fantasy • Not Rated (Kids)

Odyssey: The Mind's Eye Presents Ancient Alien

Sony, 1998, 45 mins., #LVD49927.

This DVD was not available for review. It is a CGI anthology set to music.

Ogenki Clinic Adventures ☞ see Mature/Adult
Section

Oh My Goddess! Vol. 1

AnimEigo, 2001, 87 mins., #AV201-063.
Directed by Hiroaki Goda. Screenplay by
Naoko Hasegawa. Based on the manga
series by Kosuke Fujishima in *Afternoon
Magazine.*

Little did Keiichi realize that a wrong
number could lead to so much trouble! When the college student dials
for pizza, he accidentally manages to
call the Goddess Helpline and speak to Belldandy, a real
live goddess who offers to grant him one wish. Keiichi,
thinking it is a joke, wishes she would be his girlfriend.
Belldandy appears to grant his wish and become his
steady. However, once he has a real live woman in tow,
Keiichi is too shy to make any moves. Disgusted by his
inability to be a suitable boyfriend to Belldandy, her sisters—the goddesses Urd and Skuld—appear to cause
trouble. Skuld tries to help the romance blossom, while
the youngest sister Urd thinks it's degrading for Belldandy to be with Keiichi. As with most romantic comedies, there are more hijinks than anything else. *Oh My
Goddess!* is a lot of fun with the charm of *I Dream of Jean-
nie* mixed with a likable teen WB type cast.

Oh My Goddess! debuted in 1993, and spanned multiple OVAs, a television series, and a set of *The Adventures
of Mini-Goddess* anime featuring small versions of Belldandy, Skuld, and Urd (see listings for that title and *Ah!
My Goddess: The Movie*). This DVD contains the first
three episodes of the *Oh My Goddess!* series, as well as
commentary by the U.S. voice director and major voice
actors. Another cool feature is the "Dub Your Own Version," which features music and sound effects but no
vocal track, while the "Silent Movie Version" features
music and sound effects with English subtitles. This
makes it one DVD that any *Oh My Goddess!* fan can't be
without. [JMC]

SPECIAL FEATURES Commentary Track with Cast and Crew • Dub
Your Own Version • Silent Movie Version • Character and Art
Galleries • Easter Eggs TECHNICAL FEATURES Fullscreen (1.33:1) •
Subtitles/CC: Eng. • Languages: Jap., Eng. dub • Sound:
Dolby Digital 2.0 • Keepcase • 1 Disc • Region 1, 2, 4 GENRE &
RATING Fantasy/Girls • Not Rated (Teens)

Oh My Goddess! Vol. 2

AnimEigo, 2001, 69 mins., #AV201-064.
Directed by Hiroaki Goda. Screenplay by
Naoko Hasegawa. Based on the manga
series by Kosuke Fujishima in *Afternoon
Magazine.*

Keiichi and Belldandy seem cursed.
Whenever the pair get close, evil Bugs
escape into the Earth and cause chaos.
The Lord is angry about the bugs and
has recalled Belldandy to Heaven to prevent further
episodes. Her sisters Skuld and Urd are frantically working to find a solution to the Bug problem before Belldandy is forced to return to Heaven forever. Belldandy
has two days to erase herself from Keiichi's life and her
sisters have two days to save her. Is there enough time, or
is this the end of Belldandy's days with Keiichi?

It's a frantic search for the cure, as this volume concludes the *Oh My Goddess!* OVA. This DVD contains
episodes four and five of this cute, imaginative series.

SPECIAL FEATURES Commentary Track with Cast and Crew • Dub
Your Own Version • Silent Movie Version • Character and Art
Galleries • Clean Credits • Easter Eggs TECHNICAL FEATURES
Fullscreen (1.33:1) • Subtitles/CC: Eng. • Languages: Jap.,
Eng. dub • Sound: Dolby Digital 2.0 • Keepcase • 1 Disc •
Region 1–6 GENRE & RATING Fantasy/Girls • Not Rated (Teens)

Oliver and Company [Special Edition]

Disney, 2002, 74 mins., #25047. Directed
by George Scribner. Screenplay by Jim
Cox, Timothy J. Disney, James Mangold.
Based on the book *Oliver Twist* by
Charles Dickens.

Oliver is an orphaned kitten adrift in
the streets of New York. Befriended
by the rascally Dodger, a mutt who
runs with a gang of pickpocket dogs,
Oliver is eventually adopted by a little rich girl named
Jenny. But Oliver and Jenny are soon caught in the kidnapping plot of the villainous Sykes. Now it's up to
Dodger and all the rest of Oliver's canine pals to brave
Sykes's Dobermans and foil the kidnapper's plans . . .
even if it means a harrowing chase through New York's
dangerous streets.

This 1988 feature film—Disney's twenty-seventh full-
length animated feature—was a huge financial and critical success, and led directly into other highly successful
creations such as *The Little Mermaid.* Part of its appeal was
the music by well-known singers such as Bette Midler,
Billy Joel, Huey Lewis, and Ruth Pointer. One of the
songs was written by Howard Ashman, who was just
starting work on *Mermaid* as well. The film was also the
first Disney creation to have its own computer-anima-
tion department (though *The Great Mouse Detective* was

the first to use much CGI), resulting in about eleven minutes of footage—mostly mechanical equipment and cars—interspersed with the hand-drawn animation.

The DVD features a plethora of extras, one of which deals with the history of Disney's use of animals as protagonists. There are also two cartoon shorts starring Pluto: the Oscar-winning "Lend a Paw" (1941) and "Puss Cafe" (1950). While *Oliver and Company* is charming and fun, some scenes are fairly scary, so concerned parents may want to watch with younger children. And it is amusing that since Disney has digitally edited cigars and cigarettes out of some of their other shorts and features, the prominent cigars in this film made it through unscathed.

SPECIAL FEATURES "Making of" Featurette • Character and Art Galleries • Production Notes • Trailers • Promotional Footage • Sing-Alongs • Other Title Trailers TECHNICAL FEATURES Widescreen (1.66:1 enhanced for 16x9) • Subtitles/CC: Eng. • Languages: Eng., Fren. dub, Span. dub • Sound: Dolby Digital Surround 5.1 • Keepcase • 1 Disc • Region 1 GENRE & RATING Animals/Music/Adventure • Rated G

Oliver Twist

Liberty International, 2001, 69 mins., #LIP 0112. Directed by Richard Slapczynski. Adapted by John Palmer. Based on the book *Oliver Twist* by Charles Dickens.

Young orphan Oliver Twist toils in the seedy and wretched nineteenth century workhouses. As a boy, he escapes the workhouse—and an abusive mortician—and falls in with a pack of thieves and pickpockets. Led by the charismatic Artful Dodger, the gang is overseen by Fagin, master of thieves. Oliver's adventures take him toward potential redemption, but he's soon drawn back into trouble and danger with Fagin's group.

A 1982 production by Burbank Films Australia, this depressing and gloomy tale is relatively faithful to its roots. The animation is a bit jumpy in spots, and Oliver's big eyes make him look like either an alien or a Walter Keane painting. Scenes of whipping, hanging, guns, and snuff-snorting seem a little out-of-place in an animation project aimed at children, even if they're consistent with the original story. The DVD is no-frills, but the picture is well presented.

SPECIAL FEATURES Oliver's Map (Scene Jumps) TECHNICAL FEATURES Fullscreen (1.33:1) • Languages: Eng., Fren. dub, Span. dub • Sound: Dolby Digital 2.0, Dolby Digital 5.1 • Keepcase • 1 Disc • Region 1–6 GENRE & RATING Historical/Drama • Not Rated (Kids)

Oni Tensei: The Demon Collection ☞ see
Mature/Adult Section

Operavox

Image, 2000, 184 mins., #ID6974S4DVD. Directed by Valeri Ugarov, Natalia Dabizha, Mario Cavalli, Graham Ralph, Gary Hurst, Barry J. C. Purves. Based on the music of Wolfgang Amadeus Mozart, Gioacchino Rossini, Georges Bizet, Richard Wagner, Giacomo Puccini, and Giuseppe Verdi.

What would you get if you took six numbers sung by the Welsh National Opera, gave them to another half-dozen of England's most original animators, and didn't put any limitations on the animation styles used to bring them to life? You'd have *Operavox*, an extravagant mix of short films, full of visual and aural flourishes that viewers will love. Although some may compare the results to Disney's *Fantasia*, this isn't quite fair; the short films here are all approximately a half hour in length, and the directors and producers weren't hampered by "family first" age restrictions.

"The Magic Flute" leads the pack, with flat-looking surreal cel animation telling the tale of young lovers trying to prove they belong together. "The Barber of Seville" is an elaborate stop-motion version of the tale in which the barber Figaro and the rich Count Almaviva vie for Rosina's love. "Carmen" uses animated paintings over rotoscoped live-action (presented 1.85:1 widescreen) to tell the tragic story of a beautiful gypsy girl.

"Das Rheingold" is an ethereal and Bakshi-esque version of the tale in which a powerful gold ring is stolen, while Puccini's "Turandot" uses Eastern designs and watercolored backgrounds to tell a story in which a Chinese princess riddles her suitors, only to be presented with an equally puzzling riddle by an exiled prince. Finally, "Rigoletto" again showcases richly detailed stop-motion to tell the story of a court jester who is also an overprotective father. Although devoid of any extra features, the long running time—and beauty of the work contained herein—make this an excellent disc for animation and music fans.

SPECIAL FEATURES None TECHNICAL FEATURES Widescreen (1.85:1, for "Carmen" only) • Fullscreen (1.33:1) • Languages: Eng., Ital. • Sound: Dolby Digital 2.0 • Snapcase • 1 Disc • Region 1–6 GENRE & RATING Music/Adventure/Romance • Not Rated (Kids)

Original Dirty Pair: Girls With Guns [#1]

ADV Films, 2001, 125 mins., #DOD/001. Directed by Masayoshi Tanidabe. Script by Hiroyuki Hoshiyama, Koichi Kasamoto, Hiroki Sonoda. Based on the novels by Haruka Takachiho.

Depending on who you talk to, the beautiful but destructive Kei and Yuri are known as the "Lovely Angels" or "The Dirty Pair." The bikini-clad duo use highly unorthodox and oftentimes dangerous methods to complete a job, but even though the damage and destruction isn't always their fault, they do have a lot of fun causing it. They're Trouble Consultants for the World Welfare and Works agency, catching criminals, checking up on problems, and completing almost any task if the price is right. Plus, they blow things up . . . a lot. Whether it's crushing a rebellion of convicts on a prison world, chasing after a prototype battle robot bent on destroying the universe, defending "God" when he's accused of nasty things on a religious planet, catching baby mobsters, or attempting to convince a rogue World Welfare and Works Agent to return to the fold, the Dirty Pair are on the case!

In 1989, a ten-episode OVA series of *Dirty Pair* was released, which included new uniforms, ships, and other slight changes. Nanmo, a staple in the preceding *Dirty Pair* TV shows and OVAs, wasn't present, and this version of the series follows a continuity independent of others. Still, this is a fun DVD collection, even if the artwork is a bit flat and dull in places.

Girls with guns might seem like every guy's fantasy, but there is plenty of fun, action, and adventures to appeal to female viewers as well. Kei and Yuri are outrageous and entertaining. This DVD contains the first five episodes of the 1987 series. [JMC]

See also the entry for *Dirty Pair Flash*.

SPECIAL FEATURES Trailer • Clean Credits • Other Title Trailers TECHNICAL FEATURES Fullscreen (1.33:1) • Subtitles/CC: Eng. • Languages: Jap., Eng. dub • Sound: Dolby Digital 2.0 • Keepcase • 1 Disc • Region 1, 2, 4 GENRE & RATING Science Fiction/Cheesecake/Action • Rated 15+

Original Dirty Pair: Damsels in Destruction [#2]

ADV Films, 2001, 125 mins., #DOD/002. Directed by Masayoshi Tanidabe. Script by Yasushi Hirano, Hideki Sonoda, Yumiko Tsukamoto, Seiji Hirano, Hiroyuki Hoshiyama. Based on the novels by Haruka Takachiho.

Kei and Yuri are working on a number of assignments for the World Welfare and Works Association. First it's

more bang for the buck as the girls go up against a counterfeit ring. Then when a disgruntled former associate returns looking to bust some wings, the Lovely Angels are in for a fight like no other. Next, enjoy some adventures in babysitting as the duo discovers a cryogenic chamber housing some deep, dark secrets. Then they find themselves up against a group of warriors with red eyes. Are they devils looking to bring down some angels? Finally the Dirty Pair become space truckers to solve murders on a space station, but will they discover the killer or become the next victims?

This DVD contains the final five action-packed episodes of the 1989 series. [JMC]

SPECIAL FEATURES Trailer • Clean Credits • Other Title Trailers TECHNICAL FEATURES Fullscreen (1.33:1) • Subtitles/CC: Eng. • Languages: Jap., Eng. dub • Sound: Dolby Digital 2.0 • Keepcase • 1 Disc • Region 1, 2, 4 GENRE & RATING Science Fiction/Cheesecake/Action • Rated 15+

Origins of Film, The [Box Set]

Image, 2001, 564 mins., #ID9807UMDVD. This box set features a trio of discs, each split into two parts, examining the origins of film styles: African American Cinema I and II, First Women Filmmakers, The Gangster Film, The Fantasy Feature, and American Animation. Twenty-one short films are presented, made between 1900 and 1921. All are in black and white, and all are silent. The films and shorts contained here are from the Library of Congress archive holdings, and each was restored and given a new musical score.

The first of the shorts is "The Enchanted Drawing," made in (or before) 1900 by Thomas Edison and animated by J. Stuart Blackton. It is not animation in the strictest sense, but shows the building blocks of what was to come. As the disc progresses, there are examples of claymation, stop motion, paper cutouts, pen and ink, and even chalk animation styles. There are a few Krazy Kat shorts, as well as adventures of The Katzenjammer Kids and other comic strip stars of the era. There is also a pair of Winsor McCay segments.

Although the box set may be pricey for animation fans, it includes some very rare material, and is a must for serious animation historians. Some of the shorts herein contain racially offensive stereotypes; common in those early days, they are jarring in today's world.

SPECIAL FEATURES Insert: Liner Notes TECHNICAL FEATURES Fullscreen (1.33:1) • Languages: Eng. • Sound: Dolby Digital 2.0 • Cardboard Box with 3 Keepcases • 3 Discs • Region 1–6 GENRE & RATING Anthology/Historical • Not Rated (Kids)

Orphen: Spell of the Dragon [#1]

ADV Films, 2001, 75 mins., #DOP/001. Directed by Hiroshi Watanabe. Screenplay by Mayori Sekijima, Masashi Kubota. Based on the novels by Yoshinobu Akita.

Orphen is one of the best sorcerers that anyone's ever seen, but he isn't interested in studying at a school and casting simple spells. He's on a quest to find the Bloody August, a dragon unlike any other, that was once his human friend Azalie. Unfortunately, his old school didn't like someone with so much potential leaving their ranks, so they've sent staff members off on their own quest to return Orphen to the fold. Besides searching for Bloody August and magical items that will help free her, Orphen now must avoid his old teachers! Teamed up with an earnest boy named Majic, who wants to be Orphen's apprentice, and a willful girl, Cleao, an heiress with an attitude, Orphen sets off to find the dragon, restore his friend, and battle his teachers and anyone else who gets in the way.

Set in a medieval-looking time and place, *Orphen* is a popular anime based on a series of fantasy novels. The *Orphen* television series lasted two seasons, for a total of forty-seven episodes. Besides watching and reading adventures of the *Orphen* gang, fans can also play Orphen in a variety of computer and video game formats.

Although the story is somewhat predictable, this DVD—containing the first three episodes from the original *Orphen* anime series—sets the stage for events to come, and is intriguing enough to leave viewers wanting more. [JMC]

SPECIAL FEATURES Character and Art Galleries • Clean Credits • Other Title Trailers TECHNICAL FEATURES Fullscreen (1.33:1) • Subtitles/CC: Eng. • Languages: Jap., Eng. dub • Sound: Dolby Digital 2.0 • Keepcase • 1 Disc • Region 1 GENRE & RATING Fantasy/Adventure • Rated 12+

Orphen: Supernatural Powers [#2]

ADV Films, 2001, 75 mins., #DOP/002. Directed by Hiroshi Watanabe. Screenplay by Mayori Sekijima, Masashi Kubota. Based on the novels by Yoshinobu Akita.

Life as an adventurer isn't the fairy tale Cleao dreamed it would be. In fact, she finds it quite boring, which is why she convinces Majic to join her on a monster hunt. She's heard tales of a creature near a resort, so the pair go to learn if the legend is fact or fiction. Then the group encounters a tribe whose quest in life is to kill all sorcerers. Tough luck for Orphen and Majic. Majic gets nabbed by the tribe and it's up to Orphen and Cleao to rescue the young apprentice before he becomes a statistic.

This disc contains episodes #4–6, and is filled with battles and unlikely allies as the quest for Bloody August progresses. [JMC]

SPECIAL FEATURES Character and Art Galleries • Clean Credits • Other Title Trailers TECHNICAL FEATURES Fullscreen (1.33:1) • Subtitles/CC: Eng. • Languages: Jap., Eng. dub • Sound: Dolby Digital 2.0 • Keepcase • 1 Disc • Region 1 GENRE & RATING Fantasy/Adventure • Rated 12+

Orphen: Ruins and Relics [#3]

ADV Films, 2001, 75 mins., #DOP/003. Directed by Hiroshi Watanabe. Screenplay by Mayori Sekijima, Masashi Kubota. Based on the novels by Yoshinobu Akita.

Secret origins are revealed, as we learn about Orphen's past and details of his relationship with Azalie. On the quest to help Bloody August, and between bouts with possessed toys and former allies, Orphen recalls meeting nine-year-old Azalie at the Tower of Fangs when he was only four. He reveals how they grew up together, how his feelings for her changed, and how he last saw her in human form at the age of nineteen. The two were tasked with finding artifacts, relics, and ruins, one of which changed Azalie into a dragon and set in motion the dangerous chain of events that have now led Orphen to his current quest.

The third volume of Orphen is a character-driven history lesson containing episodes #7–9. It furthers the mystery and complexities surrounding the legend of the woman who became Bloody August. [JMC]

SPECIAL FEATURES Character and Art Galleries • Clean Credits • Other Title Trailers • Easter Egg TECHNICAL FEATURES Fullscreen (1.33:1) • Subtitles/CC: Eng. • Languages: Jap., Eng. dub • Sound: Dolby Digital 2.0 • Keepcase • 1 Disc • Region 1 GENRE & RATING Fantasy/Adventure • Rated 12+

Orphen: Mystere [#4]

ADV Films, 2002, 125 mins., #DOP/004. Directed by Hiroshi Watanabe. Screenplay by Mayori Sekijima, Masashi Kubota. Based on the novels by Yoshinobu Akita.

The cast learns never to play with dolls, especially deadly killer dolls able to adapt to spells cast against them. Orphen has his hands full with an assassin toy and has to use every trick he's learned to get the upper hand. Later, the gang's back on their quest to find a cure for Azalie. However, the answers and spell they seek may lie within the confines of the Tower of Fangs. Now they must invade Orphen's old school, find the Book of Shadows, and leave before anyone—or anything—discovers them.

This part of the magical journey ups the ante for danger, and the disc provides a hefty five episodes instead of the usual three! [JMC]

SPECIAL FEATURES Character and Art Galleries • Trailer • Promotional Footage • Clean Credits • Other Title Trailers • Easter Egg TECHNICAL FEATURES Fullscreen (1.33:1) • Subtitles/CC: Eng. • Languages: Jap., Eng. dub • Sound: Dolby Digital 2.0 • Keepcase • 1 Disc • Region 1 GENRE & RATING Fantasy/Adventure • Rated 12+

Orphen: The Soul Stealers [#5]

ADV Films, 2002, 125 mins., #DOP/005. Directed by Hiroshi Watanabe. Screenplay by Mayori Sekijima, Masashi Kubota. Based on the novels by Yoshinobu Akita.

Orphen is searching for Rox Roe, the only sorcerer who knows the spell to trap the dragon and free Azalie from its control, but Bloody August will do anything to stop Orphen. The group's troubles are just beginning, with demons, weird bug creatures, and exploding volcanoes barring their success. Any one of those things might do Bloody August's job for it, and even if Orphen and the gang make it through this gauntlet, they might be too spent to defend against the skills and power of Bloody August. Is this the end of our heroes? And is one of the group a liar? Watch for an unexpected plot twist!

This penultimate DVD contains episodes #15–19 and includes some all-new material in a recap episode that will leave both regular and new viewers satisfied. [JMC]

SPECIAL FEATURES Character and Art Galleries • Promotional Footage • Clean Credits • Other Title Trailers TECHNICAL FEATURES Fullscreen (1.33:1) • Subtitles/CC: Eng. • Languages: Jap., Eng. dub • Sound: Dolby Digital 2.0 • Keepcase • 1 Disc • Region 1 GENRE & RATING Fantasy/Adventure • Rated 12+

Orphen: The Third Talisman [#6]

ADV Films, 2002, 125 mins., #DOP/006. Directed by Hiroshi Watanabe. Screenplay by Mayori Sekijima, Masashi Kubota. Based on the novels by Yoshinobu Akita.

Orphen and his friends are nearing the end of their adventures, but they must translate the set of mysterious runes in the Room of Knowledge or all may be lost. Meanwhile, two trolls try to heal the dragon, just in case Orphen isn't victorious. Orphen's enemy Flameheart is determined not to allow our heroes to achieve victory, but Cleao might be the one who can save Orphen and the dragon!

The final five episodes of this magical series are presented on this DVD.

SPECIAL FEATURES Interview with Cast and Crew • Character and Art Galleries • Clean Credits • Other Title Trailers TECHNICAL

FEATURES Fullscreen (1.33:1) • Subtitles/CC: Eng. • Languages: Jap., Eng. dub • Sound: Dolby Digital 2.0 • Keepcase • 1 Disc • Region 1 GENRE & RATING Fantasy/Adventure • Rated 12+

Osmosis Jones

Warner, 2001, 95 mins., #21323. Directed by Peter Farrelly, Bobby Farrelly. Written by Marc Hyman.

Frank isn't in the best of health, much to the concern of his preteen daughter Shane. He's a couch potato, eats all sorts of junk, and is probably the most unhygienic man on the planet outside of his best friend, Bob. But is he entirely to blame? They say our bodies are "temples," but in this story, Frank's body is a *city*, complete with a corrupt mayor and your average joe blood cells that are just trying to get by. One of those corpuscles is white blood cell Osmosis Jones, laughingstock of the local law enforcement. Nothing this suave character tries to do ever seems to go as smoothly as he talks. But he gets a chance to redeem himself when he gets assigned to assist a cold tablet, Drix, in stopping what *seems* to be just a cold. Further investigation by Osmosis leads him to believe that something more sinister than a cold virus is at work. Can he and Drix purge Frank of this deadly threat?

An extremely well-animated but also extremely *disgusting* live-action and animated film from 2001, *Osmosis Jones* features Bill Murray as Frank and the voice of Chris Rock as Osmosis. Listen also for voices by William Shatner, Laurence Fishburne, and Brandy Norwood. The movie surprises with its witty dialogue and touching scenes. Children will love "gross anatomy" humor and well-designed characters, and adults will appreciate the sophisticated aspects of the story. Younger children, however, may be frightened by the movie's extreme—albeit cartoonish—violence.

The DVD has loads of extras, including commentary by the director, and several cool segments. The menus are also full of clever puns—just like the movie. [WM]

SPECIAL FEATURES "Making of" Featurettes • Commentary Track with Director • Deleted Scenes • Trailer • Game • Easter Eggs TECHNICAL FEATURES Widescreen (2.35:1 enhanced for 16x9) • Subtitles/CC: Eng., Fren. • Languages: Eng., Fren., Span. • Sound: Dolby Digital Surround 5.1 • Snapcase • 1 Disc • Region 1 GENRE & RATING Live/Comedy • Rated PG

Otaku No Video

AnimEigo, 2001, 100 mins., #AV201-066. Directed by Takeshi Mori. Screenplay by Toshio Okada.

Kubo's an ordinary college student. He plays tennis, has an active social life, lots of friends, and a cute girl-friend. Then one day a chance encounter with an old high school acquaintance named Tanaka changes Kubo's life forever. Tanaka's an "otaku," meaning his life revolves around anime, manga, model building, and science fiction films. Eager to indoctrinate Kubo into the joys of otakudom, Tanaka brings Kubo into his circle of anime-obsessed friends. Slowly, Kubo leaves his former life behind to become not just an otaku, but King of the Otaku. With Tanaka at his side, Kubo starts a company making garage kits (models of anime characters), which quickly grows into an industry powerhouse. While their otaku kingdom seemingly expands without limit, calamity looms on the horizon.

This 1982 mockumentary and 1985 sequel are the fictionalized story of the founding of Gainax, one of Japan's most respected animation studios. Its harsh treatment of otaku earns *Otaku No Video* a mixed reception among anime fans, where it may hit a little too close to home. Nevertheless, the film's hilarious send-up of otaku culture can't be denied. The clever mix of animation and live action "Portraits of Otaku" makes for outstanding comedy, though those who aren't familiar with the phenomenon of otaku and its place in Japanese society may find some aspects of the film difficult to understand.

The DVD contains some nudity and adult situations, so parents are warned. [BR]

SPECIAL FEATURES Character and Art Galleries • Trailer • Liner Notes • Easter Egg TECHNICAL FEATURES Fullscreen (1.33:1) • Subtitles/CC: Eng. • Languages: Jap. • Sound: Dolby Digital 2.0 • Keepcase • 1 Discs • Region 1 GENRE & RATING Live/Comedy • Not Rated (Teens)

Outlaw Star: DVD Collection 1

Bandai, 2000, 225 mins., #0820. Directed by Mitsuru Hongo. Written by Katsuhiko Chiba. Based on characters created by Hiroyuki Hataike, and the manga series by Takehiko Ito in *Ultra Jump*.

In a galaxy where the military and space pirates struggle for control, Gene Starwind yearns to make a name for himself in space as an outlaw. Gene and his young, mechanically inclined partner Jim Hawking accept a job from a mysterious client who soon reveals herself as a notorious outlaw who has stolen an advanced spaceship developed to search for the Galactic Leyline, an enigmatic treasure left by an ancient civilization. Kei pirates bent on finding the Leyline pursue the trio, and when the dust clears, a comrade is dead.

Gene is left as captain of the Outlaw Star, joined by an unlikely crew of Jim, Melfina, a bio-android who doubles as the ship's navigation system, and two deadly women: Aisha Clan Clan, a ferocious but sometimes silly cat-girl of the Ctarl-Ctarl Empire who wants the treasure of the Leyline for herself, and "Twilight" Suzuka, an assassin waiting for a chance to kill Gene without distraction. Together the group embarks on a frenetic journey across space to discover the Outlaw Star's secret purpose and Melfina's origins under constant threat from pirates and rival outlaws.

Adopted for Japanese television in 1998, *Outlaw Star* caught the eye of Cartoon Network, which brought the show's intriguing cast of characters, intense action, and well-conceived story to American television in 2000. Takuya Saito's distinctive character design lends itself well to *Outlaw Star*'s crisp, fluid animation and brisk pace. Not to be outdone, composer Ko Otani puts together an extraordinary music score, marked by moody orchestral movements, jazzy licks, and a soulful end theme song.

This two-disc set contains episodes #1–9, and has occasional use of mature language and moderate violence. See also *Angel Links* for a related series. [BR]

SPECIAL FEATURES Character and Art Galleries • Clean Credits • Other Title Trailers TECHNICAL FEATURES Fullscreen (1.33:1) • Subtitles/CC: Eng. • Languages: Jap., Eng. dub • Sound: Dolby Digital Surround 2.0 • Multikeepcase • 2 Discs • Region 1 GENRE & RATING Science Fiction/Adventure • Rated 13+

Outlaw Star: DVD Collection 2

Bandai, 2000, 225 mins., #0821. Directed by Mitsuru Hongo. Written by Katsuhiko Chiba. Based on characters created by Hiroyuki Hataike, and the manga series by Takehiko Ito in *Ultra Jump*.

Gene enters the Outlaw Star in the Heifong Space Race, but rival pirates are more interested in killing Gene and his crew than competing with them. Meanwhile, Lord Hazanko, leader of the Kei pirates, has sent elite assassin group Anten Seven to kill Gene. Shimi, the first of the Anten, confronts Gene in a bloody duel that unifies the crew in defiance of the pirates. The crew then teams with a salty aging outlaw who needs help chasing his personal "white whale." As the secrets of Melfina and her connections to the Outlaw Star and the Galactic Leyline start to reveal themselves, Aisha and Gene (yes, Gene) compete in a contest to determine the strongest woman in the universe.

Episodes #10–18 are included on this hefty two-disc set. [BR]

SPECIAL FEATURES Character and Art Galleries • Clean Credits • Other Title Trailers TECHNICAL FEATURES Fullscreen (1.33:1) • Subtitles/CC: Eng. • Languages: Jap., Eng. dub • Sound: Dolby Digital Surround 2.0 • Multikeepcase • 2 Discs • Region 1 GENRE & RATING Science Fiction/Adventure • Rated 13+

Outlaw Star: DVD Collection 3

Bandai, 2001, 200 mins., #0822. Directed by Mitsuru Hongo. Written by Katsuhiko Chiba. Based on characters created by Hiroyuki Hataike, and the manga series by Takehiko Ito in *Ultra Jump.*

Private Security Forces mistake the crew for pirates and Jim has an unlikely love interest cut short by battle with Hanmyo, the second of the Anten Seven. Soon after, Gene and crew discover ancient ruins as the enemy battles for Melfina's heart. Gene infiltrates a high-gravity prison to get the last clue to the Leyline's location, and then the crew takes a break (as do the sensibilities of the show's creators) on a vacation planet where clothing is strictly optional. Tan lines gone, the Outlaw Star races to the Leyline only to find their enemies waiting. Melfina's secrets reveal themselves while Gene and crew battle the remaining Anten Seven assassins.

The *Outlaw Star* epic comes to a close with a decisive, deadly battle with Lord Hazanko that leaves you wishing for a sequel. This two-disc set, containing episodes #19–26, features nudity, some mature language, and moderate violence. [BR]

SPECIAL FEATURES Character and Art Galleries • Clean Credits • Other Title Trailers • Easter Egg TECHNICAL FEATURES Fullscreen (1.33:1) • Subtitles/CC: Eng. • Languages: Jap., Eng. dub • Sound: Dolby Digital Surround 2.0 • Multikeepcase • 2 Discs • Region 1 GENRE & RATING Science Fiction/Adventure • Rated 13+

Outlaw Star: The Perfect Collection [Box Set]

Bandai, 2002, 650 mins.

This 3-disc boxed set was not available for review.

P

Pagemaster, The

20th Century Fox, 2002, 75 mins., #2003495. Live Action Directed by Joe Johnston. Animation Directed by Maurice Hunt. Story by David Kirschner, David Casci. Screenplay by David Casci, David Kirschner, Ernie Contreras.

Timid young Richard Tyler escapes from a storm into a library with a very strange librarian. Richard is soon swept into the world of books, and set on a journey of adventure accompanied by three magical book companions: Adventure, Fantasy, and Horror. On his travels, he crosses paths with characters from *Dr. Jekyll and Mr. Hyde*, *Moby Dick*, *Treasure Island*, and more. Will he find his lost courage?

Macauley Culkin was the selling point of this live-action/animated feature film in 1994. Culkin played the live Richard, and voiced the animated Richard once he entered the world of books. Other voice actors included Christopher Lloyd, Patrick Stewart, Whoopi Goldberg, Leonard Nimoy, and voice actor god Frank Welker.

The DVD is double-sided, with the widescreen version on one side, and the fullscreen version on the other. For kids who can't get enough of Harry Potter, or those not yet old enough to see the *Potter* films without nightmares, *The Pagemaster* is a nice G-rated flick with the message that reading is a good thing. And that message, in itself, is also a good thing.

SPECIAL FEATURES "Making of" Featurette • Trailers • Music Video • Other Title Trailers TECHNICAL FEATURES Widescreen (1.85:1 enhanced for 16x9) • Fullscreen (1.33:1) • Subtitles/CC: Eng., Span. • Languages: Eng., Fren. dub • Sound: Dolby Digital Surround 5.1 • Keepcase • 1 Disc • Region 1 GENRE & RATING Live/Fantasy • Rated G

Panda! Go Panda!

Pioneer, 2000, 75 mins., #10521. Directed by Isao Takahata. Screenplay by Hayao Miyazaki.

Five-year-old Mimiko has it made. While her grandmother is away at a funeral, the surprisingly resourceful little girl has the run of the house. It isn't long before she finds a friendly pair of pandas in her backyard. The father panda is affable and chatty, and his son seems eager to make friends with Mimiko. Papa panda is so upset to find that Mimiko is actually an orphan that he declares that he shall be her father, and Mimiko herself can play mother to the little panda ("Panny"). The trio spend their days whimsically, going on picnics, striking up a marching band, and making friends with a tiger cub at the circus.

This wonderfully unpretentious family movie is an early theatrical outing by Hayao Miyazaki, the animation grandmaster who would go on to direct classics like *Princess Mononoke*. The animation was excellent for its time and is in surprisingly good shape—the two stories certainly don't look like they were animated back in 1972. All told, this DVD is an excellent family feature, and an obvious prototype for some of Miyazaki's later family films. Serious animation fans will love it, but small children will love it even more.

This DVD contains both of the theatrical short films, "Panda Family" and "The Circus in the Rain." The dubbed version also contains some new, more polished-sounding music instead of the dated original soundtrack. [MT]

SPECIAL FEATURES Creator Bios • Character and Art Galleries • Original Opening TECHNICAL FEATURES Fullscreen (1.33:1) • Subtitles/CC: Eng. • Languages: Jap., Eng. dub • Sound: Dolby Digital 2.0 • Keepcase • 1 Disc • Region 1 GENRE & RATING Animals/Family • Rated 3+

Parade Parade ☛ see Mature/Adult Section

Patlabor 1: The Movie

Manga Entertainment, 2000, 100 mins., #Manga4054-2. Directed by Mamoru Oshii. Script by Kazunori Ito. Based on the manga series by Masami Yuki in *Shonen Sunday Comics.*

In the future, giant robots called Labors are used for projects such as construction and military operations. A select few are used with Police Force's Special Vehicle Division as Patrol Labors, or Patlabors, to catch criminals and those misusing technology. Things are going great until a group of rogue Labors begin causing destruction and damage instead of repairing things. Two of the Patlabor officers, Noah Izumi and Azuma Shinohara, are trying to figure out why technology is turning against them. In their investigation they find ties to the new Hyper Operating System and, after its creator commits suicide, the pair realizes that the HOS system is corrupting all the Labors it touches. But their knowledge might have come too late; their own Patlabors are scheduled to receive the Hyper Operating System upgrade! Now, the two must prove the existence of a conspiracy to spread the corrupt system before all Labors are changed, but will they be able to combat the enemy and cure a virus whose roots are on a floating tower in Tokyo Bay?

This 1990 *Patlabor* film followed the successful 1988 OVA and 1989 television launches of the series. Filled with slight Biblical references and cynical political commentary on society, this character-driven and dialogue-heavy DVD contains enough action, intrigue, and mystery to keep most fans guessing and anxious to see what happens next. [JMC]

SPECIAL FEATURES Trailer • Other Title Trailers • Easter Eggs
TECHNICAL FEATURES Widescreen (1.85:1) • Subtitles/CC: Eng. • Languages: Jap., Eng. dub • Sound: Dolby Digital 5.1 • Keepcase • 1 Disc • Region 1, 2, 4 GENRE & RATING Robots/Action • Not Rated (Teens)

Patlabor 2: The Movie

Manga Entertainment, 2000, 100 mins., #Manga4055-2. Directed by Mamoru Oshii. Script by Kazunori Ito. Based on the manga series by Masami Yuki in *Shonen Sunday Comics.*

Japan is on the brink of chaos and war, and some parties welcome the apocalypse. When terrorist acts happen a little too close to home and threaten to cause anarchy and panic in Tokyo, the Patlabor team is called to investigate. Their investigation leads them to trouble as the person behind these attacks is Nagumo's former teacher, lover, and one of the founders of the Patlabors! Now Nagumo is torn. Will she be able to do her job and bring him to justice, or will old feelings color her actions?

This anime is a bit long in places, and is much more political than its predecessor. The DVD does not feature many extras, but the presentation is fine. [JMC]

SPECIAL FEATURES Trailer • Other Title Trailers • Easter Eggs
TECHNICAL FEATURES Widescreen (1.85:1) • Subtitles/CC: Eng. • Languages: Jap., Eng. dub • Sound: Dolby Digital 5.1 • Keepcase • 1 Disc • Region 1, 2, 4 GENRE & RATING Robots/Action • Not Rated (Teens)

Patlabor: The Mobile Police—The TV Series Vol. 1

U.S. Manga Corps, 2001, 120 mins., #USMD2069. Directed by Naoyuki Yoshinaga. Screenplay by Kazunori Ito, Mamoru Oshii, Hiroyuki Hoshiyama. Based on the manga series by Masami Yuki in *Shonen Sunday Comics.*

In the future, Tokyo's Metropolitan Police Department activates a special unit to combat techno-threats, terrorists, monsters, and more. These Mobile Police are known as Patrol Labors or Patlabors, and their drivers are an odd ensemble. There's rookie girl Noa Izumi, rich kid Asuma Shinohara, cool Captain Kiichi Gotu, large-sized Hiromi Yamazaki, firepower fanatic loudmouth Isao Ota, and others. Unfortunately for them, Section Two gets the outmoded Labors, while Section One gets the newest models. But that doesn't stop Noa and Asuma and the others from fighting crime to the best of their abilities.

Combining the cop-show characterization of *Hill Street Blues* with giant robots, *Patlabor* debuted in 1988 on OVA, and followed up with a television series in 1989. It quickly gained popularity due to its humor and cynicism, mixed with realistic characters with whom audiences could identify. The TV series is funnier than the movies. Also note that USMC spells some names slightly differently from Manga Entertainment.

This DVD collects the first five episodes of the TV series: "Ingram Animated"; "Kanuka Appears"; "Speed Vehicles Department 2"; "Goto Demon Mountain!"; and "Labor X-10, Out of Control!"

SPECIAL FEATURES Director Bio • Character Bios • Character and Art Galleries • DVD-ROM Features: Art, Scripts, Episode Guide, Bios • Other Title Trailers TECHNICAL FEATURES Fullscreen (1.33:1) • Subtitles/CC: Eng. • Languages: Jap., Eng. dub • Sound: Dolby Digital 2.0 • Keepcase • 1 Disc • Region 1 GENRE & RATING Robots/Action • Rated 3+

Patlabor: The Mobile Police—The TV Series Vol. 2

U.S. Manga Corps, 2002, 125 mins., #USMD2172. Directed by Naoyuki Yoshinaga. Screenplay by Michiko Yokote, Naoto Kimura, Kazunori Ito, Mamoru Oshii.

NOTE: This DVD arrived too late for a full review. The following text is promotional copy provided by the releasing company:

"Not just another Girl-Loves-Giant-Robot movie! Everybody loves Alphonse—a giant robot with huge guns to match! But technology marches on, and his police officer pilot may be forced to abandon him for a newer model. She'll have to prove that Alphonse is still strong enough, big enough, and cute enough to stay on the force. Together, they'll rescue a famous politician, hunt down a pesky demon, and solve a national conspiracy . . . all while causing worse trouble along the way!"

This disc contains episodes #6–10.

SPECIAL FEATURES "Making of" Featurette • Text Interview with Screenwriter • Character Bios • Character and Art Galleries • Promotional Footage • DVD-ROM Features: Art, Scripts, Character Bios • Other Title Trailers TECHNICAL FEATURES Fullscreen (1.33:1) • Subtitles/CC: Eng. • Languages: Jap., Eng. dub • Sound: Dolby Digital 2.0 • Keepcase • 1 Disc • Region All GENRE & RATING Robots/Action • Rated 3+

Peanuts Classic: Holiday Collection [Box Set]

Paramount, 2000, 150 mins., #15614.

This box set features the commercially available keepcase editions of *It's The Great Pumpkin, Charlie Brown*; *A Charlie Brown Thanksgiving*; and *A Charlie Brown Christmas*. It does not feature any extras. See individual entries for the Special and Technical Features listings.

TECHNICAL FEATURES Cardboard Box with 3 Keepcases • 3 Discs • Region 1 GENRE & RATING Holiday/Family • Not Rated (All Ages)

Pebble and the Penguin, The

MGM/UA, 2001, 74 mins., #905403. Directed by Don Bluth, Gary Goldman. Screenplay by Rachel Koretsky, Steve Whitestone.

A shy and nerdy penguin named Hubie must prove his love to his sweetheart, Marina, by presenting her with a pebble during the Full Moon Mating Ceremony (an actual practice among real-life Adelie penguins in Antarctica). Also vying for Marina's attention is Hubie's polar opposite, the buff and studly Drake, who throws Hubie into the sea before the special pebble can be given to Marina. Now Hubie and his rebellious friend Rocko must brave humans who capture them, killer whales, and leopard seals to help Hubie win his true love.

Don Bluth's Irish production company animated this film for 1995 release, but it was the last of that studio's creations. Featuring songs by Barry Manilow and voice talent by Tim Curry, Martin Short, and Jim Belushi, the film sounds pleasant enough, and it's really hard to do anything wrong with penguins. Most adults won't be as charmed by the cute film as their young ones will, but hopeless romantics and the kiddie brigade will adore the characters and the messages about true love, perseverance, and romance.

While the DVD picture is fine, the DVD has unfortunately only been released in a full-frame transfer, rather than the film's original widescreen form. But comparisons to the widescreen laserdisc version have shown that more information is given at the top and bottom, even if the sides have been trimmed, so viewers aren't completely cheated.

SPECIAL FEATURES Trailer • Other Title Trailers • Inserts: Character Notes TECHNICAL FEATURES Fullscreen (1.33:1 full frame) • Subtitles/CC: Eng., Fren. • Languages: Eng., Fren. dub • Sound: Dolby Digital Surround 5.1 • Keepcase • 1 Disc • Region 1 GENRE & RATING Music/Animal/Family • Rated G

Perfect Blue ☛ see Mature/Adult Section

Pet Shop of Horrors: Special Edition ☛ see Mature/Adult Section

Pet's Dragon [Gold Collection]

Disney, 2001, 129 mins., #19576. Directed by Don Chaffey. Screenplay by Malcolm Marmorstein. Story by Seton I. Miller, S. S. Field.

Poor Pete is an orphan who runs away from his nasty guardians, escaping to a Maine fishing town with his "imaginary" friend: a large green and purple dragon named Elliott, who stays invisible most of the time! Pete meets Nora, a woman who lives in a lighthouse with her father as she waits for her fiancé to return home to her. But what happens when Elliott's existence is revealed, and cruel people set out to imprison and exploit him?

This 1977 film is a mixture of live-action elements and animation (Elliott is animated), and it attempted to impress theater audiences in the same vein as *Mary Poppins*. Unfortunately, female lead Helen Reddy has little of Julie Andrews's screen presence or charisma, and neither the story nor the music were up to the levels of the previous classic (although one of the songs, "Candle on the Water," was nominated for a 1977 Academy Award). Mickey Rooney is fun as Nora's father, though. The animation itself is fine for the period (Don Bluth supervised it), but it seems quaint and a bit dated in today's CGI-heavy world.

The DVD contains the complete film (as far as is known), not the several shorter versions that had been used for feature rerelease over the years. The disc also has a nice series of extra features, including a featurette about monsters, another about the "Plausible Impossible," and a 1982 excerpt about the making of the film. There's also a 1946 animated short, "Lighthouse Keeping," starring Donald Duck.

SPECIAL FEATURES "Making of" Featurettes • Character and Art Galleries • Production Notes • Trailers • Game • Easter Egg TECHNICAL FEATURES Widescreen (1.66:1 enhanced for 16x9) • Subtitles/CC: Eng., Fren. • Languages: Eng. • Sound: Dolby Digital 5.1 • Keepcase • 1 Disc • Region 1 GENRE & RATING Live/Music/Fantasy • Rated G

Peter Pan [Collector's Edition]

Digital Versatile Disc, 1999, 49 mins., #179. Screenplay by Paul Leadon. Based on the play and book by James M. Barrie.

After retrieving his lost shadow from the Darling house, Peter Pan brings Wendy, Michael, and John Darling to the magical Never Land. Peter is the boy who never grew up, and the kids soon find themselves having adventures with Tinker Bell the fairy, the Lost Boys, Tiger Lily and her Indians, and the dastardly pirates. But one man threatens the lives of Peter Pan, the Lost Boys, and the Darlings: the one-handed pirate leader, Captain Hook!

Produced by Burbank Films Australia, this is a lackluster adaptation of the original play and novel that audiences have loved since early in the 20th century. The character designs are fairly simplistic and ugly (especially for Captain Hook), and the voice work—including a lisping Wendy, a jive-sounding African pirate, and a barking dog that is barely heard—is pathetic. The script keeps the bare bones plot points, but almost none of the original dialogue. This version is *not* a trip to Never Land.

As with other DVD Ltd. releases, there is a bio of the author on the disc.

SPECIAL FEATURES Author Bio • Game TECHNICAL FEATURES Fullscreen (1.33:1) • Languages: Eng. • Sound: Dolby Digital 5.1, DTS • Keepcase • 1 Disc • Region All GENRE & RATING Fantasy/Family/Adventure • Not Rated (All Ages)

Peter Pan [Limited Issue]

Disney, 1999, 77 mins., #18786. Directed by Hamilton Luske, Cyde Geronimi, Wilfred Jackson. Story by Ted Sears, Bill Peet, Joe Rinaldi, Erdman Penner, Winston Hibler, Milt Banta, Ralph Wright. Based on the play and book by James M. Barrie.

The magical boy Peter Pan uses some of Tinker Bell's fairy dust to allow Wendy, Michael, and John Darling to fly. Soon, it's off to Never Land, where the Darlings join Peter's clan of Lost Boys, who all plan to never grow up. The Lost Boys—and especially Peter—are hated by Captain Hook, whose hand Peter once fed to a crocodile. Luckily, that croc also swallowed a clock, so Hook can hear whenever the creature comes near, hoping for another bite.

Released in 1953, Disney's fourteenth animated feature film takes many liberties with its source material, while still *appearing* to hew closely to the storyline of Barrie's play and book. Most of the changes were made for tone reasons; the original story is often dark and verging on gloomy at times. Still, the animation is glorious, and the Marilyn Monroe–esque Tinker Bell design has made many children and adults believe in fairies (even though she was *not* based on the blonde actress).

As with other early Disney features, a live-action version of the film was shot first, providing animators with a guide to make the characters' movements realistic. Hans Conried, who voiced the dastardly Captain Hook, also played him in the unseen live version. The music in the feature is extremely engaging and natural, though PC types might cringe a bit at the depiction and savage-speak of the Indians, especially in the song "What Makes the Red Man Red?"

This DVD is strictly no-frills, and is on moratorium.

SPECIAL FEATURES None TECHNICAL FEATURES Fullscreen (1.33:1) • Subtitles/CC: Eng. • Languages: Eng., Fren. dub • Sound: Dolby Digital Surround 4.0 • Keepcase • 1 Disc • Region 1 GENRE & RATING Music/Fantasy/Family • Rated G

Peter Pan [Special Edition]

Disney, 2002, 77 mins., #21620. Directed by Hamilton Luske, Cyde Geronimi, Wilfred Jackson. Story by Ted Sears, Bill Peet, Joe Rinaldi, Erdman Penner, Winston Hibler, Milt Banta, Ralph Wright. Based on the play and book by James M. Barrie.

Disney's 1953 film is given the deluxe treatment with this disc, which features a restored and remastered print, as well as a plethora of extras. One "making of" featurette is newly produced, while another is a vintage 1952 short. The commentary track is hosted by Roy Disney, and features droll recollections from original animators Frank Thomas, Ollie Johnston and Marc Davis, as well as historian Leonard Maltin. A handful of other extras are more appealing for kids.

This DVD gets another high recommendation for not only families, but animation lovers in general, and anyone who believes in fairies.

NOTE: This DVD is now on moratorium.

SPECIAL FEATURES "Making of" Featurettes • Commentary Track with Animators • Character and Art Galleries • Sing-Along • Storybook • Game • Other Title Trailers TECHNICAL FEATURES Fullscreen (1.33:1) • Subtitles/CC: Eng. • Languages: Eng., Fren. dub, Span. dub • Sound: Dolby Digital 5.1 • Keepcase • 1 Disc • Region 1 GENRE & RATING Music/Fantasy/Family • Rated G

Peter Pan in Return to Never Land

Disney, 2002, 73 mins., #25274. Directed by Robin Budd. Screenplay by Temple Mathews. Based on the characters created in the book by Sir James M. Barrie.

When Jane's father goes off to fight in World War II, London is wrecked by bombing. Hiding in a shelter with her mother—once known as Wendy Darling—her brother, and her dog, Nana II, Jane is frustrated with Wendy's tales of Peter Pan and Never Land. Seeing the world crumble around her, Jane is a realist who has no time for fantasy. But when Captain Hook and his pirates fly into town to kidnap Wendy, nabbing Jane in the process, the girl soon learns that magic is real. Back in Never Land, Jane is saved by Peter Pan and Tinker Bell, and she's soon adventuring with the Lost Boys. But pursuing them all is Captain Hook, who himself is being chased by a clever orange octopus.

Given a perfunctory theatrical release in 2002, *Peter Pan in Return to Never Land* is a sequel to the 1953 Disney film. Unfortunately, at times, it feels like an inferior remake. The London scenes are excellent and filled with peril and conflict, and Jane seems like a very interesting character. But once the story shifts to Never Land, the plot practically mirrors the original, and comes up short by comparison. Artistically, although Hook and his pirates look about the same, Peter has been drawn to be more elastic and cartoony, while full-figured Tinker Bell has definitely been hitting the fairy diet pills. And what's up with the Lost Boys, who've apparently lost their brains?

The DVD has some traditional extras, along with a pair of deleted scenes with introductions. *Peter Pan in Return to Never Land* isn't bad, but as the first fifteen minutes show, it could have been so much better.

NOTE: This DVD is now on moratorium.

SPECIAL FEATURES Deleted Scenes • Music Video • Storybook •

Games • DVD-ROM Features: Sampler • Other Title Trailers TECHNICAL FEATURES Widescreen (1.66:1 enhanced for 16x9) • Subtitles/CC: Eng. • Languages: Eng., Fren. dub, Span. dub • Sound: Dolby Digital Surround 5.1 • Keepcase • 1 Disc • Region 1 GENRE & RATING Music/Adventure • Rated G

Peter Rabbit Collection, The [Vol. 1: Flopsy Bunnies/Pigling Bland]

GoodTimes, 2002, 53 mins., #05-81195. Directed by Dave Unwin, Tony Guy, Mike Stuart. Written by Dianne Jackson. Based on the books and stories by Beatrix Potter.

In "The Tale of the Flopsy Bunnies and Mrs. Tittlemouse," Benjamin Bunny marries his cousin, Flopsy Bunny, and the resultant six little Flopsy Bunnies are soon causing mischief all over the glen. Will Mrs. Tittlemouse be able to tame them? In "The Tale of Pigling Bland," it looks as if bacon is in their future, unless Pigling Bland and Pig-Wig can escape from Mr. Piperson!

Bookended by live-action segments, these 1993 British adaptations of Beatrix Potter's beloved stories are delightful, charming, and sweet. Although the animation is a bit simplified, it even resembles the original Potter book illustrations, with watercolor hues and washes and fine linework. The DVD is no-frills, but it is recommended for families.

The DVD was also included in a two-disc box set, *The World of Peter Rabbit and Friends: Vol. 2.*

SPECIAL FEATURES None TECHNICAL FEATURES Fullscreen (1.33:1) • Subtitles/CC: Eng. • Languages: Eng. • Sound: Dolby Digital 2.0 • Keepcase • 1 Disc • Region 1 GENRE & RATING Animals/Family • Not Rated (All Ages)

Peter Rabbit Collection, The [Vol. 2: Samuel Whiskers/Tom Kitten]

GoodTimes, 2002, 53 mins., #05-81196. Directed by Dave Unwin, Mike Stuart. Written by Dianne Jackson. Based on the books and stories by Beatrix Potter.

In "The Tale of Samuel Whiskers or the Roly-Poly Pudding," three little kittens get into mischief. Mittens and Moppet hide in some flour barrels, but Tom climbs up into the chimney, where he meets Samuel Whiskers, a hungry rat who wants to eat a cat! In "The Tale of Tom Kitten and Jemima Puddle-Duck," Tom, Moppet, and Mittens all try to stay out of trouble in anticipation of their mother's upcoming tea party. But the arrival of someone with big whiskers could set Jemima Puddle-Duck all awhirl.

Like others in this DVD series, this has a live-action

intro, and some wonderfully sweet animation and story-telling. The DVD was also included in a two-disc box set, *The World of Peter Rabbit and Friends: Vol. 2.*

SPECIAL FEATURES None TECHNICAL FEATURES Fullscreen (1.33:1) • Subtitles/CC: Eng. • Languages: Eng. • Sound: Dolby Digital 2.0 • Keepcase • 1 Disc • Region 1 GENRE & RATING Animals/Family • Not Rated (All Ages)

Peter Rabbit Collection, The [Vol. 3: Peter Rabbit/Mr. Tod]

GoodTimes, 2002, 51 mins., #05-81197. Directed by Geoff Dunbar. Written by Dianne Jackson. Based on the books and stories by Beatrix Potter.

The best-known hero of Beatrix Potter's stories gets two adventures on this DVD. In "The Tale of Peter Rabbit and Benjamin Bunny," the two playful rabbit cousins get loose in Mr. McGregor's garden. Then, in "The Tale of Mr. Tod," Mr. Tod kidnaps a trio of Flopsy Bunnies, and Peter and Benjamin follow Tommy Brock, a wily badger, to find and rescue them.

More delightful animation and storytelling are found on this DVD, which again features live-action intros.

The DVD was also included in a two-disc box set, *The World of Peter Rabbit and Friends: Vol. 1.*

SPECIAL FEATURES None TECHNICAL FEATURES Fullscreen (1.33:1) • Subtitles/CC: Eng. • Languages: Eng. • Sound: Dolby Digital 2.0 • Keepcase • 1 Disc • Region 1 GENRE & RATING Animals/Family • Not Rated (All Ages)

Peter Rabbit Collection, The [Vol. 4: Two Bad Mice/Tiggy-Winkle/Tailor]

GoodTimes, 2002, 78 mins., #05-81198. Directed by Roger Mainwood, Geoff Dunbar, Jack Stokes. Written by Dianne Jackson. Based on the books and stories by Beatrix Potter.

A trio of tales make up this final disc in the Beatrix Potter animated stories. In "The Tale of Two Bad Mice and Johnny Town-Mouse," you might think you know what happens when a city mouse and a country mouse visit each other, but the real story is presented here. In "The Tale of Mrs. Tiggy-Winkle and Mr. Jeremy Fisher," kindly shrew washerwoman Mrs. Tiggy-Winkle helps Lucille find her lost handkerchief and listens to froggy Jeremy Fisher tell of his tales of adventure while fishing. Finally, in "The Tailor of Gloucester," some mice lend their sewing talents to help an elderly tailor make a beautiful coat for the Mayor of Gloucester, who is to be wed on Christmas morning!

With a trio of tales instead of a duo, this DVD is a

good value for families seeking sweet stories and pleasant animation. The DVD was also included in a two-disc box set, *The World of Peter Rabbit and Friends: Vol. 1.*

SPECIAL FEATURES None TECHNICAL FEATURES Fullscreen (1.33:1) • Subtitles/CC: Eng. • Languages: Eng. • Sound: Dolby Digital 2.0 • Keepcase • 1 Disc • Region 1 GENRE & RATING Animals/Family • Not Rated (All Ages)

Phantom Quest Corp.: Perfect Collection

Pioneer, 2000, 140 mins., #11491. Directed by Koichi Chigira, Morio Asaka, Takuji Endo. Screenplay by Asami Watanabe, Tatsuhiko Urahata, Satoshi Kimura.

It's the '90s in Japan and businesses have it tough . . . even specialized businesses like the Phantom Quest Corp. Their president is the sexy redhead Ayaka Kisaragi. She's willing to do the work of finding and stopping restless spirits, as long as it doesn't interrupt her party time. Working with her is the low-key detective Kozo Karino, who seems to mainly be hanging around because he has the hots for Ayaka. Mamoru Shimesu keeps track of the incoming business and the books, like any good elementary school boy should. Other members of the firm include an exorcist and a firestarter. Can Phantom Quest Corp. take on the vampires, demons, and ghosts that torment Tokyo and manage to stay out of the red?

This could be the first OVA series ever with a lipstick that turns into a glowing sword. But, hey, Ayaka's better at wielding it than singing karaoke. Released in 1994, this series is a fun romp into the supernatural with some comedy thrown in for good measure. The animation is pretty good, as are the jazzy opening and ending themes. It's a good night's entertainment, especially if you're looking for something along the lines of *Buffy the Vampire Slayer* or *Ghostbusters.*

The DVD contains all four episodes of the series. It also has some neat extras like a selection of translated computer screens, signs and business cards. Also, a behind-the-scenes Easter egg lies waiting to be discovered. There is some playful brief nudity and some of the monsters can be a bit scary for young viewers. [RJM]

SPECIAL FEATURES Character and Art Galleries • Clean Credits • Other Title Trailers • Easter Egg TECHNICAL FEATURES Fullscreen (1.33:1) • Subtitles/CC: Eng. • Languages: Jap., Eng. dub • Sound: Dolby Digital 2.0 • Keepcase • 1 Disc • Region 1, 4 GENRE & RATING Horror/Comedy • Rated 13+

Photon: The Idiot Adventures

U.S. Manga Corps, 2000, 180 mins., #USMD1880. Directed by Koji Masunari. Script by Yosuke Kuroda, Katsumi Hasegawa.

Photon Earth is a seemingly ordinary kid. He works hard in his village, he enjoys playing, and he's very protective of his longtime friend, the obnoxious, pink-haired Aun. Photon is also almost completely indestructible and boasts the strength of a superhero. When Aun runs off in pursuit of her favorite pop idol, Photon is enlisted to bring her back. He ends up intercepting a crashed spaceship, rescuing its damsel-in-distress pilot in the process. All this gets Photon and Aun unwittingly caught up in a series of Machiavellian galactic political maneuvers, as the galaxy's twisted Emperor seeks to use the idiotic warrior Papacha to both unseat the galactic princess and reveal Photon's hidden power. Photon, for his part, just wants to protect his old and new friends and enjoy a nice meal.

The animation is great, but the story is all over the place in this good-natured sci-fi comedy from one of the original creators of *Tenchi Muyo!* The series' story greedily swipes from a number of sources, including *Star Wars* and *Superman*, to create its fairly predictable plot. The result is a 1997 OVA series with fantastic animation and funny characters, but not a whole lot else. *Photon* tries to make up for this shortcoming by throwing in some entertaining scenes of cartoonish violence and lots of gratuitous nudity, but the essential feel of the show is still light and insubstantial.

This DVD contains all six of the *Photon* OVA episodes that were produced. [MT]

SPECIAL FEATURES Cast Clips • DVD-ROM Features: Art, Scripts • Other Title Trailers TECHNICAL FEATURES Fullscreen (1.33:1) • Subtitles/CC: Eng. • Languages: Jap., Eng. dub • Sound: Dolby Digital 2.0 • Keepcase • 1 Disc • Region 1–6 GENRE & RATING Science Fiction/Comedy • Rated 13+

Pigeon (And More) Within: Animation by Emily Hubley

Image, 2002, 59 mins., #ID1478PIDVD. Directed by Emily Hubley.

Like the collections of her parents Faith and John Hubley's work, this collection of seven short films produced by Emily Hubley showcases a wide array of animation styles. Most are expressionistic and simplistic, produced with crayons, watercolor, and traditional cel animation. But these films are not as much about the specific slickness of animation as they are about expressions of the feelings in the music and narration.

"Pigeon Within" (2000) shows a girl encountering what could be her guardian angel, while "One Self: Fish/Girl" (1997) listens in on the diary entries of a young girl. "Delivery Man" (1982) finds a girl discussing fears about doctors and the death of her father, and "The Tower" (1984) teams Emily up with Georgia Hubley for a story about victimization. "Enough" (1993) features a search for a magical fish, while "Blake Ball" (1988) refocuses the words of WIlliam Blake through a game of baseball. Finally, "Her Grandmother's Gift" (1995) is a primer about menstruation, with grandma passing down information to her granddaughter.

Fans should look for further Hubley family work under the *Art and Jazz in Animation: The Cosmic Eye* and *The Hubley Collection* listings.

SPECIAL FEATURES None TECHNICAL FEATURES Fullscreen (1.33:1) • Languages: Eng. • Sound: Dolby Digital 1.0 • Keepcase • 1 Disc • Region 1–6 GENRE & RATING Anthology • Not Rated (Kids)

Pilot Candidate: The Academy [#1]

Bandai, 2001, 75 mins., #1855. Directed by Mitsuru Hongo. Written by Akira Oketani, Miho Sakai. Based on the manga series by Yukiru Sugisaki in *Comic Gam.*

Thousands of years in the future, when humanity is under attack from evil mysterious aliens known only as Victim, it's up to a group of teen pilots to save the day. The pilots are all students at a prestigious academy, who go through a rigorous training for a chance to pilot one of five mechs, the only devices capable of harming the Victim. The mechs, powerful battle robots known as Ingrids or Goddesses, must merge with their young pilots and form a bond. This bond remains intact until the pilot dies, retires, or is surpassed by another pilot. Each mech also has a teen technician who provides repairs and other upgrades as needed. Children from many space stations are being tested and gathered at GOA Space Academy to see if they have the skills to pilot or repair one of the mechs. Zero Enna, Hiead Gnr, Clay Cliff Fortran, Roose Sawamura, Yamagi Kushida, and Erts Cocteau are a few of the teens training to be mech pilots, but the competition is fierce and, sometimes, deadly. The fate of the universe and humanity rests in the hands of these young students.

Pilot Candidate is a twelve-part anime series released in 2001 in Japan. The following year, Cartoon Network aired episodes of this series during its "Midnight Run" block. This initial DVD contains episodes #0–2. Unfortunately, the subtitles are actually "dubtitles," transcriptions of the English script rather than the Japanese script.

A rushed and predictable anime with elements from

many other "mechs must merge with humans to save the universe" anime and sci-fi series, *Pilot Candidate* has a bland cast, uneventful subplots, and little in the way of character development. After viewing several episodes, only a few names of characters, out of the tons introduced, can be easily recalled. The CGI sequences are also poorly integrated into the 2D animation. If you have acute insomnia, this is the anime for you. [JMC]

SPECIAL FEATURES "Welcome to GOA" clip • Clean Credits • Other Title Trailers TECHNICAL FEATURES Fullscreen (1.33:1) • Subtitles/CC: Eng. • Languages: Jap., Eng. dub • Sound: Dolby Digital 2.0 • Keepcase • 1 Disc • Region 1 GENRE & RATING Robots/Science Fiction/Action • Rated 13+

Pilot Candidate: Training [#2]

Bandai, 2001, 75 mins., #1856. Directed by Mitsuru Hongo. Written by Akira Oketani, Miho Sakai. Based on the manga series by Yukiru Sugisaki in *Comic Gam.*

Now that the teens have passed the initiation and show the potential to actually be pilots, their teachers have a special curriculum in mind. They want to begin training each pilot and seeing just who has the right stuff for this intense job. Each navigator is introduced to a repair technician and given a guided tour of a mech. Using virtual reality to simulate combat and other situations, the pilots are able to merge with a mech and gain invaluable experience, but will the rigorous training discourage or motivate them?

Although a little more information is revealed about a few of the characters, the second DVD, containing episodes #3–5, is still suffering from too many characters and not enough character development, the same problem that was prevalent throughout the first installment. There isn't a lot of reason to be vested in these characters or care if one of them is hurt, maimed, or worse. [JMC]

SPECIAL FEATURES "Making of" Voice Actor Featurette • Interview with Director • Other Title Trailers TECHNICAL FEATURES Fullscreen (1.33:1) • Subtitles/CC: Eng. • Languages: Jap., Eng. dub • Sound: Dolby Digital 2.0 • Keepcase • 1 Disc • Region 1 GENRE & RATING Robots/Science Fiction/Action • Rated 13+

Pilot Candidate: Working Together [#3]

Bandai, 2001, 75 mins., #1857. Directed by Mitsuru Hongo. Written by Akira Oketani, Miho Sakai. Based on the manga series by Yukiru Sugisaki in *Comic Gam.*

The aftermath of a Victim attack leaves a pilot gravely injured and the threat of another impending battle makes finding a replacement an immediate necessity. The freshman pilots are all anxious, each hoping for a shot at piloting an Ingrid in battle against the vile aliens. But the teens soon discover they don't have to travel to space to make a difference as another Victim attacks near the school and both pilots and mechanics work together to help defend and protect their friends and classmates. The battle hits home and the pilots realize this isn't a game, but a matter of life and death, in this penultimate disc containing episodes #6–8. [JMC]

SPECIAL FEATURES "Making of" Voice Actor Featurette • Interview with Director • Other Title Trailers TECHNICAL FEATURES Fullscreen (1.33:1) • Subtitles/CC: Eng. • Languages: Jap., Eng. dub • Sound: Dolby Digital 2.0 • Keepcase • 1 Disc • Region 1 GENRE & RATING Robots/Science Fiction/Action • Rated 13+

Pilot Candidate: The Test [#4]

Bandai, 2001, 75 mins., #1858. Directed by Mitsuru Hongo. Written by Akira Oketani, Miho Sakai. Based on the manga series by Yukiru Sugisaki in *Comic Gam.*

While most of the pilots are training and vying for a spot as mech pilot, Zero is using hypnosis to try and unravel his past and the mysteries surrounding it. He begins to believe that another world, untouched by the Victim, might exist. Meanwhile a massive Victim offensive is launched against this world that brings all candidates, trainers, technicians, and anyone even remotely associated with the academy into the battle. Armed with weapons that are definitely outclassed by the Victim's armory, these people stand poised to defend their world or die.

We're left with an ending that isn't really an ending in the final volume of this series, containing episodes #9–11. It all ends with a cliffhanger that leaves no closure or resolution, and we will quite probably have no chance to ever see if anyone survives the Victim attack. Even if the story wasn't that compelling to begin with, it's still annoying not to know how it all played out. [JMC]

SPECIAL FEATURES "Making of" Voice Actor Featurette • Interview with Director TECHNICAL FEATURES Fullscreen (1.33:1) • Subtitles/CC: Eng. • Languages: Jap., Eng. dub • Sound: Dolby Digital 2.0 • Keepcase • 1 Disc • Region 1 GENRE & RATING Robots/Science Fiction/Action • Rated 13+

Ping Pong Club, The: Make Way For [#1]

Software Sculptors, 2002, 120 mins., #USSDVD-6193. Directed by Masami Hata. Screenplay by Tsunehisa Ito, Yoshiro Sasa, Kenji Terada, Sukehiro Tomita. Based on the manga series by Minoru Furuya in *Young Magazine*.

NOTE: This DVD arrived too late for a full review. The following text is promotional copy provided by the releasing company:

"Dirty jokes, girl trouble, and other dumb things—these are the trials and tribulations of the boys' Ping Pong Club. Only one passion truly fires their souls: the glorious sport of Ping Pong! Unfortunately, tragedy strikes when the girls' team conquers the gym, leaving our heroes humiliated and homeless. Foul play may be the only way for the boys to get back on top. Luckily, it's the only way they know how to play. Join these not-so-lovable losers as they face their worst enemies—themselves!"

SPECIAL FEATURES Commentary Track by Characters • Trailer • Promotional Footage • Clean Credits • DVD-ROM Features: Art, Scripts, Character Bios • Other Title Trailers TECHNICAL FEATURES Fullscreen (1.33:1) • Subtitles/CC: Eng. • Languages: Jap., Eng. dub • Sound: Dolby Digital 2.0 • Keepcase • 1 Disc • Region 1 GENRE & RATING Comedy • Rated 16+

Ping Pong Club, The: Love and Comedy (Die! Die! Die!) [#2]

Software Sculptors, 2002, 100 mins., #USSDVD-6195. Directed by Masami Hata. Screenplay by Tsunehisa Ito, Yoshiro Sasa, Kenji Terada, Sukehiro Tomita. Based on the manga series by Minoru Furuya in *Young Magazine*.

NOTE: This DVD arrived too late for a full review. The following text is promotional copy provided by the releasing company:

"Something amazing has happened: Maeno and the boys' Ping Pong Club have actually started practicing! Watch and laugh as our heroes fight their way through Ping Pong Camp to meet their opponents: an all-female Ping Pong team! But how can any girl learn to love such pathetic losers as these? Cringe in terror as our heroes pull inane and outrageous stunts for a chance at the ladies. All's fair in love and Ping Pong, and Ping Pong is definitely war!"

SPECIAL FEATURES "How to Play Ping Pong" Clip • Trailer • Promotional Footage • Clean Credits • DVD-ROM Features: Art, Scripts, Character Bios • Other Title Trailers TECHNICAL FEATURES Fullscreen (1.33:1) • Subtitles/CC: Eng. • Languages: Jap., Eng. dub • Sound: Dolby Digital 2.0 • Keepcase • 1 Disc • Region 1 GENRE & RATING Comedy • Rated 16+

Ping Pong Club, The: Losers' Club [#4]

Software Sculptors, 2001, 180 mins., #SSDVD-6178. Directed by Masami Hata, Takashi Tanasawa, Toshiaki Kanbara, Kenichiro Watanabe, Yukio Takahashi, Futa Morita, Raisen Hanyu, Tanasawa Takahashi, Toshiaki Tanazawa. Screenplay by Sukehiro Tomita, Yoshiro Sasa, Tsunehisa Ito. Based on the manga series by Minoru Furuya in *Young Magazine*.

Inachu Junior High has a table tennis club comprised of several players; Kinoshita and Takeda are handsome, but the other four male members are geeks. The quartet includes: Maeno and Izawa, whose skill at disguises are far surpassed by their lechery; Tanabe, a blond American exchange student with bad body odor, a hairy chest, and a huge belly button; and Tanaka, a short boy with a huge head and an unusual interest in animals. Kyoko, an easily offended and often angry girl, completes the group. The club constantly finds ways to get into trouble, whether it's by playing "doctor" to the school's female students or allowing perverted Maeno to take the place of an elderly performer's ventriloquist dummy. Another story has a club member stealing dues money to feed animals, but there's a twist ending.

A 1995 TV series in Japan, *The Ping Pong Club* is often compared to *South Park*, but it owes just as much—or more—to *Beavis and Butt-Head*. The twelve-minute stories are full of crude humor that involves sex, flatulence, urination, defecation, violence, voyeurism, and more. Your ability to enjoy the humor will depend largely on whether you find these topics intrinsically funny, as the wry social commentary and blistering satire often present in *South Park* is missing here. Crude jokes are just meant to be crude jokes. The ugly art and character designs will also likely put off some viewers.

Inexplicably, Software Sculptors/Central Park Media have chosen to release the first DVD containing material halfway through the show's run. "Losers' Club" and "Goes for Broke" comprise episodes #23–34 of the series. With a lot of exposed male genitalia, the material almost rates inclusion in the Mature/Adult section, but stays just shy of the mark.

SPECIAL FEATURES Character Bios • Trailer • Clean Credits • DVD-ROM Features: Scripts • Other Title Trailers TECHNICAL FEATURES Fullscreen (1.33:1) • Subtitles/CC: Eng. • Languages: Jap., Eng. dub • Sound: Dolby Digital Surround 5.1 • Keepcase • 1 Disc • Region All GENRE & RATING Comedy • Rated 16+

Ping Pong Club, The: Rots in Hell [#5]

Software Sculptors, 2001, 180 mins., #SSDVD-6179. Directed by Kenichiro Watanabe, Raisen Hanyu, Yukio Takahashi, Takashi Tanasawa, Toshiaki Tanazawa. Screenplay by Yoshiro Sasa, Tsunehisa Ito, Kenji Terada, Sukehiro Tomita. Based on the manga series by Minoru Furuya in *Young Magazine*.

Kinoshita is horrified when the club members come to a sleepover, wearing his sister's underwear and raiding his parent's condoms. Later, the boys all take a bath together and hatch a peeping plan. Then, Tanaka reveals his destiny as a "Panty Master," and three members decide to prove they're tough enough to survive the trials that Japanese people in the past had to endure. And a new junior high school principal brings trouble.

More raunchy humor, gross-outs, tastelessness, and other weirdness occur in this volume, which assembles the segments "Assorted Shorts" and "Rots in Hell," comprising the final TV episodes #35–47. As with the previous disc, there's three hours of material, so if you like this kind of humor, this is a great value for your money.

SPECIAL FEATURES Character Bios • Production Notes • DVD-ROM Features: Scripts • Other Title Trailers TECHNICAL FEATURES Fullscreen (1.33:1) • Subtitles/CC: Eng. • Languages: Jap., Eng. dub • Sound: Dolby Digital Surround 5.1 • Keepcase • 1 Disc • Region All GENRE & RATING Comedy • Rated 16+

Pink Floyd: The Wall ☞ see Mature/Adult Section

Pink Panther Cartoon Collection, The: Jet Pink

MGM/UA, 2001, 51 mins., #907435. Directed by Art Davis, Hawley Pratt, Friz Freleng, Gerry Ciniquy, Sid Marcus. Written by Lee Mishkin, John W. Dunn, Sid Marcus, Dave Detiege.

The Pink Panther stars in his first collection of seven cartoon shorts, in which he faces a relentless cuckoo clock, accidentally powers up a jet plane, cavorts with sheep, plays with his pet rock, attempts to build a house, battles a painter, crosses a busy street, and faces a snorting bull.

Although most people think that he began in cartoons, the Pink Panther actually first appeared in the opening credits of Blake Edwards 1964 bumbling spy film, *The Pink Panther*. There, he became forever identified with Henry Mancini's slinky theme song, and became popular enough that United Artists engaged animation studio Depatie-Freleng to produce dozens of

animated shorts that preceded all of their films for the latter half of the 1960s. NBC licensed the cartoons for a series in 1969, and some versions of the show ran on NBC, ABC, and, in syndication, into the 1990s!

This collection includes "The Pink Pfink," the debut cartoon, which won an Oscar for Best Animated Short Subject in 1964. Others include: "In the Pink of the Night" (1969); "Jet Pink" (1967); "Little Beaux Pink" (1968); "Pet Pink Pebbles" (1981); "The Pink Blueprint" (1966); "Think Before You Pink" (1969); and "Toro Pink" (1979). Most of the cartoons have no dialogue, though a few have laugh tracks or minor amounts of text. The transfer from film is to DVD is mostly nice, though the colors are a little too vibrant in spots.

SPECIAL FEATURES Inserts: Booklet with History Notes TECHNICAL FEATURES Fullscreen (1.33:1) • Subtitles/CC: Eng. • Languages: Eng., Fren. dub • Sound: Dolby Digital 2.0 • Keepcase • 1 Disc • Region 1 GENRE & RATING Comedy/Espionage • Not Rated (All Ages)

Pinocchio [Gold Collection]

Disney, 1999, 88 mins., #18665. Directed by Ben Sharpsteen, Hamilton Luske. Story by Ted Sears, Otto Englander, Webb Smith, William Cottrell, Joseph Sabo, Erdman Penner, Aurelius Battaglia. Based on the book by Carlo Lorenzini (aka Collodi).

Woodcarver Gepetto wants a son so badly that he carves a puppet that resembles a boy, and calls him Pinocchio. One magical night, the Blue Fairy brings Pinocchio to life, but he won't ever get to become a real living boy unless he proves he can learn valuable virtues such as bravery, unselfishness, and more. Accompanied by Jiminy Cricket—a diminutive umbrella-toting insect who acts as his conscience—Pinocchio sets out on a series of adventures and misadventures that will teach him lessons. Will he be able to escape from a wicked puppet-show slavedriver and later, the creepy Pleasure Island? How will he free Gepetto from the belly of Monstro the whale? Will Pinocchio ever get to become a real boy?

Disney's second animated feature film is widely hailed as a masterpiece of animation, and truthfully, there is little argument from any camp. Combining a strong story with lush art and highly detailed backgrounds, the 1940 film also featured some truly magical music; both the score and the theme song "When You Wish Upon a Star" won Academy Awards in 1940. The only downside is that the feature contains some scary sequences that might be tough for young children to take.

The DVD has almost no extras, but the picture and soundtrack were restored for the film's sixtieth anniversary. The disc is now on moratorium.

SPECIAL FEATURES Trailer • Other Title Trailers TECHNICAL FEATURES

Fullscreen (1.33:1) • Subtitles/CC: Eng. • Languages: Eng., Fren. dub • Sound: Dolby Digital 2.0 • Keepcase • 1 Disc • Region 1 GENRE & RATING Music/Fantasy/Family • Rated G

Pinocchio [Limited Edition]

Disney, 1999, 88 mins., #18665. Directed by Ben Sharpsteen, Hamilton Luske. Story by Ted Sears, Otto Englander, Webb Smith, William Cottrell, Joseph Sabo, Erdman Penner, Aurelius Battaglia. Based on the book by Carlo Lorenzini (aka Collodi).

This DVD is the exact same release as the Gold Collection, with the exception that the labels on the keepcase and DVD itself both say "Limited Edition" instead of "Gold Collection." The disc is also now on moratorium.

SPECIAL FEATURES Trailer • Other Title Trailers TECHNICAL FEATURES Fullscreen (1.33:1) • Subtitles/CC: Eng. • Languages: Eng., Fren. dub • Sound: Dolby Digital 4.0 • Keepcase • 1 Disc • Region 1 GENRE & RATING Music/Fantasy/Family • Rated G

Pippi Longstocking: Pippi's Adventures on the South Seas

HBO, 2000, 69 mins., #91704. Directed by Clive Smith. Screenplay by Catharina Stackleberg, Frank Nissen, Ken Sobol. Based on the series of books by Astrid Lindgren.

Red-pigtailed Pippi Longstocking is the strongest girl in the world, and there's nothing she likes better than to have adventures. So when a sailing ship arrives in the nearly frozen harbor of her hometown, Pippi is delighted to learn that the Captain is her long-lost father! She soon joins him aboard sailing the South Seas. Along the way, Pippi and her father's crew encounter pirates and pearl poachers, as well as stowaways and castaways!

This 2000 feature is a co-production between Canadian and Swedish animators. It features cute and lively animation, nice voice work, and spritely musical numbers. Had it been given a theatrical run in more than seventy-three U.S. theaters, it might have fared better than it did, but audiences now have a chance to watch it at home on DVD. The disc has basically no extra features (except one trailer for *Babar*), but it's still a perfectly fun affair that will be especially popular with young girls.

SPECIAL FEATURES Other Title Trailer TECHNICAL FEATURES Fullscreen (1.33:1) • Subtitles/CC: Eng., Fren., Span. • Languages: Eng. • Sound: Dolby Digital 2.0 • Snapcase • 1 Disc • Region 1 GENRE & RATING Music/Adventure/Girls • Rated G

Pixar 15th Anniversary Box Set

Disney, 2001, 271 mins., #24347-1.

This box set features the commercially available keepcase "basic" editions of *Toy Story*, *Toy Story 2*, and *A Bug's Life*. See individual entries for the Special and Technical Features listings. Note that the title of *Pixar 15th Anniversary Box Set* is not presented anywhere on the box itself, but was used for solicitations and ordering.

TECHNICAL FEATURES Cardboard Box with 3 Keepcases • 3 Discs GENRE & RATING CGI/Comedy/Insects/Toys • Rated G

Planetary Traveler

Wellspring, 2000, 40 mins., #WHE73001. Directed by Jan C. Nickman.

A mysterious alien race known as the Phlieg were once Planetary Travelers, exploring the galaxy and its worlds in their spaceships. Now, only one of them is left, a creature named Sumoc. Aboard his ship, we travel to world upon world, viewing the alien landscapes from high in the air as he swoops above them.

The original CGI film of *Planetary Traveler* was a landmark, as it was the first such feature to be produced entirely on desktop computers, with CGI imagery showing the visually stunning landscapes as original music soothes the senses. Two-time Emmy award winning director/producer Jan C. Nickman (who also worked on the early CGI hit *The Mind's Eye*) created this film, working for two years with top visual artists.

The DVD features an entirely remastered print and new Surround Sound, as well as a number of extras: profiles of the alien worlds visited, information about the Phlieg and their ships, and much more. One of the more cohesive CGI and music hybrids, *Planetary Traveler* is definitely a good DVD to view if you want to escape to other realms.

SPECIAL FEATURES Director Interview • Crew Profiles • Planetary and Alien Culture Profiles • Production Notes • Trailer TECHNICAL FEATURES Fullscreen (1.33:1) • Subtitles/CC: Fren., Germ., Jap., Kor., Span. • Languages: Eng. • Sound: Dolby Digital 5.1 • Keepcase • 1 Disc • Region All GENRE & RATING CGI/Music/Anthology • Not Rated (Kids)

Plastic Little ☛ see Mature/Adult Section

Please Save My Earth

Pioneer, 2000, 180 mins., #D-PS001. Directed by Kazuo Yamazaki. Screenplay by Kazuo Yamazaki. Based on the manga series by Saki Hiwatari in *Hana To Yume*.

Alice Sakaguchi is a Japanese high school student whose dreams are haunted by memories of being an alien scientist on the moon! But when two of her classmates come to her with the same dream—that they are also a part of the team of seven alien scientists watching over the Earth—reality begins to warp around Alice. The mystery deepens as more of the scientists are discovered, and it seems clear that Alice and the others have somehow been reborn on Earth, after living past lives on the moon. But could their dreams be telling them something? Who is the seventh scientist? What is their destiny? And what happened to them in the past?

Based on a twenty-one-volume manga series, *Please Save My Earth* was presented as a 1993 OVA series of six parts. The animation is beautiful and realistic, and the music is pleasant and relaxing as well; both of them complement the intriguing, slightly complex plot and solid dialogue. Some fans have complained that the ending seems rushed, and that too much was left out of the story from the manga original.

The DVD contains all six chapters, and some nice background material that—the viewer is hereby cautioned—should *not* be read until after viewing the entire half-dozen episodes. Neither the thirty-minute music video or later "movie version" of the story is on the disc, however.

SPECIAL FEATURES Character Bios • Production Notes & FAQ • Clean Credits • Other Title Trailers TECHNICAL FEATURES Fullscreen (1.33:1) • Subtitles/CC: Eng. • Languages: Jap., Eng. dub • Sound: Dolby Digital Surround 2.0 • Keepcase • 1 Disc • Region 1 GENRE & RATING Science Fiction/Mystery/Romance • Rated 13+

Pleasure Pack ☞ see Mature/Adult Section

Plymptoons: The Complete Works of Bill Plympton

Slingshot, 1999, 60 mins., #DVD9815. Directed by Bill Plympton. Written by Bill Plympton.

Bill Plympton's animation is one of the most easily recognizable styles put to film. Using colored-pencil drawings, he showcases the metamorphosis of man or woman into something bizarre and yet still humanesque.

Bodies are constantly in motion, with limbs or features moving; a man might put his hand and arm into his mouth and pull his head inside out, then place his lips on top like a hair bow.

Plympton's highly stylized shorts made him the darling of the animation film festivals, and after winning a 1987 Academy Award for the short "Your Face," the independent animator became much more in demand, producing commercials and two feature films: *The Tune* and *I Married a Strange Person!* (see entries). But this DVD, containing nineteen of his shorts, shows that it took a while for the artist's style to evolve into itself. Early work from 1968 and 1977 is childlike; most of the featurettes were made between 1985 and 1991 and are in the traditional style.

While Plympton's work is fun to watch, seeing so much of it in a row without any coherent plot makes it a chore to absorb this entire disc at once. Even hardcore fans will have a better time if they break it up over multiple viewings.

SPECIAL FEATURES None TECHNICAL FEATURES Fullscreen (1.33:1) • Languages: Eng. • Sound: Dolby Digital 2.0 • Keepcase • 1 Disc • Region All GENRE & RATING Anthology/Humor • Not Rated (Teens)

Pocahontas

Madacy, 1999, 30 mins.

This DVD was not available for review.

Pocahontas [Gold Collection]

Disney, 2000, 81 mins., #19579. Directed by Mike Gabriel, Eric Goldberg. Screenplay by Carl Binder, Susannah Grant, Philip LaZebnik.

In the year 1607, the English have come to the New World, and Jamestown settler Captain John Smith has caught the eye of Pocahontas, the daughter of the Native American Chief Powhatan. But the English are led by the greedy Governor Ratcliffe, who comes to believe that the Native Americans are his enemy. Much to the consternation of her father and her tribe, the strong-willed Pocahontas continues to consort with Smith, teaching him about the beauty in nature just around the Virginia riverbend. But as tensions mount between the settlers and the Native Americans, can Pocahontas gain wisdom from the wise Grandmother Willow tree and bring peace to the very different cultures?

Released in 1995, *Pocahontas* wasn't quite the success Disney hoped it would be, largely due to an overstuffed summer movie season with multiple kids' movies. Historians also mocked the film for its almost complete lack of historical accuracy. Unfortunately, in their zeal to wag fingers, those critics missed the fact that this animated fantasy has some *great* voice work and music. More importantly, the character designs—especially for the ultra-hot Pocahontas—and backgrounds were stupendous, making the film a visual treat.

The DVD contains a pair of music videos, including one for the 1995 Oscar-winning "Colors of the Wind" (the film also won the Oscar for Best Score), and it also contains a relative rarity among DVDs: a "Theatre-Vision" voice track narrates and describes the film for the visually impaired! Despite the G rating, the romance and violence might make this more reasonable for older viewers. If you haven't watched *Pocahontas*—and can ignore the historical inaccuracies—this is a gorgeous film.

SPECIAL FEATURES Trailer • Music Videos • Storybook • Game • Other Title Trailers • Inserts: "Fun with Nature" Booklet TECHNICAL FEATURES Widescreen (1.66:1) • Subtitles/CC: Eng., TheatreVision • Languages: Eng., Fren. dub, Span. dub • Sound: Dolby Digital Surround 5.1 • Keepcase • 1 Disc • Region 1, 4 GENRE & RATING Music/Historical/Adventure • Rated G

Pocahontas II: Journey to a New World [Gold Collection]

Disney, 2000, 73 mins., #19598. Directed by Bradley Raymond, Tom Ellery. Screenplay by Allen Estrin, Cindy Marcus, Flip Kobler.

Some time has passed, and John Smith escapes after being charged with treason for his actions against Ratcliffe. The rotund Governor appeals to King James to send an army back to the New World to deal with the fearsome savages. The King requests that an ambassador from the Native American tribe be brought to England to discuss the matter, and Pocahontas and her warrior protector soon depart for the British Isles. But once in the courts of King James, Pocahontas must adopt the ways of "civilization" if she is to save her people. How will John Smith come back into her life? And how will Pocahontas outwit the scheming Ratcliffe?

A direct-to-video feature, *Pocahontas II* bears even less resemblance to real history than its predecessor. In fact, it's best to just consider this as much of a fantasy as *Peter Pan* or *Snow White*. The animation is not quite as strong, though many of the pretty character designs are kept. But the courts and streets of England aren't as gorgeous and lush as the unspoiled wilderness seen in the first film; thankfully, we see snow-covered nature during the film's first third. Vocal work and music are fine, though not up to the award-winning standards of the original.

The DVD contains a handful of extras, including the 1937 *Silly Symphonies* episode, "Little Hiawatha."

SPECIAL FEATURES Trailer • Music Video • Read-Along • Games • Other Title Trailers TECHNICAL FEATURES Widescreen (1.66:1) • Subtitles/CC: Eng. • Languages: Eng., Fren. dub, Span. dub • Sound: Dolby Digital Surround 5.1 • Keepcase • 1 Disc • Region 1 GENRE & RATING Music/Historical/Adventure • Rated G

Pokémon: I Choose You! Pikachu! [#1]

Pioneer/Viz, 1998, 75 mins., #PIKA-01DVD. Directed by Kunihiko Yuyama, Masamitsu Hidaka, Yoshitaka Fujimoto. Screenplay by Atsuhiro Tomioka, Takeshi Shudo, Hideki Sonoda, Junji Takegami.

Ash is a young boy in the town of Pallet who wants to learn to capture and train Pocket Monsters, or Pokémon, strange and magical little creatures who share the world alongside humans. Unfortunately, Ash oversleeps on the fateful day he is to be given a training manual and his first Pokémon. Ash is forced to take Pikachu, a yellow mouse-like creature that has the power to shock. Pikachu doesn't want to obey Ash initially, but when a Spearow attack leaves Pikachu injured, Ash fights to protect his new friend. With their close relationship now established, Pikachu helps Ash catch many other Pokémon, all so he can become the world's best Pokémon trainer. But sinister forces are conspiring against them in the person of Team Rocket—a duo named Jessie and James—who are intent on stealing as many rare and valuable Pokémon as they can! Luckily, Ash is also befriended by feisty girl Misty.

Debuting on Japanese television in 1997, *Pokémon* tied in to a popular Nintendo game and a massive marketing drive. Children loved the world in which they could collect cute and cuddly creatures and pit them against each other. The following year, *Pokémon* debuted in the U.S. with another huge marketing and advertising push, and the series became a runaway success. Parents were soon falling prey to their kids' plaintive wails for more *Pokémon* toys, trading cards, games, and the like. But at least the TV series was free . . . until its "gotta catch them all" release on video and DVD. *Pokémon* imitators followed suit, and the series is credited for bringing anime into mainstream America more than any property since *Akira* (and since it is a series for kids, it far surpassed *that* more adult film in licensing value alone).

As a series, *Pokémon* is cutely animated, though repetitive animation and excessive use of speed-line backgrounds show a genuine lack of artistry and desire to pump out as much product in as little time as possible. In addition to the full-length "Pokc-Rap," which describes all 150 known Pokémon!—the DVD contains the first three episodes of the series: "I Choose You! Pikachu!"; "Pokémon Emergency!"; and "Ash Catches a Pokémon."

SPECIAL FEATURES Music Video TECHNICAL FEATURES Fullscreen

(1.33:1) • Languages: Eng. • Sound: Dolby Digital 2.0 • Keepcase • 1 Disc • Region 1 GENRE & RATING Adventure/Kids • Not Rated (Kids)

Pokémon: The Mystery of Mount Moon [#2]

Pioneer/Viz, 1999, 75 mins., #PIKA-02DVD. Directed by Kunihiko Yuyama, Masamitsu Hidaka, Yoshitaka Fujimoto. Screenplay by Atsuhiro Tomioka, Takeshi Shudo, Hideki Sonoda, Junji Takegami.

In the forest, Ash, Misty, and Pikachu are confronted by a mysterious young samurai who challenges them. Then, in Pewter City, Ash decides to join the Pokémon League Championships, but first he must earn a Boulder Badge by defeating a Pokémon Gym Leader named Brock. But if he beats Brock, he'll destroy Brock's family. What will Ash do? Then, it's off to Mt. Moon to search for the Moon Stone, but eco-disasters are happening in the caves there and Pokémon are being depleted.

This DVD contains episodes #4–6: "Challenge of the Samurai"; "Showdown in Pewter City"; and "Clefairy and the Moon Stone."

SPECIAL FEATURES Music Video • Inserts: Mini Comic TECHNICAL FEATURES Fullscreen (1.33:1) • Languages: Eng. • Sound: Dolby Digital 2.0 • Keepcase • 1 Disc • Region 1 GENRE & RATING Adventure/Kids • Not Rated (Kids)

Pokémon: The Sisters of Cerulean City [#3]

Pioneer/Viz, 1999, 75 mins., #PIKA-03DVD. Directed by Kunihiko Yuyama, Masamitsu Hidaka, Yoshitaka Fujimoto. Screenplay by Atsuhiro Tomioka, Takeshi Shudo, Hideki Sonoda, Junji Takegami.

Ash goes to defeat the Cerulean Gym Leader to gain another badge, but encounters three swimming sisters and a strange aquarium instead. What link do they have to Misty? Then, on the way to Vermilion City, Ash encounters A.J., a Pokémon collector who has had 98 consecutive victories! That dwarfs Ash's ten wins, but the scrappy Ash may yet prevail. Later, Ash overhears news about a Pokémon Seminar that could get him into the Pokémon Leagues earlier.

This DVD contains episodes #7–9: "The Water Flowers of Cerulean City"; "The Path to the Pokémon League"; and "The School of Hard Knocks."

SPECIAL FEATURES Music Video • Insert: Mini Comic TECHNICAL FEATURES Fullscreen (1.33:1) • Languages: Eng. • Sound: Dolby Digital 2.0 • Keepcase • 1 Disc • Region 1 GENRE & RATING Adventure/Kids • Not Rated (Kids)

Pokémon: Poké-Friends [#4]

Pioneer/Viz, 1999, 75 mins., #PIKA-04DVD. Directed by Kunihiko Yuyama, Masamitsu Hidaka, Yoshitaka Fujimoto. Screenplay by Atsuhiro Tomioka, Takeshi Shudo, Hideki Sonoda, Junji Takegami.

Ash, Misty, and Brock arrive at a forgotten village where a sweet girl cares for injured Pokémon, but Team Rocket may be hot on their trail. Then, Ash tries to help an abandoned Pokémon named Charmander, but is initially rebuffed. And when a group of Squirtles joins forces with Team Rocket, Pikachu is captured and Misty is threatened.

This DVD contains episodes #10–12: "Bulbasaur and the Hidden Village"; "Charmander—The Stray Pokémon"; and "Here Comes the Squirtle Squad."

SPECIAL FEATURES Music Video • Inserts: Mini Comic, Trading Card TECHNICAL FEATURES Fullscreen (1.33:1) • Languages: Eng. • Sound: Dolby Digital 2.0 • Keepcase • 1 Disc • Region 1 GENRE & RATING Adventure/Kids • Not Rated (Kids)

Pokémon: Thunder Shock! [#5]

Pioneer/Viz, 1999, 75 mins., #PIKA-05DVD. Directed by Kunihiko Yuyama, Masamitsu Hidaka, Yoshitaka Fujimoto. Screenplay by Atsuhiro Tomioka, Takeshi Shudo, Hideki Sonoda, Junji Takegami.

Ash and his friends meet a lighthouse keeper who is awaiting the arrival of a never-before-seen Pokémon, but Team Rocket may spoil the party. Then, finally in Vermilion City, Ash must face a brutal trainer named Marcus, while Pikachu has to trade shocks with the more powerful Raichu. Later, Ash and lots of other Pokémon trainers go on a free trip on a cruise ship, but when Team Rocket shows up, it ceases being the Love Boat and devolves into the Titanic!

This DVD contains episodes #13–15: "Mystery at the Lighthouse"; "Electric Shock Showdown"; and "Battle Aboard the St. Anne."

SPECIAL FEATURES Music Video • Inserts: Mini Comic, Trading Card TECHNICAL FEATURES Fullscreen (1.33:1) • Languages: Eng. • Sound: Dolby Digital 2.0 • Keepcase • 1 Disc • Region 1 GENRE & RATING Adventure/Kids • Not Rated (Kids)

Pokémon: Seaside Pikachu [#6]

Pioneer/Viz, 1999, 75 mins., #PIKA-06DVD. Directed by Kunihiko Yuyama, Masamitsu Hidaka, Yoshitaka Fujimoto. Screenplay by Atsuhiro Tomioka, Takeshi Shudo, Hideki Sonoda, Junji Takegami.

The St. Anne is sinking fast, and Ash and his friends may be trapped underwater with Team Rocket. How will James's mistreatment of one of their Pokémon affect their future? Washed up on an island, Ash's team and Team Rocket soon encounter a giant-sized Pikachu and other surprises. Then, a girl offers Ash a lot of money to exterminate a Tentacool, but Misty won't have anything to do with the plan.

This DVD contains episodes #16–18: "Pokémon Shipwreck"; "Island of the Giant Pokémon"; and "Tentacool and Tentacruel." Note that another episode, "Beauty and the Beach," should have been included in this sequence, but since James has an inflatable bikini, it was not aired in America.

SPECIAL FEATURES Music Video TECHNICAL FEATURES Fullscreen (1.33:1) • Languages: Eng. • Sound: Dolby Digital 2.0 • Keepcase • 1 Disc • Region 1 GENRE & RATING Adventure/Kids • Not Rated (Kids)

Pokémon: Psychic Surprise [#7]

Pioneer/Viz, 1999, 75 mins., #PIKA-07DVD. Directed by Kunihiko Yuyama, Masamitsu Hidaka, Yoshitaka Fujimoto. Screenplay by Atsuhiro Tomioka, Takeshi Shudo, Hideki Sonoda, Junji Takegami.

In a seaside town celebrating a Summer's End festival, both Brock and James see a ghostly girl, and they vow to get to the truth behind her story. Back on the water, mating season for the Butterfree means that Ash may lose one of his Pokémon to love, but the interference of Team Rocket may have tough consequences. Then, in Saffron City, Ash encounters much danger with a mysterious innocent girl who is also an evil trainer.

This DVD contains episodes #19–21: "The Ghost of Maiden's Peak"; "Bye Bye Butterfree"; and "Abra and the Psychic Showdown."

SPECIAL FEATURES Music Video TECHNICAL FEATURES Fullscreen (1.33:1) • Languages: Eng. • Sound: Dolby Digital 2.0 • Keepcase • 1 Disc • Region 1 GENRE & RATING Adventure/Kids • Not Rated (Kids)

Pokémon: Primeape Problems [#8]

Pioneer/Viz, 1999, 75 mins., #PIKA-08DVD.

In the woods, Ash and company encounter a tower that's haunted by ghosts. Is one of them a Pokémon? Then, Ash returns to Saffron City to face Sabrina again, but her tricks are too much for them, and ghostly intervention may be their only hope. Later, encountering a Mankey in the woods, Ash gets his Pokémon hat stolen. But that's nothing compared to the trouble Team Rocket finds when a scorned Mankey becomes a Primeape!

This DVD contains episodes #22–24: "Tower of Terror"; "Haunter vs. Kadabra"; and "Primeape Goes Bananas."

SPECIAL FEATURES None TECHNICAL FEATURES Fullscreen (1.33:1) • Languages: Eng. • Sound: Dolby Digital 2.0 • Keepcase • 1 Disc • Region 1 GENRE & RATING Adventure/Kids • Not Rated (Kids)

Pokémon: Fashion Victims [#9]

Pioneer/Viz, 1999, 75 mins., #PIKA-09DVD.

In Celadon City, perfume is most important, and those that don't like it—like Ash—aren't welcome. Ash must dress in drag to try to get his next badge, but a deadly fire may send his plans up in smoke. In Hop Hop Hop Town, children are missing, and it has something to do with two sleep-inducing Pokémon named Drowzee and Hypno. Then, on Scissor Street, it's time for Pokémon makeovers.

This DVD contains episodes #25–27: "Pokémon Scent-Sation!"; "Hypno's Naptime"; and "Pokémon Fashion Flash."

SPECIAL FEATURES None TECHNICAL FEATURES Fullscreen (1.33:1) • Languages: Eng. • Sound: Dolby Digital 2.0 • Keepcase • 1 Disc • Region 1 GENRE & RATING Adventure/Kids • Not Rated (Kids)

Pokémon: Fighting Tournament [#10]

Pioneer/Viz, 1999, 75 mins., #PIKA-10DVD.

Lots of comic violence as Hitmonchan faces other Pokémon in the P-1 Grand Prix. Then, in Gringy City, Pikachu is sick, but power and water seem to be out at the Pokémon Center. What could Pokémon in the sewers have to do with it? And another environmentally friendly message is imparted when Ash and his friends encounter some Digletts in the forest who are trying to stop the building of a dam that threatens their ecosystem.

This DVD contains episodes #28–30: "The Punchy Pokémon"; "Sparks Fly for Magnemite"; and "Dig Those Diglett!"

SPECIAL FEATURES None TECHNICAL FEATURES Fullscreen (1.33:1) • Languages: Eng. • Sound: Dolby Digital 2.0 • Keepcase • 1 Disc • Region 1 GENRE & RATING Adventure/Kids • Not Rated (Kids)

Pokémon: The Great Race [#11]

Pioneer/Viz, 1999, 75 mins., #PIKA-11DVD.

In a ninja building, Ash has a ferocious battle to win the Soul badge, but the arrival of Team Rocket might blow all his plans. Thinking they've reached the Safari Zone, Ash and his friends are surprised to find they're on a Pokémon ranch instead, and they're pulled into competing in a Pokémon race. Then, once they've reached the Safari Zone, Ash's group encounters a young boy who's been raised by the Kangaskhan. Are the people who show up really his parents, or are they Pokémon poachers?

This DVD contains episodes #31–33: "The Ninja Poke-Showdown"; "The Flame Pokémon-athon!"; and "The Kangaskhan Kid." Note that another episode, "Legend of Dratini," should have been included after this sequence, but since it had realistic guns in it, it was not aired in America.

SPECIAL FEATURES Inserts: Mini Comic TECHNICAL FEATURES Fullscreen (1.33:1) • Languages: Eng. • Sound: Dolby Digital 2.0 • Keepcase • 1 Disc • Region 1 GENRE & RATING Adventure/Kids • Not Rated (Kids)

Pokémon: Pikachu Party [#12]

Pioneer/Viz, 1999, 75 mins., #PIKA-12DVD.

On their way across a very long bridge to deliver medicine to sick Pokémon, Ash and his friends encounter trouble in the form of a bike gang who were once friends with Team Rocket. In an old theater, a girl named Duplica uses her talent for pretending to be other people to stage entertainment, but her Pokémon, Ditto, can't change its face. Later, in the forest, Pikachu finds all of its fellow Pikachu. Now that it has a home, will it leave Ash?

This DVD contains episodes #34–36: "The Bridge

Bike Gang"; "Ditto's Mysterious Mansion"; and "Pikachu's Goodbye." Note that the episode "Electric Hero Porygon" should have been included before "Pikachu's Goodbye," but this is the infamous episode that gave 700 Japanese children seizures due to flickering images. Needless to say, it has not been rereleased.

SPECIAL FEATURES None TECHNICAL FEATURES Fullscreen (1.33:1) • Languages: Eng. • Sound: Dolby Digital 2.0 • Keepcase • 1 Disc • Region 1 GENRE & RATING Adventure/Kids • Not Rated (Kids)

Pokémon: Wake Up Snorlax! [#13]

Pioneer/Viz, 2000, 75 mins., #PIKA-13DVD.

A little boy is forced to abandon his Eevee by his brothers because he doesn't want to make it evolve. And Team Rocket comes close to capturing all the Pokémon! Then, a sleeping Snorlax and a bunch of thorns are blocking the water supply to a small town. If Ash and his friends can't wake up the Snorlax, crops will die. And in Dark City, two Pokémon gyms and their competitiors are engaging in very bad behavior, battling to see which of them will be the "official" gym.

This DVD contains episodes #37–39: "The Battling Eevee Brothers"; "Wake Up Snorlax!"; and "Showdown at Dark City."

SPECIAL FEATURES Inserts: Mini Comic TECHNICAL FEATURES Fullscreen (1.33:1) • Languages: Eng. • Sound: Dolby Digital 2.0 • Keepcase • 1 Disc • Region 1 GENRE & RATING Adventure/Kids • Not Rated (Kids)

Pokémon: Jigglypuff Pop [#14]

Pioneer/Viz, 2000, 75 mins., #PIKA-14DVD.

A failed carnival magician causes Pokémon hypnotism and unwittingly unleashes destruction, even as Charmander begins to evolve. Then, in a town that doesn't have a Pokémon Center, Ash and the group meet a girl whose Pokémon is too weak to evolve, and a smitten Meowth tries to help. And in Neon Town, everyone is cranky because they can't sleep. If Ash can make the sore-throated forest creature Jigglypuff sing, the town might be able to go to sleep.

This DVD contains episodes #40–42: "The March of the Exeggutor Squad"; "The Problem with Paras"; and "The Song of Jigglypuff." Note that Jigglypuff is also a character in some Super Smash Bros. games.

SPECIAL FEATURES Inserts: Mini Comic TECHNICAL FEATURES Fullscreen (1.33:1) • Languages: Eng. • Sound: Dolby Digital

2.0 • Keepcase • 1 Disc • Region 1 GENRE & RATING Adventure/Kids • Not Rated (Kids)

Pokémon: Charizard!! [#15]

Pioneer/Viz, 2000, 75 mins., #PIKA-15DVD.

In Grandpa Canyon, the group is sent to the Land of the Lost and meets ancient Pokémon including the Aerodactyl. But is it real or a dream? Then, Pikachu gets sick eating an apple whole, and other Pokémon are in an accident, but medical help may be difficult when Team Rocket interferes with the doctor. And what secrets of James's past will be revealed when a strange road sign leads to an inheritance and a woman named Jessiebell?

This DVD contains episodes #43–45: "Attack of the Prehistoric Pokémon"; "A Chansey Operation"; and "Holy Matrimony."

SPECIAL FEATURES Inserts: Mini Comic TECHNICAL FEATURES Fullscreen (1.33:1) • Languages: Eng. • Sound: Dolby Digital 2.0 • Keepcase • 1 Disc • Region 1 GENRE & RATING Adventure/Kids • Not Rated (Kids)

Pokémon: Totally Togepi [#16]

Pioneer/Viz, 2000, 75 mins., #PIKA-16DVD.

After chasing a Farfetch'd in the woods, Misty battles a young Pokémon thief. Then, Ash gets a Pokémon upgrade from Professor Oak, and the egg gained in the Aerodactyl episode hatches, revealing a new life form that is very attached to Misty. And when it's Bulbasaur's time to evolve, it decides it doesn't want to . . . but circumstances—and another Bulbasaur—may force the evolution.

This DVD contains episodes #46–48: "So Near Yet So Farfetch'd"; "Who Gets to Keep Togepi?" and "Bulbasaur's Mysterious Garden."

SPECIAL FEATURES Inserts: Mini Comic TECHNICAL FEATURES Fullscreen (1.33:1) • Languages: Eng. • Sound: Dolby Digital 2.0 • Keepcase • 1 Disc • Region 1 GENRE & RATING Adventure/Kids • Not Rated (Kids)

Pokémon: Picture Perfect [#17]

Pioneer/Viz, 2000, 90 mins., #PIKA-17DVD.

In the forest, Ash's team encounters a running man who is being chased by a Growlithe, and they think he's a thief. But it's really a police officer training the Growlithe in the K-9 police squad! Then, a photographer named Snap may secretly be working for Team Rocket when he takes pictures of Pikachu . . . or is he really working against them? And later, Ash and Team Rocket enroll in a school from which they'll be able to enter the Pokémon League without getting all the badges. But the tests are harder than they realize. Finally, a fake breeding center for Pokémon lures Ash and his group into a confrontation with new Team Rocket members Butch and Cassidy.

This extra-length DVD contains the four episodes #49–52: "The Case of the K-9 Caper!"; "Pokémon Paparazzi"; "The Ultimate Test"; and "The Breeding Center Secret." Note that these were the last episodes aired of *Pokémon*'s first season in the U.S.

SPECIAL FEATURES Inserts: Mini Comic TECHNICAL FEATURES Fullscreen (1.33:1) • Languages: Eng. • Sound: Dolby Digital 2.0 • Keepcase • 1 Disc • Region 1 GENRE & RATING Adventure/Kids • Not Rated (Kids)

Pokémon: Water Blast! [#18]

Pioneer/Viz, 2000, 70 mins., #PIKA-18DVD.

Sailing toward Cinnibar Island, Ash and friends meet Gary, and learn that the Pokémon gym has been dismantled due to an overwhelming tourist trade! Will Pikachu get fried by Magmar's Fire Blast attack? The battle is joined by Team Rocket, but the ensuing trouble causes a volcanic explosion! Later, the group takes a trip to Squirtle Island to help a Wartortle, but the affair ends in a messy encounter with Jigglypuff!

This DVD contains episodes #55–57: "Riddle Me This"; "Volcanic Panic"; and "Beach Blank-Out Blastoise."

SPECIAL FEATURES Inserts: Flicker Card TECHNICAL FEATURES Fullscreen (1.33:1) • Subtitles/CC: Eng. • Languages: Eng. • Sound: Dolby Digital Surround 2.0 • Keepcase • 1 Disc • Region 1 GENRE & RATING Adventure/Kids • Not Rated (Kids)

Pokémon: Our Hero Meowth [#19]

Pioneer/Viz, 2000, 70 mins., #PIKA-19DVD.

Princess Day at the mall means that Misty and Jessie are gonna have a throw-down Poké-battle to win fabulous prizes. Then, during a school visit, Ash and company meet a little boy who was once saved by a wild Meowth. Will Team Rocket do the right thing? Later, Misty takes Horsea back to the Cerulean City gym, where she's talked into performing in her sisters' water ballet!

This DVD contains episodes #53, 54, 58: "Princess vs. Princess"; "The Purr-fect Hero"; and "The Misty Mermaid."

SPECIAL FEATURES Inserts: Flicker Card TECHNICAL FEATURES Fullscreen (1.33:1) • Subtitles/CC: Eng. • Languages: Eng. • Sound: Dolby Digital Surround 2.0 • Keepcase • 1 Disc • Region 1 GENRE & RATING Adventure/Kids • Not Rated (Kids)

Pokémon: The Final Badge [#20]

Pioneer/Viz, 2000, 70 mins., #PIKA-20DVD.

A space ship crashes in the woods, releasing some Clefairy, who kidnap Pikachu to power their new ship! In Viridian City, it's a battle to the finish between Gary, Ash, Giovanni, and Team Rocket. Plus, a new and very rare Pokémon is introduced, named Mewtwo (this episode preceeds *Pokémon: The First Movie*). Then, circus attraction Mr. Mime can create invisible walls, but is he Ash's friend or foe?

This DVD contains episodes #59–61: "Clefairy Tales"; "The Battle of the Badge"; and "It's Mr. Mime Time."

SPECIAL FEATURES Inserts: Flicker Card TECHNICAL FEATURES Fullscreen (1.33:1) • Subtitles/CC: Eng. • Languages: Eng. • Sound: Dolby Digital Surround 2.0 • Keepcase • 1 Disc • Region 1 GENRE & RATING Adventure/Kids • Not Rated (Kids)

Pokémon: The Po-Ké Corral! [#21]

Pioneer/Viz, 2000, 70 mins., #PIKA-21DVD.

Jesse wants to capture a Jynx who masqueraded as Santa Claus and took her favorite doll when she was younger. But will Team Rocket capture the real Santa instead? Then, Ash's group is trapped in the snow, but Team Rocket hasn't fared any better. Will they all become Poké-popsicles? And Ash and his teammates go back to Professor Oak's lab, where Ash learns that he'll have to work harder to make the Pokémon League tournament. But when the pesky Tauros run rampant, Ash may lose some momentum.

This DVD contains Special #1–2 and episode #62: "Holiday Hi-Jynx"; "Snow Way Out"; and "Showdown at the Po-Ké Corral." The specials take place before #47, though original plans had them set in the mid-30s.

SPECIAL FEATURES Inserts: Flicker Card TECHNICAL FEATURES Fullscreen (1.33:1) • Subtitles/CC: Eng. • Languages: Eng. • Sound: Dolby Digital Surround 2.0 • Keepcase • 1 Disc • Region 1 GENRE & RATING Adventure/Kids • Not Rated (Kids)

Pokémon: Hang Ten, Pikachu [#22]

Pioneer/Viz, 2000, 70 mins., #PIKA-22DVD.

Everyone goes to Seafoam Islands for a little vacation time, with Misty and Brock surfing and Ash trying to find out why Slowpoke evolves into a Slowbro. Then, a huge wave called Humunga Dunga is coming in and Ash and another Pikachu owner meet. But when Team Rocket captures both Pikachus, can Ash and Victor surf to the rescue? Back home working in a garden, Ash discovers a plant that makes Pokémon paralyzed, and Brock falls for the pretty greenhouse owner, Florinda.

This DVD contains episodes #63–65: "The Evolution Solution"; "The Pi-Kihuna"; and "Make Room for Gloom."

SPECIAL FEATURES Inserts: Flicker Card TECHNICAL FEATURES Fullscreen (1.33:1) • Subtitles/CC: Eng. • Languages: Eng. • Sound: Dolby Digital Surround 2.0 • Keepcase • 1 Disc • Region 1 GENRE & RATING Adventure/Kids • Not Rated (Kids)

Pokémon: Show Time! [#23]

Pioneer/Viz, 2000, 70 mins., #PIKA-23DVD.

Famous movie director Spielbug is making a film called "Pokémon in Love," and he needs someone to co-star with Wigglytuff, a tough Pokémon. Could Psyduck have a future in film? When Ash and friends go to Hollywood for the premiere of the movie, Meowth remembers his time growing up there, when things were tough. And Ash and Brock try to find super Pokémon trainer Master Bruno of the Elite Four, but they learn that not everyone they look up to deserves their respect.

This DVD contains episodes #66–68: "Lights, Camera, Quack-tion"; "Go West, Young Meowth"; and "To Master the Onixpected."

SPECIAL FEATURES Inserts: Flicker Card TECHNICAL FEATURES Fullscreen (1.33:1) • Subtitles/CC: Eng. • Languages: Eng. • Sound: Dolby Digital Surround 2.0 • Keepcase • 1 Disc • Region 1 GENRE & RATING Adventure/Kids • Not Rated (Kids)

Pokémon: Into the Arena [#24]

Pioneer/Viz, 2000, 70 mins., #PIKA-24DVD.

When they dig up some ancient artifacts, Ash and his friends also unleash a giant Gengar. How will Jigglypuff save the day? Then, Ash hasn't completed his training, but he plans to go to the Pokémon League and do his best. Now if only he could recover his badges, stolen by Team Rocket! Later, Ash is one of the people who gets to bring the torch into the Pokémon League tournament stadium, but Team Rocket intrudes again.

This DVD contains episodes #69–71: "The Ancient Puzzle of Pokemopolis"; "Bad to the Bone"; and "All Fired Up!"

SPECIAL FEATURES Inserts: Flicker Card TECHNICAL FEATURES Fullscreen (1.33:1) • Subtitles/CC: Eng. • Languages: Eng. • Sound: Dolby Digital Surround 2.0 • Keepcase • 1 Disc • Region 1 GENRE & RATING Adventure/Kids • Not Rated (Kids)

Pokémon: Round One! [#25]

Pioneer/Viz, 2001, 70 mins., #PIKA-25DVD.

Entered into the Pokémon League competition, Ash is sent into the first of four arenas: the water arena. Will Krabby, a new Pokémon he just acquired, help him win? In the rock arena, Ash uses a Squirtle, then gets his Pokémon stolen by Team Rocket, then shivers his way into the ice arena using Pikachu. Gary gets bad news in the fourth round, and Ash is very nervous. While Team Rocket engage in some shifty salesmanship in the stadium, Ash and his Pokémon face an undefeated Bellsprout.

This DVD contains episodes #72–74: "Round One—Begin!"; "Fire and Ice"; and "The Fourth Round Rumble."

SPECIAL FEATURES Inserts: Flicker Card TECHNICAL FEATURES Fullscreen (1.33:1) • Subtitles/CC: Eng. • Languages: Eng. • Sound: Dolby Digital Surround 2.0 • Keepcase • 1 Disc • Region 1 GENRE & RATING Adventure/Kids • Not Rated (Kids)

Pokémon: Friends and Rivals [#26]

Pioneer/Viz, 2001, 70 mins., #PIKA-26DVD.

Trapped in an elevator, Ash and his Pokémon become friends with Richie, a boy who later helps stop Team Rocket from getting away with stolen Pokémon. Too bad that Richie is Ash's opponent in the sweet-sixteen round in the Indigo Leagues! Then Team Rocket kidnaps Ash in an attempt to stop him from getting to the competition. And then the unthinkable happens—Ash loses. Will Richie lose his sixth battle as well? And will their friendship survive?

This DVD contains episodes #75–77: "A Friend in Deed"; "Friend and Foe Alike"; and "Friends to the End." For some reason, after this disc Pioneer and Viz decided to relaunch the *Pokémon* DVD line with *The Johto Journeys* stories, skipping over episodes #78–116.

SPECIAL FEATURES Inserts: Flicker Card TECHNICAL FEATURES Fullscreen (1.33:1) • Subtitles/CC: Eng. • Languages: Eng. • Sound: Dolby Digital Surround 2.0 • Keepcase • 1 Disc • Region 1 GENRE & RATING Adventure/Kids • Not Rated (Kids)

Pokémon: Adventures on the Orange Islands! [#27]

Pioneer/Viz, 2002, 250 mins., #11598. Directed by Masamitsu Hidaka.

NOTE: This DVD arrived too late for a full review. The following text is promotional copy provided by the releasing company:

"Ash and his friend depart for the Orange Islands. While they may leave some old friends behind and meet some new friends, Ash and Pikachu continue their wild adventures on Ash's quest to become the best Pokémon Master!"

This disc contains a whopping twelve episodes, #78 and #81–91.

SPECIAL FEATURES Other Title Trailers TECHNICAL FEATURES Fullscreen (1.33:1) • Subtitles/CC: Eng. • Languages: Eng. dub • Sound: Dolby Digital • Keepcase • 1 Disc • Region 1 GENRE & RATING Adventure/Kids • Not Rated (Kids)

Pokémon—The Johto Journeys: A Brand New World [JJ#1]

Pioneer/Viz, 2001, 70 mins.,
#11525/PIKA-39DVD.

On their way to sign up for the Johto League, Ash, Misty and Brock discover a Totodile has been kidnapped, and Team Rocket may be behind the dastardly deed. Later, Ash defeats a young trainer, but Team Rocket convinces the baseball fan that Ash threw him a foul Pokéball. Finally, Heracrosses are destroying the forests, and Ash and friends must stop them before an ecological disaster.

This DVD contains episodes #117–19: "Don't Touch That 'Dile"; "The Double Trouble Header"; and "A Sappy Ending." This disc contains the first trio of episodes from *Pokémon*'s third season, airing in the U.S. beginning October 2000.

SPECIAL FEATURES Inserts: Flicker Card TECHNICAL FEATURES Fullscreen (1.33:1) • Subtitles/CC: Eng. • Languages: Eng. • Sound: Dolby Digital Surround 2.0 • Keepcase • 1 Disc • Region 1 GENRE & RATING Adventure/Kids • Not Rated (Kids)

Pokémon—The Johto Journeys: Midnight Guardian [JJ#2]

Pioneer/Viz, 2001, 70 mins.,
#11526/PIKA-40DVD.

In one small valley, the tusked Donphan are used to sniff out precious amberite stones, but Team Rocket naturally wants to use them to steal the gems. Later, Ash enters a dense forest with a half-trained Hoothoot guide, and the group gets lost among the scary illusions there. And once they exit the forest, the friends decide to relax at the city of Flowender. It's almost time for the Flowender Festival, where live stage acts and the Pokémon Exhibition will take place. What talents will the Pokémon exhibit?

This DVD contains episodes #120–22: "Roll On, Pokémon!"; "Illusion Confusion"; and "Flower Power."

SPECIAL FEATURES Inserts: Flicker Card TECHNICAL FEATURES Fullscreen (1.33:1) • Subtitles/CC: Eng. • Languages: Eng. • Sound: Dolby Digital Surround 2.0 • Keepcase • 1 Disc • Region 1 GENRE & RATING Adventure/Kids • Not Rated (Kids)

Pokémon—The Johto Journeys: Mission Spinarak [JJ#3]

Pioneer/Viz, 2001, 70 mins.,
#11541/PIKA-41DVD.

Officer Jenny is determined to stop the Black Arachnid and the thieves that are plaguing the city. Using her spidery Spinarak, Jenny intends to web up the evil forces. Later, Ash's group enters Palm Hills, a neighborhood of huge mansions. They soon meet a female Snubbull who is unhappy living in luxury . . . and sad about her upcoming wedding to an ugly Snubbull. And when Brock helps an injured Stantler fawn, you can be sure that Team Rocket has some dastardly plans.

This DVD contains episodes #123-25: "Spinarak Attack"; "Snubbull Snobbery"; and "The Little Big Horn."

SPECIAL FEATURES Inserts: Flicker Card TECHNICAL FEATURES Fullscreen (1.33:1) • Subtitles/CC: Eng. • Languages: Eng. • Sound: Dolby Digital Surround 2.0 • Keepcase • 1 Disc • Region 1 GENRE & RATING Adventure/Kids • Not Rated (Kids)

Pokémon—The Johto Journeys: Snow Rescue [JJ#4]

Pioneer/Viz, 2001, 70 mins.,
#11542/PIKA-42DVD.

When he meets a wild Chikorita, Ash isn't sure whether he needs to save it from Team Rocket or itself. Then, Professor Oak wants a GS Ball delivered, but it's stolen by a Quagsire! Later, Pokémon trainer Ariel and her group of Ledyba rescue Ash and his group from Team Rocket, but Jessie and James manage to steal Ariel's whistle, which she uses to control the Ledybas.

This DVD contains episodes #126-28: "The Chikorita Rescue"; "Once in a Blue Moon"; and "The Whistle Stop."

SPECIAL FEATURES Inserts: Flicker Card TECHNICAL FEATURES Fullscreen (1.33:1) • Subtitles/CC: Eng. • Languages: Eng. • Sound: Dolby Digital Surround 2.0 • Keepcase • 1 Disc • Region 1 GENRE & RATING Adventure/Kids • Not Rated (Kids)

Pokémon—The Johto Journeys: Flying Ace [JJ#5]

Pioneer/Viz, 2001, 70 mins., #11557/PIKA-43DVD.

After Blissey gives Team Rocket all the food in a Pokémon Center, the two thieves must confront their consciences. Then, Ash and his group are in Violet City, where they meet a teacher from the Pokémon Academy and help out with some classes. But what happens when Pikachu falls prey to a young thief? Plus, Team Rocket masquerades as surveyors from the Pokémon Bureau, and they confiscate Pikachu. Can Falkner, the Violet City gym leader and flying Pokémon master, help rescue Pikachu?

This DVD contains episodes #129–31: "Ignorance is Blissey"; "A Bout with Sprout"; and "Fighting Flyer with Fire"

SPECIAL FEATURES Inserts: Flicker Card TECHNICAL FEATURES Fullscreen (1.33:1) • Subtitles/CC: Eng. • Languages: Eng. • Sound: Dolby Digital Surround 2.0 • Keepcase • 1 Disc • Region 1 GENRE & RATING Adventure/Kids • Not Rated (Kids)

Pokémon—The Johto Journeys: Fire Power [JJ#6]

Pioneer/Viz, 2001, 70 mins., #11558/PIKA-44DVD.

Misty's Pokémon is a crybaby Marill, and its bawling is making everyone batty! Then, Team Rocket develops a new superweapon called the Arbotank. Too bad that Togepi and a Sentret take it for a joyride. And Ash takes Charizard to the Charicific Valley to meet other dragons, but they get a chilly reception when Charizard is deemed too weak by the others.

This DVD contains episodes #133–35: "For Crying Out Loud"; "Tanks a Lot!"; and "Charizard's Burning Ambitions."

SPECIAL FEATURES Inserts: Flicker Card TECHNICAL FEATURES Fullscreen (1.33:1) • Subtitles/CC: Eng. • Languages: Eng. • Sound: Dolby Digital Surround 2.0 • Keepcase • 1 Disc • Region 1 GENRE & RATING Adventure/Kids • Not Rated (Kids)

Pokémon—The Johto Journeys: Team Green! [JJ#7]

Pioneer/Viz, 2001, 70 mins., #11569/PIKA-45DVD.

The annual Sunflora contest is coming up, but Ash's new friend can't get her Sunflora to compete. Then, Ash has some problems with Chikorita and takes it to Nurse Joy, an expert on Pokémon psychology. Could Chikorita be jealous of Pikachu? And how does Team Rocket's robot made out of recycled tires figure into the story? Finally, the group encounters the featherweight Pokémon called a Hoppip, who helps a girl named Mariah make weather predictions. Will they help an Oddish learn to float and fly like the Hoppips?

This DVD contains episodes #136, 132, 137: "Grin to Win!"; "Chikorita's Big Upset"; and "Foul Weather Friends."

SPECIAL FEATURES Inserts: Flicker Card TECHNICAL FEATURES Fullscreen (1.33:1) • Subtitles/CC: Eng. • Languages: Eng. • Sound: Dolby Digital Surround 2.0 • Keepcase • 1 Disc • Region 1 GENRE & RATING Adventure/Kids • Not Rated (Kids)

Pokémon—The Johto Journeys: Crimson Warrior [JJ#8]

Pioneer/Viz, 2001, 70 mins., #11570/PIKA-48DVD.

In a forest outside of Azalea Town, Ash and his friends meet Gligarman, a pudgy purple superhero who commands a Gligar to stop Team Rocket's evil plans. Then, Little Mary has lost her Mareep and doesn't know where to find them. Ash and friends do: Team Rocket has captured Mary's Mareep flock! Plus, a Pokémon dojo named Shingo deems Ash unworthy of battle based on his computer's extensive Pokémon database.

This DVD contains episodes #138–40: "The Superhero Secret"; "Mild 'n Wooly"; and "Wired for Battle!"

SPECIAL FEATURES Inserts: Flicker Card TECHNICAL FEATURES Fullscreen (1.33:1) • Subtitles/CC: Eng. • Languages: Eng. • Sound: Dolby Digital Surround 2.0 • Keepcase • 1 Disc • Region 1 GENRE & RATING Adventure/Kids • Not Rated (Kids)

Pokémon—The Johto Journeys: Azalea Adventures [JJ#9]

Pioneer/Viz, 2001, 70 mins., #11596/PIKA-47DVD.

In the deep forest, Ash and friends meet a sore loser boy who warns them not to try to catch a Cyndaquil. But they'll soon be too busy escaping from a giant Meowth robot, powered by Team Rocket! Then, in Azalea Town, a drought has made everyone thirsty, but if Ash and his friends can help the Slowpokes in the Slowpoke Well, water may run freely again. Plus, our heroes soon learn that specialized Pokéballs can be made using colored apricorns, but picking them in the forest is easier said than done. Ball maker Kurt asks to keep the mysterious GS ball to study it, and Ash lets him.

This DVD contains episodes #141–43: "Good 'Quil Hunting"; "A Shadow of a Drought"; and "Going Apricorn!"

SPECIAL FEATURES Inserts: Glow-in-the-Dark Sticker TECHNICAL FEATURES Fullscreen (1.33:1) • Subtitles/CC: Eng. • Languages: Eng. • Sound: Dolby Digital Surround 2.0 • Keepcase • 1 Disc • Region 1 GENRE & RATING Adventure/Kids • Not Rated (Kids)

Pokémon—The Johto Journeys: Buggy Boogie [JJ#10]

Pioneer/Viz, 2001, 70 mins., #11597/PIKA-48DVD.

On to the Azalea Town Gym to earn his next badge, Ash discovers the gym is set up like a forest! But he must battle Bugzy, the Gym leader, and his insectoid Pokémon. Can Cyndaquil muster up the firepower needed to win? And what about those new Pokéballs that Kurt made for them? Later, Ash helps a young trainer in need of some more training; he's run off his own Farfetch'd, and Team Rocket is on the path to capture it! Plus, at the Pokémon Swap Meet in Palmpona, Ash and friends meet a young Pokémon trainer with a Wobbuffet for which nobody wants to trade, and Jessie causes something unexpected to happen.

This DVD contains episodes #144–46: "Gettin' the Bugs Out"; "A Farfetch'd Tale"; and "Tricks of the Trade."

SPECIAL FEATURES Inserts: Glow-in-the-Dark Sticker TECHNICAL FEATURES Fullscreen (1.33:1) • Subtitles/CC: Eng. • Languages: Eng. • Sound: Dolby Digital Surround 2.0 • Keepcase • 1 Disc • Region 1 GENRE & RATING Adventure/Kids • Not Rated (Kids)

Pokémon—The Johto Journeys: The Squirtle Squad [JJ#11]

Pioneer/Viz, 2002, 70 mins., #11646/PIKA-49DVD.

The Fire and Rescue Grand Prix is coming, and it's a firefighting competition for water-based Pokémon. Soon, Squirtle has to pep up the Squirtle Squad as they face Team Wartortle, a Golduck team, and Team Rocket's flamethrowing giant robot! Then, Ash and the group help out at a Wooper preschool. Plus, taking the Onix Tunnel through a mountain is supposed to shorten their route to Goldenrod City, but it leads to a bizarre confrontation between Ash's group, Team Rocket, the Onix, a Snubbull, Meowth, and Jigglypuff.

This DVD contains episodes #150, 147, 148: "The Fire-ing Squad"; "No Big Woop!"; and "Tunnel Vision."

SPECIAL FEATURES Inserts: Glow-in-the-Dark Sticker TECHNICAL FEATURES Fullscreen (1.33:1) • Subtitles/CC: Eng. • Languages: Eng. • Sound: Dolby Digital Surround 2.0 • Keepcase • 1 Disc • Region 1 GENRE & RATING Adventure/Kids • Not Rated (Kids)

Pokémon—The Johto Journeys: Midnight Heroes [JJ#12]

Pioneer/Viz, 2002, 70 mins., #11647/PIKA-50DVD.

Food is being stolen by Pokémon, and Ash sets out to find out why. It all leads to the Houndour, and a battle between the Golem and the Houndour pack leader. Plus, Ash and Misty both try to capture a Totodile, leading them to battle it out to see who will be the dancing Pokémon's new master. And a beautiful trainer named Mickey has a very tough Skarmory, making her virtually undefeatable. Can Ash get Cyndaquil fired up to win?

This DVD contains episodes #149, 152, 153: "Hour of the Houndour"; "The Totodile Duel"; and "Hot Matches!"

SPECIAL FEATURES Inserts: Glow-in-the-Dark Sticker TECHNICAL FEATURES Fullscreen (1.33:1) • Subtitles/CC: Eng. • Languages: Eng. • Sound: Dolby Digital Surround 2.0 • Keepcase • 1 Disc • Region 1 GENRE & RATING Adventure/Kids • Not Rated (Kids)

Pokémon—The Johto Journeys: Ursaring Rampage [JJ#13]

Pioneer/Viz, 2002, 70 mins., #11678/PIKA-51DVD.

Ash's dancing Totodile falls in love with a singing Azumarill, but she doesn't return his affection. Can unlucky-in-love Brock help? The creature is still unsuccessful in having its feelings requited when Team Rocket kidnaps the Pokémon before Totodile's eyes. Next, Ash wants to capture a Noctowl—a rare Pokémon indeed—but the creature's hypnotic abilities turn everything into an illusion for the young Trainer. Finally, Team Rocket and Ash's team are forced to work together when they're all trapped in the woods by a herd of angry Ursaring!

This DVD contains episodes #154, 151, 156: "Love, Totodile Style"; "Fowl Play"; and "Forest Grumps."

SPECIAL FEATURES Inserts: Glow-in-the-Dark Sticker TECHNICAL FEATURES Fullscreen (1.33:1) • Subtitles/CC: Eng. • Languages: Eng. • Sound: Dolby Digital Surround 2.0 • Keepcase • 1 Disc • Region 1 GENRE & RATING Adventure/Kids • Not Rated (Kids)

Pokemon—Johto League Champions: Collector's Edition [JJ#14]

Pioneer/Viz, 2002, 150 mins., #10489. Directed by Masamitsu Hidaka. Written by Takeshi Shudo, Junji Takegami, Yukiyoshi Ohashi, Hideki Sonoda, Atsuhiro Tomioka, Shinzo Fujita, Shoji Yonemura.

NOTE: This DVD arrived too late for a full review. The following text is promotional copy provided by the releasing company:

"Our heroes continue their journey to the Johto League Championship! Ash and his beloved Pokémons encounter tough and skillful opponents as well as brand new Pokémons while they travel from Goldenrod City to Ecruteak City."

This disc contains episodes #158–64 from the fourth TV season.

SPECIAL FEATURES Other Title Trailers TECHNICAL FEATURES Fullscreen (1.33:1) • Subtitles/CC: Eng. • Languages: Eng. dub • Sound: Dolby Digital • Keepcase • 1 Disc • Region 1 GENRE & RATING Adventure/Kids • Not Rated (Kids)

Pokémon: Mewtwo Returns

Warner, 2001, 63 mins., #22142. Directed by Masamitsu Hidaka. Written by Takeshi Shudo.

Continuing to explore the Johto region, Ash and his friends are dismayed when Team Rocket once again captures Pikachu. As they search for him, they find a hidden area where Mewtwo and other bio-engineered superclone Pokémon have made a refuge. But the evil Giovanni wants to recapture Mewtwo, and he'll sacrifice all the other superclones to get his way!

A direct-to-video sequel to *Pokémon: The First Movie*, this 1999 project is darker in tone than its TV counterparts. It features some strong action sequences, and the angry Mewtwo can be a bit intimidating for younger viewers. The brevity actually helps the film, as most of the generally padded fight scenes are shorter.

The DVD contains the textless opening of the *Johto League Champions* TV series, as well as a widescreen animated short that tells the creepy "The Uncut Story of Mewtwo's Origin."

SPECIAL FEATURES Clean Credits • Trailer • Other Title Trailers TECHNICAL FEATURES Fullscreen (1.33:1) • Subtitles/CC: Eng., Fren., Span. • Languages: Eng. dub, Fren. dub, Span. dub • Sound: Dolby Digital Surround 2.0 • Snapcase • 1 Disc • Region 1 GENRE & RATING Adventure/Kids • Not Rated (Kids)

Pokémon: The First Movie—[#1]

Warner, 2001, 96 mins.

This DVD was not available for review.

Pokémon: The Movie 2000 [#2]

Warner, 2001, 102 mins., #18620. Directed by Kunihiko Yuyama. Written by Takeshi Shudo.

A Pokémon collector causes nature to go awry when he captures three very rare and legendary Pokémon: Articuno. Zapdos. and Moltres, the Gods of Ice, Lightning, and Fire! Ash and his friends join with Team Rocket to return three glass balls to their proper place, even as Earth's weather turns violent and deadly. Can Ash save the world?

Subtitled "The Power of One," this 1999 feature film was Japan's third highest grossing anime feature! The film is heavy on the environmental messages, but is short on traditional TV-style Pokémon fighting. Fans have complained that the Japanese musical score was replaced, partially by youthful pop groups whose spotlight probably lasted a shorter time than the film itself.

The film is preceded on DVD (as it was in theaters) by the short film "Pikachu's Rescue Adventure." Unfortunately, it's a twenty-minute sequence with almost no human vocals, meaning the viewer will go catatonic listening solely to the "cute" warbling and sounds of the various Pokémon in the story.

SPECIAL FEATURES Music Videos • Other Title Trailers TECHNICAL FEATURES Fullscreen (1.33:1 pan-and-scan) • Subtitles/CC: Eng., Fren. • Languages: Eng. dub, Fren. dub • Sound: Dolby Digital Surround 5.1 • Snapcase • 1 Disc • Region 1 GENRE & RATING Adventure/Kids • Rated G

Pokémon 3—The Movie [#3]

Warner, 2001, 91 mins., #21251. Directed by Kunihiko Yuyama. Written by Takeshi Shudo, Hideki Sonoda.

Eight-year-old Molly's father was investigating the mysterious Unown, a group of twenty-six Pokémon whose shapes correspond to the English alphabet. But after he disappeared, the Unown take Molly under their protection, with one of them—a lionlike creature named Entai—acting as her surrogate father. Meanwhile, the Unown create a crystal shell around Molly's towering home. Molly really wants a mother, but when Entai kidnaps Ash Ketchum's mother, the Pokémon group comes to her rescue. Can Ash and his friends—including Team Rocket—defeat the unstoppable Unown, and maybe even rescue Molly's father?

Subtitled "Spell of the Unknown," this 2000 feature was released in Japan subtitled as "Emperor of the Crystal Tower." While the lead characters are all cel-animated, much of the crystal settings and other work are CGI, and the effect doesn't always work well. Still, the story is probably one of Pokémon's most interesting and effective ever. Unfortunately, almost ten minutes have been cut from the original Japanese version, and the picture was cropped down from 1.85:1 widescreen to 1.33:1.

The DVD contains a large array of extras, including a full-feature commentary, as well as the Johto Pokerap, the Japanese trailer for the fourth *Pokémon* film, and more. Also included is the short "Pikachu and Pichu," with the popular yellow characters spotlit in a silly tale in which they're lost in the big city. Fans will enjoy the hordes of Pokémon, though parents may groan at the obvious marketing ploy.

SPECIAL FEATURES "Making of" Featurette • Commentary Track by American Director and Producer • Production Notes • Trailers • Promotional Footage • Music Video • Inserts: Card, Decoder Flicker Coin TECHNICAL FEATURES Fullscreen (1.33:1 pan-and-scan) • Subtitles/CC: Eng., Fren. • Languages: Eng. dub, Fren. dub • Sound: Dolby Digital Surround 5.1 • Snapcase • 1 Disc • Region 1 GENRE & RATING Adventure/Kids • Rated G

Popeye

Digital Disc Entertainment, 45 mins., #519.

This DVD was not available for review. The company is out of business.

Popeye: 18 Fun-Filled Cartoons!!

Image, 2000, 120 mins., #ID5848RHDVD. Based on the comic strip *Thimble Theatre* by Elzie Segar.

Yet another group of cool *Popeye* cartoons showcasing the spinach-eating Popeye the Sailor Man, skinny girlfriend Olive Oyl, hamburger-loving best friend Wimpy J. Wellington, baby Swee' Pea, mortal enemy Bluto, and nephews Peepeye, Pupeye, and Pipeye.

This collection of eighteen shorts include: "The Spinach Bowl"; "Pedal Powered Popeye"; "Olive's Shining Hour"; "The Loneliness of the Long Distance Popeye"; "Popeye's Self Defense"; "The Umpire Strikes Back"; "The Decathlon Dilemma"; "Take Me Out to the Brawl Game"; "Olive Goes Dallas"; "The Great Speckled Whale"; "Shark Treatment"; "Popeye the Sleepwalker"; "A Goon Gone Gooney"; "Popeye Goes Sailing"; "Pappy Falls in Love"; "Ships that Pass in the Fright"; "Popeye Snags the Seahag"; and "The Game."

Unfortunately, these aren't the vintage *Popeye* cartoons from your grandparents' childhood; these are from Hanna-Barbera's *The All-New Popeye Hour,* which ran on CBS from 1978 to 1981. As such, they're a bit toothless, since violence then was meant to be toned down. But the comedy quotient was upped, and the color animation style is arguably many notches higher then its predecessor. The transfer quality is also good. Just be warned that these are not the vintage *Popeye*s. See *70 Years of Popeye* for the older episodes.

SPECIAL FEATURES None TECHNICAL FEATURES Fullscreen (1.33:1) • Languages: Eng. • Sound: Dolby Digital 1.0 • Snapcase • 1 Disc • Region 1 GENRE & RATING Comedy • Not Rated (All Ages)

Powerpuff Girls, The: Powerpuff Bluff [#1]

Warner, 2001, 140 mins., #H1684. Directed by Craig McCracken, Genndy Tartakovsky, John McIntyre. Written by Dave Smith, John McIntyre, Chris Savino, Don Shank, Cindy Morrow, Rob Renzetti, Cindy Banks, Mike Stern, Clayton Morrow, Genndy Tartakovsky.

When Professor Utonium mixes up a special concoction in his laboratory, he creates three pint-sized girl superheroes: Bubbles, Blossom, and Buttercup. But life in Townsville is no picnic for the tiny tots, as super villains such as turban-wearing monkey Mojo Jojo, purple-furred Fuzzy Lumpkin, spoiled Princess, and others attempt to wreak evil deeds on the populace. Each day, the girls must save the world before bedtime!

The Powerpuff Girls debuted in 1998 on the Cartoon Network, quickly becoming a sensation not just among kids, but also among older audiences who enjoyed watching the uber-cute girls kick butt (and who got some of the jokes that went above youngsters' heads). The series was created by Craig McCracken, based on an early short film he did called "The Whoopass Girls." One two-part episode was quickly nominated for an Emmy Award, and *Powerpuff* licensing became a smash hit. The cool primary-colored visuals, chirpy fun dialogue, and action should keep *The Powerpuff Girls* fighting crime for some time to come.

This disc contains ten episodes. In "Cat Man Do" (#10a), the girls rescue a cat from a bad guy's lair, but he turns out to be a kitty with hypnotic mind control powers (and the voice of Mark Hamill)! Then in "Uh-Oh Dynamo" (#13), the girls battle a giant Fish Balloon with the help of a giant robot, but the toll on Tokyo Townsville is high. In "Mr. Mojo's Rising" (#7b), the professor is kidnapped by a monkey with an oversized brain who is attempting to steal the Powerpuff Girls' powers. Three criminals impersonate the Girls in "Powerpuff Bluff" (#1b), ruining the reputations of Townsville's heroes. In "Bubblevicious" (#9a), an Emmy-nominated episode, Bubbles decides to go hardcore like her sisters instead of being the cute one.

In "Monkey See, Doggie Do" (#2a), Mojo Jojo is back, and he's using the Anubis jewels to turn citizens into dogs! When the Professor starts dating again in "Mommy Fearest" (#2b), what is Ima Goodlady's secret? In "Telephonies" (#6a), the Gang Green Gang is making crank calls, and the Powerpuff Girls don't appreciate the pranks! An evil mime turns Townsville black and white in "Mime for a Change" (#11b). Finally, the second part of the Emmy-nominated episode, "Bare Facts" (#9b) shows the Powerpuff Girls rescuing the Mayor, with differing animation styles showing the story from each girl's point of view. A bonus "Sheep in the Big City" (not the advertised "Courage the Cowardly Dog") episode rounds out the DVD collection.

Besides being offered as a single DVD, the disc was also included as part of a 2001 "Powerpuff Girls Power Pack" set, along with the other three discs in the series.

SPECIAL FEATURES Character Bios TECHNICAL FEATURES Fullscreen (1.33:1) • Subtitles/CC: Eng. • Languages: Eng. • Sound: Dolby Digital 5.1 • Snapcase • 1 Disc • Region 1 GENRE & RATING Girls/Superheroes • Not Rated (Kids)

Powerpuff Girls, The: Down 'N' Dirty [#2]

Warner, 2001, 125 mins., #H1685. Directed by Genndy Tartakovsky, Randy Myers, John McIntyre, Craig McCracken. Written by Clayton Morrow, Cindy Morrow, Paul Rudish, Charlie Bean, Genndy Tartakovsky, Chris Savino, Lynne Naylor, Dave Smith, Don Shank, Rob Renzetti.

Ten more terrific episodes make up this second DVD collection of *The Powerpuff Girls*, collecting shows from seasons 1–2. "Birthday Bash" (#16a) shows the girls celebrating their birthday and foiling the plots of Mojo Jojo, Princess, and the Amoeba Boys all at the same time! In the second Emmy-nominated episode, "Beat Your Greens" (#17a), alien broccoloids need to be chopped. The origin of Princess Morebucks is revealed in "Stuck Up, Up and Away" (#14a). The Gang Green Gang goes to kindergarten in "School House Rocked" (#14b), only to unleash trouble on Pokey Oaks. And in "Los Dos Mojo" (#19b), Bubbles gets hit on the head and thinks she's Mojo Jojo!

The girls go after the sleep-inducing Sandman in "Dream Scheme" (#18a), but he really just wants some dream time to himself. In "Just Another Manic Mojo" (#11a), the big-brained monkey wants to use his new giant laser, but the girls are ruining everything while they search for their ball! In the second half of the second Emmy-nominated episode, Pokey Oaks Kindergarten gets stinky in "Down 'n' Dirty" (#17b) after Buttercup refuses to bathe. Will Mojo Jojo turn Princess into a Powerpuff Girl in "Mo Job" (#21a)? And new superhero Major Man is taking over for the girls in Townsville in "Major Competition" (#7a), and they don't like it. A bonus "Courage the Cowardly Dog" (not the advertised "Sheep in the Big City") episode rounds out the DVD collection.

Besides being offered as a single DVD, the disc was also included as part of a 2001 "Powerpuff Girls Power Pack" set, along with the other three discs in the series.

SPECIAL FEATURES Character Bios • Game TECHNICAL FEATURES Fullscreen (1.33:1) • Subtitles/CC: Eng. • Languages: Eng. • Sound: Dolby Digital 5.1 • Snapcase • 1 Disc • Region 1 GENRE & RATING Girls/Superheroes • Not Rated (Kids)

Powerpuff Girls, The: The Mane Event [#3]

Warner, 2001, 133 mins., #H1730. Directed by John McIntyre, Genndy Tartakovsky, Craig McCracken, Randy Myers. Written by Dave Smith, Lynne Naylor-Reccardi, Paul Rudish, John McIntyre, Chris Savino, Don Shank, Kevin Kaliher, Clayton Morrow, Chris Reccardi.

When the sisters "do" her hair, Blossom becomes the laughingstock of Townsville in "The Mane Event" (#27a). And lest you think it has anything to do with porn, rest assured that "Boogie Frights" (#5a) tells the story of the girls vs. the Boogie Man, who wants to cause an eclipse so he can keep dancing all night! In "Slumbering with the Enemy" (#26b), the girls are throwing a slumber party, and Mojo Jojo gets an invite to come in drag as Mojesha!

Then, Blossom discovers new powers to make things chilly on a hot day in "Ice Sore" (#8b), but it doesn't make her sisters very happy. The girls manage to create a fourth Powerpuff Girl named Bunny in "Twisted Sister" (#24a), but she can't tell the good guys from the bad guys. And in "Somethings a Ms." (#26a), Seduca returns to seduce Townsville's Mayor. Two non-advertised extra episodes are available in the "Adventures in Townsville" interactive section: "Power Lunch" (#36b) and "Helter Shelter" (#36a), in which the girls battle the Gang Green Gang yet again and help a baby whale.

Of most interest to *Powerpuff Girls* fans is the DVD's extras including the original *Powerpuff Girls* pilot, "The Whoopass Girls"! Intros and full commentary by creator Craig McCracken are supplemented by the "alternate angle" option that allows you to see the pilot in pencil test form! Two of the episodes feature commentary tracks—by the Mayor and Mojo Jojo, *in character*! There are lots of other extras to keep viewers occupied for a while. For fans, this DVD is a winner!

Besides being offered as a single DVD, the disc was also included as part of a 2001 "Powerpuff Girls Power Pack" set, along with the other three discs in the series.

SPECIAL FEATURES Commentary Tracks by Mojo Jojo, the Mayor, and Craig McCracken • Character Bios • Unaired Pilot and Episodes • Trailer • Promotional Footage • Music Video • Games • Other Title Trailers • Easter Egg TECHNICAL FEATURES Fullscreen (1.33:1) • Subtitles/CC: Eng. • Languages: Eng., Fren., Span. • Sound: Dolby Digital 5.1 • Snapcase • 1 Disc • Region 1 GENRE & RATING Girls/Superheroes • Not Rated (Kids)

Powerpuff Girls, The: Meet the Beat-Alls [#4]

Warner, 2001, 120 mins., #H1927. Directed by Robert Alvarez, John McIntyre, Craig McCracken, Randy Myers, Genndy Tartakovsky. Written by Craig McCracken, Lauren Faust, Dave Smith, Clayton Morrow, Lynne Naylor-Reccardi, Kevin Kaliher, Cindy Morrow, Paul Rudish, Chris Savino, Michael Stern.

Fans of the Beatles will absolutely love the title episode of this DVD. In "Meet the Beat-Alls" (#39b), Mojo Jojo, Princess Morebucks, Fuzzy Lumpkins, and drag queen villain Him all team up as the Beat-Alls (aka "The Bad Four"). They might just defeat the Powerpuff Girls, if Asian monkey Moko Jono—Mojo Jojo's new love interest—doesn't break up the band—er, supervillain group. The story, dialogue, and music are jam-packed with Beatles music references, with even more of them on the Mojo Jojo commentary track on the DVD! Roger Jackson, the voice of the killer in the *Scream* movies, voices Sergeant Pepper here. This was the third Emmy-nominated episode of the series.

Others on this disc include "Jewel of the Aisle" (#32a) in which a crook posing as Lucky Captain Rabbit King hides a jewel in a cereal box . . . the very box that Professor Utonium buys for the girls! Femme Fatale gives the girls a lesson in sexism in "Equal Fights" (#38b), while Bubbles is forced to wear glasses in "Bubblevision" (#30a). A nerd who collects Powerpuff Girl memorabilia decides to make the real girls a part of his collection in "Collect Her" (#15a), and Princess buys Townsville in "Bought and Scold" (#30b), so that, as Mayor, she can make crime legal! Finally, Buttercup falls for the leader of the Gang Green Gang in "Buttercrush" (#4a), but he takes advantage of her affections.

Note that the first pressing of this DVD had a computer virus on the DVD-ROM portion, so the disc was recalled, destroyed, and re-pressed without the virus.

Besides being offered as a single DVD, the disc was also included as part of a 2001 "Powerpuff Girls Power Pack" set, along with the other three discs in the series.

SPECIAL FEATURES "Making of" Featurette: Music Video and Movie • Commentary Track by the Mayor and Mojo Jojo • Music Video • DVD-ROM Features: Screensaver, Games TECHNICAL FEATURES Fullscreen (1.33:1) • Subtitles/CC: Eng. • Languages: Eng., Fren., Span. • Sound: Dolby Digital 5.1 • Snapcase • 1 Disc • Region 1 GENRE & RATING Girls/Superheroes • Not Rated (Kids)

Powerpuff Girls Movie, The

Warner, 2002, 73 mins., #23016. Directed by Craig McCracken. Written by Charlie Bean, Lauren Faust, Craig McCracken, Paul Rudish, Don Shank.

How did the Powerpuff Girls get their start? Well, everyone knows that Professor Utonium made them out of sugar, spice, and everything nice . . . plus a little accidental Chemical X. But how is their origin tied into that of evil monkey Mojo Jojo? When the Professor is locked up, the young superpowered girls are befriended by Mojo. Soon, he's manipulating them to help him in his wicked schemes against Townsville and the world. Will Blossom, Buttercup, and Bubbles realize how truly naughty Mojo Jojo is in time to stop him and his army of sinister simians?

Released theatrically in 2002, *The Powerpuff Girls Movie* updates the strengths of the series with some bigger and bolder animation, a touch of CGI here and there, and a booming soundtrack. Fans will find everything to love here, if only Warner had put the film itself onto the DVD properly. Instead, the widescreen version has been both pan-and-scanned and squeezed to get a cramped and less-attractive fullscreen image. Phooey!

Other aspects of the DVD are fun, including narration for the menus, a commentary track by the series creator, and some "interview" segments (with new animation) and scene-specific commentaries by Blossom, Buttercup, and Bubbles, Mojo Jojo, and the Mayor. There's also some behind-the-scenes material, alternate and deleted scenes, and more. Also included is a *Dexter's Laboratory* short called "Chicken Scratch."

SPECIAL FEATURES "Making of" Featurettes • Commentary Track by Director • Interviews with Characters • Scene-Specific Commentary by Characters • Deleted and Alternate Scenes • Trailer • Promotional Game Footage • DVD-ROM Features: Games, Online Trading Cards • Other Title Trailers TECHNICAL FEATURES Fullscreen (1.33:1) • Subtitles/CC: Eng., Fren., Span. • Languages: Eng., Fren. dub, Span. dub • Sound: Dolby Digital Surround 5.1 • Snapcase • 1 Disc • Region 1 GENRE & RATING Comedy/Superhero/Girls • Rated PG

Power Stone: Mystery of the Stones [#1]

ADV Films, 2001, 100 mins., #DPS/001. Directed by Kenichiro Watanabe, Jun Takada, Kenichi Araki. Scripts by Mark Askwith, Howard Ryshpan, Sukehiro Tomita, Masashi Yokoyama, Yukiyoshi Ohashi, Kenji Yasuda.

Edward Falcon is a young man with a dream of becoming a world-class fighter, but when his father, Pride Falcon—who left him as a boy—sends him a package con-

taining an unassuming rock, his whole world get turned upside down. It is a Power Stone that can transform him into a powerful fighting robot. Before long Falcon finds himself surrounded by friends and enemies, all with a keen interest in the stone. To solve the mysteries of the stone, Falcon must find his world-traveling father, which he might do . . . if he can keep from ogling every girl in town.

Released as a television series in 1999 and based on the CAPCOM video game of the same name, *Power Stone* is an action series for early teens. While spending more time on the personality traits of its characters than on action, it does have some solid fighting scenes, especially when Falcon uses the stone. A mildly interesting story for anyone beyond its intended age group, *Power Stone* is fairly well done when considering its intended audience.

With episodes #1–4 on this DVD, the animation is acceptable but hardly awe-inspiring. Likewise, the soundtrack lacks anything special but matches the production as a whole. There is no objectionable material on the disk with the exception of some shots that linger a bit too long on Rouge's barely clothed breasts. All in all, *Power Stone* will be welcomed by its intended audience but contains little for those either much younger or older. [GP]

SPECIAL FEATURES Other Title Trailers TECHNICAL FEATURES Fullscreen (1.33:1) • Languages: Eng. dub • Sound: Dolby Digital 2.0 • Keepcase • 1 Disc • Region 1 GENRE & RATING Action/Adventure/Robots • Rated 12+

Power Stone #2: Battle Training! [#2]

ADV Films, 2002, 100 mins., #DPS/002. Directed by Jun Matsumoto, Tatsuya Ishihara, Kenichiro Watanabe, Tenji Yasuda. Scripts by Mark Askwith, Howard Ryshpan, Sukehiro Tomita, Masashi Yokoyama, Kenichi Araki.

Falcon decides to master the Power Stone, but first, he must deal with Cassie's marriage plans. Falcon then travels to Wood Land searching for his father who has sent him another Power Stone. There he meets Wang Tang, and together they must meet the challenge of Mt. Min-min. Just when things seem in hand, Falcon and company encounter the pirate Kraken—who also has a Power Stone!

This disk, containing episodes #5–8, sees some significant developments as Falcon begins to make friends on his quest to understand the Power Stones. [GP]

SPECIAL FEATURES Other Title Trailers TECHNICAL FEATURES Fullscreen (1.33:1) • Languages: Eng. dub • Sound: Dolby Digital 2.0 • Keepcase • 1 Disc • Region 1 GENRE & RATING Action/Adventure/Robots • Rated 12+

Power Stone: Dangerous Journeys [#3]

ADV Films, 2002, 100 mins., #DPS/003. Directed by Kenichiro Watanabe, Hiroshi Yamamoto, Kazuhiro Yamashita, Masahiko Murata, Jun Matsumoto. Scripts by Mark Askwith, Howard Ryshpan, Sukehiro Tomita, Yukiyoshi Ohashi, Masashi Yokoyama, Kenichi Araki.

Falcon, Ryoma, and Rouge journey to Fire Land. Once there they run into some bad luck as they try to solve the mystery of the Oracle. But, when things get too hot to handle, Rouge's crystal ball reveals itself for what it truly is. Back on his father's trail, Falcon ventures to Gold Land and meets the massive Gunrock, who has sad news about Falcon's father. Going to his father's rescue, Falcon finds himself in a pile of trouble.

In this volume of *Power Stone*, containing episodes #9–13, things gets more complicated as romance creeps into the story. [GP]

SPECIAL FEATURES Other Title Trailers TECHNICAL FEATURES Fullscreen (1.33:1) • Languages: Eng. dub • Sound: Dolby Digital 2.0 • Keepcase • 1 Disc • Region 1 GENRE & RATING Action/Adventure/Robots • Rated 12+

Power Stone: The Search Continues [#4]

ADV Films, 2002, 100 mins., #DPS/004. Directed by Tatsuya Ishihara, Yashiko Shima, Kunitoshi Okajima, Takahi Ikehata. Scripts by Mark Askwith, Howard Ryshpan, Masashi Yokoyama, Sukehiro Tomita, Kenichi Araki, Yukiyoshi Ohashi.

Tracing the steps of his father, Falcon travels to Moon Land. There he finds the land racked by an unnatural drought. Falcon, Rouge, and Ryoma, accompanied by the ninja girl Ayame and her cross-dressing big brother Mitsue (who has serious eyes for Falcon), must face Kraken to set things right. Then it's off to Soil Land, but en route Rouge and Ayame are kidnapped. Falcon and Ryoma try to rescue the girls, but this time the Stones may not even the odds.

In this volume, featuring episodes #14–17, the action picks up as Falcon begins to master the Power Stone. [GP]

SPECIAL FEATURES Other Title Trailers TECHNICAL FEATURES Fullscreen (1.33:1) • Languages: Eng. dub • Sound: Dolby Digital 2.0 • Keepcase • 1 Disc • Region 1 GENRE & RATING Action/Adventure/Robots • Rated 12+

Power Stone: Friends and Enemies [#5]

ADV Films, 2002, 100 mins., #DPS/005. Directed by Hiroshi Yamamoto, Kenichiro Watanabe, Kazuya Komai. Scripts by Mark Askwith, Howard Ryshpan, Sukehiro Tomita, Masashi Yokoyama, Yukiyoshi Ohashi, Sukehiro Tomita.

Using the Power Stones, Edward Falcon helps the Old West–style town of Dulustown, which has fallen under attack by Indians. But is the town sheriff hiding something? Later, in Aqua Land, Falcon and his friends must face the evil pirate Kraken and his bumbling goons. And what happens when Falcon meets his idol, a fearsome fighter named Valgas? Will Valgas help or hurt him?

This penultimate volume contains episodes #18–21.

SPECIAL FEATURES Other Title Trailers TECHNICAL FEATURES Fullscreen (1.33:1) • Languages: Eng. dub • Sound: Dolby Digital 2.0 • Keepcase • 1 Disc • Region 1 GENRE & RATING Action/Adventure/Robots • Rated 12+

Power Stone: The Last Battlefield [#6]

ADV Films, 2002, 125 mins., #DPS/006. Directed by Kenichiro Watanabe, Jun Matsumoto, Vian, Tatsuya Ishihara . Scripts by Mark Askwith, Howard Ryshpan, Sukehiro Tomita, Masashi Yokoyama, Kenichi Araki, Yukiyoshi Ohashi.

Two of the Power Stones are stolen by his enemies, and Edward Falcon tries to help his friends find their Stones. Falcon's father has been found, but what does he have to do with the future of the Stones? Valgas might be the thief of the Stones, but the truth lies in the Dark Land, where monsters attack the adventurers, dark magic spells are cast, and a supreme evil awaits them!

The final *Power Stone* disc contains five episodes, numbered #22–26. There's a bit of a jarring shift in story as the episodes continue, almost as if last-minute changes were made in the plot.

SPECIAL FEATURES Other Title Trailers TECHNICAL FEATURES Fullscreen (1.33:1) • Languages: Eng. dub • Sound: Dolby Digital 2.0 • Keepcase • 1 Disc • Region 1 GENRE & RATING Action/Adventure/Robots • Rated 12+

Presenting Felix the Cat

Image, 1999, 119 mins., #ID5532BKDVD. Another collection of vintage black and white cartoons stars Felix the Cat, an adventurous scamp whose tail helped him out of many a problem. Felix was created by Pat Sullivan, Otto Messmer, and John King. The collection begins with "Paramount Magazine" from 1919, which contained the short "Feline Follies," the introduction of Felix (originally called Tom).

Also included on the disc are the following fifteen shorts: "Felix Saves the Day" (1922); "Felix in the Swim" (1922); "Felix Turns the Tide" (1922); "Felix Lends a Hand" (1922); "Felix Minds the Kid" (1922); "Felix in the Bone Age" (1922); "Felix the Ghost Breaker" (1923); "Felix Wins Out" (1923); "Felix Revolts" (1923); "Felix Gets Broadcasted" (1923); "Felix in Hollywood" (1923); "Felix in Fairyland" (1923); "Felix Out of Luck" (1924); "Felix Goes A-Hunting" (1923); and "Felix Finds 'Em Fickle" (1924).

The transfer quality varies widely: some shorts are nearly flawless, others painful to watch due to scratches and nicks. The shorts are accompanied by an original organ score by Dave Wickersham.

See also *Felix!* and *Felix the Cat: Collector's Edition.*

SPECIAL FEATURES None TECHNICAL FEATURES Fullscreen (1.33:1 windowboxed) • Subtitles/CC: Eng. • Sound: Dolby Digital 2.0 • Snapcase • 1 Disc • Region 1 GENRE & RATING Animals/Comedy • Not Rated (All Ages)

Prince of Egypt, The [Signature Selection]

DreamWorks, 1999, 99 mins., #84853. Directed by Brenda Chapman, Steve Hickner, Simon Wells. Written by Philip Lazebnik. Based on the Book of Exodus.

Set adrift in a basket in the river by his mother, baby Moses is raised as the son of Pharaoh Seti. He grows up alongside his stepbrother Ramses, and although the two share some sibling rivalry, they are the best of friends. But destiny will soon tear the two apart, as Moses learns of his secret past . . . and determines that he will heed the will of God and free the Hebrew slaves from Egypt. Ramses, now the Pharaoh, cannot allow his brother to succeed.

The Prince of Egypt is DreamWorks' first animated film, and the first project created by executive producer Jeffrey Katzenberg after his acrimonious exit from Disney. The film is true to Biblical and historical roots, while being careful not to push any specific religious agenda or dogma. Music plays a strong role in the film, from Hans Zimmer's Oscar-nominated score to Stephen Schwartz's songs. One song, "When You Believe," won an Academy Award in 1998.

But the backbone of the picture is the animation, which is some of the richest and most lush ever put on screen. Some moments are simply breathtaking, including the parting of the Red Sea, a series of hieroglyphics coming to life, or God's scourges on Egypt. The scope and wonder of the animated images is aided significantly by CGI work, but it is so seamlessly integrated that it's hard to tell cels from pixels. There is little in American animation—or elsewhere—that can compare to the stunning vistas and effects on screen in this film.

Parents are warned that there is a significant amount of violence in the film, whether from Egyptian slavers and soldiers or from divine forces. Young children will probably not be able to handle scarier scenes, and slightly older children might need to discuss elements with adults after viewing.

The DVD is loaded with extras, many about the making of the film. Oddly, for a film that values music so highly, there are no music video selections. Still, that's small quibble for a disc that gets the highest marks in every other category. Highly recommended!

Besides being offered as a single DVD, the disc was also included as part of a pack set, with *Joseph: King of Dreams.*

SPECIAL FEATURES "Making of" Featurettes • Commentary Track with Directors • Cast & Crew Bios • Character and Art Galleries • Production Notes • Trailers • Promotional Footage • Other Title Trailers • Inserts: Liner Notes TECHNICAL FEATURES Widescreen (1.85:1 enhanced for 16x9) • Subtitles/CC: Eng. • Languages: Eng. • Sound: Dolby Digital Surround 2.0, Dolby Digital 5.1 • Keepcase • 1 Disc • Region 1 GENRE & RATING Music/Historical/Religious • Rated PG

Prince of Egypt, The [DTS]

DreamWorks, 2000, 99 mins., #84667. Directed by Brenda Chapman, Steve Hickner, Simon Wells. Written by Philip Lazebnik. Based on the Book of Exodus.

This DVD is the same as the traditional DVD, with the exception that it has an added DTS soundtrack. The cover text has been altered slightly to reflect this, and the keepcase is black instead of gold.

SPECIAL FEATURES "Making of" Featurettes • Commentary Track with Directors • Cast & Crew Bios • Character and Art Galleries • Production Notes • Trailers • Promotional Footage • Other Title Trailers • Inserts: Liner Notes TECHNICAL FEATURES Widescreen (1.85:1 enhanced for 16x9) • Subtitles/CC: Eng. • Languages: Eng. • Sound: Dolby Digital Surround 2.0, DTS • Keepcase • 1 Disc • Region 1 GENRE & RATING Music/Historical/Religious • Rated PG

Prince of the Nile: The Story of Moses

Madacy, 1999, 30 mins.

This DVD was not available for review.

Princess Mononoke

Disney, 2000, 134 mins., #19300. Directed by Hayao Miyazaki. Screenplay by Hayao Miyazaki.

In medieval Japan, something is terribly wrong in the forest. Young Ashitaka must defend his village from a boar demon with writhing snakes for flesh that barrels out of the woods, threatening to kill all in its path. The warrior prince manages to bring down the horrible monster and save his people, but not before an infectious curse is passed from the beast to his arm. To save himself and the forest, Ashitaka embarks on a quest to discover the reason for nature's imbalance and the anger within the former boar-god that drove it mad. Along the way, Ashitaka is ensnared in a battle for the forest's soul between fierce white spirit-wolves and the followers of Lady Eboshi, who are industrializing their village to produce iron and gunpowder. Ashitaka meets San, a feral young girl also known as Princess Mononoke. Raised by the wolf god Moro, she ferociously fights to repel the momentum of human advance. As San and Ashitaka fall in love, the battle lines between spirit and humanity, nature and technology are drawn.

Widely hailed as one of the great achievements of Eastern animation, *Princess Mononoke*'s Japanese release set box office records. Hayao Miyazaki and Studio Ghibli created a masterpiece in this 1997 film, which took three years to complete. Graceful and lush, *Princess Mononoke* is what animation is all about: creating worlds, characters, and grand fables that cannot be conveyed by live action. *Mononoke*'s depiction of nature's spirit and fury against those who would contain it is unforgettable.

The English-language adaptation is by popular fantasy and comic book author Neil Gaiman, who worked with the framework of the complete film to recraft the story. While some anime fans quibbled with the revised story and name-actor voice talent used for the U.S. theatrical release, few complained that the gorgeous animation—uncensored—was finally available for American audiences. Purists have the option of captions that show the English-language script or the literal translation of the Japanese dialogue.

A "featurette" of interviews with the voice actors for the film's English language release, including Gillian Anderson, Minnie Driver, Jada Pinkett Smith, and Billy Bob Thornton, is among the few extras on the *Mononoke* disc. [BR]

SPECIAL FEATURES "Making of" Featurette • Trailer TECHNICAL FEATURES Widescreen (1.85:1 enhanced for 16x9) • Subtitles/CC: Eng. • Languages: Jap., Eng. dub, Fren. dub • Sound: Dolby Digital 5.1 • Keepcase • 1 Disc • Region 1 GENRE & RATING Historical/Fantasy • Rated PG-13

Princess Nine: First Inning! [#1]

ADV Films, 2001, 125 mins., #DPN/001. Directed by Tomomi Mochizuki. Screenplay by Hiro Maruyama, Hiroaki Kitajima.

Ryo Hayakawa dreams of become a professional baseball player like her father. In the sexist world of sports, it is a dream that she thinks could never come true (girls are supposed to play softball, not baseball). Enter Ms. Himuro, the head of prestigious Kisaragi High and mysterious friend of Ryo's late father. After scouting Ryo, Ms. Himuro decides to grant Ryo a full baseball scholarship to Kisaragi High. But, her plan isn't to have Ryo play on the boys' team or to start a girls' league—she wants to build a team to compete with the boys on their own turf and win the national tournament.

First released on Japanese television in 1999, *Princess Nine* is a serious drama. Its characters are very human and endure sexism, ridicule, and mockery as individuals; as a nine-member team, they pursue their goals. Part of what makes *Princess Nine* so attractive is that it is so different from your run-of-the-mill anime. No robots, no scantily clad space vixens, no evil empires, no sorcery, just good writing and believable characters with a dream.

Princess Nine is a well-directed series that doesn't rely on flashy content to entertain. The animation is smooth but not exceptional. The picture is crisp and clear. The soundtrack is uneventful but fits the mood of any given scene. All in all, this first volume in the series, which includes episodes #1–5, is very story-driven and shows just how far a series can go on a good script. [GP]

SPECIAL FEATURES Character Statistics • Clean Credits • Other Title Trailers TECHNICAL FEATURES Fullscreen (1.33:1) • Subtitles/CC: Eng. • Languages: Jap., Eng. dub • Sound: Dolby Digital 2.0 • Keepcase • 1 Disc • Region 1 GENRE & RATING Baseball/Girls • Rated 12+

Princess Nine: Double Header! [#2]

ADV Films, 2002, 100 mins., #DPN/002. Directed by Tomomi Mochizuki. Screenplay by Takao Kawaguchi, Hiro Maruyama, Hiroaki Kitajima.

As the group starts to come together, the Princesses are still four girls short of a team, and they begin an all-out attempt to recruit the needed players. Meanwhile, Ms. Himuro must appease Kisaragi High's Board of Trustees as they express their anger at the decision to start an all-girl baseball team without their consultation. Ryo also has problems off the field as she must face the jealous hatred of Izumi, daughter of Ms. Himuro and the school's high-profile tennis star.

Comprising episodes #6–10, this DVD sees a lot of character development as new players are added and the emotions—and baseballs—fly. One extra includes a segment on how to cook oden, a form of fish stew. [GP]

SPECIAL FEATURES Character Statistics • Clean Credits • Cooking Segment • Other Title Trailers TECHNICAL FEATURES Fullscreen (1.33:1) • Subtitles/CC: Eng. • Languages: Jap., Eng. dub • Sound: Dolby Digital 2.0 • Keepcase • 1 Disc • Region 1 GENRE & RATING Baseball/Girls • Rated 12+

Princess Nine: Triple Play! [#3]

ADV Films, 2002, 100 mins., #DPN/003. Directed by Tomomi Mochizuki. Screenplay by Hiro Maruyama, Takaaki Kawaguchi.

With one position left to fill, and their first game coming up, the last person the Princesses expect steps up to the plate. Also, people have begun whispering about Ryo's father, and she begins to ask some hard questions about the man she never knew. Behind the scenes, the High School Baseball Association is planning to destroy the Princesses' hopes of competing, but a powerful friend steps in and sets things to rights.

This DVD, with episodes #11–15, sees the girls working to overcome their own personal demons and fears. Once again, the writing makes *Princess Nine* shine. [GP]

SPECIAL FEATURES Cast Bios • Japanese Baseball History • Clean Credits • Other Title Trailers TECHNICAL FEATURES Fullscreen (1.33:1) • Subtitles/CC: Eng. • Languages: Jap., Eng. dub • Sound: Dolby Digital 2.0 • Keepcase • 1 Disc • Region 1 GENRE & RATING Baseball/Girls • Rated 12+

Princess Nine: Strike Zone! [#4]

ADV Films, 2002, 100 mins., #DPN/004. Directed by Tomomi Mochizuki. Screenplay by Susumu Ishubashi, Takaaki Kawaguchi, Hiro Maruyama.

Viewers were left on a bit of a cliffhanger last episode, and here it's resolved. But even as it seems acceptance will buoy the Princesses' hopes, secrets are revealed and wedges are driven into relationships. The Parents Association wants to shut down the baseball program, and the media is giving all sorts of attention to the girls. While it goes to Yoko's head, Izumi is less seduced by fame. But a reporter

digs up a baseball scandal that Ryo's father was involved in twenty years ago! Will the sins of the father spoil his daughter's future?

Episodes #16–19 deal with the scandal and its aftermath, and give lots more room for character development and interaction. And more cliffhangers are on the way!

SPECIAL FEATURES Cast Bios • Karaoke • Clean Credits • Other Title Trailers TECHNICAL FEATURES Fullscreen (1.33:1) • Subtitles/CC: Eng. • Languages: Jap., Eng. dub • Sound: Dolby Digital 2.0 • Keepcase • 1 Disc • Region 1 GENRE & RATING Baseball/Girls • Rated 12+

Princess Nine: Bases Loaded! [#5]

ADV Films, 2002, 100 mins., #DPN/005. Directed by Tomomi Mochizuki. Screenplay by Hiro Maruyama, Takaaki Kawaguchi.

It's time for the Princesses to go to a special training camp in the mountains, but they're still reeling from events in the previous disc. Now, at a co-ed camp, their hearts are going to be as engaged as their other muscles, and romance will blossom. But if the team breaks training—even if it's for love—what will the consequences be?

The penultimate *Princess Nine* disc collects episodes #20–23.

SPECIAL FEATURES Cover Art • Clean Credits • Other Title Trailers TECHNICAL FEATURES Fullscreen (1.33:1) • Subtitles/CC: Eng. • Languages: Jap., Eng. dub • Sound: Dolby Digital 2.0 • Keepcase • 1 Disc • Region 1 GENRE & RATING Baseball/Girls • Rated 12+

Princess Nine: Grand Slam [#6]

ADV Films, 2002, 125 mins., #DPN/006. Directed by Kaoru Suzuki, Susumu Ishizaki, Shinya Hanai, Tomomi Mochizuki. Screenplay by Hiro Maruyama, Takao Kawaguchi.

NOTE: This DVD arrived too late for a full review. The following text is promotional copy provided by the releasing company:

"The quest for Koshien explodes in a furious series of games that leave the Princesses gasping for breath, yet in the end the team holds true. Now they must meet their greatest challenge, for not only are they up against the one school they had hoped to never face, but they must finally come to terms with their true feelings. For the team. For each other. And for the people they love. Ten girls become women, forged into diamonds on the field of dreams, in the spectacular final volume of *Princess Nine!*"

SPECIAL FEATURES Cover Art • Clean Credits • Other Title Trailers TECHNICAL FEATURES Fullscreen (1.33:1) • Subtitles/CC: Eng. • Languages: Jap., Eng. dub • Sound: Dolby Digital 2.0 • Keepcase • 1 Disc • Region 1 GENRE & RATING Baseball/Girls • Rated 12+

Prisoner of Zenda, The [Collector's Edition]

Digital Versatile Disc, 2000, #180. Based on the novel by Anthony Hope.

This DVD was not available for review.

Project A-Ko

Image, 1999, 86 mins., #4640.

This DVD was not available for review. It is out of print.

Project A-Ko: Collector's Series

U.S. Manga Corps, 2002, 86 mins., #USMD2185. Directed by Katsuhiko Nishijima. Script by Yuji Moriyama, Katsuhiko Nishijima, Tomoko Kawasaki. Story by Katsuhiko Nishijima, Kazumi Shirasaka.

NOTE: This DVD arrived too late for a full review. The following text is promotional copy provided by the releasing company:

"This anime classic is now digitally remastered! It's the not-too-distant future, and a metropolis flourishes in the crash site of an alien spacecraft. A-ko, a teenager growing up in this city, enjoys the life of an ordinary schoolgirl . . . along with incredible superhuman strength! But her carefree days are numbered. Her school rival, B-ko, is not content to live in the shadows any longer. A-ko's super-powers and good fashion sense may not be a match for B-ko's evil genius and Mega-Powered Fighting Robots of Doom!"

The second disc is the *Project A-Ko* original soundtrack.

SPECIAL FEATURES "Making of" Featurettes • Commentary by Co-Writer/Designer • Interview with Co-Writer/Designer • Fan Art Gallery • Manga-to-Film Comparison • Trailers • Promotional Footage • Music Videos • DVD-ROM Features: Art, Scripts, Manga • Other Title Trailers TECHNICAL FEATURES Fullscreen (1.33:1) • Subtitles/CC: Eng. • Languages: Jap., Eng. dub • Sound: Dolby Digital 2.0 • Multikeepcase • 2 Discs • Region All GENRE & RATING Comedy/Science Fiction • Rated 13+

Project A-Ko: Love and Robots [#1]

U.S. Manga Corps, 2001, 180 mins., #USMD 2054. Directed by Yuji Moriyama. Screenplay by Takao Koyama, Tomoko Kawasaki, Yuji Moriyama.

A-Ko Magami is a sixteen-year-old girl at Graviton High School, but she's no ordinary girl: she inherited superstrength, speed, and invulnerability from her parents. B-Ko Daitokuji is a rich girl who is obsessed with C-Ko, and will fight A-Ko until C-Ko is hers. B-Ko's father is a suave mustachioed man who designs weapons for the military. C-Ko Kotobuki is a happy child—except when she's bawling—with a secret past. She likes A-Ko, but hates B-Ko. All of the characters face wacky plots with aliens, giant robots, romantic love triangles, hostile occult takeovers, and C-Ko's alien mother.

This DVD contains the OVA movies #2–4: "The Plot of the Daitokuji Financial Group" (1987); "Cinderella Rhapsody" (1988); and "Final" (1989). While the original *Project A-Ko* from 1986 was full of parody, slapstick, and silliness, this later version lacks the punch and verve of its predecessor. Fans also complained about the music, which is very 1980s-sounding and contributes to the slower, duller pace. Those who wish to avoid big-eyed cuteness and super-deformed characters would do well to run away before C-Ko melts their retinas. While not a disappointment, neither does *Project A-Ko* garner a ringing endorsement for fun either.

SPECIAL FEATURES Character Bios • Deleted Scenes • Manga Art • Promotional Footage • Music Videos • DVD-ROM Features: Art, Scripts, Lyrics TECHNICAL FEATURES Fullscreen (1.33:1) • Subtitles/CC: Eng. • Languages: Jap., Eng. dub • Sound: Dolby Digital Surround 2.0 • Keepcase • 1 Disc • Region 1–6 GENRE & RATING Comedy/Science Fiction • Rated 13+

Project A-Ko: Uncivil Wars [#2]

U.S. Manga Corps, 2001, 104 mins., #USMD 2072. Directed by Katsuhiko Nishijima. Screenplay by Katsuhiko Nishijima, Tomoko Kawasaki, Yuji Kawahara.

As if the previous stories never happened, now A-Ko and B-Ko are slightly competitive friends who work as bounty hunters in space; when a ship crashes out of the sky, C-Ko emerges to complicate their lives. Soon, they're battling against space pirate kidnappers Gash, Liza, and Gail—plus the galactic police—to keep C-Ko safe, but what secrets does their uber-cute always-bawling charge hide? The pirates want C-Ko to meld with the soul of long-dead evil sorceress Xena, and the universe may be destroyed if they succeed!

The final *A-Ko* two-parter is from a 1990 OVA, here titled "Project A-Ko Vs. Battle 1: Grey Side" and "Project A-Ko Vs. Battle 2: Blue Side." As noted above, the story and characters bear almost no resemblance to their earlier versions, except visually. The parody element is less apparent as well, and the humor becomes more about blowing things up and such, although when Xena inhabits C-Ko, there are some funny dichotomies in the dark vs. light personalities. Still, fans looking for *A-Ko* will find her here in name only.

SPECIAL FEATURES Character Bios • Character and Art Galleries • Trailer TECHNICAL FEATURES Fullscreen (1.33:1) • Subtitles/CC: Eng. • Languages: Jap., Eng. dub • Sound: Dolby Digital Surround 2.0 • Keepcase • 1 Disc • Region 1–6 GENRE & RATING Comedy/Science Fiction • Rated 13+

Project Arms: The Claws That Catch [#1]

VIZ/Pioneer, 2002, 75 mins., #DPA01. Directed by Junichi Takaoka. Based on the manga series by Ryoji Minagawa, Kyoichi Nanatsuki in *Shonen Sunday*.

NOTE: This DVD arrived too late for a full review. The following text is promotional copy provided by the releasing company:

"The claws that catch . . . Ryo Takatsuki, Hayato Shingu, Takeshi Tomoe—three boys, three accidents, three ARMS. Nanomachines designed to be the ultimate integrated weaponry, ARMS are insanely powerful . . . and, in inexperienced hands, often out of control. Now a powerful, secret organization is after the only living samples of this technology, and the strangely enhanced assassins who have been sent to get them are ready to kill anyone who gets in their way."

This disc contains episodes #1–3.

SPECIAL FEATURES Character and Art Galleries • Storyboards • Trailer • Clean Credits • Other Title Trailers TECHNICAL FEATURES Fullscreen (1.33:1) • Subtitles/CC: Eng. • Languages: Jap., Eng. dub • Sound: Dolby Digital • Keepcase • 1 Disc • Region 1 GENRE & RATING Robots/Science Fiction/Action • Rated 13+

Prostashino [Sour Cream Village]

Jove/Stellar.

This DVD was not available for review. It is a Russian-language disc.

Psychic Force

Image, 2002, 64 mins., #ID1060TIDVD. Directed by Fujio Yamauchi. Screenplay by Hiroyuki Kawasaki, Kenichi Onuki, Katsuhiko Takayama.

The near future is a dark age for psychics. The Army is experimenting with young psychics in the hopes of creating elite soldiers. Keith Evans escapes a military compound and is taken in by the Griffith family, but when the military tracks him down, he leaves, along with his new friend, Burn Griffith. Later, Keith appears to have joined the army of Noah, a group of psychics determined to separate themselves from humanity and build a safer place. Noah is led by the mysterious Wong, but his motives are unknown, even to those who read minds. What will Keith sacrifice in the bid to build a psychic Utopia, and will Burn stop him or help him?

Hardly an original premise, the two-OVA *Psychic Force* series from 1998 was based on characters from an arcade fighting game. Feeling a bit like *Firestarter, Mai the Psychic Girl,* or other "government pursues psychics" storylines, the stories are nonetheless entertaining. The art is expressive and fluid, with just enough realism to balance out the wildly impossible hair.

The DVD has a number of extras, perhaps the most interesting of which is a fifteen-minute segment from "Psychic Junky Fair 3" in Tokyo, an event where 700 fans watched panel discussions, live voice-reenactments, and a costume contest, all based on *Psychic Force.* The disc also features an isolated music and sound effects track, still (unfortunately) a rarity on DVD.

SPECIAL FEATURES "Making of" Featurette • Trailer • Promotional Footage • Isolated Music Track TECHNICAL FEATURES Fullscreen (1.33:1) • Subtitles/CC: Eng. • Languages: Jap., Eng. dub • Sound: Dolby Digital 2.0, Dolby Digital 5.1 • Keepcase • 1 Disc • Region 1 GENRE & RATING Science Fiction/Action • Not Rated (Teens)

Psychic Wars

Manga Entertainment, 2002, 60 mins., #MANGA4059-2. Directed by Tetsuo Imazawa. Screenplay by Yasushi Ishikura. Based on the novel by Yasuake Kadota.

A woman claiming to have a 5,000-year-old cancer visits surgeon Ukyo Retsu. She tells him of a message from the gods she received when visiting a strange temple and of a great war that is to come. Ukyo hardly believes her story, but when he removes the tumor, it continues to grow. Seeking answers, he visits the temple and finds an idol resembling the woman. Suddenly, the idol emits a strange light engulfing Ukyo. Five thousand years ago good triumphed over evil. Now, the power to defend humanity from this ancient enemy has passed to a new guardian—Ukyo.

Released in 1991, *Psychic Wars* has a very thin, overly dramatic storyline with hardly a single twist after the first five minutes. What there is of a storyline is difficult to follow, as it jumps about in a misguided attempt to appear sophisticated. Likewise, its presentation and development of the characters could have easily been much better.

Psychic Wars's other ailments are the result of poor production. The animation is sometimes stiff and jerky and at other times missing completely: lingering stills—with no place in the story—account for a fourth of the film. The soundtrack is also unimpressive, as is the picture quality. In short, *Psychic Wars* is a campy, cliché-filled flick with shallow writing and occasional nudity, all produced in a very dated style on a low budget. It's an animated *Rosemary's Baby,* only without the baby, the characters, or the script. [GP]

SPECIAL FEATURES Other Title Trailers TECHNICAL FEATURES Fullscreen (1.33:1) • Subtitles/CC: Eng. • Languages: Jap., Eng. dub • Sound: Dolby Digital Surround 5.1 • Keepcase • 1 Disc • Region 1 GENRE & RATING Horror/Action • Not Rated (Teens)

Puppet Films of Jiri Trnka, The

Image, 2000, 156 mins., #ID9005ASDVD. Directed by Jiri Trnka.

What is it about the Czech that they produce so many memorable stop-motion animators? Decades before Jan Svankmajer began plying his creepy trade, Jiri Trnka was creating stop-motion and puppet short films that told stories from around the world, often in gorgeous and haunting detail. The first half of this disc offers five short films, ranging from eleven to twenty-one minutes each: "Story of the Bass Cello" (1949) tells Anton Chekhov's story about a bass player whose clothes are stolen while he bathes, and the women he meets because of it; "The Song of the Prairie" (1949) is a romantic parody of America's Wild West; "The Merry Circus" (1951) features paper cut-outs and stop motion; "A Drop Too Much (1954) relates the woeful tale of a motorcyclist who drinks too much; and "The Hand" (1965), Trnka's final film, finds a live-action hand ordering a puppet creator to change his art.

The biggest and best-known draw for the disc is *The Emperor's Nightingale,* a sixty-seven-minute 1948 film that adapts Hans Christian Andersen's fairy tale with Chinese settings. Boris Karloff narrated the English-language version, which was released to U.S. theaters in 1951 and restored for video release in 1996. A newly produced

twelve-minute documentary, "Jiri Trnka: Puppet Animation Master," completes the disc, giving a view of the man behind the magic and a look at his life as a children's book artist before becoming a filmmaker.

SPECIAL FEATURES None TECHNICAL FEATURES Fullscreen (1.33:1) • Languages: Czech, Eng. dub • Sound: Dolby Digital 1.0 • Snapcase • 1 Disc • Region 1 GENRE & RATING Stop Motion/Puppet • Not Rated (Kids)

Puppet Princess

Anime Works, 2001, 43 mins., #AWDVD-0112. Animation Directed by Hirotoshi Takaya, Tsutomu Susuki. Script by Junichi Miyashita. Based on the manga series by Kazuhiro Fujita in *Shonen Sunday.*

The 16th century is an age of civil war in Japan, where a reckless ninja named Yasaburo is his clan's only survivor. One day he meets Princess Rangiku, a girl whose family was decimated by the forces of General Karimata. Now, they want the strange puppets that Rangiku's father created—and which she carries in a huge box on her back—and they'll kill anyone who gets in their way. But is Yasaburo scared? Not at all. If it's a fight Karimata wants, blood will be spilled.

Blood is the operative term in this 2000 OVA. From its opening scenes to its end, *Puppet Princess* is full of blood and gore. Combine this with the angular, unattractive animation designs, and you have a disc that most fans will find unpleasant to watch. Yasaburo is a bit of a wisecracker, so he brings some much-needed humor to the plot, and the writers are to be commended for coming up with surprisingly creepy and weird story elements (hard to do in the realm of anime).

If it isn't obvious from the above, this DVD is not intended for younger audiences. Despite the 16+ rating, it almost lands itself in the Mature/Adult category; the brief nudity is nothing compared to the gore and genuinely disturbing moments with the puppets.

SPECIAL FEATURES Outtakes • Other Title Trailers TECHNICAL FEATURES Fullscreen (1.33:1) • Subtitles/CC: Eng. • Languages: Jap., Eng. dub • Sound: Dolby Digital 2.0 • Keepcase • 1 Disc • Region 1 GENRE & RATING Historical/Martial Arts/Action • Rated 16+

Puppetoon Movie, The

Image, 2000, 79 mins., #ID5865ALDVD. Directed by George Pal. Written by Arnold Leibovit.

Another of Europe's greatest stop-motion and puppet animators is Hungarian-born animator and director George Pal, whose "Puppetoons" were popular with audiences from 1933 to 1947, prior to his leap to directing live-action films. *The Puppetoon Movie* is a 1987 collection of eleven of Pal's shorts, including newly filmed introductions by Gumby, Pokey, and Arnie the Dinosaur. Entries in the film include: "The Little Broadcast" (1935); "The Philips Broadcast of 1938" (1938); "Hoola Boola" (1941); "South Seas Sweethearts" (1938); "The Sleeping Beauty" (1935); "Tulips Shall Grow" (1942), a film about the Nazi attack on Holland; "Together in the Weather" (1946); "John Henry and the Inky Poo" (1946), a short that has been praised as one of the first to treat African-Americans with dignity; "Philips Cavalcade" (1938); "Jasper in a Jam" (1946); and "Tubby the Tuba" (1947), in which a little horn wants its song heard!

A dozen extra "Puppetoons" are also included on the disc, though three are repeats from the movie. The other toons are: "What Ho She Bumps" (1937); "Mr. Strauss Takes a Walk" (1943); "Olio for Jasper" (1946); "Jasper's Derby" (1946); "Ether Symphony" (1936); "Aladdin and the Magic Lamp" (1947); "The Magic Atlas" (1935); "Jasper and the Haunted House" (1942); and "The Ship of the Ether" (1935).

Pal's films include work by Ray Harryhausen and Willis O'Brien (creator of *King Kong*) among others, and the shorts are all dazzling, bright, and impressively packed with detail. The miniature figures are meticulously costumed, and dozens of sets make their worlds come alive. The only negative element on this disc is that some may find the "Jasper" shorts racially offensive; despite the accolades he got for the "John Henry" short, Pal did get later criticism for some stereotyped elements of "Jasper" that in today's more enlightened times seem insensitive to African Americans.

The Puppetoon Movie has a handful of interesting extras, and music by Charlie Barnet, Peggy Lee, and Louis Armstrong, among others. Watch for a salute at the end of the film, featuring stop-motion characters from film, television, and advertising all raising a cheer for George Pal. See how many you can name. The Pillsbury Doughboy, Mr. Peanut, Curious George, Speedy Alka Seltzer, a Gremlin . . .

See also *The Fantasy Film Worlds of George Pal.*

SPECIAL FEATURES Interview with Animator • Photo Galleries • Trailer TECHNICAL FEATURES Fullscreen (1.33:1) • Subtitles/CC: Eng. • Languages: Eng. • Sound: Dolby Digital Surround 5.1 • Snapcase • 1 Disc • Region 1 GENRE & RATING Stop Motion/Puppet • Rated PG

Pure Love ☞ see Mature/Adult Section

Q

Queen Emeraldas

ADV Films, 1999, 60 mins., #DVDQE001. Directed by Yuji Asada. Screenplay by Mugi Kamio. Based on the manga series by Reiji Matsumoto.

In the interstellar trade routes of the far future, piracy is still an inevitability. An army of Efressian warships terrorizes cargo fleets, but ends up raising the ire of the legendary space pirate Emeraldas when they use her calling card—the skull and crossbones. She attacks, and her powerful ship makes a mockery of the Efressian forces. The Efressian commander, Eldomain, wants revenge against Emeraldas; even more dangerously, Emeraldas's cutting remarks and devastating attacks wound the ego of Efressian Queen Luda, who decides that Emeraldas must be stamped out to preserve her own status. As the Efressians plot their counterattack, Emeraldas is surprised when a young stowaway, Hiroshi Umino, appears on her ship, looking for answers of his own.

Queen Emeraldas is an almost painfully straightforward outing from Reiji Matsumoto, famed creator of *Captain Harlock, Maetel Legend*, and many other popular science fiction epics. All of the usual pieces are in place—Emeraldas is the swashbuckling, seemingly invincible heroine; Hiroshi is the usual angry, impetuous kid; and Luda and Eldomain are suitable straight villains. Queen Emeraldas looks great—modern animation is very kind to Matsumoto's classic character designs—but the story is so simple and predictable that regular science fiction fans might be bored. Still, Matsumoto fans will find *Queen Emeraldas* irresistible.

This DVD contains both of the two 1998 *Queen Emeraldas* OVA episodes. The disc looks good, but there isn't much in the way of extras. [MT]

SPECIAL FEATURES Other Title Trailers TECHNICAL FEATURES Fullscreen (1.33:1) • Subtitles/CC: Eng., Span. • Languages: Jap., Eng. dub, Fren. dub • Sound: Dolby Digital 5.1 • Keepcase • 1 Disc • Region 1–6 GENRE & RATING Science Fiction/Action • Not Rated (Teens)

Quest for Camelot

Warner, 2001, 86 mins., #16607. Directed by Frederik Du Chau. Screenplay by Kirk DeMicco, William Schrifrin, Jacqueline Feather, David Seidler. Based on the novel *The King's Damosel* by Vera Chapman.

Years after rogue knight Ruber kills her father, young Kayley wishes she could be a Knight of the Round Table in Camelot. When Ruber sends a griffin to steal the sword Excalibur, the beast drops it into a dangerous forest. Kayley sets out to recover the sword and return it to Camelot before Ruber can take over the kingdom. She's aided by a blind squire named Garrett, who has a strange affinity with nature, and a two-headed dragon named Devon and Cornwall. Will they triumph over Ruber's evil henchmonsters?

One wishes that this 1998 Warner Bros. film were more of a doozy than a snoozy. There's little wrong with the film that a good story couldn't fix, but what story there is takes forever to establish. The animation—incorporating nice CGI work—is charming, the character designs pleasant, and the voice work is strong, with stars such as Eric Idle, Gary Oldman, Jane Seymour, Pierce Brosnan, and Sir John Gielgud chiming in. But the story is predictable and thin.

The songs are mostly gorgeous. One song, "The Prayer" (performed by both Celine Dion and Andrea Bocelli), was used in the 2002 Olympics, perhaps a first for an animated cartoon. There is an isolated music track for the whole film, which removes the lyrics from some songs during the closing credits. The disc is doublesided, with the second side loaded with extras. Included are scenes showing how the film was created and vocals recorded, plus CGI animation tests, histories of Warner's animation, and a wide selection of trailers.

SPECIAL FEATURES "Making of" Featurettes • Production Notes • CGI Tests • Trailer • Promotional Footage • Music Video • Other Title Trailers TECHNICAL FEATURES Widescreen (1.85:1) • Subtitles/CC: Eng., Fren. • Languages: Eng., Fren. dub • Sound: Dolby Digital Surround 5.1 • Snapcase • 1 Disc • Region 1 GENRE & RATING Music/Fantasy/History • Rated G

R

Rainbow Fish, The

These *Rainbow Fish* titles, from Sony, were not available for review: *The Rainbow Fish* (with the short "Dazzle the Dinosaur."); *Fintastic Fun in Neptune Bay; Tails from the Sea; The Three Fishkateers; Undersea Adventures* [3 disc set with bonus CD].

Rancou Choukyo: Orgy Training ☛ see

Mature/Adult Section

Ranma 1/2 The Movie: Big Trouble in Nekonron China [#1]

Viz/Pioneer, 1998, 74 mins., #V-RMD001. Directed by Shuji Iuchi. Screenplay by Shuji Iuchi, Shigeru Yanagawa, Ryota Yamaguchi. Based on the manga series by Rumiko Takahashi in *Shonen Sunday.*

A strange girl named Lychee shows up one day with her pet elephant Jasmine looking for revenge on Happosai, the lecherous old panty-stealing martial artist who long ago gave half of a legendary happiness-granting scroll to her great-grandmother. Generations later, Lychee has the scroll, but the prince promised to the scroll bearer still hasn't showed up. Sick of waiting, Lychee momentarily lets the scroll fall into the hands of Akane, Ranma's fiancée. Not surprisingly, Prince Kirin arrives just then to sweep the lucky holder of the scroll off her feet. Now Ranma and the gang must follow the prince to Nekonron, China, to save Akane and fulfill Lychee's destiny.

Ranma 1/2 features the adventures of Ranma Saotome and his father, Genma. After they're exposed to a magical pool, they are cursed to change shape whenever they get wet: Ranma becomes a girl, and Genma becomes a large panda! Ranma has to keep his sex changes a secret, which he does by posing as his own sister when he's a she. Wacky hijinks ensue. The long-running TV series began in 1989, and went for 161 episodes, two movies, and nine OVAs!

This disc contains the 1994 movie, yet another amusing trip through the wacky world of *Ranma 1/2.* There are plenty of hijinks to go around in this incarnation of the Ranma bunch. *Big Trouble* is a laid–back slapstick comedy adventure with enough action to keep things moving. The disc also features very handy character bios to help uninitiated viewers figure out who's who in the sometimes-complicated universe of *Ranma 1/2.*

Note that this DVD is available in two different case configurations, both numbered #V-RMD001. One is a CD jewel case that is held in a DVD-sized cardboard sleeve. The other case is a traditional keepcase. [BR]

SPECIAL FEATURES Character Bios • Character and Art Galleries • Synopsis • Deleted Scenes: Original Ending • Trailer TECHNICAL FEATURES Fullscreen (1.33:1) • Subtitles/CC: Eng. • Languages: Jap., Eng. dub • Sound: Dolby Digital 2.0 • Keepcase/Box with Jewel Case • 1 Disc • Region 1 GENRE & RATING Comedy/Fantasy/Martial Arts • Not Rated (Teens)

Ranma 1/2 The Movie 2: Nihao My Concubine [#2]

Viz/Pioneer, 1998, 60 mins., #V-RMD002. Directed by Shuji Iuchi. Screenplay by Shuji Iuchi, Shigeru Yanagawa, Ryota Yamaguchi. Based on the manga series by Rumiko Takahashi in *Shonen Sunday.*

It was just supposed to be a nice cruise on Kuno's yacht, but Ranma and the gang get shipwrecked on a tropical island instead. But, hey, things could be worse. At least they get to hang out on the beach all day. But before you can say P-chan, all the girls start disappearing. The remaining guys (and Cologne) decide to use girl-type Ranma as bait. It works, and the kidnapper turns out to be a young prince named Toma, who is collecting girls to compete in a series of silly contests—the winner becoming his bride. It also just so happens that Toma has magic water that will turn any creature into a man . . . forever. That's just what our cursed hero could use! So Ranma turns into his girl type and enters the contest. Will he forget to rescue Akane and the rest of the girls? Does he even care?

It's wacky mayhem on a tropical island in this 1992 theatrical outing. It's really more of the same goofy antics and silly action. The enhanced cleavage of the updated character designs and plethora of skimpy outfits will please fans of the female cast. There is some brief, bouncy nudity and of course the required nude panda scene as well. The violence is all done in a silly, carefree way. The bottom line is, if you like *Ranma*, you'll probably enjoy this film. [RJM]

SPECIAL FEATURES Character Bios • Character and Art Galleries • Trailer • "Love Battles" Map • Easter Eggs TECHNICAL FEATURES Fullscreen (1.33:1) • Subtitles/CC: Eng. • Languages: Jap., Eng. dub • Sound: Dolby Digital 2.0 • Keepcase • 1 Disc • Region 1 GENRE & RATING Comedy/Fantasy/Martial Arts • Not Rated (Teens)

Ranma 1/2: OAV Series [Box Set]

Viz/Pioneer, 2000, 375 mins., #D-RBS01. Directed by Junji Nishimura. Screenplay by Ryota Yamaguchi. Based on the manga series by Rumiko Takahashi in *Shonen Sunday*.

Ranma Saotome and the rest of the gang are back for all kinds of wacky adventures. But really, did you expect anything else from our gender-bending hero? These three DVDs have it all. You want demonic possession? You want a cook-off between Ranma and Akane? You want more Tendo sisters? You want a giant Phoenix stuck on Kuno's head? You got it. And if those stories don't sound strange enough, how about a doll that swaps bodies with Akane, making our tough heroine into a little wooden toy about 6 in. tall? It's all the crazy situations and martial arts action you expect from this series.

The real highlight of this 1990s OVA series is the high quality of the animation. All these episodes look great. As far as story goes, it's all typical *Ranma*. Most of the stories on these discs are pretty self-contained, and nothing is really resolved in terms of Ranma and Akane's relationship. This doesn't tie any loose ends or reveal any secrets. But you'll have a good time and get some chuckles out of this group of stories.

The set itself does include a whole bunch of *Ranma* music videos, most of which have clean opening and ending credits. All the violence in the series is silly martial arts action, but there is some brief-but-harmless nudity as well. And don't forget that every episode includes at least one scene with a nude panda.

Note that this DVD is available in two different case configurations, both numbered #D-RBS01. One is a clear plastic sleeve that opens at the top and bottom. The other case is a clear plastic box. [RJM]

SPECIAL FEATURES Text Interview with Creator • Character Bios • Character and Art Galleries • Trailer • Clean Credits TECHNICAL FEATURES Fullscreen (1.33:1) • Subtitles/CC: Eng. • Languages: Jap., Eng. dub • Sound: Dolby Digital 2.0 • Plastic Sleeve

with Foldout Case • 3 Discs • Region 1 GENRE & RATING Comedy/Fantasy/Martial Arts • Not Rated (Teens)

Ranma 1/2: Random Rhapsody—Who Do? Voodoo [#1]

Viz/Pioneer, 2001, 78 mins., #DRRR01. Directed by Junji Nishimura. Written by Trish Ledoux, Terry Klassen. Based on the manga series by Rumiko Takahashi in *Shonen Sunday*.

Kodachi gets the shock of her life when she learns a secret about the relationship she has with the principal, plus Kuno's worst nightmare is realized. Then, creepy, geeky, voodoo-practicing Hikaru Gosunkugi moves to town and gets a crush on Akane. Too bad for Ranma, who Gosunkugi thinks is standing in his way. But Ranma's biggest challenge to date comes when he must face a master of martial arts calligraphy, but Ranma's handwriting is awful!

This DVD contains the debut episodes of season six, #113–15.

SPECIAL FEATURES None TECHNICAL FEATURES Fullscreen (1.33:1) • Subtitles/CC: Eng. • Languages: Jap., Eng. dub • Sound: Dolby Digital 2.0 • Keepcase • 1 Disc • Region 1 GENRE & RATING Comedy/Fantasy/Martial Arts • Not Rated (Teens)

Ranma 1/2: Random Rhapsody—The Way We're Not [#2]

Viz/Pioneer, 2001, 78 mins., #DRRR02. Directed by Junji Nishimura. Written by Trish Ledoux, Terry Klassen. Based on the manga series by Rumiko Takahashi in *Shonen Sunday*.

Ranma and Akane are caught in a battle between the principal and a crazy old man who runs a secret store hidden deep within Furinkan High. Then, Ranma might be able to cure his curse on a secluded mountain, if he can trust the also-cursed Ryoga and Mousse. And family fights aren't much fun when Ranma and his father have a falling-out and Ranma is disowned. Ryoga becomes Genma's new disciple, but where does that leave Akane?

This DVD contains the season six episodes #116–18.

SPECIAL FEATURES None TECHNICAL FEATURES Fullscreen (1.33:1) • Subtitles/CC: Eng. • Languages: Jap., Eng. dub • Sound: Dolby Digital 2.0 • Keepcase • 1 Disc • Region 1 GENRE & RATING Comedy/Fantasy/Martial Arts • Not Rated (Teens)

Ranma 1/2: Random Rhapsody— Watermelon Beach [#3]

Viz/Pioneer, 2001, 78 mins., #DRRR03. Directed by Junji Nishimura. Written by Trish Ledoux, Terry Klassen. Based on the manga series by Rumiko Takahashi in *Shonen Sunday*.

Kasumi and Dr. Tofu go on a date and bring the family to an amusement park, leading to an escapade that includes arcade games, go-cart races, and an unwanted guest. Then, the girls of Furinkan High are being stalked by someone who's playing malicious pranks . . . and Ranma is the prime suspect! Next, the Tendo Dojo group takes a vacation to a local beach, but when Kuno washes up on shore wearing a watermelon on his head and suffering from amnesia, the mystery must be solved!

This DVD contains the season six episodes #119–21.

SPECIAL FEATURES None TECHNICAL FEATURES Fullscreen (1.33:1) • Subtitles/CC: Eng. • Languages: Jap., Eng. dub • Sound: Dolby Digital 2.0 • Keepcase • 1 Disc • Region 1 GENRE & RATING Comedy/Fantasy/Martial Arts • Not Rated (Teens)

Ranma 1/2: Random Rhapsody—The Demon from Jusenkyo [#4]

Viz/Pioneer, 2001, 78 mins., #DRRR04. Directed by Junji Nishimura. Written by Trish Ledoux, Terry Klassen. Based on the manga series by Rumiko Takahashi in *Shonen Sunday*.

Someone is stalking all the people who visited the cursed springs at Jusenkyo, Ranma comes under attack, and Akane is kidnapped. What does the winged monster Ranma faces have to do with a youth who wields pantyhose? Then, Sentaro shows up again, wanting Ranma and Akane's help to rescue his kidnapped grandmother.

This DVD contains the season six episodes #122–24.

SPECIAL FEATURES None TECHNICAL FEATURES Fullscreen (1.33:1) • Subtitles/CC: Eng. • Languages: Jap., Eng. dub • Sound: Dolby Digital 2.0 • Keepcase • 1 Disc • Region 1 GENRE & RATING Comedy/Fantasy/Martial Arts • Not Rated (Teens)

Ranma 1/2: Random Rhapsody—Wacky Winter Wonderland [#5]

Viz/Pioneer, 2001, 78 mins., #DRRR05. Directed by Junji Nishimura. Written by Trish Ledoux, Terry Klassen. Based on the manga series by Rumiko Takahashi in *Shonen Sunday*.

It's Christmas time, but where has Ranma gone? Will Akane and the others find him/her in time? Next, Ryoga is attacked outside the Tendo Dojo by a ferocious snow beast. What does the creature have to do with a little girl passed out in the snow? Later, Akane is injured during gym class and hospitalized, but Ranma and Akane are fighting and he can't figure out how to apologize.

This DVD contains the season six episodes #125–27.

SPECIAL FEATURES None TECHNICAL FEATURES Fullscreen (1.33:1) • Subtitles/CC: Eng. • Languages: Jap., Eng. dub • Sound: Dolby Digital 2.0 • Keepcase • 1 Disc • Region 1 GENRE & RATING Comedy/Fantasy/Martial Arts • Not Rated (Teens)

Ranma 1/2: Random Rhapsody— Pandamonium [#6]

Viz/Pioneer, 2001, 78 mins., #DRRR06. Directed by Junji Nishimura. Written by Trish Ledoux, Terry Klassen. Based on the manga series by Rumiko Takahashi in *Shonen Sunday*.

At an exhibit of cursed Chinese artwork, Ranma's fight with his father unleashes a trio of demons into the world. But as the others fight two of the demons, Ranma must contend with a girl demon— in the form of a childlike doodle of a panda who wants to date him! Then, Genma (in panda form) tumbles off a cliff and hits his head. When he awakens, he's in a feudal village in the past, where familiar faces worship him as the "Lucky Panda." And when Ranma and others go to a quaint seaside village, they must face a mysterious octopus pot and its cook.

This DVD contains the season six episodes #128–30.

SPECIAL FEATURES None TECHNICAL FEATURES Fullscreen (1.33:1) • Subtitles/CC: Eng. • Languages: Jap., Eng. dub • Sound: Dolby Digital 2.0 • Keepcase • 1 Disc • Region 1 GENRE & RATING Comedy/Fantasy/Martial Arts • Not Rated (Teens)

Ranma 1/2: Random Rhapsody—Ukyo's Secret Sauce [#7]

Viz/Pioneer, 2002, 78 mins., #DRRR07. Directed by Junji Nishimura. Written by Trish Ledoux, Terry Klassen. Based on the manga series by Rumiko Takahashi in *Shonen Sunday.*

Ukyo has kept her special okonomiyaki sauce aside for ten years to ferment, but somehow, Ranma has ruined it! Akane grows jealous, and soon Akane and Ranma have to pretend to be married. Later, after Akane reads lyrics to an old song aloud, the ghost of a teenage girl appears, leading Kuno to search for a hidden treasure that will free the girl's restless spirit.

This DVD contains the season six episodes #131–33.

SPECIAL FEATURES None TECHNICAL FEATURES Fullscreen (1.33:1) • Subtitles/CC: Eng. • Languages: Jap., Eng. dub • Sound: Dolby Digital 2.0 • Keepcase • 1 Disc • Region 1 GENRE & RATING Comedy/Fantasy/Martial Arts • Not Rated (Teens)

Ranma 1/2: Random Rhapsody—For the Love of Akane [#8]

Viz/Pioneer, 2002, 78 mins., #DRRR08. Directed by Junji Nishimura. Written by Trish Ledoux, Terry Klassen. Based on the manga series by Rumiko Takahashi in *Shonen Sunday.*

Gosunkugi gets a set of magic paper dolls that can force someone to follow their owner's bidding. Will he use them on Akane? Then, Ryoga meets a young boy named Satori who can read minds. What happens when Satori stalks Akane at the Tendo Dojo . . . and Ranma arrives? And finally, Happosai launches his plan to get Ranma to obey, but the magic backfires and the two of them are stuck together—literally—and nothing can pull them apart!

This DVD contains the final episodes of season six, #134–36.

SPECIAL FEATURES None TECHNICAL FEATURES Fullscreen (1.33:1) • Subtitles/CC: Eng. • Languages: Jap., Eng. dub • Sound: Dolby Digital 2.0 • Keepcase • 1 Disc • Region 1 GENRE & RATING Comedy/Fantasy/Martial Arts • Not Rated (Teens)

Ranma 1/2: The Digital Dojo [TV Anime Season One Box Set]

Viz/Pioneer, 2001, 450 mins., #DRTV1BS. Directed by Tsutomu Shibayama. Screenplay by Yoshio Urasawa. Based on the manga series by Rumiko Takahashi in *Shonen Sunday.*

Genma Saotome has made a decision. He will take his son Ranma to visit his old and dear friend Son Tendo. The purpose of the journey is for Ranma to choose a wife from among Tendo's three daughters, Kasumi, Nabiki, and Akane. Not relishing the idea of an arranged marriage, the girls are relieved to see Ranma is a girl, but their relief is short lived when they learn that a little water can change that. In order to move things along, the fathers decide that Ranma will marry the youngest girl, the fiery Akane. Both Ranma and Akane couldn't be more unhappy, but while at each others' throats, they may just learn to love to hate each other.

Ranma 1/2: The Digital Dojo is a four-DVD set containing episodes #1–18 that make up the first season of the popular television series, which first aired in Japan in 1993. From its gender-changing premise to its energetic execution, *Ranma 1/2* is a romantic comedy that is pleasant, amusing, and full of unusual and interesting characters.

Ranma 1/2 frequently has scenes with frontal female nudity and the type of adult situations you'd expect when someone changes gender at the drop of a hat (or a drop of water). Though not exactly cutting-edge animation, the work certainly gets the job done. The picture clarity on the disc is good, though nothing exceptional, while the soundtrack is bouncy and catchy. Overall, it is the humorous stories and situations that make *Ranma 1/2* such an entertaining series. [GP]

SPECIAL FEATURES Clean Credits TECHNICAL FEATURES Fullscreen (1.33:1) • Subtitles/CC: Eng. • Languages: Jap., Eng. dub • Sound: Dolby Digital 2.0 • Cardboard Box with 4 Keepcases • 4 Discs • Region 1 GENRE & RATING Comedy/Fantasy/Martial Arts • Not Rated (Teens)

Ranma 1/2: Anything Goes Martial Arts [TV Anime Season Two Box Set]

Viz/Pioneer, 2002, 550 mins., #DRTV2BS. Directed by Koji Sawai. Screenplay by Toshiki Inoue, Hiroshi Toda, Yoshiyuki Suga, Hisashi Tokimura, Kazuhito Hisajima, Aya Matsui, Hiroyuki Kawasaki, Hiroko Naka. Based on the manga series by Rumiko Takahashi in *Shonen Sunday.*

NOTE: This DVD set arrived too late for a full review. The following text is promotional copy provided by the releasing company:

"This box set contains the entire twenty-two-episode second season, and continues to develop the on-going storylines of Ranma Saotome and Akane Tendo, their families, and introduces even more of the series' zany cast of characters. Get to know the infamous Golden Pair of the high school combat figure skating world; Mikado 'Emperor' Sanzenin; Azusa Shiratori, the girl who gives anything 'cute' a bad name (before taking it home); Sasuke, loyal ninja manservant to high school swordsman Tatewaki 'Blue Thunder' Kuno; Cologne, the hundreds-of-years-old leader of the same Chinese Amazon tribe that introduced the sassy Shampoo; Mousse, the near-sighted master of hidden weapons and all things avian; Happosai, panty stealing master of both Ranma and Akane's fathers; plus a host of others."

SPECIAL FEATURES (disc 5) Voice Actor Bios • Character and Art Galleries • Clean Credits • Other Title Trailers TECHNICAL FEATURES Fullscreen (1.33:1) • Subtitles/CC: Eng. • Languages: Jap., Eng. dub • Sound: Dolby Digital • Cardboard Box with 5 Keepcases • 5 Discs • Region 1 GENRE & RATING Comedy/Fantasy/Martial Arts • Not Rated (Teens)

Ranma 1/2: Hard Battle [TV Anime Season Three Box Set]

Viz, 2002, 600 mins., #DRTV3BS. Directed by Koji Sawai. Screenplay by Michiko Yokote, Shigeru Hosokawa, Yoshiyuki Suga, Kazuhito Hisajima, Hiroko Naka. Based on the manga series by Rumiko Takahashi in *Shonen Sunday*.

NOTE: This DVD set arrived too late for a full review. The following text is promotional copy provided by the releasing company:

"This box set contains the entire twenty-four-episode third season of *Ranma 1/2*. Ranma comes face to face with some of his greatest adversaries yet. There's Ukyo, a friend from his childhood who bears a mysterious grudge; Tsubasa, the incredibly persistent suitor who comes chasing after Ukyo (and Ranma . . . and Akane); a secret Jusenkyo society that punishes transgressors to the 'rules' of the magical springs; a pair of Amazon 'sisters' who pack a mean punch; plus magic soap, magic mirrors, and more!"

SPECIAL FEATURES (disc 5) Voice Actor Bios • Character and Art Galleries • Clean Credits • Other Title Trailers TECHNICAL FEATURES Fullscreen (1.33:1) • Subtitles/CC: Eng. • Languages: Jap., Eng. dub • Sound: Dolby Digital • Cardboard Box with 5 Keepcases • 5 Discs • Region 1 GENRE & RATING Comedy/Fantasy/Martial Arts • Not Rated (Teens)

Ranma 1/2 Ranma Forever: Initiation Nite [#1]

VIZ/Pioneer, 2002, 78 mins., #DRRF01. Directed by Junji Nishimura. Screenplay by Kazuhito Hisajima, Shigeru Hosokawa, Michiko Yokote, Hiroko Naka, Naoto Kimura, Yoshiyuki Suga, Ryota Yamaguchi. Based on the manga series by Rumiko Takahashi in *Shonen Sunday*.

NOTE: This DVD arrived too late for a full review. The following text is promotional copy provided by the releasing company:

"With the first three episodes of the final season, follow Ranma into a mixed bag of nuts and another season of hilarious mishaps! In 'Tatewaki Kuno, Acting Principal,' the principal is off on an inspection tour, and he's put his seventeen-year-old son, Tatewaki Kuno, in charge. As they say, the coco-nutcase never falls far from the tree. In 'Howling at the Moon,' Ranma is told the Tendo Dojo will lose its successor if he doesn't win, so Ranma trains hard for an upcoming contest. But 'kick-the-can' may be just another way to say 'kick-the-Ranma!' It's really just thuggery, Tendo Dojo–style. Then, in 'Nihao! It's the Jusenkyo Guide,' he claims he's just on a sightseeing tour, but surely the Jusenkyo Guide hasn't come all the way from China just for that. Could his surprise visit have something to do with Ranma and Genma's mishap at Jusenkyo Spring?"

SPECIAL FEATURES None TECHNICAL FEATURES Fullscreen (1.33:1) • Subtitles/CC: Eng. • Languages: Jap., Eng. dub • Sound: Dolby Digital • Keepcase • 1 Disc • Region 1 GENRE & RATING Comedy/Fantasy/Martial Arts • Not Rated (Teens)

Ranma 1/2 Ranma Forever: From the Depths of Despair [#2]

VIZ/Pioneer, 2002, 78 mins., #DRRF02. Directed by Junji Nishimura. Screenplay by Kazuhito Hisajima, Shigeru Hosokawa, Michiko Yokote, Hiroko Naka, Naoto Kimura, Yoshiyuki Suga, Ryota Yamaguchi. Based on the manga series by Rumiko Takahashi in *Shonen Sunday*.

NOTE: This DVD arrived too late for a full review. The following text is promotional copy provided by the releasing company:

"It's the second trio of episodes from the final season. In 'Pick-a-Peck o' Happosai,' a pack of magical, powerful cards has fallen into the wrong hands, and now Happosai is even more of a pain than before! It was bad enough when there was just the one of him—now there are six! Then, in 'From the Depths of Despair, Part I,' Ryoga's new move has got Ranma on the run. The construction-specific 'Breaking Point' technique was bad enough, and that only worked on rocks! Can Ranma get away fast enough? And finally, in 'From the Depths of Despair, Part II,' to perfect the dangerous 'Shishi Hoko-Dan' technique, Ryoga must travel to the depths of despair . . . where he lives most of the time anyway. But why is Ranma trying to make Ryoga even more miserable?"

SPECIAL FEATURES None TECHNICAL FEATURES Fullscreen (1.33:1) • Subtitles/CC: Eng. • Languages: Jap., Eng. dub • Sound: Dolby Digital • Keepcase • 1 Disc • Region 1 GENRE & RATING Comedy/Fantasy/Martial Arts • Not Rated (Teens)

Real Bout High School: Enter the Samurai Girl [#1]

TokyoPop, 2002, 100 mins., #TPDV-1372. Directed by Shinichi Tokairin. Script by Aya Matsui, Yukio Mishina. Based on the manga series by Reiji Saiga, Sora Inoue in *Dragon Magazine*.

Ryoko Mitsurugi is more than just your run-of-the-mill pretty high school girl. She's a brutal, top-of-the-line street fighter with an attitude. At other schools this might be a problem, but at Real Bout High School, home of the K-Fighting system, Ryoko is not only a celebrity but the school's champion K-Fighter. The K-Fighting system was designed to allow students to resolve their differences through personal combat, and at this school Ryoko is the best of the best. Things take an unexpected turn, however, when, in the midst of a K-Fight, Ryoko is transported to an alternate dimension to fight evil on behalf of the whole planet.

Real Bout High School debuted on Japanese television in 2001. What the series lacks—character and plot development is slow—it more than makes up for in action. A host of characters in all different shapes, sizes, and fighting styles are all looking to take down the story's heroine. As episodes #1–4 progress on this debut DVD, Ryoko not only struggles with her fellow students but also with the turmoil of simply being a teenager.

Real Bout High School's strongest suit comes in its animation and character designs. Extremely well-animated with smooth-flowing action and sweeping camera angles, the look is top-notch. The character designs are highly detailed with bold colors. *Real Bout* also sports a plateful of cheesecake in the form of plentiful panty shots, but no real nudity. There are also a host of extras to please the fans. [GP]

SPECIAL FEATURES Trailers • Promotional Footage • Outtakes • Other Title Trailers • Inserts: Liner Notes TECHNICAL FEATURES Fullscreen (1.33:1) • Subtitles/CC: Eng. • Languages: Jap., Eng. dub • Sound: Dolby Digital 2.0 • Keepcase • 1 Disc • Region 1 GENRE & RATING Martial Arts/Action/Fantasy • Rated 13+

Real Bout High School: Netherworld Battle [#2]

Tokyopop, 2002, 75 mins., #TPDV-1382. Directed by Shinichi Tokairin. Script by Hideki Mitsui, Aya Matsui, Yukio Mishina. Based on the manga series by Reiji Saiga and Sora Inoue in *Dragon Magazine*.

NOTE: This DVD arrived too late for a full review. The following text is promotional copy provided by the releasing company:

"Ryoko, the modern-day samurai girl and #1 fighter of Daimon High, must now take on her widest range of adversaries yet: from magical waitresses to a dominant trio of new enemies—Akitaka, Nanase, and Setsura. Add the mysterious dimension of Solvania, and even a K-Fight cooking contest, and things are about to get real interesting for this samurai girl."

This disc contains episodes #5–7.

SPECIAL FEATURES "Making of" Featurettes • Interview with Voice Actress • Character and Art Galleries • Outtakes • Clean Credits • Other Title Trailers • Inserts: Liner Notes TECHNICAL FEATURES Fullscreen (1.33:1) • Subtitles/CC: Eng. • Languages: Jap., Eng. dub • Sound: Dolby Digital • Keepcase • 1 Disc • Region 1 GENRE & RATING Martial Arts/Action/Fantasy • Rated 13+

Real Bout High School: Strange Journeys [#3]

Tokyopop, 2002, 75 mins., #TPDV-1422. Directed by Shinichi Tokairin. Script by Aya Matsui, Yukio Mishina. Based on the manga series by Reiji Saiga and Sora Inoue in *Dragon Magazine*.

NOTE: This DVD arrived too late for a full review. The following text is promotional copy provided by the releasing company:

"For the Samurai Girl, Ryoko, things are never easy. Even when on summer vacation at the beach, she runs across a haunted island, and a trio of vicious enemies return. From there, things get even more 'dramatic' with the return of Oyster Lulu, her worst nightmare. Finally, things seem to ease up for the weary warrior, only for her to realize that a new battle begins . . . only this time, it's a battle of the heart."

This disc contains episodes #8–10.

SPECIAL FEATURES "Making of" Featurettes • Interview with Voice Actress • Character and Art Galleries • Outtakes • Clean Credits • Other Title Trailers • Inserts: Liner Notes TECHNICAL FEATURES Fullscreen (1.33:1) • Subtitles/CC: Eng. • Languages: Jap., Eng. dub • Sound: Dolby Digital • Keepcase • 1 Disc • Region 1 GENRE & RATING Martial Arts/Action/Fantasy • Rated 13+

ReBoot: To Mend and Defend [#1]

ADV Films, 2000, 90 mins., #DVDRB/001. Directed by Steve Ball, J. Falconer, James Boshier, Michaela Zabranska, Mark Schiemann. Written by Marv Wolfman, Len Wein, Dan DiDio, Ian Pearson. Story by Gavin Blair, Ian Pearson, Phil Mitchell, Michael Skorey.

Ever wonder why your personal computer has errors or glitches or any other of the problems users are plagued with? Check with the residents of Mainframe City for answers in the intriguing computer-generated series, *ReBoot*. The series includes a likable cast of good guys—Enzo and Dot, Matrix, Frisket, AndrAIa, Phong, and the Binomes, to name a few—versus bad guys Megabyte, Hack, Slash, Hexadecimal, and Scuzzy. Megabyte is a dastardly computer virus trying to take over Mainframe City and use it for his own nefarious ends. The guardian hero is Enzo, a former protégé of Bob, the original protector of Mainframe City, who is now trapped in cyberspace. It's Enzo's duty to protect his friends, fix problems within Mainframe, and stop any viruses, including Megabyte and his warping game cubes. The game cubes trap residents and reboot them as characters in a variety of wild video games. There they remain trapped until rescued by a guardian. Enzo must save the residents and restore order, but as a fledgling guardian, does he have the confidence and means to pull it off?

Created in 1994 by Mainframe Entertainment, *ReBoot* lasted for four seasons on television, and was the first 100% computer-generated television series. ABC aired it beginning in 1996 as part of its Saturday morning lineup and in 1999 the series began airing on the Cartoon Network.

This data-filled DVD contains the first four episodes of season three: #24–27. To indoctrinate viewers unfamiliar with *ReBoot*, ADV included final scenes from the second season and a brief summary of seasons one and two to get viewers up to speed. Other cool extras will also please fans. [JMC]

SPECIAL FEATURES Character and Art Galleries • Animation Tests • Season Overviews • Game Guide • Other Title Trailers • Inserts: Character Bios TECHNICAL FEATURES Fullscreen (1.33:1) • Languages: Eng. • Sound: Dolby Digital Surround 2.0 • Keepcase • 1 Disc • Region 1 GENRE & RATING CGI/Science Fiction/Action • Rated (All Ages)

ReBoot: The Net [#2]

ADV Films, 2001, 90 mins., #DVDRB/002. Directed by Ezekiel Norton, Owen Hurley, Steve Bell, James Boshier, J. Falconer. Written by Christy Marx, D. C. Fontana, Dan DiDio, Adria Budd. Story by Gavin Blair, Ian Pearson, Phil Mitchell, Michael Skorey.

Our heroes are pitted against a variety of computer baddies in this action-packed collection filled with pop culture references to movies and TV shows such as *Star Trek, The Prisoner, Six Million Dollar Man,* and *Star Wars,* to name a few. Enzo and AndrAIa go through four games in an attempt to find Bob and get back home. Each time they help the local residents fight against oppression, learn how to get along, and overcome almost any obstacle. They prove themselves to be true heroes, and even when faced with villainous duplicates of themselves, they're able to persevere.

This second collection of season three—containing episodes #28–31—introduces elements such as the daemon virus, which is an integral part of season four. [JMC]

SPECIAL FEATURES Character Bios • Character and Art Galleries • Animation Tests • Game Guide • Other Title Trailers • Inserts: Character Bios TECHNICAL FEATURES Fullscreen (1.33:1) • Languages: Eng. • Sound: Dolby Digital Surround 2.0 • Keepcase • 1 Disc • Region 1 GENRE & RATING CGI/Science Fiction/Action • Rated (All Ages)

ReBoot: The Web [#3]

ADV Films, 2001, 90 mins., #DVDRB/003. Directed by Michael Ferraro, Ezekiel Norton, Andrew Duncan, J. Falconer, Owen Hurley. Written by Christy Marx, Len Wein, Marv Wolfman. Story by Gavin Blair, Ian Pearson, Phil Mitchell, Michael Skorey, Christy Marx, Dan DiDio, Phil Mitchell, Len Wein, Marv Wolfman.

Enzo and AndrAIa hook up with some software pirates. In exchange for the pirates' freedom, their captain, Capacitor, offers to help them find and rescue Bob. They set off with the crew of the *Saucy Mare* to surf the World Wide Wilderness in hopes of finding their friend. But when a creature attacks and injures the *Saucy Mare,* the duo is sidetracked in an attempt to heal the ship. And just when things can't get any worse, a group of demented sprites attacks! Can our heroes fight off all their enemies, or is time running out?

This exciting edition features episodes #32–35. In it, our heroes move one step closer to finding Bob. [JMC]

SPECIAL FEATURES Character and Art Galleries • Animation Tests • Other Title Trailers • Inserts: Character Bios TECHNICAL FEA-

TURES Fullscreen (1.33:1) • Languages: Eng. • Sound: Dolby Digital Surround 2.0 • Keepcase • 1 Disc • Region 1 GENRE & RATING CGI/Science Fiction/Action • Rated (All Ages)

ReBoot: The Viral Wars [#4]

ADV Films, 2001, 90 mins., #DVDRB/004. Directed by Stephen Cooper, Steve Ball, Mark Schiemann, Andrew Duncan. Written by Katherine Lawrence, Len Wein, Marv Wolfman, Ken Pontac. Story by Gavin Blair, Ian Pearson, Phil Mitchell, Michael Skorey, Katherine Lawrence, Len Wein, Marv Wolfman.

The group finally comes home, but it isn't quite what they remember it to be; evil forces running rampant have all but destroyed Mainframe. Enzo, Bob, and AndrAIa are shocked to see how much devastation Megabyte and his wicked followers have caused. Now the group must go to war with Megabyte, but with so much loss and damage, even the winners might ultimately be losers.

This powerful conclusion to season three is one not to be missed. Filled with action, heartache, and tough decisions, the final episodes #36–39 are some of the most memorable of this computer-generated series. [JMC]

SPECIAL FEATURES Character and Art Galleries • Promotional Footage • Other Title Trailers • Inserts: Character Bios TECHNICAL FEATURES Fullscreen (1.33:1) • Languages: Eng. • Sound: Dolby Digital Surround 2.0 • Keepcase • 1 Disc • Region 1 GENRE & RATING CGI/Science Fiction/Action • Rated (All Ages)

Recess Christmas: Miracle on Third Street

Disney, 2001, 65 mins., #22951. Directed by Howy Parkins. Written by Paul Germain, Joe Ansolabehere.

The fourth-graders of Third Street Elementary may be troublemakers sometimes, but they won't ruin Principal Prickly's holiday . . . will they? Driving in the cold snow, Prickly and his two faculty passengers, Miss Finster and Miss Grotke, recount tales of naughtiness and niceness about T.J. and his friends. Whether it's T.J. as "Principal for the Day," the Thanksgiving canned food drive, or a nightmarish baby-sitting eve, the kids are unpredictable. But what will happen at the big Christmas pageant?

This direct-to-video feature was released for the holiday season in 2001, capitalizing on the theatrical and video/DVD success of *Recess: School's Out*. Like episodes of the series, it contains charm and humor that will appeal to adults and children alike, as well as some corny singing from Robert Goulet and a *Recess* rendition of Jingle Bells. The DVD also has a fun trio of slideshows—

on Mistletoe, Santa and the Chimney, and Christmas Lights—presented by three of the kids.

SPECIAL FEATURES Slide Shows • Other Title Trailers TECHNICAL FEATURES Fullscreen (1.33:1) • Subtitles/CC: Eng. • Languages: Eng. • Sound: Dolby Digital Surround 5.1, DTS • Keepcase • 1 Disc • Region 1 GENRE & RATING Holiday/Comedy/Adventure • Not Rated (All Ages)

Recess: School's Out

Disney, 2001, 84 mins., #21945. Directed by Chuck Sheetz. Screenplay by Jonathan Greenburg. Story by Joe Ansolabehere, Paul Germain, Jonathan Greenburg.

Third Street Elementary's finally out for summer vacation, and all the kids are looking forward to months of fun. But T.J. Detweiler's plans are spoiled when all the kids get to go to summer camp but him. Boredom comes to an end when T.J. sees a weird green light coming from the school. No one believes him but Principal Prickly, but he's disintegrated when he tries to investigate. Now T.J. must gather his friends from camp and face the laser-wielding, ninja-fighting, possibly alien terrors that have invaded their school in a plot to create a permanent winter!

Disney's *Recess* debuted on television in 1997 and quickly became a staple of both ABC's Saturday mornings and UPN and cable's daily lineups. The adventures of the fourth-grade classmates are humorous enough for both kids and adults; grown audiences will be reminded of some of the trials and tribulations they went through in their youth as well. This 2001 film is the first feature for the cast, and it has some more complex animation and subtle CGI work in it.

The DVD has a wide variety of cool extra features on it, including a trippy music video by Robert Goulet and a digital comic book. Since no one throws dodgeballs at you or pushes you off the swings, this *Recess* is much more fun for all ages than the real recess ever was!

SPECIAL FEATURES "Making of" Featurette • Creator Fun Facts • Digital Comic Book • Trailer • Music Videos • Game • DVD-ROM Features • Other Title Trailers TECHNICAL FEATURES Widescreen (1.66:1 enhanced for 16x9) • Subtitles/CC: Eng. • Languages: Eng., Span. dub • Sound: Dolby Digital Surround 5.1 • Keepcase • 1 Disc • Region 1 GENRE & RATING Comedy/Adventure • Rated G

Record of Lodoss War

Image, 1998, 290 mins., #ID4411CTDVD.

This two-disc DVD set was not available for review. It is out of print.

Record of Lodoss War: Chronicles of Heroic Knight DVD Collection [Box Set]

U.S. Manga Corps, 2000, 620 mins., #USMD 2008. Directed by Yoshihiro Takamoto. Script by Katsumi Hasegawa.

To the south of the continent of Alecrast lies a land people call Lodoss, the accursed island.... So says the legend at the beginning of each episode. Five years ago, six heroes saved the land, but now a familiar evil has reared its head again, and Lodoss will need defending once more. Mercenaries mix with elves, mages with mundanes, and for a new group of adventurers the battles against the Black Knight, dark sorcerers, mad goddesses, and fire-filled demon dragons, may be their last.

Chronicles of Heroic Knight is the final television series in the *Record of Lodoss War* chronicles, begun in 1990 (collected on Image's out of print disc) after its beginnings as a serialized role-playing game in 1986. *Chronicles*, released in 1998, was set five years after the original series, and featured most of the main characters, as well as beefed-up roles for secondary characters. The animation is stylistically excellent for this type of series, neither pushing the boundaries nor seeming low-budget. The character designs and settings are a cross between medieval, feudal, and fantasy, meaning lots of capes and big shoulders.

Those who hate super-deformed material will want to stay away from the pre-credit endings of most episodes; those who like it will want to skip directly there (with only two chapter stops per episode, that's not difficult). The box set contains all twenty-seven television episodes on four discs, which are only available in the box set, not separately. Although there is a wealth of DVD-ROM material on disc A, the actual DVD supplemental material is woefully small. *Record of Lodoss War: Chronicles of Heroic Knight* will be popular with fantasy lovers and role-playing gamers, but it's unlikely to convert many new fans.

See also the tie-in project, *Legend of Crystania*.

SPECIAL FEATURES Character and Art Galleries • Comics • DVD-ROM Features: Art, Scripts, Reviews, Comics, Information Guide • Other Title Trailers • Inserts: Liner Note Booklet TECHNICAL FEATURES Fullscreen (1.33:1) • Subtitles/CC: Eng. • Languages: Jap., Eng. dub • Sound: Dolby Digital 2.0 • Box with 4 Keepcases • 4 Discs • Region All GENRE & RATING Fantasy/Action • Not Rated (Teens)

Record of Lodoss War DVD Collection

U.S. Manga Corps, 2002, 355 mins., #USMD2184. Directed by Akinori Nagao-ka, Shigeto Makino, Katsuhisa Yamada, Taiji Ryu, Kazunori Mizuno, Akio Sakai, Hiroshi Kawasaki. Screenplay by Mami Watanabe, Kenichi Kanemaki.

NOTE: This DVD set arrived too late for a full review. The following text is promotional copy provided by the releasing company:

"Newly remastered and repackaged with new features! Lodoss, the accursed island, has long been a haven for monsters and witchcraft. Now, as the old kingdoms topple, ravaged by war, a dark wizard seeks to wake an ancient evil. To vanquish this threat, fate draws a party of six heroes: Warrior, Elf, Wizard, Dwarf, Cleric, and Thief. Together, they will encounter untold dangers and wonders beyond imagination. Join the quest. The battle for Lodoss has begun!"

These discs contains episodes #1-13.

SPECIAL FEATURES Convention Featurette • Character Bios • Character and Art Galleries • Manga-to-Film Comparison • Promotional Footage • Spell Casting Scenes • DVD-ROM Features: Art, Scripts, Manga • Other Title Trailers • Inserts: Booklet TECHNICAL FEATURES Fullscreen (1.33:1) • Subtitles/CC: Eng. • Languages: Jap., Eng. dub • Sound: Dolby Digital 2.0 • Cardboard Sleeve with Fold-Out Case • 2 Discs • Region All GENRE & RATING Fantasy/Action • Rated 13+

Red Hawk: Weapon of Death

Manga Entertainment, 2002, 90 mins., #MANGA4114-2. Supervising Direction by Jung Yul Hwang. Written by Ju Wan So, Sang Wol Ji. Based on the comic book series *Red Hawk*.

The land of Chungwon is under siege by a gang of marauders known as the Camelia Blossoms. Although all of its members are deadly, a sub-group known as "Five Dragons" is taught secret and very lethal—martial arts moves. Two brothers—Danlyong and Muklyong—decide to break away from the Dragons and the Blossoms, but the group won't let them leave unscathed. Although Danlyong gets away, the gang takes over the mind and body of Muklyong and turns him into the ultimate weapon. Three years later, a young girl goes out to find a legendary fighter, a man who hates the outlaws that prey on people, a man who is rumored to be able to fly like the bird of prey that often accompanies him, a man whose own brother now fights for evil. But will Danlyong, the Red Hawk, be able to defeat and ultimately kill his own sibling?

Red Hawk is a feature-length project from 1995, based

on a popular Korean comic book series of the same name. The animation is nice in spots, pedestrian in others. The designs for *Red Hawk* are excellent, especially the lead character's mask, which can't help but remind savvy comic book readers of a similar mask on Hawkman.

The DVD contains only a small number of extras, but the film is letterboxed. Those looking for something different in their martial arts action fare won't find too much original in this story, but they'll at least find the familiar elements done well.

SPECIAL FEATURES Character Bios • Character and Art Galleries • Trailer • Other Title Trailers TECHNICAL FEATURES Widescreen (1.66:1) • Subtitles/CC: Eng. • Languages: Eng. dub • Sound: Dolby Digital Surround 5.1 • Keepcase • 1 Disc • Region 1 GENRE & RATING Martial Arts/Action • Not Rated (Teens)

Rembrandt Films' Greatest Hits

Image, 2000, 59 mins., #ID9000AASDVD.

This collection of short films by Prague's Rembrandt Studios features twelve cartoons including one Oscar winner and multiple nominees. The winner is "Munro," a story about a four-year-old drafted into the Army, written by famed cartoonist Jules Feiffer. Two entries in the "Self-Help Series" are nominees, including "Self Defense for Cowards" and "How to Avoid Friendship," while two others in this section are just fun: "How to Win on the Thruway" and "How to Live with a Neurotic Dog."

"Anatole" adapts the beloved children's book by Eve Titus, while the pilot shorts "Terr'ble Tessie!" and "Big Sam and Punky" will have viewers chuckling. Rembrandt's signature character is Nudnik, star of a world-syndicated television series, *The Nudnik Show*. Three Nudnik shorts are presented, including one Oscar nominee. Finally, "The Frozen Logger" is a love story between a waitress and the titular woodsman.

The disc features no extras, but the selection of cartoons is top-notch and fun. Unfortunately, the transfer is not great, with washed-out colors on some shorts, video glitches, and other problems. Art styles vary widely.

SPECIAL FEATURES None TECHNICAL FEATURES Fullscreen (1.33:1) • Languages: Eng. • Sound: Dolby Digital 1.0 • Snapcase • 1 Disc • Region 1 GENRE & RATING Anthology/Comedy • Not Rated (Kids)

Rescuers Down Under, The [Gold Collection]

Disney, 2000, 77 mins., #18667. Directed by Hendel Butoy, Mike Gabriel. Screenplay by Jim Cox, Karey Kirkpatrick, Byron Simpson, Joe Ranft. Based on characters in books by Margery Sharp.

Bernard and Bianca, the mice adventurers from the Rescue Aid Society are back, with new friend Wilbur the albatross (brother to Orville). This time, a boy named Cody befriends a magnificent golden eagle in the Australian Outback. When a poacher sets his sights on the bird, Cody's call for help is answered by Bernard, Bianca, and Wilbur. Lots of adventure, breathtaking escapes, and harrowing rescues ensue.

Released in 1990, *The Rescuers Down Under* was a sequel to the 1977 hit, *The Rescuers* (making it Disney's first animated feature sequel). Disney's twenty-ninth feature-length animated film did respectably at the box office—bringing in $27 million—but was not a big enough hit to generate further sequels or a TV spin-off. The animation is solid, especially Glen Keane's work on the golden eagle. There is some early CGI animation in the film as well, and the project was the first in which Disney did not use any clear acetate cels for the animation, moving the "ink and paint" process fully onto computers. The voice cast includes Bob Newhart, Eva Gabor, John Candy, and George C. Scott.

The DVD has a few extras, and a nice transfer.

SPECIAL FEATURES Trailer • Storybook • Game • Other Title Trailers • Inserts: Booklet TECHNICAL FEATURES Widescreen (1.66:1 enhanced for 16x9) • Subtitles/CC: Eng. • Languages: Eng., Fren. dub, Span. dub • Sound: Dolby Digital Surround 4.0 • Keepcase • 1 Disc • Region 1, 4 GENRE & RATING Animals/Adventure • Rated G

Return of the King, The

Warner, 2001, 97 mins., #576. Directed by Arthur Rankin, Jr., Jules Bass. Screenplay by Romeo Muller. Based on the novels *The Hobbit* and *The Return of the King* by J.R.R. Tolkien.

Frodo Baggins and his friend Samwise have undertaken a mission to return the evil Ring to Mordor, where it will be destroyed in the raging fires of Mount Doom. If the two hobbits don't succeed in their mission, all of Middle Earth may fall under the reign of evil. But danger bars their path, from the slithering Gollum to orcs and more. And then there's the matter of the Ring itself, which may possess Frodo and drive him mad before he can finish his journey....

In 1980, Rankin-Bass produced this ABC television

follow-up to their 1977 *Hobbit* project. The same art styles and some of the same designs were used for this version—which took nothing from Ralph Bakshi's *Lord of the Rings* project—and even some of the same voice actors returned. Here, Orson Bean voiced Frodo instead of Bilbo Baggins, but Gandalf the Grey was once again played by John Huston, and one-named Theodore returned to give Gollum his gravelly tones.

Some Tolkien fans will be comforted to note that unlike *The Hobbit*, this is not a musical, but others will complain that too much of the book has been left out of the script. The DVD contains a nice transfer of the film, and a few minor historical extras.

This disc was also included as part of a 2001 three-pack set, its keepcase packaged with *The Hobbit* and *Lord of the Rings*.

SPECIAL FEATURES Tolkien Bio • Director Filmography TECHNICAL FEATURES Fullscreen (1.33:1) • Subtitles/CC: Eng. • Languages: Eng., Fren. dub, Span. dub • Sound: Dolby Digital 1.0) • Snapcase • 1 Disc • Region 1 GENRE & RATING Fantasy/Adventure • Not Rated (Kids)

Return to Treasure Island, The

Liberty International, 2001, 72 mins., #LIP 0116. Directed by Victor Andrianko. Screenplay by Julie Aiken, Ronald Schmidt. Based on the novel by Robert Louis Stevenson.

Drawn into a world of pirates, buried treasure, and more, young Jim Hawkins finds himself sailing the seas aboard the *Hispaniola* with an odd collection of sailors and treasure hunters. But the crew of the ship is full of pirates, and they take over the vessel, led by the one-legged scoundrel cook, Long John Silver. Jim manages to escape to the island, where he is helped by castaway Jim Gunn. Can they find the treasure, rescue his friends, and stop the pirates?

Robert Louis Stevenson's classic tale has been told a few times in animated form on television before, but this semi-comic version is a 1992 Ukrainian production. The art is overly stylized, with large potato-noses on nearly everyone, and bright, gaudy colors. The voice work is annoying. The DVD contains one of the worst transfers I've seen yet, with ghost images, artifacts, stutters, and more. It's only worth a look if you like the classic story, or want to see one of the few Ukrainian-animated properties on the market.

SPECIAL FEATURES Treasure Map: Scene Jump TECHNICAL FEATURES Fullscreen (1.33:1) • Languages: Eng. dub • Sound: Dolby Digital 2.0, Dolby Digital 5.1 • Keepcase • 1 Disc • Region 1–6 GENRE & RATING Historical/Adventure/Pirates • Not Rated (Kids)

Revolutionary Girl Utena: The Movie

Software Sculptors, 2001, 87 mins., #SSDVD-6182. Directed by Kunihiko Ikuhara. Screenplay by Yoji Enokido. Based on the manga series by Chiho Saito in *Ciao*.

Utena Tenjo is a student at Otori School, an exclusive private academy where she hopes to escape her troubled past. Fascinated and strangely attracted to the school's large group of fencing competitors, Utena senses something different about some of her classmates. Wandering the school's lavish gardens one day, she spies a white rose among a sea of red. When Utena bends to pick the bud, however, the blossom becomes a ring that grants her entrance to a furtive group of duelists who battle for possession of Anthy Himemiya, a beautiful, delicate young woman also known as the Rose Bride. Perhaps detecting a shared repudiation of the tribulations faced by adolescent girls, Utena befriends Anthy and fights valiantly to defend her from an eager and skilled crop of duelists seeking sexual conquest, power, and escape from their ordinary lives. In a sea of allegorical images and free-flowing storytelling, Utena and Anthy make a climactic attempt to escape the world of Otori after Utena undergoes a perplexing transformation.

Revolutionary Girl Utena: The Movie is a fanciful, airy fable, animated in rich colors and flowing movements. Elaborate symbolism, deeply layered visuals, and multi-faceted character relationships carry this sometimes sexually charged, often baffling film through director Kunihiko Ikuhara's majestic world. The 1999 film was supposed to be the finale to the story following the television series.

This disc contains a director's commentary, which is comforting when you can't figure out what's going on. [BR]

SPECIAL FEATURES "Making of" Featurette • Commentary Track with Director • Character and Art Galleries • Trailers • Promotional Footage • Fan Art • Games • DVD-ROM Features: Art, Scripts • Other Title Trailers • Easter Eggs TECHNICAL FEATURES Widescreen (1.85:1) • Subtitles/CC: Eng. • Languages: Jap., Eng. dub • Sound: Dolby Digital 2.0 • Keepcase • 1 Disc • Region 1 GENRE & RATING Action/Swordplay/Fantasy • Rated 13+

Revolutionary Girl Utena: The Movie [Limited Edition]

Software Sculptors, 2001, 87 mins. Directed by Kunihiko Ikuhara. Screenplay by Yoji Enokido. Based on the manga series by Chiho Saito in *Ciao*.

This edition is the early release volume, issued in a limited edition pink case, with an extra DVD that includes Central Park Media trailers.

SPECIAL FEATURES "Making of" Featurette • Commentary Track with Director • Character and Art Galleries • Trailers • Promotional Footage • Fan Art • Games • DVD-ROM Features: Art, Scripts • Other Title Trailers • Easter Egg TECHNICAL FEATURES Widescreen (1.85:1) • Subtitles/CC: Eng. • Languages: Jap., Eng. dub • Sound: Dolby Digital 2.0 • Keepcase • 1 Disc • Region 1 GENRE & RATING Action/Swordplay/Fantasy • Rated 13+

Revolutionary Girl Utena: The Rose Collection #1

Software Sculptors, 1999, 170 mins., #SSDVD-6041. Directed by Kunihiko Ikuhara. Story by Chiho Saito. Based on the manga series by Chiho Saito in *Ciao*.

Meet Utena Tenjo, the pretty pink-haired heroine of Otori Academy. Not only is she good-looking, and great at fencing and sports, but she's fun to hang out with, too. Did I mention she wants to be a prince? It seems that Utena met a handsome prince when she was much younger. He gave her a ring with a rose seal on it and promised it would lead her to him. She was so impressed with the prince that she made it her ambition to become one as well. And a prince-in-training might be just what this school needs. The student council is engaged in mysterious activity with something (or someone) called End of the World. All Utena has to do is duel each member of the student council for the hand of the Rose Bride. Anthy Himemiya is the Rose Bride, a shy girl with glasses who seems to be hiding a secret. Utena befriends Anthy, but the duels threaten to tear them apart. Can Utena keep her new friend, keep her grades up, and be a prince all at the same time?

This TV series was released in 1997, directed by one of the creators of the *Sailor Moon* series. But don't let that sway your decision to watch or pass over this series. This show has a style all its own. The plot itself starts out simply enough; it's a coming-of-age story for our main character and her friends. But symbolism abounds and this mythic tale will either intrigue you or leave you scratching your head. Some viewers find the repetition of scenes and music annoying. Others will find the '70s rock opera–esque dueling music to be distracting. The funny thing is, the more you watch, the more the whole thing seems to work.

The first seven television episodes are on this debut disc. It's enough to give you a good taste of the style of the series. Watch this show in Japanese with subtitles, as the English dub is very rough, and takes away from the experience. *Utena* is not a show for younger *Sailor Moon* fans. It's got some lesbian overtones, and Anthy gets slapped around quite a bit. The fencing duels (at this point) are not bloody, however. [RJM]

SPECIAL FEATURES Music Videos • Other Title Trailers • Easter Egg TECHNICAL FEATURES Fullscreen (1.33:1) • Subtitles/CC: Eng. • Languages: Jap., Eng. dub • Sound: Dolby Digital 2.0 • Keepcase • 1 Disc • Region All GENRE & RATING Action/Swordplay/Fantasy • Not Rated (Teens)

Revolutionary Girl Utena: The Rose Collection #2

Software Sculptors, 2000, 144 mins., #SSDVD-6079. Directed by Kunihiko Ikuhara. Story by Chiho Saito. Based on the manga series by Chiho Saito in *Ciao*.

Utena may technically be engaged to the Rose Bride, Anthy Himemiya, but she's the only one who just wants to be Anthy's friend. Still, she must defend her title as Duelist Champion in order to protect Anthy from the members of the Student Council, who are all Duelists as well and have their own plans for the Rose Bride. To make matters worse, could Student Council President Toga really be Utena's long-lost prince? Will she have to fight him to defend her friend's freedom? And what is Utena to do with Toga's half-mad sister, Nanami, who hates anyone who takes her precious brother's attention away from her?

This DVD carries on the series' usual bizarre mix of outrageous humor and dark intrigue with six episodes, for hours of viewing pleasure! The DVD also has some nice extras, such as the option to watch videos of several songs. Those who are uncomfortable with lesbian innuendo, however, may want to avert their eyes. [WM]

SPECIAL FEATURES Music Videos • DVD-ROM Features: Art, Scripts • Other Title Trailers TECHNICAL FEATURES Fullscreen (1.33:1) • Subtitles/CC: Eng. • Languages: Jap., Eng. dub • Sound: Dolby Digital 2.0 • Keepcase • 1 Disc • Region 1–6 GENRE & RATING Action/Swordplay/Fantasy • Not Rated (Teens)

RG Veda

U.S. Manga Corps, 2001, 90 mins., #USMD 2065. Directed by Hiroyuki Ebata, Takamasa Ikegami. Screenplay by Nanase Okawa. Based on the manga series by CLAMP.

The "Lord of Heaven" was betrayed by his wife and her lover, now an evil tyrant who has ruled the land for 300 years. But legend foretells that six mystical warriors will end the reign of the despot. Five of them have gathered together and faced foes and adversity with their astonishing powers, but they must find the sixth fighter to fulfill their destiny.

Released in 1991 as a two-part OVA, *RG Veda* is based on manga (and elements of Hindu myth and Buddhist philosophies). The manga origins are important to remember, as the animated version doesn't so much end as much as it begins. The discovery of the final warrior and the sextet's fight against evil forces are barely begun when the story ends, forcing fans who want to know what happens next to read the comics.

The animation is very nice, with overly pretty fantasy settings, and lots and lots of large-and-lovely hairstyles on the big-eyed characters. Those searching for a complete fantasy story should bypass this offering, but fans of CLAMP and animated fantasy will want to give the DVD a try, even if it's certain to leave them wanting more.

SPECIAL FEATURES Character Bios • Story Notes • Trailer • DVD-ROM Features: Art, Scripts • Other Title Trailers TECHNICAL FEATURES Fullscreen (1.33:1) • Subtitles/CC: Eng. • Languages: Jap., Eng. dub • Sound: Dolby Digital 2.0 • Keepcase • 1 Disc • Region 1 GENRE & RATING Fantasy/Adventure • Rated 13+

Rhea Gall Force

Digital Versatile Disc, 2001, 60 mins.

This DVD was not available for review.

Richard Scarry's Best ABC Video Ever! [#1]

Sony Wonder, 2001, 30 mins., #LVD 51301. Directed by Tony Eastman. Written by Emily Perl Kingsley and Sharon Lerner. Based on the books by Richard Scarry.

NOTE: This DVD arrived too late for a full review. The following text is promotional copy provided by the releasing company:

"Join Huckle Cat, Lowly Worm, and all their friends for Alphabet Day at the Busytown School. Huckle and his classmates present the alphabet in the context of twenty-six charming stories, each emphasizing familiar words beginning with each letter. Children will laugh at the antics of Banana Gorilla, Sergeant Murphy, and the other beloved Richard Scarry characters as they learn their alphabet."

Note that although the disc cover claims it is closed captioned, it is not.

SPECIAL FEATURES Other Title Trailers TECHNICAL FEATURES Fullscreen (1.33:1) • Languages: Eng. • Sound: Dolby Digital • Keepcase • 1 Disc • Region 1 GENRE & RATING Music/Educational • Not Rated (All Ages)

Richard Scarry's Best Busy People Video Ever! [#2]

Sony Wonder, 2001, 30 mins., #LVD 51302. Directed by Tony Eastman. Written by Ellen Weiss. Based on the books by Richard Scarry.

NOTE: This DVD arrived too late for a full review. The following text is promotional copy provided by the releasing company:

"Join Huckle Cat, Lowly Worm, and all the other delightful Richard Scarry characters in the Busytown playground as they take turns answering every child's favorite question: 'What do you want to be when you grow up?' Children will love learning all about the exciting jobs—from farmers and firefighters to teachers and truck drivers—that keep Busytown bustling everyday. Charming animation and original music, including a 'Busy People' theme song, will have children laughing and singing along."

Note that although the disc cover claims it is closed captioned, it is not.

SPECIAL FEATURES Other Title Trailers TECHNICAL FEATURES Fullscreen (1.33:1) • Languages: Eng. • Sound: Dolby Digital • Keepcase • 1 Disc • Region 1 GENRE & RATING Music/Educational • Not Rated (All Ages)

Richard Scarry's Best Counting Video Ever! [#3]

Sony Wonder, 2001, 30 mins., #LVD 51303. Directed by Tony Eastman. Written by Emily Perl Kingsley and Sharon Lerner. Based on the books by Richard Scarry.

NOTE: This DVD arrived too late for a full review. The following text is promotional copy provided by the releasing company:

"Children will love helping Lily Bunny count from 1 to 20! 'Tra La La, 1, 2, 3, Come Along and Count With Me,' is the song that Lily sings as she starts off on her counting adventure. Along the way, she meets Huckle Cat, Lowly Worm, Wrong-Way Roger, Bananas Gorilla, and many other delightful Richard Scarry characters who each help her find funny things to count. Learning to count has never been more fun."

Note that although the disc cover claims it is closed captioned, it is not.

SPECIAL FEATURES Other Title Trailers TECHNICAL FEATURES Fullscreen (1.33:1) • Languages: Eng. • Sound: Dolby Digital • Keepcase • 1 Disc • Region 1 GENRE & RATING Music/Educational • Not Rated (All Ages)

Richard Scarry's Best Learning Songs Video Ever! [#4]

Sony Wonder, 2001, 30 mins., #LVD 51304. Directed by Tony Eastman. Written by Ellen Weiss. Based on the books by Richard Scarry.

NOTE: This DVD arrived too late for a full review. The following text is promotional copy provided by the releasing company:

"Join Huckle Cat and all his friends as they put on a backyard show that's full of songs and surprises. Children will laugh and learn, and will want to join in the fun as their favorite characters from Busytown sing about letters, shapes, numbers, and much, much more! They'll delight in hearing old favorites like 'The Alphabet Song' and 'If You're Happy and You Know It' as well as equally irresistible new tunes that will have them singing along."

Note that although the disc cover claims it is closed captioned, it is not.

SPECIAL FEATURES Other Title Trailers TECHNICAL FEATURES Fullscreen (1.33:1) • Languages: Eng. • Sound: Dolby Digital • Keepcase • 1 Disc • Region 1 GENRE & RATING Music/Educational • Not Rated (All Ages)

Richard Scarry's Best Silly Stories and Songs Video Ever! [#5]

Sony Wonder, 2002, 30 mins., #LVD 51305. Directed by Tony Eastman. Based on the books by Richard Scarry.

NOTE: This DVD arrived too late for a full review. The following text is promotional copy provided by the releasing company:

"Huckle Cat and Lowly Worm have just taken a very silly storybook out of the Busytown library. Each hilarious adventure comes to life as Huckle reads about absent-minded Mr. Rabbit, mixed-up Mr. Fixit, and Pa Pig's unforgettable ride through Busytown. Children will laugh with and learn from this irresistible collection of silly songs and original sing-along songs, including 'At the Library' and 'Stop, Look, and Listen.'"

Note that although the disc cover claims it is closed captioned, it is not.

SPECIAL FEATURES Other Title Trailers TECHNICAL FEATURES Fullscreen (1.33:1) • Languages: Eng. • Sound: Dolby Digital • Keepcase • 1 Disc • Region 1 GENRE & RATING Music/Educational • Not Rated (All Ages)

Richard Scarry's Best Sing-Along Mother Goose Video Ever! [#6]

Sony Wonder, 2002, 30 mins., #LVD 51306. Directed by Tony Eastman. Written by Emily Perl Kingsley and Sharon Lerner. Based on the books by Richard Scarry.

NOTE: This DVD arrived too late for a full review. The following text is promotional copy provided by the releasing company:

"Join Huckle Cat on his adventure through Mother Gooseland. Huckle is looking for his old friend, Lowly Worm, and along the way he meets lots of new friends, like Old Mother Hubbard, Little Miss Muffet, Wee Willie Winkie, and even Mother Goose herself! Children will love singing along with these classic nursery rhymes, including 'Mary Had a Little Lamb,' 'Hey, Diddle, Diddle,' 'Old King Cole,' and many more."

Note that although the disc cover claims it is closed captioned, it is not.

SPECIAL FEATURES Other Title Trailers TECHNICAL FEATURES Fullscreen (1.33:1) • Languages: Eng. • Sound: Dolby Digital • Keepcase • 1 Disc • Region 1 GENRE & RATING Educational • Not Rated (All Ages)

Riding Bean

AnimEigo, 2002, 46 mins., #AV202-100. Directed by Yasuo Hasegawa. Story by Kenichi Sonoda. Based on the manga series by Kenichi Sonoda.

Robbing banks, smuggling drugs, and moving other contraband can be pretty hazardous to the common criminal's health. Bean Bandit offers his services to these lowlifes as a courier; in his heavily armored, tricked-out sports car, the Roadbuster, Bean is practically impossible to catch. On a fairly normal bank robbery job, Bean and his partner Rally find themselves double-crossed by their mysterious clients. This is a mistake; Bean's not easy to kill nor easy to shake, and he's intent on chasing the bad guys through the streets of Chicago to get his revenge.

Riding Bean has been available on VHS for many years prior to its release on DVD; as such, it's regarded as something of a classic. Longevity isn't the only factor, though—the fact is, *Riding Bean* is action-packed and directed with wit and style. Its relatively short running time also makes it easy to watch this one-shot 1989 OVA over and over. *Riding Bean* takes place in an absolutely picture-perfect rendering of Chicago, right down to the American-produced background music. Interestingly, supporting character Rally Vincent would later be repurposed (and recolored!) by the creator/writer for the *Gunsmith Cats* series.

This DVD contains the complete forty-five-minute OVA. It should be noted that the trailer included is actually for the Japanese DVD release, and is not the trailer for the show's original release in Japan. [MT]

SPECIAL FEATURES Character and Art Galleries • Trailer • Inserts: Liner Notes, Lyrics TECHNICAL FEATURES Fullscreen (1.33:1) • Subtitles/CC: Eng. • Languages: Jap., Eng. dub • Sound: Dolby Digital 2.0 • Keepcase • 1 Disc • Region 1 GENRE & RATING Action/Crime • Not Rated (Teens)

Ripping Friends, The

Trimark, 2002, 80 mins., #VM8003D.

This DVD was not available for review.

Road to El Dorado, The

DreamWorks, 2000, 89 mins., #86545. Directed by Eric "Bibo" Bergeron, Don Paul. Written by Ted Elliott, Terry Rossio.

Tulio and Miguel are a pair of slick con men who think they may have lucked into the map to El Dorado, the legendary City of Gold. Things don't look good for them initially, as they're locked in the brig of a Spanish explorer ship, but they eventually escape and wash up—with their horse—on the shores of the new world. There, they actually do stumble onto El Dorado, where a crafty and devious high priest named Tzekel-Kan declares them gods. It's all part of the priest's plan to oust the chief of the city, and when he's done, Tzekel-Kan has ominous plans for his "gods." Tulio and Miguel love the attention at first, but soon learn they must accept help from beautiful native girl Chel . . . or El Dorado—and their own lives—may be in danger!

A 2000 feature film, *The Road to El Dorado* is a hip and pleasant confection that is entirely predictable from beginning to end. What makes the trip enjoyable is the camaraderie between its two leads, and excellent voice acting all around—from such notables as Kevin Kline, Kenneth Branagh, Rosie Perez, and Armand Assante. The humor is fun, and the songs—by Elton John and Tim Rice—are mostly unobtrusive. Designs based largely on the Mayan civilization are cool and realistically tactile.

Although most of it has the look of traditional cel animation, *The Road to El Dorado* is a true hybrid of styles.

Traditional animators and CGI animators worked in the same department, using new computer programs to "paint" unfinished backgrounds, warp leaves or sails with movement, and render crashing oceans and other liquids. Even the lead characters were created in a mixture of formats.

As with most DreamWorks releases, the DVD is chock full of extras. Perhaps the coolest and most unusual of them is a "Color Script" with commentary, which walks the viewer through the art—concept, paintings, storyboards, roughs—for many major sequences of the film. Despite its "been there done that" script, *The Road to El Dorado* is charming, and will win audiences over if given the chance.

SPECIAL FEATURES "Making of" Featurette • Commentary Track by Directors • Cast & Crew Filmographies • Character and Art Galleries with Commentary • Production Notes • Trailer • Storybook • Music Video • DVD-ROM Features: Games, Coloring Pages • Insert: Liner Notes TECHNICAL FEATURES Widescreen (1.85:1 enhanced for 16x9) • Subtitles/CC: Eng. • Languages: Eng. • Sound: Dolby Digital Surround 2.0, Dolby Digital Surround 5.1, DTS • Keepcase • 1 Disc • Region 1 GENRE & RATING Music/Adventure/Comedy • Rated PG

Robbie the Reindeer: Hooves of Fire

Warner, 2001, 95 mins., #E1583. Directed by Richard Goleszowski. Written by Andy Riley, Kevin Cecil, Richard Curtis.

Poor Robbie the Reindeer is too chubby and too lazy to get a job on Santa's sleigh team. And he doesn't even have a glowing red nose! Donner is a psychotherapist reindeer whose heart yearns for Robbie's attention, even if he doesn't notice. Blitzen is the evil leader of the sleigh team, and he doesn't like Robbie at all. Vixen is the superficial femme fatale of the group, while Prancer has gotten way too fat because of excessive partying. And as if things weren't bad enough among the North Pole's reindeer, Santa Claus doesn't want to wear the red and white suit, but he has no fashion sense at all!

If *Robbie the Reindeer* sounds a little daft, it's because this 1999 stop-motion production was animated by some of the Aardman guys who gave the world *Wallace and Gromit*, and scripted by the award-winning writers of *Bridget Jones's Diary* and *Notting Hill*. Mix in music by Seal, Mark Knopfler, Vangelis, and the Three Tenors, and you've got one of the strangest and funniest holiday specials ever produced.

If you need any other excuse to buy this short-run disc (the special itself is only thirty minutes), look for over an hour of extras including commentary and other cool elements. The special features menu takes a bit to master, but it will be worth it. And your money will go to a good cause; BBC Worldwide is giving 100% of their profits to the Comic Relief charity!

SPECIAL FEATURES "Making of" Featurette • Commentary Track by Director • Cast Bios • Character Bios • Character and Art Galleries • Animatics • Other Title Trailers TECHNICAL FEATURES Widescreen (1.85:1 enhanced for 16x9) • Subtitles/CC: Eng. • Languages: Eng. • Sound: Dolby Digital 2.0, Dolby Digital 5.1 • Snapcase • 1 Disc • Region 1 GENRE & RATING Holiday/Comedy • Not Rated (Kids)

Robin Hood [Collector's Edition]

Digital Versatile Disc, 1999, 50 mins., #167. Animation Directed by Warwick Gilbert. Script by Eddy Graham.

England is in a dark time since King Richard left to fight in the Crusades, leaving his brother, Prince John, in charge. John's thuggish partner, the Sheriff of Nottingham, collects taxes and tariffs for him, but no one can collect the love of Maid Marion, whom John desires. Often foiling the Prince's plans is Robin Hood of Sherwood Forest and his band of green-clad Merry Men, who steal from the rich and give to the poor. But the sheriff and the prince are scheming to lure Robin out of hiding and gain the hand of Marion in marriage. . . .

This retelling of the classic English legend was created by Burbank Films Australia in 1985. The designs for characters are simple, but not overly cartoony. The film itself has a gritty look, but it appears to have come from the original animation, not the transfer. While relatively true to the best-known version of the Robin Hood tale, the story skimps on archery, not unslinging its arrows until more than halfway through. Still, this is enjoyable enough, and one of Burbank Films Australia's best efforts. Oddly enough, the cover shows Robin Hood dressed in red!

SPECIAL FEATURES Myth Notes • Game TECHNICAL FEATURES Fullscreen (1.33:1) • Languages: Eng. • Sound: Dolby Digital 5.1, DTS • Keepcase • 1 Disc • Region All GENRE & RATING Historical/Adventure • Not Rated (Kids)

Robin Hood [Gold Collection]

Disney, 2000, 83 mins., #19692. Directed by Wolfgang Reitherman. Story by Larry Clemmons. Based on story and character concepts by Ken Anderson.

England is at war, and the throne is currently occupied by a greedy and corrupt lion, Prince John. He is taxing Nottingham's townsfolk more than they can bear, and they have little choice but to pay him. That is, little choice until the roguish Robin Hood and his band of Merry Men make

the scene! Robin disrupts all of John's plans, whether at an archery contest or in his attempts to woo Maid Marion. But can the crafty Robin stay out of John's clutches long enough for King Richard to return?

Released in 1973, Disney's *Robin Hood* changed the entire cast to animals, anthropomorphizing Robin into a fox, Marion into a vixen, and various Merry Men into bears and other woodland creatures. The effect is charming, and gives the already adventurous tale much humor. Disney's famed "Nine Old Men" contributed much to the animation, direction, and designs, all of which are top-notch, as are the songs. Watch for a bit of reused animation in the scene where Maid Marion dances in the woods; it replicates a scene from *Snow White*! Kids and adults will probably love the sulking thumb-sucking Prince John more than foxy, often-disguised Robin, but a good villain is hardly a failing.

Robin Hood was the biggest box office hit that Disney had at the time of its release. The DVD contains an excellent transfer of the film and a handful of extras. If you haven't seen this lesser-publicized gem, do yourself a favor and enjoy it. The DVD also features a Mickey Mouse short from 1933, "Ye Olden Days."

SPECIAL FEATURES Storybook • Sing-Along • Game • Other Title Trailers TECHNICAL FEATURES Fullscreen (1.33:1) • Subtitles/CC: Eng. • Languages: Eng., Fren. dub, Span. dub • Sound: Dolby Digital 1.0 • Keepcase • 1 Disc • Region 1 GENRE & RATING Music/Historical/Adventure • Rated G

Robotech: The Macross Saga—First Contact [#1]

ADV Films, 2001, 150 mins., #DRT/001. Directed by Ippei Kuri. Written by Gregory Snegoff, Robert Barron, Greg Finley, Steve Kramer, Mike Reynolds, Tao Will, Ardwight Chamberlain, Jason Klassi.

In 1999 an armored alien spaceship crashes to Earth near Macross Island in the South Pacific. Over the following decade, scientists and the military have studied its complex "Robotech" technology, even as the threat of invasion from space has ended the Global War and brought about the United Earth Government. In 2009, the ship—now called *Super Dimensional Fortress One* (*SDF-1*) —is relaunched under the command of Captain Henry J. Gloval. The celebrating public doesn't know that Earth is about to be attacked by the Zentraedi, a race of giant warriors. Soon, Rick Hunter, Lisa Hayes, and others in the Robotech Defense Force are battling aliens in deep space!

In episode #1, "Booby Trap," the scientists of Macross Island prepare to launch SDF-1. But a second ship nears Earth, carrying the Zentraedi. The SDF-1 automatically fires at the Zentraedi ship, launching its crew into an intergalactic war. In "Countdown" (#2), fighter jock

Rick Hunter meets charming Lynn Minmei on the deserted streets of Macross City, and tries to impress her with his flying abilities. While Captain Gloval prepares to take the untested SDF-1 into battle against the Zentraedi, Rick destroys one of the alien mecha aircraft and is the first human to see a Zentraedi alive! In "Space Fold" (#3), Rick and Minmei make it back aboard the SDF-1 and Rick trades in his morphing Veritech fighter for his old plane. Captain Gloval attempts an emergency hyperspace jump with the SDF-1, but the resulting space-fold pocket takes Macross Island with it! Now, the SDF-1 and Macross Island are both orbiting Pluto! In "The Long Wait" (#4), Rick and Minmei wander lost aboard the immense SDF-1 and the survivors of Macross City are brought aboard, too. In "Transformation" (#5), as the citizens of Macross City adapt to their new life on the alien ship, Rick is conflicted about becoming a warrior with the Robotech forces. Orbiting Earth, the Zentraedi discover troubling links between Earth and an ancient race of short creatures they know as "Micronians." And a Zentraedi ship is dispatched to attack the suddenly transforming SDF-1. In "Blitzkrieg" (#6), the newly configured SDF-1 repels the Zentraedi armada and hides in the rings of Saturn, but not without cost to Macross City. Rick joins the Robotech Defense Force and becomes a Veritech fighter pilot, working under Lisa Hayes. And Captain Gloval learns that the fold system generator may have distorted the space/time continuum!

Each disk can be purchased separately, but fans would be better off getting the three-disk box sets known as *The Robotech Legacy Collection*. The third disk in each set is called Elements of Robotechnology, and each volume is full of supplemental materials including making of featurettes, audio commentary, animation model sheets, promotional films, unaired episodes, and more! See entries for details.

This DVD contains episodes #1–6.

SPECIAL FEATURES Other Title Trailers TECHNICAL FEATURES Fullscreen (1.33:1) • Languages: Eng. dub • Sound: Dolby Digital 2.0 • Keepcase • 1 Disc • Region 1 GENRE & RATING Science Fiction/Robots • Not Rated (Kids)

Robotech: The Macross Saga—Transformation [#2]

ADV Films, 2001, 150 mins., #DRT/002. Directed by Ippei Kuri. Written by Gregory Snegoff, Robert Barron, Greg Finley, Steve Kramer, Mike Reynolds, Tao Will, Ardwight Chamberlain, Jason Klassi.

The galactic saga continues in episode #7, "Bye-Bye Mars," when Breetai, the leader of the Zentraedi attack forces, calls in reinforcements—the ruthless warlord Khyron and his fleet. And, near Mars, the SDF-1 discovers that observation post Sara Base is

destroyed along with Lisa Hayes's fiancé who was stationed there. In "Sweet Sixteen (#8), the SDF-1 continues to orbit Mars, but Khyron's troops keep assaulting it. Meanwhile, Rick is given the Medal of Valor and command of a squad, but all he can think about is Minmei's birthday party. In "Miss Macross" (#9), Macross City holds a beauty pageant to boost morale, and Minmei wins the title of Miss Macross. Watching the broadcast, the Zentraedi are aghast that the Micronians (humans) mingle their sexes.

This DVD contains episodes #7–12.

SPECIAL FEATURES Other Title Trailers TECHNICAL FEATURES Fullscreen (1.33:1) • Languages: Eng. dub • Sound: Dolby Digital 2.0 • Keepcase • 1 Disc • Region 1 GENRE & RATING Science Fiction/Robots • Not Rated (Kids)

Robotech: The Macross Saga—Homecoming [#3]

ADV Films, 2001, 150 mins., #DRT/003. Directed by Ippei Kuri. Written by Gregory Snegoff, Robert Barron, Greg Finley, Steve Kramer, Mike Reynolds, Tao Will, Ardwight Chamberlain, Jason Klassi, Jim Wager, Steve Flood.

The epic continues when, in episode #13, "Blue Wind," Rick, Lisa, Max, and Ben are back aboard *SDF-1* and they report on the Zentraedi and what they've learned about protoculture. Minmei becomes a singing star, and Rick feels left out. Meanwhile, the trio of Zentraedi spies enjoy life among the Micronians. In "Gloval's Report" (#14), Captain Gloval prepares to make a report to his superiors on Earth, telling them everything that has happened in the two years since the *SDF-1* departed the planet.

This DVD contains episodes #13–18.

SPECIAL FEATURES Other Title Trailers TECHNICAL FEATURES Fullscreen (1.33:1) • Languages: Eng. dub • Sound: Dolby Digital 2.0 • Keepcase • 1 Disc • Region 1 GENRE & RATING Science Fiction/Robots • Not Rated (Kids)

Robotech: The Macross Saga—Battlefront [#4]

ADV Films, 2001, 150 mins., #DRT/004. Directed by Ippei Kuri. Written by Gregory Snegoff, Robert Barron, Greg Finley, Steve Kramer, Mike Reynolds, Jim Wager, Steve Flood.

The action continues in episode #19, "Bursting Point," as Captain Gloval tries to relocate Macross City's civilian population to Earth's North American Ontario quadrant. The beautiful Zentraedi warrior Miriya is shrunk to Micronian size to stalk Max, and Lynn Kyle preaches peace, an intriguing concept to the three Zentraedi spies. In "Paradise Lost" (#20), An explosion has wiped out an Earth city and the government exiles the *SDF-1* and its inhabitants from Earth forever. Breetai is put back in charge and he asks for an Imperial Class fleet of over one million ships!

This DVD contains episodes #19–24.

SPECIAL FEATURES Other Title Trailers TECHNICAL FEATURES Fullscreen (1.33:1) • Languages: Eng. dub • Sound: Dolby Digital 2.0 • Keepcase • 1 Disc • Region 1 GENRE & RATING Science Fiction/Robots • Not Rated (Kids)

Robotech: The Macross Saga—War and Peace [#5]

ADV Films, 2001, 150 mins., #DRT/005. Directed by Ippei Kuri. Written by Gregory Snegoff, Robert Barron, Greg Finley, Steve Kramer, Mike Reynolds, Jim Wager, Steve Flood.

Things get personal in episode #25, "Wedding Bells," when Miriya fails in her attempt to kill Max. When she asks him to kill her, he proposes instead! The first wedding between a human and a Zentraedi is historically significant, and Captain Gloval addresses the crowd, calling for peace. Dolza orders the Zentraedi to attack, but Miriya helps the Veritech fighter pilots cripple their enemy without killing them.

This DVD contains episodes #25–30.

SPECIAL FEATURES Other Title Trailers TECHNICAL FEATURES Fullscreen (1.33:1) • Languages: Eng. dub • Sound: Dolby Digital 2.0 • Keepcase • 1 Disc • Region 1 GENRE & RATING Science Fiction/Robots • Not Rated (Kids)

Robotech: The Macross Saga—Final Conflict [#6]

ADV Films, 2001, 150 mins., #DRT/006 Directed by Ippei Kuri. Written by Gregory Snegoff, Robert Barron, Greg Finley, Steve Kramer, Mike Reynolds, Jim Wager, Steve Flood.

In episode #31, "Khyron's Revenge," Khyron attacks and steals the last protoculture chamber. Because he can use it to restore discontented Zentraedi to their giant warrior size, Khyron regains many deserters. Meanwhile, Admiral Gloval and Exedore ponder the history of the Zentraedi race. In "Broken Heart" (#32), Khyron kidnaps Minmei and Kyle and offers to return them in exchange for the hulk of the *SDF-1*. Rick and Lisa launch operation "Star Saver" and lead the Veritech forces against the Zentraedi troops. Their rescue works, and Minmei finally awakens to her feelings for Rick even as he leaves for battle.

This DVD contains episodes #31–36. It is the final volume of *The Macross Saga*.

SPECIAL FEATURES Other Title Trailers TECHNICAL FEATURES Fullscreen (1.33:1) • Languages: Eng. dub • Sound: Dolby Digital 2.0 • Keepcase • 1 Disc • Region 1 GENRE & RATING Science Fiction/Robots • Not Rated (Kids)

Robotech: The Macross Saga—Complete Collection

ADV Films, 2002, 900 mins., #DRT/BX8.

This multikeepcase set includes the six *Robotech: The Macross Saga* discs exactly as they appeared in the individual editions. See individual entries for the Special and Technical Features listings.

TECHNICAL FEATURES Multikeepcase • 6 Discs • Region 1 GENRE & RATING Science Fiction/Robots • Not Rated (Kids)

Robotech: The Masters—A New Threat [#7]

ADV Films, 2001, 150 mins., #DRT/007. Directed by Ippei Kuri. Written by Gregory Snegoff, Robert Barron, Greg Finley, Steve Kramer, Mike Reynolds, Tao Will, Ardwight Chamberlain, Jason Klassi.

In the year 2031, half-breed Dana Sterling and Bowie Grant, Claudia Grant's nephew, are graduating from the United Earth Forces Military Academy. The world's societies are unstable, aggressive, and feudal, with many cities sealed to prevent radiation contamination. Other cities are rebuilt, such as New Macross City. The Robotech Masters soon arrive in the space above Earth, to reclaim the *SDF-1* and its protoculture matrix. The Zentraedi Holocaust barely fifteen years past, Dana and her squadron friends are quickly embroiled in the Second Robotech War.

In episode #37, "Dana's Story," Dana and Bowie graduate, but Bowie doesn't want to remain in the military. Meanwhile, the Robotech Masters have arrived to reclaim their lost protoculture factory. In "False Start" (#38), Dana's squadron, the Southern Cross Defense Corps, prepares for battle, but Dana runs afoul of Lt. Crystal and is thrown in the brig. Given another chance, Dana and her squadron defend Earth against the Robotech Masters, and the battle ends in a draw. Dana is promoted but is troubled by alien visions.

This DVD contains episodes #37–42. It is the first volume of *The Masters*.

SPECIAL FEATURES Other Title Trailers TECHNICAL FEATURES Fullscreen (1.33:1) • Languages: Eng. dub • Sound: Dolby Digital 2.0 • Keepcase • 1 Disc • Region 1 GENRE & RATING Science Fiction/Robots • Not Rated (Kids)

Robotech: The Masters—Revelations [#8]

ADV Films, 2001, 150 mins., #DRT/008. Directed by Ippei Kuri. Written by Gregory Snegoff, Robert Barron, Greg Finley, Steve Kramer, Mike Reynolds, Tao Will, Ardwight Chamberlain, Jason Klassi.

In episode #43, "Prelude to Battle," the 15th Squad prepares to go on another dangerous mission, this time to explore the downed Robotech mothership. Bowie is arrested and confined to a guardhouse, but he's freed in time to join the mission as Veritech hovertanks battle the bioroids. In "The Trap" (#44), Dana's ATAC group discovers a biomechanical operation inside the alien ship that seems to create androids. Bowie meets a beautiful alien woman named Musica, but after helping him defeat some sentries, she runs away. The Robotech Masters trap the 15th Squad, but Dana's soldiers escape, capturing a bioroid on the way.

This DVD contains episodes #43–48.

SPECIAL FEATURES Other Title Trailers TECHNICAL FEATURES Fullscreen (1.33:1) • Languages: Eng. dub • Sound: Dolby Digital 2.0 • Keepcase • 1 Disc • Region 1 GENRE & RATING Science Fiction/Robots • Not Rated (Kids)

Robotech: The Masters—Counterattack [#9]

ADV Films, 2001, 150 mins., #DRT/009. Directed by Ippei Kuri. Written by Gregory Snegoff, Robert Barron, Greg Finley, Steve Kramer, Mike Reynolds, Tao Will, Ardwight Chamberlain, Jason Klassi.

The Masters saga begins with episode #49, "A New Recruit," in which Zor is inducted into the Southern Cross army and assigned to the 15th Squad in hopes that his memory will return and he'll have important tactical information. Other recruits won't accept Zor, even though Dana does. The Robotech Masters watch the reawakening of Zor's emotions and memory with concern. In "Triumvirate" (#50), the United Earth Defense Force launches a full assault on the armada of the Robotech Masters, but they've been forewarned by Zor's internal spy transmissions. Left behind, Dana and the 15th ATAC go to the wreck of the *SDF-1* to try to stimulate Zor's memory. Zor notices a trio of strange flowers that are somehow linked to the alien lifeforce.

This DVD contains episodes #49–54.

SPECIAL FEATURES Other Title Trailers TECHNICAL FEATURES Fullscreen (1.33:1) • Languages: Eng. dub • Sound: Dolby Digital 2.0 • Keepcase • 1 Disc • Region 1 GENRE & RATING Science Fiction/Robots • Not Rated (Kids)

Robotech: The Masters—Final Solution [#10]

ADV Films, 2001, 150 mins., #DRT/010. Directed by Ippei Kuri. Written by Gregory Snegoff, Robert Barron, Greg Finley, Steve Kramer, Mike Reynolds, Tao Will, Ardwight Chamberlain, Jason Klassi.

The saga continues in episode #55, "Dana in Wonderland," with the 15th Squad scattering into the Robotech mothership in flight from Zor and his sentries. As the humans run, they learn that the androids are actually biogenetic clones, and that contact with humans awakens their emotions and thoughts. Bowie helps Musica learn to rebel against the Masters, but the 15th Squad is all captured! In "Crisis Point" (#56). the Robotech Masters have captured the humans, but Zor Prime is missing and considered unstable. Musica finds Zor and helps him come to terms with his past. The two then help the 15th Squad escape, and Zor almost makes the ultimate sacrifice for his Earth friends.

This DVD contains episodes #55–60. It is the final volume of *The Masters*.

SPECIAL FEATURES Other Title Trailers TECHNICAL FEATURES Fullscreen (1.33:1) • Languages: Eng. dub • Sound: Dolby Digital 2.0 • Keepcase • 1 Disc • Region 1 GENRE & RATING Science Fiction/Robots • Not Rated (Kids)

Robotech: New Generation—The Next Wave [#11]

ADV Films, 2002, 175 mins., #DRT/011. Directed by Ippei Kuri. Written by Gregory Snegoff, Robert Barron, Greg Finley, Steve Kramer, Mike Reynolds, Tao Will, Ardwight Chamberlain, Jason Klassi.

In the year 2033, the parasitic Invid race has invaded Earth, led by a queen known as the Regis. Cities have been leveled by the various wars, and humanity is scattered across the planet. The surviving humans are used in work camps to harvest Invid flowers and process protoculture. From space—where his Expeditionary Forces are searching for the Robotech Masters' homeworld—Admiral Rick Hunter has sent a group of Veritech squadron fighters to Earth to free what's left of humanity from the tyrannical protoplasmic creatures. In "New Generation," a ragtag group of human freedom fighters will make their way across a shattered world to win Earth back for humankind.

Lieutenant Scott Bernard leads a doomed Veritech squadron against the Invid, then teams up with an Earth youth named Rand to find an area known as Reflex Point so that he can kill the Invid Regis. Along the way, they are befriended by the tough orphan, Annie, and a mysterious female cyclone rider who saves them from Invid shock troopers. The group picks up another ally in a singer named Yellow Dancer (who is secretly a transvestite), and a man named Lunk. Scott's group of resistance fighters can't use Lunk's working Veritech Alpha fighter, but they can stage a raid on an Invid protoculture storage unit. Though not without difficulties with the law and the Invid, the group gets away with the badly needed protoculture.

This third series of *Robotech* episodes combines minor footage from the previous series with lead footage from *Genesis Climber Mospeada*, a 1983 Japanese television show. The stories here are significantly different from their predecessors, with Scott's group operating on a guerilla-fighting basis. There's also a touch of "Old West"–style storytelling as the team makes its way across a ruined world and meets townsfolk in settlements. Some of the stories are thus more human-oriented than mecha-fighting science fiction. The first volume of *New Generation*, this DVD contains episodes #61–67.

SPECIAL FEATURES Other Title Trailers TECHNICAL FEATURES Fullscreen (1.33:1) • Languages: Eng. dub • Sound: Dolby Digital 2.0 • Keepcase • 1 Disc • Region 1 GENRE & RATING Science Fiction/Robots • Not Rated (Kids)

Robotech: New Generation—Counter Strike [#12]

ADV Films, 2002, 150 mins., #DRT/012. Directed by Ippei Kuri. Written by Gregory Snegoff, Robert Barron, Greg Finley, Steve Kramer, Mike Reynolds, Tao Will, Ardwight Chamberlain, Jason Klassi.

Scott's group comes to a town where a group of Expeditionary Forces soldiers seems to have nothing to fear from the Invid. At Reflex Point, the Invid Regis is concerned that human resistance fighters could destroy the Genesis Pits and their Invid larvae. Stumbling into one of those very pits, Scott and his allies are trapped with dinosaurs, Invid, and monsters! The Regis creates a biogenetic woman with a psychic link to the Invid mother, and she joins Scott's group. They soon invade an Invid mountain fortress, then must hide in a cave to evade Invid shock troopers. And when Rand falls into a pit containing the hallucinogenic spores of the Invid Flower of Life, he learns of the Invid's plans to plug themselves into Earth's evolutionary chain!

With lots of action and a few choice revelations, this DVD contains episodes #68–73.

SPECIAL FEATURES Other Title Trailers TECHNICAL FEATURES Fullscreen (1.33:1) • Languages: Eng. dub • Sound: Dolby Digital 2.0 • Keepcase • 1 Disc • Region 1 GENRE & RATING Science Fiction/Robots • Not Rated (Kids)

Robotech: New Generation—Genesis [#13]

ADV Films, 2002, 150 mins., #DRT/013. Directed by Ippei Kuri. Written by Gregory Snegoff, Robert Barron, Greg Finley, Steve Kramer, Mike Reynolds, Tao Will, Ardwight Chamberlain, Jason Klassi.

The freedom fighters hide out in a jungle, where they discover a group of primitive outcasts that worships the Invid. Scott teaches them the truth, and they help the rebels to fight the aliens. Meanwhile, the Regis creates a prince and princess out of the protoplasm—human in form, but with Invid instincts—and sends them to find out why his previous simulagent spy among the humans is malfunctioning. That spy, Marlene, starts to recall her memories as the group crosses a snowy mountain range. Word comes from Admiral Hunter's Expeditionary Force that a major offensive on the Invid is planned from space. And in the deserted city of Denver, emotions boil to the surface.

In the next-to-last disc in the *Robotech* saga, this DVD contains episodes #74–79.

SPECIAL FEATURES Other Title Trailers TECHNICAL FEATURES Fullscreen (1.33:1) • Languages: Eng. dub • Sound: Dolby Digital 2.0 • Keepcase • 1 Disc • Region 1 GENRE & RATING Science Fiction/Robots • Not Rated (Kids)

Robotech: New Generation—Hollow Victory [#14]

ADV Films, 2002, 150 mins., #DRT/014. Directed by Ippei Kuri. Written by Gregory Snegoff, Robert Barron, Greg Finley, Steve Kramer, Mike Reynolds, Tao Will, Ardwight Chamberlain, Jason Klassi.

While the group bonds at Annie's birthday celebration, bad news looms. A rogue cyborg soldier has killed his fellow squadmembers, but the shocking truth behind his actions will give Rook pause. Arriving in New York City—where the humans and the Invid uneasily coexist—the rebel group is endangered, and Marlene learns she's an Invid. The group finally arrives at Reflex Point, but the Expeditionary Forces have beaten them there. Unfortunately, the Invid have decimated the humans. Can the small group of heroes hold off the Invid long enough for reinforcements from Rick Hunter's main Robotech force to arrive?

The final volume of *Robotech*, this DVD contains episodes #80–85. The storyline wraps up, while still leaving threads open for the planned sequel series. For more about that series, see *The Robotech Legacy: Collection 3—Macross Saga*.

SPECIAL FEATURES Other Title Trailers TECHNICAL FEATURES Fullscreen (1.33:1) • Languages: Eng. dub • Sound: Dolby

Digital 2.0 • Keepcase • 1 Disc • Region 1 GENRE & RATING Science Fiction/Robots • Not Rated (Kids)

Robotech Legacy, The: Collection 1—Macross Saga [Box Set]

ADV Films, 2001, 375 mins., #DRT/BX1.

This box set contains the two commercially available keepcase editions of *Robotech: The Macross Saga #1–2*.

The set also contains a third keepcase and disc titled *Robotech Extra: Macross Saga 1—Elements of Robotechnology*. This disc contains a plethora of extra features and is only available in the box set. Included is the original *Codename Robotech* feature (a seventy-three-minute introduction to the series given to TV stations, comprising bits from the first thirteen episodes edited together); an audio commentary on the history of *Robotech* by series developer/producer Carl Macek (the vocal track is on *Codename Robotech*); model sheets; and lots of international clips in French, Spanish, Italian, and Portuguese. See individual entries for the Special and Technical Features listings.

SPECIAL FEATURES Commentary Track by Producer • Character and Art Galleries • International Footage • Other Title Trailers • Inserts: Liner Notes • Easter Egg TECHNICAL FEATURES Fullscreen (1.33:1) • Languages: Eng. dub • Sound: Dolby Digital 2.0 • Cardboard Box with 3 Keepcases • 3 Discs • Region 1 GENRE & RATING Science Fiction/Robots • Not Rated (Kids)

Robotech Legacy, The: Collection 2—Macross Saga [Box Set]

ADV Films, 2001, 325 mins., #DRT/BX2.

This box set contains the two commercially available keepcase editions of *Robotech: The Macross Saga #3–4*.

The set also contains a third keepcase and disc titled *Robotech Extra: Macross Saga 2—Elements of Robotechnology II*. This disc contains more extra features and is only available in the box set. Included is a promotional video for the *Robotech* toy line; *Robotech* toy commercials; character biographies; more international clips (French, Spanish, Italian, Portuguese); more model sheets; a cover gallery for Comico's *Robotech* comic book line; and a Texas cable access program in which producer Carl Macek was interviewed. See individual entries for the Special and Technical Features listings.

SPECIAL FEATURES Producer Interview • Character Bios • Character and Art Galleries • Promotional Footage • International Footage • Other Title Trailers • Inserts: Liner Notes TECHNICAL FEATURES Fullscreen (1.33:1) • Languages: Eng. dub • Sound:

Robotech Legacy, The: Collection 3—Macross Saga [Box Set]

ADV Films, 2001, 375 mins., #DRT/BX3.

This box set contains the two commercially available keepcase editions of *Robotech: The Macross Saga #5–6*.

The set also contains a third keepcase and disc titled *Robotech Extra: The Sentinels—Elements of Robotechnology III*. This disc contains a plethora of extra features and is only available in the box set. Included is the original *Robotech II: The Sentinels* feature-length film (a seventy-three-minute film created from the animation done for an aborted *Sentinels* TV project); an audio commentary on *Robotech II: The Sentinels* by producer Carl Macek (the vocal track is over the top of the feature); more model sheets and preproduction art; more international clips in French, Spanish, Italian, Portuguese; a promotional sales reel for *Robotech II: The Sentinels*; and character biographies from *Robotech II: The Sentinels*. See individual entries for the Special and Technical Features listings.

SPECIAL FEATURES Commentary Track by Producer • Character Bios • Character and Art Galleries • Promotional Footage • International Footage • Other Title Trailers • Inserts: Liner Notes • Easter Egg TECHNICAL FEATURES Fullscreen (1.33:1) • Languages: Eng. dub • Sound: Dolby Digital 2.0 • Cardboard Box with 3 Keepcases • 3 Discs • Region 1 GENRE & RATING Science Fiction/Robots • Not Rated (Kids)

Robotech Legacy, The: Collection 4—Masters [Box Set]

ADV Films, 2001, 315 mins., #DRT/BX4.

This box set contains the two commercially available keepcase editions of *Robotech: The Masters #7–8*.

The set also contains a third keepcase and disc titled *Robotech Extra: Masters 1—Elements of Robotechnology IV*. This disc contains a plethora of extra features and is only available in the box set. Included are the original openings and closings from all three shows that comprise the *Robotech* saga; animation and model sheets; a cover gallery for Comico's *Robotech* comic book line; and more international clips (French, Spanish, Italian, Portuguese). See individual entries for the Special and Technical Features listings.

SPECIAL FEATURES Character and Art Galleries • Promotional

Footage • International Footage • Other Title Trailers • Inserts: Liner Notes TECHNICAL FEATURES Fullscreen (1.33:1) • Languages: Eng. dub • Sound: Dolby Digital 2.0 • Cardboard Box with 3 Keepcases • 3 Discs • Region 1 GENRE & RATING Science Fiction/Robots • Not Rated (Kids)

Robotech Legacy, The: Collection 5—Masters [Box Set]

ADV Films, 2001, 330 mins., #DRT/BX5.

This box set contains the two commercially available keepcase editions of *Robotech: The Masters #9–10*

The set also contains a third keepcase and disc titled *Robotech Extra: Masters 2—Elements of Robotechnology V.* This disc contains a host of extra features and is only available in the box set. Included is the original *Robotech* pilot (never released); preproduction art for *Robotech II: The Sentinels*; an early music video; storyboards and animatics; and lots of international clips (French, Spanish, Italian, Portuguese). See individual entries for the Special and Technical Features listings.

SPECIAL FEATURES Character and Art Galleries • Storyboards • Promotional Footage • Music Video • International Footage • Other Title Trailers • Inserts: Liner Notes TECHNICAL FEATURES Fullscreen (1.33:1) • Languages: Eng. dub • Sound: Dolby Digital 2.0 • Cardboard Box with 3 Keepcases • 3 Discs • Region 1 GENRE & RATING Science Fiction/Robots • Not Rated (Kids)

Robotech Legacy, The: Collection 6—New Generation [Box Set]

ADV Films, 2002, 405 mins., #DRT/BX6.

This box set contains the two commercially available keepcase editions of *Robotech: New Generation #11–12*.

The set also contains a third keepcase and disc titled *Robotech Extra: New Generation 1—Elements of Robotechnology VI.* This disc contains a plethora of extra features and is only available in the box set. Included is the unaired pilot for *Genesis Climber Mospeada* (an English-language version that eventually became episode #61 of *Robotech*); promotional footage for the *Robotech* toy lines; preproduction art; a cover gallery for Comico's *Robotech: The New Generation* comic book line; and more international clips (French, Spanish, Italian, Portuguese). See individual entries for the Special and Technical Features listings.

SPECIAL FEATURES Character and Art Galleries • Promotional Footage • International Footage • Other Title Trailers • Inserts: Liner Notes TECHNICAL FEATURES Fullscreen (1.33:1) • Languages: Eng. dub • Sound: Dolby Digital 2.0 • Cardboard

Box with 3 Keepcases • 3 Discs • Region 1 GENRE & RATING Science Fiction/Robots • Not Rated (Kids)

Robotech Legacy, The: Collection 7—New Generation [Box Set]

ADV Films, 2002, 480 mins., #DRT/BX7.

This last box set contains the two commercially available keepcase editions of *Robotech: The Macross Saga #13–14*.

The final set also contains a third keepcase and disc titled *Robotech Extra: New Generation 2—Elements of Robotechnology VII.* This disc contains one last selection of extra features and is only available in the box set. Included is cut footage from some of the original Japanese series that did not make it into the *Robotech* reconfiguration; a gallery of *Robotech* licensed merchandise and toys; video footage from Robocon 10, a convention celebrating *Robotech*'s tenth anniversary; clips from various *Robotech* video games; and the ever-present international clips (French, Spanish, Italian, Portuguese). See individual entries for the Special and Technical Features listings.

SPECIAL FEATURES Merchandising Galleries • Convention Footage • Deleted Scenes • Video Game Clips • International Footage • Other Title Trailers • Inserts: Liner Notes • Easter Eggs TECHNICAL FEATURES Fullscreen (1.33:1) • Languages: Eng. dub • Sound: Dolby Digital 2.0 • Cardboard Box with 3 Keepcases • 3 Discs • Region 1 GENRE & RATING Science Fiction/Robots • Not Rated (Kids)

Rob Roy [Collector's Edition]

Digital Versatile Disc, 2000, 48 mins., #181. Animation directed by Warwick Gilbert. Screenplay by Rob Mowbray. Based on the novel by Sir Walter Scott.

Scotland in the 18th century is a dangerous country, where noblemen vie for the attention of England's King George I, and dangerous scoundrels and brigands roam the countryside perpetrating violence and thievery. But the Highlands have a hero in dashing rogue Rob Roy MacGregor, an honorable man who will lead his countrymen to revolt against the cruel king.

It's hard to take this 1987 production by Burbank Films Australia—based on the 1818 novel about real Scottish rogue Robert MacGregor—very seriously. For starters, the simplistic art style isn't very realistic or expressive of the gritty story. There is very little actual Scottish music anywhere in the soundtrack. And as if to pound a hobnail into the coffin further, the voice work includes some of the worst Scottish accents ever put to film. Most viewers will find that haggis leaves a better taste in their mouth than this feature.

SPECIAL FEATURES Author Bio • Game TECHNICAL FEATURES Fullscreen (1.33:1) • Languages: Eng. • Sound: Dolby Digital 5.1, DTS • Keepcase • 1 Disc • Region All GENRE & RATING Historical/Adventure • Not Rated (Kids)

Rock-A-Doodle

HBO, 1999, 75 mins., #90701. Directed by Don Bluth. Screenplay by David N. Weiss.

A little boy named Edmond—who lives in the real live-action world—is turned into a cartoon kitten by the evil Grand Duke of Owls, a character from a storybook. The Grand Duke wants to stop the sun from shining. Pulled into the animated storybook, Edmond makes friends with a number of other animals and sets out on a quest to get the help of Chanticleer, the rooster who can make the sun shine again. But will Chanticleer leave his life as a rock-and-roll star to stop the Grand Duke's evil plans?

Don Bluth has had lots of interesting ideas and lots of not-so-interesting ideas in his animated feature film career. This falls more into the "what-was-he-thinking?" category, even as it half-heartedly entertains. Voiced by country star Glen Campbell, Chanticleer is a thinly disguised Elvis Presley, meaning lots of rockabilly songs, rooster pompadours, and swooning chickens. But the characters and designs seem old hat, and the story somewhat uninvolving.

The DVD transfer is soft, muting the bright colors and frenetic action a bit. For those who like chickens, Bluth, or Elvis, this is a must-see; others will likely be bewildered.

SPECIAL FEATURES Trailer TECHNICAL FEATURES Fullscreen (1.33:1) • Languages: Eng., Fren. dub, Span. dub • Sound: Dolby Digital Surround 2.0, Dolby Digital Surround 5.1 • Snapcase • 1 Disc • Region 1 GENRE & RATING Music/Animals/Fantasy • Rated G

Roger Ramjet: Hero of Our Nation [#1]

Image, 2002, 83 mins., #ID1253HRDVD. Directed by Fred Crippen. Written by Gene Moss, Jim Thurman.

Roger Ramjet is a patriotic "daredevil, flying fool, and all-around good guy." Not quite a superhero (even if he dresses like one), Ramjet is a scientist turned aviator who leads the American Eagle Squadron, a group of jet-flying children named Yankee, Doodle, Dan, and Dee. Together, they fight the dreaded menace of Noodles Romanoff and the agents of N.A.S.T.Y. (The National

Association of Spies, Traitors, and Yahoos), Red Dog the Pirate, Jacqueline Hyde, the Solenoid Robots, and Roger's rival Lance Crossfire, as well as assorted other non-patriotic baddies. And when he needs to have a bit more power, Roger can take a Proton Energy Pill to gain the strength of twenty atom bombs for twenty seconds!

Syndicated in 1965, Roger Ramjet was a satirical and sly precursor to the live-action Batman series, and a good companion to *Rocky and His Friends* (aka Rocky and Bullwinkle). Full of bad puns, hyperbole, pop culture references, and non sequiturs, Roger Ramjet appealed to adults just as much as it did to kids. With its five-minute episodes, the stories were forced to be snappy and sly, and unrelenting patriotism was the order of the day.

According to some animation historians, the fact that Roger Ramjet was not shown much after its initial syndication package ended was probably due to the pill-popping "drug use" of the hero! But to read that motivation into the character really takes some twisting, and a viewer's time would be better spent laughing and enjoying the emotive tones of a pre–*Space Ghost* Gary Owens as the title character.

The DVD contains fifteen episodes: "Dr. Evilkisser"; "The Shaft"; "Baseball"; "The Pirates"; "Drafted"; "TV Crisis"; "Revolution"; "Miss America"; "The Race"; "Jack the Nipper"; "Ma Ramjet"; "Hi Noon"; "Bank Robbers"; "Dumb Waiter"; and "Skydiving." A ten-minute clip segment with partial episodes features commentary by star Gary Owens.

SPECIAL FEATURES Commentary by Gary Owens • Bumper Segments • Insert: Episode Guide TECHNICAL FEATURES Fullscreen (1.33:1) • Languages: Eng. • Sound: Dolby Digital 1.0 • Keepcase • 1 Disc • Region 1–6 GENRE & RATING Comedy/Action • Not Rated (Kids)

Roger Ramjet: Man of Adventure [#2]

Image, 2002, 82 mins., #ID1255HRDVD. Directed by Fred Crippen. Written by Gene Moss, Jim Thurman.

Roger Ramjet and his kids are back to fight for the American Way again. Whether the job is surfing space as an astronaut, facing down a werewolf or flying tea saucers, racing skateboards to win a date, or rescuing comedians from robots, Roger has lots to do. Plus, mom comes to visit, a pair of jet boots gives lift, Roger finds out why American coffee tastes so bad, a trip through time yields a meeting with Leonardo da Vinci, and a surfing contest gets everyone wet.

The DVD contains fifteen more five-minute Roger Ramjet episodes: "Monkey"; "Orbit"; "Werewolf"; "Flying Saucers"; "Skateboards"; "Long Joan Silver"; "Comics"; "Jet Boots"; "Hollywood"; "Treasure in Sierra's Mattress"; "Coffee"; "Time Machine"; "Pool";

"Ancestors"; and "Surf Nuts." The commentary by Gary Owens and five bumper segments are the same as those from the first disc.

SPECIAL FEATURES Commentary by Gary Owens • Bumper Segments • Insert: Episode Guide TECHNICAL FEATURES Fullscreen (1.33:1) • Languages: Eng. • Sound: Dolby Digital 1.0 • Keepcase • 1 Disc • Region 1–6 GENRE & RATING Comedy/Action • Not Rated (Kids)

Rolie Polie Olie: The Great Defender of Fun

Disney, 2002, 75 mins., #25000. Directed by Ron Pitts. Written by Nadine van der Velde. Based on the books by William Joyce.

NOTE: This DVD arrived too late for a full review. The following text is promotional copy provided by the releasing company:

"Get ready to blast off for out-of-this-world fun in Olie's first-ever full-length movie. It's little sister Zowie's birthday, and everybody's gearing up for the party. But there's a storm cloud overhead: space pirate Gloomius Maximus (voiced by James Woods) is out to plunder all the happiness out of the whole galaxy. Can Olie and his friends find a way to defeat Gloomius' evil plot and save then universe from being un-fun-erated?

"Join Olie and a stellar cast of memorable characters in this song-filled, visually dazzling outer space adventure. *Rolie Polie Olie: The Great Defender of Fun* boldly goes where no one in Polieville has gone before!"

SPECIAL FEATURES Galaxy Map • Games • Coloring Pages • Other Title Trailers • Easter Egg TECHNICAL FEATURES Fullscreen (1.33:1) • Subtitles/CC: Eng. • Languages: Eng. • Sound: Dolby Digital Surround 5.1 • Keepcase • 1 Disc • Region 1 GENRE & RATING CGI/Music/Imagination • Rated G

Ronin Warriors: The Call [#1]

Bandai, 2002, 100 mins. (each side), #1950. Directed by Masashi Ikeda, Mamoru Hamazu. Screenplay by Jinzo Toriumi, Yuki Onishi, Masanori Oka, Saburo Ebinuma, Yuji Watanabe, Hideki Sonoda, Tomoko Nakaya, Kun Iwasaki.

A millennium ago a terrible dark lord from another dimension tried to enslave a planet. One lone warrior was able to fend him off and trap him in a deep sleep. But Lord Talpa's just received his wake-up call, and he definitely got up on the wrong side of the bed. Now he's decided the planet needs a new ruler: him. With the fabled warrior gone, Lord Talpa and his army, the Dynasty, think they've got it easy. That's just because the group hasn't met the Ronin Warriors yet. Ryu, Rowen, Sai, Sage, and Kento are five teenagers banded together

in samurai armor that enhances their natural abilities, who are ready, willing, and—hopefully—able to give Lord Talpa a run for his money. Aided by Ryu's white tiger, a mysterious monk known as the Ancient, and their friend Mia, a young woman knowledgeable in legends, lore, and the mysteries surrounding the Ronin's armor, this group hopes to defend their planet or die trying.

First airing in 1988, *Ronin Warriors* was a popular anime series lasting for thirty-nine episodes and three OVAs. In 1999 episodes of this series began airing on the Sci-Fi Channel, and the Cartoon Network added it to their Toonami line in 2000. The series is fairly violent, and is probably not appropriate for young viewers.

The DVD contains episodes #1–4. It's the best of both worlds as the double-sided disc gives viewers the option of watching the original Japanese series, *Legendary Armor Samurai Troopers* (subtitled in English), or its English-only counterpart, *Ronin Warriors*. It's interesting to see the edits, changes, and additions that took place from one version to the next. [JMC]

SPECIAL FEATURES Reversible Cover TECHNICAL FEATURES Fullscreen (1.33:1) • Subtitles/CC: Eng. • Languages: Jap., Eng. dub • Sound: Dolby Digital Surround 2.0 • Keepcase • 1 Disc • Region 1 GENRE & RATING Action/Adventure/Fantasy • Rated 13+

Ronin Warriors: Rescue Operations [#2]

Bandai, 2002, 100 mins. (each side), #1951. Directed by Masashi Ikeda, Mamoru Hamazu. Screenplay by Jinzo Toriumi, Yuki Onishi, Masanori Oka, Saburo Ebinuma, Yuji Watanabe, Hideki Sonoda, Tomoko Nakaya, Kun Iwasaki.

With the world suffering at the hands of Lord Talpa's evil demons, Ryu sets off to find the other Ronin, so that together they can save the planet. The road to gather allies is tough, as he soon discovers. First, after fighting a demon, he finds Sage, but no sooner do the pair get acquainted than they decide to split up to more quickly find the next two Ronin, Kento and Sai. Gathering their other allies, the quartet set off in search of the fifth legendary warrior, but a master of illusion tricks the teens into fighting each other instead of the enemy. Will they be able to regain their senses and find the last Ronin?

Every great group of heroes has to start somewhere, and this DVD, containing episodes #5–8, shows how Ryu went about finding and meeting most of the other Ronin Warriors. As with the previous double-sided discs, one side is the English-only version, *Ronin Warriors*, while the other side is the original Japanese series, *Legendary Armor Samurai Troopers* (subtitled in English). [JMC]

SPECIAL FEATURES Reversible Cover TECHNICAL FEATURES Fullscreen (1.33:1) • Subtitles/CC: Eng. • Languages: Jap., Eng. dub •

Sound: Dolby Digital Surround 2.0 • Keepcase • 1 Disc • Region 1 GENRE & RATING Action/Adventure/Fantasy • Rated 13+

Ronin Warriors: Warriors Reunited! [#3]

Bandai, 2002, 100 mins. (each side), #1952. Directed by Masashi Ikeda, Mamoru Hamazu. Screenplay by Jinzo Toriumi, Yuki Onishi, Masanori Oka, Saburo Ebinuma, Yuji Watanabe, Hideki Sonoda, Tomoko Nakaya, Kun Iwasaki.

Ryu and Kento are searching for Rowen within the Dynasty when they're discovered and sent off into space. Talpa hopes that will kill the legendary warriors, but instead of destroying the teens, it reunites them with Rowen, who was trapped in the Earth's atmosphere. Now the five fighters are together again and ready to take on Talpa's Dynasty. The Ronin Warriors invade the Dynasty, ready to do anything to save Earth, but they're terribly outnumbered and magically outclassed. Will they be able to fulfill their mission and prevent Talpa from conquering the Earth, or by going to his turf have they unknowingly played right into his master plan?

Taking the battle to the source is the theme of this action-packed DVD containing episodes #9–12. As with the previous double-sided discs, one side is the English-only counterpart, *Ronin Warriors*, while the other side is the original Japanese series, *Legendary Armor Samurai Troopers* (subtitled in English). [JMC]

SPECIAL FEATURES Reversible Cover TECHNICAL FEATURES Fullscreen (1.33:1) • Subtitles/CC: Eng. • Languages: Jap., Eng. dub • Sound: Dolby Digital Surround 2.0 • Keepcase • 1 Disc • Region 1 GENRE & RATING Action/Adventure/Fantasy • Rated 13+

Ronin Warriors: The Shadow of Doom [#4]

Bandai, 2002, 100 mins. (each side), #1953. Directed by Masashi Ikeda, Mamoru Hamazu. Screenplay by Jinzo Toriumi, Yuki Onishi, Masanori Oka, Saburo Ebinuma, Yuji Watanabe, Hideki Sonoda, Tomoko Nakaya, Kun Iwasaki.

The warriors prepare to assault Talpa's castle, but their strategy is a mess. Separated by the evil Talpa, the seeds of doubt are planted into the minds of the heroes; is their armor really a force for evil? But help may come from the strangest place . . . one of Talpa's own warlords!

This DVD contains episodes #13–16. As with the previous double-sided discs, one side is the English-only version, *Ronin Warriors*, while the other side is the original Japanese series, *Legendary Armor Samurai Troopers* (subtitled in English).

SPECIAL FEATURES Reversible Cover TECHNICAL FEATURES Fullscreen (1.33:1) • Subtitles/CC: Eng. • Languages: Jap., Eng. dub • Sound: Dolby Digital Surround 2.0 • Keepcase • 1 Disc • Region 1 GENRE & RATING Action/Adventure/Fantasy • Rated 13+

Ronin Warriors: The Hardest Battle [#5]

Bandai, 2002, 100 mins. (each side), #1955. Directed by Masashi Ikeda, Mamoru Hamazu. Screenplay by Jinzo Toriumi, Yuki Onishi, Masanori Oka, Saburo Ebinuma, Yuji Watanabe, Hideki Sonoda, Tomoko Nakaya, Kun Iwasaki.

NOTE: This DVD arrived too late for a full review. The following text is promotional copy provided by the releasing company:

"Ryo and the other Warriors confront Talpa again, and once again, Talpa seems to have the upper hand. After Talpa quickly absorbs the others and their powers, Ryo and White Blaze are all that stand against the forces of doom and the conquest of the Earth!"

This disc contains episodes #17–20.

SPECIAL FEATURES Reversible Cover TECHNICAL FEATURES Fullscreen (1.33:1) • Subtitles/CC: Eng. • Languages: Jap., Eng. dub • Sound: Dolby Digital • Keepcase • 1 Disc • Region 1 GENRE & RATING Action/Adventure/Fantasy • Rated 13+

Ronin Warriors: Arise, New Armor! [#6]

Bandai, 2002, 100 mins. (each side), #1954. Directed by Masashi Ikeda, Mamoru Hamazu. Screenplay by Jinzo Toriumi, Yuki Onishi, Masanori Oka, Saburo Ebinuma, Yuji Watanabe, Hideki Sonoda, Tomoko Nakaya, Kun Iwasaki.

NOTE: This DVD arrived too late for a full review. The following text is promotional copy provided by the releasing company:

"*Ronin Warriors* tells the story of four young men gifted with the powers of the elements within their armor suits and thrust into battle against a seemingly invincible enemy, the might Talpa. This time, it's Round Two of Ryo's battle against Sarenbou! Still after the White Armor, Sarenbou attacks again with ferocious intent! Interestingly, he is accompanied by his own tiger, Black Blaze. As the tigers battle, their masters do so as well. When all looks lost, White Blaze saves his master, but at a great cost. Now, even after recovering from the latest attack, a new enemy shows up to test them! "

This disc contains episodes #21–24.

SPECIAL FEATURES Reversible Cover TECHNICAL FEATURES Fullscreen (1.33:1) • Subtitles/CC: Eng. • Languages: Jap., Eng. dub • Sound: Dolby Digital 2.0 • Keepcase • 1 Disc • Region 1 GENRE & RATING Action/Adventure/Fantasy • Rated 13+

Ronin Warriors: The Evil Priestess [#7]

Bandai, 2002, 100 mins. (each side), #1956. Directed by Masashi Ikeda, Mamoru Hamazu. Screenplay by Jinzo Toriumi, Yuki Onishi, Masanori Oka, Saburo Ebinuma, Yuji Watanabe, Hideki Sonoda, Tomoko Nakaya, Kun Iwasaki.

NOTE: This DVD arrived too late for a full review. The following text is promotional copy provided by the releasing company:

"The Ancient has appeared to the Warriors in a dream, telling them that they must all work hard and hone their powers! Has the time finally come for the final battle? The warriors split up and begin their training, but Talpa is waiting for them. One by one, the Warriors fall prey to Talpa's henchmen until there are only two of them left. And then, the evil Lady Kayura appears to deal with the last two Warriors. . . ."

This disc contains episodes #25–28.

SPECIAL FEATURES Reversible Cover TECHNICAL FEATURES Fullscreen (1.33:1) • Subtitles/CC: Eng. • Languages: Jap., Eng. dub • Sound: Dolby Digital • Keepcase • 1 Disc • Region 1 GENRE & RATING Action/Adventure/Fantasy • Rated 13+

Ronin Warriors: A New Ally [#8]

Bandai, 2002, 100 mins. (each side), #1957. Directed by Masashi Ikeda, Mamoru Hamazu. Screenplay by Jinzo Toriumi, Yuki Onishi, Masanori Oka, Saburo Ebinuma, Yuji Watanabe, Hideki Sonoda, Tomoko Nakaya, Kun Iwasaki.

NOTE: This DVD arrived too late for a full review. The following text is promotional copy provided by the releasing company:

"The identity of the Ancient is revealed. Ryo and Rowen, the two Warriors left standing in the fight against Talpa, continue their difficult quest. One of Kayura's tricks backfires, and the two warriors find themselves in Arago's realm. However, Arago servant Dara lies in wait for them. And to make matters worse, they're plotting to possess the Inferno Armor! But during the battle, Kayura starts to wonder why she's fighting so hard against Ryo. . . ."

This disc contains episodes #29–32.

SPECIAL FEATURES Reversible Cover TECHNICAL FEATURES Fullscreen (1.33:1) • Subtitles/CC: Eng. • Languages: Jap., Eng. dub • Sound: Dolby Digital • Keepcase • 1 Disc • Region 1 GENRE & RATING Action/Adventure/Fantasy • Rated 13+

Roughnecks: Starship Troopers Chronicles— The Pluto Campaign [#1]

Columbia/TriStar, 2002, 97 mins., #06174. Directed by Audu Paden, Christopher Berkeley, David Hartman, Jay Olivia, Sam Liu. Written by Duane Capizzi, Marsha F. Griffin, Thomas Pugsley, Greg Klein, Jennifer Levin, Michael Kramer. Based on the novel by Robert A. Heinlein.

A group of young Starship Troopers roams the galaxy, assigned to take out infestations of alien "bugs"—Arachnid Forces—which threaten all life. Members of the Alpha Team "Razak's Roughnecks" include tough-guy Rico, telepathic Jenkins, and fearless female soldier Flores. When they travel to Pluto, they find that the plasma-shooting bugs are threatening research outposts there. Rico soon risks his life for his fellow soldiers, even as a reporter must learn to defend himself against new flying bugs. A new intelligence officer gives them a chilling mission: enter the Bug's underground incubation center and capture a live Plasma Bug!

Although the look and designs of *Roughnecks: Starship Troopers Chronicles* are based on the 1997 feature film directed by Paul Verhoeven, the story and characters are much closer to Robert A. Heinlein's original novel than the movie was. The series debuted on television in the fall of 1999, and is entirely computer-generated, making it one of the first projects to try to use CGI for lots of human characters. Of course it helps that many of them are dressed in armor, and the battle-heavy series lends itself to odd lighting, but the animators did a fine job.

The DVD contains the first five episodes of the TV series, edited together to create a cohesive whole. The beginning and end credit sequences for each individual episode have been removed, except at the start and end of the story. While the series is exceedingly violent—it is about war, after all—it doesn't even come close to the ultra-violence of the film.

SPECIAL FEATURES Character and Art Galleries • Other Title Trailers TECHNICAL FEATURES Fullscreen (1.33:1) • Subtitles/CC: Eng., Chin., Fren., Kor., Port., Span., Thai • Languages: Eng., Fren. dub, Port. dub, Span. dub • Sound: Dolby Digital Surround 2.0, Dolby Digital 5.1 • Keepcase • 1 Disc • Region 1, 3, 4 GENRE & RATING CGI/Science Fiction/Insects • Not Rated (Teens)

Roughnecks: Starship Troopers Chronicles— The Hydora Campaign [#2]

Columbia/TriStar, 2002, 96 mins., #07495. Directed by David Hartman, Vincent Edwards, Andre Clavel, Sam Liu. Written by Steve Berman, Dan Gordon, Dave Clark, Andrew Robinson, Jules Dennis. Based on the novel by Robert A. Heinlein.

The Troopers follow a "Transport Bug" back to the watery world of Hydora, hoping to destroy the enemy bugs' home base. But they're soon attacked by a new form of bug, a barbed mosquito-like insect. Carmen is in trouble when she tries to evacuate wounded soldiers, and Jenkins is incapacitated by an acid-tipped barb as the Roughnecks try to rout a Rippler nest. Two squads disappear, leading to a fight against giant beetles, and the Roughnecks are captured . . .

The DVD contains the episodes #6–10 of the TV series, edited together to create a cohesive whole. One commentary track includes producers, directors, writers, and the composer, while a second technical commentary track is from the crew from CGI companies such as Foundation Imaging.

SPECIAL FEATURES Commentary Tracks by Producers, Crew, and CGI Artists • Cast and Crew Filmographies • Character and Art Galleries • Trailers TECHNICAL FEATURES Fullscreen (1.33:1) • Subtitles/CC: Eng., Chin., Fren., Kor., Port., Span., Thai • Languages: Eng., Fren. dub, Port. dub, Span. dub • Sound: Dolby Digital 5.1 • Keepcase • 1 Disc • Region 1, 3, 4 GENRE & RATING CGI/Science Fiction/Insects • Not Rated (Teens)

Roughnecks: Starship Troopers Chronicles— The Tophet Campaign [#3]

Columbia/TriStar, 2002, 95 mins., #06889. Directed by Alan Caldwell, Michael Chang, Jay Oliva, Sean Song. Written by Jon Weisman, Cary Bates, Michael Reaves, Greg Weisman, Lydia Marano. Based on the novel by Robert A. Heinlein.

On the planet of Tophet, the Roughnecks meet an advanced species they call the "Skinnies." But if what the aliens tell them is true—that the bugs couldn't adapt to their climate and died—where are all the dead bugs? It's clear the Skinnies are hiding something, but meanwhile the Roughnecks must accept help from a new Trooper that's a cyborg! When mind-control from the bugs is discovered, who will be able to free their thoughts?

The DVD contains the episodes #11–15 of the TV series, edited together to create one complete storyline. One commentary track includes producers, directors, the

vice president of creative affairs, and a story editor, while a second technical commentary track is from the crew of CGI companies such as Flat Earth and Foundation Imaging.

SPECIAL FEATURES Commentary Tracks by Producers, Crew, and CGI Artists • Cast and Crew Filmographies • Character and Art Galleries • Trailers • Easter Egg TECHNICAL FEATURES Fullscreen (1.33:1) • Subtitles/CC: Eng., Chin., Fren., Kor., Port., Span., Thai • Languages: Eng., Fren. dub, Port. dub, Span. dub • Sound: Dolby Digital 5.1 • Keepcase • 1 Disc • Region 1, 3, 4 GENRE & RATING CGI/Science Fiction/Insects • Not Rated (Teens)

Roughnecks: Starship Troopers Chronicles— The Tesca Campaign [#4]

Columbia/TriStar, 2002, 96 mins., #07496. Directed by Jay Olivia, Sean Song, Alan Caldwell. Written by Tom Pugsley, Greg Klein, Tony Schillaci, Steve Melching, Geoff Miller. Based on the novel by Robert A. Heinlein.

T'Phai, one of the Skinnies, encounters some bad feelings when he is assigned to help the Roughnecks as they storm Zegema Beach. But later, Rico and T'Phai learn they must work together after squad members disappear in the jungle on Tesca Nemerosa, and attacks by Giant Spider Bugs, Control Bugs, and Tanker Worms commence! Rico is hurt and placed into a regeneration tank, but his warnings of dangerous bug movements go unheeded . . .

The DVD contains the episodes #16–20 of the TV series, edited together to create a complete story. The single commentary track includes producers, directors, and a story editor.

SPECIAL FEATURES Commentary Track by Producers, Directors, and Story Editor • Cast and Crew Filmographies • Production Photos • Trailer • Other Title Trailers TECHNICAL FEATURES Fullscreen (1.33:1) • Subtitles/CC: Eng., Chin., Fren., Kor., Port., Span., Thai • Languages: Eng., Fren. dub, Port. dub, Span. dub • Sound: Dolby Digital 5.1 • Keepcase • 1 Disc • Region 1, 3, 4 GENRE & RATING CGI/Science Fiction/Insects • Not Rated (Teens)

Roughnecks: Starship Troopers Chronicles— The Homefront Campaign [#5]

Columbia/TriStar, 2002, 96 mins.

This DVD was not available for review. It contains episodes #21–25.

Roughnecks: Starship Troopers Chronicles— The Klendathu Campaign [#6]

Columbia/TriStar, 2002, 96 mins.

This DVD was not available for review. It contains episodes #26–30.

Roujin Z

Image, 1998, 80 mins., #ID4409CTDVD. Directed by Hiroyuki Kitakubo. Screenplay by Katsuhiro Otomo.

Welcome to near-future Japan. The Ministry of Public Welfare has come up with a great new machine, the Z-001. It's a bed with a built-in supercomputer and it's set to revolutionize home care for the elderly. Unfortunately, the machine doesn't care about comfort, or that it makes the poor senior citizen feel like he's no longer human. The creators don't care that the machine has a small nuclear-powered engine. But student nurse Haruko Mihashi cares about Mr. Takazawa, the elderly man who becomes the human guinea pig for this technological "miracle." When Haruko receives a distress call from the poor man, she springs into action with some fellow students to smuggle Mr. Takazawa and the Z-001 away. What follows has to be seen to be believed, as the Ministry and then the military chase after the fugitive superbed. But just where is it taking Mr. Takazawa anyway?

This over-the-top theatrical film was released in 1991 and tackles the very real problem of future care for senior citizens. But it does so in a satiric and semi-comic way that leaves some people wondering if they should laugh or feel sorry for poor Takazawa. It's an interesting concept that works pretty well. The colors look a bit lighter and less vibrant than what you usually see in Japanese animation. But this movie isn't your typical story and so the difference in style seems to fit just fine.

The English dub script is quite different from the Japanese script, so you might want to stick with the more accurate Japanese-language track. There is some brief nudity, but nothing really offensive in this movie, other than some language. [RJM]

SPECIAL FEATURES None TECHNICAL FEATURES Widescreen (1.66:1) • Subtitles/CC: Eng. • Languages: Jap., Eng. dub • Sound: Dolby Digital 2.0 • Snapcase • 1 Disc • Region 1 GENRE & RATING Medical/Comedy/Robots • Rated PG-13

Roujin Z [Special Widescreen Edition]

Central Park, 2002, 87 mins.

This DVD was not available for review. It is a remastered rerelease.

Royal Space Force: The Wings of Honneamise

Manga Entertainment, 2000, 125 mins., #MANGA4012-2. Directed by Hiroyuki Yamaga. Screenplay by Hiroyuki Yamaga.

This movie covers the first journey into space by humans from another world. Shirotsugh Lhadatt (Shiro for short) is a young man whose ambition was to be a pilot of high-speed aircraft, but because of poor grades ended up in the Royal Space Force. Unfortunately the Space Force is considered a joke by the rest of the military. Shiro himself agrees, until he meets Riquinni Nonderaiko, a young woman whose faith in God changes Shiro's perspective. But just when the Space Force seems to be taking off (no pun intended), an opposing government decides that the Royal Space Force must be stopped, and Shiro becomes a target. Now the Space Force must rush to get the spaceship completed and Shiro must swiftly complete his training to become the first pilot.

This theatrical production was released in 1987 by the famous Japanese studio Gainax. The production design and visuals are stunning, even by today's standards. An entire alternate world was created and realized for this film and it takes multiple viewings to absorb it all. The story itself isn't bad, but some viewers might find it lacking or too slow moving.

This DVD does contain a commentary track by the director Hiroyuki Yamaga, as well as the original short that was used to pitch the film. Unfortunately it isn't the best transfer you'll see, and it doesn't do the visuals justice. There is an attempted rape scene in the film and some brief nudity, marking this for older audiences. But the serious science fiction elements and political allegories are what really make *Royal Space Force: The Wings of Honneamise* gel for older viewers. [RJM]

SPECIAL FEATURES Commentary Track with Director • Character and Art Galleries • Deleted Scene • Promotional Footage • Other Title Trailers • Inserts: Liner Notes • Easter Eggs TECHNICAL FEATURES Widescreen (1.85:1 enhanced for 16x9) • Subtitles/CC: Eng. • Languages: Jap., Eng. dub • Sound: Dolby Digital 5.1 • Keepcase • 1 Disc • Region 1, 2, 4 GENRE & RATING Science Fiction/Action • Not Rated (Teens)

Rudolph the Red-Nosed Reindeer: The Movie

GoodTimes, 1999, 84 mins., #05-81059. Directed by Bill Kowalchuk. Written by Michael Aschner.

Rudolph is a young reindeer who is laughed at because of his glowing nose. He runs off into the arctic wilderness, where he is befriended by a polar bear. Later, Rudolph helps save pretty doe Zoey, who has been captured by the villainous Ice Queen Stormella. Along the way, Rudolph just happens to help Santa save Christmas!

The animated story of Rudolph is so ingrained in the collective public consciousness that it's hard to understand why this new version of the tale was created for video and DVD release. At least GoodTimes got it right two years later when they hired the same writer and director to create a sequel to the beloved 1964 stop-motion version of *Rudolph*. That's not to say this film doesn't have some charm, but most of it seems borrowed from elsewhere. A veteran cast of Hollywood actors voice the characters, including John Goodman as Santa, Eric Idle as a cat, Bob Newhart as the polar bear, Whoopi Goldberg as Stormella and—heaven help us—Richard Simmons as an elf.

The animation is just above acceptable, but not enjoyable for older audiences. Kids may like it, however. The DVD is mostly no frills, with the 2.0 stereo sound helping the nine songs (including one from Paul McCartney) sound their best. For a much better Rudolph sequel, see the 2001 release below.

SPECIAL FEATURES Trailer TECHNICAL FEATURES Widescreen (1.78:1 enhanced for 16x9) • Subtitles/CC: Eng., Fren., Span. • Languages: Eng., Fren. dub, Span. dub • Sound: Dolby Digital 2.0 • Snapcase • 1 Disc • Region 1 GENRE & RATING Holiday/Music/Family • Not Rated (Kids)

Rudolph the Red-Nosed Reindeer

Sony Wonder, 2002, 52 mins., #LVD 54339. Directed by Larry Roemer. Written by Romeo Muller. Based on a story by Robert May.

NOTE: This DVD arrived too late for a full review. The following text is promotional copy provided by the releasing company:

"Christmas has been cancelled! Or, at least it will be if Santa Claus can't find a way to guide his sleigh through a fierce blizzard. Fortunately for him, there's Rudolph the Red-Nosed Reindeer! Shunned by the other reindeer because of his glowing nose, Rudolph becomes a hero when he guides Santa through the storm and enables him to deliver Christmas presents to all. This digitally remastered version features the renowned original music score known the world over."

What the PR doesn't say is that all the favorite characters from the Island of Misfit Toys are here too, as well as Hermey the Elf, Yukon Cornelius, and the Abominable Snow Monster.

SPECIAL FEATURES Interview with Producer • Promotional Footage • Sing-Along • Game • Other Title Trailers TECHNICAL FEATURES Fullscreen (1.33:1) • Subtitles/CC: Eng. • Languages: Eng., Span. dub • Sound: Dolby Digital • Keepcase • 1 Disc • Region 1 GENRE & RATING Holiday/Stop-Motion/Music • Not Rated (All Ages)

Rudolph the Red-Nosed Reindeer and the Island of Misfit Toys

GoodTimes, 2001, 74 mins., #05-81236. Directed by Bill Kowalchuk. Written by Michael Aschner.

Rudolph the Red-Nosed Reindeer doesn't look thirty-seven years old, but it's been that long since his television debut. He's still friends with Hermey, the elf dentist, big-bearded prospector Yukon Cornelius, the scary/cute Abominable Snowman Bumbles, and cute girl reindeer Clarice. This time out, Christmas is threatened by a trenchcoat-wearing bad guy called the Toy Taker! After the mysterious villain steals all of Santa's toys—jeopardizing Christmas—Rudolph and his pals set out to find out where the playthings have gone. Look for a plus-sized Hippo Queen to take part in the story as well, while the familiar Snowman narrates.

This CGI cartoon is a sequel to the stop-motion 1964 NBC TV special, *Rudolph the Red-Nosed Reindeer*, and features many of the same characters. With much of the charm of its original—but with updated technology—this *Rudolph* features the voices of Jamie Lee Curtis, Richard Dreyfuss, and Rick Moranis. Unfortunately, none of the original voice actors were used. Still, kids will love this tale. The only negative is one element of the plot: Parents may want to chat with their kids about not going away with nice strangers who offer gifts, as some of the toys do with the Toy Taker.

The feature-length DVD has quite a number of very short extras, including a featurette on "Maya Technology," the CGI system used for this digital version, and a four-minute commentary by the director. Seven new holiday songs are featured, along with Tony Bennett's version of the classic Rudolph song.

SPECIAL FEATURES "Making of" Featurettes • Cast Filmographies • Trailer • DVD-ROM Features: Printable Holiday Cards • Easter Egg TECHNICAL FEATURES Fullscreen (1.33:1) • Subtitles/CC: Eng. • Languages: Eng. • Sound: Dolby Digital 2.0, Dolby Digital 5.1 • Keepcase • 1 Disc • Region 1 GENRE & RATING Holiday/Music/Family • Not Rated (Kids)

Rugrats Movie, The

Paramount, 1999, 79 mins., #333997.

This DVD was not available for review. This disc was also included as part of a two-pack set, its keepcase packaged with *Rugrats in Paris: The Movie*.

Rugrats in Paris: The Movie

Paramount, 2001, 80 mins., #33672.

This DVD was not available for review. This disc was also included as part of a two-pack set, its keepcase packaged with The *Rugrats Movie*.

Ruin Explorers

ADV Films, 2000, 120 mins., #DVDRE/001. Directed by Takeshi Mori. Screenplay by Takeshi Mori.

A ruin explorer is a thrill-seeking treasure hunter willing to take any and all risks to obtain rare treasures and artifacts. The catgirl Fam and her human best friend Ihrie are ruin explorers with a less-than-glorious track record, partly due to the curse haunting them both. Fam, a great sorceress, can't remember a spell to save her life. Ihrie, also a skilled mage, turns from woman to mouse when she uses magic. Together, they search for the Ultimate Power, a magical artifact that can break the curse and grant them riches beyond their wildest dreams. When the pair meets up with the unscrupulous treasure seeker Galuf—who claims to have a map to the Ultimate Power—they form an unlikely alliance and set off, not knowing that another team, magician Rasha and strongman Migel, have the same goals. It seems everyone wants the Ultimate Power, but no one wants it for unselfish reasons, except Prince Lyle. He needs it to fight the evil Rugodorull, a sorcerer who destroyed his land and wants to enslave the earth. When these hapless thrill-seekers meet the noble prince, will they all team up to fight the good fight, or will it still be everyone for him- or herself?

Ruin Explorers first saw life in 1995 as a series of four thirty-minute OVAs, based on role-playing segments by Kunihiko Tanaka in *RPG Magazine*. Although there aren't a lot of unique characters or scenes presented in this tale, what's fun about it is that this archetypical cast eventually takes on a life of its own, turning the familiar into an engaging and enjoyable story.

This DVD collects the whole saga in one convenient place. [JMC]

SPECIAL FEATURES Character and Art Galleries • Other Title Trailers TECHNICAL FEATURES Fullscreen (1.33:1) • Subtitles/CC: Eng. • Languages: Jap., Eng. dub • Sound: Dolby Digital 2.0 • Keepcase • 1 Disc • Region 1 GENRE & RATING Fantasy/Adventure • Not Rated (Teens)

Rurouni Kenshin: Wandering Samurai—The Legendary Swordsman [#1]

Anime Works, 2000, 100mins., #RKDVD-2000. Directed by Kazuhiro Furuhashi. Screenplay by Michiru Shimada, Yoshiyuki Suga. Based on the manga series by Nobuhiro Watsuki in *Shonen Jump*.

The Meiji Revolution marked the end of shogun and samurai in Japan. Now, though, the revolutionaries are as corrupt as those who used to be in power, and foreign influences are creating even more change in the land. Kenshin Himura is an ex-assassin and legendary swordsman who now wanders the land, but when he meets the lovely Kaoru Kamiya, everything changes. He helps her find a killer at her fencing school—a man who is masquerading as "Battosai the Manslayer," the assassin Kenshin once was—and then aids the townspeople who are being bullied by the police. Later, a mercenary named Sanosuke Sagara challenges Kenshin to a fight, and the swordsman cannot back down. . . .

Debuting in 1996 on television, *Rurouni Kenshin* was a fairly direct adaptation of its manga source material. In fact, the first sixty-two episodes came from specific manga arcs. Several of the characters (including Kenshin himself) were based on historical figures. The show has occasional comedy, usually in the form of Kenshin's goo-goo eyes for Kaoru or klutziness when she's around. While that works at times, it is a bit distracting from the semi-seriousness of the main story. Designs are simple and functional, but it is the detailed swordfight and martial arts battle scenes where the show shines best.

This DVD contains episodes #1–4. There's nothing in here that pre-teens and up can't watch, though a word of warning about the opening credits song: flee!

Note that the movie and OVA series that ended the storyline were collected by ADV under the name *Samurai X*. See entries for those titles.

SPECIAL FEATURES Character Bios • Character and Art Galleries • Liner Notes • Clean Credits • Other Title Trailers TECHNICAL FEATURES Fullscreen (1.33:1) • Subtitles/CC: Eng. • Languages: Jap., Eng. dub • Sound: Dolby Digital 2.0 • Keepcase • 1 Disc • Region 1 GENRE & RATING Martial Arts/Action • Rated 13+

Rurouni Kenshin: Wandering Samurai—Battle in the Moonlight [#2]

Anime Works, 2000, 100 mins., #RKDVD-2001. Directed by Kazuhiro Furuhashi. Screenplay by Yoshiyuki Suga, Michiru Shimada. Based on the manga series by Nobuhiro Watsuki in *Shonen Jump*.

Sanosuke and Kenshin duel, with both weapons and words, but they soon learn that they have much in common. Then, the police ask Kenshin for help tracking down a serial killer who is offing Imperialist politicians. Kaoru is taken hostage by the killer, whose motivations are tied to Kenshin's past as Battosai. And later, when a woman named Megumi, who is being chased by drug dealers, asks for Kenshin and Sanosuke's help, they come up against the Oniwaban Group . . . a powerful force.

This DVD contains episodes #5–8.

SPECIAL FEATURES Character Bios • Character and Art Galleries • Liner Notes • Clean Credits • Outtakes TECHNICAL FEATURES Fullscreen (1.33:1) • Subtitles/CC: Eng. • Languages: Jap., Eng. dub • Sound: Dolby Digital 2.0 • Keepcase • 1 Disc • Region 1–6 GENRE & RATING Martial Arts/Action • Rated 13+

Rurouni Kenshin: Wandering Samurai—The Shadow Elite [#3]

Anime Works, 2000, 100 mins., #RKDVD-2002/2003. Directed by Kazuhiro Furuhashi. Screenplay by Yoshiyuki Suga, Michiru Shimada. Based on the manga series by Nobuhiro Watsuki in *Shonen Jump*.

Megumi is hiding a secret that could get her killed—and another that causes Sanosuke grief—but when she sacrifices herself to keep the Kamiya school safe, Kenshin and Sanosuke decide to raid Kanryu's camp to save her. But first they must get past a man skilled in ninja illusions and another fighter who has the ability to nullify Kenshin's speed and powers. Who will be the "strongest man"? And later, a young waitress is being blackmailed, and Kenshin and young protégé Yahiko decide to help her.

This DVD contains episodes #9–12. Note that although the spine is labeled #RKDVD-2003, this is actually #RKDVD-2002 (as it says on the disc itself).

SPECIAL FEATURES Character and Art Galleries • Liner Notes • Fan Art Contest Rules • Other Title Trailers TECHNICAL FEATURES Fullscreen (1.33:1) • Subtitles/CC: Eng. • Languages: Jap., Eng. dub • Sound: Dolby Digital 2.0 • Keepcase • 1 Disc • Region 1 GENRE & RATING Martial Arts/Action • Rated 13+

Rurouni Kenshin: Wandering Samurai—False Prophet [#4]

Anime Works, 2000, 125 mins., #RKDVD-2003. Directed by Kazuhiro Furuhashi. Screenplay by Yoshiyuki Suga, Nobuaki Kishima. Based on the manga series by Nobuhiro Watsuki in *Shonen Jump*.

Kaoru's newest student at the school is big trouble. He's a sumo wrestler who has managed to anger the entire assemblage at his old sumo school. Will Kenshin and Sanosuke still fight when the fight gets heavy? And now that Megumi is a country doctor and not involved with opium smugglers, things can go smoothly, right? Wrong. A faith healer means to get rid of her by any means necessary. Then, in a two-part story, Kenshin must aid a retired manslayer—who was once Sanosuke's teacher—when old enemies return. Plus, Yahiko goes to the circus, but he finds that Marimo, the human bullet, has become the target of a rival show!

This DVD contains five episodes instead of the usual four, comprising #13–17.

SPECIAL FEATURES Fan Art Gallery • Liner Notes • Outtakes TECHNICAL FEATURES Fullscreen (1.33:1) • Subtitles/CC: Eng. • Languages: Jap., Eng. dub • Sound: Dolby Digital 2.0 • Keepcase • 1 Disc • Region 1 GENRE & RATING Martial Arts/Action • Rated 13+

Rurouni Kenshin: Wandering Samurai—Renegade Samurai [#5]

Anime Works, 2001, 125 mins., #RKDVD-2004. Directed by Kazuhiro Furuhashi. Screenplay by Nobuaki Kishima, Mitsuru Shimada, Michiko Yokote. Based on the manga series by Nobuhiro Watsuki in *Shonen Jump*.

When Yahiko is tricked into stealing Kenshin's infamous reverse-blade sword, how will the ex-assassin defend himself against Gohei Hiruma's hired killers? Then in a three-part story, Kenshin meets a young apprentice who is being taught a deadly fighting technique by his surrogate father, an undefeated manslayer. But the man wants to use "borrowed" wealth to fund a new revolution. Kenshin must help Yutaro see the truth about his teacher. Later, Kenshin and the others take their first steam-powered train ride, only to get caught in a robbery!

This DVD contains the five episodes #18–22.

SPECIAL FEATURES Liner Notes • Clean Credits • Other Title Trailers TECHNICAL FEATURES Fullscreen (1.33:1) • Subtitles/CC: Eng. • Languages: Jap., Eng. dub • Sound: Dolby Digital 2.0 • Keepcase • 1 Disc • Region 1 GENRE & RATING Martial Arts/Action • Rated 13+

Rurouni Kenshin: Wandering Samurai—The Flames of Revolution [#6]

Anime Works, 2001, 125 mins., #RKDVD-2005. Directed by Kazuhiro Furuhashi. Screenplay by Yoshiyuki Suga, Mitsuru Shimada. Based on the manga series by Nobuhiro Watsuki in *Shonen Jump*.

When a comrade from his past contacts Sanosuke with a plan to avenge fallen friends, Sanosuke turns against those who trust him. Kenshin must face his friend in battle once again, and one of them may not survive. And in a three-part story, Kenshin is swept up into the world of piracy and drug-runners, all without the help of his friends.

This DVD contains the five episodes #23–27. This sequence completes the first story arc for the series, known as the Tokyo arc.

SPECIAL FEATURES Character and Art Galleries • Liner Notes • Outtakes • Other Title Trailers • Easter Egg TECHNICAL FEATURES Fullscreen (1.33:1) • Subtitles/CC: Eng. • Languages: Jap., Eng. dub • Sound: Dolby Digital 2.0 • Keepcase • 1 Disc • Region 1 GENRE & RATING Martial Arts/Action • Rated 13+

Rurouni Kenshin: Legend of Kyoto—Shadow of the Wolf [#7]

Anime Works, 2001, 100 mins., #RKDVD-2006. Directed by Kazuhiro Furuhashi. Screenplay by Yoshiyuki Suga, Mitsuru Shimada. Based on the manga series by Nobuhiro Watsuki in *Shonen Jump*.

Kenshin is having flashbacks of previous battles, specifically those against Hajime Saito. Little does he suspect that Saito has been hired to kill him, but when Sanosuke gets in the way, blood is spilled! Another assassin, Akamatsu, faces Kenshin in battle, while Saito disguises himself to gain access to Kaoru's school. Soon, Kenshin and Saito engage in a deadly battle that brings out the Battosai beast in Kenshin. How does Saito's attack relate to the Secretary of Defense and the political future of Japan? And what surprise role will Kenshin play in it? After a political assassination rocks the city—and on the eve of a year of refuge at Kaoru's dojo—Kenshin makes a fateful decision.

This DVD contains episodes #28–31. Episode #30 is a brutal turning point for the series.

SPECIAL FEATURES Liner Notes • Original Epilogue • Clean Credits • Outtakes • Other Title Trailers TECHNICAL FEATURES Fullscreen (1.33:1) • Subtitles/CC: Eng. • Languages: Jap., Eng. dub • Sound: Dolby Digital 2.0 • Keepcase • 1 Disc • Region 1 GENRE & RATING Martial Arts/Action • Rated 13+

Rurouni Kenshin: Legend of Kyoto—Ice Blue Eyes [#8]

Anime Works, 2001, 100 mins., #RHDVD-2007. Directed by Kazuhiro Furuhashi. Screenplay by Yoshiyuki Suga, Mitsuru Shimada. Based on the manga series by Nobuhiro Watsuki in *Shonen Jump*.

Wandering the countryside again, Kenshin meets up with a crafty female thief named Misao Makimachi. They soon are involved with saving a village that has been overtaken by Shishio's henchman Senkaku. Meanwhile, Sanosuke decides to go after Kenshin, but a battle with Saito changes those plans. But that doesn't stop Kaoru and Yahiko from traveling after Kenshin on their own.

This DVD contains episodes #32–35.

SPECIAL FEATURES Liner Notes • Outtakes • Other Title Trailers TECHNICAL FEATURES Fullscreen (1.33:1) • Subtitles/CC: Eng. • Languages: Jap., Eng. dub • Sound: Dolby Digital 2.0 • Keepcase • 1 Disc • Region 1 GENRE & RATING Martial Arts/Action • Rated 13+

Rurouni Kenshin: Legend of Kyoto—Heart of the Sword [#9]

Anime Works, 2001, 100 mins., #RKDVD-2008. Directed by Kazuhiro Furuhashi. Screenplay by Yoshiyuki Suga, Mitsuru Shimada. Based on the manga series by Nobuhiro Watsuki in *Shonen Jump*.

Kenshin, Misao, Saito, and a villager named Eiji are all determined to bring down Shishio, who is revealed to have also been an assassin alongside Battosai. But Kenshin will have to defeat the brutish Senkaku—and the emotionless Sojiro—if he wants to stop Shishio. Meanwhile, Sanosuke meets a failed priest who seems to command the legendary Ho-riki technique, channeling the earth spirits. Will the priest train Sanosuke, and what secret agenda does he have? And Kenshin relates to Misao exactly why he's not happy about returning to Kyoto, and encounters a deadly swordsman.

This DVD contains episodes #36–39.

SPECIAL FEATURES Liner Notes • Clean Credits • Outtakes • Other Title Trailers TECHNICAL FEATURES Fullscreen (1.33:1) • Subtitles/CC: Eng. • Languages: Jap., Eng. dub • Sound: Dolby Digital 2.0 • Keepcase • 1 Disc • Region 1 GENRE & RATING Martial Arts/Action • Rated 13+

Rurouni Kenshin: Legend of Kyoto—Between Life and Death [#10]

Anime Works, 2001, 100 mins., #RKDVD-2009. Directed by Kazuhiro Furuhashi. Screenplay by Yoshiyuki Suga, Mitsuru Shimada. Based on the manga series by Nobuhiro Watsuki in *Shonen Jump*.

When he was young, Kenshin abandoned his training to become the killer Battosai, but when he reunites with his former master, Seijuro Hiko, he determines to finish his training, no matter what the cost. Thief Misao reveals to Yahiko and Kaoru what the stakes of Kenshin's current undertakings are, and what his actions might mean to Japan's future. A man named Aoshi Shinomori is also on Kenshin's trail, and he's connected to Misao, who learns a secret about Kenshin from Kaoru. Shishio's motivations are revealed, as well as the reason he wraps his body in bandages, and he makes a pact with Aoshi. And a death he's responsible for will change Kenshin forever . . .

This DVD contains episodes #40–43.

SPECIAL FEATURES Liner Notes • Clean Credits • Outtakes • Other Title Trailers TECHNICAL FEATURES Fullscreen (1.33:1) • Subtitles/CC: Eng. • Languages: Jap., Eng. dub • Sound: Dolby Digital 2.0 • Keepcase • 1 Disc • Region 1 GENRE & RATING Martial Arts/Action • Rated 13+

Rurouni Kenshin: Legend of Kyoto—Faces of Evil [#11]

Anime Works, 2001, 100 mins., #RKDVD-2010. Directed by Kazuhiro Furuhashi. Screenplay by Mitsuru Shimada, Yoshiyuki Suga. Based on the manga series by Nobuhiro Watsuki in *Shonen Jump*.

Saito and Sanosuke meet again, and soon, Shishio's plan is revealed. Operation Kyoto Holocaust will see Kyoto burn, with 500 fires started at once! Shishio has a giant iron battleship named *Purgatory,* and he plans to use it against the city. Kenshin, Sanosuke, Saito, and others band together to make an assault on Shishio's ship . . .

This DVD contains episodes #44–47. According to some sources, there is apparently one episode missing from this sequence: the "real" 45th episode is a "clips show" with cute dolls of Kaoru and Yahiko recalling all of Kenshin's greatest fights.

SPECIAL FEATURES Liner Notes • Outtakes • Other Title Trailers TECHNICAL FEATURES Fullscreen (1.33:1) • Subtitles/CC: Eng. • Languages: Jap., Eng. dub • Sound: Dolby Digital 2.0 • Keepcase • 1 Disc • Region 1 GENRE & RATING Martial Arts/Action • Rated 13+

Rurouni Kenshin: Legend of Kyoto—Blind Justice [#12]

Anime Works, 2001, 125 mins., #RKDVD-2011. Directed by Kazuhiro Furuhashi. Screenplay by Mitsuru Shimada, Yoshiyuki Suga. Based on the manga series by Nobuhiro Watsuki in *Shonen Jump*.

Kenshin, Sanosuke, and Saito have come to a temple to take care of the Shishio problem once and for all. But to get to the villain, they'll have to fight their own ex-friends and comrades . . . including the failed priest who once taught Sanosuke! Saito must face Usui, a blind fighter who is among the last of the dreaded Shinsengumi. And Kenshin must face Aoshi in a final battle to the death! Is there a chance Kenshin can redeem Aoshi and bring him back to the woman he once loved, Misao the thief? And what has become of Misao, Kaoru, and Yahiko, who are fighting their own battles?

This DVD contains the five episodes #48–52.

SPECIAL FEATURES Liner Notes • Clean Credits • Outtakes • Other Title Trailers TECHNICAL FEATURES Fullscreen (1.33:1) • Subtitles/CC: Eng. • Languages: Jap., Eng. dub • Sound: Dolby Digital 2.0 • Keepcase • 1 Disc • Region 1 GENRE & RATING Martial Arts/Action • Rated 13+

Rurouni Kenshin: Legend of Kyoto—Innocence and Experience [#13]

Anime Works, 2001, 125 mins., #RKDVD-2012. Directed by Kazuhiro Furuhashi. Screenplay by Mitsuru Shimada, Yoshiyuki Suga. Based on the manga series by Nobuhiro Watsuki in *Shonen Jump*.

The giant Fuji has brought destruction down on Kenshin and his friends, but the arrival of Kenshin's superpowered former master, Seijuro Hiko, may save the day. But Kenshin must now face boy assassin Sojiro if he wants to get to Shishio (does this guy have endless henchmen or what?). But Sojiro is known as the "Tenken" because his sword skills seem to be a present from the gods. How can Kenshin prevail?

This DVD contains episodes #53–57.

SPECIAL FEATURES Liner Notes • Outtakes • Other Title Trailers TECHNICAL FEATURES Fullscreen (1.33:1) • Subtitles/CC: Eng. • Languages: Jap., Eng. dub • Sound: Dolby Digital 2.0 • Keepcase • 1 Disc • Region 1 GENRE & RATING Martial Arts/Action • Rated 13+

Rurouni Kenshin: Legend of Kyoto—Fire Requiem [#14]

Anime Works, 2002, 125 mins., #RKDVD-2013. Directed by Kazuhiro Furuhashi. Screenplay by Yoshiyuki Suga. Based on the manga series by Nobuhiro Watsuki in *Shonen Jump*.

The final battle is finally here, and the fate of the Meiji Era hangs in the balance. Five men are soon to be joined in combat: Kenshin Himura, Sanosuke Sagara, Hajime Saito, Aoshi Shinomori, and Makoto Shishio. Foes will become allies as all the skills of the past are employed. In the end, it doesn't matter whether one used to be the most skilled assassin or the most feared or the strongest. What matters is who will be standing at the end of the clash . . . Kenshin or Shishio?

This DVD contains episodes #58–62, which wrap up the Kyoto storyline.

SPECIAL FEATURES Liner Notes • Outtakes • Attack List • Character Messages • Other Title Trailers TECHNICAL FEATURES Fullscreen (1.33:1) • Subtitles/CC: Eng. • Languages: Jap., Eng. dub • Sound: Dolby Digital 2.0 • Keepcase • 1 Disc • Region 1 GENRE & RATING Martial Arts/Action • Rated 13+

Rurouni Kenshin: Tales of the Meiji—Firefly's Wish [#15]

Anime Works, 2002, 100 mins., #RKDVD-2014. Directed by Kazuhiro Furuhashi. Screenplay by Mitsuru Shimada, Yoshiyuki Suga. Based on the manga series by Nobuhiro Watsuki in *Shonen Jump*.

The ghosts of the Revolution have been put to rest, and Kenshin and his friends try to get back to a normal life at Kaoru's Kamiya dojo. But first, Kenshin and Kaoru must deal with a love that haunts Kenshin from his past. Later, young Yahiko is mistaken for a foreign prince, and Sanosuke discovers a dog that might lead him to a treasure!

This DVD contains episodes #63–66. Since the manga adapted for the first sixty-two episodes was not yet complete when production began on these episodes, an entirely new series of "filler" stories was used.

SPECIAL FEATURES Liner Notes • Outtakes • Other Title Trailers TECHNICAL FEATURES Fullscreen (1.33:1) • Subtitles/CC: Eng. • Languages: Jap., Eng. dub • Sound: Dolby Digital 2.0 • Keepcase • 1 Disc • Region 1 GENRE & RATING Martial Arts/Action • Rated 13+

Rurouni Kenshin: Tales of the Meiji—Son of God [#16]

Anime Works, 2002, 100 mins., #RKDVD-2015. Directed by Kazuhiro Furuhashi. Screenplay by Michiru Shimada, Zoshi Shia. Based on the manga series by Nobuhiro Watsuki in *Shonen Jump*.

In a storyline known as the Shimabara Saga, Kenshin must confront an apprentice swordsman who is using the astonishing Hiten Mitsurugi fighting style to disrupt the peace. A new revolutionary army is forming, but how can Kenshin and his friends fight against them when their ideals seem to be related to truth and justice?

This DVD contains episodes #67–70.

SPECIAL FEATURES Liner Notes • Clean Credits • Outtakes • Other Title Trailers TECHNICAL FEATURES Fullscreen (1.33:1) • Subtitles/CC: Eng. • Languages: Jap., Eng. dub • Sound: Dolby Digital 2.0 • Keepcase • 1 Disc • Region 1 GENRE & RATING Martial Arts/Action • Rated 13+

Rurouni Kenshin: Tales of the Meiji—Holy War [#17]

Anime Works, 2002, 100 mins., #RKDVD-2016. Directed by Kazuhiro Furuhashi. Screenplay by Michiru Shimada. Based on the manga series by Nobuhiro Watsuki in *Shonen Jump*.

The beginning of the war continues, as Shogo Amakusa, the self-proclaimed "Son of God," begins a revolution with his army. As Sanosuke rescues a holy woman, a blinded Kenshin struggles to do good. He may have to act quickly, as some of the faithful revolutionaries are planning to crucify their leader!

This DVD contains episodes #71–74.

SPECIAL FEATURES Liner Notes • Clean Credits • Outtakes • Other Title Trailers TECHNICAL FEATURES Fullscreen (1.33:1) • Subtitles/CC: Eng. • Languages: Jap., Eng. dub • Sound: Dolby Digital 2.0 • Keepcase • 1 Disc • Region 1 GENRE & RATING Martial Arts/Action • Rated 13+

Rurouni Kenshin: Tales of the Meiji—Fall from Grace [#18]

Anime Works, 2002, 100 mins., #RKDVD-2017. Directed by Kazuhiro Furuhashi. Screenplay by Michiru Shimada, Yoshiyuki Suga, Kazuhiro Furuhashi. Based on the manga series by Nobuhiro Watsuki in *Shonen Jump*.

With Kenshin still blind and Shogo wounded by a bullet, the two must battle to decide the fate of the people in this conclusion to the Shimabara Saga. The army and revolutionaries have given a one-hour truce, and the two martial artists must fully commit to an attack against each other, taking the Hiten Mitsurugi combat style further than it has ever gone before.

This DVD contains episodes #75–78.

SPECIAL FEATURES Liner Notes • Outtakes • Other Title Trailers TECHNICAL FEATURES Fullscreen (1.33:1) • Subtitles/CC: Eng. • Languages: Jap., Eng. dub • Sound: Dolby Digital 2.0 • Keepcase • 1 Disc • Region 1 GENRE & RATING Martial Arts/Action • Rated 13+

Rurouni Kenshin: Tales of the Meiji— Dreams of Youth [#19]

Anime Works, 2002, 100 mins., #RKDVD-2018. Directed by Kazuhiro Furuhashi. Screenplay by Akemi Omode. Based on the manga series by Nobuhiro Watsuki in *Jump Comics*.

NOTE: This DVD arrived too late for a full review. The following text is promotional copy provided by the releasing company:

"Kenshin and the others meet Daigoro, a young man with a western education. Daigoro has been rejected by Kaishu, a famous teacher, who has been active since the times of the Revolution. Kaoru steps in, and the Kamiya Dojo gets a new student. Kenshin suspects that something is amiss, however, and he uncovers a strange conspiracy leading back to the Tokugawa Era. A powerful group of outlaws, the Beni Aoi, believe that Kaishu is the heir of the Tokugawa fortune, and they won't let him or Daigoro live in peace until it is uncovered!"

This DVD contains episodes #79–82.

SPECIAL FEATURES Liner Notes • Clean Credits • Outtakes • Other Title Trailers • Easter Egg TECHNICAL FEATURES Fullscreen (1.33:1) • Subtitles/CC: Eng. • Languages: Jap., Eng. dub • Sound: Dolby Digital • Keepcase • 1 Disc • Region 1 GENRE & RATING Martial Arts/Action • Rated 13+

Rurouni Kenshin: Tales of the Meiji— Soulless Knights [#20]

Anime Works, 2002, 100 mins., #RKDVD-2019. Directed by Kazuhiro Furuhashi. Screenplay by Yoshiyuki Suga. Based on the manga series by Nobuhiro Watsuki in *Shonen Jump*.

In the past, a wounded Yutaro Tsukayama promised to return to Tokyo—after a trip to Germany—to finish his duel with young Yahiko. Now, he has returned to the Kamiya Dojo, rejoining with friends. Will he keep his vow to Yahiko? And what

about the mystical order of Germanic soldiers that followed Yutaro to the city? Kenshin, Yutaro, and the others must face a ninja squad and other adversities.

This DVD contains episodes #83–86.

SPECIAL FEATURES Liner Notes • Clean Credits • Outtakes • Other Title Trailers TECHNICAL FEATURES Fullscreen (1.33:1) • Subtitles/CC: Eng. • Languages: Jap., Eng. dub • Sound: Dolby Digital 2.0 • Keepcase • 1 Disc • Region 1 GENRE & RATING Martial Arts/Action • Rated 13+

Rurouni Kenshin: Tales of the Meiji—A Shinobi's Love [#21]

Anime Works, 2002, 100 mins., #RKDVD-2020. Directed by Kazuhiro Furuhashi. Screenplay by Yoshiyuki Suga. Based on the manga series by Nobuhiro Watsuki in *Jump Comics*.

NOTE: This DVD arrived too late for a full review. The following text is promotional copy provided by the releasing company:

"Yutaro and the others are on the trail of Meldars, a deadly swordsman from Germany. Meldars's ambition knows no end as he searches for the legendary Divine Elixir, said to grant eternal life. Enlisting the help of Misanagi and her Sanada Ninja clan, the Germans prepare for a final confrontation with Kenshin and the others. The tragedy begins when Meldars's Lieutenant, Schneider, finds himself attracted to the ninja, Misanagi. When the Germans plan a lethal double-cross, Schneider will have to choose between his feelings and his loyalty to the Fatherland."

This DVD contains episodes #87–90.

SPECIAL FEATURES Liner Notes • Clean Credits • Outtakes • Other Title Trailers TECHNICAL FEATURES Fullscreen (1.33:1) • Subtitles/CC: Eng. • Languages: Jap., Eng. dub • Sound: Dolby Digital • Keepcase • 1 Disc • Region 1 GENRE & RATING Martial Arts/Action • Rated 13+

Rurouni Kenshin: Tales of the Meiji—End Song [#22]

Anime Works, 2002, 100 mins., #RKDVD-2021. Directed by Kazuhiro Furuhashi. Screenplay by Masashi Sogo. Based on the manga series by Nobuhiro Watsuki in *Jump Comics*.

NOTE: This DVD arrived too late for a full review. The following text is promotional copy provided by the releasing company:

"As the end of Kenshin's legend draws near, the scarred swordsman meets an opponent like none other. Saeki Mizu is a master of Feng Shui, a mysterious form of Chinese astrology that prevents him from ever being defeated by a sword! During the time of the Tokugawa, there were two competing families who taught the art of Feng Shui, the Kaze and the Mizu families. Before the slighted Mizu family topples the Meiji government, Kenshin must join forces with Jinpu Kaze, whose family knowledge is the only defense against their powers."

This DVD contains episodes #91–95.

SPECIAL FEATURES Liner Notes • Outtakes • Other Title Trailers • Easter Egg TECHNICAL FEATURES Fullscreen (1.33:1) • Subtitles/CC: Eng. • Languages: Jap., Eng. dub • Sound: Dolby Digital • Keepcase • 1 Disc • Region 1 GENRE & RATING Martial Arts/Action • Rated 13+

Saber Marionette J: DVD Collection 1

Bandai, 2001, 225 mins., #0515. Directed by Masami Shimoda. Based on the novels by Satoru Akahori in *Dragon Magazine* and *Dragon Jr.*

In the future when mankind is looking for other inhabitable planets, a terrible accident causes the destruction of an interstellar spacecraft and only six men survive. The men—Donatello of Romania, Harold from Russia, Jones of the U.S., Wang from China, Ieyasu of Japan, and Faust from Germany—land on Terra II and colonize it. The planet has no women, save for emotionless female androids called marionettes. Unknown to the other four, Ieyasu and Faust create six special components called the "maiden circuit" that can grant sentience and emotions to six marionettes. They divide the marionettes up and keep their existence a secret for centuries. Meanwhile the men break off into different areas, clone themselves, and colonize the world. A few hundred years later, strife has developed among the nations, especially between Faust's land of Gartlant and Ieyasu's Japoness. A Japoness teen stumbles across a few of the marionettes with the maiden circuit: Lime, Cherry, and Bloodberry. The three are immediately smitten with the lad, and consider Otaru their master. When he's in danger or his friends are in trouble, they'll do anything they can to help.

The *Saber Marionette J* saga was based on Satoru Akahori's work in *Dragon Magazine*. The anime premiered in 1995 and spanned several different series, including three OVAs, as well as video games and toys. Although considered a treat by some and quite popular with *new* anime fans, the story is lacking in depth and a little unrealistic, even for anime. There is quite a bit of double-entendre comedy—which, combined with the premise—aims the series squarely toward hormonally charged teen male audiences.

This first two-disc DVD is bit slow paced. It contains episodes #1–9 of the *Saber Marionette J* series. [JMC]

SPECIAL FEATURES Character Bios • Character and Art Galleries • Music Video • Other Title Trailers • Easter Egg TECHNICAL FEATURES Fullscreen (1.33:1) • Subtitles/CC: Eng. • Languages: Jap., Eng. dub, Span. dub • Sound: Dolby Digital Surround 2.0 • Multikeepcase • 2 Discs • Region 1 GENRE & RATING Action/Girls • Rated 13+

Saber Marionette J: DVD Collection 2

Bandai, 2001, 220 mins., #0516. Directed by Masami Shimoda. Based on the novels by Satoru Akahori in *Dragon Magazine* and *Dragon Jr.*

Otaru, Bloodberry, Lime, and Cherry are looking to shut down Faust's master computer. They enter his land and discover most residents lead pitiful existences crushed by Faust's cruel reign. They want to help a resistance group overcome his tyranny, but Faust has marionettes of his own . . . and his Saber Dolls might be too much for Otaru and the Saber Marionettes to overcome.

The second two-disc collection contains episodes #10–17, revealing more information about the maiden circuits and about their role in the advancement of life on Terra II. [JMC]

SPECIAL FEATURES Character Bios • Character and Art Galleries • Music Video • Other Title Trailers • Easter Egg TECHNICAL FEATURES Fullscreen (1.33:1) • Subtitles/CC: Eng. • Languages: Jap., Eng. dub, Span. dub • Sound: Dolby Digital Surround 2.0 • Multikeepcase • 2 Discs • Region 1 GENRE & RATING Action/Girls • Rated 13+

Saber Marionette J: DVD Collection 3

Bandai, 2001, 220 mins., #0517. Directed by Masami Shimoda. Based on the novels by Satoru Akahori in *Dragon Magazine* and *Dragon Jr.*

Faust's Saber Dolls are kicked out of their homeland for failing to get the maiden circuit. They journey to Japoness to try and get the circuit from the Saber Marionettes and win favor with Faust again. In the heat of this battle, the marionettes become aware of their true role on this planet—a role that will either unite Terra II or drive the wedges between nations even deeper.

Enemies become allies as they all have a common goal in the final two-disc collection of *Saber Marionette J,* which contains episodes #18–25 of the television series. The conclusion, although it answers a lot of questions, still has too many unbelievable parts—even for anime. [JMC]

SPECIAL FEATURES Character Bios • Character and Art Galleries • Music Video • Other Title Trailers • Easter Eggs TECHNICAL FEATURES Fullscreen (1.33:1) • Subtitles/CC: Eng. • Languages: Jap., Eng. dub, Span. dub • Sound: Dolby Digital Surround 2.0 • Multikeepcase • 2 Discs • Region 1 GENRE & RATING Action/Girls • Rated 13+

Saber Marionette J: Again—Plasmatic Crisis

Bandai, 2002, 170 mins., #0575. Directed by Masami Shimoda. Screenplay by Masayori Sekijima, Satoru Akahori, Kenichi Kanemaki. Based on the novels by Satoru Akahori in *Dragon Magazine* and *Dragon Jr.*

After Faust is defeated, he's sorry and heads off to explore the world. With Gartlant no longer a threat, Otaru and the marionettes decide to open up a restaurant and try to lead some kind of normal existence. Speaking of leading a normal existence, Faust realized he was wrong to raise his marionettes as slaves and wants them to have a chance as "regular" beings. He sends Luchs, Panther, and Tiger to Otaru to learn the average ways of the world and how to act around others. He wants them to learn positive social skills and figures Otaru's gang the best bet for this to happen. Although apprehensive at first, the rival marionettes learn to get along and things look pretty good for our group—which always means trouble. While traveling, Faust finds an empty canister that contained a very special marionette with an awesome power that's greater than all the previous marionettes. He's worried about the gang so he goes back to warn them. The new marionette, Marine, has already arrived, but no one is sure if she's friend or foe.

This wacky two-disc set contains the entire *Saber Marionette J* OVAs in one place and is much better than the *SMJ Collections.* There are a few extras included, but the funniest is the collection of commercials from the series. [JMC]

SPECIAL FEATURES Character and Art Galleries • Trailer • Promotional Footage • Clean Credits • Other Title Trailers • Inserts: Episode Guide TECHNICAL FEATURES Fullscreen (1.33:1) • Subtitles/CC: Eng. • Languages: Jap., Eng. dub, Span. dub • Sound: Dolby Digital Surround 2.0 • Multikeepcase • 2 Discs • Region 1 GENRE & RATING Action/Girls • Rated 13+

Saber Marionette J to X: Program One

Bandai, 2002, 125 mins., #0490. Directed by Hiyoko Sayama. Based on the novels by Satoru Akahori in *Dragon Magazine* and *Dragon Jr.*

Life is good for Otaru. He's organizing the high point of Japoness Culture—the Sanja Fair—a job he's wanted since he was a little boy. Most of the marionettes have good jobs and are happy, and there hasn't been too much trouble for a while. However, all good things must come to an end and some people want to rain on Otaru's parade—uh—Fair. Since Gartlant fell from power and its people were able to make choices on their own, some have decided to migrate to different lands. A lot found homes in Japoness and have decided that the annual Sanja Fair should include some things they enjoy, like Christmas, but Christmas has never been a part of the festival. Otaru must decide which traditions to incorporate and why. Plus there's even more trouble when the marionettes, after mishearing a conversation about the first female clones almost being ready, believe Otaru will soon want to get rid of them. Now Otaru must both convince them they're still necessary and please everyone of Japoness with his Fair choices. Plus, Faust returns, and the Shiritaki Alliance may mean trouble . . .

Set an unspecified time after *Saber Marionette J Again,* this disc contains the first episodes, #1–5, of the *Saber Marionette J to X* saga, broadcast on Japanese television in 1998. The animation is credible but not fantastic, and some fans have complained that too much obvious CGI was utilized. Similarly, the general consensus among fandom is that the English-language voices are abysmal, and the Japanese voice track is a must.

The DVD might be confusing to first timers in the *Saber Marionette J* world because it does little to introduce the characters and history of the series, assuming all viewing it will be familiar with the mythos. [JMC]

SPECIAL FEATURES Clean Credits • Other Title Trailers TECHNICAL FEATURES Fullscreen (1.33:1) • Subtitles/CC: Eng. • Languages: Jap., Eng. dub • Sound: Dolby Digital Surround 2.0 • Keepcase • 1 Disc • Region 1 GENRE & RATING Action/Girls • Rated 13+

Saber Marionette J to X: Program Two

Bandai, 2002, 125 mins., #0491. Directed by Hiyoko Sayama. Based on the novels by Satoru Akahori in *Dragon Magazine* and *Dragon Jr.*

This disc, containing episodes #6–10, is filled with a variety of girl problems. First, after a bad date with Otaru, Bloodberry is crushed and runs away to join the circus. Can Otaru convince her to return and leave the Big Top behind? Then Cherry finds a baby clone and must decide whether to hide it herself or turn it back in to the proper authorities. Finally Lime gets the spotlight in a few episodes dealing with her fairy friend that only she can see, and some other ecological problems threatening not only Japoness, but all of Terra II. [JMC]

SPECIAL FEATURES Interview with Character Designer • Other Title Trailers • Inserts: Episode Guide TECHNICAL FEATURES Fullscreen (1.33:1) • Subtitles/CC: Eng. • Languages: Jap., Eng. dub • Sound: Dolby Digital Surround 2.0 • Keepcase • 1 Disc • Region 1 GENRE & RATING Action/Girls • Rated 13+

Saber Marionette J to X: Program Three

Bandai, 2002, 125 mins., #0492. Directed by Masami Shimoda. Based on the novels by Satoru Akahori in *Dragon Magazine* and *Dragon Jr.*

Lorelei is the key to Terra II's future, but she's been kidnapped by Gettel, who announces the rebirth of the country of Gartlant. Otaru plans to save Lorelei, but he finds that he's facing Faust again! When Faust orders his marionettes to attack Otaru, will they obey, or rebel against their former master? The battle is soon joined, with a surprise ally waiting in the wings. Plus, who will Otaru take with him on vacation when he wins a trip to Xian? All the marionettes want to go. . . .

This third DVD collection of episodes contains #11–14.

SPECIAL FEATURES Interview with Character Designer • Character and Art Galleries • Other Title Trailers • Inserts: Episode Guide TECHNICAL FEATURES Fullscreen (1.33:1) • Subtitles/CC: Eng. • Languages: Jap., Eng. dub • Sound: Dolby Digital Surround 2.0 • Keepcase • 1 Disc • Region 1 GENRE & RATING Action/Girls • Rated 13+

Saber Marionette J to X: Program Four

Bandai, 2002, 100 mins., #0493. Directed by Masami Shimoda. Based on the manga series by Satoru Akahori in *Dragon Magazine* and *Dragon Jr.*

NOTE: This DVD arrived too late for a full review. The following text is promotional copy provided by the releasing company:

"Otaru, Lime, Cherry, Bloodberry, and friends have a new adventure ahead of them, but with new adventure comes new enemies. Otaru and the Marionettes have arrived in Xian and are beginning to enjoy their well-deserved vacation, despite the fact that Hanagata has managed to tag along. However, Otaru suddenly collapses with a burning fever. When the doctor advises that the cure must be gathered from plants in the surrounding countryside, Lime, Cherry, and Bloodberry selflessly go on a quest to save Otaru. When Otaru wakes from his illness, five days have passed, the Marionettes have disappeared, and he's been branded an international terrorist by the Xian government! Now, Otaru must find the others and clear his name before it's too late."

This disc contains episodes #15–18.

SPECIAL FEATURES "Making of" Featurettes • Other Title Trailers • Inserts: Episode Guide TECHNICAL FEATURES Fullscreen (1.33:1) • Subtitles/CC: Eng. • Languages: Jap., Eng. dub • Sound: Dolby Digital • Keepcase • 1 Disc • Region 1 GENRE & RATING Action/Girls • Rated 13+

Sabrina: The Animated Series—Sabrina's World

Trimark, 2001, 90 mins., #VM7716D. Directed by Scott Heming. Written by Gary Apple, Jan Strnad, Jeanmarie Williams, Don Gillies.

Sabrina Spellman is not yet the teenage half-witch seen in the live-action television series from which this series was spun off. Here, she's a preteen girl with a penchant for getting into interesting situations with her magical powers. She's often accompanied by her talking cat, Salem, or her two magical aunts, Hilda and Zelda, not to mention her non-magical friend Harvey and rich-girl rival Gem. In one story, Sabrina has to rescue Salem from shooting off into space in the space shuttle, and in another, she must stop Salem from baring his claws at a witch-kitty. Next, Sabrina bewitches a handsome piano teacher, and later learns that love often means getting your heart broken . . . even if you have magic powers.

Based on the comic book character debuting in Archie Comics in 1962, Sabrina was a regular on the animated *The Archies* in 1969–70, then soloed in *Sabrina and the Groovie Ghoulies* in 1970. She starred in a CBS *Sabrina the Teen-Age Witch* series from 1971 to 1974, and NBC rebroadcast episodes in a series called *Sabrina, Superwitch* in 1977. *Sabrina* first appeared in modern-era form as a live-action Showtime telefilm in spring 1996, and was followed that fall by a long-running sitcom on ABC, and later, the WB.

Although the live show features Melissa Joan Hart in the title role, the 1999 animated show features her younger sister, Emily, as the voice of Sabrina. Melissa voices both Zelda and Hilda, who are cursed to be teenagers in the series, and she does live-action introductory segments for this DVD. The animation is simplistic and cute, full of bright colors. Kids will love it.

SPECIAL FEATURES Game • Other Title Trailers TECHNICAL FEATURES Fullscreen (1.33:1) • Subtitles/CC: Eng., Span. • Languages: Eng., Span. dub • Sound: Dolby Digital 2.0 • Keepcase • 1 Disc • Region 1 GENRE & RATING Comedy/Fantasy/Girls • Not Rated (Kids)

Sailor and the 7 Ballz ☞ see Mature/Adult Section

Sailor Moon: A Heroine is Chosen [#1]

ADV Films, 2002, 135 mins., #DMN/001. Directed by Junichi Sato. Based on the manga series by Naoko Takeuchi in *Nakayoshi*.

After a talking black cat has a conversation with fourteen-year-old Serena, her life will never be the same! The feline, Luna, reveals Serena to be the fabled Moon Princess; it was her duty to protect the Earth from the forces of darkness, even if she was afraid and unsure. In times of trouble, Serena uses a magic locket to transform from a klutzy crybaby into the champion of love and justice, Sailor Moon. Joined by her friends the Sailor Scouts—Sailor Mars, Mercury, Jupiter, and Venus—and her boyfriend, Darien (aka the mysterious Tuxedo Mask), she fights the evil Negaverse's Queen Beryl and her minions. But can these teenagers successfully combat the forces of darkness from out of this world?

A delightfully poignant manga series by Naoko Takeuchi, *Sailor Moon* began in 1992 as a television series and lasted through five incarnations, with 200 episodes total. *Sailor Moon* also saw life in three OVAs, a few live-action adventures, several video games, and is rumored to be returning in a new *Sailor Moon X* series. Thanks to DIC, U.S. audiences were introduced to *Sailor Moon* in 1994, albeit in a sanitized version. In 1998 the Cartoon Network began airing episodes daily as part of its afternoon Toonami line. Filled with a likable cast that doesn't

always initially win, this series has charm and imagination, and proves that you don't have to be the smartest, prettiest, or most talented to be a hero. The animation is cutesy at times, and drenched with rainbow-bright colors, but the transformation sequences have fans all their own.

The first six episodes of *Sailor Moon* are presented in this charming collection, setting the stage and introducing the initial players in the saga. [JMC]

SPECIAL FEATURES Other Title Trailers TECHNICAL FEATURES Fullscreen (1.33:1) • Languages: Eng. • Sound: Dolby Digital Surround 2.0 • Keepcase • 1 Disc • Region 1 GENRE & RATING Action/Girls • Not Rated (Kids)

Sailor Moon: Sailor Scouts to the Rescue [#2]

ADV Films, 2002, 135 mins., #DMN/002. Directed by Junichi Sato. Based on the manga series by Naoko Takeuchi in *Nakayoshi*.

Six more battles against the villains from the evil Negaverse are presented in this volume, giving even the most dedicated travelers reason to stay at home. Demonic buses take riders to another dimension instead of their next stop, amusement park attractions turn deadly, a relaxing cruise causes more than seasickness, a quiet park becomes the site of a nefarious Negaforce plot—and Sailor Moon and pals go right to the heart of each problem. Will these beautiful heroes be able to stop the spread of darkness?

This DVD contains episodes #7–12 of the *Sailor Moon* TV series, and introduces us to Sailor Mars, as well as the beginning of Serena's attraction to Darien. [JMC]

SPECIAL FEATURES Other Title Trailers • Inserts: Trading Card TECHNICAL FEATURES Fullscreen (1.33:1) • Languages: Eng. • Sound: Dolby Digital Surround 2.0 • Keepcase • 1 Disc • Region 1 GENRE & RATING Action/Girls • Not Rated (Kids)

Sailor Moon: The Man in the Tuxedo Mask [#3]

ADV Films, 2002, 135 mins., #DMN/003. Directed by Junichi Sato. Based on the manga series by Naoko Takeuchi in *Nakayoshi*.

The Negaverse tries to possess a variety of people from different walks of life and use their talents to invade Earth. Dressmakers, photographers, precocious nine-year-olds, cartoon animators, and even princesses aren't safe from the Negaverse's manipulations! Can Sailor Moon and the Scouts stop all those innocents before they commit unspeakable crimes? Plus Sailor Moon is totally confused when her pal Tuxedo Mask starts committing acts of evil. Is he a creep dressed to the nines, or is there another reason for his dastardly deeds?

Containing episodes #13–18, this action-packed DVD volume furthers the serial and soap opera feel of *Sailor Moon*, while providing excellent characterization and depth to its cast. [JMC]

SPECIAL FEATURES Other Title Trailers TECHNICAL FEATURES Fullscreen (1.33:1) • Languages: Eng. • Sound: Dolby Digital Surround 2.0 • Keepcase • 1 Disc • Region 1 GENRE & RATING Action/Girls • Not Rated (Kids)

Sailor Moon: Secret of the Sailor Scouts [#4]

ADV Films, 2002, 135 mins., #DMN/004. Directed by Junichi Sato. Based on the manga series by Naoko Takeuchi in *Nakayoshi*.

This revealing DVD contains the origins of the Sailor Scouts' powers and shows the true deadly evil of Queen Beryl. When one of Queen Beryl's generals turns against the dark monarch, the consequences are major, and one of Serena's best friends might pay the ultimate price for his betrayal. Then the Scouts face a deadlier version of the Negaverse, and even the newest Scout, Sailor Jupiter, might not be enough to turn the tide in upcoming battles. Have the Scouts met their match or can they overcome even the vilest of adversaries?

One of the most remarkable things about *Sailor Moon* is that sometimes the good guys lose . . . and lose big. This poignant collection of episodes #19–24 contains a heartfelt goodbye guaranteed to make even the most stoic of viewers a little misty-eyed. [JMC]

SPECIAL FEATURES Other Title Trailers TECHNICAL FEATURES Fullscreen (1.33:1) • Languages: Eng. • Sound: Dolby Digital Surround 2.0 • Keepcase • 1 Disc • Region 1 GENRE & RATING Action/Girls • Not Rated (Kids)

Sailor Moon: Introducing Sailor Venus! [#5]

ADV Films, 2002, 135 mins., #DMN/005. Directed by Junichi Sato. Based on the manga series by Naoko Takeuchi in *Nakayoshi*.

Sailor Moon is jealous, and the green-eyed monster may cause her some problems in her fight against evil. Speaking of which, she and her fellow Sailors must contend with the nasty monsters of Zoycite, who want to capture the Rainbow crystals. And joining them in their fight against Queen Beryl is Sailor Venus, but not everyone is sure she's on the side of right!

Another sextet of episodes is presented on this DVD with #25–30.

SPECIAL FEATURES Other Title Trailers TECHNICAL FEATURES Fullscreen (1.33:1) • Languages: Eng. • Sound: Dolby Digital Surround 2.0 • Keepcase • 1 Disc • Region 1 GENRE & RATING Action/Girls • Rated All Ages

Sailor Moon: Adventure Girls! [#6]

ADV Films, 2002, 135 mins., #DMN/006. Directed by Junichi Sato. Based on the manga series by Naoko Takeuchi in *Nakayoshi*.

Lots of complications for the Sailor Scouts leave them asking "Can't a Sailor Scout get a break?" Defending the planet is supposed to take a back seat to their "real" lives at times, but a stint at a ghoulish finishing school may ruin their moods and their manners, and a bad hair day really gets them cranky. Not even a family vacation goes smoothly, and an avalanche means no more skiing for Serena and the gang.

Episodes #31–36 fill up this DVD with Sailor power.

SPECIAL FEATURES Other Title Trailers TECHNICAL FEATURES Fullscreen (1.33:1) • Languages: Eng. • Sound: Dolby Digital Surround 2.0 • Keepcase • 1 Disc • Region 1 GENRE & RATING Action/Girls • Not Rated (Kids)

Sailor Moon: Fight to the Finish! [#7]

ADV Films, 2002, 135 mins., #DMN/007. Directed by Junichi Sato. Based on the manga series by Naoko Takeuchi in *Kodansha Monthly*.

NOTE: This DVD arrived too late for a full review. The following text is promotional copy provided by the releasing company:

"You think you have problems? Things are bad enough for Sailor Moon when the evil Queen Beryl tries to recapture the Rainbow Crystals, but the forces of the Negaverse finally manage to break into our universe! Now, the Sailor Scouts have to face off against both Beryl and her 'doom and gloom' girls. And if that's not bad enough, there are newer and even tougher villains just waiting to take over from Beryl!"

This disc contains six episodes.

SPECIAL FEATURES Other Title Trailers TECHNICAL FEATURES Fullscreen (1.33:1) • Languages: Eng. • Sound: Dolby Digital • Keepcase • 1 Disc • Region 1 GENRE & RATING Action/Girls • Not Rated (Kids)

Sailor Moon: The Doom Tree Strikes! [#8]

ADV Films, 2002, 135 mins., #DMN/008. Directed by Junichi Sato. Based on the manga series by Naoko Takeuchi in *Kodansha Monthly*.

NOTE: This DVD arrived too late for a full review. The following text is promotional copy provided by the releasing company:

"It came to conquer the Earth, and only Sailor Moon and the Sailor Scouts can stop it! As the evil Anne and Alan continue to scheme up new ways to steal the Earth's energy for the Doom Tree, will the combined power of all the Sailor Scouts be enough? The power of friendship will be tested as never before when our planet's mightiest protectors join forces in their greatest battles yet!"

This disc contains six episodes.

SPECIAL FEATURES Other Title Trailers TECHNICAL FEATURES Fullscreen (1.33:1) • Languages: Eng. • Sound: Dolby Digital • Keepcase • 1 Disc • Region 1 GENRE & RATING Action/Girls • Not Rated (Kids)

Sailor Moon: The Return of the Doom Tree [#9]

ADV Films, 2002, 135 mins., #DMN/009. Directed by Junichi Sato. Based on the manga series by Naoko Takeuchi in *Kodansha Monthly*.

NOTE: This DVD arrived too late for a full review. The following text is promotional copy provided by the releasing company:

"It's girl power to the rescue as Sailor Moon and the Sailor Scouts continue to fight the evil minions of the Doom Tree. Forced to find new victims to feed the monstrous vegetable's ever-increasing appetite for energy, Alan and Anne concoct their most diabolical scheme yet! Can Serena and the Scouts stop them in time, or will all their friends at school become veggie snacks?"

This disc contains six episodes.

SPECIAL FEATURES Other Title Trailers TECHNICAL FEATURES Fullscreen (1.33:1) • Languages: Eng. • Sound: Dolby Digital • Keepcase • 1 Disc • Region 1 GENRE & RATING Action/Girls • Not Rated (Kids)

Sailor Moon: The Trouble with Rini [#10]

ADV Films, 2002, 135 mins., #DMN/010. Directed by Junichi Sato. Based on the manga series by Naoko Takeuchi in *Kodansha Monthly*.

NOTE: This DVD arrived too late for a full review. The following text is promotional copy provided by the releasing company:

"Serena's obnoxious new cousin is just the beginning of a new set of problems for Sailor Moon! The invaders from the Negamoon continue in their attempts to foil Sailor Moon, but fortunately, the Sailor Scouts are up to the task. However, when the Nega-baddies come up with the evil plan of using Serena's greatest fear against her, can even the mighty Sailor Moon triumph against them?"

This disc contains six episodes.

SPECIAL FEATURES Other Title Trailers TECHNICAL FEATURES Fullscreen (1.33:1) • Languages: Eng. • Sound: Dolby Digital • Keepcase • 1 Disc • Region 1 GENRE & RATING Action/Girls • Not Rated (Kids)

Sailor Moon: The Ties That Bind [#11]

ADV Films, 2002, 135 mins., #DMN/011. Directed by Junichi Sato. Based on the manga series by Naoko Takeuchi in *Nakayoshi*.

NOTE: This DVD arrived too late for a full review. The following text is promotional copy provided by the releasing company:

"Rubeus and the evil sisters from the Negamoon are back and they're pulling out all the stops in a furious series of new attacks! Between his last evil sisters and his new ally, Emerald, it looks like Rubeus may finally have Serena cornered. But don't count Earth's greatest heroine out yet because she's a got a few aces up her own sleeve, including a brand new Sailor Scout!"

This disc contains six episodes.

SPECIAL FEATURES Other Title Trailers TECHNICAL FEATURES Fullscreen (1.33:1) • Languages: Eng. • Sound: Dolby Digital 2.0 • Keepcase • 1 Disc • Region 1 GENRE & RATING Action/Girls • Not Rated (Kids)

Sailor Moon: The Wrath of Emerald [#12]

ADV Films, 2002, 135 mins., #DMN/012. Directed by Junichi Sato. Based on the manga series by Naoko Takeuchi in *Nakayoshi*.

NOTE: This DVD arrived too late for a full review. The following text is promotional copy provided by the releasing company:

"Poor Serena! From hanging out in bakery shops to falling in love, there are so many things for a young girl to do when she's not in school. Unfortunately, the evil Rubeus and Emerald are keeping Sailor Moon and the Sailor Scouts so busy that there's not much time left for a little fun on the side! Whether it's dealing with tainted Love Bracelets or combating evil viruses, the Sailor Scouts will have their hands full."

This disc contains six episodes.

SPECIAL FEATURES Other Title Trailers TECHNICAL FEATURES Fullscreen (1.33:1) • Languages: Eng. • Sound: Dolby Digital 2.0 • Keepcase • 1 Disc • Region 1 GENRE & RATING Action/Girls • Not Rated (Kids)

Sailor Moon R: The Movie—Uncut Special Edition

Pioneer, 2000, 60 mins., #PISA-0001V. Directed by Kunihiko Ikuhara. Screenplay by Sukehiro Tomita. Based on the manga series by Naoko Takeuchi in *Nakayoshi.*

When Serena, better known as Sailor Moon, and her friends the Sailor Scouts enjoy a romp through the public gardens, they learn that a pretty flower can also be deadly. The Kisenian Blossom is draining the people of Tokyo of their energy! In the meantime, Serena has something new to cry over—the appearance of a strange young man, Fiore, who claims to be an old friend of her boyfriend, Darien. Who is he really, and what has he to do with this latest threat?

The first *Sailor Moon* movie hit the screens in Japan in 1993, during season R of the TV series. It stands alone from the series, but seems, in essence, to be just another TV episode, complete with the message that friendship can overcome all obstacles (even if that obstacle is an oversized alien flower!). Still, if you like the series, you won't be disappointed. The DVD allows American audiences to finally see Sailor Moon in her true, uncensored context. The English dub may have "tweaked" the story to fit with the American version of the series, but the subtitled edition keeps the old names, Usagi (Serena), Mamoru (Darien), and such, as well as the original humor, such as the hints that there may be something more between Darien and Fiore than just friendship.

The extras on the DVD are nothing special, mostly things you get just by watching the movie itself, but the character bios may prove informative for those who haven't been exposed to the Japanese version before. Some fans also know this story as "The Promise of the Rose." [WM]

SPECIAL FEATURES Character Bios • Character and Art Galleries • Alternate Opening • Music Video TECHNICAL FEATURES Fullscreen (1.33:1) • Subtitles/CC: Eng. • Languages: Jap., Eng. dub • Sound: Dolby Digital 2.0 • Keepcase • 1 Disc • Region 1 GENRE & RATING Action/Girls • Rated 13+

Sailor Moon S: Heart Collection I

Pioneer, 2001, 165 mins., #11474. Directed by Kunihiko Ikuhara. Screenplay by Sukehiro Tomita, Shigeru Yanagawa, Katsuyuki Sumizawa, Megumi Sugihara, Yoji Enokido. Based on the manga series by Naoko Takeuchi in *Nakayoshi*.

Professor Tomoe and his Death Busters want to conquer the world and steal everyone's pure hearts to harness the power within and open a gateway to a deadly dimension that will easily conquer the earth. New Sailor Scouts Neptune, Uranus, and Pluto appear, but they seem to have an agenda of their own. They're searching for three mysterious objects, but won't reveal what they intend to do with them. Plus they seem just as content to battle the other Scouts as they are to fight alongside them! Rini, Sailor Mini Moon, the future daughter of Darien and Serena, seems to have made a new friend in a sickly girl named Hotaru, but the child hides a deep, dark secret. Is she connected to the Kaorinite and the Death Busters? If need be, can Rini fight her new best friend?

If you've only seen the dubbed version of *Sailor Moon S* the Cartoon Network first aired in 1999, you're missing a few key things. Sailors Neptune and Uranus were not cousins, but lovers. However homosexuality is often altered in U.S. airings of anime. Also in the original airings, all the Scouts believed Haruka (Sailor Uranus's civilian ID) was a man and flirted, but this also was changed for American audiences. On this disc, the original versions are presented.

With each new season of *Sailor Moon*, the Scouts face a deeper and darker evil, but also make more allies. The S season is no exception to this rule. This introduction to the S Universe contains seven original uncensored episodes of *Sailor Moon S* (English episodes #83–89/Japanese episodes #90–96). [JMC]

SPECIAL FEATURES Character and Art Galleries • Clean Credits • Reversible Cover TECHNICAL FEATURES Fullscreen (1.33:1) • Subtitles/CC: Eng. • Languages: Jap., Eng. dub • Sound: Dolby Digital 2.0 • Keepcase • 1 Disc • Region 1 GENRE & RATING Action/Girls • Rated 13+

Sailor Moon S: Heart Collection II

Pioneer, 2001, 145 mins., #11475. Directed by Kunihiko Ikuhara. Screenplay by Megumi Sugihara, Sukehiro Tomita, Yoji Enokido, Katsuyuki Sumizawa. Based on the manga series by Naoko Takeuchi in *Nakayoshi*.

The Death Busters have decided that the Sailor Scouts contain the pure hearts they're searching for, so the girls become the new targets. Are the Inner Scouts powerful enough to fight off the dark forces of Professor Tomoe? And when Usagi's broach—the object she uses to transform into Sailor Moon—falls off after she and Darien are attacked by a demon, will the fourteen-year-old be able to defend her pure heart from Kaorinite's heart snatchers, or is this the end of Sailor Moon and Serena?

Almost every Inner Scout—Mars, Mercury, Jupiter, and Venus—gets a turn in the spotlight in this character-driven DVD. It contains the next six uncut episodes in the *Sailor Moon S* saga U.S. episodes #90–95/Japanese episodes #97–102). Plus, a little more is revealed about the motivations of Neptune and Uranus, when each is teamed up with another Scout and they are forced to work together. [JMC]

SPECIAL FEATURES Character and Art Galleries • Clean Credits • Reversible Cover TECHNICAL FEATURES Fullscreen (1.33:1) • Subtitles/CC: Eng. • Languages: Jap., Eng. dub • Sound: Dolby Digital 2.0 • Keepcase • 1 Disc • Region 1 GENRE & RATING Action/Girls • Rated 13+

Sailor Moon S: Heart Collection III

Pioneer, 2001, 145 mins., #11476. Directed by Kunihiko Ikuhara. Screenplay by Shigeru Yanagawa, Megumi Sugihara, Yoji Enokido, Katsuyuki Sumizawa. Based on the manga series by Naoko Takeuchi in *Nakayoshi*.

Sailor Mini Moon unexpectedly returns to train with the Inner Scouts and learn social skills. Meanwhile Sailor Jupiter, upset because her attacks on the demons have been having no effect, goes off alone to train, but will she be able to get a power boost? Then, secrets of how Uranus and Neptune met are revealed when a demon attacks the woman who introduced them. Next, one of Rini's crushes is the target of the Death Busters. Finally, the Scouts in their civilian identities are invited to a grand mansion, but the Death Busters crash the party. Can the Scouts defeat them in time to still have an evening of fun?

An interesting note on this DVD containing six uncensored episodes (U.S. episodes #96–101/Japanese

episodes #103–8) is that when the last episode aired in the U.S. the references to Serena being drunk were all removed, even though she drank the alcohol thinking it was regular punch! [JMC]

SPECIAL FEATURES Character and Art Galleries • Alternate Opening • Reversible Cover TECHNICAL FEATURES Fullscreen (1.33:1) • Subtitles/CC: Eng. • Languages: Jap., Eng. dub • Sound: Dolby Digital 2.0 • Keepcase • 1 Disc • Region 1 GENRE & RATING Action/Girls • Rated 13+

Sailor Moon S: Heart Collection IV

Pioneer, 2001, 145 mins., #11477. Directed by Kunihiko Ikuhara. Screenplay by Sukehiro Tomita, Yoji Enokido, Shigeru Yanagawa, Megumi Sugihara. Based on the manga series by Naoko Takeuchi in *Nakayoshi*.

The Outer Scouts—Neptune, Uranus, and Pluto—think the Inner Scouts—Mercury, Venus, Mars, and Jupiter—are hindering their task of finding the magic Talismans (which, when combined, will create the Holy Grail). However, even though the two groups bicker, they are able to discover the hearts that hold the keys to the Grail and its rightful wielder, Sailor Moon. Using the Talisman, she's able to defeat another member of the Death Busters. The group of girls seems to have a breather, but it won't last long. Professor Tomoe has more villains waiting in the wings to fight the Sailor Scouts. However his dark dealings are unknown to his frail daughter Rini's new best friend Hotaru.

This action-packed DVD contains six uncut episodes (U.S. episodes #102–7/Japanese episodes #109–14). [JMC]

SPECIAL FEATURES Character and Art Galleries • Alternate Opening • Reversible Cover TECHNICAL FEATURES Fullscreen (1.33:1) • Subtitles/CC: Eng. • Languages: Jap., Eng. dub • Sound: Dolby Digital Surround 2.0 • Keepcase • 1 Disc • Region 1 GENRE & RATING Action/Girls • Rated 13+

Sailor Moon S: Heart Collection V

Pioneer, 2001, 145 mins., #11478. Directed by Kunihiko Ikuhara. Screenplay by Yoji Enokido, Megumi Sugihara, Shigeru Yanagawa, Katsuyuki Sumizawa. Based on the manga series by Naoko Takeuchi in *Nakayoshi*.

The father of Rini's new friend Hotaru is secretly the evil behind the recent heart-stealings and the mastermind controlling the Death Busters! Hotaru is unaware of his evil doings. She's also doesn't know that housed within herself is the power of Sailor Saturn, and also the destructive will of the Messiah of Silence, a being whose emergence will signal the apocalypse! A line is drawn between the Inner and Outer Scouts as Sailor Moon and the Inners want to save Hotaru at any cost; Rini can't bear the idea of her friend being hurt. The Outers want to kill Hotaru so the Messiah of Silence will never emerge.

Tough choices have to be made in the six original episodes (U.S. episodes #108–13/Japanese episodes #115–20) contained in this penultimate collection of *Sailor Moon S*. [JMC]

SPECIAL FEATURES Character and Art Galleries • Alternate Opening • Reversible Cover TECHNICAL FEATURES Fullscreen (1.33:1) • Subtitles/CC: Eng. • Languages: Jap., Eng. dub • Sound: Dolby Digital Surround 2.0 • Keepcase • 1 Disc • Region 1 GENRE & RATING Action/Girls • Rated 13+

Sailor Moon S: Heart Collection VI

Pioneer, 2001, 165 mins., #11479. Directed by Kunihiko Ikuhara. Screenplay by Shigeru Yanagawa, Sukehiro Tomita, Megumi Sugihara, Yoji Enokido. Based on the manga series by Naoko Takeuchi in *Nakayoshi*.

The Death Busters have been collecting pure heart energy to awaken the Messiah of Silence. After they steal Rini's heart, it is enough to cause the Messiah to possess Hotaru, launching her/its attempt to destroy the world! Now, the Scouts are in a race against time to defeat the Messiah before the apocalypse can come to pass. But can eight Soldiers whose combined power barely beat the Death Busters defeat someone with the supposed power of God?

The final heart-pounding disc contains seven uncensored episodes (U.S. episodes #114–20/Japanese episodes #121–27). As with all the other installments of the *Sailor Moon* series, this one ends with just as much action, adventure, and emotion as it begins. Nothing in *Sailor Moon S* is a disappointment, and it is the epitome of shojo anime in many fans' opinion. [JMC]

SPECIAL FEATURES Character and Art Galleries • Reversible Cover TECHNICAL FEATURES Fullscreen (1.33:1) • Subtitles/CC: Eng. • Languages: Jap., Eng. dub • Sound: Dolby Digital Surround 2.0 • Keepcase • 1 Disc • Region 1 GENRE & RATING Action/Girls • Rated 13+

Sailor Moon S: The Movie—Uncut Special Edition

Pioneer, 2000, 60 mins., #PISA-0002V. Directed by Hiroki Shibata. Screenplay by Sukehiro Tomita. Based on the manga series by Naoko Takeuchi in *Nakayoshi*.

It's winter break and time for fun and snow flurries for Serena and the gang. Unfortunately, when Snow Queen Kaguya decides to turn up the global air conditioning, the Sailor Scouts end up fighting the storm of their lives! Things are made worse when their mentor, the cat Luna, has an accident. Who is the young man that saved her? Is he the reason she's giving her male cat-friend, Artemis, the cold shoulder? How can Luna help the Scouts defeat this new threat when she's got a bad case of puppy—uh, kitty—love?

The second of the Sailor Scout's big-screen adventures debuted in 1994, during season S, and included the Outer Scouts (Uranus, Neptune, and Pluto) in minor roles. Once again, it's basically a stand-alone episode of the TV series, but still a good one. Die-hard fans may find that the dub version falls a little flat with regard to the story. Otherwise, the movie stays true to the heart of the TV series, with dazzling special effects, slapstick humor, beautiful character designs, and fights that leave you on the edge of your seat!

The only worthwhile extra feature on the DVD (aside from the option to view the film in the original Japanese with subtitles) is the character guide, and then only for viewers who aren't already familiar with the franchise. But the movie is all you really need to enjoy this DVD. Some fans also know this story as "Hearts in Ice." [WM]

SPECIAL FEATURES Character Bios • Character and Art Galleries • Production Notes • Alternate Opening & Closing • Easter Egg TECHNICAL FEATURES Fullscreen (1.33:1) • Subtitles/CC: Eng. • Languages: Jap., Eng. dub • Sound: Dolby Digital 2.0 • Keepcase • 1 Disc • Region 1 GENRE & RATING Action/Girls • Rated 13+

Sailor Moon Super S: Pegasus Collection I

Pioneer, 2002, 145 mins., #11652. Directed by Kunihiko Ikuhara. Screenplay by Yoji Enokido, Megumi Sugihara, Ryota Yamaguchi, Motoki Yoshimura. Based on the manga series by Naoko Takeuchi in *Nakayoshi*.

The dark forces Sailor Moon and the Sailor Scouts face this time around are the Dead Moon Circus, a triad of evil villains nicknamed the "Amazon Trio" (Hawk's Eye, Fish Eye, and Tiger's Eye). The villains are searching for the mythical Pegasus and a fabled Golden Crystal. If they possess its power, they can free their mistress, the villainous Queen Nephrenia, from her trap within a mirror. Nephrenia wants to conquer this world and remake it into her kingdom. The Dead Moon Circus targets good people, then traps them and uses a mirror to steal their "good dreams," because in the purest of dreams is supposed to lie Pegasus and the Golden Crystal. Sailor Moon, Sailor Mini Moon, and the Scouts must cancel this Circus's performance before innocent lives are lost.

The *Super S* season of *Sailor Moon* introduces Diana, Rini's pet kitten from the future, and Artemis and Luna's future child. Criticized by some as the worst season of *Sailor Moon*, the Super S season has a fairy tale feel and a playfulness that most viewers couldn't relate to. However, if you're into magic, romance, and adventures into the unknown, then this is the anime for you. It is written more to attract the core shojo audience, girls age five to twelve, but still has that same *Sailor Moon* flavor.

The Cartoon Network aired the *Super S* season in 2000, but this mystical DVD contains the first six uncut episodes of that season, (U.S. episodes #121–26/Japanese episodes #128–33) including uncensored footage not aired on U.S. television. [JMC]

SPECIAL FEATURES Alternate Opening • Reversible Cover TECHNICAL FEATURES Fullscreen (1.33:1) • Subtitles/CC: Eng. • Languages: Jap., Eng. dub • Sound: Dolby Digital Surround 2.0 • Keepcase • 1 Disc • Region 1 GENRE & RATING Action/Girls • Rated 13+

Sailor Moon Super S: Pegasus Collection II

Pioneer, 2002, 145 mins., #11713. Directed by Kunihiko Ikuhara. Screenplay by Ryota Yamaguchi, Yoji Enokido, Megumi Sugihara, Motoki Yoshimura, Mutsumi Nakano. Based on the manga series by Naoko Takeuchi in *Nakayoshi.*

Can the Sailor Scouts defend two best-selling authors from the deadly Amazon Trio? Then, can Rini protect her teacher from a villain trying to steal her pure dreams? Plus, what happens when Serena's boyfriend Darien has to move in with Rei after his apartment is trashed? When the Dead Moon Circus attacks Rei, Serena must put aside her jealousy to save her friend. Next, the triad attacks a popular mechanic, hoping her spirit is the purest and that Pegasus lies within her dreams. Can the Sailor Scouts stop them before they give her a permanent tune-up?

This action-packed DVD tells another modern fairy tale, as the group protects their friends, their honor, and sometimes their adversaries from the evil Dead Moon Circus. It contains six uncensored episodes (U.S. episodes #127–32/Japanese episodes #134–39).

SPECIAL FEATURES Karaoke Opening • Reversible Cover TECHNICAL FEATURES Fullscreen (1.33:1) • Subtitles/CC: Eng. • Languages: Jap., Eng. dub • Sound: Dolby Digital Surround 2.0 • Keepcase • 1 Disc • Region 1 GENRE & RATING Action/Girls • Rated 13+

Sailor Moon Super S: Pegasus Collection III

Pioneer, 2002, 145 mins., #11715. Directed by Kunihiko Ikuhara, Junichi Sato, Takuya Igarashi, Yuji Endo, Noriyo Sasaki, Hiroki Shibata, Harume Kosaka. Screenplay by Motoki Yoshimura, Ryota Yamaguchi, Megumi Sugihara, Yoji Enokido. Based on the manga series by Naoko Takeuchi in *Kodansha Monthly.*

NOTE: This DVD arrived too late for a full review. The following text is promotional copy provided by the releasing company:

"The Amazon Trio continues their search for the Pegasus, targeting fashion designers, ballet instructors, and others with pure dreams. Sailor Moon keeps struggling against the Dead Moon Circus, but when they target Sailor Venus and Sailor Mercury, are they closing in on Chibi-Usa? How long can Chibi-Usa keep her Pegasus dream a secret? Meanwhile, when a Pegasus begins causing trouble around the city, can they continue to trust it?"

This disc contains six uncut episodes.

SPECIAL FEATURES Clean Credits • Inserts: Mini Poster • Reversible Cover TECHNICAL FEATURES Fullscreen (1.33:1) • Subtitles/CC: Eng. • Languages: Jap., Eng. dub • Sound: Dolby Digital 1.0 • Keepcase • 1 Disc • Region 1 GENRE & RATING Action/Girls • Rated 13+

Sailor Moon Super S: Pegasus Collection IV

Pioneer, 2002, 145 mins., #11716. Directed by Kunihiko Ikuhara, Junichi Sato, Yuji Endo, Konosuke Uda, Hiroki Shibata, Takuya Igarashi. Screenplay by Megumi Sugihara, Ryota Yamaguchi, Yoji Enokido. Based on the manga series by Naoko Takeuchi in *Kodansha Monthly.*

NOTE: This DVD arrived too late for a full review. The following text is promotional copy provided by the releasing company:

"The Amazon Trio has until the next full moon to capture the Pegasus or Zirconia, the leader of the Dark Moon Circus, will change them back into animals. However, when Fish Eye targets Mamoru (Tuxedo Mask), she falls in love! Finally understanding the value of dreams, Fish Eye conceals the location of the Pegasus only to have her partners target Usagi! Ultimately, the Amazon Trio fail in their mission only to receive an unexpected reward. However, for Sailor Moon, the danger continues now that the Amazon Quartet begin the hunt."

This disc contains six uncut episodes.

SPECIAL FEATURES Sing-Along • Inserts: Mini Poster • Reversible Cover TECHNICAL FEATURES Fullscreen (1.33:1) • Subtitles/CC: Eng. • Languages: Jap., Eng. dub • Sound: Dolby Digital 1.0 • Keepcase • 1 Disc • Region 1 GENRE & RATING Action/Girls • Rated 13+

Sailor Moon Super S: Pegasus Collection V

Pioneer, 2002, 145 mins., #11717. Directed by Kunihiko Ikuhara, Harume Kosaka, Noriyo Sasaki, Yuji Endo, Konosuke Uda, Takuya Igarashi. Screenplay by Megumi Sugihara, Motoki Yoshimura, Ryota Yamaguchi. Based on the manga series by Naoko Takeuchi in *Kodanasha Monthly*.

NOTE: This DVD arrived too late for a full review. The following text is promotional copy provided by the releasing company:

"Sailor Evolution! From a young athlete trying to overcome a childhood phobia to a starving artist pursuing his skills, there is no pure dream that the Amazon Quartet won't try to corrupt! Fortunately, as the challenges grow, so do the Sailor Soldiers. Unfortunately, some challenges don't come from the Dead Moon Circus, and while Rei tries to cope with sudden fame, Mako-chan and Minako struggle against each other over love!"

This disc contains six uncut episodes.

SPECIAL FEATURES Original Opening • Inserts: Mini Poster • Reversible Cover TECHNICAL FEATURES Fullscreen (1.33:1) • Subtitles/CC: Eng. • Languages: Jap., Eng. dub • Sound: Dolby Digital 1.0 • Keepcase • 1 Disc • Region 1 GENRE & RATING Action/Girls • Rated 13+

Sailor Moon Super S: The Movie—Uncut Special Ed.

Pioneer, 2000, 60 mins., #PISA-0003V. Directed by Hiroki Shibata. Screenplay by Yoji Enokido. Based on the manga series by Naoko Takeuchi in *Nakayoshi*.

Someone is kidnapping the children of Tokyo! Can Sailor Moon and the Sailor Scouts save them before Badiyanu uses their dreams to make her Black Dream Hole large enough to swallow the earth, trapping everyone in nightmares for all eternity? The candy lure of her pied-piping minions makes "sweet dreams" take on a whole new meaning! Can Sailor Mini Moon learn to use her powers in time to help, or will she be caught with the other children? Can she trust her new friend, or is he a piper trying to lure her into danger?

The third and final Sailor Moon movie debuted in Japanese theaters in 1995, along with the short movie, *Ami-chan no Hatsukoi*, which featured Amy, better known

as Sailor Mercury. Unfortunately, the DVD does not contain the short, nor does it have much in the way of extras. Thankfully, the uncut movie makes up for what the DVD lacks. Rini, aka Sailor Mini Moon, is Serena's daughter from a future timeline, living with the teenage Serena (aka Sailor Moon) and her family. The movie provides a prime example of the mother-daughter bond that makes Serena and Rini more than just pretend-sisters that fight like real siblings. The film also hits the mark with stunning battle sequences.

If you watch the subtitled version, note the sexual innuendo between Neptune and Uranus, an example of how much anime is changed for American sensibilities. In Japan, there are strong hints that they are lesbian lovers—it's even suggested that Uranus can change sex—but in the American version, they are "cousins." Fans may be disappointed by the lack of screen-time for the Outer Scouts, but overall the movie retains the original series' humor, tense fight scenes, and poignant portrayals of friendship. Some fans also know this story as "Black Dream Hole." [WM]

SPECIAL FEATURES Character Bios • Character and Art Galleries • Alternate Opening TECHNICAL FEATURES Fullscreen (1.33:1) • Subtitles/CC: Eng. • Languages: Jap., Eng. dub • Sound: Dolby Digital 2.0 • Keepcase • 1 Disc • Region 1 GENRE & RATING Action/Girls • Rated 13+

Sailor Moon: The Movies—The Dream Set: Uncut Special Edition [Trilogy DVD Box Set]

Pioneer, 2000, 180 mins., #11607.

This box set contains the three *Sailor Moon* movies exactly as they appeared in the individual keepcase editions. See individual entries for the Special and Technical Features listings.

TECHNICAL FEATURES • Cardboard Box with 3 Keepcases • 3 Discs GENRE & RATING Action/Girls • Rated 13+

Sailor Victory

Anime Works, 2001, 60 mins., #AWDVD-0196. Directed by Katsuhiko Nishijima. Script by Kenichi Kanemaki.

Five friends—Kiyomi, Shizuka, Reiko, Mika, and Mami—fight crime and the forces of darkness in Mikado City. Using their giant ninja battle robots, Gion, Momoyama, and Sagano, the team of Sailor Victory hopes to overcome the evil Margarita and stop her and a corrupt city official's plans to destroy the city and its residents. However, it might be too big a task for this quintet of heroes to accomplish alone. It appears as if all the young women have to rely on is each other, especially given their uneasy association with the local police. While avoiding the law officials who view them as hindrances and have little use for their assistance, Sailor Victory must uncover Margarita's plans and stop them before she sets in motion her nefarious plan.

The story for Sailor Victory came from a computer game, *Graduation*, in which five teens don't know which career to choose after graduation, and the player got to guide each girl to her perfect future career. The game became an anime series in 1994. The last two episodes of the *Graduation* anime series were repackaged, renamed, and presented in this DVD collection as *Sailor Victory*.

Although not terribly original, a combination of cheesy mecha, shojo, and sci-fi anime series, there are a few unique parts that make *Sailor Victory* worth a try. It is a fun, alternative look at life in a sci-fi setting. [JMC]

SPECIAL FEATURES Other Title Trailers TECHNICAL FEATURES Fullscreen (1.33:1) • Subtitles/CC: Eng. • Languages: Jap., Eng. dub • Sound: Dolby Digital 2.0 • Keepcase • 1 Disc • Region 1 GENRE & RATING Action/Girls • Rated 13+

Saint Tail: Thief of Hearts [#1]

Tokyopop, 2001, 75 mins., #TPDV-982. Directed by Yukio Okazaki, Hitoyuki Matsui, Yasuichiro Yamamoto, Shinji Sakaki. Scripts by Hiroshi Kashiwabara, Shinzo Fujita, Yuichi Higurashi. Based on the manga series by Megumi Tachikawa.

One of the best concepts to use the legend of Robin Hood, Saint Tail is a precocious preteen thief who steals from other criminals and returns the items to their rightful owners. By day Meimi is a student at St. Paulia's Catholic school, but by night she uses her skills and charm as a hero. Unfortunately, some others don't view Saint Tail that way. The local police want to stop her at any cost, even going so far as to let a young boy, Asuka Jr., Meimi's classmate and junior detective, take a shot at catching the crook. But how can you catch someone if she's just doing God's will? Aided by her best friend and sister-in-training, Seira, who hears confessions of parishioners or learns of crimes and then informs Meimi of the details, Saint Tail attempts to rob from the guilty and return to the innocent. However, can she stay one step ahead of the police and her crush, the junior detective?

Created in 1995 by Megumi Tachikawa, *Saint Tail* is a successful manga and anime series. Spanning forty-three episodes, this delightful magical girl series is sure to be a hit with any family and should appeal to viewers of all ages. Her catch phrase "It's Showtime!" before she transforms is cute and the sequence itself is on par with the best magical change scenes.

This initial DVD from 2001 contains the first three episodes and does a fine job of introducing our protagonist, her antagonists, and a lot of other key players. [JMC]

SPECIAL FEATURES Character and Art Galleries • Other Title Trailers • Inserts: Liner Notes TECHNICAL FEATURES Fullscreen (1.33:1) • Subtitles/CC: Eng. • Languages: Jap., Eng. dub • Sound: Dolby Digital 2.0 • Keepcase • 1 Disc • Region 1–6 GENRE & RATING Action/Girls • Not Rated (Kids)

Saint Tail: It's Show Time! [#2]

Tokyopop, 2001, 100 mins., #TPDV-1142. Directed by Kazunori Tanahashi, Raisen Hanyu, Shinichiro Yamamoto, Hitoyuki Matsui. Scripts by Yuichi Higurashi, Shoji Yonemura, Shinzo Fujita, Yuichi Higarashi. Based on the manga series by Megumi Tachikawa.

The first item on Saint Tail's agenda is a wedding veil, but she can't recapture it without consequences; if she does as requested, she may ruin her secret identity's chances at true love. Then when a precious doll goes missing, Saint Tail risks her own safety to return the toy, even though the attempt will put her right in the middle of a police trap. Next she must catch an art thief, return the work, and avoid Asuka Jr. and his new ally, Rina. Finally the three teens tangle over an ancient weapon, but is it authentic or just the latest in a long line of traps to catch Saint Tail?

Collecting episodes #4–7, this magical girl anime proves that sometimes two wrongs *do* make a right, especially if the second wrong has to do with the lovely thief Saint Tail. [JMC]

SPECIAL FEATURES Character and Art Galleries • Outtakes • Other Title Trailers • Inserts: Liner Notes TECHNICAL FEATURES Fullscreen (1.33:1) • Subtitles/CC: Eng. • Languages: Jap., Eng. dub • Sound: Dolby Digital 2.0 • Keepcase • 1 Disc • Region 1 GENRE & RATING Action/Girls • Not Rated (Kids)

Saint Tail: Spring Love [#3]

Tokyopop, 2002, 100 mins., #TPDV-1172. Directed by Naoto Kanda, Shinji Sakai, Yukio Okazaki, Hideaki Oba, Kazunori Tanahashi. Scripts by Shoji Yonemura, Toshimichi Okawa, Yuichi Higurashi. Based on the manga series by Megumi Tachikawa.

When a baseball player's lucky glove is nicked by a young girl, the guilty party seeks Saint Tail's aid in returning the property. Then things heat up for Meimi as new rival Rina seems convinced Meimi is the magical thief Saint Tail. Can Saint Tail out-think and out-trick Rina, or is her career as heroine finished? Finally, what happens when Meimi's transformation is caught on film? Will she be able to retrieve the pictures or will her famous "It's Showtime!" be uttered in a new light as her identity is exposed?

The addition of Rina to the cast brings romantic tensions, strained friendships, and adds other touches of realism to make the third volume of *Saint Tail*, containing episodes #8–11, a fun, entertaining addition to anime DVD collections. [JMC]

SPECIAL FEATURES Character and Art Galleries • Outtakes • Other Title Trailers TECHNICAL FEATURES Fullscreen (1.33:1) • Subtitles/CC: Eng. • Languages: Jap., Eng. dub • Sound: Dolby Digital 2.0 • Keepcase • 1 Disc • Region 1 GENRE & RATING Action/Girls • Not Rated (Kids)

Saint Tail: Moonlight [#4]

Tokyopop, 2002, 100 mins., #TPDV-1182. Directed by Yasuichiro Yamamoto, Hitoyuki Matsui, Shinji Sakai, Osamu Nabeshima. Scripts by Toshimichi Okawa, Hiroshi Hashimoto, Shoji Yonemura, Shinzo Fujita. Based on the manga series by Megumi Tachikawa.

When a bully steals a pet lizard, Saint Tail must overcome her fear of slimy things to return it to its rightful owner. Then a supposedly magical mirror is stolen and the lovely thief must catch the criminals before they—or it—cracks. Plus, when a motorcycle is nabbed, will Saint Tail become a hot-rod mamma to get it back? Then, when a lovestruck boy takes the object of his affection's doll, then has it stolen out from under him by a mischievous puppy, can Saint Tail help him get the prize back before he ruins his chance at love?

Thrills, chills, and motorcycle spills entertain in another magically fun DVD containing episodes #12–15. [JMC]

SPECIAL FEATURES Clean Credits • Other Title Trailers TECHNICAL FEATURES Fullscreen (1.33:1) • Subtitles/CC: Eng. • Languages: Jap., Eng. dub • Sound: Dolby Digital 2.0 • Keepcase • 1 Disc • Region 1 GENRE & RATING Action/Girls • Not Rated (Kids)

Saint Tail: Justice! [#5]

Tokyopop, 2002, 175 mins., #TPDV-1212. Directed by Hideaki Oniwa, Yukio Okazaki, Yasuichiro Yamamoto, Shinji Sakai, Hitoyuki Matsui, Yukio Okazaki. Scripts by Sozo Tonami, Masahiro Yokotani, Yuichi Higurashi, Naoko Ito, Shinzo Fujita. Based on the manga series by Megumi Tachikawa.

Special dinners, love letters, steel weathercocks, keys, bird's eggs, and harmonicas are some of the objects Saint Tail must find and return to their rightful owners in this charming volume. No challenge is too great for our lovely thief, although she is still pursued by Asuka Jr., the police, and her rival in and out of costume, Rina. Still, Saint Tail ignores the danger and forges ahead, seeking to aid victims and rescue lost items.

The DVD content changes a little as we're blessed with seven episodes of *Saint Tail*, #16–22, for the same great price! Tokyopop apparently heard fan demand and gave more bang for the buck. [JMC]

SPECIAL FEATURES Cast Bios & Filmographies • Other Title Trailers TECHNICAL FEATURES Fullscreen (1.33:1) • Subtitles/CC: Eng. • Languages: Jap. • Sound: Dolby Digital 2.0 • Keepcase • 1 Disc • Region 1 GENRE & RATING Action/Girls • Not Rated (Kids)

Sakura Diaries ☞ see Mature/Adult Section

Sakura Wars

ADV Films, 1999, 120 mins., #DVDSW001. Directed by Takaaki Ishiyama. Screenplay by Hiroyuki Kawasaki.

In 1919, a war is raging across the country as the forces of Hell are attempting to take over the world. Nothing seems to be able to stop the demons except for powerful mecha developed by Kanzaki Heavy Industries. A group of skilled young women from all over the world, gifted with strong spirits and abilities, have been chosen to pilot the Uba Spirit Armor. Kanna, Maria, Iris, Sumire, Sakura, and Ri make up the Flower Brigade. The group goes through a series of tests to see if they can control the armor and complete basic tasks. Their leader bases them out of a theater, and to keep their cover, the girls must learn to act, sing, and dance, so that everyone thinks the girls are really performers, not protectors. Between voice lessons and dance lessons, the Flower Brigade logs some actual combat time, taking out stray demons and smaller forces. However, when a powerful group of Hellraisers attacks, will the Flower Brigade's training truly be enough to save the city and themselves?

Although magical girls piloting mechas isn't a new concept, it was interesting to see how the characters evolved and adapted to showcase their skills in order to be a better commander for their Uba Spirit Armor. The anime also did a lot of character development in a short amount of time, a tough task for anyone to pull off, but *Sakura Wars* manages the job nicely.

Based on a popular series of Sega video games from 1996, this DVD contains the first four episodes of the original OVA series. Some fans may be bothered by the many historical inaccuracies, but this is a series with demons and robots, so if viewers can accept that, they should be able to deal with some anachronisms. [JMC]

SPECIAL FEATURES Other Title Trailers TECHNICAL FEATURES Fullscreen (1.33:1) • Subtitles/CC: Eng. • Languages: Jap., Eng. dub • Sound: Dolby Digital 2.0 • Keepcase • 1 Disc • Region 1–6 GENRE & RATING Robots/Steampunk/Action • Not Rated (Teens)

Sakura Wars: Return of the Spirit Warriors [#1]

ADV Films, 2002, 90 mins., #DSW/002. Directed by Susumu Kudo. Screenplay by Hiroyuki Kawasaki. Story by Oji Hiroi.

NOTE: This DVD arrived too late for a full review. The following text is promotional copy provided by the releasing company:

"The year is 1919. The World barely survived the first Demon War, and the next is about to begin. Conventional weapons won't cut it, neither will conventional soldiers. Humanity needs the few, the proud, the pure: the Spirit Warriors. Recruited from around the world, these women are beautiful both inside and out, but can they master their steam-powered spirit weapons in time? This is the world of Sakura Wars.

"Captain Ohgami is leaving. Changes in the Flower Division rock the Imperial Flower Combat Troupe. Friendship, loyalty, and teamwork are the binding forces of the spirit warriors. Captain Ohgami reflects over his adventures with the Imperial Flower Combat Troupe as he prepares to depart for a new assignment, but turbulent winds are brewing. For more than one member of the Division, the coming storms could mean disaster; an evil voice from the past, the pressures of stardom, and the advent of cinema threaten to break up the Troupe!"

This disc contains three episodes.

SPECIAL FEATURES Character Bios • Character and Art Galleries • Promotional Artwork • Promotional Footage • Clean Credits • Other Title Trailers • Inserts: Poster, Interview TECHNICAL FEATURES Fullscreen (1.33:1) • Subtitles/CC: Eng. • Languages: Jap., Eng. dub • Sound: Dolby Digital • Keepcase • 1 Disc • Region 1 GENRE & RATING Robots/Steampunk/Action • Rated 7+

Sakura Wars: Wedding Bells [#2]

ADV Films, 2002, 90 mins., #DSW/003. Directed by Susumu Kudo. Screenplay by Hiroyuki Kawasaki. Story by Oji Hiroi.

NOTE: This DVD arrived too late for a full review. The following text is promotional copy provided by the releasing company:

"Captain Ohgami is leaving the Imperial Flower Combat Troupe, and it's clear he may not be the only one who's saying farewell. But whom is Sakura marrying? And why does it seem she herself is against the wedding? Can the Imperial Troupe rescue her before it's too late? Does she even want to be rescued? For Sakura, returning home is a demanding journey. Can she reconcile herself to the death of her father, whose destiny compelled him to give his life in the Demon Wars? And what about her own destiny? Will she carry on the Shinguji legacy? Find out in the awesome conclusion of Sakura Wars!"

This disc contains three episodes.

SPECIAL FEATURES Character Bios • Character and Art Galleries • Promotional Artwork • Promotional Footage • Clean Credits • Other Title Trailers • Inserts: Poster, Interview TECHNICAL FEATURES Fullscreen (1.33:1) • Subtitles/CC: Eng. • Languages: Jap., Eng. dub • Sound: Dolby Digital • Keepcase • 1 Disc • Region 1 GENRE & RATING Robots/Steampunk/Action • Not Rated (Teens)

Saludos Amigos [Gold Collection]

Disney, 2000, 75 mins., #19602. Sequences Directed by Bill Roberts, Jack Kinney, Hamilton Luske, Wilfred Jackson. Story by Homer Brightman, Ralph Wright, Roy Williams, Harry Reeves, Dick Huemer, Joe Grant.

Donald Duck is touring the mountainside at Lake Titicaca when he must travel across a rope bridge. His llama is more than a bit stubborn, but when planks of the bridge start to fall away, Donald gets frantic. Later, Pedro is a young airplane who must fill in for his father delivering the mail in Chile, but a wayward buzzard, a grumpy mountain, and a not-quite-full tank of gas might mean trouble. Then, Goofy tries to become a gaucho (cowboy), with limited success. And finally, Donald Duck is given a samba-dancing tour of South America by a tropical bird, as a watercolor paintbrush fills in gorgeous backgrounds wherever they go.

In the World War II era, with the nation in conflict with Europe and Japan, entertainment became fascinated with a "safe" culture down the South American way. Walt Disney was one of those enthralled by Latin charms, and he brought a plane full of staff members on a tour of the continent to generate a series of stories based there. Since the trip was filmed in 16mm, Disney used the live-action touring segments as a travelogue between the four animated short films. The result, *Saludos Amigos,* was released in 1943 as Disney's sixth full-length feature film (though it had been released in South America in 1942).

Although nicely animated, *Saludos Amigos* is a bit disjointed, hopping back and forth between live-action travelogue and cartoon shorts. The best of the lot is the Goofy segment, which has some surreal fun with slow-motion and screen dissolves. The title song was nominated for an Academy Award.

The DVD contains the complete film, which was never rereleased in theaters, even though segments were shown on television. The meager extras on the disc include a thirty-three-minute featurette called "South of the Border with Disney," which contains more footage of the South American tour.

SPECIAL FEATURES "Making of" Featurette • Trailer • Other Title

Trailers TECHNICAL FEATURES Fullscreen (1.33:1) • Subtitles/CC: Eng. • Languages: Eng., Span. dub • Sound: Dolby Digital 2.0 • Keepcase • 1 Disc • Region 1, 4 GENRE & RATING Humor/Family • Rated G

Samurai: Hunt for the Sword

Anime Works, 2001, 60 mins., #AWDVD-0104. Directed by Masahiro Sekino. Screenplay by Mitsuhiro Yamada.

In the era known as the Tokugawa period, young Shinjuro is the son of a samurai master. When his father departs on a mission, Shinjuro is left in charge of his dojo, but the students don't want him as their teacher. But Shinjuro isn't alone for long, as a group of busty, chirpy girls come to live with him. But as a challenge against the Tokugawa government becomes real, Shinjuro and the others must protect their town. What secrets in the past lead Shinjuro into conflict with Mikage and the Shuhei School? And who will find the Mizuchi sword, an ancient and exceptionally powerful weapon?

Released as a two-part OVA in 1999, *Samurai: Hunt for the Sword* is based on a Japanese video game. The project has a lot of digital production, with excellent color and nice character animation. The script doesn't try too hard to impart a message, and yet it's more interesting and complex—and humorous—than your average-game-turned-anime project. It's too bad the series is so short.

The DVD contains an excellent film transfer.

SPECIAL FEATURES Outtakes • Other Title Trailers TECHNICAL FEATURES Fullscreen (1.33:1) • Subtitles/CC: Eng. • Languages: Jap., Eng. dub • Sound: Dolby Digital 2.0 • Keepcase • 1 Disc • Region 1 GENRE & RATING Martial Arts/Comedy • Rated 13+

Samurai Jack: The Premiere Movie

Warner, 2002, 90 mins., #H1902. Directed by Genndy Tartakovsky. Written by Paul Rudish, Genndy Tartakovsky.

In the distant past, a young prince is sent away to become a samurai warrior. But when he returns to face his foe, the villainous shape-shifter Aku, the samurai is mystically flung into the far future. Now, the strong and silent hero must fight battles in a time in which he'll never belong, even as he attempts to return to the past to stop Aku's evil. Called "Jack" by those he meets in the future, the samurai faces down Aku's henchmen-robots, weird monsters, bounty hunters, and more.

First debuting on the Cartoon Network in 2001, *Samurai Jack* is best known for two things: its minimalist visuals and its sparse dialogue. The art and character designs are angular and highly stylized, with eclectic Eastern visual influences (Aku is based on a Sri Lankan demon mask). The animators decided to work without the black outlines traditional in animation for decades, instead using color against color. There are also split-screen moments and other visual tricks. As for the dialogue, Jack is seldom talkative, but everyone else talks enough for him.

It's hard to say who will like *Samurai Jack* more, kids or adults. It's violent, but the sword-fighting and destruction is usually against robots. And while the plots are not terribly adult, some fans have noted a touch of Akira Kurosawa evoked in the tone of the series, and the humor is fun. The DVD contains the opening origin storyline for *Samurai Jack*, as well as an unaired (at the time of the DVD release) episode, in which Jack meets an obnoxious Scotsman on the run from Aku. A ten-minute documentary with creator Genndy Tartakovsky explores the themes and genesis of the series.

SPECIAL FEATURES "Making of" Featurettes • Character and Art Galleries • DVD-ROM Features: Game, Screensaver • Other Title Trailers TECHNICAL FEATURES Fullscreen (1.33:1) • Languages: Eng., Span. dub • Sound: Dolby Digital 2.0, Dolby Digital 5.1 • Snapcase • 1 Disc • Region 1 GENRE & RATING Martial Arts/Action/Comedy • Not Rated (Kids)

Samurai X ☞ see Mature/Adult Section

Santa and the Three Bears

Diamond Entertainment, 2001.

This DVD was not available for review.

Santa and the Three Bears/The Little Christmas Burro

Marengo Films, 2000, 72 mins., #MRG-0014. Directed by Tony Benedict, Vic Atkinson. Written by Tony Benedict, Christine Atkinson.

In Yellowstone National Park, two bear cubs named Nikomi and Chinook really want to see Santa Claus. They keep putting off hibernation to wait for him, so mama bear asks a friendly park ranger for help. He's planning to impersonate Santa Claus until a blizzard snows him in. Will the real Santa Claus save the day? Then, a tiny burro is present for a miraculous event when it travels to Bethlehem and witnesses the birth of baby Jesus.

Santa and the Three Bears was a 1970 feature film that was cut from sixty-three minutes to a shorter running time for television in later years. The live-action introductory sections star Hal Smith. *The Little Christmas Burro* was a 1978 TV special originally called "The Little Brown Burro," narrated by Lorne Greene.

The DVD features a barely adequate transfer of the film, with sometimes-bleeding colors, a soft focus, and shifting light levels. Still, this pair of stories is a pleasant diversion for children and nostalgic parents who may have seen them on TV in their own younger days.

SPECIAL FEATURES None TECHNICAL FEATURES Fullscreen (1.33:1) • Languages: Eng. • Sound: Dolby Digital 2.0 • Keepcase • 1 Disc • Region 1–6 GENRE & RATING Holiday/Family • Not Rated (All Ages)

Santa Claus Is Comin' to Town/ The Little Drummer Boy

Sony Wonder, 2002, 85 mins., #LVD 54402. Directed by Arthur Rankin, Jr., Jules Bass. Teleplay by Romeo Muller.

NOTE: This DVD arrived too late for a full review. The following text is promotional copy provided by the releasing company:

"A holiday favorite filled with good cheer, this delightful story tells how Kris Kringle got his start as the world's most famous gift-giver by struggling to bring toys and happiness to the children of Sombertown. This remastered version is a classic tale loved by all. Features narration and songs by Fred Astaire, and the voice of Mickey Rooney.

"In *The Little Drummer Boy*, a touching Christmas classic, an evil man kidnaps a young, orphaned Drummer Boy. After he escapes, he searches for his camel, and finds him witnessing the birth of the baby Jesus. Having no gift for him, he gives the only thing he has—a song on his drum."

Note that although the disc cover claims it is closed captioned, it is not.

SPECIAL FEATURES None TECHNICAL FEATURES Fullscreen (1.33:1) • Languages: Eng., Span. dub • Sound: Dolby Digital • Keepcase • 1 Disc • Region 1 GENRE & RATING Holiday/Music • Not Rated (All Ages)

Santa's Stories: Santa's First Christmas/Santa and the Tooth Fairies

BMG, 2000, 52 mins., #75517-45735-9. Directed by Les Orton, Vincent Monluc. Written by Robin Lyons, Andrew Offiler. Script by Franciose Gaspari.

Ever wonder what Santa Claus was like as a little boy? Now you can learn the answer as Santa tells us about his sixth year, when he found his elf workers, trained his famous reindeer, and learned how to deliver presents to good boys and girls all over the world. Then, a letter reaches Santa too late, and it appears as if young Hans won't get what he wanted for Christmas. But Santa has a few good friends, and a deal with the Tooth Fairies may help get Hans his present before midnight!

Running twenty-five minutes, *Santa's First Christmas* has a traditional, if overcute, animation style full of bright colors and big eyes. By contrast, the twenty-seven-minute 1991 *Santa and the Tooth Fairies* has a watercolor/colored pencil book-illustration feel belying its foreign creation (it's a French production, while its predecessor came from Germany). Both are pleasant holiday fare for kids of all ages.

SPECIAL FEATURES None TECHNICAL FEATURES Fullscreen (1.33:1) • Languages: Eng. • Sound: Dolby Digital 2.0, Dolby Digital Surround 5.1 • Keepcase • 1 Disc • Region 1–6 GENRE & RATING Holiday/Family • Not Rated (All Ages)

Santo Bugito—Vol. 1

Image, 2000, 116 mins., #ID8503KCDVD. Directed by Bob Hathcock, Nort Virgien. Story by Lane Raichert, Jono Howard, Arlene Klasky. Written by Lane Raichert, Mark Hoffmeier, Jono Howard, Arlene Klasky.

In the desert town of Santo Bugito, Texas, the bugs rule the Earth. All kinds of insects make their home in the dusty town, eating trash, talking trash, and being trash. Carmen and Paco De La Anthchez are a romantic pair of ants who own the popular restaurant Santa Bugito's Cocina, while other odd townsbugs include Rosa the butterfly (whose cocooned husband she carries), suffering artist-termite Eaton Woode, Mr. Mothmeyer, slobby houseflies Clem and Burt, indestructible Lencho Fleabondigas, and tough vegetarian Ralph the Lady Bug. Watch as they deal with killer bees, bloodsucking mosquito lawyers, hungry dragonflies at the Talent Fair, and more.

Santa Bugito is six-legged humor with a Tex-Mex flair, created by Arlene Klasky, cofounder of animation studio Klasky-Csupo. The Latin comedy was inspired by Klasky's own children, who were both repulsed and fascinated by insects. The wacky series debuted on CBS in 1995, but only ran for one season. The eclectic voice cast included such '70s film and TV stars as William Sanderson, Cheech Marin, Joan Van Ark, Henry Gibson, and George Kennedy, and the music was by Mark Mothersbaugh of DEVO fame. The animation style was as intricate—and odd—as its insect subject matter.

The debut DVD features five episodes: "Load o' Bees"; "Sue City"; "Splitsville"; "Cupid vs. Clem"; and "How to Eat People and Make Friends."

SPECIAL FEATURES Inserts: Episode Guide TECHNICAL FEATURES Fullscreen (1.33:1) • Languages: Eng., Span. dub • Sound: Dolby Digital 2.0 • Snapcase • 1 Disc • Region 1 GENRE & RATING Insects/Comedy • Not Rated (Kids)

Santo Bugito—Vol. 2

Image, 2000, 92 mins., #ID8728KCDVD. Directed by Bob Hathcock, Nort Virgien. Story by Lane Raichert, Jono Howard, Ken Koonce, Michael Merton. Written by Lane Raichert, Michael Price, Ken Koonce, Michael Merton, Mark Hoffmeier, Jono Howard, Arlene Klasky.

Amelia becomes a superheroine named "Buzzing-Around Woman" after a series of thefts, but it doesn't stop suspicious townbugs from throwing each other into jail! Then, Carmen breaks an antenna and is put out of commission. As other bugs try to fill in for her at the restaurant, they discover just how tough her job really is. And later, when Carmen and Paco try to take a second honeymoon, the town sends out a search party, sure that they're in trouble! Finally, a sultry arachnid dancer catches all of Santa Bugito's men in her web and prepares to have a feast.

The four episodes on this DVD are: "Swiped"; "The Carmen Tango"; "Lost Cause"; and "A Widow Goes a Long Way."

SPECIAL FEATURES Inserts: Episode Guide TECHNICAL FEATURES Fullscreen (1.33:1) • Languages: Eng., Span. dub • Sound: Dolby Digital 2.0 • Snapcase • 1 Disc • Region 1 GENRE & RATING Insects/Comedy • Not Rated (Kids)

Santo Bugito—Vol. 3

Image, 2000, 92 mins., #ID8729KCDVD. Directed by Nort Virgien, Bob Hathcock. Story by Lane Raichert, Mark Hoffmeier, Michael Price. Written by Michael Price, Lane Raichert, Mark Hoffmeier.

When he is evicted from his home by his parents until he eats his first victim, a young wolf spider comes to Santa Bugito with one wish: to stay a vegetarian! Then, three cockroaches open a competing restaurant across the street from the Cocina, and they're fighting dirty. Plus, a bitter pirate aphid comes to town, gunning for Ralph. And finally, a clumsy caterpillar busboy could mean the ruin of the Cocina if a miracle doesn't occur.

The final four episodes of the *Santa Bugito* series are presented on this DVD: "The Carnivore Kid"; "Buenos Roaches!"; "My Name is Revenge"; and "Bugged Bug."

SPECIAL FEATURES Inserts: Episode Guide TECHNICAL FEATURES Fullscreen (1.33:1) • Languages: Eng., Span. dub • Sound: Dolby Digital 2.0 • Snapcase • 1 Disc • Region 1 GENRE & RATING Insects/Comedy • Not Rated (Kids)

Schoolhouse Rock! Special 30th Anniversary Edition

Disney, 2002, 283 mins., #23048.

Anyone watching ABC television on Saturday mornings from 1972 forward is likely to be familiar with *Schoolhouse Rock*, a series of ninety-second-to-three-minute musical interludes that made education fun in between programs. The series began as "Multiplication Rock," with "Grammar Rock" following in the 1973 season, "American Rock" hitting in 1974, ""Bicentennial Rock" in 1976, "Science Rock" in 1978, and "Body Rock" in 1979 (which had nothing to do with the breakdancing movie of the same title). The series won four Emmy Awards during its time on the air.

This two-disc set contains all forty-six shorts, including some never-released-on-video segments, loads of behind-the-scenes and historical footage, puzzles, games, favorite countdowns, and even an all-new song! Now you can listen to "Conjunction Junction"; "I'm Just a Bill"; "Lolly, Lolly, Lolly Get Your Adverbs Here!" "Interplanetary Janet"; and "The Shot Heard 'Round the World" as often as you like. Retro-cool doesn't get much more fun than this TV favorite.

SPECIAL FEATURES "Making of" Featurette • Commentary Track • Crew Bios • Deleted Scenes • Promotional Footage • Jukebox Features • Music Videos • Games • Other Title Trailers • Inserts: Liner Notes, Lyrics • Easter Eggs TECHNICAL FEATURES Fullscreen (1.33:1) • Subtitles/CC: Eng. • Languages: Eng. • Sound: Dolby Digital Surround 5.1 • Multikeepcase • 2 Discs • Region 1 GENRE & RATING Music/Education • Not Rated (Kids)

Scooby-Doo and the Alien Invaders

Warner, 2000, 80 mins.

This DVD was not available for review.

Scooby-Doo and the Cyber Chase

Warner, 2001, 89 mins., #H1746. Directed by Jim Stenstrum. Written by Mark Turosz.

The Mystery Inc. gang attempts to capture the Phantom Virus, but the computer virus sucks them into a game based on their own adventures! Trapped within the game, the gang must negotiate ten creepy levels, including the moon, a Coliseum, the prehistoric era, and more! Later, they're faced with some of the spookiest villains from the past, and they must find a box of Scooby Snacks or the game will be over. Will they get help from an unexpected source . . . their own cyber-counterparts?

A direct-to-video production, *Scooby-Doo and the Cyber Chase* updates the Scooby gang into thoroughly modern times, while still maintaining ties to its origins. Funnier than some of the other Scooby-features, this gives all the cast members a place in the story, offers some bouncy tunes (the theme is by the B-52s), and at its best brings the Mystery Inc. gang face-to-face with their 1970s counterparts. Those who enjoy the "old school" *Scooby Doo* will no doubt enjoy this story, as will fans of *Tron*, to which this story owes a debt of gratitude.

The DVD has some fun extras, including a spot-the-differences game called "Virtual Detective." Be sure to stick around after the credits for another look at some favorite moments.

SPECIAL FEATURES "Making of" Featurette • Trailer • Music Video • Game • Other Title Trailers • Inserts: Game Clues TECHNICAL FEATURES Fullscreen (1.33:1) • Subtitles/CC: Eng., Fren., Span. • Languages: Eng. • Sound: Dolby Digital Surround 5.1 • Snapcase • 1 Disc • Region 1 GENRE & RATING Mystery/Comedy • Not Rated (Kids)

Scooby-Doo and the Ghoul School

Warner, 2002, 90 mins.

This DVD was not available for review.

Scooby-Doo and the Reluctant Werewolf

Warner, 2002, 91 mins., #H1878. Directed by Ray Patterson. Written by Jim Ryan.

Count Dracula wants to enter a car into the Monster Car Race, but he doesn't have a driver. He zaps Shaggy and Scooby-Doo to Transylvania and transforms Shaggy into a werewolf! Ruh-roh! Now Shaggy and Scooby must run the creepiest race ever, out-driving and outscaring such other ghouls and monsters as Frankenstein, the Mummy, Dreadonia, Repulsa, Bone-jangles, Dr. Jekyll and Mr. Hyde, and others.

Don't look for the other Mystery Inc. friends in this adventure, though Scrappy-Doo and Shaggy's "adoring but liberated" girlfriend, Googie, do show up. Originally titled "Scooby and the Reluctant Werewolf" (without the "Doo"), this was a part of *Hanna-Barbera's Superstar 10* package for syndication, airing in 1988. The animation resembles the mid-vintage *Scooby*, but the story relies mostly on "wacky" car hijinks. Your enjoyment level for this DVD will depend on how much you enjoy these kinds of hijinks.

SPECIAL FEATURES How to Draw Scooby Doo • Music Video • Games • DVD-ROM Features: Games • Other Title Trailers • Inserts: Word Game TECHNICAL FEATURES Fullscreen (1.33:1) • Subtitles/CC: Eng., Fren., Span. • Languages: Eng., Fren. dub, Span. dub • Sound: Dolby Digital 2.0 • Snapcase • 1 Disc • Region 1 GENRE & RATING Mystery/Comedy • Not Rated (Kids)

Scooby-Doo and the Witch's Ghost

Warner, 2001, 77 mins., #H1487. Directed by Jim Stenstrum. Written by Rick Copp, David Goodman, Davis Doi, Glenn Leopold.

Zoinks! It looks as if the Mystery Inc. gang has finally run into a real ghost! When they're invited to the New England home of famous horror writer Ben Ravencroft, they discover that the town is haunted. As the Autumn Harvest Festival gets underway, Ben's ancestor Sarah begins haunting, but are the mummies and monster turkeys her doing? Is she a healer or a witch? Scooby and the others are on the case....

This direct-to-video feature makes fun of its roots in the opening, and the characters have ditched the bellbottoms and ascots. Tim Curry voices Ravencroft, and his sinister tones are always a plus. The theme song this time out is by country croonster Billy Ray Cyrus, and one of the Go-Gos sings in the cartoon band called "The Hex Girls." Even though the ghosts are real and the supernatural scenes are spooky in this DVD adventure, youngsters won't be too frightened.

SPECIAL FEATURES "Making of" Featurette • Character Bios • Music Video • Game • Other Title Trailers TECHNICAL FEATURES Fullscreen (1.33:1) • Languages: Eng., Fren. dub, Port. dub, Span. dub • Sound: Dolby Digital Surround 5.1 • Snapcase • 1 Disc • Region 1 GENRE & RATING Mystery/Comedy • Not Rated (Kids)

Scooby-Doo Goes Hollywood

Warner, 2002, 90 mins.

This DVD was not available for review.

Scooby-Doo on Zombie Island

Warner, 2001, 77 mins., #H1424. Directed by Jim Stenstrum. Screenplay by Glenn Leopold. Story by Glenn Leopold, Davis Doi.

Mystery Inc. has split up, frustrated that they've never found any real supernatural occurrences or ghosts. Shaggy and Scooby are customs agents, Velma owns a mystery bookstore, Daphne is the star of a TV show, and Fred is her producer. But when Daphne decides to put on a special "Haunted America" show, Fred reunites the old gang for fun and adventure. On a supposedly haunted island in a Louisiana bayou, they search for the ghost of Moonscar the pirate, but the danger is very real this time. Ghostly pirates, cat creatures, and shambling zombies are just a few of the scares in store for Scooby and the gang!

This 1998 project revamped the *Scooby-Doo* franchise, updating it for a new generation. The characters haven't really aged, but at least they changed their wardrobes a bit (all except Shaggy). The producers made the animation designs more realistic as well, and updated the music into the '90s. Some parents may not appreciate the disturbing and scary "real" monsters, but longtime fans will find themselves enjoying the old gang without the retro feel. The DVD has a few fun extras, including a short "Making of" documentary.

SPECIAL FEATURES "Making of" Featurette • Character Bios • Trailer • Game • Other Title Trailers TECHNICAL FEATURES Fullscreen (1.33:1) • Languages: Eng., Fren. dub, Port. dub, Span. dub • Sound: Dolby Digital Surround 5.1 • Snapcase • 1 Disc • Region 1 GENRE & RATING Mystery/Comedy • Not Rated (Kids)

Scooby-Doo Meets Batman

Warner, 2002, 82 mins.

This DVD was not available for review.

Scooby-Doo's Original Mysteries

Warner, 2000, 100 mins., #H1565. Directed by Joseph Barbera, William Hanna. Story by Ken Spears, Joe Ruby, Bill Lutz.

Fred, Daphne, Velma, Shaggy, and the great dane Scooby-Doo travel the country in their Mystery Machine van, solving mysteries, debunking ghosts, exposing fake monsters, and generally meddling in the affairs of villains (who would have gotten away with it if it hadn't been for those pesky kids!). Whether they're unmasking a knightly art-swindler, investigating a ghost ship, rearranging a counterfeit ring, or pouncing on a pack of dog-nappers, the Mystery Inc. gang is on the case!

Seeing the end of the cartoon superhero boom in 1969, CBS children's programming executive Fred Silverman asked Hanna-Barbera to come up with a new show. He wanted it to have comic teenagers like *The Archies*, and suggested that it resemble one of his favorite sitcoms, *Dobie Gillis*. Beyond that, he wanted it to have mysteries and scares, like his favorite radio shows. Once the human quartet was in place, the network asked H-B to ramp up the role of the dog, which Silverman named after a phrase from the Frank Sinatra song "Strangers in the Night."

Scooby-Doo, Where Are You? (a nod to another TV show, *Car 54, Where Are You?*) debuted in 1969 and hasn't really left the air since. Various versions of the show have aired under at least seventeen different titles, and Scooby has teamed up with Sonny and Cher, Batman, the Three Stooges, and more!

This DVD features the first five classic *Scooby-Doo, Where Are You?* cartoons in excellent condition: "What a Night for a Knight"; "Hassle in the Castle"; "A Clue for Scooby-Doo"; "Mine Your Own Business"; and "Decoy for a Dognapper." Anyone who has ever loved the phrases "Zoinks!," "Jinkies!," or "Ruh-Roh!" will have to own these classics of modern pop culture.

SPECIAL FEATURES Music Video • Music Jukebox • Game • Recipes TECHNICAL FEATURES Fullscreen (1.33:1) • Languages: Eng., Fren. dub, Span. dub • Sound: Dolby Digital 2.0 • Snapcase • 1 Disc • Region 1 GENRE & RATING Mystery/Comedy • Not Rated (Kids)

Scooby-Doo's Spookiest Tales

Warner, 2001, 110 mins., #H1759. Directed by Charles A. Nichols, Joseph Barbera, William Hanna. Story by Larz Bourne, Dick Conway, Willie Gilbert, Duane Poole, Haskell Barkin, Tom Dagenais, Tony DiMarco, Dave Ketchum, Norman Maurer, Dick Robbins, Dalton Sandifer, Ken Spears, Joe Ruby, Bill Lutz.

The Mystery Inc. gang is back on the case, with more creepy crooks and foul fiends. Even Scooby-Dum is along to help out. A birthday party at Great Skull Island becomes a stake-out when vampires are spotted, while later, a fortune-teller and some monsters search for treasure. Then, on a ski trip, the gang encounters a snow ghost, a Tibetan temple, and a scary toboggan ride. Finally, a zombie and a witch are haunting Swamp's End, and the pumpkin-topped Headless Horseman rides his way into terror.

Three episodes on this DVD are from the first season of *Scooby-Doo, Where Are You?*: "A Gaggle of Galloping Ghosts"; "That's Snow Ghost"; and "Which Witch is Which?" The other two are from 1976's *The Scooby-Doo/DynoMutt Hour*: "Vampire, Bats, and Scaredy Cats" and "The Headless Horseman of Halloween." Although some viewers may like Scooby-Dum (voiced by Daws Butler) more than the later Scrappy-Doo, others may find him just as much of a waste of ink and paint. All the episodes are in excellent condition, and the DVD transfer is just fine.

SPECIAL FEATURES Character Bios • Game • Other Title Trailers TECHNICAL FEATURES Fullscreen (1.33:1) • Languages: Eng., Fren. dub, Span. dub • Sound: Dolby Digital 2.0 • Snapcase • 1 Disc • Region 1 GENRE & RATING Mystery/Comedy • Not Rated (Kids)

Scooby-Doo! Winter Wonderdog

Warner, 2002.

This DVD was not available for review.

Secret Adventures of Tom Thumb, The

Palm Pictures/Manga Entertainment, 1998, 70 mins., #800 635 587-2. Directed by Dave Borthwick. Written by Dave Borthwick.

A miniature clay baby is created—not born—to human parents who live in the poor section of a rat-infested town. Little Tom Thumb is the only kid of his size until ominous government agents kidnap him and take him to a laboratory. There, he is aided by a lizard-like creature as he finds the horrific secrets of his genetically engineered origins. The pair escapes to the outer world, where Tom discovers a colony of people his own size. One of them, Jack the Giant Killer, is determined to bring down the big humans who created them. Tom joins Jack in his mission. . . .

It would be hard to find a more bizarre film than this one; only the work of Jan Svankmajer or the Brothers Quay even come close. The film was released in 1993, and won sixteen film awards, mostly in foreign countries. Animation is a constant throughout the film, even in the live-action segments. The actors were filmed in a herky-jerky style that made them into animated figures to be manipulated by the director. Tom, Jack, and other characters are filmed with claymation and stop-motion effects.

The Secret Adventures of Tom Thumb will polarize viewers. It is extremely unsettling to watch, and yet mesmerizing at the same time. Those who want something ultra-weird and mind-blowing will love it; those who want something safer, more traditional, and less horrific will loathe it. The DVD also contains a short by the same production team, the 1996 short, "The Saint Inspector."

SPECIAL FEATURES Producer Bios • Awards Listing • Trailer • Other Title Trailers • Inserts: Liner Notes TECHNICAL FEATURES Fullscreen (1.33:1) • Languages: Eng. • Sound: Dolby Digital Surround 2.0 • Keepcase • 1 Disc • Region 1 GENRE & RATING Live/Stop Motion/Surreal • Not Rated (Teens)

Secret of Anastasia, The

UAV Entertainment, 1997, 90 mins., #40089. Directed by Lee Lan. Written by Mark Zaslove, Ken Koonce, Michael Merton.

Anastasia is the youngest princess of Imperial Russia, but after the revolution, she goes into hiding. Years later, Anastasia's only friends are four magical musical instruments. Setting out to prove her identity to the world, Anastasia gains two suitors—the dashing Ikonovich and the worldly Prince Paul—but one of them isn't the man he appears to be.

What dastardly deeds will happen when Anastasia proves her identity to her grandmother?

The second feature on this disc is *Snow White and the Magic Mirror*, and in the story, the Queen is once again Snow White's wicked stepmother. Snow White has a beauty that won't quit, so the Queen sends her off to the woods. There, she becomes surrogate mother/wife to seven dwarves until the Queen decides to feed her a poisoned apple to get rid of her once and for all.

Although the UAV producers were cashing in on Fox's Don Bluth-created *Anastasia* for the main title's momentum, it's still astonishing to see how many story elements are similar, especially the "you'll know it's her by a song" element. And while there's barely a few seconds of anything remotely resembling historical accuracy, the story has cute moments and fanciful designs. The version of *Snow White* is similarly cute, bland, and non-offensive. Although neither can hold a candle to its big-budget competitor, kids might enjoy this DVD if the others are unavailable.

SPECIAL FEATURES Trailer • Other Title Trailers TECHNICAL FEATURES Fullscreen (1.33:1) • Languages: Eng. • Sound: Dolby Digital 2.0 • Snapcase • 1 Disc • Region 1 GENRE & RATING Music/Fantasy • Not Rated (All Ages)

Secret of NIMH, The

MGM, 1998, 82 mins., #907037. Directed by Don Bluth. Story Adapted by Don Bluth, John Pomeroy, Gary Goldman, Will Finn. Based on the novel *Mrs. Frisby and the Rats of NIMH* by Robert C. O'Brien.

A widowed mouse, Mrs. Brisby, must move her family before Farmer Fitzgibbon's spring plowing destroys their home. But her son is deathly ill, and Mrs. Brisby is forced to seek help in her quest. She finds aid from an addle-brained crow, a fearsome Great Owl, other mice, and even the rats who come from nearby NIMH. Along the way, she must gain a magical amulet and fend off a ferocious cat, and when she finds out the secret of NIMH, her world will change.

Released in 1982, *The Secret of NIMH* is considered by many to be the best feature produced by Don Bluth, or at least among the best (it's also his first feature after leaving Disney with coproducers Gary Goldman and John Pomeroy). The animation is meticulous and detailed, with magical and scary imagery intermingling with animal-eye views of the world beneath our feet. The story is affecting, touching, and sincere, pulling at the heart with Mrs. Brisby's unwavering love for her family. The film is as impressive for adult audiences as it is for young ones, with multilayered character motivations evident throughout much of the story. And Dom DeLuise is delightful as Jeremy the crow.

The only reason to not wholeheartedly recommend

this DVD is that it is modified from its widescreen original version into a fullscreen version. One can only hope that MGM will eventually reissue this classic in its original form.

SPECIAL FEATURES Trailer • Inserts: Booklet TECHNICAL FEATURES Fullscreen (1.33:1) • Subtitles/CC: Eng., Fren. • Languages: Eng. • Sound: Dolby Digital Surround 2.0 • Keepcase • 1 Disc • Region 1 GENRE & RATING Animals/Adventure/Family • Rated G

Secret of NIMH 2, The: Timmy to the Rescue

MGM, 2001, 68 mins., #1001608. Directed by Dick Sebast. Written by Sam Graham and Chris Hubbell. Based on the novel *Mrs. Frisby and the Rats of NIMH* by Robert C. O'Brien.

Thorn Valley needs a hero, and young Timothy Brisby may be just the mouse. He must go through lots of training to become the hero he needs to be, or he'll never be able to challenge NIMH as they try to recapture the intelligent rats. Along the way to a rescue, he gets help from a familiar crow, a caterpillar, and a pretty young girl mouse. But will a nasty cat be the smallest of his troubles . . . or the biggest?

This 1998 film is one of the most unnecessary sequels made by a major U.S. studio. The only returning member of the creative team is Dom DeLuise as the voice of Jeremy the crow, and the new production team has cannibalized the original for a lackluster and barely entertaining sequel. The animation is serviceable, but the best thing in the film is Eric Idle, voicing the villainous Martin.

Although kids will no doubt enjoy this DVD, older viewers will be disappointed all the way around.

SPECIAL FEATURES Trailer TECHNICAL FEATURES Fullscreen (1.33:1) • Subtitles/CC: Fren., Span. • Languages: Eng., Fren. dub, Span. dub • Sound: Dolby Digital 5.1 • Keepcase • 1 Disc • Region 1 GENRE & RATING Music/Animals/Adventure • Rated G

Serial Experiments: Lain—Navi [#1]

Pioneer, 1999, 100 mins., #PIDA-2231V. Directed by Ryutaro Nakamura, Joie Matsuura, Akihiko Nishiyama. Screenplay by Chiaki J. Konaka.

Lain is a quiet and unassuming schoolgirl. When she takes an interest in computers, her father gets her a brand new Navi (a computer). That's when her life changes. Lain receives an email from a girl at school that reads, "I just abandoned my body. I still live here." Confused, Lain learns at school the following day that the girl had committed

suicide—before the email was sent to Lain. Drawn to find out more, Lain begins to delve into the world of the "Wired," a global network similar to the Internet. Is anybody what they seem? In fact, do they even exist?

First airing on Japanese television in 1998, *Serial Experiments: Lain* is not a timid look into a possible future. It is a bold, disturbing look into a future that should be feared and avoided. With exceptional writing, *Lain*'s character development and storyline are paced with deliberate care, and nothing is revealed either too early or too late. This first disc in the series contains episodes #1–4 and lays the groundwork for this extraordinary tale.

Serial Experiments: Lain is a disturbing look into the human psyche, and is probably not suitable for young viewers. *Lain*'s animation is top-notch, as is the art it brings to life with a high degree of screen clarity. As for the soundtrack, *Lain* has one of the most gripping scores in anime. With haunting tunes and techno-punk tracks, the series has yielded several CDs. *Serial Experiments: Lain* is simply at the top of the anime pyramid in virtually every area. [GP]

SPECIAL FEATURES Character and Art Galleries • Promotional Footage • Easter Egg TECHNICAL FEATURES Fullscreen (1.33:1) • Subtitles/CC: Eng. • Languages: Jap., Eng. dub • Sound: Dolby Digital 2.0 • Keepcase • 1 Disc • Region 1, 4 GENRE & RATING Science Fiction/Cyberspace • Rated 16+

Serial Experiments: Lain—Knights [#2]

Pioneer, 1999, 75 mins., #PIDA-2232V. Directed by Johie Matsuura, Akihiko Nishiyama, Masahiko Murata. Screenplay by Chiaki J. Konaka.

Lain discovers that a hacker group called the Knights may be the cause of a string of recent suicides. As she drills deeper into the Wired to discover the Knights' secrets, Lain's forward and confident alter-self is becoming more brazen, and the lines between Lain's physical world and the Wired start to blur.

In this second disc of the series, containing episodes #5–7, there are critical developments in Lain's story. She begins to understand more about the Wired but less about herself when she is asked, "Are those people who you live with really your parents?" [GP]

SPECIAL FEATURES Character and Art Galleries • Clean Credits • Easter Egg TECHNICAL FEATURES Fullscreen (1.33:1) • Subtitles/CC: Eng. • Languages: Jap., Eng. dub • Sound: Dolby Digital 2.0 • Keepcase • 1 Disc • Region 1, 4 GENRE & RATING Science Fiction/Cyberspace • Rated 16+

Serial Experiments: Lain—Deus [#3]

Pioneer, 1999, 75 mins., #PIDA-2233V. Directed by Shigeru Ueda, Akihiko Nishiyama, Masahiko Murata. Screenplay by Chiaki J. Konaka.

Lain begins to lose friends as she withdraws from society and spends more time in the Wired. What friends remain are stunned as it appears Lain is stealing and revealing their deepest secrets. But it isn't Lain, exactly. Lain's parents also reveal a secret, one Lain isn't prepared for.

On this DVD, episodes #8–10 take the story much deeper, as Lain can hardly even tell the difference between herself and her alter-self. In fact, she starts to doubt which one is the "real" Lain when she meets a man who calls himself God. [GP]

SPECIAL FEATURES Character and Art Galleries • Promotional Footage • Clean Credits • Easter Egg TECHNICAL FEATURES Fullscreen (1.33:1) • Subtitles/CC: Eng. • Languages: Jap., Eng. dub • Sound: Dolby Digital 2.0 • Keepcase • 1 Disc • Region 1, 4 GENRE & RATING Science Fiction/Cyberspace • Rated 16+

Serial Experiments: Lain—Reset [#4]

Pioneer, 1999, 75 mins., #PIDA-2233V. Directed by Joie Matsuura, Shigeru Ueda, Ryutaro Nakamura. Screenplay by Chiaki J. Konaka.

As Lain's power in the Wired grows, she decides to face off against God himself. Lain knows the end is near, but she also knows that she has the power to decide what that end will be. Will the physical world die or will she reset everything to a time before her and without her? Lain wonders, "Isn't the only real way to die to be forgotten?"

Things come to a head in this, the final DVD of the series, containing episode #11–13. This is the thrilling conclusion to the *Lain* series. If you thought things seemed dark before—you ain't seen nothin' yet! [GP]

SPECIAL FEATURES Character and Art Galleries • Promotional Footage • Clean Credits • Easter Egg TECHNICAL FEATURES Fullscreen (1.33:1) • Subtitles/CC: Eng. • Languages: Jap., Eng. dub • Sound: Dolby Digital 2.0 • Keepcase • 1 Disc • Region 1, 4 GENRE & RATING Science Fiction/Cyberspace • Rated 16+

Serial Experiments: Lain Lunch Box Limited Edition [Box Set]

Pioneer, 1999, 325 mins.

This limited-edition box set features the commercially available keepcase editions of *Serial Experiments: Lain*, packed within a metal lunchbox. Also included is a four-song CD by Boa, featuring the opening theme. This edition was limited to 3,000 copies. See individual entries for the Special and Technical Features listings.

TECHNICAL FEATURES • Metal Lunchbox with CD • 4 Discs GENRE & RATING Science Fiction/Cyberspace • Rated 16+

Serial Experiments: Lain DVD Box Set

Pioneer, 1999, 325 mins., #11608.

This box set features the commercially available keepcase editions of *Serial Experiments: Lain*. It does not feature any extras. See individual entries for the Special and Technical Features listings.

TECHNICAL FEATURES • Cardboard Box with Blue Plastic Slipcase and Four Keepcases • 4 Discs GENRE & RATING Science Fiction/Cyberspace • Rated 16+

Sex Demon Queen ☞ see Mature/Adult Section

Shadoan: Kingdom II

Digital Leisure, 2000, #SPS 001. Animation Directed by Kevin Ryniker. Concept by Rick Dyer.

Long ago, the Five Kingdoms were united under the rule of the Argent Kings, but their order of Great Wizards eventually led to their downfall at the hands of Torlock, a powerful and evil mage. But Torlock's rule of the land could not be complete until he reunited the five fragments of the mystical amulet known as "The Hand." Now, Prince Lathan Kandor has teamed up with beautiful Iscar Princess Grace Delight to reunite the five pieces and overthrow Torlock. But to do this, Lathan must brave Shadoan, Torlock's land of shadows, and serpent men. . . .

Shadoan is a sequel to the arcade game "Thayer's Quest." The interactive game features much animation and alternate story possibilities, with the ability to start at Apprentice or Wizard level of play. The DVD is also compatible with Sony Playstation 2 systems.

SPECIAL FEATURES Insert: Game Notes and Hints TECHNICAL FEATURES Fullscreen (1.33:1) • Subtitles/CC: Chin., Fren., Germ., Jap., Kor., Span. • Languages: Eng. • Sound: Dolby Digital 2.0, DTS • Keepcase • 1 Disc • Region 1–6 GENRE & RATING Fantasy/Adventure/Interactive • Rated E

Shadow Raiders: Uncommon Hero [#1]

ADV Films, 2001, 90 mins., #DSR001 Directed by Colin Davies, Phil Mitchell, Mark Sawers, Mark Schiemann, Dwayne John Beaver. Written by Len Wein, Christy Marx, Marv Wolfman, Ken Pontac.

The deadly Beast planet has made its quest to destroy as many solar systems as possible, by conquering a planet, absorbing it, and using its power to increase the Beast planet. When it destroys planet Tek, that world's sole survivor, Princess Tekla, sets off to warn other planets of the impending threat. She's pursued by attack drones of the Beast planet and shot down on the Ice planet. She meets and saves the life of a miner, Graveheart, but is gravely injured. Before she dies, she tells him of her mission and implores him to unite the four planets, Ice, Rock, Fire, and Bone, to stand against the Beast planet, before their universe is destroyed as well. The four planets haven't been at peace for centuries and each has a reason for not trusting the others within their system. Plus, Graveheart is a commoner, trying to convince nobility from across his galaxy to trust him and band together against an unseen evil. Will Graveheart and his allies be able to unite the planets and defend against the Beast from another universe?

Shadow Raiders—or *War Planets* as it was sometimes called in the U.S.—began life in 1998 as a series of toys from Trendmaster. The animated series made its computer generated debut that same year and lasted two seasons. In 2000 Cartoon Network aired various episodes as part of its Toonami block.

Collecting the initial four episodes of *Shadow Raiders*, the first volume introduces viewers to the conflict, the protagonists, and the antagonists, in a sci-fi battle of the planets unlike most of the usual offerings. [JMC]

SPECIAL FEATURES Character Bios • Animation Models • Promotional Footage • Other Title Trailers TECHNICAL FEATURES Fullscreen (1.33:1) • Languages: Eng. • Sound: Dolby Digital 2.0 • Keepcase • 1 Disc • Region 1 GENRE & RATING CGI/Science Fiction • Not Rated (Kids)

Shadow Raiders: A Dangerous Enemy [#2]

ADV Films, 2001, 90 mins., #DSR002 Directed by Anthony Atkins, Owen M. Hurley, Andrew Duncan, Vladimir Stefoff. Written by Christy Marx, Ken Pontac, Katherine Lawrence, Marv Wolfman.

The fledgling alliance might not last long enough to face the Beast planet, especially since one of their most devious agents, Lamprey, has possessed Tekla and is using her body as a vessel to wreak havoc. First he tries to assassinate Graveheart, next he convinces the Bone planet ruler the alliance is plotting against him, and then he frames Jade for a terrible crime! Can Tekla free herself in time to help Jade? The Ice planet also has problems when Blokk, a drone of the Beast planet, kidnaps Zera in an effort to prove the King has more loyalty to his family than his people. When the king chooses his daughter's life over the planet, what penalty will his people demand?

The disc containing episodes #5–8 continues the lush computer-generated exploration of the spoils of war. [JMC]

SPECIAL FEATURES Character Bios • Animation Models • Promotional Footage • Other Title Trailers TECHNICAL FEATURES Fullscreen (1.33:1) • Languages: Eng. • Sound: Dolby Digital 2.0 • Keepcase • 1 Disc • Region 1 GENRE & RATING CGI/Science Fiction • Not Rated (Kids)

Shadow Raiders: Final Hours [#3]

ADV Films, 2001, 90 mins., #DSR003. Directed by George Samilski, Raul Inglis, Craig McEwen, James E. Taylor, James Boshier. Written by Christy Marx, Marv Wolfman, Len Wein, Steve Cuden.

Graveheart, Tekla, and Jade are hoping to convince planet Rock to join them before the Beast planet turns them into pebbles. Then the Ice princess and Fire king are on a diplomatic mission when they crash-land on the dead world of Remora and make a startling discovery. They're attacked by Beast drones, but manage to escape and warn the Alliance that Remora is a base for the Beast planet. The Alliance attacks Remora, but the Beast planet reveals secrets of its own as the dead world is transformed into a battle planet with weapons, defenses, and, quite possibly, more than enough power to defeat the Alliance. Is this the end of our heroes?

Containing the final parts of season one, episodes #9–13, this character-driven DVD has some of the most dramatic episodes of the series. [JMC]

SPECIAL FEATURES Character Bios • Animation Models • Promotional Footage • Other Title Trailers TECHNICAL FEATURES Fullscreen (1.33:1) • Languages: Eng. • Sound: Dolby Digital

2.0 • Keepcase • 1 Disc • Region 1 GENRE & RATING CGI/Science Fiction • Not Rated (Kids)

Shadow Raiders: Alliance Attacks! [#4]

ADV Films, 2001, 90 mins., #DSR004. Directed by Owen Hurley, Steve Ball, J. Falconer, Andrew Duncan. Written by Christy Marx, Marv Wolfman, Ken Pontac, Dan DiDio.

Tekla and Zera are able to help steer the Ice planet out of the path of the Beast planet, but their actions throw the Fire planet into the path of danger, since it becomes the new object of the Beast's appetite. Can a bickering Alliance put aside their squabbles to aid this world and others within their solar system suffering from these wars . . . or will the Beast planet win without really having to fight?

A revealing DVD containing episodes #14–17, these stories show the characters learning the value of friends and partners, instead of following the "every sentient for himself" theory. [JMC]

SPECIAL FEATURES Character Bios • Animation Models • Promotional Footage • Other Title Trailers TECHNICAL FEATURES Fullscreen (1.33:1) • Languages: Eng. • Sound: Dolby Digital 2.0 • Keepcase • 1 Disc • Region 1 GENRE & RATING CGI/Science Fiction • Not Rated (Kids)

Shadow Raiders: New Worlds! [#5]

ADV Films, 2001, 90 mins., #DSR005. Directed by Craig McEwen, George Roman Samilski, Raul Inglis, Mark Sawers. Written by Emma Bull, Will Shetterly, Brooks Watchel, Art Holcomb, Gillian Horvath.

The Alliance discovers a new planet at the end of their solar system, but can they convince the residents of planet Sand to join them against the Beast planet? Then, the argumentative girl heroines are encouraged to take a night off and relax. What secrets will each reveal when the tension is off? Next, our heroes discover a dead planet and plan on using it to trick, trap, and destroy the Beast planet, but will this big boom leave a dent on the battle world?

Two new worlds are discovered in this collection of episodes #18–21, and our heroes use both to their advantage against the Beast's weapons. [JMC]

SPECIAL FEATURES Character Bios • Animation Models • Promotional Footage • Other Title Trailers TECHNICAL FEATURES Fullscreen (1.33:1) • Languages: Eng. • Sound: Dolby Digital 2.0 • Keepcase • 1 Disc • Region 1 GENRE & RATING CGI/Science Fiction • Not Rated (Kids)

Shadow Raiders: Final Conflict [#6]

ADV Films, 2001, 110 mins., #DSR006. Directed by Owen Hurley, Steve Ball, Sebastian Brodin, James E. Taylor, Anthony Atkins George Roman Samilski. Written by Christy Marx, Marv Wolfman, Dan DiDio, Ken Pontac.

Discovering whole new worlds isn't all it's cracked up to be, especially if the new one happens to be a prison planet. When Graveheart crash-lands his ship on the world and the occupants get separated, each group meets a different faction of the planet's populace and unknowingly becomes involved in a civil war. Can they convince the residents to give peace a chance and team up against the Beast planet before it's too late?

The last hurrah! The big battle! The final five action-packed episodes #22–26 are contained on this DVD. The story gets *some* closure, but also leaves you wishing there had been a third season. [JMC]

SPECIAL FEATURES Character Bios • Animation Models • Promotional Footage • Other Title Trailers TECHNICAL FEATURES Fullscreen (1.33:1) • Languages: Eng. • Sound: Dolby Digital 2.0 • Keepcase • 1 Disc • Region 1 GENRE & RATING CGI/Science Fiction • Not Rated (Kids)

Shadow Skill

Manga Entertainment, 2001, 135 mins., #MANGA4081-2. Directed by Hiroshi Negishi. Script by Masanori Sekijimo, Mayori Sekijima. Based on the manga series by Megumu Okada in *Comic Gamma*.

In a world where almost everyone is either a warrior or a mercenary, the top fighters gather in gladiator-like combat using skills and powers to best one another in the hope of achieving an ultimate warrior position, a Sevalle. Elle is a Sevalle and she uses a technique called the Shadow Skill to best her many opponents. Her adopted brother, Gau Ban, is also trying to learn the Shadow Skill to become a skilled combatant like his sister. His training and attempts at mastery of the Shadow Skill fall under the attention of Scarface, one of the legendary Sevalles. Scarface is always looking for a worthy adversary and Gau wonders if he'll ever be able to challenge him. Speaking of challenges, outside of scheduled arenas of combat, there are always seedy types, demons, and unsavory creatures looking to pick a fight to increase their own talents and eliminate some of the competition. As the group journey through the land, secrets about their past, present, and possible future unfold, but will the knowledge help Gau master the Shadow Skill and achieve his goals?

Based on the intricate five-part manga created by Megumu Okada in 1992, *Shadow Skill* was first animated in 1995 and 1996 as a series of OVAs, then saw life as a twenty-six-part TV series in 1998. Manga released the videos as parts 1 and 2, and on the advice of fans, has rearranged their order for the DVD, making the latter one into *Shadow Skill: The Movie* and the former part into *Shadow Skill: Epilogue*.

While this gives the disc more closure and a solid flow, it doesn't help the content; the anime is much less complex than its manga origins, reducing the story significantly. [JMC]

SPECIAL FEATURES Character Bios • Character and Art Galleries • Trailer • Other Title Trailers • Inserts: Character Bios TECHNICAL FEATURES Fullscreen (1.33:1) • Subtitles/CC: Eng. • Languages: Jap., Eng. dub • Sound: Dolby Digital Surround 2.0, Dolby Digital 5.1 • Keepcase • 1 Disc • Region 1, 2, 4 GENRE & RATING Fantasy/Action • Not Rated (Teens)

Shamanic Princess: The Complete

Central Park, 2001, 180 mins., #USMA 2040. Directed by Mitsuru Hongo, Hiroyuki Nishimura. Script by Hiroyuki Nishimura, Asami Watanabe.

Tiara is a mystical warrior who has come from the Guardian World. Her mission: retrieve a stolen talisman from a renegade named Kagetsu. Disguising herself as an ordinary schoolgirl by day, she is soon sparring with a childhood friend named Lena. As Tiara finds out more about Kagetsu's motivations for stealing the Throne of Yord, the purposes behind her mission become murky. Whose side should she really take in the mystic battles?

The six-part 1996 OVA series has an unusual structure; the final two episodes are actually prequels to the first four episodes! As such, viewers might be confused by the circuitous path of the story. As for the art, if you can get past the absolutely gigantic eyes and hair, you'll enjoy the hyper-detailed backgrounds (the setting looks like a 19th-century European villa), as well as the excellent modeling and shading on the characters. Fans of manga from CLAMP will likely love this series.

The DVD features all six episodes in an excellent transfer. But be warned that the non-linear story flow may take some getting used to.

SPECIAL FEATURES Artist Bio • Character Bios • Trailers • DVD-ROM Features: Art, Scripts, Bios, Reviews • Other Title Trailers TECHNICAL FEATURES Fullscreen (1.33:1) • Subtitles/CC: Eng. • Languages: Jap., Eng. dub • Sound: Dolby Digital 2.0 • Keepcase • 1 Disc • Region 1 GENRE & RATING Fantasy/Girls • Rated 13+

Sherlock Holmes in the 22nd Century: The Fall and Rise of Sherlock Holmes

Trimark, 2002, 78 mins.

This DVD was not available for review.

Sherlock Hound: Case File I

Pioneer, 2002, 125 mins. (each side), #11720. Directed by Hayao Miyazaki, Kyosuke Mikuriya. Scripts by Hayao Miyazaki, Yoshihisa Araki, Tsunehisa Ito. Based on the detective stories by Sir Arthur Conan Doyle.

Sherlock Hound is the best dog detective in the world. Aided by his assistant, John Watson, whom he met on a cruise ship, the two pooches set out to solve mysteries, crimes, and anything else that piques their interest. Professor Moriarty and his bumbling assistants are the key archenemies, but the good Hound and Watson are also plagued by other conundrums and problems. Pirates, pilfered paintings, counterfeit coins, kidnapped housekeepers, and stolen gems are just some of the items Hound and Holmes must recover in order to clear falsely accused innocents, capture guilty parties, and set the records straight. Will these great detectives be able to outthink their adversaries and solve all the crimes in time?

Created in 1984 by Hayao Miyazaki, *Sherlock Hound* is this talented creator's reimagining of the Sherlock Holmes mythos presented in a canine version. The anime was originally made in conjunction with Italian partners, so it was created in English first since that language was easiest to translate into Italian and Japanese. The series lasted twenty-six episodes, and two OVAs were produced using existing episodes and some additional footage.

This DVD contains episodes #1–5 and is presented on a two-sided DVD-10. The English and Japanese versions are on opposite sides of each disc, and the English version contains 30–60 seconds more footage per episode than the digitally remastered Japanese version. [JMC]

SPECIAL FEATURES Inserts: Liner Notes TECHNICAL FEATURES Fullscreen (1.33:1) • Subtitles/CC: Eng. • Languages: Jap., Eng. dub • Sound: Dolby Digital 1.0 • Keepcase • 1 Disc • Region 1 GENRE & RATING Historical/Detective • Rated 7+

Sherlock Hound: Case File II

Pioneer, 2002, 125 mins. (each side), #11721. Based on the detective stories by Sir Arthur Conan Doyle.

Sherlock Hound matches wits with his archenemy—the nefarious Professor Moriarty—in three mind-racking adventures. Besides playing head games with Moriarty, Hound and Watson must find a person kidnapped by pirates before the swabbies make him walk the deck. The dog detective must also solve a mystery related to the past of his housekeeper when saboteurs keep throwing monkey wrenches in the British Postal Airlines. Can Hound put a few kinks in their plans before they ground the planes permanently?

This DVD contains episodes #6–10. Like the first volume, the slightly longer English version is on one side, with the Japanese version on the other side. [JMC]

SPECIAL FEATURES Inserts: Liner Notes TECHNICAL FEATURES Fullscreen (1.33:1) • Subtitles/CC: Eng. • Languages: Jap., Eng. dub • Sound: Dolby Digital 1.0 • Keepcase • 1 Disc • Region 1 GENRE & RATING Historical/Detective • Rated 7+

Sherlock Hound: Case File III

Pioneer, 2002, 100 mins. (each side), #11722. Directed by Hayao Miyazaki, Kyosuke Mikuriya. Scripts by Hayao Miyazaki, Yoshihisa Araki, Tsunehisa Ito. Based on the detective stories by Sir Arthur Conan Doyle.

NOTE: This DVD arrived too late for a full review. The following text is promotional copy provided by the releasing company:

"221 Baker Street has gone to the dogs! Based upon Sir Arthur Conan Doyle's detective stories, *Sherlock Hound* delivers an inspiring introduction of these classic mysteries to new audiences. The wonderful storytelling and signature directing styles from Japan's best talents such as Hayao Miyazaki, repopulate Sherlock Holmes' world with anthropomorphic dogs and a light touch suitable for all audiences! *Case File III* contains: 'The Sovereign Gold Coin,' 'The Stormy Getaway,' 'The Runaway Freight Car,' and 'The Coral Lobster.'"

Note: Extras are in the Episodes menu, not in a sub-menu of their own.

SPECIAL FEATURES Clean Credits • Inserts: Mini Poster, Liner Notes TECHNICAL FEATURES Fullscreen (1.33:1) • Subtitles/CC: Eng. • Languages: Jap., Eng. dub • Sound: Dolby Digital 1.0 • Keepcase • 1 Disc • Region 1 GENRE & RATING Historical/Detective • Rated 7+

Sherlock Hound: Case File IV

Pioneer, 2002, 100 mins. (each side), #11723. Directed by Hayao Miyazaki, Kyosuke Mikuriya. Scripts by Hayao Miyazaki, Yoshihisa Araki, Tsunehisa Ito. Based on the detective stories by Sir Arthur Conan Doyle.

NOTE: This DVD arrived too late for a full review. The following text is promotional copy provided by the releasing company:

"221 Baker Street has gone to the dogs! Based upon Sir Arthur Conan Doyle's detective stories, Sherlock Hound delivers an inspiring introduction of these classic mysteries to new audiences. *Case File IV* contains episodes #15–18: 'The Golden Statue of Great Burglar,' 'The Secret of the Sacred Cross Sword,' 'The Adventure of Thames Monster,' and 'The Adventure of the Three Students.'"

Note: Extras are in the Episodes menu, not in a sub-menu of their own.

SPECIAL FEATURES Promotional Footage • Inserts: Mini Poster, Liner Notes TECHNICAL FEATURES Fullscreen (1.33:1) • Subtitles/CC: Eng. • Languages: Jap., Eng. dub • Sound: Dolby Digital 1.0 • Keepcase • 1 Disc • Region 1 GENRE & RATING Historical/Detective • Rated 7+

Sherlock Hound: Case File V

Pioneer, 2002, 100 mins. (each side), #11724. Directed by Hayao Miyazaki, Kyosuke Mikuriya. Scripts by Hayao Miyazaki, Yoshihisa Araki, Tsunehisa Ito. Based on the detective stories by Sir Arthur Conan Doyle.

NOTE: This DVD arrived too late for a full review. The following text is promotional copy provided by the releasing company:

"221 Baker Street has gone to the dogs! Based upon Sir Arthur Conan Doyle's detective stories, Sherlock Hound delivers an inspiring introduction of these classic mysteries to new audiences. *Case File V* contains: 'The Rosetta Stone,' 'The White Silver Getaway,' 'The Disappearance of the Splendid Royal Horse,' and 'Disturbance, The World Flight Championship!'"

Note: Extras are in the Episodes menu, not in a sub-menu of their own.

SPECIAL FEATURES Character and Art Galleries • Inserts: Mini Poster, Liner Notes TECHNICAL FEATURES Fullscreen (1.33:1) • Subtitles/CC: Eng. • Languages: Jap., Eng. dub • Sound: Dolby Digital 1.0 • Keepcase • 1 Disc • Region 1 GENRE & RATING Historical/Detective • Rated 7+

Sherlock Hound: Case File VI

Pioneer, 2002, 100 mins. (each side), #11725. Directed by Hayao Miyazaki, Kyosuke Mikuriya. Scripts by Hayao Miyazaki, Yoshihisa Araki, Tsunehisa Ito. Based on the detective stories by Sir Arthur Conan Doyle.

NOTE: This DVD arrived too late for a full review. The following text is promotional copy provided by the releasing company:

"221 Baker Street has gone to the dogs! Based upon Sir Arthur Conan Doyle's detective stories, Sherlock Hound delivers an inspiring introduction of these classic mysteries to new audiences. *Case File VI* contains: 'The Secret of the Parrot,' 'The Bell of Big Ben,' 'The Priceless French Doll,' and 'The Missing Bride Affair.'"

Note: Extras are in the Episodes menu, not in a sub-menu of their own.

SPECIAL FEATURES Character and Art Galleries • Inserts: Mini Poster, Liner Notes TECHNICAL FEATURES Fullscreen (1.33:1) • Subtitles/CC: Eng. • Languages: Jap., Eng. dub • Sound: Dolby Digital 1.0 • Keepcase • 1 Disc • Region 1 GENRE & RATING Historical/Detective • Rated 7+

Shinesman: The Special Duty Combat Unit

Anime Works, 2000, 60 mins., #AWSD-VD-0087. Directed by Shinya Sadamitsu. Script by Hideki Sonoda. Based on the manga series by Minamu Tachibana in *Comic Bokke*.

Hiroya Matsumoto is the newest employee of a top trading firm. His love of superhero shows is soon noticed by his boss, Ms. Sakakibara, and before he knows it, Matsumoto is drafted into Shinesman, his company's own superhero team! Shinesman battles alien monsters just like the heroes on kiddie shows, but the twist is that these monsters are also agents from rival corporations. Only Shinesman, the Special Duty Combat Unit, has what it takes to vanquish evil, save the world, and guarantee profitability for the company by the end of the fiscal year!

Shinesman is a fairly obvious parody of the sentai (battle team) genre of stories that spawned the original *Power Rangers*, among many other shows. The relatively mediocre animation and trite storyline is aided greatly by the numerous jokes and gags—the team's enemies are humorously incompetent, and each Shinesman sports amusingly unthreatening attacks like "tie-clip bomb" and "business card attack." The humor is compounded by the exceptional English dub, which introduces even more puns and wisecracks to the story's dialogue. Altogether, *Shinesman* is a nice, broadly entertaining parody.

The DVD contains both OVA episodes. Disappointingly, the disc is light on extras. [MT]

SPECIAL FEATURES Character and Art Galleries • Other Title Trailers TECHNICAL FEATURES Fullscreen (1.33:1) • Subtitles/CC: Eng. • Languages: Jap., Eng. dub • Sound: Dolby Digital 2.0 • Keepcase • 1 Disc • Region 1–6 GENRE & RATING Science Fiction/Comedy • Rated 3+

Shrek

DreamWorks, 2001, 93 mins., #89012. Directed by Andrew Adamson, Vicky Jenson. Written by Ted Elliott, Terry Rossio, Joe Stillman, Roger S. H. Schulman. Based on the book by William Steig.

Deep in the swamp lives a large green ogre named Shrek, but his solitary existence is shattered when the diminutive Lord Farquaad forces all fairy tale creatures out of his kingdom and exiles them to the swamp. To get his home back, Shrek—accompanied by a talking donkey—agrees to rescue an enchanted princess from a dragon-guarded castle. Neither Shrek nor Farquaad could guess the princess's terrible secret . . .

One of the funniest comedy features ever animated, 2001's *Shrek* pokes great fun at fairy tales and Disney, even managing to teach a lesson about judging others by their looks in a non-preachy manner. Star voice talents in the feature include Mike Myers, Eddie Murphy, Cameron Diaz, and John Lithgow. The CGI work is excellent, with an amazingly tactile look for most of the characters and backgrounds.

The two-DVD set is loaded with eleven hours of extra material (just about every conceivable extra is here), some of it quite hilarious. *Shrek* is appropriate for most ages, with some humor that will go over young audience's heads.

SPECIAL FEATURES "Making of" Featurettes • Commentary Track with Filmmakers • Cast and Crew Bios • Character Interviews • Character and Art Galleries • Production Notes • Deleted Scenes • Storyboards • Trailers • Promotional Footage • Music Videos • Outtakes • Games • DVD-ROM Features: "ReVoice" Karaoke, Games • Other Title Trailers • Inserts: Liner Notes • Easter Eggs TECHNICAL FEATURES Widescreen (1.78:1) • Fullscreen (1.33:1) • Subtitles/CC: Eng., Fren., Span. • Languages: Eng., Fren. dub, Span. dub • Sound: Dolby Digital Surround 2.0, Dolby Digital Surround 5.1, DTS • Keepcase • 2 Discs • Region 1 GENRE & RATING CGI/Fantasy/Comedy • Rated PG

Shusaku ☞ see Mature/Adult Section

Shusaku Replay ☞ see Mature/Adult Section

Silent Mobius: Earth Under Attack [#1]

Bandai, 2002, 225 mins., #1170. Directed by Hideki Tonokatsu. Based on the manga series by Kia Asamiya in *Comic Comp.*

Ninety percent of the human race was destroyed in 2004. Now, twenty years later, humanity is rebuilding and trying to defend itself against the alien invaders known as Lucifer Hawk from the Nemesis. These creatures make sporadic trips to Earth, causing untold destruction, and then leave, until they need something from our planet again. To fight the Lucifer Hawk, one of the residents of the high-tech city of Tokyo, Rally Cheyenne, has created a police group named the AMP (Attacked Mystification Police). Composed solely of strong women—the cyborg Kiddy, the Shinto priestess Nami, the psychic Yuki, the visionary Lebia, and a newcomer, the mysteriously powered Katsumi Liqueur—the AMP is ready, willing, and able to take on Nemesis invaders and any other problems that pop up. Katsumi wasn't sure she wanted to join the AMP forces until Rally revealed information about the death of her father and his connection to the event that triggered the destruction of most of Earth's populace. Will this new information solidify Katsumi with the AMP and can these women, even with her added powers, defeat the evil extraterrestrials?

Silent Mobius was created by Kia Asamiya and became an animated series in 1991. Spanning twenty-six episodes, the dark sci-fi police drama introduced viewers to a somber world rebuilding after an incident destroyed most of its population.

This character-driven cyberpunk DVD presents the first nine episodes. Some focus solely on each woman, allowing team relationships to develop at a natural pace. The story also provides lots of thrills, chills, and goosebumps, as the evil Nemesis have a creep factor plus ten. [JMC]

SPECIAL FEATURES Clean Credits • Other Title Trailers • Inserts: Character Bios, Foldout Poster, Mini-Comic • Reversible Cover TECHNICAL FEATURES Fullscreen (1.33:1) • Subtitles/CC: Eng. • Languages: Jap., Eng. dub • Sound: Dolby Digital) • Multikeepcase • 2 Discs • Region 1 GENRE & RATING Science Fiction/Cyberpunk/Fantasy • Rated 13+

Silent Mobius: Twists of Fate [#2]

Bandai, 2002, 225 mins., #1171. Directed by Hideki Tonokatsu. Based on the manga series by Kia Asamiya in *Comic Comp.*

As the battle against the Lucifer Hawk continues, alliances begin to shift among characters. Roy and Katsumi are drawn to each other, while new members of AMP bring more complications. Rally's sister Rosa arrives and reveals secrets about Rally, and obnoxious young Elementor Lum Cheng may help the team if she doesn't drive them crazy first. And is one of the AMP team members secretly manipulating the others?

Episodes #10–18 make up this twin-DVD set, bringing more hyper-detailed cyberpunk action for the female cast.

SPECIAL FEATURES Clean Credits • Other Title Trailers • Inserts: Character Bios, Mini-Comic • Reversible Cover TECHNICAL FEATURES Fullscreen (1.33:1) • Subtitles/CC: Eng. • Languages: Jap., Eng. dub • Sound: Dolby Digital • Multikeepcase • 2 Discs • Region 1 GENRE & RATING Science Fiction/Cyberpunk/Fantasy • Rated 13+

Silent Mobius: Dark Destiny [#3]

Bandai, 2002, 200 mins., #1172. Directed by Hideki Tonokatsu. Based on the manga series by Kia Asamiya in *Comic Comp.*

NOTE: This DVD arrived too late for a full review. The following text is promotional copy provided by the releasing company:

"Has Katsumi truly embraced the Lucifer Hawk blood that flows in her veins? Her friends, hurt and angry by her sudden departure, try to go on with life as they know it. But everything is different now that Katsumi's gone. So when she suddenly returns to their ranks, is she really the same Katsumi they knew, or is she merely masquerading as her former self, waiting for the right time to strike? If Katsumi is evil and the gates of Nemesis open, the Earth will be overrun by the Lucifer Hawk. Do the women of AMP have what it takes to protect the Earth, even if it means killing their best friend? The final battle is at hand . . ."

These discs contains episodes #19–26.

SPECIAL FEATURES Karaoke • Other Title Trailers • Inserts: Character Bios, Mini Comic • Reversible Cover TECHNICAL FEATURES Fullscreen (1.33:1) • Subtitles/CC: Eng. • Languages: Jap., Eng. dub • Sound: Dolby Digital • Multikeepcase • 2 Discs • Region 1 GENRE & RATING Science Fiction/Cyberpunk/Fantasy • Rated 13+

Silent Night: The Story of the First Christmas

Madacy, 2000.

This DVD was not available for review.

Silent Service

U.S. Manga Corps, 2001, 100 mins., #USMD 1730. Directed by Ryosuke Takahashi. Written by Soji Yoshikawa. Based on the manga series by Kaiji Kawguchi in *Comic Morning*.

The *Sea Bat* is a secret advanced nuclear submarine built using Japanese technology and American designs. As a gesture of goodwill, the U.S. Navy invites a Japanese crew to pilot the vessel on its maiden voyage. But Kaieda, the calculating Japanese captain of the sub, mutinies along with his crew, attacks pursuing U.S. Navy vessels and declares the submarine *Yamato* an independent nation. Using the threat of nuclear warheads supposedly smuggled aboard by the Japanese, the sub brings the Pacific Fleet and the U.S. military to its knees. Risking war with the United States, the Japanese government must decide whether to ally itself with the *Yamato*, or help the Americans reclaim or destroy its renegade vessel.

This fervently nationalistic answer from Japan to American military dominance may be factually absurd, but its existence shows an increasing level of discomfort in Japan with the role the United States plays in world politics. *Silent Service* has its share of entertaining action and well-animated sea battles. However, the depiction of U.S. Navy vessels being decimated and sunk, while not overly brutal or graphic, will likely not sit well with some viewers, especially in the wake of September 11th.

Besides being offered as a single DVD, the disc was also included as part of a 2002 "Combat Pack" set, along with *Area 88*. [BR]

SPECIAL FEATURES Character Bios • DVD-ROM Features: Art, Scripts, Synopsis • Other Title Trailers TECHNICAL FEATURES Fullscreen (1.33:1) • Subtitles/CC: Eng. • Languages: Jap., Eng. dub • Sound: Dolby Digital 2.0 • Keepcase • 1 Disc • Region 1 GENRE & RATING Military/Action • Rated 13+

Simpsons, The: The Complete First Season

Fox, 2001, 300 mins., #200900. Directed by David Silverman, Wesley Archer, Gregg Vanzo, Kent Butterworth, Rich Moore, Milton Gray, Brad Bird. Written by Mimi Pond, Jon Vitti, Jay Kogen, Wallace Wolodarsky, Al Jean, Mike Reiss, John Swartzwelder, Sam Simon, Matt Groening, George Meyer.

Anyone who isn't familiar with the basic cast of America's most famous animated family, the Simpsons, here's a scorecard: Homer Simpson is the duncelike patriarch who works at a nuclear power plant; Marge is the blue-haired mama who tries to keep the peace; Bart is the bratty ten-year-old boy; Lisa is the ultra-smart eight-year-old vegetarian saxophone-playing girl; Maggie is the pacifier-sucking baby; and Santa's Little Helper is the rail-thin dog. But that's only scratching the immediate surface of the cast of characters in Springfield, where the yellow-skinned Simpsons live. From the evil Mr. Burns, to Principal Skinner, to bartender Moe, to TV's Krusty the Clown . . . the adventures of *The Simpsons* are a dysfunctional funhouse.

Created in 1987 as interstitial segments on *The Tracey Ullman Show*, *The Simpsons* was the brainchild of comic strip creator Matt Groening. Fox gave the family a half-hour prime-time slot just before Christmas 1989, unsure that the series would last beyond the thirteen episodes initially ordered. But audiences loved the yellow family, and kids especially took to Bart, who became a cause celebre for right-wing religious zealots who wailed that Bart's actions—and the series itself—would destroy the moral fabric of families throughout the country. The protests only brought the series more attention and higher ratings, as viewers embraced the satire. Today, the series has won nineteen Emmy Awards—and numerous other awards—and at fourteen seasons, *The Simpsons* has claimed the title of longest-running animated primetime series in history (and the longest-running sitcom on TV)!

The three-disc boxed set contains all thirteen first season episodes of *The Simpsons*, but that's not all. In addition to commentary on each episode, there are annotated scripts for four shows, unaired scenes from "Some Enchanted Evening" (#13), outtakes, animatics, a BBC Special called "America's First Family," an ABC News report on the Bart Simpson controversy, over a hundred sketches and stills, and even one of the Ullman shorts, "Good Night Simpsons."

This DVD set is a must-have item for any *Simpsons* fan and, indeed, belongs on the shelf of almost every animation fan.

SPECIAL FEATURES Commentary Track by Creator • Character and Art Galleries • Unaired and Deleted Scenes • Storyboards and Animatics • Promotional Footage • Outtakes • Scripts • International Footage • Inserts: Episode Guide Booklet • Easter Eggs TECHNICAL FEATURES Fullscreen (1.33:1) • Subtitles/CC: Eng., Span. • Languages: Eng., Fren. dub • Sound: Dolby Digital Surround 5.1 • Foldout Box with Cardboard Slipcase • 3 Discs • Region 1 GENRE & RATING Comedy • Not Rated (Kids)

Simpsons, The: The Complete Second Season [DVD Collector's Edition]

Fox, 2002, 506 mins., #2003715. Directed by David Silverman, Rich Moore, Wes Archer, Mark Kirkland, Jim Reardon. Written by David M. Stern, Jon Vitti, John Swartzwelder, Jay Kogen, Wallace Wolodarsky, Edgar Allan Poe, Sam Simon, Ken Levine, David Isaacs, Jeff Martin, George Meyer, Nell Scovell, Al Jean, Mike Reiss, Steve Pepoon, Brian K. Roberts.

Simpsons mania hit America during the series's second season, in 1990–91. Many of the series' staples were introduced during this season, including the "Treehouse of Terror" Halloween concept, news anchor Kent Brockman, groundskeeper Willie, Ralph Wiggum, and Comic Book Guy. The twenty-two stories include Bart's attempt to not fail fourth grade, Bart sending his dog to obedience school, Homer's hair growth, Bart's daredevil skateboard stunts, Marge's campaign against violence in cartoons, a flashback to Homer and Marge's first meeting, a fight over a rare Radioactive Man comic book, and the first appearance of a Beatle—Ringo Starr—on the series.

The four-disc boxed set contains all twenty-two episodes, with commentary tracks on each one! There are also interviews, behind-the-scenes material, and clips of Bart at the American Music Awards and of The Simpsons presenting at the Emmy Awards. This is another winner that will be a must-buy for any *Simpsons* fan, or lover of intelligent comedy.

SPECIAL FEATURES "Making of" Featurettes • Commentary Track by Creator and Crew • Interviews with Creator and Crew • Character and Art Galleries • Unaired and Deleted Scenes • Storyboards and Animatics • Promotional Footage • Music Videos • Outtakes • Scripts • International Footage • Inserts: Episode Guide Booklet • Easter Eggs TECHNICAL FEATURES Fullscreen (1.33:1) • Subtitles/CC: Eng., Span. • Languages: Eng., Fren. dub • Sound: Dolby Digital Surround 5.1 • Foldout Box with Cardboard Sleeve • 4 Discs • Region 1 GENRE & RATING Comedy • Not Rated (Kids)

Sin: The Movie

ADV Films, 2000, 60 mins., #DVDSN001. Directed by Yasunori Urata. Screenplay by Ryoma Kaneko, Kensei Date.

An elite police force known as HARDCORPS is trained to handle cases too dangerous and out-of-the-ordinary for the local law enforcement agencies. When a band of mutated mindless creatures appear causing havoc and killing innocent people, it's up to the HARDCORPS, led by Colonel John Blade, to save the day. The creatures are pursuing a small girl and are able to mutate others just by touching them. When Blade's partner is possessed, he must kill him to rescue the girl. His partner's sister, JC, arrives looking for answers, which seem to lie within the mysterious SinTEK Enterprises and its owner, Elexis Sinclaire. Sinclaire is manipulating DNA and creating those mutant creatures to be the perfect soldiers, not just to conquer the world, but the galaxy as well! There's one thing that can stop Sinclaire's creations though: the small child Blade rescued seems to hold the key to Sinclaire's victory. But once the villain kidnaps the girl to achieve her goals, it's up to Blade, JC, and the rest of HARDCORP to rescue her and defeat Sinclaire before the universe suffers.

Sin is a 2000 coproduction between the American ADV Films and Ritual Entertainment, plus Japan-based Phoenix Entertainment. The animated feature is based on a video game. The animation was produced to an American voice track, then dubbed for Japan. The animation for the show is solid, though not overly original, while the music stands out nicely and feels theatrical.

Unlike other anime, the *Sin* DVD contains two separate English-subtitled scripts that viewers have the option of reading while listening to the Japanese audio; one reflects the main English script (version 1), while the other translates the Japanese version of the story (version 2). [JMC]

SPECIAL FEATURES "Making of" Featurettes • Character Bios • Character and Art Galleries • Trailer • Other Title Trailers TECHNICAL FEATURES Fullscreen (1.33:1) • Subtitles/CC: Eng. • Languages: Jap., Eng. dub • Sound: Dolby Digital Surround 2.0 • Keepcase • 1 Disc • Region 1–6 GENRE & RATING Science Fiction/Action • Not Rated (Teens)

Sinbad: Beyond the Veil of Mists

Trimark, 1999, 85 mins., #VM7480D. Directed by Evan C. Ricks, Alan Jacobs. Screenplay by Jeff Wolverton.

Princess Serena unwittingly helps an exiled wizard gain access to the palace, whereupon he takes her father's place. To save her father and restore the kingdom, Serena must get an antipotion from a place at the end of the world, through the legendary Veil of Mists. She enlists the brave adventurer and hero Sinbad to sail with her into the Mists to reach her goal. On their journey, they will face monsters, magic, giant spiders, and a world beneath the sea. . . .

This 1999 production claims to be the first 3D motion-capture CGI feature ever animated. Motion capturing is similar to old-style rotoscoping, except that instead of filming live-action segments and having animators trace over them, actors are wired up to computers and their movements are digitally recorded to create 3D characters. The effect gives a slightly more lifelike appearance to the humans, although the texturing of skin and hair still gives away their computerized roots. The CGI backgrounds and monsters are mostly cool, especially the giant undersea creatures. The voice cast is excellent, with Leonard Nimoy playing the villain, Brendan Fraser voicing Sinbad, and Mark Hamill and John Rhys-Davies chiming in as well.

An interesting experiment, *Sinbad: Beyond the Veil of Mists* will appeal to kids and adults, as well as to fans of unique CGI animation.

SPECIAL FEATURES Trailer • Other Title Trailers TECHNICAL FEATURES Widescreen (1.85:1) • Subtitles/CC: Eng., Fren., Span. • Languages: Eng. • Sound: Dolby Digital 2.0 • Keepcase • 1 Disc • Region 1 GENRE & RATING CGI/Fantasy • Rated G

Sins of the Sisters ☞ see Mature/Adult Section

Skeleton Warriors:

BMG, 2000, 90 mins., #75517. Animation Directed by Sue Peters. Written by Steve Cuden, Eric Lewald, Julia Jane Lewald, Len Uhley.

After the Lightstar Crystal is split into two pieces, LuminiCity is plunged into eternal darkness. The heroic Prince Justin Lightstar and his band of Skeleton Hunters known as the "Legion of Light" represent the side of right, while the evil Baron Dark and his army of Skeleton Warriors are out to destroy humanity. Unfortunately, the Skeleton Warriors can turn humans into creatures like themselves, even if the transformation is somewhat reversible. And when Baron Dark captures Lightstar and Talyn, it appears that brother Grimskull may have betrayed them. But appearances can be deceiving in a world of darkness. . . .

This 1994 CBS television series was commissioned in the wake of *X-Men*'s success and the increasing popularity of morbid action figures and toy lines. Designs and concept art were by comic book creators Frank Brunner and Neal Adams, among others. But they couldn't overcome a clichéd story and standard characters; the series lasted one season.

Three episodes are collected on this DVD: "Flesh and Bone"; "Heart and Soul"; and "Trust and Betrayal."

SPECIAL FEATURES None TECHNICAL FEATURES Fullscreen (1.33:1) • Languages: Eng. • Sound: Dolby Digital 2.0, Dolby Digital 5.1 • Keepcase • 1 Disc • Region 1–6 GENRE & RATING Horror/Fantasy/Action • Not Rated (Kids)

Slayers, The: DVD Collection [Box Set]

Software Sculptors, 2000, 600 mins., #SSDVD-6136. Directed by Takashi Watanabe, Makoto Sokuza, Osamu Yokota, Masato Sato, Johei Matsuura, Susumu Ishi, Yoshiaki Iwasaki, Eiichi Sato, Takashi Kobayashi, Kazu Yokota, Hiromi Tamano, Arohiko Tadano. Screenplay by Takao Koyama. Based on the short stories by Hajime Kanzaka in *Dragon Magazine.*

Enter a world of sword and sorcery with the ferocious redheaded swordswoman/magician, Lina Inverse. With her—because he'd get lost otherwise—is the blonde and air-headed Gourry, master of the sword. Together they will journey across a fantasy landscape, mixing it up with dangerous monsters and power-mad sorcerers. Along the way they'll befriend all kinds of crazy characters and take on dangerous foes like Dark Lord Shabranigdo. Just how does Lina stay alive through it all? Is it skill, talent, luck, or good looks? Call it a mix of all the above, but just don't call her short. Lina's got a nasty spell called Dragon Slave, and let's just say that those who have lived after she cast it are still charred.

This fantasy/comedy series debuted in 1995 and spawned several follow-ups and even a motion picture or two. The animation isn't bad for a television series, but this one seems to be really stretching a fun premise to its limits. It's pretty much a one-joke series, with some great episodes, but overall the adventure is rather bland, and the comedy seems to be trying a bit too hard.

All twenty-six episodes of the first season are available in this box set. The set also includes lots of extras, including some interviews with the English cast on the DVD-ROM extras. Can an anime action series really live up (down?) to its suggested 3+ age limit? *The Slayers* is mostly full of wacky violence against monsters and other typical sword-and-sorcery foes. The only sexual content is a few comments on Lina's less-than-ample cleavage. [RJM]

SPECIAL FEATURES Cast Text Interviews • Cast Bios • Character Clips • Character and Art Galleries • Manga • Big Apple Anime Fest Clip • DVD-ROM Features: Art, Scripts, Bios, Manga, Cast Interviews • Other Title Trailers TECHNICAL FEATURES Fullscreen (1.33:1) • Subtitles/CC: Eng. • Languages: Jap., Eng. dub • Sound: Dolby Digital 2.0 • Cardboard Box with 4 Keepcases • 4 Discs • Region 1 GENRE & RATING Fantasy/Comedy • Rated 3+

Slayers, The: DVD Collection [Box Set—Remastered]

Software Sculptors, 2002, 600 mins., #SSDVD-6198.

This box set contains the same contents as the 2000 edition, except that the audio tracks have been remastered and the cover art for Disc A has been reversed. See previous entry for the Special and Technical Features listings.

TECHNICAL FEATURES Cardboard Box with 4 Keepcases • 4 Discs GENRE & RATING Fantasy/Comedy • Rated 3+

Slayers, The: Next DVD Collection

Software Sculptors, 2000, 600 mins., #SSDVD-6137. Directed by Hidekazu Sato, Ko Matsuzono, Yoshiaki Iwasaki, Seiji Mizushima, Kazu Yokota, Takashi Kobayashi, Shigeharu Takahashi, Shigeto Makino, Shunji Yoshida, Takeshi Yamaguchi, Makoto Sokuza, Heisaku Wada. Screenplay by Katsuhiko Chiba, Jiro Takayama, Norihisa Okamoto, Katsumi Hasegawa, Yasunori Yamada, Seiko Watanabe. Based on the short stories by Hajime Kanzaka in *Dragon Magazine.*

Supercute shorty sorceress Lina Inverse is back for more action, along with her simpleminded sidekick Gourry Gabriev, hyper-klutzy friend Amelia, and angsty golem Zelgadis. First, Lina must beat a monster, then get the better of some body-building bandits. And when she finally decides on a place to eat, the "dragon meat" isn't fit for a pig's trough. An adventure soon ensues in which Lina and her friends go "fishing" for a fresh lake dragon, but what—or who—will they use as bait? And in Amelia's city of white magic, her father has been assassinated! Does green-haired sorceress Martina have anything to do with it, or comedic character Xellos?

Then Lina goes looking for a mysterious book of spells known as the Claire Bible, but she soon crosses swords with a pair of twin sisters who want the same book. Will their differences really be decided by singing? Finally, a showdown with the Demon Dragon King is in the offing, all to capture the Claire Bible. When the Hellmaster kidnaps Gourry, what will Lina risk in a city of ghosts to save her stupid friend?

This four-DVD set collects the popular second season of *The Slayers*, episodes #27–52. The plots, character designs, and satire are in the same mold as the first season. Watch for episode #40 as a comedy highlight.

SPECIAL FEATURES Cast Interviews • Character Clips • Character and Art Galleries • Manga • DVD-ROM Features: Art, Scripts, Manga, Bios, Reviews • Other Title Trailers TECHNICAL FEATURES

Fullscreen (1.33:1) • Subtitles/CC: Eng. • Languages: Jap., Eng. dub • Sound: Dolby Digital 2.0 • Cardboard Box with 4 Keepcases • 4 Discs • Region 1–6 GENRE & RATING Fantasy/Comedy • Rated 3+

Slayers, The: Try DVD Collection

Software Sculptors, 2002, 598 mins., #SSDVD-6169. Directed by Takashi Watanabe. Screenplay by Jiro Takayama. Based on the short stories by Hajime Kanzaka in *Dragon Magazine.*

Romance takes a backseat to humor as the adventures of Lina Inverse continue. Lina and her friends set sail for new adventures—literally—until the ship capsizes. Accompanying them is a young woman named Filia, who hides a dragon-sized secret even as they plan to return her to her home. Then, the demons and beast-men attack. Later, two kingdoms are always fighting, but if Lina can gather talismans from them, she can stop an otherworldly invasion. How does a pair of star-crossed lovers fit into the situation?

After a battle, Lina wakes up in Wonderland . . . or at least it seems that way since animals are talking and people have vegetable heads! Has Gourry turned into a girl as well? Then, Almayce the Overworlder has succeeded in opening the gateway to the other dimension, paving the way for the evil Dark Star to come forth. Lina and her allies must gather all their strength and power to stop the villain from destroying the world!

The third—and final—television season is gathered on this DVD, collecting episodes #53–78. Anthropomorphic fans will enjoy some of the scenes, as will those who enjoy slapstick humor with their sword-swinging fantasy.

SPECIAL FEATURES "Making of" Featurette • Character Clips • Character and Art Galleries • Manga • Deleted Scenes • DVD-ROM Features: Art, Scripts, Bios, Manga, Reviews • Other Title Trailers TECHNICAL FEATURES Fullscreen (1.33:1) • Subtitles/CC: Eng. • Languages: Jap., Eng. dub • Sound: Dolby Digital 2.0 • Cardboard Box with 4 Keepcases • 4 Discs • Region 1 GENRE & RATING Fantasy/Comedy • Rated 3+

Slayers: The Book of Spells

ADV Films, 2000, 75 mins., #DVDSL002. Directed by Hiroshi Watanabe. Screenplay by Kazuo Yamazaki. Based on the short stories by Hajime Kanzaka in *Dragon Magazine.*

Slayers follows the adventures of a fantastic sorcerer with a fiery attitude and heroic nature named Lina Inverse. Lina's seeking treasure, fame, and fortunes anywhere and everywhere. She's joined on her adventures by a beautiful but naughty witch named

Naga the Serpent. Together the two get into all sorts of trouble, but almost always manage to come out on top. This dynamic duo has three grand adventures. First, the pair is in hot water when a mad scientist wants to perform some unscheduled and unorthodox operations on Lina. She and Naga must stop his devious plans before they wind up with one too many heads or other body parts. Next, the two promise to help a young boy become a member of the Royal Guard, but he might not be royal—or, for that matter, guard—material. Can they work miracles or will the only knight this kid sees be the one after it gets dark? Finally they're up against an evil sorcerer who stole a magical mirror that makes the exact opposite of anyone whose reflection it casts. What disasters await when Lina finds herself in front of the mirror?

Although the trio of OVAs that makes up *Slayers: The Book of Spells* were released in 1996, after the animated television series, the stories officially occur *before* the animated series. Filled with lots of sight and sound gags as well as a fair amount of cheesecake, this is an anime series for the early teen crowd. Look in the Special Features section for extensive production art galleries with characters and backgrounds. [JMC]

SPECIAL FEATURES Character and Art Galleries • Trailers • Easter Egg TECHNICAL FEATURES Fullscreen (1.33:1) • Subtitles/CC: Eng. • Languages: Jap., Eng. dub • Sound: Dolby Digital 2.0 • Keepcase • 1 Disc • Region 1, 2, 4 GENRE & RATING Fantasy/Comedy • Rated 12+

Slayers: The Motion Picture

ADV Films, 2000, 75 mins., #DVDSL002. Directed by Hiroshi Watanabe. Script by Kazuo Yamazaki. Based on the short stories by Hajime Kanzaka in *Dragon Magazine.*

It's time to enter the world of *Slayers* and that means swords, sorcery, and someone making a joke about Lina's lack of cleavage. That's right, Lina Inverse, the vertically challenged, magically powerful adventurer stars in her first theatrical outing. And with her is the tall, buxom-but-ditzy Nahga. Together they are on a journey to the island of Mipross, where they must take on a dangerous foe. But don't let the seriousness of the plot frighten you. Goofy comedy abounds. There are stone dragons to be conjured (if they can remember the spell) and hot springs to visit. And what is in it for our heroes? Wealth? You bet! Fame? Got some of that too. But for Lina the promise of increasing her bust might be too good to pass up!

The Slayers went on their first theatrical venture in 1995. It's actually a step up from the television series in almost every way. The animation is better, the writing is better, the comedy is better, and the action is better. There is a carefree adventuring spirit in this, as well as a

nice self-mocking attitude that works well for these characters and story. The plot never really takes itself seriously (something that plagued the first season of the television series). Best of all, if you've never seen any *Slayers* before, you can watch this and follow it just fine. There is no Gourry in this movie, but Nagha is the perfect replacement foil for Lina.

The English cast on this DVD does a very good job. Nagha's psychotic laugh is mirrored almost perfectly in English (not an easy feat). The print is pretty good. There is lots of cleavage bouncing around in this movie, but no real nudity to scare parents, and all the action is done in a silly over-the-top manner. [RJM]

SPECIAL FEATURES Character Bios • Character and Art Galleries • Trailers • Other Title Trailers TECHNICAL FEATURES Widescreen (1.85:1) • Subtitles/CC: Eng., Span. • Languages: Jap., Eng. dub • Sound: Dolby Digital 2.0 • Keepcase • 1 Disc • Region 1–6 GENRE & RATING Fantasy/Comedy • Not Rated (Teens)

Slight Fever Syndrome: Complete ☛ see
Mature/Adult Section

Snowman, The/Father Christmas

Columbia Tri-Star, 1998, 54 mins., #03227. Directed by Dianne Jackson, Dave Unwin. Written by Richard Briggs. Based on the books by Richard Briggs.

A boy in New England makes a snowman, and when the snowman comes to life, holiday adventures begin! Whether flying up among the clouds over snow-covered landscapes or joining in country dances in the woods, the snowman is a wonderful companion. And in a second story, a rather tired Santa shares with viewers what he does the rest of the year: travel! After leaving France and Scotland, Santa goes to Las Vegas on vacation to get a tan and gamble a bit, all before returning to the North Pole for the Christmas season again.

Two classic children's books by Raymond Briggs are adapted into short films by British animators. *The Snowman* is done with colored pencil, giving it a meticulously hand-drawn look. The short was nominated for an Academy Award in 1982. *Father Christmas* is produced in traditional cel animation, but the designs and bold colors are a delight.

This gentle and fun holiday collection is appropriate for all ages, isn't treacly, and doesn't push either consumerism or religious elements. It could well become a holiday favorite at your household.

SPECIAL FEATURES None TECHNICAL FEATURES Fullscreen (1.33:1) • Languages: Eng. • Sound: Dolby Digital Surround 2.0 • Keepcase • 1 Disc • Region 1 GENRE & RATING Holiday/Family • Not Rated (Kids)

Snow White and the Seven Dwarfs: Platinum Edition

Disney, 2001, 84 mins., #22254. Directed by David Hand, Perce Pearce, Larry Morey, William Cottrell, Wilfred Jackson, Ben Sharpsteen. Story Adaptation by Ted Sears, Otto Englander, Earl Hurd, Dorothy Ann Blank, Richard Creedon, Dick Richard, Merrill De Maris, Webb Smith.

Orphaned as a child, Snow White is a menial servant at the Queen's castle. So when the vain Queen asks her Magic Mirror who the fairest in the land is, and the mirror tells her it's Snow White, you can understand that the Queen isn't very happy. The Queen orders a huntsman to take Snow into the forest and kill her, but he lets her go instead. After befriending the forest animals, Snow White comes to the very messy cottage of seven dwarfs, and she cleans it for them, becoming a surrogate mother/wife for the diminutive miners. But the Queen has found out that Snow White is still alive, and the wicked monarch is determined to get rid of the "fairest one" forever. Using dark magic, she creates a very poisonous apple and sets out into the forest to tempt her rival to take one bite. . . .

Released in December of 1937 by RKO, *Snow White and the Seven Dwarfs* was Walt Disney's first full-length animated film. To say that it's an unparalleled classic is probably not high enough praise, but it's certainly one of the standards by which all animation has been measured since. The human characters are naturalistic and based on real people, whereas the animals, dwarfs, and witch characters are given lifelike-yet-still-cartoony designs and presence. The music was nicely integrated into the film, including the blocking, pacing, and editing of scenes.

Snow White and the Seven Dwarfs had a major effect on the entire movie industry of the time. The film itself was dubbed and translated into dozens of languages, although some (such as England) restricted it to older audiences due to some truly scary imagery with the Queen. Other studios raced to do their own animated epic. And the $1,480,000 film became a blockbuster, earning an estimated $4.2 million (1937 dollars) in North America alone! Film restorations in 1987 and 1993 helped clean the film, and eight theatrical reissues made it one of the most successful animated films of all time.

The two-DVD set is nothing short of amazing. The first disc contains the film itself, a section on the restoration of the feature, a game/tour of the mines with "Dopey's Wild Ride," a sing-along, and a newly recorded expanded version of "Someday My Prince Will Come" by Barbra Streisand. A guided tour by Angela Lansbury and Roy Disney supplements the experience, which also includes audio commentary, a thirty-eight-minute "Making of" featurette, and a *Silly Symphony* short, "The Goddess of Spring" (1934).

The second disc features a 3D "tour" of the Queen's castle, with thousands of pages of preliminary art, designs, layouts, backgrounds, and more. A historical timeline hosted by eight celebrities tracks Disney's history from *Snow White*'s debut forward. There are sections with camera tests and live-action reference, information about the original Brothers Grimm fairy tale, storyboard-to-film comparisons, three abandoned concepts, restoration elements, five deleted scenes, film premiere footage, trailers, publicity segments, radio broadcasts and commercials, and even a deleted song! Be sure to let the front menu sit for a while after you highlight each section, as the Magic Mirror will make droll comments the longer you wait.

If you're reading this book, you should already own *Snow White*. If you don't, buy it the next time you're at a store. In terms of importance to animation history, it is unparalleled; in terms of the DVD experience, only *Akira* comes close to this bounty of riches.

NOTE: This DVD is now on moratorium.

SPECIAL FEATURES "Making of" Featurettes • Commentary Track • Character and Art Galleries • Production Notes • Deleted Scenes and Songs • Restoration Featurette • Storyboards • Trailers • Promotional Footage • Radio Spots • Music Videos • Games • Other Title Trailers • DVD-ROM Features • Inserts: Booklet • Easter Eggs TECHNICAL FEATURES Fullscreen (1.33:1) • Subtitles/CC: Eng. • Languages: Eng., Fren. dub • Sound: Dolby Digital 1.0, Dolby Digital Surround 5.1 • Multikeepcase • 2 Discs • Region 1 GENRE & RATING Music/Fantasy/Family • Rated G

Sol Bianca: The Legacy—Lost Treasures [#1]

Pioneer, 2000, 70 mins., #PIDA-2361V. Directed by Hiroyuki Ochi. Written by Hideki Mitsui.

Meet the all-female crew of the *Sol Bianca*. Each of these sexy pirates is named after a month. There's the brave captain, April; Jani, the tough-talking muscle gal; June, the computer wiz; Feb the sultry booze-swilling party girl; and Mayo the stowaway. Together these gals get enmeshed in a search for a lost planet (called Earth) and more treasure than you can shake a cutlass at. But first they have to survive attacks by the Blue Comets and their mysterious leader. Then they have to figure out a puzzle based on some old Earth text called *The Divine Comedy*. If you're looking for a female space pirate adventure in the distant future, then this is for you.

This OVA series was released in 1999 and explores a premise that sounds like a sci-fi/action fan's dream. Mix in all-computerized animation and you should have a surefire winner, right? Well, things don't seem to come together quite as they should. Visually the animation is impressive, melding 3D and 2D. But the way the characters are handled is just kind of clunky, especially in the few comic moments that occur. It's good no-brain entertainment, but most viewers will likely be left wanting a bit more.

This DVD has an awesome 5.1 surround track that works great with the visuals in the two episodes presented. You also get a music video as an extra as well. Some slick menus round out the whole presentation. [RJM]

SPECIAL FEATURES Character and Art Galleries • CGI Animation Tests • Trailer • Music Video TECHNICAL FEATURES Fullscreen (1.33:1) • Subtitles/CC: Eng. • Languages: Jap., Eng. dub • Sound: Dolby Digital 2.0, Dolby Digital 5.1 • Keepcase • 1 Disc • Region 1, 4 GENRE & RATING Science Fiction/Action/Girls • Rated 13+

Sol Bianca: The Legacy—Separation [#2]

Pioneer, 2000, 68 mins., #PIDA-2362V. Directed by Hiroyuki Ochi. Written by Hideki Mitsui.

The girls of the Sol Bianca take on a strange alien creature that is hunting down the crew. It's up to Jani to get the biggest gun she can find and take out the creature before it kills anyone. But is she going to run out of ammo first? The second episode pits the clashing personalities of April and Feb against each other. Stir in some man trouble and you've got a bad concoction. This episode contains a pretty impressive space battle.

Much like the contents of the previous DVD, these two episodes just don't quite mesh. It's got impressive animation and sound, but a weak script and plot. Viewers won't find themselves getting pulled in to the whole situation, and instead will be just waiting around for the next cool action sequence to occur. [RJM]

SPECIAL FEATURES Character and Art Galleries • Trailer • Music Video TECHNICAL FEATURES Fullscreen (1.33:1) • Subtitles/CC: Eng. • Languages: Jap., Eng. dub • Sound: Dolby Digital 2.0, Dolby Digital 5.1 • Keepcase • 1 Disc • Region 1, 4 GENRE & RATING Science Fiction/Action/Girls • Rated 13+

Sol Bianca: The Legacy—Going Home [#3]

Pioneer, 2001, 66 mins., #10340. Directed by Hiroyuki Ochi. Written by Hideki Mitsui.

It's the conclusion of the *Sol Bianca* saga and that means a huge climactic battle and revelations about the fates of Earth and our heroines. But the big question is: how many ships will be blown up, and how skimpy will the pirate outfits get?

All the story elements get wrapped up in these final two episodes of the series, although there's nothing too

surprising or exciting. The visuals and sound continue to be strong in this series, while the characters and plot remain weak. If you're looking for some good explosions and hot girls wielding guns, then this is the OVA for you. If you're looking for a really good space adventure, *Outlaw Star* gets a better recommendation. [RJM]

SPECIAL FEATURES Character and Art Galleries • Music Video TECHNICAL FEATURES Fullscreen (1.33:1) • Subtitles/CC: Eng. • Languages: Jap., Eng. dub • Sound: Dolby Digital 2.0, Dolby Digital 5.1 • Keepcase • 1 Disc • Region 1, 4 GENRE & RATING Science Fiction/Action/Girls • Rated 13+

Sonic the Hedgehog: Super Sonic

Trimark, 2002, 85 mins., #VM7919D. Directed by Dick Sebast. Written by Jules Dennis, Pat Allee and Ben Hurst.

He's little, he's blue, and he's a hedgehog that runs really fast. He's Sonic the Hedgehog, and he's working with the Freedom Fighters to free Mobotropolis—and the world of Mobius—from the tyranny of the evil Dr. Robotnik. First up, Sonic takes an undercover trip to the city to search for a missing microchip. Then, Robotnik clones Princess Sally and sends her to spy on the Freedom Fighters. Later, Sonic agrees to race Speed Bot in the city, but it's all a clever plot to capture Sonic. And finally, Sally takes on a dangerous mission even as the other Freedom Fighters try to reprogram Robotnik's droids!

Based on the arcade game by SEGA, *Sonic the Hedgehog* debuted in September 1993 as an ABC series, and a completely separate (though with the same creative team) syndicated series called *Adventures of Sonic the Hedgehog*. The animation is acceptable for what it is, but anyone over the age of eight will likely be bored to tears by the stories.

The DVD features four adventures: "Super Sonic"; "Sonic and Sally"; "Sonic Racer"; and "Sonic Boom."

SPECIAL FEATURES Game • Other Title Trailers TECHNICAL FEATURES Fullscreen (1.33:1) • Subtitles/CC: Eng. • Languages: Eng. dub • Sound: Dolby Digital 2.0 • Keepcase • 1 Disc • Region 1 GENRE & RATING Animals/Adventure • Not Rated (Kids)

Sonic the Hedgehog: The Movie

ADV Films, 1999, 60 mins., #DVDHH/001. Directed by Kazunori Ikegami. Original Story by Masashi Kubota.

Sonic is back with more races to run, and the villainous Dr. Robotnik has dastardly plans yet again, starting with Hyper Metal Sonic, a robot version of the hedgehog! But when the Robot Generator is sabotaged, all life on the planet is in jeopardy. Will Sonic be forced to work alongside his archenemy, at the behest of the President's daughter, Sara?

The "Blue Blur" based on the SEGA game is back, this time with a pair of 1996 Japanese-produced OVAs, combined into a "film" for the U.S. market. There's nothing exceptional about the project, though it does sometimes look a bit better than its television counterpart. If you're a fan of *Sonic*, here's another helping.

SPECIAL FEATURES Character Bios • Character and Art Galleries • Other Title Trailers TECHNICAL FEATURES Fullscreen (1.33:1) • Subtitles/CC: Eng., Span. • Languages: Jap., Eng. dub • Sound: Dolby Digital 2.0 • Keepcase • 1 Disc • Region 1–6 GENRE & RATING Animals/Adventure • Not Rated (Kids)

Sorcerer Hunters, The: Magical Encounters [#1]

ADV Films, 2001, 165 mins., #DSH001. Directed by Koichi Mashimo. Script by Hiroyuki Kawasaki, Masaharu Amiya. Based on the manga series by Satoru Akahori and Rei Omishi in *Dengeki Comic Gao*.

When evil sorcerers threaten to enslave and abuse innocents, the Sorcerer Hunters must track them down, free the victims, and defeat the villains. Sounds like a simple enough task for a trained team of professionals, but Big Mama's last line of Sorcerer Hunters are a little . . . unorthodox. The five Hunters comprise brothers Marron and Carrot Glace, the latter of whom unknowingly houses a dangerous beast within him; sisters Chocolate and Tira Misu, who dress in S/M gear; and strong savvy muscleman, Gateau Mocha. Although they might not seem like the best choice for the job given their squabbles, taunts, and jeers, in dangerous situations they band together like none other and get the job done. Dragons, forbidden flowers, evil sorceresses, deadly vacation spots, and virgin sacrifices are just some of the problems our quintet have to deal with in order to uphold their vows to protect and defend the innocent.

Sorcerer Hunters made its animated series debut in 1995 and lasted for twenty-six episodes and three OVAs. It's funny to see heroes with faults and flaws, and get to watch how they develop, grow, and change from one-dimensional to three-dimensional characters. As to why the Hunters are all named after desserts, who knows?

This initial DVD (the only one to feature a "The" in the title) contains the first seven episodes of the *Sorcerer Hunters* saga and introduces all the key cast and themes prevalent throughout this wacky, zany, outrageous series. [JMC]

SPECIAL FEATURES Character Bios • Trailer • Other Title Trailers TECHNICAL FEATURES Fullscreen (1.33:1) • Subtitles/CC: Eng. • Languages: Jap., Eng. dub • Sound: Dolby Digital 2.0 • Keep-

case • 1 Disc • Region 1 GENRE & RATING Fantasy/Comedy • Rated 15+

Sorcerer Hunters: Magical Desires [#2]

ADV Films, 2001, 165 mins., #DSH002. Directed by Koichi Mashimo. Script by Hiroyuki Kawasaki, Noboru Aikawa, Masaharu Amiya, Chinatsu Hojo. Based on the manga series by Satoru Akahori and Rei Omishi in *Dengeki Comic Gao*.

Can evil repent? When a terrible sorcerer appears to be doing good deeds for a town, the Sorcerer Hunters must determine if he's truly turned over a new leaf or if he has more nefarious goals. Next, they learn some secrets of Gateau's past and about his former partner, Opera. Then, the gang investigates a gambling hall where the stakes are literally life or death. Later, the quintet stumbles across orphaned brothers, longing for new parents. Can they help the boys? An encounter with a peeved dragon gets them trapped inside a wacky fairy tale where anything can and does happen. Finally, townspeople ask for help, but then change their mind when the Hunters arrive. But what really caused the change?

Another seven humorous adventures of the *Sorcerer Hunters* are presented on this DVD, chronicling episodes #8–14. [JMC]

SPECIAL FEATURES Character Bios • Clean Credits • Other Title Trailers • Inserts: Liner Notes TECHNICAL FEATURES Fullscreen (1.33:1) • Subtitles/CC: Eng. • Languages: Jap., Eng. dub • Sound: Dolby Digital 2.0 • Keepcase • 1 Disc • Region 1 GENRE & RATING Fantasy/Comedy • Rated 15+

Sorcerer Hunters: Magical Contests [#3]

ADV Films, 2001, 150 mins., #DSH003. Directed by Koichi Mashimo. Script by Hiroyuki Kawasaki, Satoru Akahori, Katsuhiko Takayama, Chinatsu Hojo, Noboru Aikawa. Based on the manga series by Satoru Akahori and Rei Omishi in *Dengeki Comic Gao*.

Big Mama's archenemy, the dastardly sorcerer Zaha Torte, returns to wreak havoc with her newest group of Sorcerer Hunters. Torte is one of the most powerful magicians in the universe and even with Big Mama's power, plus their combined skills, the group might not be able to stop his evil quest . . . or even protect themselves. Especially since, unknown to the Sorcerer Hunters, Torte has hired one of the best assassins around to eliminate them from the mix.

This penultimate collection—of episodes #15–20—introduces a very interesting bad guy and takes the series on a decidedly more serious road, at least for a few shows. [JMC]

SPECIAL FEATURES Character Bios • Trailer • Other Title Trailers TECHNICAL FEATURES Fullscreen (1.33:1) • Subtitles/CC: Eng. • Languages: Jap., Eng. dub • Sound: Dolby Digital 2.0 • Keepcase • 1 Disc • Region 1 GENRE & RATING Fantasy/Comedy • Rated 15+

Sorcerer Hunters: Magical Battles [#4]

ADV Films, 2001, 150 mins., #DSH004. Directed by Koichi Mashimo. Script by Hiroyuki Kawasaki, Yasuhiko Takayama. Based on the manga series by Satoru Akahori and Rei Omishi in *Dengeki Comic Gao.*

The Sorcerer Hunters doubt they can beat Zaha Torte, but they're not ones to shirk responsibilities, so they go after the villain. What follows is an epic battle spanning almost three full episodes, revealing many secrets, and bringing the series to a nice conclusion. In a battle like this, with the stakes so high, even in victory there's bound to be losses. And more than a little cheesecake.

Sorcerer Hunters comes to its conclusion on this DVD containing the final six episodes, #21–26. [JMC]

SPECIAL FEATURES Character Bios • Trailer • Other Title Trailers TECHNICAL FEATURES Fullscreen (1.33:1) • Subtitles/CC: Eng. • Languages: Jap., Eng. dub • Sound: Dolby Digital 2.0 • Keepcase • 1 Disc • Region 1 GENRE & RATING Fantasy/Comedy • Rated 15+

Sorcerer on the Rocks

ADV Films, 2002, 60 mins., #DCV/001. Directed by Kazuhiro Ozawa. Screenplay by Hiroyuki Kawasaki. Based on the manga series by Satoru Akahori in *Comic Gao.*

Long ago, in a land called the Spooner Continent, warlords ruled, and the sorcerers employed by them brought forth unimaginable atrocities and horrors. Having shrugged off those evil times, the people now live free, but from time to time an evil magician rears his head and must be put down. When this happens, they call Shibas Scotch, a warrior-wizard bounty hunter, who, for a large price, will do battle on their behalf. But times aren't what they used to be, and in order to pay off his debts, Shibas responds to a "Hero Wanted" ad that leads him on a comedic and epic path to defeat evil—and pay the bills.

This two-part OVA, first released in 1999, is a funny tongue-in-cheek sword-and-sorcery adventure. The storyline, though not too deep, entertains well. *Sorcerer on the Rocks* also takes the time to develop its characters, especially the depraved Shibas, which adds nicely to the story and keeps it from running too shallow. *Sorcerer on the Rocks* has good solid animation that, while not

exceptional, is above average with sharp clear pictures. The soundtrack is also better than average but not exactly ready for the Top 40. *Sorcerer on the Rocks* also has lots of nudity, violence, the demeaning of women, and prostitution, so concerned parties are hereby warned.

In the final analysis, this DVD is good for some laughs, but it somehow leaves viewers feeling as though they've only seen part of a longer series. [GP]

SPECIAL FEATURES Game • Other Title Trailers TECHNICAL FEATURES Fullscreen (1.33:1) • Subtitles/CC: Eng. • Languages: Jap., Eng. dub • Sound: Dolby Digital 2.0 • Keepcase • 1 Disc • Region 1 GENRE & RATING Fantasy/Comedy • Rated 15+

Soul Hunter—Vol. 1: Taikobo's Mission

ADV Films, 2001, 125 mins., #DHT001. Directed by Junji Nishimura. Script by Atsuhiro Tomioka, Masashi Sogo, Koji Veda. Based on the manga series by Ryu Fujisaki in *Shonen Jump.*

The High Council of the Immortals has decided that it is time to rid the mortal world of the evil immortal souls that have been wreaking havoc on Earth. The Council's plan is to send an emissary to capture the souls and seal them away for eternity. But, capturing the most dangerous souls ever born is a dangerous mission, one nobody on the high council cares to handle personally. Enter Taikobo, an immortal not held in very high esteem. He's careless, lazy, and clumsy. The council decides that he is the perfect choice—if he doesn't survive, there's still an up-side! Joined by his hippo-like spiritual beast Sibuxiang, Taikobo sets out to hunt down the souls on his list and maybe make an ally or two, so he isn't splattered by some of his more formidable opponents.

First released in 1999, the *Soul Hunter* series is an amusing, well-written tale based loosely on an old Chinese ghost story. It is well drawn, and animated with either bright colors or somber tones, depending on the mood of the moment. It also has a well-done soundtrack, though it lacks any discernible hits.

With interesting characters developed over time, comical sidelines, and no fear of stepping into the dramatic when the storyline calls for it, *Soul Hunter* does a far better job in the entertainment department than most anime. It has some violent content, but nothing too disturbing. The DVD contains episodes #1–5 and is a pretty solid anime, suitable for young and old alike. [GP]

SPECIAL FEATURES Cast Bios • Character Bios & Chart • Production Notes: Translator & Historical • Glossary • Clean Credits • Other Title Trailers • Inserts: Glossary TECHNICAL FEATURES Fullscreen (1.33:1) • Subtitles/CC: Eng. • Languages: Jap., Eng. dub • Sound: Dolby Digital 2.0 • Keepcase • 1 Disc • Region 1 GENRE & RATING Fantasy/Adventure • Rated 12+

Soul Hunter—Vol. 2: All the Queen's Men

ADV Films, 2002, 100 mins., #DHT/002. Directed by Junji Nishimura, Hiroshi Morioka. Script by Atsuhiro Tomioka, Tetsuo Tanaka, Koji Veda. Based on the manga series by Ryu Fujisaki in *Shonen Jump.*

As Taikobo continues on his mission , he makes two new allies. Then, faced with a match against the formidable Raishinshi, Taikobo uses his special "get drunk" technique to win the day. Meanwhile, at the Emperor's court, the evil Dakki has defeated the Four Great Lords and casts her evil gaze on the Emperor's family. The honorable Bunchu and Ko Hiko will do their best to stop her, but do they really have a chance?

In volume two, containing episodes #6–10, the story continues to develop, and new characters are added as things become a bit more dramatic. [GP]

SPECIAL FEATURES Cast Bios • Character Bios & Chart • Production Notes: Translator • Glossary • Clean Credits • Other Title Trailers • Inserts: Glossary TECHNICAL FEATURES Fullscreen (1.33:1) • Subtitles/CC: Eng. • Languages: Jap., Eng. dub • Sound: Dolby Digital 2.0 • Keepcase • 1 Disc • Region 1 GENRE & RATING Fantasy/Adventure • Rated 12+

Soul Hunter—Vol. 3: The Spoils of War

ADV Films, 2002, 100 mins., #DHT/003. Directed by Junji Nishimura, Akira Shimizu, Yukihiro Matsushita, Hiroshi Morioka. Script by Masashi Sogo, Atsuhiro Tomioka, Tetsuo Tanaka, Koji Veda. Based on the manga series by Ryu Fujisaki in *Shonen Jump.*

The loyal Ko Hiko tries to spirit away the two princes and protect them from the evil Dakki, whose demon allies are in hot pursuit. Meanwhile, Taikobo tries to catch up so that he and his group can bring their powerful, mystical weapons to bear and save the future of the Yin dynasty. But, catching the princes may not be as difficult as surviving the day. Plus, back at the palace, Dakki sows more discord, and heads begin to roll.

This DVD, containing episodes #11–15, sees a more dramatic turn in the storyline as Taikobo must race to save the princes. [GP]

SPECIAL FEATURES Cast Bios • Character Bios & Chart • Production Notes: Translator • Glossary • Trailer • Other Title Trailers • Inserts: Glossary TECHNICAL FEATURES Fullscreen (1.33:1) • Subtitles/CC: Eng. • Languages: Jap., Eng. dub • Sound: Dolby Digital 2.0 • Keepcase • 1 Disc • Region 1 GENRE & RATING Fantasy/Adventure • Rated 12+

Soul Hunter—Vol. 4: Game of Kings

ADV Films, 2002, 100 mins., #DHT/004. Directed by Junji Nishimura, Akira Shimizu, Makoto Sokuza, Yukihiro Matsushita, Hiroshi Morioka. Script by Masashi Sogo, Atsuhiro Tomioka. Based on the manga series by Ryu Fujisaki in *Shonen Jump.*

Taikobo and Lord Ki Sho must work fast if they are to save the Yin dynasty, not to mention the entire nation, from extermination. As Taikobo fumbles in his diplomatic efforts to strike an alliance with the northern armies, he might accidentally start a new war instead! Meanwhile, Bunchu sends four emissaries to crush the rising dissension, and, without the backup of the Western military, only one thing remains between the Shisei and the destruction of the West— Taikobo.

The plot thickens as Taikobo's mission is in jeopardy on this DVD containing episodes #16–19. [GP]

SPECIAL FEATURES Cast Bios • Character Bios & Chart • Production Notes: Translator • Glossary • Other Title Trailers • Inserts: Glossary TECHNICAL FEATURES Fullscreen (1.33:1) • Subtitles/CC: Eng. • Languages: Jap., Eng. dub • Sound: Dolby Digital 2.0 • Keepcase • 1 Disc • Region 1 GENRE & RATING Fantasy/Adventure • Rated 12+

Soul Hunter—Vol. 5: City of Fire

ADV Films, 2002, 100 mins., #DHT/005. Directed by Junji Nishimura, Hiroyuki Yokoyama, Akira Shimizu, Makoto Sokuza. Script by Koji Veda, Tetsuo Tanaka. Based on the manga series by Ryu Fujisaki in *Shonen Jump.*

Two armies face each other, but they appear to be caught in a standoff. Taikobo and his allied forces of the North and West want to bring about a new Chinese dynasty, but Bunchu and the Emperor's army support the Yin princes, who now have enhanced immortal powers! But even as war appears imminent, the evil Dakki looses a ravening monster on the capital city. Taikobo makes a choice about his future as a War Minister and the Immortal assigned to Project Soul Hunt. And then, battle rages on....

A series of flashbacks illuminates some history in the complex story, but three of the four episodes contained on this penultimate DVD volume are heavily action-oriented.

SPECIAL FEATURES Cast Bios • Character Bios & Chart • Production Notes: Translator • Glossary • Other Title Trailers • Inserts: Glossary TECHNICAL FEATURES Fullscreen (1.33:1) • Subtitles/CC: Eng. • Languages: Jap., Eng. dub • Sound: Dolby Digital 2.0 • Keepcase • 1 Disc • Region 1 GENRE & RATING Fantasy/Adventure • Rated 12+

Soul Hunter—Vol. 6: The One that Got Away

ADV Films, 2002, 125 mins., #DHT/006. Directed by Hiroyuki Matsushita, Hiroyuki Yokoyama, Akira Shimizu, Makoto Sokuza, Hiroshi Morioka. Script by Atsuhiro Tomioka, Masashi Sogo, Koji Veda. Based on the manga series by Ryu Fujisaki in *Shonen Jump*.

Is the battle truly over? Has Taikobo really won against Dakki? Not if Dakki's restless soul has anything to say about it! When spies are revealed, Taikobo confronts those above him about the real object of Project Soul Hunt, and what he learns from the unabridged Book of Souls will cause him to doubt all his loyalties. If Taikobo now does what he knows is the right thing, mankind could be exterminated in a final conflict. But what other choice does he have?

While the battle seemed over with the previous volume, things take a surprising turn in this final DVD, which collects episodes #21–26.

SPECIAL FEATURES Cast Bios • Character Bios & Chart • Production Notes: Translator and Historical • Glossary • Other Title Trailers • Inserts: Glossary TECHNICAL FEATURES Fullscreen (1.33:1) • Subtitles/CC: Eng. • Languages: Jap., Eng. dub • Sound: Dolby Digital 2.0 • Keepcase • 1 Disc • Region 1 GENRE & RATING Fantasy/Adventure • Rated 12+

Soul Taker, The: The Monster Within [#1]

Pioneer, 2002, 75 mins., #11698. Directed by Shintaro Inokawa, Yasuhiro Takemoto. Script by Masashi Kubota, Kenichi Araki.

Life would be normal for seventeen-year-old Kyosuke Date if it wasn't for the fact that he's been murdered—by his own mother! Despite this, he soon comes back to life, and realizes that he's gained some terrible powers. As a result, Kyosuke is quickly caught up in a struggle between two rival factions—the Kirihara Group, a corporation that rules most of the world, and the Hospital Organization, a bizarre gathering of superhuman rogue doctors bent on "curing" the world's problems. Kyosuke gains some unlikely allies, but comes to realize that his sister has been kidnapped—and only the powers of his new alter-ego, the SoulTaker, can unravel the mystery.

Visually, *Soul Taker* is nothing short of dazzling, a wildly colorful and mind-bendingly hallucinogenic thrill ride. The show's constant use of oversaturated colors, dark outlines, and religious symbols makes it irresistible, at least visually. The plot is another story. The series' creators took it upon themselves to deliberately make *Soul Taker* as cryptic and strange as possible. This makes the show both intriguing and frustrating; the plot is coherent, but *very* difficult to follow. Beyond that, *Soul Taker* is very much a superhero show—the SoulTaker itself, while boasting incredible supernatural powers, is essentially a good guy in a costume, and his adversaries are a gallery of grotesques that would fit in just fine in superhero comics. *Soul Taker* is a quality show, but be ready to reconcile the intense visuals, weird plot, and costumed-hero trappings.

The *Soul Taker* DVD is technically very interesting. Unlike most anime TV shows, *Soul Taker* was filmed in anamorphic widescreen—in other words, with a 16:9 ratio, just like Hollywood movies. The DVD preserves this aspect ratio perfectly, and also includes a fairly common smattering of extras. The disc contains episodes #1–3 of the thirteen-episode series. There's also a nifty sixteen-page *Soul Taker* encyclopedia booklet in the keepcase, and a shiny metallic-tinted cover. [MT]

SPECIAL FEATURES Character and Art Galleries • Clean Credits • Inserts: Encyclopedia Booklet TECHNICAL FEATURES Widescreen (1.85:1 enhanced for 16x9) • Subtitles/CC: Eng. • Languages: Jap., Eng. dub • Sound: Dolby Digital Surround 2.0 • Keepcase • 1 Disc • Region 1, 4 GENRE & RATING Superhero/Action/Surreal • Rated 16+

Soul Taker, The: Flickering Faith [#2]

Pioneer, 2002, 75 mins., #11699. Directed by Matsuo Asami, Kenji Nakamura, Yasuhiro Takemoto. Script by Sumio Uetake, Masashi Kubota, Mayori Sekijima.

Kyosuke, along with his new allies Shiro and Komugi, continues his search for "flickers," living fragments of his lost sister's soul. The trio clashes openly with the Kirihara Group, and Kyosuke himself ends up in a life-or-death battle with Dr. Richard Vincent, the leader of the Hospital Organization. Kyosuke is powerful in his transformed state as the SoulTaker—but Dr. Vincent transforms into the SoulCrusher, an even more powerful mutant!

This DVD continues the quality anamorphic widescreen presentation of the previous volume. It contains episodes #4–6. [MT]

SPECIAL FEATURES Character and Art Galleries • Clean Credits • Toy Designs TECHNICAL FEATURES Widescreen (1.85:1 enhanced for 16x9) • Subtitles/CC: Eng. • Languages: Jap., Eng. dub • Sound: Dolby Digital Surround 2.0 • Keepcase • 1 Disc • Region 1, 4 GENRE & RATING Superhero/Action/Surreal • Rated 16+

Soul Taker, The: Blood Betrayal [#3]

Pioneer, 2002, 75 mins., #11700. Directed by Kiyoshi Fukumoto, Yoshio Suzuki. Script by Keiichi Araki, Sumio Uetake, Mayori Sekijima.

Kyosuke Date, the SoulTaker, continues to uncover new secrets about his origins. He finds out the true identities of his mother and father, and subsequent events cause him to fly into a rage and seek out his father to fight him again. But his search is derailed by yet another enemy—an unknown entity called the SoulAnubis.

More visually cool widescreen superheroics make up this DVD, containing episodes #7-9. [MT]

SPECIAL FEATURES Character and Art Galleries • Clean Credits • Sing-Along • Inserts: Sticker TECHNICAL FEATURES Widescreen (1.85:1 enhanced for 16x9) • Subtitles/CC: Eng. • Languages: Jap., Eng. dub • Sound: Dolby Digital Surround 2.0 • Keepcase • 1 Disc • Region 1, 4 GENRE & RATING Superhero/Action/Surreal • Rated 16+

Soul Taker, The: The Truth [#4]

Pioneer, 2002, 100 mins., #11701. Directed by Shintaro Inokawa, Minoru Ohara, Ko Matsuzono. Script by Sumio Uetake, Keiichi Araki, Masashi Kubota, Mayori Sekijima.

The journey of Kyosuke Date and his allies to rescue his sister, Runa, meets its end on the moon. There, Kyosuke discovers the terrible truth about himself, about his mother and father, and about his sister. The pot is stirred even more by the continued interference of the Kirihara Group, and the possible involvement of an alien! As Kyosuke's ally Shiro confronts his sister (the leader of the Kirihara Group), Kyosuke must choose between saving his own sister and setting off Armageddon.

This final DVD ends a visually rich but head-scratching widescreen presentation, with episodes #10–13 wrapping up the TV series. [MT]

SPECIAL FEATURES Character and Art Galleries • Clean Credits • Sing-Along TECHNICAL FEATURES Widescreen (1.85:1 enhanced for 16x9) • Subtitles/CC: Eng. • Languages: Jap., Eng. dub • Sound: Dolby Digital Surround 2.0 • Keepcase • 1 Disc • Region 1, 4 GENRE & RATING Superhero/Action/Surreal • Rated 16+

South Park ☛ see Mature/Adult Section

South Park: Bigger, Longer and Uncut ☛ see Mature/Adult Section

Space Ace

Digital Leisure, 1999, #24719-99003. Created by Don Bluth and Rick Dyer

Space Ace is the defender of truth, justice, and the planet Earth. His toughest foe is the evil blue-skinned Commander Borf, whose Infanto-Ray can turn anyone back into a child. When Borf kidnaps Kimberly, Ace (and his Infanto-alter ego Dexter) must blast his way through dozens of adventures—with dogs, robots, trash compactors, and aliens—to save her and stop Borf from enslaving Earth.

Space Ace was a 1983 arcade-style laserdisc game that featured fun graphics by the animation team headed by Don Bluth and including Gary Goldman, John Pomeroy, and Rick Dyer. The popular game was a segment on the second season of CBS's Saturday morning TV series, *Saturday Supercade*, but that's not that's collected here. This DVD contains the game itself with all the animation footage present. In "watch mode," you can view the game as a semi-complete science fiction adventure story, from beginning to end. In "play mode," you can use the DVD remote to control the character's choices, which leads to alternate story possibilities.

An excellent picture transfer—and the chance to play the game without continually depositing quarters—will bring happiness to older fans. There's also a set of vintage interviews with Don Bluth and Rick Dyer, the game's cocreators, and some news clips. Unfortunately, the DVD will not play on some Toshiba, Samsung, and Aiwa machines, so if that's your brand, be warned.

SPECIAL FEATURES Interview Clips • Other Title Trailers • Insert: Liner Notes and Game Hints TECHNICAL FEATURES Fullscreen (1.33:1) • Languages: Eng. • Sound: Dolby Digital 2.0 • Keepcase • 1 Disc • Region 1–6 GENRE & RATING Science Fiction /Adventure/Interactive • Rated 6+

Space Battleship Yamato: The Movie

Voyager, 2002, 135 mins., #69071-00619. Directed by Toshio Masuda. Written by Keisuke Fujikawa, Eiichi Yamamoto.

In 2199, Earth is in danger, and humanity lives in underground cities. But radiation from the earlier nuclear attacks from Planet Gamilus is seeping downward, and the contamination may eradicate humankind soon. The converted battleship *Yamato* is launched with newly created wave engines, and it sets out on a course for Iscandar, a planet that has a neutralizer—Cosmo Cleaner-D—that can clean the radiation from Earth's atmosphere and make the planet livable again. But the trip is 148,000 light years, and Earth only has one year left. With perils aplenty along the way, will the brave crew of the *Yamato* make it to Iscandar and back in time?

A 1977 feature film, *Space Battleship Yamato: The Movie* was a briefer version of the *Space Battleship Yamato* television series (see entries for *Star Blazers*). The animation is a bit quaint compared to today's anime, but it has a solid picture and an entertaining story.

Extras on the DVD include a hyper-informative translated program book from the theatrical release, alternate footage created for a 1978 Japanese TV airing, a history of the *Yamato/Star Blazers* phenomenon and more. Couple this with an excellent transfer and you've got a fan favorite in the making.

SPECIAL FEATURES Character and Art Galleries • Production Notes & Program Book • Alternate Scenes • Trailer • Promotional Materials TECHNICAL FEATURES Fullscreen (1.33:1) • Subtitles/CC: Eng. • Languages: Jap. • Sound: Dolby Digital 1.0 • Snapcase • 1 Disc • Region 1–6 GENRE & RATING Science Fiction/Action • Not Rated (Kids)

Space Jam [Video Version]

Warner, 1997, 87 mins., #16400.

This DVD was not available for review. It is the early release with a purple cover. See rerelease review below.

Space Jam [Enhanced Edition]

Warner, 2000, 88 mins., #18317. Directed by Joe Pytka. Written by Leo Benvenuti, Steve Rudnick, Timothy Harris, Hershel Weingrod.

What happens when one of the real world's biggest basketball players meets one of the animation world's biggest stars? Michael Jordan exits reality and enters the WB-zone, where he is drafted to help Bugs Bunny, Daffy Duck, Porky Pig, Elmer Fudd, Sylvester, Tweety, Speedy Gonzalez, the Tazmanian Devil, Foghorn Leghorn, and Yosemite Sam as they face off against the Nerdlucks in a wacky interstellar basketball game.

This 1996 live-action/animated combo appeared to be a marketing cash cow waiting to be milked, as it combined sports and cartoons into a project that would appeal to adults and kids. Michael Jordan is comfortable in the lead role of himself, interacting with his toon co-stars but rarely overacting with them. The familiar Warner characters are all present, acting like their "classic" cartoon selves, and always prone to anarchy in the name of humor. Technically, the film is excellent, exceeding the

earlier *Who Framed Roger Rabbit* and other predecessors. Cynical viewers and those who don't like sports are advised that this may not be the best film for them, but the movie accomplishes exactly what it sets out to do; mixing zany cartoon humor and oversized courtsmanship to sink a basket.

This DVD release has a blue cover, making it easy to tell apart from the earlier version. Although elements such as a music-only track and a commentary track by the director, Bugs Bunny, and Daffy Duck are very nice, it's unfortunate that Warner didn't release the original widescreen version on this disc instead of the pan-and-scan version.

SPECIAL FEATURES Commentary Track by Director and Characters • Cast Bios • Character Bios • Production Notes • Trailer • Music Videos • Isolated Score • Other Title Trailers TECHNICAL FEATURES Fullscreen (1.33:1) • Subtitles/CC: Eng., Fren., Span. • Languages: Eng., Fren. dub, Span. dub • Sound: Dolby Digital 5.1 • Snapcase • 1 Disc • Region 1 GENRE & RATING Live/Comedy/Sports • Rated PG

Space Pirate Mito: Vol. 1—Call Me Mom

Anime Works, 2002, 100 mins., #AWDVD-0234. Directed by Takashi Watanabe. Screenplay by Fumihiko Shimo.

NOTE: This DVD arrived too late for a full review. The following text is promotional copy provided by the releasing company:

"Honor thy mother and firepower! Mito isn't just another space pirate, she's a three-foot-tall childlike alien with enough guts to outshine a supernova. Known as the galaxy's most dangerous criminal, Mito lays it down on the Galactic Patrol who track her every move. But behind the ferocious façade lies a mother's love. Her earthbound son, Aoi, has no idea about his mother's infamous career, or even what she really looks like. This unsuspecting boy is in for an adventure that will bring him to all corners of the universe, with the first working mom to carry a pulse rifle!"

This disc contains episodes #1–4.

SPECIAL FEATURES Clean Credits • Other Title Trailers TECHNICAL FEATURES Fullscreen (1.33:1) • Subtitles/CC: Eng. • Languages: Jap., Eng. dub • Sound: Dolby Digital • Keepcase • 1 Disc • Region 1 GENRE & RATING Science Fiction/Comedy • Rated 7+

Space Travelers: The Animation

Media Blasters, 2001, 60 mins., #AWDVD-0114. Directed by Takashi Ui. Script by Katsuhiko Koide.

In the New Cosmic Century 038, an unknown alien civilization has destroyed the Earth Civilization Sphere's defensive fleet, installed an Orbital Ring System around the planet, and cut humanity off from its colonies. Now, the Space Travelers—a group of space pirates and smugglers—may be mankind's only hope. But when they smuggle items for the underground Liberation Army, one of those containers may hold the key to humanity's future.

Space Travelers was the name of a 2000 live-action Japanese movie about bank robbers, which included snippets of a fictional anime, the bandits' favorite cartoon show. The producers were soon working on this animated follow-up, which showed the complete version of the story. While the budget is clearly low, and the herky-jerky mix of traditional animation mixed with CGI makes for varied viewing, the show is a pretty adept handling of all of the science fiction anime clichés.

The DVD contains two commercials for the project, which show an image or two from the live-action movie that inspired it.

SPECIAL FEATURES Promotional Footage • Other Title Trailers TECHNICAL FEATURES Widescreen (1.85:1) • Subtitles/CC: Eng. • Languages: Jap., Eng. dub • Sound: Dolby Digital 2.0 • Keepcase • 1 Disc • Region 1 GENRE & RATING Science Fiction/Action • Rated 7+

Spaceship Agga Ruter ☞ see Mature/Adult Section

Spawn [Todd McFarlane's] ☞ see Mature/Adult Section

Speed Racer: The Movie

Pioneer, 2001, 68 mins., #DVD11521. Directed by Peter Fernandez, Jack Schleh. Written by Peter Fernandez, Robert D. Buchanan.

The dashing young Speed Racer constantly competes in international car races, using his signature vehicle, the powerful and gimmick-laden Mach V. His usual entourage consists of his girlfriend, Trixie, as well as her little brother and his pet monkey. As he grapples with the mysterious Racer X (actually Speed's brother Rex, as the narration breath-

lessly reminds us), Speed is forced to take on a variety of baddies, including an anti-car rabble-rouser and a gigantic behemoth of an automobile.

This DVD is actually made up of three episodes of the original *Speed Racer* cartoon: "The Car Hater" and the two-part "The Race Against the Mammoth Car." The animation is absolutely terrible in this product of the '60s, but the memorable character and color design, witty direction, and entertainingly silly English dub make the show so entertaining that it still endures today. "The Car Hater" is nothing special, but "Mammoth Car" is excellent, with amusingly punchy dialogue and some great action scenes.

On its face, this DVD is a good buy for fans of retro anime—the remainder of the *Speed Racer* TV series has been published on DVD, but it's exceedingly difficult to find. What really makes this DVD worthwhile is the audio commentary track by Peter Fernandez (voice of Speed and the dub director) and Corinne Orr (voice of Trixie). The pair makes pithy comments about the lousy plot, Fernandez regales the audience with stories about the slipshod nature of dubbing the series, and the duo generally hams it up. Other than that, the video and audio quality is merely adequate. The DVD is now out of print. [MT]

SPECIAL FEATURES Commentary Track with Actors • Mach V Specs and Demonstration • Music Video • Game • Easter Eggs TECHNICAL FEATURES Fullscreen (1.33:1) • Languages: Eng. • Sound: Dolby Digital 2.0 • Keepcase • 1 Disc • Region 1–6 GENRE & RATING Racing/Adventure • Not Rated (Kids)

Spider-Man: The Return of the Green Goblin

Buena Vista, 2002, 79 mins., #28128. Directed by Bob Shellhorn. Written by James Grieg. Story by John Semper. Teleplay by Robert N. Skir, Marty Isenberg, Mark Hoffmeier, John Semper, Larry Brody, Meg McLaughlin. Based on the comic book series published from Marvel Comics.

A brilliant researcher is accidentally turned into The Spot, the living embodiment of a portal to other dimensions. When Spider-Man confronts the Spot, the result yields unstable vortexes that could swallow New York! Then, the Hobgoblin almost strands Spidey in another dimension, while the Kingpin engineers the return of the Green Goblin. When the Green Goblin kidnaps Mary Jane and flies her to the top of the Brooklyn Bridge, what tragedy awaits the wall-crawler and his lady love? Finally, Spider-Man and J. Jonah Jameson must work together to exonerate Robbie Robertson and save him from Tombstone.

This DVD includes episodes #37, and 40–42 of the third season of Spider-Man in 1996. Despite the numbering (the episodes were originally aired out of order) these four stories follow each other in sequence. The disc also includes a two-part story from the classic 1967 *Spider-Man*: "The Terrible Triumph of Dr. Octopus" and "Magic Malice." There are a number of clips from the ever-enthusiastic Stan Lee. The only complaint Spider-fans might have is that the airbrushed menu art is absolutely hideous.

SPECIAL FEATURES Interview and Introductions with Creator • Character Bios • Game • Other Title Trailers TECHNICAL FEATURES Fullscreen (1.33:1) • Subtitles/CC: Eng. • Languages: Eng., Span. dub • Sound: Dolby Digital 2.0 • Keepcase • 1 Disc • Region 1 GENRE & RATING Super-Hero/Action • Not Rated (Kids)

Spider-Man: The Ultimate Villain Showdown

Disney, 2002, 79 mins., #25898. Directed by Yosi Cyatani, Eun Byung Kim, Eel Kim, Young Duk Kim. Story by John Semper. Teleplay by Mark Hoffmeier, Elliott S. Maggin, Meg McLaughlin, John Semper, Marty Isenberg, Robert Skir, Doug Booth. Based on the comic book series published from Marvel Comics.

While on a high-school field trip to a laboratory, teenage bookworm Peter Parker is bitten by a radioactive spider. He soon gains superhuman abilities that mimic those of a spider and puts on a costume to fight crime. But there are more superpowered villains than there are heroes, and Spidey is soon tangling with the likes of the Green Goblin, the Lizard, Sandman, and the Kingpin.

Spider-Man burst onto the comic book scene in 1962, created by Stan Lee with artist Steve Ditko. His first animated adventures came with an ABC series in 1967, best known for its limited animation and ultra-catchy theme song. Numerous other *Spider-Man* animated series aired in the 1970s and 1980s. In 1994, hot off the success of the *X-Men* cartoon, Fox Children's Network debuted a *Spider-Man* one-shot special that was really just meant to whet the appetite for the early-1995 series.

With realistic artwork and shading and multilevel, character-oriented scripts, the Fox version of *Spider-Man* was one of the closest to the comics version ever produced. It was also generally entertaining, and very popular with the viewers and comic book fans.

This DVD includes four episodes, #29–32, from the second and third season in 1996. In one of them, Spider-Man tells his origin to a young girl and engages in a battle with Dr. Octopus, then the Green Goblin is born, and finally, a hero called the Rocket Racer helps Spidey stop a group of thugs in a bizarre gyro-wheel. The disc also has live. intros by Stan Lee, a Rogue's Dossier file of Spidey's toughest villains, and the thirty-ninth episode of the classic 1967 *Spider-Man*, "The Origin of Spider-Man."

SPECIAL FEATURES "Making of" Featurette • Commentary Track • Character Bios • Trailer • Promotional Footage • Games • Other Title Trailers • Easter Eggs TECHNICAL FEATURES Fullscreen (1.33:1) • Subtitles/CC: Eng. • Languages: Eng., Span. dub • Sound: Dolby Digital 2.0 • Keepcase • 1 Disc • Region 1 GENRE & RATING Superhero/Action • Not Rated (Kids)

Spike and Mike's Classic Festival of Animation

Slingshot, 2001, 110 mins., #SDVD9148.

Whether you want something mild or something mad, the world's most famous rotating animation anthology is here on DVD. Animation styles present include traditional cel, CGI, stop-motion, paper cut-outs, colored pencil, pastel, claymation, puppets, and more. The fourteen shorts included on this disc are: "Bambi Meets Godzilla"; "Ah, Pook is Here"; "Slim Pickings"; "Monkey vs. Robot"; "Tightrope"; "Chicken Coup"; "Nose Hair"; "Graveyard Jamboree with Mysterious Mose"; "Barflies"; "Panther"; "Bsss"; "The Queens Monastery"; "Fruhling"; and "Son of Bambi Meets Godzilla."

In 1977, Craig "Spike" Decker and Mike Gribble founded a company to promote underground bands, using retro animation as filler. Over the years, the animated shorts they gathered eclipsed their other work in popularity, and they began a *Festival of Animation*. They showcased work by not-yet-award-winning creators such as Tim Burton, Nick Park, Will Vinton, Bill Plympton, and many others. In 1990, they produced a spin-off, *Spike and Mike's Sick and Twisted Festival of Animation*, to show all the risque, revolting, and "adult" toons they had.

Most of the material included on this DVD is appropriate for kids, though some are rather twisted, and black humor abounds. Although this might be a bit much to handle in one sitting at home, it makes a great party disc. Of the running time, nearly half of it is given to supplemental material, including behind-the-scenes footage, commentaries, concepts, extensive bios and filmographies, and more.

There are three versions of this DVD: the original was released by Lumivision in 1998; the second was rereleased by Slingshot in 1999; and the third is this disc, rereleased again in 2001.

SPECIAL FEATURES "Making of" Featurette • Commentary Track • Crew Bios & Filmographies • Character Bios • Character and Art Galleries • Production Notes • Storyboards • Trailers • Promotional Footage • Sing-Alongs • Other Title Trailers • Inserts: Liner Notes TECHNICAL FEATURES Fullscreen (1.33:1) • Languages: Eng. • Sound: Dolby Digital Surround 2.0 • Keepcase • 1 Disc • Region 1–6 GENRE & RATING Anthology • Not Rated (Teens)

Spike and Mike's Sick and Twisted Festival of Animation ☛ see Mature/Adult Section

Spirit: Stallion of the Cimarron [Widescreen]

DreamWorks, 2002, 83 mins.

This DVD was not available for review.

Spirit: Stallion of the Cimarron [Full Screen]

DreamWorks, 2002, 83 mins.

This DVD was not available for review.

SpongeBob SquarePants: Nautical Nonsense/Sponge Buddies [#1]

Paramount, 2002, 123 mins., #87679. Animation Directed by Edgar Larrazabla, Tom Yasumi, Sean Dempsey, Alan Smart, Walt Dohrn, Paul Tibbitt, Fred Miller, Andrew Overtoom. Written by Paul Tibbitt, Peter Burns, Aaron Springer, Erik Wiese, Mr. Lawrence, Sherm Cohen, Vincent Waller, David Fain, Jay Lender, Dan Povenmire, C. H. Greenblatt, Merriwether Williams, Steve Fonti, Chris Mitchell, Tim Hill, Walt Dohrn, Mark O'Hare.

The deep blue waters of the Pacific Ocean have never been funnier than in the adventures of yellow sea sponge SpongeBob SquarePants and his friends. SpongeBob rips his pants at Mussel Beach but everyone thinks it was on purpose as a joke, then cranky neighbor Squidward accidentally gets frozen and lands in the future! Plus, Sandy Cheeks gets homesick for Texas, Squidward's spooky tales starts scaring even himself, and sea onion breath is scaring everyone away from SpongeBob and starfish buddy Patrick. Later, Squidward tries to recuperate after an accident, but jellyfishing doesn't help, SpongeBob eats an exploding pie, and a caterpillar-turned-butterfly is terrorizing Bikini Bottom! Finally, SpongeBob befriends Plankton, but Plankton plots to steal a secret recipe, and Squidward accidentally propels SpongeBob's clubhouse into the middle of the sea.

Nickelodeon debuted the bizarrely funny *SpongeBob SquarePants* in the summer of 1999, created by Stephen Hillenburg. Both kids and adults loved the eternally optimistic SpongeBob and the eclectic cast of characters around him, driving the show to high ratings. The series has had a variety of guest celebrity voices, including Tiny Tim, Ernest Borgnine and Tim Conway (as aged superheroes Mermaid Man and Barnacle Boy), Charles Nelson Reilly, Ween, and John Rhys-Davies, among others.

Ten episodes of *SpongeBob SquarePants* are included on this disc, which also features a music video of the Violent Femmes singing the series theme song! There's also a cool feature called "Backstage Pants," in which viewers can go "backstage" during the episodes to learn more about the cast, crew, and characters, plus five informative featurettes about the making of the series.

SPECIAL FEATURES "Making of" Featurette • Production Notes • Music Video • Other Title Trailers • Inserts: Episode Guide
TECHNICAL FEATURES Fullscreen (1.33:1) • Languages: Eng. • Sound: Dolby Digital 2.0 • Keepcase • 1 Disc • Region 1
GENRE & RATING Comedy • Not Rated (Kids)

SpongeBob SquarePants: Halloween [#2]

Paramount, 2002, 112 mins., #87690. Directed by Sean Dempsey, Walt Dohrn, Paul Tibbitt, Aaron Springer. Written by Paul Tibbitt, Peter Burns, Walt Dohrn, Mr. Lawrence, Merriwether Williams, Steve Fonti, Chris Mitchell, Sherm Cohan, Aaron Springer, C. H. Greenblatt, Kent Osborne.

The silliness continues in this holiday-themed volume that has five spooky sea tales, plus five non-spooky stories. In the spooky quintet, SpongeBob masquerades as the Flying Dutchman, then uses a magic pencil to create a Frankenstein "SpongeDoodle" of himself. Then, has Squidward become a ghost? And what about Plankton's evil robot? Later, SpongeBob is turned into a SpongeSnail!

In the non-spooky tales, SpongeBob is going crazy trying to find out what's in Gary's secret box, plus Squidward forms the guys into a band to play at the Bubble Bowl. SpongeBob begins working at the Chum Bucket, then befriends a stray sea horse. Finally, SpongeBob and Patrick enjoy adventures in a giant box . . . until they're carted out with the garbage!"

If you enjoy this silly nautical-themed series, here's more fun for you!

SPECIAL FEATURES Music Video • Game • Other Title Trailers
TECHNICAL FEATURES Fullscreen (1.33:1) • Languages: Eng. • Sound: Dolby Digital • Keepcase • 1 Disc • Region 1 GENRE & RATING Comedy/Underwater • Not Rated (Kids)

Spriggan

ADV Films, 2002, 90 mins., #DSP/001. Directed by Hirotsugu Kawasaki. Screenplay by Hirotsugu Kawasaki, Yasutaka Ito. Based on the manga series by Hiroshi Takashige and Ryoji Minagawa in *Shonen Sunday*.

Archeology is none of your business. So says ARCAM, a secret global cabal backed by a team of elite superwarrior Spriggan soldiers charged with protecting humanity from its own curiosity about lost civilizations. When the remnants of Noah's Ark are discovered buried deep within Mt. Ararat in Turkey, ARCAM springs into action. But this mission won't be easy. The wrecked ship emits a lethal burst of energy soon after its discovery, attracting the attention of the Pentagon, which rushes to obtain the destructive power of the artifact for the United States military. High school student and Spriggan Yu Ominae travels to Turkey to assist fellow ARCAM soldiers and Spriggan Jean with securing the Ark. As he arrives, Yu is confronted by the Pentagon's own secret forces, supported by a duo of supersoldiers, Fattman and Little Boy, and led by an all-powerful young boy named Colonel MacDougall. With the future of humanity in the balance, the two sides lock horns in a vicious, bloody battle for control of the Ark.

Released in 1998, *Spriggan* hurtles into action right out of the starting blocks and doesn't take a breath until the end credits roll. Richly detailed backgrounds and animation help to create a truly exciting action film. Along with great action, however, come common complaints. Not much attention is paid to keeping the plot tight and the film's dialogue is largely empty, especially disappointing when considering the voice-over track was recorded before animating the movie, an unusual practice in anime.

The DVD features a couple of extras—and a widescreen transfer—including a commentary track by the ADR voice director. [BR]

SPECIAL FEATURES Commentary Track by Voice Directors • Character and Art Galleries • Other Title Trailers • Easter Egg TECHNICAL FEATURES Widescreen (1.85:1 enhanced for 16x9) • Languages: Jap., Eng. dub • Sound: Dolby Digital 5.1 • Keepcase • 1 Disc • Region 1 GENRE & RATING Science Fiction • Rated PG

Spring and Chaos

Tokyopop, 2001, 67 mins., #TPV-872. Directed by Shoji Kawamori. Written by Shoji Kawamori. Based on the stories and poems of Kenji Miyazawa.

Kenji Miyazawa went to school to become a geologist, but his mind was occupied with more than the study of Earth. Allegorical poems of heaven, water, time, space, matter, and spirit flow from Miyazawa's pen, but his genius is unrecognized and unappreciated. His failures as a commercially viable writer and as a teacher in a rural high school weigh heavily on Miyazawa as his father expresses unrelenting disappointment. As his beloved sister slowly dies, the poet painfully tries to swallow his idealism and struggles to earn a living teaching his impoverished neighbors modern farming techniques. He fails at this too, but

though his ideas are ridiculed and rejected, Miyazawa resigns himself to toil until others share his vision.

Like the poet it memorializes, *Spring and Chaos* speaks in the abstract. It's beautiful and ethereal, infused with rich meaning and symbolism, but its unbound narrative makes the film difficult to follow. A remarkable combination of computer and hand-drawn animation shows the breathtaking level of artistry that Japanese animation has attained, but be prepared to watch the movie more than once to fully follow it.

This disc comes with several fun features, including a brief biography of Miyazawa, an art gallery, and interviews with sound director and producer Atsumi Tashiro and writer/director Shoji Kawamori. There's also an eight-page booklet with bios and poems. If you think your head is swimming after watching the film, just wait until you hear Kawamori tell you he decided to make all the characters in the film cats because the late poet hated them.

An original version of this disc was released in May 2001, but it was quickly remastered and rereleased in September 2001. [BR]

SPECIAL FEATURES Interviews with Director/Writer and Sound Director • Poet Bio • Poet Documentary • Crew Bios and Filmographies • Trailer • Inserts: Booklet) TECHNICAL FEATURES Fullscreen (1.33:1) • Subtitles/CC: Eng., Chin., Fren., Germ., Kor., Span. • Languages: Jap., Eng. dub • Sound: Dolby Digital 2.0 • Keepcase • 1 Disc • Region 1–6 GENRE & RATING Biography/Cats/Poetry • Not Rated (Kids)

Sprite: Between Two Worlds ☞ see
Mature/Adult Section

Spy of Darkness ☞ see Mature/Adult Section

Star Ballz ☞ see Mature/Adult Section

Star Blazers: Series 1—The Quest for Iscandar: Part I

Voyager, 2001, 125 mins., #69071-0001-9. Directed by Reiji Matsumoto. Screenplay by Keisuke Fujikawa, Eiichi Yamamoto.

The Earth is at a turning point in the year 2199. Bombed by the alien Gamilons, the surface is uninhabitable, and mankind lives underground in subterranean cities. The radiation is seeping down, though, and mankind will have to take drastic measures if it is to survive. Luckily, they receive a message from the stars: the aliens of far-away planet Iscandar will give them technology—the Cosmo DNA machine—to neutralize the radiation contamination, if they come to get it. Mankind soon refits an aging battleship, the *Yamato*, to travel the 148,000 light years through space to Iscandar, and it is soon launched as the Space Battleship *Argo*. The crew—known as Star Force—is a diverse lot, but they all want to make sure that Earth is saved. In space, they face attacks from the Gamilon fleets, and other dangers. They also must deal with alien races, radiation poisoning, a cyborg among the crew, a bitter feud, and a romance, and early on, the *Argo* is caught in the gravitational pull of Jupiter . . . not to mention the crossfire from the Gamilon base!

Debuting in 1974 on Japanese television, *Star Blazers* was created by Yoshinobu Nishizaki, Reiji Matsumoto, and Eiichi Yamamoto. The original planned story was to be fifty-two episodes, but disastrously meager ratings meant that the series was soon cut back to twenty-six for its first season. In 1977, after the worldwide popularity of *Star Wars* made space operas cool again, *Star Blazers* was given a compilation feature and a new movie, then relaunched in 1978 for a second TV season. It would last for three seasons total, plus numerous OVAs, TV movies, and theatrical features.

The design work by Reiji Matsumoto is fabulous; much simpler than today's designs, but detailed enough to create an entire worldview. Although it had some trademark anime elements, *Star Blazers* was also fairly realistic in its art style, giving it an easy cross-over appeal to American and worldwide audiences who weren't used to other series' big eyes, big hair, speed lines, and super-deformed silliness. Today, although the series looks a bit dated, many fans regard it as the best sweeping epic in space opera history.

The DVD is dubbed in English and features no subtitles or Japanese voice track. Although the packaging lists the disc as containing episodes #1–5 (and contains the titles on the inside), the episodes have been edited together with the front and end credits only used once. The picture quality is a bit grainy, but certainly watchable.

Note that a revised version of *Star Blazers: Series 1—The Quest for Iscandar: Part I* DVD was included as part of the *Star Blazers: DVD Collection—The Quest for Iscandar: Series I* [Box Set].

SPECIAL FEATURES None TECHNICAL FEATURES Fullscreen (1.33:1) • Languages: Eng. dub • Sound: Dolby Digital 2.0 • Keepcase • 1 Disc • Region 1–6 GENRE & RATING Science Fiction/Action • Not Rated (Kids)

Star Blazers: Series 1—The Quest for Iscandar: Part II

Voyager, 2001, 100 mins., #69071-0002-9. Directed by Reiji Matsumoto. Screenplay by Keisuke Fujikawa, Eiichi Yamamoto.

The *Argo* stops at Saturn's moon, Titan, to mine ore for its journey, but a surprise awaits them. Then, the ship is shot down by the Gamilons and sinks into the frozen ice of Pluto. The crew must launch an attack on the Gamilon base on Pluto, but time is running short for the ship. Can it break free of its icy prison and make it to the edge of the solar system, and if so, what about the Gamilon blockade?

The second DVD in this series features a revamped menu, and the choice to watch episodes #6–9 with the credits (though those credits all come from a separate file and are the same for each). There is also a handful of extras, including a scene cut out when the show was brought to America.

SPECIAL FEATURES Character Bios • Deleted Scenes • Promotional Footage • Inserts: Episode Guide TECHNICAL FEATURES Fullscreen (1.33:1) • Languages: Eng. dub • Sound: Dolby Digital 2.0 • Keepcase • 1 Disc • Region 1–6 GENRE & RATING Science Fiction/Action • Not Rated (Kids)

Star Blazers: Series 1—The Quest for Iscandar: Part III

Voyager, 2001, 90 mins., #69071-0003-9. Directed by Reiji Matsumoto. Screenplay by Keisuke Fujikawa, Eiichi Yamamoto.

The *Argo* prepares to leave the solar system, and goodbyes are exchanged. Meanwhile, Emperor Desslok and his Gamilon troops are plotting the destruction of the *Argo*, setting a deadly minefield in its path, and later, an energy net and a sea of fire. And what will happen when young Derek Wildstar sees his first Gamilon pilot after the *Argo* captures him?

This DVD contains episodes #10–13, plus a technical guide to the interior deck configuration of the *Argo*, with lots of art.

SPECIAL FEATURES Art Galleries (Argo) • Promotional Footage • Inserts: Episode Guide TECHNICAL FEATURES Fullscreen (1.33:1) • Languages: Eng. dub • Sound: Dolby Digital 2.0 • Keepcase • 1 Disc • Region 1–6 GENRE & RATING Science Fiction/Action • Not Rated (Kids)

Star Blazers: Series 1—The Quest for Iscandar: Part IV

Voyager, 2001, 100 mins., #69071-0004-9. Directed by Reiji Matsumoto. Screenplay by Keisuke Fujikawa, Eiichi Yamamoto.

Deep space is fraught with danger, including a massive space storm that threatens the *Argo* and a dimensional vortex that could trap them forever! Gamilon General Lysis attacks, with the intent of wiping out Star Force, and later, on planet Beeland, Nova and IQ-9 are captured by Bee people and put in danger. And as the *Argo* nears Lysis's Gamilon base, a space monster is unleashed!

This DVD contains episodes #14–17, plus an extensive overview of the Gamilon Empire, including sections on History, Personnel, Spacefleet, Fighter Craft, Bases, Weapons, and Mecha!

SPECIAL FEATURES Character Bios • Character and Art Galleries • Historical Notes • Promotional Footage • Inserts: Episode Guide TECHNICAL FEATURES Fullscreen (1.33:1) • Languages: Eng. dub • Sound: Dolby Digital 2.0 • Keepcase • 1 Disc • Region 1–6 GENRE & RATING Science Fiction/Action • Not Rated (Kids)

Star Blazers: Series 1—The Quest for Iscandar: Part V

Voyager, 2001, 100 mins., #69071-0005-9. Directed by Reiji Matsumoto. Screenplay by Keisuke Fujikawa, Eiichi Yamamoto.

Near Balan, the halfway point in their journey to Iscandar, the *Argo* is trapped by a space fortress and its shattering Graviton wave. Then, a crewmember gets bad news from Earth and he plans to desert the ship and return home . . . at any cost. Later, will General Lysis use Balan's artificial sun to destroy his enemies? And if that doesn't work, the entire Gamilon fleet is lined up and ready to fight the Star Force crew!

This DVD contains episodes #18–21, plus a look at the Equipment Manifest of the Star Force and the *Argo*, as well as an art-heavy guide to friends and enemies.

SPECIAL FEATURES Character Bios • Character and Art Galleries • Promotional Footage • Inserts: Episode Guide TECHNICAL FEATURES Fullscreen (1.33:1) • Languages: Eng. dub • Sound: Dolby Digital 2.0 • Keepcase • 1 Disc • Region 1–6 GENRE & RATING Science Fiction/Action • Not Rated (Kids)

Star Blazers: Series 1—The Quest for Iscandar: Part VI

Voyager, 2001, 112 mins., #69071-0006-9. Directed by Reiji Matsumoto. Screenplay by Keisuke Fujikawa, Eiichi Yamamoto.

If the crew of the *Argo* can defeat General Lysis and the Gamilon fleet, they might make it to Iscandar in time to save Earth. But even if they destroy the enemy fleet, Planet Gamilon and its leader, Desslok, are still ahead, and the aliens are determined to stop the *Argo* from reaching Queen Starsha and her radiation-cleansing Cosmo DNA machine! With time running out and the Gamilons gunning for them, it's going to be a very rough battle for Star Force.

The final DVD of the first season of *Star Blazers* contains episodes #22–26, as well as an interactive map of the Star Force's journey from Earth to Iscandar and back (beware of the spoilers within).

SPECIAL FEATURES Interactive Map with Art Galleries and Historical Notes • Promotional Footage • Inserts: Episode Guide TECHNICAL FEATURES Fullscreen (1.33:1) • Languages: Eng. dub • Sound: Dolby Digital 2.0 • Keepcase • 1 Disc • Region 1–6 GENRE & RATING Science Fiction/Action • Not Rated (Kids)

Star Blazers: DVD Collection—The Quest for Iscandar: Series I [Box Set]

Voyager, 2001, 627 mins., #69071-0099-9.

This boxed set features the commercially available keepcase editions of *Star Blazers: Series 1—The Quest for Iscandar*. The DVD for *Part I* is completely revised from the individual version, however, and is exclusive to this set. Besides featuring a new cover, this DVD contains a newly redesigned menu that allows for episode-by-episode chapter stops, as well as a history of the Earth vs. Gamilon conflict and a visual technical guide to the *Argo*.

The boxed set also contains a special twenty-four-page full-color booklet with lots of background material about the *Star Blazers* series.

SPECIAL FEATURES (Part I only) Art Galleries • Historical Notes • Promotional Footage • Inserts: Booklet, Episode Guide TECHNICAL FEATURES Fullscreen (1.33:1) • Languages: Eng. dub • Sound: Dolby Digital 2.0 • Cardboard Box with 6 Keepcases • 6 Discs • Region 1–6 GENRE & RATING Science Fiction/Action • Not Rated (Kids)

Star Blazers: Series 2—The Comet Empire: Part I

Voyager, 2001, 112 mins., #69071-0021-9. Directed by Reiji Matsumoto. Screenplay by Keisuke Fujikawa, Eiichi Yamamoto.

The year is 2201, and Earth is blooming again, having reversed the effects of the Gamilon radiation. But that doesn't mean that the planet is safe from more alien attacks. From deep space, a white comet hurtles through space, laying waste to the planets and civilizations it encounters. It isn't a comet at all, but a powerful space fortress from the Comet Empire, an alien race bent on destruction. Against orders, Derek Wildstar, Nova, Dr. Sane, Mark Venture, and the rest of Star Force launch the *Argo* again, to bravely save another world . . . unaware they will soon be facing a new enemy. And lurking in league with the Comet Empire is Desslok of Gamilon . . .

Star Blazers was revived for a second season in 1978—called *Space Battleship Yamato 2* in Japan—with much of the same production, design, and animation crews of the earlier debut season. Most fans agree that this season featured some of the strongest writing, plotting, and characterization of the series. This DVD begins those adventures, with episodes #1–5 also containing a better quality picture than *Series I*. More of the extensive extra features include information and art about the crew of the *Argo* and the history of Earth circa A.D. 2201.

SPECIAL FEATURES Character Bios • Character and Art Galleries • Historical Notes • Promotional Footage • Inserts: Episode Guide TECHNICAL FEATURES Fullscreen (1.33:1) • Languages: Eng. dub • Sound: Dolby Digital 2.0 • Keepcase • 1 Disc • Region 1–6 GENRE & RATING Science Fiction/Action • Not Rated (Kids)

Star Blazers: Series 2—The Comet Empire: Part II

Voyager, 2002, 90 mins., #69071-0022-9. Directed by Reiji Matsumoto. Screenplay by Keisuke Fujikawa, Eiichi Yamamoto.

When forces from the Comet Empire attack the planet Brumas, Star Force and the Space Marines respond. Once the alien threat is found, the Earth Defense Commander calls off the warrant for the "mutinous" members of the *Argo*. But while the *Argo* deals with stealth sub-space submarines, the obnoxious Sgt. Knox and his Marines aren't getting along well with the *Argo*-nauts. A distress call is traced to the planet of Telezart—about 40,000 light years from Earth—and the villainous General Torbuck lures the *Argo* into a space cyclone that accelerates time, rapidly aging the ship and everyone aboard it! And later, a Comet Empire pilot is captured and interrogated, but he escapes and takes drastic measures. . . .

The second DVD in this series contains episodes #6–9. It also has video interviews with the voice actors for Wildstar and Desslok, a look at the technology inside the *Argo*, an updated Equipment Manifest for the Star Forces, and spoiler-filled features on Desslok and the Gamilons!

SPECIAL FEATURES Interview with Voice Actors • Character Bios • Character and Art Galleries • Historical Notes • Promotional Footage • Inserts: Episode Guide TECHNICAL FEATURES Fullscreen (1.33:1) • Languages: Eng. dub • Sound: Dolby Digital 2.0 • Keepcase • 1 Disc • Region 1–6 GENRE & RATING Science Fiction/Action • Not Rated (Kids)

Star Blazers: Series 2—The Comet Empire: Part III

Voyager, 2002, 90 mins., #69071-0023-9. Directed by Reiji Matsumoto. Screenplay by Keisuke Fujikawa, Eiichi Yamamoto.

Desslok is planning the defeat of the Star Force, but General Torbuck trumps him by catching the *Argo* in a magnetic meteor cloud that knocks out their systems. Then, Gamilon General Garrot unleashes a swarm of starflies—which are infected with bacteria that corrode metal—on the *Argo*. Plus, Star Force learns that Desslok is still alive. When the *Argo* docks in a hollow asteroid for repairs, they're caught in a trap! And what kind of political conspiracies are transpiring between Prince Zordar, General Dire, Princess Invidia, and Desslok? Will the enemy plots wipe them out before Star Force can defeat them?

In addition to episodes #10–13 of the second season, this disc contains the second part of the voice actor interviews, as well as a full (spoiler-filled) briefing on the Comet Empire, with sections on Masters and Underlings, the Fleet, and the Arsenal.

SPECIAL FEATURES Interview with Voice Actors • Character Bios • Character and Art Galleries • Historical Notes • Promotional Footage • Inserts: Episode Guide TECHNICAL FEATURES Fullscreen (1.33:1) • Languages: Eng. dub • Sound: Dolby Digital 2.0 • Keepcase • 1 Disc • Region 1–6 GENRE & RATING Science Fiction/Action • Not Rated (Kids)

Star Blazers: Series 2—The Comet Empire: Part IV

Voyager, 2002, 90 mins., #69071-0024-9. Directed by Reiji Matsumoto. Screenplay by Keisuke Fujikawa, Eiichi Yamamoto.

On Telezart, the Star Force finally meets the mysterious Trelaina, but she holds a powerful secret and a dark past that relates to the destruction of all life on her planet except herself. Can Mark Venture convince her to join the fight against the Comet Empire . . . a fight she can probably single-handedly win? Invidia plots even further against Desslok, trying to turn Prince Zordar against him. It would appear that it's all going to end badly for the Comet Empire. . . .

This disc contains episodes #14–17, as well as features on the Comet Empire's Gatlantis City Fortress, as well as background on Trelaina and Planet Telezart. Two voice actors are featured: the voices of Mark Venture and Nova.

SPECIAL FEATURES Interview with Voice Actors • Character Bios • Character and Art Galleries • Historical Notes • Promotional Footage • Inserts: Episode Guide TECHNICAL FEATURES Fullscreen (1.33:1) • Languages: Eng. dub • Sound: Dolby Digital 2.0 • Keepcase • 1 Disc • Region 1–6 GENRE & RATING Science Fiction/Action • Not Rated (Kids)

Star Blazers: Series 2—The Comet Empire: Part V

Voyager, 2002, 90 mins., #69071-0025-9. Directed by Reiji Matsumoto. Screenplay by Keisuke Fujikawa, Eiichi Yamamoto.

The Comet Empire prepares its fleets for a final attack, even as the Earth Defense Forces prepare to rendezvous at Titan. Desslok escapes Invidia's plot and regains his flagship. As the *Argo* passes the planet Brumas, Sgt. Knox memorializes lost friends, and finds an enemy base filled with weapons! Then, the EDF orders a preemptive strike against the Comet Empire, with Captain Gideon's carrier leading the attack. A massive space battle erupts, and not everyone is going to make it out alive. . . .

The conflict reaches a head in episodes #18–21, with episode #20 a fan favorite. The extras include more of the Mark Venture/Nova voice actor interviews, plus information and art on the Earth Defense Forces crews/personnel and fleets.

SPECIAL FEATURES Interview with Voice Actors • Character Bios • Character and Art Galleries • Historical Notes • Promotional Footage • Inserts: Episode Guide TECHNICAL FEATURES Fullscreen (1.33:1) • Languages: Eng. dub • Sound: Dolby Digital 2.0 • Keepcase • 1 Disc • Region 1–6 GENRE & RATING Science Fiction/Action • Not Rated (Kids)

Star Blazers: Series 2—The Comet Empire: Part VI

Voyager, 2002, 112 mins., #69071-00269. Directed by Reiji Matsumoto. Screenplay by Keisuke Fujikawa, Eiichi Yamamoto.

NOTE: This DVD arrived too late for a full review. The following text is promotional copy provided by the releasing company:

"If Zordar's plot should work, he'll destroy the universe! All of Earth's warships, even the flagship *Andromeda*, have fallen in battle against the might of the Comet Empire. Now, only the Star Force remains to stop Prince Zordar. But before they can rejoin the battle, they must face Desslok of Gamilon, who is determined to destroy them forever. Even if the Star Force survives this challenge, they must still defeat a foe that has conquered entire galaxies! This is what it's all been leading up to: the decisive battle of the entire *Star Blazers* saga!"

This disc contains episodes #22–26.

SPECIAL FEATURES Tactical and Interactive Maps TECHNICAL FEATURES Fullscreen (1.33:1) • Languages: Eng. dub • Sound: Dolby Digital 2.0 • Keepcase • 1 Disc • Region 1–6 GENRE & RATING Science Fiction/Action • Not Rated (Kids)

Star Warp'd: Special Edition

Synapse, 2002, 32 mins.

This DVD was not available for review.

Steel Angel Kurumi ☞ see Mature/Adult Section

Stories from My Childhood: Vol. 1

Image, 1999, 159 mins., #ID5521FJDVD. Directed by L. Atamanov, M. Tsehanovsky, V. Tsehanovsky, R. Kachanov. Screenplay by A. Grebner, L. Atamanov, N. Erdman, E. Reese, L. Trauberg, Kir Buliechov. Based on the fairy tales of Hans Christian Andersen and the book by Kir Buliechov.

In "The Snow Queen," brave young Gerta defies the frigid Snow Queen to rescue her friend, Kai. Then, in "The Wild Swans," a witch transforms eleven princes into swans, and their sister, Princess Eliza, must save them. And in "Alice and the Mystery of the Third Planet," a futuristic young girl and her father travel the universe to find exotic animals for Earth's Intergalactic Animal Preserve.

This series of stories was animated by Russia's Soyuzmultfilm over the last several decades. In 1995, Mikhail Baryshnikov worked with Films by Jove to bring a collection of the tales to PBS, then to video. The animation on most of them is excellent, often feeling rotoscoped due to the natural actions of the characters (on "Alice," it's almost psychedelic). A wide variety of Hollywood stars have lent their voices for the soundtracks; on this volume, you'll hear Kathleen Turner, Mickey Rooney, Kirsten Dunst, Cathy Moriarty, Jim Belushi, and Harvey Fierstein. Be warned that these tales have not been sanitized for American audiences. There are some creepy and scary elements that could frighten youngsters. But these are recommended for those who delight in strong animation and fanciful fairy tales.

SPECIAL FEATURES None TECHNICAL FEATURES Fullscreen (1.33:1) • Languages: Eng. dub, Fren. dub, Span. dub • Sound: Dolby Digital 2.0 • Snapcase • 1 Disc • Region 1–6 GENRE & RATING Fantasy/Anthology • Not Rated (Kids)

Stories from My Childhood: Vol. 2

Image, 1999, 120 mins., #ID5522FJDVD. Directed by I. Ivanov-Vano, D. Babichenko. Screenplay by I. Ivanov-Vano, A. Vokov, N. Erdman, L. Tolstaya. Based on the fairy tale by Peter Yershov and on "Adventures of Buratino" by Alexi Tolstoy.

In "Ivan and His Magic Pony," a young country boy owns a magic horse that allows him to go on a trio of adventures at the behest of a greedy king, collecting a firebird, a seamaiden, and a special ring from the ocean's floor. Then, Alexi Tolstoy's adaptation of Collodi's 17th-century novel into "Pinocchio and the Golden Key" is given a Fleischer-esque animated treatment, telling both delightful and dangerous stories with the world's most famous puppet boy.

Another collection of fantastic animated stories by Soyuzmultfilm Studio, this set features voices by Rob Lowe, Hector Elizondo, and Bill Murray, among others.

SPECIAL FEATURES None TECHNICAL FEATURES Fullscreen (1.33:1) • Languages: Eng. dub, Fren. dub, Span. dub • Sound: Dolby Digital 2.0 • Snapcase • 1 Disc • Region 1–6 GENRE & RATING Fantasy/Anthology • Not Rated (Kids)

Stories from My Childhood: Vol. 3

Image, 1999, 128 mins., #ID5523FJDVD. Directed by Ivan Aksenchuk, I. Ivanov-Vano, R. Kachanov, V. Broomberg, Z. Broomberg. Screenplay by A. Sazhin, S. Marshak, N. Erdman, R. Kachanov, T. Gabbe. Based on the stories and books by Charles Perrault, V. Kataev, and E. Labule.

The traditional fairy tale story of "Cinderella" is followed by an animated version of "House on Chicken Legs," which relates the tale of forest witch Baba Yaga. It features music from Mussorgsky's "Pictures from an Exhibition." In "Twelve Months," a peasant girl finds spring flowers in the midst of winter, while in "The Snow Girl," an elderly couple creates a little girl using snow and magic. Rounding out the disc is "Wishes Come True," in which a grumpy-but-pleasant lumberjack gains the power to grant wishes, and a similar story in "The Last Petal," in which a young girl who loves to count gains a magical flower with seven wishes for its seven petals.

These six stories feature a stunning array of animation, plus wonderful vocal work by Amanda Plummer, Lolita Davidovich, Sarah Jessica Parker, Kathleen Turner, Martin Sheen, and Bobcat Goldthwait.

SPECIAL FEATURES None TECHNICAL FEATURES Fullscreen (1.33:1) • Languages: Eng. dub, Fren. dub, Span. dub • Sound: Dolby Digital 2.0 • Snapcase • 1 Disc • Region 1–6 GENRE & RATING Fantasy/Anthology • Not Rated (Kids)

Stories from My Childhood: Vol. 4

Image, 1999, 128 mins., #ID5524FJDV. Directed by L. Atamanov, B. Stepantsev, I. Ivanov-Vano, L. Milchin, A. Snzhko-Blotskaya. Screenplay by G. Grebner, B. Parin, B. Stepantsev, I. Ivanov-Vano, L. Milchin, V. Shklovski. Based on the fairy tales by S. Aksakov and E. Hoffman.

It would be hard to rival Disney's version of the beloved story, but Soyuzmultfilm's version of "Beauty and the Beast: A Tale of the Crimson Flower" has stunning Indian and Persian backgrounds and settings and rotoscope-like figure work, making it a beautiful alternative. "The Nutcracker" follows, telling the famous Christmas tale in less-pretty artwork, and in "The Golden Rooster," a czar makes a pact with a magician and falls in love with a beautiful princess. Then, in "The Prince, the Swan, and the Czar Saltan," a czar tricked into casting out his wife and newborn son is reunited with his family.

Voices for this gorgeously produced final volume include Amy Irving, Tim Curry, Robert Loggia, Shirley MacLaine, Timothy Dalton, Gregory Hines, and others. On a trivia note, Tim Curry plays the Beast in this story and a villain in the Beast's home in *Beauty and the Beast: The Enchanted Christmas* (see entry).

SPECIAL FEATURES None TECHNICAL FEATURES Fullscreen (1.33:1) • Languages: Eng. dub, Fren. dub, Span. dub • Sound: Dolby Digital 2.0 • Snapcase • 1 Disc • Region 1–6 GENRE & RATING Fantasy/Anthology • Not Rated (Kids)

Strange Dawn: Strange World [#1]

Urban Vision, 2002, 92 mins., #UV1076. Directed by Junichi Sato. Screenplay by Michiko Yokote. Based on the manga series by Hajime Miyakawa in *Young King Ours*.

The queen of Guriania has called two high school girls to her world, thinking them powerful warriors who can help defend her kingdom from the evil Barujitans. The bewildered students, Emi and Yuko, definitely do not have superpowers, or the inclination to fight in someone else's civil war. The two are just concerned with returning to their world and leaving this mixed-up fairy tale place behind. The girls meet strange little people who take them to the village of Bellzagle and laud them as the "Legendary Protectors," but the villagers are leery of believing two gawky, mean-spirited girls are the heroes of myth. One of the villagers, Shal, believes in them and desperately wants them to save his land. However, since the teens insist they're not heroes and just want to go home, Shal, followed by Reka and Mani, leaves the village and attempts to help Emi and Yuko discover their true path back to Earth. Will their quest lead to home or more danger?

Although this has cute art and is supposedly for viewers of all ages, parents are hereby warned; this anime contains violence, hints at rape (to touch toes is equivalent to having sex and one character pushes another onto a bed and tries to take off her shoes so he can touch her toes), and numerous mentions of bathrooms, peeing, and washing unmentionables, to name a few. Those acts make this an anime suitable more for the teen crowd, not the tiny tots as the Lil'Visions imprint on the Urban Visions release might suggest.

This DVD contains episodes #1–4 of the 13-part animated television series created in 2000. [JMC]

SPECIAL FEATURES Character and Art Galleries • Other Title Trailers • Inserts: Stickers, Character Bio, Episode Guide TECHNICAL FEATURES Fullscreen (1.33:1) • Subtitles/CC: Eng. • Languages: Jap., Eng. dub • Sound: Dolby Digital 5.1 • Keepcase • 1 Disc • Region 1 GENRE & RATING Fantasy/Adventure • Not Rated (Teens)

Strange Dawn: Strange Journeys [#2]

Urban Vision, 2002, 70 mins., #UV1077. Directed by Junichi Sato. Screenplay by Michiko Yokote. Based on the manga series by Hajime Miyakawa in *Young King Ours*.

Yuko is doing little to endear herself to her non-human companions as she continues to complain, argue, and gripe about being stranded in this

world. Her friend Emi, on the other hand, is beginning to accept their fate and find out about the world around them and the reasons for the civil unrest. As she discovers more about the villager's plight, Emi wants to help them however possible. Can she convince Yuko to quit thinking about herself for a few moments and help these tiny titans out?

The second volume of *Strange Dawn* contains episodes #5–7, and continues the journey of Emi and Yuko to escape this odd world and return to the Earth they know and love. [JMC]

SPECIAL FEATURES Trailer • Other Title Trailers • Inserts: Episode Guide TECHNICAL FEATURES Fullscreen (1.33:1) • Subtitles/CC: Eng. • Languages: Jap., Eng. dub • Sound: Dolby Digital 5.1 • Keepcase • 1 Disc • Region 1 GENRE & RATING Fantasy/Adventure • Not Rated (Teens)

Strange Love ☛ see Mature/Adult Section

Strawberry Eggs: 1st Quarter—Make-Up Exam [#1]

Pioneer, 2002, 100 mins., #11817. Directed by Yuji Yamaguchi. Screenplay by Yasuko Kobayashi, Mutsumi Nakano.

NOTE: This DVD arrived too late for a full review. The following text is promotional copy provided by the releasing company:

"A cross-dressing teacher? Hibiki Amawa needs a job. If he wants to avoid being shot by his landlady, Hibiki has to get a job teaching at the local high school. Unfortunately, this high school only accepts female teachers. This new dramatic comedy is about a man's goal to fulfill his desire to teach, in conflict with a school's strict traditions and his own male image."

This disc contains episodes #1–4.

SPECIAL FEATURES Character Bios • Character and Art Galleries • Clean Credits • Other Title Trailers • Inserts: Mini Poster, Liner Notes • Easter Egg TECHNICAL FEATURES Fullscreen (1.33:1) • Subtitles/CC: Eng. • Languages: Jap., Eng. dub • Sound: Dolby Digital 2.0 • Keepcase • 1 Disc • Region 1 GENRE & RATING School/Girls • Rated 13+

Strawberry Eggs: 2nd Quarter—Pop Quiz [#2]

Pioneer, 2002, 75 mins., #11818. Directed by Yuji Yamaguchi, Megumi Yamamoto, Akira Miyata. Screenplay by Yasuko Kobayashi, Mutsumi Nakano. Based on the manga series by Kentaro Miura.

NOTE: This DVD arrived too late for a full review. The following text is promotional copy provided by the releasing company:

"How far will he go to be a woman? It's time for the school physical! Apparently, the students aren't the only ones required to be tested. How will Hibiki get out of this one? Next, when tempers flare between the students, their long-standing friendships are at risk. Still, that hardly seems like trouble after the school's director decides to play matchmaker and sets Hibiki up with the perfect man! Becoming a great teacher was never meant to be this difficult . . . or this weird!"

This disc contains episodes #5–7.

SPECIAL FEATURES Character Bios • Character and Art Galleries • Promotional Footage • Clean Credits • Other Title Trailers • Inserts: Mini Poster, Liner Notes • Easter Egg TECHNICAL FEATURES Fullscreen (1.33:1) • Subtitles/CC: Eng. • Languages: Jap., Eng. dub • Sound: Dolby Digital • Keepcase • 1 Disc • Region 1 GENRE & RATING School/Girls • Rated 13+

Strawberry Eggs: 3rd Quarter—School Spirit [#3]

Pioneer, 2002, 75 mins., #11819. Directed by Yasuhiro Minami, Hideki Okamoto, Shintaro Itoga. Screenplay by Yasuko Kobayashi, Mutsumi Nakano, Hideki Shirane. Based on the manga series by Kentaro Miura.

NOTE: This DVD arrived too late for a full review. The following text is promotional copy provided by the releasing company:

"All's Fair in Love and War! It's students vs. teachers, when a student is accused of the theft of a teacher's paycheck! Will Hibiki's students respect him if he doesn't stand up for their rights? Unfortunately, Hibiki has to worry more about his students loving him too much when the class goes on a school camping trip and a couple of his students become a little too forward in expressing their . . . ahem . . . love? Who will be the first to confess their secret love? What is a teacher to do?"

This disc contains episodes #8–10.

SPECIAL FEATURES Character and Art Galleries • Promotional Footage • Other Title Trailers • Inserts: Mini Poster, Liner Notes TECHNICAL FEATURES Fullscreen (1.33:1) • Subtitles/CC: Eng. • Languages: Jap., Eng. dub • Sound: Dolby Digital •

Keepcase • 1 Disc • Region 1 GENRE & RATING School/Girls • Rated 13+

Street Fighter Alpha: The Movie

Manga Entertainment, 2001, 120 mins., #MANGA4061-2. Directed by Shigeyasu Yamauchi. Script by Reiko Yoshida.

Featuring a score of familiar characters as well introducing some new ones to the *Street Fighter* mythos, *Street Fighter Alpha* picks up some time after the gang met. Ken is returning to see Ryu after learning the master who trained them both has died. Ryu's been having some problems fighting his inner demons; he worries that he will succumb to the Dark Hado, an amazingly strong evil power that resides within him and consumed and killed his father. A young boy named Shun, claiming to be Ryu's brother, arrives from South America for the new street fighting tournament. At the contest, Shun exhibits powers similar to the Dark Hado. The group learns from Chun Li that the villainous Sadler has been kidnapping street fighters, draining their energy, and using it in his plan for world domination. He nabs Shun in an attempt to force Ryu to work with him. Now the street fighter must decide; to save a brother he never knew he had, will Ryu join the forces of darkness within him?

A sequel to the *Street Fighter II V* series, this story contains the two 1999 OVAs called *Street Fighter Zero*. For those who beat the Street Fighter game and were left feeling "this is it?" *Street Fighter Alpha* brings a resolution and conclusion with more heart and soul. Although this movie might not appeal to the average anime fan, gamers and fans of the fight genre will find this right up their alley. The DVD features extensive cast and crew interviews. [JMC]

SPECIAL FEATURES "Making of" Featurette • Interviews with Cast and Crew • Trailer • Japanese Closing Credits • Other Title Trailers • Easter Egg TECHNICAL FEATURES Fullscreen (1.33:1) • Subtitles/CC: Eng. • Languages: Jap., Eng. dub • Sound: Dolby Digital 2.0, Dolby Digital 5.1 • Keepcase • 1 Disc • Region 1, 2, 4 GENRE & RATING Martial Arts/Action • Not Rated (Teens)

Street Fighter II: The Animated Movie

Sony, 1997, 96 mins., #LVD49753.

This DVD was not available for review.

Street Fighter II V: Vol. 1

Manga Entertainment, 2001, 172 mins., #MANGA4069-2. Directed by Gisaburo Sugii. Screenplay by So Sotoyama, Masumi Hirayanagi, Naoyuki Sakai, Shinichi Tokairin.

They're big. They're beefy. They're ready to beat up some bad guys and have fun doing it. Join Ken and Ryu, two heroes from the videogame series, *Street Fighter*. They mix it up with all kinds of evildoers in their quest to perfect the ultimate fighting technique. Along the way they'll meet other game characters including the tough American Guile, the muscular Fei Long, and the perky Chun Li. Dangerous criminal syndicates have their eyes on our heroes. They want to use them or bump them off. But it's not going to be that easy. These guys are master martial artists.

This 1995 TV series fleshed out the characters introduced in the video game, allowing fans to get to know them a bit. If you are a fan of *Street Fighter* or enjoy shows with lots of hand-to-hand combat, then you'll enjoy this disc. Viewers looking for a bit more meat to their animation might be disappointed. There is some repetition of scenes here and there, but nothing too annoying.

The DVD is a good transfer of the series, containing the first eight episodes. There's also an odd full version of the repetitive opening theme over a still picture. Although this is fairly violent, it's not overly offensive, save for some pretty realistic bone-crunching sounds and body hits. There's also a scene of the two heroes jumping into a pool together sans clothing. [RJM]

SPECIAL FEATURES Trailer • Music Video • Other Title Trailers • Inserts: Synopsis • Easter Egg TECHNICAL FEATURES Fullscreen (1.33:1) • Subtitles/CC: Eng. • Languages: Jap., Eng. dub • Sound: Dolby Digital 2.0 • Keepcase • 1 Disc • Region 1, 2, 4 GENRE & RATING Martial Arts/Action • Not Rated (Teens)

Street Fighter II V: Vol. 2

Manga Entertainment, 2001, 172 mins., #MANGA4070-2. Directed by Gisaburo Sugii. Screenplay by Naoyuki Sakai, Katsumi Ono.

If you're looking for more scenes of men rolling around on the ground and getting their shirts ripped off, then this is the series for you. Ryu and Ken continue on their quest to discover ultimate fighting techniques. But that pesky criminal syndicate isn't done with them yet. Ryu gets thrown into prison and Ken has to dig up evidence to set his pal free. Then it's off to India to find more wisdom in the form of martial arts guru, Dhalsim. The disc wraps up with the dynamic duo heading off to Spain

with Chun Li to take in the sights and attend an award ceremony. But there's more going on than meets the eye.

This DVD locks in seven more episodes of *Street Fighter*. If you've enjoyed the show so far, this disc delivers more of the same. [RJM]

SPECIAL FEATURES Trailer • Music Video • Other Title Trailers • Inserts: Synopsis TECHNICAL FEATURES Fullscreen (1.33:1) • Subtitles/CC: Eng. • Languages: Jap., Eng. dub • Sound: Dolby Digital 2.0 • Keepcase • 1 Disc • Region 1, 2, 4 GENRE & RATING Martial Arts/Action • Not Rated (Teens)

Street Fighter II V: Vol. 3

Manga Entertainment, 2001, 172 mins., #MANGA4071-2. Directed by Gisaburo Sugii. Screenplay by Naoyuki Sakai, Kenya Sawada.

Ken and Ryu are back and it's time for some more brawling. Vega, the handsome Spanish bullfighter, is locked in mortal battle with Ken, while Ryu practices his powerful new technique. But who is this lurking in the background? Why, it's none other than the evil overlord of the *Street Fighter* universe, Bison! What could he be plotting? Finally, the lovely and deadly Cammy makes her appearance, with lots of leg and cleavage for some viewers to enjoy. She's got one thing on her mind: killing Chun Li's father. It's not personal, just business.

You want seven more episodes? This DVD has them. However things seem to go down a bit in the entertainment department, mostly because of the annoying overuse of flashbacks. When they flashback to stuff that happened five minutes ago, it gets a bit repetitive. [RJM]

SPECIAL FEATURES Music Video • Other Title Trailers • Inserts: Synopsis TECHNICAL FEATURES Fullscreen (1.33:1) • Subtitles/CC: Eng. • Languages: Jap., Eng. dub • Sound: Dolby Digital 2.0 • Keepcase • 1 Disc • Region 1, 2, 4 GENRE & RATING Martial Arts/Action • Not Rated (Teens)

Street Fighter II V: Vol. 4

Manga Entertainment, 2001, 196 mins., #MANGA4072-2. Directed by Gisaburo Sugii. Screenplay by Naoyuki Sakai, Kenya Sawada.

It's the final set of stories for Ken and Ryu, and you know it's going to be one big ol' brawl. Bison has done some evil things to Ryu and Chun Li, but don't fret because help is on the way. American buddy Guile shows up with a partner, and they infiltrate Bison's lair and start to make a mess. And don't forget Cammy, and her mission to kill. Can our Hong Kong action star save the day? It's a whole bunch of powering-up and beating-up in this final disc of *Street Fighter II V.* And they even left room for a sequel.

This disc is a step down from the previous one. Lots of flashbacks. Lots of powering up. And Chun Li stands around looking wicked and doing nothing. Than there's the main villain, Bison, whose sole purpose seems to be to laugh like a nut and glow. The fighting is OK but it relies heavily on stock footage from previous battles. All in all, episodes #22–29 represent a weak ending to a show that started out decently enough. [RJM]

SPECIAL FEATURES Music Video • Other Title Trailers • Inserts: Synopsis • Easter Egg TECHNICAL FEATURES Fullscreen (1.33:1) • Subtitles/CC: Eng. • Languages: Jap., Eng. dub • Sound: Dolby Digital 2.0 • Keepcase • 1 Disc • Region 1, 2, 4 GENRE & RATING Martial Arts/Action • Not Rated (Teens)

Street Sharks: Shark Bait/Action Man in Space

Trimark, 2002, 140 mins.

This DVD was not available for review.

Super Atragon

ADV Films, 2002, 100 mins., #DSA/001. Directed by Kazuyoshi Katayama, Mitsuo Fukuda. Script by Nobuaki Kishima. Based on the novel by Shunro Oshikawa.

NOTE: This DVD arrived too late for a full review. The following text is promotional copy provided by the releasing company:

"Our armed forces are helpless. The world's navies destroyed. Man's only hope is an untried weapon. Get ready for a non-stop onslaught of high-tech action as metal leviathans collide in the ultimate war of super science in Super Atragon. Moments after an atomic bomb falls over Hiroshima, a secret Japanese submarine sails into battle against its American counterpart, and both are lost to history. Some fifty years later, a special UN task force sent to investigate unusual phenomenon in Antarctica is threatened by a mysterious black cylinder until the reappearance of the long-lost Japanese sub. However, the incident in the Antarctic is only the first round in a cataclysmic battle of wills between two descendants of an ancient race dwelling within the Earth. Standing against them is a single, amazing ship, the *RA*, a Yamato–class battle sub secretly rebuilt after its supposed destruction in World War II."

SPECIAL FEATURES Other Title Trailers TECHNICAL FEATURES Fullscreen (1.33:1) • Subtitles/CC: Eng. • Languages: Jap., Eng. dub • Sound: Dolby Digital • Keepcase • 1 Disc • Region 1 GENRE & RATING Science Fiction/Action • Rated 15+

Super Dimension Fortress Macross Box Set [#1–9]

AnimEigo, 2002, 900 mins., #AV001-250. Directed by Kenichi Matsuzaki, Noboru Ishiguro, Sukuhiro Tomita, Hiroshi Onogi, Hiroyuki Hoshiyama, Shoji Kawamori.

In 1999, a giant spacecraft crash lands on an island, and the resulting conflict between Earth's nations over the ship—known as "Macross"—begins. Ten years later, the "Unification Wars" have ended, and mankind is governed by the Earth United Nations Government. The Macross ship, now called *Super Dimension Fortress-1* or *SDF-1,* is about to be relaunched, but Earth is soon to be in conflict with invading aliens known as the Zentraedi. Numerous fighter pilots and humans—including Ichijo Hikaru, Major Ray Focker, and Lynn Minmay—are caught up in the battle. The *SDF-1* crew accidentally folds space and warps far away, and as they travel back toward Earth, they engage the Zentraedi in space battles and more.

If the storyline to *Super Dimension Fortress Macross* sounds familiar, that's because you've probably read about it already under ADV's *Robotech: The Macross Saga* (see entries). In 1985, U.S. producer Carl Macek took the 1982 *SDF Macross* television series and shaped it—and two other completely unrelated series—into his U.S. *Robotech* release. But while *Super Dimension Fortress Macross* has many story similarities to *Robotech* and features most of the same animation, there are big differences in the stories and motivations. The series was a huge success in Japan, given its songs (Minmay's voice actress Mari Iijima became a singing star) and its transforming mecha planes known as the Valkyries, which were a big hit on toy shelves.

The nine-disc DVD set is handsomely packaged in a black and white box, with matching bold-graphic keepcases. Each keepcase also includes an insert with information about the series, complete with art. The picture quality is excellent for its age, with a very nice use of stereo sound. Although there are no dubbed English-language versions of the shows, each disc has a music-and-sound-effects-only track with subtitles, allowing industrious fans to stage their own dubbing sessions.

All thirty-six episodes of *Super Dimension Fortress Macross* are included in this special set, allowing *Macross* fans their choice of seeing the shows in their original form. Either as *SDF Macross* or as *Robotech*, the series remains one of the most popular in anime history.

SPECIAL FEATURES Inserts: Liner Notes, Episode Guides, Lyrics, Character Bios and Art, Mecha Art • Easter Eggs TECHNICAL FEATURES Fullscreen (1.33:1) • Subtitles/CC: Eng. • Languages: Jap. • Sound: Dolby Digital 2.0 • Cardboard Box Set with 9 Keepcases • 9 Discs • Region 1 GENRE & RATING Science Fiction/Action • Not Rated (Kids)

Super Dimension Fortress Macross—Macross Set #1

AnimEigo, 2002, 300 mins., #AV002-230.

This box set includes the first three *Super Dimension Fortress Macross* discs (containing episodes #1–12) exactly as they appeared in the previously released *Super Dimension Fortress Macross Box Set*. See that entry for the Special and Technical Features listings.

TECHNICAL FEATURES Cardboard Box Set with 3 Keepcases • 3 Discs • Region 1 GENRE & RATING Science Fiction/Action/Robots • Not Rated (Kids)

Super Dimension Fortress Macross—Macross Set #2

AnimEigo, 2002, 300 mins., #AV002-231.

This box set includes the second trio of *Super Dimension Fortress Macross* discs (containing episodes #13–24) exactly as they appeared in the previously released *Super Dimension Fortress Macross Box Set*. See that entry for the Special and Technical Features listings.

TECHNICAL FEATURES Cardboard Box Set with 3 Keepcases • 3 Discs • Region 1 GENRE & RATING Science Fiction/Action/Robots • Not Rated (Kids)

Super Dimension Fortress Macross—Macross Set #3

AnimEigo, 2002, 300 mins., #AV002-232.

This box set includes the final trio of nine *Super Dimension Fortress Macross* discs (containing episodes #25–36) exactly as they appeared in the previously released *Super Dimension Fortress Macross Box Set*. See that entry for the Special and Technical Features listings.

TECHNICAL FEATURES Cardboard Box Set with 3 Keepcases • 3 Discs • Region 1 GENRE & RATING Science Fiction/Action/Robots • Not Rated (Kids)

Super Grand Prix

Liberty International, 2001, 90 mins., #LIP0101. Adaptation Written by L. Michael Haller, Collins Walker.

Aspiring pro racer Sean Corrigan can't seem to catch a break. Repeated accidents both on and off the track have earned him the nickname "Crash," and despite a lucrative contract with a Japanese auto manufacturer, he's having trouble living up to his potential. Help comes in the form of a mysterious masked benefactor, who pushes Corrigan to try harder, along with his new mechanic, Patty, who inspires him to race again. Before he knows it, the young driver is competing at Monte Carlo, the famous all-day road rally in Monaco.

Super Grand Prix is actually a ninty-minute movie version of the 1977 TV series *Hawk of the Grand Prix*. It sums up the first third of the TV series. While the film suffers badly from a lousy film transfer and low-quality animation, the realistic cars and appearance by a real-life Grand Prix champion make it worth a look.

Unfortunately, the DVD is nothing to crow about. As stated above, the image quality is horribly grainy, and the only audio tracks included are an exceedingly hokey dub and a muffled Spanish-language track. Even the end credits are cut off! For racing show completists only. [MT]

SPECIAL FEATURES None TECHNICAL FEATURES Fullscreen (1.33:1) • Languages: Eng. dub, Span. dub • Sound: Dolby Digital 2.0 • Keepcase • 1 Disc • Region All GENRE & RATING Racing/Action • Not Rated (Kids)

Superman [Max Fleischer's]

Winstar, 1998, 100 mins., #WHE73010. Directed by Dave Fleischer. Story by Seymour Kneitel, Isidore Sparber, Bill Turner, Ted Pierce, Carl Meyer, Dan Gordon, Jay Morton. Based on the DC Comics character created by Jerome Siegel and Joe Schuster.

This disc contains the first nine of the Fleischer Brothers *Superman* theatrical shorts from 1941 to 1942. For a description of the history of these cartoons, see *The Complete Superman Collection [Diamond Anniversary Edition]*.

Episode titles include: "Superman: The Mad Scientist"; "The Mechanical Monsters"; "Electronic Earthquake"; "Billion Dollar Limited"; "The Arctic Giant"; "The Bulleteers"; "The Magnetic Telescope"; "Volcano"; and "Terror on the Midway." The disc also includes a 1936 bonus cartoon by Fleischer, "Play Safe," as well as a demonstration of the restoration techniques used on the Fleischer cartoons. While the digital restoration makes the cartoons look good and the colors vibrant, the fact that the episodes are split over two DVDs makes them a bit less cost-effective than either of the two Image discs.

Besides being offered as a single DVD, the disc was also included as part of a pack set, along with *Superman: The Lost Episodes.*

SPECIAL FEATURES Production Notes • Synopsis • Restoration Demo • Other Title Trailers TECHNICAL FEATURES Fullscreen (1.33:1) • Languages: Eng. • Sound: Dolby Digital 2.0, Dolby Digital 5.1 • Keepcase • 1 Disc • Region 1–6 GENRE & RATING Superhero/Adventure • Not Rated (All Ages)

Superman Cartoons of Max and Dave Fleischer, The

Image, 1998, 147 mins., #ID4388BRDV. Directed by Dave Fleischer, Seymour Kneitel, Isidore Sparber, Dan Gordon. Story by Seymour Kneitel, Isidore Sparber, Bill Turner, Ted Pierce, Carl Meyer, Dan Gordon, Jay Morton, Robert Little. Based on the DC Comics character created by Jerome Siegel and Joe Schuster.

This disc contains all seventeen of the *Superman* cartoons produced by Max and Dave Fleischer from 1941 to 1943. The disc has functionally the same contents as the later 2000 disc from Image, *The Complete Superman Collection [Diamond Anniversary Edition]* (see entry). The biggest difference between the two is the addition of a 1944 *Private Snafu* cartoon parody by Dave Fleischer, "Snafuperman."

Of all the *Superman* discs, this one probably has some of the cleanest images, without any date subtitles (as *The Complete Superman Collection* has). Unfortunately, it lacks all the historical data on the Winstar discs.

SPECIAL FEATURES None TECHNICAL FEATURES Fullscreen (1.33:1) • Languages: Eng. • Sound: Dolby Digital Mono • Snapcase • 1 Disc • Region 1–6 GENRE & RATING Superhero/Adventure • Not Rated (All Ages)

Superman: The Lost Episodes [Max Fleischer's]

Winstar, 1999, 100 mins., #WHE73029. Directed by Seymour Kneitel, Isidore Sparber, Dan Gordon. Story by Bill Turner, Carl Meyer, Jay Morton, Robert Little. Based on the DC Comics character created by Jerome Siegel and Joe Schuster.

This disc contains eight more of the Fleischer Brothers *Superman* theatrical shorts from 1942 to 1943. For a description of the history of these cartoons, see *The Complete Superman Collection [Diamond Anniversary Edition].*

Episode titles include: "Japoteurs"; "Showdown"; "Eleventh Hour"; "Destruction Inc."; "The Mummy Strikes"; "Jungle Drums"; "The Underground World";

and "Secret Agent." The disc also includes a 1944 bonus *Mighty Mouse* cartoon, "Wolf! Wolf!" as well as a demonstration of the restoration techniques used on the *Superman* cartoons. While the digital restoration makes the cartoons look good and the colors vibrant, the fact that the episodes are split over two DVDs makes them a bit less cost-effective than either of the two Image discs.

Besides being offered as a single DVD, the disc was also included as part of a pack set, along with *Superman [Max Fleischer's].*

SPECIAL FEATURES Production Notes • Synopsis • Restoration Demo • Other Title Trailers TECHNICAL FEATURES Fullscreen (1.33:1) • Languages: Eng. • Sound: Dolby Digital 2.0, Dolby Digital 5.1 • Keepcase • 1 Disc • Region All GENRE & RATING Superhero/Adventure • Not Rated (All Ages)

Superman vs. The Monsters and Villains

GoodTimes, 2002, 77 mins., #05-81318. Based on the DC Comics character created by Jerome Siegel and Joe Schuster.

This disc contains nine of the Fleischer Brothers *Superman* theatrical shorts from 1941 to 1943. For credits and a description of the history of these cartoons, see the entry for *The Complete Superman Collection [Diamond Anniversary Edition].*

Episode titles include: "The Arctic Giant"; "The Mechanical Monsters"; "Electronic Earthquake"; "Superman: The Mad Scientist"; "The Underground World"; "The Bulleteers"; "Billion Dollar Limited"; "The Mummy Strikes"; and "The Magnetic Telescope." The image is pretty decent, if a bit soft-edged, but the soundtrack is muted and it echoes in spots. The opening credit sequences are window-boxed.

SPECIAL FEATURES None TECHNICAL FEATURES Fullscreen (1.33:1) • Languages: Eng. • Sound: Dolby Digital 2.0 • Keepcase • 1 Disc • Region All GENRE & RATING Superhero/Adventure • Not Rated (All Ages)

Superman vs. Nature and War

GoodTimes, 2002, 65 mins., #05-81319. Based on the DC Comics character created by Jerome Siegel and Joe Schuster.

This disc contains eight of the Fleischer Brothers *Superman* theatrical shorts from 1941–43. For credits and a description of the history of these cartoons, see the entry for *The Complete Superman Collection [Diamond Anniversary Edition].*

Episode titles include: "Volcano"; "Jungle Drums"; "Destruction Inc."; "Eleventh Hour"; "Secret Agent"; "Japoteurs"; "Showdown"; and "Terror on the Midway."

As with the other GoodTimes disc, the image is pretty decent, if a bit soft-edged, but the soundtrack is muted and it echoes in spots. The opening credit sequences are window-boxed.

SPECIAL FEATURES None TECHNICAL FEATURES Fullscreen (1.33:1) • Languages: Eng. • Sound: Dolby Digital 2.0 • Keepcase • 1 Disc • Region All GENRE & RATING Superhero/Adventure • Not Rated (All Ages)

Super Mario Bros. Super Show, The: Mario's Greatest Movie Moments

Trimark, 2002, 85 mins., #VM 7922D. Directed by Dan Riba, John Grusd. Written by Kevin O'Donnell, Cassandra Schafhausen, Phil Harnage, Perry Martin.

Mario and Luigi are two Italian plumbers who are suddenly transported out of Brooklyn and into the Mushroom Kingdom. While there, they constantly have to rescue Princess Toadstool from King Koopa and his lackeys. Villains they face include spaghetti-sauce vampire Kount Koopula, cheese monster Koopenstein, hot-air-breathing Koop-Zilla, mecha-monster Robo-Koopa, and more.

The Super Mario Bros. Super Show debuted in syndication in 1989, then on NBC the following year. The characters were from a popular Nintendo video game, and the series was devoid of any but the most basic internal logic. In other words, if you like bright colors, nonsensical characters and names, and adventures that have no logic, then *Pokémon*—excuse me, *Super Mario Bros.*—is right up your alley.

Despite what it says on the packaging, the disc features six episodes of the Marios: "Robo-Koopa"; "Toad Warriors"; "Raiders of the Lost Mushroom"; "Count Koopula"; "Mario Meets Koop-Zilla"; and "Koopenstein." It also contains two *The Adventures of Zelda* episodes, a series that was a segment of the original *The Super Mario Bros. Super Show*: "The Missing Link" and "Kiss and Tell."

SPECIAL FEATURES Game TECHNICAL FEATURES Fullscreen (1.33:1) • Subtitles/CC: Eng. • Languages: Eng. • Sound: Dolby Digital 2.0 • Keepcase • 1 Disc • Region 1 GENRE & RATING Adventure/Humor • Not Rated (Kids)

Sword for Truth ☞ see Mature/Adult Section

Sword in the Stone, The [Gold Collection]

Disney, 2001, 79 mins., #19691. Directed by Wolfgang Reitherman. Story by Bill Peet. Based on the book by T. H. White.

Wart is an unlucky squire who one day happens to bump into Merlin the Magician in the woods. Merlin undertakes to train the boy in the ways of magic, which puts Wart in the path of the evil Madame Mim, a sorceress. But later, Wart must return to his duties as a squire for his foster father, Sir Ector, and his older foster brother, Sir Kay. At a jousting tournament, Wart forgets Kay's sword, but as he runs through the woods to get the missing weapon, he spies a sword in a stone. Wart draws the sword and returns to the tournament, only to be informed that whoever pulled the sword is the rightful King of England!

Released in 1963, *The Sword in the Stone* was the next-to-last animated feature film that Walt Disney personally oversaw. The film featured an often-realistic drawing style, though Wart's magical training and the sorcery battles between Madame Mim and Merlin gave lots of screen time to funny animals and fanciful elements. Heavy on dialogue, the film has lots of wit, much of it from Merlin or his pet owl, Archimedes. The film did OK in theaters, but was not a perennial hit for Disney, nor did it inspire much merchandising.

As with all Disney DVDs, the picture transfer is excellent, and there are quite a number of very cool extras. These include a vintage segment about magic from a 1957 Disney show, a deleted song from the film by the Sherman Brothers, sing-alongs, and a pair of vintage shorts: Mickey Mouse in "The Brave Little Tailor" (1938) and Goofy in "Knight for a Day" (1946).

SPECIAL FEATURES "Making of" Music Featurette • Character and Art Galleries • Production Notes • Promotional Footage • Sing-Alongs • Other Title Trailers TECHNICAL FEATURES Fullscreen (1.33:1) • Subtitles/CC: Eng. • Languages: Eng., Fren. dub, Span. dub • Sound: Dolby Digital 5.1 • Keepcase • 1 Disc • Region 1, 4 GENRE & RATING Music/Adventure/Historical • Rated G

T

Tales Trilogy, The ☛ see Mature/Adult Section

Tangerine Bear, The

Artisan, 2000, 48 mins., #10402. Directed by Bret King. Teleplay by Betty Paraskevas. Based on the book by Betty Paraskevas.

Pity the poor teddy bear whose smile was accidentally sewn on upside-down at the factory. No one buys him at Christmas, and he's shipped off to a second-hand store run by kindly Mr. Winkle. There he sits until the sun fades his fur to a tangerine color, earning him the nickname Tangie. The bear soon makes friends with other misfit toys in the window, including a jack-in-the-box, a bent-nosed bird in a cuckoo clock, a mermaid clock, a blue monkey, and others. Together, the toys learn that they are special because they are different, and they form their own family.

This story practically defines the word "sweet," but in a non-saccharine manner. The animation is cute but not cloying, and an all-star cast of sitcom voices appear, including Tom Bosley, Marlon Wayans, David Hyde Pierce, Jonathan Taylor Thomas, Jenna Elfman, and Howie Mandel. The whole story is narrated by country star Trisha Yearwood, who also sings two new holiday songs.

Kids will love this DVD, and parents will like the messages about individuality and the value of friendship. There are even a handful of extras, including a bunch of fun facts about Teddy Bears.

SPECIAL FEATURES "Making of" Featurette • Cast Filmographies • Trailer • Games • Inserts: Liner Notes TECHNICAL FEATURES Fullscreen (1.33:1) • Languages: Eng. • Sound: Dolby Digital 2.0 • Keepcase • 1 Disc • Region 1 GENRE & RATING Fantasy/Family • Not Rated (All Ages)

Tarzan

Disney, 2000, 88 mins., #18150. Directed by Kevin Lima, Chris Buck. Screenplay by Tab Murphy, Bob Tzudiker, Noni White. Based on *Tarzan of the Apes* by Edgar Rice Burroughs.

When his parents are killed, a young baby is raised by a clan of apes. Young Tarzan—as the boy is known—is accepted by everyone except the clan leader, his foster-father. His best friends are Terk, a girl ape, and Tantor, a neurotic elephant. As he grows into a man, Tarzan becomes one with the jungle, learning to communicate with animals of all types. And then, other humans come to the land. Jane and her father are there to study the ways of the simians, but the evil men who brought them conspire to capture the apes instead! Even as Tarzan and Jane fall in an unlikely love, Tarzan must save his adopted family and friends from the humans. . . .

Released in summer 1999, *Tarzan* wasn't the huge hit Disney hoped for, but it was a solid performer. *Tarzan* had been the subject of forty-seven previous movie adaptations, but this was the first animated version. Interestingly enough, original author Edgar Rice Burroughs had considered an animated film, once writing to his son that, "The cartoon must be good. It must approximate Disney excellence."

Burroughs's desire for excellence is realized onscreen. The animation is slick and at times even breathtaking, combining traditional 2D characters with a 3D CGI jungle environment (using a new process known as "Deep Canvas"). When Tarzan "surfs" through the trees and vines, viewers go on a roller coaster ride of greenery with him. Vocal work is also top-notch, with Glenn Close, Minnie Driver, Brian Blessed, and Rosie O'Donnell voicing the lead characters, and Lance Henriksen turning in a bone-chilling performance as clan leader Kerchak.

The film features five songs by Phil Collins, but they are background songs, not sung by the characters. They express the feelings and thoughts of the characters, without putting words directly in their mouths. Collins rerecorded the songs in five different languages, two of which are heard on alternate language tracks (French and Spanish).

The *Tarzan* DVD has a couple of cool extra features (though not nearly as many as the *Collector's Edition*), which, when combined with the lush and detailed film, make this an excellent addition to a DVD collection.

NOTE: This DVD is now on moratorium.

SPECIAL FEATURES "Making of" Music Featurette • Trailer • Music Video • Read-Along • Games • DVD-ROM Features: Game • Other Title Trailers TECHNICAL FEATURES Widescreen (1.66:1 enhanced for 16x9) • Subtitles/CC: Eng., Span. • Languages: Eng., Fren. dub, Span. dub • Sound: Dolby Digital 5.0 • Keepcase • 1 Disc • Region 1, 4 GENRE & RATING Adventure/Action • Rated G

Tarzan [Collector's Edition]

Disney, 2000, 88 mins., #19320. Directed by Kevin Lima, Chris Buck. Screenplay by Tab Murphy, Bob Tzudiker, Noni White. Based on *Tarzan of the Apes* by Edgar Rice Burroughs.

Another in the line of Disney's collector's series, this set of *Tarzan* discs offers hours of special behind-the-scenes features, tracking the development of the film from start to finish. The first disc contains the widescreen version of the film with a commentary track by the producer and directors, as well as the same material that's on the normal edition. There is an additional audio track that describes the onscreen action in detail for the visually impaired!

The second disc is a comprehensive look at the roots of *Tarzan*, with early tests and presentation reels, research footage from Africa, character creation, 3D digital Deep Canvas, and multiple-angle production progression. Plus there are features on digital production, music, story and editorial, and publicity, as well as three abandoned scenes. As with others in Disney's collector's editions, the *Tarzan* set is an excellent deconstruction of the making of the film. The producers certainly have a reason to beat their chests and let out a hearty Tarzan yodel.

SPECIAL FEATURES "Making of" Featurettes • Commentary Tracks by the Producer and Directors • Character and Art Galleries • Production Notes • Abandoned Sequences • Storyboards • Story Treatment • Trailers • Promotional Footage • Music Videos • Read-Along • Games • Descriptive Audio Track for the Visually Impaired • DVD-ROM Features: Game • Other Title Trailers TECHNICAL FEATURES Widescreen (1.66:1 enhanced for 16x9) • Subtitles/CC: Eng., Span. • Languages: Eng., Fren. dub, Span. dub • Sound: Dolby Digital 5.0 • Multikeepcase • 2 Discs • Region 1, 4 GENRE & RATING Adventure/Action • Rated G

Tarzan and Jane

Disney, 2002, 70 mins., #23975. Directed by Steve Loter. Written by Bill Motz, Bob Roth. Based on the books by Edgar Rice Burroughs.

While pondering a good gift for her first anniversary with Tarzan, Jane Porter takes a trip down memory lane to adventures of the recent past. First, there was a visit from the three stuffy British women with whom she attended finishing school who are all appalled at her "rough ways." Later, Tarzan aids some diamond hunters, until he's double-crossed, leading to Jane, her father, and Tarzan being trapped inside a bubbling volcano! Finally, a dashing pilot crashes back into Jane's life, but he's hiding a secret.

Sapping almost every bit of enjoyment out of the concepts and designs of the 2000 feature film, this direct-to-video release is a disappointment. The characters are all brightly animated over muted and murky backgrounds, meaning they don't appear to have any weight, and the "realistic" shading that attempts to make up for this layering problem only makes the visuals worse. The scene where Tarzan surfs on the molten lava is a low-budget and pale version of his vine-surfing scenes in the original film. Kids may like it, but older *Tarzan* fans will want to catch the first vine away from this dud.

SPECIAL FEATURES Music Video • Interactive Story • Games • Other Title Trailers TECHNICAL FEATURES Widescreen (1.66:1 enhanced for 16x9) • Subtitles/CC: Eng. • Languages: Eng., Fren. dub • Sound: Dolby Digital Surround 5.1 • Keepcase • 1 Disc • Region 1 GENRE & RATING Adventure/Action • Rated G

Teachers Pet ☞ see Mature/Adult Section

Tekkaman Blade II [Complete Collection]

Urban Vision, 2001, 180 mins., #UV1071. Directed by Hideki Tonokatsu. Written by Hiroyuki Kawasaki.

Tekkaman Blade II is a fast-paced action anime that begins ten years after the original series with the building of a new Tekkaman team equipped with more advanced weaponry. Not only must they be ready to face their powerful enemy Radham, but, in the end, they will be forced to deal with the bitter reality of their own history. Fortunately, they will not have to face these "ghosts" of their technology alone as Tekkaman Blade, thought to be long dead or perhaps simply a myth, returns to bring his legendary power to bear.

First released in 1994, *Tekkaman Blade II* progresses through the three "stages" that comprise the entire six-part OVA series, a sequel to the original 1975 TV series and the 1992 revival. The atmosphere of the anime changes noticeably from a somewhat light and occasionally humorous feeling in the beginning to a darker, more fast-paced mood as the very human characters struggle not only to find their places in the action, but are also faced with the realities of death and war.

Extremely well animated, with flashes of true mastery of the art, and with an outstanding Dolby 5.1 soundtrack, this digitally remastered anime is sure to please fans of the power-suit genre. There is some brief nudity as the female Tekkamen make their transformations. *Tekkaman Blade II* is not only a real treat for fans of the old series but the story is laid out so that "first-timers" can enjoy it equally as well. [GP]

SPECIAL FEATURES Fan Art Galleries • Other Title Trailers • Inserts: Tech Notes TECHNICAL FEATURES Fullscreen (1.33:1) • Subtitles/CC: Eng. • Languages: Jap., Eng. dub • Sound: Dolby Digital 5.1 • Keepcase • 1 Disc • Region 1 GENRE & RATING Robots/Science Fiction • Not Rated (Teens)

Tekken: The Motion Picture

ADV Films, 1999, 60 mins., #DVDTK001. Directed by Kunihisa Sugishima. Screenplay by Ryota Yamaguchi.

The Mishima Conglomerate is up to no good and Hong Kong International Police agent Jun Kazama knows it. Invited to a martial arts tournament by the head of the Conglomerate himself, Heihachi Mishima, Jun heads off to a secret island with memories of the past haunting her. Years prior, Jun watched Heihachi throw his young son Kazuya off a cliff to test his toughness. Scarred forever by his father's cruelty, Kazuya seeks revenge at the Conglomerate tournament. A cast of fighters with an assortment of motives battle across difficult terrain and unlikely odds as the tournament forges on. Will Jun uncover the Conglomerate's clandestine plans? Will Kazuya get his revenge and kill his father before his adopted brother unleashes his secret weapons?

Tekken: The Motion Picture is fairly entertaining, but isn't terribly unique or memorable. Fans of the video game may be disappointed by the limited cast of characters that appear in the film, but the fight scenes are well animated and accompanied by a high-energy audio track of rock bands.

The disc includes character biographies and a gallery of still art from the film. The fighting can get a bit violent, but not enough to warrant keeping the kids away. [BR]

SPECIAL FEATURES Character Bios • Character and Art Galleries • Trailers • Other Title Trailers TECHNICAL FEATURES Fullscreen (1.33:1) • Subtitles/CC: Eng., Span. • Languages: Jap., Eng. dub, Fren. dub • Sound: Dolby Digital 5.1 • Keepcase • 1 Disc

• Region All GENRE & RATING Martial Arts/Action • Not Rated (Teens)

Televoid

Simitar, 1997, 60 mins., #7320.

Skully is a skeleton who is bored with television. But when he clicks on an unknown channel, he is sucked into the Televoid. In this land of CGI, he witnesses living nightmares such as robots with guns for heads, organic tunnels, bizarre machines, spaceship thrill-rides, a tour of an ancient Egyptian pyramid, mad scientists, and more.

Another in the line of CGI anthologies, *Televoid* attempts to be freaky for freakiness's sake. The music is moody and creepy at times, and at others boring gothic/new age material. And although the stop-motion Skully and a few segments are fun, the program loses coherency by constantly jumping back to Skully mid-segment. Often, just when a segment starts to get interesting, the picture will go back to Skully watching, then off to some new segment.

The audience for *Televoid* is clearly the stoner goth teenager demographic, so if that's what you're into—or you just like creepy CGI—track down this out-of-print DVD.

SPECIAL FEATURES None TECHNICAL FEATURES Widescreen (multi-aspect) • Fullscreen (1.33:1) • Languages: Eng. • Sound: PCM Stereo • Box Sleeve with Jewel Case • 1 Disc • Region All GENRE & RATING CGI/Anthology • Not Rated (Kids)

Tenamonya Voyagers

Bandai, 2000, 100 mins., #1520. Directed by Akiyuki Shinbo. Written by Ryoei Tsukimura, Masashi Kubota.

It's the distant future and intergalactic cops are hunting down powerful space pirate syndicates. For the pretty, bespectacled teacher Ayako Hanabishi, her trip was supposed to be the start of a wonderful career at a new school. For Wakana Nanamiya, the trip began with a full athletic scholarship. For Peraila, whose fiery hair matches her fiery personality, her trip was a way to sneak off-world. These three women are stuck together whether they like it or not, all because Peraila has this little problem: She's a wanted criminal and space pirate. Of course the police are after her, with their most persistent and dangerous female detective leading them, and so are the heads of the intergalactic crime syndicate. Can the three girls escape from the clutches of the determined space detective and the syndicate hit men?

This four-episode OVA was released in 1999. It's a mix of goofy comedy, girls in revealing outfits, and space police action. The whole mix works pretty well for an evening of entertainment. The animation is fluid and seems to have some computer work in it. The only real downside to this series is that it never really gets to a conclusion. But the episodes you do get are perfect no-brain fun.

The transfer on this DVD is pretty impressive. It's a recent series, so it looks clean. You get a bonus art gallery that features many of the revealing outfits from the series. There is a high cheesecake factor, and some brief nudity. [RJM]

SPECIAL FEATURES Character and Art Galleries • Clean Credits • Other Title Trailers TECHNICAL FEATURES Fullscreen (1.33:1) • Subtitles/CC: Eng. • Languages: Jap., Eng. dub • Sound: Dolby Digital Surround 2.0 • Keepcase • 1 Disc • Region 1 GENRE & RATING Science Fiction/Cheesecake/Comedy • Rated 13+

Tenchi Forever! The Movie

Pioneer, 1999, 95 mins., #PIVA-1392V. Directed by Hiroshi Negishi. Screenplay by Masaharu Ayano.

After yet another one of Ayeka and Ryoko's fights, Tenchi walks into the mountains and disappears. Consumed with concern, the two girls join forces and search tirelessly all over Japan for their missing friend. Ryoko finally locates Tenchi in Tokyo, where the two girls take jobs as waitresses. Strangely, Tenchi looks several years older and lives with a mysterious girl named Haruna. He appears to have slipped into an alternate world, having lost all memory of his friends and family. Tenchi loves Haruna, but something doesn't seem right. Before Tenchi is lost forever, Ryoko and Ayeka must fight to draw Tenchi back to reality.

This 1999 film was billed as the third and last of the *Tenchi* movies, and the close of the *Tenchi Muyo!* franchise. Appropriately, the movie is a mature, somber rendering of the classic *Tenchi* characters in appearance, dialogue, and action. There's no comedic romp in this film to put *Tenchi* fans at ease. The film wraps up the tale with an emotional love story and a conclusion that answers some questions posed by the series.

This disc features a sparkling clear THX audio track and more explicit nudity and sex scenes than one might expect in a *Tenchi* movie. [BR]

SPECIAL FEATURES Character and Art Galleries • Trailers • Easter Egg TECHNICAL FEATURES Widescreen (1.85:1 enhanced for 16x9) • Subtitles/CC: Eng. • Languages: Jap., Eng. dub • Sound: Dolby Digital 5.1 • Keepcase • 1 Disc • Region 1, 4 GENRE & RATING Romance/Comedy/Action • Not Rated (Teens)

Tenchi in Tokyo: A New Start [#1]

Pioneer, 1999, 100 mins., #PIDA-7121V. Directed by Yoshiro Takamoto. Script by Pratanasu.

In modern-day Japan, Tenchi is a young man living outside Tokyo with his father and grandfather. There is also a whole bunch of girls living in his house. There's Ryoko, the rowdy blue-haired space pirate. Purple-haired Space-princess Ayeka and her sweet little sister Sasami have taken up residence with their pet the rabbit/cat Ryo-Oki. Two space police, the serious Kiyone and the bumbling blonde Mihoshi, are also there. And rounding out the group is the greatest scientist in the galaxy, the pink-haired Washu. Now for some reason or another these girls are all very attached to Tenchi, which makes it hard for the poor boy to do anything alone. So when the opportunity comes up for him to travel to Tokyo, he jumps at it. Now he's off in the big city, going to school and even catching the eye of the pretty but shy Sakuya. But the peace can't last, as the alien girls start showing up and chaos ensues.

This disc contains four episodes of the 1997 television series. This is the third separate incarnation of the *Tenchi* series and it begins to feel like the producers are stretching a by-now familiar premise to its limit. The animation style is completely different and much more cartoonish. The characters often go from normal to super-deformed at the drop of a hat. The music is reminiscent of *Scooby-Doo* background material. On the other hand, this disc does contain some very funny situations and introduces the most normal girl in the *Tenchi* canon, Sakuya. She actually seems to be the perfect fit for our hero.

Being a recent series, the DVD transfer is nice and clean. There is nothing really offensive in this series, except for some cartoon violence and brief nudity. [RJM]

SPECIAL FEATURES Character and Art Galleries TECHNICAL FEATURES Fullscreen (1.33:1) • Subtitles/CC: Eng. • Languages: Jap., Eng. dub • Sound: Dolby Digital 2.0 • Keepcase • 1 Disc • Region 1 GENRE & RATING Romance/Comedy/Action • Rated 13+

Tenchi in Tokyo: A New Friend [#2]

Pioneer, 1999, 75 mins., #PIDA-7122V. Directed by Yoshiro Takamoto. Script by Pratanasu.

This disc contains one of the funniest episodes in the series. In "Money! Money! Money!" the girls realize that they have no money to live on their own, so they attempt to get jobs in Tokyo. Of course comedy ensues as each girl attempts to work . . . and runs into Tenchi (who is trying to ignore them). "Play Date" features Sasami and her new pal Yugi, and something is definitely up here. The final episode is the first of a two-parter that shows how all the alien girls came to live on earth and why they are crazy about Tenchi. [RJM]

SPECIAL FEATURES Character and Art Galleries TECHNICAL FEATURES Fullscreen (1.33:1) • Subtitles/CC: Eng. • Languages: Jap., Eng. dub • Sound: Dolby Digital 2.0 • Keepcase • 1 Disc • Region 1 GENRE & RATING Romance/Comedy/Action • Rated 13+

Tenchi in Tokyo: A New Legend [#3]

Pioneer, 1999, 75 mins., #PIDA-7123V. Directed by Yoshiro Takamoto. Script by Pratanasu.

The two-part episode concludes in this disc. "Tenchi Anniversary" finishes the tale of how the girls arrive on Earth and get involved with Tenchi. During a celebration, Sakuya arrives, and things get a bit ugly. The next episode, "The Guardians of Old," is about the discovery of large wooden guardians. Fans of *El Hazard* might recognize a character from that series in this episode. "Ryoko's Big Date" follows the space pirate and her date with Tenchi. Of all the alien girls, she might be the one with some chemistry with Tenchi. Well-handled, this is one of the best and more serious shows in the series. [RJM]

SPECIAL FEATURES Promotional Footage • Clean Credits TECHNICAL FEATURES Fullscreen (1.33:1) • Subtitles/CC: Eng. • Languages: Jap., Eng. dub • Sound: Dolby Digital 2.0 • Keepcase • 1 Disc • Region 1, 4 GENRE & RATING Romance/Comedy/Action • Rated 13+

Tenchi in Tokyo: A New Enemy [#4]

Pioneer, 1999, 75 mins., #PIDA-7124V. Directed by Yoshiro Takamoto. Script by Pratanasu.

We know that Yugi is trying to split up Tenchi and the girls, so now she gets to work and her first target is . . . Ryo-Oki? "Moon Mission" has the characters journeying to the moon to find their faithful cabbit, who turns out to be not so faithful: She's fallen in love with another cabbit from the moon. In "Stupid Cupid," Yugi makes a clone of Tenchi's dad and has him try to keep Sakuya and Tenchi together. But he's just not cut out for the task. The final episode of the disc is "The Eye of the Destroyer," which focuses on Ryoko and Yugi's plan to get her away from Tenchi's group. [RJM]

SPECIAL FEATURES Music Video TECHNICAL FEATURES Fullscreen

(1.33:1) • Subtitles/CC: Eng. • Languages: Jap., Eng. dub • Sound: Dolby Digital 2.0 • Keepcase • 1 Disc • Region 1, 4 GENRE & RATING Romance/Comedy/Action • Rated 13+

Tenchi in Tokyo: A New Love [#5]

Pioneer, 1999, 75 mins., #PIDA-7125V. Directed by Yoshiro Takamoto. Script by Pratanasu.

This disc has three solid episodes that mix the best of the comedy and drama together. The show hits its stride here, but after this climax, things start to go downhill. "Tokyo or Bust!" follows Ayeka and Sasami as they try to journey to Tokyo to see Tenchi without the rest of the girls finding out. They run into a tough biker chick who seems to want to help them . . . or does she? "Love Match" begins a two-part school festival story, giving you not only wacky festival hijinks, but some wrestling action to boot. The final episode on the disc, "Carnival!" wraps things up. So much happens to poor Tenchi and Sakuya; can he forgive his alien girls this time? [RJM]

SPECIAL FEATURES Promotional Footage • Music Video TECHNICAL FEATURES Fullscreen (1.33:1) • Subtitles/CC: Eng. • Languages: Jap., Eng. dub • Sound: Dolby Digital 2.0 • Keepcase • 1 Disc • Region 1, 4 GENRE & RATING Romance/Comedy/Action • Rated 13+

Tenchi in Tokyo: A New Challenge [#6]

Pioneer, 1999, 75 mins., #PIDA-7126V. Directed by Nobuhiro Takamoto. Screenplay by Sumio Uetake, Masashi Kubota, Hideki Mitsui. Script by Pratanasu.

This disc completes Yugi's plan of driving Tenchi away from his alien pals and into the arms of Sakuya. But what does the sweet girl have to do with the main villain? "Drifting Away" occurs right after the events of the festival. Ryoko, after seeing Tenchi and Sakuya together, decides that she had better leave the planet and return to piracy. "Game Over" follows Ryoko and her new and improved life of crime with Hotsuma (Yugi's henchman). Meanwhile, the Galaxy Police organization promotes both Kiyone and Mihoshi. Then, in "The Lonely Princess," Ayeka loses her cool and wants things to return to normal, but no one seems to want to cooperate. [RJM]

SPECIAL FEATURES Character and Art Galleries TECHNICAL FEATURES Fullscreen (1.33:1) • Subtitles/CC: Eng. • Languages: Jap., Eng. dub • Sound: Dolby Digital 2.0 • Keepcase • 1 Disc • Region 1, 4 GENRE & RATING Romance/Comedy/Action • Rated 13+

Tenchi in Tokyo: A New Career [#7]

Pioneer, 1999, 75 mins., #PIDA-7127V. Directed by Nobuhiro Takamoto. Screenplay by Yoshimichi Hosoi, Hideki Mitsui. Script by Pratanasu.

Things are coming to a climax in *Tenchi in Tokyo*. "Old Friends" follows Kiyone and Mihoshi as they go undercover into Ryoko and Hotsuma's hideout. Can the old friends come to an understanding? "Real Friends?" is all about fun in the sun, and a summer vacation. But when Washu comes up with some interesting information on Yugi, Sasami doesn't want to believe that her new friend is the person that Washu claims she is. "Sakuya's Secret" begins to unravel the mystery behind Sakuya. She isn't what she seems to be, but does she really have feelings for Tenchi? [RJM]

SPECIAL FEATURES Character and Art Galleries TECHNICAL FEATURES Fullscreen (1.33:1) • Subtitles/CC: Eng. • Languages: Jap., Eng. dub • Sound: Dolby Digital 2.0 • Keepcase • 1 Disc • Region 1, 4 GENRE & RATING Romance/Comedy/Action • Rated 13+

Tenchi in Tokyo: A New Ending [#8]

Pioneer, 2000, 75 mins., #PIDA-7128V Directed by Nobuhiro Takamoto. Screenplay by Yoshimichi Hosoi, Masashi Kubota, Sumio Uetake, Mayori Sekijima. Script by Pratanasu.

This final disc of *Tenchi in Tokyo* has four episodes and wraps up all the situations. Things are a little less wacky and almost seem out of tone with the rest of series. Sakuya is unmasked and her true nature is revealed. Yugi unleashes her final plot and abducts Sasami. It's up to Tenchi and the gang to put aside their differences and take on Yugi. But do they even have a chance?

This incarnation of the *Tenchi* story is one of the weakest. Much of it seems to have been taken from the second and third movies. Sakuya is a great character and the one girl fans might have wanted Tenchi to end up with, but her handling lacks the emotional punch the creators seem to be going for. Finally, most of the series is more comedic than action-packed, meaning that when viewers get to "the final battle" section of the story, it just seems a bit flat. While the series could be fun, it just doesn't come together often enough to work. [RJM]

SPECIAL FEATURES Character and Art Galleries • Clean Credits TECHNICAL FEATURES Fullscreen (1.33:1) • Subtitles/CC: Eng. • Languages: Jap., Eng. dub • Sound: Dolby Digital 2.0 • Keepcase • 1 Disc • Region 1, 4 GENRE & RATING Romance/Comedy/Action • Rated 13+

Tenchi Muyo! DVD Ultimate Edition

Pioneer, 1999, 420 mins., #PIDA-1001V. Directed by Hiroki Hayashi, Kenichi Yatagai. Screenplay by Toshio Henmi, Yasue Funami.

Young Tenchi Masaki lives with his dopey father and spends his days helping his stately grandfather manage the family temple. One day, he steals the keys to an old shrine where an ancestor of his was alleged to have defeated a demon. He enters the shrine and finds a mysterious sword, but in doing so breaks the seals imprisoning the demon. But as it turns out, the demon is really a space pirate in exile named Ryoko, and she's quite fond of Tenchi. Before the bewildered young man has a chance to react, alien princesses Ayeka and Sasami descend from the skies, followed by the brainless space policewoman Mihoshi and genius inventor Washu. All of these attractive young women end up living with Tenchi, who finds out that he's really the heir to the throne of Jurai, a planet across the galaxy. Not surprisingly, Tenchi has absolutely no idea what to do with his newfound powers and harem of beautiful girls.

If the fact that Tenchi is surrounded by pretty girls who all like him seems familiar, it's because *Tenchi Muyo!* (which literally means "No Need for Tenchi," among other things) actually started the anime trend that has since been repeated in popular fare like *Hand Maid May* and *Love Hina*. This thirteen-episode 1992 OVA series is an affable and charming situation comedy that ended up spawning a slew of sequels and imitators. It's easy to see why; the characters are well-defined, the stories fun and engaging, and the animation is excellent. *Tenchi Muyo!* has aired on the Cartoon Network and remains popular today.

This box set is a good example of how DVDs should be handled. It features completely remastered audio and video, which results in a beautiful-looking release with a deafening THX audio mix. All thirteen episodes are in the set, which also includes an extra "Tenchi Encyclopedia" disc, chock full of facts and figures about the series (split into four areas: Personal Files, Visual Records, Geographical Data, and Secret Files). Pioneer gave *Tenchi Muyo!* the royal treatment with this release, and it shows. [MT]

SPECIAL FEATURES Character Bios • Character and Art Galleries • Production Notes • Pencil Tests • Digital Comics • Trailer • Promotional Footage • Other Title Trailers • Easter Egg TECHNICAL FEATURES Fullscreen (1.33:1) • Subtitles/CC: Eng. • Languages: Jap., Eng. dub • Sound: Dolby Digital 2.0 • Foldout Case with Plastic Slipcover • 3 Discs • Region 1, 4 GENRE & RATING Romance/Comedy/Action • Not Rated (Teens)

Tenchi the Movie: Tenchi Muyo in Love

Pioneer, 1997, 95 mins., #PIDA-1390V. Directed by Hiroshi Negishi. Written by Ryoei Tsukimura, Hiroshi Nigeshi.

Tenchi and his alien girls star in their first full-fledged movie, which takes place after the events of the *Tenchi Universe* television series. Tenchi's at home watching some home movies of his mom back in 1970 when he begins to disappear. Yep, he becomes transparent and starts to cry out in pain . . . you know, the usual. Scientific genius Washu discovers that supercriminal Kain has escaped from Galaxy Police headquarters and has traveled back in time to kill Tenchi's mother. Why is he picking on Tenchi? That and other secrets are revealed when the whole gang travels back in time and tries to stop Kain. Can Ryoko and Ayeka stop fighting over Tenchi long enough to cooperate? Will Mihoshi make a good teacher? How good is Kiyone's shooting? Will Sasami and Ryo-Oki be cute enough to save the day? Watch this disc and find out.

This 1996 movie is big and bold. It's got some great visuals, and features some classic *Tenchi* moments. But it's missing something, mostly the fun character interaction that made the OVA series and the first television series so entertaining. The plot is your basic *Terminator* meets *Tenchi* tale. Time travel storylines can be hard to pull off effectively, and this one just doesn't do the job. The producers were clearly going for the "wow" factor, and they achieve it at times, but the movie eventually loses its charm and ends up pretty, but cold.

This is a great print, especially for an early DVD title, and it has a 5.1 audio track that will wow you. This move has brief nudity and some violence , but if you watched the OVA series and weren't offended, this will be just fine. [RJM]

SPECIAL FEATURES Interview with Composer • Text Interview with Directors • Composer Bio • Trailers • Promotional Footage • Original Japanese Closing • Song Lyrics • Episode Guide • Easter Egg TECHNICAL FEATURES Widescreen (1.85:1 enhanced for 16x9) • Subtitles/CC: Eng. • Languages: Jap., Eng. dub • Sound: Dolby Digital 5.1 • Keepcase • 1 Disc • Region 1, 4 GENRE & RATING Romance/Comedy/Action • Not Rated (Teens)

Tenchi the Movie 2: The Daughter of Darkness

Pioneer, 1998, 60 mins., #PIDA-7075V. Directed by Satoshi Kimura. Written by Naoko Hasegawa.

On a midsummer night long ago on the planet Jurai, a young Yosho met an odd creature who tried to give him a gift. But before he could reciprocate the creature's kindness, royal guards chased her off. Years later, a young girl named Mayuka appears at the Masaki house calling Tenchi her father. Predictably, Ryoko and Ayeka erupt in fits of jealousy, fomented by Washu's confirmation that Mayuka's DNA shows that Tenchi really is the girl's dad. Mayuka's mysterious origins begin to reveal themselves as it becomes clear she's a tool of the demon Yuzuha who seeks to bring Tenchi to her Nightmare World so she can get her revenge. Tenchi is soon in a struggle to save himself, while also fighting to save his supposed daughter.

This disc includes the "Tenchi Encyclopedia," which is chock full of the ins and outs of the many incarnations of the *Tenchi Muyo!* world and its characters. Even if you're familiar with *Tenchi Muyo!*, there's interesting stuff in the here, broken down into sections for Tenchi's Garden, House of Jurai, Galaxy Police, Jewels, and Subspace Network. [BR]

SPECIAL FEATURES Massive Tenchi Encyclopedia with Bios and Art • Trailers • Promotional Footage • Easter Eggs TECHNICAL FEATURES Widescreen (1.85:1 enhanced for 16x9) • Subtitles/CC: Eng., Jap. • Languages: Jap., Eng. dub • Sound: Dolby Digital 5.1 • Keepcase • 1 Disc • Region 1, 4 GENRE & RATING Romance/Comedy/Action • Not Rated (Teens)

Tenchi Universe: On Earth I [#1]

Pioneer, 2000, 100 mins., #110461. Directed by Hiroshi Negishi. Screenplay by Ryoei Tsukimura, Satoru Nishizono, Yosuke Kuroda, Yosuke Kuroda.

Poor, shy Tenchi Masaki has problems communicating with girls his own age, so what's he going to do when five female aliens end up in his life and begin developing feelings for him? As if living in the family shrine with his father and grandfather weren't tough enough, now he has to deal with alien houseguests! A space pirate named Ryoko, the galaxy cop named Mihoshi trying to bring her in, wayward space princess Ayeka, her little sister Sasami, and a mad scientist named Washu all take up residence in the Masaki household. The extraterrestrial teens cause conflicts, trouble, and lots of laughs. All the girls—even preteen Sasami—develop crushes on Tenchi and fight for his attention. Besides breaking up cat-fights and keeping the girls from destroying his home, Tenchi becomes involved in galactic-sized problems as other aliens are looking for some of the girls for nefarious reasons of their own.

Tenchi Universe is a collection of the second season of the popular *Tenchi Muyo!* TV series. The *Tenchi* saga began life as a series of OVAs in 1992. The popularity of the OVAs led to the development of three different anime series, a manga series, more OVAs, and several video games.

This DVD contains episodes #1–4 and introduces the main characters. It gives viewers a taste of the zaniness to come, and more than adequately provides all the pertinent information necessary to enjoy future episodes of the series. [JMC]

SPECIAL FEATURES Character Bios • Character and Art Galleries • Clean Credits TECHNICAL FEATURES Fullscreen (1.33:1) • Subtitles/CC: Eng. • Languages: Jap., Eng. dub • Sound: Dolby Digital 2.0 • Keepcase • 1 Disc • Region 1, 4 GENRE & RATING Romance/Comedy/Action • Rated 13+

Tenchi Universe: On Earth II [#2]

Pioneer, 2000, 75 mins., #10462. Directed by Hiroshi Negishi. Screenplay by Ryoei Tsukimura.

Respecting your local police is awfully hard when the resident space officer is a bumbling ditz. Mihoshi was the object of ridicule and scorn from her peers, and her partner, Galaxy cop Kiyone, was overjoyed when Mihoshi disappeared. Kiyone isn't thrilled, though, when her boss orders her to go find Mihoshi, and she heads to Earth. Once she finds Mihoshi, though, will it be off again to protect the galaxy, or will Kiyone find more than she bargained for on Earth?

This DVD contains episodes #5–7 and introduces Kiyone, one of the more serious women in Tenchi's life. [JMC]

SPECIAL FEATURES Character Bios • Character and Art Galleries • Clean Credits TECHNICAL FEATURES Fullscreen (1.33:1) • Subtitles/CC: Eng. • Languages: Jap., Eng. dub • Sound: Dolby Digital 2.0 • Keepcase • 1 Disc • Region 1, 4 GENRE & RATING Romance/Comedy/Action • Rated 13+

Tenchi Universe: On Earth III [#3]

Pioneer, 2000, 75 mins., #10463. Directed by Hiroshi Negishi. Screenplay by Ryoei Tsukimura, Yosuke Kuroda.

Why do all mad scientists insist on playing Dr. Frankenstein at one time or another? Washu tries to create life but her experiment goes horribly astray. When she creates a robot in her image, it gets a mix of brains and per-sonality from both Washu and Mihoshi. How's the gang going to stand up against a crazy air-headed robot? As if facing Washu's monster isn't trouble enough, the group gets visitors from outer space, a terrible bounty hunter named Naga, who's looking to collect the price on Ryoko's head.

Robots, bounty hunters, and aliens, oh my! The third *Tenchi Universe* DVD collects episodes #8–10, the end of the "On Earth" saga. [JMC]

SPECIAL FEATURES Character Bios • Character and Art Galleries • Clean Credits TECHNICAL FEATURES Fullscreen (1.33:1) • Subtitles/CC: Eng. • Languages: Jap., Eng. dub • Sound: Dolby Digital 2.0 • Keepcase • 1 Disc • Region 1, 4 GENRE & RATING Romance/Comedy/Action • Rated 13+

Tenchi Universe: Time and Space Adventures [#4]

Pioneer, 2000, 75 mins., #10464. Directed by Hiroshi Negishi. Screenplay by Ryoei Tsukimura.

All scientists spend their time thinking of creations to help mankind and better the human race. Mad scientists think about stuff like that too, except for the helping and bettering parts. Washu invented the Dimensional Cause and Effect controller to grant the user's wishes, but she plans to be the only user! However, an experiment with the controller goes horribly wrong and Tenchi, Sasami, Mihoshi, Kiyone, Ayeka, and Washu find themselves blinking through time and space in a variety of roles. The characters wind up in different times, planets, themes, and situations. Each woman gets to live out her fantasy—or in some cases fantasies—but they're not all the girls hoped they would be. Ryoko goes from being a devil to a gangster, Bonnie to Tenchi's Clyde. Kiyone becomes a world famous private detective. Mihoshi is a "perfect" housewife, and Sasami transforms into her ideal self, Pretty Sami, a superheroine. It's a wild, zany, outrageous adventure, filled with camp, lightheartedness, and other factors that make *Tenchi* a consistently fun adventure.

Besides throwing the cast through dimensions and showing them that wish fulfillment might not be all it's cracked up to be, this series also included the first appearance of Pretty Sami, an alternative version of Sasami from the OVAs, who hadn't appeared in this "reality" yet.

Containing the fan-favorite three-part "Time and Space Adventures," this hysterical collection of episodes #11–13 is one not to be missed. [JMC]

SPECIAL FEATURES Character Bios • Character and Art Galleries • Promotional Footage TECHNICAL FEATURES Fullscreen (1.33:1) • Subtitles/CC: Eng. • Languages: Jap., Eng. dub • Sound: Dolby Digital 2.0 • Keepcase • 1 Disc • Region 1, 4 GENRE & RATING Romance/Comedy/Action • Rated 13+

Tenchi Universe: Space I [#5]

Pioneer, 2000, 75 mins., #10465. Directed by Hiroshi Negishi. Screenplay by Ryoei Tsukimura.

Kiyone finally gets a new assignment from headquarters and is able to leave Earth and her former partner Mihoshi behind. Tenchi and pals want to throw her a good-bye party, but there's hardly time as Ryoko, Ayeka, and Sasami are kidnapped by the underlings of Emperor Yosho. He's the new ruler of Ayeka and Sasami's home planet, Jurai, and he's trying to solidify his role as ruler by eliminating the competition. He frames Ayeka and Sasami as traitors who supposedly conspired with Ryoko to ruin their planet. It's guilt by association as Kiyone, Mihoshi, Washu, and soon, Tenchi, find themselves on the most-wanted list across the galaxy. Determined to rescue their friends, the gang sets off to free Ayeka, Sasami, and Ryoko. But can a group of teens from across the galaxy outsmart the Jurai Military and the Galaxy Police?

The beginning of the *Tenchi Muyo in Space* saga is on this action-packed DVD, filled with revelations, betrayals, and great escapes. Tenchi and pals are in for the battle of their young lives across the galaxy and viewers have a front row seat.

Although some of the humor and camp is still present, this part of the *Tenchi* story is of a more serious nature. Collected on this DVD are episodes #14–16, the beginning of the Great Jurai Conspiracy. [JMC]

SPECIAL FEATURES Character Bios • Character and Art Galleries • Inserts: Finger Puppets TECHNICAL FEATURES Fullscreen (1.33:1) • Subtitles/CC: Eng. • Languages: Jap., Eng. dub • Sound: Dolby Digital 2.0 • Keepcase • 1 Disc • Region 1, 4 GENRE & RATING Romance/Comedy/Action • Rated 13+

Tenchi Universe: Space II [#6]

Pioneer, 2001, 75 mins., #10466. Directed by Hiroshi Negishi. Screenplay by Yosuke Kuroda, Naoko Hasegawa, Masamichi Sekijima.

Traveling through the galaxy as fugitives is tough, especially when you run low on supplies and the ship needs repairs. The easily tempted Ryoko goes shopping, but will she buy necessities or whatever catches her eye? Then Sasami meets and befriends a young ghost from a "dead" ship near theirs, but is she truly a friend? Finally a pair of delinquents steals the ship and unknowingly alerts the Galaxy Police to Tenchi and his friends' position. Now the gang has to avoid the police *and* recover their ship!

This DVD contains episodes #17–19. [JMC]

SPECIAL FEATURES Character Bios • Character and Art Galleries

TECHNICAL FEATURES Fullscreen (1.33:1) • Subtitles/CC: Eng. • Languages: Jap., Eng. dub • Sound: Dolby Digital 2.0 • Keepcase • 1 Disc • Region 1, 4 GENRE & RATING Romance/Comedy/Action • Rated 13+

Tenchi Universe: Space III [#7]

Pioneer, 2001, 75 mins., #11467. Directed by Hiroshi Negishi. Screenplay by Ryoei Tsukimura, Yosuke Kuroda.

The gang's trying to raise funds to repair their ship, again, so they enter a swimsuit competition. But money might be the least of their concerns when Nagi returns, still trying to collect the bounty on Ryoko's head. Then, as they near Jurai, the group splits up at a checkpoint and tries to discover information. They're soon in way over their head, but can a mysterious stranger pull their fat out of the collective fire? Then, the gang's fighting for their lives in space against the Jurai forces, when the stranger directs them to a safe haven and tells them to revive two legendary knights, Azaka and Kamidake.

This character-driven DVD containing episodes #20–22 adds a few more members to the cast and reveals some interesting surprises. [JMC]

SPECIAL FEATURES Character Bios • Character and Art Galleries TECHNICAL FEATURES Fullscreen (1.33:1) • Subtitles/CC: Eng. • Languages: Jap., Eng. dub • Sound: Dolby Digital 2.0 • Keepcase • 1 Disc • Region 1, 4 GENRE & RATING Romance/Comedy/Action • Rated 13+

Tenchi Universe: The Last Battle [#8]

Pioneer, 2001, 100 mins., #10468. Directed by Hiroshi Negishi. Screenplay by Ryoei Tsukimura.

Tenchi learns he's part of the royal bloodline of Jurai and maybe the only one able to restore peace and order to the planet in turmoil. The emperor of Jurai battles the evil Kagato and is defeated. Then Kagato kidnaps Akane and has plans of his own for the princess. Tenchi vows to rescue Akane no matter what the cost. Ryoko is terrified, thinking the inexperienced Tenchi will die if he faces Kagato. She begs him to forget Jurai and leave with her now. He refuses, so she helps him and the two knights get to the surface of Jurai. Ryoko's gravely injured in the process and flies off, leaving Tenchi and the knights to battle their way into Kagato's stronghold. The knights sacrifice themselves in order for Tenchi to make it to Kagato. Kagato challenges Tenchi to a sword fight, and the fate of Jurai, Akane, and, perhaps, the galaxy, now rests on the shoulders of the teenager. Is Tenchi up for the battle or will this be the end of our hero?

Although filled with lots of action, seriousness, and drama, the series does end on a high note. The final episode of the series ties up loose ends quite nicely . . . at least until the next series, and the movies, and . . .

This powerful DVD contains the final four episodes, #23–26 and was later made into an OVA with more footage added to the fight scene between Tenchi and Kagato. [JMC]

SPECIAL FEATURES Character Bios • Character and Art Galleries • Inserts: Finger Puppets TECHNICAL FEATURES Fullscreen (1.33:1) • Subtitles/CC: Eng. • Languages: Jap., Eng. dub • Sound: Dolby Digital 2.0 • Keepcase • 1 Disc • Region 1, 4 GENRE & RATING Romance/Comedy/Action • Rated 13+

Tenchi Universe: The Complete DVD Box Set

Pioneer, 2001, 800 mins., #11605.

This box set contains all eight commercially released keepcase editions in an illustrated cardboard box. See individual entries for the Special and Technical Features listings.

TECHNICAL FEATURES Cardboard Box with 8 Keepcases • 8 Discs • Region 1, 4 GENRE & RATING Romance/Comedy/Action •

Rated 13+

Terry Pratchett's Discworld: Wyrd Sisters [#1]

Acorn Media, 2000, 140 mins., #54961-83749. Directed by Jean Flynn. Adapted by Martin Jameson. Based on the novel by Terry Pratchett.

On the back of an immense star turtle are four giant elephants, which carry on their shoulders a place known as Discworld. On this world lives a very human civilization, except that magic and magical creatures are a part of everyday life. A trio of witches known as the Wyrd Sisters—not a name they like much—is entrusted to take care of a murdered king's baby, but the resulting chaos sees them accused of evil-doing, not to mention dealing with guest appearances by Charlie Chaplin and the Marx Brothers!

Terry Pratchett's *Discworld* series was called "the finest set of pure comedies the genre has yet seen" in *The Encyclopedia of Science Fiction*. Beginning with *The Color of Magic* in 1983, Pratchett has written over two dozen *Discworld* novels and companion books, of which *Wyrd Sisters* (1988) was the sixth. In 1996, *Discworld* was animated in England and aired on television as a mini-series. The result had some wonderful voice work—including Christopher Lee as Death—but the animation itself is rather simplistic and doesn't give the characters much weight. Some fans have complained that seeing Pratchett's humor onscreen is nowhere near as much fun as reading it. Your mileage may vary.

The DVD contains the complete production of *Wyrd Sisters*, as well an introduction to the series, "Welcome to Discworld."

SPECIAL FEATURES Character Bios • Creator Bio • Storyboards • Book Listing TECHNICAL FEATURES Fullscreen (1.33:1) • Languages: Eng. • Sound: Dolby Digital 2.0 • Keepcase • 1 Disc • Region 1–6 GENRE & RATING Fantasy/Adventure/Comedy • Not Rated (Teens)

Terry Pratchett's Discworld: Soul Music [#2]

Acorn Media, 2001, 175 mins., #54961-46229. Directed by Jean Flynn. Adapted by Martin Jameson. Based on the novel by Terry Pratchett.

On Discworld, the skeletal figure of Death rides a horse named Binky, and he has a teenage granddaughter, Susan. So when Death decides to take a holiday, leaving Susan in charge of his duties, you can imagine that things might not go well. Especially when she becomes involved with Buddy, a teenage boy who longs to form a rock band. He does so, with the help of a magical guitar, a rocky troll, and a horn-playing dwarf. Hilarity ensues.

As mentioned in the previous entry, Terry Pratchett's *Discworld* series was adapted for British television in 1996–97. *Soul Music* was the seventeenth book in the series, released in 1994. The storyline—and music played by Buddy's band—is full of rock music trivia and homages. Those versed in '60s and '70s rock will get most of the humor; younger audiences might be left a bit in the dark.

The DVD contains the complete production of *Soul Music*, as well as a longer introduction to the series, "Welcome to Discworld." An extensive interview with creator Pratchett shows how pleased he was with the series and how faithful to its concepts he felt the animation was.

SPECIAL FEATURES Interview with Terry Pratchett • Cast Filmographies • Character Bios • Creator Bio • Storyboards • Book Listing TECHNICAL FEATURES Fullscreen (1.33:1) • Languages: Eng. • Sound: Dolby Digital 2.0 • Keepcase • 1 Disc • Region All GENRE & RATING Fantasy/Adventure/Comedy • Not Rated (Teens)

Thief and the Cobbler, The

Alliance Atlantis.

This DVD was not available for review. It was a Canadian release that was distributed as a cereal promotion!

This Metal Mind

Simitar, 1997, 40 mins., #7200.

This CGI anthology DVD was not available for review. The company is out of business.

Thomas and Friends: Best of Thomas [#1]

Anchor Bay, 2001, 46 mins., #DV11952. Directed by David Mitton. Adapted by Britt Allcroft. Based on the book series by the Rev. W. Awdry.

The Island of Sodor is a happy place, with farms, a harbor for fishing, a coal mine and quarry, and lots of roads and viaducts. But what it has the most of are trains! Sir Topham Hatt is the superintendent of the railway, and from the Station, he makes sure everything runs smoothly. Two young trains are very friendly: Thomas is a bit fussy and overeager, but he always pulls through, while James is very shiny and red and has a bit of a cocky attitude. Other friends include Harold the helicopter, Cranky the crane, Bulstrode the bad-tempered sea barge, and more.

Thomas the Tank Engine has been a star of children's books for around fifty years. In 1984, Britt Allcroft decided to bring *Thomas the Tank Engine and Friends* to life for British television; it later came to the United States to show on PBS in conjunction with spin-off series *Shining Time Station*. At first the series was hosted by Ringo Starr, then George Carlin, and eventually, Alec Baldwin. The *Thomas* segments are a cross between live-action models, puppetry, and stop-motion animation; often, the actions are created with miniature train models/puppets and live backgrounds and environments, but stop-motion is used in some cases to change the expression on a train's face.

This kid-friendly disc has eight *Thomas*-related short episodes, as well as four sing-alongs, three games, and a nifty twelve-page book with a chart showing all the trains, tractors, cars, boats, and other vehicles on Sodor Island.

SPECIAL FEATURES Character Bios • Sing-Alongs • Read-Alongs • Games • Other Title Trailers • Inserts: Booklet TECHNICAL FEATURES Fullscreen (1.33:1) • Languages: Eng. • Sound: Dolby Digital Surround 2.0 • Keepcase • 1 Disc • Region 1–6 GENRE & RATING Puppets/Trains/Education • Not Rated (All Ages)

Thomas and Friends: Best of James [#2]

Anchor Bay, 2002, 46 mins., #DV12103. Directed by David Mitton. Adapted by Britt Allcroft. Based on the book series by the Rev. W. Awdry.

Best known for his shiny red coat and his high-falutin' attitude, James likes to think of himself as a Really Splendid Engine. But as kids everywhere know, James really has a heart of gold to go with his big smile, and he always does the right thing.

This disc contains eight stories spotlighting James—as told by George Carlin—as well as four sing-alongs, three games, and a different twelve-page book from the one in *Best of Thomas*. And to delight young ruffians everywhere, it also includes temporary tattoos of Thomas and James!

SPECIAL FEATURES Character Bios • Sing-Alongs • Read-Alongs • Games • Other Title Trailers • Inserts: Booklet, Temporary Tattoo TECHNICAL FEATURES Fullscreen (1.33:1) • Languages: Eng. • Sound: Dolby Digital Surround 2.0 • Keepcase • 1 Disc • Region 1–6 GENRE & RATING Puppets/Trains/Education • Not Rated (All Ages)

Thomas and Friends: Make Someone Happy [#3]

Anchor Bay, 2002, 35 mins., #DV12109. Directed by Britt Allcroft. Story by Britt Allcroft, David Mitton. Based on the book series by the Rev. W. Awdry.

More train adventures commence with Thomas and his friends, James, Gordon, Percy, and others. Whether helping to build a playground for special children or delivering important packages, the trains all learn that working together and making others happy also serves to make themselves happy!

Six episodes are narrated by Alec Baldwin, and fans will enjoy two more sing-alongs and biographies of their favorite trains.

SPECIAL FEATURES Character Bios • Sing-Alongs • Other Title Trailers TECHNICAL FEATURES Fullscreen (1.33:1) • Languages: Eng. • Sound: Dolby Digital Surround 2.0 • Keepcase • 1 Disc • Region 1–6 GENRE & RATING Puppets/Trains/Education • Not Rated (All Ages)

Thomas and Friends: Best of Percy [#4]

Anchor Bay, 2002, 48 mins., #DV12168.

This DVD was not available for review.

Thomas and Friends: Races, Rescues and Runaways and other Thomas Adventures [#5]

Anchor Bay, 2002, 37 mins., #DV12169.

This DVD was not available for review.

Thomas and Friends: Cranky Bugs and Other Thomas Stories [#6]

Anchor Bay, 2002, 37 mins., #DV12170.

This DVD was not available for review.

Thomas and the Magic Railroad

Columbia/TriStar, 2001, 84 mins., #05426. Directed by Britt Allcroft. Written by Britt Allcroft. Based on the book series by the Rev. W. Awdry.

The Island of Sodor has always been a happy place, but sometimes bad things happen even to good trains. The evil Diesel #10 plans to use his powerful claw to wreck the other trains in an effort to control the ever-smaller supply of magical gold dust. A plucky young girl and her grandfather come to help Thomas, Mr. Conductor, and the other trains, before Diesel #10 can derail their futures!

Released in the summer of 2000, *Thomas and the Magic Railroad* was the first feature film for the *Thomas* cast. Starring Alec Baldwin as Mr. Conductor, the film used a variety of techniques to bring its story to life. Traditional model work was done for most of Thomas's scenes, although some scenes were filmed with CGI. Computer animation also enabled the human characters to interact with the trains, and added elements like the Magic Railroad and the important sparkling gold dust.

Kids and adult fans are likely to be just as enchanted with the *Thomas* movie as they are with the PBS series. The DVD features an ultra-crisp print and a handful of extras.

SPECIAL FEATURES Cast Filmographies • Deleted Scenes • Trailer • Other Title Trailers • Inserts: Liner Notes TECHNICAL FEATURES Fullscreen (1.33:1) • Subtitles/CC: Eng., Span. • Languages: Eng., Span. dub • Sound: Dolby Digital Surround 2.0 • Keepcase • 1 Disc • Region All GENRE & RATING Live/CGI/Puppets/Trains • Rated G

Those Who Hunt Elves: Ready, Set, Strip! [#1]

ADV Films, 2001, 150 mins., #DTW/001. Directed by Kazuyoshi Katayama. Screenplay by Masaharu Amiya, Masafumi Kubota, Yasutomo Yamada. Based on the manga series by Yutaka Yagami in *Dengeki Comic Gao.*

Junpei, Airi, and Ritsuko find themselves transported to an alternate universe, along with their T-74 tank. In their efforts to learn what's happened, they seek out the wisdom of elves. Attempting to send them back home, the High Elf Celsia performs an incantation. But when she is interrupted, the spell is fragmented and spread across the land as tattoos appearing on the bodies of female elves. The humans' only hope is to mount their tank and travel across the land, stripping every elf maiden they come across. With luck and determination, they might find all the missing pieces and go home.

First aired in 1998 on late-night Japanese television, *Those Who Hunt Elves* is a series that doesn't get too deep with the writing. That aside, it is witty, and at times hilarious, as the characters get to know each other and ponder why the young female elves are reluctant to strip on command. Additionally, each of the main players has an unhealthy obsession with something (Junpei with curried rice, Airi with herself, and Ritsuko with the tank) that adds up to laughs as episodes #1–6 progress on this DVD.

With attractive art and animation, as well as a fitting soundtrack and a decent job of voice acting, *Those Who Hunt Elves* measures up well against other anime. As you might expect, the series does have scenes with nude female elves, but it's not nearly as gratuitous as it sounds. All told, *Those Who Hunt Elves* is an entertaining and fun disc to watch. [GP]

SPECIAL FEATURES Character and Art Galleries • Clean Credits • Other Title Trailers • Inserts: VHS Cover Art TECHNICAL FEATURES Fullscreen (1.33:1) • Subtitles/CC: Eng. • Languages: Jap., Eng. dub, Span. dub • Sound: Dolby Digital 2.0 • Keepcase • 1 Disc • Region 1, 2, 4 GENRE & RATING Fantasy/Adventure/ Cheesecake • Rated 12+

Those Who Hunt Elves: Elf Stripping for Fun and Profit [#2]

ADV Films, 2002, 150 mins., #DTW/002. Directed by Kazuyoshi Katayama. Screenplay by Masaharu Amiya, Masafumi Kubota, Yasunori Yamada. Based on the manga series by Yutaka Yagami in *Dengeki Comic Gao.*

In their efforts to find the missing pieces of the spell they need to get home, our heroes Junpei, Airi, and Ritsuko continue to strip every elf that is unfortunate enough to get in their way. But the importance of their mission has changed a little. If they aren't sent home soon, both this world and Earth may be destroyed in an extra-large bang. Containing episodes #7–12, the *Those Who Hunt Elves* series comes to an exciting conclusion as the High Elf Celsia joins with our heroes and the clothes fly for the benefit of man and elf alike. [GP]

SPECIAL FEATURES Character and Art Galleries • Trailer • Other Title Trailers TECHNICAL FEATURES Fullscreen (1.33:1) • Subtitles/CC: Eng. • Languages: Jap., Eng. dub, Span. dub • Sound: Dolby Digital 2.0 • Keepcase • 1 Disc • Region 1, 2, 4 GENRE & RATING Fantasy/Adventure/Cheesecake • Rated 12+

3x3 Eyes: Collectors Edition

Pioneer, 2001, 270 mins., #10501. Directed by Daisuke Nishio, Kazuhisa Takenouchi, Seiko Sayama, Shigeru Nishiyama. Screenplay by Yuzo Takada, Kazuhisa Takenouchi, Akinori Endo. Based on the manga series by Yuzo Takada in *Young Magazine Weekly*.

Teenager Yakumo Fuji is the son of an explorer who was lost in Tibet. Unbeknownst to Yakumo, his dying father sent Pai to find him. Though she looks like a pudgy sixteen-year-old Tibetan girl, Pai is the physical vessel that holds the last of the Sanjiyan Unkara, powerful three-eyed demons. When the two teens collide—literally—Pai absorbs Yakumo's soul into her body, leaving him an immortal zombie. Pai wants to become fully human, but she must find the Statue of Ningen (Humanity) to do so. With Yakumo's help, and her own formidable demonic powers, Pai sets off on her quest.

This OVA series debuted in 1991 and 1992. Disc One is titled "Immortals" and contains the first four OVA episodes of the series: "Transmigration"; "Yakumo"; "Sacrifice"; and "Straying." Fans had to wait until 1995 to view the second part of the story, taking place four years later, with Pai still on a quest to become human, but now lacking the memory of ever having been a demon. Disc Two, titled "Legend of the Divine Demon," features the final three OVA chapters: "Descent"; "The Key"; and "The Return."

Popular with fans—who regularly beg for future animated installments to match the long-running manga series—*3X3 Eyes* is an enjoyable mixture of horror, comedy, and an odd romance. Much gore is shown whenever the zombie Yakumo is dispatched, so those with weak stomachs might beware.

SPECIAL FEATURES Cast Credits • Art Galleries • Insert; Temporary Tattoo • Easter Egg TECHNICAL FEATURES Fullscreen (1.33:1) • Subtitles/CC: Eng. • Languages: Jap., Eng. dub • Sound: Dolby Digital Stereo 2.0 • Multikeepcase • 2 Discs • Region 1 GENRE & RATING Horror/Comedy/Romance • Rated 16+

3-2-1 Penguins!—Trouble on Planet Wait-Your-Turn [Episode #1]

Big Ideas, 2002, 30 mins., #BIDVD2002. Directed by Ron Smith. Written by Mike Nawrocki, Phil Vicsher, Jeff Parker, Ron Smith, Nathan Carlson, Phil Loller.

Jason and Michelle Conrad are a pair of fraternal twins who are stuck at their grandmum's cottage for vacation, instead of going to SpaceCamp. Jason is miserable, especially when the video game console his parents bought for them can't be connected to the ancient TV. Grandmum tries to get them to learn patience, but later, they sneak into the attic, where they find a giant telescope and play with a toy spaceship and penguins. Soon, Jason is shrunk to small size and goes on a mission with spacefaring penguins named Zidgel, Midgel, Fidgel, and Kevin. They try to help a planet full of sentient vacuum cleaners whose planet has cut ahead of the others and will soon plunge into the sun.

This fully CGI series is aimed at a younger market than the *VeggieTales* series from the same creators (see entries). It has some cute and gentle humor, and hammers home lessons about manners and virtues with little subtlety. There are also a number of non-denominational religious references to the Bible and God. The animation and voice work are excellent.

The DVD itself is meager when it comes to the show itself, which is only a half-hour long. However, the extras are plentiful, and kids are likely to spend more than a half hour on them.

SPECIAL FEATURES Commentary Track by Penguins • Character Bios • Character and Art Galleries • Progression Reels • Promotional Footage • Music Video • Karaoke • Games • Recipes • How To Draw • DVD-ROM Features: Games • Other Title Trailers • Easter Eggs TECHNICAL FEATURES Fullscreen (1.33:1) • Subtitles/CC: Eng. • Languages: Eng. • Sound: Dolby Digital Surround 5.1 • Keepcase • 1 Disc • Region 1 GENRE & RATING CGI/Comedy/Science Fiction • Not Rated (Kids)

3-2-1 Penguins!—The Cheating Scales of Bullamanka [Episode #2]

Big Ideas, 2002, 60 mins., #BIDVD2003. Directed by Ron Smith. Written by Mike Nawrocki, Ron Smith. Story by Phil Vicsher.

This time out, Michelle goes into the wild blue yonder with the spacegoing flightless birds. She must play a game against the cheating Lizard King to save the Bandicoot King. Along the way, she'll learn that playing by the rules is important, especially when the game is Squid-Tac-Toe.

More cute jokes include some breaking of the fourth wall, clever wordplay, and some characters that could have come from a Dr. Seuss book. There's also more semireligious moralizing, more excellent CGI work, and lots of extra materials.

SPECIAL FEATURES Commentary Track by Penguins • Character Bios • Character and Art Galleries • Progression Reels • Promotional Footage • Music Video • Karaoke • Games • Recipes • How To Draw • DVD-ROM Features: Games • Other Title Trailers • Easter Eggs TECHNICAL FEATURES Fullscreen (1.33:1) • Subtitles/CC: Eng. • Languages: Eng. • Sound: Dolby Digital Surround 5.1 • Keepcase • 1 Disc • Region 1 GENRE & RATING CGI/Comedy/Science Fiction • Not Rated (Kids)

3-2-1 Penguins!—The Amazing Carnival of Complaining [Episode #3]

Big Idea, 2002, 60 mins., #BIDVD2000. Directed by Ron Smith. Written by Mike Nawrocki, Ron Smith with Tom Owens. Story by Phil Vischer, Mike Nawrocki, Ron Smith.

While Michelle and Grandmum sow seeds out in the garden, it's Jason's turn back aboard the Penguin spaceship. He gets to accompany them to Uncle Blobb's Amazing Carnival of Complaining, but it isn't nearly as much fun as it sounds. Why is Blobb sowing the seeds of discontent and turning the Penguins into complaining drones?

Heavier on the Biblical references than the previous discs, this is a less-pleasant episode, if only because everyone is in a bad mood. But as the show says, nobody likes to be around a complainer, so I'll just add that the extras are the usual batch of fun.

SPECIAL FEATURES Commentary Track by Penguins • Character Bios • Character and Art Galleries • Progression Reels • Promotional Footage • Music Video • Karaoke • Games • Recipes • How To Draw • DVD-ROM Features: Games • Other Title Trailers • Easter Eggs TECHNICAL FEATURES Fullscreen (1.33:1) • Subtitles/CC: Eng. • Languages: Eng. • Sound: Dolby Digital Surround 5.1 • Keepcase • 1 Disc • Region 1 GENRE & RATING CGI/Comedy/Science Fiction • Not Rated (Kids)

3-2-1 Penguins!—Runaway Pride at Lightstation Kilowatt [Episode #4]

Big Idea, 2002, 30 mins., #BIDVD2004. Directed by Ron Smith. Written by Tim Hodge, Ron Smith. Story by Keith Lango.

It's Michelle's turn to adventure with the penguins yet again. This time, they need to work as a team to help repair Lightstation Kilowatt, or the *F.S.S. Emperor* cargo ship may crash into a giant cosmic reef. What will this

adventure teach her about pride, and about asking others for help?

Like others in this series, this disc is full of fun extras, moral lessons, gentle humor, and imaginative CGI.

SPECIAL FEATURES Character Bios • Character and Art Galleries • Storyboards • Progression Reels • Promotional Footage • Music Video • Karaoke • Games • Recipes • How To Draw • DVD-ROM Features: Games • Other Title Trailers • Easter Eggs TECHNICAL FEATURES Fullscreen (1.33:1) • Subtitles/CC: Eng. • Languages: Eng. • Sound: Dolby Digital Surround 5.1 • Keepcase • 1 Disc • Region 1 GENRE & RATING CGI/Comedy/Science Fiction • Not Rated (Kids)

Three Caballeros, The

Disney, 2000, 72 mins., #19599. Directed by Norman Ferguson, Clyde Geronimi, Jack Kinney, Bill Roberts, Harold Young. Story by Homer Brightman, Ernest Terrazzas, Ted Sears, Bill Peet, Ralph Wright, Elmer Plummer, Roy Williams, William Cottrell, Del Connell, James Bodrero.

Donald Duck gets a film projector as a birthday gift, and begins watching movies from South America. First, he sees the story of a penguin that doesn't like the Antarctic and travels to warmer climates, then an aracuan bird walks out of the movie screen to greet Donald. Later, a young boy uses a flying donkey to win some races. Then, Donald looks at a pop-up book on Brazil, and his old parrot pal Joe Carioca drags him inside the book, whereupon he falls in love. Finally, while listening to Mexican music, Donald and Joe meet a charro rooster named Panchito, who shows them the wonders of Mexico, giving Donald a chance to ogle some beach beauties and engage in a mock bullfight.

If it sounds like *The Three Caballeros* is a sequel to *Saludos Amigos*, you're entirely correct. *The Three Caballeros* was released in 1945, the seventh feature-length animated film from Disney (and the first to follow *Saludos Amigos*). It would have been released closer to its predecessor, but the events of the Second World War made it difficult to obtain color prints. *The Three Caballeros* is fast-paced, but it's almost hallucinatory in its stream-of-consciousness imagery. A wide variety of Latin music (sixteen songs!) and dance styles are showcased, including several revolutionary sequences where Donald dances and interacts with live-action senoritas (a throwback to Disney's earlier *Alice in Cartoonland* shorts and a precursor to *Mary Poppins* and *Pete's Dragon*). There is also live-action travelogue footage from multiple South American countries.

One of Disney's most psychedelic films, *The Three Caballeros* looks and sounds great on DVD. Two extra cartoons are also included: Donald Duck in "Don's Fountain of Youth" (1953) and Pluto in "Pueblo Pluto" (1949).

SPECIAL FEATURES Trailer • Other Title Trailers TECHNICAL FEATURES
Fullscreen (1.33:1) • Subtitles/CC: Eng. • Languages: Eng.,
Fren. dub, Span. dub • Sound: Dolby Digital 2.0 • Keepcase •
1 Disc • Region 1, 4 GENRE & RATING Music/Comedy/Family •
Rated G

Three Little Pigs, The

Madacy, 1999, 30 mins.

This DVD was not available for review.

Three Musketeers, The [Collector's Edition]

Digital Versatile Disc, 1999, #171.

This DVD was not available for review.

Three Stooges, The: Cartoon Classics [#1]

Rhino, 2002, 113 mins., #R2 976040.
Directed by Eddie Bernds, Eddie
Rehberg, Sam Cornell, Dave Detiege.
Written by Jack Miller, Sam Cornell, Art
Diamond, Warren Tufts, Cecil Beard, Bar-
bara Chain, Jack Kinney, Nick George, Pat
Kearin, Homer Brightman, Lee Orgel,
Dave Detiege.

The Three Stooges engage in a never-
ending set of slapstick, whether
they're pretending to be soldiers, campers, bakers, fisher-
men, dentists, janitors, decorators, golfers, or hunters.
Which Stooges would it be though? That would be
Larry Fine, Moe Howard, and Curly Joe DeRita (that
latter one the fourth "third Stooge").

The Stooges filmed forty live-action segments to
open and close the 156 five-minute episodes of the 1965
syndicated series *The New Three Stooges*. While the
humor reflected the trio's film work, the violence was
toned down a bit. The project was in development for
quite a while, with a pilot called *The Three Stooges Scrapbook* predating it. Once aired, *The New Three Stooges* was
hampered by the small number of live-action segments;
viewers who had seen one of them rerunning might
tune out, not realizing that the show that followed had
new cartoons.

After fans endured years of bad-looking public
domain versions of these toons on video, Rhino released
authorized cleaned-up versions of the shows on video
and DVD. This volume features four full episodes that are
new digital transfers from 16mm film, as well as an interview with the show's supervising producer.

SPECIAL FEATURES Interview with Supervising Producer TECHNICAL
FEATURES Fullscreen (1.33:1) • Languages: Eng., Span. dub •
Sound: Dolby Digital 2.0 • Keepcase • 1 Disc • Region 1
GENRE & RATING Comedy • Not Rated (All Ages)

Three Stooges, The: Cartoon Classics [#2]

Rhino, 2002, 112 mins., #R2 976074.
Directed by Eddie Bernds, Eddie
Rehberg, Sam Cornell, Dave Detiege.
Written by Jack Miller, Sam Cornell, Art
Diamond, Warren Tufts, Cecil Beard, Bar-
bara Chain, Jack Kinney, Nick George, Pat
Kearin, Homer Brightman, Lee Orgel,
Dave Detiege.

Four more episodes of *The New Three
Stooges* include the comedy trio as
campers, caretakers, golfers, salesmen, prospectors, elec-
tricians, and barbers. As with the previous volume, these
are new prints from 16mm film, and all four episodes
feature a quartet of live-action bumper segments.

SPECIAL FEATURES None TECHNICAL FEATURES Fullscreen (1.33:1) •
Languages: Eng., Span. dub • Sound: Dolby Digital 2.0 •
Keepcase • 1 Disc • Region 1 GENRE & RATING Comedy • Not
Rated (All Ages)

Thumbelina

Delta Entertainment, 2001, 41 mins., #82
101. Screenplay by Leonard Lee. Based
on the story by Hans Christian Andersen.

As a reward for her goodness, a magician gives widow Hobbs a magic barley seed. The seed grows and grants
the widow's wish, eventually growing
her a tiny daughter, whom she names
Thumbelina. But the new mama
already has one creature dependent on her—a pig
named Percival—who grows insanely jealous of the
attention that Thumbelina is getting. Percival arranges to
have a bullfrog kidnap the little girl, and Thumbelina is
soon launched into a magical series of adventures in the
swamp as she attempts to return home.

One of the latest releases by Burbank Animation Studios Australia, this 2000 story looks better than the
majority of their earlier product, even including some
unobtrusive CGI work. The biggest drawback to the
story is the voice of Thumbelina, which recalls all the
awful "little girl" voices you may have heard in animated
or adult films.

SPECIAL FEATURES None TECHNICAL FEATURES Fullscreen (1.33:1) •
Languages: Eng. • Sound: Dolby Digital 2.0 • Keepcase • 1
Disc • Region All GENRE & RATING Fantasy/Family • Not Rated
(All Ages)

Thumbelina

Warner, 1999, 86 mins., #2002928. Directed by Don Bluth, Gary Goldman. Screenplay by Don Bluth. Based on the story by Hans Christian Andersen.

A lonely childless woman gets a magic barley corn seed from a good witch and grows a tiny daughter named Thumbelina. But even though she's happy on the farm, Thumbelina longs to have adventures. When she meets a royal fairy, Prince Cornelius, she's enchanted, and they seem fated to be together. Unfortunately, Thumbelina is kidnapped by some show-business toads, and must later deal with a scheming ugly beetle, and her unwitting engagement to a mole! Will interspecies romance force Thumbelina into a life she never wanted, or will Prince Cornelius and a coterie of animal and insect friends help save the day?

Thumbelina was Don Bluth's final production for his own animation studio in Ireland, but the 1994 theatrical release bombed in movie houses, bringing in a paltry $11 million. It's unclear why the film didn't perform well, as it's entirely accessible to audiences, features some of Bluth's wonderfully naturalistic human figure animation, gorgeous fairy effects, and some interesting animal designs. The voice cast is good, including Jodi Benson, Carol Channing, John Hurt, June Foray, and Gilbert Gottfried. Cynics will likely blame the failure on the music of Barry Manilow, who wrote the feature's seven songs, but they're mostly perfectly serviceable (though one of them—"Marry the Mole"—won a Golden Raspberry award for worst song).

This double-sided DVD contains the widescreen version of *Thumbelina* on one side, and the pan-and-scan version on the other side. The standard-frame version does cut quite a bit off the sides, but offers a little bit more image on the bottom of the frame. Unfortunately, the disc does not include the *Animaniacs* short that preceded the theatrical exhibitions.

SPECIAL FEATURES Trailer TECHNICAL FEATURES Widescreen (1.85:1 enhanced for 16x9) • Fullscreen (1.33:1) • Subtitles/CC: Eng., Fren. • Languages: Eng., Fren. dub • Sound: Dolby Digital Surround 2.0 • Snapcase • 1 Disc • Region 1 GENRE & RATING Music/Fantasy/Family • Rated G

Thumbelina

Fox, 2002, 86 mins., #2002928. Directed by Don Bluth, Gary Goldman. Screenplay by Don Bluth. Based on the story by Hans Christian Andersen.

Fox's rerelease of *Thumbelina* is almost exactly the same as the Warner version; it even includes both the widescreen and pan-and-scan versions. The picture is not noticeably different, either. The only major alteration appears to be the addition of two TV spots instead of the theatrical trailer (an advertised "Making of" segment is nowhere to be found). Which version you buy therefore depends on your interest in extras.

SPECIAL FEATURES Promotional Footage • Other Title Trailers TECHNICAL FEATURES Widescreen (1.85:1 enhanced for 16x9) • Subtitles/CC: Eng., Span. • Languages: Eng. • Sound: Dolby Digital Surround 2.0 • Keepcase • 1 Disc • Region 1 GENRE & RATING Music/Fantasy/Family • Rated G

Thunderbirds: Set 1

A&E Video, 2001, 312 mins., #AAE-70159. Directed by Alan Pattillo, Desmond Saunders, David Elliot, David Lane. Teleplay by Gerry Anderson, Sylvia Anderson, Alan Fennell, Dennis Spooner.

In the year 2063, an American billionaire astronaut and his five sons run a secret global organization named International Rescue (I.R.) from a Pacific Island base. Their primary equipment consists of five supercraft called Thunderbirds. Many of the hour-long episodes devote the first half to a particular disaster, with the second half being I.R.'s attempts to save the day. Although always visually fascinating, those weaned on MTV or video games may find the show's pacing slow for what's touted as an action series. However, characters get killed and wounded (with "bleeding"), and some of the principals smoke cigars and cigarettes, making the level of "reality" very high for a puppet show.

Thunderbirds was created in 1965 by famed British husband-and-wife team Gerry and Sylvia Anderson, shot in "Supermarionation"—that is, all the parts are played by marionettes! The show is a must-see for miniature buffs, from dollhouse fans to G.I. Joe enthusiasts. The series features miniature sets, props, vehicles, and special effects that were state-of-the-art at the time and hold up extremely well today. The craftsmen involved would later work on *Space: 1999* and *Star Wars*. *Thunderbirds* toys and related items remain the most popular TV memorabilia ever produced in England and have become a huge hit in Japan.

The initial DVD features six uncut, hour-long episodes, beginning with "Trapped in the Sky," the series intro, which is surprisingly flat and doesn't show off all the vehicles seen in the title sequence. In "Pit of Peril," I.R. utilizes its most visually interesting craft, the Mole (its nose is a large drill so it can "drive" underground). "City of Fire" spends too much time with an obnoxious family trapped in the basement of a burning megaskyscraper, while in "Sunprobe," a space mission gone awry means lots of footage of astronauts sitting in cockpits. "The Uninvited" is a gem about I.R. saving captives from a mysterious people living under a pyramid; they wipe out their ancient civilization, but according to their logic, it's okay, because the "Zombites" were bad guys. Finally, "The Mighty Atom" has an uncharacteristically intense opener depicting a nuclear meltdown.

The DVDs show off the vibrant, colorful 1960s art direction and details such as "perspiration" on the marionettes, as well as the strings used to operate them! It also includes a 1965 featurette. [PVG]

SPECIAL FEATURES "Making of" Featurette • Production Stills Photo Gallery TECHNICAL FEATURES Fullscreen (1.33:1) • Languages: Eng. • Sound: Dolby Digital 2.0, Dolby Digital 5.1 • Cardboard Box with 2 Keepcases • 2 Discs • Region 1 GENRE & RATING Marionettes/Science Fiction • Not Rated (Kids)

Thunderbirds: Set 2

A&E Video, 2001, 312 mins., #AAE-70162. Directed by Alan Pattillo, Desmond Saunders, David Elliot, David Lane. Teleplay by Dennis Spooner, Martin Crump, Alan Pattillo, Alan Fennell.

The second DVD features six uncut, hour-long episodes, including: "Vault of Death," a rare character piece focusing on I.R.'s London agents; "Operation Crash-Dive," a sequel to the first episode, this time with more vehicles and action; "Move and You're Dead," a great off-format story with a Spanish guitar score, it places an I.R. pilot in peril . . . with his grandma; "Martian Invasion," in which trouble on the set of a science fiction film is a nice premise, but it is, unfortunately, flatly executed; "Brink of Disaster," in which greedy Americans doom a monorail; and "The Perils of Penelope," which is heavy on espionage, light on disaster, and features more monorail action.

The extras on this DVD include the same "Making of" short that was included with *Thunderbirds: Set 1.* [PVG]

SPECIAL FEATURES "Making of" Featurette • Production Stills Photo Gallery TECHNICAL FEATURES Fullscreen (1.33:1) • Languages: Eng. • Sound: Dolby Digital 2.0, Dolby Digital 5.1 • Cardboard Box with 2 Keepcases • 2 Discs • Region 1 GENRE & RATING Marionettes/Science Fiction • Not Rated (Kids)

Thunderbirds: Set 3

A&E Video, 2001, 312 mins., #AAE-70329. Directed by Desmond Saunders, David Elliot, David Lane. Teleplay by Dennis Spooner, Alan Fennell, Donald Robertson.

Six more uncut, hour-long episodes are on this DVD, featuring: "Terror in New York City," in which a famous skyscraper collapses into rubble while

stunned I.R. members watch events unfold on live TV (of course, this episode takes on new resonance in the wake of the World Trade Center disaster of 2001); "End of the Road," a soap opera featuring comings and goings at I.R., with a disaster tied in; "Day of Disaster," in which all I.R. characters get screen time while saving a sunken spacecraft; "Edge of Impact," containing a recycled subplot from "End of the Road" that isn't helped by added action; "Desperate Intruder," in which I.R. goes treasure-hunting, complete with cool sunken ruins; and finally, "30 Minutes After Noon" wherein arson in a downtown office building provides an opportunity for elaborate urban set pieces . . . plus robots! [PVG]

SPECIAL FEATURES "Making of" Featurette • Production Stills Photo Gallery TECHNICAL FEATURES Fullscreen (1.33:1) • Languages: Eng. • Sound: Dolby Digital 2.0, Dolby Digital 5.1 • Cardboard Box with 2 Keepcases • 2 Discs • Region 1 GENRE & RATING Marionettes/Science Fiction • Not Rated (Kids)

Thunderbirds: Set 4

A&E Video, 2001, 312 mins., #AAE-70332. Directed by Desmond Saunders, David Elliot, David Lane. Teleplay by Dennis Spooner, Martin Crump, Alan Pattillo, Alan Fennell, Donald Robertson.

The fourth set of *Thunderbirds* episodes includes six more uncut, hour-long episodes. In "The Impostors," the heroes face evil twins and hillbilly agents (what more can you ask for?). "The Man from M.I.5," is an espionage episode without much action, while "Cry Wolf" is a good showcase for I.R. vehicles, in which two kids get a tour of I.R.'s base, then get trapped in a mine.

"Danger at Ocean Deep," a sea rescue, sadly, doesn't involve I.R.'s submarine, and a lackluster "The Duchess Assignment" features ho-hum casinos and kidnapping schemes. Finally, "Attack of the Alligators" is a great gothic swamp story with real, live crocodiles terrorizing our puppet heroes! [PVG]

SPECIAL FEATURES Production Stills Photo Gallery TECHNICAL FEATURES Fullscreen (1.33:1) • Languages: Eng. • Sound: Dolby Digital 2.0, Dolby Digital 5.1 • Cardboard Box with 2 Keepcases • 2 Discs • Region 1 GENRE & RATING Marionettes/Science Fiction • Not Rated (Kids)

Thunderbirds: Set 5

A&E Video, 2002, 260 mins., #AAE-70434. Directed by Alan Pattillo, Desmond Saunders, David Elliott. Teleplay by Alan Pattillo, Alan Fennell, Donald Robertson.

The fifth *Thunderbirds* set features only five uncut, hour-long episodes, including: "The Cham-Cham," in which the broadcast of a rock group's hit song causes airline crashes; "Security Hazard," a clips show framed by a boy's trip to Tracy Island; "Atlantic Inferno," an action-packed pyrotechnics showcase; "Path of Destruction," in which a clear-cut logging vehicle goes berserk; and "Alias Mr. Hackenbacker," featuring a fashion show with designs by Sylvia Anderson. [PVG]

SPECIAL FEATURES Production Stills Photo Gallery TECHNICAL FEATURES Fullscreen (1.33:1) • Languages: Eng. • Sound: Dolby Digital 2.0, Dolby Digital 5.1 • Cardboard Box with 2 Keepcases • 2 Discs • Region 1 GENRE & RATING Marionettes/Science Fiction • Not Rated (Kids)

Thunderbirds: Set 6

A&E Video, 2002, 220 mins., #AAE-70437. Directed by Brian Burgess, Desmond Saunders. Teleplay by Tony Barwick, Alan Pattillo.

In this final Thunderbirds set, one disc has three uncut, hour-long episodes: "Lord Parker's 'Oliday," which features threats from deadly solar technology; "Ricochet," in which disaster befalls an orbiting pirate broadcasting station; and "Give or Take a Million," the show's Christmas episode.

On the other disc are two featurettes: "The Brains Behind *Thunderbirds*" is an hour-long clip show framed by new video material of character Brains providing the viewers with "biographies" of the people and vehicles of International Rescue. "The Making of *Thunderbirds*" is a rare black-and-white short made in 1965 (different from the one included in the first two volumes), containing interviews with Gerry and Sylvia Anderson as well as the great special effects wizard Derek Meddings. It features fascinating glimpses into the production of this well-crafted show. [PVG]

SPECIAL FEATURES Creator Bio • Character Bios • Production Stills Photo Gallery • Technical History of Thunderbirds TECHNICAL FEATURES Fullscreen (1.33:1) • Languages: Eng. • Sound: Dolby Digital 2.0, Dolby Digital 5.1 • Cardboard Box with 2 Keepcases • 2 Discs • Region 1 GENRE & RATING Marionettes/Science Fiction • Not Rated (Kids)

Tigger Movie, The

Disney, 2000, 77 mins., #19302. Directed by Jun Falkenstein. Story by Eddie Guzelian. Screenplay by Jun Falkenstein. Based on the characters created in books by A. A. Milne.

Deep in the Hundred Acre Wood, Winnie the Pooh and his friends are all happy. Happiest among them is the bouncy Tigger, but he's beginning to wonder if being the only Tigger is *really* the best. Who is his family? Where did he come from? At the suggestion of Roo, Tigger writes a letter to his family, and Pooh, Owl, Eeyore, and Kanga all send him a reply, forging the signatures of his "family." But their plan to help their friend backfires as Tigger becomes certain that his real family is coming to visit. How will Tigger's friends help him realize that even if he is the "onliest one" that he doesn't need to be the loneliest one, and that he still has family in them?

A 2000 theatrical release from Disney, *The Tigger Movie* feels more like a direct-to-DVD release due to the animation, which is perfectly acceptable for TV, but wasn't great on the big screen. But you aren't watching it on the big screen if you're getting the DVD, are you? Expect lots of orange onscreen in this Fall-feeling feature, which has seven bouncy, fun, and singable songs. There's a bit of jarring modernism in one song when Jerry Springer and Marilyn Monroe–esque versions of Tigger pop up, but the moment will likely only bother Pooh purists.

The biggest concern for parents will likely be the messages it sends to children. Very young ones might be depressed by Tigger's feelings of loneliness, but adopted children of all ages might have more of a negative reaction to the main story about the search for a "real" family.

The DVD is loaded with some fun features, including the beautiful Kenny Loggins theme song, and a section telling kids how they can create their own family trees!

SPECIAL FEATURES Music Video • Sing-Along • Storybook • Games • How to Make a Family Tree • Other Title Trailers • Easter Egg TECHNICAL FEATURES Widescreen (1.66:1 enhanced for 16x9) • Subtitles/CC: Eng. • Languages: Eng., Fren. dub, Span. dub • Sound: Dolby Digital 5.1 • Keepcase • 1 Disc • Region 1, 4 GENRE & RATING Animals/Family • Rated G

Time Masters

Image, 2000, 79 mins., #ID9061SIDVD. Directed by Rene Laloux. Screenplay by Rene Laloux, Moebius. Based on the novel *L'Orphelin de Perdide* by Stefan Wul.

Piel is a young boy marooned on the planet of Perdide. Mercenary Jaffar, a friend of Piel's father, tries to rescue the boy from the planet. But along the way, he encounters the Blue Comet, sexless winged beings, and other dangerous space travelers. Can Jaffar stop the uncaring and evil Masters of Time from turning back time?

Released in 1982 in France, *Time Masters* (known there as *Les Maitres du Temps*) was adapted from a science fiction novel, and directed by the same man who helmed the weirdly trippy *Fantastic Planet* (see entry). The designs for the space opera film are by famed French comic book artist Jean Giraud, better known as "Moebius." While the animation is striking because of Moebius's designs, the production feels leaden at times, mostly due to the meandering story. For fans of Moebius or Laloux, this is a must, but others might want to rent it before buying it.

SPECIAL FEATURES None TECHNICAL FEATURES Fullscreen (1.33:1) • Subtitles/CC: Eng. • Languages: Fren. • Sound: Dolby Digital 1.0 • Snapcase • 1 Disc • Region 1–6 GENRE & RATING Science Fiction • Not Rated (Teens)

Titan A.E.: Special Edition

Fox, 2000, 95 mins., #2000924. Directed by Don Bluth, Gary Goldman. Story by Hans Bauer, Randall McCormick. Screenplay by Ben Edlund, John August, Joss Whedon.

In the year 3028 an alien race comes to earth. They are called the Drej and they aren't here to be our friends. In one fell swoop they completely obliterate earth. Nothing is left. But humans, being humans, do escape and manage to create a living in the universe (even though they are considered lowlifes by the other inhabitants). It's in this time a young man named Cale is living, doing menial tasks that are considered beneath other beings. He meets Korso, the human captain of the starship *Valkyrie*, and an old friend of his father. It seems that Cale's dad had created something called the *Titan*, a ship hiding a valuable secret. Cale has the map leading to the *Titan* in his hand, and together with the sexy and tough Akima, the intelligent but bumbling Gune, the snotty Preed, and the trash-talking Stith, they search out the *Titan* before the Drej can find it.

Titan A.E. hit theaters in the summer of 2000 and

while it wasn't a commercial success it is a solid, entertaining, sci-fi adventure. The plot is your standard hero coming of age story, but the visuals are impressive, even if the CGI and the 2D animation sometimes work at cross-purposes. The voice acting is top notch, by names such as Matt Damon, Drew Barrymore, Janeane Garofalo, and Nathan Lane. The songs from the top forty artists do end up overpowering some scenes and pull you out of the movie. But that's about the worst thing in the film. It's not deep, but it's a good story and worth seeing.

This DVD is impressive. Not only is the print outstanding, but you also get deleted scenes and a nice still gallery of concept and design art. To top it off, you get a director's commentary that is insightful and entertaining. There is some violence and spaceship combat, but the action is on the same level as a *Star Wars* film. [RJM]

SPECIAL FEATURES "Making of" Featurette • Commentary Track with Director • Character and Art Galleries • Deleted Scenes • Trailers • Promotional Footage • Music Video • DVD-ROM Features: Game • Other Title Trailers TECHNICAL FEATURES Widescreen (2.35:1 enhanced for 16x9) • Subtitles/CC: Eng., Span. • Languages: Eng., Fren. dub • Sound: Dolby Digital Surround 2.0. Dolby Digital 5.1, DTS • Keepcase • 1 Disc • Region 1 GENRE & RATING CGI/Science Fiction • Rated PG

Tokio Private Police: Complete ☛ see

Mature/Adult Section

Tokyo Babylon

NuTech, 1999, 105 mins., #DVD154. Directed by Koichi Chigira. Script by Yoshihiko Urahata, Hiroaki Jinno. Based on the manga series by CLAMP.

Shinji Nagumo is building skyscrapers in the city, but everyone around him keeps dying. But are the deaths accidental or planned? That's what psychic medium Subaru Sumeragi intends to find out. But given that the sister of a dead man is already conjuring a demon to take revenge on Nagumo, the man's luck may run out before Subaru finds the answers. Then, a serial killer is stalking women aboard the subways. Enter Mirei Hidaka, a psychic postcognitive who can see the secrets of events after they've happened. But as she gets closer to the identity of the killer—with the help of Subaru—Hidaka's own life is put in jeopardy!

Released as two OVAs in 1992 and 1994, *Tokyo Babylon* adapts characters from a popular manga serial by CLAMP. The moody animation works well for the stories, and is almost duochromatically heavy on blacks and reds. The stories aren't overly original, and yet their sense of murder-mystery suspense and the occult are strong. The gay relationship between Subaru and Seishiro Sakurazuka—present in the manga—is downplayed significantly here.

The DVD features a good picture, but no extras of interest. Note that Subaru also appears in *X: The Movie* (see entry).

SPECIAL FEATURES Other Title Trailers TECHNICAL FEATURES Fullscreen (1.33:1) • Subtitles/CC: Eng. • Languages: Jap., Eng. dub • Sound: Dolby Digital 2.0 • Keepcase • 1 Disc • Region All GENRE & RATING Martial Arts/Action • Not Rated (Teens)

Tokyo Project, The

Anime Works, 2001, 60 mins., #AWDVD-0122. Directed by Masao Yamazaki. Script by Masao Yamazaki. Original Story by Bugyoshi Minamimachi.

The four members of the Rutz Detective Agency are Keiko, Akira, Kumiko, and Junpei. They've solved crimes before, but they never intended to get involved in a deadly game of military cover-ups and political espionage. But when a computer disc falls into their hands at a concert—containing compromising information about many high-ranking politicians and plans for a new military weapon—their lives are in danger. They're soon facing government thugs, superweapons controlled by artificial intelligence, and more!

This 1999 OVA is well-drawn and shadowy, appropriate for its suspenseful story. While the robotic super-weapons seem a little out of place, this is anime, so it makes as much sense as strip club scenes do in live-action American movies. The DVD contains the requisite English- and Japanese-language tracks. The Japanese track is an easy PG, while the English track has enough swearing in it to bump this disc's rating up to 16+! Unfortunately, curse words are about the only extras on the DVD.

SPECIAL FEATURES Other Title Trailers TECHNICAL FEATURES Fullscreen (1.33:1) • Subtitles/CC: Eng. • Languages: Jap., Eng. dub • Sound: Dolby Digital 2.0 • Keepcase • 1 Disc • Region 1 GENRE & RATING Suspense/Action • Rated 16+

Tokyo Revelations

Manga Entertainment, 2002, 60 mins., #MANGA4082-2. Directed by Osamu Yamazaki. Script by Mamiya Fujimura. Original Story by Kazuya Suzuki, Chiaki Mikishioma.

Aboard an airliner, a white-haired boy unleashes invisible demons with a computer spell. The plane explodes, but the boy—Akito Kobayashi—survives, pledging allegiance to a demon. Using his satanic software, Akito plans to collect more magnetite—the essence of the human soul—thus allowing devils to walk the Earth once more! But after Akito enrolls in school, one of his classmates, Kojiro Soma, begins to see something slightly different about the boy he once knew, and another classmate may contain all the necessary magnetite. Now, bookish Kojiro is fated to face the ultimate demon in a fight to save Tokyo and the world!

Based on a computer game and novel, *Tokyo Revelations* was released as a two-part series in 1995. The animation is mostly realistic for the male characters, but overly fantastical for the female characters. The English voice dubbing is particularly nice. There is some nudity and very minor gore, but the supernatural themes should probably mark this one as off-limits for young viewers. The DVD transfer is nice, but there are no real extras

SPECIAL FEATURES Other Title Trailers TECHNICAL FEATURES Fullscreen (1.33:1) • Subtitles/CC: Eng. • Languages: Jap., Eng. dub • Sound: Dolby Digital 2.0, Dolby Digital Surround 5.1 • Keepcase • 1 Disc • Region 1 GENRE & RATING Supernatural/Cyberpunk • Not Rated (Teens)

Tom and Jerry's Greatest Chases

Warner, 2000, 101 mins., #65306. Directed by William Hanna, Joe Barbera.

Tom is a grey house cat that is very resourceful but very testy, especially when it comes to Jerry, a mischievous brown mouse who delights in teasing Tom. But even if Tom and Jerry do chase each other around and play all sorts of destructive pranks on one another, they really do care. Would Tom really eat Jerry? Would Jerry really allow Tom to get hurt? Not a chance, or this long-running series would be over!

Tom and Jerry were some of the earliest—and longest-lived—creations of William Hanna and Joe Barbera. The cat and mouse starred in about 200 theatrical cartoons, from 1939 to 1967, then in multiple television series from 1965 syndication to ABC TV in 1975, and all the way into the 1990s on Fox. Despite popular belief, the pair was not always silent, though they rarely spoke until later years. The animated violence was always harmless—due to cartoon character resiliency—although modern-day censors have toned down the material ("The Little Orphan" on this disc has reportedly been trimmed).

This DVD contains fourteen cartoon shorts from throughout the *Tom and Jerry* film oeuvre: "Yankee Doodle Mouse" (1952); "Solid Serenade" (1946); "Tee for Two" (1945); "Mouse in Manhattan" (1945); "Zoot Cat" (1944); "Dr. Jekyll and Mr. Mouse" (1947); "The Cat Concerto" (1946, an Academy Award winner); "The Little Orphan" (1948, another Academy Award winner); "Salt Water Tabby" (1947); "Kitty Foiled" (1948); "Johann Mouse (1953, another Academy Award winner);

"Jerry's Diary" (1949); "Jerry and the Lion" (1950); and "Mice Follies" (1954).

The disc also contains a very cool bonus: a ten-minute segment from the 1944 live-action film *Anchors Aweigh*, which features Gene Kelly and Jerry dancing together in a cartoon kingdom!

SPECIAL FEATURES Dance Excerpt TECHNICAL FEATURES Fullscreen (1.33:1) • Languages: Eng. • Sound: Dolby Digital 2.0 • Snapcase • 1 Disc • Region 1 GENRE & RATING Animals/Comedy • Not Rated (All Ages)

Tom and Jerry: The Magic Ring

Warner, 2001, 62 mins., #65550. Directed by James Tim Walker. Written by Tim Cahill, Julie McNally.

After a young wizard leaves a powerful magic ring under Tom's protection, Jerry manages to get the bauble stuck on his head! Tom tries to catch Jerry, but the now-magical mouse runs off to the city, where his actions cause chases and slapstick mayhem. Tom has to catch Jerry and remove the ring before even more misery can happen, but if he had problems catching his counterpart before, how will he catch the magical mouse now?

The world's favorite cat and mouse team returns for this direct-to-video feature released for the Christmas 2001 season. Director Walker tries hard to replicate the feel of the Hanna-Barbera shorts, but that's part of the problem, as the film plays out like a really long extended gag. Youngsters will no doubt love the show with its flashy and funny moments, but parents may long to see some of the original toons for shorter doses of the same mirth.

Luckily for those who want older material, the DVD also contains two vintage cartoons: "The Flying Sorceress" (1956) and "Haunted Mouse" (1965). There are a number of other fun extras to keep kids occupied.

SPECIAL FEATURES "Making of" Featurette • How To Draw Tom and Jerry • Trivia • Trailer • Games • Other Title Trailers TECHNICAL FEATURES Fullscreen (1.33:1) • Subtitles/CC: Eng., Fren., Span. • Languages: Eng., Fren. dub, Span. dub • Sound: Dolby Digital 5.0 • Snapcase • 1 Disc • Region 1–4 GENRE & RATING Animals/Comedy • Not Rated (All Ages)

Tom and Jerry: The Movie

Warner, 2002, 84 mins., #T8055. Directed by Phil Roman. Screenplay by Dennis Marks.

Once upon a time, an evil guardian named Pristine Figg kept her little girl, Robyn Starling, locked away in an attic. Tom and Jerry help Robyn escape so that she can find her missing father, but the job won't be easy with dastardly lawyer Lickboot and pet prison warden Dr. Applecheeks hot on their tails. Tom and Jerry must forge alliances with other animals in the city, the country, and even on the sea if they're going to survive this cat-and-mouse chase.

With the tagline "After years of fighting, they finally found something worth fighting for . . . each other," Turner Entertainment unleashed *Tom and Jerry: The Movie* on the public in 1993. It was a sign that this was a kinder and gentler duo, but as the trailer warned, they not only talked now, they were positively chatty . . . and their voices were horrific and grating! The animation is fine, and the music is actually pretty good (it should be since it's by Broadway and film vets Henry Mancini and Leslie Bricusse), but neither the story nor the updated Tom and Jerry feel quite right.

This tenderized vittle will be perfect for kids and those who feel that the originals were too violent, but for fans of the original, the DVD has two more vintage toons: "The Invisible Mouse" (1947) and "Just Ducky" (1953).

SPECIAL FEATURES How To Draw Tom and Jerry • Trailer • Game • Other Title Trailers TECHNICAL FEATURES Fullscreen (1.33:1) • Subtitles/CC: Eng., Fren., Port., Span. • Languages: Eng., Fren. dub, Port. dub, Span. dub • Sound: Dolby Digital 2.0 • Snapcase • 1 Disc • Region 1–4 GENRE & RATING Music/Animals/Comedy • Not Rated (All Ages)

Tommy and the Computoys: The Story [#1]

Image, 1999, 85 mins., #ID5561M3DVD. Directed by Marcel Nottea. Story by Marcel Nottea.

Tommy is a little boy that lives in the virtual world inside a computer. He soon learns that using his own computer, he can create a second virtual world full of magical friends known as the Computoys. He soon engages in a variety of adventures with his Computoys, including stories with space stations and interstellar pirates, circuses, the juggling Pigasso, dancing snails and vegetables, floating paintbrushes, and more.

If it weren't for the narration by Tommy—and the regular appearance of Tommy, who looks vaguely like Pinocchio—this project would resemble one of the more adult CGI anthologies. There's almost no story to speak of, except Tommy introducing things he's created on his computer. The feature is meant to be educational, and it does teach a few things about computers, but it would be going a bit far to say much solid information can be gleaned from the DVD.

Mostly, *Tommy and the Computoys* seems to be an exercise in barely competent computer animation that's designed to stimulate the imagination with weird images. Not that the stimulation of imagination is a bad thing, but this is such a weird project that it's hard to review in any linear way. This could be recommended for any tech-head youngsters or adults who enjoy—ahem—altered states.

SPECIAL FEATURES None TECHNICAL FEATURES Fullscreen (1.33:1) • Languages: Eng. • Sound: Dolby Digital 2.0 • Snapcase • 1 Disc • Region 1–6 GENRE & RATING CGI/Music/Anthology • Not Rated (Kids)

Tommy and the Computoys Sing-Along [#2]

Image, 1999, 59 mins., #ID5560M3DVD. Directed by Marcel Nottea.

Tommy is back, and he's created more musical oddities with his computer animation. This time, he and his Computoys are presenting twenty-one songs—some familiar, some newer—with bizarre and imaginative graphics to go along with them. Songs include "This Old Man"; "I'm a Little Teapot"; "Itsy Bitsy Spider"; "Old MacDonald"; and even "The Old Lady" (generally known as "There Was an Old Lady Who Swallowed a Fly").

The CGI animation is no better in this volume than in the first volume, but young audiences will likely still enjoy it. The one element that doesn't track is that the songs are supposed to be sing-alongs, but there are no lyrics or captions for singers (of any age) to follow along with, making the segments more like music videos.

SPECIAL FEATURES None TECHNICAL FEATURES Fullscreen (1.33:1) • Languages: Eng. • Sound: Dolby Digital 2.0 • Snapcase • 1 Disc • Region 1–6 GENRE & RATING CGI/Music/Anthology • Not Rated (Kids)

Tom Sawyer

MGM/UA, 2000, 89 mins., #908393. Directed by Paul Sabella. Written by Patricia Jones, Donald Reiker. Based on the novel by Mark Twain.

Tom Sawyer is a mischievous boy who lives in Illinois near the banks of the Mississippi River. His best friend is Huckleberry Finn, and the two of them delight in pranks and tricks. They're also sweet on Becky Thatcher, the new girl in school. When Tom and Huck set out to find buried treasure, they discover more than they bargained for. Barely escaping the claws of Injurin' Joe, the massive grizzly bear that terrorizes the town, Tom and Huck eventually find adventure and excitement down the river . . . and is that treasure in the secret hideout?

There are two things that make this 1999 production

of *Tom Sawyer* different from any other version of Mark Twain's famous tale: first, all the characters have been anthropomorphized into animals; and second, country music stars provide almost all of the voices. Listen for Hank Williams Jr., Lee Ann Womack, Rhett Akins, and Waylon Jennings, alongside old pros Betty White and Don Knotts. The animation isn't quite theatrical quality, but it's better than most direct-to-video projects.

Older audiences will enjoy this *Tom Sawyer* as much as their young 'uns, especially if they're country music lovers. The DVD offers a nice stereo version of some of the catchy songs.

SPECIAL FEATURES Cast Photos and Art • Inserts: Stickers TECHNICAL FEATURES Fullscreen (1.33:1) • Subtitles/CC: Fren., Span. • Languages: Eng. • Sound: Dolby Digital Surround 5.1 • Keepcase • 1 Disc • Region 1 GENRE & RATING Music/Animals/Adventure • Rated G

Tom Sawyer [Collector's Edition]

Digital Versatile Disc, 1999, 51 mins., #172.

This DVD was not available for review.

Toothbrush Family, The: A Visit from the Tooth Fairy

Celebrity, 1999, 85 mins.

This DVD was not available for review.

Toy Story

Disney, 2001, 81 mins., #22336. Directed by John Lasseter. Screenplay by Joss Whedon, Andrew Stanton, Joel Cohen, Alec Sokolow. Original Story by John Lasseter, Pete Docter, Andrew Stanton, Joe Ranft.

Little boy Andy has a roomful of toys that come to life when he's out of the room. The leader of the toys is much-beloved cowboy doll Woody, but on Andy's birthday, Woody is displaced. The new favorite is Space Ranger Buzz Lightyear, a toy that lights up, extends wings from his backpack, and more. But Buzz thinks he's a real Space Ranger, not a toy. Woody tries to get rid of his rival, or at the very least, prove to Buzz that he really is just a plaything. But Woody and Buzz fall into the hands of Andy's neighbor, Sid, a boy who delights in torturing and destroying toys. Even with the help of mutant toys created from dismantled playthings, can Buzz and Woody escape unharmed?

Released in 1995, *Toy Story* was the first fully computer-animated feature film. Technically brilliant, the feature was the work of Pixar; the studio spent seven years working on the film! Although the human characters show the limitations of the medium, the three-dimensionality of the toys and their environments is breathtaking. Voice work is sublime, with turns by Tim Allen, Tom Hanks, Annie Potts, John Ratzenberger, and Don Rickles, among others. The script is fresh, funny, poignant, and most of all, evocative of youthful imagination.

The music and songs by Randy Newman were some of the best of his career, and he was nominated for both Best Score and Best Song Academy Awards. Director John Lasseter was presented with a Special Achievement Academy Award for his groundbreaking work with the CGI film. Made for $30 million, *Toy Story* grossed over $350 million in theaters worldwide, even prior to its video and DVD release!

Because the original film is digital, its transfer to DVD is excellent. The sound quality is superb as well, and the freeze-frame and zoom features on your DVD player will allow you to check out all the in-jokes that appear throughout the movie (look at bookcases and labels especially). The Oscar-winning short film *Tin Toy* (also by Pixar) is presented as well. This is another must-have DVD, though which version you'll get is a question. See the following entries for other options (and see *Pixar 15th Anniversary Box Set*).

SPECIAL FEATURES None TECHNICAL FEATURES Widescreen (1.77:1 enhanced for 16x9) • Subtitles/CC: Eng. • Languages: Eng., Fren. dub, Span. dub • Sound: Dolby Digital 5.1 • Keepcase • 1 Disc • Region 1, 4 GENRE & RATING Toys/Comedy/Adventure • Rated G

Toy Story 2

Disney, 2001, 95 mins., #22337. Directed by John Lasseter, Lee Unkrich, Ash Brannon. Screenplay by Andrew Stanton, Rita Hsiao, Doug Chamberlin, Chris Webb. Original Story by John Lasseter, Pete Docter, Ash Brannon, Andrew Stanton.

When Andy goes away to summer camp, leaving some of his toys behind, Woody gets toynapped by Al of Al's Toy Barn. Al has been assembling a whole set of toys from *Woody's Playhouse* to sell to the highest bidder, and Woody is the last piece of the collection. Woody soon discovers that he was once a TV star, and he's befriended by spunky cowgirl Jessie, a horse named Bullseye, and the prospector Stinky Pete. Buzz Lightyear launches a rescue mission to reclaim Woody, with Hamm the piggy bank, Rex the dinosaur, Slinky Dog, and Mr. Potato Head along to help.

Although originally intended as a direct-to-video sequel, *Toy Story 2* was upgraded to feature film status and released in 1999. With four years of software advances in their hands, the CGI animators at Pixar delivered an even more vibrant and realistic world for the toys. It helped that they were working from an excel-

lent script that had real moments of drama and action mixed in with the comedy. With its poignant backstory about the relationship between toys and their owners, the film also managed to presciently pinpoint the eBay mentality of selling toy collectibles at a time when online auctions had just become firmly implanted in the public consciousness.

Toy Story 2 was both a critical and financial success, with most critics and audiences agreeing that the feature was actually *better* than its beloved predecessor. This was in part likely due to everyone who had worked on the first film being inspired to greater glory. Randy Newman returned again for an excellent score and songs, and the entire voice cast reconvened, joined this time by Wayne Knight, Joan Cusack, and others. And most of the creative team from Pixar—most importantly John Lasseter, hailed as the "Disney of the new millennium"—returned as well.

The DVD for *Toy Story 2* features another digital transfer, as well as a choice of viewing the feature in widescreen or fullscreen images. The Academy Award–nominated short *Luxo Jr.* is also included, as are a round of animated "bloopers" prepared for the film.

SPECIAL FEATURES Outtakes • Other Title Trailers TECHNICAL FEATURES Widescreen (1.77:1 enhanced for 16x9) • Fullscreen (1.33:1) • Subtitles/CC: Eng. • Languages: Eng. • Sound: Dolby Digital 5.1 • Keepcase • 1 Disc • Region 1, 4 GENRE & RATING Toys/Comedy/Adventure • Rated G

Toy Story 2 Pack

Disney, 2002, 176 mins., #20992.

This set contains *Toy Story* and *Toy Story 2* exactly as they appeared in the individual keepcase editions, except here the discs are packaged in a double-keepcase. See individual entries for the Special and Technical Features listings.

TECHNICAL FEATURES Multikeepcase • 2 Discs GENRE & RATING Toys/Comedy/Adventure • Rated G

Toy Story: The Ultimate Toy Box [Box Set]

Disney, 2002, 546 mins., #18668.

To call *Toy Story* a work of genius is barely an overstatement. When it's paired with its arguably superior sequel, *Toy Story 2*, "work of genius" becomes an understatement. In this three-disc gorgeously packaged box set, the collection is positively heavenly.

Animation fans young and old, cinephiles, critics, animators, and anybody with the slightest interest in the medium will find much to love in this jam-packed DVD set. The first disc contains the widescreen version of *Toy Story*, as well as a highly entertaining commentary track, making-of features, an isolated track for the film's sound effects, and specially animated interviews with the film's stars, Woody and Buzz! The second disc contains *Toy Story 2* in widescreen, audio commentary, and another sound effects-only track.

The third disc in this set contains an exhaustive look at both *Toy Story* and *Toy Story 2* from preproduction up through release. Along the way are history details on story, treatment, and script, plus early test reels of CGI, storyboards, editing, and design. There are explorations of each character and setting, with concept, character, and location artwork. There's production featurettes on character animation, shading, shot-building, production progression, special effects, and more, as well as additional features on the music, sound, voice actors, director and crew, and advertising/trailer campaigns for the films. As if that weren't enough, how about some deleted scenes, a guide to hidden jokes, and alternate animation? Even the box is fun, with cel-style art on the plastic slipcover, and wire-frame models of the art on the shiny silver metallic box!

It's hard to imagine improving on *Toy Story* and *Toy Story 2*, but *Toy Story: The Ultimate Toy Box* does a fantastic job of extending the feelings, adventure, and fun of these animation landmarks.

SPECIAL FEATURES "Making of" Featurettes • Commentary Track with Filmmakers • Cast and Crew Bios • Character Interviews • Character and Art Galleries • Production Notes • Deleted Scenes and Abandoned Sequences • Storyboards • Story Treatment • Trailers • Promotional Footage • Music Videos • Outtakes • Isolated Sound Effects Tracks • International Footage • Other Title Trailers • Inserts: Liner Notes • Easter Eggs TECHNICAL FEATURES Widescreen (1.77:1 enhanced for 16x9) • Subtitles/CC: Eng. • Languages: Eng., Fren. dub • Sound: Dolby Digital 5.1 • Cardboard Box with Plastic Cover and 3 Keepcases • 3 Discs • Region 1 GENRE & RATING Toys/Comedy/Adventure • Rated G

Toy Town Story Adventures, The

Brentwood, 2001, 60 mins., #44096-9. Directed by Hendrick Baker. Written by S. G. Hulme Beaman.

Toy Town is full of all sorts of interesting characters including the talking Larry the Lamb, the constantly sleeping town Mayor, and a town wizard. The characters engage in a series of adventures, putting on shows, camping by the duck pond as scouts, and more.

The animation in *The Toy Town Story Adventures* is all stop-motion, although some paper cutouts seem to be in evidence. The characters all look vaguely like nutcrack-

ers. The series was created in England, and though its storylines are a bit bizarre, it is appropriate for all ages. The DVD contains five short stories with a fairly good transfer. Also included is a live-action *Little Rascals* short, "Came the Brawn."

SPECIAL FEATURES DVD Dictionary • Movie Trivia Game TECHNICAL FEATURES Fullscreen (1.33:1) • Languages: Eng. • Sound: Dolby Digital Surround 2.0 • Keepcase • 1 Disc • Region 1–6 GENRE & RATING Toys/Comedy/Adventure • Rated G

Transformers: Villains—The Ultimate Doom [#1]

Rhino, 2001, 66 mins., #R2970049. Directed by John Walker. Written by Douglas Booth, Earl Kress, Donald F. Glut, Leo D. Paur, Alfred A. Pegal, Reed Robbins, Larry Strass, Peter Salas.

Far off in space, on the planet of Cybertron, the good Autobots (led by Optimus Prime) are engaged in a never-ending battle against the evil Decepticons (led by Megatron). Both sides have the ability to change their robotic forms into cars, planes, or other vehicles. In the year 2005, the Transformers leave Cybertron and bring their battle to Earth, where both sides gain human allies. By the time of the adventures on this DVD—"The Ultimate Doom, Part 1–3"—Dr. Arkeville has helped the Decepticons capture Sparkplug, into which has been installed the experimental hypno-chip, designed by Arkeville to control the minds of humanity. But to achieve their goals of building more Energon cubes with the human slaves, Megatron must bring Cybertron into Earth's orbit! The results are catastrophic, devastating the planet. Now the Autobots and their human allies must fight the Decepticons, their human slaves, and the very forces of nature that threaten to tear Earth asunder!

Based on a line of transforming toys by Hasbro, *Transformers* remains one of the most popular series of the 1980s. A U.S./Japan coproduction, the show began syndication in September 1984, and continued for several seasons (it began in Japan in 1985). A sequel series, *Transformers: Generation II,* in 1993 was just thirteen of the original episodes with added CGI footage. The series gained a new popularity with reruns on the Sci-Fi Channel in the 1990s, and experienced a nostalgia-inspired rebirth on DVD and in the comic book and toy world in 2002.

The animation in *Transformers* is better than most of the fare of that time, and the stories and characterizations were better than was expected for a show about transforming robots. Unfortunately, this DVD features a worn print that shows some scratching in the transfer, and although the packaging lists a time of 150 minutes, it's a miserly sixty-six minutes, instead. Fans were resentful, especially given that this trilogy of stories is one of the best-loved of the series' run. Rhino did a better job with the *Transformers [First Season]* discs, and the third volume of that set contains the same episodes as this disc, plus others (see entry).

SPECIAL FEATURES None TECHNICAL FEATURES Fullscreen (1.33:1) • Languages: Eng. • Sound: Dolby Digital 5.1 • Keepcase • 1 Disc • Region 1 GENRE & RATING Robots/Science Fiction • Not Rated (Kids)

Transformers: Heroes—The Rebirth [#2]

Rhino, 2001, 66 mins., #R2970050. Directed by Jaeho Hong. Written by David Wise.

As before, the Earth is still a battleground in the ongoing struggle between the supertechnological transforming Autobots and Decepticons. But the battle doesn't just end on our planet, as it still rages on Cybertron, and on Nebulos. As the Decepticons prepare to attack Autobot City en masse—to steal the key to the Plasma Energy Chamber where the Autobots were forged—Nebulons are being joined with Autobots to become a new breed of Transformer known as Headmasters. But when an entire city of the Hive is transformed into a powerful Decepticon superbot, the good Optimus Prime will have to take drastic measures to ensure that evil does not win!

This DVD contains the last three episodes of the original *Transformers* series run, known as "The Rebirth, Episodes #1–3." The shows are complete, with full episode previews and recaps, although the commercial bumpers are not included. The picture quality is better than the *Villains* disc, and this season has not (yet) been collected. Once again, the packaging incorrectly lists the time as 150 minutes, and it is sixty-six minutes long.

SPECIAL FEATURES None TECHNICAL FEATURES Fullscreen (1.33:1) • Languages: Eng. • Sound: Dolby Digital 5.1 • Keepcase • 1 Disc • Region 1 GENRE & RATING Robots/Science Fiction • Not Rated (Kids)

Transformers: Vol. 1 [First Season]

Rhino, 2002, 118 mins., #R2 976034. Directed by John Gibbs, Terry Lennon. Written by George Arthur Bloom.

Escaping the planet of Cybertron in a spaceship, the good Autobots are seeking new reserves of energy, but they are attacked by the evil Decepticons. The resulting battle forces the Transformers to crash land on Earth, where, thankfully, their ability to change into cars and planes is considered a plus, even if their war against the

Decepticons isn't. The Decepticons quickly try to force humans to make the Energon cubes they need for power, and they establish an undersea base from which they hope to create a "space bridge" back to Cybertron. And although the Autobots have the upper hand now, what will happen when the evil Megatron arrives on Earth?

Rhino begins its DVD releases of the first season of the syndicated *Transformers* series from 1984 with this volume. The picture is better than the 2001 single *Transformer* releases, and the disc features a generous five episodes instead of only three. And even the commercial bumpers are included! The episodes are: "More Than Meets the Eye, Parts 1–3"; "Transport to Oblivion"; and "Roll for It."

SPECIAL FEATURES None TECHNICAL FEATURES Fullscreen (1.33:1) • Languages: Eng. • Sound: Dolby Digital 2.0, Dolby Digital Surround 5.1 • Keepcase • 1 Disc • Region 1 GENRE & RATING Robots/Science Fiction • Not Rated (Kids)

Transformers: Vol. 2 [First Season]

Rhino, 2002, 118 mins., #R2 976035. Directed by Terry Lennon, John Walker. Written by Douglas Booth, Earl Kress, Donald F. Glut, Leo D. Paur, Alfred A. Pegal, Reed Robbins, Larry Strass, Peter Salas.

During a Decepticon attack, Optimus Prime is badly damaged. To repair their leader, a group of Autobots must go back to Cybertron to get a part, but this leaves the other Autobots vulnerable to the Decepticons. Then, the Decepticons discover an ancient Transformer named Skyfire buried in the ice at the North Pole. Will he help them drain Earth's energy? When the Autobots discover dinosaur fossils, they decide to create the Dinobots, but the new machines are mentally unstable. As the Decepticons ready an ancient crystal to power their new weapon, will the Dinobots ally themselves with evil?

Five more complete first-season episodes of *Transformers* are included in their production order, not the order in which they originally aired. The episodes include: "Divide and Conquer"; "Fire in the Sky"; "S.O.S. Dinobots"; "Fire on the Mountain"; and "War of the Dinobots."

SPECIAL FEATURES None TECHNICAL FEATURES Fullscreen (1.33:1) • Languages: Eng. • Sound: Dolby Digital 2.0, Dolby Digital Surround 5.1 • Keepcase • 1 Disc • Region 1 GENRE & RATING Robots/Science Fiction • Not Rated (Kids)

Transformers: Vol. 3 [First Season]

Rhino, 2002, 118 mins., #R2 976035. Directed by Terry Lennon, John Walker. Written by Douglas Booth, Earl Kress, Donald F. Glut, Leo D. Paur, Alfred A. Pegal, Reed Robbins, Larry Strass, Peter Salas.

An attack on a Maharajah was a diversion so that the Decepticons could attack the Ark and capture Sparkplug. A hypno-chip is installed in the captive Autobot, which will turn him—and humans—into slaves of the Decepticons. The Decepticons have a dangerous plan to bring Cybertron into Earth's orbit! The results are catastrophic, devastating the planet. Now the Autobots and their human allies must fight the Decepticons, their human slaves, and the very forces of nature that threaten to tear Earth asunder! What could possibly force Optimus Prime and Megatron to team up? Then, the Decepticons have another ally in the new Transformers, the Insecticons. And finally, Megatron challenges Optimus Prime to a fight, but if the good Autobot loses, all of the Autobots will be forced to leave Earth!

The final six first-season episodes of *Transformers* are included complete, in their production order, not the order in which they originally aired. The episodes include: "The Ultimate Doom: Brainwash"; "The Ultimate Doom: Search"; "The Ultimate Doom: Revival"; "Countdown to Extinction"; "A Plague of Insecticons"; and "Heavy Metal War."

SPECIAL FEATURES None TECHNICAL FEATURES Fullscreen (1.33:1) • Languages: Eng. • Sound: Dolby Digital 2.0, Dolby Digital Surround 5.1 • Keepcase • 1 Disc • Region 1 GENRE & RATING Robots/Science Fiction • Not Rated (Kids)

Transformers: Season 1 [Box Set]

Rhino, 2002, 490 mins., #R2976039

This DVD box set was not available for review. It contains the first three volumes of the series, as well as an exclusive fourth disc of special features.

Transformers: Season Two, Part 1 [Box Set]

Rhino, 2002, 715 mins., #R2 976046. Directed by Norm McCabe, Bob Shellhorn, Karen Peterson, Bob Kirk, Bob Treat, Tom Ray, Margaret Nichols, Bob Matz, Al Kouzel, Andy Kim. Written by Donald F. Glut, Larry Parr, Douglas Booth, David Wise, George Hampton, Mike Moore, Earl Kress, Sylvia Wilson, Richard Milton, Dick Robbins, Bryce Malek, Dennis Marks, David Gottlieb, Herb Englehardt, Antoni Zalewski, Larry Strass.

NOTE: This DVD arrived too late for a full review. The following text is promotional copy provided by the releasing company:

"Earth is the battleground, control of the universe is the prize. And the only defense is an army of Autobots able to transform into massive fighting machines as powerful as their enemy—the deadly Decepticons. When an erupting volcano revives the dormant cargo of a spaceship that crashed four million years ago, two types of Transformers emerge: the power-hungry Decepticons and the honorable Autobots. Join the struggle in these high-energy original episodes from the popular animated TV series."

The DVD box set contains the first half of the extended second season of the series, with twenty-four episodes in chronological order. Titles include: "Autobot Spike"; "Changing Gears"; "City of Steel"; "Attack of the Autobots"; "Traitor"; "The Immobilizer"; "The Autobot Run"; "Atlantis, Arise!"; "Day of the Machines"; "Enter the Nightbird"; "A Prime Problem"; "The Core"; "The Insecticon Syndrome"; "Dinobot Island Part 1"; "Dinobot Island Part 2"; "The Master Builders"; "Auto Berserk"; "Microbots"; "Megatron's Master Plan Part 1"; "Megatron's Master Plan Part 2"; "Desertion of the Dinobots Part 1"; "Desertion of the Dinobots Part 2"; "Blaster Blues"; and "A Decepticon Raider in King Arthur's Court";

Note that although the 3D CGI animation on the menus is nice, you'll likely get tired of waiting for it to finish before you can accomplish anything on the menu.

SPECIAL FEATURES Interview with Voice Actors and Writer • BotCon 2002 Documentary • Mistake Reel • Inserts: Episode Guide Booklet, Mini-Cels, Trading Card TECHNICAL FEATURES Fullscreen (1.33:1) • Languages: Eng. • Sound: Dolby Digital 2.0, Dolby Digital Surround 5.1 • Foldout Box • 4 Discs • Region 1 GENRE & RATING Robots/Science Fiction • Not Rated (Kids)

Transformers: The Movie

Rhino, 2000, 86 mins., #R2 976644. Directed by Nelson Shin. Written by Ron Friedman.

It's 2005 and the evil Decepticons have nearly defeated the heroic Autobots after years of battle. Sensing the end is near, the Autobots' leader Optimus Prime orders a desperate, last-ditch mission to Earth to retrieve enough resources to keep hope alive. Unfortunately for the Autobots, a spy sent by Megatron, the Decepticon commander, is watching the plan unfold. Soon a ruthless Decepticon ambush leaves many Autobots destroyed and the remainder in disarray. In a memorable turn of events, the Autobot chain of command is tragically cut, and the Matrix of leadership is passed to a new generation. The rookie leader, Ultra Magnus, is immediately put to the test as the planet-devouring Unicron teams with Megatron to capture the Matrix and utterly destroy the Autobots.

Though bolstered by the immense success of the *Transformers* line of toys and syndicated cartoon, this 1986 movie was a box office failure. On disc, however, *Transformers: The Movie* is a nostalgic bit of entertainment with an unusual voice cast including Eric Idle, Judd Nelson, Leonard Nimoy, and (in one of his final roles) Orson Welles. The animation was groundbreaking in 1986, and is still appealing today. But there's no forgetting the era in which Transformers was made, as the soundtrack screams 1980s, with even Weird Al Yankovic providing a track. One of the songs was even reworked for the recording studio scene in *Boogie Nights*! [BR]

SPECIAL FEATURES Interview with Composer • Storyboards TECHNICAL FEATURES Fullscreen (1.33:1) • Languages: Eng. • Sound: Dolby Digital 5.1 • Keepcase • 1 Disc • Region 1 GENRE & RATING Robots/Science Fiction • Rated PG

Treasure Island

Image, 1999, 86 mins., #ID5706PZDVD. Directed by Dino Athannassiou. Written by Barbara Slade, Marty Isenberg, Robert N. Skir, Matthew Malach, Frank Kerr, Jules Dennis, Richard Meuller, Jimmy Hibbert, Chris Trengove. Based on the novel by Robert Louis Stevenson.

Young Jim Hawkins is a dog who is given an old sea chart that's actually a treasure map to loot buried on an island. But when Jim and his friends go on a journey, their ship is overtaken by pirates, and the peg-legged fox named Long John Silver is their leader. Soon, Jim and his friends—including a girl cat who has served as Long John's cook for years—are on an island of magic, mystery, and danger. Can they outwit, outthink, and outplay the pirates to become the survivors of Treasure Island? Or will the volcano be the death of everyone?

Robert Louis Stevenson's classic is anthropomorphized in this 1993 British telefilm, and the effect is cute, even if it takes a little of the dangerous edge off the story. But then the original plot has really been so altered that it's almost another story entirely. The art designs and voice work are wonderful, making this one of the best feature-length releases that hasn't come from a major studio. Preteens will enjoy it a bit more than youngsters, but adults won't have a difficult time watching it alongside them. The DVD is strictly no-frills, but the picture transfer is excellent.

SPECIAL FEATURES None TECHNICAL FEATURES Fullscreen (1.33:1) • Languages: Eng. • Sound: Dolby Digital 2.0 • Snapcase • 1 Disc • Region 1–6 GENRE & RATING Historical/Animals/Pirates • Not Rated (Kids)

Treasure Island [Collector's Edition]

Digital Versatile Disc, 2000, 46 mins., #184. Animation Directed by Warwick Gilbert. Written by Paul Leadon. Based on the novel by Robert Louis Stevenson.

When he gets a treasure map from an old sea dog at the Admiral Benbow Inn , young Jim Hawkins is bound for adventure. Jim and his friends, Squire Trelawney and Dr. Livesey, board a sailing ship to search for the buried treasure, unaware that the ship has a partially pirate crew. Danger ensues when Hawkins learns of a planned mutiny by Long John Silver. On the island, Jim finds a marooned sailor, his friends find an old stockade, and the battle for the island—and whatever treasures it contains—begins.

Produced by Burbank Films Australia in 1987, this is a fairly faithful adaptation of the Stevenson book, complete with the mixed messages of friendship from Silver to Jim, and some deadly violence. The animation and voice work are some of the best produced by this studio, earning this a recommendation for adventure and pirate fans. As with other DVD, Ltd. releases, there is a bio of the author on the disc.

SPECIAL FEATURES Author Bio • Game TECHNICAL FEATURES Fullscreen (1.33:1) • Languages: Eng. • Sound: Dolby Digital 5.1, DTS • Keepcase • 1 Disc • Region All GENRE & RATING Historical/Adventure/Pirates • Not Rated (Kids)

Treasure Island

Warner, 90 mins., #14498.

This DVD was not available for review.

Treasures from the American Film Archives: 50 Preserved Films [Box Set]

Image, 2000, 642 mins., #9706.

This 4-DVD boxed set was not available for review. It contains examples of early animation.

Triangle ☞ see Mature/Adult Section

Trigun: The $$60,000,000,000 Man [#1]

Pioneer, 2000, 100 mins., #PIMT-0001V. Directed by Satoshi Nishimura. Story by Yasuke Kuroda. Based on the manga series by Yasuhiro Nightow in *Young King Ours.*

In a world where the desert rules and humans have barely made an existence for themselves, a new danger arrives. His name is Vash the Stampede and he's so dangerous that a 60,000,000,000 double dollar reward is out for his capture . . . dead or alive. He is known as the Humanoid Typhoon, mostly because he destroyed a whole city single-handedly. Very few have seen his face and lived to tell the tale. He's a threat to humanity, not to mention the biggest insurance liability on this whole lump of sand. And that is why Meryl Stryfe and Milly Thompson from Bernardelli Insurance Society have been sent to find him and minimize damage. That's a good idea in theory, except no one knows what the heck Vash looks like. All they can find is a skinny blond guy who claims to be Vash. Look at the doughnut-eating freak. He couldn't possibly be the Humanoid Typhoon . . . could he?

This disc starts viewers off with four episodes from this 1998 television series. It's a great mix of comedy and action that will keep fans of both space adventures and westerns satisfied. The visuals are a stand-out; not only are the weapons in this series very creative (and have unique sound design) but the villains come with an assortment of weird heads. The great soundtrack is a melding of rock, blues, and techno. As the series progresses, it changes tone a bit as well; the first half of the series is a character study of Vash, and the second half is when the real bullets begin to fly.

Not only is the fan-favorite show itself entertaining, but the discs have some of the best menus ever seen on anime DVDs. Also, the English dub is one of the better ones out there. The voice actor for Vash is top notch. There is some rough language and violence, so parents might not want little cowpokes around. But for everyone over twelve years of age, *Trigun* is gun-slinging goofy sci-fi fun! [RJM]

SPECIAL FEATURES Character and Art Galleries TECHNICAL FEATURES Fullscreen (1.33:1) • Subtitles/CC: Eng. • Languages: Jap., Eng. dub • Sound: Dolby Digital 2.0 • Keepcase • 1 Disc • Region 1 GENRE & RATING Action/Western/Science Fiction • Rated 13+

Trigun: Lost Past [#2]

Pioneer, 2000, 75 mins., #PIMT-0002V. Directed by Satoshi Nishimura. Story by Yasuke Kuroda. Based on the manga series by Yasuhiro Nightow in *Young King Ours.*

Three more western/sci-fi adventures await you on this disc of *Trigun.* At this point things seem pretty non-linear. Is this simply the adventures of Vash "the goofball" Stampede and the Insurance Girls? Watch carefully and see if you can figure out how long it takes him to actually fire his gun. "Hard Puncher" features a whole town crazy with bounty-hunting fever. Look out Vash! "Lost July" features a sexy scientist who

hires Vash to protect her, but what is really going on? "B.D.N." offers both the start of a real cliffhanger and one of the flashiest villains in the series! [RJM]

SPECIAL FEATURES Character and Art Galleries: Mechanical TECHNICAL FEATURES Fullscreen (1.33:1) • Subtitles/CC: Eng. • Languages: Jap., Eng. dub • Sound: Dolby Digital 2.0 • Keepcase • 1 Disc • Region 1 GENRE & RATING Action/Western/Science Fiction • Rated 13+

Trigun: Wolfwood [#3]

Pioneer, 2000, 75 mins., #PIMT-0003V. Directed by Satoshi Nishimura. Story by Yasuke Kuroda. Based on the manga series by Yasuhiro Nightow in *Young King Ours.*

The sand-steamer cliffhanger concludes in "And Between the Wasteland and the Sky," with an old-fashioned shoot out between Vash and the neon villain. "Murder Machine" introduces one of the more popular regulars in the series, Nicholas Wolfwood. He claims to be a priest, and he does have a giant metal cross, but check out how much heat this guy is packing! Wolfwood and Vash are going to need all the bullets they've got, because something is waiting for them in the desert. The last episode on the DVD is called "Quick Draw," and it pits Wolfwood against Vash in a gun-slinging contest. [RJM]

SPECIAL FEATURES Character and Art Galleries: Weapons TECHNICAL FEATURES Fullscreen (1.33:1) • Subtitles/CC: Eng. • Languages: Jap., Eng. dub • Sound: Dolby Digital 2.0 • Keepcase • 1 Disc • Region 1 GENRE & RATING Action/Western/Science Fiction • Rated 13+

Trigun: Gung-Ho Guns [#4]

Pioneer, 2000, 75 mins., #PIMT-0004V. Directed by Satoshi Nishimura. Story by Yasuke Kuroda. Based on the manga series by Yasuhiro Nightow in *Young King Ours.*

Halfway through the series, and things really start getting interesting. In "Escape from Pain," Vash is going after a bounty himself, and his personality has totally changed to boot! He's as cold and cruel as some of the villains that have gone after him. Can Wolfwood and the Insurance Girls stop him before he does something he'll regret? "Diablo" introduces the first of the Gung-Ho Guns, a set of deadly assassins. He's a man who has spent his entire life training to do one thing: kill Vash the Stampede. And speaking of our goofball hero, "Vash the Stampede" is basically a recap/clips episode narrated by Meryl as she tries to put the many aspects of Vash together and make sense of the guy. It's a nice breather before things get really nasty in the next disc. [RJM]

SPECIAL FEATURES Character and Art Galleries: Toys and Villains TECHNICAL FEATURES Fullscreen (1.33:1) • Subtitles/CC: Eng. • Languages: Jap., Eng. dub • Sound: Dolby Digital 2.0 • Keepcase • 1 Disc • Region 1 GENRE & RATING Action/Western/Science Fiction • Rated 13+

Trigun: Angel Arms [#5]

Pioneer, 2000, 75 mins., #PIMT-0005V. Directed by Satoshi Nishimura. Story by Yasuke Kuroda. Based on the manga series by Yasuhiro Nightow in *Young King Ours.*

A family argument starts out this fifth disc of *Trigun*. "Little Arcadia" deals with generation gaps and family ties. We also see that family means a great deal to Milly (even more than pudding). "Demon's Eye" introduces another fan-favorite member of the Gung-Ho Guns. Is there any way Vash can defeat the deadly gaze of the Demon Eye? And just how dangerous is the mysterious Legato Bluesummers? The final episode reveals not only the secret of the title, *Trigun*, but a horrifying truth. Vash must face two Gung-Ho Guns, while keeping himself from doing more harm to others. "Fifth Moon" really proves this series to be not just purely entertaining stories but something more solid as well. [RJM]

SPECIAL FEATURES Clean Credits TECHNICAL FEATURES Fullscreen (1.33:1) • Subtitles/CC: Eng. • Languages: Jap., Eng. dub • Sound: Dolby Digital 2.0 • Keepcase • 1 Disc • Region 1 GENRE & RATING Action/Western/Science Fiction • Rated 13+

Trigun: Project Seeds [#6]

Pioneer, 2001, 75 mins., #10288. Directed by Satoshi Nishimura. Story by Yasuke Kuroda. Based on the manga series by Yasuhiro Nightow in *Young King Ours.*

For those fans thirsting for more history behind Vash, the wait is over on this *Trigun* DVD. "Rem Saverem" not only shows just how Vash got onto this sandy world, but how humans in general ended up there as well. Why is a person named Knives important to Vash's story? "Goodbye for Now" brings viewers back to the present and to the sad fate of Vash the Stampede. Will Wolfwood be able to bring him out of this funk? The final episode, "Hangfire," deals with two families locked in battle. Once again, Vash and Wolfwood get involved. These guys just don't know when to quit. [RJM]

SPECIAL FEATURES Character and Art Galleries: Seeds • Japanese DVD Covers TECHNICAL FEATURES Fullscreen (1.33:1) • Sub-

titles/CC: Eng. • Languages: Jap., Eng. dub • Sound: Dolby Digital 2.0 • Keepcase • 1 Disc • Region 1 GENRE & RATING Action/Western/Science Fiction • Rated 13+

Trigun: Puppet Master [#7]

Pioneer, 2001, 75 mins., #10289. Directed by Satoshi Nishimura. Story by Yasuke Kuroda. Based on the manga series by Yasuhiro Nightow in *Young King Ours.*

"Flying Ship" introduces a new element of Vash's past, and it has something to do with a space ship hanging in midair. There, Vash and Wolfwood find a group of people that have not known the pain of living on the dusty world below. Can such a society continue when the violence is brought to them? "Out of Time" answers that question, as Gung-Ho Guns follow Vash onto the floating city and all hell breaks loose. "Alternative" features another Gung-Ho Gun and one of the turning points in the series. Things are going to go bad for some of the favorite characters from here on in. [RJM]

SPECIAL FEATURES Character and Art Galleries: Villains • Japanese VHS Covers • Inserts: Chromium Cover Card TECHNICAL FEATURES Fullscreen (1.33:1) • Subtitles/CC: Eng. • Languages: Jap., Eng. dub • Sound: Dolby Digital 2.0 • Keepcase • 1 Disc • Region 1 GENRE & RATING Action/Western/Science Fiction • Rated 13+

Trigun: High Noon [#8]

Pioneer, 2001, 100 mins., #10290. Directed by Satoshi Nishimura. Story by Yasuke Kuroda. Based on the manga series by Yasuhiro Nightow in *Young King Ours.*

Four final episodes are featured in this disc of *Trigun*. Vash has come a long way from the bumbling man Meryl and Milly first met. Now, it's a face-off between Vash and the power behind the Gung-Ho Guns. But getting to that showdown will cost lives and loves. And when it comes down to it, can Vash turn his back on everything he holds dear . . . even if it is to stop a madman who wants to cleanse this world and start all over again?

Trigun may be a real surprise for viewers. It starts off entertaining enough, but the character of Vash the Stampede is really fleshed out and carries the series. Wolfwood also fares pretty well in the character development area. Only the Insurance Girls and the Gung-Ho Guns don't become three dimensional. This series combines comedy, action, and drama very well. It's got a great visual style and is almost better the second time you watch it. And the DVDs really do have great menus; a different one for each volume! Saddle up on this adventure: *Trigun* is a trip worth taking. [RJM]

SPECIAL FEATURES Character and Art Galleries • Japanese Laserdisc Covers • Clean Credits • Easter Egg TECHNICAL FEATURES Fullscreen (1.33:1) • Subtitles/CC: Eng. • Languages: Jap., Eng. dub • Sound: Dolby Digital 2.0 • Keepcase • 1 Disc • Region 1 GENRE & RATING Action/Western/Science Fiction • Rated 13+

Trigun: The Complete DVD Box Set

Pioneer, 2001, 650 mins., #11606.

This box set contains the eight *Trigun* volumes almost exactly as they appeared in the individual keepcase editions. The only difference is the keepcase volume numbering for #1–5: #1 is now #10283; #2 is now #10284; #3 is now #10285; #4 is now #10286; and #5 is now #10287.

See individual entries for the Special and Technical Features listings.

TECHNICAL FEATURES Cardboard Box with 8 Keepcases • 8 Discs • Region 1 GENRE & RATING Action/Western/Science Fiction • Rated 13+

Troll in Central Park, A

Fox, 2002, 76 mins., #2002932. Directed by Don Bluth, Gary Goldman. Screenplay by Stu Krieger.

Stanley is a troll who lives in a world of trolls, but he's a bit different. Not only is he more human-looking than his counterparts, but he's also got a green thumb . . . literally! His magical thumb allows him to instantly grow flowers that can move on their own, but they can't move him out of the way fast enough to escape from Queen Gnorga. She hates flowers, so she exiles Stanley to the world of the humans, and he takes up residence in New York's Central Park. But there, Stanley becomes friends with Gus and his baby sister, Rosie. Peace and love bloom in pretty colors . . . until Gnorga decides to unleash some magic on New York!

This 1993 production of Don Bluth's Irish animation studio is probably the least inspired of his career. The designs are ugly, the songs flat, and even the voice work by Dom DeLuise, Cloris Leachman, and Charles Nelson Reilly feels as old as the actors. Cute, cloying, and annoying, *A Troll in Central Park* will feel more like A Mugging in Central Park if you buy it or if it is viewed by anyone over the age of two.

The disc is supposed to be double-sided, with a fullscreen version on one side and the widescreen on the other. However, since the fullscreen-labeled side repeatedly locked up the reviewer's DVD player, this could not be confirmed. The cover advertises the inclusion of the theatrical trailer and a featurette as well, but unless they're on the fullscreen side, they don't exist either.

SPECIAL FEATURES Other Title Trailers TECHNICAL FEATURES Widescreen (1.77:1 enhanced for 16x9) • Fullscreen (1.33:1) • Subtitles/CC: Eng., Span. • Languages: Eng. • Sound: Dolby Digital Surround 2.0 • Keepcase • 1 Disc • Region 1 GENRE & RATING Music/Fantasy • Rated G

Tron

Disney, 1998, 96 mins., #14256. Directed by Steven Lisberger. Screenplay by Steven Lisberger.

Kevin Flynn has invented a number of computer games, but he's recently been fired from Encom, the computer company he worked for. His rival, Alan, invented the program Tron for Encom as a security protocol, meant to watch for illegal hacking and to oversee the Master Control Program. Dillenger stole many of Flynn's game programs in the past, and now runs Encom. When Dillenger locks everyone out of the Encom system due to Flynn's attempts at hacking, Alan and his girlfriend, Lora, help Flynn sneak into the building. Flynn is sucked into the virtual world of Tron, where an electronic civilization lives, and deadly light-cycle races solve conflicts. Will Flynn be able to beat the Master Control Program, whose lieutenant Sark is the avatar of the evil Dillenger? If so, Flynn will have to win at all the games he invented . . . but which Sark has perfected.

In 1982, Disney released *Tron* to a public that was wild about video games, but still years away from virtual reality systems. The film presciently described things about computers that we take for granted these days: the Internet, virtual reality, hacking, firewalls, etc. The film was first shot in live-action, with all the "virtual world" computer scenes shot in black and white with the actors working against blackscreens. The live footage was then composited with early CGI, with all background elements, lightcycles, and other devices added in. For the distinctive glowing lines on the costumes and headgear, the film was shipped to Japan, where animators hand-animated each frame of the film!

As much as it was a technological success—and managed to come out at the same time as the video game boom—*Tron* failed to capture the hearts (and wallets) of audiences. Although it wasn't a failure, it didn't perform nearly as well as Disney had hoped it would. Some blamed the simplistic story, but the real blame probably is due to the inability to tell good guys apart from bad guys in the black-and-neon virtual world. Audiences didn't know who they were rooting for, even if the good guys glowed blue and the bad guys glowed red.

This initial DVD release of *Tron* contains an excellent copy of the film, with a booming soundtrack. This edition will suit some viewers, but hardcore fans—and technojunkies who grew up after *Tron* was released—are better served by the *20th Anniversary Collector's Edition* (see entry below).

SPECIAL FEATURES Trailer • Other Title Trailers TECHNICAL FEATURES Widescreen (2.35:1) • Subtitles/CC: Eng. • Languages: Eng., Fren. dub, Span. dub • Sound: Dolby Digital 5.0 • Keepcase • 1 Disc • Region 1 GENRE & RATING Live/CGI/Science Fiction • Rated PG

Tron [20th Anniversary Collector's Edition]

Disney, 2002, 96 mins., #23569. Directed by Steven Lisberger. Screenplay by Steven Lisberger.

This two-disc set of *Tron* is a techno-geek's best friend, delving deeper into the making of this seminal CGI film more than most viewers would have thought possible. An extensive "The Making of *Tron*" documentary runs eighty-eight minutes, almost as long as the film itself! There's also a commentary track by the writer/director, producer, and visual effects supervisors, and deleted scenes introduced by the film's star, Bruce Boxleitner.

Beyond that, there are tons of production photos (including many that weren't used for the archival laser disc edition), storyboard-to-film comparisons, animation tests, demo reels, publicity material, and even deleted music from the score! And to top it all off, this version has higher resolution since it has been enhanced for 16x9 screens, and features a remixed six-channel digital surround audio track. If you liked *Tron*, or want to see a pioneer in the CGI field at its best, this is the set to get.

SPECIAL FEATURES "Making of" Feature • Commentary Track with Filmmakers • Character and Art Galleries • Production Notes • Deleted Scenes and Music • Storyboards • Trailer • Promotional Footage • Other Title Trailers TECHNICAL FEATURES Widescreen (2.35:1 enhanced for 16x9) • Subtitles/CC: Eng., Fren., Span. • Languages: Eng. • Sound: Dolby Digital Surround 5.1 • Keepcase • 1 Disc • Region 1, 4 GENRE & RATING Live/CGI/Science Fiction • Rated PG

Trumpet of the Swan, The

Columbia/TriStar, 2001, 75 mins., #05847. Directed by Richard Rich, Terry L. Noss. Screenplay by Judy Rothman Rofe. Based on the book by E. B. White.

Triplets are born to a proud pair of Trumpeter Swans, but one of them is a bit different. Louie is a mute, unable to talk or trumpet. Other swans tease him, and he can't compete against his much-louder rival, Boyd, when they both try to win the affection of beautiful Serena. But when Louie meets a young human boy and his teacher at a camp, hope begins, and when his father gets Louie a trumpet, he finally finds his voice. Louie becomes a musical star, and learns that his talents just might help him get the girl.

Released in 2000, *The Trumpet of the Swan* was barely a blip in theaters, despite its production pedigree and an all-star cast of voices that includes Jason Alexander, Mary Steenburgen, Seth Green, Reese Witherspoon, and Carol Burnett. The film is based on one of the bestselling children's books of all time (or so the promo says), and though it's been updated to more modern times, the feel of the original story is kept. Unlike many animated features, none of the characters are orphans or orphaned, and the story is generally positive and heartwarming from beginning to end. Alexander's vocal performance is the best element of the film, but the designs are nice, the animation appropriate (if a bit rushed at times), and the music—by jazz artist Marcus Miller and guest star Little Richard—is uplifting.

The DVD is double-sided, with the widescreen version on one side, and the fullscreen version on the other.

SPECIAL FEATURES Trailers • Game • DVD-ROM Features: Game, Coloring Pages, Puppets • Other Title Trailers TECHNICAL FEATURES Widescreen (1.77:1 enhanced for 16x9) • Fullscreen (1.33:1) • Subtitles/CC: Eng., Fren., Span. • Languages: Eng., Fren. dub • Sound: Dolby Digital Surround 2.0, Dolby Digital 5.1 • Keepcase • 1 Disc • Region All GENRE & RATING Music/Animals • Rated G

Tsukikage Ran: Carried by the Wind [#1]

Bandai, 2002, 100 mins., #1930. Directed by Akitaro Daichi. Screenplay by Akitaro Daichi, Michiko Yokote, Mamiko Ikeda.

In the Edo period, a lonely female samurai named Ran loves only one thing more than fighting with her sword, and that's drinking sake. Her partner is the mysterious Chinese girl, Lady Meow of the Iron Cat Fist, who is great at martial arts but a bit clumsy and loud. Together the pair travel the land, wandering from town to town and conflict to conflict, with Ran always drinking sake wherever she can find it.

Airing on Japanese television in 2000, *Tsukikage Ran* is a parody of samurai movies and shows, but it's largely considered a parody because the roles of samurai and sidekick—usually male characters—are played by women. The series has been compared to *Xena, Warrior Princess*, and the comparison is not far off base. With strong clean animation, a nice English dub track, and an interesting soundtrack, it's a good bet that if you were a fan of *Xena*, you'll also like *Tsukikage Ran*.

The DVD has a couple of nice extras, with quite a bit

of historical material to place the settings and character in context. Picture and sound are excellent.

SPECIAL FEATURES Character and Art Galleries • Liner Notes • Promotional Footage • Other Title Trailers • Inserts: Historical Notes TECHNICAL FEATURES Fullscreen (1.33:1) • Subtitles/CC: Eng. • Languages: Jap., Eng. dub • Sound: Dolby Digital 2.0 • Keepcase • 1 Disc • Region 1 GENRE & RATING Martial Arts/Comedy • Rated 13+

Tsukikage Ran: Carried by the Wind— Shocking Secrets! [#2]

Bandai, 2002, 75 mins., #1931. Directed by Akitaro Daichi. Screenplay by Akitaro Daichi, Michiko Yokote, Mamiko Ikeda.

NOTE: This DVD arrived too late for a full review. The following text is promotional copy provided by the releasing company:

"Our heroine Ran is still saddled with her erstwhile sidekick, Meow. Together, they continue traveling the countryside looking for wrongs to right, and of course, sake! When Meow is scouted by a "modeling" agent, things don't seem quite right and it's up to Ran to figure what it is. When a string of robberies is committed, all fingers point toward our heroic heroines! Can the two clear their names, and help a poor inventor on the verge of discovering electricity?"

This disc contains episodes #5–7.

SPECIAL FEATURES Character and Art Galleries • Production Notes • Other Title Trailers • Inserts: Liner Notes TECHNICAL FEATURES Fullscreen (1.33:1) • Subtitles/CC: Eng. • Languages: Jap., Eng. dub • Sound: Dolby Digital • Keepcase • 1 Disc • Region 1 GENRE & RATING Martial Arts/Comedy • Rated 13+

Tune, The

Image, 1997, 80 mins., #ID41880CDVD.

This DVD was not available for review. It is now on moratorium.

Turbulence

Sony, 1997, 25 mins., #LVD49922.

This DVD was not available for review. It is an abstract CGI-and-music anthology.

20,000 Leagues Under the Sea [Collector's Edition]

Digital Versatile Disc, 1999, 50 mins., #173. Directed by Warwick Gilbert, Geoff Collins. Screenplay by Stephen MacLean. Based on the book by Jules Verne.

The waters off the coast of 1886 New England are treacherous; ships are being destroyed by something monstrous out at sea. Marine expert Professor Pierre Aronnax accompanies a crew of sailors out into the deep blue yonder to find what is causing the destruction. What he and tough swabbie Ned Land find is that it's not fully a "what" but also a "who." Captain Nemo has constructed an immense and powerful submarine called the *Nautilus*. Can Land and Aronnax stop Nemo, and will they want to once they find out his true goals?

Produced by Burbank Films Australia in 1985, this adaptation of Jules Verne's 1870 novel is a decent primer for kids who might be encouraged to read the book. Not nearly as exciting as Disney's 1954 live-action version, this *Leagues* suffers a bit from cartoonish figure animation mixed with more lush backgrounds. Points go to the DVD producers for including information on Verne's life and real nautiluses—both living undersea creatures and submarines—through history.

SPECIAL FEATURES Author Bio • Game TECHNICAL FEATURES Fullscreen (1.33:1) • Languages: Eng. • Sound: Dolby Digital 5.1, DTS • Keepcase • 1 Disc • Region All GENRE & RATING Historical/Adventure • Not Rated (All Ages)

Twilight of the Dark Master: Collectors Edition ☞ see Mature/Adult Section

Twin Angels ☞ see Mature/Adult Section

Twin Signal

Media Blasters, 2001, 90 mins., #AWDVD-0102. Directed by Takashi Sogabe. Screenplay by Kuniaki Yamashita. Based on the manga series by Sachi Oshimizu in *Shonen Gan-Gan*.

Robotics expert Dr. Otoi builds a new robot named Signal—who looks like a teenage boy—to function as an older brother for his grandson, Nobuhiko. Signal is very powerful, but a malfunction means that every time Nobuhiko sneezes, Signal turns into Chibi Signal, a super-deformed baby-like creature!

Chibi Signal loves chocolate and is very cute, but he isn't very powerful. That's too bad, because Pulse, one of Otoi's earlier creations, has been reprogrammed to kill Signal, and he's packing some serious firepower!

Three OVA episodes of *Twin Signal* were released in 1995, and all three of them are collected on this DVD. The plot is fairly simple and the humor is on the level of most sitcoms. The animation is competent, but super-deformed faces and expressions abound, not to mention the hyper-cutesy Chibi Signal. If you like SD stuff, here it is in spades, but if not, stay away.

SPECIAL FEATURES Character and Art Galleries • Game • Other Title Trailers • Easter Egg TECHNICAL FEATURES Fullscreen (1.33:1) • Subtitles/CC: Eng. • Languages: Jap., Eng. dub • Sound: Dolby Digital 2.0 • Keepcase • 1 Disc • Region 1 GENRE & RATING Humor/Robots • Rated 13+

Twisted Tales of Felix the Cat, The

BMG, 2000, 90 mins., #75517 45716-9. Directed by Chris Bartleman, Blair Peters, Lynne Naylor, Phil Robinson, Timothy Berglund, Milton Knight, Dominic Polcino, Robin Steele. Story by Martin Olsen, Timothy Berglund, Jeremy Kramer. Written by Martin Olsen, Jeremy Kramer, Lynne Naylor, Stephan DeStefano, Phil Robinson, Bob Koch, Timothy Berglund, Milton Knight, Michael Polcino, Dominic Polcino, Christopher Moeller, Robin Steele, Christian Roman.

Felix climbs back out of retirement for new adventures, most of which are stranger than any he ever had in the past. He helps detective crow Shamus H. Gold solve the case of the petrified cheese in Egypt, then deals with disaster when the Bermuda Triangle descends on New York City. What happens when Felix jumps onto a movie screen with his favorite starlet? Or when he gets put in jail? And even weirder, can you guess what madness will occur when Martians abduct Felix?

In the fall of 1995, after creating a series of fifty bumpers for the previous season, studio Film Roman produced a new series for CBS called *The Twisted Tales of Felix the Cat*. The series tried its best to emulate the look and feel of the original theatrical cartoons, even though they were now in color and Felix had a voice. Reportedly the most expensive cartoon Film Roman produced (and this from a company that also produced *The Simpsons!*), *Twisted Tales* lasted two seasons, with fifty-eight cel-animated, CGI, and even live-action shorts produced.

This DVD features ten stories: "The Petrified Cheese"; "Manhattan Triangle"; "Now Playing Felix"; "Jailhouse Shock"; "The Sludge Kings Parts 1 and 2"; "Mars Needs Felix"; "Space Time Twister"; "Guardian Idiot"; "Step Right Up"; and "Don't String Me Along." Each of them is full of highly stylized and surreal come-dy. The series clearly intended to live up to its title. And it succeeds.

See also entries for *Felix!* and *Felix the Cat*.

SPECIAL FEATURES None TECHNICAL FEATURES Fullscreen (1.33:1) • Languages: Eng. • Sound: Dolby Digital 2.0, Dolby Digital 5.1 • Keepcase • 1 Disc • Region 1–6 GENRE & RATING Comedy/Animals • Not Rated (Kids)

2000-Year-Old Man, The

Rhino, 2002, 26 mins., #R2 2168. Directed by Leo Salkin. Written by Carl Reiner, Mel Brooks.

This half-hour television special aired on CBS in 1975. It featured an interviewer (Carl Reiner) talking with a man who had lived for 2,000 years (Mel Brooks), with the elder man recounting stories from two millennia of "the old days." Included are stories about William Shakespeare, Robin Hood, and the origins of singing and marriage. The improvised dialogue was recorded before a live studio audience, and later animated. While the animation is fairly simple and looks dated, it accomplishes its job.

SPECIAL FEATURES None TECHNICAL FEATURES Fullscreen (1.33:1) • Languages: Eng. • Sound: Dolby Digital 1.0 • Snapcase • 1 Disc • Region 1 GENRE & RATING Comedy • Not Rated (Teens)

Ultimate 3-D Collection [Box Set]

Slingshot, 2001, 234 mins.

This DVD box set was not available for review. It features a cardboard box with the keepcase editions of *Alien Adventure*, *Haunted Castle*, and the non-animated *Encounter in the Third Dimension*.

Ultraman II

Digital Multimedia, 1997, 84 mins., #00143. Animation Directed by Hiroshi Jinzenji. Story by Hiroyasu Yamaura.

Young pilot Hikari was transported to another dimension, where he agrees to let the power of Ultraman use his body to defend Earth. Now he can transform into a red-and-white-clad hero with the power to grow to giant size. All the better to fight monsters and outer-space aliens! When the Earth Defense isn't able to handle the otherworldly attacks, Ultraman will use his superpowers and martial arts to bring peace to the world!

Ultraman first appeared in a live-action television series in 1966, and the popular hero was brought to animated form in 1979. Several *Ultraman* series, videos, and even films followed. This DVD collects four episodes of one of the series (it's unclear which one, but this version was produced in 1983) into a "movie," which basically means there is only one set of credits at the front and end. The animation is acceptable, but it's standard fare, almost Western-looking. The transfer is fine, though the sound is weak.

SPECIAL FEATURES None TECHNICAL FEATURES Fullscreen (1.33:1) • Languages: Eng. • Sound: Dolby Digital 1.0 • Keepcase • 1 Disc • Region All GENRE & RATING Robots/Science Fiction • Not Rated (Kids)

Uncensored Bosko: Vol. 1

Image, 2000, 96 mins., #ID9572BKDVD.

Bosko is a cartoon boy who can do anything. His body twists and contorts, talks back to his animator, splits into lots of little Boskos, sings, dances, and more! He has a girlfriend named Honey, and a dog named Bruno.

Bosko was the creation of Hugh Harman and Rudolf Ising for Warner Bros. Developed to counter Disney's success with Mickey Mouse and the *Silly Symphonies* series, Bosko had eerily similar adventures and became the star of the newly created *Looney Tunes* series. Harman and Ising were less concerned with originality than in putting out the animated shorts as quickly as possible; indeed, some of Bosko's animators would later recall orders from Harman to directly copy the plots and animation of Disney's shorts! *Bosko* first appeared in 1929, and stayed at Warner Bros until 1933, when a spat over money meant that Harman and Ising took their creation with them to MGM. The shows are rarely seen today due to their inherent politically incorrect attitude: there are many racial stereotypes, not the least of which is Bosko himself, who appears to be an African-American boy in old-style blackface makeup.

This DVD collects public domain copies of the *Bosko* shorts from throughout the run (pulled from the 1950s TV syndication package), including the rarely seen pilot. The quality is called "remarkable" on the packaging, but it's actually quite poor, even factoring in the age of the prints. The picture has even been cropped slightly, and the soundtrack is very low and full of static and hisses. Still, this is the only place these cartoons have ever been collected on DVD, and they do have historical value, so historians should take note.

The fourteen selections on this disc are: "Bosko the Talk-Ink Kid" (1929, the pilot); "Congo Jazz" (1930); "Big Man from the North" (1931); "Ups 'N Downs" (1931); "Yodeling Yokels" (1931); "The Tree's Knees" (1931); "Bosko the Doughboy" (1931); "Bosko's Fox Hunt" (1931); "Battling Bosko" (1931); "Sinkin' in the Bathtub (1930, the debut cartoon); "Hold Anything"

(1930); "Box Car Blues" (1930); "Ain't Nature Grand" (1931); and "Dumb Patrol" (1931).

SPECIAL FEATURES Other Title Trailers TECHNICAL FEATURES Fullscreen (1.33:1) • Languages: Eng. • Sound: Dolby Digital 1.0 • Snapcase • 1 Disc • Region 1–6 GENRE & RATING Anthology/Historical/Comedy • Not Rated (Teens)

Uncensored Bosko: Vol. 2

Image, 2000, 90 mins., #ID9573BKDVD.

Thirteen more unexpurgated black and white adventures of Bosko and his pals make up this second DVD. The episodes include: "Bosko's Holiday" (1931); "Bosko Shipwrecked" (1931); "Bosko's Soda Fountain" (1931); "Bosko at the Zoo" (1932); "The Booze Hangs High" (1930); "Big-Hearted Bosko" (1932); "Bosko and Bruno" (1930); "Bosko's Party" (1931); "Bosko's Dog Race" (1931); "Bosko at the Beach" (1931); "Bosko's Store" (1931); "Bosko and the Lumberjack" (1931); "Bosko and Honey" (1932). This disc and the previous volume together contain all of the 1930–32 Bosko shorts. The 1933 shorts and MGM years have not been collected on DVD.

SPECIAL FEATURES None TECHNICAL FEATURES Fullscreen (1.33:1) • Languages: Eng. • Sound: Dolby Digital 1.0 • Snapcase • 1 Disc • Region 1–6 GENRE & RATING Anthology/Historical/Comedy • Not Rated (Teens)

Underdog: Collector's Edition [#1]

Sony Wonder, 2000, 75 mins., #LVD 55406.

When humble and lovable Shoe Shine Boy hears cries of "Help!" he rushes off to change into the super-powered Underdog. Using strength, flight, and a few other powers, Underdog takes on arch-villains such as evil scientist Simon BarSinister, mob boss Riff Raff, the Marbleheads, and others. Often, Underdog must rescue Sweet Polly Purebread, a blond bombshell TV reporter. But when danger threatens, our heroic canine will soon be present. "Have no fear; Underdog is here!"

Debuting on NBC in 1964, Underdog soon became a hit. In 1965, when a giant Underdog balloon appeared in the Macy's Thanksgiving Day Parade, his status as an American icon was assured. Each half-hour show was split up, with other animated shorts by the same production crew filling the rest of the time. Underdog featured simple plots and repetitive animation and storylines, but almost forty years later, it retains a thrilling charm that will bring smiles to the faces of older fans and younger viewers alike.

Sony Wonder has done a nice job with this initial Underdog DVD. It features three seventeen-minute episodes (including the final show), plus four five-minute shorts, including the pilot, and a never-rerun-since-the-'60s show. The transfers range from pretty good to excellent, with the colors and soundtrack holding up astonishingly well. There is also a cool interview with Underdog's cocreator in which he reveals who the characters were based on and the origins of the Macy's balloon. There are also opening credit clips from the seven rotating series that shared Underdog's half-hour: Tennessee Tuxedo, Commander McBragg, Tooter Turtle, Go-Go Gophers, The Hunter, The King and Odie, and Klondike Kat.

Note that although the disc cover claims it is closed captioned, it is not.

SPECIAL FEATURES Interview with Cocreator • Archival Introductions • Sing-Along • Games • DVD-ROM Features: Screen Savers, Audio Clips • Other Title Trailers • Easter Egg TECHNICAL FEATURES Fullscreen (1.33:1) • Subtitles/CC: Eng. • Languages: Eng. • Sound: Dolby Digital • Keepcase • 1 Disc • Region 1 GENRE & RATING Comedy/Superhero • Not Rated (Kids)

Underdog: Collector's Edition [#1]

Sony Wonder, 2002, 75 mins.

This DVD was not available for review. The contents are exactly the same as the 2000 version, but it features a different white cover, matching the design of Underdog: Nemesis [#3].

Underdog Chronicles, The [#2]

Sony Wonder, 2001, 105 mins., #LVD 54063.

Simon BarSinister sets loose the TickleFeather Machine on the city, so that he can rule the world. Then, Riff Raff and his crew decide to steal a famous painting, whether Underdog is guarding it or not. And in a fan-favorite episode called "Zot," an alien space princess has her eyes on Underdog, and her father, King Klobber, wants her to have a strong husband. Could a ray-gun wedding be in the offing?

This second DVD isn't quite the quality package that the first one was. There is only a trio of Underdog episodes, plus four-minute episodes of Tennessee Tuxedo, Commander McBragg, Tooter Turtle, Go-Go Gophers, The Hunter, The King and Odie, and Klondike Kat. Unfortunately, the presentation is shoddier, with missing credits or altered title cards. There are some cute menus though, and more cool interview time with Underdog's cocreator.

Note that although the disc cover claims it is closed captioned, it is not.

SPECIAL FEATURES Interview with Cocreator • Storyboards • DVD-ROM Features: Screen Savers, Audio Clips • Other Title Trailers TECHNICAL FEATURES Fullscreen (1.33:1) • Subtitles/CC: Eng. • Languages: Eng. • Sound: Dolby Digital • Keepcase • 1 Disc • Region 1 GENRE & RATING Comedy/Superhero • Not Rated (Kids)

Underdog Chronicles, The [#2]

Sony Wonder, 2002, 105 mins.

This DVD was not available for review. The contents are exactly the same as the 2001 version, but it features a different red cover, matching the design of *Underdog: Nemesis [#3]*.

Underdog: Nemesis [#3]

Sony Wonder, 2002, 81 mins., #LVD 54257.

Underdog faces the wicked witch of Pickyoon to save Sweet Polly, then confronts a trio of ghost-like Silver Thieves on this third Underdog DVD. Unfortunately, the *Underdog* segments continue to get shorter, with only two seventeen-minute episodes here. The disc also contains two episodes each of *Commander McBragg, Go-Go Gophers, The King and Odie*, and *Klondike Kat*, and one episode each of *Tennessee Tuxedo, Tooter Turtle*, and *The Hunter*.

Note that although the disc cover claims it is closed captioned, it is not.

SPECIAL FEATURES DVD-ROM Features: Screen Savers, Audio Clips • Other Title Trailer TECHNICAL FEATURES Fullscreen (1.33:1) • Subtitles/CC: Eng. • Languages: Eng. • Sound: Dolby Digital • Keepcase • 1 Disc • Region 1 GENRE & RATING Comedy/Superhero • Not Rated (Kids)

Underdog Box Set

Sony Wonder, 2002, 261 mins.

This DVD box set was not available for review. It features a cardboard box with the 2002 keepcase editions of *Underdog: Collector's Edition, The Underdog Chronicles*, and *Underdog: Nemesis*.

Urotsukidoji ☛ see Mature/Adult Section

Urusei Yatsura Movie 2: Beautiful Dreamer

U.S. Manga Corps, 1998, 90 mins., #USMD 1728. Directed by Mamoru Oshii. Screenplay by Mamoru Oshii. Based on the manga series by Rumiko Takahashi in *Shonen Sunday*.

It seems like another day in the life of the crazy cast of *Urusei Yatsura*. Ataru is being a perv. Mendo is yelling like a madman and waving his sword around. Shinobu is trying to ignore everyone, and Lum is blissfully happy to be with her friends. And why shouldn't Lum be happy? It's the day of the school festival after all. But wasn't it the school festival yesterday, and the day before that, and the day before that? Soon, everyone begins to realize that something bizarre is going on. Time and space seem to have no meaning and reality is warped (or more warped than usual). But can Ataru stop being a dork long enough to figure it all out? And how the heck did Mendo get a tank?

This movie was released in theaters in 1984, and is actually a refreshing change of pace from the typical *Urusei Yatsura* antics. The plot is a mind bender, but handled very well. The characters keep their familiar personalities and designs, but it works fine with this situation. The animation in general is much better than the television series. Beyond that, this movie also has a great visual style that keeps you feeling like you are in a dream. And when it comes down to it, it's a fun movie that, for some fans, may have the best story of all the *Urusei Yatsura* tales. The DVD doesn't have the best print of the film, but it's not bad either. There is some brief nudity and slapstick violence, but nothing offensive. [RJM]

SPECIAL FEATURES Character Clips • Historical Notes • Other Title Trailers • Inserts: Liner Notes on Back of Cover Sleeve TECHNICAL FEATURES Fullscreen (1.33:1) • Subtitles/CC: Eng. • Languages: Jap., Eng. dub • Sound: Dolby Digital 2.0 • Keepcase • 1 Disc • Region All GENRE & RATING Comedy/Science Fiction • Not Rated (Teens)

Urusei Yatsura: TV Series 1

AnimEigo, 2000, 100 mins., #AV000-101. Based on the manga series by Rumiko Takahashi in *Shonen Sunday*.

Ataru Moroboshi's family and friends see him as a big loser, but the young man is about to be given a chance to save the Earth. Aliens called Oni have arrived and they have challenged the Earth to a duel . . . in the form of a game of tag. Earth's champion—for reasons that puzzle everyone—is Ataru. The Oni champion is the cute and sexy Princess Lum. Now all Ataru has to do is chase a pretty girl in a bikini and touch her horns. Well, there is one small problem: she can fly. When Ataru actually wins, his girlfriend promises to marry him, but soon, Lum thinks Ataru is going to marry *her* instead, and she begins living in his closet! The stage is set for one of the wackiest stories ever animated, and that's not even mentioning all the wild and crazy secondary characters that start showing up. Pull plots from Japanese myths and legends and toss them in the blender with some cultural references and aliens . . . you'll get *Urusei Yatsura*.

Urusei Yatsura first appeared in 1981 and is one of the most popular television series in Japan. The creator later made the wacky martial arts comedy *Ranma 1/2*. The animation is a bit dated now, but the character designs are very cute. The stories are all good no-brain fun, an aspect even reflected in the series title, which means "Those Obnoxious Aliens."

One of the interesting things about this show is that each episode is actually two different stories, so viewers get a total of eight mini-stories on one disc. This DVD set comes with a set of liner notecards to help guide the Western viewer with some of the more obscure Japanese references and in-jokes. The cards also serve as an introduction to Japanese culture, so that curious viewers might be intrigued to find out more. The show is completely subtitled, as this would be a difficult dub to pull off well. There is some brief nudity and some sexual innuendo, but most of it is done in a completely playful way. All in all, *Urusei Yatsura* is like a very funny anime-induced fever dream. [RJM]

SPECIAL FEATURES Inserts: Liner Note Cards TECHNICAL FEATURES Fullscreen (1.33:1) • Subtitles/CC: Eng. • Languages: Jap. • Sound: Dolby Digital 2.0 • Keepcase • 1 Disc • Region 1 GENRE & RATING Comedy/Science Fiction • Not Rated (Teens)

Urusei Yatsura: TV Series 2

AnimEigo, 2000, 100 mins., #AV000-102. Based on the manga series by Rumiko Takahashi in *Shonen Sunday*.

Lum and the gang return for more wacky adventures in this disc. The first episode, "Sakura, Raving Beauty of Mystery," introduces the school nurse/Shinto priestess. Of course she's a sexy older woman that Ataru can't resist. And just when you thought it was safe to play with voodoo dolls, it's time to think again. Take a look at "Voodoo Dolls of Vengeance" and you'll understand. Then, Lum's old friend from Neptune, Oyuki, arrives and takes up residence with the Moroboshis in "Neptune Is Beyond My Closet." Plus, a mirror mishap unleashes a devil that Cherry can't exorcize, a mishap on an airline flight puts the gang among the dinosaurs, and Ataru finds a way to insulate himself from Lum's electrical zaps. [RJM]

SPECIAL FEATURES Inserts: Liner Note Cards TECHNICAL FEATURES Fullscreen (1.33:1) • Subtitles/CC: Eng. • Languages: Jap. • Sound: Dolby Digital 2.0 • Keepcase • 1 Disc • Region 1 GENRE & RATING Comedy/Science Fiction • Not Rated (Teens)

Urusei Yatsura: TV Series 3

AnimEigo, 2000, 100 mins., #AV000-103. Based on the manga series by Rumiko Takahashi in *Shonen Sunday*.

The good old-fashioned holiday episode "Pitter Patter Christmas" is a two-parter, and is one of the best episodes on this disc. Another good one is "Ataru Genji Goes to the Heian Capital," a retelling of the classic Japanese story "The Tale of Genji," with an *Urusei Yatsura* time-traveling baby-napping twist. Then, the "Battle Royal of Love" features a disco, a wild bear, and demon-summoning gone horribly wrong. By the end of the episode viewers will have disco fever too!

Later, Princes Kurama of the Karasutengu (crow goblins) picks Ataru as a suitable mate, but only if she can completely remake him. And Kurama's father promises to tutor Ataru in swordsmanship in exchange for lessons on becoming a babe magnet. [RJM]

SPECIAL FEATURES Inserts: Liner Note Cards TECHNICAL FEATURES Fullscreen (1.33:1) • Subtitles/CC: Eng. • Languages: Jap. • Sound: Dolby Digital 2.0 • Keepcase • 1 Disc • Region 1 GENRE & RATING Comedy/Science Fiction • Not Rated (Teens)

Urusei Yatsura: TV Series 4

AnimEigo, 2000, 100 mins., #AV000-104. Based on the manga series by Rumiko Takahashi in *Shonen Sunday*.

If the Bradys can go to Hawaii for vacation, then what's to stop the *Urusei Yatsura* crew from taking a trip to the islands as well? Two tales in Hawaii include "Hawaiian Swimsuit Thief," the title of which makes the plot self-explanatory. And in "Full Course from Hell," Cherry and Sakura take an "all you can eat" challenge.

Introduced in this disc in "Mendo Brings Trouble" is the amazingly rich and snobby Mendo Shutaro, and Lum uses high-tech astrology to see if Mendo would be a better mate for her than Ataru. The Chinese Gods of Luck have a grudge match at the end of winter, and a new teacher at school brings new problems. And wrapping up the disc is a meeting of the mothers of Lum, Ataru, and Mendo, in "Terrifying Visiting Day." If you thought *your* mom could be a pain, you haven't seen anything yet! [RJM]

SPECIAL FEATURES Inserts: Liner Note Cards TECHNICAL FEATURES Fullscreen (1.33:1) • Subtitles/CC: Eng. • Languages: Jap. •

Sound: Dolby Digital 2.0 • Keepcase • 1 Disc • Region 1
GENRE & RATING Comedy/Science Fiction • Not Rated (Teens)

Urusei Yatsura: TV Series 5

AnimEigo, 2000, 100 mins., #AV000-105.
Based on the manga series by Rumiko
Takahashi in *Shonen Sunday*.

The final disc in this set contains
some of the most random stories and
characters you'll ever see. The first
episode puts a mysterious camera in
Mendo's hands. You've got to see
"The 4D Camera" to believe it. Lum's
childhood friend (or foe), Ran, is introduced in "Girl's
Day," and she's out for revenge. "The Tearful Diary of
Tomorrow" puts too much temptation into Ataru's
hands, since it is literally a book from the future. Plus, an
alien baby pops up in Mendo's locker, Ataru accidentally
sells his soul, and the school gets sleepy thanks to two
spirits. The final episode, "Peach-Blossom Poetry Contest," pits Ataru against a Poetry wizard to improvise the
best poem about peach blossoms.

Urusei Yatsura is a mix of totally absurd and slapstick
humor. It bases much of its comedy on Japanese culture
and language, so as a result, some Western viewers might
feel a bit alienated. But the characters are likable and the
situations that occur can be hilarious. It's worth your
time to check out a few episodes of the show. Most people who give it a shot end up becoming big fans of Lum
and company. [RJM]

SPECIAL FEATURES Inserts: Liner Note Cards TECHNICAL FEATURES
Fullscreen (1.33:1) • Subtitles/CC: Eng. • Languages: Jap. •
Sound: Dolby Digital 2.0 • Keepcase • 1 Disc • Region 1
GENRE & RATING Comedy/Science Fiction • Not Rated (Teens)

Urusei Yatsura: TV Series 6

AnimEigo, 2001, 100 mins., #AV001-106.
Based on the manga series by Rumiko
Takahashi in *Shonen Sunday*.

In "The Duel! Ataru versus Ataru,"
when Ataru eats a magic melon, he
splits into a polite Ataru and a not-so-
polite Ataru. Then, Ataru lets loose a
dream demon when he falls asleep in
class in "Wake Up to a Nightmare."
And if you are confused as to the story so far, Mrs.
Moroboshi recaps the series' first forty-two episodes in
"Urusei Yatsura All-Star All-Out Attack!" Kaede, the
ninja girl, makes her debut in "The School Excursion!
Run Kunoichi!," which also features a pack of baby ninjas. Finally, in "The Great Space Matchmaking Operation," Lum's father plays matchmaker, involving a
unicorn boy, a winged woman named Primu, and the
Prince of the Underground, among other bizarre aliens.

This DVD volume contains TV episodes #41–44 and
two special *Urusei Yatsura* episodes, originally airing in
March–April 1982. With this volume, the episodes started to be longer in length as well, meaning only four sto-
ries/episodes for future volumes. The disc also contains
two "Kansai Electric Public Service Announcements."

SPECIAL FEATURES Promotional Footage • Insert: Liner Notes
TECHNICAL FEATURES Fullscreen (1.33:1) • Subtitles/CC: Eng. •
Languages: Jap. • Sound: Dolby Digital 2.0 • Keepcase • 1
Disc • Region 1 GENRE & RATING Comedy/Science Fiction • Not
Rated (Teens)

Urusei Yatsura: TV Series 7

AnimEigo, 2001, 100 mins., #AV001-107.
Based on the manga series by Rumiko
Takahashi in *Shonen Sunday*.

During a trip to the outdoors in "The
Big Springtime Picnic Uproar!" Ataru
is captured by a lizard creature and
discovers a mermaid, while Lum and
the group stumble upon a buried
UFO! Mind-switching earmuffs get
Ataru and JariTen in enough trouble that they pay attention to the title, "Beware of Earmuffs!" And what's with
the caterpillar that keeps eating and growing at school?
Find out in "Fly Imo!" Finally, in "Ten's Love," JariTen is
in lust with Sakura. Will a double date with Lum and
Ataru help matters?

This DVD volume contains TV episodes #45–49,
originally airing in April–May 1982. As mentioned on
the previous volume, the stories are now longer, with
dual plots.

SPECIAL FEATURES Insert: Liner Notes TECHNICAL FEATURES
Fullscreen (1.33:1) • Subtitles/CC: Eng. • Languages: Jap. •
Sound: Dolby Digital 2.0 • Keepcase • 1 Disc • Region 1
GENRE & RATING Comedy/Science Fiction • Not Rated (Teens)

Urusei Yatsura: TV Series 8

AnimEigo, 2001, 100 mins., #AV001-108.
Based on the manga series by Rumiko
Takahashi in *Shonen Sunday*.

A vampire strikes in "What a Dracula!" but why are Ataru and Lum helping him snack on Ran? Then, Lum
goes back in time to reform young
Ataru, but he follows her to the past
in "Lum's Education Lecture Course
for Boys." JariTen and Ataru are both interested in a
flower shop girl in "From the Gardenia, with Love," but
JariTen's experiments give the plant sentience! Lastly, Ataru dates a new girl at school who is cursed by a
bad weather spirit in "A Beautiful Girl Brings Rain."

This DVD volume contains TV episodes #50–53,
originally airing in May–June 1982.

SPECIAL FEATURES Insert: Liner Notes TECHNICAL FEATURES
Fullscreen (1.33:1) • Subtitles/CC: Eng. • Languages: Jap. •
Sound: Dolby Digital 2.0 • Keepcase • 1 Disc • Region 1
GENRE & RATING Comedy/Science Fiction • Not Rated (Teens)

Urusei Yatsura: TV Series 9

AnimEigo, 2001, 100 mins., #AV001-109.
Based on the manga series by Rumiko
Takahashi in *Shonen Sunday*.

Poor JariTen loses his horn and his
powers in "Gimme Back My Horn!"
But when Ran curses the horn—
thinking it's Lum's—the situation gets
thorny for Ten. And in "Shocking
Library—Quiet, Please!" Ataru helps
out at the school library, and meets some very familiar
literary characters. Lum finally goes to school in "Mr.
Hanawa Arrives! It's the Springtime of Youth!" just in
time for a new teacher and the tryouts for the volleyball
team. And in "Goblin in Distress, Yearning for People," a
blue goblin with a penchant for water takes up residence
at one of Mendo's hotels, then Ataru's house!

This *Urusei Yatsura* DVD volume contains TV episodes
#54–57, originally airing in June 1982.

SPECIAL FEATURES Insert: Liner Notes TECHNICAL FEATURES
Fullscreen (1.33:1) • Subtitles/CC: Eng. • Languages: Jap. •
Sound: Dolby Digital 2.0 • Keepcase • 1 Disc • Region 1
GENRE & RATING Comedy/Science Fiction • Not Rated (Teens)

Urusei Yatsura: TV Series 10

AnimEigo, 2001, 100 mins., #AV001-110.
Based on the manga series by Rumiko
Takahashi in *Shonen Sunday*.

Ran tries to steal Ataru away from
Lum by making him sick, prompting
the interference of Sakura in "Darling's Had It This Time!" Then, Rei
comes to school hungry and disrupts
everyone in "Rei Returns! The Big
Study-Hall Panic!!" Next, teacher Onsen-mark tells
about a mysterious phantom man who stole his girlfriend in the past, and the same phantom—older and fat-
ter—shows up again in "The Coming of the Mysterious
Mantle!?" Then, Ran and Lum begin creating duplicates
of Ataru in "Steal Darling! The Copy Operation!!"

This *Urusei Yatsura* DVD volume contains TV episodes
#58–61, originally airing in July and August of 1982.

SPECIAL FEATURES Insert: Liner Notes TECHNICAL FEATURES
Fullscreen (1.33:1) • Subtitles/CC: Eng. • Languages: Jap. •
Sound: Dolby Digital 2.0 • Keepcase • 1 Disc • Region 1
GENRE & RATING Comedy/Science Fiction • Not Rated (Teens)

Urusei Yatsura: TV Series 11

AnimEigo, 2001, 100 mins., #AV001-111.
Based on the manga series by Rumiko
Takahashi in *Shonen Sunday*.

Lum and Ataru go out on a date, but
it turns out to be anything but normal
in "Thrilling Summer Date." Ataru,
Lum, and Shinobu then run afoul of a
watermelon god, while a party gets
crashed by a weepy lizard-goblin in
"Goodbye, So Long, Summer Days." A typhoon has
everyone panicking and packing, but Lum thinks a capsule she has might be the safe antidote in "Panic in a
Typhoon." Then, JariTen and Lum accidentally get drunk
and cause problems, all because their race has no tolerance for alcohol! Their drunken rampage happens in
"Drunkard's Boogie."

Episodes #62–65 of *Urusei Yatsura* make up this DVD
volume. The shows originally aired in August–September 1982.

SPECIAL FEATURES Inserts: Liner Note Cards TECHNICAL FEATURES
Fullscreen (1.33:1) • Subtitles/CC: Eng. • Languages: Jap. •
Sound: Dolby Digital 2.0 • Keepcase • 1 Disc • Region 1
GENRE & RATING Comedy/Science Fiction • Not Rated (Teens)

Urusei Yatsura: TV Series 12

AnimEigo, 2001, 100 mins., #AV001-112.
Based on the manga series by Rumiko
Takahashi in *Shonen Sunday*.

Misuzu is half cat/half woman, but a
kiss from Ataru or JariTen could turn
her fully into one or the other in
"The Terror of Meow." After Ataru
complains about Lum, she leaves
Earth, prompting the others to search
for her in "After You've Gone." All of Lum's alien and
magical friends decide to visit her at school, just before
Ataru and Mendo disappear in "Lum's Class Reunion."
Then, the teachers want the kids to stop sneaking away
from school for fast food in "Lunchtime Eat-Out'ers
Gather Around."

Episodes #66–69 of *Urusei Yatsura* make up this DVD
volume. The 67th episode, "After You've Gone," was
voted the best *Urusei Yatsura* episode in a Japanese survey.
The shows originally aired in September–October 1982.

SPECIAL FEATURES Inserts: Liner Note Cards TECHNICAL FEATURES
Fullscreen (1.33:1) • Subtitles/CC: Eng. • Languages: Jap. •
Sound: Dolby Digital 2.0 • Keepcase • 1 Disc • Region 1
GENRE & RATING Comedy/Science Fiction • Not Rated (Teens)

Urusei Yatsura: TV Series 13

AnimEigo, 2001, 100 mins., #AV001-113. Based on the manga series by Rumiko Takahashi in *Shonen Sunday*.

When Ataru constructs a bizarre bird out of prehistoric fossils, Lum brings it to life with disastrous results in "Terror! The Deserted Fossil Ground's Mystery." Then, goblin girl Kurama tries to get Mendo to be her mate in "Princess Kurama—A New Challenge." JariTen's alien toothache seems to be spreading like a plague in "The Terrifying Cavity Wars." Next, Mendo's younger sister Ryoko has the hots for Ataru, and Mendo and Lum are horrified in "The Mendo Siblings."

Episodes #70–73 of *Urusei Yatsura* make up this DVD volume. The shows originally aired in November 1982.

SPECIAL FEATURES Inserts: Liner Note Cards TECHNICAL FEATURES Fullscreen (1.33:1) • Subtitles/CC: Eng. • Languages: Jap. • Sound: Dolby Digital 2.0 • Keepcase • 1 Disc • Region 1 GENRE & RATING Comedy/Science Fiction • Not Rated (Teens)

Urusei Yatsura: TV Series 14

AnimEigo, 2001, 100 mins., #AV001-114. Based on the manga series by Rumiko Takahashi in *Shonen Sunday*.

Why is there a huge white Kotatsu half-ghost cat blocking the stairway at Ataru's home? Find out in "There's a Cat on the Stairs." A magical bird helped by Ataru changes into a raccoon and tries unsuccessfully to return the kindness in "Can a Raccoon Repay a Favor?!" And what kind of person would take the hellish job of attendant at an alien bath house? That would be Ataru, in "The Do-or-Die Subspace Part-Time Job." Finally, Lum's dimensional doors give everyone new identities in fictional worlds, but some of them are forgetting who they are, in "The Big Year-End Party that Lum Organized!"

Episodes #74–77 of *Urusei Yatsura* make up this DVD volume. The shows originally aired in December 1982.

SPECIAL FEATURES Inserts: Liner Note Cards TECHNICAL FEATURES Fullscreen (1.33:1) • Subtitles/CC: Eng. • Languages: Jap. • Sound: Dolby Digital 2.0 • Keepcase • 1 Disc • Region 1 GENRE & RATING Comedy/Science Fiction • Not Rated (Teens)

Urusei Yatsura: TV Series 15

AnimEigo, 2001, 100 mins., #AV001-115. Based on the manga series by Rumiko Takahashi in *Shonen Sunday*.

Ataru and the others play roles in an ancient Japanese story that involves a legendary swordsman and a giant monkey in "Bad Boy Musashi: A Success Story." After a massive snowball fight, JariTen seeks revenge in the classroom, but the teacher has demanded complete silence in "We'll Risk Our Lives During Classtime!" And why does Lum's father come to live with her? Could it be because mother has kicked him out of the house? Find out the hilarious answer in "Domestic Quarrel—To Eat or To Be Eaten?!" Then, Ataru and Lum go on a ski trip, but Lum isn't happy that the winner of a ski contest gets a romantic prize in "Steal the Kiss of Miss Snow Queen!"

Episodes #78–81 of *Urusei Yatsura* make up this DVD volume. The shows originally aired in January–February 1983.

SPECIAL FEATURES Inserts: Liner Note Cards TECHNICAL FEATURES Fullscreen (1.33:1) • Subtitles/CC: Eng. • Languages: Jap. • Sound: Dolby Digital 2.0 • Keepcase • 1 Disc • Region 1 GENRE & RATING Comedy/Science Fiction • Not Rated (Teens)

Urusei Yatsura: TV #1–5 [Box Set]

AnimEigo, 2000, 500 mins., #AV001-201.

This box set contains *Urusei Yatsura* volumes #1–5 exactly as they appeared in the individual keepcase editions. It was originally available via the AnimEigo website, prior to these volumes being released individually. See individual entries for the Special and Technical Features listings.

TECHNICAL FEATURES Cardboard Box with 5 Keepcases • 5 Discs • Region 1 GENRE & RATING Comedy/Science Fiction • Not Rated (Teens)

Urusei Yatsura: TV #6–10 [Box Set]

AnimEigo, 2001, 500 mins., #AV001-202.

This box set contains *Urusei Yatsura* volumes #6–10 exactly as they appeared in the individual keepcase editions. It was originally available via the AnimEigo website, prior to these volumes being released individually. See individual entries for the Special and Technical Features listings.

TECHNICAL FEATURES Cardboard Box with 5 Keepcases • 5 Discs

• Region 1 GENRE & RATING Comedy/Science Fiction • Not
Rated (Teens)

Urusei Yatsura: TV #11–15 [Box Set]

AnimEigo, 2001, 500 mins., #AV001-203.

This box set contains *Urusei Yatsura*
volumes #11–15 exactly as they
appeared in the individual keepcase
editions. It was originally available via
the AnimEigo website, prior to these
volumes being released individually.
See individual entries for the Special
and Technical Features listings.

TECHNICAL FEATURES Cardboard Box with 5 Keepcases • 5 Discs
• Region 1 GENRE & RATING Comedy/Science Fiction • Not
Rated (Teens)

V

Vampire Hunter D: Special Edition ☞ see

Mature/Adult Section

Vampire Hunter D: Bloodlust ☞ see

Mature/Adult Section

Vampire Princess Miyu: Initiation [TV #1]

Tokyopop, 2001, 75 mins., #TPDV-972.
Directed by Toshiki Hirano. Written by
Toshiki Hirano. Based on the manga
series by Narumi Kakinouchi.

Miyu was born a vampire princess
with a curse. She has the duty of traveling the world seeking Shinma,
shape-shifting vampires and monsters
loose on earth, and returning them to
their realm, the Dark. She's joined in her quest by Larva,
a former evil Shinma who tried to kill her, but whom
she was able to overpower, bite, and change his mind
about his place in this world. Larva now acts as her
guardian as the pair try to fulfill Miyu's obligation to dis-
pel the Shinma. Until Miyu can complete this task, she's
forced to live life as an eternal thirteen-year-old, roam-
ing the earth, never at peace. The two face more than evil
demons; they also face former friends of Larva who are
hell bent on returning him to the fold and breaking the
spell they think Miyu has on him.

Vampire Princess Miyu, a successful manga series, was
created in 1988 by Narumi Kakinouchi and initially saw
life as four OVAs. In 1997, it became a successful twenty-
five-episode anime series. The animation is strong and
moody. This haunting DVD contains the first three television episodes and is named "Initiation" for a good reason: It initiates viewers into the life of Miyu and the
specific problems she's going to face. However be
warned that *Vampire Princess Miyu* is a bit repetitive since
almost every episode deals with finding a Shinma,
defeating it, and moving on. [JMC]

SPECIAL FEATURES Character and Art Galleries • Other Title Trailers • Inserts: Liner Notes, Episode Guide TECHNICAL FEATURES
Fullscreen (1.33:1) • Subtitles/CC: Eng. • Languages: Jap.,

Eng. dub • Sound: Dolby Digital 2.0 • Keepcase • 1 Disc •
Region 1–6 GENRE & RATING Horror/Action • Not Rated (Teens)

Vampire Princess Miyu: Haunting [TV #2]

Tokyopop, 2001, 100 mins., #TPDV-1132.
Directed by Toshiki Hirano. Written by
Toshiki Hirano. Based on the manga
series by Narumi Kakinouchi.

Miyu learns that a lot of people entering a wooded area never return, and
she believes a Shinma is responsible.
Then, a missing movie is scary, but
not because it's a horror film. Miyu
investigates to find out what secrets are held on the
bloody silver screen. Then, an evil Shinma double of
Miyu is out ruining Miyu's reputation. Can the Vampire
Princess put a stop to the Shinma while she still has some
friends left? Finally, Miyu meets a few siblings with
supernatural powers who've been shunned by family and
friends and taken to a life on the road. Are these the
friends to end Miyu's loneliness, or just another tragic
encounter?

Miyu faces more Shinma in the second volume, containing episodes #4–7 of this eerie anime series, which
introduces Reiha, someone whom Miyu isn't sure is a
friend or a foe. [JMC]

SPECIAL FEATURES Character and Art Galleries • Clean Credits •
Other Title Trailers • Inserts: Liner Notes, Episode Guide TECH-
NICAL FEATURES Fullscreen (1.33:1) • Subtitles/CC: Eng. • Lan-
guages: Jap., Eng. dub • Sound: Dolby Digital 2.0 • Keepcase
• 1 Disc • Region 1 GENRE & RATING Horror/Action • Not Rated
(Teens)

Vampire Princess Miyu: Illusion [TV #3]

Tokyopop, 2002, 100 mins., #TPDV-1262.
Directed by Toshiki Hirano. Written by
Toshiki Hirano. Based on the manga
series by Narumi Kakinouchi.

Lucky red shoes might be bringing
danger instead of good fortune, since
Miyu suspects they have ties to the
Shinma. A couple become obsessed
with a cat, but is the feline just lovable

or it something more sinister? A vacation by the lake brings with it some uninvited company. Can Miyu and Reiha get rid of these Shinma party crashers? Finally, a murdered killer returns to life with a new identity and the determination to lead a different life. But can he escape from his past sins?

Nothing is as it seems in this third ghostly volume of *Vampire Princess Miyu*, collecting episodes #8–11. [JMC]

SPECIAL FEATURES Clean Credits • Other Title Trailers • Inserts: Liner Notes TECHNICAL FEATURES Fullscreen (1.33:1) • Subtitles/CC: Eng. • Languages: Jap., Eng. dub • Sound: Dolby Digital 2.0 • Keepcase • 1 Disc • Region 1 GENRE & RATING Horror/Action • Not Rated (Teens)

Vampire Princess Miyu: Mystery [TV #4]

Tokyopop, 2002, 125 mins., #TPDV-1292. Directed by Toshiki Hirano. Written by Toshiki Hirano. Based on the manga series by Narumi Kakinouchi.

First Miyu must learn if a mysterious rich woman is just a lonely recluse or a Shinma who is luring people into her lair and then disposing of them. More secrets of Larva are revealed when he's lured onto a ghost ship by a Shinma who is hoping to return the reformed Larva to his evil ways. Finally, Miyu meets Yuiri, another Shinma hunter, but will the two work together or will Miyu become the next target for Yuiri?

It's a Larva-licious collection as we learn more about Miyu's man-Friday in episodes #12–16. [JMC]

SPECIAL FEATURES Clean Credits • Other Title Trailers • Inserts: Liner Notes TECHNICAL FEATURES Fullscreen (1.33:1) • Subtitles/CC: Eng. • Languages: Jap., Eng. dub • Sound: Dolby Digital 2.0 • Keepcase • 1 Disc • Region 1 GENRE & RATING Horror/Action • Not Rated (Teens)

Vampire Princess Miyu: Dark Love [TV #5]

Tokyopop, 2002, 125 mins., #TPDV-1302. Directed by Toshiki Hirano. Written by Toshiki Hirano. Based on the manga series by Narumi Kakinouchi.

When Miyu discovers a loving human and Shinma relationship, will she do her duty or leave the couple in peace? Then can Miyu rescue a man compelled to build homes for Shinma before he wastes his life away in their service? A famous doll-maker hires a young assistant who may be more than meets the eye. Is she just an overeager employee, or a Shinma in disguise? A young girl wants Miyu's help to rouse her father from the daze he's been in. Miyu discovers a Shinma may be responsible for his mood and works to banish the demon. Finally, Miyu must rescue a woman

from a trio of Shinma terrorizing a town and planning on making the girl their bride.

This penultimate spooky DVD collects episodes #17–21 of *Vampire Princess Miyu*. [JMC]

SPECIAL FEATURES Character and Art Galleries • Clean Credits • Other Title Trailers • Inserts: Liner Notes TECHNICAL FEATURES Fullscreen (1.33:1) • Subtitles/CC: Eng. • Languages: Jap., Eng. dub • Sound: Dolby Digital 2.0 • Keepcase • 1 Disc • Region 1 GENRE & RATING Horror/Action • Not Rated (Teens)

Vampire Princess Miyu: The Last Shinma [TV #6]

Tokyopop, 2002, 125 mins., #TPDV-1312. Directed by Toshiki Hirano. Written by Yuji Hayami. Based on the manga series by Narumi Kakinouchi.

NOTE: This DVD arrived too late for a full review. The following text is promotional copy provided by the releasing company:

"In a flashback, unaware of her true identity, Miyu is living as a normal girl with her mother. But a stray Shinma tribe is plotting to kill Miyu off before she awakens! Then, stray Shinma are dying mysteriously, and Miyu suspects Reiha, but can't understand why. Later, Tokiya is given the power of Shinma, and returns to Tokiwadai as an assassin with the mission of killing Miyu. Then, in order to protect her friends, Miyu must reveal her true identity to Chisato and the others. Finally, Larva is trapped in a mysterious place and is confronted by the mighty bird Shinma, Shidon."

This disc contains episodes #22–26.

SPECIAL FEATURES Character and Art Galleries • Trailer • Other Title Trailers • Inserts: Liner Notes TECHNICAL FEATURES Fullscreen (1.33:1) • Subtitles/CC: Eng. • Languages: Jap., Eng. dub • Sound: Dolby Digital • Keepcase • 1 Disc • Region 1 GENRE & RATING Horror/Action • Not Rated (Teens)

Vampire Princess Miyu: Vol. 1

AnimEigo, 2001, 50 mins., #AV201-070. Directed by Toshihiro Hirano. Screenplay by Noboru Aikawa. Based on the manga series by Narumi Kakinouchi.

Himiko is a spiritualist who doesn't always believe in her work. But soon enough, in the old world city of Kyoto—Japan's former capital—she discovers a wave of vampire attacks and the demonic hordes of the Shinma. While trying to exorcise a child thought possessed, Himiko comes into confrontation with Miyu, a teenage girl who is, in reality, a vampire. And there's something even weirder about her hulking, silent companion. Are they friends or foes of humanity? Later, Himiko and Miyu are both drawn into the life of a school boy whose classmates are mysteriously disappearing, replaced by strange dolls.

This DVD contains the first two *Vampire Princess Miyu* OVAs from 1988, predating the television series. The animation holds up well, and the gothic, moody stories are intriguing. Episode titles are "Unearthly Kyoto" and "A Banquet of Marionettes." The DVD includes a "signs–only" caption option for translation of all text and signage during the series.

SPECIAL FEATURES Character and Art Galleries • Other Title Trailers • Inserts: Liner Notes TECHNICAL FEATURES Fullscreen (1.33:1) • Subtitles/CC: Eng. • Languages: Jap., Eng. dub • Sound: Dolby Digital 2.0 • Keepcase • 1 Disc • Region 1 GENRE & RATING Horror/Action • Not Rated (Teens)

Vampire Princess Miyu: Vol. 2

AnimEigo, 2001, 55 mins., #AV201-071. Directed by Toshihiro Hirano. Screenplay by Noboru Aikawa. Based on the manga series by Narumi Kakinouchi.

Himiko and Miyu strike an uneasy bargain, in which Himiko will gain some valuable knowledge about herself in exchange for her help in defeating the Shinma. Their first battle is against an armored monster that seems connected to a beautiful young man. Plus, Himiko learns the twisted origins of Larva, Miyu's silent sidekick. And later, in Himiko's childhood home town of Kamakura, the true connections between Miyu and Himiko are made clear as secrets of both their pasts are brought to light.

This second DVD contains the third and fourth OVAs of the 1988–89 series, which would be brought to television almost a decade later. Episode titles are "Fragile Armor" and "Frozen Time." Look for a humorous *non*-liner note card inserted with the disc. The image gallery is a repeat from the first disc, and the DVD again includes a "signs–only" caption option.

SPECIAL FEATURES Character and Art Galleries TECHNICAL FEATURES Fullscreen (1.33:1) • Subtitles/CC: Eng. • Languages: Jap., Eng. dub • Sound: Dolby Digital 2.0 • Keepcase • 1 Disc • Region 1 GENRE & RATING Horror/Action • Not Rated (Teens)

Vampire Wars ☞ see Mature/Adult Section

Vandread: Enemy Engaged! [#1]

Pioneer, 2002, 100 mins., #11651. Directed by Takeshi Mori. Screenplay by Atsuhiro Tomioka.

Several generations after a colony ship left earth for a new home, a schism has developed between the colonists. At some point, the males and the females were separated, and as a result, they've formed their own insular societies. Not surprisingly, the men and women are now deeply suspicious of each other, and the two societies wage war constantly. Hibiki Tokai is a mechanic who's very low on the social totem pole in the male society, the Tarak Empire. To impress his friends, Hibiki tries to steal a Vanguard, one of the Tarak's bipedal combat machines. But before he knows it, Hibiki finds himself in the middle of a devastating fight between the Tarak and the Mejale (female) forces. In the end, a catastrophic warp accident occurs, and Hibiki finds himself stranded with two other men on a ship full of women, and surrounded by unknown enemies. Which will the men find more terrifying—the enemies, or the women?

Vandread seems dopey on its face, but it's actually remarkably entertaining. The series sets up a "battle of the sexes" scenario, but suddenly diverts and becomes a straightforward comedy-tinged action series. There's more social tension than sexual, and most of the characters are distinctive and likeable. With its attractive characters, flashy computer animation, and easy-to-follow story, Vandread is a highly accessible series.

This DVD is presented in widescreen, though it's not the high-resolution anamorphic widescreen seen on some DVDs. The disc contains episodes #1–4 of this thirteen-episode TV series, along with a fairly standard set of extras. [MT]

SPECIAL FEATURES Character and Art Galleries • Promotional Footage • Clean Credits • Inserts: Trading Cards TECHNICAL FEATURES Widescreen (1.85:1) • Subtitles/CC: Eng. • Languages: Jap., Eng. dub • Sound: Dolby Digital 2.0 • Keepcase • 1 Disc • Region 1 GENRE & RATING CGI/Science Fiction • Rated 13+

Vandread: Nirvana [#2]

Pioneer, 2002, 75 mins., #11704. Directed by Takeshi Mori. Screenplay by Atsuhiro Tomioka.

Hibiki and his friends have adjusted to dealing with their new female captors/co-workers. But problems remain—the warp accident has caused some very strange side effects in the crew's ship, the *Nirvana*, and enemies are still all around. Most terrifying, though, is the fact that Dita, one of the Mejale's pilots, is quite fond of Hibiki. She wants to make friends with him, which he simply can't handle. Among the crew's discoveries is the fact that Hibiki's bipedal Vanguard robot can combine with Dita's sleek Dread fighter, creating an entirely new and extremely powerful weapon.

This DVD continues the decent widescreen presentation of the first disc. The DVD contains episodes #5–7 of this thirteen-episode TV series, along with a fairly standard set of extras. [MT]

SPECIAL FEATURES Character and Art Galleries • Promotional Footage • Clean Credits • Inserts: Trading Cards TECHNICAL FEATURES Widescreen (1.85:1) • Subtitles/CC: Eng. • Languages: Jap., Eng. dub • Sound: Dolby Digital 2.0 • Keepcase • 1 Disc • Region 1 GENRE & RATING CGI/Science Fiction • Rated 13+

Vandread: Great Expectations [#3]

Pioneer, 2002, 75 mins., #11705. Directed by Takeshi Mori. Screenplay by Atsuhiro Tomioka.

The *Nirvana* continues to fight its way toward home, and the strange relationships between the ship's female crew and their male guests continue to blossom. On an abandoned spacebound colony, the group meets Rabat, a rapacious space pirate who may not be entirely friendly to their cause. Along with him, they grapple with other threats, such as more alien adversaries and the prospect of exchanging Christmas presents.

This DVD continues the same widescreen presentation of the first disc, for episodes #8–10. [MT]

SPECIAL FEATURES Character and Art Galleries • Promotional Footage • Clean Credits TECHNICAL FEATURES Widescreen (1.85:1) • Subtitles/CC: Eng. • Languages: Jap., Eng. dub • Sound: Dolby Digital 2.0 • Keepcase • 1 Disc • Region 1 GENRE & RATING CGI/Science Fiction • Rated 13+

Vandread: Pressure [#4]

Pioneer, 2002, 75 mins., #11706. Directed by Takeshi Mori. Screenplay by Atsuhiro Tomioka.

The rocky social relationship between the men and women of the *Nirvana* finally reaches its breaking point—just in time for the aliens to attack again. The women's refusal to work with the men comes at exactly the worst time, and the *Nirvana* ends up running away. All Hibiki has to do to win back the trust of his allies is destroy the enemy force—but can he do it himself?

Episodes #11–13 of the TV series are presented in widescreen. The series is continued in *Vandread: The Second Stage*. [MT]

SPECIAL FEATURES Character and Art Galleries • Promotional

Footage • Clean Credits TECHNICAL FEATURES Widescreen (1.85:1) • Subtitles/CC: Eng. • Languages: Jap., Eng. dub • Sound: Dolby Digital 2.0 • Keepcase • 1 Disc • Region 1 GENRE & RATING CGI/Science Fiction • Rated 13+

Vandread: The Second Stage—Survival [#1]

Pioneer, 2002, 100 mins., #11832. Directed by Takeshi Mori, Yoshimasa Hiraike, Toshiyuki Kato, Makoto Bessho. Script by Atsuhiro Tomioka, Natsuko Takahashi, Takeshi Mori.

NOTE: This DVD arrived too late for a full review. The following text is promotional copy provided by the releasing company:

"Eat or be Eaten! The discovery of a drifting escape capsule leads to new threats to the survival of the *Nirvana*, two new members of the crew, and the secret to the Alien's origin! The Aliens continue to adapt themselves and attack the *Nirvana* in new ways. As the crew struggles against these developments the *Nirvana* itself undergoes a transformation and a tragedy causes the unthinkable—Bart grows up."

This disc contains episodes #1–4.

SPECIAL FEATURES Clean Credits • Promotional Footage • Other Title Trailers TECHNICAL FEATURES Widescreen (1.85:1) • Subtitles/CC: Eng. • Languages: Jap., Eng. dub • Sound: Dolby Digital • Keepcase • 1 Disc • Region 1 GENRE & RATING CGI/Science Fiction • Rated 13+

Vandread: The Second Stage—Sacrifice [#2]

Pioneer, 2002, 100 mins., #11833. Directed by Takeshi Mori, Yu Ko, Yoshimasa Hiraike, Tatsuya Abe. Script by Atsuhiro Tomioka, Natsuko Takahashi.

NOTE: This DVD arrived too late for a full review. The following text is promotional copy provided by the releasing company:

"The shocking appearance of an Alien version of the *Nirvana* crushes the *Nirvana*'s attack on an alien mothership! As the battle continues, severe injuries to key personnel cause tempers to flare as the humans become more desperate. Then a valiant sacrifice inspires the crew's resolve to challenge the Aliens and leads to a new Vandread evolution! Meanwhile, the male-female tension continues to provide distractions and entertainment that helps the crew cope with their stressful situation."

This disc contains episodes #5–7.

SPECIAL FEATURES Character and Art Galleries • Clean Credits • Other Title Trailers • Inserts: Trading Cards TECHNICAL FEATURES Widescreen (1.85:1) • Subtitles/CC: Eng. • Languages: Jap., Eng. dub • Sound: Dolby Digital • Keepcase • 1 Disc • Region 1 GENRE & RATING CGI/Science Fiction • Rated 13+

Vandread: The Second Stage—Special Collector's Box [Box Set]

Pioneer, 2002, 100 mins., #11844.

This cardboard box set is sized to fit eight volumes of *Vandread* and *Vandread: The Second Stage*, but it contains only volume #1 of *Vandread: The Second Stage*, plus an insert to fill out the rest of the box. Collectors CAN fill out their own boxed collection. See individual entries for the Special and Technical Features listings.

TECHNICAL FEATURES Cardboard Box with 1 Keepcase • 1 Disc
GENRE & RATING CGI/Science Fiction • Rated 13+

VeggieTales: Lyle the Kindly Viking

Big Ideas, 2001, 45 mins., #80688-61009. Directed by Tim Hodge, Marc Vulcano. Written by Phil Vischer, Eric Metaxas, Tim Hodge, Marc Vulcano.

Archibald Asparagus decides that he and the French Peas can produce a better program of vegetable entertainment, full of classy music and staging. His idea is to produce the world's first all-vegetable production of William Shakespeare's Hamlet—or is that "Omelet"?—followed by a "lost" musical of "Lyle the Kindly Viking." But Archie is uptight, the French Peas aren't the best assistants, and Bob the Tomato, Larry the Cucumber, and Junior all learn that sharing is important.

The *VeggieTales* series is an all-CGI show that promises "Sunday Morning Values, Saturday Morning Fun!" And fun they are. Extremely well animated, clever, and often very funny, the entertainment value for kids and adults is very high. In "Omelet," the prince declares about his omelet made from the last eggs in the kingdom, "The last poor yolks, I'll chew them well, Horatio!" The voice talent is excellent, and the music good and clever. In fact, *VeggieTales* appears to be almost a modern vegetable version of *The Muppet Show*, albeit with a few religious/moral values thrown in ("God says he likes it when we share our blessings") alongside an end-credits Old Testament verse.

The DVD contains a few extras that are both informative and fun. The only problem with the disc is the lack of captions, which would be helpful during some of the multi-voice song sequences, and would allow for more of the quick jokes to be digested. But that's a small quibble for a delightful series. See also *Larryboy* for more *VeggieTales* fun.

SPECIAL FEATURES Director and Creator Interviews • Story Reels
• Music Video • Other Title Trailers TECHNICAL FEATURES

Fullscreen (1.33:1) • Languages: Eng. • Sound: Dolby Digital Surround 2.0, Dolby Digital 5.1 • Keepcase • 1 Disc • Region 1 GENRE & RATING Music/Vegetables/Comedy • Not Rated (All Ages)

VeggieTales: The Ultimate Silly Song Countdown

Big Ideas, 2001, 43 mins., #80688-61309. Directed by Tom Bancroft. Written by Mike Nawrocki.

The *VeggieTales* series has always included Silly Songs, but which ones are the silliest of all? Here's a chance to find out, as The Pirates Who Don't Do Anything (Larry the Cucumber, Pa Grape, and Mr. Lunt) host a countdown show, after tabulating votes from the fans with their "Astonishing Contraption of Silliness." The songs in the countdown include: "Endangered Love"; "The Dance of the Cucumber"; "Larry's High Silk Hat"; "The Water Buffalo Song"; "The Yodeling Veterinarian of the Alps"; "The Song of the Cebu"; "Do the Moo Shoo"; "His Cheeseburger"; "Love My Lips"; "The Pirates Who Don't Do Anything"; and "The Hairbrush Song."

With eleven songs and interstitial elements, this disc certainly lives up to its title. Combine the fun songs with a bunch of extras, one karaoke sing-along, and four funny Easter eggs, and you've got another enjoyable DVD.

SPECIAL FEATURES Commentary Track by Creators • Creator Interviews • Deleted Scenes • Story Reels • Sing-Along • Other Title Trailers • Easter Eggs TECHNICAL FEATURES Fullscreen (1.33:1) • Languages: Eng. • Sound: Dolby Digital Surround 2.0, Dolby Digital 5.1 • Keepcase • 1 Disc • Region 1 GENRE & RATING Music/Vegetables/Comedy • Not Rated (All Ages)

VeggieTales: Rack, Shack and Benny [#3]

Big Idea, 2002, 60 mins., #2079. Directed by Phil Vischer. Written by Phil Vischer.

The Nezzer Chocolate Factory is throwing a celebration because they've sold two million chocolate bunnies! But when the company president tells the workers they can eat all the chocolate bunnies that they want to as a reward, tummy troubles are on the way. Luckily, Rack, Shack, and Benny remember a Bible story and lesson their parents taught them about peer pressure, and save the day.

More excellent computer animation, silly plots, non-denominational religious morals, and talking vegetables are served up on this disc. There's also a host of really cool extras, including a briefly amusing feature that allows you to switch the character voices around.

SPECIAL FEATURES "Making of" Featurette • Commentary Track by Creators • Character and Art Galleries • Storyboards • Story Reel • Promotional Art • Voice Switcher • Karaoke • DVD-ROM Features: Game • Other Title Trailers • Easter Eggs TECHNICAL FEATURES Fullscreen (1.33:1) • Languages: Eng. • Sound: Dolby Digital Surround 2.0, Dolby Digital 5.1 • Keepcase • 1 Disc • Region 1 GENRE & RATING Music/Vegetables/Comedy • Not Rated (All Ages)

VeggieTales: Josh and the Big Wall! [#4]

Big Idea, 2002, 60 mins., #2089. Directed by Phil Vischer, Chris Olsen. Written by Phil Vischer.

The *VeggieTales* crew tackles the retelling of a story from the Bible with typical fun. This time it's the story of the walls of Jericho, and of the Israelites journey toward the Promised Land. But it's tough going, especially when the nasty French Pea guards atop the walls of Jericho are lobbing purple slushies onto the departing vegetables!

Although this—clearly—has a more religious agenda than many of the other *VeggieTales* stories, it doesn't preach any particular religion, and hews more to generalized moral lessons. But in the midst of the Bible stories are some very funny moments, including the bizarre and silly tune, "The Song of the Cebu." Once again, Big Ideas doesn't skimp on the DVD extras, one of which is an amusing look at the perils of translating the series to a live-action stage show with inflatable costumes.

SPECIAL FEATURES "Making of" Featurette • Commentary Track by Creators • Character and Art Galleries • Storyboards • Story Reel • Promotional Art • Promotional Footage • Voice Switcher • Karaoke • DVD-ROM Features: Game • Other Title Trailers • Easter Eggs TECHNICAL FEATURES Fullscreen (1.33:1) • Languages: Eng. • Sound: Dolby Digital 5.1 • Keepcase • 1 Disc • Region 1 GENRE & RATING Music/Vegetables/Comedy • Not Rated (All Ages)

Venus 5: The Inma Ball/Labyrinth of the Inma ☞ see Mature/Adult Section

Venus Wars, The

U.S. Manga Corps, 1998, 104 mins., #USMD 1743. Directed by Yoshikazu Yasuhiko. Screenplay by Yuichi Sasamoto, Yoshikazu Yasuhiko. Based on the manga series by Yoshikazu Yasuhiko.

The planet Venus is completely uninhabitable. But that's what science fiction is for—and in this science fiction story, Venus has been colonized and terraformed into a livable, if barren, planet. The trouble

is, Venus is controlled by two kingdoms, Ishtar and Aphrodia, which are constantly at odds with each other. The story centers on a young resident of Aphrodia named Hiro. Hiro's a simple young man—he likes his girlfriend, he likes racing his "Battlebike," and he likes hanging out with his friends, mostly fellow Battlebike racers. Feisty young war correspondent Susan Sommers arrives just in time for full-fledged war to break out between the kingdoms, and in the ensuing turmoil Hiro and his friends have a lot to think about. They all realize that war is inherently destructive—but is retaking their city and their freedom something worth fighting for?

The Venus Wars is an odd duck. It was originally produced as a direct-to-video film, but ended up being shown in theaters. It's almost entirely the product of a single creator, an obsessive character designer who almost single-handedly defined the look of the 1980s in the seminal *Mobile Suit Gundam* series. The movie's plot is unexceptional—Hiro's profound thoughts about war mostly ring hollow—but it's still worthwhile for the tremendous scenes of action and heavy combat, which are lavishly animated and detailed.

The DVD is an early product of Central Park Media, so it's merely adequate, technically, and lacking almost completely in extras. But the disc contains the full 100-minute widescreen feature film. [MT]

SPECIAL FEATURES Character and Battle Clips • Other Title Trailers • Inserts: Liner Notes on Inside Cover TECHNICAL FEATURES Widescreen (1.85:1) • Subtitles/CC: Eng. • Languages: Jap., Eng. dub • Sound: Dolby Digital 2.0 • Keepcase • 1 Disc • Region All GENRE & RATING Science Fiction/Action • Not Rated (Teens)

Very Classic Christmas, A

Roan Group/Troma, 2001.

This DVD was not available for review.

Very Private Lesson ☞ see Mature/Adult Section

Vicious ☞ see Mature/Adult Section

Video Girl Ai

Viz/Pioneer, 2001, 180 mins., #DVGAS. Directed by Mizuho Nishikubo. Screenplay by Satoru Akahori, Mayuri Sekijima, Kuniaki Yamashita. Based on the manga series by Masakaza Katsura.

Heartbroken and dismayed, Yota Moteuchi is wandering the streets when he comes across a video store he's never seen before. Entering the store, he browses until he sees a tape titled "Video Girl

Ai." Once Yota gets home, he puts the tape in his VCR and a girl appears—Ai. In short order she comes out of the television and into his life, literally. As Yota grapples with what's happened to him, he finds his life taking a new and unexpected turn for the better as beautiful Ai sets her own love aside to help Yota live his dreams. But, Ai's time with Yota is limited, since the tape will reach an end sooner or later. Will Yota find all of his dreams of romance fulfilled or will he find something else he never expected?

All six OVAs included on this disc were first released in 1992. Since then the *Video Girl Ai* series has found a place among the classics of anime. As the characters and their personalities develop, the excellent writing really shows. The storyline is so aware of human nature that the characters in this series could almost be people you know.

Not especially shining in art, animation, or soundtrack by today's standards, this decade-old anime still stands tall primarily due to its script and voice acting. *Video Girl Ai* is about adult situations and does have some nudity. One of the first romantic drama/comedies ever seen in the anime medium by western audiences, *Video Girl Ai* has earned its reputation as a solid DVD. [GP]

SPECIAL FEATURES Text Interview with Director • Character and Art Galleries • Insert: Liner Notes TECHNICAL FEATURES Fullscreen (1.33:1) • Subtitles/CC: Eng. • Languages: Jap., Eng. dub • Sound: Dolby Digital Surround 2.0 • Keepcase • 1 Disc • Region 1 GENRE & RATING Romance/Comedy • Not Rated (Teens)

Virgin Fleet

U.S. Manga Corps, 2001, 90 mins., #USMD 2029. Directed by Masahiro Hosoda. Script by Yasuhiro Imagawa.

What if your superabilities were based on your virginity? For the girls in Virgin Fleet, that's a big question. Trained at a military base to use weapons and psychic energy, the girls once helped win a world war between the Confederacy and the Federation. Now, as peace settles in, the girls are learning more about their powers and each other. Healthy competition between the girls is one thing, but what happens when they want more? The most powerful of them, Shiokaze, wants love and marriage, but the Federation is rumbling again, and the girls of Virgin Fleet may not scare them anymore . . .

If this 1991 trio of episodes seems familiar, it's because it rehashes plot elements from previous series, including creator Oji Hiroi's own *Sakura Wars*. The animation is nice—especially some water battles and the sepia-tinted movie-reel style flashbacks—but there's not much to the plot, and much is taken at face value with no explanation. Oddly for anime, and despite the title of this show,

there's hardly any cheesecake material. But there are some cool biplanes and aeronautical battles.

Besides being offered as a single DVD, the disc was also included as part of a 2002 "Girlpower Pack" set, along with *Gall Force*.

SPECIAL FEATURES DVD-ROM Features: Art, Scripts • Other Title Trailers TECHNICAL FEATURES Fullscreen (1.33:1) • Subtitles/CC: Eng. • Languages: Jap., Eng. dub • Sound: Dolby Digital 2.0 • Keepcase • 1 Disc • Region 1 GENRE & RATING Action/Adventure/Girls • Rated 13+

Virus: Virus Buster Serge—Vol. 1

Manga Entertainment, 2002, 96 mins., #MANGA4123-2. Directed by Masami Obari. Script by Masami Obari, Seiji Tanda, Jiro Kaneko, Tomoyasu Okubo, Kiyotsugu Mizugami. Based on the manga series in *Gekkan Ace Next*.

NOTE: This DVD arrived too late for a full review. The following text is promotional copy provided by the releasing company:

"Neo Hong Kong, 2097: Genetic Engineering and Advanced Cybernetics have successfully fused man and machine. But alongside this new technology, mankind faces an insidious new threat . . . The Virus. Artificially enhanced humans and intelligent supercomputers operate as one using biological software. But the same technology that has allowed man and machine to merge has made both susceptible to digital viruses capable of controlling their hosts.

"The last line of defense against this insidious foe is an elite task force known as S.T.A.N.D. Equipped with state-of-the-art armored cybernetic battle gear, only this special law enforcement arm can deal with virus-infected war machines. When a mysterious stranger known as Serge appears on the scene and displays unique fighting abilities, he is invited to join the team. But what is the secret behind Serge's phenomenal strength and skill, and what dark secret does his past really hold?"

This disc contains episodes #1–4.

SPECIAL FEATURES Character Bios • Character and Art Galleries • Promotional Footage • Other Title Trailers TECHNICAL FEATURES Fullscreen (1.33:1) • Subtitles/CC: Eng. • Languages: Jap., Eng. dub • Sound: Dolby Digital 2.0, Dolby Digital Surround 5.1 • Keepcase • 1 Disc • Region 1 GENRE & RATING Robots/Science Fiction • Not Rated (Teens)

Voltage Fighter Gowcaizer

Image, 1999, 90 mins., #ID4408CTDVD.

This DVD was not available for review. It is out of print.

Voogie's Angel

Anime Works, 2001, 90 mins., #AWDVD-0109. Directed by Masami Obari, Aoi Takeuchi. Script by Aoi Takeuchi.

The year is New Western Calendar 202, and Earth has been overtaken by an unknown alien lifeform. A hundred years later, a group of biomechanically engineered girls may be the last hope for mankind, which now lives below the sea in aqua-bases. Known as "Voogie's Angel," the group includes the spirited Voogie, motherly Midi, the hard-hitting Rebecca, the innocent Merrybell, and the pensive Shiori. They aren't robots or marionettes, but they're not exactly human either. Aboard their intelligent warship *Strikemeyer*, the girls set out to kick some alien booty!

Debuting as an OVA series in 1997, each of the three chapters of *Voogie's Angel* is a bit different. The first story is more action and comedy, while the second is much more violent. The third features extensive black-and-white flashback footage showing the girls before they became "reborn" as enhanced cyborgs. Art is nice throughout—aside from the huge eyes on the girls and a few goofy faces early on. The animation really shines in the flashback footage. There's also quite a bit of cool technology and backgrounds on display. Unfortunately, the DVD is no-frills.

SPECIAL FEATURES Other Title Trailers TECHNICAL FEATURES Fullscreen (1.33:1) • Subtitles/CC: Eng. • Languages: Jap., Eng. dub • Sound: Dolby Digital 2.0 • Keepcase • 1 Disc • Region 1 GENRE & RATING Science Fiction/Action/Girls • Rated 13+

Waking Life ☛ see Mature/Adult Section

Walking with Dinosaurs

BBC Video/Fox, 2000, 230 mins., #2000040. Directed by Jasper James.

In the Late Triassic period, 220 million years ago, the Earth was still recovering from a mass extinction, and surviving reptiles battled and eventually thrived. Into the Jurassic period, dinosaurs grew to larger sizes on land and sea. By the time of the Cretaceous period, the dinosaurs had also taken to the sky, but harsh changes in climate meant they must continue to evolve. And as the Cretaceous came to an end, a giant meteor and problems in the environment signaled the end of dinosaurs, even the monstrous Tyrannosaurus Rex!

Narrated by Kenneth Branagh, this 1999 project was aired in the U.S. on the Discovery Channel. The show combines fantastically detailed CGI dinosaurs—and sometimes animatronic puppets—with live nature backgrounds, creating a realistic and believable prehistoric world. The first disc contains the main *Walking with Dinosaurs* program, complete with the option to watch it with the "Picture in Picture" feature turned on. With this activated, a secondary screen pops up regularly with alternate footage, additional paleontological information, or producer commentary. The second disc contains an extensive "making of" documentary, as well as a pair of promotional spots for the series.

There are two nearly identical versions of *Walking with Dinosaurs*: Fox released its version in April 2000, and Warner rereleased the title in September 2000. This DVD is highly recommended for anyone with an interest in dinosaurs, and is appropriate for children to adults, though it gets a little scary at times. It's much more educational than *Jurassic Park*, but loaded with just as much (or more) dino-fun! See also *Allosaurus: A Walking with Dinosaurs Special* (the second in the series) and *Walking with Prehistoric Beasts* (third in the series).

SPECIAL FEATURES "Making of" Featurette • Picture in Picture Program • Promotional Footage • Insert: Timeline TECHNICAL FEATURES Widescreen (1.85:1 enhanced for 16x9) • Subtitles/CC: Eng., Span. • Languages: Eng. • Sound: Dolby Digital Surround 2.0 • Foldout Multicase with Cardboard Sleeve • 2 Discs • Region 1 GENRE & RATING CGI/Dinosaurs/History • Not Rated (Kids)

Walking with Prehistoric Beasts

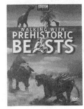

BBC Video/Fox, 2002, 300 mins., #E1589. Directed by Jasper James.

Like the two programs that came before it—*Walking with Dinosaurs* and *Allosaurus: A Walking with Dinosaurs Special*—this program is narrated by Kenneth Branagh and aired in six parts on the Discovery Channel in 2001. As before, the show combines fantastically detailed CGI saber-toothed tigers, wooly mammoths—and sometimes animatronic puppets and real actors as prehistoric men—with live nature backgrounds, creating a realistic and believable prehistoric world.

The first disc contains six half-hour episodes that show a day in the life of creatures from the post-dinosaur era, whether it's saber-toothed tigers or the heavily armored Glyptodons, the tall bird-like Gastronis, or a primitive whale. The second disc contains all the "making of features," including two separate fifty-minute behind-the-scenes documentaries, a wide selection of photos and storyboards, and text and comparison charts for those who wish a closer factual view of the subject.

Utterly engrossing and beautifully crafted, this is an important—and fun—historical and scientific exploration of a seldom seen subject. Parents might want to keep little cave-kids out of the room for some parts, as the violent hunting scenes could scare them, and the mating scenes could prompt some interesting questions (one of which might well be what the animators said to people who asked about their project: "Oh, I'm CGI-animating wooly mammoths humping!").

SPECIAL FEATURES "Making of" Featurettes • Interviews with Production Personnel • Beast Fact Files • Photo Galleries • Storyboards • Other Title Trailers TECHNICAL FEATURES Widescreen (1.85:1 enhanced for 16x9) • Subtitles/CC: Eng., Span. • Languages: Eng. • Sound: Dolby Digital 2.0 • Foldout Multicase with Cardboard Sleeve • 2 Discs • Region 1 GENRE & RATING CGI/Dinosaurs/History • Not Rated (Kids)

Wallace and Gromit: The First Three Adventures

BBC/Fox, 1999, 84 mins., #4112596. Directed by Nick Park. Written by Nick Park

English inventor Wallace and his irrepressible dog Gromit star in their first three adventures on this DVD. Released a year prior to the BBC/Warner disc, *The Incredible Adventures of Wallace and Gromit*, this one contains most of the same features as that disc (see listing for synopsis). The episodes included are "A Grand Day Out"; "The Wrong Trousers"; and "A Close Shave." Look for a few of the same extras, including behind-the-scenes footage, four early animated works, and British TV "bumper segments."

This disc is now out of print, and is mainly of interest only to collectors, since the material has been duplicated—and bettered—on the later disc. If you find this one, however, the cartoons themselves are just as brilliant and wonderful. And for more work by Nick Park and cohorts, see *Chicken Run* and *Robbie the Reindeer*.

SPECIAL FEATURES "Making of" Featurette TECHNICAL FEATURES Fullscreen (1.33:1) • Subtitles/CC: Eng., Span. • Languages: Eng. • Sound: Dolby Digital 2.0 • Keepcase • 1 Disc • Region 1 GENRE & RATING Stop Motion/Animal/Comedy • Not Rated (All Ages)

Walt Disney Animated Anthology [Box Set]

Disney, 1999.

This DVD box set was not available for review. It is on moratorium. It was a cardboard box containing the commercially available keepcase editions of the following nine titles: *Pinocchio, 101 Dalmatians, Hercules, Mulan, Lady and the Tramp, Peter Pan, The Lion King II: Simba's Pride, The Jungle Book*, and *The Little Mermaid*.

Walt Disney Treasures: Behind the Scenes at the Walt Disney Studio [Limited Edition Tin]

Disney, 2002, 240 mins., #28070.

If you've ever wanted to take a trip behind the scenes at Walt Disney Studios during its prime, this DVD set is the place to do it. With Leonard Maltin introductions for each segment, there is a huge amount of archival material and footage on display here, some of it never seen by the public, and much of it never seen in color.

Disc One includes "A Trip through the Walt Disney Studio," a twelve-minute short made in 1937 for RKO staffers, which can be viewed with running informational subtitles. Next up is the public version of the RKO tour with "How Walt Disney Cartoons Are Made," an eight-minute segment from 1939. But the bulk of the disc is taken up by the live-action and animated feature *The Reluctant Dragon* from 1941. The film was a financial necessity for Disney to stay in business during World War II, though the public and critics felt cheated that it was more of a behind-the-scenes look at Disney; the animated sequences were only a small part of the feature. "Leonard Maltin's Studio Tour" offers a look at the Burbank lot from 1954 to modern day, while other extras include storyboards and art.

Disc Two features a trio of *Disneyland* TV episodes, filmed in color but aired in black and white. On this disc, most of the footage is restored to color. The three forty-nine-minute shows are "The Story of the Animated Drawing" (1955); "The Plausible Impossible" featuring a cut scene from *Snow White* (1956); and "Tricks of Our Trade" (1957). Extras include an art and photo gallery and an Australian radio program from 1946 that features lots of Disney interviewees.

As with others in this series, the box is tin, with an individual number stamped on the cover of each of the 125,000 sets. Inside is a multikeepcase with the two discs. Picture and sound quality are mostly excellent thanks to extensive restoration of the prints. Disney buffs or animation historian will want this in their collection.

SPECIAL FEATURES "Making of" Featurettes • Art Galleries • Storyboards • Promotional Footage • Other Title Trailers • Inserts: Liner Notes, Postcard TECHNICAL FEATURES Fullscreen (1.33:1) • Subtitles/CC: Eng. • Languages: Eng. • Sound: Dolby Digital • Metal Case with Multikeepcase • 2 Discs • Region 1 GENRE & RATING Live/Comedy/Family • Not Rated (All Ages)

Walt Disney Treasures: Mickey Mouse in Black and White [Limited Edition Tin]

Disney, 2002, 256 mins., #25847.

For a look at the history of Mickey Mouse, Walt Disney's signature character, see *Walt Disney Treasures: Mickey Mouse in Living Color*. This two-disc set actually predates that set in content, but it was released just as this book was being finished.

As with others in this series, Leonard Maltin provides an introduction and historical notes to the many features on these discs. Thirty-four *Mickey Mouse* cartoons are presented with 1928's "Steamboat Willie" and "Plane Crazy" (the first-released and first-created episode, respectively) leading the pack. The shorts run up to 1935 with "Mickey's Service Station," though a missing toon is actually the final black-and-white *Mickey* short.

The shorts can be viewed alphabetically or chronologically, and extras include scripts and storyboards for "Steamboat Willie" and "Mickey Steps Out," and an eighteen-minute featurette on famed animators Frank Thomas and Ollie Johnston. There's also a pencil test for "The Mail Pilot," storyboard sketch sequences from nineteen of the shows, and a poster gallery with commentary by Maltin.

Like the other *Walt Disney Treasures*, the box is tin, with an individual number stamped on the cover of each of the 125,000 sets. Inside is a multikeepcase with the two discs.

SPECIAL FEATURES "Making of" Featurettes • Art Galleries • Storyboards • Pencil Tests • Promotional Materials • Other Title Trailers • Inserts: Liner Notes, Postcard • Easter Egg TECHNICAL FEATURES Fullscreen (1.33:1) • Subtitles/CC: Eng. • Languages: Eng. • Sound: Dolby Digital • Metal Case with Multikeepcase • 2 Discs • Region 1 GENRE & RATING Animals/Comedy/Family • Not Rated (All Ages)

Walt Disney Treasures: Mickey Mouse in Living Color [Limited Edition Tin]

Disney, 2001, 227 mins., #21541.

The most famous creation of Walt Disney is Mickey Mouse, the four-fingered, round-eared, shorts-wearing rodent who starred in the first ever synchronized sound cartoon, "Steamboat Willie," in 1928. Mickey would go on to immense international fame in cartoons and licensing, and, later, television and theme parks. But before he became an unabashed corporate icon, Mickey was an impish chap who often got himself into trouble.

This collection features the color *Mickey Mouse* theatrical shorts from 1935 to 1938, complete and uncensored. Disney himself provides the voice of Mickey, and many of the cartoons guest-starred Minnie Mouse, Donald Duck, Goofy, and Pluto. The lavish images on display are wonderful—dancing decks of cards, flying bands, ghosts—and the artistry is all the more impressive when viewers remember that this was all hand-drawn animation!

Disc One contains an introduction by Disney/film historian Leonard Maltin, five 1935 cartoons and some pencil-test footage from three episodes, as well as all nine 1936 shorts. There's also a "Parade of Award Nominees" segment from 1932, which is an animated short shown only at the Academy Awards banquet and that featured Mickey in color three years before his theatrical color debut! Disc Two contains all seven 1937 shorts (from United Artists and RKO) and all five 1938 shorts. There's also a behind-the-scenes discussion by Maltin, and each disc has a special Easter egg.

The discs are attractively packaged in this limited edition set. The box is tin, with an individual number stamped on the cover of each of the 150,000 sets. Inside is a multikeepcase with the two discs. Picture quality is mostly excellent thanks to extensive restoration of the prints, and all prints include the original title credits and endings. All in all, this is a wonderful addition to the library of any family, Disney buff, or animation historian.

SPECIAL FEATURES "Making of" Featurette • Art Galleries • Trailer • Inserts: Liner Notes, Postcard) • Easter Eggs TECHNICAL FEATURES Fullscreen (1.33:1) • Subtitles/CC: Eng. • Languages: Eng. • Sound: Dolby Digital 2.0 • Metal Case with Multi-Keepcase • 2 Discs • Region 1 GENRE & RATING Animals/Comedy/Family • Not Rated (All Ages)

Walt Disney Treasures: Silly Symphonies [Limited Edition Tin]

Disney, 2001, 305 mins., #23087.

In the early days of theatrical animation, Walt Disney wanted to do an animated anthology series like Paul Terry's *Aesop's Fables*, but he wanted to base it around something other than traditional stories. At the suggestion of musical director Carl Stalling, Disney created *Silly Symphonies* in 1928. The first short was "The Skeleton Dance," animated by Ub Iwerks and directed by Disney. The series would eventually last for seventy-four short films, ending in 1939 with "The Ugly Duckling."

This two-disc set collects thirty-seven of the *Silly Symphonies* shorts with gorgeous digitally restored imagery and sound. Disc One features nineteen cartoons from the era, including eight that feature commentary and introductions by Disney/film historian Leonard Maltin. Disc Two has another eighteen shorts, with more Maltin commentary, as well as a supplemental section on the music of *Silly Symphonies*, souvenirs of the series from the Disney Archives, and an art gallery. The shorts are broken down into categories of Fables and Fairy Tales, Favorite Characters, Leonard Maltin's Picks, Accents on Music, and Nature on the Screen.

Among the selections on these discs are Academy Award winners "Flowers and Trees" (1932, also the first color cartoon); "The Three Little Pigs" (1933); "The Tortoise and the Hare" (1934); "The Country Cousin" (1936); "The Old Mill" (1937); and "The Ugly Duckling" (1939). Other spectacular stories include the Hollywood insider-ish "Who Killed Cock Robin?"; the gorgeous "Water Babies"; and "The Wise Little Hen," which debuted a new character named Donald Duck. Many of the shorts also introduced innovative new animation techniques and technologies.

There are two problems with this set. First, the plethora of Easter eggs—most of which feature Walt Disney's later television introductions—are haphazardly arranged, and one of the advertised cartoons, "The Practical Pig," is *only* available as an Easter egg. Secondly, at least one of the cartoons, "The Three Little Pigs," has been censored and altered, removing a potentially offensive Jewish stereotype that was in the original short. A short bit of footage from the censored scene is visible in Leonard Maltin's introduction.

As with the *Mickey Mouse* set, the discs are attractively packaged in this limited edition set. The box is tin, and each of the 150,000 sets has an individual number stamped on the cover. Inside is a multikeepcase with the two *Silly Symphonies* discs. This is an enticing collection, which—with the unfortunate exception of the censorship—is another wonderful addition to the library of any family, Disney buff, or animation historian.

SPECIAL FEATURES Music Featurette • Memorabilia Featurette • Art Galleries • Trailer • Inserts: Liner Notes, Postcard • Easter Eggs TECHNICAL FEATURES Fullscreen (1.33:1) • Subtitles/CC: Eng. • Languages: Eng. • Sound: Dolby Digital 2.0 • Tin Box with Keepcase • 1 Disc • Region 1, 4 GENRE & RATING Animals/Comedy/Family • Not Rated (All Ages)

Walt Disney Treasures: The Complete Goofy [Limited Edition Tin]

Disney, 2002, 326 mins., #25844.

One of Disney's most enduring creations is Goofy, a lanky accident-prone character who started life as Dippy Dawg in 1932's "Mickey's Revue," then played sidekick to Mickey Mouse and Donald Duck before his first starring role in 1939's

theatrical short "Goofy and Wilbur." In voice and manner, Goofy lived up to his name, but he eventually became a beloved star in his own right.

Leonard Maltin introduces these archival volumes that feature most—though not all, despite the title—of Goofy's cartoons. Forty-six *Goofy* shorts are spread over the two discs, and the menus allow them to be played alphabetically or chronologically (from 1939 to 1961). The discs also contain a six-minute history of Goofy, another six-minute featurette on Pinto Colvig, the original voice of Goofy, and a fourteen-minute discussion with Bill Farmer, Goofy's modern-day voice. There are also sections on movie posters, character art from 1940 to 1953, and even a gallery of *Goofy* comic books and memorabilia.

Despite a handful of omissions (a few team-ups with Donald Duck and some educational films), *The Complete Goofy* is another winner in the *Walt Disney Treasures* line. Picture and sound have been remastered, and due to its humor, this set will be of interest to families as well as historians. As with others in this series, the box is tin, with an individual number stamped on each of the 125,000 sets. Inside is a multikeepcase with the two discs.

SPECIAL FEATURES "Making of" Featurettes • Interview with Voice Actor • Art Galleries • Promotional Materials and Memorabilia • Other Title Trailers • Inserts: Liner Notes, Postcard TECHNICAL FEATURES Fullscreen (1.33:1) • Subtitles/CC: Eng. • Languages: Eng. • Sound: Dolby Digital • Metal Case with Multikeepcase • 2 Discs • Region 1 GENRE & RATING Animals/Comedy/Family • Not Rated (All Ages)

Wanderers, The: El Hazard TV Series—The Adventure Begins [#1]

Pioneer, 2001, 175 mins., #11634. Directed by Katsuhito Akiyama. Screenplay by Ryoei Tsukimura, Hideki Sonoda, Katsumi Hasegawa.

On Earth Makoto is a boy genius with lots of friends and ideas. Jinnai is jealous of his classmate and always tries to mess up his inventions. While Makoto's working on a machine in science club, Jinnai tampers with it and unknowingly opens up a dimensional rift that transports the boys and other people in the school to the mysterious world of El Hazard. Most of the students and faculty wind up separated from the others. Jinnai finds himself in the epicenter of the Bugrom Empire. He quickly becomes a military leader within its army and stages many battles. His sister Nanami isn't sure where she is either, but manages to take on some odd jobs to get money, while still seeking answers to where she is and how she can return to Earth. Makoto and his teacher, Mr. Fujisawa, while in Roshtaria, stumble across a princess under attack from evil forces. They help Princess Rune Venus, but some-how—through miscommunication—wind up in her dungeon as prisoners, not at her table as heroes. They get things straightened out, but they still long to be home. The two are advised to seek out the three princesses to help them return to their own world. But even if they're able to find a way home, it's possible that not everyone who was transported to El Hazard will want to join them.

The Wanderers: El Hazard first began airing in 1996. This twenty-six-part anime series is based on the seven *El Hazard: The Magnificent World* OVAs with additional plotting added to stretch out the storylines and fill time. Unfortunately, at times, it feels stretched too thin.

This introductory DVD contains episodes #1–7 of the TV series. [JMC]

SPECIAL FEATURES Character and Art Galleries • Reversible Cover TECHNICAL FEATURES Fullscreen (1.33:1) • Subtitles/CC: Eng. • Languages: Jap., Eng. dub • Sound: Dolby Digital 2.0 • Keepcase • 1 Disc • Region 1, 4 GENRE & RATING Fantasy/Adventure • Rated 13+

Wanderers, The: El Hazard TV Series—The Ultimate Weapon [#2]

Pioneer, 2001, 150 mins., #11635. Directed by Katsuhito Akiyama. Screenplay by Katsumi Hasegawa, Isao Shizutani, Jiro Takayama.

Makoto and Mr. Fujisawa are adjusting to life in El Hazard, but they still miss home. By luck, Nanami, who has taken a job at the local shrine, discovers the pair and realizes she's not alone in El Hazard. When her boss Miss Miz takes off for a while, Nanami sees a money-making opportunity and transforms the shrine into a water park. But after all the water is drained from the surrounding region, the neighbors are not pleased with Nanami and her park is shut down. Makoto and the Princesses' forces are also stopped during their search for a powerful artifact. It is a weapon, now in the human form of Ifurita, who has chosen Jinnai and joined up with the Bugrom Empire.

The second outrageous installment of *The Wanderers* contains episodes #8–13. [JMC]

SPECIAL FEATURES Character and Art Galleries • Clean Credits • Reversible Cover • Easter Egg TECHNICAL FEATURES Fullscreen (1.33:1) • Subtitles/CC: Eng. • Languages: Jap., Eng. dub • Sound: Dolby Digital 2.0 • Keepcase • 1 Disc • Region 1 GENRE & RATING Fantasy/Adventure • Rated 13+

Wanderers, The: El Hazard TV Series—The Winds of War [#3]

Pioneer, 2002, 175 mins., #11634. Directed by Katsuhito Akiyama. Screenplay by Katsumi Hasegawa, Ryoei Tsukimura, Jiro Takayama, Hideki Sonoda.

Princess Rune has told Makoto a story about the legendary snow, so he and others go out to see the event. Jinnai, hearing rumors of something "legendary," goes seeking it on his own, not realizing it's just the weather. Then more secrets of the three priestesses and the rivalries between the triad are revealed as more alliances arereformed. Finally, Jinnai captures Nanami and Princess Rune and brings them back to his kingdom. Makoto, Fujisawa, and a few friends go off to rescue the girls, but even with the Eye of God, can they stand up to Jinnai, Ifurita, Jinnai's forces?

Episodes #14–20 are contained on this magical and penultimate DVD. [JMC]

SPECIAL FEATURES Character and Art Galleries • Reversible Cover • Easter Egg TECHNICAL FEATURES Fullscreen (1.33:1) • Subtitles/CC: Eng. • Languages: Jap., Eng. dub • Sound: Dolby Digital 2.0 • Keepcase • 1 Disc • Region 1 GENRE & RATING Fantasy/Adventure • Rated 13+

Wanderers, The: El Hazard TV Series—Final Adventures [#4]

Pioneer, 2002, 150 mins., #11637. Directed by Katsuhito Akiyama. Screenplay by Ryoei Tsukimura, Kazuhisa Onishi, Mitsuhiro Yamada.

The battle to rescue the princess and restore order to Rhostaria continues. As the war rages between the two forces, Makoto and his friends arrive to challenge Jinnai and free the prisoners. While the armies fight, Makoto faces off against Jinnai in a sword fight. Angered at being bested by his rival again, Jinnai gets the Eye of God and joins it with Ifurita, thinking he will have the ultimate weapon. Instead, unknown to the greedy teen, he has activated a sequence set to cause massive destruction to El Hazard! Will this be the end of that magical world or can all the forces work together to save the planet?

The final exciting action-filled volume of *The Wanderers* contains episodes #21–26, and brings a nice sense of closure to the series and characters. [JMC]

SPECIAL FEATURES Reversible Cover TECHNICAL FEATURES Fullscreen (1.33:1) • Subtitles/CC: Eng. • Languages: Jap., Eng. dub • Sound: Dolby Digital 2.0 • Keepcase • 1 Disc • Region 1 GENRE & RATING Fantasy/Adventure • Rated 13+

Watership Down

Warner, 2002, 92 mins., #37501. Directed by Martin Rosen. Screenplay by Martin Rosen. Based on the novel by Richard Adams.

A community of rabbits lives happily in their warren in the English countryside. But soon, a group of them leave their home, fearing it is threatened by the coming of man . . . and other dangers. Fiver's visions foretell doom, but the group—which includes Bigwig, Blackberry, Hazel, and a seagull ally named Kehaar—will encounter dangers in their search for a peaceful life in the hills. Dogs, cats, hawks, owls, badgers, and another community of rabbits led by the evil General Woundwort will stand in their way. But will the predators win, or will the rabbits triumph in their search for freedom?

Released in 1978, *Watership Down* is an amazingly faithful adaptation of the novel by Richard Adams. With lush watercolor backgrounds and flat cel-work for the main characters, the animation varies. Done in several different styles for different sequences, its attempts at realism in most scenes and surrealism in others works nicely. The British voice cast is exceptional, with John Hurt as the brave Hazel. There are many allegorical elements to the deep story, including explorations of fascism and dictatorship, and the price of progress and freedom.

The DVD features a nice print of the film, though with a few audio hisses. And while this is highly recommended for adult audiences who want a rich, transcendent animated story, it is *not* recommended for children. There are many horrific, brutal, and graphic scenes that will give sensitive minds nightmares. But for those old enough to understand the emotional tale, you'll find one of the best animated feature films released to date.

SPECIAL FEATURES Author Bio • "Bunny Talk" Glossary • Trailer TECHNICAL FEATURES Widescreen (1.85:1) • Subtitles/CC: Eng., Fren., Port., Span. • Languages: Eng., Fren. dub • Sound: Dolby Digital Surround 2.0 • Snapcase • 1 Disc • Region 1, 4 GENRE & RATING Animals/Drama • Rated PG

Water Babies, The

MGM, 2002, 76 mins., #1003822. Directed by Lionel Jeffries. Screenplay by Michael Robson. Based on the book by Charles Kingsley.

NOTE: This DVD arrived too late for a full review. The following text is promotional copy provided by the releasing company:

"When twelve-year-old Tom jumps into a swirling stream, he is suddenly swept away to a fantastical place filled with music, excitement and colorful characters. Frolicking with the fish, singing with the squid, and cavorting with the crabs, Tom is as happy as a clam . . . until he grows lonesome for his friends back home. To get to solid ground, Tom must find the Water Babies—a group of fun-loving children who live far across the ocean. For only the Water Babies can take Tom to the great Lord of the Sea, the one creature powerful enough to make his every wish come true!"

This feature film from 1978 has been pan-and-scanned from its original widescreen image. Besides being offered as a single DVD, the disc was also included as part of a 2002 two-pack set, its keepcase banded back-to-back with *The Care Bears Movie*.

SPECIAL FEATURES Trailer • Other Title Trailers TECHNICAL FEATURES Fullscreen (1.33:1) • Subtitles/CC: Eng., Fren., Span. • Languages: Eng. • Sound: Dolby Digital 1.0 • Keepcase • 1 Disc • Region 1 GENRE & RATING Live/Music/Fantasy • Not Rated (Kids)

Weather Report Girl ☞ see Mature/Adult Section

Welcome to Pia Carrot ☞ see Mature/Adult Section

Welcome to Pia Carrot 2 ☞ see Mature/Adult Section

Westward Ho [Collector's Edition]

Digital Versatile Disc, 2000, #185.

This DVD was not available for review.

Wet Shorts: The Best of Liquid Television

Sony, 1997, 90 mins., #LVD48435.

This DVD was not available for review.

What-a-Mess

Image, 2000, 128 mins., #ID8500LNDVD. Directed by Timothy Forder. Adapted by Timothy Folder. Based on the children's books by Frank Muir and Joseph Wright.

Prince Amir of Kinjan should be royalty, but you'd hardly know that the scruffy little Afghan puppy whom everyone calls "What-a-Mess" was born of royal blood. It could be because of the ducks and other creatures that live in his hair, the leaves in his fur, dirt on his coat, disheveled features, or penchant for rummaging through the garbage or piles of cast-offs. Whether chasing the Cat-Next-Door or feuding with spoiled Little Poppet, What-a-Mess is happy to play and frolic, sometimes with real friends, other times with imaginary ones.

Based on a series of children's books, this version of *What-a-Mess* was created and animated in England in 1989–90, and is not the DIC version that debuted in interstitials on ABC in 1994 prior to a one-season series in 1995. Creator/writer Frank Muir narrates each of the short programs. The animation style is reminiscent of the book illustrations, and has an interestingly washed-out watercolor look. Watch for lots of bizarre little non sequitur jokes put in the background for older audiences, such as the flies with the heads of Abbott and Costello, floating baseballs with aliens in them, and other strangeness.

Thirteen charming, droll, and short cartoons are featured on this volume, which will likely become a favorite of any family that has dogs . . . and even some that don't.

SPECIAL FEATURES Inserts: Theme Song Lyrics TECHNICAL FEATURES Fullscreen (1.33:1) • Languages: Eng. • Sound: Dolby Digital 1.0 • Snapcase • 1 Disc • Region 1–6 GENRE & RATING Animals/Comedy • Not Rated (All Ages)

When Dinosaurs Roamed America

Artisan, 2001, 90 mins., #12029. Directed by Pierre de Lespinois. Written by Georgann Kane.

Dinosaurs didn't just roam foreign countries, as you'll learn in this Discovery Channel special; they also roamed America! Driving pick-up trucks, listening to country music, eating apple pie and attending baseball games with . . . sorry, lost track of reality there for a moment. But given the CGI dino-marvels on display here, reality is a bendable concept. Here, you'll see how dinosaurs lived and moved in prehistoric America, as well as get information from paleontologists and scientists. From the Dilophosaurus to the T-Rex to the Stegosaurus to the Triceratops . . . get ready for a lizard-skinned adventure in the U. S. of A. (even without the baseball and apple pie).

Another production aired on the Discovery Channel in 2001, *When Dinosaurs Roamed America* is similar to BBC's *Walking with Dinosaurs* in that it uses live-action backgrounds combined with CGI dinosaurs to tell its stories. But whereas that other series used storytelling and narration to reveal history, this program has a more documentary feel, with on-camera experts, 3D cross-sections of the dinosaurs, and more. It also has a sly sense of humor in a few scenes and title cards. But using John Goodman as narrator is a bit odd.

Kids may love the special if they're interested in dinos,

but there is a bit of violence and blood. The DVD picture is excellent, and there is a whole herd of extra features. While the CGI is not as realistic as that in *Walking with Dinosaurs*, this special is still an excellent look at an era we'll never see in reality.

SPECIAL FEATURES "Making of" Featurettes • Paleontologist and Animator Text Interviews • Crew Bios • CGI Art Gallery • Dinosaur Notes • Music Video • Game TECHNICAL FEATURES Widescreen (1.85:1 enhanced for 16x9) • Subtitles/CC: Eng. • Languages: Eng. • Sound: Dolby Digital 2.0, Dolby Digital 5.1 • Keepcase • 1 Disc • Region 1 GENRE & RATING CGI/Dinosaurs/History • Not Rated (Kids)

When Dinosaurs Ruled

These *When Dinosaurs Ruled* titles, from Madacy, were not available for review: *At the Ends of the Earth; Birth of the Giants; Ground Zero; The Land that Time Forgot; The Real Jurassic Park; When Dinosaurs Ruled* [Box Set].

Where on Earth Is Carmen Sandiego: Time Traveler

Trimark, 2001, 60 mins., #VM7858D. Directed by Joe Barruso. Story by Joe Barruso. Written by Wendell Morris, T. R. Sheppard, Dennis O'Flaherty, Sean Roche, Doug Molitor.

Carmen Sandiego may well be the greatest thief the world has ever known, stealing priceless artifacts from around the world. Chasing after her are Ivy and Zack, a brother-and-sister team who work for the Acme Detective Agency. Luckily the two are very smart, and always manage to figure out the clues that Carmen leaves behind at the scenes of her crimes. The crime-busting siblings have their hands full this time when Carmen unveils her newest invention, a time machine. Carmen manages to change her future so that she's the hero and Ivy and Zack are wanted criminals, but they soon follow her to ancient Rome, where Carmen plans to steal the Colosseum!

Based on the best-selling educational CD-ROM game from 1985, *Carmen Sandiego* finally debuted on television in 1994. Though it had been in development for three years for CBS, it eventually aired on Fox. The series combines decent animation with educational snippets; the Acme Detective kids solve Carmen's crimes by gaining knowledge. Also interesting is the fact that the show is played as a computer game, with live-action "players" interacting at times with Carmen. The series won an Emmy award during its debut year, for Outstanding Animated Program. Stage and screen star Rita Moreno does a great job as the voice of Carmen Sandiego.

The DVD contains a three-part adventure called

"Labyrinth." Unfortunately, the advertised mission from the CD-ROM game does not appear to be on the disc.

SPECIAL FEATURES Trailer • Game • Other Title Trailers TECHNICAL FEATURES Fullscreen (1.33:1) • Subtitles/CC: Eng. • Languages: Eng. • Sound: Dolby Digital Surround 5.1 • Keepcase • 1 Disc • Region 1 GENRE & RATING Adventure/Game • Rated 6+

Who Framed Roger Rabbit

Disney, 1999, 104 mins., #18140. Directed by Robert Zemeckis. Screenplay by Jeffrey Price, Peter Seaman. Based on the book *Who Censored Roger Rabbit?* by Gary K. Wolf.

Detective Eddie Valiant is hired to find out what's going on with the lovely toon Jessica Rabbit, since her husband Roger Rabbit is too distracted—with fears that she's having an affair—to work in the cartoons properly. But Eddie hates toons, and the case is leading him further and further into their wacky territory. Soon, Eddie has to go to Toontown, the animated ghetto on the outskirts of Hollywood. There, he faces blackmail, horny hyenas, murder, talking cabs, and a plot that will change the future of Los Angeles forever!

It's hard to describe the impact that 1988's *Who Framed Roger Rabbit* had on the film industry, but its technical genius is evident in nearly every frame. Combining live-action and animation in an unprecedentedly real manner, *Who Framed Roger Rabbit* left all its predecessors in the ink-and-paint dust, and paved the way for today's live/CGI feature film blockbusters. The film garnered four Academy Awards, including Best Visual Effects, Best Film Editing, and a Special Achievement Award. The feature also saw the first ensemble cast of cartoons from a variety of studios (Disney, Warner Bros., MGM, Fleischer, and Universal), with Donald Duck and Daffy Duck on stage at the same time, and appearances by Betty Boop, Woody Woodpecker, Bugs Bunny, and more.

The road to *Who Framed Roger Rabbit* was a long one, with the feature in development since 1981. The $45 million film was also the first joint project with Steven Spielberg's Amblin, but Disney was so concerned about the PG-rated material that they distanced themselves as much as possible, debating whether to allow Disney characters in the film, and eventually releasing it under the Touchstone banner. Of course, once the film became a hit, Disney embraced it wholeheartedly.

The DVD is entirely no-frills, and has been censored in several spots (this is ironic, given the original title of the book on which the film was based): Baby Herman no longer makes an obscene gesture when walking underneath a woman's skirt, some adult graffiti is missing, and the infamous panty-less sequence with Jessica Rabbit has been excised as well. The release is also miss-

ing the new four-minute sequence that was animated for CBS's 1991 airing. If any Disney DVD release is crying out for an extended multidisc special edition, it's *Who Framed Roger Rabbit* . . . and Disney is planning to release a two-disc set in March 2003.

Still, it's hard to find a funnier zeitgeist of animation for kids and adults alike, and there has yet to be such a wide-ranging feast for animation fans in the years since its release. *Who Framed Roger Rabbit* is one of the animation world's classics.

SPECIAL FEATURES Other Title Trailers TECHNICAL FEATURES Widescreen (1.85:1) • Subtitles/CC: Eng. • Languages: Eng., Fren. dub • Sound: Dolby Digital 5.1 • Keepcase • 1 Disc • Region 1 GENRE & RATING Live/Comedy/Detective • Rated PG

Wicked City: Special Edition ☛ see Mature/Adult Section

Wild Cardz

U.S. Manga Corps, 1999, 50 mins., #USMD 1830. Directed by Yasuchika Nagaoka. Screenplay by Studio Ox, Yasuchika Nagaoka, Hiromitsu Amano, Hideki Sonoda, Yoshimichi Hosoi.

It is a world similar to ours, only extremely goofy. And when extremely goofy criminals attempt to break the law, who are you gonna call? Extremely goofy superheroines! That's the Crown Knights: Jo Diamonds can run at extremely high speeds; Casa Clubs is a master of hand-to-hand combat and has superstrength; Coco Hearts uses good old fashioned magic to defeat enemies; and Sunday Spades is the leader, and holder of the mysterious Trump Power. Now these four girls are up against another form of entertainment . . . no, not video games. Can the Crown Knights stop the giant flying chess pieces with destructive capabilities that appear and start tearing everything apart? And what happens if someone tries to shuffle the deck?

It would appear that an extreme sugar high was involved in the making this two-episode OVA series. It was released in 1997 and seems to be the start of a full-fledged series, but you only get two episodes on this DVD. This is a hyper-cute, superspazzy series, but it's all sparkle and pop on the surface and not much else. If a viewer is in the mood for something over the top and fun, this is a good night's rental. But don't expect *Wild Cardz* to reveal the secrets of the universe. Also, watch the Japanese-language track since the English track is more annoying than cute. Anything offensive? Just some bouncing chests and short skirts. [RJM]

SPECIAL FEATURES Voice Actor Clips • Other Title Trailers TECHNICAL FEATURES Fullscreen (1.33:1) • Subtitles/CC: Eng. • Languages: Jap., Eng. dub • Sound: Dolby Digital 2.0 • Keepcase

• 1 Disc • Region All GENRE & RATING Fantasy/Action/Cheese-cake • Rated 13+

Wind in the Willows, The/The Willows in Winter

GoodTimes, 1999.

This DVD was not available for review. It is out of print.

Wind in the Willows [Collector's Edition]

Digital Versatile Disc, 2000, 49 mins., #186. Animation Directed by Warwick Gilbert. Screenplay by Leonard Lee. Based on the book by Kenneth Grahame.

Bored with life underground, Mole tunnels upward to see the world. He soon meets a new friend named Rat, as well as the scholarly Badger, and the reckless and wealthy motor-car-driving Mr. Toad. What happens when Mole gets lost in the Wild Woods in the winter? And when Toad is impris-oned, will the evil weasels cause problems at Toad Hall?

Wind in the Willows was originally conceived as a series of bedtime stories for Kenneth Grahame's son, but Gra-hame turned them into a book in 1908. Eighty years later, in 1988, Burbank Films Australia produced this ani-mated version. Previous versions included an ABC spe-cial in 1987, a British puppet version in 1989, and Disney's *The Adventures of Ichabod and Mr. Toad* in 1949 (see entry). The Australian version is well animated, with the studio's traditionally wonky human designs looking just fine for the simpler animal characters. Transfer and sound are both good. As with other DVD Ltd. releases, there is a bio of the author on the disc.

SPECIAL FEATURES Author Bio • Game TECHNICAL FEATURES Fullscreen (1.33:1) • Languages: Eng. • Sound: Dolby Digital Surround 5.1, DTS • Keepcase • 1 Disc • Region All GENRE & RATING Animals/Adventure • Not Rated (Kids)

Wind Named Amnesia, A

U.S. Manga Corps, 1999, 80 mins., #USMD 1749. Directed by Kazuo Yamazaki. Script by Kazuo Yamazaki, Yoshiaki Kawajiri. Based on the novel by Hideyuki Kikuchi.

This apocalyptic tale takes place in the United States. Civilization has come to an end, but not because of war or epidemic. All it took was a lit-tle wind, a wind that carried away all the memories of humankind. The wind blew and everyone fell asleep. When they awoke they all had amnesia. No speech. No government. No law. Nothing. In this world a young man named Wataru wanders. He has somehow regained

his memory, and when he runs into the beautiful but mysterious Sophia, he is excited to find someone else who has too. The two go on a cross-country journey to find out what kind of state the world is in, but following them is a large security robot that seems to think Wataru is a criminal. The journey reveals to them the depths to which mankind has sunk, and also shows that maybe the world is better because of the wind. But how did the wind happen? How did Wataru and Sophia remain untouched?

A 1993 feature film, *A Wind Named Amnesia* is a strong movie, with a solid and involving story. The animation is very well done and mixes light and shadow in really interesting ways. And while the apocalyptic theme has been done before, there are some very interesting twists along the way. This is definitely worth seeing, especially if viewers are looking for a good story instead of no-brain action. There is some nudity, sexual situations, and violence in the movie, but teen audiences will be able to handle it. [RJM]

SPECIAL FEATURES Cast Clips • Mecha Clips • Other Title Trailers TECHNICAL FEATURES Fullscreen (1.33:1) • Subtitles/CC: Eng. • Languages: Jap., Eng. dub • Sound: Dolby Digital 2.0 • Keep-case • 1 Disc • Region All GENRE & RATING Drama/Action/Mys-tery • Not Rated (Teens)

Winnie the Pooh: A Very Merry Pooh Year

Disney, 2002, 65 mins., #27588. Directed by Gary Katona, Ed Wexler, Jamie Mitchell. Written by Brian Hohfield, Ted Henning, Karl Geurs, Mark Zaslove. Based on the books by A. A. Milne.

It's close to holiday time for the denizens of the Hundred Acre Wood, and after everyone makes out their wish list to Santa, Pooh decides he needs to add something to the list. But when he retrieves it, there's only one more day until Christmas; how will he ever get it to Santa in time? Will he spoil his friend's Christmas? Then, as New Year's Eve approaches, every-one makes a resolution to change. But why is Roo bouncing and Tigger not? Why is Pooh gloomy and Eeyore gleeful and hungry for honey? Oh, bother.

Although Disney bills this as a "brand-new" full-length adventure, almost half of it is the 1991 TV special (previously released on video) *Winnie the Pooh and Christmas Too*. That flashback segment features more tra-ditional textured artwork, whereas the newly produced animation on this disc looks brighter and more flat. Still, *Winnie the Pooh* fans will delight in the further adven-tures of their favorite characters. But be warned that a smiling Eeyore is a bit creepy, and may give the wee ones nightmares.

For those who really want Pooh in their home for the holidays, the "Enchanted Environment" extra is a shot of

Pooh's living room with crackling fire and Christmas music playing.

SPECIAL FEATURES Sing-Alongs • Games • Enchanted Environment • Other Title Trailers TECHNICAL FEATURES Fullscreen (1.33:1) • Subtitles/CC: Eng. • Languages: Eng., Fren. dub, Span. dub • Sound: Dolby Digital 2.0 • Keepcase • 1 Disc • Region 1 GENRE & RATING Music/Animals/Adventure • Rated G

Winnie the Pooh: Frankenpooh and Spookable Pooh

Disney, 2002, 70 mins., #26298. Directed by Ken Kessel, Terence Harrison. Written by Bruce Talkington, Carter Crocker, Evelyn A-R Gabai. Based on the books by A. A. Milne.

A quintet of Halloween adventures brings spooky happenings to the Hundred Acre Wood. Dr. Von Piglet creates a giant honey-eating bear in "The Monster Frankenpooh." Pooh and the others go ghost-busting in "Things That Go Piglet in the Night." And have Pooh and Piglet really landed on a moon full of honey in "Pooh Moon," or is something more spooky going on? Exploring Christopher Robin's attic, Piglet is magically transported to medieval times where he must face a dragon in "A Knight to Remember." And finally, nightmares have Piglet afraid to go to sleep in "Rock-a-Bye Pooh Bear," and his friends must help him.

Previously released as two separate videos, this DVD contains modern-day animation from *The New Adventures of Winnie the Pooh* TV series. The stories range from six to twenty-two minutes, and shouldn't scare young viewers at all.

SPECIAL FEATURES Sing-Along • Game • Other Title Trailers • Inserts: Trick or Treating Tips TECHNICAL FEATURES Fullscreen (1.33:1) • Subtitles/CC: Eng. • Languages: Eng. • Sound: Dolby Digital • Keepcase • 1 Disc • Region 1 GENRE & RATING Animals/Adventure • Not Rated (Kids)

Wizard of Oz, The: Rescue of the Emerald City

Trimark, 2002, 63 mins.

This DVD was not available for review.

Words Worth ☞ see Mature/Adult Section

World of Peter Rabbit and Friends, The: Vol. 1 [Box Set]

GoodTimes, 2002, 131 mins., #05-83087.

This box set contains two discs exactly as they appeared in the individual keepcase editions, with no extras. The discs included are: *The Peter Rabbit Collection [Vol. 3: Peter Rabbit/Mr. Tod]* and *The Peter Rabbit Collection [Vol. 4: Two Bad Mice/Tiggy-Winkle/Tailor]*. See individual entries for Special and Technical Features.

TECHNICAL FEATURES Cardboard Box with 2 Keepcases • 2 Discs GENRE & RATING Animals/Family • Not Rated (All Ages)

World of Peter Rabbit and Friends, The: Vol. 2 [Box Set]

GoodTimes, 2002, 104 mins., #05-83088.

This box set contains two discs exactly as they appeared in the individual keepcase editions, with no extras. The discs included are: *The Peter Rabbit Collection [Vol. 1: Flopsy Bunnies/Pigling Bland]* and *The Peter Rabbit Collection [Vol. 2: Samuel Whiskers/Tom Kitten]*. See individual entries for Special and Technical Features.

TECHNICAL FEATURES Cardboard Box with 2 Keepcases • 2 Discs GENRE & RATING Animals/Family • Not Rated (All Ages)

World's Greatest Animation, The

Image, 1998, 105 mins., #ID4530JFDVD.

It's always a dicey proposition to call something "World's Greatest," but these sixteen animated shorts are the cream of the awards crop. Most have either won or been nominated for Academy Awards. Winners include: "Special Delivery" (1978), about a dead mailman; "Every Child" (1979) about a repeatedly abandoned baby; "The Fly" (1980), which shows life from an insect's point of view; "Crac" (1981), about a rocking chair in Montreal; "Tango" (1982), a repetitive selection with photos of humans; "Sundae in New York" (1983), a claymation musical piece about New York; "Charade" (1984), with characters acting out movie titles; "Anna and Bella" (1985), with two sisters reminiscing about their lives; "A Greek Tragedy" (1986), about a trio of female statues coming to life; "Balance" (1989), featuring creepy stop-motion figures; and "Creature Comforts" (1990), with claymation zoo animals directed by *Wallace and Gromit*'s Nick Park.

Others on the disc that were "just nominees" include: "Technological Threat" (1988), which features early CGI; "The Cat Came Back" (1988), an infamous Canadian film; "Your Face" (1987) with colored pencil animation by Bill Plympton; "The Big Snit" (1985), in which a game-playing couple ignores the world around them; and "The Great Incognito" (1982) with claymation directed by Will Vinton. These toons are mostly suitable for all ages, though a few have some brief cartoony nudity in them.

SPECIAL FEATURES None TECHNICAL FEATURES Widescreen (multi-aspect) • Languages: Eng. • Sound: Dolby Digital 1.0) • Keepcase • 1 Disc • Region 1–6 GENRE & RATING Anthology • Not Rated (Teens)

Wrath of the Ninja: The Yotoden Movie

 Central Park, 1999, 87 mins., #USMD 1778. Directed by Osamu Yamazaki. Screenplay by Sho Aikawa. Based on the novel by Jo Toriumi.

It is the age of civil wars, and warlords battle for power and control of Japan. Three schools train the best ninja fighters for these warlords: Kasumi, Hyuga, and Hagakure. One of the warlords is Nobunaga Oda, and he is consorting with demons that can only be harmed by three powerful weapons. Those weapons are each held by one of the clans. When Lord Oda's unholy armies slaughter the Kasumi Clan, young ninja girl Ayame takes to the shadows with the mystical dagger. She must join with two renegade ninja, Sakon and Ryoma, who possess the sacred sword and spear. But can this trio of shadow warriors and their united weapons defeat the demons and fulfill the Prophecy of the Enchanted Swords?

Three *Yotoden* OVAs were released in 1987 and edited together to make this feature-length story. Unfortunately, almost forty-five minutes of footage was excised—while new footage was put in—and even the quartet of deleted scenes on the disc don't make up for the missing plot elements. The animation is sharp and mostly realistic, although the '80s-era hair makes the men and women look interchangeable. Voice and sound work are nice. Story elements from this were later "borrowed" for projects like *Ninja Scroll*.

Featuring some very bloody battles with demon warriors, plus some brief nudity, this disc almost edges into the Mature category. The DVD picture quality is excellent.

SPECIAL FEATURES Character Clips • Deleted Scenes • Other Title Trailers • Insert: Liner Notes on Inside Cover TECHNICAL FEATURES Fullscreen (1.33:1) • Subtitles/CC: Eng. • Languages: Jap., Eng. dub • Sound: Dolby Digital 2.0 • Keepcase • 1 Disc • Region All GENRE & RATING Supernatural/Martial Arts/Action • Not Rated (Teens)

X

X [One]

Pioneer, 2002, 95 mins., #11824. Directed by Yoshiaki Kawajiri, Takuji Endo, Hideo Hayashi, Koji Aritomi, Ko Matsuo. Based on the original manga by CLAMP in *Asuka Comic.*

NOTE: This DVD arrived too late for a full review. The following text is promotional copy provided by the releasing company:

"Two choices, two sides, one future . . . Two groups of supernaturally powered warriors begin a prophetic battle to shape the future—a clash that will rock the foundations of the planet! The Dragons of Earth swear to purge humanity from the world, while the Dragons of Heaven are the last hope of all mankind. One young man holds the key to the Earth's destiny."

This disc contains the TV episodes #1–3 and episode #0 "An Omen."

SPECIAL FEATURES Trailer • Other Title Trailers • Inserts: 24-page Character Guide Booklet • Reversible Cover TECHNICAL FEATURES Fullscreen (1.33:1) • Subtitles/CC: Eng. • Languages: Jap., Eng. dub • Sound: Dolby Digital 2.0 • Cardboard Slipcase with Keepcase • 1 Disc • Region 1 GENRE & RATING Science Fiction/Fantasy/Action • Rated 16+

X [Two]

Pioneer, 2002, 75 mins., #11825. Directed by Yoshiaki Kawajiri. Based on the original manga by CLAMP in *Asuka Comic.*

NOTE: This DVD arrived too late for a full review. The following text is promotional copy provided by the releasing company:

"Unable to accept the truth behind his mother's death, Kamui visits Hinoto, the dreamseer for the Dragons of Heaven. He refuses to believe her prophecy—that he is the key to the Earth's fate! She pleads with him to try and change the future she foresees. As Kamui ponders his options, the Dragons of Earth start attacking Tokyo!"

This disc contains the TV episodes #4–6.

SPECIAL FEATURES Interview with Director • Other Title Trailers • Reversible Cover TECHNICAL FEATURES Fullscreen (1.33:1) • Subtitles/CC: Eng. • Languages: Jap., Eng. dub • Sound: Dolby Digital 2.0 • Cardboard Slipcase with Keepcase • 1 Disc • Region 1 GENRE & RATING Science Fiction/Fantasy/Action • Rated 16+

X: Dragons of Earth—Special Collector's Box [Box Set]

Pioneer, 2002, 100 mins., #11823.

This cardboard box set is sized to fit eight volumes of *X*, but it contains only volume #1, plus an insert to fill out the rest of the box. Collectors can fill out their own boxed collection. See individual entries for the Special and Technical Features listings.

TECHNICAL FEATURES Cardboard Box with 1 Keepcase • 1 Disc GENRE & RATING Fantasy/Horror/Action • Rated 16+

X [The Movie] ☛ see Mature/Adult Section

X-Men: Reunion/Out of the Past/No Mutant Is an Island [#1]

Universal, 2001, 70 mins., #21366. Directed by Richard Bowman, Larry Houston. Written by Len Wein, Michael Edens, Sandy Scesny. Based on the comic book series from Marvel Comics.

The world fears them, but that doesn't mean that mutants have all turned their backs on humanity. Under the tutelage of Professor Charles Xavier, one of the world's most powerful telepaths, a group of heroic mutants known as the X-Men fights for truth and justice for Homo sapiens and Homo superior alike! They include optic-blast-firing Cyclops, claw-wielding Wolverine, power-leeching Rogue, weather-controlling Storm, bombastic Jubilee, power-psychic Jean Grey, and others.

In "Reunion, Parts 1 and 2," Xavier, the X-Men, and

Magneto are in the Savage Land, where they team up with Ka-Zar and Shanna to battle Mr. Sinister and the Mutates. Then, in "Out of the Past, Parts 1 and 2," Wolverine finds out that his ex-lover, Yuriko, is now the cyborg known as Lady Deathstrike. When she and her Reavers discover a Shi'ar ship buried in the Morlock tunnels underneath New York, they lure the X-Men to their doom, only to discover a greater evil in the gaseous M'Kraan Spirit Drinker! Finally, in "No Mutant Is an Island," a grieving Cyclops leaves the X-Men and strikes out on his own. At the orphanage where he was raised, he rekindles an old friendship and helps a young mutant fight an evil conspiracy.

The X-Men were created in 1963 by Stan Lee and Jack Kirby, but they became most popular in a successful revival in 1975's *Giant Size X-Men #1*. Although they had guest-starred in a few animated series based on other Marvel Comics characters—and a 1989 pilot—the "children of the atom" made it big in 1992–93 on Fox. The *X-Men* series lasted five successful seasons, with episodes #25–28 and #66 coming from seasons 2, 3, and 5.

The animation is better-than-average—and it looks good on DVD—but it's the multilayered characters and stories that really make the few *X-Men* DVDs worthwhile. But what's with the awful covers that don't feature any main heroic characters?

SPECIAL FEATURES None TECHNICAL FEATURES Fullscreen (1.33:1) • Subtitles/CC: Eng., Fren., Span. • Languages: Eng. • Sound: Dolby Digital Surround 2.0 • Keepcase • 1 Disc • Region 1 GENRE & RATING Superheroes/Action • Not Rated (Kids)

X-Men: Sanctuary/Weapon X, Lies and Videotape/Proteus

Universal, 2001, 69 mins., #21367. Directed by Larry Houston. Written by Steven Melching, David McDermott, Jeff Saylor, Bruce Reid Schaefer, LuAnne Crocker. Based on the comic book series from Marvel Comics.

In "Sanctuary, Parts 1 and 2," Magneto plans to transport all mutants who want to leave Earth to an orbiting asteroid sanctuary where they can live their lives in peace. But when Fabian Cortez gains control of Asteroid M and its massive nuclear arsenal, the X-Men are implicated in Magneto's apparent demise! Then, in "Weapon X, Lies, and Videotape," Wolverine is aided by the Beast as he faces his past in the ruins of the top-secret Weapon X laboratory. There, they find Sabretooth and others, suffering from the same symptoms as Wolverine. Finally, in "Proteus, Parts 1 and 2," the son of scientist Moira McTaggert finally demonstrates his mutant powers. He becomes Proteus, a spectacularly strong telepath who sees the X-Men as enemies. He then targets his father, a prominent politician, and the X-Men must stop him.

These five episodes, #48–52, are from the fourth season of *X-Men*. The disc is fine, but the cover is even worse than the first one. Why spotlight guest-star Hulk over Wolverine?

SPECIAL FEATURES None TECHNICAL FEATURES Fullscreen (1.33:1) • Subtitles/CC: Eng., Fren., Span. • Languages: Eng. • Sound: Dolby Digital Surround 2.0 • Keepcase • 1 Disc • Region 1 GENRE & RATING Superheroes/Action • Not Rated (Kids)

X-Men: The Phoenix Saga

Universal, 2000, 109 mins., #21119. Directed by Larry Houston. Written by Michael Edens, Mark Edwards Edens. Based on the comic book series from Marvel Comics.

In "The Phoenix Saga, Pt. I: Sacrifice," the X-Men must stop Eric the Red, a merciless Shi'ar emissary, from attacking the Eagle One space station.

But afterward, aboard the *Starcore* space shuttle, a strange alien energy envelops Jean Grey. In "Pt. II: Dark Shroud," Jean Grey emerges from beneath the waters of New York Harbor as the more-powerful Phoenix. Meanwhile, Professor X is losing control of his darker side, and retreats to Muir Island, where he meets the alien princess, Lilandra. In "Pt. III: Cry of the Banshee," the X-Men and Banshee must stop Black Tom Cassidy, Juggernaut, and Eric the Red from kidnapping Lilandra. Then, in "Pt. IV: Starjammers," the X-Men are transported to Lilandra's ship, where they must protect the all-powerful M'Kraan crystal. Not only is Emperor D'Ken after the crystal, but so are Corsair and his ragtag group of crystal thieves known as the Starjammers. Finally, in "Pt. V: Child of Light," D'Ken gains control of the M'Kraan crystal and begins to suck the life from the solar system! Only one member of the X-Men is powerful enough to stop him, but what will the cost be for Phoenix?

"The Phoenix Saga" storyline is one of the early cosmic storylines from the *X-Men* comic book that made readers sit up and take notice that something daring was happening in the series. The storyline adapted for this five-parter from the show's third season (1994) actually came from X-Men #100–108 (1976–77), written by Chris Claremont and drawn by Dave Cockrum, John Byrne, and Terry Austin. As in the comics, the cartoon show later did the multipart "The Dark Phoenix Saga," in which Jean Grey turns to evil.

The DVD is a nice set-up—though the reds bleed a bit much—but once again, the cover designer must have been smoking illegal substances; neither Magneto nor the Sentinels appear in this storyline!

SPECIAL FEATURES None TECHNICAL FEATURES Fullscreen (1.33:1) • Subtitles/CC: Eng. • Languages: Eng., Fren. dub • Sound: Dolby Digital Surround 2.0 • Keepcase • 1 Disc • Region 1 GENRE & RATING Superheroes/Action • Not Rated (Kids)

Xena, Warrior Princess: Death in Chains

Slingshot, 2000, #BDVD9301. Directed by Andrew Taylor. Written by Anthony O'Conner.

Xena is a warrior princess who was once a ruthless killer, but now travels the countryside to redeem herself by doing good deeds. She's accompanied on her travels by good friend Gabrielle. This time out, Gabrielle's got a new boyfriend named Talus, but he's dying. Bummer. However, King Sisyphus has trapped Celesta, the Death Goddess, and as long as she's in chains—or dead—everyone is granted eternal life! Sounds cool, except that the Olympian Gods have decreed that mortals can't live forever, and evil things don't die either. Xena and Gabrielle must find a way to free death, whether they want to or not.

Based on the popular 1995–2001 syndicated action series, this *Xena* story is a "Multipath Adventure," which is a cross between a video game and traditional storytelling. As viewers watch the story, they are presented with choices of action every few minutes. Each choice (made using the DVD remote) branches the story off into a new direction, meaning there are multiple outcomes and storylines for the characters. The animation is rough 3D CGI, which will probably be fine for video game enthusiasts, but might hurt the eyes of traditional animation fans. Still, the movements of Xena and Gabrielle seem surprisingly close to their live-action counterparts, and the voice of Xena even sounds like Lucy Lawless.

SPECIAL FEATURES Other Title Trailers TECHNICAL FEATURES Widescreen (1.85:1) • Languages: Eng. • Sound: Dolby Digital 5.1 • Keepcase • 1 Disc • Region 1–6 GENRE & RATING Interactive/Fantasy/Action • Not Rated (Teens)

Xena, Warrior Princess: Girls Just Want to Have Fun

Slingshot, 2000, #BDVD9116. Directed by Andrew Taylor. Written by Anthony O'Conner.

Xena and Gabrielle are back for another rousing adventure. This time out, Bacchus—who used to be the God of Wine—has changed from merry to menacing. He's created an army of Bacchae, demonic fanged vixens who are attacking villages throughout the land, killing everyone except the young girls they lure into their coven. With the help of Zeus and bumbling Joxer, Xena and Gabby must stop the Bacchae before they themselves become servants of the evil Bacchus!

This is another "Multipath Adventure," with branching story choices. Like its predecessor, the animation is rough 3D CGI appropriate for video games.

SPECIAL FEATURES Other Title Trailers TECHNICAL FEATURES Widescreen (1.85:1) • Languages: Eng. • Sound: Dolby Digital 5.1 • Keepcase • 1 Disc • Region 1–6 GENRE & RATING Interactive/Fantasy/Action • Not Rated (Teens)

Yamamoto Yohko, Starship Girl: The Perfect Collection

Right Stuf, 2001, 175 mins., #RSDVD9010. Based on the novels by Taku Shoji, Takashi Akaishizawa

In the future, wars are no longer waged by armies but by teams of pilots fighting in non-fatal battles to settle disputes between opposing civilizations. Earth, or—as it's called a thousand years from now—Terra, has been losing battle after battle to the Ness team, the Red Snappers. But the Terra team has a plan: go back into the past (the present time) and recruit crack female pilots from video arcades. Enter Yamamoto Yohko, the best of the best with reflexes and intuition to spare. With Yohko on the team, flying a brand new X-29 fighter that only she can handle, Terra's fortunes of war have turned. However, the Red Snappers aren't about to take it lying down!

Yamamoto Yohko, Starship Girl contains two three-episode OVAs. The first OVA covers Yohko's recruitment and training as a Starship Girl. The second covers the Terra team and their battles against Ness. While the plot is developed very slowly, the writing is solid and the characters interesting. The story itself becomes more and more entertaining as the episodes continue, but don't expect it to get too deep.

The character designs for *Yamamoto Yohko* are both attractive and interesting, and they match well with the quality animation. Its soundtrack—which has spawned a CD—is also more interesting than you would expect and suits the stories and action well. The picture is clear and vivid. With only a smattering of harsh language, there is little objectionable material. Sometimes silly, sometimes serious, *Yamamoto Yohko, Starship Girl* is always amusing. [GP]

SPECIAL FEATURES Character and Art Galleries • Outtakes TECHNICAL FEATURES Fullscreen (1.33:1) • Subtitles/CC: Eng. • Languages: Jap., Eng. dub • Sound: Dolby Digital 2.0 • Keepcase • 1 Disc • Region 1–6 GENRE & RATING Science Fiction/Action/Comedy • Rated 15+

Year Without a Santa Claus, The

Warner, 2000, 125 mins., #537. Directed by Arthur Rankin, Jr., Jules Bass. *Santa* Teleplay by William Keenan. Based on the book by Phyllis McGinley. *Rudolph* and *Nestor* written by Romeo Muller.

In *The Year Without a Santa Claus*, Santa feels that the world has lost the proper holiday spirit and decides to skip Christmas. Can Mrs. Claus and the elves reawaken the jolly holiday magic in Santa? How will the Snowmiser and the Heatmiser play a role in the proceedings? Then, in *Rudolph's Shiny New Year*, Santa and Rudolph come to the rescue when Baby New Year runs away and Father Time has to stop the world on December 31 permanently if they can't find the babe! Finally, in *Nestor, the Long Eared Christmas Donkey*, a donkey with extremely long ears is the runt of the pack, until he gets chosen to guide Mary and Joseph to a certain stable in Bethlehem.

All three of these perennial holiday shows are stop-motion "animagic" specials by Rankin-Bass. All debuted on ABC: *Year Without* was in 1974; *Rudolph's* was in 1976; and *Nestor* was in 1977. Mickey Rooney is the voice of Santa in *Year Without*, while Red Skelton narrates *Rudolph's*. Warner made the right choice in teaming these three beloved holiday specials onto one disc instead of three separate discs. Picture and sound are both nice, and families should enjoy the stories and music.

SPECIAL FEATURES None TECHNICAL FEATURES Fullscreen (1.33:1) • Subtitles/CC: Eng., Fren. • Languages: Eng. • Sound: Dolby Digital 1.0 • Snapcase • 1 Disc • Region All GENRE & RATING Stop Motion/Holiday/Music • Not Rated (All Ages)

Yellow Submarine

MGM/UA, 1999, 90 mins., #907508. Directed by George Dunning. Screenplay by Lee Minoff, Al Brodax, Jack Mendelsohn, Erich Segal. Story by Lee Minoff.

The Beatles go to the undersea world of Pepperland, a musical kingdom that is under attack by the Blue Meanies, creatures who worship order and hate music. The Beatles are soon enmeshed in a battle for songs, love, and creativity, against such bizarre day-glo creatures as Robin the butterfly stomper, Snapping Turtle Turk, the Apple Bonkers, the Terrible Flying Glove, and more.

The Fab Four were not directly involved in the writing or voice work of this 1968 release, but the film does feature their songs and likenesses (and they do appear in a brief sequence at the end). Instead, sound-alike voice actors were used, and the eleven-month production began without a finished script or storyboards! The designers and animators on the film decided that a surrealistic and psychedelic approach would be best for the project, with styles changing every few minutes. The animators used a variety of techniques, from photos to cel work to rotoscoping, and even achieved some effects by changing the film stock used within scenes. In addition to several of their older songs, the Beatles contributed four original tunes to the production: "It's All Too Much," "Only a Northern Song," "All Together Now," and "Hey Bulldog."

Yellow Submarine is highly regarded by most Beatles fans, and has been extensively restored for this DVD release. Accompanied by a nice selection of extras—including a newly restored stereo mix on an isolated music track that has all the incidental music as well as the songs themselves—the film itself is shown in widescreen, and the colors are vibrant and dazzling. A seventeen-minute "Making of" documentary, plus interviews with surviving voice actors, animators, and a cowriter, gives viewers insight into the creation of this surreal film. To call *Yellow Submarine* a milestone in animation might invite jeers, but it really is an astonishing portrait of the music, humor, and attitudes of the psychedelic era of the late 1960s.

SPECIAL FEATURES "Making of" Featurette • Commentary Track by Production Supervisor • Interviews with Voice Cast and Crew • Character, Art, and Photo Galleries • Deleted Scenes • Storyboards • Trailer • Isolated Music Score • Inserts: Liner Notes • Easter Eggs TECHNICAL FEATURES Widescreen (1.66:1) • Subtitles/CC: Eng., Fren., Jap., Port., Span. • Languages: Eng. • Sound: Dolby Digital 2.0, Dolby Digital 5.1 • Keepcase • 1 Disc • Region 1–4 GENRE & RATING Pyschedelia/Music • Rated G

Young Cinematographer

USA Films/Polygram, 1998.

This DVD was not available for review. It is an anthology featuring fifteen short films by kids.

Ys: Book One

AnimeWorks, 2002, 102 mins., #AWDVD-0226. Directed by Jun Kimaya. Screenplay by Tadashi Hayakawa.

NOTE: This DVD arrived too late for a full review. The following text is promotional copy provided by the releasing company:

"Esteria is an island country that once flourished with great riches and promise. But the hands of evil have taken hold and monsters now cover the country and torment its people. An unsuspecting adventurer by the name of Adol Christen has been drawn into the great conflict that has beset the island. He sets off on a quest to save this desperate and plagued land . . . a land once known as the great utopia of Ys."

Despite its nice cover art, the touted "Retro Game Interface" for the disc menu is ugly. But it's perhaps appropriate for this based-on-a-game series.

SPECIAL FEATURES Character Bios • Episode Map • Item (Prop) Notes • Games • Outtakes • Other Title Trailers TECHNICAL FEATURES Fullscreen (1.33:1) • Subtitles/CC: Eng. • Languages: Jap., Eng. dub • Sound: Dolby Digital • Keepcase • 1 Disc • Region 1 GENRE & RATING Fantasy/Action • Rated 13+

Yu-Gi-Oh! The Heart of the Cards—Vol. 1

4 Kids/Funimation, 2002, 64 mins., #FN-05452. Directed by Kunihisa Sugihima. Written by Junji Takegami, Masashi Sogo, Shin Yoshida. Based on the manga series by Kazuki Takahashi and Studio Dice in *Weekly Shonen Jump.*

NOTE: This DVD arrived too late for a full review. The following text is promotional copy provided by the releasing company:

"*Yu-Gi-Oh!* follows the adventures of Yugi and his buddies—Joey, Tristan, and Tea—who spend most of their free time playing the coolest new game ever, 'Duel Monsters.' When Yugi's grandfather gave Yugi an old Egyptian artifact called the 'Millennium Puzzle,' Yugi pieced the puzzle together and was infused with incredible mystical powers. With the help of his friends, his belief in the heart of the cards, and the mysterious power of his Millennium Puzzle, Yugi sets out on the adventure of a lifetime!

"Yugi and his friends are in awe of his grandpa's collection of Duel Monster cards, but when #1 ranked Duelist and ruthless tycoon Kaiba kidnaps grandpa to get the rare Blue Eyes White Dragon card, Yugi must face Kaiba in the Ultimate Duel Monsters showdown and avenge his gramps! Then, Yugi and friends take a break from honing their card playing skills to watch Weevil and Rex Raptor compete in the Duel Monsters Regional Championship. When Yugi opens a package from Duel Monsters creator, Maximillion Pegasus, Yugi is forced to face him in the mysterious Shadow Realm where all the monsters and magic are real. Yugi loses, and Pegasus claims grandpa's soul as his prize. Yugi must travel to the Duelist Kingdom and Pegasus's tournament if he is ever to see his grandpa again.

"Finally, Yugi gives up one of his own star chips so Joey can board the boat bound for the Duelist Kingdom and duel to save his sister's eyesight. Meanwhile, Tea and Tristan stowaway to join their friends. But when word spreads that Yugi was the one who defeated World Champion Kaiba, the cheat Weevil tries to cripple Yugi's deck by tossing his best cards overboard just as they reach the island."

This disc contains episodes #1–3.

SPECIAL FEATURES Character Bios • Music Video • Promotional Footage • Other Title Trailers TECHNICAL FEATURES Fullscreen (1.33:1) • Subtitles/CC: Eng. • Languages: Eng. dub, Span. dub • Sound: Dolby Digital • Keepcase • 1 Disc • Region 1 GENRE & RATING Fantasy/Action • Not Rated (Kids)

Yu-Gi-Oh! Into the Hornet's Nest [#2]

4 Kids/Funimation, 2002, 60 mins.

This DVD was not available for review.

Yu-Gi-Oh! Attack from the Deep—Vol. 3

4 Kids/Funimation, 2002, 64 mins., #FN-05472. Directed by Kunihisa Sugihima. Written by Junji Takegami, Masashi Sogo, Shin Yoshida. Based on the manga series by Kazuki Takahashi and Studio Dice in *Weekly Shonen Jump.*

NOTE: This DVD arrived too late for a full review. The following text is promotional copy provided by the releasing company:

"The fisherman duelist Mako, the master of the Sea Deck, baits Yugi into a duel on his own Sea playing field for a home field advantage. Can Yugi adapt to these new settings to turn the tide of battle? Then, if Yugi is eliminated from the tournament, Kaiba Corporation's crooked Board of Directors will transfer control of the company from Kaiba to Pegasus! Kaiba's younger brother, Mokuba, challenges Yugi to a duel not only to protect his brother's company but to regain their honor! Is Pegasus successfully manipulating possible allies against each other?

"Later, Yugi must duel a magical doppelganger of Kaiba, created from the greed and power lust Yugi wiped from Kaiba's soul. But with his best cards resting at the bottom of the ocean, Yugi must discover a new strategy if he's to survive fake Kaiba's powerful Blue Eyes White Dragon!"

This disc contains episodes #7–9.

SPECIAL FEATURES Character Bios • Music Video • Promotional Footage • Other Title Trailers TECHNICAL FEATURES Fullscreen (1.33:1) • Subtitles/CC: Eng. • Languages: Eng. dub, Span. dub • Sound: Dolby Digital • Keepcase • 1 Disc • Region 1 GENRE & RATING Fantasy/Action • Not Rated (Kids)

Yu-Gi-Oh! Give Up the Ghost—Vol. 4

4 Kids/Funimation, 2002, 64 mins., #FN-05482. Directed by Kunihisa Sugihima. Written by Junji Takegami, Masashi Sogo, Shin Yoshida. Based on the manga series by Kazuki Takahashi and Studio Dice in *Weekly Shonen Jump.*

NOTE: This DVD arrived too late for a full review. The following text is promotional copy provided by the releasing company:

"Yugi defeats the Blue Eyes White Dragon, but there are two more waiting in the wings! Will the real Kaiba reach Yugi in time to help beat this impersonator? Then, Joey decides to battle Rex Raptor without his friends' help to prove that he is man enough to take care of Serenity on his own. But as Rex Raptor destroys Joey's best Duel Monsters, will Tristan's card remind him that with his friends he is never alone in battle?

"Later, Joey duels valiantly, but Rex Raptor has unleashed his secret weapon: the Red Eyes Black Dragon! Joey must figure out the secret of Yugi's gift, the Time Wizard card, without Yugi's help or he's taking the next boat out of the Duelist Kingdom!"

This disc contains episodes #10–12.

SPECIAL FEATURES Character Bios • Music Video • Other Title Trailers TECHNICAL FEATURES Fullscreen (1.33:1) • Subtitles/CC: Eng. • Languages: Eng. dub, Span. dub • Sound: Dolby Digital • Keepcase • 1 Disc • Region 1 GENRE & RATING Fantasy/Action • Not Rated (Kids)

Yu Yu Hakusho: The Movie/Ninku: The Movie

Anime Works, 2001, 120 mins., #AWDVD-0195. Directed by Noriyuki Abe. Script by Shinichi Ohashi, Hiroshi Hashimoto. *Yu Yu Hakusho* is based on the manga series by Yoshihiro Togashi in *Young Jump*. *Ninku* is based on the manga series by Koji Kiriyama in *Shonen Jump*.

Yusuke Urameshi's vacation ends early when his diminutive boss Koenma is kidnapped. Just when he thought he could take a break from his job as a Spirit World detective, he's dragged back to work to save Koenma, who was the one who brought him back to life after a fatal accident. Before setting Koenma free, however, the demon Garuga demands Yusuke turn over the Lord of the Underworld's Golden Seal. Yusuke acquiesces, or does he? With the seal in hand, Yusuke must summon all his strength and spirit energy to save Koenma and escape alive.

The Ninku are a legendary group of fighters, but their fame doesn't bring fortune. Times are tough, so the Ninku head to a small town in search of jobs. But when they get there, they find a group of Ninku impostors receiving a hero's welcome! Hired as lackeys for the Ninku imitators, the gang watches with glee as a pack of evil demons besieges the town, propelling the fakers into action.

This double-feature DVD contains two brief (30 mins.) movies that probably wouldn't warrant their own discs. From 1993, *Yu Yu Hakusho: The Movie* is amusing, but seems more like an episode of the television series than a stand-alone film. Fast action and clever fight scenes are highlights of the film. From 1995 (while the TV series was still on the air), *Ninku: The Movie* features a very unusual-looking group of characters in a fairly ordinary situation. While the film is a good introduction to the *Ninku* cast, it's predictable and a bit too short.

With the exception of some mild fantasy violence, this disc is appropriate for all ages. The disc is truly a double feature; the cover is flippable and features all the copyright information on each side! [BR]

SPECIAL FEATURES Other Title Trailers TECHNICAL FEATURES Widescreen (1.85:1) • Subtitles/CC: Eng. • Languages: Jap., Eng. dub • Sound: Dolby Digital 2.0 • Keepcase • 1 Disc • Region 1 GENRE & RATING Action/Martial Arts/Fantasy • Rated 7+

Yu Yu Hakusho

These *Yu Yu Hakusho* titles, from Funimation, were not available for review: *Yusuke Lost, Yusuke Found* [#1]; *Artifacts of Darkness* [#2]; *A New Apprentice* [#3—Uncut]; *A New Apprentice* [#3—Edited]; *The Gate of Betrayal* [#4— Uncut]; *The Gate of Betrayal* [#4—Edited]; *The Beasts of Maze Castle* [#5—Uncut]; *The Beasts of Maze Castle* [#5—Edited]; *Seven Ways to Die* [#6—Uncut]; *Seven Ways to Die* [#6—Edited]; *Rescue Yukina* [#7—Uncut]; *Rescue Yukina* [#7—Edited]; *The Dark Tournament Begins* [#8—Uncut]; *The Dark Tournament Begins* [#8—Edited].

Z

Z-Mind

Bandai, 2002, 150 mins., #1570. Directed by Yasuhiro Matsumura. Screenplay by Fuyunori Gobu.

Meet a typical Japanese family in the late 1970s. There's an amusingly grumpy dad, an alarmingly huge mom, a feisty grandma, an older brother, and the centerpiece of the family and the series: four teenage daughters named Ayame, Renge, Sumire, and Satsuki. Unknown at first, the sisters have some special powers that a certain agency finds desirable; after a thwarted kidnapping attempt, an old family friend, Mr. Peckinpah, arrives to explain the story. In short, the earth is secretly under attack by aliens . . . and the only people with the correct psychic profile to pilot earth's counterweapon are the three oldest daughters of the family! Not surprisingly, the secret weapon is a giant, combining robot! Oh no, not that old plot again!

To its credit, Z-Mind—released in 1999 in Japan—is reasonably entertaining and well animated. While some recently produced anime shows have taken it upon themselves to mimic the style of 1970s robot shows like Voltron, the retro Z-Mind doesn't stop there; it actually takes place in the 1970s! Add in a creepy race of bad guys and a mysterious hero who looks just like the hero from every other '70s robot anime, and you've got a good-natured but generic spoof. Z-Mind isn't any great shakes, but fans of battling giant robots will see its appeal.

The DVD is reasonably well produced. It's packed with all six OVA episodes, which might explain the occasional video artifacting. The extras on the disc are fairly scant, but also included is a reversible cover, which allows fans to change the package to feature the cute girl of their choice. Anime companies know their audience, after all. [MT]

SPECIAL FEATURES Art Gallery • Clean Credits • Other Title Trailers • Reversible Cover • Easter Egg TECHNICAL FEATURES Fullscreen (1.33:1) • Subtitles/CC: Eng. • Languages: Jap., Eng. dub • Sound: Dolby Digital Surround 2.0 • Keepcase • 1 Disc • Region 1 GENRE & RATING Robots/Science Fiction/Girls • Rated 13+

Zenki Saga 1

Anime Works, 2001, 325 mins., #EFDVD-8902. Directed by Hiroyuki Yokoyama. Screenplay by Ryota Yamaguchi. Based on the manga series by Kikuhide Tani and Yoshihiro Kuroiwa in Shonen Jump.

High priest Ozuno knows that the guardian demon Zenki can barely be controlled, so he seals the destructive creature away. A thousand years pass, and Japan is once again beset by all manner of demons and nasty spirits, all coming from the 108 Seeds of Evil. Chiaki is a direct descendant of the priest Ozuno, and she knows the forbidden spell that can unleash Zenki. But will Chiaki have enough power to control Zenki once he's free? To make matters worse, when he's not fighting other demons, Zenki decides to live in the Ozuno family temple in the form of an annoying super-deformed little version of himself. Thankfully, Chiaki has a guardian bracelet that keeps Zenki from harming her; it also enables her to transport him to her when she's in danger, and shows him that he needs her help to retain his muscular adult form.

First aired in 1995 in Japan, Zenki has a formulaic premise, but coasts along on interesting characters and good execution of its predictable demon-of-the-week stories. The cast grows on Chiaki's side to include a handy grandmother, Chiaki's brother, and some local clerics. The animation style is a bit too angular and busy; just looking at the art on the DVD covers gives you an idea of how cluttered the screen might look if that art were in motion. There's also quite a bit of goofy and super-deformed moments, not just with Zenki himself.

The two-disc DVD set contains the initial thirteen Zenki episodes. Fans might prefer the subtitled version, as the dub cuts out quite a bit of material.

SPECIAL FEATURES Other Title Trailers TECHNICAL FEATURES Fullscreen (1.33:1) • Subtitles/CC: Eng. • Languages: Jap., Eng. dub • Sound: Dolby Digital 2.0 • Keepcase • 1 Disc • Region 1 GENRE & RATING Supernatural/Action • Rated 13+

Zenki Saga 2

Anime Works, 2002, 325 mins., #EFDVD-8907. Directed by Hiroyuki Yokoyama. Screenplay by Ryota Yamaguchi. Based on the manga series by Kikuhide Tani and Yoshihiro Kuroiwa in *Shonen Jump*.

The evil Karuma is powerful enough that help is needed. A mysterious sorcerer, Soma Miki, is able to stand against the more-powerful Anju, but soon Chiaki and Zenki are thrown 800 years back in time! There, Chiaki must battle some of her own ancestors—including one that looks like her—and Zenki must transform again to gain enough strength to challenge Karuma's ancient powers. Can they wrest the Golden Axe from the Golden Dragon? And if they change the timeline in the past, will Karuma somehow gain the advantage in the present?

Episodes #14–26 of *Zenki* are collected in this two-DVD set, which completes the first season of the series with an all-out battle and a stronger collection of story arcs.

SPECIAL FEATURES Other Title Trailers TECHNICAL FEATURES Fullscreen (1.33:1) • Subtitles/CC: Eng. • Languages: Jap., Eng. dub • Sound: Dolby Digital 2.0 • Keepcase • 1 Disc • Region 1 GENRE & RATING Supernatural/Action • Rated 13+

Zenki Saga 3

Anime Works, 2002, 325 mins., #EFDVD-8914. Directed by Junichi Nishimura, Hiroyuki Yokoyama. Screenplay by Ryota Yamaguchi. Based on the manga series by Kikuhide Tani and Yoshihiro Kuroiwa in *Shonen Jump*.

NOTE: This DVD arrived too late for a full review. The following text is promotional copy provided by the releasing company:

"The Tree of Karuma may be firewood, but the dark side of the human heart is still a home for demons. New evil and demonic objects called the Seeds of Karuma, have appeared. Only with the help of Zenki's brother, Goki, and newfound friends, Miss Kazue and Professor Kouri, will Chiaki be able to awaken the Ultimate form of the guardian spirit, Zenki, and face the Beasts of Karuma. This double DVD pack contains the complete third season."

SPECIAL FEATURES Other Title Trailers TECHNICAL FEATURES Fullscreen (1.33:1) • Subtitles/CC: Eng. • Languages: Jap., Eng. dub • Sound: Dolby Digital • Multikeepcase • 2 Discs • Region 1 GENRE & RATING Supernatural/Action • Rated 13+

Zoids: The Battle Begins [#1]

Pioneer, 2002, 88 mins., #11761.

On the faraway planet Zi, youthful junk dealer Bit Cloud unexpectedly finds himself swept up in a battle between the Blitz Team and the Tiger Team, competitors in an event that uses Zoids—mechanical animals—to do battle. The Liger Zero, a Zoid thought unusable, responds to Bit, and he's eventually invited to join the Blitz team. The team faces a variety of opponents, including sniper Naomi Flugel, the arrogant Harry Champ, and the enigmatic Backdraft Group, as they battle their way to the top of the heap.

For such an obvious toy tie-in, *Zoids* is surprisingly sophisticated. The story is very simple, but features a strong cast of characters and a surprisingly rich story. The character design and animation is simple at best, but it's aided greatly by the look of the Zoids themselves, which are all cel-shaded computer graphics models. This gives the series a polished, distinctive look. Also of note is the fact that this series is actually the *second Zoids* TV series (the first was broadcast in the U.S., and has not yet seen DVD release). This *Zoids* is a 1999 Japanese children's show, but adults may find themselves drawn in by its likable characters and decent stories.

Unfortunately, the DVD production of *Zoids* is extremely poor. The lack of inclusion of a Japanese audio track isn't surprising for a children's video release, but *Zoids* just looks bad. The picture is fuzzy and full of video artifacts, and the discs are all almost completely devoid of extras (even the opening credits are missing). This disc contains episodes #1–4 of the twenty-six-episode TV series. [MT]

SPECIAL FEATURES Character Bios • Promotional Footage • Insert: Mini-Comic TECHNICAL FEATURES Fullscreen (1.33:1) • Languages: Eng. dub • Sound: Dolby Digital 2.0 • Keepcase • 1 Disc • Region 1 GENRE & RATING Robots/Science Fiction/Action • Rated 7+

Zoids: The High-Speed Battle [#2]

Pioneer, 2002, 88 mins., #11762.

The adventure continues for Bit, Leena, and the Blitz Team. This time, they face a variety of enemies, including a mercenary in a high-speed Zoid, a gigantic elephant Zoid, a gang of desert raiders known as the Sand Stingrays, and tornados that strike during a battle with the Tigers Team.

As with the previous disc, this DVD features substandard video and audio quality, as well as completely lacking a Japanese audio track. This disc contains Zoids episodes #5–8 and a "Score Book" that shows that the Blitz team always wins, no matter what. [MT]

SPECIAL FEATURES Character Bios • Promotional Footage • Zoids Score Sheet • Insert: Chrome Sticker TECHNICAL FEATURES Fullscreen (1.33:1) • Languages: Eng. dub • Sound: Dolby Digital 2.0 • Keepcase • 1 Disc • Region 1 GENRE & RATING Robots/Science Fiction/Action • Rated 7+

Zoids: The Coliseum Battle [#3]

Pioneer, 2002, 88 mins., #11763.

When the Blitz Team takes on the Backdraft Team, could they be facing their first defeat? Plus, Harry's sister tries to convince him to stop Zoids fighting. Then, when Backdraft uses a bunch of tough Zoid-eating War Sharks, Jamie comes up with a dangerous plan to defeat them. And once the Blitz Team is moved up to class "A" battles, they're put at odds with the tough Lightning Team. Finally, two Blitzers are abducted by the Backdraft Team and forced to duke it out against an old foe . . . at the Coliseum!

Zoids episodes #9–12 plus a couple of extras make up the contents of this disc.

SPECIAL FEATURES Character Bios • Promotional Footage • Zoids Score Sheet • Insert: Chrome Sticker TECHNICAL FEATURES Fullscreen (1.33:1) • Languages: Eng. dub • Sound: Dolby Digital 2.0 • Keepcase • 1 Disc • Region 1 GENRE & RATING Robots/Science Fiction/Action • Rated 7+

Zoids: The Supersonic Battle [#4]

Pioneer, 2002, 88 mins., #11764.

NOTE: This DVD arrived too late for a full review. The following text is promotional copy provided by the releasing company:

"Dr. Toros replaces Jamie's Ptera Striker with a Raynos that his father used to pilot, and he helps the Blitz Team as the 'Wild Eagle.' Leena is haunted by a spooky story of the Chainsaw Man on the internet, and receives email implying that she and her Zoid friends are the next victims. Then, Dr. Leon returns with a Whale King transport Carrier outfitted with an antigravity weapon, and Oscar, Jamie's father, also returns! Finally, Leon appears with the Red Blade Liger and teams up with Naomi to challenge the Blitz team!"

This disc contains episodes #13–16.

SPECIAL FEATURES Character Bios • Promotional Footage • Zoids Score Sheet • Inserts: Chrome Sticker TECHNICAL FEATURES Fullscreen (1.33:1) • Languages: Eng. dub • Sound: Dolby Digital 2.0 • Keepcase • 1 Disc • Region 1 GENRE & RATING Robots/Science Fiction/Action • Rated 7+

Zoids: The Shadow Battle [#5]

Pioneer, 2002, 110 mins., #11765. Directed by Takao Kato.

NOTE: This DVD arrived too late for a full review. The following text is promotional copy provided by the releasing company:

"Dr. Laon continues to cause trouble as he challenges the Blitz team to a battle and plots his revenge with Harry against Dr. Toros. Yet, not all troubles on the battlefield remain between the Zoids as Harry's robot Benjamin falls in love with a judge! Can Harry and Bit help him out? Then, against Stoller in his Elephander, Bit equips Liger with the heavy Panzer battle armor, but no amount of armor will protect the Blitz team against betrayal when one of their old friends joins the Backdraft team!"

This disc contains five episodes.

SPECIAL FEATURES Character Bios • Promotional Footage • Zoids Score Sheet • Inserts: Chrome Sticker TECHNICAL FEATURES Fullscreen (1.33:1) • Languages: Eng. dub • Sound: Dolby Digital 2.0 • Keepcase • 1 Disc • Region 1 GENRE & RATING Robots/Science Fiction/Action • Rated 7+

Zone of the Enders Z.O.E.: Idolo [#1]

ADV Films, 2002, 55 mins., #DZE/001. Directed by Tetsuya Watanabe. Script by Shin Yoshida.

It's A.D. 2167. Do you know where your space colonists are? Humanity is spread throughout the solar system and beyond, and violence is commonplace. A group of Martian mecha pilots aren't treated well by the Earth soldiers of the UN Space Force, and the situation is symptomatic of widespread Earth's oppression. Second Lieutenant Radium Lavans and Sergeant Viola Gyunee are pulled into a plot in which the Martians are developing an Orbital Frame, an ultrapowerful, almost-indestructible mecha weapon designed to cause mass destruction on Earth. But even as he bonds with the suit, Lavans becomes more and more filled with rage and doubt; is he changing, or is the mecha changing him? Then, the UNSF raids the project thanks to a spy, and Radium is left with only one alternative . . . even if it pits him against both Martian and Earth military forces!

A very new release, *Zone of the Enders* first appeared as both an OVA and a TV series in April 2001. The series has realistic designs for its human characters, and gorgeous backgrounds and settings. Unfortunately, the mecha all has a seen-it-before feel, which is heightened at times by some CGI work. The story, which is entertaining—and sometimes unpredictable—is based on a PlayStation game, but the game takes place five years after the events in the anime.

The DVD contains the first OVA. Extras include some nice interviews with the director (which hilariously opens with a dead serious, "I'm not the type to think much while I work"), chief character designer, and other character and mecha designers, as well as a timeline and art.

SPECIAL FEATURES Crew Interviews • Character and Art Galleries • Timeline • Other Title Trailers TECHNICAL FEATURES Fullscreen (1.33:1) • Subtitles/CC: Eng. • Languages: Jap., Eng. dub • Sound: Dolby Digital 2.0, Dolby Digital 5.1 • Keepcase • 1 Disc • Region 1 GENRE & RATING Robots/Science Fiction/Action • Rated 15+

Zone of the Enders Z.O.E.: Dolores, i— Countdown to Destiny! [#1]

ADV Films, 2002, 125 mins., #DZE/002. Directed by Tetsuya Watanabe. Script by Masanao Akahoshi, Shin Yoshida.

NOTE: This DVD arrived too late for a full review. The following text is promotional copy provided by the releasing company:

"The planets are on the brink of war, but the only thing hard-working, hard-drinking, all-American cargo hauler James Links wants is to reconcile with his estranged wife. But when he discovers the Orbital Frame Dolores aboard his carrier ship *Ender*, the entire Links clan is plunged into mystery, murder and mayhem! Earth wants her; Mars wants her; everybody wants Dolores except the one man who has her. Blast off with a crew of unlikely heroes in the high-speed interplanetary adventure *Zone of the Enders*!"

This disc contains five episodes.

SPECIAL FEATURES "Making of" Featurette • Character and Art Galleries • Clean Credits • Other Title Trailers TECHNICAL FEATURES Fullscreen (1.33:1) • Subtitles/CC: Eng. • Languages: Jap., Eng. dub • Sound: Dolby Digital 2.0 • Keepcase • 1 Disc • Region 1 GENRE & RATING Robots/Science Fiction/Action • Rated 15+

Zoids: The Coliseum Battle [#3]

Pioneer, 2002, 88 mins., #11763.

When the Blitz Team takes on the Backdraft Team, could they be facing their first defeat? Plus, Harry's sister tries to convince him to stop Zoids fighting. Then, when Backdraft uses a bunch of tough Zoid-eating War Sharks, Jamie comes up with a dangerous plan to defeat them. And once the Blitz Team is moved up to class "A" battles, they're

put at odds with the tough Lightning Team. Finally, two Blitzers are abducted by the Backdraft Team and forced to duke it out against an old foe . . . at the Coliseum!

Zoids episodes #9–12 plus a couple of extras make up the contents of this disc.

SPECIAL FEATURES Character Bios • Promotional Footage • Zoids Score Sheet • Insert: Chrome Sticker TECHNICAL FEATURES Fullscreen (1.33:1) • Languages: Eng. dub • Sound: Dolby Digital 2.0 • Keepcase • 1 Disc • Region 1 GENRE & RATING Robots/Science Fiction/Action • Rated 7+

Zoids: The Supersonic Battle [#4]

Pioneer, 2002, 88 mins., #11764.

NOTE: This DVD arrived too late for a full review. The following text is promotional copy provided by the releasing company:

"Dr. Toros replaces Jamie's Ptera Striker with a Raynos that his father used to pilot, and he helps the Blitz Team as the 'Wild Eagle.' Leena is haunted by a spooky story of the Chainsaw Man on the internet, and receives email implying that she and her Zoid friends are the next victims. Then, Dr. Leon returns with a Whale King transport Carrier outfitted with an antigravity weapon, and Oscar, Jamie's father, also returns! Finally, Leon appears with the Red Blade Liger and teams up with Naomi to challenge the Blitz team!"

This disc contains episodes #13–16.

SPECIAL FEATURES Character Bios • Promotional Footage • Zoids Score Sheet • Inserts: Chrome Sticker TECHNICAL FEATURES Fullscreen (1.33:1) • Languages: Eng. dub • Sound: Dolby Digital 2.0 • Keepcase • 1 Disc • Region 1 GENRE & RATING Robots/Science Fiction/Action • Rated 7+

Zoids: The Shadow Battle [#5]

Pioneer, 2002, 110 mins., #11765. Directed by Takao Kato.

NOTE: This DVD arrived too late for a full review. The following text is promotional copy provided by the releasing company:

"Dr. Laon continues to cause trouble as he challenges the Blitz team to a battle and plots his revenge with Harry against Dr. Toros. Yet, not all troubles on the battlefield remain between the Zoids as Harry's robot Benjamin falls in love with a judge! Can Harry and Bit help him out? Then, against Stoller in his Elephander, Bit equips Liger with the heavy Panzer battle armor, but no amount of armor will protect the Blitz team against betrayal when one of their old friends joins the Backdraft team!"

This disc contains five episodes.

SPECIAL FEATURES Character Bios • Promotional Footage • Zoids Score Sheet • Inserts: Chrome Sticker TECHNICAL FEATURES Fullscreen (1.33:1) • Languages: Eng. dub • Sound: Dolby Digital 2.0 • Keepcase • 1 Disc • Region 1 GENRE & RATING Robots/Science Fiction/Action • Rated 7+

Zone of the Enders Z.O.E.: Idolo [#1]

ADV Films, 2002, 55 mins., #DZE/001. Directed by Tetsuya Watanabe. Script by Shin Yoshida.

It's A.D. 2167. Do you know where your space colonists are? Humanity is spread throughout the solar system and beyond, and violence is commonplace. A group of Martian mecha pilots aren't treated well by the Earth soldiers of the UN Space Force, and the situation is symptomatic of widespread Earth's oppression. Second Lieutenant Radium Lavans and Sergeant Viola Gyunee are pulled into a plot in which the Martians are developing an Orbital Frame, an ultrapowerful, almost-indestructible mecha weapon designed to cause mass destruction on Earth. But even as he bonds with the suit, Lavans becomes more and more filled with rage and doubt; is he changing, or is the mecha changing him? Then, the UNSF raids the project thanks to a spy, and Radium is left with only one alternative . . . even if it pits him against both Martian and Earth military forces!

A very new release, *Zone of the Enders* first appeared as both an OVA and a TV series in April 2001. The series has realistic designs for its human characters, and gorgeous backgrounds and settings. Unfortunately, the mecha all has a seen-it-before feel, which is heightened at times by some CGI work. The story, which is entertaining—and sometimes unpredictable—is based on a PlayStation game, but the game takes place five years after the events in the anime.

The DVD contains the first OVA. Extras include some nice interviews with the director (which hilariously opens with a dead serious, "I'm not the type to think much while I work"), chief character designer, and other character and mecha designers, as well as a timeline and art.

SPECIAL FEATURES Crew Interviews • Character and Art Galleries • Timeline • Other Title Trailers TECHNICAL FEATURES Fullscreen (1.33:1) • Subtitles/CC: Eng. • Languages: Jap., Eng. dub • Sound: Dolby Digital 2.0, Dolby Digital 5.1 • Keepcase • 1 Disc • Region 1 GENRE & RATING Robots/Science Fiction/Action • Rated 15+

Zone of the Enders Z.O.E.: Dolores, i— Countdown to Destiny! [#1]

ADV Films, 2002, 125 mins., #DZE/002. Directed by Tetsuya Watanabe. Script by Masanao Akahoshi, Shin Yoshida.

NOTE: This DVD arrived too late for a full review. The following text is promotional copy provided by the releasing company:

"The planets are on the brink of war, but the only thing hard-working, hard-drinking, all-American cargo hauler James Links wants is to reconcile with his estranged wife. But when he discovers the Orbital Frame Dolores aboard his carrier ship *Ender*, the entire Links clan is plunged into mystery, murder and mayhem! Earth wants her; Mars wants her; everybody wants Dolores except the one man who has her. Blast off with a crew of unlikely heroes in the high-speed interplanetary adventure *Zone of the Enders*!"

This disc contains five episodes.

SPECIAL FEATURES "Making of" Featurette • Character and Art Galleries • Clean Credits • Other Title Trailers TECHNICAL FEATURES Fullscreen (1.33:1) • Subtitles/CC: Eng. • Languages: Jap., Eng. dub • Sound: Dolby Digital 2.0 • Keepcase • 1 Disc • Region 1 GENRE & RATING Robots/Science Fiction/Action • Rated 15+

MATURE/
ADULT FILMS

ABOUT THIS SECTION

Most DVD or video guides make no distinction between their listings of titles for all ages and titles intended for mature viewers. I felt that since a large portion of the entries in this book are aimed at children, younger viewers, and families, it would be inappropriate to put *Beast City* on the same page as *Beauty and the Beast*. Then, too, I felt it would be censorship not to include *all* animated titles. Thus, my publisher and I decided that all titles labeled Mature or Adult, or rated R or X, would be placed in this separate section.

Warning: The DVD box covers reproduced in this section are quite small and do not portray actual naked bodies or explicit sexual activities, but they are indeed suggestive and, to some, potentially offensive. Parents who don't want their children to look in this section are encouraged to tape the pages together or take other proactive steps, while still understanding the importance of this anticensorship stance.

So be forewarned: this section contains some sexually graphic terms and descriptions. I have tried to keep all text to a PG rating, but there are a few points I'd like to cover before you begin reading.

First, not all the titles in this section are sexually explicit. Some are political in nature, others are rated R because they offended someone on the Motion Picture Association of America's ratings board. I consider the *South Park* movie to be near the pinnacle of comedic animation, but its deserved R rating places it in this section.

Second, although I specify homosexual or lesbian acts in some of the listings that follow, this is not for reasons of homophobia. I am openly gay myself. I call attention to these acts because some people may wish to search them out and others may wish to avoid them. Note that the same "call outs" were done for religious themes in the main portion of this book.

Third, many of the reviews of explicit DVDs have a "laundry list" of sexual acts contained within. Again, this is to help people who do—or do not—want to view such acts find the appropriate DVD.

Finally, people who have not viewed Japanese pornography before may be shocked to learn that the vast majority of the titles available on DVD feature the rape of women by men, women, demons, tentacled monsters, and more. Many also feature very child-like characters engaging in sex.

This element may disturb many viewers, so I have clearly listed the titles that feature rape or characters that appear to be underage (U.S. packaging for these titles always says "19-year-old" and often mentions "college" instead of high school).

Japanese attitudes regarding repression of sexuality as it relates to anime and manga are discussed clearly in several books, including Helen McCarthy and Jonathan Clements' *The Erotic Anime Movie Guide* and Patrick Drazen's *Anime Explosion! The What? Why? and Wow! of Japanese Animation.*

Affairs, The

Kitty, 2001, 35 mins., #KVDVD-0111. Directed by Mitsuhiro Yoneda, Sai Imazaki. Script by Rokurota Marabe, Sai Imazaki.

In "Office Affairs," Ono has a tough job and a girlfriend who's a bit jealous. She's got good reason to be, since Ono's new female manager Sugiyama has more on her mind than company economics. She wants Ono . . . and what she wants, she's going to get. Then, in "Co-Ed Affairs," a group of school girls decide to use their new video camera to explore their bodies and each other.

A 1996 video, "Office Affairs" is poorly animated with much of the action in still-frames and off-panel sex (duo and group) that is uninspired. "Co-Ed Affairs" has better animation, with much solo and lesbian sex on display, as well as a touch of watersports.

SPECIAL FEATURES Other Title Trailers TECHNICAL FEATURES Fullscreen (1.33:1) • Subtitles/CC: Eng. • Languages: Jap., Eng. dub • Sound: Dolby Digital 2.0 • Keepcase • 1 Disc • Region 1 GENRE & RATING Adult/Anthology • Rated 18+

Akira

Pioneer, 2001, 124 mins., #11538. Directed by Katsuhiro Otomo. Screenplay by Katsuhiro Otomo, Izo Hashimoto. Based on the manga series by Katsuhiro Otomo in *Young Magazine*.

The year is 2019, and Neo Tokyo has been rebuilt after the cataclysmic explosion that destroyed it in July 1988. Although it's now preparing to host the next Olympic Games, the city is overrun by dissent, both political and social. Beneath the glittering towers are people used to poverty and despair. Tetsuo is a teenage member of a biker gang headed by his longtime friend Kaneda. One evening, while they race and rumble with rival gang The Clowns, Tetsuo gets into an accident, almost hitting a child who looks like an aged man. Tetsuo is taken into custody by the military, and they begin to experiment on him.

An angry Kaneda searches for his friend, allying himself with Kai and Ryu, members of a resistance group that opposes the military. But Kaneda is also searching for the fabled entity known as Akira, who may be responsible for Tokyo's first destruction. When Tetsuo's immense latent psychic powers begin to manifest, what will be the outcome for the military, his friends, and the rebuilt city?

Released theatrically in the summer of 1988 in Japan, and in 1989 in the U.S., *Akira* is generally credited with bringing the world of anime to the general public. The success of the film certainly paved the way for greater acceptance of anime and animation as a serious adult entertainment form; after all, *Akira* could never be shown on Saturday morning.

Akira features some mind-blowing gore and some brief nudity, enough to earn it an R rating in the U.S. But most of the violence comes in service to the story, showcasing just what kind of rage an untrained mind with immense psychic powers might unleash. And while the story is not particularly groundbreaking in either theme or execution, the dazzling animation is astounding. Produced in a time when computer animation was still in its infancy, *Akira* manages to accomplish things with traditional cel animation that are still unrivaled today.

Although a previous video release of *Akira* is available, Pioneer's DVD releases of the feature are completely remastered. Everything about the discs is top-notch, from a crisp and clear digitally remastered picture to a closer-to-the-Japanese English dub that has fans cheering. Although fans debate whether or not *Akira* is the best anime film ever produced, the fact that the debate still rages over a decade since its release is telling enough. While it may or may not be *the* best, *Akira* remains one of the most influential and technically excellent anime films ever.

SPECIAL FEATURES Translation Capsule Feature. TECHNICAL FEATURES Widescreen (1.78:1) • Subtitles/CC: Eng. • Languages: Jap., Eng. dub • Sound: Dolby Digital Surround 5.1 • Keepcase • 1 Disc • Region 1 GENRE & RATING Thriller/Science Fiction • Rated R

Akira: The Special Edition

Pioneer, 2001, 124 mins., #11568. Directed by Katsuhiro Otomo. Screenplay by Katsuhiro Otomo, Izo Hashimoto. Based on the manga series by Katsuhiro Otomo in *Young Magazine*.

This two-DVD set contains not only the same disc as in the single edition, but a second disc chock full of extras. The 4,500 images in the gallery section alone stand as an unrivaled selection in the world of DVDs (viewing them at two seconds apiece would take two-and-a-half hours!). Additional materials include the "Akira Production Report," a forty-eight-minute featurette about the making of the film, plus a half-hour interview with the director, twenty minutes on the sound and music, fourteen minutes on the digital restoration, and more! For cinephiles and hardcore anime fans, this is the version of *Akira* to get.

SPECIAL FEATURES "Making of" Featurettes • Director Interview • Cast Filmographies • Glossary • Character and Art Galleries • Production Notes • Storyboards • Trailer • Promotional Footage • Restoration Featurettes • Translation Capsule Feature • Insert: Liner Notes TECHNICAL FEATURES Widescreen (1.78:1 enhanced for 16x9) • Subtitles/CC: Eng. • Languages: Jap., Eng. dub • Sound: Dolby Digital Surround 5.1 • Keepcase with Cardboard Slipcover • 2 Discs • Region 1 GENRE & RATING Thriller/Science Fiction • Rated R

Akira: The Limited Edition Tin

Pioneer, 2001, 124 mins., #11537. Directed by Katsuhiro Otomo. Screenplay by Katsuhiro Otomo, Izo Hashimoto. Based on the manga series by Katsuhiro Otomo in *Young Magazine*.

This tin was released in a limited edition of 100,000 copies, so there are a lot of them on the market, though they can be hard to track down. A cardboard holder cradles the metal case, which is painted a dark blue-black, with embossed silver-and-red lettering. The interior discs are the same as in the Special Edition, but the clear holders are overlaid on beautiful shots of Neo Tokyo's cityscape. The edition also featured a temporary tattoo. Although it is a numbered edition, there is no numbering on the case or the contents.

SPECIAL FEATURES "Making of" Featurettes • Director Interview • Cast Filmographies • Glossary • Character and Art Galleries • Production Notes • Storyboards • Trailer • Promotional Footage • Restoration Featurettes • Translation Capsule Feature • Insert: Temporary Tattoo, Liner Notes TECHNICAL FEATURES Widescreen (1.78:1 enhanced for 16x9) • Subtitles/CC: Eng. • Languages: Jap., Eng. dub • Sound: Dolby Digital Surround 5.1 • Metal Box • 2 Discs • Region 1 GENRE & RATING Thriller/Science Fiction • Rated R

Angel Cop: The Collection

Manga Entertainment, 2000, 160 mins., #4063-2. Directed by Ichiro Itano. Screenplay by Noboru Aikawa, Ichiro Itano. Based on the manga series by Taku Kitazaki, Itano Ichiro in *Newtype*.

In the 1990s, Japan has become a target for terrorism, so the powers-that-be have set up the Special Security Force. All officers on the force have a license to kill with no questions asked. The newest member is Angel, but she's soon embroiled in a war against psychics (who might be tied to the government), cyborgs, political double-crossing, and a vigilante.

Cyberpunk action junkies will like this; the story is exceedingly—in many places gratuitously—violent. Dark and gritty, it attempts to have mystery, but the characters are too often in service only to kill or be killed. All six hard-as-diamonds OVA episodes are included on this DVD, which also contains explicit language, nudity, and mature situations. There's also a limited anti-American and anti-Jewish sentiment that creeps into the dialogue, though it's more prevalent in the subtitles of the Japanese version than it is in the dubbed version.

SPECIAL FEATURES Weblinks • Other Title Trailers • Insert: Liner Notes TECHNICAL FEATURES Widescreen (1.66:1) • Subtitles/CC: Eng. • Languages: Jap., Eng. dub • Sound: Dolby Digital Surround 2.0 • Keepcase • 1 Disc • Region 1, 2, 4 GENRE Mature/Police/Action/Science Fiction

Angel of Darkness

SoftCel, 2002, 100 mins., #DAD/001. Directed by Kazuma Muraki. Story by Yukihiro Makino.

Atsuko and Sayaka are two lesbian schoolgirls who attend a prestigious women's academy, but the institution holds a secret that relates to demonic sacrifices of young women! Now, they must face demons with the help of miniature elves. Then, the school is in danger from a professor who raises plants that feed on young women. But this isn't any mean green mother from outer space, these plants are demonic!

This 1990s-era OVA series has some very nice backgrounds and pleasant Western-style animation designs. As might be expected by the plot, there's plenty of lesbianism, SM, fetish gear, and rape by demons, elves, trolls, and plants.

SPECIAL FEATURES Other Title Trailers TECHNICAL FEATURES Fullscreen (1.33:1) • Subtitles/CC: Eng. • Languages: Jap. • Sound: Dolby Digital 2.0 • Keepcase • 1 Disc • Region 1 GENRE & RATING Adult/Schoolgirl • Rated 18+

Angels in the Court: Vol. 1

NuTech, 2001, 28 mins., #558. Directed by Satoru Sumisaki. Script by Muto Yasuyuki .

The volleyball team of Aota Academy is made up of voluptuous girls, and their coach, Akira Motoura, a former All-Japan ace player, can barely keep his fantasies under control. He wants the new girl, buxom Nanase Morimura, a mysterious transfer student. Nanase is a killer volleyball player, but only if sufficiently excited before entering the court. Soon, it's not only teammate Nao who responds to the coach's desires.

Brightly colored, sometimes funny, and cheerful, this sports porn features American dub voices by adult film stars Shayla LeVeaux and Haven. The sex is all consensual, and there are group scenes. The flip side of the DVD contains a whole bunch of preview trailers.

SPECIAL FEATURES Photo Galleries • Character and Art Galleries • Other Title Trailers TECHNICAL FEATURES Fullscreen (1.33:1) • Subtitles/CC: Eng. • Languages: Jap., Eng. dub • Sound: Dolby Digital 2.0 • Keepcase • 1 Disc • Region 1 GENRE & RATING Adult/Sports

Angels in the Court: Vol. 2

NuTech, 2001, 28 mins., #559. Directed by Satoru Sumisaki. Script by Muto Yasuyuki.

When Coach Motoura saves Kozue from being raped in the park, he goes missing! But even as the team searches for him, they have a big championship match coming up for which they must prepare. And while Nao does her best to keep everyone focused, without the coach's special input, Nanase is a disastrous player.

More group sex, lesbianism, and cheerful girl's volleyball make up this short disc. The extras are the same as in volume #1, and the disc is once again double-sided with previews.

SPECIAL FEATURES Photo Galleries • Character and Art Galleries • Other Title Trailers TECHNICAL FEATURES Fullscreen (1.33:1) • Subtitles/CC: Eng. • Languages: Jap., Eng. dub • Sound: Dolby Digital 2.0 • Keepcase • 1 Disc • Region 1 GENRE Adult/Sports

Angels in the Court [Box Set]

NuTech, 2001, 56 mins., #560.

This box set features the two commercially available keepcase editions of *Angels in the Court* in a cardboard box. It does not feature any additional extras. See individual entries for the Special and Technical Features listings.

TECHNICAL FEATURES Cardboard Box with 2 Keepcases • 2 Discs • Region 1 GENRE

Adult/Sports

Anime Fiction: Vol. 1

Digital Anime, 2002, 45 mins.

If you've always wanted to see your favorite anime characters doing the dirty deed, welcome to this porn parody series. In three eight-minute segments, plus seven two-minute clips, you'll see sexual parodies of *Cowboy Bebop, Love Hina, Fushigi Yugi, Gundam*, and others.

The animation includes some CGI work, but is very basic in general. Most of the movements are repetitive, and the "bonus clips" of thirteen snippets don't even go that far; they're mostly the camera panning past still artwork!

SPECIAL FEATURES None TECHNICAL FEATURES Fullscreen (1.33:1) • Languages: Eng. • Sound: Dolby Digital 2.0 • Keepcase • 1 Disc • Region All GENRE Adult/Parody/Anthology

Anime Fiction: Vol. 2

Digital Anime, 2002, 45 mins., #23154-10040.

Another grouping of short sex "parodies" includes four eight-minute shorts, plus twelve extra two-minute scenes and the "bonus" art clips. This time out, look for the *Ronin Warriors* to get involved in a group scene, and in non-anime, Wolverine, Storm, and Rogue—three of the *X-Men* cast—get jiggy with it. All this, plus some bondage and demon sex.

SPECIAL FEATURES None TECHNICAL FEATURES Fullscreen (1.33:1) • Languages: Eng. • Sound: Dolby Digital 2.0 • Keepcase • 1 Disc • Region All GENRE Adult/Parody/Anthology

Baoh

AnimEigo, 2002, 50 mins., #AV202-062. Directed by Hiroyuki Yokoyama. Screenplay by Kenji Terada. Based on the manga series by Araki Hirohiko in *Shonen Jump Comics*.

A secret organization has created a genetically engineered parasitic virus code-named "BAOH." Unfortunately for him, young Hashizawa Ikuro is infected, turning him into a virtually indestructible bio-weapon. Although he escapes with the aid of a young precognitive girl, Ikuro is forced to fight for his freedom from the organization's agents and the BAOH virus itself!

Hyper-extreme gore and violence against humans and animals will bother some viewers, but *Baoh's* animation includes a nice multi-shadowed look. Similar in tone to *Guyver* and *Genocyber*, *Baoh* is probably best for those who like nasty thrills with little plot. The DVD presents the 1989 OVA, with minor extras.

SPECIAL FEATURES Character Galleries • Insert: Character Notes, Song Lyrics TECHNICAL FEATURES Fullscreen (1.33:1) • Subtitles/CC: Eng. • Languages: Jap., Eng. dub • Sound: Dolby Digital 2.0 • Keepcase • 1 Disc • Region 1 GENRE Mature/Action/Horror

Battle Angel

ADV Films, 1999, 60 mins., #DVDBA001. Directed by Masami Obari. Screenplay by Jiro Takayama, Masaharu Amiya. Based on the manga series "Gunm" by Kishuro Yukito in *Business Jump*.

Alita is a cyborg repaired by cybernetics expert Daisuke Ido after he finds what's left of her body in a scrapyard. She becomes a bounty hunter, but her missing past nags at her.

This DVD contains the 1993 episodes "Rusty Angel" and "Tears Sign," the only two animated OVAs taken from the popular manga graphic novel line "Gunm." The story condenses some of the earliest manga plots and features some violence and nudity. Some fans have complained that the end credit sequences on each episode do not play correctly on the DVD.

This DVD was not available for review. It is currently on moratorium.

Beast City

Anime 18, 2002, 90 mins., #AI8D-1834. Directed by Shinichi Watanabe. Script by Yuri Kanai. Based on the manga series by Naomi Hayakawa.

The year is "201X AD" in Tokyo City, and a tough woman named Mina stops a demonic rape in an alley. Mina is a vampire herself (known here as a "Draculon"), but she hates the sex-starved Beasts that are running rampant. Armed with her Beast-Hunter Sword, Mina tracks down and destroys the creatures of evil . . . when she's not breaking into apartments and sucking the blood from sleeping-but-aroused men. She soon faces Karma, a demon who feed on endorphins, and whose "furniture" consists of women tied up in restrictive poses.

"Vampire Madonna" and "Awakening of the Beast," two of the 1990 *Beast City* OVAs, are collected in this volume, which features some rather disturbing demon imagery. The story is mostly predictable, though Mina and her two small charges are unusual "heroes." There is grotesque demon rape, lesbianism, and bondage.

SPECIAL FEATURES Character Bios • Character and Art Galleries • Storyboards • Trailer • Anime Featurette • DVD-ROM Features: Art, Scripts • Other Title Trailers TECHNICAL FEATURES Fullscreen (1.33:1) • Subtitles/CC: Eng. • Languages: Jap., Eng. dub • Sound: Dolby Digital 2.0 • Keepcase • 1 Disc • Region 1–6 GENRE & RATING Adult/Horror • Rated 18+

Behind the Music That Sucks—Vol. 1: Pure Energy! Pure Rock!

Heavy, 2000, 50 mins. Series produced by Heavy.com.

A parody of VH1's *Behind the Music* program, this limited-animation series is also low on intelligence, but it's good for a few guilty laughs. A collection of shorts, the "animation" largely consists of blinking eyes and moving mouths. The humor, in turn, is offensive to just about everyone, and includes jokes about sex, death, drugs, ethnicity, sexual orientation, and musical talent. That's not to say some of the jokes aren't funny—and/or cruel—but that is a warning for those who might be easily offended.

Volume #1 contains such rock, hard rock, goth rock, and hair rock bands as Marilyn Manson, Limp Bizkit, Nine Inch Nails, Bon Jovi, Stryper, Smashing Pumpkins, Kiss, Kid Rock, Garbage, and AC/DC. A couple of bonus clips include the mildly funny "American Suck Countdown." The DVD was advertised as available as a part of a five-disc box set, but it's not clear if the set was released or if it is available any longer.

SPECIAL FEATURES Bonus Clips. TECHNICAL FEATURES Fullscreen (1.33:1) • Languages: Eng. • Sound: Dolby Digital 2.0 • Keepcase • 1 Disc • Region 1 GENRE Mature/Music/Parody/Anthology

Behind the Music That Sucks—Vol. 2: Cherry Poppin' Pop Stars!

Heavy, 2000, 50 mins. Series produced by Heavy.com.

Another volume in the limited-animation parody of VH1's *Behind the Music* program, this disc contains such boy band, divas, and one-hit wonders as Britney Spears, Backstreet Boys, Shania Twain, Christina Aguilera, N'Sync, Sisqo, Bloodhound Gang, Hanson, and Chumbawamba. The bonus clip is a rerun of the "American Suck Countdown" from Volume #1. The DVD was advertised as available as a part of a five-disc box set, but it's not clear if the set was released or if it is available any longer.

SPECIAL FEATURES Bonus Clips. TECHNICAL FEATURES Fullscreen (1.33:1) • Languages: Eng. • Sound: Dolby Digital 2.0 • Keepcase • 1 Disc • Region 1 GENRE Mature/Music/Parody/Anthology

Behind the Music That Sucks—Vol. 3: Hairy Women of Rock!

Heavy, 2001, 50 mins. Series produced by Heavy.com.

More limited-animation parodies of VH1's *Behind the Music* program, including Mariah Carey, Christina Aguilera, Melissa Etheridge, Barbra Streisand, and others.

This DVD was not available for review. The DVD was advertised as available as a part of a five-disc box set, but it's not clear if the set was released or if it is available any longer.

SPECIAL FEATURES Bonus Clips. TECHNICAL FEATURES Fullscreen (1.33:1) • Languages: Eng. • Sound: Dolby Digital 2.0 • Keepcase • 1 Disc • Region 1 GENRE Mature/Music/Parody/Anthology

Behind the Music That Sucks—Vol. 4: Killin' Cops and Hip-Hop!

Heavy, 2000, 50 mins. Series produced by Heavy.com.

The fourth volume in the limited-animation parody of VH1's *Behind the Music* program, this disc contains such rap, hip-hop, gangsta, and rock bands as Puff Daddy, Dr. Dre, Will Smith, Eminem, Tupac, LL Cool J, Kid Rock, Limp Bizkit, and Insane Clown Posse. The bonus clip is a drug-oriented story called "Munchyman and Fatty." The DVD was advertised as available as a

part of a five-disc box set, but it's not clear if the set was released or if it is available any longer.

SPECIAL FEATURES Bonus Clips. TECHNICAL FEATURES Fullscreen (1.33:1) • Languages: Eng. • Sound: Dolby Digital 2.0 • Keepcase • 1 Disc • Region 1 GENRE Mature/Music/Parody/Anthology

Behind the Music That Sucks—Vol. 5: Poor Dumb Loser Bastards

Heavy, 2001, 50 mins. Series produced by Heavy.com.

The final volume of limited-animation parodies of VH1's "Behind the Music" program.

This DVD was not available for review. The DVD was advertised as available as a part of a five-disc box set, but it's not clear if the set was released or if it is available any longer.

SPECIAL FEATURES Bonus Clips. TECHNICAL FEATURES Fullscreen (1.33:1) • Languages: Eng. • Sound: Dolby Digital 2.0 • Keepcase • 1 Disc • Region 1 GENRE Mature/Music/Parody/Anthology

Best of Kitty, The: Vol. 1

Kitty, 2000, 120 mins., #KVDVD-0081. Directed by Masanori Suzuki, Kan Fukumoto, Takashi Kawamura. Written by Hideaki Kushi, Wataru Amano, Ryusei.

This DVD contains three 1996 OVAs. The first, the forty-five-minute "Orchid Emblem," features an ex-DEA agent named Rei-Lan who becomes lovers with the crime lord who raped her, gets a matching dragon tattoo, and then can't be satisfied without him. Animation is standard, with lesbianism and rape, but the script is dull.

In the forty-five-minute "Advancer Tina," the year is 3113, and Earth is long dead. Mankind now lives throughout the solar system, with "Advancer" scouts helping to make sure potential homeworlds are inhabitable. Enter Tina Owen and the rest of her crew, who are hoping to commute their jail sentences by undertaking the dangerous mission. What awaits them is a creature like that from an *Alien* film, which uses its tentacles to rape all the women. The animation is tremendously Western-looking.

The final selection is the twenty-nine-minute "Battle Team Lakers Ex," a mish-mash about aliens who look like pretty girls that come to Earth and use their power to defend the planet from an evil space dominatrix named Dieana. Plus, there's monsters, mecha, and swords, and all the girls go ga-ga after the nerdy guy. The art is cutesy, the story is cliché to the point of parody, and the sex isn't very interesting, even with bondage and lesbianism added.

SPECIAL FEATURES Character and Art Galleries • Other Title Trailers TECHNICAL FEATURES Fullscreen (1.33:1) • Subtitles/CC: Eng.

• Languages: Jap., Eng. dub • Sound: Dolby Digital 2.0 • Keepcase • 1 Disc • Region 1 GENRE & RATING Adult/Anthology • Rated 18+

Best of Kitty, The: Vol. 2

Kitty, 2002, 105 mins., #KVDVD-0210. Directed by Yukihiro Makino, Komari Yukino, Yorihisa Uchida. Script by Komari Yukino, Ryoei Tsukimura.

Another trio of short porn anime OVAs makes up this disc. The twenty-nine-minute "Wake Up, Aria!" from 1998 features a girl named Aria who goes to Golden Breast Island to attend a distinguished music school. But it's just a front for the headmaster and mistress who enslave and sexually abuse the female students. The animation is disturbingly kiddy-oriented, and the story features much rape and demon sex.

In the thirty-eight-minute "Legend of Reyon" from 1986, ancient warriors do battle in a fantasy setting. The animation is interesting, with a nice use of color—though there is some super-deformed footage; this one has demons, tentacles, bondage, and even transsexualism.

The third segment, the thirty-minute "Balthus (Tia's Radiance)" from 1988, factory workers try to revolt against their oppressive master, Morlock. Lovers Eud and Tia escape, but are caught, whereupon Eud is imprisoned and Tia is raped. The animation on this is well above par, with a trippy, realistic, steampunk design sense. This short alone makes the disc worth viewing, even if only on a technical level.

SPECIAL FEATURES Other Title Trailers TECHNICAL FEATURES Fullscreen (1.33:1) • Subtitles/CC: Eng. • Languages: Jap., Eng. dub • Sound: Dolby Digital 2.0 • Keepcase • 1 Disc • Region 1 GENRE & RATING Adult/Anthology • Rated 18+

Best of Kitty, The: Vol. 3

Kitty, 2002, 140 mins., #KVDVD-0213. Directed by Shunji Yoshida, Shigeru Yazaki, Mitsuo Kusakabe. Script by Shunji Yoshida, Kazuhiko Godo, Naruhiko Ta-tsumiya. "My Fair Masseuse" based on the manga series by Naruo Kuzukawa in *Young Champion*. "Chimera" based on the manga series by Asami Tojo.

In the forty-one-minute "My Fair Masseuse" from 1996, Moko really enjoys her life as a masseuse/house prostitute, even though it generally involves old men. That's too bad for the frustrated guy who's trying to get to know her better. This comedy has some super-deformed moments. On the plus side, all the sex is consensual; on the negative, much of it is with geriatrics or geeks.

With a title like "Sexorcist" (1996), you'd expect demon rape, and you'll get it. You'll also get robot rape in this thirty-nine-minute story about 22nd-century advanced robots called silhouettes. There's lots of virtual reality and some gladiator arena battles, all wrapped up in this game-based OVA from 1996. It has acceptable animation.

Finally, in the forty-eight-minute "Chimera" from 1997, Rei is an assassin for the Hong Kong underworld kingpin who killed her parents. Sounds like a recipe for rape, violence, bondage, SM, and lesbianism. The animation is almost Western, but more angular than most anime.

SPECIAL FEATURES Other Title Trailers TECHNICAL FEATURES Fullscreen (1.33:1) • Subtitles/CC: Eng. • Languages: Jap., Eng. dub • Sound: Dolby Digital 2.0 • Keepcase • 1 Disc • Region 1 GENRE & RATING Adult/Anthology • Rated 18+

Best of Kitty, The: Vol 4

Kitty, 2002, 105 mins., KVDVD-0219. Directed by Akihiro Okuzawa, Teruaki Murakami, Yoshitaka Fujimoto. Screenplay by Hiroshi Ishii, Rokurota Marabe, Ken Oketani. "Bondage House" based on the manga series by Takushi Fukada. "Sins of the Flesh" based on the manga series by Tsuyoshi Tamaoki. "Erotic Torture Chamber" based on the book by Piace Hoshino.

A private detective who isn't afraid to get his hands—or anything else—dirty rescues a girl from rape in the twenty-eight-minute "Bondage House," a 1999 story that has animation that's far too cutesy for the bondage, rape, and drug use contained therein. Then, in the thirty-one-minute "Sins of the Flesh" from 1999, a young painter who wants to devote his life to the church is seduced by a girl . . . or is she a demoness? Viewers won't care, as this is a very boring OVA.

Fantasy fans will like the forty-five-minute "Erotic Torture Chamber" from 1994, wherein a land of dragons and knights is being conquered by a king. Too bad he's targeted a princess to become his sex slave. Serviceable animation includes bondage, rape, fetishwear, and lesbianism.

SPECIAL FEATURES Character and Art Galleries • Other Title Trailers TECHNICAL FEATURES Fullscreen (1.33:1) • Subtitles/CC: Eng. • Languages: Jap., Eng. dub • Sound: Dolby Digital 2.0 • Keepcase • 1 Disc • Region 1–6 GENRE & RATING Adult/Anthology • Rated 18+

Best of the Web #1, The

M2K, 2001, 88 mins., #BE1DV401. Produced by www.alwaysi.com.

This collection of short films from alwaysi.com contains three animated segments. "Wild Safari Jackass" is a pointless and much-too-long (five parts!) parody of TV's Crocodile Hunter. The weirdest of the lot is "Broken" a creepy and ultragory claymation story in which a child watches his parents get violently killed. Finally, "Portait of the Sand" follows a CGI woman and child as they approach something in the desert.

Although the live-action films are mostly harmless and acceptable for teens, the "Broken" short puts this collection firmly into the Mature category.

SPECIAL FEATURES Weblinks TECHNICAL FEATURES Fullscreen (1.33:1) • Languages: Eng. • Sound: Dolby Digital 2.0 • Snapcase • 1 Disc • Region All GENRE Mature/Anthology

Best of the Web #2, The

M2K, 2001, 73 mins., #BE2DV401.

This collection of shorts from camp chaos.com includes several profane-but-funny cartoons making fun of Metallica and their battle against Napster, parodying *Cops, Who Wants to Be a Millionaire?* and the charity song "We Are the World." There's also a very nasty *Survivor* parody entitled "They Shoved a Camera Right up My A★★!" Two political toons include a spot-on look at President Bush's election, and a crude "Monkey for President" short.

The remainder of the twenty-four tracks include more Metallica clips, some pointless and gory "Puke 'n' Chunder" episodes, "Safari Kingdom" set in a schoolyard, a crazed sports announcer, ads for nipple clamps, and a singing old geezer. This is a very uneven collection, with some laugh-out-loud segments mixed in among a lot of not-very-funny flotsam.

SPECIAL FEATURES None TECHNICAL FEATURES Widescreen (multiple aspect) • Languages: Eng. • Sound: Dolby Digital 2.0 • Keepcase • 1 Disc • Region All GENRE & RATING Mature/Anthology/ Humor

Best of the Web #3, The

M2K, 2001, 81 mins., #BE3DV401. Produced by www.bijouflix.com.

This collection of shorts from bijouflix.com is quite a mixed bag, as it consists of both new and (presumably) public domain material. Animated clips include two episodes of "A.D.D. Man," plus Ray Harryhausen's stop-motion "King Midas" from the 1950s. "The Flocculus" is a CGI toon, while "Ricky and Lucy Go to Hell" is a1950s animated and live-action TV ad for Phillip Morris cigarettes (starring Lucille Ball and Ricky Ricardo). There are a handful of other animated bits, including some drive-in theater warnings.

Much of the material is for older audiences, though some is for all ages. And although it isn't animated, the best segment on the DVD is a hilarious thirteen-minute short called "Mattress of Solitude," in which Superman goes to a hotel to take a weekend off.

SPECIAL FEATURES Weblinks TECHNICAL FEATURES Fullscreen (1.33:1) • Languages: Eng. • Sound: Dolby Digital 2.0 • Snapcase • 1 Disc • Region All GENRE Mature/Anthology

Best of Zagreb Film, The: Nudity Required

Image, 2000, 59 mins., #ID9004ASDVD.

More animated short subjects from the Yugoslavian animation studio Zagreb Films are collected in this DVD volume (see main section for other *The Best of Zagreb Film* titles). The seven shorts include some nudity in each, though it's mostly incidental and rarely at all sexual.

In "Way to Your Neighbor," a man prepares to go to his office, while the Oscar-nominated "Satiemania" (featuring the music of Eric Satie) shows lives in the big city—including in a brothel—in charcoal and colored pencil animation. "Album" features a woman reminiscing about her life as she thumbs through a photo album, with more pencil and charcoal art. In the funny "Plop," a cartoony lothario picks a woman up, ostensibly for sex, but the punchline reveals something more humorous. Sports fans might like "The Match," in which a soccer match is related to other things, including nude women and brief gay male sex. An old man finds company with a blow-up friend in "Dream Doll." And finally, a vampiric mouse bites a nude female cat in "Mousferatu" and gets more than he bargained for.

SPECIAL FEATURES None TECHNICAL FEATURES Fullscreen (1.33:1) • Languages: Eng. • Sound: Dolby Digital 1.0 • Snapcase • 1 Disc • Region 1–6 GENRE Mature/Anthology

Bible Black

Kitty, 2002, 60 mins., #KVDVD-0206. Directed by Kazuyuki Honda. Screenplay by Yasuyuki Muto.

At one inconspicuous university, a girl was sacrificed to a demon twelve years ago. But she made a pact with the demon, and now sexual Hell on Earth has arrived. It starts when a love-struck Minase uses a forbidden spell to seduce the most popular girl at school. But the magic gets out of control, and students all over the campus are engaging in perverse sex. What answers does the mysterious school nurse hold, and why is she only helping female students?

A relatively recent production based on a PC game, *Bible Black* features realistic and uncensored animation. There's a gory blood sacrifice of a girl at the beginning, plus lots of consensual and non-consensual sex, and some transsexual scenes.

SPECIAL FEATURES Other Title Trailers TECHNICAL FEATURES Fullscreen (1.33:1) • Subtitles/CC: Eng. • Languages: Jap., Eng. dub • Sound: Dolby Digital 2.0 • Keepcase • 1 Disc • Region 1 GENRE Adult/Supernatural/School

Big Wars

Image/U.S. Manga Corps, 1998, 71 mins., #ID4410CTDVD. Directed by Issei Kume. Screenplay by Kazui Koide.

Mars has been tamed by humanity, its dusty red surface terraformed and colonized. But now an alien race known as "The Gods" has come to stop humankind's further progress into space. Among the weapons at the Gods' disposal is a plague that allows them to control the minds of humans, turning soldiers against each other as the battle wages. Aboard the *Battleship Aoba*, Captain Akuh and his crew are on a secret mission that could turn the tide of the war, but betrayal from within, in the beautiful form of Lieutenant Darsa, may be coming soon.

This 1993 OVA (later released for a brief theatrical run) is a nice militaristic set piece, with strong action and science fiction elements. It has great character animation visuals and mechanical design, though the backgrounds are a weak point at times and the plot is rather thin. The story is full of intense graphic violence, and quite a bit of nudity and sexual situations (the first sign of alien mind control is nymphomaniac tendencies). It's rare that anime gets the widescreen treatment, but this DVD has it. Recommended mainly for military fans.

SPECIAL FEATURES None TECHNICAL FEATURES Widescreen (1.85:1)

• Subtitles/CC: Eng. • Languages: Jap., Eng. dub • Sound: Dolby Digital Stereo 2.0 • Snapcase • 1 Disc • Region 1–6 GENRE Mature/Action/Science Fiction

Biohunter: Special Edition

Urban Vision, 2001, 60 mins., #UV1066. Directed by Yuzo Sato. Written by Yoshiaki Kawajiri. Based on the manga series by Fujihiko Hosono in *Comic Burger*.

The "Demon Virus" is spreading, and people infected with it are genetically changed into horrible monsters. One such creature is terrorizing Tokyo, using its demonic powers to make lunch of women's livers. Two molecular biologists, "Bio Hunters" Komada and Koshigaya, are on the trail of the beast, and they've got some help from a famous psychic who knows who the monster is and where it will strike next. But what happens if the creature gets to the psychic and his granddaughter first? Komada is infected with the virus, but luckily he can control the transformations to his benefit. Will he be able to stop the virus from spreading across Tokyo?

Although the creatures aren't technically vampires or zombies, the effect is the same in this 1995 OVA. Extreme violence and gore, plus some nudity, make this one for mature audiences only, but those who like live-action creature features like *From Dusk Till Dawn* and *John Carpenter's Vampires* will likely suck this up. The DVD transfer is slick, showcasing the slightly above-average animation to its best effect. Calling it a "Special Edition" when it has so few extras is a stretch, but horror fans will get their money's worth and likely not complain.

SPECIAL FEATURES Storyboards • Trailer • Other Title Trailers • Insert: Liner Notes TECHNICAL FEATURES Fullscreen (1.33:1) • Subtitles/CC: Eng. • Languages: Jap., Eng. dub • Sound: Dolby Digital Surround 5.1 • Keepcase • 1 Disc • Region 1 GENRE Mature/Horror/Demons/Vampires

Black Jack

Manga Entertainment, 2001, 90 mins., #4018-2. Directed by Osamu Dezaki. Screenplay by Eto Mori, Osamu Dezaki. Based on the manga series by Osamu Tezuka in *Shonen Champion*.

Black Jack is an unlicensed surgeon with the hands of an angel. He can fix your problems, but the price will be high. So what happens when he discovers the secret behind the growing number of people with superpowers? These superhumans first came to prominence during the 2000 Olympics, but when they burn out, they end up at the Brane Company's medical center. Pharmaceutical executive Jo Carroll coerces Black Jack to discover why the superhumans are deteriorating; it's personal to her because she herself developed the Endorph-A drug that may have caused humanity's next evolutionary step!

Traditional cel animation and computer graphics are combined in this bloody, horrific, and tense psychological thriller. This is one of the first (if not the only) animated projects I've seen that has a medical consultant, but given the number of close-up graphic operations on-screen it was necessary. Still, those with weak stomachs are forewarned that much blood is spilt, sprayed, and vomited in the name of medicine and entertainment.

The DVD contains a gorgeous transfer of the film, showcasing the lush and baroque noirish designs and camera tricks employed by the animators. Still, some will be put off by the slow storytelling and lack of humor, meaning there's little respite from the gory tension.

SPECIAL FEATURES Trailer • Other Title Trailers TECHNICAL FEATURES Widescreen (1.85:1) • Subtitles/CC: Eng. • Languages: Jap., Eng. dub • Sound: Dolby Digital 2.0, Dolby Digital Surround 5.1 • Keepcase • 1 Disc • Region 1 GENRE Mature/Thriller/Medical

Black Magic M66

Manga Entertainment, 2001, 48 mins., #4080-2. Directed by Masamune Shirow, Hiroyuki Kitakubo. Screenplay by Masamune Shirow. Based on the manga by Masamune Shirow.

In the near future, a helicopter containing two prototype military robots is brought down and its cargo disappears. The missing robots are deadly M66 units, and they soon attack a military base on a mission to kill the teenage granddaughter of their creator. Caught in the midst of the military firefight is freelance video journalist Sybel, but curiosity may be the death of the photographer.

The first Masamune Shirow project to be animated, this 1987 OVA (based on the *Black Magic* manga storyline "Booby Trap") is essentially a retread of *The Terminator*; military robots run amok and their makers vainly attempt to control their technology. While it has some great action and nice animation, even if the animation lines are thin in places, *Black Magic M66* will likely only engage fans who want action but little story. Besides the violence, there's also a bit of nudity, so this is appropriate for older viewers only. The DVD's picture is a bit jumpy, which, combined with the thin linework, creates a bit of eyestrain.

This was Shirow's only project as writer, director, and (by way of the manga) designer. The project went tremendously over budget, and other difficulties forced

the creator to divorce himself from future animated adaptations of his work.

SPECIAL FEATURES Character Bios • Other Title Trailers TECHNICAL FEATURES Fullscreen (1.33:1) • Subtitles/CC: Eng. • Languages: Jap., Eng. dub • Sound: Dolby Digital 2.0, Dolby Digital Surround 5.1 • Keepcase • 1 Disc • Region 1, 2, 4 GENRE Mature/Science Fiction/Thriller

Blackmail, The: Vol. 1—Tomorrow Never Ends

NuTech, 2001, 30 mins., #561. Directed by Katsuma Kanazawa. Script by Kancho Taifu, Teruaki Momoi.

Asuka Akiyama is in love, but she confides her secret to the wrong person. The next thing she knows, she's being blackmailed by the threat of exposure of a pornographic picture. What will the blackmailer do, and how will Asuka and her friends suffer . . . or fight back?

Standard animation is made unusual in some spots by the lack of the black outlines and the use of computer shading. Two of the American dub voices are by adult film stars Tabitha Stevens and Misty Rain. There is lesbianism, bondage, and rape, and an overall nasty tone to this entire series. This 2001 series is based on a PC game. The flip side of the DVD contains a whole bunch of preview trailers.

SPECIAL FEATURES Photo Galleries • Character and Art Galleries • Other Title Trailers TECHNICAL FEATURES Fullscreen (1.33:1) • Subtitles/CC: Eng. • Languages: Jap., Eng. dub • Sound: Dolby Digital 2.0 • Keepcase • 1 Disc • Region 1 GENRE Adult/Revenge

Blackmail, The: Vol. 2—Tomorrow Never Ends

NuTech, 2001, 28 mins., #562. Directed by Katsuma Kanazawa. Script by Kancho Taifu, Teruaki Momoi.

Yumiko Miyazaki will have her revenge on Aya Yuki, and she promises to make her sorry for even being born a woman! The plot of vengeance will involve Asuka and her friends . . . and not even Asuka's family will be safe!

More standard animation, more lesbianism, more nastiness, and more rape. And on the flip side of the DVD, more previews!

SPECIAL FEATURES Photo Galleries • Character and Art Galleries • Other Title Trailers TECHNICAL FEATURES Fullscreen (1.33:1) • Subtitles/CC: Eng. • Languages: Jap., Eng. dub • Sound: Dolby Digital 2.0 • Keepcase • 1 Disc • Region 1 GENRE Adult/Revenge

Blackmail, The: Vol. 3—Tomorrow Never Ends

NuTech, 2001, 29 mins., #563. Directed by Katsuma Kanazawa. Script by Teruaki Momoi.

Asuka isn't aware that her mother and sister are in danger at home. As all the players converge on Asuka's house, some are trying to help, while others have evil and lustful intentions. The series ends with more rape, degradation, bondage, and lesbianism. Look for previews on the flip side of the DVD.

SPECIAL FEATURES Photo Galleries • Character and Art Galleries • Other Title Trailers TECHNICAL FEATURES Fullscreen (1.33:1) • Subtitles/CC: Eng. • Languages: Jap., Eng. dub • Sound: Dolby Digital 2.0 • Keepcase • 1 Disc • Region 1 GENRE Adult/Revenge

Blackmail, The: Tomorrow Never Ends [Box Set]

NuTech, 2001, 87 mins., #564.

This box set features the three commercially available keepcase editions of *The Blackmail* in a cardboard box. It does not feature any additional extras. See individual entries for the Special and Technical Features listings.

TECHNICAL FEATURES Cardboard Box with 3 Keepcases • 3 Discs • Region 1 GENRE Adult/Revenge

Blood: The Last Vampire

Manga Entertainment, 2001, 48 mins., #4078-2. Directed by Hiroyuki Kitakubo. Screenplay by Kenji Kamiyama.

Secret government agents recruit a young girl named Saya, the last remaining original vampire, to help them track demonic creatures at the Yokota Air Force Base. Since she looks like a schoolgirl, Saya enrolls in the base's school. She soon finds herself embroiled in battles against undead classmates. But when the demon menace (called "Teropterids") is loosed on the military complex, not even a formidable vampire girl with a sword may be enough to stop the destruction.

A top-notch horror feature from 2000, *Blood's* storyline is micro-thin, but the engaging visuals, fantastic lighting, lush orchestral soundtrack, and 3D CGI backgrounds mixed with 2D characters make for a stunning ride. The nearly silent lead character is surly and mean;

think *Buffy the Vampire Slayer's* Spike as a schoolgirl and you've got the point. There is a lot of blood and gore, including violence against children.

The DVD features a number of extras, including a twenty-one-minute making-of feature (almost half the length of the forty-eight-minute OVA itself!). My only complaint here is that the interviewer too often intrudes on his subject's speeches with "uh-huhs." Viewers should also be aware that some of the story's dialogue in the English dubbed version is spoken in Japanese. Also note that although the DVD sleeve lists a running time of eighty-three minutes, this is quite an inflation (even factoring in the extras).

Though *Blood's* plot is simple and feels unfinished, the look of this project on DVD makes it a must for serious horror fans.

SPECIAL FEATURES "Making of" Featurette • Character and Art Galleries • Trailer • DVD-ROM Features: Wallpaper, Screen Saver, Trailer • Easter Egg TECHNICAL FEATURES Widescreen (1.85:1 enhanced for 16x9) • Subtitles/CC: Eng. • Languages: Jap., Eng. dub • Sound: Dolby Digital Surround 2.0, Dolby Digital Surround 5.1 • Keepcase • 1 Disc • Region 1, 2, 4 GENRE Mature/Horror/Action

Bondage Mansion [Vanilla Series, Vol. 1]

Critical Mass, 2002, 60 mins., #CMDVD6980. Animation directed by Isao Tanagida. Screenplay by Rokurota Marabe.

Yukio Mimura is a rich, pampered, nice guy. But when he fulfills his father's dying wish and allows cousin Hayato to move into the family mansion, things begin to get ugly. Hayato knows all the family's dirty sado-masochistic secrets, and he blackmails Yukio into an SM contest. The first of them to "break" Yukio's girlfriend Reika will get all the family money and the mansion. What torments must Reika endure?

A newer two-part OVA from Japan, *Bondage Mansion* doesn't fit the title *"Vanilla Series"* at all (in the SM world, "vanilla" means plain ordinary non-SM sex). It also doesn't inspire in the animation department; the artwork is simple, and the backgrounds are wimpy. But for those into bondage, rape, watersports, and enemas, here's a disc that's tailor-made for you.

SPECIAL FEATURES Character and Art Galleries TECHNICAL FEATURES Fullscreen (1.33:1) • Subtitles/CC: Eng. • Languages: Jap., Eng. dub • Sound: PCM Audio • Keepcase • 1 Disc • Region 1–6 GENRE Adult/Fetish

Bondage Queen Kate: Complete

Kitty, 2001, 90 mins., #KVDVD-0123. Directed by Takashi Asami. Script by Yuji Kishino.

Kate is a policewoman with the Federal Space Army Security Police. Her first big undercover assignment is to find out who is kidnapping and raping the young women of the desert planet Doune. But to get into the lair of the gang, Kate may have to get into a few compromising outfits . . . and positions.

This two-OVA 1994 series is really more story-driven than sex-driven, despite the setup. The art is standard, if a bit cartoony and flavorless. For a title with "bondage" in it, this is not really a kinky fetish film, though there is some bondage and rape. There is, however, an uncomfortable amount of demeaning of the female characters.

SPECIAL FEATURES Other Title Trailers TECHNICAL FEATURES Fullscreen (1.33:1) • Subtitles/CC: Eng. • Languages: Jap., Eng. dub • Sound: Dolby Digital 2.0 • Keepcase • 1 Disc • Region 1 GENRE & RATING Adult/Science Fiction • Rated 18+

Bride of Darkness

Kitty, 2002, 60 mins., #KVDVD-0204. Directed by Aranpo. Screenplay by Osamu Kudo.

In a mansion in Japan, Sanshiro secretly spies on the daughter of his master, Momoyo. But he can never have her, because he is the lowly son of a servant, and she has a fiancé, Yoichiro, who will soon return to take her to England forever. But once Yoichiro comes back, something bad is in the air, and Momoyo's older divorced sister, the maid, and others are soon driven by unnatural lust. Could the lust and sadism be the result of demons and possession?

With very gothic designs and backgrounds, this historical hentai is unusual in both look and storytelling. The characters are deeper and more interesting than usual, and several of the sexual encounters are consensual. On the other hand, there is SM, rape, demon rape, and tentacle rape, so it's still too edgy to watch with your parents.

SPECIAL FEATURES Other Title Trailers TECHNICAL FEATURES Widescreen (1.85:1) • Subtitles/CC: Eng. • Languages: Jap., Eng. dub • Sound: Dolby Digital 2.0 • Keepcase • 1 Disc • Region 1 GENRE & RATING Adult/Drama/Horror • Rated 18+

Buttobi CPU: I Dream of Mimi

Right Stuf, 2001, 90 mins.

This DVD was not available for review.

Campus [Vanilla Series, Vol. 3]

Critical Mass, 2002, 60 mins., #CMDVD6982. Animation Directed by Shinichi Omata. Screenplay by Rokurota Marabe.

NOTE: This DVD arrived too late for a full review. The following text is promotional copy provided by the releasing company:

"The dream of the past and an improbable future . . . Night after night, Takakage's dreams take him away to another life. A life where a very special girl named Ayame is the central part of his life. Yet every morning he awakens to the disappointment of reality where his dream girl is only a faint memory. If only she was more than just a dream . . .

"When Takakage has his fortune read, his perception of reality drastically changes. It seems that his dreams are more than just mere fantasy! He did, in fact, live 400 years before! Through the mists of time, spirits move freely and mysteriously. Souls who were once drawn together tend to draw together again. And, lovers can reappear in places where they are least expected!"

SPECIAL FEATURES Character and Art Galleries • Other Title Trailers TECHNICAL FEATURES Fullscreen (1.33:1) • Subtitles/CC: Eng. • Languages: Jap., Eng. dub • Sound: Dolby Digital • Keepcase • 1 Disc • Region 1 GENRE Adult/Fantasy

Cartoon Noir

First Run Features, 2000, 83 mins., #20229-90948.

Although the title of this compilation might lead you to expect tough detectives and tougher girls, that's not what you'll find here. "Noir" here means "black," with a lot of dark, black and white animated shorts. Most are international toons, from England, Czechoslovakia, Poland, Portugal, and elsewhere. All are dramatic, without a hint of humor.

"The Story of the Cat and the Moon" has a cat exploring the city at night, with black and white art reminiscent of comic book artist Mike Mignola. "Club of the Discarded" is a stop-motion piece with mannequins in an abandoned building playing the harp, listening to the radio, and "living," until more hip mannequins are dumped in with them. "Ape" is a charcoal and airbrush short about a married couple arguing over their dinner of cooked monkey.

"Gentle Spirit" is a sepia-toned story that looks as if it was painted on cheesecloth. Based on a Dostoyevsky story, it's about a woman and a mysterious man who menaces her. Five alien abductions are discussed in "Abductees," which uses a variety of art styles mixed with live action. Finally, in "Joy Street," a depressed woman meets her spiritual guide in the form of a molded ashtray monkey that comes to life, but is he too late to stop her from committing suicide?

SPECIAL FEATURES None TECHNICAL FEATURES Fullscreen (1.33:1) • Languages: Eng. • Sound: Dolby Digital 2.0 • Keepcase • 1 Disc • Region 1–6 GENRE Mature/Anthology

Clerks Uncensored

Miramax, 2001, 130 mins., #21707. Directed by Chris Bailey, Nick Filippi, Steve Loter. Written by Dave Mandel, Kevin Smith, Scott Mosier, Brian Kelley.

Dante and Randal work at the Quick Stop and RST Video stores next door to each other. Jay and Silent Bob hang out in front, selling fireworks, illegal substances, or cooking up bizarre schemes. Match these slackeresque characters against the evil billionaire Leonardo Leonardo who moves in across the road, and you've got a hilarious series that was never given a chance to survive.

Based on Kevin Smith's live-action low-budget 1994 feature film, the *Clerks* animated series was a midseason replacement on ABC in 2000. Unfortunately, only two episodes were aired before it was axed. All six complete episodes are on this two-disc DVD set, complete and uncensored. Besides the six main episodes, the discs feature commentaries, live-action intros by Jason Mewes and Kevin Smith (in character as Jay and Silent Bob), animatics for each story and more.

The series is hilarious and completely irreverent, with elements of parody, social satire, burlesque, and bumbling physical comedy. *Clerks* ranks with *The Simpsons* and *South Park* as one of the strongest mature humor series ever produced for American television.

SPECIAL FEATURES "Making of" Featurettes • Commentary Track by Producers and Stars • Character and Art Galleries • Storyboards • Promotional Footage • DVD-ROM Features: Scripts, Storyboards, Character Bios • Easter Egg TECHNICAL FEATURES Fullscreen (1.33:1) • Subtitles/CC: Eng. • Languages: Eng. • Sound: Dolby Digital Surround 2.0 • Multisnapcase • 2 Discs • Region 1 GENRE & RATING Comedy/Parody • Rated R

Complete Adventure Kid, The

Anime 18, 2001, 115 mins., #A18D-2088. Directed by Yoshitaka Fujimoto. Written by Atsushi Yamatoya. Based on the manga series by Toshio Maeda.

When construction workers dig up an ancient computer outside the house of nineteen-year-old Norikazu, the young computer game whiz tries to activate the machine. Instead, he releases the spirit of the angry creator that is trapped inside it. The ghost of Masago wants revenge, and he brings Norikazu and his girlfriend, Midori, through time and cyberspace in the process. They soon find themselves in World War II, Hell, and other nasty places.

This three-part 1993 OVA series is pretty bad. The voice "actress" playing Midori is awful. The story bounces all over the place. And the vast array of featured rapes almost defies categorization: zombies, biotentacles, cybercreatures, soldiers, elves, and demons all force their unwanted attentions on female characters. There's also some fetishwear in later scenes.

Although most Anime 18 titles include it, this DVD is the first Anime 18 title reviewed that has the short featurette on the "Anime Artform" that explains all about school uniforms, multicolored hairstyles, big eyes, and the absence of pubic hair in most anime. Too bad it couldn't inform us why awful projects like *Adventure Kid* get created.

SPECIAL FEATURES Character Bios • Character and Art Galleries • Anime Featurette • Game • DVD-ROM Features: Art, Scripts • Other Title Trailers TECHNICAL FEATURES Fullscreen (1.33:1) • Subtitles/CC: Eng. • Languages: Jap., Eng. dub • Sound: Dolby Digital 2.0 • Keepcase • 1 Disc • Region 1 GENRE & RATING Adult/Comedy/Horror • Rated 18+

Conspirators of Pleasure

Kino, 1999, 97 mins., #K146DVD. Directed by Jan Svankmajer. Written by Jan Svankmajer.

Czechoslovakian stop-motion animator Jan Svankmajer is at it again, and this time he's using his bizarre imagery to follow six city dwellers as they prepare to indulge in their personal fetishes. There's a man who buys a porn magazine and decides to build a chicken head and costume so he can ravish the old woman across the hall. There's the postal delivery woman with a thing for making balls of bread and stuffing them up her nose. One man makes hands, while a handyman is into fingercots and fur. It's all told with a minimum of dialogue, mostly ambient sound. Created in 1996, the eighty-three-minute feature takes forty-two minutes to get to the stop-motion material, but it's pretty much non-stop (so to speak) from there.

A second Svankmajer short is also included on the disc. The fourteen-minute 1993 film "Food" is another weird look at the three main meals, using live actors in a stop-motion film style. The Breakfast section is about coin-operated people who become food dispensers. In the Lunch section, two men try to get a waiter's attention at a restaurant and, failing to, start to devour the flowers, plate, table, their clothes, and more. Dinner, finally, melds the concepts and shows people devouring body parts.

While neither part of this disc is overly smutty, there is a smattering of nudity, and a whole heaping helping of weirdness.

SPECIAL FEATURES None TECHNICAL FEATURES Fullscreen (1.33:1) • Languages: Eng. dub • Sound: Dolby Digital 2.0 • Keepcase • 1 Disc • Region 1–6 GENRE Mature/Live/Stop-Motion

Cool Devices: Operations 1–4

NuTech, 2000, 98 mins., #450. Directed by Osamu Shimokawa, Megumi Saki, Hiroshi Matsuda, Akira Nishimori. Story by Mon-Mon, Hiroyuki Utatane, Proton-saurus, Yumisuke Kotoyoshi. "Curious Fruit" based on the manga series by Mon-Mon.

Cool Devices is actually the umbrella title for a series of completely unrelated porn shorts (about eleven minutes each) that were first released on video in 1996 in Japan. The art styles vary wildly, but what's consistent is a complete tone of degradation for the female characters, and in a few cases, the males. The series explores almost every sexual taboo, from incest to bestiality to watersports. One of the nastiest of the hentai series on the market, this is not for the faint of heart.

"Curious Fruit" tells the story of a woman who spots another woman being fetishistically degraded at a bar, and she soon follows in her high-heeled steps, into a world of bondage and tentacle rape. Then, in "Sacred Girl," a boy who lives a fantasy life through a series of hidden cameras begins an incestuous relationship with his sister and gets involved in group activities.

A trio of connected shorts are: "Lover Doll," about human "pets"; "Winter Swimsuit," about a girl menaced by a man; and "Enema," which is rather self-explanatory. Finally, "Kirei" reveals the group sex, lesbianism, and bondage that take place at an idyllic beach vacation spot.

Unlike other NuTech releases, these DVDs are not double-sided with preview trailers.

SPECIAL FEATURES Character and Art Galleries TECHNICAL FEATURES Fullscreen (1.33:1) • Subtitles/CC: Eng. • Languages: Jap. • Sound: Dolby Digital 2.0 • Keepcase • 1 Disc • Region All GENRE Adult/Anthology/Fetish

Cool Devices: Operations 5–8

NuTech, 2000, 97 mins., #451. Directed by Kan Matsuda, Yuma Nakamura, Jiro Hijikata, Yukihiro Makino. Story by PIL, Toboku Akutagawa, Konodonto. "Slave Warrior Maya" based on the manga series by Konodonto.

More bizarre and depraved erotica highlight this volume, which contains one of the fan-favorite episodes of the series. In "Seek 1" and "Seek 2: SM Queen Saki," viewers get to see young Saki debased repeatedly, in scenes of fetish, incest, SM; and an electro-torture scene that had censors squirming. "Seek" was based on a PC video game.

A fan-favorite, "Yellow Star" is essentially a precursor to *Kite*, telling the story of a detective who uses the ultimate date-rape drug on young women. Will he use it on his own step-daughter? Finally, in "Slave Warrior Maya," a far-off planet has a legend of a Druid Warrior who will one day arise and vanquish evil. Could that warrior be the woman who is captured by lizard-people and raped by the robot king?

Unlike other NuTech releases, these DVDs are not double-sided with preview trailers.

SPECIAL FEATURES Character and Art Galleries TECHNICAL FEATURES Fullscreen (1.33:1) • Subtitles/CC: Eng. • Languages: Jap. • Sound: Dolby Digital 2.0 • Keepcase • 1 Disc • Region All GENRE Adult/Anthology/Fetish

Cool Devices: Operations 9–11

NuTech, 2000, 81 mins., #452. Directed by Yukihiro Makino, Hiro Asano, G. T. Story by Konodonto, Persian Soft, Mon-Mon. "Slave Warrior Maya" based on the manga series by Konodonto. "Fallen Angel Rina" based on the manga series by Mon-Mon.

The depraved hentai series comes to an end with three final stories. "Slave Warrior Maya 2" finds the previously tortured woman now in better standing . . . and sporting a new appendage! Will she escape back to Earth, or will she be tortured once again? Then, in "Binding," Masaki Hishino is a writer who awakens on a train to find his wallet and luggage missing. He follows a mysterious woman to a house where a group of women await. But after sunset, the women become something else, and begin to torture Masaki in ways he never expected. After so much degradation of women, it's surprising to see the man on the bottom in this segment.

The final *Cool Devices* story is "Fallen Angel Rina," in which a once-popular idol singer discovers that her father owes lots of favors. She's soon forced to be more and more degraded, or her father's reputation will be destroyed.

Unlike other NuTech releases, these DVDs are not double-sided with preview trailers.

SPECIAL FEATURES Character and Art Galleries TECHNICAL FEATURES Fullscreen (1.33:1) • Subtitles/CC: Eng. • Languages: Jap. • Sound: Dolby Digital 2.0 • Keepcase • 1 Disc • Region All GENRE Adult/Anthology/Fetish

Cool Devices: Operations [Box Set]

NuTech, 2000, 276 mins., #453.

This box set features the three commercially available keepcase editions of *Cool Devices—Operations*, in a cardboard box. It does not feature any additional extras. See individual entries for the Special and Technical Features listings.

TECHNICAL FEATURES Cardboard Box with 3 Keepcases • 3 Discs • Region All GENRE Adult/Anthology/Fetish

Crimson Wolf

Image, 1998, 60 mins., #ID4652SEDVD. Directed by Shoichi Masuo. Written by Shoichi Masuo, Yasuhito Kikuchi, Isamu Imakake.

When archeologists revive the legacy of Genghis Khan, three untested warriors may be all that protects humankind from an army of darkness. If only every spy agency in the world weren't trying to kill them! The reportedly incoherent story contains graphic violence and sex.

This DVD was not available for review. It is out of print.

Demon Beast Invasion: 1 and 2

Anime 18, 2000, 93 mins., #A18D-2006. Directed by Jun Fukuda. Script by Joji Maki. Based on the manga series by Toshio Maeda.

The Demon Beasts left Earth 100 million years ago, but they've just returned to claim the planet. They will accomplish this by breeding with human females to create monstrous demon-human hybrids capable of helping the invasion. Female operatives from the Interplanetary Observation Agency plan to stop the demons by any means necessary. But can agent Muneto help save nineteen-year-old Kayo after she is raped and impregnated by a possessed lover? And if not, what horrors will her spawn wreak?

Based on a story by Toshio Maeda—familiar to demon

rape fans for the *Urotsukidoji* series (see entries)—the 1990 series *Demon Beast Invasion* is shocking mostly due to its inclusion of pregnancy and motherhood in the mix of savage demon rape. Audiences inured to tentacle scenes might still be bothered by the attacking demons's desire for mother, and with the rather underage look of most of the animated women. With a lower budget, poor character designs, and a lesser musical score than *Urotsukidoji*, this series doesn't look or sound quite as good, and the Japanese vocal work is largely done by Japanese porn stars.

SPECIAL FEATURES Anime Artform • DVD-ROM Features: Art, Scripts, Manga • Other Title Trailers TECHNICAL FEATURES Fullscreen (1.33:1) • Subtitles/CC: Eng. • Languages: Jap., Eng. dub • Sound: Dolby Digital 2.0 • Keepcase • 1 Disc • Region 1, 4 GENRE & RATING Adult/Horror • Rated 18+

Demon Beast Invasion: 3 and 4

Anime 18, 2001, 90 mins., #A18D-2075. Directed by Juki Yoma. Screenplay by Wataru Amano. Based on the manga series by Toshio Maeda.

Kayo's demonic offspring has caused mass destruction, and the female trio from the Interplanetary Observation Agency comes to town to stop the beast. It's hunting down friends of Kayo and raping them with his tentacles. But the girls from IOA may be out of their league!

This second volume of *Demon Beast Invasion* actually features a finale of sorts, though the series did continue for two more "episodes." There's a bit more plot this time out, as well as emotional conflicts.

SPECIAL FEATURES Anime Artform • Manga • DVD-ROM Features: Art, Scripts, Manga • Other Title Trailers TECHNICAL FEATURES Fullscreen (1.33:1) • Subtitles/CC: Eng. • Languages: Jap., Eng. dub • Sound: Dolby Digital 2.0 • Keepcase • 1 Disc • Region 1 GENRE & RATING Adult/Horror • Rated 18+

Demon Beast Invasion: 5 and 6

Anime 18, 2001, 90 mins., #A18D-2076. Directed by Jun Fukuda. Screenplay by Wataru Amano. Based on the manga series by Toshio Maeda.

Kayo's demonic offspring seemed to have been vanquished, but it rises again. Now it's loose in Hong Kong, and looking to find its mother. Along the way, it takes over the bodies of underworld gangsters, and sets a trap for Kayo. Lured to the trap, Kayo and Muneto are attacked, but the IOA agents are on the job, and gunfire erupts. What will happen when Muneto learns that the IOA doesn't plan to save Kayo . . . it plans to kill her? And later, what does El

Niño have to do with the emergence of an island monster that resembles Kayo's offspring?

Tentacle rape meets El Niño. Only in the world of hentai.

SPECIAL FEATURES Anime Artform • Manga • DVD-ROM Features: Art, Scripts, Manga • Other Title Trailers TECHNICAL FEATURES Fullscreen (1.33:1) • Subtitles/CC: Eng. • Languages: Jap., Eng. dub • Sound: Dolby Digital 2.0 • Keepcase • 1 Disc • Region 1 GENRE & RATING Adult/Horror • Rated 18+

Demon Beast Invasion: DVD Collection [Box Set]

Anime 18, 2001, 273 mins., #A18D-2077.

This box set features the three commercially available keepcase editions of *Demon Beast Invasion* in a cardboard box. It does not feature any additional extras. See individual entries for the Special and Technical Features listings.

TECHNICAL FEATURES Cardboard Box with 3 Keepcases • 3 Discs • Region 1 GENRE & RATING Adult/Horror • Rated 18+

Demon Warrior Koji

Anime 18, 2001, 120 mins., #A18D-2033. Directed by Yasunori Urata. Screenplay by Takao Kawaguchi. Based on the manga series by Toshio Maeda.

A demonic monster is killing in the city, but thankfully, there's a team of people who can stop it. Enter Koji Yamada, a man-demon stuntman, accompanied by a pretty young psychic with a morbid mind. They're part of a motley group of extranormal humans that investigates sex murders under the watch of Police Chief Kanzaki. Together, they stand a chance of unraveling the careful patterns of the murders and catching the demon. But in this case, the victims are men, and the clues are pointing to a seemingly innocent girl!

Another Toshio Maeda title means more demon rapes and horror sex. This DVD combines three 1999 OVAs, offering the entirety of the series on one disc. There's a bit less of the traditional meanness to the story—much of the sex is consensual—though the designs are uglier than normal. There's much bloody violence, as well as some rape and bondage.

SPECIAL FEATURES Creator Bio • Character Bios • Anime Artform • DVD-ROM Features: Art, Scripts • Other Title Trailers TECHNICAL FEATURES Fullscreen (1.33:1) • Subtitles/CC: Eng. • Languages: Jap., Eng. dub • Sound: Dolby Digital 2.0 • Keepcase • 1 Disc • Region 1–6 GENRE & RATING Adult/Horror • Rated 18+

Desert Island Story X, The: Vol. 1

NuTech, 2001, 24 mins., #568. Directed by Katsuma Kanazawa. Script by Mirin Muto.

When Toko's father's yacht is hijacked by escaped fugitives, the girls on board struggle to gain control before the boat is caught in a severe storm. Eventually, almost all the girls end up on the beach of a deserted island. Toko, Ayaka, Natsuno, Flora, and Yuka think they have made their way to freedom, but their friend Hitomi is still in the clutches of the sadistic hijackers. Can even Gilligan and the Skipper save them?

Based on a PC game, this 1998 series is demon and tentacle-free, but it still features lots and lots of rape and bondage. The English voice dub includes work by adult film stars Miko Lee and Dayton Rains. The disc is double-sided, with the second side containing previews. Why NuTech chooses to put the previews on the second side when the front only contains a twenty-four-minute show is a mystery.

And Gilligan and the Skipper do *not* show up in this series. That was a joke, son.

SPECIAL FEATURES Photo Galleries • Character and Art Galleries • Other Title Trailers TECHNICAL FEATURES Fullscreen (1.33:1) • Subtitles/CC: Eng. • Languages: Jap., Eng. dub • Sound: Dolby Digital 2.0 • Keepcase • 1 Disc • Region 1 GENRE Adult/Shipwreck Drama

Desert Island Story X, The: Vol. 2

NuTech, 2001, 25 mins., #569. Directed by Katsuma Kanazawa. Script by Mirin Muto.

First it was Hitomi that was in the clutches of the bad guys, and now, when Natsuno tries to go back to the yacht, she's caught as well. And wouldn't you know it, she's soon tied up and getting her nipples pierced! This never happened to Ginger and Mary Anne!

More rape and bondage, with some lesbianism and piercing thrown in for flavor. As with others in the series, the disc is double-sided, with the second side containing previews.

SPECIAL FEATURES Photo Galleries • Character and Art Galleries • Other Title Trailers TECHNICAL FEATURES Fullscreen (1.33:1) • Subtitles/CC: Eng. • Languages: Jap., Eng. dub • Sound: Dolby Digital 2.0 • Keepcase • 1 Disc • Region 1 GENRE Adult/Shipwreck Drama

Desert Island Story X, The: Vol. 3

NuTech, 2001, 25 mins., #570. Directed by Katsuma Kanazawa. Script by Mirin Muto.

Yuka secretly makes a deal with the hijackers in order to save herself, but it costs Flora dearly. And poor Natsuno pleads for help, but Aoki has other plans for her. More rape and some plot twists on this double-sided disc, with the second side containing previews.

SPECIAL FEATURES Photo Galleries • Character and Art Galleries • Other Title Trailers TECHNICAL FEATURES Fullscreen (1.33:1) • Subtitles/CC: Eng. • Languages: Jap., Eng. dub • Sound: Dolby Digital 2.0 • Keepcase • 1 Disc • Region 1 GENRE Adult/Shipwreck Drama

Desert Island Story X, The: Vol. 4

NuTech, 2001, #571.

This DVD was not available for review.

Desert Island Story X, The [Box Set]

NuTech, 2001, 100 mins., #572.

This box set features the four commercially available keepcase editions of *The Desert Island Story X* in a cardboard box. It does not feature any additional extras. See individual entries for the Special and Technical Features listings.

TECHNICAL FEATURES Cardboard Box with 4 Keepcases • 4 Discs • Region 1 GENRE Adult/Shipwreck Drama

Desert Island Story XX, The: Vol. 1—The Music Box

NuTech, 2001, 27 mins., #573. Directed by Katsuma Kanazawa. Script by Katsuma Kanazawa.

A laboratory on an island explodes; there are only nine survivors: six women and three men. Isolated and without any means of communication, the women are horrified to find out the labs' experiments involved mental transference and mind control! You can bet that the unscrupulous men will soon start using it on the women. . . .

Popular enough to merit a sequel, *The Desert Island Story* continues with more rape and bondage. Adult film stars Ava Vincent and Jewel De'Nyle provide voices. As with other NuTech titles, the disc is double-sided, with the second side containing previews.

SPECIAL FEATURES Photo Galleries • Character and Art Galleries • Other Title Trailers TECHNICAL FEATURES Fullscreen (1.33:1) • Subtitles/CC: Eng. • Languages: Jap., Eng. dub • Sound: Dolby Digital 2.0 • Keepcase • 1 Disc • Region 1 GENRE Adult/Shipwreck Drama

Desert Island Story XX, The: Vol. 2—The Necklace

NuTech, 2001, 27 mins., #574. Directed by Katsuma Kanazawa. Script by Katsuma Kanazawa.

The girls try to find a way to escape the island, but they keep falling prey to the men. Evil Matsui is reinvigorated in a youthful body, and he sets upon Shiori to rape her, until someone intercedes. But the lines between predator and prey are blurring, and Mio begins to wonder if the girls aren't just as dangerous as the boys.

More rape and some lesbianism on this disc, which includes the double-side of preview trailers.

SPECIAL FEATURES Photo Galleries • Character and Art Galleries • Other Title Trailers TECHNICAL FEATURES Fullscreen (1.33:1) • Subtitles/CC: Eng. • Languages: Jap., Eng. dub • Sound: Dolby Digital 2.0 • Keepcase • 1 Disc • Region 1 GENRE Adult/Shipwreck Drama

Desert Island Story XX, The: Vol. 3—The Piano

NuTech, 2001, 27 mins., #575. Directed by Katsuma Kanazawa. Script by Katsuma Kanazawa.

Matsui has been killed, and Ikegami thinks he's next to go. So, what's he do? He rapes a girl, while planning to rape yet another girl! And then he's dead meat, leaving only one man left alive on the island. But it appears as if Hiroki has multiple personalities, and the girls may not be safe just yet!

More rape, bondage, lesbianism, and some grotesquely colored male appendages on this disc, which includes the double-side of preview trailers.

SPECIAL FEATURES Photo Galleries • Character and Art Galleries • Other Title Trailers TECHNICAL FEATURES Fullscreen (1.33:1) • Subtitles/CC: Eng. • Languages: Jap., Eng. dub • Sound: Dolby Digital 2.0 • Keepcase • 1 Disc • Region 1 GENRE Adult/Shipwreck Drama

Desert Island Story XX, The: Vol. 4—The Ribbon

NuTech, 2001, 28 mins., #576. Directed by Katsuma Kanazawa. Script by Katsuma Kanazawa.

Hiroki's mind is fractured, and he's channeling the dead Professor Todokoro, who was in charge of the island laboratory's horrifying experiments. Now, Hiroki plans to ravage all the girls . . . and worse! Can the girls turn the table on their oppressor?

The finale of the series features more rape and brutality, plus previews on side two.

SPECIAL FEATURES Photo Galleries • Character and Art Galleries • Other Title Trailers TECHNICAL FEATURES Fullscreen (1.33:1) • Subtitles/CC: Eng. • Languages: Jap., Eng. dub • Sound: Dolby Digital 2.0 • Keepcase • 1 Disc • Region 1 GENRE Adult/Shipwreck Drama

Desert Island Story XX, The [Box Set]

NuTech, 2001, 109 mins., #577.

This box set features the four commercially available keepcase editions of *The Desert Island Story XX* in a cardboard box. It does not feature any additional extras. See individual entries for the Special and Technical Features listings.

TECHNICAL FEATURES Cardboard Box with 4 Keepcases • 4 Discs • Region 1 GENRE Adult/Shipwreck Drama

Devil Hunter Yohko: The Complete Collection—Vol. 1

ADV Films, 2002, 105 mins., #DY/001. Directed by Katsuhisa Yamada, Tetsuro Aoki, Hisashi Abe. Screenplay by Sukehiro Tomita, Hisaya Takabayashi, Katsuhisa Yamada.

A teen girl finds out that she's heir to superhuman powers to fight evil and slay demons. Sound familiar? It's not Buffy Summers, it's Yohko Mano! As she turns sixteen, Yohko becomes the target of attack by demons, vampires, hellfire, zombies, witches, incubi, and other denizens of ickiness.

The short-lived 1992 series is released in a two-disc collection containing all the episodes, plus a special extended version of the initial series. This was the first anime released in America by ADV Films, and a commentary track by ADV executives and producers details not only information about the film but historical information about the company and anime fandom in the U.S. Lots of nudity and sexual situations, plus comedic violence and horror, this is like an adult version of *Buffy*, except sweeter than most hentai.

SPECIAL FEATURES Commentary Track by Producers • Art Galleries • Trailer • Promotional Footage • Music Video TECHNICAL FEATURES Fullscreen (1.33:1) • Subtitles/CC: Eng. • Languages: Jap., Eng. dub • Sound: Dolby Digital 2.0 • Multikeepcase • 2 Discs • Region 1 GENRE & RATING Mature/Horror/Comedy • Rated 17+

Devil Hunter Yohko: The Complete Collection—Vol. 2

ADV Films, 2002, 120 mins., #DY/002. Directed by Junichi Sakata, Akiyuki Shinbo. Script by Tatsuhiko Urahata.

Young demon fighter Yohko is back for more wacky weirdness and monster-slaying, aided by her ancient grandmother. When the demon Tokima plots to open the demonic dimensional portal to Earth, Yohko must assemble some help to fight him. And later, another Devil Hunter makes the scene, and she's determined to be the only Devil Hunter in town. It's Buffy vs. Faith to the . . . er, it's Yohko and her doppelganger cousin, Ayako, in a final battle!

This DVD set features one disc with the final two *Devil Hunter Yohko* OVAs, as well as the "Super Music Special: 4-Ever!" It includes seven music clips, with some live-action singers, super-deformed chibi moments, and other fun. A second DVD has the entire ADV catalogue of titles with seventy-one anime preview trailers and seven live-action trailers! And if that wasn't enough, there's also a twenty-four-minute *Excel Saga* episode, and a fourteen-minute *Steel Angel Kurumi* show.

SPECIAL FEATURES Clean Credits • Trailer • Promotional Footage • Other Title Trailers TECHNICAL FEATURES Fullscreen (1.33:1) • Subtitles/CC: Eng. • Languages: Jap., Eng. dub • Sound: Dolby Digital 2.0 • Multikeepcase • 2 Discs • Region 1 GENRE & RATING Mature/Horror/Comedy • Rated 17+

Devil Lady, The: The Awakening [#1]

ADV Films, 2003, 125 mins., #DDL/001. Directed by Toshiki Hirano. Screenplay by Chiaki Konaka. Based on the manga series by Go Nagai.

NOTE: This DVD arrived too late for a full review. The following text is promotional copy provided by the releasing company:

"Jun has always been different from everyone else—the life of a fashion model is unlike anything else in the world. But she has no idea how different she is . . . until a mysterious stalker throws her head-first into a brutal confrontation with the supernatural! From Go Nagai, the master of animated horror, comes a harrowing odyssey through the twisted maze that is Jun's new life. By day a beautiful, shy fashion plate. By night a terrifying vision of demonic power. It's full-tilt gothic horror as Jun, as the Devil Lady, does battle with a demonic army threatening to destroy mankind!"

This disc contains episodes #1–5 and is a DVD-only release.

SPECIAL FEATURES Character and Art Galleries • Trailer • Clean Credits • Other Title Trailers • Inserts: Monster Cards TECHNICAL FEATURES Fullscreen (1.33:1) • Subtitles/CC: Eng. • Languages: Jap. Eng. dub • Sound: Dolby Digital 2.0 • Keepcase • 1 Discs • Region 1 GENRE & RATING Mature/Horror • Rated 17+

Devil Man

Manga Entertainment, 2000, 120 mins., #MANGA4050-2. Directed by Tsutomu Iida. Script by Go Nagai, Tsutomu Iida. Based on the manga series by Go Nagai in *Shonen Magazine.*

In "The Birth," young Akira is experiencing a cataclysmic change in his world. His parents are missing, his pet rabbit has been killed, and now he finds out that he can save mankind from demons, but only if he bonds with a demon himself. Since he is an innocent, he should be able to control his demon side. But is his friend, Ryo Asuka, really on his side, or is he hiding a darker self?

Then, in "Demon Bird," demons who were trapped in glacial ice are freed, and Ryo and Akira/Devilman may be all that stand in their way in defense of mankind. Akira's girlfriend is attacked by a water demon even as Devilman fights another hellish fiend. But those battles are nothing compared to the conflict with the demon bird Siren that stands in Devilman's future!

Devilman (its Japanese title) began as a TV series in 1972, adapted from the work of Go Nagai, and featuring a weird mixture of superhero action and horror. In 1987, the concept was revisited for a two-part OVA series, which is what's contained on this disc. Although the look of the series is retro, and the OVA stories are similar to some of the TV episodes, the character designs are different, and the gore and sex quotient are obviously pumped up. Fans may not like the fact that there's *only* the English-language track—and it's extremely profanity-filled—but this is likely to be the only DVD version released.

SPECIAL FEATURES Creator Bio • Character and Art Galleries • Trailer • Other Title Trailers TECHNICAL FEATURES Fullscreen (1.33:1) • Languages: Eng. dub • Sound: Dolby Digital Sur-

round 5.1 • Keepcase • 1 Disc • Region 1, 2, 4 GENRE Adult/Horror

Dirty Duck

New Concorde, 2001, 70 mins., #NH2143U D. Directed by Charles Swenson. Written by Charles Swenson.

Willard Eisenbaum is an insurance adjuster who leads a quiet life until he meets Dirty Duck at a tattoo parlor. The two soon embark on a tour of the city with drugs, sex, and debauchery as their goals. They'll meet the jivest African-Americans, the nelliest gays, and the sleaziest women before they're done.

Although this tremendously dated 1975 film shares the same name, it is *not* based on Bobby London's "Dirty Duck" character as seen in *National Lampoon* and *Playboy.* Instead, the creative minds behind the feature film project were rock performers Howard Kaylan and Mark Volman (aka Flo and Eddie), the founder of the Turtles and members of Frank Zappa's Mothers of Invention. It's astonishing to know that Kaylan and Volman—who also perform songs in the film—later went on to do music and songs for *Strawberry Shortcake* and *The Care Bears*! Writer/director Charles Swenson also later worked for a younger set, working on the *Rugrats* series for Nickelodeon.

But don't go into this film thinking that it's in any way for kids, no matter what its pedigree. It's as sleazy as the title suggests; it's also fairly pointless and barely entertaining. The ultra-grainy print oddly helps the retro feel, but you'll likely enjoy it only as an arcane piece of animation history . . . or if you view it while partaking of mind-altering substances.

SPECIAL FEATURES Creator Bios • Trailer • Other Title Trailers TECHNICAL FEATURES Fullscreen (1.33:1) • Languages: Eng. • Sound: Dolby Digital 2.0 • Keepcase • 1 Disc • Region 1 GENRE Mature/Comedy/Animals

Doomed Megalopolis

ADV Films, 2002, 175 mins., #DDM/001. Directed by Kazuyoshi Katayama, Koichi Chigira, Kazunari Kume, Masashi Ikeda. Screenplay by Akinori Endo. Based on the novel by Hiroshi Aramata.

NOTE: This DVD set arrived too late for a full review. The following text is promotional copy provided by the releasing company:

"Set in Tokyo during the first decades of the 20th century, *Doomed Megalopolis* tells the story of the powerful mystic Kato's obsession with the conquest of Tokyo, 'the greatest city on earth.' But Kato's actions awaken the long-dead spirit Masakato, the legendary guardian of Tokyo. Unable to stand along against Masakato's power, the calculating Kato uses an innocent woman as an unsuspecting pawn in the hope of producing an off-spring capable of challenging Tokyo's mystical protector. But Kato never counted on the effect that a team of unlikely heroes would have on his sinister plans. Nor could he anticipate the destruction his spells would cause for the millions of innocent citizens of Tokyo . . .

"A classic struggle between good and evil, *Doomed Megalopolis* takes place in the context of a devastating earthquake that destroyed much of Tokyo in 1923. The tale posits an alternate cause for that destruction, putting a supernatural spin on the actual event."

These discs contains OVAs #1–4.

SPECIAL FEATURES Other Title Trailers TECHNICAL FEATURES Fullscreen (1.33:1) • Subtitles/CC: Eng. • Languages: Jap., Eng. dub • Sound: Dolby Digital • Multikeepcase • 2 Discs • Region 1 GENRE & RATING Mature/Horror/Action * Rated 17+

Dragon Rider

Kitty, 2002, 60 mins., #KVDVD-0223. Directed by Katsuma Kanazawa . Screenplay by Tetsuya Oishi. Based on the manga series by Fujisango in *Comic Papipo*.

NOTE: This DVD arrived too late for a full review. The following text is promotional copy provided by the releasing company:

"Rike, a real dragon knight, leaves his lover so that he can quest for his very own dragon. When he discovers the dragon, Karin, he finds that she is not only a giant fire-breathing lizard, but she also has the power to transform into a beautiful blond girl! When his former lover, Princess Lilia, sees the two of them together, she becomes mad with jealousy. A group of demonic creatures senses her dark feelings, and uses them to seduce her with power."

SPECIAL FEATURES Other Title Trailers TECHNICAL FEATURES Fullscreen (1.33:1) • Subtitles/CC: Eng. • Languages: Jap., Eng. dub • Sound: Dolby Digital • Keepcase • 1 Disc • Region 1 GENRE & RATING Adult/Fantasy • Rated 18+

EL: Vol. 1

Nutech, 2002, 26 mins., #586. Directed by Katsuma Kanazawa. Written by Elf (pseudonym for Masato Hiruda).

A 2030 nuclear war leaves much of humanity dead from radiation poisoning. A domed city known as the Megaro Earth Project might be the last hope of mankind. But the terror-ist group known as Black Widow—led by the mysteri-ous Mr. Gimmick—plans to stop the MEP. But the good guys have their own counter-terrorist group known as Sniper Control, led by sexy redhead lady sniper EL. She's sometimes involved with pop idol Parsley, whom she saved from a Black Widow attack once. But when a young Black Widow woman named Natsuki is captured by the Snipers, they torture her for information.

This 2000–2001 series consisted of two OVAs. The picture transfer is excellent, and the animation is pretty good. Obvious care was taken to design a futuristic world that looks reasonable, with many social questions arising from the plot addressed even if in very brief ways. The story and plot are slick and sometimes even surprising. Although there are rape sequences, most of the rapists are shot, providing some measure of vengeance; unfortunately, the torture-for-information sequences might bother sensitive viewers almost as much. There is some lesbianism as well, and adult film stars Shelbee Myne and Lola provide voices.

The disc is double-sided, with previews on the flip side.

SPECIAL FEATURES Photo Galleries • Character and Art Galleries • Other Title Trailers TECHNICAL FEATURES Fullscreen (1.33:1) • Subtitles/CC: Eng. • Languages: Jap., Eng. dub • Sound: Dolby Digital 2.0 • Keepcase • 1 Disc • Region All GENRE & RATING Adult/Science Fiction

EL: Vol. 2

Nutech, 2002, 26 mins., #587. Directed by Katsuma Kanazawa. Written by Elf (pseudonym for Masato Hiruda).

Chris is accused of being a Black Widow, while the already-interrogat-ed Natsuki has lost her mind. Later, after Parsley seduces her, EL is cap-tured and put under the Black Widow's own form of sexual interro-gation techniques.

With an ending that's not entirely obvious, and some touches of *The Matrix*, this two-parter climaxes well (so to speak). There's more torture, SM, rape, and lesbianism, and a series of previews on the second side of the disc.

SPECIAL FEATURES Photo Galleries • Character and Art Galleries • Other Title Trailers TECHNICAL FEATURES Fullscreen (1.33:1) • Subtitles/CC: Eng. • Languages: Jap., Eng. dub • Sound: Dolby Digital 2.0 • Keepcase • 1 Disc • Region All GENRE & RATING Adult/Science Fiction

EL [Box Set]

Nutech, 2002, 52 mins., #588.

This box set features the two commercially available keepcase editions of *EL* in a cardboard box. It does not feature any additional extras. See individual entries for the Special and Technical Features listings.

TECHNICAL Cardboard Box with 2 Keepcases • 2 Discs • Region All GENRE Adult/Science Fiction

Evil Toons

Retro Media, 2001, 86 mins., #RMED011. Directed by Fred Olen Ray. Screenplay by Sherman Scott (aka Fred Olen Ray).

Four girls are dropped off at a mansion for the weekend to earn $100 each for cleaning the place for its new owners. But when a creepy old book is delivered to the house at midnight, an ancient monster emerges from its pages to menace and attack the women. Is the evil toon going to kill them, or turn them into something more undead?

This 1990 ultra-cheapy B-movie was conceived as a *Who Framed Roger Rabbit*–style live film mixed with animation, but director Fred Olen Ray was unable to secure as much financing as he wanted. Thus, the animated monster appears in only a handful of scenes, usually to rip some B-movie starlet's clothes off and bite them. The animation is barely credible, but it tops the awful "acting" and dialogue. But for those who love trash cinema, this is apparently a classic, as it has been translated into multiple languages. A friend summed it up best by saying that "watching *Evil Toons* requires alcohol."

There are a number of cool extras on the DVD, including a funny, lengthy live-action intro by Fred Olen Ray and an entertaining "making of" section. There's also a surprising offer for fans to get a free animation cel from the film (with four coupons from RetroMedia DVDs)!

SPECIAL FEATURES "Making of" Featurette • Photo Gallery • Trailer • Promotional Footage • Music Video • Outtakes • Games • DVD-ROM Features • Other Title Trailers • Inserts: Liner Notes TECHNICAL FEATURES Fullscreen (1.33:1) • Languages: Eng. • Sound: Dolby Digital 2.0 • Keepcase • 1 Disc • Region 1 GENRE Mature/Live/Horror

Excel Saga, Vol. 1: The Weirdness Has Begun

ADV Films, 2002, 125 mins., #DEX001. Directed by Shinichi Watanabe. Screenplay by Hideyuki Kurata, Yosuke Kuroda. Based on the manga series by Koshi Rikdo in *Young King Ours*.

Describing *Excel Saga* is a bit difficult. It's a parody of anime, spy films, the world of manga cartooning, and much more. Excel is an outrageous agent for ACROSS, a small organization bent on conquering the city of F, or at least bringing it under control. Joined by the equally beautiful agent, Hyatt (who can't seem to stay alive no matter how many times she comes back from the dead), and her pet dog, Mensch, Excel sometimes engages in bounty hunting to supplement her income. Along the way, there are (to quote ADV's own words): "your complete daily requirements of Martian princesses, afro-wearing action heroes, mysterious government agencies, space butlers, deranged comic book authors, androgynous prisoners in iron masks, annoying roommates, removable moustaches, and a generous supply of adorably cute aliens bent on galactic domination."

See why it's hard to explain this one? Consider it *Austin Powers* meets *Airplane* meets *South Park*. So, is *Excel Saga* funny? Yep. Even for non-Japanese audiences, the humor works, if only in a "what the hell?" kind of way. Witness a dog singing the end credit song about being eaten, or the video piracy warning that starts the disc (do *not* skip it!). The DVD also features "AD Vid-Notes," a pop-up feature that explains cultural references for non-Japanese audiences. And be sure to read the closing credits for each of the five episodes carefully. Humor is hard; cross-cultural humor is harder. *Excel Saga* hits the right funny bones.

SPECIAL FEATURES AD Vid-Notes Pop-Up Feature • Art Galleries • Video Piracy Warnings • Trailer • Clean Credits • Other Title Trailers TECHNICAL FEATURES Fullscreen (1.33:1) • Subtitles/CC: Eng. • Languages: Jap., Eng. dub • Sound: Dolby Digital 2.0 • Keepcase • 1 Discs • Region 1 GENRE & RATING Mature/Comedy • Rated 17+

Excel Saga, Vol. 2: Missions Improbable

ADV Films, 2002, 100 mins., #DEX/002. Directed by Shinichi Watanabe. Screenplay by Yosuke Kuroda, Hideyuki Kurata. Based on the manga series by Koshi Rikdo in *Young King Ours*.

NOTE: This DVD arrived too late for a full review. The following text is promotional copy provided by the releasing company:

"Their motto is 'Do or Die!' (Well, at least they got

the dying part covered.) When the plan to conquer the city isn't going well, Lord Ilpalazzo doesn't get mad, he just gets ACROSS . . . his crack team of Excel and Hyatt, that is. Of course, maybe this is one crack team of special agents that might be doing better if they weren't actually on crack. And now that there's a rival secret organization whose goal is to protect the city, things are going to be tougher than ever. Especially since their opponents may actually have a competent agent on their side! There's lots of totally pointless violence and senseless mayhem ahead as opposing forces collide in the second sense-numbing volume of *Excel Saga!*"

SPECIAL FEATURES AD Vid-Notes Pop-Up Feature • Art Galleries • Video Piracy Warnings • Promotional Footage • Other Title Trailers • Easter Eggs TECHNICAL FEATURES Fullscreen (1.33:1) • Subtitles/CC: Eng. • Languages: Jap., Eng. dub • Sound: Dolby Digital 2.0 • Keepcase • 1 Discs • Region 1 GENRE & RATING Mature/Comedy • Rated 17+

Excel Saga, Vol. 3: When Excels Strike (Out)

ADV Films, 2002, 100 mins., #DEX/003. Directed by Shinichi Watanabe. Screenplay by Yosuke Kuroda, Hideyuki Kurata. Based on the manga series by Koshi Rikdo in *Young King Ours.*

NOTE: This DVD arrived too late for a full review. The following text is promotional copy provided by the releasing company:

"Excel Excel, secret agent and agent of disaster, and her trustworthy (although decidedly unhealthy) fellow agent Hyatt are back, and once again they're out to conquer the city of F for the glory of the secret ideological agency of ACROSS! Whether they're up against murderous monkeys, possessed detectives, or men with excessively inflamed anuses, you can bet they'll give it their all or die trying. In fact, you can usually bet on the latter. The most deranged duo to ever dangle their derrières in the naked face of death return in the almost all new (contains 10% recycled material) and excruciatingly hilarious third volume of *Excel Saga.*"

By the way, the "Mint" in the "Find the Mint" game on this disc is a urinal freshener!

SPECIAL FEATURES Text Interview with Director • AD Vid-Notes Pop-Up Feature • Video Piracy Warnings • Art Galleries • Game • Recipes • Other Title Trailers TECHNICAL FEATURES Fullscreen (1.33:1) • Subtitles/CC: Eng. • Languages: Jap., Eng. dub • Sound: Dolby Digital 2.0 • Keepcase • 1 Discs • Region 1 GENRE & RATING Mature/Comedy • Rated 17+

Excel Saga, Vol. 4: Doing Whatever It Takes!

ADV Films, 2002, 100 mins., #DEX/004. Directed by Shinichi Watanabe. Screenplay by Yosuke Kuroda, Hideyuki Kurata. Based on the manga series by Koshi Rikdo in *Young King Ours.*

NOTE: This DVD arrived too late for a full review. The following text is promotional copy provided by the releasing company:

"Yes, the producers of the most demented anime ever produced are getting desperate, so in order to keep up the ratings, Excel and Hyatt find themselves facing new, Highly Merchandisable Characters, gimmick episodes and even Sexual Jeopardy (I'll take 'lesbian android overtures for $100, Alex!'). It's all in the service of Il Palazzo and ACROSS as our favorite set of social misfits once again plunge into the breach as the plot sickens . . . er, thickens . . . in the fourth incredibly bizarre volume of *Excel Saga!*"

This disc contains four episodes.

SPECIAL FEATURES Character and Art Galleries • AD Vid-Notes Pop-Up Feature • Video Piracy Warnings • Alternate Credits • Promotional Footage • Other Title Trailers TECHNICAL FEATURES Fullscreen (1.33:1) • Subtitles/CC: Eng. • Languages: Jap. Eng. dub • Sound: Dolby Digital 2.0 • Keepcase • 1 Discs • Region 1 GENRE & RATING Mature/Comedy • Rated 17+

Fencer of Minerva: The Emergence [#1]

U.S. Manga Corps, 2001, 135 mins., #USMD 2030. Directed by Tadayoshi Kusaka. Screenplay by Yuji Kishino.

In the fantasy kingdom of Doria, two children—the King's son Sho and the daughter of a Royal Guardsman, Diana—are separated in a palace coup, and Sho is thought dead. Diana is raised as a princess by her father, the new King, and twelve years later, is destined to be married. But while disguised in the city streets, she rescues a mistreated sex slave, and heads out of the city. The two women are captured and subjected to torture, until the grown-up Sho arrives and saves them from the nomads. But how will Sho take his revenge on the kingdom, and what will Diana's fiancé do to get her back?

Three episodes of this 1995 series are presented on this DVD. According to some sources, some of the adult material has actually been edited out from the first episode, even though this is an adult title (though even that is debatable; the package lists 16+ and then notes that it's not suitable for anyone under 18). The animation is nicely detailed, though the soundtrack is a bit quiet, and the English dub is pretty bad. There's much violence, bondage, rape, and lesbianism.

SPECIAL FEATURES Character Bios • Character and Art Galleries • Trailer • DVD-ROM Features: Art, Scripts, Bios • Other Title Trailers TECHNICAL FEATURES Fullscreen (1.33:1) • Subtitles/CC: Eng. • Languages: Jap., Eng. dub • Sound: Dolby Digital 2.0 • Keepcase • 1 Disc • Region 1–6 GENRE & RATING Mature/Fantasy • Rated 16+

Fencer of Minerva: The Tempest [#2]

U.S. Manga Corps, 2001, 90 mins., #USMD 2057. Directed by Tadayoshi Kusaka. Screenplay by Yuji Kishino.

It's been three months since the kingdom of Doria was saved, and now Diana is revered through the land as the beautiful Slave Queen. Alliances with the nomads and the merchants have helped the economy. But behind the scenes, there is more betrayal and skullduggery afoot. When assassins attack the new King, Diana may soon be subjected to more nastiness, unless she and Sho can make new plans.

The fourth and fifth OVAs are presented here, and the animation features a cartoonier look with brighter colors and less detailed backgrounds. As might be expected, there's bondage, consensual slavery, and lesbianism.

SPECIAL FEATURES Character Bios • DVD-ROM Features: Art, Scripts) • Other Title Trailers TECHNICAL FEATURES Fullscreen (1.33:1) • Subtitles/CC: Eng. • Languages: Jap., Eng. dub • Sound: Dolby Digital 2.0 • Keepcase • 1 Disc • Region 1–6 GENRE & RATING Mature/Fantasy • Rated 16+

Five Card

These *Five Card* titles, from NuTech, were not available for review: *Five Card: Vol. 1; Five Card: Vol. 2; Five Card: Vol. 3; Five Card: Vol. 4;* and *Five Card* [Box Set].

Flashback

These *Flashback* titles, from NuTech, were not available for review: *Flashback: Game #1; Flashback: Game #2; Flashback: Game #3;* and *Flashback* [Box Set].

Fritz the Cat

MGM/UA, 2001, 79 mins., #1002730. Directed by Ralph Bakshi. Screenplay by Ralph Bakshi. Based on the comic books and characters of Robert Crumb.

Fritz is a college-aged cat who decides to embark on a series of adventures into the forbidden life on the edge. He engages in group sex, then helps start a full-scale race riot between the police (portrayed as pigs) and African-

Americans (portrayed as crows). Constantly on the run from the cops, Fritz goes road-tripping with a biker rabbit and his donkey girlfriend, gets involved with radicals and psychedelic drugs, and eventually decides that of all the hedonistic opportunities open to him, sex is the best.

Released in 1972, *Fritz the Cat* was the first animated feature film to receive the dreaded (at that time) X rating, and there were police seizures and public protests at some theaters showing the film. Writer/director Ralph Bakshi based the film on characters and situations from underground comics by Robert Crumb; the cranky cartoonist later disavowed the film. While shocking for the time—negative publicity helped make it popular enough to earn $25 million—*Fritz the Cat* seems tremendously old-school today. Not only are the language and art dated, but the racial depictions offend, and the gratuitous violence just seems mean-spirited.

Still, this DVD represents a true historic landmark, and those interested in Crumb, the career of Bakshi, or animation history should be interested in picking it up. It spawned a later sequel, *The Nine Lives of Fritz the Cat* (see entry).

SPECIAL FEATURES Trailer TECHNICAL FEATURES Widescreen (1.85:1 enhanced for 16x9) • Subtitles/CC: Eng., Fren., Span. • Languages: Eng., Fren. dub, Span. dub • Sound: Dolby Digital 2.0 • Keepcase • 1 Disc • Region 1 GENRE & RATING Mature/Satire/Animals • Rated X

General Chaos Uncensored Animation

Manga Entertainment, 1999, 74 mins., #602-004-003-2.

With twenty-three short films and a variety of familiar faces on camera, this collection could be another volume of *Spike and Mike's Sick and Twisted Festival of Animation*. But it isn't. Really! Sure there are S and M favorites like Mike Grimshaw and Rob Filbrandt's "Quiet Please," "Sittin' Pretty," and "Deep Sympathy." And yes, Bill Plympton clocks in with seven morphing segments of "Sex and Violence."

But there are also a gaggle of newcomers using cel animation, stop-motion, claymation, and more to get their adults-only shorts onto the bill. From a cracker-addicted parrot to a Gothic mansion where grisly scientific transplants are taking place, from a woman strapping on enhancements for a night of debauchery to the masturbatory '60s rock group the Meatles . . . lots of humor and more than a few gross-outs can be yours on this DVD.

SPECIAL FEATURES Trailer • Other Title Trailers • Inserts: Liner Notes TECHNICAL FEATURES Fullscreen (1.33:1) • Languages: Eng. • Sound: Dolby Digital 2.0 • Keepcase • 1 Disc • Region All GENRE Mature/Anthology

Golden Boy: Treasure Hunt [#1]

ADV Films, 2002, 75 mins., #DGB/001. Directed by Hiroyuki Kitakubo. Written by Tatsuya Egawa. Based on the manga series by Tatsuya Egawa.

Student Kintaro Oe is as lucky as can be. As he rides his bicycle across the highways of Japan, he finds odd jobs and lots of sex. In "Computer Lesson," he swaps software and hardware with the president of an all-female software company. Then, in "Temptation of the Maiden" he stuffs a few ballots in the process of taking on the daughter of a tough politician. Finally, in "Danger! The Virgin's First Love," Kintaro must cope with an innocent noodle maker's daughter who wants to cook up some fun.

This 1995 OVA series is very goofy and funny, with extremely nice, realistic animation, and a likable lead character. And despite its preoccupation with sex, there's not a huge amount of nudity; just lots of sex talk and implications. There's fetishwear, toilet-seat sniffing, and even a humorous gay kiss! Plus, the DVD contains a rather good dub that actually complements the character, though the subtitles will show the original Japanese translation. *Golden Boy* is an enjoyably naughty series, and a cleansing relief from all the violence and rape-filled hentai.

SPECIAL FEATURES Character and Art Galleries • Clean Credits • Trailer • Other Title Trailers • Easter Egg TECHNICAL FEATURES Fullscreen (1.33:1) • Subtitles/CC: Eng. • Languages: Jap., Eng. dub • Sound: Dolby Digital 2.0 • Keepcase • 1 Disc • Region 1 GENRE & RATING Mature/Comedy • Rated 17+

Golden Boy: Bound for Glory [#2]

ADV Films, 2002, 90 mins., #DGB/002. Directed by Hiroyuki Kitakubo. Written by Tatsuya Egawa. Based on the manga series by Tatsuya Egawa.

Kintaro Oe is back on his bike, trekking throughout the country to take odd jobs. This time out, he joins a swim team to meet a female Olympic swimmer in "Swimming in the Sea of Love," and ends up helping her teach kids. Then, in "Balls to the Wall," he challenges a beautiful female motorcycle racer (who really likes her hard, throbbing engine) to a race. But how can he win on his bicycle? And in the funniest segment of the whole series, he gets a job at an animation studio in "Animation Is Fun." But when he tries to cook and clean, he only gets into trouble.

The final three *Golden Boy* OVAs are included on this disc, and fans should really have fun with them, especially the final story.

SPECIAL FEATURES Character and Art Galleries • Clean Credits •

Trailer • Other Title Trailers TECHNICAL FEATURES Fullscreen (1.33:1) • Subtitles/CC: Eng. • Languages: Jap., Eng. dub • Sound: Dolby Digital 2.0 • Keepcase • 1 Disc • Region 1 GENRE & RATING Mature/Comedy • Rated 17+

Golgo 13: Queen Bee—Special Edition

Urban Vision, 2001, 60 mins., #UV1069. Directed by Osamu Dezaki. Screenplay by Akihiro Tago, Matt Aichir. Based on the manga series by Takao Saito in *Big Comic*.

Golgo 13 is the world's most notorious assassin, and he'll take on any job for the right amount of money. This time out, it's assassin versus assassin, as he gets a bead on his latest target: Sonia the Queen Bee, a nymphomaniac and the leader of a South American guerilla liberation army. She's planning on offing a high-profile U.S. presidential candidate, unless he can stop her first. But once he's deep into the mission, Golgo is caught in the middle of twists, turns, drugs, plots for revenge, and double-crosses!

Golgo 13 began in the pages of manga in 1969 and has been produced ever since, with over 120 volumes published! Extraordinarily popular, it's only been made into two anime films, with *Queen Bee* (1988) the second. This features slick, detailed, Americanized animation, and lots of sex and often-gratuitous violence. Most of the characters may be stick-figures to be blown away, but the plotting is intricate and strong, and the gun-play action is barely rivaled in the field.

The DVD features a rare commentary track, as well as a remixed 5.1 soundtrack for both the English and Japanese versions. If you like guns and girls, but have always felt James Bond was a little too stuffy, *Golgo 13* may be your new favorite.

SPECIAL FEATURES Commentary Track with Director and Executive Producer (Japanese language) • Other Title Trailers TECHNICAL FEATURES Fullscreen (1.33:1) • Subtitles/CC: Eng. • Languages: Jap., Eng. dub • Sound: Dolby Digital 5.1 • Keepcase • 1 Disc • Region 1 GENRE Mature/Thriller

Gonad the Barbarian: Search for Uranus

VCA, 76 mins.

This DVD was not available for review.

Haitoku no Shoujyo: Family of Debauchery

NuTech, 2002, 29 mins., #677. Directed by Mikan Fuyukawa. Screenplay by Jinmu. Based on the manga series by Atushi Tachibana.

Lured to a private mansion to act as a tutor for young Yuki, the chaste Hiroko is drugged, then put into bondage. Hiroko is soon at the mercy of Yuki and older sister Shizuki, who plan to use her as a human sex toy. And then, Yuki reveals something surprising . . .

With a very short running time, this one has quite a bit of action, with bondage, lots of lesbianism, and cross-dressing. Despite the presence of a dog on the cover, it does not feature bestiality. It's probably a best buy for anyone with a fetish for maid's outfits. The disc is double-sided, with previews on side two.

SPECIAL FEATURES Character and Art Galleries • Other Title Trailers TECHNICAL FEATURES Fullscreen (1.33:1) • Subtitles/CC: Eng. • Languages: Jap., Eng. dub • Sound: Dolby Digital 2.0 • Keepcase • 1 Disc • Region All GENRE Adult/Fetish

Happy Tree Friends: Vol. 1—First Blood

Mondo Media, 2003, 141 mins., #1388-7. Directed by Rhode Montijo, Aubrey Ankrum. Written by Warren Graff, Rhode Montijo, Kenn Navarro, Mark Fiorenza, Paul Allen, Mark Giglio, Jason Sadler.

Cuddles, Giggles, Toothy, Lumpy, and Nutty . . . they all seem like such cute, cuddly, lovable cartoon animals. You just want to hug them and squeeze them until their eyes pop out and their limbs fall off. The denizens of Happy Tree Friends love to have everyday adventures, but they always end up going horribly wrong. Playing ball with Pop leads to a deadly encounter with a helicopter, while a spin on the merry-go-round ends with viscera strewn all over the playground. Not even disco dancing is safe from bloody dismemberment, and you can bet that the ol' swimming hole has deadly denizens of the deep just below the surface. Babble and cutely coo all you want, Happy Tree Friends . . . your days are numbered!

Astonishingly popular since its debut online in December 2000, Happy Tree Friends is the brainchild of Rhode Monitjo and Aubrey Ankrum. Featured as part of a series of animated shorts at www.mondominishows.com, Happy Tree Friends quickly gained in popularity worldwide, garnering a choice spot in Spike and Mike's Sick and Twisted Festival of Animation.

The DVD was originally offered online in 2002 from Mondo Media in a cardboard package, but the 2003 edition contains the same material under a different cover.

There are 14 main episodes, plus a bonus episode, the pilot show, and a "Pop-Corn" trivia-info story. Each episode also features complete commentary and storyboard comparisons, and you can control the fate of favorite characters in four interactive "Smoochies" (the sickest of which are the Easter Smoochies). You'll want to check out every menu page of the disc as well; each has a plastic-packaged Happy Tree Friends action figure, all of which have an action feature if you wait for 30 seconds or so.

Demented and delicious, Happy Tree Friends combines cute cartoon animals with gore and violence in a hilarious and perverse manner. No other cartoon goes quite this far into twisted shocker territory yet still retains innocence and mainstream appeal. This DVD is the perfect party disc, and will make a wonderful addition to any animation collection for mature viewers who like just a little bit of (rabid) bite to their humor.

SPECIAL FEATURES Commentary Track by Creators • Character and Art Galleries • Character Bios • Storyboards TECHNICAL FEATURES Fullscreen (1.33:1) • Languages: Eng. • Sound: Dolby Digital 2.0 • Keepcase • 1 Disc • Region 1 GENRE Mature/Comedy/Animals

Heat for All Seasons, A

Kitty, 2002, 90 mins., #KVDVD-0207. Directed by Rion Kujo. Screenplay by Rokurota Marabe. Original Story by KID.

College student Masato is really trying to pay attention to his studies, especially since he wants to be a novelist. While working a summer job in Namiekaze City, he runs into a woman named Chihiro, whom he knew back in junior high school. They eventually have sex together, the first time for each of them. Later, Masato is tempted by Rie, Miku, and Kanna, and he isn't helped much by his superstud co-worker Oka. If only Masato could get his mind off sex, he'd be an ace student!

This recent trio of OVAs is nicely drawn, with cutesy art and bright colors. Unlike most hentai, all of the sex in the series is consensual, and some of it is even very sweet. This is the type of hentai that a couple could share together, though the Japanese subtitles will offer a much sweeter story than the coarser English dub.

SPECIAL FEATURES Other Title Trailers TECHNICAL FEATURES Fullscreen (1.33:1) • Subtitles/CC: Eng. • Languages: Jap., Eng. dub • Sound: Dolby Digital 2.0 • Keepcase • 1 Disc • Region 1 GENRE & RATING Adult/Romance • Rated 18+

Heavy Metal [Special Edition]

Columbia TriStar, 1999, 90 mins., #3929.

This DVD was not available for review.

Heavy Metal 2000

Columbia TriStar, 2000, 88 mins., #05267. Directed by Michael Lemire, Michael Coldewey. Screenplay by Robert Payne Cabeen. Based on the graphic novel by Kevin Eastman, Simon Bisley, Eric Talbot.

Julie is a warrior whose father and sister live on the planet Eden, redesignated FAKK2 (Federation Assigned Kitogenic Killzone) after evil Captain Tyler razes the planet. Julie's father is killed, and Tyler takes her sister hostage. Tyler wants the key to eternal life, and he's gone insane. Now Julie must track him across the galaxy, shooting at him—and even seducing him—to retrieve her sister and stop the madman from gaining immortality.

Released in 1981, the original *Heavy Metal* was a cult classic, combining rock music and animation full of sex, blood, and mature themes adapted from the *Heavy Metal* comic series. Almost twenty years later, the sequel was also based on comic book work by Kevin Eastman and artists Simon Bisley and Eric Talbot, but it's a sequel in name only. Eastman had made a fortune cocreating the *Teenage Mutant Ninja Turtles*, and had later married Amazonian *Playboy* model and B-movie actress Julie Strain. *Heavy Metal 2000* is his animated love letter to Strain. Not only does she portray the lead character (vocally and in art designs), but the male sidekick role is modeled after Eastman, and her sister is modeled after a Strain protégé.

Vanity production or not, *Heavy Metal 2000* doesn't live up to its predecessor in the sex and blood quotas, but it features some nice animation (both traditional and CGI), with hyperdetailed technical backgrounds that sometimes overshadow the foreground figures. The rock music and sound effects are ear-bleedingly loud, but fans will likely enjoy the workout their speakers will get. Most of the nudity is of the topless variety, including some sex-bots.

The DVD features some cool extras, including a "Julie Strain, SuperGoddess" featurette that paints a warm and funny portrait of the very tall, well-endowed actress. There's also a featurette on voice talent, and an isolated music score.

SPECIAL FEATURES "Making of" Featurettes • Character and Art Galleries • Animatic Comparisons • Animation Tests • Trailer • Isolated Score • Other Title Trailers TECHNICAL FEATURES Widescreen (1.85:1 enhanced for 16x9) • Subtitles/CC: Eng., Fren., Port., Span. • Languages: Eng., Fren. dub, Port. dub, Span. dub • Sound: Dolby Digital Surround 3. Dolby Digital Surround 5.1 • Keepcase • 1 Disc • Region 1, 4 GENRE & RATING Mature/Science Fiction/Action • Rated R

Heavy Metal/Heavy Metal 2000 [Box Set]

Columbia TriStar, 2000, 178 mins.

This DVD set was not available for review. It contains both commercially available keepcase editions, with no extras.

Heavy Traffic

MGM/UA, 2000, 76 mins., #10000979. Directed by Ralph Bakshi. Written by Ralph Bakshi.

Michael is a twenty-four-year-old pinball-playing virgin who wants to be a cartoonist. He lives with his always-fighting Italian father and Jewish mother. He eventually gets involved with Carole, a cool African-American bartender, and the plot begins to meander as they wander the city. Meet the legless amputee dwarf bouncer, the masochistic drag queen Snowflake, and more, as Carole and Michael move on down the road.

In 1973, *Heavy Traffic* was released as the follow up to Bakshi's *Fritz the Cat* (see entry). This time, all the characters are human, though their caricatures are far from anything resembling reality. Some of the art is realistic, some of it features photo backgrounds, some is highly cartoony, and the ending is live-action. As for the story, let's just say that even on mind-altering substances it might not make sense. There is lots of violence, a very minor amount of sex, and surprisingly, almost no drugs. This may be because some scenes in the movie were reanimated in 1974 so that *Heavy Traffic* could get its original X rating rescinded for an R, to double-bill with *The Nine Lives of Fritz the Cat* (see entry). This DVD presents the censored R-rated version.

Potential viewers are warned that the film features some very offensive stereotypes of African-Americans, Jews, and gays, and some major misogyny, but at least the amputee is generally treated with some respect. Still, *Heavy Traffic* is awfully unpleasant and dysfunctional.

SPECIAL FEATURES Trailer TECHNICAL FEATURES Fullscreen (1.33:1) • Subtitles/CC: Fren., Span. • Languages: Eng. • Sound: Dolby Digital 2.0 • Keepcase • 1 Disc • Region 1 GENRE & RATING Mature/Drama • Rated R

House of Morecock, The

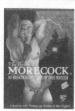

Greenwood Cooper/10% Productions, 2001, 60 mins., #D2019. Directed by Joe Phillips. Written by Joe Phillips, R. J. Zebley, B. Colt, Darren Catheart.

Jonas Morecock is an adventurer whose investigations into the paranormal always seem to land him in a highly sexual situation. The twist? Jonas is gay, but thankfully, he finds lots of lusty men—and monsters—in his travels. In eight segments, Jonas leaves the pampered safety of Morecock Manor to meet the Loch Ness Monster, a Ghostly Miner, the Chupacabra, Bigfoot, aliens and the agents of The SeX Files, monstrous Gogeerah, Moby Dick, and an angel and devil in the Afterlife!

Created as web-based animation, the four-minute adventures of Jonas are the work of popular comic book artist Joe Phillips, whose gay-themed cards, calendars, and refrigerator magnets all reflect a happy sensuality. *The House of Morecock* is no exception to this theme; there's no violence, and everything's consensual. Phillips also uses a variety of ethnicities for his models, thus widening the appeal of his men. The art style is streamlined and clean, realistic at all times except for the once-per-episode super-deformed moment just before the sex starts.

The DVD also includes a fun little "Behind the Toons" short that traces Jonas's career in Hollywood, including some fun Fleischeresque black and white footage. *The House of Morecock* is a rare "happy porn" disc, and is the first gay-themed animated adult DVD on the market. It's recommended for all open-minded viewers.

SPECIAL FEATURES Interview with Director • Character and Art Galleries • Trailer • Promotional Footage • Music Clips TECHNICAL FEATURES Fullscreen (1.33:1 boxed) • Languages: Eng. • Sound: Dolby Digital 2.0 • Keepcase • 1 Disc • Region All GENRE Adult/Gay/Supernatural

I Married a Strange Person!

Universal, 2000, 73 mins., #20768. Directed by Bill Plympton. Written by Bill Plympton, P. G. Vey.

Grant Boyer has changed, and his wife Keri is noticing it. A strange growth on his neck has given him the power to make his sexual fantasies into reality. Whether it's turning breasts into balloon animals or forcing military tanks to copulate, Grant's mind is wandering further and further into strange territories. Can Keri save her marriage and her husband, before the outer world discovers his abilities?

Bill Plympton's sketchy, constantly morphing colored pencil art is given the movie-length treatment here. Plympton takes the act of sex and humorizes, with lightbulbs inserting themselves into sockets, shoes humping, birds mating, pencils sharpening, and more. Then there are the sentient blades of grass and movable mounds of cellulite. Some cute and funny songs will further amuse audiences, but be warned that this is a very bizarre film.

SPECIAL FEATURES Trailer TECHNICAL FEATURES Fullscreen (1.66:1) • Subtitles/CC: Eng. • Languages: Eng. • Sound: Dolby Digital 2.0 • Keepcase • 1 Disc • Region 1 GENRE Mature/Comedy

Imma Youjo: The Erotic Temptress—Vol. 1: What the Wise Stranger Fears

NuTech, 2000, 44 mins., #455. Directed by Kanenari Tokiwa.

Wherever Maya goes, erotic madness follows. An anomalous force of nature—sexually speaking—Maya exits one town, leaving its residents in a violent sexual frenzy, and makes her way to a city. There, she falls prey to some thugs, then is taken inside a massive tower in the center of town. What is the secret of the being known as Chaos . . . and why are all the city's voluptuous young women inside the tower as well?

A five-part OVA series from 2000, *Imma Youjo* has a bit of a plot, and is longer than most hentai OVAs. There's also some espionage, bondage, and rape by demons, tentacles, and a cyborg! Like other NuTech releases, the second side of the DVD features trailers and previews. The picture quality is excellent, but viewers will definitely have one major gripe: the menu is extremely difficult to use.

SPECIAL FEATURES Character and Art Galleries • Other Title Trailers TECHNICAL FEATURES Fullscreen (1.33:1) • Subtitles/CC: Eng. • Languages: Jap. • Sound: Dolby Digital 2.0 • Keepcase • 1 Disc • Region 1–6 GENRE Adult/Supernatural

Imma Youjo: The Erotic Temptress—Vol. 2: Making the Woman Perfect

NuTech, 2000, 48 mins., #456. Directed by Kazumasa Muraki.

Maya is back, but it's not the same Maya. In this story, an android craftsman named Ichiro creates the most exceptional female androids known to man. His customers include the world's richest men, and a popular sex club. And then, using illegal parts, Ichiro manages to create Maya, the most perfect female droid ever. Once he has made her, Ichiro refuses to give Maya up, and he decides to leave with her. But at what cost?

It's not clear if "Maya" is supposed to be a sex avatar of some sort, or if using the name for the central female character is a flimsy narrative device to hang an anthology series on. Regardless, with echoes of *Blade Runner*, this OVA is a bit more interesting than the other episodes of *Imma Youjo*. In addition to the rape and bondage, there's also some cybersex and lesbianism, and consensual sex with old men. And nary a demon or tentacle in sight! The DVD's second side offers more previews, and the disc itself has a much better menu than the first volume.

SPECIAL FEATURES Character and Art Galleries • Other Title Trailers TECHNICAL FEATURES Fullscreen (1.33:1) • Subtitles/CC: Eng. • Languages: Jap. • Sound: Dolby Digital 2.0 • Keepcase • 1 Disc • Region 1–6 GENRE Adult/Science Fiction

Imma Youjo: The Erotic Temptress—Vol. 3: The Paths Less Traveled

NuTech, 2000, 41 mins., #457. Directed by Kazumasa Muraki.

Feudal Japan is a rough place to be a woman, especially if you're young Maya, a servant girl for an exiled noblewoman. When two warrior knights hold the promise of a rescue, Maya is excited. But who are the two witchy women hidden away in the mountainside, and what danger will they be to the knights? Will a spider-demon devour them all alive?

A third version of Maya is presented in this volume, with some minor changes to the previous character designs. There's the much-too-common rape and lesbianism, and some really creepy moments of rape with the female spider-demon. Ick. As with the other *Imma Youjo* discs, there are previews on side two.

SPECIAL FEATURES Character and Art Galleries • Other Title Trailers TECHNICAL FEATURES Fullscreen (1.33:1) • Subtitles/CC: Eng. • Languages: Jap. • Sound: Dolby Digital 2.0 • Keepcase • 1 Disc • Region 1–6 GENRE Adult/Supernatural

Imma Youjo: The Erotic Temptress—Vol. 4: Within the Lie, Once Told

NuTech, 2000, 49 mins., #458. Directed by Kazumasa Muraki.

Jumping into the Dark Ages of Europe, the age of witch hunts is at its peak. An evil count is torturing women of the medieval kingdom into confessing they're witches, and then burning them at the stake. But a military man named Mayatola interferes with the hunts, until his secret is discovered. Mayatola is really a girl named Maya, and her treachery against the Count and the King's plans leads to accusations that she, too, is a witch!

The most brutal and sadistic episode of *Imma Youjo*, this one has lots of rape, bondage, and very nasty torture. Not much to recommend here. The second side of the disc contains trailers.

SPECIAL FEATURES Character and Art Galleries • Other Title Trailers TECHNICAL FEATURES Fullscreen (1.33:1) • Subtitles/CC: Eng. • Languages: Jap. • Sound: Dolby Digital 2.0 • Keepcase • 1 Disc • Region 1–6 GENRE Adult/Medieval

Imma Youjo: The Erotic Temptress—Vol. 5: The Extent of Their Collections

NuTech, 2000, 44 mins., #459. Directed by Kazumasa Muraki.

Maya takes a job as a maid at a luxurious mansion owned by some sort of artist. The job seems relatively easy, until the secret of the basement is discovered. That's where the Master of the house is building his harem of sex slaves to be kept for corrupt depravities . . . or to be sold to other houses. Will Maya and her friend Tomoka be forced into sexual slavery?

The finale of the *Imma Youjo* series has yet another different design for Maya, and lots of bondage, rape, SM, and lesbianism. It's also a bit boring. Side two has trailers.

SPECIAL FEATURES Character and Art Galleries • Other Title Trailers TECHNICAL FEATURES Fullscreen (1.33:1) • Subtitles/CC: Eng. • Languages: Jap. • Sound: Dolby Digital 2.0 • Keepcase • 1 Disc • Region 1–6 GENRE Adult/Sadism

Imma Youjo: The Erotic Temptress [Box Set]

NuTech, 2000, 226 mins., #460.

This box set features the five commercially available keepcase editions of *Imma Youjo: The Erotic Temptress* in a cardboard box. It does not feature any additional extras. See individual entries for the Special and Technical Features listings.

TECHNICAL FEATURES Cardboard Box with 5 Keepcases • 5 Discs • Region 1–6 GENRE Adult/Supernatural/Science Fiction/Sadism

Immoral Sisters: Two Premature Fruits—Night One: "Madonna Debauched"

NuTech, 2002, 30 mins., #600. Directed by Roku Iwata. Written by Osamu Momoi. Original Story by Elf (pseudonym for Masato Hiruda).

Taketo and his father, Nogawa, are determined to sexually out-perform each other. Taketo engineers a car accident with a housewife named Yuki, and when she is unable to pay the settlement, he begins his conquest of her. Nogawa—who is both the owner/president of Nogawa Industries and the school principal—goes after Yuki's two daughters, Rumi and Tomoko, using his secretary to help break them into sexual debauchery.

Since blackmail is the source of most of the sex in this series, the sex is more consensual than in most hentai, but the youthful appearance of Rumi and Tomoko is cause for discomfort for many viewers. Still, the animation is very realistic and attractive, and the character designs are nice. The stories also include lesbianism and incest, and the disc is double-sided with previews. Adult film stars Holly Hollywood and Jenna Haze provide two of the voices, as well as a selection of nasty photos.

SPECIAL FEATURES Photo Galleries • Character and Art Galleries • Other Title Trailers TECHNICAL FEATURES Fullscreen (1.33:1) • Subtitles/CC: Eng. • Languages: Jap., Eng. dub • Sound: Dolby Digital 2.0 • Keepcase • 1 Disc • Region 1 GENRE Adult/Drama

Immoral Sisters: Two Premature Fruits—Night Two: "The Fallen Good Student"

NuTech, 2002, 30 mins., #601. Directed by Roku Iwata. Written by Osamu Momoi. Original Story by Elf (pseudonym for Masato Hiruda).

More of the same story as in the first part, as Taketo and Yuki engage in more lustful behavior. Nogawa makes another play for the two sisters, getting them to do just what he wants. More lesbianism, incest, and semi-consensual sex, and another B-side of previews.

SPECIAL FEATURES Photo Galleries • Character and Art Galleries • Other Title Trailers TECHNICAL FEATURES Fullscreen (1.33:1) • Subtitles/CC: Eng. • Languages: Jap., Eng. dub • Sound: Dolby Digital 2.0 • Keepcase • 1 Disc • Region 1 GENRE Adult/Drama

Immoral Sisters: Two Premature Fruits—Night Three: "Drowning in Love and Pleasure"

NuTech, 2002, 32 mins., #602. Directed by Roku Iwata. Written by Osamu Momoi. Original Story by Elf (pseudonym for Masato Hiruda).

The intertwined plots of Taketo and Nogawa come together as the girls attempt to take some of the sexual pressure off their mother, resulting in a big group sex scene to end the series. In this very nicely animated conclusion, look for more lesbianism, incest, and semi-consensual sex, and another B-side of previews.

SPECIAL FEATURES Photo Galleries • Character and Art Galleries • Other Title Trailers TECHNICAL FEATURES Fullscreen (1.33:1) • Subtitles/CC: Eng. • Languages: Jap., Eng. dub • Sound: Dolby Digital 2.0 • Keepcase • 1 Disc • Region 1 GENRE Adult/Drama

Immoral Sisters: Two Premature Fruits [Box Set #1–3]

NuTech, 2002, 92 mins., #603.

This box set features the three commercially available keepcase editions of *Immoral Sisters: Two Premature Fruits* in a cardboard box. It does not feature any additional extras. See individual entries for the Special and Technical Features listings.

TECHNICAL FEATURES Cardboard Box with 3 Keepcases • 3 Discs • Region 1 GENRE Adult/Drama

Inma Seiden: The Legend of the Beast of Lust—Episode #1

NuTech, 2002, 29 mins., #589. Directed by Kan Fukumoto. Screenplay by Katsuma Kanazawa.

At the private Otori Academy, two related families struggle for control. The principal of the Academy plans to bring the king from the land of Death to our realm, but to do this, he must allow demons to rape the women of the school. With each rape that occurs, a sigil map appears on the victim's body, bringing the principal's evil plans one step closer to fruition. Senna is raped by one of the demons, and her friend, Mao, bands with other teen girls and some teachers to fight the horrifying possible future. . . .

Inma Seiden was released as a series of OVAs in 2001,

and it features a bit more plot and characterization than most demon rape series. Set mainly in the daytime, it still manages to look dark due to muted art. Besides the demon and tentacle rape, there's also bondage. The disc is double-sided, with previews.

SPECIAL FEATURES Character and Art Galleries • Other Title Trailers TECHNICAL FEATURES Fullscreen (1.33:1) • Subtitles/CC: Eng. • Languages: Jap., Eng. dub • Sound: Dolby Digital 2.0 • Keepcase • 1 Disc • Region All GENRE Adult/Supernatural

Inma Seiden: The Legend of the Beast of Lust—Episode #2

NuTech, 2002, 27 mins., #590. Directed by Kan Fukumoto. Screenplay by Katsuma Kanazawa.

Mao is enraged over Senna's rape, and wants revenge. Hitomi, Himiko, and Kaori are all determined to get to the bottom of the conspiracy at the Academy. Who is the man in the iron mask? What will the female demon, Ken, do to Mao? And then, Mao is attacked by the demon king. . . .

This disc has more demon rape, with a side of lesbianism thrown in, plus a B-side of previews.

SPECIAL FEATURES Character and Art Galleries • Other Title Trailers TECHNICAL FEATURES Fullscreen (1.33:1) • Subtitles/CC: Eng. • Languages: Jap., Eng. dub • Sound: Dolby Digital 2.0 • Keepcase • 1 Disc • Region All GENRE Adult/Supernatural

Inma Seiden: The Legend of the Beast of Lust—Episode #3

NuTech, 2002, 30 mins., #591. Directed by Kan Fukumoto. Screenplay by Katsuma Kanazawa.

Mao is in shock, but alive, and while Suzune is worried about Mao, she also needs to worry about getting out of the Academy alive herself! All the conspiracies and demonic threats come to an explosive tentacle-filled climax in this final DVD volume, which includes more demon rape, plus previews on side two.

SPECIAL FEATURES Character and Art Galleries • Other Title Trailers TECHNICAL FEATURES Fullscreen (1.33:1) • Subtitles/CC: Eng. • Languages: Jap., Eng. dub • Sound: Dolby Digital 2.0 • Keepcase • 1 Disc • Region All GENRE Adult/Supernatural

Inma Seiden: The Legend of the Beast of Lust [Box Set]

NuTech, 2002, 90 mins., #593.

This box set features the three commercially available keepcase editions of *Inma Seiden: The Legend of the Beast of Lust* in a cardboard box. It does not feature any additional extras. See individual entries for the Special and Technical Features listings.

TECHNICAL FEATURES Cardboard Box with 3 Keepcases • 3 Discs • Region All GENRE Adult/Supernatural

Inmu: Feast of Victims—Vol. 1: 1st and 2nd Nights

NuTech, 2002, 28 mins., #549. Directed by Misumi Ran. Script by Yoshioka Takao. Original Story by Pink Pineapple.

Two short adventures, each held together by their violent sexual plots . . . and a mysterious semi-naked woman in a mask. In the first story, Yumi is molested on a train, and she begins to feel that the attacker is stalking her, until the masked woman offers her a very odd form of therapy. In the second story, a nasty female fashion designer humiliates and fires a male employee, then is warned by the masked woman. Soon, the ex-employee kidnaps the designer and forces public degradation and humiliation on her.

Well, this is an unpleasant mix here in this 2001 OVA series. There's demon rape, human rape, bondage, and non-consensual SM. What is most disturbing is that one of the rapists looks like Microsoft CEO Bill Gates! Adult film star Asia Carrera not only does one of the English voices, she also provides a revealing little mini-documentary about herself.

SPECIAL FEATURES Interview with Voice Actress • Photo Galleries • Character and Art Galleries • Other Title Trailers TECHNICAL FEATURES Fullscreen (1.33:1) • Subtitles/CC: Eng. • Languages: Jap., Eng. dub* Sound: Dolby Digital 2.0 • Keepcase • 1 Disc • Region 1 GENRE Adult/Sadism

Inmu: Feast of Victims—Vol. 2: 3rd and 4th Nights

NuTech, 2002, 28 mins., #550. Directed by Misumi Ran. Script by Yoshioka Takao. Original Story by Pink Pineapple.

The masked woman is back, with more tales to tell. Izumi Hinagawa is a lesbian on the swim team, and she has the hots for teammate Aki Sakuragi. But what lurks below the waters of lust? In the next story, a woman opens a strange box from an antique shop, and wakes up in a dungeon where she is raped repeatedly. How did she get there, and are the increasingly horrifying rapes real or fantasy?

More of the same contained in the first disc, this has human rapes, demon rapes, mechanical tentacle rapes, and lesbianism. Viewers who like this material might be frustrated that the stories are so short, but others might wonder why it was animated at all.

SPECIAL FEATURES Interview with Voice Actress • Photo Galleries • Character and Art Galleries • Other Title Trailers TECHNICAL FEATURES Fullscreen (1.33:1) • Subtitles/CC: Eng. • Languages: Jap., Eng. dub* Sound: Dolby Digital 2.0 • Keepcase • 1 Disc • Region 1 GENRE Adult/Sadism

Inmu: Feast of Victims [Box Set]

NuTech, 2001, 56 mins., #551.

This box set features the two commercially available keepcase editions of *Inmu: Feast of Victims* in a cardboard box. It does not feature any additional extras. See individual entries for the Special and Technical Features listings.

TECHNICAL FEATURES Cardboard Box with 2 Keepcases • 2 Discs • Region 1 GENRE & RATING Adult/Sadism

Inmu 2: The Wandering Flesh Slave

These *Inmu 2: The Wandering Flesh Slave* titles, from NuTech, were not available for review: *Vol. 1—1st and 2nd Nights; Vol. 2—3rd and 4th Nights;* and *Inmu 2: The Wandering Flesh Slave* [Box Set].

Kamyla

These *Kamyla* titles, from NuTech, were not available for review: *Kamyla Vol. 1; Kamyla Vol. 2;* and *Kamyla* [Box Set].

Karakuri Ninja Girl, Book 1: Escaped Ninjas Triple Love

NuTech, 2002, 28 mins., #612. Directed by Sukizo Sabage. Script by Akira Takano. Original story by Ryo Ramiya.

Fawn Bell and Moon Shadow decide that the life of the ninja is not for them, so they leave their clan. But the Ninja Clan—led by Madam Devil Grace—isn't about to let them go so easily. But even Grace isn't prepared for the oddness of the two lovers, and they're soon banished to the city. But then, female ninja Morning Mist arrives, and she wants her ex-girlfriend to return. . . .

Humorous adventure hentai is a rarity, so viewers looking for a lighter side will want to check out *Karakuri.* A grocery store scene is a funny stand-out, and the art looks an awful lot like *Slayers,* with super-deformed elements thrown in. Despite its comedic elements, *Karakuri* still has rape and bondage, as well as lesbianism and pixelated male organs. Adult film stars Alexa Rae and Trisha Uptown lend their voices, and the second side of the disc has numerous trailers.

SPECIAL FEATURES Photo Galleries • Character and Art Galleries • Other Title Trailers TECHNICAL FEATURES Fullscreen (1.33:1) • Subtitles/CC: Eng. • Languages: Jap., Eng. dub • Sound: Dolby Digital 2.0 • Keepcase • 1 Disc • Region 1 GENRE Adult/Martial Arts

Karakuri Ninja Girl, Book 2: Ninja Girl Strikes Back—The Honey Hell

NuTech, 2002, 28 mins., #613. Directed by Sukizo Sabage. Script by Akira Takano. Original story by Ryo Ramiya.

Morning Mist does her best to come between Fawn Bell and Moon Shadow, but will Mist's sacred card help immobilize the object of her lust?

More campy humor in the second volume of Karakuri is supported by the lack of a rape scene. Viewers will get lesbianism and invisible or censored male organs though. The disc also includes another flip side of trailers.

SPECIAL FEATURES Photo Galleries • Character and Art Galleries • Other Title Trailers TECHNICAL FEATURES Fullscreen (1.33:1) • Subtitles/CC: Eng. • Languages: Jap., Eng. dub • Sound: Dolby Digital 2.0 • Keepcase • 1 Disc • Region 1 GENRE Adult/Martial Arts

Karakuri Ninja Girl [Box Set]

NuTech, 2002, 56 mins., #614.

This box set features the two commercially available keepcase editions of *Karakuri Ninja Girl*, in a cardboard box. It does not feature any additional extras. See individual entries for the Special and Technical Features listings.

TECHNICAL FEATURES Cardboard Box with 2 Keepcases • 2 Discs • Region 1 GENRE Adult/Martial Arts

Karen

NuTech, 2002, 25 mins., #674. Directed by Shinichi Shimizu. Screenplay by Dansu Ban.

Ryo thought that being captain of the male cheer squad would be fun, but she soon finds out the nasty side of the game. First she must cheer perfectly while she has a sex toy inserted inside her, then the rugby captain rapes and humiliates her. Then the female cheerleaders rape her. Then the rest of the rugby team rapes her.

Karen is a 2002 OVA that has been quickly shuttled over to the U.S. The animation is clear and strong, with more of the anatomical correctness that is now legally allowed to Japanese hentai artists. The disc is all about humiliation and rape, with group scenes and lesbianism thrown in.

SPECIAL FEATURES Art Galleries • Other Title Trailers TECHNICAL FEATURES Fullscreen (1.33:1) • Subtitles/CC: Eng. • Languages: Jap., Eng. dub • Sound: Dolby Digital 2.0 • Keepcase • 1 Disc • Region 1 GENRE Adult/Sports

Kimera

ADV Films, 2002, 45 mins., #DKM/001. Directed by Hazu Yokota. Screenplay by Henichi Hanemaki. Based on the manga series by Kazuma Kodaka.

NOTE: This DVD arrived too late for a full review. The following text is promotional copy provided by the releasing company:

"For centuries, there have been legends of 'devils' walking the Earth, feeding off the blood of humans. However, the truth behind these vampiric legends has remained a mystery until now. Strange 'lifepods' have crashed in the western mountains, bringing with them supernatural beings previously found only in the realm of folklore and fantasy. Vampires walk the Earth, at war with humanity and each other, driven by the most terrifying of genetic imperatives! Like wasps seeking a spider, they have come to this planet for only one purpose: to perpetuate their species. To save mankind, Kimera must die!"

SPECIAL FEATURES Other Title Trailers TECHNICAL FEATURES Fullscreen (1.33:1) • Subtitles/CC: Eng. • Languages: Jap., Eng. dub • Sound: Dolby Digital • Keepcase • 1 Disc • Region 1 GENRE & RATING Mature/Horror • Rated 17+

Kite: Director's Cut

Kitty, 2002, 51 mins. #KVDVD-0202. Directed by Yasuomi Umezu. Script by Yasuomi Umezu.

Sawa is a young girl whose parents were brutally murdered years ago. Taken in by Akai, the detective assigned to the case, she grows to be his lover and his protégé as the years go by. But behind the scenes, he has trained her to be a cold-blooded assassin, using special exploding bullets to take out those who think they're above the law. But what will happen when little miss vigilante starts showing interest in another boy? And what is the secret that detective Akai never wants her to learn?

With six added minutes of explicit sex scenes that weren't in the general release DVD, this *Kite* is still a bit censored from the 1998 OVA series (because the underage sex elements would not fly with U.S. audiences). However, it does feature immense amounts of blood, gore, and nudity. Unlike the regular version of *Kite*, this disc features no real extras.

SPECIAL FEATURES Other Title Trailers TECHNICAL FEATURES Fullscreen (1.33:1) • Subtitles/CC: Eng. • Languages: Jap., Eng. dub • Sound: Dolby Digital 2.0 • Keepcase • 1 Disc • Region 1 GENRE & RATING Adult/Action/Adventure—Rated 18+

Koihime: Vol. 1—The Love

NuTech, 2001, 29 mins., #565. Directed by Masaki Shinichi. Script by Yoshioka Takao. Original Story by Elf (pseudonym for Masato Hiruda).

When college student Musashi, returns to his Grandmother's village for a vacation, he takes a trip back to his past as well. There, four beautiful girls—Nami, Anzu, Suzaku, and Mayuki—remember him from their childhood, when they had played games together. Musashi and Nami have a wonderful night of sex, but Anzu wants Musashi as well. . . .

Wow! A fully consensual hentai series! Not a bit of rape or demons here, just consensual sex between lovers. The art is only average, tending toward goofy at times.

The series was released in Japan in 2000. The DVD features trailers on side two, and voice work from adult film stars Kobe Tai and Houston.

SPECIAL FEATURES Photos • Art Galleries • Other Title Trailers TECHNICAL FEATURES Fullscreen (1.33:1) • Subtitles/CC: Eng. • Languages: Jap., Eng. dub • Sound: Dolby Digital 2.0 • Keepcase • 1 Disc • Region 1 GENRE Adult/Romance

Koihime: Vol. 2—The Princess

NuTech, 2001, 28 mins., #566. Directed by Masaki Shinichi. Script by Yoshioka Takao. Original Story by Elf (pseudonym for Masato Hiruda).

When Musashi's affairs with Nami and Anzu are discovered, he is in danger. Why are the villagers calling his female friends princesses? And what mystical powers do some of them possess?

More happy, healthy, consensual sex here, with a hint of magical peril thrown into the mix. If there's a complaint, it's that this ends too quickly. The DVD contains more previews on the second side.

SPECIAL FEATURES Photos • Art Galleries • Other Title Trailers TECHNICAL FEATURES Fullscreen (1.33:1) • Subtitles/CC: Eng. • Languages: Jap., Eng. dub • Sound: Dolby Digital 2.0 • Keepcase • 1 Disc • Region 1 GENRE Adult/Romance

Koihime [Box Set]

NuTech, 2001, 57 mins., #567.

This box set features the two commercially available keepcase editions of *Koihime*, in a cardboard box. It does not feature any additional extras. See individual entries for the Special and Technical Features listings.

TECHNICAL FEATURES Cardboard Box with 2 Keepcases • 2 Discs • Region 1 GENRE Adult/Romance

Kokudo Oh: The Black Eye King

These *Kokudo Oh: The Black Eye King* titles, from NuTech, were not available for review: *Kokudo Oh: The Black Eye King Vol. 1*; *Kokudo Oh: The Black Eye King Vol. 2*; *Kokudo Oh: The Black Eye King Vol. 3*; *Kokudo Oh: The Black Eye King Vol. 4*; and *Kokudo Oh: The Black Eye King [Box Set]*.

LA Blue Girl: Vols. 1 and 2

NuTech/Anime18, 1999, 90 mins.

This DVD was not available for review.

LA Blue Girl 1 and 2 [Remastered]

Anime 18, 2002, 90 mins., #A18D-2182.

NOTE: This DVD arrived too late for a full review. The following text is promotional copy provided by the releasing company:

"Sex Ninjas Must Die! Miko Mido answers the call of the wild, to become a mistress of martial arts sexcraft. In these erotic episodes, Miko discovers that she is the last in a line of supernatural sex ninjas. Now, this delectable demon slayer is all that stands between humanity and the perverted hordes of the underworld. It won't be easy—these depraved demons are ready to turn a few tricks of their own. It'll be a whammin', slammin' battle as she thrashes the monsters in carnal combat!"

This disc contains the same episodes as the original release, but these have been remastered for better picture. There is also a new slate of extras. See review for *LA Blue Girl* volumes #3 and #4 for historical information on this series.

SPECIAL FEATURES Interviews with Creators • Character and Art Galleries • Promotional Footage • Manga • Anime Featurette • DVD-ROM Features: Art, Scripts, Manga • Other Title Trailers TECHNICAL FEATURES Fullscreen (1.33:1) • Subtitles/CC: Eng. • Languages: Jap., Eng. dub • Sound: Dolby Digital 2.0 • Keepcase • 1 Disc • Region 1 GENRE & RATING Adult/Supernatural • Rated 18+

LA Blue Girl: Vols. 3 and 4

NuTech/Anime18, 1999, 85 mins., #867. Directed by Kan Fukumoto, Rino Yanagikaze. Script by Megumi Ichiyanagi.

Half-demon girl Miko wants to be a ninja, but when she arrives to train at the secret village of the Miroku clan, she finds it in shambles. Now she must face traitors and demons, track down a special sword, save her father, and more. Even with the help of young ninja girl Yaku, Miko might not be strong enough, especially when one of the villains turns her against her new ally. . . .

This notorious 1992 hentai series was based on ideas by Toshio Maeda, and his brand of necro-eroticism is very much in evidence here. A man is bound and forced into sex, women are bound and raped by demons, tentacles, and mecha-tentacles. And a particularly grotesque sequence features rape with a spiked sex toy. Between the violence and the youthful appearance of the females and their genitalia, it's no wonder this got stopped by British censors and raised eyebrows in the U.S.

The DVD features the "about anime" short, as well as trailers. A "remastered" version has also been released.

SPECIAL FEATURES Anime Featurette • Other Title Trailers TECHNICAL FEATURES Fullscreen (1.33:1) • Subtitles/CC: Eng. • Languages: Jap., Eng. dub • Sound: Dolby Digital 2.0 • Keepcase • 1 Disc • Region All GENRE Adult/Supernatural

LA Blue Girl 3 and 4 [Remastered]

Anime 18, 2002, 90 mins., #A18D-2183.

This disc contains the same episodes as the original release, but these have been remastered for better picture. There is also a new slate of extras.

SPECIAL FEATURES Interviews with Creators • Character and Art Galleries • Promotional Footage • Manga • Anime Featurette • DVD-ROM Features: Art, Scripts, Manga • Other Title Trailers TECHNICAL FEATURES Fullscreen (1.33:1) • Subtitles/CC: Eng. • Languages: Jap., Eng. dub • Sound: Dolby Digital 2.0 • Keepcase • 1 Disc • Region 1 GENRE & RATING Adult/Supernatural • Rated 18+

LA Blue Girl: Vols. 5 and 6

NuTech/Anime 18, 1999, 97 mins., #868. Directed by Kan Fukumoto, Rino Yanagikaze. Script by Megumi Ichiyanagi.

Miko, the half-demon ninja sex-warrior, goes back to school, but she's got a rival in Fubuki Kai. The popular girl is just as tough as Miko, and she wants to know the Miroku clan's secret for getting into the Shikima realm. Then, Miko's attempt to live a normal life are interrupted by frightening dreams . . . and the fact that her classmates—and her mother—are all being abducted by monsters!

Two more OVAs from 1993 wrap up the main portion of this series, though it was followed by live-action films and a sequel series (see entry for *Lady Blue*). It's more of the same, though part 5 has a very grainy transfer, and part 6 has very bright colors. The animation is poor, with little resemblance to reality. There's lesbianism, bondage, demon rape, tentacle rape, and mecha-tentacle rape.

SPECIAL FEATURES Anime Featurette • Other Title Trailers TECHNICAL FEATURES Fullscreen (1.33:1) • Subtitles/CC: Eng. • Languages: Jap., Eng. dub • Sound: Dolby Digital 2.0 • Keepcase • 1 Disc • Region All GENRE Adult/Supernatural

LA Blue Girl 5 and 6 [Remastered]

Anime 18, 2002, 105 mins., #A18D-2194.

This disc contains the same episodes as the original release, but these have been remastered for better picture. There is also a new slate of extras.

SPECIAL FEATURES Interviews with Creators • Character and Art Galleries • Promotional Footage • Manga • Anime Featurette • DVD-ROM Features: Art, Scripts • Other Title Trailers TECHNICAL FEATURES Fullscreen (1.33:1) • Subtitles/CC: Eng. • Languages: Jap., Eng. dub • Sound: Dolby Digital 2.0 • Keepcase • 1 Disc • Region 1 GENRE & RATING Adult/Supernatural • Rated 18+

LA Blue Girl [Box Set]

NuTech/Anime 18, 1999, 273 mins.

This box set contains all three commercially available keepcase editions of *LA Blue Girl*, with no extras.

This DVD set was not available for review.

LA Blue Girl [Remastered Box Set]

Anime 18, 2002, 285 mins.

This box set contains all three commercially available keepcase editions of *LA Blue Girl [Remastered]*, with no extras.

This DVD set was not available for review.

LA Blue Girl Returns: Demon Seed

Anime 18, 2002, 60 mins., #A18D-2152. Directed by Hiroshi Ogawa, Yoshitaka Fujimoto. Script by Megumi Hitotsuyanagi.

NOTE: This DVD arrived too late for a full review. The following text is promotional copy provided by the releasing company:

"A new saga for *LA Blue Girl*! A deadly sex ninja trained in the carnal arts, Miko is hot to deal out heavy martial arts mistreatment to any demon who threatens her. But when the monsters target her sexy sister for a little family fun, Miko really sees red! Who is the stronger sexual slayer, our hedonistic heroine, or the preternatural perverts of the underworld? It's time for Miko to show these supernatural sex fiends who wears the pants in this business . . . no one!"

SPECIAL FEATURES Commentary Track with Creators • Character and Art Galleries • Promotional Footage • Storyboards • Anime Featurette • DVD-ROM Features: Art, Scripts • Other Title Trailers TECHNICAL FEATURES Fullscreen (1.33:1) • Subtitles/CC: Eng. • Languages: Jap., Eng. dub • Sound: Dolby

Digital 2.0 • Keepcase • 1 Disc • Region 1 GENRE & RATING Adult/Supernatural • Rated 18+

Lady Blue

Anime 18, 2001, 120 mins., #A18D-1835. Directed by Kan Fukumoto. Screenplay by Megumi Ichiryu. Original story by Toshio Maeda.

Miko Mido is back, and she's in college. There, she meets Hidemasa, the man of her dreams! But Fubuki Kai is jealous, and secrets about Hidemasa's family begin to emerge. What could antique flutes have to do with 400-year-old demonic alliances, crossbred marriages, and clan warlords? And what curses will the playing of the flutes bring in modern times?

This four-part OVA sequel from 1996 is a bit more story-driven than its predecessor, though it's just as nasty in its depictions of sexuality. The animation is a bit better than earlier volumes of *LA Blue Girl*, though it is goofy at times, and styles often clash. For those keeping track, it features lesbianism, demon rape, tentacle rape, and even vampires! Oddly, it also features lots of flute music.

The DVD is well produced and includes more extras than almost any other adult release.

SPECIAL FEATURES Creator Bio • Anime Featurette • Character Bios • Character and Art Galleries • Production Notes • Deleted Scenes • Storyboards • Trailers • DVD-ROM Features: Art, Scripts • Other Title Trailers TECHNICAL FEATURES Fullscreen (1.33:1) • Subtitles/CC: Eng. • Languages: Jap., Eng. dub • Sound: Dolby Digital 2.0 • Keepcase • 1 Disc • Region 1 GENRE Adult/Supernatural

Leatherman

These *Leatherman* titles, from NuTech, were not available for review: *Leatherman: Vol. 1*; *Leatherman: Vol. 2*; and *Leatherman* [Box Set].

Lesson of Darkness

Kitty, 2002, 45 mins., #KVDVD-0215. Directed by Tsutomu Yabuki. Screenplay by Goro Shiraoka.

In 1920's-era Tokyo, beautiful women are found dead, their bodies turned into lifeless husks. College girl Miho has felt like she's being stalked ever since she got a blue stone that might have magical powers. Her friend, Azusa, seduces a professor, but he soon reveals that he's a tentacle demon! What do a black cat and a mysterious boy have to do with it all?

Marginally more stylish than most demon hentai, this 1996 production is often moody, with muted colors predominating. There's demon rape and tentacle rape, and even a hint of demon romance.

SPECIAL FEATURES Other Title Trailers TECHNICAL FEATURES Fullscreen (1.33:1) • Subtitles/CC: Eng. • Languages: Jap., Eng. dub • Sound: Dolby Digital 2.0 • Keepcase • 1 Disc • Region 1–6 GENRE & RATING Adult/Supernatural • Rated 18+

Love Lessons

Anime 18, 2002, 60 mins., #A18D-2192. Directed by Makoto Fujiaki. Screenplay by Reiji Izumo.

NOTE: This DVD arrived too late for a full review. The following text is promotional copy provided by the releasing company:

"What's your fantasy? For a price, the Trainer will shape any woman into the culmination of your most erotic fantasies. Watch the parade of beautiful females that come to him to be transformed into the ultimate object of desire. Naughty, nice, playful, or passionate, each one is eager to please, and hand-tailored to fit your needs!"

SPECIAL FEATURES Character and Art Galleries • Clean Credits • Promotional Footage • Anime Featurette • DVD-ROM Features: Art, Scripts • Other Title Trailers TECHNICAL FEATURES Fullscreen (1.33:1) • Subtitles/CC: Eng. • Languages: Jap., Eng. dub • Sound: Dolby Digital 2.0 • Keepcase • 1 Disc • Region All GENRE & RATING Adult/Fetish • Rated 18+

Luv Wave

These *Luv Wave* titles, from NuTech, were not available for review: *Luv Wave: Vol. 1*; *Luv Wave: Vol. 2*; and *Luv Wave* [Box Set].

Magic Woman M

Anime 18, 2002, 58 mins., #A18D-1876. Directed by Minekazu Hirade. Script by Hakase Ishii. Based on the manga series by Pong Nekoshita in *Monthly Fantazine*.

Meruru is a sexy young sorceress who has a secret power; at her moment of climax, her powers are at their greatest! When she gets lost in the woods, she meets ogres, fish-men, and other creepy beasts, but she must let them have their way with her to defeat them.

A two-part 1996 OVA series, *Magic Woman M* is filled with cutesy character designs that make it look like a kid's show, but it's anything but. There's bondage, lesbianism, tentacles, and the aforementioned monsters—but whether the sexual encounters are technically rape is in question given Meruru's need for power. Several extras make this DVD a bit more fun, though the advertised "character commentary" is more annoying than amusing.

SPECIAL FEATURES Joke Commentary • Character Bios • Character and Art Galleries • Character and Spell Intro Clips • Anime Featurette • DVD-ROM Features: Art, Scripts • Other Title Trailers TECHNICAL FEATURES Fullscreen (1.33:1) • Subtitles/CC: Eng. • Languages: Jap., Eng. dub • Sound: Dolby Digital 2.0 • Keepcase • 1 Disc • Region All GENRE & RATING Adult/Supernatural • Rated 18+

Maiden Diaries, The

Kitty, 2001, 120 mins., #KVDVD-0128. Directed by Hideki Takayama. Script by Oyasudo, Naoki Tsuruoka.

Foster has a secret past—was he a revolutionary, a secret service agent, or something else?—but his present is filled with women and sex . . . and submission. Foster has been hired by ultrarich railroad tycoon Dred Burton to "train" young women to be properly subservient, submissive, and open to all forms of abuse. Foster tries to fight his attraction to Clair, even as he dallies with the rest of the women in the household. But what purpose does the training and torture really serve?

This 1998 OVA series is an odd throwback to secret societies of old England, the type alluded to in Stanley Kubrick's *Eyes Wide Shut*. With realistic, attractive art, this series includes bondage, torture, rape, lesbianism, and lots of maid outfits. There are reportedly five parts to the *Maiden* series, but the second of them has apparently been excised; the four parts on this DVD are "Maiden of Desire"; "Maiden of Decadence"; "Maiden of Deception"; and "Maiden of Destruction."

SPECIAL FEATURES Other Title Trailers TECHNICAL FEATURES Fullscreen (1.33:1) • Subtitles/CC: Eng. • Languages: Jap., Eng. dub • Sound: Dolby Digital 2.0 • Keepcase • 1 Disc • Region 1 GENRE & RATING Adult/Fetish • Rated 18+

Mail Order Maiden 28: The Dutch Wife

Critical Mass, 2001, 39 mins., #CMDVD6931. Directed by Hiroshi Midoriyama. Script by Hogara Hatta. Based on the manga series by U-Jin.

Aiwa is a hopeless nerd, completely unable to attract the attentions of his dream girl, Kozue. An unexpected delivery results in a big surprise, as Aiwa soon finds himself sharing his apartment with Satomi, a blow-up doll who's a lot more high-tech than he was expecting. Satomi is blonde, buxom, intelligent, and just as sex-starved as Aiwa himself—it sounds like a dream come true. But Aiwa may not be able to satisfy Satomi's constant demands, and

how can he ever score with Kozue if Satomi is following him around?

Mail Order Maiden 28 seems like a promising sex comedy at first glance, but as is so common in hentai anime, it's dragged down by extremely shoddy animation and character artwork. Aficionados of the genre will be happy to note that *Mail Order Maiden 28* is uncensored, but there really isn't very much to look at anyway. The DVD is solid enough, but also quite unexceptional. Along with the requisite woodenly acted English dub, the only extra is a photo gallery. Video and audio quality are adequate, but nothing more. [MT]

SPECIAL FEATURES Art Galleries TECHNICAL FEATURES Fullscreen (1.33:1) • Subtitles/CC: Eng. • Languages: Jap., Eng. dub • Sound: Dolby Digital Surround 3.0 • Keepcase • 1 Disc • Region All GENRE Adult/Comedy

Masquerade

Anime 18, 2002, 120 mins., #A18D-2078. Directed by Yusuke Yamamoto. Written by Ryota Yamaguchi.

NOTE: This DVD arrived too late for a full review. The following text is promotional copy provided by the releasing company:

"Gen hungers for sexy women, but every time he gets near them he transforms into a monster! Luckily, he's met a sexy scientist who's extremely interested in his condition. And she wants to starts a more aggressive, hands-on investigation! Can beauty tame this savage beast?"

This disc contains both OVAs.

SPECIAL FEATURES Character Bios • Character and Art Galleries • Storyboards • Anime Featurette • DVD-ROM Features: Art, Scripts, Storyboards • Other Title Trailers TECHNICAL FEATURES Fullscreen (1.33:1) • Subtitles/CC: Eng. • Languages: Jap., Eng. dub • Sound: Dolby Digital • Keepcase • 1 Disc • Region All GENRE & RATING Adult/Horror • Rated 18+

MeiKing [Vanilla Series, Vol. 2]

Critical Mass, 2002, 120 mins., #CMDVD6981. Animation Directed by Hideo Okazaki. Screenplay by Rokurota Marabe. Story by Nikukyuu.

When a young shepherd named Cain Asbell follows a sheep into a cave, he finds a fairy named Elise trapped there. He helps her, and she sends him to rescue Princess Charlotte. Cain is now a Lord of Norland with a shot at a magnificent future; if he makes his country the most prosperous in five years, he'll be able to marry Charlotte and become a rich king! Along the path to riches, Cain encounters bandits and slavers, as well as a bevy of beautiful women—including a tough warrior woman who'll do anything he wants. . . .

A part of the 1999 *Vanilla Series* anthology, *MeiKing* is set in a neo-medieval kingdom and features ultrastylized cartoony art and vibrant colors. There's lesbianism, bondage, and rape, but nary a demon in sight! There are lots of elves though.

SPECIAL FEATURES Art Galleries TECHNICAL FEATURES Fullscreen (1.33:1) • Subtitles/CC: Eng. • Languages: Jap., Eng. dub • Sound: Dolby Digital • Keepcase • 1 Disc • Region 1 GENRE Adult/Fantasy

Mezzo Forte [Uncut]

Kitty, 2001, 60 mins., #KVDVD-0131. Directed by Yasuomi Umezu. Script by Yasuomi Umezu.

This DVD is identical to the "mainstream" edition of *Mezzo Forte* detailed elsewhere in this book, save for one important distinction: this version contains a pair of extremely steamy, uncensored sex scenes. Judging by the construction of *Mezzo Forte*'s story, it appears that the show was deliberately produced with both a "mainstream" and this "uncut" version in mind—the sex scenes don't actually have any effect on the story. Otherwise, the DVD presentation of this two-part OVA series is identical to the regular release. [MT]

SPECIAL FEATURES Interview with Director • Storyboards • Other Title Trailers • Easter Egg TECHNICAL FEATURES Fullscreen (1.33:1) • Subtitles/CC: Eng. • Languages: Jap., Eng. dub • Sound: Dolby Digital 2.0 • Keepcase • 1 Disc • Region 1 GENRE & RATING Adult/Action • Rated 18+

Midnight Panther

Anime 18, 1999, 60 mins., #A18D-1858. Directed by Morino Yosei. Script by Morino Yosei. Based on the manga series by Yu Asagiri.

The Pussycats are a musical group who have a secret: they may be great singers, but Lou, Kei, and Sonya are also assassins! Kei can transform into a panther, while Lou has incredible strength and skills, and Sonya can seduce anyone and kill them in the throes of passion. But when the Pussycats take on the job of killing an evil king, Lou rediscovers secrets of her past that are long forgotten. This time, the murder has very personal overtones, and could change Lou's personal fortunes forever!

If the story seems oddly complex and missing elements, that's because this two-part 1988 OVA series is based on an extensive manga series. Compressed here with very few of the manga elements, *Midnight Panther*

will likely confuse many viewers. The art is ultragoofy, though the DVD picture is extraordinarily crisp. There isn't a huge amount of sex, though there is nudity and violence.

SPECIAL FEATURES Character Clips • Anime Featurette • Other Title Trailers TECHNICAL FEATURES Fullscreen (1.33:1) • Subtitles/CC: Eng. • Languages: Jap., Eng. dub • Sound: Dolby Digital 2.0 • Keepcase • 1 Disc • Region All GENRE & RATING Adult/Fantasy • Rated 18+

Mija: Beautiful Demon

NuTech, 2002, 28 mins., #675. Directed by Jun Fukuda. Original story by Saki Hosen.

Exiled lust demon Mija has come to St. Moses Academy, where she sets about bringing the lusts and carnality to the surface of everyone there. She's most interested in the female student Mayu, whom she seduces. But opposing Mija are subsitute teacher Sara Tadeshina (who's really an undercover religious agent) and Mayu's admirer, Kotaro. Will they be able to rescue Mayu from Mija's lustful advances before it's too late?

Average from beginning to end, *Mija* wasn't popular enough with Japanese audiences to warrant further OVA releases, though it's clearly set up for sequels. There's lesbianism, female and male bondage, and demon rape. The DVD is double-sided, with previews of other series on the back.

SPECIAL FEATURES Character and Art Galleries • Other Title Trailers TECHNICAL FEATURES Fullscreen (1.33:1) • Subtitles/CC: Eng. • Languages: Jap., Eng. dub • Sound: Dolby Digital 2.0 • Keepcase • 1 Disc • Region All GENRE Adult/Supernatural

Mission of Darkness

NuTech, 2001, 43 mins., #557. Directed by Kikumoto Futoshi. Script by Shunpei Narai.

A spaceship that looks a lot like a male organ approaches Earth, and soon, a strange meteorite hits the planet. Now, women all over Japan are being murdered by a tentacle, their corpses containing alien semen. The government decides to use prostitutes as "artificial hormone scatter" to lure the murderous alien monster into a trap, whereupon all the soldiers get horny and begin to have sex. Then, Venus arrives to save the day.

Sigh. This 1997 OVA is pretty much an insult to the intelligence of even the lowest knuckle-dragger. As if the giant alien beast resembling parts of the female anatomy wasn't offensive enough, there's a huge amount of demon and tentacle rape. There's also lackluster low-budget art, lack of any interesting characters, and a script that would embarrass Roger Corman. Adult film star Nicole Sheridan shows she has no shame by voicing the character of Venus. The DVD is double-sided, with previews.

SPECIAL FEATURES Photo Galleries • Character and Art Galleries • Other Title Trailers TECHNICAL FEATURES Fullscreen (1.33:1) • Subtitles/CC: Eng. • Languages: Jap., Eng. dub • Sound: Dolby Digital 2.0 • Keepcase • 1 Disc • Region 1 GENRE Adult/Science Fiction

My Life As . . . Stage 1: A Chicken

NuTech, 2002, 34 mins., #659. Directed by Akebi Haruno. Story by Hirogari Sue. Screenplay by Ippei Taira. Based on the manga series in *My Life As*.

Yasunari ran away from home six months ago, and found the perfect home life. He's kept as the sexual pet of Fumi and Rino, two girls who engage in group sex and SM with him and his female friend, Chie. Yasunari writes about his adventures in a magazine, which is found by his brother, Tomoyasu. Upset to find out that his missing brother is living a fulfilling sexual life, Tomoyasu forces himself on his tutor Serina, unaware that she's friends with Yasunari's mistresses!

Given that almost all of the characters—boys and girls—look underage, this series is one step up from kiddie porn. The sex is consensual and there is lesbianism, but most viewers are likely to be creeped out by the cutesy prepubescent character designs. Adult film stars Brittany Andrews and Aurora Snow provide some of the voices, and the DVD has preview trailers on the flip side.

SPECIAL FEATURES Photo Galleries • Character and Art Galleries • Other Title Trailers TECHNICAL FEATURES Fullscreen (1.33:1) • Subtitles/CC: Eng. • Languages: Jap., Eng. dub • Sound: Dolby Digital 2.0 • Keepcase • 1 Disc • Region All GENRE Adult/Comedy

My My Mai

U.S. Manga Corps, 2002, 86 mins., #USMD 1892. Directed by Osamu Sekita. Based on the manga series by Masakazu Yamaguchi in *Shonen Champion Comics*.

Mai runs a strange consulting service that deals with psychic problems, medical or supernatural issues, and more. First she helps find a doctor to operate on a sick girl, only to discover that the dashing Count who helps her has another personality that may "operate" on a different vibe. She also helps out a rock star who's got some odd phobias, goes

to the beach, and helps out with a case of exorcism and demonic possession.

The cute art designs are very cheesecake-oriented, and although there are few direct sexual actions, there are a lot of bust shots, panty shots, and female nudity. This four-part 1993 OVA series also features some creepy stuff, really disgusting old people, and some material that might offend Christians.

SPECIAL FEATURES Character Bios • Character and Art Galleries • Live Action Closing Credits • DVD-ROM Features: Art, Scripts • Other Title Trailers TECHNICAL FEATURES Fullscreen (1.33:1) • Subtitles/CC: Eng. • Languages: Jap., Eng. dub • Sound: Dolby Digital 2.0 • Keepcase • 1 Disc • Region All GENRE & RATING Mature/Cheesecake/Comedy • Rated 16+

Mystery of the Necronomicon

Anime 18, 2001, 128 mins., #A18D-2043. Directed by Hideki Takayama. Screenplay by Ryo Saga. Original story by Abogado Powers.

While Satoshi, a private detective, and his daughter, Asuka, are staying at a winter ski resort, someone is murdered, their skin ripped off and eyeballs removed! Satoshi is soon investigating the crimes, but he's hampered by the lack of contact with the outer world . . . at first. Slowly, a plot unravels, revealing hints of the secret of immortality, a mad scientist's plans, and the ancient evil tome, the book known as the *Necronomicon*!

Based on a computer game, this four-part 1999 OVA series has quite a bit of plot, but some viewers may feel there is too much back story; Satoshi's past is linked to his motivations and actions, but it's never clearly explained how or why. The art is attractive (if grainy), and as each character appears, their name is subtitled onscreen. However, as you'll see from the blood-soaked DVD menu, this series is a gorefest. While there is sex, including lesbianism, bondage, and blackmail rape, it's the floor-to-ceiling gore that is more shocking. Funny that the producers censor the male organs in the early episodes, and yet they feature dismembered eyes, nude bodies covered in blood, zombies, and other grisly stuff. Gotta love those double standards.

SPECIAL FEATURES Character Bios • Character and Art Galleries • Anime Featurette • Storyboards • DVD-ROM Features: Art, Scripts • Other Title Trailers TECHNICAL FEATURES Fullscreen (1.33:1) • Subtitles/CC: Eng. • Languages: Jap., Eng. dub • Sound: Dolby Digital 2.0 • Keepcase • 1 Disc • Region All GENRE & RATING Adult/Horror • Rated 18+

New Cutey Honey: Collection One

ADV Films, 2000, 115 mins. #DC/001. Directed by Yasuchika Nagaoha. Screenplay by Isao Shizuya. Based on the original manga characters created by Go Nagai in *Shonen Champion*.

In the '70s, Cutey Honey was a fantastic battle android who helped stop a bunch of bullies called Panther Claw and their leader, a dark goddess named Panther Zora from taking over the city. Now, twenty years later, she's forgotten her role as hero and is the secretary of Cosplay City's Mayor Light. When Panther Zora uses her powers in a bid to return to the world by possessing third-rate criminals, it's up to Cutey Honey to save the city—if she can remember she's a hero. Aided by Danbei and his grandson Chokkei, Cutey Honey is able to recall her past and join the fight again. With her trademarked "Honey Flash!" she rips out of her clothes and transforms from secretary into a powerful fighting machine ready and willing to take on all of Panther Zora's minions. Each of Cutey Honey's transforming chassis outfits comes equipped with weapons, tricks, and unique tools ready for battle, but will it be enough to fight demons, killer dolls, and other nasties?

Cutey Honey began life as a popular manga series in the 1970s by Go Nagai. From there it became a weekly anime series in 1973 that lasted twenty-five episodes. *Honey* disappeared for a while until she was resurrected in 1994 as *New Cutey Honey*, which spawned eight OVAs. The character designs are updated, and an all-new set of sidekicks and ancillary characters has been added.

This *New Cutey Honey* DVD contains the first four OVAs from 1994. It features nudity, violence, and adult situations. One of the coolest extras in the *Cutey Honey* DVDs are the animated phone messages. You too can have a greeting on your home answering machine from Cutey. [JMC]

SPECIAL FEATURES Character and Art Galleries • Promotional Footage • Phone Messages TECHNICAL FEATURES Fullscreen (1.33:1) • Subtitles/CC: Eng. • Languages: Jap., Eng. dub • Sound: Dolby Digital 2.0 • Keepcase • 1 Disc • Region 1 GENRE & RATING Mature/Action • Rated 17+

New Cutey Honey: Collection Two

ADV Films, 2001, 115 mins. #DC/002. Directed by Yasuchika Nagaoha. Screenplay by Isao Shizuya. Based on the original manga characters created by Go Nagai in *Shonen Champion*.

Fighting enemies with more tricks up their sleeves than a coven of wizards at a magician's convention seems to be the theme of this explosive collection. Now that Cutey Honey has defeated the evil Dolmek, all kinds of criminals are crawling out of the woodwork to become the new crimelord of Cosplay City. First a gang holds the city ransom with a terrible bomb that could erase the metropolis from the map. Next Honey is trapped by an army of zombie mannequins. Can she outsmart the dummies and prevent them from taking over Cosplay City? Next she faces a foe who can literally disappear into thin air, with nothing up his sleeve, or anywhere else for that matter!

This sleight-of-hand DVD contains the last four OVAs from 1995, which feature nudity, violence, and adult situations. [JMC]

SPECIAL FEATURES Interview with Actresses • Trailer • Promotional Footage • Music Video: Concert, Recording Session • Other Title Trailers TECHNICAL FEATURES Fullscreen (1.33:1) • Subtitles/CC: Eng. • Languages: Jap., Eng. dub • Sound: Dolby Digital 2.0 • Keepcase • 1 Disc • Region 1 GENRE & RATING Mature/Action • Rated 17+

Night Shift Nurses

Anime 18, 2002, 70 mins., #A18D-2165. Directed by Nao Okezawa. Screenplay by Ryo Saga.

NOTE: This DVD arrived too late for a full review. The following text is promotional copy provided by the releasing company:

"Open wide and say 'Ahhh.' The doctor is in! A new doctor has arrived to whip the hospital's nursing staff into shape. His lesson plan is strict, and he has no tolerance for failure, which is met with the harshest punishments imaginable. The Night Shift Nurses must learn their lessons well if they hope to please their new master—whenever and wherever he wants!"

SPECIAL FEATURES Character and Art Galleries • Trailer • Promotional Footage • Anime Featurette • DVD-ROM Features: Art, Scripts • Other Title Trailers TECHNICAL FEATURES Fullscreen (1.33:1) • Subtitles/CC: Eng. • Languages: Jap., Eng. dub • Sound: Dolby Digital 2.0 • Keepcase • 1 Disc • Region All GENRE & RATING Adult/Medical/Fetish • Rated 18+

Nightmare Campus: A Total Nightmare

Anime 18, 2000, 200 mins., #A18D-1879. Directed by Koji Yoshikawa. Screenplay by Koji Yoshikawa. Original story by Toshio Maeda.

When the ancient seal of the gods is opened, demons will return to Earth. So intones the prophecy that starts this story. Masao is a young boy whose father was a demonic creature who killed his mother while at an archeological dig. Now, he's grown up and gone to college, but he and his best friend are both demonic themselves. The school and its students are soon caught between seemingly angelic creatures who really want to harm them, and the demonic students who might save them. Along the way, lots of people transform into demons and monsters, and the school martial arts club gains superpowers to fight the evil creatures.

This five-part 1995–96 OVA series is created by Toshio Maeda, and it contains all the gruesome hall marks of his productions. There's human rape, demon rape, tentacle rape, male bondage, lesbianism, and lots of gore. The art designs are all over the place, which sometimes looks cool—like a cross between *Batman: The Animated Series* and *Lupin III*—but at other times looks bizarre, cheap, or goofy.

The DVD has a cool yearbook feature with morphing faces (from human to demon), but its functions make it impossible to tell which picture you're on, or how to get off the page. The story's supposed to be a nightmare, not the DVD functions!

SPECIAL FEATURES Morphing Yearbook • Character and Art Galleries • Anime Featurette • Trailers • DVD-ROM Features: Art, Scripts • Other Title Trailers TECHNICAL FEATURES Fullscreen (1.33:1) • Subtitles/CC: Eng. • Languages: Jap., Eng. dub • Sound: Dolby Digital 2.0 • Keepcase • 1 Disc • Region All GENRE & RATING Adult/Supernatural • Rated 18+

Nine Lives of Fritz the Cat, The

MGM/UA, 2001, 77 mins., #1002735. Directed by Robert Taylor. Written by Robert Taylor, Fred Halliday, Eric Monte. Based on the comic books and characters of Robert Crumb.

Out of college, Fritz now has a bitchy wife who harps on him constantly about being high and everything else, while his infant son causes his own brands of parental trauma. Fritz tokes some "catnip" to induce a psychedelic haze, and his astral self/soul goes out into the streets to live his other eight lives. Over the course of those lives, he psychoanalyzes a naked Adolf Hitler, dances through old newsreel clips, goes into space on a rocket, deals with racial strife with black crows, meets God in a very unlikely form, goes to Hell, and is eventually kicked out of the house by his wife, whereupon he decides that living on the streets is better.

Released in 1974, this film was completed without the involvement of either creator Robert Crumb or *Fritz the Cat*'s writer/director Ralph Bakshi. Made with a budget of $1.5 million, the film skirted much of the sexual nature of its predecessor (see entry) to gain an R rating, though jokes about Hitler and African-Americans are likely to offend, as is the rampant anti-female sexism. The director reportedly scrapped over a thousand feet of footage to add in more topical humor about Watergate, Vietnam, and the energy crisis, but he would have been better served to scrap the whole script and write something less awful. The film has the distinction of being the first animated film to compete at Cannes. Interestingly enough, the concept of Lucifer as a gay purple demon may have (unwittingly?) been the inspiration for *South Park*'s gay Satan.

SPECIAL FEATURES Trailer TECHNICAL FEATURES Widescreen (1.85:1 enhanced for 16x9) • Subtitles/CC: Eng., Fren., Span. • Languages: Eng. • Sound: Dolby Digital 2.0 • Keepcase • 1 Disc • Region 1 GENRE & RATING Mature/Satire/Animals • Rated R

Nine O'Clock Woman

Kitty, 2002, 58 mins., #KVDVD-0203. Directed by Yoshio Shirokuro. Screenplay by Reiji Izumo. Based on the manga series by Akira Goto in *Core Magazine Ururu!*.

Miki Katsuragi is the anchorwoman for the nine o'clock news, and she's got a reputation to uphold. Too bad she's a chronic masturbator! When her cue-card holder catches her using a vibrator while she's on the air, he soon blackmails her into being his sex slave. And wait until she's forced to wear remote-controlled vibrating panties while delivering the news!

Hentai doesn't get much sillier than *Nine O'Clock Woman*, even though it's presented as a drama. The art is average, but uses lots of muted pastel colors, creating a pleasing palette. Unfortunately, there's lots of repeated art, so some viewers will feel cheated. Although the back cover notes rape, most of the sex is fairly consensual (even if blackmailed) and there is a lot of sex toy usage. Viewers may be frustrated that the series appears to be continued, but no further releases have appeared.

SPECIAL FEATURES Other Title Trailers TECHNICAL FEATURES Fullscreen (1.33:1) • Subtitles/CC: Eng. • Languages: Jap., Eng. dub • Sound: Dolby Digital 2.0 • Keepcase • 1 Disc • Region 1 GENRE & RATING Adult/Drama • Rated 18+

MATURE/ADULT MATURE/ADULT MATURE/ADULT

Ninja Resurrection

ADV Films, 1999, 80 mins., #DVDNR/001. Directed by Yasunori Urata. Script by Kensei Date. Inspired by the novels of Futaro Yamada.

In the 17th century, Christians are being persecuted in Japan. The Tokugawa Shogunate bans the religion and begins to kill its believers. Those who escape death put their faith in an ancient prophecy about the Son of God returning to save them from their enemies. During this terrible time, a small child is shot in the chest and survives thanks to a metal cross he was wearing. The Christians proclaim the boy, Tokisada Shiro Amakusa, the son of God. However there is a dark side to the prophecy. If Amakusa doesn't become the leader to heaven, he will fall and become the leader to Hell. Soon he's amassed a group of followers, which angers the Shogunate. The Shogunate hires Jubei Yagyu, a ninja skilled in stealth, weapons, and fighting, to assassinate Amakusa before his influence spreads further.

You could spend half this movie's running time on fast forward and still get the gist of this long, drawn-out story. The Christian persecution in the 1600s is well known, but this telling of events leaves a lot to be desired—even for an anime.

Contrary to popular belief, this two-part 1997 OVA has nothing to do with the *Ninja Scroll* saga other than having a ninja named Jubei in it. It's an average story, with an above average amount of blood, guts, and sexual acts. If you're easily offended this is definitely not the anime for you. [JMC]

SPECIAL FEATURES Character and Art Galleries TECHNICAL FEATURES Fullscreen (1.33:1) • Subtitles/CC: Eng. • Languages: Jap., Eng. dub • Sound: Dolby Digital 2.0 • Keepcase • 1 Disc • Region 1–6 GENRE & RATING Mature/Martial Arts/Action • Rated 17+

Ogenki Clinic Adventures

Anime 18, 2000, 90 mins., #A18D-1872. Directed by Takashi Watanabe. Based on the manga series by Haruka Inui in *Play Comic*.

Dr. Ogenki runs a clinic for people with sexual problems, and he's ably aided by his buxom, scantily clad assistant, Nurse Ruko. Much wackiness ensues, with talking penises, enormous breasts, and more. One segment features a man who has "hero costume syndrome," in which he must dress up like a Batman-style hero to have sex.

Released in 1991 as a series of OVAs, *Ogenki Clinic* has completely unattractive super-deformed art, and pix-

elates some of the crotches. There's lots of fetish gear, lesbianism, bondage, and basketball-breasts. I guess some people will find this funny, but even the most permissive audiences will likely roll their eyes at the gratuitous stupidity. The DVD transfer is fine, but there is no Japanese-language track.

SPECIAL FEATURES Anime Featurette • Trailer • DVD-ROM Features: Art, Scripts, Manga • Other Title Trailers TECHNICAL FEATURES Fullscreen (1.33:1) • Subtitles/CC: Eng. • Languages: Eng. dub • Sound: Dolby Digital 2.0 • Keepcase • 1 Disc • Region All GENRE & RATING Adult/Comedy • Rated 18+

Oni Tensei: The Demon Collection

Kitty, 2002, 120 mins., #KDVD-0217. Directed by Nobuhiro Kondo. Written by Ryota Yamaguchi. Based on the manga series by Ryota Yamaguchi.

An ancient legend says that if a tattoo is drawn perfectly, it will come to life. Ema Nozomi is a girl with a tattoo of a demon on her back, but is it turning her into the demon, or allowing it to come out of another realm? Ema comes to the attention of police detective Reiko Kure when she's the only survivor of a massacre of thirteen mafia members. Reiko takes Ema to a nunnery, but the demon rapes the nun. Who is the strange tattooed man who seems to be after Ema, and is there another woman like her?

This four-part 2000 OVA series is really twisted. Above-average animation showcases bondage, human rape, demon rape, heavy gore, forced tattooing, a graphic castration, sex with a gun involved, and more. The rape of the nun and some other scenes are likely to offend religious types, but they're unlikely to watch this anyhow, right? It all ends sweetly with a lesbian kiss. The DVD features an absolutely stunning cover, with gorgeous, vibrant colors.

special features Other Title Trailers technical features Fullscreen (1.33:1) • Subtitles/CC: Eng. • Languages: Jap., Eng. dub • Sound: Dolby Digital 2.0 • Keepcase • 1 Disc • Region 1 genre & rating Adult/Supernatural • Rated 18+

Parade Parade

Kitty, 2002, 60 mins., #KDVD-0222. Animation directed by Toshimitsu Kobayashi. Screenplay by Hideyuki Kurata. Based on the manga series by Satoshi Akifuji in *Fujimi Publication*.

Kaori is an ultra popular "idol" singer, but she's hiding a secret that could destroy her . . . and only her manager Yuko knows the truth: Kaori is a hermaphroditic "she-male," with sexual characteristics of both a man and a woman! As she finishes a tour, Kaori meets her biggest fan, a lesbian named Saki. Soon, Kaori, Yuko, and Saki are involved in sexual misadventures.

Released in 1996 as two OVAs, *Parade Parade* is one of the few "she-male" (not true transsexualism) hentai titles on the market. The art is average, with a color palette of pastels, occasionally intruded upon by bright colors. There's lesbianism, fetish scenes, and a gang rape.

SPECIAL FEATURES Other Title Trailers TECHNICAL FEATURES Fullscreen (1.33:1) • Subtitles/CC: Eng. • Languages: Jap., Eng. dub • Sound: Dolby Digital 2.0 • Keepcase • 1 Disc • Region 1 GENRE & RATING Adult/Music • Rated 18+

Perfect Blue

Manga Entertainment, 2000, 81 mins., #MANG4049-2. Directed by Satoshi Kon. Screenplay by Sadayuki Murai. Based on the novel by Yoshikazu Takeuchi.

Perfect Blue follows the travails of Mima Kirigoe as she decides to give up the music business for an acting career. Mima is one-third of Cham, a pop music group of teenage girls just reaching its peak of popularity. Suffering from years of isolation as a pop star, Mima is haunted by obsessed fans, manipulative managers, and a web site that catalogues her every move in disturbing detail as she struggles to cope with the pressures of proving herself as a rookie actress on a gritty television drama. When the young girl sheds her innocent image to act out a rape scene, it marks her symbolic exit from pop stardom and her arrival as an actress. But the scripts start to parallel life, and people surrounding Mima start mysteriously dying. Reality, drama, flashback, and hallucination become difficult to distinguish as Mima increasingly encounters her own accusing image dressed in her old pop star costume. As *Perfect Blue* builds to a frightening, feverish peak of murder, paranoia, and terror, Mima must fight to maintain her sanity and escape those who want her dead.

A 1997 theatrical release with scattered U.S. screenings, *Perfect Blue* is a gripping psychological thriller that skillfully combines penetrating narrative, multiple levels of reality, and a pointed admonition about Japanese pop idol culture. While Mima's world dissolves around her, a haunting musical score and polished animation add to the enthralling package.

This disc features several extras, including a set of still images from the movie; a short film of Cham's Japanese voice actors in the studio performing the group's pop anthem; and interviews with voice actors and the film's director. Nudity, adult language, and graphic violence make this film one to keep away from the kids (unless you want to give them nightmares). [BR]

SPECIAL FEATURES Interview with Director and Actresses (Japanese and American) • Character and Art Galleries • Music Videos: Recording Session • Trailer • Other Title Trailers TECH

NICAL FEATURES Fullscreen (1.33:1) • Subtitles/CC: Eng. • Languages: Jap., Eng. dub • Sound: Dolby Digital 2.0 • Keepcase • 1 Disc • Region 1 GENRE Mature/Suspense

Pet Shop of Horrors: Special Edition

Urban Vision, 2001, 95 mins., #UV1067. Directed by Toshio Hirata. Screenplay by Yasuhiro Imagawa. Based on the manga series by Mari (Matsuri) Akino in *Mitzi Comics DX*.

A mysterious exotic pet shop in Chinatown has attracted the attention of homicide detective Leon. At the shop, he encounters the proprietor, the bizarre Count D. The Count is more than willing to explain all of the mysterious occurrences regarding the shop's customers—but as Leon hears each tale of woe, betrayal, and horror, he finds himself wondering if the strange pet shop is really the guilty party.

The plot outlined above is really just a framing device for four separate, stand-alone stories ("Daughter"; "Delicious"; "Despair"; and "Duel"). Each tale is unusually slick-looking and well directed, because it has to be; *Pet Shop of Horrors* originally ran on Japanese television in five-minute segments, making good production and tight storytelling an absolute necessity. The end result is a surprisingly absorbing and compelling set of horror stories, each using the familiar "Monkey's Paw" tale as a central theme—wonderful things happen to the pet shop's clientele, but in the end they bring tragedy upon themselves. Japanese animation doesn't have many strong horror titles, which makes this one a standout.

One unusual extra on the DVD is a commentary track by the dub director and lead actors. This makes the disc a lot more interesting, as the performers elaborate on the process of creating an English version of the show. The series includes moments of extreme violence, and some minor nudity. [MT]

SPECIAL FEATURES Commentary Track by English Director and Cast • Deleted Scenes • Trailer • Other Title Trailers • Inserts: Liner Notes TECHNICAL FEATURES Fullscreen (1.33:1) • Subtitles/CC: Eng. • Languages: Jap., Eng. dub • Sound: Dolby Digital 5.1 • Keepcase • 1 Disc • Region 1 GENRE Mature/Anthology/Horror

Pink Floyd: The Wall

Sony, 1999, 100 mins., #VD50198. Directed by Alan Parker. Animation directed by Gerald Scarfe. Written by Roger Waters.

Rock star Pink loses his mind in a Los Angeles hotel room, descending into a cascade of delusional live-action segments, symbolism-rich flashbacks, and expressive animation set to the music of Pink Floyd. At each stage of Pink's life, the people most important to him pile on abuse by withholding love, affection, and intellectual and creative freedom. To keep himself whole, Pink builds a mental "wall" against reality. In an anguished, desperate culmination of distress, Pink recalls his life and imagines himself an omnipotent commissar whose every whim is obeyed by his dutiful, mindless audiences. He recoils internally from his haunting visions, hallucinating animated allegories to his spiraling mental state and a tribunal that has the power to ultimately determine his fate.

In terms of screen time, this 1982 movie is more of a live-action rock opera than an animated film. *The Wall's* animated fare is so powerful, however, that its dark visions of marching fascist hammers, sinister metamorphic flowers, and other menacing visions have come to define the film. *The Wall* is light on dialogue and heavy on music, so fans of Pink Floyd will revel in the disc's crystal clear audio track, remastered from the original master tapes.

This disc features a high-quality print and entertaining extras like song lyric subtitles, an image gallery, two documentaries (one from 1982, the other newer), and audio commentary from the film's writer, former Pink Floyd lead singer Roger Waters and animation director Gerald Scarfe. [BR]

SPECIAL FEATURES "Making of" Featurettes • Commentary Track by Musician/Writer and Animation Director • Art and Photo Galleries • Production Notes • Deleted Scenes • Trailers • Easter Eggs TECHNICAL FEATURES Widescreen (2.35:1) • Subtitles/CC: Eng., Fren., Span. • Languages: Eng. • Sound: Dolby Digital 5.1 • Keepcase • 1 Disc • Region 1 GENRE & RATING Mature/Music/Psychedelia • Rated R

Plastic Little

ADV Films, 2002, 50 mins., #DPL001. Directed by Kinji Yoshimoto. Screenplay by Masayori Sekimoto.

While in port on the planet Yietta, Tita, the perky captain of the pet-hunting ship *Cha Cha Maru*, decides to go buy some groceries. In town Tita bumps into a girl being chased by a pack of trained assassins. Unable to resist trouble, Tita spirits her back to the Cha Cha Maru. Once aboard ship, Tita learns that the girl, Elysse Mordish, possesses a secret code, one the military needs to access a secret weapon that can control the planet, one her father died to protect. With a crew affectionate and loyal to Captain Tita (especially the female members), the *Cha Cha Maru* goes to extremes to protect its favorite new pet.

First released in 1994 as an OVA, *Plastic Little* is little more than a passable storyline designed as a vehicle for tons of dramatic action and impressive animation, and to show off the work of famed cheesecake-artist Satoshi Urushibara. That said, it does an excellent job at all three!

Plastic Little is filled with gratuitous shots of the female characters in the nude—filled! An interesting "extra" on this DVD is a "Jiggle Counter" that, once activated, will keep track of all the little bounces and jiggles expressed by the breasts of Tita and company. With bold striking colors, a clean soundtrack, and an excellent transfer to DVD, *Plastic Little* is a fun action/adventure more suited to lovers of hot anime babes than to those who love a good story. [GP]

SPECIAL FEATURES Character and Art Galleries • Storyboards • Trailer • Other Title Trailers • Jiggle Counter TECHNICAL FEATURES Fullscreen (1.33:1) • Subtitles/CC: Eng. • Languages: Jap., Eng. dub • Sound: Dolby Digital 2.0 • Keepcase • 1 Disc • Region 1 GENRE & RATING Mature/Science Fiction • Rated 15+

Pleasure Pack #1

Kitty, 2002, 58 mins., #KVDVD-0209. Directed by Rion Kujo, Yukimaro Otsubo. Screenplay by Teshujiro Ikaike. "Midnight Milk Party" based on the manga series by Piko Fujikatsu. "Tail of Two Sisters" based on the manga series by Kazu Shimao.

This DVD is an anthology featuring two unrelated short OVAs. In "Midnight Milk Party," a pretty young college girl decides to make a porn video after her graduation, but the solo act leads to more nastiness. Obsessed with sex, she's now got lots of admirers who will use blackmail or coercion to have their way with her. The animation is grainy and below average. The 1999 OVA was originally titled *Pikkoman's Devil Training*.

The second short is "Tail of Two Sisters." It tells the parallel stories of a college teacher and her sister, a student. Both of them have problems with their boyfriends, leading to hints of incest, lesbianism, and use of sex toys. At least it's all consensual.

The DVD also features a strange "stripping" feature that shows scenes from the video, and then shows the female characters' clothes vanishing. Also, the packaging credits list Teshoro Imaiki as the screenwriter of both parts, while the onscreen credits (used above) list Teshujiro Ikaike.

SPECIAL FEATURES Stripping Slideshow • Other Title Trailers TECHNICAL FEATURES Fullscreen (1.33:1) • Subtitles/CC: Eng. • Languages: Jap., Eng. dub • Sound: Dolby Digital 2.0 • Keepcase • 1 Disc • Region 1 GENRE & RATING Adult/Anthology • 18+

Pleasure Pack #2

Kitty, 2002, 60 mins., #KVDVD-0212. Directed by Takashi Minamide, Shoichiro Kamijo, Ichibai Kin. Screenplay by Teshujiro Ikaike. "Stairs" based on the manga series by Mikan R in *Core Magazine*. "Countdown to Delight" based on the manga series by Hyura Konata.

In "Stairs," Makoto is old friends with party girl Une, but he can't work up his nerve to ask her out. Then she gets pregnant, and he gets chased by Nonoka, who wants him. Nice animation helps a consensual storyline.

In "Countdown to Delight," a supposed college student named Motoki (who looks like a prepubescent boy) is trying to study, but his sister is having noisy lesbian sex in the bedroom next door. This soon leads to his own involvement in their affairs, which include bondage, SM, and sex toys. With goofy super-deformed art, and a protagonist that looks *very* underage, this verges uncomfortably close to kiddie porn.

As with the first disc, the screenwriter is credited as Teshujiro Ikaike onscreen, but Teshoro Imaiki on the packaging.

SPECIAL FEATURES Other Title Trailers TECHNICAL FEATURES Fullscreen (1.33:1) • Subtitles/CC: Eng. • Languages: Jap., Eng. dub • Sound: Dolby Digital 2.0 • Keepcase • 1 Disc • Region 1 GENRE & RATING Adult/Anthology • 18+

Pure Love

Anime 18, 2001, 62 mins., #A18D-2045. Directed by Miyo Morita. Screenplay by Miyo Morita. Original story by Libido.

In a medieval kingdom, the Queen's daughter is a nymphomaniac, and somehow it has something to do with a boy knight named Hiro who must translate a book, and entering a mysterious cave. Then they have sex, some consensual, some lesbian. That's about the extent to which any of the plot makes sense in this two-part 1998 OVA. It plays like a "Mad Lib" version of a story (add a noun, add a verb, add a sex act).

The animation is CGI, but it's pretty bad. There is an unusual airbrushed look to the backgrounds and characters, but nothing looks like it's real (even in an animated sense) and characters barely interact with each other, much less with the background elements. Add to that a

picture image in which everything shimmers like a bad video game, and you've got one of the worst hentai DVDs released to date.

SPECIAL FEATURES Anime Featurette • Character Bios • Storyboards • DVD-ROM Features: Art, Scripts • Other Title Trailers TECHNICAL FEATURES Fullscreen (1.33:1) • Languages: Jap., Eng. dub • Sound: Dolby Digital 2.0 • Keepcase • 1 Disc • Region 1 GENRE & RATING Adult/Fantasy • Rated 18+

Rancou Choukyo: Orgy Training

NuTech, 2002, 28 mins., #676. Screenplay by Saki Hosen. Based on the manga series by S. T. March.

A young man from a wealthy family has grown up hating his brutal father, who uses and abuses women (often while his son watches and pleasures himself). He goes out on a date, and tries to rape his date, then walks home depressed. He meets a girl and falls instantly in love with her, but is concerned when he finds out she's the new maid. Sure enough, father rapes the maid that night. But how will the son react? Will he stop his father, confess his love, or rape her as well?

Nasty characters rule the roost in this decidedly nonconsensual one-shot OVA. Despite its title, there are no orgies, just humiliation, domination, and rape. The animation is average. The DVD is double-sided, with previews on the flip side.

SPECIAL FEATURES Character and Art Galleries • Other Title Trailers TECHNICAL FEATURES Fullscreen (1.33:1) • Subtitles/CC: Eng. • Languages: Jap., Eng. dub • Sound: Dolby Digital 2.0 • Keepcase • 1 Disc • Region All GENRE Adult/Drama

Sailor and the 7 Ballz

MMG, 2000, 70 mins.

Sailor Moon and Tuxedo Mask are getting married and a who's who of anime is invited to Kamen Castle for the ceremony. *Sailor and the 7 Ballz* brings characters from *Dragonball Z*, *Evangelion*, *Ranma 1/2*, *Trigun*, *Fist of the North Star*, *Card Captor Sakura*, *Sailor Moon*, and several other anime favorites together in a crudely rendered orgy of silly erotica. There's no plot to speak of; characters arrive at the front door of the castle and quickly pair off to commit assorted kinky deeds. To show their dedication to the cause, the Sailor Scouts get breast implants to prepare for the event and Tuxedo Mask's castle is rigged with cameras in every nook and cranny so the voyeuristic groom won't miss a moment of action. Look for an *Austin Powers* parody as well.

Either this 2000 production is a contender for the worst piece of animation on DVD, or the appalling, lower-than-low quality is supposed to be a parody of bad animation. *Sailor and the 7 Ballz* is sometimes marketed as the latter, but don't believe it. While there is some humor value in watching choppy, awkward action and listening to exaggerated Japanese porn slang, it's not by design in this film. Everything from backgrounds to animation to voiceover is amateurish. Duck and cover! [BR]

SPECIAL FEATURES Slide Show • Other Title Trailer TECHNICAL FEATURES Fullscreen (1.33:1) • Subtitles/CC: Eng. • Languages: Jap. • Sound: Dolby Digital 2.0 • Keepcase • 1 Disc • Region 1–6 GENRE Adult/Parody

Sakura Diaries: Chapter 1

ADV Films, 2000, 90 mins., #DVDSM/001. Animation directed by Hiroyuki Yanagise, Keiji Sakai, Yoshio Usuda, Shinichiro Kajiura. Screenplay by Takefumi Terada. Based on the manga series by U-jin in *Young Sunday*.

Toma is the classic loser who tries and tries, but just never comes close to hitting the mark. He wants badly to get into Tokyo University so he won't wind up in a dead-end job, but he's having a lot of problems passing the entrance exams. He's living with his younger cousin Urara, a precocious teen who's infatuated with him (she dreams of being his lover). Sadly, Toma only has eyes for the lovely Mieko. But Mieko only dates college men, so Toma lies and says he's a student at Tokyo U. Cousin Urara isn't willing to give up the object of her affection so easily. She's determined to win Toma's heart any way she can. When all's said and done, will Toma have the object of his desire, or discover something unexpected in a place he wasn't even looking?

Chaos, comedy, drama, and romance are all ingredients in *Sakura Diaries*, a twelve-part anime series that originally aired in 1997 in Japan. The animation is pleasant, and the story is a wacky, outrageous love triangle that will raise more than a few eyebrows due to two of the participants being cousins, and due to Urara's high school age. The first controversial volume of *Sakura Diaries* contains episodes #1–3 and is definitely for mature audiences and those that won't be upset by "kissing cousins." [JMC]

SPECIAL FEATURES Other Title Trailers TECHNICAL FEATURES Fullscreen (1.33:1) • Subtitles/CC: Eng. • Languages: Jap., Eng. dub • Sound: Dolby Digital 2.0 • Keepcase • 1 Disc • Region 1–6 GENRE & RATING Mature/Romantic/Comedy • Rated 17+

Sakura Diaries: Chapter 2

ADV Films, 2000, 90 mins., #DVDSM/002. Animation directed by Masayuki Hiraoka, Shinichiro Kajiura, Noboru Koizumi, Miyako Shingu. Screenplay by Takefumi Terada. Based on the manga series by U-jin in *Young Sunday*.

Toma's the object of envy as he accompanies Mieko to a college party. However he's also the object of scrutiny as a few other students enamored with Mieko question whether he's actually a college student. Using general answers, he's able to keep his cover and continue partying, but a rival won't let the subject drop. Urara's also jealous of Toma and Mieko and has plans of her own to win Toma's heart. By confronting a drunk Toma, will Urara get what she wants or should the teen have been more careful about what she wished for?

The second pulse-racing volume of *Sakura Diaries* contains episodes #4–6 and shows us a new, darker side of Toma that proves alcohol doesn't mix well with some personalities. [JMC]

SPECIAL FEATURES Other Title Trailers TECHNICAL FEATURES Fullscreen (1.33:1) • Subtitles/CC: Eng. • Languages: Jap., Eng. dub • Sound: Dolby Digital 2.0 • Keepcase • 1 Disc • Region 1 GENRE & RATING Mature/Romantic/Comedy • Rated 17+

Sakura Diaries: Chapter 3

ADV Films, 2001, 90 mins., #DVDSM/003. Animation directed by Masayuki Yanase, Shinichiro Kajiura, Yoshio Usuda. Screenplay by Takefumi Terada. Based on the manga series by U-jin in *Young Sunday*.

After attacking Urara the night before, Toma is sincerely apologetic about his drunk actions and wants his cousin's forgiveness. She'll forgive him if he takes her out and promises to stop seeing Mieko. He agrees, but can't honor his word and soon calls Mieko. Toma has a heart-to-heart with Mieko and discusses where their relationship, if they even have one, is going. Will he get the answer he desires, or should he have been content with the fantasy?

The penultimate edition of *Sakura Diaries* containing episodes #7–9 has plenty of revelations and surprises, especially in the chat between Toma and Mieko. Most shows would choose to keep the romantic tension high and not allow major characters to discuss plot points, but this one breaks the mold. [JMC]

SPECIAL FEATURES Other Title Trailers TECHNICAL FEATURES Fullscreen (1.33:1) • Subtitles/CC: Eng. • Languages: Jap., Eng. dub • Sound: Dolby Digital 2.0 • Keepcase • 1 Disc •

Region 1 GENRE & RATING Mature/Romantic/Comedy • Rated 17+

Sakura Diaries: Chapter 4

ADV Films, 2001, 90 mins., #DVDSM/004. Animation directed by Masahiko Murata, Akira Takeuchi, Nobuyuki Takeuchi. Screenplay by Takefumi Terada. Based on the manga series by U-jin in *Young Sunday*.

After Toma chats with Mieko and gets some answers, things become even more confusing for the lad when he now starts to truly develop romantic feelings for Urara. Toma's got some tough decisions to make and things get a little more complicated when Urara's father calls from Italy with questions of his own. How will things turn out in this love triangle?

The final three episodes of this somewhat predictable romantic comedy are collected on this DVD. Although a little more closure would have been welcome, the ending sets the stage nicely for a second series. Now if only U-jin and company would produce a sequel. [JMC]

SPECIAL FEATURES Other Title Trailers TECHNICAL FEATURES Fullscreen (1.33:1) • Subtitles/CC: Eng. • Languages: Jap., Eng. dub • Sound: Dolby Digital 2.0 • Keepcase • 1 Disc • Region 1 GENRE & RATING Mature/Romantic/Comedy • Rated 17+

Sakura Diaries: Collector's Edition

ADV Films, 2001, 265 mins., #DSM100.

This two-volume set collects the previously released *Sakura Diaries* series on two DVDs, with a few new extra features.

SPECIAL FEATURES Unused Closing Theme • Trailer • Clean Credits • Other Title Trailers • Inserts: Liner Notes TECHNICAL FEATURES Multikeepcase • 2 Discs • Region 1–6 GENRE & RATING Mature/Romantic/Comedy • Rated 17+

Samurai X: Trust [#1]

ADV Films, 2000, 60 mins., #DVDSX001. Directed by Kazuhiro Furuhashi. Screenplay by Masashi Sogo. Based on the manga series by Nobuhiro Watsuki in *Jump Comics*.

A young slave boy named Shinta witnesses the cold-blooded murder of an entire slave caravan by a band of heartless bandits. Rescued and taken in by Hiko, a swordmaster, he learns the rare and deadly Hiten-Mitsurugi fighting technique. Later, outside their mountain retreat, the Meiji Restoration rocks Japan, and Shinta—now known as Kenshin—leaves his master to fight for the people. A rebel lord, impressed by the youth's swordsmanship, convinces Kenshin to become an assassin. So skilled is Kenshin that no one can touch him. Yet, on one fateful mission, a victim manages to scar Kenshin's left cheek before his death, which sets the stage for further tragedy. Kenshin is beginning to lose his soul to the endless killing. But just as he starts to slip out of touch forever, a young woman named Tomoe stumbles into him on a dark, rainy night. He takes her in and nurses her back to health, but the question of who and what she is remains.

This anime is the first 1999 OVA in the dark *Samurai X* series. The storyline precedes the popular *Rurouni Kenshin* TV series (see entries). The events portrayed in these OVAs show how Kenshin becomes the free spirit he is in the animated TV series.

If you have fond memories of Kenshin as an outrageous, happy-go-lucky character, then you might not want to watch these OVAs. They will change the way you view the character. [JMC]

SPECIAL FEATURES Character Bios • Historical Notes • Other Title Trailers • Reversible Cover TECHNICAL FEATURES Fullscreen (1.33:1) • Subtitles/CC: Eng. • Languages: Jap., Eng. dub • Sound: Dolby Digital 2.0 • Keepcase • 1 Disc • Region 1 GENRE & RATING Mature/Martial Arts • Rated 17+

Samurai X: Betrayal [#2]

ADV Films, 2000, 60 mins., #DVDSX002. Directed by Kazuhiro Furuhashi. Screenplay by Masashi Sogo. Based on the manga series by Nobuhiro Watsuki in *Jump Comics*.

When the Shogun's forces invade the rebel lord's estate, Edo goes up in flames, and Kenshin and Tomoe are forced to flee into the countryside. There, they disguise themselves as innocent farmers while they wait for a signal that it's safe to return. As the seasons change and time slips by, Kenshin finds himself letting go of the anger and despair that had gripped him and realizes that he is well suited for farming. But politics continue to churn around him, and his lord's enemies realize they must kill the deadly assassin. And what role does Tomoe play? Though Kenshin and Tomoe grow to care for one another, Tomoe's past will forever keep them apart. The ultimate betrayal awaits Kenshin as he realizes those around him aren't who he thinks they are. But will the knowledge move him to act?

Not burdened by the constraints facing an animated series that might be viewed by impressionable children, the *Samurai X* stories paint a darker, more realistic, and more poignant view of feudal Japan that is not sugar coated. [JMC]

SPECIAL FEATURES Character Bios • Screenwriter Notes • Other

Title Trailers • Reversible Cover • Easter Egg TECHNICAL FEA-
TURES Fullscreen (1.33:1) • Subtitles/CC: Eng. • Languages:
Jap., Eng. dub • Sound: Dolby Digital 2.0 • Keepcase • 1 Disc
• Region 1 GENRE & RATING Mature/Martial Arts • Rated 17+

Samurai X: The Motion Picture

ADV Films, 2001, 90 mins., #DVDSX003.
Directed by Hatsuki Tsuji. Script by
Yukiyoshi Ohashi. Based on the manga
series by Nobuhiro Watsuki in *Jump
Comics.*

Japan faces a time of change. The civil
unrest is over and a new government
has been built in the ashes of the old,
but thousands died so that the new
Meiji government could be created. After Himura Kenshin was forced to kill so many people—friends, enemies, and lovers—during the Bakumatsu, he's sworn
never to kill again. For ten years he's lived peacefully near
Tokyo as a part-time kendo instructor. He's looking to
the future and trying hard not to dwell on the past, until
it comes back to haunt him in the form of a vengeful
swordsman, Takimi Shigure. Shigure plots against the
new government. While establishing ties with Kenshin
and convincing the samurai he's a friend, he recruits a
bunch of angry young men to rise against the fledgling
government. Now Kenshin must struggle to keep his
vow of nonviolence, help his new friends, and prevent
tragic events that could have lasting repercussions.

Created in 1997 as a Japanese OVA, ADV Films
released the DVD version in 2000 to the delight of rabid
Rurouni Kenshin fans. The story occurs twelve years into
the Meiji era and there are frequent flashbacks to the
days of the Tokugawa Shogunate, when Himura Kenshin
was known as Hitokiri Battosai, which might be confusing to first timers to the world of Kenshin. [JMC]

SPECIAL FEATURES Trailer • Promotional Footage • Other Title
Trailers • Reversible Cover TECHNICAL FEATURES Widescreen
(1.85:1) • Subtitles/CC: Eng. • Languages: Jap., Eng. dub •
Sound: Dolby Digital 2.0 • Keepcase • 1 Disc • Region 1
GENRE & RATING Mature/Martial Arts • Rated 17+

Sex Demon Queen

Kitty, 2002, 30 mins., #KVDVD-0221.
Directed by Takeoshi Aoki. Screenplay by
Mitsuro Tanisato.

In a world of fantasy, sorceress Kuri
and swordswoman Linna are mercenaries who have a passion for their
work. One day, however, the two
women save a young girl from a gang
rape, thus attracting the attention of
the Sex Demon Queen and her dog-demons. The
Queen is after the two women because they have special

rings that help them fight demons, but before she takes
the rings, she means to take the women to heights of
demonic pleasure.

This is one weird OVA. There's a lot of humor, and
the pleasant animation—which includes measurements
of onscreen penises—is supergoofy at times. It's hard to
take the rapes by the dog-demons seriously because they
seem to have the heads of racoons. As if things weren't
bizarre enough, there's also some transforming armor
involved! Look for lesbianism, bondage, demon rape,
tentacle rape, and raccoon rape.

SPECIAL FEATURES Other Title Trailers TECHNICAL FEATURES
Fullscreen (1.33:1) • Subtitles/CC: Eng. • Languages: Jap.,
Eng. dub • Sound: Dolby Digital 2.0 • Keepcase • 1 Disc •
Region 1 GENRE & RATING Adult/Fantasy/Comedy • Rated 18+

Shusaku: Vol. 1—The Man's Paradise

NuTech, 2001, 27 mins., #544. Directed
by Jun Fukuda. Script by Sakura Momoi.

The Shukusei Music Academy is hiding shameful secrets in its girl's dormitory. Male manager/janitor Kato
Shusaku is determined to violate,
shame, and disgrace all the privileged
young girls who attend the academy.
Shusaku videotapes and photographs
each of the girls secretly, using the images to blackmail
them. First on his list is Kaori, who is tied up and forced
to have an enema.

This 1999 OVA series is also known as "Shameful,"
and it's based on a computer game. The animation is
average, and the subject matter—the continual rape and
degradation of schoolgirls—will make some viewers
queasy. Aside from the above-mentioned bondage, enemas, and rape, there's also lesbianism (it *is* a girl's school
after all). Adult film stars Asia Carrera and Rayveness
provide voices, and Carrera also gets a video profile. The
DVD is double sided, with previews.

SPECIAL FEATURES Voice Actress Interview • Photo Galleries •
Character and Art Galleries • Other Title Trailers TECHNICAL FEA-
TURES Fullscreen (1.33:1) • Subtitles/CC: Eng. • Languages:
Jap., Eng. dub • Sound: Dolby Digital 5.1, DTS • Keepcase •
1 Disc • Region 1 GENRE Adult/School

Shusaku: Vol. 2—The Man's Aesthetic

NuTech, 2001, 27 mins., #545. Directed
by Jun Fukuda. Script by Sakura Momoi.

Shusaku forces two students—Chiaki
and Asami—to become his sexual
slaves, but he's caught by teacher
Ayaka Minami. She soon becomes his
plaything as well, before Shusaku
moves on to quiet Nagisa and Shiho.

This second volume contains bondage, rape, a glowing yellow penis, and lesbianism. The disc has previews on the flip side.

SPECIAL FEATURES Voice Actress Interview • Photo Galleries • Character and Art Galleries • Other Title Trailers TECHNICAL FEATURES Fullscreen (1.33:1) • Subtitles/CC: Eng. • Languages: Jap., Eng. dub • Sound: Dolby Digital 5.1, DTS • Keepcase • 1 Disc • Region 1 GENRE Adult/School

Shusaku: Vol. 3—The Man's Pride

NuTech, 2001, 27 mins., #546. Directed by Jun Fukuda. Script by Sakura Momoi.

Shusaku sets a trap for the final three girls he wants to rape and disgrace—trouble-making wild girl Moeka, dreamer Eri, and the previously victimized Kaori. Now, the nasty old manager will orchestrate a concert of sexual degradation among the young music students.

Continuing the themes of the previous discs, this time there is more bondage, rape, a glowing yellow penis, and lesbianism. New in this segment is plenty of bathroom-oriented material. More previews are on side two.

SPECIAL FEATURES Voice Actress Interview • Photo Galleries • Character and Art Galleries • Other Title Trailers • Fullscreen (1.33:1) • Subtitles/CC: Eng. • Languages: Jap., Eng. dub • Sound: Dolby Digital 5.1, DTS • Keepcase • 1 Disc • Region 1 GENRE & RATING Adult/School

Shusaku [Box Set]

NuTech, 2001, 81 mins., #548. Directed by Jun Fukuda. Script by Sakura Momoi.

This box set features the three commercially available keepcase editions of *Shusaku* in a cardboard box. It does not feature any additional extras. Due to the squared-off design of these keepcases, they are almost impossible to remove from the box. Buyers might wish to substitute blank keepcases for the ones provided by NuTech. See individual entries for the Special and Technical Features listings.

TECHNICAL FEATURES Cardboard Box with 3 Keepcases • 3 Discs • Region 1 GENRE Adult/School

Shusaku Replay: Vol. 1—The First Night

NuTech, 2001, 28 mins., #552. Directed by Dasuzo Nakade. Script by Sanahiro Nukii.

Masochistic manager Kato Shusaku wasn't able to finish his evil plans of debauchery last time, but now he's back again, to disgrace, debase, and shame the girls of the Shukusi Music Academy.

A 2000 sequel to the original OVA trilogy, *Shusaku Replay* is, quite literally, more of the same. Although the writer and director are different, the characters and settings are the same, as is the depraved storyline. Shusaku's male member no longer glows yellow, but other than that, there's just more rape and lesbianism. Even Asia Carrera and Rayveness have returned for more voice work. Side two features previews.

SPECIAL FEATURES Voice Actress Interview • Photo Galleries • Character and Art Galleries • Other Title Trailers • TECHNICAL FEATURES Fullscreen (1.33:1) • Subtitles/CC: Eng. • Languages: Jap., Eng. dub • Sound: Dolby Digital 5.1, DTS • Keepcase • 1 Disc • Region 1 GENRE Adult/School

Shusaku Replay: Vol. 2—The Second Night

NuTech, 2001, 28 mins., #553. Directed by Kanbara Toshiaki. Script by Sanahiro Nukii.

Shusaku forces Moeko to perform for him, and plans a group scene with Shiho, Asami, and Nagisa. Elsewhere, a different man rapes Kaori. But who could it be?

The story continues on its nasty way, with lesbianism, bondage, rape, enemas, and watersports. Look for extensive preview trailers on side two.

SPECIAL FEATURES Voice Actress Interview • Photo Galleries • Character and Art Galleries • Other Title Trailers TECHNICAL FEATURES Fullscreen (1.33:1) • Subtitles/CC: Eng. • Languages: Jap., Eng. dub • Sound: Dolby Digital 5.1, DTS • Keepcase • 1 Disc • Region 1 GENRE Adult/School

Shusaku Replay: Vol. 3—The Third Night

NuTech, 2001, 28 mins., #554. Directed by Kanbara Toshiaki. Script by Sanahiro Nukii.

Shusaku further debases the girls of the academy, capturing it all on video and film. As usual, he forces lesbian acts, bondage, enemas, and rape upon the helpless females.

Unlike the other DVDs in the Shusaku series, this volume's only adult star voice is Asia

Carrera, since Rayveness's character was given the episode off. The B-side still contains trailers though. They didn't get to vacation with Rayveness.

SPECIAL FEATURES Voice Actress Interview • Photo Galleries • Character and Art Galleries • Other Title Trailers TECHNICAL FEATURES Fullscreen (1.33:1) • Subtitles/CC: Eng. • Languages: Jap., Eng. dub • Sound: Dolby Digital 5.1, DTS • Keepcase • 1 Disc • Region 1 GENRE Adult/School

Shusaku Replay: Vol. 4—The Fourth Night

NuTech, 2001, 28 mins., #555. Directed by Kanbara Toshiaki. Script by Sanahiro Nukii.

As Shusaku's evil plans reach a climax—seven of the girls are now his sex slaves—he turns his eyes to the last unspoiled girls of the academy. He hasn't conquered Eri yet, and she's determined to stop Shusaku once and for all.

This final volume of the series features lesbianism and rape, but it crosses one barrier not seen in any other adult volume on DVD: scatology. Wipe your shoes before it gets tracked onto the carpet, please. Side two features more DVD previews.

SPECIAL FEATURES Voice Actress Interview • Photo Galleries • Character and Art Galleries • Other Title Trailers TECHNICAL FEATURES Fullscreen (1.33:1) • Subtitles/CC: Eng. • Languages: Jap., Eng. dub • Sound: Dolby Digital 5.1, DTS • Keepcase • 1 Disc • Region 1 GENRE Adult/School

Shusaku Replay [Box Set]

NuTech, 2001, 112 mins., #556. Directed by Dasuzo Nakade, Kanbara Toshiaki. Script by Sanahiro Nukii.

This box set features the four commercially available keepcase editions of *Shusaku Replay*, in a cardboard box. It does not feature any additional extras. See individual entries for the Special and Technical Features listings.

TECHNICAL FEATURES Cardboard Box with 4 Keepcases • 4 Discs • Region 1 GENRE Adult/School

Sins of the Sisters

U.S. Manga Corps, 2002, 100 mins., #USMD2074. Based on the novel by Hide Takatori.

During the Crusades of A.D.1212, an army of children who are being transported by a ship find that they are betrayed. Sold into slavery by the Pope, the children choose death rather than slavery and perish at sea. Before his death, their leader swears he will no longer follow God but oppose him. Transformed into an angel, he reappears in modern times as a young woman named Aiko and leads a new crusade to abolish all religion. Disturbed by memories of her former life, Aiko travels back in time to rejoin the crusade and wage a battle to save the future.

First released in 1994, *Sins of the Sister* starts well enough, but the story quickly unravels, leaving the viewer confused as to what is happening. It also jumps from scene to scene failing to explain what relevance the disjointed images have to one another. After a short while there seems to be no story at all (this is partially because the first two episodes of the story have been—bizarrely—unreleased). Like the story, the animation in *Sins of the Sister* starts out good but quickly fades to average, at best. The picture is clear and crisp, but the soundtrack lacks any real inspiration.

Sins of the Sister has many scenes of not only nudity, but vicious rape and similarly disturbing acts. Those with strong religious beliefs should also know that this DVD not only attacks religion but depicts disturbing sexual acts performed by some of its leaders. To sum up, *Sins of the Sister* is short on story, short on directing, and long on potentially disturbing images, and generally a confusing flick. [GP]

SPECIAL FEATURES Trailer • Promotional Footage • DVD-ROM Features: Art, Scripts • Other Title Trailers TECHNICAL FEATURES Fullscreen (1.33:1) • Subtitles/CC: Eng. • Languages: Jap., Eng. dub • Sound: Dolby Digital 2.0 • Keepcase • 1 Disc • Region All GENRE & RATING Mature/Time Travel/Action • Rated 16+

Slight Fever Syndrome: Complete

Kitty , 2001, 90 mins., #KVDVD-0126 Directed by Fuyuzo Shirakawa. Script by Kei Aoyama. Based on the manga series by Rumi Miyamoto in *Penguin Club*.

Pretty Yuzuriha Mizuki starts off her assignment as a nurse in the local high school's infirmary with a bang—literally! Her attractiveness, youthfulness, and open-mindedness (as well as her Homer Simpson—esque powers of intelligence and logic)

quickly cause a stampede, as students and coworkers alike rush to solicit her advice . . . not to mention personal assistance in all matters sexual! But soon, not only does she face the hurdle of giving out hands–on sex advice, Ms. Mizuki also finds herself attracted to one of her male students.

Slight Fever Syndrome is an easygoing sex comedy. As is typical in the genre of pornographic anime, the animation and character design are seriously substandard in the first episode from 1996, but surprisingly, the second episode's production values improve tremendously. Since it's free of some of the genre's more disturbing elements (rape, tentacle sex), *Slight Fever Syndrome* makes a good choice for the curious hentai beginner.

The DVD contains both episodes of the two-part OVA series. Extras are minimal, but overall it's a decent product. [MT]

SPECIAL FEATURES Other Title Trailers TECHNICAL FEATURES Fullscreen (1.33:1) • Subtitles/CC: Eng. • Languages: Jap., Eng. dub • Sound: Dolby Digital 2.0 • Keepcase • 1 Disc • Region 1 GENRE & RATING Adult/Comedy • Rated 18+

South Park: Vol. 1

Warner, 1998, 100 mins., #R2 5655. Animation Directed by Eric Stough. Written by Trey Parker, Matt Stone.

Four young boys live in the quiet mountain town of South Park, Colorado. Excitable Stan Marsh, tubby Eric Cartman, neurotic Kyle Broflovski, and ill-fated Kenny McCormick may seem like any other set of youngsters, but these foul-mouthed third-graders engage in some bizarre, freakish, and tasteless adventures. And yet, at the end of every episode, the boys have "learned something today" . . . usually a moral lesson about the horrifying world that awaits them when they grow up.

When cattle are being mutilated in South Park, Cartman claims to have been abducted by aliens who subjected him to anal probes that make him fart fire. Then, on a hunting trip with Uncle Jimbo and one-armed veteran Ned, the boys must face a volcano and a mythical woods monster named Scuzzlebutt. Later, Cartman decides to bulk up for a TV appearance, only to become immense, while puppet-toting teacher Mr. Garrison tries to kill Kathy Lee Gifford. Finally, Stan finds out that his dog Sparky is gay, and learns a lesson in tolerance and history from Big Gay Al.

Creators Trey Parker and Matt Stone originally created a *South Park* pilot as a "video Christmas card," and the obscenely funny short gained them raves in Hollywood. Comedy Central won the bidding war to feature *South Park* as a series, debuting it in August 1997. The animation style looks like paper cut-outs (and *was* cut-outs in

the earliest footage) but soon became computer-animated images that *looked* like paper cut-outs.

With language that pushes every censor barrier on television already, Parker and Stone set their crew to devising stories that tweaked everything from Hollywood stars to politically correct people of almost every stripe. While one episode might offend Jewish or gay or environmentalist viewers, the next one might make them cheer; *South Park* became a *truly* equal-opportunity offender. And in doing so, it became a tremendous hit for Comedy Central and a licensing boom.

This hilarious debut DVD features the series' first four episodes: "Cartman Gets an Anal Probe"; "Volcano"; "Weight Gain 4000"; and "Big Gay Al's Big Gay Boat Ride." On that last show, listen for star George Clooney as the voice of Sparky, the gay dog! The DVD also contains live-action introductions for each episode, in which a very fey Parker and Stone chat by a fireside, reminiscing about the "very favorite" episode that follows. Watch as their dog, Old Scratch, changes size, sex, and breed from shot to shot.

Besides being offered as a single DVD, the disc was also included as part of a three-part *South Park* pack set, along with *South Park #2* and *South Park #3*.

SPECIAL FEATURES Comedy Central TV Promos TECHNICAL FEATURES Fullscreen (1.33:1) • Languages: Eng. • Sound: Dolby Digital Surround 2.0 • Snapcase • 1 Disc • Region 1 GENRE & RATING Mature/Comedy/Satire • Rated MA

South Park: Vol. 2

Warner, 1998, 100 mins., #36595. Written by Trey Parker, Matt Stone, Dan Sterling, Philip Stark.

To win a science fair, the boys will stop at nothing, even trying to get Kyle's pet elephant to mate with Cartman's pot-bellied pig. And when Stan's 102-year-old grandfather tries to get someone to help him end his miserable life, the parents of the community are too busy to notice since they're trying to get the fart-joking Terrance and Phillip show off the TV airwaves. Later, the town is caught in the middle of a zombie catastrophe at Halloween, while Kyle's Chewbacca costume isn't a hit, and Cartman can't understand why everyone's offended at his Adolf Hitler costume. Finally, on the day of Cartman's birthday, a pay-per-view fight between Jesus and Satan has everyone distracted.

This second DVD contains more live-action intros, plus episodes #5–7 and #10: "An Elephant Makes Love to a Pig"; "Death"; "Pink Eye"; and "Damien."

Besides being offered as a single DVD, the disc was also included as part of a three-part *South Park* pack set, along with *South Park #1* and *South Park #3*.

SPECIAL FEATURES Comedy Central TV Promos TECHNICAL FEATURES Fullscreen (1.33:1) • Languages: Eng. • Sound: Dolby Digital Surround 2.0 • Snapcase • 1 Disc • Region 1 GENRE & RATING Mature/Comedy/Satire • Rated MA

South Park: Vol. 3

Warner, 1998, 100 mins., #36596. Animation Directed by Eric Stough. Directed by Trey Parker. Written by Trey Parker, Matt Stone, Philip Stark.

It's Thanksgiving time, and genetically altered turkeys are rampaging in South Park, even as Cartman is mistaken for a starving Ethiopian, and a real malnourished Ethiopian boy is adopted by the quartet. Next, Barbra Streisand becomes a giant robot monster destroying the town, requiring a team of Leonard Maltin, Sidney Poitier, and Robert Smith of The Cure to destroy her! And in one of the most infamous episodes of all, Kyle shows everyone that Mr. Hankey the Christmas Poo is real, and Phillip Glass helps the school kids put on a surreal non-offensive, non-denominational holiday pageant. Finally, Mr. Garrison has plastic surgery and ends up looking like a washed-up TV star, while substitute teacher Ms. Ellen drives the boys crazy and sends Wendy Testaburger into a jealous Valentine's Day rage!

Another four episodes are presented from the series' first season, with #8–9 and #11–12: "Starvin' Marvin"; "Mecha-Streisand"; "Mr. Hankey, the Christmas Poo"; and "Tom's Rhinoplasty."

Besides being offered as a single DVD, the disc was also included as part of a three-part *South Park* pack set, along with *South Park #1* and *South Park #2*.

SPECIAL FEATURES Comedy Central TV Promos TECHNICAL FEATURES Fullscreen (1.33:1) • Languages: Eng. • Sound: Dolby Digital 2.0 • Snapcase • 1 Disc • Region 1 GENRE & RATING Mature/Comedy/Satire • Rated MA

South Park: Vol. 4

Warner, 1999, 125 mins., #36678. Directed by Trey Parker. Written by Trey Parker, David Goodman, Trisha Nixon, Matt Stone.

Cartman really wants to find out who his father is, but it seems his mother was busy with just about everyone back in the day. Will America's Stupidest Home Videos help find the answer? Actually, it's creepy Dr. Mephesto that's about to reveal the identity of Cartman's father when he's shot, plus a blizzard leaves the residents of South Park without food . . . for hours! A bonus episode of The Terrance and Phillip show has the farting Canadians facing Saddam Hussein. Then, someone in South Park is having sex with chickens, but Officer Barbrady is learning to read, so Officer Cartman comes to the rescue. And when Kyle finds out what circumcision will mean to his baby brother, the boys kidnap him, even as school counselor Mr. Mackie descends into a haze of drugs and alcohol.

The first episode on this DVD was the first season's cliffhanger finale, but when viewers tuned in for the second season opener on April 1st, they got the Terrance and Phillip show instead as a joke (fans were irate!). This disc contains episodes #13–17: "Cartman's Mom Is a Dirty Slut"; "Cartman's Mom Is Still a Dirty Slut"; "Terrance and Phillip in 'Not Without My Anus'"; "Chicken Lover"; and "Ike's Wee Wee."

Besides being offered as a single DVD, the disc was also included as part of a three-part *South Park* pack set, along with *South Park #5* and *South Park #6*.

SPECIAL FEATURES Comedy Central TV Promos TECHNICAL FEATURES Fullscreen (1.33:1) • Languages: Eng. • Sound: Dolby Digital 2.0 • Snapcase • 1 Disc • Region 1 GENRE & RATING Mature/Comedy/Satire • Rated MA

South Park: Vol. 5

Warner, 1999, 100 mins., #36679. Directed by Trey Parker. Written by Trey Parker, Matt Stone, David Goodman, Nancy M. Pimental.

The South Park dodgeball team is off to Japan for the world championships, but back at home, the school nurse's physical deformity—a fetus growing out of the side of her head—is cause for alarm, then celebration. Stan plans revenge on his Uncle Jimbo by setting him up against the Mexican Staring Frog of Southern Sri Lanka, while Jesus takes drastic steps to gain ratings for his cable access show. On a ride up a mountain, the school bus teeters off the edge of a cliff, prompting the boys to flash back to prime experiences of their young lives. And when school lets out for the year, Mr. Garrison's puppet goes missing, and the town gets the biggest snake ever for the 4th of July fireworks celebration.

A few celebrities, including Henry Winkler and Jay Leno, lend their voices to episodes #18–21: "Conjoined Fetus Lady"; "The Mexican Staring Frog of Southern Sri Lanka"; "Flashbacks"; and "Summer Sucks."

Besides being offered as a single DVD, the disc was also included as part of a three-part *South Park* pack set, along with *South Park #4* and *South Park #6*.

SPECIAL FEATURES Comedy Central TV Promos TECHNICAL FEATURES Fullscreen (1.33:1) • Languages: Eng. • Sound: Dolby Digital Surround 2.0 • Snapcase • 1 Disc • Region 1 GENRE & RATING Mature/Comedy/Satire • Rated MA

South Park: Vol. 6

Warner, 1999, 100 mins., #36679. Directed by Trey Parker. Written by Trey Parker, Matt Stone, Nancy M. Pimental, Trisha Stone, David Goodman.

When an independent film festival comes to town, the ecosystem is destroyed, bringing Mr. Hankey out of hiding. But no one expects the piece of poo to become a movie star! Later, the kids' mothers try to get the boys to all catch chicken pox, so the boys hire a prostitute to give their parents herpes. On a field trip to a planetarium, a crazed astronomer hypnotizes the kids, except for Cartman, who's trying to make a commercial for Cheesy Poofs. And when the boys build a clubhouse they have unwelcome visitors, plus Stan has to deal with the news that his parents are divorcing! Plus, look for some "Fat Abbot" cartoon segments that make Kyle say, "Cartoons are getting really dirty!"

The first episode on this volume is a savage satire of Hollywood types, and includes a poop-filled parody of *Fantasia's* "The Sorcerer's Apprentice" sequence. It also featured a song that was later remixed as a single by Chef's voice actor, Isaac Hayes. Episodes #22–25 are on this disc: "Chef's Salty Chocolate Balls"; "Chickenpox"; "Roger Ebert Should Lay Off the Fatty Foods"; and "Clubhouses."

Besides being offered as a single DVD, the disc was also included as part of a three-part *South Park* pack set, along with *South Park #4* and *South Park #5*.

SPECIAL FEATURES Comedy Central TV Promos TECHNICAL FEATURES Fullscreen (1.33:1) • Languages: Eng. • Sound: Dolby Digital Surround 2.0 • Snapcase • 1 Disc • Region 1 GENRE & RATING Mature/Comedy/Satire • Rated MA

South Park: The Chef Experience [#7]

Warner, 2000, 93 mins., #36681. Directed by Trey Parker, Eric Stough. Written by Trey Parker, Matt Stone.

Chef is sued by a record company, but some of his old rock star friends stage a concert to help him. Then, in a special, those same rock stars talk about the influence Chef had on their musical careers. Later, it looks like Chef might get married to the woman of his dreams, but the boys know there's something demonic about her. And on a field trip to Costa Rica to help save the rainforest, the kids learn just how evil the rainforest really is!

The animated "Chef Aid" and partially live-action special "Chef Aid: Behind the Menu" feature appearances by such music icons as Sir Elton John, Rick James, Meat Loaf, Ol' Dirty Bastard, Ozzy Osbourne, and others (many of whom also appeared on the soundtrack album). The DVD features episodes #27, 32, and 34—including "Succubus" and "Rainforest Schmainforest"—as well as the music video for "Chef's Salty Chocolate Balls."

SPECIAL FEATURES "Making of" Featurette TECHNICAL FEATURES Fullscreen (1.33:1) • Subtitles/CC: Eng., Fren. • Languages: Eng. • Sound: Dolby Digital Surround 2.0 • Snapcase • 1 Disc • Region All GENRE & RATING Mature/Comedy/Satire • Rated MA

South Park: Christmas in South Park [#8]

Warner, 2000, 124 mins., #37261. Directed by Trey Parker, Eric Stough. Written by Trey Parker, Nancy M. Pimental, Matt Stone, Pam Brady.

Mr. Hankey hosts a holiday special with ten musical moments with the *South Park* regulars. Then, Stan sneaks out to a holiday dinner with the Cartman family, but when prison escapee Uncle Howard shows up with cellmate Charlie Manson, the boys will find out who's naughty and nice. And when the boys get caught in the grip of Japanese Chinpokomon fever, what evil messages are being subconsciously put into their minds? And if you've ever wondered how the *South Park* tales are created, watch a fifty-one-minute British documentary called "Goin' Down to *South Park*," which reveals many secrets. Shhhh.

This holiday-themed DVD features episodes #29, 42, and 46: "Merry Christmas Charlie Manson"; "Chinpoko Mon"; and "Mr. Hankey's Christmas Classics." This last episode was also a big plug for the *South Park* Christmas album of the same name.

SPECIAL FEATURES "Making of" Featurette TECHNICAL FEATURES Fullscreen (1.33:1) • Subtitles/CC: Eng., Fren. • Languages: Eng. • Sound: Dolby Digital Surround 2.0 • Snapcase • 1 Disc • Region All GENRE & RATING Mature/Comedy/Satire • Rated MA

South Park: Timmy! [#9]

Warner, 2000, 92 mins., #37350. Directed by Trey Parker. Written by Trey Parker, Matt Stone.

After wheelchair-bound Timmy is diagnosed with Attention Deficit Disorder, all the kids get medicated into catatonia. Meanwhile, Timmy becomes front-man for the heavy metal band Lords of the Underworld. Then, the kids all move into the fourth grade, get a lazy-eyed new teacher, and travel back in time, while Mr. Garrison finally comes out as gay! The Thanksgiving play is in trouble until Cartman's Broadway connections pitch in, and Timmy thinks his turkey should star as well. And Cartman takes over the tooth fairy trade until Denver's kiddy mob boss puts the novocaine to his plans.

For its fourth season, South Park moved the kids into the fourth grade, with an updated opening and the addition of Timmy, a disabled boy in an electric wheelchair. Handicapped activists didn't raise much of a fuss as Timmy usually came out on top, even recording a single with Lords of the Underworld. This DVD collects episodes #49, 51, 59, and 61: "Timmy 2000"; "4th Grade"; "Helen Keller, The Musical"; and "The Tooth Fairy's Tats 2000."

SPECIAL FEATURES Trailer • Comedy Central TV Promos TECHNICAL FEATURES Fullscreen (1.33:1) • Subtitles/CC: Eng., Fren. • Languages: Eng. • Sound: Dolby Digital 2.0 • Snapcase • 1 Disc • Region 1 GENRE & RATING Mature/Comedy/Satire • Rated MA

South Park: Winter Wonderland [#10]

Warner, 2000, 85 mins., #37423. Directed by Trey Parker. Written by Trey Parker, Matt Stone.

Mr. Hankey is having some family problems, so Christmas is in a slump, leading the boys to make an animated video Christmas card. Then, Cartman thinks he's started puberty and Stan takes a serum from Dr. Mephesto, while Jesus tries to give people a millennium miracle. When Cartman throws a rock at "Token," the school's only minority student, he's put in jail, where he learns the error of his ways . . . and where to hide contraband best. Finally, the quartet decides to become a boy band called "Fingerbang," but who will be their fifth member?

The original *South Park* video Christmas card is excerpted in the opening episode, though it's unfortunate that the entire card wasn't included on this DVD. Episodes #47, 50, 56, 65, are included on this disc: "A Very Crappy Christmas"; "Are You There, God? It's Me, Jesus"; "Cartman's Silly Hate Crime 2000"; and "Something You Can Do with Your Finger."

SPECIAL FEATURES Trailer • Comedy Central TV Promos TECHNICAL FEATURES Fullscreen (1.33:1) • Subtitles/CC: Eng., Fren. • Languages: Eng. • Sound: Dolby Digital 2.0 • Snapcase • 1 Disc • Region 1 GENRE & RATING Mature/Comedy/Satire • Rated MA

South Park: Insults to Injuries [#11]

Warner, 2002, 88 mins., #37535. Directed by Trey Parker, Eric Stough. Written by Trey Parker, Matt Stone.

When the boys hear a swear-word rhyming with "fit" on a cop program, the poop hits the fans. High ratings result in more swearing and a confrontation with the ancient Knights of Standards and Practices. Then, Big Gay Al gets fired as a Scoutmaster even as handi-capable Jimmy sets up a rivalry with Timmy. Also, Mr. Mackey and Ms. Choksondik team up to teach sex education, and Cartman puts together a horrifying plot of revenge against an older kid.

This disc contains four of the most button-pushing episodes of the fifth season, with everything from cripple-fights to gay scouts to cannibalism shocking audiences along the way. Episodes include #66, 67, 69, and 72: "It Hits the Fan"; "Cripple Fight"; "Proper Condom Use"; and "Scott Tenorman Must Die." If you haven't jumped into the South Park pool yet, be warned that this volume is at the deep end.

SPECIAL FEATURES Promotional Footage • Other Title Trailers TECHNICAL FEATURES Fullscreen (1.33:1) • Subtitles/CC: Eng., Fren. • Languages: Eng. • Sound: Dolby Digital Surround 2.0 • Keepcase • 1 Disc • Region 1 GENRE & RATING Mature/Comedy/Satire • Rated TV-MA

South Park: Ghouls, Ghosts, and Underpants Gnomes [#12]

Warner, 2002, 88 mins., #37590. Directed by Trey Parker. Written by Trey Parker, Matt Stone, Pam Brady.

When the band Korn is going to perform in South Park, creepy pirate ghosts appear, but could Father Maxi have something to do with the mysterious goings on? Then, possessed animals and murders in the town are bad enough, but what about the evil Cartman from another dimension? The over-caffeinated Tweek fears the gnomes who are stealing his underwear, even as his parents rally against big coffee conglomerates, while later, Cartman's cool new *Dawson's Creek* Trapper Keeper becomes a horrendous monster that threatens mankind's very existence!

Timed as a Halloween release, this is one of the weakest of the *South Park* collections. However, one episode references the national election recount of 2000. What's most surprising about this is the timeliness of the topic; "Trapper Keeper," which features endless recounts in a Kindergarten Class President vote, aired November 15,

2000, just eight days after the November 7 election following which George W. Bush and Al Gore battled over the Presidential vote recount in Florida! This DVD contains episodes #28, 30, 41, and 60 from the second to the fourth seasons: "Spooky Fish"; "Underpants Gnomes"; "Trapper Keeper"; and "Korn's Groovy Pirate Ghost Mystery."

SPECIAL FEATURES Promotional Footage • Other Title Trailers TECHNICAL FEATURES Fullscreen (1.33:1) • Subtitles/CC: Eng., Fren. • Languages: Eng. • Sound: Dolby Digital Surround 5.1 • Keepcase • 1 Disc • Region 1 GENRE & RATING Mature/Comedy/Satire • Rated TV-MA

South Park: The Complete First Season

Warner, 2002, 310 mins., #137633.

The first thirteen episodes of *South Park* are collected into a box set, bringing together the first appearance of Mr. Hankey, Starvin Marvin, Big Gay Al, and many more of the small town's interesting denizens. The three disc set contains the exact same episodes as volumes #1–3 of the individual *South Park* line, as well as #13 from Vol. 4.

There are a handful of extras, including two Christmas videos, a few promos, a segment with Jay Leno from *The Tonight Show*, and a clip from the CableAce Awards. But where is the original *South Park* pilot? Where is the alternate, longer version of "Cartman Gets an Anal Probe"? Where are all the other snippets and goodies that have been making the fan bootleg circuit for years?

Lack of extras isn't the only place that Warner dropped the ball with this set. The episodes are not in the same order that the packaging lists them in, and some are not even on the correct disc! There also aren't any scene selections or breaks, meaning a skip forward gets you to the next episode. But the biggest blunder was a legal one; creators Trey Parker and Matt Stone recorded commentary tracks for the entire season, but the Warner legal department was concerned about negative remarks they made about the film *Contact* and other Warner titles. When Parker and Stone refused to allow the comments to be cut, Warner removed the commentaries.

Through an offer at www.comedycentral.com, fans could get the commentaries free of charge through March 2003 on a 5-disc CD set that can be synched with the episodes. After that date, the fate of the commentary CDs is unknown. It's too bad this snafu—and the missing extras—spoil what could have been an incredible set. As it is, *South Park: The Complete First Season* remains a barely worthy addition for longtime fans, and a nice catch-up for newcomers.

SPECIAL FEATURES Promotional Footage • Music Videos • Other Title Trailers • Easter Eggs TECHNICAL FEATURES Fullscreen (1.33:1) • Subtitles/CC: Eng., Fren., Span. • Languages: Eng.

• Sound: Dolby Digital Surround 2.0 • Foldout Box with Cardboard Sleeve • 3 Discs • Region 1 GENRE & RATING Mature/Comedy/Satire • Rated TV-MA

South Park: Bigger, Longer and Uncut

Paramount, 1999, 81 mins., #33682. Directed by Trey Parker. Written by Trey Parker & Matt Stone and Pam Brady.

When Cartman, Stan, Kyle, and Kenny sneak into the hot new Canadian film by flatulent comedy stars Terrance and Phillip—"Asses of Fire"—they learn lots of foul language and a trick for lighting gas. Unfortunately, the trick ends up killing Kenny, and the potty mouths of the boys (and other kids who rally to the movie) shock the parents of South Park into action. Soon, war is declared on Canada for all the country's ills, and Terrance and Phillip are to be executed if the boys can't rescue them. Meanwhile, in Hell, Kenny makes friends with the gay Satan, but not his lover, Saddam Hussein, who is plotting Armageddon. And did I mention it's all a musical?

Released in 1999, the *South Park* movie is one of the most brilliant pieces of animated satire ever committed to film. Despite the simplistic style of the animation itself, the story is multi-layered and complex. As in the TV show itself (see entries for show DVDs) creators Stone and Parker use the raucous take-no-prisoners tone to make some fairly pointed political statements, including some justifiable lambasting of the MPAA rating board. But the greatest elements of the film are the songs by Marc Shaiman, who spoofs everything from Busby Berkeley musicals to Disney's *The Little Mermaid* to an astonishing *Les Miserables* four-part rallying cry. The song "Blame Canada" was even nominated for a 2000 Academy Award, while another song—"Uncle F★★ka"—won an MTV movie award, even though its name couldn't be stated on television!

According to media watchdog groups, the film contains 399 profane words, 128 offensive gestures, and 221 acts of violence. The count even won the film a place in the *Guiness Book of World Records* as the record holder for the most profanity in an animated feature film (and with DVD subtitles you can finally figure out Cartman's curse-athon near the end). The film's subtitle is a joke itself; forced by the MPAA to change the title from "South Park: All Hell Breaks Loose," Stone and Parker added words that refer both to the movie. . . and to a penis.

Hilarious and shocking, inspired and politically incorrect, *South Park: Bigger, Longer and Uncut* is the best mature title on DVD, and it's not likely to be toppled from that particular throne.

SPECIAL FEATURES Trailers TECHNICAL FEATURES Widescreen (1.85:1)

• Subtitles/CC: Eng. • Languages: Eng., Fren. dub • Sound: Dolby Digital Surround 2.0, Dolby Digital 5.1 • Keepcase • 1 Disc • Region 1 GENRE & RATING Mature/Music/Comedy • Rated R

Spaceship Agga Ruter

Anime 18, 2001, 111 mins., #A18D-2079. Directed by Shigeru Yazaki. Written by Hideyuki Kurata.

Orphaned as a child and left to die in space, young Taiyo is rescued by android Kei. He grows up on her ship the Agga Ruter, and she instructs him in the ways of love. When they're captured by a beautiful space pirate (whose ship resembles a giant transparent gift box floating in space), Kei and Taiyo soon become her willing sex hostages. The pirate is a were-woman whose savage lusts can only be tamed by Taiyo's sexual healing. They're soon working together to steal a gem that used to be aboard the Agga Ruter, but the man who has hired the pirate—and who double-crosses them at the first opportunity—is the one who killed Taiyo's parents!

Released as a four-part OVA series in 1998, *Spaceship Agga Ruter* is—ahem—very similar to the various *Tenchi Muyo!* series, both in tone and character designs (not surprising, since many staffers worked on both shows). The animation is mostly attractive, but there are some really goofy moments. There's lots of sex, but none of it is rape, and there's nary a tentacle to be seen. If you want entertaining science fiction porn, here it is.

SPECIAL FEATURES Anime Featurette • Character Bios • Character and Art Galleries • Storyboards • DVD-ROM Features: Art, Scripts • Other Title Trailers TECHNICAL FEATURES Fullscreen (1.33:1) • Subtitles/CC: Eng. • Languages: Jap., Eng. dub • Sound: Dolby Digital 2.0 • Keepcase • 1 Disc • Region All GENRE & RATING Adult/Science Fiction • Rated 18++

Spawn [Todd McFarlane's]

HBO, 1997, 140 mins., #91425 Directed by Eric Radomski, John Hays. Written by Alan McElroy, Gary Hardwick. Based on the comic book series by Todd McFarlane.

Al Simmons is a CIA assassin who is murdered. Given the choice to return from the dead, Al becomes Spawn, a chain-wielding, cape-wearing, green ectoplasm-firing anti-hero who must try to redeem his soul before his time runs out. He wants to see his wife and child again, but his features are burned and scarred, and he looks like a monster. But even as Spawn starts his mission against evil—five years after his death—he finds multiple forces stand in his way: a child murderer; an ex-

boss operative; a demon clown that can morph into a monster; and the ticking time clock that his powers start every time he wields them.

In 1992, a group of popular comic book artists left Marvel Comics en masse and founded their own company, Image Comics. Biggest among them was Todd McFarlane, an ex-*Spider-Man* artist, who created a dark and bloody series called *Spawn*. The character was turned into a feature film for 1997 release, as well as an HBO series that debuted in May 1997, the first project of the HBO Animation production company.

The animation on the series is very anime-esque, with recurring motifs of fire, close-ups of eyes, pools of blood, and moving shadows. Although it is at times monochromatic, in other scenes, *Spawn* is almost unnaturally brightly colored. Voice work is decent, though without many stand-outs. Shirley Walker lays on creepy moans over her synthesized score, adding a pervasive feel of dread and terror. Although it's not rated, *Spawn* features nudity and lots of violence, so it's not appropriate for younger audiences (although too many video stores rack it with kiddie titles).

The first DVD in the series collects all six episodes of season one on a double-sided disc. There's also a very informative—and candid—running commentary track by McFarlane throughout all six shows.

SPECIAL FEATURES Commentary Track by Creator • Creator Bio & Interview • Character Bios • Character and Art Galleries • Storyboards • Other Title Trailers TECHNICAL FEATURES Fullscreen (1.33:1) • Subtitles/CC: Eng., Fren., Span. • Languages: Eng., Span. dub • Sound: Dolby Digital Surround 2.0 • Snapcase • 1 Disc • Region 1 GENRE Mature/Horror/Superhero

Spawn 2 [Todd McFarlane's]

HBO, 1998, 144 mins., #91487. Directed by Jennifer Yuh, Tom Nelson and Mike Vosburg. Written by Larry Brody, John Shirley, Victor Bumbalo, Gerard Brown, Rebekah Bradford, John Leekley. Based on the comic book series by Todd McFarlane.

The corrupt government officials want their stash of illegal weapons back, and they hire Chapel to recover them. Chapel just happens to be the mercenary who was the partner of Al Simmons (aka Spawn), and the man who murdered him as well! Terry Fitzgerald tries to investigate the missing weapons, but is framed by Jason Wynn for trying to sell them to foreign nations. Will Spawn save the man who was once his best friend and who is now married to Spawn's wife? Plus, something is preying on the homeless, and Spawn gets involved, not yet realizing he's playing into the plans of the demonic Malebolgia. And when Wynn decides to get rid of Wanda, Cyan, and Terry,

Spawn is forced to make some difficult choices, and a revelation. And then comes the showdown between Spawn and Wynn.

The second season of *Spawn* ran six episodes, from May–June 1998, and all six are included on this double-sided DVD volume. It features more violence, action, bloodshed, and a really, really long cape.

SPECIAL FEATURES Creator Bio & Interview • DVD-ROM Features: Digital Trading Card TECHNICAL FEATURES Fullscreen (1.33:1) • Subtitles/CC: Eng., Fren., Span. • Languages: Eng., Span. dub • Sound: Dolby Digital 5.1 • Snapcase • 1 Disc • Region 1 GENRE Mature/Horror/Superhero

Spawn 3: The Ultimate Battle [Todd McFarlane's]

HBO, 1999, 150 mins., #91589. Directed by Tom Nelson, Chuck Patton, Brad Rader, Mike Vosburg, Jennifer Yuh. Written by John Leekley, Rebekah Bradford. Based on the comic book series by Todd McFarlane.

Freezing time, Spawn gives some street punks the chance to turn away from violence and redeem them-selves, while Wynn visits the opium-mad Major Fosberg, the man who once tried to save Al Simmons from the demons of revenge. Cogliostro reveals his past—he was once Merlin and a hellspawn as well—and tries to help Spawn give up violence. Detectives Sam and Twitch investigate reports of a red-cloaked vigilante in the alleys of the city, while reporter Lisa Wu and Jason Wynn both independently start putting the pieces of the Al Simmons puzzle together. Spawn is framed for the shooting of a major character by a corrupt police chief. Terry provides evidence to the NSC agents that could put Wynn away, but the wily villain escapes. Lisa Wu's secret is revealed, and it could mean the end for Spawn. A female assassin is dispatched to kill Spawn, while Spawn uses his cloak to regain his human form for a short time to be reunited with his wife. Wynn tries to get hold of a mystical mask that could help him defeat his enemy. And Spawn's actions with Wanda could bring about Armageddon. . .

The third season of *Spawn* aired in one week of May 1999, and all six episodes are included on this DVD. The disc features a difficult-to-navigate menu, but is a nice production otherwise. This season won an Emmy Award in the "Outstanding Animated Program" category, a fact that is not touted anywhere on the packaging because the DVD was released prior to the awards.

SPECIAL FEATURES "Making of" Featurette • Commentary Track by Creator • Creator Bio • Music Videos TECHNICAL FEATURES Fullscreen (1.33:1) • Subtitles/CC: Eng., Fren., Span. • Languages: Eng., Span. dub • Sound: Dolby Digital Surround 2.0 • Snapcase • 1 Disc • Region 1 GENRE Mature/Horror/Superhero

Spawn: The Ultimate Collection [Box Set]

HBO, 2001, 440 mins., #99322.

This box set features the three commercially available editions of *Spawn* in a foldout cardboard box. It also features an additional DVD-ROM disc entitled "In the Mind of Todd McFarlane," which contains multiple interview segments (in one of them creator McFarlane wishes he could pass himself off as the AntiChrist), and a storyboard-to-film comparison. See individual entries for the Special and Technical Features listings of the other three discs.

SPECIAL FEATURES Interview with Creator • Storyboards TECHNICAL FEATURES Cardboard Foldout Box • 4 Discs • Region 1 GENRE Mature/Horror/Superhero

Spike and Mike's Sick and Twisted Festival of Animation

Slingshot, 1999, 99 mins., #SDVD9814.

If gross-out humor is your goal in entertainment, you've found the right DVD entry. In 1990, Craig "Spike" Decker and Mike Gribble spun off a new anthology from their popular *Classic Festival of Animation*. Featuring all of the most objectionable, violent, sexual, and just plain weird cartoons they could get their hands on, *Spike and Mike's Sick and Twisted Festival of Animation* was born. The festival thrives to this day, with old favorites and newcomers rotated in and out each summer.

This DVD volume contains thirty-five short films with multiple styles of animation, including cel, colored pencil, stop motion, and claymation. Most of the humor is either sexual or scatological, and creators include Bill Plympton, *Powerpuff Girls* creator Craig McCracken, comic book artist Brandon McKinney, and others.

Shorts included on the disc are: "No Neck Joe"; "Dumb, Big, Fat, Stupid Baby"; "Baby's New Formula"; "How to Make Love to a Woman"; "Rick the Dick"; "Shindler's Fist"; "Jurassic Fart"; "Dogpile"; "Horndog"; "Brian's Brain"; "The Cat, Cow and Beautiful Fish"; "Finger Food"; "Slaughter Day"; "Petey's Wake"; "Oh, Crappy Day"; "Triassic Parking Lot"; "Spaghetti Snot"; "Chainsaw Bob in a Cult Classic"; "Stubbs"; "Lloyd's Lunchbox"; "Wrong Hole"; "Gun, Zipper, Snot"; "Empty Roll"; "Hut Sluts"; "Wastes Away"; "Phull Phrontal Phingers"; "The Birth of Brian"; "Home Honey I'm High"; "Lloyd Loses His Lunch"; and "Illusion of Life," among others.

Lumivision released an early version of this DVD in

1998, but Slingshot rereleased it less than a year later.

SPECIAL FEATURES None TECHNICAL FEATURES Fullscreen (1.33:1) • Languages: Eng. • Sound: Dolby Digital 2.0 • Keepcase • 1 Disc • Region All GENRE Mature/Anthology

Sprite: Between Two Worlds

U.S. Manga Corps, 2001, 81 mins., #USMD 2039. Directed by Takeshi Yamaguchi. Screenplay by Tsutomu Senogai. Based on the manga series by Shinobu Arimura.

Shy, pretty Manami is a college student whose cousin calls her "Nami." Both of them are unaware that this name triggers her dual personality, and Nami is the butt-kicking, flirtatious wild side of Manami. Her rival, Chiaki, wants to create trouble for Manami, but she never figured on dealing with two women in one!

This two-part 1996 OVA features cutesy retro character designs that may have viewers expecting to see Gigantor or Speed Racer, as well. Although it initially features mainly female nudity and erotic images, there are sexual encounters as the story continues into its second half. Refreshingly free of rape, demons, and tentacles, *Sprite* might still bother some viewers with its intimations of incest and a glancing reference to fatherly sexual abuse.

SPECIAL FEATURES Character Clips • DVD-ROM Features: Art, Scripts • Other Title Trailers TECHNICAL FEATURES Fullscreen (1.33:1) • Subtitles/CC: Eng. • Languages: Jap., Eng. dub • Sound: Dolby Digital 2.0 • Keepcase • 1 Disc • Region 1 GENRE & RATING Mature/Action • Rated 16+

Spy of Darkness

Kitty, 2002, 44 mins., #KVDVD-0218. Directed by Hisashi Tomii. Script by Ginzo Choshiya, Hisashi Tomii.

The government has created a bioengineered cyborg, but the creature—called Dragon—has faulty genes when it comes to sex, making him a green-skinned sexual predator. After terrorist commandoes free Dragon, the leader of the Special Securities Service Cabinet "Q Section" accompanies two other of her top female agents to stop the bioborg. But will Anne, Shion, and Layla fall prey to the beast's savage lusts before they can stop it?

This 1997 hentai contains all the traditional elements you'd expect from the plot: rape, bondage, torture, gore, and tentacle rape. The animation is average, though it uses realistic color palettes.

SPECIAL FEATURES Other Title Trailers TECHNICAL FEATURES Fullscreen (1.33:1) • Subtitles/CC: Eng. • Languages: Jap.,

Eng. dub • Sound: Dolby Digital 2.0 • Keepcase • 1 Disc • Region 1 GENRE & RATING Adult/Action • Rated 18+

Star Ballz

MMG, 2001, 60 mins.

Another hentai parody from the group that brought the world *Sailor and the 7 Ballz*, you can probably guess which popular movie trilogy *Star Ballz* targets. The "story" mixes characters from the *Star Wars* saga with familiar agents from *The X-Files*, plus characters from *Dragon Ball Z*, *Wayne's World, Beavis and Butt-Head, Star Trek, Pokémon, Sailor Moon*, and more. This light-hearted sex romp features slightly better animation than *Sailor*, though the plot is only coherent because it's a parody of an existing plot. Still, viewers may get a few naughty giggles.

One person that didn't get naughty giggles was George Lucas, creator of *Star Wars*. Following the release of *Star Ballz* in mid-2001, Lucasfilm Ltd. sued Media Market Group Ltd., the New York producers of *Star Ballz*, for copyright and trademark infringement. The suit was filed in October, but a federal judge refused to permanently block the sale of the DVD and videos in January 2002, citing the opinion that the public would not likely confuse the parody with the real property. A temporary restraining order had been in effect from December to January.

SPECIAL FEATURES None TECHNICAL FEATURES Fullscreen (1.33:1) • Languages: Eng. dub • Sound: Dolby Digital 2.0 • Keepcase • 1 Disc • Region All GENRE Adult/Parody/Science Fiction

Steel Angel Kurumi: Angel On My Shoulder [#1]

ADV Films, 2002, 90 mins., #DKU/001. Directed by Naohito Takahashi, Kazuya Murata, Norihiko Sudo. Screenplay by Naruhisa Arakawa. Based on the manga series by Kaishaku in *Monthly Ace Next*.

While exploring a presumably abandoned house, a young and naive Nakahito finds himself face-to-face with a beautiful girl. At least, it looks like a girl. In reality she is Kurumi, a Steel Angel, the most powerful weapon system ever created. One thing leads to another, and Nakahito accidentally manages to activate her. Now awakened, the Steel Angel sees Nakahito as her only master and her true love. However, some in the military are not amused. Realizing that she will never conform to their wishes, they must now do the only thing that seems reasonable—destroy her and her master.

Steel Angel Kurumi was originally released on Japanese television in 1999. Though the storyline seems predictable (and a bit like *Tenchi Muyo!*), it manages to throw viewers enough curves—and cheesecake—to remain both interesting and entertaining. One such surprise is when Kurumi jealously refuses to let Nakahito "activate" Steel Angel Saki—she decides to do it. Saki is then born with deep, passionate, lesbian love for Kurumi.

With vibrant artwork and animation, *Steel Angel Kurumi* is a pleasure to watch. Its soundtrack is good also, but the often bouncy tunes lack any hit material. There is abundant nudity and adult situations, both serious and comical. The voice acting is above average and includes a host of ADV Film's best talent, including *Farscape's* Claudia Black in a cameo role (reciting the Onmyo Prayer prior to the menu). All in all, this disc is a solid choice and is sure to please. [GP]

SPECIAL FEATURES Interviews with Voice Actresses • Character and Art Galleries • Production Notes • Trailers • Game: Printable Fortune Teller • Other Title Trailers • Insert: Fortune Teller Game TECHNICAL FEATURES Fullscreen (1.33:1) • Subtitles/CC: Eng. • Languages: Jap., Eng. dub • Sound: Dolby Digital 2.0 • Keepcase • 1 Disc • Region 1 GENRE & RATING Mature/Science Fiction • Rated 17+

Steel Angel Kurumi: The Trouble with Angels [#2]

ADV Films, 2002, 90 mins., #DKU/002. Directed by Naohito Takahashi, Kazuya Murata, Norihiko Sudo. Screenplay by Naruhisa Arakawa. Based on the manga series by Kaishaku in *Monthly Ace Next*.

Dr. Amagi takes Kurumi, Saki, and Nakahito with her to someplace safer, but their journey by train is not an easy one. On the way, Saki takes steps to reveal her feelings for Kurumi, but the others have confusing romantic issues of their own to deal with. Meanwhile, the men of the Academy are plotting the downfall of the Steel Angels, using newly activated Steel Angels of their own. Will these new Angels destroy their "sisters?"

These six fifteen-minute episodes move the series away from sexy comedy and more into drama. The plot still doesn't seem new or ground-breaking, but it's at least establishing a bit of its own identity. There are some nice moments with the train and fireworks, and the art is very pretty, though often cartoony. The stories on this disc have lots of cheesecake elements, but not much real nudity.

SPECIAL FEATURES Live-Action Photo Shoot • Character and Art Galleries • Production Notes • Trailers • Game: Printable Fortune Teller • Other Title Trailers • Insert: Fortune Teller Game TECHNICAL FEATURES Fullscreen (1.33:1) • Subtitles/CC: Eng. • Languages: Jap., Eng. dub • Sound: Dolby Digital 2.0 • Keep-

case • 1 Disc • Region 1 GENRE & RATING Mature/Science Fiction • Rated 17+

Steel Angel Kurumi: Where Angels Fear to Tread [#3]

ADV Films, 2002, 90 mins., #DKU/003. Directed by Naohito Takahashi, Koji Fukazawa, Kazuya Murata, Norihiko Sudo. Screenplay by Naruhisa Arakawa. Based on the manga series by Kaishaku in *Monthly Ace Next*.

Karinka is the Academy's best assassin, and she has two Angel hearts to counter Kurumi's Mark II heart. But something within Kurumi's heart holds a dark and terrible power; why is she manifesting black wings? Will Nakahito be turned against his friend in an effort to stop her before she turns to evil? And who—or what—is the mysterious Mikhail?

With dark secrets about the Angel's origins revealed here, the tension in these six episodes goes up several notches. There are some super-deformed scenes, and mild nudity, which is troubling mainly because most of the lead characters look like children.

SPECIAL FEATURES Text Interviews with Crew • Live-Action Photo Shoot • Character and Art Galleries • Production Notes • Trailers • Game: Printable Fortune Teller • Other Title Trailers • Insert: Fortune Teller Game TECHNICAL FEATURES Fullscreen (1.33:1) • Subtitles/CC: Eng. • Languages: Jap., Eng. dub • Sound: Dolby Digital 2.0 • Keepcase • 1 Disc • Region 1 GENRE & RATING Mature/Science Fiction • Rated 17+

Steel Angel Kurumi: Fallen Angel [#4]

ADV Films, 2002, 90 mins., #DKU/004. Directed by Naohito Takahashi, Norihiko Sudo, Kazuya Murata, Koji Fukazawa. Screenplay by Naruhisa Arakawa. Based on the manga series by Kaishaku in *Monthly Ace Next*.

The Steel Angels have found the mysterious floating fortress of the Academy, and now they must find a way to save Nakahito. Mikhail is working on Nakahito, trying to turn him against his friends. Saki and Karinka are detained by a force field, and Dr. Amagi is also captured. It all finishes with a battle between Kurumi and Mikhail, equally matched opponents who both hide secrets.

Lots of combat and exposed secrets make up the final six episodes of the series. More stylized animation was used toward the end, heightening the emotional punch of the story. Claudia Black plays a much bigger voice role in this volume, and viewers will be pleasantly surprised to find that they've been hearing more of her than they realized. There's some minor nudity in the volume.

SPECIAL FEATURES Interview with Claudia Black and Voice Actresses • Character Bios • Character and Art Galleries • Travelogue • Production Notes • Trailers • Game: Printable Fortune Teller • Other Title Trailers • Insert: Fortune Teller Game TECHNICAL FEATURES Fullscreen (1.33:1) • Subtitles/CC: Eng. • Languages: Jap., Eng. dub • Sound: Dolby Digital 2.0 • Keepcase • 1 Disc • Region 1 GENRE & RATING Mature/Science Fiction • Rated 17+

Strange Love

U.S. Manga Corps, 2002, 74 mins., #USMD 1746. Directed by Daiji Suzuki. Screenplay by Masayori Sekijima. Based on the manga series by Hiroya Oku in *Young Jump.*

Yoshida Chizuru is a very sexy girl, but she's about to get in some trouble. It's against school policy for her to appear in TV commercials, but she's been secretly starring in an ad campaign. When one of her teachers discovers the ads, he tries to use this to his advantage with Yoshida, but he doesn't get very far. Later, Yoshida gets romantically involved with a rock star, but then she meets the girl of her dreams, Ayumi. Will the two girls become lesbian lovers?

This two-part 1997 OVA series really isn't very good. The art is vaguely realistic, but still unnatural looking, and it's not helped by the basketball-sized breasts on Yoshida. *Strange Love* is not particularly hardcore in the sexual arena, but it is definitely in the mature category.

SPECIAL FEATURES "Making of" Featurette • Character Bios • DVD-ROM Features: Art, Scripts • Other Title Trailers TECHNICAL FEATURES Fullscreen (1.33:1) • Subtitles/CC: Eng. • Languages: Jap., Eng. dub • Sound: Dolby Digital 2.0 • Keepcase • 1 Disc • Region 1 GENRE & RATING Mature/Erotic/Comedy • Rated 16+

Sword for Truth

Manga Entertainment, 2000, 51 mins., #MANGA4057-2. Directed by Osamu Dezaki. Screenplay by Takeshi Narumi. Based on the novels by Takeshi Narumi.

In the days of feudal Japan, Shuranosuke Sakaki is a ronin (a masterless samurai) who easily dispatches a ferocious giant tiger that has menaced the countryside. The tiger attack is apparently a diversion created so that a cluster of rogue Seki Ninja can abduct Princess Mayu. Impressed by his sword skills, the Tokugawa Shogunate hires Sakaki to rescue Mayu from the clan. The ninja want an antique sword in exchange for the girl, but Sakaki offers them death at the point of his own blade instead. Along the way, he fights a water demon known as a "kappa" and the hellish spirits of undead Seki Ninja!

A 1990 OVA, this single-part story is nonsensical at times, and mind-numbingly, repetitiously bloody. Fountains of crimson fluid geyser forth as heads and limbs are lopped off, bodies are disemboweled, and more. The grue relents at times to make way for a few sex scenes and use of drugs, but the viewer will be so desensitized (or traumatized) by the red haze that he may not even notice the change in the action. The animation is very naturalistic and attractive, and some of the scene changes use old-style Japanese erotic art, or reproductions thereof. If you like lots of swordplay and gore, with a dash of sex, this one's for you.

SPECIAL FEATURES Other Title Trailers TECHNICAL FEATURES Fullscreen (1.33:1) • Subtitles/CC: Eng. • Languages: Jap., Eng. dub • Sound: Dolby Digital 2.0 • Keepcase • 1 Disc • Region 1, 2, 4 GENRE Mature/Fantasy/Action

Tales Trilogy, The

Kitty, 2001, 115 mins., #KVDVD-0114. Directed by Toshiyuki Sakurai. Screenplay by Toshiyuki Sakurai. Based on the manga stories by U-Jin in *Leed Comics.*

In "Tales of Titillation," a geek tries to see panties on a school playground, a pizza delivery man gets more than he bargained for, and—in an *Ultraman* parody—a man grows to the size of a giant, sexually assaults skyscrapers, shoots corrosive sperm, and battles a Sailor Moon lookalike. In "Tales of Sintillation," a nerd is beaten up and he pleasures himself until through contrivances, a girl falls on him. Also, a female baseball catcher has a secret weapon when she crouches, a tennis coach loves looking up skirts, and some girls tell horny campfire tales. Finally, in "Tales of Misbehavior," a man gets some oral attention on a train, the little match girl shows her other wares, and a nurse administers some special medicine.

An extremely popular trio of OVAs from 1990 to 1992, *The Tales Trilogy* is supposed to be humorous, and it is—in a lowbrow *Porky's* way. All of the men are ugly and depicted unflatteringly, while most of the girls look much too young. Still, all of the sex is consensual and the whole affair is genial enough. Few of the stories have any writer or director credits, and even the U.S. voice actors use silly *nom de porn* names, such as "Willie Dickersum." If you think it's funny for someone to get a nosebleed when sexually aroused—something that happens to almost every man on the disc—this is the disc for you.

SPECIAL FEATURES Other Title Trailers TECHNICAL FEATURES Fullscreen (1.33:1) • Subtitles/CC: Eng. • Languages: Jap., Eng. dub • Sound: Dolby Digital 2.0 • Keepcase • 1 Disc • Region 1 GENRE & RATING Adult/Anthology/Comedy • Rated 18+

Teacher's Pet

Anime 18, 2001, 114 mins., #A18D-2080. Directed by Kan Fukumoto, Hiroshi Ogawa. Screenplay by Yosei Morino, Takawa Yoshioka.

A college student, Chitose, has gotten involved with Professor Haruhiko. Complicating matters is the fact that he used to go out with her sister. She's on the swim team, and he's an artist, and their affair burns hot. But when a female teacher catches them in the act, will she turn them in, or insert herself into the relationship? What do you think? This is porn after all!

Released in Japan in 1999–2000, this four-part series features nothing but happy, consensual sex, with most of the sex scenes animated in a gauzy, dreamy fashion. There's some hot wax, bondage, and lesbianism. Nothing offensive for most audiences here, unless you can understand Japanese (reportedly the dialogue strongly implies Chitose and Haruhiko are brother and sister).

SPECIAL FEATURES Anime Featurette • Character and Art Galleries • Storyboards • Clean Credits • DVD-ROM Features: Art, Scripts, Storyboards • Other Title Trailers TECHNICAL FEATURES Fullscreen (1.33:1) • Subtitles/CC: Eng. • Languages: Jap., Eng. dub • Sound: Dolby Digital 2.0 • Keepcase • 1 Disc • Region All GENRE & RATING Adult/Romance • Rated 18+

Tokio Private Police: Complete

Kitty, 2001, 656 mins., #KVDVD-0117. Directed by Shinichi Higashi. Written by Yu Yamato. Based on the novel by Tatenao Hakage.

It's 2034 in a Japan so plagued with crime, private police forces must be hired to supplement the cops' efforts. Noriko Ibuki's a tomboyish but spunky young officer with the Tokio Private Police in the notorious Ginza district. While her work has numbed her to violence and crime, one thing still scares Noriko: sex. Newly transferred to the mobile police division, Noriko finds herself teamed up with the buxom nymphomaniac Kayoko, brawny Isamu, and the mecha freak Yasuo. Right off the bat, the clothes and inhibitions drop off of everyone but Noriko and Yasuo, who's too engrossed in the new crab-cop vehicles to pay attention to the opposite sex. Will the lessons taught by Noriko's teammates cure her distaste for sex? Take a guess.

Tokio Private Police has a surprising amount of plot development for an adult film (and more than a smidgen of familiar concepts for *Patlabor* fans). The character design is high quality, as is the animation. All that attention to detail doesn't keep the disc from being lewd, lascivious, and fully uncensored, though. Be prepared for a lesbian scene and an extremely graphic rape. [BR]

SPECIAL FEATURES Other Title Trailers TECHNICAL FEATURES Fullscreen (1.33:1) • Subtitles/CC: Eng. • Languages: Jap., Eng. dub • Sound: Dolby Digital 2.0 • Keepcase • 1 Disc • Region 1 GENRE & RATING Adult/Science Fiction • Rated 18+

Triangle

Anime 18, 2001, 58 mins., #A18D-2046. Directed by Hiroyuki Makino. Script by Reni Ko. Original story by Yutaka Hidaka.

Keisuke likes Misa, a wealthy girl from another college. Keisuke's tomboyish longtime friend Rina, has a crush on Keisuke. Toshiya is a stud with the ladies, and also Keisuke's friend. Then there's big-breasted Mimi who has the hots for Keisuke after he defends her honor, and a sexy nurse who "heals" Keisuke when he's hospitalized.

This two-part 1998 hentai series is based on a computer game. It's pretty cutesy, with goofy characters and average animation. All of the sex is consensual, with no demons or tentacles in sight, and the kinkiest it gets is the use of an enema. In the most bizarre element, watch for a *Mary Poppins* homage! The DVD features a nice-enough transfer, but some viewers will be disappointed by the lack of subtitles.

SPECIAL FEATURES Anime Featurette • Character Bios • Storyboards • DVD-ROM Features: Art, Scripts, Storyboards • Other Title Trailers TECHNICAL FEATURES Fullscreen (1.33:1) • Languages: Jap., Eng. dub • Sound: Dolby Digital 2.0 • Keepcase • 1 Disc • Region 1 GENRE & RATING Adult/Romance/Medical • Rated 18+

Twilight of the Dark Master: Collector's Edition

Urban Vision, 2001, 50 mins., #UV1068. Directed by Akiyuki Shinbo. Written by Duane Dell'Amico, Tatsuhiko Urahata. Based on the manga series by Saki Okuse in *Wings*.

It's the near future, and mankind finds itself at war with a mysterious race of demons. Their only savior is apparently Tsunami Shijo, a silver-haired, effeminate man with remarkable psychic powers. Tsunami goes to work after a woman who was mauled by her lover begs him for help. The woman's lover inexplicably turned into a demon. Tsunami fights a variety of grotesque and gimmicky bad guys before encountering Takamiya, the titular dark master who's been causing all of earth's problems with demons.

Some aspects of *Twilight of the Dark Master*—the theory that demons are just byproducts of mankind's tampering with science, for example—are sort of interesting. Unfortunately, the characters are dull, the story is sluggish and impenetrable (due perhaps to a condensation from the manga), and the animation is only intermittently above average for this 1997 OVA. With its almost token use of graphic violence and nudity, *Twilight of the Dark Master* comes off as a poor man's version of more popular supernatural thrillers like *Wicked City* and *Vampire Hunter D*.

The extras on the DVD aren't really substantial enough to warrant the "Collector's Edition" tag. The only really interesting one among them is a quick film of series designer Hisashi Abe drawing the stunning cover for the DVD; it's a nice study of the artist at work. Overall, though, *Twilight of the Dark Master* is dull and silly. [MT]

SPECIAL FEATURES "Making of" Cover Art Featurette • Character and Art Galleries • Trailer • Other Title Trailers • Inserts: Character Designer Bio TECHNICAL FEATURES Fullscreen (1.33:1) • Subtitles/CC: Eng. • Languages: Jap., Eng. dub • Sound: Dolby Digital 5.1 • Keepcase • 1 Disc • Region 1, 6 GENRE Mature/Horror

Twin Angels: Vols. 1 and 2

NuTech, 1999, 87 mins., #872. Directed by Kan Fukumoto. Script by Oji Miyako.

Mai and Ai Amatsu are nineteen-year-old girls who are heir to the mantle of legendary warrior-guardians, and using their sexually charged mystical powers, they must protect the half-demon boy Onimaro from the demons of seduction. If he is seduced by the dark side, he will become more powerful than they ever imagined . . . or something like that. But when the Tenjin Shrine is compromised by evil, Mai and Ai may soon be sacrificed to the demonic lust of the Onuiyasha-Doji. Will Onimaro succumb to his demon side, or keep his human heart?

This 1995 two-part OVA is actually the sequel to the original *Twin Angels* series from 1994. The animation is often attractive, but still average, and there is some superdeformity. The story features bondage, lesbianism, and rape by humans, demons, and tentacles. The disc is double-sided, with previews on side two.

SPECIAL FEATURES Anime Featurette • Other Title Trailers TECHNICAL FEATURES Fullscreen (1.33:1) • Subtitles/CC: Eng. • Languages: Jap., Eng. dub • Sound: Dolby Digital 2.0 • Keepcase • 1 Disc • Region All GENRE Adult/Supernatural

Twin Angels: Vols. 1 and 2 [Remastered]

Anime 18, 2002, 120 mins., #A18D-2187. Directed by Kan Fukumoto. Screenplay by Oji Miyako.

This disc contains the same episodes as the original release, but these have been remastered for better picture. There is also a new slate of extras.

SPECIAL FEATURES Interviews with Producer • Character Bios • Character and Art Galleries • Promotional Footage • Anime Featurette • DVD-ROM Features: Art, Scripts • Other Title Trailers TECHNICAL FEATURES Fullscreen (1.33:1) • Subtitles/CC: Eng. • Languages: Jap., Eng. dub • Sound: Dolby Digital 2.0 • Keepcase • 1 Disc • Region 1 GENRE & RATING Adult/Supernatural • Rated 18+

Urotsukidoji: Legend of the Overfiend [#1]

Anime 18, 1999, 103 mins., #A18D-1831. Directed by Hideki Takayama. Screenplay by Noboru Aikawa. Based on the manga series by Toshio Maeda in *Wani*.

According to legend, mankind doesn't really rule the Earth. Parallel to the Human World are the worlds of the Monster Demons and the Man-Beasts. A prophecy foretells of a superbeing called the Overfiend that appears every 3,000 years, appearing through the body of a human. This creature will have the power to unite the three worlds and create a world of peace and harmony. But to do so will cause untold rape, death, and misery to mankind. Negumo is that ill-fated human. Along with his friend, the Man-Beast Amano Jyaku, and his sister Megumi, Negumo tries to keep the demonic power under control, even as creatures from the other dimensions begin to appear. The battle may destroy Tokyo, and if that happens, the rest of Earth is next. . . .

Toshio Maeda is generally credited as the man who created the "erotic grotesque" form of manga, and helped usher in the same genre in anime. *Urotsukidoji* first saw release in 1987, as multiple OVAs, though they have been edited together (and some scenes have been cut) to create this "movie" version. For the unedited version, see the entry for *Urotsukidoji: Perfect Collection*. The animation is mostly attractive, even if the subject matter is grotesque. There's much gore and blood, bondage, lesbianism, and rape by demons and tentacles. There's also a clear homoerotic subtext to one scene with a basketball player.

If demon hentai is of interest to you, *Urotsukidoji* is generally considered both the grand-daddy of them all, and one of the best in terms of story and plot.

SPECIAL FEATURES Other Title Trailers TECHNICAL FEATURES Fullscreen (1.33:1) • Languages: Jap., Eng. dub • Sound:

Dolby Digital 2.0 • Keepcase • 1 Disc • Region All GENRE & RATING Adult/Supernatural • Rated 18+

Urotsukidoji II: Legend of the Demon Womb

Anime 18, 1999, 88 mins., #A18D-1832. Directed by Hideki Takayama. Screenplay by Noboru Aikawa. Based on the manga series by Toshio Maeda in *Wani*.

During World War II, Nazi mad scientist Dr. Munnihausen used a Nazi Death Rape machine in an attempt to summon and control—or kill—the Overfiend. In the present, Munnihausen Jr. is carrying on his father's legacy, and he's found something interesting; cousin Takeaki has gotten some of Nagumo's blood after an accident, and Takeaki is now developing demonic powers of his own. Will Takeaki become a demonic overlord himself, and will he turn on his cousin and destroy him?

This portion of the series goes over-the-top with offensive material, adding Nazis to the mix. There are many more demonic rapes and tentacle rapes. This version has reportedly been heavily censored, and fans have long complained that the English dub is awful. Compare this to the version shown in the *Urotsukidoji: Perfect Collection* (see entry). There may also be some confusion for fans since the story takes place partially during the events of the first *Urotsukidoji*, partially before it, and partially after it, making it not exactly a sequel *or* a prequel. Most fans tend to view it as an alternate reality.

SPECIAL FEATURES Background Notes • Other Title Trailers TECHNICAL FEATURES Fullscreen (1.33:1) • Languages: Jap., Eng. dub • Sound: Dolby Digital 2.0 • Keepcase • 1 Disc • Region All GENRE & RATING Adult/Supernatural • Rated 18+

Urotsukidoji III: Return of the Overfiend

Central Park, 2001, 190 mins., #A18D-2035. Directed by Hideki Takayama. Script by Noboru Aikawa, Hideki Takayama, Yasuhito Yamake, Gonzo Sasazuka. Based on the manga series by Toshio Maeda in *Wani*.

In the third installment of the *Urotsukidoji* story, things take a turn toward the apocalyptic. And if it's the end of the world in Urotsukidoji, you know that means lots of demons and lots of naked women in addition to all out carnage and destruction. Only the Chojin, a god-like being, can put the world to rights. Unfortunately the forces of darkness led by Kyo-o are trying to destroy the Chojin. So Amano Jyaku, the Man-Beast from the first installment of this series, is sent out to find Kyo-o and destroy him first. Along the way Amano Jyako encoun-

ters the power-mad Caesar, his sexy daughter Alector, and evil wizard Faust manipulating events.

When creators try to make an epic tale, sometimes things can go wrong. This is one of those times. The story for this 1993 OAV series is so contrived and convoluted, you hope for it to end after only one episode. None of the characters are likable or even very well developed. And when things finally come together, you realize that you're really only in the middle of the story, without much of a pay-off. The animation goes from average to below average depending on the scene. Many of the backgrounds have a thrown-together look.

The print and sound are fine. Another downside to this disc is that there is a Japanese track but no subtitles. This is a problem considering that the English dub is pretty bad. This has some serious hardcore sex in it, most of it rape and tentacles.

Note that in the DVD extras, the Japanese Trailer is only viewable from page two of the *Urotsukidoji* History section. [RJM]

SPECIAL FEATURES Anime Featurette • Background Notes • Manga • Trailer • DVD-ROM Features: Art, Manga, History, Character Bios, Production Notes • Other Title Trailers TECHNICAL FEATURES Fullscreen (1.33:1) • Languages: Jap., Eng. dub • Sound: Dolby Digital 2.0 • Keepcase • 1 Disc • Region All GENRE & RATING Adult/Supernatural • Rated 18+

Urotsukidoji IV: Inferno Road

Anime 18, 2001, 128 mins., #A18D-1836. Directed by Hideki Takayama, Shigenori Kageyama. Screenplay by Noboru Aikawa, Yosei Shano. Based on the manga series by Toshio Maeda in *Wani*.

It's the 2020s and Earth is a wasteland. The overfiend can be overthrown by the Mad Regent, a Lord of Chaos, who is personified as a girl named Himi. She travels through the wastes of the city with Buju, the leader of the Makemono (Man-Beasts), and the elderly Man-Beast Gashim, as they attempt to find the Overfiend in Osaka. On the way, they meet some really creepy psychic kids. And Amano Jyaku, the Man-Beast, once again faces Munnihausen Jr. Is the final battle for the three worlds coming, and if so, what will the rebirth bring?

With more of the same horror, gore, violent sexuality, and dark themes as in previous volumes, this contains a two-part OVA story, and a third part that was released as a widescreen theatrical feature in some countries. As expected, there are lots of demon and tentacle rapes, and in a bid to cover new ground for horror anime, a scene of childbirth is presented! Taken as a whole, the Urotsukidoji saga has many ups and downs, but seems to postulate that there are things worse than death, and that sex is the cause of both life and death and all the horrors in between.

As with the other DVDs in this series, there are no subtitles, and the dub is pretty bad (the fact that different casts were used for different volumes may account for some of the problem).

SPECIAL FEATURES Anime Featurette • Background Notes • Manga • Trailer • DVD-ROM Features: Art, Manga, History, Character Bios, Production Notes • Other Title Trailers TECHNICAL FEATURES Multi-Aspect (1.66:1 and 1.33:1) • Languages: Jap., Eng. dub • Sound: Dolby Digital 2.0 • Keepcase • 1 Disc • Region All GENRE & RATING Adult/Supernatural • Rated 18+

Urotsukidoji Saga: Hell on Earth [Box Set]

Anime 18, 2001, 541 mins., #A18D-2037.

This box set features the four commercially available keepcase editions of *Urotsukidoji* in a cardboard box. It does not feature any additional extras. See individual entries for the Special and Technical Features listings.

TECHNICAL FEATURES Cardboard Box with 4 Keepcases • 4 Discs • Region All GENRE & RATING Adult/Supernatural • Rated 18+

Urotsukidoji: Perfect Collection

Anime 18, 2000, 250 mins., #A18D-1833. Directed by Hideki Takayama. Screenplay by Goro Sanyo, Noboru Aikawa. Based on the manga series by Toshio Maeda in *Wani*.

Responding to complaints from hentai fans, Central Park Media/Anime 18 released the two-disc *Urotsukidoji: Perfect Collection*, which contains the complete and uncensored versions of *Urotsukidoji: Legend of the Overfiend* and *Urotsukidoji II: Legend of the Demon Womb*. The five OVAs were originally released in Japan from 1987 to 1991.

On these DVDs, there are English subtitles but no dub track, a fact that most fans cheered since *Urotsukidoji*'s dub tracks are widely reviled. Disc one is 146 minutes (compared to 103 minutes in the censored version), while disc two is 98 minutes (versus the 88-minute cut version). It's safe to say that most fans will prefer this set to the other two.

SPECIAL FEATURES Creator Bio • Anime Featurette • DVD-ROM Features: Art, Manga • Other Title Trailers TECHNICAL FEATURES Fullscreen (1.33:1) • Subtitles/CC: Eng. • Languages: Jap. • Sound: Dolby Digital 2.0 • Multikeepcase • 2 Discs • Region All GENRE & RATING Adult/Supernatural • Rated 18+

Vampire Hunter D: Special Edition

Urban Vision, 2000, 80 mins., #UV1064. Directed by Toyo Ashida. Script by Yasushi Hirano. Based on the novels by Hideyuki Kikuchi.

The setting is a post-apocalyptic Earth where monsters rule. Vampire Count Magnus Lee has reappeared, bringing with him a gaggle of bloodthirsty fiends, including his daughter. The people of a nearby village offer up young Doris to be his bride, hoping to placate him into leaving them alone. But Doris won't submit willingly, and her young brother Dan won't let her go so easily. When a dampiel (half man, half vampire) named D rides into town on a cyborg steed, Doris thinks her prayers are answered. But can she really trust a man who is half monster, even if she is attracted to him? Will D be able to stop Lee? More importantly, when he learns Lee's secret, will he want to?

Originally released in 1985, *Vampire Hunter D* is considered by many to be an anime classic, an innovator that spawned many imitations. It's humorous at times, but mostly dark and rather violent, with strong language and a good deal of cheesecake. The best thing about it is D's talking hand that eats dirt and ridicules him. Like many mid-eighties sci-fi/horror films, it's notable for its time, but pales next to modern fare, including the sequel.

The DVD has some cool extras, including a "making of" featurette that anime fans should drool over, as well as beautiful conceptual art by Yoshitaka Amano. [WM]

SPECIAL FEATURES "Making of" Featurette • Character and Art Galleries • Trailer • Promotional Game Footage • Other Title Trailers TECHNICAL FEATURES Fullscreen (1.33:1) • Subtitles/CC: Eng. • Languages: Jap., Eng. dub • Sound: Dolby Digital 5.1 • Keepcase • 1 Disc • Region 1 GENRE Mature/Horror/Action

Vampire Hunter D: Bloodlust

Urban Vision, 2002, 105 mins., #UV1093. Directed by Yoshiaki Kawajiri. Screenplay by Yoshiaki Kawajiri. Based on the novels by Hideyuki Kikuchi

Charlotte is kidnapped by the vampire lord, Meier Link, and her father hires every bounty hunter he can to get her back. One of those bounty hunters is a dunpeal (spelled differently than in the first movie), a half-vampire named D. Another bounty hunter is Leila, a woman orphaned by vamps, who fights alongside the vampire-killing team known as the Markus Brothers. And if competing with them wasn't enough, D must also get past the killer Barbarois, an organization of demonic assassins sent to kill him, and Carmila, who is certainly the craziest and possibly the most bloodthirsty vampire he's ever met. And if he manages to get past all that, will Charlotte still need saving? Or will D's greatest enemy turn out to be himself?

Released in 2001 after years of anticipation, *Vampire Hunter D: Bloodlust* is among the best anime of all time. It features an excellent story, a stirring soundtrack, superb animation, and achingly beautiful designs. A dark, gothic piece, viewers should be warned that it is extremely violent, and it features strong language—and yet, neither quality detracts from the story. It is a deeply touching, haunting tale, where all the players are complex and mysterious. D and Meier Link have earned places in the annals of vampire lore.

Unfortunately, as amazing as the movie is, the DVD doesn't do it justice. Why? Because there is no Japanese-language version on the disc! At least the English version is better than most dubs, but it's disappointing for fans who enjoy seeing anime in its original state—especially since having dual-languages is supposed to be one of DVD's perks! On the upside, the DVD does have a storyboard-to-film comparison and a "making of," must-see features for animation fans. [WM]

SPECIAL FEATURES "Making of" Featurette • Storyboards • Trailer • Promotional Footage • Other Title Trailers TECHNICAL FEATURES Widescreen (1.85:1 enhanced for 16x9) • Languages: Eng. dub • Sound: Dolby Digital 5.1 • Keepcase • 1 Disc • Region 1 GENRE & RATING Mature/Horror/Action • Rated R

Vampire Wars

Manga Entertainment, 2002, 60 mins., #MANGA4060-2. Directed by Kazuhisa Takenouchi. Script by Hiroyuki Hoshiyama. Based on the novel by Kiyoshi Kasai.

A mysterious attack on a NASA project in Arizona sets off a horrifying chain of events. First, the base is destroyed by a group of unknown terrorists, then the CIA begins a secret project, code-named "Dracula," in Paris. Enter Kosaburo Kuki, a former KGB operative turned freelancer. Coerced by the head of the French Secret Service, Monsieur Lassar, to find the reason for the CIA's operations in France, Kuki soon finds himself stuck in the middle of intrigue and mayhem. The trail leads him to the beautiful actress Lamia Vindaw, who, along with Kuki, must struggle to survive the CIA, the French Secret Service, and an army of vampires not too shy to pull out a rocket launcher or two, to discover the secret that will change both of their lives.

First released as an OVA in 1991, *Vampire Wars* makes the best of its short run time to develop the lead characters and form a viable, though not too deep, plot. Still, it does a good job of keeping the story moving while reserving time for plenty of death, gore, and destruction.

Though the art and animation are only what you would expect from a feature that's over a decade old, it does have a surprising effects soundtrack that shines best when the action goes the fastest. *Vampire Wars* does contain brief nudity and the language is harsh, colorful, and very profane throughout most of the movie. In the end, fans of action, bloodshed, and devastation on a large scale will find *Vampire Wars* accommodates their tastes very well. [GP]

SPECIAL FEATURES Other Title Trailers TECHNICAL FEATURES Fullscreen (1.33:1) • Subtitles/CC: Eng. • Languages: Jap., Eng. dub • Sound: Dolby Digital Surround 5.1 • Keepcase • 1 Disc • Region 1 GENRE Mature/Horror/Action

Venus 5: The Inma Ball/Labyrinth of the Inma

NuTech, 1999, 95 mins., #869. Directed by Osamu Inoue, Kan Fukumoto. Screenplay by Wataru Amano. Based on the manga series by Jin Ara.

Five teenage girls have superpowers, and call themselves "Venus 5." They serve the Greek goddess of love, Aphrodite . . . or at least, they would if they knew that's what they were supposed to be doing. Their liaison to the goddess is a smutty talking cat, but he isn't much help. Now, Necros, the female head of the Inma Empire, plans to revive the long-slumbering sun god Apollo so that she can steal his powers. But to revive Apollo, Necros needs the sexual secretions of the Venus 5, and she'll do anything to get them.

This 1994 two-part OVA is nothing more than thinly disguised *Sailor Moon* porn, with the names changed to protect the naughty. The animation is only average, and the contents include all the traditional trappings of the "dark side" of hentai: lesbianism, bondage, and demon and tentacle rape. The disc is double-sided with previews. There is no Japanese-language track, or any subtitles.

SPECIAL FEATURES Anime Featurette • Other Title Trailers TECHNICAL FEATURES Fullscreen (1.33:1) • Languages: Eng. dub • Sound: Dolby Digital 2.0 • Keepcase • 1 Disc • Region All GENRE Adult/Supernatural

Very Private Lesson

Anime Works, 2001, 80 mins., #AWDVD-0107. Directed by Hideaki Oba. Screenplay by Hideaki Oba. Based on the manga series by Kazuto Okada in *Young Champion*.

Aya Shirakaba is a pretty female student who is fixated on her teacher, Oraku Tairaku. And while Oraku is tempted by Aya visiting his apartment in very revealing clothing, he's also engaged to be married to another teacher. And then there's the issue of Aya's father, a major crime boss in the city; he's threatened that if his daughter doesn't remain pure, Oraku will die a slow death. Now, Oraku must make it his mission to keep Aya chaste . . . a tough proposition given that she's already being chased—by half the men and women at the school!

Very Private Lesson is not really smutty enough to go into the Mature/Adult category, and yet it features lots of panty shots of underage girls, and some minor nudity, as well as intimations of whipping, bondage, and enemas (between two men, and later, three girls). The animation is very standard and rather uninspired, and there is a lot of goofy super-deformed moments. The disc features notes from the director and each cast member on their characters.

SPECIAL FEATURES Production Notes • Other Title Trailers TECHNICAL FEATURES Fullscreen (1.33:1) • Subtitles/CC: Eng. • Languages: Jap., Eng. dub • Sound: Dolby Digital 2.0 • Keepcase • 1 Disc • Region 1 GENRE & RATING Mature/Cheesecake • Rated 16+

Vicious #1

NuTech, 2002, 28 mins., #654. Directed by Sakura Harukawa. Screenplay by Hideki Mitsui. Story by Yuna Kurosaki.

Angela is a beautiful young girl who lives with her rich father. Daddy is a nasty man who forces himself on the maid, Bridget, repeatedly. Among other things, this makes Angela mad, and she's soon plotting with her lover, John the butler. What does this all have to do with the death of Angela's mother, who took a tumble down the stairs six months ago?

Vicious has some decent animation, and a creepy little story about a *very* dysfunctional household. Who is the real manipulator of the household? The disc is double-sided with previews, and adult film stars Alysin Chaynes and Alexis Amore dub the female voices.

SPECIAL FEATURES Photo Galleries • Character and Art Galleries • Other Title Trailers TECHNICAL FEATURES Fullscreen (1.33:1) • Subtitles/CC: Eng. • Languages: Jap., Eng. dub • Sound: Dolby Digital 2.0 • Keepcase • 1 Disc • Region All GENRE Adult/Suspense

Vicious #2

NuTech, 2002, 29 mins., #655. Directed by Sakura Harukawa. Screenplay by Hideki Mitsui. Story by Yuna Kurosaki.

When John becomes increasingly concerned about Bridget, and a little freaked out by Angela's possessiveness, he makes plans to leave with the maid. But then the players start getting killed, in very bloody ways. Is someone at the mansion not playing with a full deck?

Lust and murder connect in the second half of this tale, which is more suspenseful than most hentai, and entirely devoid of demons and tentacles. The disc again has a B-side full of previews.

SPECIAL FEATURES Photo Galleries • Character and Art Galleries • Other Title Trailers TECHNICAL FEATURES Fullscreen (1.33:1) • Subtitles/CC: Eng. • Languages: Jap., Eng. dub • Sound: Dolby Digital 2.0 • Keepcase • 1 Disc • Region All GENRE Adult/Suspense

Vicious [Box Set]

NuTech, 2002, 57 mins., #656.

This box set features the two commercially available keepcase editions of *Vicious*, in a cardboard box. It does not feature any additional extras. See individual entries for the Special and Technical Features listings.

TECHNICAL FEATURES Cardboard Box with 2 Keepcases • 2 Discs • Region All GENRE & RATING Adult/Suspense

Waking Life

Fox, 2002, 100 mins., #2004065. Directed by Richard Linklater. Screenplay by Richard Linklater.

Wiley Wiggins is trying to figure out what parts of life are real and what parts are a dream, so as he walks through the city, he talks with men and women. They are a wide collection of people, ranging from street philosophers to philosophy professors, drunks to train-hoppers, and their answers range from banal to insightful, reveling in coarse reality or shifting to the existential and intellectual. They expound and pontificate on what their ideas are about dreaming, waking, existence, sex, religion, time, culture, violence, identity, and much more.

Released at the Sundance Film Festival in 2001, and theatrically later in the fall, *Waking Life* is a gorgeous experiment in animation, but its pretensions will polarize audiences. Writer/director Richard Linklater shot the film in live action first in the summer of 1999 on digital video, and then edited it into a completed feature. The film was then transferred to computer for an animation team headed by Bob Sabiston, where it was rotoscoped and digitally painted.

Your enjoyment of *Waking Life* will depend on what you're seeking when you view it. The constant dialogue can be numbing, like being stuck at an after-party with two dozen semi-stoned college students, but there are some interesting concepts. But as much as Linklater and the actors want it to be, the beauty of *Waking Life* isn't in the words or characters, but in the mind-blowing animation. There's really nothing similar in the entire realm of animation, so to say the film is ground-breaking is not hyperbole. By visualizing the words without tying them to reality, the animators create an almost tactile sensation with the dialogue; conversely, muting the sound and using the imagery as visual wallpaper may be more satisfying for some viewers.

The DVD is packed with extras, including two commentary tracks, and a running text commentary feature. There are also some fascinating looks into the making of the animation, original shorts by Sabiston, and more.

SPECIAL FEATURES "Making of" Featurette • Commentary Tracks by Director, Actor, and Crew • Cast & Crew Filmographies • Production Notes/Text Commentary • Deleted Scenes • Live-Action Takes • Trailer • Animation Software Tutorial • Promotional Footage • Other Title Trailers TECHNICAL FEATURES Widescreen (1.85:1 enhanced for 16x9) • Subtitles/CC: Eng., Fren. • Languages: Eng., Span. dub • Sound: Dolby Digital Surround 5.1 • Keepcase • 1 Disc • Region 1 GENRE & RATING Mature/Drama/Existential • Rated R

Weather Report Girl

Critical Mass, 2001, 90 mins., #CMDVD6959. Directed by Kunihiko Yuyama. Based on the manga series by Tetsu Adachi in *Young Magazine.*

Keiko Nakadaiure works at a low-rated TV station, but she has much bigger dreams, and will do anything to get her shot at stardom. When the regular weather report girl goes on vacation, Keiko gets her shot, and she begins flashing her skin while doing the reports. But even as ratings—and Keiko's fame—begin to increase, the station management isn't happy with her antics. A series of "accidents" imperil Keiko, but she turns the tables on everyone . . . including Michiko Kawai, the previous weather girl, who returns to find her job in jeopardy.

This 1994 two-part OVA has some funny over-the-top moments, but it suffers from truly ugly character designs. The DVD transfer is also bad, with shimmering lines, problematic subtitles, and a menu in which it's very difficult to see the choices. In terms of content, the show is generally more suggestive and naughty, with little actual hardcore sex. There are some sex toys, and a brief bondage and SM fantasy sequence, however. A live-action version of the manga and anime, entitled *Weather Woman*, was released in 1995, and followed by a sequel, *Weather Woman Returns*.

SPECIAL FEATURES Character and Art Galleries TECHNICAL FEATURES Fullscreen (1.33:1) • Subtitles/CC: Eng. • Languages: Jap., Eng. dub • Sound: Dolby Digital Surround 3.0 • Keepcase • 1 Disc • Region All GENRE Adult/Comedy

Welcome to Pia Carrot: Vol. 1

NuTech, 2001, 28 mins., #578. Directed by Katsuma Kanazawa . Script by Katsuma Kanazawa .

Teenage boy Yusuke begins working a summer job at his father's restaurant, Pia Carrot, unaware of what fate has in store for him there. Teased by female classmate and coworker Satomi (who has a crush on him), Yusuke is also watched by the restaurant manager, a woman named Shiho. Then, Yusuke saves another waitress who has a crush on him, Reika, when she falls in an alley. Soon, he's all ready to get down to business with Reika . . . or will it be one of the other girls?

Based on a computer game, this three-part 1997 OVA series is spread across a trio of discs. The art is cutesy, and features some super-deformed moments. The sex is all consensual, and relatively tame, when it finally appears; the first nudity doesn't even happen until seventeen minutes in, and there's only one sex scene on the first DVD. Adult film stars Inari Vachs and Gina Ryder provide voices, and there's a breathy "interview" with Ryder included in the extras. The second side of the disc contains preview trailers. *Welcome to Pia Carrot* is great "soft" hentai that isn't likely to embarrass or enrage female fans; take out the explicit sex, and the series would be a conventional romantic comedy.

SPECIAL FEATURES Voice Actress Interview • Photo Galleries • Character and Art Galleries • Other Title Trailers TECHNICAL FEATURES Fullscreen (1.33:1) • Subtitles/CC: Eng. • Languages: Jap., Eng. dub • Sound: Dolby Digital 2.0 • Keepcase • 1 Disc • Region 1 GENRE & RATING Adult/Romantic/Comedy

MATURE/ADULT MATURE/ADULT MATURE/ADULT

Welcome to Pia Carrot: Vol. 2

NuTech, 2001, 28 mins., #579. Directed by Katsuma Kanazawa. Script by Katsuma Kanazawa.

Waitress Shoko admits her feelings for Yusuke to Satomi, unaware that her friend also desires their workmate. Later, Shoko and Yusuke go to a love hotel, where Shoko offers Yusuke her virginity. But Satomi sees them enter the hotel, and is jealous. Meanwhile, Shiho has to leave the restaurant due to family issues, and Yusuke tries to talk to her. They end up in bed together.

More pleasant consensual sex, with no violence or supernatural creatures of any kind, this volume of *Welcome to Pia Carrot* also features a solo scene with one character in the shower. As with other volumes, the DVD has previews on side two.

SPECIAL FEATURES Voice Actress Interview • Photo Galleries • Character and Art Galleries • Other Title Trailers TECHNICAL FEATURES Fullscreen (1.33:1) • Subtitles/CC: Eng. • Languages: Jap., Eng. dub • Sound: Dolby Digital 2.0 • Keepcase • 1 Disc • Region 1 GENRE Adult/Romantic/Comedy

Welcome to Pia Carrot: Vol. 3

NuTech, 2001, 28 mins., #580. Directed by Katsuma Kanazawa. Script by Katsuma Kanazawa.

The workers at the Pia Carrot restaurant decide to go to the beach on Okinawa at the end of the summer. Yusuke thinks the vacation will be paradise, but other factors enter into it. His father is getting remarried, but won't tell Yusuke who the bride-to-be is, while Satomi confronts Yusuke about his sex with the others. Will Yusuke kiss and make up with Satomi? It's porn. What do you think?

The final volume of the first *Welcome to Pia Carrot* series features some character development, pleasant outdoor scenery, and lesbianism. The DVD has previews of other series on side two.

SPECIAL FEATURES Voice Actress Interview • Photo Galleries • Character and Art Galleries • Other Title Trailers TECHNICAL FEATURES Fullscreen (1.33:1) • Subtitles/CC: Eng. • Languages: Jap., Eng. dub • Sound: Dolby Digital 2.0 • Keepcase • 1 Disc • Region 1 GENRE Adult/Romantic/Comedy

Welcome to Pia Carrot [Box Set]

NuTech, 2001, 84 mins., #581.

This box set features the three commercially available keepcase editions of *Welcome to Pia Carrot*, in a cardboard box. It does not feature any additional extras. See individual entries for the Special and Technical Features listings.

TECHNICAL FEATURES Cardboard Box with 3 Keepcases • 3 Discs • Region 1 GENRE Adult/Romantic/Comedy

Welcome to Pia Carrot 2: Vol. 1

NuTech, 2001, 28 mins., #582. Directed by Kan Fukumoto. Script by Morino Yosei.

It's a new year, and there's a new staff at the Pia Carrot restaurant. Koji is late for his job interview, but persistence pays off, and he's hired. Part of the reason he's hired is because manager Ryoko has a crush on him, even though waitress Azusa doesn't like him. At a welcome party, Aoi gets drunk and falls asleep, leaving Koji and Ryoko some time to get better acquainted . . . carnally.

This 1998 sequel isn't quite as pleasant as the first series, largely because it has a "been there done that" atmosphere, and all the development of earlier characters is gone. The DVD also features a very poor quality transfer, making it unpleasant to watch at times. Adult film stars Devon and Charmaine Star provide voices, and side two of the disc has trailers.

SPECIAL FEATURES Photo Galleries • Character and Art Galleries • Other Title Trailers TECHNICAL FEATURES Fullscreen (1.33:1) • Subtitles/CC: Eng. • Languages: Jap., Eng. dub • Sound: Dolby Digital 2.0 • Keepcase • 1 Disc • Region 1 GENRE Adult/Romantic/Comedy

Welcome to Pia Carrot 2: Vol. 2

NuTech, 2001, 28 mins., #583. Directed by Kan Fukumoto. Script by Morino Yosei.

On a trip to a hot springs, Koji shares a room with male waiter Jun, and is bothered when he has gay fantasies about his roommate. But later, when Jun passes out in the hot springs, Koji learns Jun's secret, and the two are soon making whoopee.

The picture quality improves with this DVD, which features nothing but consensual sex. The disc is double-sided, with previews.

SPECIAL FEATURES Photo Galleries • Character and Art Galleries • Other Title Trailers TECHNICAL FEATURES Fullscreen (1.33:1) • Subtitles/CC: Eng. • Languages: Jap., Eng. dub • Sound: Dolby Digital 2.0 • Keepcase • 1 Disc • Region 1 GENRE Adult/Romantic/Comedy

Welcome to Pia Carrot 2: Vol. 3

NuTech, 2001, 28 mins., #584. Directed by Kan Fukumoto. Script by Morino Yosei.

When Azusa's little sister Mina begins to work at the restaurant, the girl gets a crush on Koji and begins to hang around him. Koji and Azusa's relationship goes even further downhill, until they realize that maybe their antagonism is masking some sort of sexual attraction.

The final *Welcome to Pia Carrot 2* DVD has more consensual sex, with some of it outdoors under fireworks. Once again, there are trailers on the flip side of the disc.

SPECIAL FEATURES Photo Galleries • Character and Art Galleries • Other Title Trailers TECHNICAL FEATURES Fullscreen (1.33:1) • Subtitles/CC: Eng. • Languages: Jap., Eng. dub • Sound: Dolby Digital 2.0 • Keepcase • 1 Disc • Region 1 GENRE Adult/Romantic/Comedy

Welcome to Pia Carrot 2 [Box Set]

NuTech, 2001, 84 mins., #585. Directed by Kan Fukumoto. Script by Morino Yosei.

This box set features the three commercially available keepcase editions of *Welcome to Pia Carrot 2*, in a cardboard box. It does not feature any additional extras. See individual entries for the Special and Technical Features listings.

TECHNICAL FEATURES Cardboard Box with 3 Keepcases • 3 Discs • Region 1 GENRE Adult/Romantic/Comedy

Wicked City: Special Edition

Urban Vision, 2000, 82 mins., #UVIO65. Directed by Yoshiaki Kawajiri. Screenplay by Kisei Cho. Based on the novel by Hideyuki Kikuchi.

Renzaburo Taki might look like an ordinary Tokyo salaryman, but at night, he walks the dangerous line between good and evil—between the human world and the Black World, a world of demons. He's a "Black Guard," a specially trained warrior who excels at dealing with supernaturally powered enemies. This makes his life interesting, but

dangerous. He must meet up with a female agent of the Black World and escort Giuseppi Mayart, an important spiritual diplomat, to a meeting that will signify a peace treaty between the humans and the demons. Not surprisingly, there are factions that would rather not see this treaty go into effect, so they quickly move to attack Taki and his party.

Wicked City is a good movie that was released theatrically in Japan in 1987. It's clever, action-packed, visually distinctive, and fun to watch. The director gives the look of the film a cool, blue tint, which makes the action scenes (tinted red) stand out even more. The relationship between Taki and his new partner, Makie, is sexually charged, and the enemies they face are grotesque and powerful. Amusingly, through it all, Taki is still a salaryman—he talks to his boss, makes business calls, and picks up a client at the airport. *Wicked City* is a great slice of dark action, but it's certainly not one for children, since it has gore, violence, and sex.

The DVD's quality is only adequate because *Wicked City* was animated in 1986, and is starting to look like it's badly in need of digital remastering. The picture isn't *bad*, but it's a little fuzzy. The disc does feature one interesting extra, an interview with the director conducted more than ten years after the film was completed. [MT]

SPECIAL FEATURES Interview with Director • Character Bios • Trailer • Other Title Trailers • Inserts: Liner Notes TECHNICAL FEATURES Fullscreen (1.33:1) • Subtitles/CC: Eng. • Languages: Jap., Eng. dub • Sound: Dolby Digital 5.1 • Keepcase • 1 Disc • Region 1 GENRE & RATING Mature/Horror

Words Worth: Vol. 1

NuTech, 2002, 28 mins., #594. Directed by Kan Fukumoto. Script by Morino Yosei.

The tribes of Light and Shadow are at war, partly because the Words Worth tablet/monolith (which contains secrets to unlocking the universe) has been shattered, though no one knows who did it. Astral is the prince heir of the Shadow Forces, and he will soon be wed to beautiful warrior woman Sharon. But she is in lust with another, the bravest Shadow swordsman, a man named Caesar. The two of them fight against the Tribe of Light's forces together, and during the battle, Light's Sir Fabris vows to take Sharon one day . . . by force if necessary. Later, the bitter and sexually frustrated Astral picks a captured Light sorceress named Maria to torture and rape, unaware that the forces of Light are mounting a full-scale war!

Yes, the plot of this five-part game-based 1999 OVA series is a bit common as fantasy series go, but hentai fantasy isn't very common, so fans might enjoy this sword and sorcery epic. The character designs for *Words Worth* are attractive and realistic, though some goofy elements pop up from time to time. There are lots of elves, a humorous skeleton, and in the sex department, a lusty shower scene and a bound woman raped by a horse-man creature. The series features voices by adult film stars Jenna Jameson and Nikki Dial, and Jameson does a brief "interview" segment in the extras (the interviews vary, so check them out on each disc). The flip side of the DVD contains a bunch of preview trailers.

SPECIAL FEATURES Voice Actress Interview • Photo Galleries • Character and Art Galleries • Other Title Trailers TECHNICAL FEATURES Fullscreen (1.33:1) • Subtitles/CC: Eng. • Languages: Jap., Eng. dub • Sound: Dolby Digital 2.0 • Keepcase • 1 Disc • Region All GENRE Adult/Fantasy

Words Worth: Vol. 2

NuTech, 2002, 28 mins., #595. Directed by Kan Fukumoto. Script by Morino Yosei.

The Light fighters mount an assault on the Shadow stronghold. Sorceress Maria, the daughter of Sir Fabris, escapes and begins to free Light prisoners, even the sexually abused girls in the dungeons. Meanwhile, Astral saves a girl named Nina from a beast in a cave, has sex with her, then arrives in time to stop Sir Fabris from raping Sharon. But Astral is about to pay for his rape of Maria, and the mystical spell she casts has an unexpected result!

Volume #2 contains more mystical fantasy, plus more bizarre sex, including a bound woman raped by pig-men and a sex scene with a cat-girl. The disc is once again double-sided, with previews.

SPECIAL FEATURES Voice Actress Interview • Photo Galleries • Character and Art Galleries • Other Title Trailers TECHNICAL FEATURES Fullscreen (1.33:1) • Subtitles/CC: Eng. • Languages: Jap., Eng. dub • Sound: Dolby Digital 2.0 • Keepcase • 1 Disc • Region All GENRE Adult/Fantasy

Words Worth: Vol. 3

NuTech, 2002, 28 mins., #596. Directed by Kan Fukumoto. Script by Morino Yosei.

Astral has been sent to the barren wastelands by Maria's spell, but not only has he gained distance, he's also been thrown twenty years into the future, *and* he has amnesia! It sucks to be him. Having grown a beard, Astral wanders into the Kingdom of Light, where the people mistake him for Pollux, a legendary swordsman. Astral has sex with Mew, and then moves off toward the Kingdom of Shadows to discover the secret past that eludes

him. Meanwhile, Tessio and Menza are plotting some major evil once the final stone pieces of the Words Worth tablet are recovered.

Continuing the "icky creature rapists" sequences, the animators follow up the horse and pig-men with . . . demon tentacle rape! Didn't see that one coming, did you? And on the flip side of the DVD, more previews!

SPECIAL FEATURES Voice Actress Interview • Photo Galleries • Character and Art Galleries • Other Title Trailers TECHNICAL FEATURES Fullscreen (1.33:1) • Subtitles/CC: Eng. • Languages: Jap., Eng. dub • Sound: Dolby Digital 2.0 • Keepcase • 1 Disc • Region All GENRE Adult/Fantasy

Words Worth: Vol. 4

NuTech, 2002, 28 mins., #597. Directed by Kan Fukumoto. Script by Morino Yosei.

Astral is seduced by a demonic creature sent by Tessio and Menza, but he's saved by swordswoman Rita. When they open the barrier that separates the kingdoms of Light and Shadow, the older Sir Fabris reactivates his armies to attack the enemy. Astral's onetime-fiancée, Sharon, joins with Caesar to lead the armies of Shadow. Believing Astral to be an enemy, they attack him. Astral's father, King Watoshika, begins to sexually torture Rita, but Tessio and Menza use that moment to launch their own attack!

Lots of action, mistaken identities, and a bit of rape make up this penultimate volume in the *Words Worth* saga. Look for previews on the back side of the DVD.

SPECIAL FEATURES Voice Actress Interview • Photo Galleries • Character and Art Galleries • Other Title Trailers TECHNICAL FEATURES Fullscreen (1.33:1) • Subtitles/CC: Eng. • Languages: Jap., Eng. dub • Sound: Dolby Digital 2.0 • Keepcase • 1 Disc • Region All GENRE Adult/Fantasy

Words Worth: Vol. 5

NuTech, 2002, 27 mins., #598. Directed by Kan Fukumoto. Script by Morino Yosei.

Astral remembers his true identity just in time, and his sexual reunion with Sharon follows soon after. But will there be much of a future to celebrate if Tessio and Menza complete their evil plans? All of the saga's players— young and old—must somehow unite behind Astral if both kingdoms are to be saved. Will the old hatreds and rivalries be put to rest in the coming battle?

The final volume of *Words Worth* contains consensual sex, as well as a final tentacle rape sequence. Look for other title trailers on the disc's B-side.

SPECIAL FEATURES Voice Actress Interview • Photo Galleries •
Character and Art Galleries • Other Title Trailers TECHNICAL FEA-
TURES Fullscreen (1.33:1) • Subtitles/CC: Eng. • Languages:
Jap., Eng. dub • Sound: Dolby Digital 2.0 • Keepcase • 1 Disc
• Region All GENRE Adult/Fantasy

Other Title Trailers • Easter Egg TECHNICAL FEATURES
Widescreen (1.85:1) • Subtitles/CC: Eng. • Languages: Jap.,
Eng. dub • Sound: Dolby Digital 2.0, Dolby Digital 5.1 • Keep-
case • 1 Disc • Region 1, 2, 4 GENRE & RATING
Mature/Fantasy/Action • Rated R

Words Worth [Box Set]

NuTech, 2002, 140 mins., #599. Directed
by Kan Fukumoto. Script by Morino
Yosei.

This box set features the five commercially available keepcase editions
of *Words Worth* in a cardboard box. It
does not feature any additional extras.
See individual entries for the Special
and Technical Features listings.

TECHNICAL FEATURES Cardboard Box with 5 Keepcases • 5 Discs
• Region All GENRE Adult/Fantasy

X [The Movie]

Manga Entertainment, 2001, 100 mins.,
#MANGA4046-2. Directed by Rintaro.
Screenplay by Mami Watanabe, Nanase
Okawa, Rintaro. Based on the manga
series by CLAMP in *Asuka*.

It's the year 1999 and you know that
means the world is going to end. With
that premise, this story follows a
young man named Kamui Shiro and
his quest to stop the Dragons of Earth from destroying
the world. The Dragons of Earth are seven superhumans
who wield magic powers as well as standard weapons.
Against them are the Dragons of Heaven, who want to
protect earth, even if it isn't the greatest place in the
galaxy. Added to this mix is Kamui's childhood friend
Fumma, who gets recruited by the Dragons of Earth.
Fumma's little sister Kotari is going to end up being a
human sacrifice to bring about the apocalypse. The battle erupts and Tokyo gets torn apart. Can Kamui face his
childhood friend Fumma, and which one of them will
win the battle?

The visuals in this 1996 film are very well done. The
destruction of Tokyo, the horrifying dreams, and the
gruesome deaths capture the feel of apocalypse perfectly.
The sound is also very good. But in the end the story
feels rushed and simplistic. You can tell this was a much
longer manga series that was condensed into a film.

The transfer to DVD is well done, and you get a 5.1
audio track that makes the explosive battle scenes pop
off the screen. Be warned that even though *X* isn't hentai, this is not for kids. There's lots of gore, nudity, and
skimpy outfits. [RJM]

SPECIAL FEATURES Text Interview with Director • Tarot
Cards/Character Bios • Character and Art Galleries • Trailer •

Easter Eggs
Feature Films
Companies & Resources
Selected Bibliography
Index

Easter Eggs

Among the many cool features that the DVD format allows is the addition of "Easter eggs," known as "Digital Omake" to anime fans. These are hidden features that must be searched for, just as a child hunts for Easter eggs. Once found, the eggs can offer anything from special art galleries and bloopers to mini-documentaries, and more.

The following is a listing of Easter eggs for animated titles released on DVD. Note that I have not included Easter eggs that are Web links, or those that lead solely to credits for the DVD authoring crew. Many of these Easter eggs have been verified, but not all. Also realize that some eggs may only work with machines with DVD-ROM capabilities, while others may be incompatible with certain brands or older-model DVD players. For more information on Easter eggs, go to www.dvdeastereggs.com or www.animeondvd.com.

Enjoy the hunt!

Adventures of Ichabod and Mr. Toad, The [Gold Collection]
Play the Mr. Toad's Wild Ride Game. If you answer all the trivia questions correctly, you can watch a bonus 1952 cartoon, "Susie, the Little Blue Coupe."

Angel Sanctuary
Go to "Sneak Peeks" and click on the building underneath the words "Sneak Peeks." Click on the red outline for a preview of the *Utena* movie.

Antz [Signature Selection]
Go to "Special Features." On the right side of the screen in the grass is a ghostly Dreamworks logo. Click **Left Down** to get an extra credit sequence.

Appleseed
Go to "Special Features," select "Main Menu," go **Left**. When no blue cursor is onscreen, press **Enter** to see a special trailer for *Appleseed*.

Armitage III
Go to "Extras" and highlight the LD covers. Click **Right** twice (the cursor will disappear) and **Up**. Armitage's glasses should now be red. Click **Enter** for a special New Year's message from Armitage and the director.

Armitage: Dual Matrix, Armitage: Dual Matrix—Special Edition
During the end credits, press **Skip Forward** to see an extra clip of Mousse.

Berserk: Immortal Soldier [#2]
Go to "Extras," click **Left** to light up the left torch. Click **Enter** for a chibi picture of Nosferatu Zodd.

Big O, The—Vol. #4
Go to "Menu," then click **Down** then **Left** or **Right**. When the pedals underneath the feet are highlighted, click **Enter** for the Easter egg.

Blue Submarine No. 6: Blues [#1]
When playing a preview for the next episode, skip to Chapter 4 before the preview is over. This will take you to special previews of *Monkey Magic* and *Gundam 0083*.

Blue Submarine No. 6: Minasoko [#4]
Go to "Extras," then click on "DVD Credits." Click **Up** four times to highlight the question mark next to the creature's ear. Click **Enter** to view a secret image gallery.

Bob Clampett's Beany and Cecil: The Special Edition
Go to "Characters," and put your cursor on top right corner of the billboard. Press **Up** twice and the "And Friends" should be highlighted in the upper right. Click **Enter** for a special Beany announcement, followed by a slide show with photos of Bob Clampett

with celebrities such as Bob Hope, Dean Martin, and Sonny Bono.

Bubblegum Crisis: Episodes 7, 8, and Music
EGG 1: Go to "Track Listing" for music videos. Press **Right** to go to a musical slideshow.

EGG 2: Go to "Track Listing" for music videos. Click on "Credits." While the credits roll, press **Enter** for a live-action musical clip.

Bubblegum Crisis: Tokyo 2040—Leviathans [#3]
This is a tricky one. Go to "Extras" and select "Credits" twice. The cursor should be hidden. Press **Enter** to view an alternate "Extras" menu.

Cardcaptor Sakura: The Movie
EGG 1: Go to "Extras" and highlight "English Trailer." Click **Left** and the cursor will disappear. Click **Left** again, then **Up** three times and **Right** once. There should be white bars around the word "Extra" now. Press **Enter** and the menu animation will restart.

EGG 2: Do the above, and then go to "Japanese Commercial Spots." Select "15 Second TV Commercial 'C' Type." Click **Left Up Enter**, then **Down Enter** to play a video.

Ceres, Celestial Legend: Destiny [#1]
EGG 1: Go to "Extras," then "Character Profiles," then Aya's page. Highlight the right arrow and click **Up**. "Friends" will be highlighted. Click it to get a bonus screen.

EGG 2: Go to "Extras," then "Character Profiles," then Aki's page. Highlight the right arrow and click **Up**. "Gift" will highlighted. Click it to get a bonus screen.

Ceres, Celestial Legend: Past Unfound [#2]
Same eggs as DVD #1.

Ceres, Celestial Legend: C-Genome [#3]
Same eggs as DVD #1.

Chicken Run
There are twelve eggs on this DVD, each containing an interesting fact about the movie. Until highlighted, the eggs are invisible. Once highlighted, they are green or yellow and are "cracked." IMPORTANT: Once one egg is clicked, the factoid will appear along with a "Back" link. Click it and you will be taken back to the original egg. Highlight the egg again and you will go to a different factoid (they appear to be displayed randomly).

EGG 1: In the "Audio" menu, go to "2.0 Dolby" and click **Right** to find a yellow egg.

EGG 2: In the "Subtitle" menu, go to the "Main Menu" link and click **Up** to get a yellow egg.

EGG 3: In the "Special Features" menu, go to the "Main Menu" link and click **Up** to get a green egg.

EGG 4: Go to page five of "Production Notes." Go to the "Back" link and click **Right** for a green egg.

EGG 5: In "Scene Selection," go to "Scene 17" and click **Right** for a yellow egg.

EGG 6: In "Trailers/Spots" go to "Trailer 2" and click **Down** to get a green egg.

EGG 7: Go to "Cast Bios" and choose "Mel Gibson." Go to the "Forward" link, and click **Left** for a yellow egg.

EGG 8: Go to "Cast Bios" and choose "Tony Haygarth." Go to page two, go to the "Forward" link, and click **Left** for a yellow egg.

EGG 9: Go to "Cast Bios" and choose "Jane Horrocks." Go to page two, go to the "Back" link, and click **Right** for a yellow egg.

EGG 10: Go to "Cast Bios" and choose "Imelda Staunton." Go to the "Forward" link and click **Left** for a yellow egg.

EGG 11: Go to "Crew Bios" and choose "Lloyd Price." Go to page two, go to the "Back" link, and click **Right** for a yellow egg.

EGG 12: Go to "Crew Bios" and choose "Dave Alex Riddett." Go to the "Forward" link and click **Left** for a yellow egg.

For another very cool *Chicken Run* Easter egg, you must own the live-action *Gladiator* DVD. There, if you highlight the eagle on Richard Harris's armored breastplate, you'll get a special *Chicken Run* trailer, scored to the *Gladiator* theme and narrated with similar bravado.

Cowboy Bebop: 6th Session
Go to "Extras" and highlight "Image Gallery." Click **Left** six times. The red eye on Ein's visor should light up. Press **Enter** for a secret gallery of Ein art. On some machines, pressing **5** on your remote while in "Extras" will also bring up the gallery.

Crest of the Stars #1: To the Stars
Go to "Extras" and move down the options list as diamonds appear in the right column. When the Abh character appears next to "Extras," click on him to see a creditless closing. Note that this feature may only work on machines with DVD-ROM capabilities.

Crest of the Stars #2: The Politics of War
EGG 1: Go to "Extras" and move down the options list as diamonds appear in the right column. When the Abh character appears next to "Extras," click below him to see a creditless opening. Note that this feature may only work on machines with DVD-ROM capabilities.

EGG 2: Go to "Extras" and look for a dark stripe in the lower left corner. Click to the left of the stripe for an English-language trailer. Note that this feature may only work on machines with DVD-ROM capabilities.

Crest of the Stars:#3: Wayward Soldiers
Same eggs as DVD #2.

Crest of the Stars #4: Into the Unknown
EGG 1: Go to "Extras" and move down the options list as diamonds appear in the right column. When the Abh character appears next to "Extras," click on him to see a creditless opening. Note that this feature may only work on machines with DVD-ROM capabilities.

EGG 2: Same as EGG 2 in DVD #2.

EGG 3: Go to "Extras" and press **1** for the creditless opening.

EGG 4: Go to "Extras" and press **2** for two creditless endings.

EGG 5: Go to "Extras" and press **3** for an English-language trailer.

EGG 6: Go to "Extras," then to "Crest of the Stars History." Pressing **1** on the first page of any section will take you to the last page of the next section. Pressing **3** on the last page of each section will also take you to the other sections.

Dinosaur [2-Disc Collector's Edition]
EGG 1: On Disc 1, while the movie is playing, pressing **1** on the remote during specific chapters will bring up behind-the-scenes materials, as well as some alternate takes or deleted scenes. The chapters are: 1, 3, 5, 6, 10, 12, 15, 16, 18, 19, 20, 21, 25, and 26. All other eggs are on Disc 2.

EGG 2: Go to "The Production Process" and click **Right** to highlight the dinosaur head. Press **Enter** to see a five-minute clip from the 1964 broadcast of "Disneyland Goes to the World's Fair," which includes scenes of animatronic dinosaurs.

EGG 3: Go to "Creating the Characters" and click **Right** to highlight the dinosaur head. Press **Enter** to see a segment called "Render Bugs," which are essentially CGI bloopers.

EGG 4: Go to "Development" and click **Right** to highlight the dinosaur head. Press **Enter** to see a six-minute short with Walt Disney talking about the genesis of animation and showing segments of Winsor McCay's "Gertie the Dinosaur."

EGG 5: Go to "Publicity" and click **Right** to highlight the dinosaur head. Press **Enter** to see a twelve-minute educational cartoon called "Recycle Rex" made in conjunction with the California Department of Recycling!

Dirty Pair Flash: Angels in Trouble [#1]
Go to "Extras," then to "Flash Trailers," then to "Act 3." Click **Right Left Up**. Click **Enter** and you'll see the ADV trailer for *Dirty Pair Flash Mission 2*, with commentary!

Dragon Half
Go to "Mink's Journey" and click **Right** to see a hidden trailer.

Dual: Parallel Trouble Adventure— Visions [#1]
Go to "Languages" and highlight "English Subtitles." Click **Left** or **Right** then press **Enter** to see a special cartoon, or press **Down** and **Enter** to see a second cartoon.

Dual: Parallel Trouble Adventure—Student Housing [#2]
Go to "Extra Visions," then "Line Art/Designs," then go to picture #7. Click **Up Enter** for a surprise.

Dual: Parallel Trouble Adventure—Artifacts [#3]
EGG 1: Go to "Extra Visions," then "Character Data." Click **Left** or **Right** for a short cartoon.

EGG 2: Go to "Extra Visions," then "Character Data." Go to "Rara Mitsuki" and click **Up Enter** for another short cartoon. This can also be reached by clicking on Rara Mitsuki's forehead on the main "Extra Visions" page.

Dual: Parallel Trouble Adventure—One Vision [#4]
EGG 1: Go to "Extra Visions," then "Character Data." Go to page 4:8 and click **Up Enter** for a short cartoon.

EGG 2: Go to "Extra Visions," then "Line Art." Go to page 1:26 and click **Up Enter** for another short cartoon.

EGG 3: Go to Extra Visions, then Line Art. Go to page 7:46 and click **Up Enter** for another short cartoon.

EGG 4: Go to "Audio Setup," highlight "English Setup," then click **Right**. The electricity will disappear and you can select a cartoon to view.

El Hazard: The Magnificent World [DVD Box Set]
EGG 1: On Disc 1, go to "Main Menu" and highlight "Enter the Magnificent World." Click **Left Enter** to get a special greeting.

EGG 2: On Disc 1, go to "Extras," then "Also on DVD." Go to the screen with *Fushigi Yuugi* and *Tenchi Muyo!* Click **Up Enter** for a series of *El Hazard* commercials.

EGG 3: On Disc 1, go to "Extras," then "Art Gallery." Go to the fifty-sixth picture ("Springs of Arliman") and click **Up Enter** for a message from the four priestesses.

EGG 4: On Disc 2, go to "Setup," select "English Audio," and turn the subtitles off. Highlight "Subtitles," then click **Right Enter** to hear a rant.

EGG 5: On Disc 2, go to "Scene Access," then to "Sixth Night." Go to "Opening" and click **Right Enter** to hear cast commentary on the opening.

EGG 6: On Disc 2, go to "Extras," then "Line Art," and

select "Items." Go to #3 (a lamp), click **Up Enter** for a message about the priestesses' lamps.

EGG 7: On Disc 2, go to "Extras," then to "DVD Credits." While the credits play, click **Up Enter**. The credits will restart, but a character drunkenly berates you during them.

EGG 8: On Disc 2, go to "Extras," then to "Non-Credit Ending." Click **Right Enter** for some commentary over the ending.

EGG 9: On Disc 2, go to "Scene Access," then "Seventh Night." Highlight "Encounter (Reprise)" and click **Left Down Down Up Enter**. You'll hear a special message.

EGG 10: On Disc 3, go to "Extras," then to "Dimension Tables." Highlight "Real World" and click **Left Enter** for commentary about El Hazard's worlds.

EGG 11: On Disc 3, go to "Scene Access," then to "Episode 1." Highlight "Opening" and click **Right Enter** for commentary about the second OVA series opening.

EGG 12: On Disc 3, go to "Extras" and highlight "DVD Credits." Click **Left Up Up Down Enter**. An identical menu will appear. Again highlight "DVD Credits" and click **Left Down Down Up Enter**. A special message from the cast will be heard over the credits.

EGG 13: On Disc 3, let the "Main Menu" play through until the music restarts. Click **5** on your remote and a picture of caves will appear with a numeric keypad. The keypad does not appear to do anything, however.

Emperor's New Groove, The: The Ultimate Groove [2-Disc Collector's Edition]
Although not quite Easter egg material, there are some fun scenes in the Trivia Game. Make sure to get a wrong answer at least once for each question.

Escaflowne: Dragons and Destiny [#1]
Go to "Menu," highlight "Music Videos." Click **Left** and "Ni Hon Go" will appear. Clicking this enables the songs to be viewed with subtitles that are the romanized pronunciation of the Japanese-language songs.

Escaflowne: Past and Present [#4]
Go to "Setup" and change the language to Japanese and turn on subtitles. The usual song will be replaced with an instrumental piece.

Escaflowne: Forever and Ever [#8]
EGG 1: Go to "Extras" and highlight "Playstation Game Footage." Click **Left Right** and parts of a star will appear in the right corner of the menu. Click **Right Left Down** to assemble all the parts of the star. Click on it for a creditless closing.

EGG 2: During the Maaya Sakamoto concert clip, if you use your subtitle button, you can switch between the English translation and the romanized Japanese-language translation.

Ex-Driver #1: Downshift
Go to "Main Menu," go down to "E." Click **Right** to highlight "1. Downshift," and click **Enter** to see a music clip.

Fatal Fury: Double Impact
Go to "Extras" and highlight "Conceptual Drawings." Click **Right** and a cursor will appear in Terry's eye. Click **Enter** to see a deleted fight scene of Joe Higashi vs. Big Bear.

Final Fantasy: The Spirits Within [Special Edition]
EGG 1: On Disc 1, go to "Special Features," go to "DVD-ROM Content." Click **Up** twice to see cheesecake gallery of Aki art. All other eggs are on Disc 2.

EGG 2: Go to "Main Menu" and highlight "Highlights Menu." Click **Right Down**. Click on the coffin symbol to see a storyboarded romantic dinner scene.

EGG 3: Go to "Main Menu" and highlight "Play Documentary." Click **Left Down**. Click on a symbol to see Aki's 3D CGI model.

EGG 4: Go to the second page of "Highlights Menu," then to "More Boards/Blasts." Click **Up Right Right** and you'll see a small frame. Click the frame to see a Final Fantasy sequence animated to Michael Jackson's "Thriller." You're guaranteed to laugh.

EGG 5: Go to "Highlights Menu" then "Vehicle Scale Comparisons" and highlight the arrow at the bottom of the screen. Click **Right** twice and a starfish symbol will appear. Click it to see a detailed vehicle rendering slideshow.

EGG 6: Go to "Highlights Menu" then "Character Files" and highlight the arrow at the bottom of the screen. Click **Right Left** to get a circular symbol leading to more storyboards.

EGG 7: Go to the second page of "Highlights Menu" then "DVD-ROM Content" and highlight the arrow at the bottom of the screen. Click **Up Right** to get to another symbol leading to more storyboards.

Fushigi Yugi: The Mysterious Play [#2—Seiryu/Blue Box Set]
During the music videos, if you use your subtitle button, you can switch between the English translation and the romanized Japanese-language translation.

Galaxy Fraulein Yuna
Go to "Main Menu" and highlight "Languages." Click **Down** to highlight the heart, then click **Enter** to see a clean credits opening.

Gasaraki #1: The Summoning
Go to "Main Menu" and click the English-language Gasaraki logo to see ADV trailers.

Gatchaman: Collection DVD

Nothing to click here, unless you use "Scene Selection" to speed to the end. At the end of the final episode, watch all the way through the credits. At the end, the screen will go black for a bit, then a music video of the *Gatchaman* theme—using footage from the TV and OVA series—will play.

Geo-Armor: Kishin Corps [Alien Defender]

On Disc 2 , go to "Title 3." This is a seven-minute introduction to the show, most of it live action!

Geobreeders

Go to the end credits of Episode 2. What follows is a commercial for *Cat Energizer*, featuring some familiar anime faces.

Getter Robo: Resurrection [Armageddon #2]

Go to "Extras" then "Behind the Scenes." Highlight "Genki/Dr. Cohen" then click **Right** to highlight the robot at the bottom of the screen. Press **Enter** for an odd interview with the ADR "dub" director.

Gokudo #2: Magician Extraordinaire

Go to "Trailers" then click **Up**. When the yellow ball is highlighted, click to see clean credits.

Gundam Wing: The Movie—Endless Waltz [Special Edition]

Go to "Extras" then "Credits." The background music is the full-length version of "White Reflection."

Hand Maid May: Maid to Order [#1]

EGG 1: Go to "Appendix Menu," highlight "Movie Appendix" then click **Up**. If the upper left corner video is playing, click **Enter** to show the clean credits opening.

EGG 2: Go to "Appendix Menu," highlight "Kasumi File:1," then click **Up**. If the upper right corner video is playing, click **Enter** to show the clean credits closing.

Hand Maid May: Product Recall [#2]

EGG 1: Go to "Appendix Menu" and then click **Up Enter** to play a new clean credits closing.

EGG 2: Go to "Appendix Menu" and then click **Up Right Enter** to see an art gallery.

Hand Maid May: Memory Failure [#3]

EGG 1: Go to "Appendix Menu," highlight "Movie Appendix," then click **Up**. If the upper left corner video is highlighted, click **Enter** to show the clean credit opening for Episode 11.

EGG 2: Go to "Appendix Menu," highlight "Kasumi File:1," then click **Up**. If the upper right corner video is highlighted, click **Enter** to show the clean credit closing for Episode 10.

Haunted Junction

On Disc 2, go to the second page of "Scene Select" (with Episodes #10–12). Go to #12, click **Down**, and the cursor will disappear off screen. Click **Enter** and a good-bye from Miss Hanako will appear. You can also access it by clicking **Up** when the cursor highlights the opening of chapter 10, or you can go to chapter 5 and press "Title 11."

His and Her Circumstances: The Appearance of a Normal Life [#1]

Go to the episode previews and click **Play**. Use the **Angle** button on your remote to toggle between the live action Japanese and American voice actresses.

His and Her Circumstances: Love and War Under the Cherry Blossoms [#2]

Go to the episode previews and click **Play**. Use the **Angle** button on your remote to toggle between the live action Japanese and American voice actresses.

Irresponsible Captain Tylor, The: Leave This to Me [TV #1]

EGG 1: The Easter eggs are literally a game to find—a target-shooting game. On the main menu, you must use your **Up**, **Down**, **Right**, and **Left** keys to target the moving ships. If you click **Enter** when the target is over the ship, you get one of four special short animation or artwork montages.

EGG 2: From "Bonus Menu," go to "Web Links." Click on "URL" then **Up**. When "Taylor" changes colors, press **Enter** to see clean credits and other alternate footage.

Irresponsible Captain Tylor, The: Did Somebody Say Luck? [TV #2]

Same eggs as DVD #1.

Irresponsible Captain Tylor, The: Little Azalyn, Eh? [TV #3]

Same eggs as DVD #1.

Irresponsible Captain Tylor, The: Let's Go! [TV #4]

Same eggs as DVD #1.

Jubei-Chan: Ninja Girl—Secret of the Lovely Eyepatch: A Legend Reborn [#1]

EGG 1: Go to "Extras" and click **5**. The black-and-white Jubei art will be highlighted. Click **Enter** to see an art gallery at the end of each episode.

EGG 2: After viewing the above, you will see a scene that does not appear at the end of an episode. Click **Down** four or five times and a super-deformed version of some animators will appear.

Jubei-Chan: Ninja Girl—Secret of the Lovely Eyepatch: Basic Ninja Training [#2]

EGG 1: Go to "Extras" and click **Down** until the eye-patch lights up. Press **Enter** for an Art Gallery.

EGG 2: On the first image in the above gallery (Yagyu on the eyepatch), click **Down** five times for more super-deformed animation staffers.

Jubei-Chan: Ninja Girl—Secret of the Lovely Eyepatch: Heart of Steel [#3]

Go to "Extras" and click **Down** until the logo on the face lights up. Press **Enter** for an Art Gallery.

Jubei-Chan: Ninja Girl—Secret of the Lovely Eyepatch: Final Showdown! [#4]

Go to "Extras" and click **Down** on a signpost toward the bottom of the screen. Click **Left Right** until the black-and-white Jubei art is highlighted. Click **Enter** to go to another Art Gallery.

Key: The Metal Idol #2—Dreaming

On some players, while in "Extras," pushing **2** will access a FAQ that was included on Disc 1.

Larryboy: The Cartoon Adventures—The Angry Eyebrows

Each egg is decorated to look like Larryboy—a green egg with Larry's plunger-mask on it.

EGG 1: Go to "Secret Room Stuff," click on the egg at the bottom of the screen to see a pencil test.

EGG 2: Go to "Secret Room Stuff," go to "Fun!," and click on the egg at the bottom of the screen to see Larry's Plane Cockpit.

EGG 3: Go to "Promo Materials," click on the egg at the bottom of the screen to see a "top swapper" illustration.

Larryboy: The Cartoon Adventures—Leggo My Ego [#2]

EGG 1: Go to "Bonus Materials," highlight "Behind the Scenes" and click **Up** for a "Silly Literature with Larry" voice-actor clip.

EGG 2: Go to "Bonus Materials," Go to "Behind the Scenes," highlight the "Back" button, and click **Right** for clips with Cocreator/Director and a voice actor.

EGG 3: Go to "Bonus Materials," go to "Fun!," highlight "Bumblyburg Bios," and click **Right** for another voice-actor clip.

Lost Universe: Vol. 5—Wanted Union of Evil

Go to "Main Menu," highlight "Trailers," and click **Left**. Logo will turn blue. Click **Enter** to get clean opening and closing credits.

Lost Universe: Vol. 6—It's His Duty to Kick Some Booty

Go to "Main Menu," highlight "Trailers" and click **Left**.

Logo will turn green. Click **Enter** to get new opening and closing credits with Japanese text.

Macross Plus: Vol. 1—Parts 1 and 2

Play the movie, then skip forward all six chapters. When the second part starts, skip six chapters again. A trailer will play.

Macross Plus: Vol. 2—Parts 3 and 4

Same egg as DVD #1.

Magic Knight Rayearth #1: Daybreak

Select "English Audio," then "Character Profiles." Some of the characters will now greet you in English. This option does not work on the Japanese audio track.

Maze [DVD Collection—Box Set]

Go to "Special Features," then "Meet the Characters," then "Mill." Highlight "Meet the Characters" and click **Up**. If Mill's name is highlighted, click **Enter** to get a special Mill sequence.

Mezzo Forte

Go to "Extras," highlight middle storyboard, click **Right**. If scar on man is highlighted, click **Enter** to hear some dubbing outtakes.

Mobile Suit Gundam 0083: Stardust Memory [#1]

Go to "Options" and select "English 5.1 Audio." The opening and closing credits are now the translated VHS credits, complete with less-sharp images and the title spelled "Suits" instead of "Suit."

Mobile Suit Gundam Wing: Operation 1

At 5:14 into episode #3, a file of Hiro's is scrolling on the screen. The text is actually a help file for a TWAIN driver to access a scanner within Adobe Photoshop.

Monkeybone

Go to "Audio Set-Up" and click **Right**. Monkeybone will appear holding a sign that says "Watch the Organ Harvest." Click **Enter** to see a behind-the-scenes clip.

Monsters, Inc.

All eggs are on Disc 2.

EGG 1: Go to "Humans Only," then through the "Pixar" door. Highlight the Monsters, Inc. eyeball and then click **Left**. Select the paper airplane to watch the Paper Airplane Contest.

EGG 2: Go to "Humans Only," then watch the entire "Tour" (skip through it with the remote if you like, but you'll miss some cool stuff). You'll see a screen of new doors at the end. Most of them lead to fun extras such as art, short animation clips, tour bloopers, an early test scene, and more.

EGG 3: Go to "Monsters Only" and click on the Monsters, Inc. eye logo at the right of the "Menu" screen for the "Charades" trailer. Note that this trailer can also be found in the "Release" section in the "Humans Only" area.

EGG 4: Go to "Monsters Only"and click on the Monsters, Inc. eye logo above Celia's shoulder. A monkey gathering easter eggs will appear, leading to a message from the film director and some funny "dailies" footage from the film.

Neon Genesis Evangelion—Collection 0:1 [Remastered]
Go to "Extras," click **Up** to highlight "Extras." Click **Enter** to see clean credits.

Neon Genesis Evangelion—Collection 0:4
Go to "Extras," then "Character Bios," and go to the final screen (Angel #11, Ireul). Click on the empty space where the "Continue" button is on earlier pages to go to a bio of the 6th Angel, Gaghiel. Alternately, you can click **1** on the keypad on the final screen to go to the same page.

Neon Genesis Evangelion—Collection 0:5
Go to "Extras," then "Character Bios," and go to the final screen. Click on the empty space where the "Continue" button is on earlier pages to go to a bio of Eva 03. Click "Forward" for a bio of the 13th Angel, Bardiel.

Neon Genesis Evangelion—Collection 0:6
Go to "Extras," then "Character Bios," and go to the final screen (the 14th Angel, Zeruel). Click on the empty space where the "Continue" button is on earlier pages to go to an info page about NERV Site 2.

Neon Genesis Evangelion—Collection 0:7
EGG 1: Go to "Extras," then "Character Bios," and go to the final screen. Click on the empty space where the "Continue" button is on earlier pages to go to a bio of the 17th Angel.

EGG 2: Go to "Magi Data Files" and highlight "Shigeru." Wait ten seconds for flash pictures of women in bikinis.

Neon Genesis Evangelion—Collection 0:8
Go to "Extras," then "Character Bios," and go to the final screen. Click on the empty space where the "Continue" button is on earlier pages to go to a bio of Adam, the apprentice, and more info about the 15th and 16th Angels.

Oh My Goddess! Vol. 1
EGG 1: Go to "Extras," then choose one of the following: "Dub-Your-Own," "Silent," or "Commentary." Highlight "Chapter One," then click **Down Right Down Right Up Enter**. You will see an advertisement with some artwork.

EGG 2: Go to "Subtitles" and highlight "English Audio/English Subtitles." Click **Left Right Right**

Down Enter to see an ad for *Oh My Goddess!* merchandise.

EGG 3: To view clean endings on all three episodes, start watching the ending. Then turn off the subtitles and switch to **Angle 2**.

Oh My Goddess! Vol. 2
EGG 1: Same first egg as DVD #1.

EGG 2: Go to "Episodes," highlight "Episode 5." Click **Down Right Enter**. You will see a photo gallery of members of Goddess Family Club—the Japanese voice actresses for the series—promoting their CD.

Orphen: Ruins and Relics [#3]
Go to "Main Menu," highlight "Languages," then click **Left**. A rune on Orphen's wrist should light up. Click it to see a funny behind-the-scenes segment with the voice actors.

Orphen: Mystere [#4]
Go to "Main Menu," go to "Extras," click **Up**, then **Enter** for some dubbing outtakes. Alternately, go to "Main Menu," highlight "Episode 10," then click **Left**. Click on the rune below Orphen's hands.

Osmosis Jones
EGG 1: Go to "Smelly Feetures/Special Features," then click **Left** to highlight the "Gas Next Exit" freeway sign. Click **Enter** to get a short movie clip.

EGG 2: Go to "Lunguages/Languages," then click "Continue." Click **Up** to highlight Drix's head, then **Enter** for a montage clip.

EGG 3: Go to "Frank's Gross Anatomy," then to "The Earl of Hurl." Click **Up** to highlight the "Funny Bone." Click **Enter** for a gross-out scene.

EGG 4: Go to "Audio/Subtitles." At "Subtitles," click "Next" until you reach the final choice with Bill Murray's insides pictured. Click **Up Enter** to see another clip.

Otaku no Video
Go to "Images." Click the "Title" button on your DVD remote, not the "Menu" button. You'll see a special clip.

Outlaw Star: DVD Collection 3
On Disc 2, go to "Extras" and play "Textless Ending #2." While it's playing, click "Next" and the Ending #1 song will play.

Patlabor 1: The Movie
EGG 1: Go to "Audio/Subtitles," highlight "Japanese Stereo" and click **Left**. Press **Enter** to see a trailer for *Patlabor*.

EGG 2: Go to "Special Features," highlight "Manga DVD Catalog," and click **Left**. Press **Enter** to see another trailer.

EGG 3: This must be accessed after the other two or you will get a restricted warning. Go to "Special Features," go to "Manga DVD Catalog," and highlight "Patlabor 1 & 2." Click **Left Enter** to see a third trailer.

If using Title and Chapter selections, these can also be chosen at Title 12 Chapter 1, Title 11 Chapter 1, and Title 4 Chapter 1.

Patlabor 2: The Movie
Same eggs as DVD #1.

Pete's Dragon [Gold Collection]
Play the "Find Elliot Game" and get all the answers correct. Your prize is a short documentary about dragons.

Phantom Quest Corp.: Perfect Collection
Go to "Extra Stuff" and play the "Non-Credit Opening." While it plays, click "Previous" to skip back to Title 3, Chapter 1. This will show a clean credits opening, plus a twenty-two-minute animation and voice-actor dubbing session. Alternate methods to reach this include clicking "Stop" on the disc, then going to "Title." Select "Title 3" or "Title 3-1." Another option is to go to "Extra Stuff" and clicking **7 3 Enter**. These methods may not work for all DVD players.

Powerpuff Girls, The: The Mane Event [#3]
Go to the "Adventures in Townsville" map, then to "Craig's House." While watching the "Whoopass Girls" pilot, select **Angle** on your DVD remote. You will see the pencil test version of the pilot cartoon.

Ranma 1/2 The Movie 2: Nihao My Concubine [#2]
Go to "Viz Video Information" and find the peach to the left of the wheel. Click it for a special scene.

Revolutionary Girl Utena: The Movie
When the disc is first started and the "FBI Warning" screen is visible, click **Forward** to see a selection of clips from the movie.

Revolutionary Girl Utena: The Movie [Limited Edition]
Egg is the same as on the regular release.

Revolutionary Girl Utena: The Rose Collection #1
Play the "English Audio" track. Go to "Episode #7" and play the opening for an instrumental version of the song.

Robotech Legacy, The: Collection 1—Macross Saga [Box Set]
On the bonus disc *Robotech Extra: Macross Saga 1—Elements of Robotechnology*, you can switch to a third unlisted audio track that features an isolated music/effects–only track, perfect for dubbing your own scenes.

Robotech Legacy, The: Collection 3—Macross Saga [Box Set]
On the bonus disc *Robotech Extra: The Sentinels—Elements of Robotechnology III* you can switch to a third unlisted audio track that features another isolated music/effects-only track, perfect for dubbing your own scenes.

Robotech Legacy, The: Collection 7—New Generation [Box Set]
EGG 1: On the bonus disc *Robotech Extra: New Generation 2—Elements of Robotechnology VII*, go to "Main Menu," highlight "International Clips," click **Down**. Click on the upside-down triangle at the bottom of the screen to see a short TV promo trailer.

EGG 2: Go to "Merchandise Gallery," go to "Toys" and highlight "Revell Models." Click **Left** to spotlight a figure, and **Enter** to see an old toy commercial.

Rolie Polie Olie: The Great Defender of Fun
Go to "Bonus Features," click **Up** to highlight the planet. Click **Enter** to see a new character from the TV series, but don't blink.

Roughnecks: Starship Troopers Chronicles—The Tophet Campaign [#3]
Go to "Special Features," highlight "Play Movie," click **Left**. When a blue spot appears in the reactor, click **Enter** for a presentation showing the progression from storyboard to completed CGI.

Royal Space Force: The Wings of Honneamise
EGG 1: Go to "Special Features," highlight "Art and Music," click **Up**. When the "Manga" logo is highlighted, press **Enter** to see the English trailer for *Wings of Honneamise*.

EGG 2: Go to "Web Links" and click **Up Enter** to see a trailer for *Sputnik 7*.

Rudolph the Red-Nosed Reindeer and the Island of Misfit Toys
Wait until the credits are completed for a short scene of the elf dentist at work.

Rurouni Kenshin: Wandering Samurai—The Flames of Revolution [#6]
Go to "Extras," go to "Liner Notes," and click **Left**. When the egg appears, click **Enter** for a preview trailer of the Kyoto Saga. This is also accessible as Track 26.

Rurouni Kenshin: Tales of the Meiji—Dreams of Youth [#19]
Go to "Extras," go to "Liner Notes," and click **Left**. When a gravestone appears, click **Enter** to get a music video from the Shimabara Arc.

Rurouni Kenshin: Tales of the Meiji—End Song [#22]

Go to "Extras," go to "Liner Notes," go to "Shiki," and click **Left**. When the word "Anime" lights up, click **Enter** to get a special announcement for the boxed set and more.

Saber Marionette J: DVD Collection 1

On Disc 2, play the Music Video. Switch subtitle tracks while watching: Track 1 is an Englsh translation; Track 2 is a romanized version; and Track 3 has Japanese characters.

Saber Marionette J: DVD Collection 2

On Disc 2, play the "Cherry Musical Circuit Music Video." Switch subtitle tracks while watching: Track 1 is an English translation; Track 2 is a romanized version; and Track 3 has Japanese characters.

Saber Marionette J: DVD Collection 3

All eggs are on Disc 1.

EGG 1: Let the "Main Menu" animation run twice, then click the red orb at the upper right. You will get a live-action segment with popular Japanese voice actress Megumi Hayashibara. An alternate way to highlight the red orb is to go to "Setup," then exit back to "Main Menu." Go to "Play" and click **Right**. The orb should light up.

EGG 2: Let the "Main Menu" animation run twice, then click the red orb at the upper right. Click **Up Down** to highlight the "J" on the Saber Marionette J logo. Click **Enter** to see clean credits. An alternate way to view the clean credits is go to "Title #12."

Sailor Moon S: The Movie—Uncut Special Edition

Go to "Extra Stuff," then highlight "Transformation Scenes." Click **Left** to turn forehead moon red and click **Enter** to see Luna's transformation.

Schoolhouse Rock! Special 30th Anniversary Edition

EGG 1: On Disc 1, go to "Setup Menu." Highlight the smiling man doodle and click **Enter** to see a section on artist Tim Yohe. Clicking on each sketch on the page leads to more sketches and some music.

EGG 2: On Disc 2, go to "Main Menu." Highlight the water fountain on the right wall and click **Enter** to flood the hall. You'll see a few familiar characters shortly.

EGG 3: On Disc 2, go to "Main Menu." Highlight the light switch on the left and click **Enter**. The hallway will go dark, then a familiar skeleton and some fun animation will follow.

EGG 4: On Disc 2, go to "Main Menu." Highlight the word "Credit" on the "Extra Credit" banner at the top.

Click **Enter** to see fifty-nine pages of credits for the songs!

EGG 5: On Disc 2, go to "Earn Your Diploma." If you pass five tests on the subjects of America, Grammar, Science, Money, and Multiplication, and solve the word scramble puzzles, you'll be able to view an all-new song called "Exercise Your Right to Vote."

Serial Experiments: Lain—Navi [#1]

EGG 1: Go to "Main Menu" and click **Up**. Click on the letter that lights up (either the second "E" in Experiments or the "I" in Lain) for a secret animation.

Serial Experiments: Lain—Knights [#2]

EGG 1: Go to "Main Menu" and click **Up**. Click on the eyes for a secret animation.

EGG 2: Go to "Main Menu," highlight "Play," and click **Left**. When the cursor disappears, click **Enter** for a chibi Lain animation.

Serial Experiments: Lain—Deus [#3]

Go to "Main Menu" and click **Left**. When some buttons/emblems on Lain's shirt are highlighted, click **Enter** for an animation.

Serial Experiments: Lain—Reset [#4]

Go to "Main Menu," highlight "Play," and click **Left**. Click on the eyes for a secret animation.

Shrek

EGG 1: On both discs, go to "Main Menu," then "Special Features." Highlight "Main Menu" at the bottom of the screen. Click **Up** to highlight the Gingerbread Man's gumdrop buttons. Click **Enter** to get a "Shrek Fun Fact." There are multiple facts, shown at random.

EGG 2: On Disc Two, go to "Main Menu," highlight "Play," and click **Up**. When a musical note appears, click **Enter** to go to "Shrek Karaoke." This is also available on Disc 1, and seen after the credits on Disc 2.

EGG 3: Play Title 11 for a short DTS clip.

EGG 4: Titles 22 and 23 have music videos by Baja Men and Smash Mouth.

Simpsons, The: The Complete First Season

EGG 1: On Disc 3, go to the second page of "Extra Features," then go to "Art of the Simpsons." Highlight "Extra Features" and click **Left**. When Bart's comic book is highlighted, click **Enter** for a gallery of Simpsons magazine covers.

EGG 2: On Disc 3, go to the second page of "Extra Features," then highlight the "Some Enchanted Evening Script." Click **Left** to highlight Bart's shirt, then click **Enter** to see a 1990 ABC News report on the Bart Simpson T-shirt controversy.

Simpsons, The: The Complete Second Season [DVD Collector's Edition]

EGG 1: On Disc 1, go to "Language Selection" for "Two Cars in Every Garage and Three Eyes on Every Fish." Click on Blinky to get an animated thank you note.

EGG 2: On Disc 3, go to "Language Selection" for "Bart's Dog Gets an F." Click on the piece in the dog's mouth to get a sketch. Click on the head in the sketch to see another sketch.

EGG 3: On Disc 3, go to "Main Menu" for "Old Money" and click on Grandpa's fez to see a sketch.

EGG 4: On Disc 3, go to "Language Selection" for "Brush with Greatness." Click on the painting for a sketch.

EGG 5: On Disc 4, go to "Language Selection" for "Three Men and a Comic Book." Click on the Comic Book Guy's paper slip for a sketch.

EGG 6: On Disc 4, go to "Language Selection" for "Blood Feud." Click on Olme's eyes for some Homer lay-out sketches. Click on the post-it note for more sketches.

EGG 7: On Disc 4, go to the storyboards for "Bart Gets an F" in the "Special Features" section. Click until you find a storyboard with a post-it note on it. Click on the post-it for a deleted sequence.

Note that eggs hidden in the "Language Selection" menus can also be reached by highlighting "More" and clicking **Right Enter.**

Slayers: The Book of Spells

Go to "Main Menu" and highlight "Jeffery's Knighthood." Click **Left Enter** to see an ADV music video.

Snow White and the Seven Dwarfs: Platinum Edition

EGG 1: On Disc 1, go to "Main Menu." Don't do anything. Just wait. The mirror will start making sarcastic comments at you.

EGG 2: On Disc 1, go to "Set-Up," then "Audio." Under "Spoken Language" select "French." Now, all text in the film—the storybook at the start, the Queen's spells, and even the dwarf's bed signs—will be in French!

EGG 3 : On Disc 2, go to "Main Menu" and highlight the cauldron at lower left. Click **Right** to highlight the apple. Click it to find text menus for all the "Special Features."

Speed Racer: The Movie

EGG 1: Play the Trivia Game and answer five questions correctly. Once you win, instead of pressing "Next," click **Up**. Click **Enter** on the Mammoth Car and you'll get three 1950s animated TV commercials (for paint, bug spray, and milk).

EGG 2: Answer all ten questions on the Trivia Game cor-

rectly, and you'll be rewarded with an animated cartoon from the 1957 TV series *Colonel Bleep.*

Spider-Man: The Ultimate Villain Showdown

EGG 1: Go to "Main Menu," then "Setup," then "Spoken Languages." Highlight "Setup," then click **Up**. Click **Enter** on the spider and you'll get to hear *Spider-Man* cocreator Stan Lee discussing villain Dr. Doom.

EGG 2: Go to "Main Menu," then "Setup," then "Captions." Highlight "Setup," then click **Up**. Click **Enter** on the spider and you'll hear Stan Lee reveal his favorite superhero.

Spriggan

Go to "Main Menu" and highlight "Special Ops." Click **Right** to highlight "Control C.S." Click **Enter** to see the *Spriggan* trailer.

Strawberry Eggs: 1st Quarter—Make-Up Exam [#1]

Go to "Main Menu" and click on any page, then go back to "Main Menu." Highlight "Begin Class" and click **Right** twice, **Down** six times, and **Left** twice. A line should appear under "Extra Credit." Click **Left** again, then **Enter** to see a humorous clip. Some machines may allow you to access this by pressing **2 4** on your DVD remote while on the Main Menu.

Strawberry Eggs: 2nd Quarter—Pop Quiz [#2]

Go to "Main Menu" and click on any page, then go back to "Main Menu." Highlight "7th Period." Click **Left Down Right Right Down Up Left Left Enter**. You will see a "What if" scene connecting to a scene in the seventh episode.

Street Fighter Alpha: The Movie

Go to "Special Features," then "Weblink." Click on the Manga symbol, and the Japanese trailer will play.

Street Fighter II V: Vol. 1

Let the Main Menu play for a while and watch the upper left window. Eventually a girl will appear there for a short scene.

Street Fighter II V: Vol. 4

Go to "Extras" and click on the Manga symbol, and the U.S. trailer for *Street Fighter II V* will play.

Super Dimension Fortress Macross Box Set [#1–9]

EGG 1: On all discs, go to "Settings" and highlight "Subtitles Off/Japanese Audio." Click **Left Enter** to see a test pattern. Woohoo!

EGG 2: On Disc 8, go to "Main Menu" and highlight "Lonely Song." Click **Left Enter** to see a music video. Alternately, when in "Main Menu," click **8** on your DVD remote for the same video.

EGG 3: On Disc 9, go to "Episode 35." During the show,

use your DVD remote to go to a third audio track *and* a second subtitle track. Both tracks continue into Episode 36.

EGG 4: On Disc 9, go to "Settings" and highlight "Main Menu." Click **Down Enter** to see a slideshow with fifty-two character and mecha designs.

Super Dimension Fortress Macross—Macross Set #1
All discs have same first egg as listed in the Box Set.

Super Dimension Fortress Macross—Macross Set #2
All discs have same first egg as listed in the Box Set.

Super Dimension Fortress Macross—Macross Set #3
All discs have same first egg as listed in the Box Set. Discs 8 and 9 have the same eggs as listed in the Box Set.

Tenchi Forever! The Movie
Go to "Language/Subtitles," then "DVD Credits," then "English Credits." You can now view the movie credits in English.

Tenchi Muyo! DVD Ultimate Edition
Go to "Main Menu" and click **12** (or **10 2**) to go to a "Meet Pioneer" section with super-deformed chibi cartoons of Pioneer staff-members. An alternate route is to go to Title 4.

Tenchi the Movie: Tenchi Muyo in Love
Go to "Main Menu" and click on the Japanese characters at the bottom left corner. The menu will change to Japanese, and the bottom left-hand corner will now say "English Menu" if you want to switch back.

Tenchi the Movie 2: The Daughter of Darkness
EGG 1: While watching the film, click the **Angle** button on your DVD remote. This will occasionally bring up artwork and stills of characters. Keep **Angle 2** going through the credits to see an alternate Japanese closing credit sequence.

EGG 2: While accessing any of the Menu options, a complete instrumental track from the movie soundtrack will play in 5.1 surround.

3x3 Eyes: Collectors Edition
On Disc 2, select "Extras," then "Actors," then "Megumi." Click **Right** to find a hidden art gallery.

3-2-1 Penguins!—Trouble on Planet Wait-Your-Turn [Episode #1]
EGG 1: Go to "Promo Materials," then "Larryboy Trailer." Click **Right** for a live-action clip of penguins.

EGG 2: Go to "Hey Kids!!" then move your cursor to

the "Back" button at the bottom. Click **Right** to see a trippy Penguin kaleidoscope.

3-2-1 Penguins!—The Cheating Scales of Bullamanka [Episode #2]
EGG 1: Go to "Promo Materials," then "Larryboy Trailer." Click **Right** for another live-action clip of penguins.

EGG 2: Go to "Hey Kids!!" then move your cursor to the "Back" button at the bottom. Click **Right** to see a different trippy Penguin kaleidoscope.

EGG 3: Go to "Features and Fun," highlight "ROM Stuff," and click **Left** for voice-actor clip

3-2-1 Penguins!—The Amazing Carnival of Complaining [Episode #3]
EGG 1: Go to "Promo Materials," then "Larryboy Trailer." Click **Right** for yet another live-action clip of penguins.

EGG 2: Go to "Hey Kids!!" then move your cursor to the "Back" button at the bottom. Click **Right** to see another trippy Penguin kaleidoscope.

EGG 3: Go to "Features and Fun," highlight "ROM Stuff," and click **Left** for an Art Director clip.

3-2-1 Penguins!—Runaway Pride at Lightstation Kilowatt [Episode #4]
EGG 1: Go to "Promo Materials," then "Larryboy Trailer #1." Click **Right** for a clip of the Director and a preview of future episodes.

EGG 2: Go to "Hey Kids!!" then move your cursor to the "Back" button at the bottom. Click **Left** to see a Director clip.

EGG 3: Go to "Features and Fun," highlight "Hey Kids!!," and click **Left** for a Director clip.

Tigger Movie, The
Play the Trivia Game and get all the answers right. If you do, you'll be rewarded with a five-minute documentary on the history of *Winnie the Pooh*.

Toy Story: The Ultimate Toy Box [Box Set]
EGG 1: Go to Chapter 14 of Toy Story 2 and find Buzz Lightyear's speech. Switch to the French audio track. Instead of the American National Anthem in the background, you'll hear Randy Newman's "One World Anthem."

EGG 2: On Disc 2, access Title 4 to see trailers for *Dinosaur*, *The Emperor's New Groove*, and *Fantasia 2000*. If you click Title 5, you get the same trailers, plus clips for Disney's California Adventure Theme Park and *Buzz Lightyear of Star Command*.

EGG 3: On Disc 3, go to "*Toy Story 2*," then go to "Story," then go to "Jessie's Song." Click **Left** and a question mark will appear. Click **Enter** for a special message and an outtake.

EGG 4: On Disc 3, go to "*Toy Story 2*," then go to "History," then go to "The Continuing World of *Toy Story*." Skip through the video to the end for a new menu called "Links." Here you'll be able to see some story reels and extra cartoon clips.

Trigun: High Noon [#8]
Go to "Scene Selection," then go to "Chapter Select" for "Episode 26." Find the headline that says "Cat Found!" Click the headline for some concept art.

Twin Signal
Go to "Extras," then go to "Dress-Up Signal." Put the wedding dress on Signal, and when it's on him, click the dress again. This will take you to a set of dubbing outtakes.

Underdog: Collector's Edition [#1]
Go to Title 19 or Track 19 for preview trailers.

VeggieTales: The Ultimate Silly Song Countdown
Go to "Chapter Selections." On each page of the selections, press **9** on your remote. You will see the following eggs:

On Page 1–4, an extra "Oh Santa" Silly Song;

On Page 5–8, an extra "Lost Puppies" Silly Song;

On Page 9–12, the Official Voting Results;

On Page 13–16, a Japanese version of "Hairbrush Song" Silly Song.

VeggieTales: Rack, Shack, and Benny [#3]
EGG 1: Go to "Features," then to "Promo Materials." Highlight "Larryboy Trailer" and click **Left** on the vegetable to get a cocreator biography.

EGG 2: Go to "Features," then to "Behind the Scenes." Highlight "Concept Art" and click **Right** on the vegetable to get a silly ad.

VeggieTales: Josh and the Big Wall! [#4]
EGG 1: Go to "Features," then "Promo Materials." Highlight "Larryboy Trailer" and click **Right** on the vegetable to get a blooper scene.

EGG 2: Go to "Features," then "Behind the Scenes." Highlight "From Screen to Stage" and click **Right** on the vegetable to get extra concept art.

Walt Disney Treasures: Mickey Mouse in Black and White [Limited Edition Tin]
On Disc 1, go to "Bonus Material," highlight "Register Your DVD" and click **Up** to highlight Mickey's cowboy hat; then click **Enter.** You'll get to see a sing-along and a newsreel.

Walt Disney Treasures: Mickey Mouse in Living Color [Limited Edition Tin]
EGG 1: On Disc 1, highlight "1936" and click **Right.**

Mickey's ears and head will change colors. Click **Enter** to see a clip from a vintage TV show of Walt Disney discussing Mickey Mouse.

EGG 2: On Disc 2, highlight "1938" and click **Up.** Mickey's head should appear near an "O." Click **Enter** to see a bonus cartoon—"Mickey's Surprise Party"—shown *only* at the 1939 World's Fair!

Walt Disney Treasures: Silly Symphonies [Limited Edition Tin]
EGG 1: On Disc 1, go to "Main Menu," then "Leonard's Picks," and highlight "Three Little Pigs." Click **Up** twice to highlight "Leonard." Click **Enter** to see Walt Disney introduce the "Wynken, Blynken and Nod" cartoon.

EGG 2: On Disc 1, go to "Main Menu," then click **Up** to highlight the "S." Click **Enter** to see Walt Disney introduce the "The Grasshopper and the Ants" cartoon.

EGG 3: On Disc 1, go to "Main Menu," then "Favorite Characters." Click **Up** from "The Wise Little Hen" to highlight a chick. Click **Enter** to see Walt Disney introduce the "Who Killed Cock Robin?" cartoon.

EGG 4: On Disc 1, go to "Main Menu," then go to page two of "Fables and Fairy Tales." Highlight "Lullaby Land," then click **Left.** When Ambrose the Cat's sword is lit, click **Enter** to see Walt Disney introduce the "Water Babies" cartoon.

EGG 5: On Disc 1, go to "Captions" and click **Down** twice to highlight the water baby on the left. Click **Enter** to see Walt Disney introduce "The Practical Pig" cartoon.

EGG 6: On Disc 2, go to "Nature on Screen." Highlight "Mother Pluto" and click **Right.** When the star on a rabbit's cheek is highlighted, click **Enter** to see Walt Disney introduce "The Old Mill" cartoon.

EGG 7: On Disc 2, go to "Accent on Music." Highlight "Music Land," and click **Left.** When the saxophone's hat is highlighted, click **Enter** to see Walt Disney introduce the "Farmyard Symphony" cartoon.

The Wanderers: El Hazard TV Series—The Ultimate Weapon [#2]
Go to "Main Menu" and highlight "Extras." Click **Left Down Up Enter** to see a brief animation.

The Wanderers: El Hazard TV Series—The Winds of War [#3]
Go to "Main Menu," then "Extras," and highlight "DVD Credits." Click **Right Right Up Left.** When the word "Extras" changes colors, click **Enter** to get an image gallery with fifteen pieces of art.

Yellow Submarine
There are numerous eggs on the Main Menu, all available by clicking on different parts of the submarine.

They are all either dialogue or music clips. Here's a guide:

The four Beatles heads have dialogue clips.

The four portholes have dialogue clips from other characters.

The lines above the four Beatles heads have dialogue clips.

The periscope has a music clip from *Yellow Submarine*.

The fantail of the sub has a music clip from *Help!*

Z-Mind
Go to "Extras," highlight "Trailers," and click **Down** twice. When part of the robot is highlighted, click **Enter** on the top right part, then click **Enter** on all parts in counter-clockwise order. Do this twice and all four parts should change to red. Click **Enter** again and you'll get a special trailer for *Melty Lancer*.

MATURE/ADULT SECTION

Blood: The Last Vampire
Go to "Menu," then click **Right**, and three logos will appear. Each contains trailers and other clips.

Clerks Uncensored
Nothing to click here. Just wait. On "Main Menu," let the dog walk by four times. On his fourth pass, he will urinate on Silent Bob (creator Kevin Smith).

Excel Saga, Vol. 2: Missions Improbable
OK, gentle readers, I'm only going to do this once. There are so many Easter eggs on this disc that it would take over a page to list them. I'm not kidding. There are a *lot*. More than a few baskets. So, I'll suggest you check out the listing at www.animeondvd.com/discdata/digital_omake.php to find out how to view them all. Here's a small sample of what you'll find:

EGG 1: In "Main Menu," click the folder in the upper left corner for a Menchi Dogs Commercial.

EGG 2: In "Main Menu," click the folder in the upper right corner for a clip of a laughing man.

EGG 3: In "Scene Selection" for Episode #7, click the folder in the lower right corner for a Menchi Chow Commercial.

EGG 4: In "Language Selection," click the folder in the lower middle for a clip of Excel and a toilet.

EGG 5: In "Language Selection," select "L-E," then highlight "Main," go down, and click **Enter** to see the menu flip.

EGG 6: In "Language Selection," select "L-ES," then highlight "Main," go down, and click **Enter** to see a Spenchi advertisement

EGG 7: In "Extras," click the skull in the lower middle to see a character get electrocuted.

EGG 8: In "Extras," click the left folder in the lower left to see a randomly chosen production sketch.

EGG 9: In "Extras," click the right folder in the lower left to see a randomly chosen production sketch.

EGG 10: In "Extras," click the folder in the lower right to see a Menchi Soup Commercial.

Golden Boy: Treasure Hunt [#1]
Go to "Extras," highlight "Clean Closing Animation," and click **Left** to see a preview for Episode 4.

Mezzo Forte [Uncut]
Go to "Extras," highlight the middle storyboard, and click **Right**. When the man's scar is highlighted, click **Enter** to hear some dubbing outtakes.

Pink Floyd: The Wall
Almost every page of the menu system has a small picture in the corner. To access this, click **9** on your remote; each page will play a different sound or music clip

Samurai X: Betrayal [#2]
Go to "Main Menu" and click **Left** to see a trailer for *Samurai X: Trust [#1]*.

South Park: The Complete First Season
EGG 1: On Disc 1, go to "Languages," highlight "Espanol," then go **Left**. Wendy's face will change. Click **Enter** for a brief joke.

EGG 2: On Disc 2, go to "Languages," highlight "Espanol," then go **Left**. Death's hand will change. Click **Enter** for a brief joke.

EGG 3: On Disc 1, go to "Special Features," highlight "CableAce Awards," then go **Right**. Damien's eyes will change. Click **Enter** for a brief joke.

EGG 4: On Disc 3, go to "Languages" and click on the "Who Is Cartman's Father" link. It will highlight any of the characters below. Click on any of them for a brief joke.

X [The Movie]
Go to "Main Menu" and highlight the Manga Video logo. Click **Enter** to play the trailer for *Blood: The Last Vampire*.

Feature Films

Despite the huge number of DVDs in this volume, very few of them are full-length theatrical films made by American studios. Most are television series, direct-to-video projects, foreign projects, theatrical shorts, or anime.

The first list below is a complete "official" listing of Disney's animated theatrical films, in order of release, with DVD availability indicated next to the DVD release year. (Occasionally, DVDs are pulled from the market and placed "On Moratorium"; if you are shopping for a DVD, you can usually check a disc's status on the Internet at one of the addresses in the following section "Companies & Resources.")

The second, shorter list shows theatrical releases that Disney does not consider to be a part of its "Full Length Animation Features" line.

The third list is a complete listing of all U.S.-made feature films that have been released on DVD.

OFFICIAL DISNEY THEATRICAL RELEASES

Snow White and the Seven Dwarfs (1937), 2001—On Moratorium

Pinocchio (1940), 1999—On Moratorium

Fantasia (1940), 2000

Dumbo (1941), 2001

Bambi (1942)

Saludos Amigos (1943), 2000

The Three Caballeros (1945), 2000

Make Mine Music (1946), 2000

Fun and Fancy Free (1947), 2001

Melody Time (1948), 2000

The Adventures of Ichabod and Mr. Toad (1949), 2001

Cinderella (1950)

Alice in Wonderland (1951), 2001

Peter Pan (1953), 1999, 2002—On Moratorium

Lady and the Tramp (1955), 1999—On Moratorium

Sleeping Beauty (1959)

101 Dalmatians (1961), 1999—On Moratorium

The Sword in the Stone (1963), 2001

The Jungle Book (1967), 1999—On Moratorium

The Aristocats (1970), 2000

Robin Hood (1973), 2000

The Many Adventures of Winnie the Pooh (1977), 2002

The Rescuers (1977)

The Fox and the Hound (1981), 2000

The Black Cauldron (1985), 2001

The Great Mouse Detective (1986), 2002

Oliver and Company (1988), 2002

The Little Mermaid (1989), 1999—On Moratorium

The Rescuers Down Under (1990), 2000

Beauty and the Beast (1991), 2002

Aladdin (1992)

The Lion King (1994)

Pocahontas (1995), 2000

The Hunchback of Notre Dame (1996), 2002

Hercules (1997), 2001

Mulan (1998), 1999—On Moratorium

Tarzan (1999), 2000—On Moratorium

Fantasia/2000 (2000), 2000

The Emperor's New Groove (2001), 2001

Atlantis: The Lost Empire (2001), 2002

Lilo and Stitch (2002), 2002

Treasure Planet (2002)

OTHER DISNEY
THEATRICAL RELEASES
(by year of theatrical release)

Song of the South (1946)—Suppressed (release unlikely)

Mary Poppins (1964), 1998, 2001

Bedknobs and Broomsticks (1971), 2001

Pete's Dragon (1977), 2001

Tron (1982), 1998, 2002

Who Framed Roger Rabbit (1988), 1999

The Nightmare Before Christmas [Tim Burton's] (1993), 2001

A Goofy Movie (1995), 2000

Toy Story (1995), 2001

James and the Giant Peach (1996), 2001

A Bug's Life (1998), 2000

Toy Story 2 (1999), 2001

Dinosaur (2000), 2002

The Tigger Movie (2000), 2000

Recess: School's Out (2001), 2001

Monsters Inc. (2001), 2002

Peter Pan in Return to Never Land (2002), 2002—On Moratorium

U.S. THEATRICAL RELEASES
(by year of theatrical release)

Gulliver's Travels (1939), 1999, 2000, 2001, 2002

Mad Monster Party (1967), 2002

Yellow Submarine (1968), 1999

Fritz the Cat (1972), 2001

Charlotte's Web (1973), 2001

Heavy Traffic (1973), 2000

Dirty Duck (1975), 2001

The Nine Lives of Fritz the Cat (1974), 2001

The Lord of the Rings (1978), 2001

Watership Down (1978), 2002

The Water Babies (1979), 2002

American Pop (1981), 1998

Heavy Metal (1981), 1999

Pink Floyd: The Wall (1982), 1999

The Secret of NIMH (1982), 1998

The Care Bears Movie (1985), 2002

Transformers: The Movie (1986), 2000

G.I. Joe: The Movie (1987), 2000

The Puppetoon Movie (1987), 2000

The Land Before Time (1988), 1999

All Dogs Go to Heaven (1989), 2001

Evil Toons (1990), 2001

Rock-A-Doodle (1991), 1999

Ferngully: The Last Rainforest (1992), 2002

The Tune (1992), 1997—On Moratorium

Batman: Mask of the Phantasm (1993), 1999

Tom and Jerry: The Movie (1993), 2002

A Troll in Central Park (1993), 2002

The Pagemaster (1994), 2002

Thumbelina (1994), 1999, 2002

Balto (1995), 2002

The Pebble and the Penguin (1995), 2001

All Dogs Go to Heaven 2 (1996), 2001

Beavis and Butt-Head Do America (1996), 2002

Space Jam (1996), 1997, 2000

Anastasia (1997), 1999

Pippi Longstocking (1997), 2000

Antz (1998), 1999

The Prince of Egypt (1998), 1999, 2000

Quest for Camelot (1998), 2001

The Rugrats Movie (1998), 1999

The Iron Giant (1999), 1999

The King and I (1999), 1999

South Park: Bigger, Longer, and Uncut (1999), 1999

The Adventures of Rocky and Bullwinkle (2000), 2000

Chicken Run (2000), 2000

Heavy Metal 2000 (2000), 2000

The Road to El Dorado (2000), 2000

Thomas and the Magic Railroad (2000), 2001

Titan A.E. (2000), 2000

Final Fantasy: The Spirits Within (2001), 2001, 2002

Monkeybone (2001), 2002

Osmosis Jones (2001), 2002

Jimmy Neutron: Boy Genius (2001), 2002

Shrek (2001), 2001

The Trumpet of the Swan (2001), 2001

Waking Life (2001), 2002

Ice Age (2002), 2002

Spirit: Stallion of the Cimarron (2002), 2002

Companies & Resources

Provided in this section are two types of resources for finding out about animated titles on DVD. The first is a list of the releasing companies for all titles included in this book (if they're still in business).

Following that is a listing of Web sites that are good resources for building an excellent Animation on DVD collection. The listings are far from exhaustive; follow the links on almost any of these sites to find many other cool sites (note that web site addresses change frequently).

RELEASING COMPANIES

Acorn Media
www.acornmedia.com

ADV Films/AD Vision Films
www.advfilms.com

A&E
www.aande.com

Alliance Atlantis
www.AllianceAtlantis.com

Alpha Omega Publications
www.aop.com

Anchor Bay
www.anchorbayentertainment.com

Anime 18
(see also Central Park Media, Software Sculptors, U.S. Manga Corps)

www.anime18.com

AnimEigo
www.animeigo.com

AnimeWorks
(see also Kitty Media, Media Blasters)
www.media-blasters.com

Ariztical/Culture Q
www.ariztical.com

Artisan
www.artisanent.com

Bandai Entertainment
www.bandai-ent.com

BBC
www.bbc.co.uk

BFS Entertainment
www.bfsent.com

Big Idea
www.bigidea.com

Blackboard Entertainment
(Minnesota Orchestra Visual Entertainment)
www.mnorch.org

BMG Special Products
www.bmge.com

Brentwood/Eclipse
No website available

Buena Vista Home Entertainment
(see also Disney, Miramax)
www.bvhe.com

Celebrity Home Entertainment
www.celebhomeent.com

Central Park Media
(see also Anime 18, Software Sculptors, U.S. Manga Corps)
www.centralparkmedia.com

Columbia Tristar Home Entertainment
(see also Sony, Sony Wonder)
www.sonypictures.com/cthe/index_ie.html

Critical Mass
(see also Right Stuf International)
www.rightstuf.com

Delta Entertainment/Laserlight
www.deltamusic.com

Digital Leisure
www.digitalleisure.com

Digital Versatile Disc
(see also NuTech Entertainment)
www.digitalversatiledisc.com

Disney
(see also Buena Vista, Miramax)
http://disney.go.com/disneyvideos/ddvd.html

DreamWorks SKG
www.dreamworks.com

DVD International
www.dvdinternational.com

Facets MultiMedia
www.facets.org

First Run Features
www.firstrunfeatures.com

4Kids Entertainment
www.4KidsEntertainment.com

Fox/20th Century Fox
www.tcfhe.com

Front Row Entertainment
www.frontrowent.com

Funimation
www.funimation.com

Goodtimes
www.goodtimes.com

HBO
www.hbo.com

Heavy.Com
www.heavy.com

Hen's Tooth
No website available

HIT Entertainment
www.hitentertainment.com

Image Entertainment
www.image-entertainment.com

Jove/Films by Jove, Inc.
www.jovefilm.com

Kino International
www.kino.com

Kitty Media
(see also AnimeWorks, Media Blasters)
www.kittymedia.com

Koch Entertainment
www.kochint.com

Liberty International
www.libertyinteractive.com

Lions Gate Films
(see also Trimark)
www.lionsgatefilms.com

The Living Scriptures
www.livingscriptures.com

Madacy
www.madacy.com

Manga Entertainment
www.manga.com

Marengo Films
www.marengofilms.com

Media Blasters
(see also AnimeWorks, Kitty Media)
www.media-blasters.com

MGM/Metro Goldwyn Mayer
www.mgm.com

Miramax
(see also Buena Vista Home Entertainment, Disney)
www.miramax.com

MMG Anime
www.mmganime.com

Mondo Media
www.happytreefriends.com

Multimedia 2000/M2K
www.m-2k.com

Naxos
www.naxosusa.com

New Concorde
www.concorde-newhorizons.com

NuTech Entertainment
(see also Digital Versatile Disc)
www.nutechdvd.com

Paramount
www.paramount.com

Pioneer
www.pioneeranimation.com

Ralph Edwards Productions/Steeplechase
www.annabelleswish.com/ralph.html

Retro Media
www.retromedia.org

Rhino
www.rhino.com

Right Stuf International
(see also Critical Mass)
www.rightstuf.com

Slingshot Entertainment
www.slingshotent.com

SoftCel Pictures
www.softcelpics.com

Software Sculptors
(see also Anime 18, Central Park Media, U.S. Manga Corps)
www.centralparkmedia.com

Sony Entertainment
(see also Columbia Tristar Home Entertainment, Sony Wonder)
www.spe.sony.com

Sony Wonder
(see also Columbia Tristar Home Entertainment, Sony)
www.sonywonder.com

SVE/Churchill Media/Clearvue
www.svemedia.com
www.clearvue.com

Synch-Point
www.synch-point.com

Tai Seng Video
www.taiseng.com

10% Productions
www.10percent.com

Time-Life
www.timelife.com

TokyoPop
www.tokyopop.com

TriMark
(see also Lion's Gate Entertainment)
www.lgecorp.com

Troma
www. troma.com

UAV Entertainment
www.uavco.com

Universal Studios
http://homevideo.universalstudios.com

Urban Vision
www.urban-vision.com

USA Home Video
No website available

U.S. Manga Corps
(see also Anime 18, Central Park Media, Software Sculptors)
www.centralparkmedia.com

VCA
www.vcapix.com

View Video
www.view.com

Viz Communications
www.viz.com

Voyager
www.starblazers.com

Warner Bros.
www.warnerbros.com

Whirlwind Media
www.whirlwinddvd.com

Wellspring Media/Winstar/Fox Lorber
www.wellspring.com

Xenon Pictures
www.xenonpictures.com

RESOURCES

Anime on DVD
The best resource for this material on the web.
www.animeondvd.com

Anime Castle
Site for a large warehouse-style anime retailer.
www.animecastle.com

Anime Nation
Links, news, and merchandise.
www.AnimeNation.com

Anime Prime
Has a useful section on edited material.
www.animeprime.com

Animetric
Reviews, links, discussions, wallpaper.
www.animetric.com

Digitally Obsessed!
In-depth reviews include information on image and sound transfers.
www.digitallyobsessed.com

DVD Easter Eggs
The best site for Easter eggs.
www.dvdeastereggs.com

DVD Price Search
Has search engines to help you find the best prices.
www.dvdpricesearch.com

Right Stuf International
Industry news and merchandise.
www.rightstuf.com

Suncoast
Major national retailer site with extensive inventory and store-finder search.
www.suncoast.com

Selected Bibliography

The following books, magazines, and newspapers were of great help in preparing the entries in this book. Many of the books provide fascinating overviews of animation history, artists, and studios. Others will guide readers through the general world of DVDs, or provide further information on anime and manga. I have not listed individual editions of all the magazines and newspapers I referred to as they are too numerous to mention.

BOOKS

Baricordi, Andrea, Massimiliano De Giovanni, Andrea Pietroni, Barbara Rossi, and Sabrina Tunesi. *Anime: A Guide to Japanese Animation (1958–1988)*. Montreal: Protoculture, 2000.

Brooks, Tim, and Earle Marsh. *The Complete Directory to Prime Time Network TV Shows 1946–Present*. New York: Ballantine Books, 1999.

Cabarga, Leslie. *The Fleischer Story*. New York: Da Capo Press, 1988.

Clements, Jonathan, and Helen McCarthy. *The Anime Encyclopedia: A Guide to Japanese Animation Since 1917*. Berkeley: Stone Bridge Press, 2001.

Erickson, Hal. *Television Cartoon Shows: An Illustrated Encyclopedia, 1949 through 1993*. North Carolina: McFarland, 1995.

Halas, John. *Masters of Animation*. London: BBC Books, 1987.

Hyatt, Wesley. *The Encyclopedia of Daytime Television*. New York: Billboard, 1997.

Kilmer, David. *The Animated Film Collector's Guide: Worldwide Sources for Cartoons on Videotape and Laserdisc*. Sydney: John Libbey and Co., 1999.

Ledoux, Trish, editor. *Anime Interviews: The First Five Years of "Animerica, Anime and Manga Monthly" (1992–97)*. San Francisco: Cadence Books, 1997.

Lenburg, Jeff. *The Encyclopedia of Animated Cartoons*. New York: Facts on File, 1991.

———. *The Encyclopedia of Animated Cartoons*. 2nd edition. New York: Checkmark Books, 1999.

Maltin, Leonard. *The Disney Films*. 4th editon. New York: New American Library, 1987.

———. *Of Mice and Magic: A History of American Animated Cartoons*. Revised and updated edition. New York: Disney Editions, 2000.

Mayo, Mike, editor. *Videohound's DVD Guide*. Michigan: Visible Ink, 2001.

———, ed. *Videohound's DVD Guide Book 2*. Michigan: Gale Group, 2002.

McCarthy, Helen. *The Anime Movie Guide*. New York: The Overlook Press, 1996.

———. *Hayao Miyazaki: Master of Japanese Animation*. Berkeley: Stone Bridge Press, 1999.

——— and Jonathan Clements. *The Erotic Anime Movie Guide*. New York: The Overlook Press, 1999.

Poitras, Gilles. *Anime Essentials: Every Thing a Fan Needs to Know*. Berkeley: Stone Bridge Press, 2001.

Pratt, Doug. *Doug Pratt's DVD-Video Guide*. New York: Harber Electronic Publishing, 1999.

Rovin, Jeff. *Adventure Heroes: Legendary Characters from Odysseus to James Bond*. New York: Facts on File, 1994.

Schodt, Frederik L. *Manga! Manga! The World of Japanese Comics*. Tokyo: Kodansha International, 1984.

———. *Dreamland Japan: Writings on Modern Manga*. Berkeley: Stone Bridge Press, 1996.

Thompson, Nathaniel. *DVD Delirium: The International Guide to Weird and Wonderful Films on DVD!* Volume 1. London: Fab Press, 2002.

MAGAZINES AND NEWSPAPERS

Animated Life (U.S.)

Animation Magazine (U.S.)

Animato! The Animation Fan's Magazine (U.S.)

Anime Invasion (U.S.)

AnimeFantastique (U.S.)

Animerica (U.S.)

Comics Buyer's Guide (U.S.)

The DVD Guide (U.S.)

Manga Mania/Manga Max (U.K.)

Protoculture Addicts (Canada)

Toon Magazine (U.S.)

Total DVD (U.K.)

Wild Cartoon Kingdom (U.S.)

Index

This index, like the DVD title listing in the main text, is alphabetized on a word-by-word basis. Titles beginning with numerals, like *3x3 Eyes*, are listed as if the numerals were spelled out.

VIEWING NOTES

VIEWING NOTES

VIEWING NOTES

VIEWING NOTES

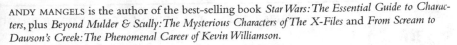

ANDY MANGELS is the author of the best-selling book *Star Wars: The Essential Guide to Characters*, plus *Beyond Mulder & Scully: The Mysterious Characters of The X-Files* and *From Scream to Dawson's Creek: The Phenomenal Career of Kevin Williamson*.

He is also the coauthor (with Michael A. Martin) of *Star Trek: The Next Generation, Section 31—Rogue; Star Trek: Deep Space Nine, Mission: Gamma—Cathedral; Roswell: Skeletons in the Closet*; the upcoming pair of *Star Trek: Starfleet Corps of Engineers—Ishtar Rising* e-books; the upcoming *Star Trek: Lost Era—The Sundered* novel; the upcoming *Roswell: Pursuit* and *Roswell: Turnabout* novels; and several more future *Star Trek* book projects.

Andy Mangels has written for *The Hollywood Reporter, The Advocate, Just Out, Cinescape, Gauntlet, Dreamwatch, Sci-Fi Universe, SFX, Anime Invasion, Outweek, Frontiers, Portland Mercury, Comics Buyer's Guide*, and scores of other entertainment and lifestyle magazines. He has also written licensed material based on properties by Lucasfilm, Paramount, New Line Cinema, Universal Studios, Warner Bros., Microsoft, Abrams-Gentile, and Platinum Studios.

His comic-book work has been published by DC Comics, Marvel Comics, Dark Horse, Wildstorm, Image, Innovation, WaRP Graphics, Topps, and others, and he was the editor of the award-winning *Gay Comics* anthology for eight years. He has also written DVD Supplemental Material and Liner Notes for Anchor Bay. He is currently writing the upcoming *Dragon's Lair* comic book series (based on the game and DVD reviewed in this book) for MVCreations.

In what little spare time he has, he likes to country dance and collect uniforms and Wonder Woman memorabilia. He lives in Portland, Oregon, with his longtime partner, Don Hood, and their dog, Bela.

Visit Andy Mangels's Web site at www.andymangels.com

Our special thanks to MARK HAMILL, who graciously provided the Foreword to this book. . . . Mark Hamill has done hundreds of voice-overs for cartoons as diverse as *The Simpsons, The Ren and Stimpy Show, Time Squad, Spider-Man, Little Mermaid, Family Guy*, and *Joseph: King of Dreams*. He's the Joker on *Batman: The Animated Series, Superman, Batman Beyond, Justice League*, and the *Batman* features *Mask of the Phantasm* and *Return of the Joker*. He is executive producer, cocreator, voice director, and performer for AMC's animated satire *The Wrong Coast*.

His on and off-Broadway work includes *The Elephant Man, Room Service, Amadeus* (as well as the first national tour), *The Nerd*, and *Harrigan 'n' Hart* (Drama Desk Nomination as "Outstanding Actor in a Musical"), which he originated at the Goodspeed Opera. As of this writing he is in rehearsal for *Six Dance Lesson in Six Weeks*, a new Broadway play.

He also created *The Black Pearl* (a Dark Horse comic series and graphic novel), which he cowrote with Eric Johnson.

Mark Hamill's films include Sam Fuller's *The Big Red One, Slipstream, Walking across Egypt, Hamilton*, and *Reeseville*. He is also remembered as the guy with the crush on his sister in George Lucas's original *Star Wars* trilogy.

Philadelphia-based illustrator CHRISTOPHER TAYLOR has been putting pencil to Bristol professionally for over ten years. Most notable among his numerous clients are DC Comics and DarkHorse comics. His favorite anime are *Neon Genesis Evangelion* and *Outlaw Star*.

Christopher Taylor's personal website can be viewed at http://marknemesis.homestead.com/OP1.html.

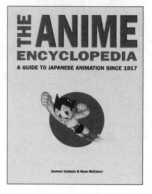